THE OPERATIONS OF THE IRISH HOUSE OF COMMONS, 1613–48

Studies presented to the International Commission for the
History of Representative and Parliamentary Institutions

Volume CVI
2023

Études présentées à la Commission Internationale
pour l'Histoire des Assemblées d'États

The operations of the Irish House of Commons, 1613–48

BRÍD McGRATH

FOUR COURTS PRESS
in association with
THE IRISH LEGAL HISTORY SOCIETY

Set in EhrhardtMT Pro 10.5pt/12.5pt by
Carrigboy Typesetting Services for
FOUR COURTS PRESS LTD
7 Malpas Street, Dublin 8, Ireland
www.fourcourtspress.ie
and in North America for
FOUR COURTS PRESS
c/o IPG, 814 N Franklin St, Chicago, IL 60610

References to this publication should cite the publisher as Four Courts Press
in association with the Irish Legal History Society.

A catalogue record for this title is available
from the British Library.

ISBN 978-1-84682-814-0

Printed in England
by CPI Antony Rowe Ltd, Chippenham, Wilts.

Do mo mhuintir, le grá, Simon, Oisín agus Sibéal,
agus i ndíl chuimhne ár James Casey An Clochán,
Paddy McNamee, Ceannanas Mór agus Frank Casey, Mullach Íde.

Contents

Illustrations

Tables

Abbreviations

Add.	Additional
Anal. Hib.	*Analecta Hibernica*
APC	*Acts of the privy council of England, 1542–1631*, 46 vols (1890–1964).
ARL	Armagh Robinson Library
Bennett, *Bandon*	George Bennett, *The history of Bandon and the principal towns in the west riding of County Cork* (Cork, 1869).
BL	The British Library, London
Bodl. Lib.	The Bodleian Library, Oxford
Borlase, *History*	Edmund Borlase, *The history of the execrable Irish rebellion* (London, 1680).
Cal. Carew	J.S. Brewer and William Bullen (eds), *Calendar of the Carew manuscripts, 1600–1623, preserved in the Archiepiscopal Library at Lambeth, 1515–1624*, 6 vols (London, 1867–73).
Cal. S.P. Dom.	Robert Lemon, et al. (ed.), *Calendar of State Papers preserved in the Public Record Office, Domestic Series, 1547–1695*, 81 vols (London, 1856–1972).
Cal. S.P. Ire.	H.C. Hamilton, et al. (eds), *Calendar of State Papers, Ireland, 1509–1670*, 24 vols (1860–1912).
Caulfield (ed.), *Cork*	Richard Caulfield (ed.), *Council book of the Corporation of Cork* (Guildford, 1876).
Caulfield (ed.), *Youghal*	Richard Caulfield (ed.), *Council book of the Corporation of Youghal* (Guildford, 1878).
Clarke, *Old English*	Aidan Clarke, *The Old English in Ireland, 1625–42* (London, 1966).
Cokayne, *Baronetage*	G.E. Cokayne (ed.), *Complete baronetage*, 6 vols (London, 1900–9).
Commons' Jn. Ire.	*Journals of the House of Commons of the kingdom of Ireland, 1613–1791*, 28 vols (Dublin, 1753–91).
CPRI	James Morrin (ed.), *Calendar of the patent and close rolls of chancery in Ireland, Henry VIII–Elizabeth*, 3 vols (Dublin, 1861–3).
Curtis Clayton (ed.), *Council book*	Margaret Curtis Clayton (ed.), *The council book for the province of Munster,* c.*1599–1649* (Dublin, 2008).
Dennehy, *Parliament*	Coleman A. Dennehy, *The Irish parliament, 1613–1689: the evolution of a colonial institution* (Manchester, 2019).
Deputy Keeper's Report	*The reports of the deputy keepers of the Public Records Office and keepers of the State Papers in Ireland*, 52 vols (Dublin, 1868–1921).

DIB	Dictionary of Irish biography
ed./eds	editor/editors
Edwards (ed.), 'Chichester'	R.D. Edwards (ed.), 'Letter book of Sir Arthur Chichester, 1612–14', *Anal. Hib.*, 8 (1938), 3–178.
EHR	*English Historical Review*
esp.	especially
Falkiner, *Essays*	Caesar Litton Falkiner, *Essays relating to Ireland: biographical, historical and topographical* (London, 1909).
fo./fos.	folio/folios
Foster, 'Painful labour'	Elizabeth Read Foster, 'The painful labour of Mr Elsyng', *Transactions of the American Philosophical Society*, new series, 62:8 (1972), 1–69.
FSL	The Folger Shakespeare Library, Washington DC.
G.E.C., *Peerage*	G.E. Cokayne and V. Gibbs (eds), *Complete peerage of England, Scotland, Ireland, Great Britain and the United Kingdom*, 13 vols (London, 1910–40).
Gilbert (ed.), *C.A.R.*	J.T. Gilbert (ed.), *Calendar of ancient records of Dublin*, 18 vols (Dublin, 1889–1922).
Grosart (ed.), *Lismore Papers*	Alexander B. Grosart (ed.), *The Lismore Papers*, 2 series, 10 vols (London, 1886–8).
Hakewill, *Modus*	William Hakewill, *Modus tenendi parliamentum or the old manner of holding parliaments in England* (London, 1671).
Hasler (ed.), *History of parliament*	P.W. Hasler (ed.), *The history of parliament: the House of Commons, 1558–1603*, 3 vols (London, 1981).
Hawkyard, *Commons*	Alasdair D. Hawkyard, *The House of Commons, 1509–1558: personnel, procedure, precedent and change* (Oxford, 2016).
HL, HP	Huntington Library, Hastings Papers
HMC	Historical Manuscripts Commission
HRC	The Harry Ransom Centre for the Humanities, Austin, Texas
Hughes, *Patentee Officers*	James L. Hughes, *Patentee officers in Ireland, 1173–1826* (Dublin, 1960).
IESH	*Irish Economic and Social History*
IG	*The Irish Genealogist*
IHS	*Irish Historical Studies*
IJ	*The Irish Jurist*
Inq. cancel. Hib. repert.	*Inquisitionum in officio rotulorum cancellariae Hiberniae asservatarum repertorium*, 2 vols (Dublin, 1826–9).
Jackson (ed.), 'Document'	Brian Jackson (ed.), 'A document on the parliament of 1613 from St Isidore's College, Rome', *Anal. Hib.*, 33 (1986), 47–58.

JCHAS	*The Journal of the Cork Historical and Archaeological Society*
JRSAI	*The Journal of the Royal Society of Antiquaries of Ireland*
JWSEIAS	*The Journal of the Waterford and South-East of Ireland Archaeological Society*
KCA	Kilkenny Corporation Archives
Knowler (ed.), *Letters and dispatches*	William Knowler (ed.), *The earl of Strafford's letters and dispatches*, 2 vols (London, 1739).
Liber Mun. Pub. Hib.	Rowley Lascelles, *Liber Munerum Publicorum Hiberniae*, Vol. 1 (London, 1824).
LJI	*Journals of the House of Lords of Ireland, 1634–1800*, 8 vols (Dublin, 1779–1800).
Lodge, *Desiderata Curiosa*	John Lodge, *Desiderata Curiosa Hibernia*, 2 vols (Dublin, 1732).
Lodge, *Peerage*	John Lodge, *The peerage of Ireland, revsd by M. Archdall*, 7 vols (Dublin, 1789).
LPL	Lambeth Palace Library
McGrath, 'Bio. dict.'	Bríd McGrath, 'A biographical dictionary of the membership of the Irish House of Commons, 1640–1641', 2 vols (PhD, University of Dublin, 1998).
McGrath, 'Electoral strategy'	Bríd McGrath, 'Thomas Wentworth's Irish electoral strategy', *PER*, 41:1 (March, 2021), 24–41.
McGrath, 'Membership'	Bríd McGrath, 'The membership of the Irish House of Commons, 1613–1615' (MLitt, University of Dublin, 1987).
McGrath (ed.), *Clonmel*	Bríd McGrath (ed.), *The minute book of the Corporation of Clonmel, 1608–1649* (Dublin, 2006).
McGrath (ed.), *Coleraine*	Bríd McGrath (ed.), *Acts of the Corporation of Coleraine, 1623–1669* (Dublin, 2017).
Merick, *Compendious collection*	John Merick, *Compendious collection and breefe abstract of all the auncient English statutes (from the beginning of Magna Charta) which now are in force within this kingdom of Ireland* (Dublin, 1617).
Misc.	Miscellaneous
Moynes (ed.), *Annual letters*	Vera Moynes (ed.), *Irish Jesuit annual letters, 1604–1674*, 2 vols (Dublin, 2019).
MS/MSS	Manuscript/Manuscripts
NAI	The National Archives of Ireland, Dublin
NAS	The National Archives of Scotland, Edinburgh
Neale, *House*	J.E. Neale, *The Elizabethan House of Commons* (2nd ed., London, 1976).
NLI	The National Library of Ireland, Dublin

NLI, GO	The National Library of Ireland, Dublin, Genealogical Office
Oxford DNB	Oxford dictionary of national biography
p./pp	page/pages
Parl. Hist.	*Parliamentary History*
PER	*Parliament, Estates and Representation*
Proc. RIA	*The Proceedings of the Royal Irish Academy*
PRONI	The Public Records Office of Northern Ireland, Belfast
RIA	The Royal Irish Academy, Dublin
Rot. Pac. Jac.	*Irish patent rolls of James I: facsimile of the Irish record commission's calendar prepared prior to 1830* (Dublin, 1966).
Routledge, 'Journal'	F.J. Routledge, 'Journal of the Irish House of Lords in Sir John Perrot's parliament (3 May 1585–13 May 1586)', *EHR*, 29:113 (Jan., 1914), 104–17.
Rushworth (ed.), *Tryal*	John Rushworth (ed.), *The tryal of Thomas, earl of Strafford* (2nd ed., London, 1700).
s.a.	*sub anno* (under the year)
Scobell, *Memorials*	Henry Scobell, *Memorials of the method and manner of proceedings in parliament, in passing bills* (London, 1670).
Smith, *Stuart*	David L. Smith, *The Stuart parliaments, 1603–1689* (London, 1999).
SP	State Papers
TCD	Trinity College Dublin
Thrush and Ferris (eds)	Andrew Thrush and John P. Ferris (eds), *The history of parliament: the House of Commons, 1604–1629*, 6 vols (Cambridge, 2010).
TNA	The National Archives of the United Kingdom, London
Trans. Kilkenny Arch. Soc.	*The Transactions of the Kilkenny Archaeological Society*
UCC	University College Cork
UCD	University College Dublin

Acknowledgments

THE AUTHOR OF ANY ACADEMIC BOOK incurs many debts and it is a pleasure to record my appreciation of and thanks to all those institutions and individuals who have helped me in this long and thoroughly enjoyable endeavour.

First, I wish to thank the following libraries for the research fellowships which enabled me to consult their valuable resources and made me so welcome as a research fellow: Archbishop Marsh's Library, Dr Edward Worth Library, Bodleian Library, University of Oxford, Centre Cultural Irlandais, Paris, Harry Ransom Center, University of Texas at Austin, Huntington Library, San Marino and the Moore Institute for Research in the Humanities and Social Studies, University of Galway.

No scholar can work without access to primary and secondary sources which are carefully collected, curated and made available by expert librarians and archivists. I am grateful to the staff of the following archives and libraries who allowed me to use their resources for this book and for their courtesy at all times: Archives National, Paris; Armagh Robinson Library; Bibliotheque National de France, Paris; Birr Castle; British Library; Cambridge University Library; Carlow County Library; Cork City and County Archives; Folger Shakespeare Library, Washington DC; Gilbert Library, Dublin City Council; Inner Temple Library; Kilkenny City Archives; King's Inns; Lincolnshire Record Office; The Morgan Library and Museum, New York; Library of Congress, Washington DC; National Archives of Ireland; National Library of Ireland; Nottingham Record Office; Royal Irish Academy; Trinity College Dublin and University College Cork. Special thanks to the Earl and Countess of Rosse for their warm welcome and interest in my use of their manuscripts; to Konstantin Ermolin, Sophie Evans and Siobhán FitzPatrick in the Royal Irish Academy Library; Jason McElligott; the late Muriel McCarthy and their colleagues in Archbishop Marsh's Library; Elizabethanne Boran in the Dr Edward Worth Library and Aisling Lockhart in the Manuscripts Reading Room in Trinity College Dublin.

Special thanks also to those who provided images for this volume, and retained their copyright, including Ballyfin Demesne, Hunt Museum, King's Inns, Lydiard House Museum, Swindon, Marsh's Library, National Library of Ireland, National Gallery of Ireland, National Trust, Shannon Heritage, Ulster Museum, Valence House Museum and the owners of portraits in private collections. I am grateful to my colleagues in the Department of History, Trinity College Dublin, for their friendships and great support.

I am grateful to the following colleagues for useful discussions and references, answering obscure queries, helpful comments on drafts of chapters, translating quotations in languages with which I am not familiar and other kindnesses: David Brown, Josep Capdeferro, Aidan Clarke, Peter Crooks, Coleman Dennehy, Scott

Duvall, Brigham Young University, David Edwards, Mark Empey, Gerard Farrell, Stephen Hand, Jason Harris, Joel Herman, Paul Hunneyball, Neil Johnston, Ruth M. Karras, Allan Kennedy, Colum Kenny, Stuart Kinsella, Hannes Kleineke, Simon Lewis, Patrick Little, John McCafferty, Alastair Mann, Annaleigh Margey, Alan Marshall, James McGuire, Hiram Morgan, Rachel Moss, Elaine Murphy, Tadhg Ó hAnnracháin, Michelle O'Riordan, Micheál Ó Siochrú, Stephen Roberts, Paul Smith, Clodagh Tait, Ricard Torra-Prat, Jacqueline van den Bergh, Ciarán Wallace, Mike Webb, Bodleian Library and John Young.

For encouragement and in many cases hospitality on my research trips I am grateful to Jane Alden, Julia Barrett, the late and much missed Charles Benson, Meg Bent, Danielle Byrne, Daniel Carey, David Ditchburn, Adrian Empey, Tim Harris, Brendan Kane, Linda Kiernan Knowles, Pádraig Lenihan, Gráinne McLaughlin, William Molesworth, John Morrill, Ortrun Peyn, Gerit Quealy, Paul Seaward, Joe Woods and my cousin Henry Casey.

I have been very fortunate in having publishers in both the Irish Legal History Society and Four Courts Press, Robert Marshall and Martin Fanning, who were at every stage encouraging, patient and interested. I am equally grateful for James McGuire's very careful reading of the drafts, his suggestions which added to the precision of the book and saved me from many errors, and for his advice, encouragement and courtesy over so many years.

Special thanks to David Heffernan who put smacht on my footnotes, carefully checked and formatted the text, compiled the index and saved me from many other errors; I am of course responsible for any which remain. I am also grateful to the Trinity Trust for a grant to support the copy-editing of this book.

Heartfelt thanks also to the wonderful Roberta Fleming, whose regular food-drops and support allowed me to finish this book. Her price is above rubies.

My greatest debt is to my supervisor, collaborator, mentor and dear friend, the late Aidan Clarke, who taught me to be a historian, was always ready for a chat, a long, detailed discussion on any and every aspect of early modern Ireland, a pint and hilarious stories. Laoch a bhí ann, agus ní bhéidh a leithéid arís ann.

My husband Simon and our wonderful children Oisín and Sibéal insisted on a history-free family life, which kept me grounded and constantly reminded me that there are some things more important than history (although fewer than they think). Finally, my uncles James and Frank Casey and Paddy McNamee took a huge interest and pride in my scholarly work and gave me unstinting encouragement, love and support. The dedication is a small recognition of their part in my life.

Introduction

THE STORY OF PARLIAMENTS is the history of the relationship between the state and its people and the balance between their interests and rights. Parliaments are social, economic, political, legal and cultural bodies, representative of and answerable to their communities and their business affects every area of life. Parliament's existence implies a polity – a recognized state, political community and civil government – clear functions and powers, a means of summoning and ending them and selecting their membership, a culture of representation, including public acceptance of their role and authority and the extent to which their conclusions were binding on their communities, and a means of recording, communicating and implementing their decisions. As the polity changes, so does the community, the way in which parliament works and the meaning of representation. When the community is strong and cohesive, parliament tends to be representative, respected, valued and effective; when it is weak and divided, so is parliament and tensions in the wider political community find expression there.

Representative assemblies were important institutions in European political life through the medieval and early modern periods. Their role was established in the Middle Ages as 'a single institution which united representatives from across the country to negotiate with the monarch over taxation, to submit their common grievances to the royal government, and to petition the king's officers to legislate binding solutions to their problems.'[1] By the early modern period, European assemblies, whether called parliaments, estates, diets, Cortes, Sjem, tag or other names, were 'occasions when, for a variety of reasons, rulers met with representatives of [local] power groups, who in turn represented a wide range of social, political, sectional and local interests', including economic, military and religious, among other stakeholders.[2] Many countries also had local or provincial estates with an important role in their communities.

These assemblies had different forms, memberships, powers and functions and frequency of meetings, arising from their medieval origins. Some were unicameral, others bi-cameral; some, like the French Estates General and Castilian Corts, included only urban representatives, excluding the rural population. Many assemblies had representatives whose decisions bound their communities, while others, like the Dutch estates, sent delegates with no power to make agreements without referring back to their communities. The English and Irish parliaments were revenue-raising legislatures with consultative and judicial functions; the Scottish Estates had consultative, legislative and financial functions, but no judicial role. The Dutch estates did not legislate, nor did the French Estates General,

1 Christopher Fletcher, 'Political representation' in Christopher Fletcher, et al. (eds), *Government and political life in England and France, c.1300–c.1500* (Cambridge, 2015), pp 217–39.
2 Michael Graves, *The parliaments of early modern Europe* (Harlow, 2001), p. 2.

which was a consultative and revenue-raising body, with no legislative or judicial role. The Polish Sejm was perhaps the most representative and also elected the monarch.[3] Both the English and French bodies had a role in debating succession to the throne in the sixteenth century and the 1613 Irish parliament's first statute recognized King James VI and I's accession to the Irish throne, as provided for in the 1541 Act of Kingly Title. The frequency of meetings was also variable, depending on the country and its politics; some assembled often, others rarely.[4]

State-building was the paramount political project in early modern Europe and this affected the relationship between the crown and its peoples and between the centre and locality. These relationships had to be carefully handled, especially in composite monarchies whose constituent nations had different laws, political structures, languages and cultures. The Tudors needed to find a balance between the powers of central government and local requirements and traditions in England, Wales and Ireland, incorporating Wales into the English state and creating a kingdom of Ireland; the Stuarts had to negotiate additional changes when James VI inherited the English and Irish thrones and the Scottish political axis moved from Edinburgh. With the 1541 Act of Kingly Title, and especially after the union of the crowns in 1603, Ireland's position as one of three kingdoms under the same monarch, each with its own distinct representative assemblies, body of laws and operations, was not unique. The Hispanic monarchy had to manage Castile, Aragon, Catalonia and Valencia, each of whose Corts had different structures, membership, powers, languages, traditions and operations. Monarchs of single states did not escape the dilemma of reconciling local and central relationships; the increasingly centralizing French state had to respect and accommodate local laws, structures and traditions, including the regional Coutume (customary law) and provincial estates, as well as the national Estates General. As European states expanded into other continents, representative bodies developed there too, although they were not national bodies, any more than the provincial estates in France or the Netherlands.

Parliaments were and are evolving organizations with a long history, but the early modern period was when they acquired the forms, membership and powers they retained through the eighteenth century. The political, military and economic situation and climate change that produced the Little Ice Age in early modern Europe have been described as the 'general crisis of the seventeenth century' and they set the context for politics everywhere.[5] Most European representative assemblies lost out to crown control in the seventeenth century; the English parliament and Polish Sejm were exceptions and they ended the period with enhanced roles and powers albeit through different traditions and membership.[6]

3 Graves, *Parliaments*, pp 100–3.

4 For the impact of varying origins and frequency of meetings, see Deborah Boucoyannis, *Kings as judges: power, justice and the origins of parliament* (Cambridge, 2021).

5 Eric Hobsbawm, 'The general crisis of the European economy in the 17th century', *Past & Present*, 5 (May, 1954), 33–53; Geoffrey Parker, *Global crisis: war, climate change and catastrophe in the seventeenth century* (New Haven, 2013).

The opposite was true in Ireland, where parliament became ostensibly more national and representative, but in fact resumed its medieval role as an assembly operating in the narrow interests of a small colonial elite of a different ethnic origin to the majority population and also practicing a different religion. Ireland's closest equivalent is Catalonia whose royally-appointed administration was increasingly managed by Castilians and its 'Kingless Corts' were the counterpart of the Confederation of Kilkenny's General Assembly.[7]

Early modern states faced a combination of distinct but interrelated trends that provoked tension between rulers and their subjects and eventually played out in parliaments reluctantly summoned to resolve pressing difficulties, but rarely given the opportunity to be effective. The 1614 Estates General was called during a power struggle between the regent, Queen Marie de Medici, and a group of French nobles who believed that their claims to political rights and privileges during the monarch's minority would be recognized by the Estates. They were not called to effect change, but to provide window-dressing to outflank Henri, Prince of Condé, and were unable to achieve any effective results, owing to the difficulties inherent in their structure, composition and powers, exacerbated by rivalry between the various estates. Its lack of a role in ensuring the resolution of grievances demonstrated its powerlessness; it had no genuine bargaining power and despite the hard work of its deputies, was doomed to ineffectiveness.[8] Lord Deputy Thomas Wentworth summoned the Irish parliament as an instrument of state, not as a possible partner in government.[9]

The centrality of the monarchy, the importance of religion in public and private lives and the role of representative assemblies as institutions of state remained constant, but were affected by changes in society as they sought to negotiate solutions to the pressures these developments created. The root of much of the difficulty was rulers' need for money to support the administration of increasingly centralized states, especially in composite monarchies, monarchs' lavish lifestyles and generosity to favourites and religious tensions. In many countries, these changes were accompanied by population pressure, with rising prosperous middle classes seeking a role in society; much of the financial burden of the expanding state fell on them, provoking resistance and defiance. These pressures and the greater numbers of these middle-class MPs led to the development of parliament's role, growing co-operation between parliaments in composite monarchies and the sacralization of parliamentary procedures, treating them as sacrosanct as a defence-

6 Robert Frost, 'The roads not taken: liberty, sovereignty and the idea of the republic in Poland–Lithuania and the British Isles, 1550–1660', *Transactions of the Royal Historical Society*, 32 (2022), 93–112.

7 Graves, *Parliaments*, pp 91–4.

8 J.M. Hayden, *France and the Estates General of 1614* (Cambridge, 1974), pp 214–18; Roger Chartier, 'La convocation aux Etats de 1614, note sur les formes politiques' in Roger Chartier and Denis Ricet (eds), *Representation & vouloir politiques autour des Etats-Generaux de 1614* (Paris, 1982), pp 53–61.

9 Terry Clavin, 'Wentworth, Sir Thomas', *DIB*.

mechanism against a state that sought to control parliament. Ireland proved the exception to these trends, although it experienced their effects, most notably as a country that received many immigrants whose interests were privileged by the state over the native elites and by stark religious differences.

Demands for money strained relations between monarchs and their subjects – 'a need for money this intense was liable to take priority over all other needs and therefore to be pursued in a potentially arbitrary spirit.'[10] Parliamentary taxes supplied only a small proportion of early modern European states' finance and assemblies that met rarely could provide even less. As only parliament could grant subsidies, monarchs sought extra-parliamentary sources of finance, including granting monopolies on commodities and fines, which, added to the burden of heavy taxation, created resentment and financial difficulties at local level. In Ireland and Scotland, parliamentary taxation became more important, although still inadequate for the state's needs.[11] Citizens accepted the need to support the state financially but resented the continuous demands for money, the means by which it was raised inside and outside parliament and the uses to which it was put; they also expected some concessions in return. Persistent demands for money to pay for wars was just one 'of a wide and varying combination of financial and economic, political, religious and social problems which impacted on the fortunes and fate of parliaments in the early and mid-seventeenth century.'[12] Infrequent meetings prevented them from playing a role in redressing grievances, which multiplied outside their sittings, creating a well of apprehension and resentment before sessions at which substantial taxes would be demanded.

Monarchs regarded the defence of the realm as the highest priority, whereas estates were concerned about those they represented, their historic rights and liberties and constitutions and their economic, social, legal and political rights. Traditional military obligations, frequently 40 days' service annually (but in Catalonia as in Ireland, only when the king or his deputy was present), had not kept pace with the significant developments in military technology, which led to more frequent and longer wars, requiring standing armies and navies with dramatically increased permanent costs on the crown, including ships, soldiers' wages and standard equipment previously provided by individuals. These additional recurring costs outpaced traditional systems for raising money and produced demands for greater financial support within and outside parliaments with consequent resistance from taxpayers. The strains across the 1624–6 English parliament, Catalan Corts and Sardinian parliament were all due in at least some part to the need to finance wars. As Geoffrey Parker notes, 'considerations of national security, as usual, overrode taxpayers' protests', but more critically,

10 Conrad Russell, *Unrevolutionary England, 1603–1642* (London, 1990), p. 124.

11 Julian Goodare, 'Parliamentary taxation in Scotland, 1560–1603', *Scottish Historical Review*, 68:185 (April, 1989), 23–52; J.H. Elliott, *The revolt of the Catalans: a study in the decline of Spain* (Cambridge, 1984), pp 215ff.

12 Graves, *Parliaments*, p. 127.

parliamentarians in all countries could not comprehend the amounts needed, and as Conrad Russell commented, 'even where they recognized the royal needs [parliamentarians] tended to think that these needs did not override the liberties and privileges of their own communities' (or of parliament).[13] Coleman Dennehy notes 'the need to finance war is one factor, if not the single primary factor, explaining the growth of parliaments in medieval and early modern Ireland – as it is for virtually all other states of the time', but although the crown desperately needed financial support, Irish Tudor subsidies were of very limited value. While their value rose substantially under Lord Deputy Arthur Chichester and especially Wentworth, only the latter's second parliament was summoned to raise money for a war, and that conflict was not in Ireland.[14] As Dennehy notes, that logic suggests that the wars in Ireland in the 1640s would have enhanced parliament's role and operations, especially given the part it played in Wentworth's downfall, but in fact the reverse was true. Given the power struggles between crowns and representative assemblies, the leverage parliamentarians could exert during emergencies and monarchs' determination to yield as little as possible, only states whose rulers and assemblies were able to co-operate were likely to prosper to their mutual advantage.

Monarchs and estates were not natural adversaries – most people saw strength in the co-operation and unity of the king and community, within and outside estates. Assemblies did not seek to increase their own power at royal expense but tried to avoid making commitments that were inconsistent with their own priorities. Difficulties turned into crises when the normal systems failed to resolve problems and rulers refused to consult the community about the grievances to be redressed. However, monarchs frequently regarded representative assemblies with aversion – the Spanish King Philip IV's description of them as 'pernicious at all times and in all monarchies' expressed a commonly held view – and they were often not summoned as partners in resolving difficulties, or if called, many were ill-equipped to contribute if their powers were limited, where they were unable to work together or where governments tried to control and manipulate them.[15] In the 1576 Estates at Blois, the prominent Huguenot Philippe de Mornay appealed for unity and tolerance:

> Considerons donc que nous sommes tous hommes, tous Chrestiens, tous Francois, tous amateurs de nous mesmes, de l'Eglise, de la Patrie, croians en un Dieu, confessans un Christ, desirans une reformation en cet Estat …

13 Geoffrey Parker, *The military revolution: military innovation and the rise of the west, 1500–1800* (Cambridge, 1988), pp 12, 45–81, esp. pp 61ff; Russell, *Unrevolutionary England*, p. 128.

14 Coleman A. Dennehy, 'The Irish parliament after the rebellion, 1642–48' in Patrick Little (ed.), *Ireland in crisis: war, politics and religion, 1641–50* (Manchester, 2019), pp 100–18. For more on the subject of financing military campaigns, see chapter eight of the present volume. Raymond Gillespie, 'Chichester, Arthur', *DIB*.

15 Conard Russell. 'Monarchies, wars, and estates in England, France, and Spain, *c.*1580–*c.*1640', *Legislative Studies Quarterly*, 7:2 (1982), 205–20; Graves, *Parliaments*, pp 115–55 (quotation on p. 122).

> L'Estat est compose de deux Religions. Si on ne les permet toutes deux libres, il nous faut r'entrer en la guerre … Nous avons tous, long temps a, souhaité les Estat pour le r'establissement de ce Royaume.

He also appealed to 'gentils-hommes, ecclesiastiques, marchands, laboureurs' to join together to protect the peace.[16] His words had a prophetic ring, as events in Europe, including Ireland, were to show.

Key points of tension in the three Stuart kingdoms included money, religion, social advancement, access to or exclusion from power or influence, autocratic government by the monarch or his local governors or administrators, over-taxation and the enrichment of individuals at the expense of the wider community. Impositions and grievances took different forms in each kingdom. In England they took the shape of ship money, forced loans and distraint of knighthood, among others and in Scotland levies for building the parliament house and King Charles I's 1633 coronation. Ireland experienced unfair billeting of soldiers and cess (military tax), extortionate fees from officials and churchmen, confiscation of land through plantations, depredations of the Court of Wards and exploitation of insecure land titles despite repeated payments to guarantee the same titles failing to secure them. In addition, under Wentworth they also faced monopolies, punitive and unfairly assessed subsidies, arbitrary government with extrajudicial judgments, all exacerbated by religious and ethnic tensions. In all three kingdoms, religious tensions exacerbated all the other grievances, with serious consequences for the monarch and citizens.

It was natural for parliaments, the accepted forums for consultation between monarchs and their subjects, to be summoned during crises, as states sought their citizens' consent to solutions to national difficulties, including financial support. In a sense, every early modern parliament met at a time of some crisis or at least tension between the state and its citizens and their summoning inspired optimism, apprehension and caution as to their likely outcome and fuelled vigorous competition for seats. The earl of Cork, Richard Boyle's response to the English Short Parliament's dissolution encapsulates public faith in assemblies' potential to resolve tensions and disappointment when they did not do so – 'This doleful Tuesdaie, the parlament was dissolved before any act was paste, to my great greefe of heart, as also the deep sorrow of many good subiects.'[17]

16 'Let us consider that we are all men, all Christians, all Frenchmen, all lovers of ourselves, our church, our country, believing in one God, confessing one Christ, desiring a reformation in this state … The state is composed of two religions. If we do not allow both to be free, we will have to return to war … We have all hoped that the state would re-establish the realm', appealing to 'gentlemen, churchmen, merchants, labourers.': Phillipe de Mornay, *Memoires de Messire Phillippes de Mornay* (s.l., 1624), pp 57–8.

17 Entry for 5 May 1640, Grosart (ed.), *Lismore Papers*, v, p. 136. For a similar expectation that the Scottish Estates would 'setle this distracted Natione and pute ane End [to] all our greiffes and feares', see John R. Young, *The Scottish parliament, 1639–1661: a political and constitutional analysis* (Edinburgh, 1996), p. 1.

It was the monarch's role to summon parliament, but some refused to do so, or only after other options had failed, and they prorogued or dissolved those that proved recalcitrant. This accumulated more numerous and deeper grievances, making possible solutions more drastic and engendering mistrust between the crown and its subjects in future parliaments. It was anticipated, for example, that the Estates General in France would be called, especially on the occasion of the king's majority, but it was not summoned (although suggested) during the Fronde between 1648 and 1653. Other countries managed differently: from 1477 the Dutch estates could summon itself and in 1571 Brabant's provincial states met in emergency session in Brussels and levied troops on their own authority for protection. They also summoned the estates of the other provinces to join them and the States General opened peace talks at Ghent.[18] In the absence of an effective monarch, or a breakdown in relations, the question of who had authority to call a parliament was a fraught one but assemblies not convened by monarchs appeared in many early modern states during this period, although this naturally raised questions about their legitimacy and powers. The English Lord Treasurer, William Cecil, Lord Burghley's 'Bill for the Queen's safety' of 1584 planned to recall the last parliament in the event of Queen Elizabeth I's death to decide on the succession and the Duc de Mayenne, Charles of Lorraine of the powerful House of Guise, summoned the Estates General during the interregnum in 1593. The Polish–Lithuanian Sejm managed affairs during interregnums.[19]

When divisions between monarchs and assemblies were too deep to be resolved, subjects gained control of parliaments while continuing to seek agreement with the ruler, or established counter states with representative assemblies while 'rump' parliaments continued to sit. As crises occurred at times of hardship, when monarchs and subjects were already under pressure to maintain or at least resist measures that would worsen their positions, reaching agreement was more difficult and divisions between monarchs and their administrations and parliament were frequently exacerbated, not lessened, by crises, as rulers sought support while granting as little as possible in return and parliamentarians used their powers to defend their positions. The stage was set for confrontation and what could have been points of contact and cooperation became occasions of enduring and increasingly entrenched conflict within and between states. Resolving tensions was especially difficult in composite kingdoms where the centre of power, geography and cultural distance limited the possibility of negotiating directly with the monarch and where national assemblies had different powers, structures, memberships and priorities. The Castilian Corts became increasingly important to the Hispanic monarchy, but this placed strains between its members and the cities they represented, until they received *plena potestas* in 1632, but it also led to problems in managing the other national assemblies. One assembly's

18 Geoffrey Parker, *Spain and the Netherlands, 1559–1659: ten studies* (London, 1979), p. 118.
19 Smith, *Stuart*, pp 9–10; H[enrico] C[aterino] Davila, *The historie of the civill warres of France* (London, 1647), pp 1187, 1191; Frost, 'The roads not taken'.

response to royal demands could strengthen or weaken the bargaining power of the others; the Catalan political community closely observed proceedings in the 1626 Aragonese and Castilian Corts and in Valencia. Wentworth engineered the Irish parliament's compliance in March 1640 as an example to the Short Parliament in England, although this strategy was unsuccessful and the assemblies in all three Stuart kingdoms co-operated to protect their communities against the crown's overreach of its powers against its subjects.

The increasing tendency towards centralizing power favoured the models of the dominant central kingdom. Ireland's experience was similar to other peripheral states within composite monarchies, attempting to maintain its independence and relevance in a transformed political environment where priority was always given to the central kingdom, England, which also generally contributed most to the state's coffers and whose political and cultural norms were assumed to be applicable to Ireland and to a lesser extent Scotland. England and Ireland's political community had no representation outside parliaments but the disputants in Catalonia and syndic of Agen (local estates in southwest France) had the right to speak between Corts/Estates. Continental estates had committees which remained in office during recesses and many, like the Irish parliament, had control of collection of taxes.[20] Revolts in Scotland, Ireland, Catalonia and Portugal within two short years in 1638–40 demonstrate the excessive pressure put on outlying regions which had already suffered penal taxation and other financial demands over the previous decade.

Monarchs tried to control assemblies through their electoral strategies, selection of speakers and location, but they were not always successful, as the attempt to move the Catalan Corts to Lleida in western Catalonia in 1626 demonstrated.[21] Marie de Medici made strenuous, successful attempts to influence the elections to the 1614 Estates General, concentrating on areas where her opponents were strongest, e.g., Condé, and where Huguenots were most numerous; a majority of crown officials was returned, including Lieutenants General, the most important local officials in France; Roger Chartier notes that 'elire n'implique ici ni libre vote ni loi de majorité' (election does not imply either a free vote or a majority).[22]

Assemblies that had been summoned initially for short sessions, including the 1640 Irish parliament and the English Long Parliament continued to sit and the dynamic of their work and processes altered in response to increasing divisions, using their powers to the full and instigating new practices and mechanisms to fulfil their representative, legislative, judicial and financial functions.[23] Some, like the Scottish Estates and the Catalan Corts, sat in defiance

20 Graves, *Parliaments*, pp 115–55.
21 Elliott, *Revolt of the Catalans*, pp 215–16.
22 In France, most estates were provincial (estates particular), not national. Chartier, 'La convocation aux Etats de 1614'; Elliott, *Revolt of the Catalans*, pp 215–16.
23 Bodl. Lib., Bankes MS 55/65, Commission 27 January 1640, provided that parliament should sit for nine months only; in the event it sat for eight years.

of royal orders. The English and Scottish parliaments' perceptions of themselves and their role within the state in the 1640s and 1650s changed significantly and they acted with increasing autonomy, especially when laws requiring triennial parliaments were passed in those kingdoms, an option not open to their Irish counterpart.

The Irish parliament existed from at least 1264, but until the mid-sixteenth century it sought to represent and serve only the colonial Lordship of Ireland.[24] While the Lordship initially covered much of Ireland, by the fifteenth century it had shrunk to the 'four loyal shires' of the Pale (Dublin, Kildare, Louth and Meath) and a number of important largely coastal towns.[25] The Irish parliament's transformation began in 1494 when the assembly summoned under Lord Deputy Edward Poynings passed acts that incorporated all current English statute law into Irish legislation.[26]

As crown control expanded again in the sixteenth and early seventeenth centuries, the Irish state, political community and nature of representation again changed. The century between the 1541 Act of Kingly Title (33 Hen. VIII, c. 1), which created the kingdom of Ireland, and the outbreak of the 1641 rebellion saw parliament's transformation into a national body with very different membership, operations and traditions. This radically altered its relationship with the crown and local communities. Brendan Bradshaw claimed for the 1541 parliament the distinction of first meriting the description 'national' and he traces the development of a sense of national identity to the Old English who proposed the Act of Kingly Title and went out of their way to welcome the Gaelic Irish and sought to assimilate them into the new kingdom. However, this policy rapidly changed to coercion and parliament became a point of conflict between the crown and the political community, rather than a point of contact.[27]

The 1613 parliament was the first with a genuinely national membership, if not a truly representative one. The subsequent assemblies included increasing numbers of New English members supporting the administration, with a shrinking Catholic membership drawn from the native, largely Catholic, political community. Between 1642 and 1648 parliament reverted again to a body which represented only a small element of Ireland's population, again a beleaguered largely colonial institution of largely different ethnic composition to the rest of the country and

24 For a discussion on the evolving constitutional and political thinking of the Lordship, see Peter Crooks, 'The structure of politics in theory and practice, 1210–1541' in Brendan Smith (ed.), *The Cambridge history of Ireland*, vol. 1, *600–1550* (Cambridge, 2018), pp 441–68.

25 Steven G. Ellis, 'Citizenship and the state in Ireland: from medieval Lordship to early modern kingdom' in Steven G. Ellis (ed.), *Enfranchising Ireland? Identity, citizenship and state* (Dublin, 2018), pp 19–32; Coleman A. Dennehy, 'Representation in later medieval and early modern Ireland' in Mario Damen, et al. (eds), *Political representation: communities, ideas and institutions (c.1200–c.1690)* (Leiden, 2018), pp 85–105 provides a useful summary of this process.

26 Aidan Clarke, 'The history of Poynings' Law, 1615–41', *Irish Historical Studies*, 18:70 (1972), 207–22.

27 Brendan Bradshaw, *The Irish constitutional revolution of the sixteenth century* (Cambridge, 1979), p. 240; *idem*, 'The beginnings of modern Ireland' in Brian Farrell (ed.), *The Irish parliamentary tradition* (Dublin, 1973), pp 68–87.

an almost entirely Protestant body.[28] The 1654 Cromwellian settlement's transformation of Ireland's ethnic, social, religious, economic and political landscape was not reversed at the Restoration and the post-1660 Irish parliament was indisputably a national body, but for a very different nation to that of 1613 or 1641; it was an almost entirely Protestant body with a much more limited representational nature, governing in the interests of Protestant Ireland rather than the country as a whole, despite the fact that a majority of the Irish population adhered to the Catholic religion. Only the Catholic peers in the upper house continued to provide religious diversity after 1661, but the absence of their co-religionists in the Commons limited their effectiveness.[29]

Early modern Ireland was transformed through an aggressive programme of Anglicization and colonization and its parliament's history reflects these wider political, social, economic and demographic changes. For the first time, parliament represented the entire country and its inhabitants; Gaelic chieftains accepted the monarchy and English norms of representation and central and local government structures and systems. Parliament's operations were increasingly brought into line with English practice, superseding Irish customs and traditions. However, while its membership and procedures changed and its proceedings reflected the policies, priorities and characters of successive lords deputy, parliament continued to challenge the crown's view of Ireland as a subordinate polity and strove to protect its role in representing its communities, with varying levels of success.

This book deals with the Irish House of Commons' composition, membership, transformation, powers and operations between 1613 and 1648; it concerns itself with politics or the House of Lords only as they affected the Commons' development and work. Historians' choice of starting and ending points are frequently somewhat arbitrary, but not in this case. James' only parliament met between 1613 and 1615; Charles I's parliaments sat from 1634 to 1635, and 1640 to 1648; another parliament summoned for 1628 was aborted because of procedural errors.

The Irish state, political community and parliament experienced enormous changes from the first known Irish parliament in 1264 until the 1800 Act of Union, but Ireland's transformation under the Tudors and early Stuarts established the state's form, the character and extent of its political community and parliament's representative nature, powers and operations until its demise at the end of the eighteenth century. Despite their infrequency and sitting for possibly only 424 days over 35 years, the early Stuart parliament's decisions about its membership, operations, culture and powers and the profound changes the crown enforced in Ireland's constitution, character and society endured for the following century-and-a-half.[30]

28 Bríd McGrath, 'The recruiter returns to the Irish parliament, 1642–1648' in Little (ed.), *Ireland in crisis*, pp 119–37.

29 Jane Ohlmeyer, *Making Ireland English: the Irish aristocracy in the seventeenth century* (London, 2012), pp 136, 337–41, 608–13.

30 Bradshaw, *Irish constitutional revolution*, p. 240; Dennehy, *Parliament*, p. 94. Gaps in the records, especially between 1642 and 1648, make an accurate tally impossible.

The study of parliaments, especially in the early Stuart period, has engaged Irish scholars much less than their colleagues in other countries and the exceptional level of research on early modern English parliaments has not been replicated for Ireland. H.G. Richardson and G.O. Sayles, Art Cosgrove and Philomena Connolly's extraordinary work on medieval parliaments, followed by Steven Ellis for the fifteenth century and Victor Treadwell, David B. Quinn and Brendan Bradshaw's research on individual Tudor parliaments, have transformed our understanding of those assemblies, but the early Stuart Irish parliament has been little studied, apart from Michael Perceval-Maxwell's *The outbreak of the Irish rebellion of 1641*, Coleman Dennehy's research on representation and parliament's records, officers and institutional development and this author's work on membership and elections.[31]

Scholars, such as Bradshaw, Ciaran Brady, Nicholas Canny, Aidan Clarke, David Edwards, Brendan Kane, Michael MacCarthy-Morrogh, Micheál Ó Siochrú, Quinn and Treadwell, among many others, have changed our understanding of early modern Ireland's transformation in every aspect of its culture, economy, government, politics and religion by painstaking attention to primary sources, but most have paid little attention to parliament and many important works of scholarship largely ignore the institution, although Ireland's transformation could not have been effected without it. Canny, in both *The Elizabethan conquest of Ireland: a pattern established, 1565–1576* and *Making Ireland British*, and Brady's *The chief governors: the rise and fall of reform government in Tudor Ireland* barely mention parliament.[32]

Much of the work done on medieval and early modern Irish parliaments, apart from Cosgrove, Ellis and Dennehy's studies, has paid little attention to the process of political participation and MPs' connections with their communities.[33] While

31 H.G. Richardson, 'The Irish parliament rolls of the fifteenth century', *EHR*, 58:232 (Oct., 1943); H.G. Richardson and G.O. Sayles, *The Irish parliament in the Middle Ages* (London, 1952); Art Cosgrove, 'Parliament and the Anglo-Irish community: the declaration of 1460' in Art Cosgrove and J.I. McGuire (eds), *Historical Studies XIV: parliament and community* (Belfast, 1983), pp 25–41; Philomena Connolly (ed.), *Statute rolls of the Irish parliament, Richard III–Henry VIII* (Dublin, 2002); Bradshaw, 'Beginnings'; Victor Treadwell, 'The Irish parliament of 1569–71', *Proc. RIA*, 65C (1966–7), 55–89; *idem*, 'Sir John Perrott and the Irish parliament of 1585–6', *Proc. RIA*, 85C (1985), 259–308; Brendan Bradshaw, 'The opposition to the ecclesiastical legislation in the Irish reformation parliament', *IHS*, 16:63 (March, 1969), 285–303; David B. Quinn, 'Government printing and the publication of the Irish statutes in the sixteenth century', *Proc. RIA*, 49C (1943–4), 45–129; *idem*, 'The bills and statutes of the Irish parliaments of Henry VII and Henry VIII', *Anal. Hib.*, 10 (July, 1641), 71–169; *idem*, 'The Irish parliamentary subsidy in the fifteenth and sixteenth centuries', *Proc. RIA*, 42C (1934–5), 219–46. Please see the bibliography for McGrath's work on parliaments. For the absence of scholarship on early Stuart Irish parliaments, see Dennehy, *Parliament*, pp 1–5.

32 Ciaran Brady, *The chief governors: the rise and fall of reform government in Tudor Ireland, 1536–1588* (Cambridge, 1994), although he does mention Nicholas Walsh's speech in parliament 1586 (p. 212). Nicholas Canny, *The Elizabethan conquest of Ireland: a pattern established, 1565–1576* (Hassocks, 1976); *idem*, *Making Ireland British, 1580–1650* (Oxford, 2001), pp 268–9, 275, 280, 292, 297, 405–10, 566.

33 Cosgrove, 'Parliament and the Anglo-Irish community'.

invaluable studies of individual Tudor parliaments explored their politics and the minutiae of MPs' political participation, no specific study has been done on parliaments' role in Anglicizing Ireland, the dominant political project of that period. This book aims to fill that gap by examining parliament's membership and operations in the context of the Irish political community and how MPs' work affected those it was intended to represent, and to replicate for Irish parliaments the work done by Alastair Hawkyard and John Neale on English Tudor parliaments and by David Smith on the Stuart ones, discussing its structure, membership, operations and development, its relations with its communities and its role in Anglicizing Ireland.[34] The process of transformation was completed by the end of the seventeenth century, but the foundations were laid under the Tudors and early Stuarts and every institution of state played a part; the experience of Tudor parliaments framed attitudes to that institution and to elections in the early Stuart period.

Bradshaw's seminal *Irish constitutional revolution of the sixteenth century* considers parliament within the context of the transformation of the colony into a kingdom and the priorities of the English government. He described the movement that grew in Ireland among a 'reforming milieu of experienced observers among the leading officials' and the patrician class of Irish towns. This movement, based on humanist scholarship, proposed a commonwealth model, sought the assimilation of the native Irish through the extension of the English common-law, land-holding models and national and local government systems, but after a strong initial attempt the crown failed to build on this model.[35] Perceval-Maxwell's study of the work of the 1640–41 parliament shows it reasserting its power to fulfil its legislative, judicial and representative roles and striving to redress individual and collective grievances through an improbable temporary coalition of Old English and Gaelic members with disaffected New English settlers. However, the latter failed to sustain the alliance once the immediate aim of overthrowing Lord Deputy Wentworth was achieved, in co-operation with the English parliament.[36]

Despite the strict constitutional position of two ostensibly equal kingdoms under the same monarch, the crown's role in certifying any legislation to be introduced into the Irish parliament and the English courts' willingness to exercise jurisdiction in Irish cases were *de facto* limitations on Ireland's position as a sovereign polity. The Irish parliament's subordination to England through Poynings' Law meant that it did not have the same status as the English assembly and as Ireland was increasingly governed by English Protestant crown servants rather than men of Irish origin, who were largely Catholic, tensions inevitably developed between the native political community and the crown.

34 Hawkyard, *Commons*; Neale, *House*.
35 Jon G. Crawford, *Anglicizing the government of Ireland: the Irish privy council and the expansion of Tudor rule, 1556–1578* (Dublin, 1993), pp 24–5.
36 Michael Perceval-Maxwell, *The outbreak of the Irish rebellion of 1641* (Dublin, 1994).

Parliament became the civic forum in which this disharmony most obviously played out.[37]

It is a truism that the Tudor and Stuart state-building programme intended to establish an Anglicized Ireland, with similar (Protestant) religious, and economic, legal and judicial and land-holding systems, social structures, geographical boundaries and linguistic and cultural attributes on both islands; parliament had a critical role to play in this transformation but while initial efforts were successful, the replacement of the policy of assimilation by coercion fatally undermined this programme and the growing number of English settlers whose interests were privileged over the rights of the native community subverted the process. Given the increasing Anglicization of the administration in which Englishmen with no long-term interest in or sympathy for Ireland replaced the traditional Old English community as crown officials, the stage was set for conflict.[38] The Palesmen's support for advancing administrative reform and extending crown control over the entire island was moderated by their concern to maintain their own position and the small size of their community on which the required money was increasingly levied as the only place where finance could be raised. The 1522 parliament refused the financial measures necessary to finance the overall reform of the Lordship, because the colony was unable to meet the high cost.

Between the late 1530s and mid-1550s, the crown engaged in an ambitious programme of assimilation through reconciliation in which parliament had a central role. All the traditional English governmental structures necessary to summon parliament (chancery, counties, local government officials such as sheriffs and chief officers in towns) and execute its decisions (the office of the master of the rolls and the courts) were in place, at least in the part of Ireland in which the king's writ ran. Henry VIII's leading minister of the 1530s, Thomas Cromwell, carefully managed the 1536–7 parliament, which involved a legislative programme devised in London.[39] This was possible only because Poynings' Law was suspended. But it also required negotiation and bargaining with MPs and concessions from the crown to reconcile members' interests with the draft legislation.[40] The high point of the policy of assimilation was seen in 1541, when the Act of Kingly Title was passed, peers of Gaelic origin were created for the first time and parliament was the forum for drawing Gaelic chieftains into an English judicial process; Gaelic land-holding systems were transformed through chiefs' surrendering their lands to the crown which regranted them under English tenures.

37 Ciaran Brady, 'Court, castle and country: the framework of government in Tudor Ireland' in Ciaran Brady and Raymond Gillespie (eds), *Natives and newcomers: essays on the making of Irish colonial society, 1534–1641* (Dublin, 1986), pp 22–49; Ciaran Brady, 'Conservative subversives: the community of the Pale and the Dublin administration, 1556–1586' in Patrick J. Corish (ed.), *Historical Studies XV: radicals, rebels and establishments* (Belfast, 1985), pp 11–32.

38 Crawford, *Anglicizing* (Dublin, 1993).

39 Howard Leithead, 'Cromwell, Thomas, earl of Essex', *Oxford DNB*.

40 Bradshaw, 'Opposition'; *idem*, *Irish constitutional revolution*, pp 78–9, 148–52.

The Old English community supported the Henrician Lord Deputy Anthony St Leger's management of the 1541 parliament in the following decade:

> let their heads [of the Gaelic clans] with the rest of the lords of the realm be persuaded to assemble all in one place, to the intent that there in open parliament not only those statutes which heretofore divided them asunder may be quite abrogated. But also that henceforth that both Irish and English may be joined in one [?regimen] of true and faithful subjects.

And that they would 'receive the execution of their Grace's laws, as an indifferent arbiter throughout the whole realm, to decide forever the controversies and variances depending between them for land and otherwise', noting that laws they would agree to in parliament would be applied equally to all subjects.[41]

From the mid-1550s, assimilation gave way to coercion and the crown's attitude to parliament changed from one based on accommodation and bargaining to an increasingly aggressive attempt to control its membership and operations, provoking mistrust between the crown and the native political community, with a growing reliance on illegal electioneering and dirty tricks on the administration's part and a dependence on parliament as a bulwark to defend their interest by the Old English and, increasingly, Gaelic Irish. The original plans for the 1556–7 parliament intended to hold sessions in Limerick, Athlone and Armagh or Dundalk, where local leaders were to participate in devising a system of government for their regions, tailored to local conditions and assimilated into the central administration. However, the assimilation policy was abandoned and parliament met briefly in Dublin, recognized Queen Mary I as queen, repealed the reformation legislation and confiscated the lands of the Gaelic Irish in Laois and Offaly.[42] Thereafter, royal authority was enforced through systematic dispossession and coercion. Parliament's central role is shown by even the most radical constitutional changes being effected by statute; this required the crown to control the assembly and explains the administration's energetic and often illegal electioneering and dubious manoeuvring. Brady's description of the Tudor parliaments' 'highly exclusive and unrepresentative' nature, whose effectiveness was limited by 'the continuing restrictions of Poynings' Law and its control by a predominantly non-native executive', seriously overstates the administration's dominance, as parliament's proceedings between 1560 and 1585 demonstrate.[43]

The plan to Anglicize Ireland, however, was not intended to create another England in which the subject's rights and liberties were guaranteed by statute and common law. Statute, the highest form of law, represented the formal 'assent of the whole realm' through parliament and 'common law, *lex non scripta,* was the product of time, continuous usage and the quiet and common consent of the people', serving two vital functions:

41 Brendan Bradshaw (ed.), 'A treatise for the reformation of Ireland, 1554–55', *IJ*, 16 (1981), 299–315.
42 Bradshaw, *Irish constitutional revolution*, pp 274–5.
43 Brady, 'Court, castle and country'.

> provid[ing] guidelines for the courts in both civil and criminal matters affecting the protection and transfers of properties of all sorts and the penalties for temporal offences. Second, and even more important, the common law provided the foundations for all of the most cherished liberties of English people ... the rights ... not to be taxed or subjected to laws without his consent and not to be deprived of life, liberty or property without due process of law, included an accused's right to a jury trial.[44]

As most famously enunciated by Sir John Davies, attorney general and speaker of the 1613 parliament, the extension of English common and statute law over the whole country after the end of the Nine Years War (*c.*1594–1603) would replace the 'arbitrary' Brehon law with a 'regimen in which the existence of a body of known law administered through equally known due processes would confer upon subjects certain fixed rights and protections.' Despite the fine rhetoric, Davies and others had no intention that this would be the result of extending the 'benefits' of the common law to Ireland. Whereas the Tudors initially embraced the possibility of extending English statutes to Ireland, under the Stuarts, led by Davies as the most important legal officer after the chancellor, the crown used judge-based law and arbitrary judgments to supersede statute law to justify changes in government policy on land law and the lawful expropriation of Irish land in their own interests and those of other New English settlers. All the institutions of the state, including parliament, were bent to that end.[45]

Parliaments' infrequency and limited functioning due to Poynings' Law and the increasing presence of official nominees as MPs facilitated this development, leaving the native Irish population without the protection of the law by an administration that claimed its primacy. An increasing reluctance to involve the native political community in decision-making and a determination to promote the New English Protestant community and to restrict opportunities of economic, social and political advancement to them, adversely affected parliament and its operations. Both statute and common law were increasingly made by extra-parliamentary means, including acts of state (law made by proclamation) and 'judge-made' law, and parliament's judicial function was largely taken over by the privy council, which sat as a court. What Davies started continued under Chichester's successors, and, as Clarke noted, 'subverted what it purported to exalt', initially only to the disadvantage of the native population, but increasingly, under Wentworth, at the expense of anyone who opposed him in any way.[46]

44 Jack P. Greene, 'Introduction: empire and liberty' in Jack P. Greene (ed.), *Exclusionary empire: English liberty overseas, 1600–1900* (Cambridge, 2010), pp 1–24.

45 Hans Pawlisch, *Sir John Davies and the conquest of Ireland: a study in legal imperialism* (Cambridge, 1985). See Aidan Clarke's review of this book in *IHS*, 25:97 (May, 1986) 99–101. Crawford, *Anglicizing*, based on Pawlisch, pp 245–6. Robert Armstrong, 'Davies, Sir John', *DIB*. Additional details on Davies are provided in Appendix 3.

46 The quotation is from Aidan Clarke's review of Hans Pawlisch's book in *IHS*, 25:97 (May, 1986), 99–101; McGrath, 'Electoral strategy'.

Wentworth admitted as much to his fellow privy councillor and the soon-to-be English Secretary of State, Sir Henry Vane, comparing the effect that a programmatic confiscation of Englishmen's estates such as the planned plantations of Connacht and Ormond was to involve would have in England.[47]

The traditional mainly Old English judges were succeeded by New English Protestant ones: the last Catholic judge until James II's reign, Sir John Everard, the highly respected second justice of the king's bench, resigned in 1607, refusing to take the oath of supremacy. From the sixteenth century, sheriffs increasingly were Protestant, despite many lacking the necessary qualifications for the role, although early Stuart deputies appointed Catholic sheriffs especially for collecting parliamentary subsidies and both Henry Cary, first Viscount Falkland, who served as viceroy of Ireland between 1622 and 1629, and Wentworth did so also in election years to give the impression of even-handedness.[48] Catholic chief magistrates and recorders, towns' legal officers, were deposed between 1611 and 1624 for refusing the oath of supremacy and commissions of the peace incrementally excluded Catholics. However, while the Popish Recusants Act of 1605 (3 Jac. I, c. 4), and the Oath of Allegiance Act of 1609 (7 Jac. I, c. 6), required English MPs to swear the oaths of supremacy and allegiance before the Lord Steward prior to entering parliament, no oaths were required of Irish MPs despite rumours carefully spread before the 1613 parliament, intended, unsuccessfully, to deter Catholics from contesting elections, until 21 June 1642 and then by resolution of the entirely Protestant 'rump' Commons, not by statute.[49]

The Irish parliament survived because it was the only constitutional means for transacting some business, including taxation and primary legislation. However, this was precisely the reason the crown sought to control it and why it was the native political community's only, if infrequent, bulwark against further encroachment and exploitation. Canny contends that the Old English experience in 1613–5 proved to them that they had lost dominance in parliament, but this is not borne out either by the history of that parliament, where the government's majority was so narrow that Catholics were able to hold their own and their insistence between 1627 and 1633 on the need to summon parliament. The conduct of the 1634 elections, and what we know of the 1628 ones, shows that Catholics vigorously contested them, rejected Wentworth's nominees, achieved greater success than anticipated and selected their own candidate for speaker.[50] Moreover, Canny's interpretation ignores the fact that only the deputy had the constitutional right to propose a parliament. The late 1630s were a low time for

47 Wentworth to Vane, 30 May 1639, in Canny, *Making Ireland British*, p. 284; Malcolm Smuts, 'Vane, Sir Henry', *Oxford DNB*.

48 McGrath, 'Electoral strategy'; Robert Armstrong, 'Cary, Henry, 1st Viscount Falkland', *DIB*. On Everard, see Appendix 3.

49 Hawkyard, *Commons*, p. 92.

50 Canny, *Making Ireland British*, p. 407; Clarke, *Old English*, pp 53–61; Cork to Dorchester, 8 Dec. 1630, in Aidan Clarke, Bríd McGrath and David Edwards (eds), *A lord justice's letterbook: the earl of Cork's letterbook, 1629–1633* (Dublin, forthcoming), no. 93; McGrath, 'Electoral strategy'.

confidence in parliament's powers, but this did not dilute the Irish political community's commitment to the institution and its role nor their belief in its potential to redress grievances. While MPs on both sides who suffered from Wentworth's viciousness refused to stand in elections in 1640, many rejoined parliament through by-elections from November 1640 onwards, while also working hard to use the institution to assert their rights and redress individual and collective grievances and campaign for constitutional change.[51]

Lack of sources is frequently cited as a reason for the absence of detailed studies of Irish history in general and early modern parliaments in particular, but in fact, a wide range of scattered sources is available to study the early modern Irish parliament, the attitudes of those who summoned, staffed, managed and worked in it and lived with the results of its work and how MPs conducted their business. They are, though, mainly to be found outside national collections and traditional parliamentary archives.

Unfortunately, there was no central archive of Irish parliamentary records such as the English House of Lords' repository established by the 1590s and the material which survived the very poor record-keeping in the medieval, early modern and later periods in Ireland was destroyed in the notorious 1922 Public Record Office fire, including the magnificent parliamentary journals and the indentures of elections. The Virtual Record Treasury of Ireland project now attempts to provide access to manuscripts and transcripts which were destroyed in that fire which are found in other repositories.[52] The admittedly incomplete and biased official records of commissions, elections, statutes and journals are published, but while most sources for the early modern Irish parliament are unpublished and difficult to source, they certainly exist. As Bradshaw reflected 'the story can be pieced together only incompletely and by an immense output of time and labour, sifting through archival collections for the occasional nugget.' More positively, he also noted:

> We need not doubt that this particular game is worth the effort, for here we are working not on some isolated aspect of the jigsaw of sixteenth-century Ireland but on the broad background contours which give the scene in the foreground its perspective.[53]

Writing this book required searching in many countries through innumerable sources apparently unrelated to the Irish parliament but which provide crucial evidence for its membership and work. While we certainly lack the richness of the manuals, letters, parliamentary diaries, pamphlets, petitions, reports and especially

51 Bríd McGrath, 'The Irish elections of 1640–1641' in Ciaran Brady and Jane Ohlmeyer (eds), *British interventions in early modern Ireland* (Cambridge, 2005), pp 186–206.

52 The Virtual Record Treasury of Ireland, at www.virtualtreasury.ie [accessed 15 Dec. 2022].

53 For example, Bradshaw, 'Beginnings'; Treadwell, 'Irish parliament of 1569–71'; Bradshaw, 'Opposition'; Andrew Thrush, 'The House of Lords' records repository and the clerk of the parliaments' house: a Tudor achievement', *Parl. Hist.*, 21:3 (2002), 367–73; Foster, 'Painful labour'.

speeches and other records available for Catalonia, England, Scotland and France *inter alia*, there is a multitude of rich primary sources for Ireland, albeit scattered in archives throughout Ireland, England, America and France, among other places. Considerable effort is required to locate them but the results justify Bradshaw's optimism and confirm that there is no lack of sources for early modern Irish parliamentary history.

While the early Stuart period is the first for which we have official Commons' journals (the three surviving contemporary fair copies of the 1613–15 Commons' journals are held in separate collections in Irish libraries, with the clerk's original notes in the National Archives of the United Kingdom), a wealth of other records survive, much of which has never previously been used for Irish parliamentary history. These include the papers of the English attorney general from 1634 through to early 1641, Sir John Bankes (*plate 27*), whose careful reviews of draft legislation highlight both the English privy council's ignorance of Irish affairs and the poor drafting standards of the crown's lawyers in Ireland.[54] They also contain the commissions for both of Wentworth's parliaments. Records of individual elections, payments of MPs' wages, draft bills, public and private, survive to supplement the printed statutes and journals and letters provide valuable evidence of attitudes to parliament and to its business. As parliament's decisions affected everyday life, records of its business are found in places which, at first glance, seem improbable. Accounts of elections are found in municipal records, family histories, a contemporary diary, a reform treatise and a complaint from a corrupt sheriff in a family archive. Copies of a few election returns are held in family papers, although the reason for their transcription is obscure.[55] Receipts for wages are found in published corporation records, but also in Kilkenny Corporation Archive, while the copy of another is found in French documents that were apparently used to prove the nobility of a 'Wild Geese' family. The 1615 clergy subsidies bill was located in a collection of material relating to Convocation, in the mistaken belief that it had been passed. The considerable informal and formal migration into early modern Ireland by English, Welsh, Scots, French, Dutch, Germans and others created legal tangles. English and Welshmen had full citizenship but others had no rights of residency or to hold or inherit property, including Englishmen who had been born outside the monarch's dominions and Scots born before 1603. Naturalization that provided these rights could only be achieved by private acts of parliament, which were not automatically included in the published statutes; however, bills introduced to the 1634 parliament have survived and were subsequently published. Even more intriguingly, information on the Dutchman James Martin's attempt to achieve naturalization in 1641 and his negotiations with Catholic and Protestant MPs is found only in his inquisition post mortem from

54 Christopher W. Brooks, 'Bankes, Sir John', *Oxford DNB*.
55 Bríd McGrath, 'Athboy's election returns 1640 and 1641', *Riocht na Midhe*, 21 (2010), 65–72.

the 1650s.[56] Finally, petitions and documents relating to parliament are preserved in family papers. Taken together, these provide ample sources for a study of the operations of the early Stuart Irish House of Commons.

Chapter one describes the development of the medieval Irish parliament and its transformation under the Tudors, setting the scene for the rest of the book. It notes some of the differences between the English and Irish parliaments; traditionally, discussion has focused on Poynings' Law's constraining effects but the differences were wider and deeper than those imposed by that statute. The second chapter reviews the wide range of records available for early modern Irish parliaments and the following one discusses parliament's powers, comparing them briefly with other countries. Chapter four examines the theories of representation in Ireland, attitudes to parliament and MPs' relations with their constituencies. The fifth chapter discusses parliament's summoning, the nature and extent of constituencies and electorates and the electoral process. Chapter six explores the culture of parliament, including its location and layout, material culture and the changing nature of its ceremonial under Wentworth. Chapter seven describes parliament's operations, specifically legislation and its mechanisms for attempting to redress grievances. Chapter eight considers the economics of parliament, including its cost, MPs' wages, taxation in the form of subsidies and officials' fees and the next chapter examines parliament's personnel, including its officers and MPs. Chapter ten discusses lawyers in and around parliament and chapter eleven looks at parliament's response to crises. The appendixes include a list of the copies of the surviving manuscript parliamentary journals, a submission to the 1634 parliament from the inhabitants of Munster and biographical accounts of MPs who were lawyers.

56 TNA, MS C. 86/1; W.A. Shaw (ed.), *Letters of denization and acts of naturalisation for aliens in England and Ireland, 1603–1700* (Lymington, 1911), pp xxiii, 49–52, 332; Inquisition post mortem of James Martin, RIA, MS 14/C/2, pp 183–5.

CHAPTER ONE

State, community and parliament: the development of the Irish parliament under the Tudors

THE TUDORS' ACCESSION and their state-building agenda transformed Ireland and its political community through a determined process of reform and Anglicization of which the changes instigated by Lord Deputy Sir Edward Poynings in the 1490s might be seen as the precursor.[1] Parliament was an instrument of this reform and its development reflected the changes wrought by the Tudors in Ireland. The early Stuart Irish parliament built on the Tudors' achievements to become the foundation stone of Ireland's constitutional and administrative order. Its membership expanded and nature changed and over time it acquired the form, powers and organizational capacity that it possessed until the Act of Union in 1800. The gradual and incremental process by which this transformation was achieved moved from assimilation to coercion and produced a very different Irish political community to that which had originally been envisaged. The tensions engendered within the state were played out in parliament's elections and proceedings.

The English and Irish medieval and early modern parliaments were evolving institutions lacking the 'rigidity of membership', powers and procedures they later acquired for England and Wales in the sixteenth century and for Ireland in the following one.[2] Both experienced expansion and reform under the Tudors, in some ways becoming more similar, but in other respects their development was very different. Many reforms were common to both kingdoms – the expulsion of proctors, abbots and priors, the development of committees and acceptance of parliament's right to decide on its own membership – but others were unique and most followed from Tudor state-building, the Reformation and the creation of the kingdom of Ireland in 1541. Catholics' exclusion from the English parliament following the 1559 Act of Supremacy was unique to that kingdom and while Irish recusants were barred from many official positions, they were not excluded from the lower house until 1642, a decision of dubious legality effected by resolution of the Commons, not by legislation. Charles I contested this at the time and there was no statutory exclusion until 1691.[3]

1 David Beresford, 'Poynings, Sir Edward', *DIB*.

2 Phil Bradford and Alison K. McHardy (eds), *Proctors for parliament: clergy, community and politics, c.1248–1539*, 2 vols (York, 2017–18), ii, p. liv.

3 2 Eliz., c. 1, 2; Alan Ford, 'The Protestant reformation in Ireland' in Brady and Gillespie (eds), *Natives and newcomers*, pp 50–74; McGrath, 'Recruiter returns'.

Unique Irish reforms included the rationalization of constituencies and resolving constraints on their creation, but one of the most far-reaching changes, Poynings' Law, occurred before either the Reformation or the establishment of the kingdom of Ireland. The 1494 parliament passed legislation that incorporated all current English statutes into Irish law, extended English seals' jurisdiction to Ireland, required Irish peers to wear the same parliamentary robes as their English counterparts and changed parliament's official language from French to English. Most famously, it enacted Poynings' Law under which the deputy and council had to write to the monarch listing reasons for summoning parliament and submit bills to England for prior approval, before obtaining a commission to call parliament. The process by which these statutes were enacted is unclear, although Bradshaw describes parliament as having been bullied into passing them, but their effect was explicitly to affirm the Irish government's subordination to the English one and significantly to reduce the frequency of Irish parliaments and this law led to other constitutional innovations.[44]

Key additional factors in changing the Irish state were the consistent employment of Englishmen as governors after the end of the dominance of the earls of Kildare as deputies in 1534 and the demise of the Gaelic lordships of Connacht and Ulster through the Composition of Connacht and their defeat in the Nine Years War, which gave the crown control over all of Ireland for the first time. Many changes had crystallized by 1536–7, but more were to follow:

> The Kildare supremacy was at an end ... The medieval concept of parliament as a place for redress of what were very often private grievances had given way to the concept of the public or common good [at least for the English colony], while the procedural changes resulting from Poynings' Act meant a higher degree of control over the actions of parliament.[55]

Attitudes to and interpretations of Poynings' Law changed with political circumstances and direct evidence is scarce, but at the time it was generally welcomed by the political community as a it curtailed the Irish executive but this view changed as Wentworth used it to control parliament and restrict its functions.[6]

Since 1264 parliament sought to represent and operate for the king's lieges within the geographically small and ethnically restricted Lordship. The establishment of the kingdom marked a radical change in Ireland's constitutional position and over time expanded its political community to include all its inhabitants, the Gaelic and Gaelicized Irish beyond the Pale and increasingly, English, Welsh and Scottish settlers. Bradshaw's claim that St Leger's 1541

4 Bradshaw, *Irish constitutional revolution*. For records in French from the parliamentary rolls, see Marsh's Library, MS Z3.2.5, pp 1–27.

5 Connolly (ed.), *Statute rolls*, p. xxii.

6 Clarke, 'History of Poynings' Law'.

assembly was the first 'national' Irish parliament is true in that it was the first for the kingdom and tried to engage elites outside the English Lordship by including a small number of peers of Irish origin and meeting outside Dublin after a very small opening session in the capital, but the 1613 body was actually the first with a genuinely national membership, if not a truly representative one.[7]

Irish colonial institutions were inevitably based on English models, although all were 'to a greater or lesser extent, modified by their passage across the Irish sea into a much different environment'; parliament's membership, structure and operations reflected the state of the English colony, but this community was more diverse than has generally been appreciated. Cosgrove summarized the differences between the English and Irish medieval parliaments as their size, membership and the communities they represented but these distinctions can be overstated and ignore deeper dissimilarities, such as its inward-looking nature, the monarch's absence, the varying importance of parliament's legislative and judicial functions, the nature and position of clerical proctors, different constituency types, how these were created, the means by which parliamentary representation was extended and the ability of members to resign.[8] Most differences were dissolved or modified in the Tudor period, but not the Irish parliament's inward focus, the monarch's absence or the continuing presence of Catholic members, while the increasing numbers of settlers added a religious and ethnic dimension missing from the English body. Irish MPs' ability to resign their seats, unlike their English counterparts, also affected membership and attendance.

The medieval Irish Commons was proportionately significantly smaller than the English and its size fluctuated greatly depending on the state of the Lordship and matters under consideration. The English Commons had 250 members in the late fourteenth and early fifteenth centuries, 290 in 1510, 398 in 1558, 402 in 1559 and 474 by 1603.[9] The eighteenth-century archivist and historian, John Lodge, who saw the original Irish writs of return, which were destroyed in 1922, noted that 20, including 4 from Dublin County, were summoned in March 1374, but 54 eight months later, 62 in 1377 and 58 in 1380 and 1382.[10] A maximum of 46 MPs was summoned in 1494, of whom between 24 and 34 attended. The sheriffs of Cork, Kilkenny, Limerick and Cross Wexford, the seneschal of the Liberty of Wexford and the towns of Youghal and Wexford sent no writs of return and both MPs for Waterford City and County and one each from Meath, Drogheda and

7 Bradshaw, *Irish constitutional revolution*, p. 240; Ellis, 'Citizenship'; Dennehy, 'Representation in later medieval and early modern Ireland', provides a useful summary of this process.

8 Cosgrove, 'Parliament and the Anglo-Irish community'.

9 J.S. Roskell, 'The composition of the House of Commons', at https://www.historyofparliamentonline.org/volume/1386-1421/survey/v-composition-house-commons [accessed 4 March 2019]; 'Members, 1509–1558', at https://www.historyofparliamentonline.org/research/members/members-1509-1558 [accessed 4 March 2019]; 'Constituencies, 1558–1603', at https://www.historyofparliamentonline.org/research/constituencies/constituencies-1558-1603 [accessed 19 Feb. 2021].

10 Turlough O'Riordan, 'Lodge, John', *DIB*.

Kilkenny City failed to attend, as did lords Delvin, Dunsany, Killeen and Slane, the abbots of Dunbrody and Tintern and very many clerical proctors. Many, if not most, Munster lords had not appeared for some time. The absences are telling, as while the Munster members may have been reluctant to travel to Drogheda to attend, the failure of Leinster representatives to appear indicates a deeper level of either lack of interest or resistance to the crown.[11] The absence of between a quarter and a half of those eligible to attend indicates that parliament had lost relevance even to its own political community, but also helps to explain how easily Poynings could persuade perhaps as few as 12 MPs into passing the law that bears his name. It is unclear how many MPs were present to pass the Act that the king of England, his heir and successors be kings of Ireland (33 Hen. VIII, c.1, generally known as the Act for the Kingly Title), but there were clearly far fewer than in 1536–7, given the absence of abbots and proctors and the loss of some Wexford seats (instanced below). Several peers and quite possibly many others entitled to attend did not appear until the second session. Despite its limited membership and even smaller attendance, decisions made by the medieval and early Tudor Irish parliaments bound all subsequent inhabitants of Ireland.

The Lordship naturally had many connections with England, but while professing constant loyalty to the crown, it also stressed its own separate nature. This focus on its position as a colony led to its inward-looking focus as it had no role in many of the functions played by English and other European representative assemblies, such as royal succession and marriages and foreign wars, although the Act for the Kingly Title was a clear statement of the English monarchy in Ireland and Mary's, James I's and Charles II's accessions were recognized in acts of the Irish parliament.[12] English monarchs almost never visited Ireland, which they managed through governors who summoned and held parliaments. Subjects' frequent recourse to the crown, often over the governor's head, was a feature of Irish political life until Lord Deputy Thomas Wentworth banned travel from Ireland without his licence in 1633, thereby avoiding his predecessors' fate of having his position constantly undermined at Court. Men from Ireland occasionally attended the English parliament and a steady stream of Irish business was discussed at English assemblies in the middle of King Edward I's reign, although this later subsided.[13] Sir Maurice Eustace's acceptance speech as speaker in 1640 noted the attendance of delegates from Ireland to the English parliament under the Edwards.[14] The Irish parliament sent agents to the king in England and

11 John Lodge's parliamentary register, *Liber Mun. Pub. Hib.*, vii, p. 161; John Lodge, *Sketches of the history of Poynings' Law and of the usage of parliament in Ireland* (Dublin, 1780), pp 18–19; Steven G. Ellis, 'Parliament and community in Yorkist and Tudor Ireland' in Cosgrove and McGuire (eds), *Historical Studies XIV*, pp 43–68; BL, Add. MS 4,797, fos. 109v–10. The lack of so many Wexford MPs suggests that New Ross was also not represented, if it was already a parliamentary borough.

12 33 Hen. VIII, c. 1; 3 & 4 Philip and Mary, c. 14; 12 Jac. I, c. 1; 13 Car. II, c. 1.

13 Richardson and Sayles, *Irish parliament in the Middle Ages*, pp 61–2.

14 *Commons' Jn. Ire.*, 20 March 1640; Terry Clavin, 'Eustace, Sir Maurice', *DIB*. For further details on Eustace, see Appendix 3.

to its English counterpart in 1359, 1385, 1421 and 1440 at least, but these delegations travelled at the Irish parliament's request. When King Edward III ordered the Irish Commons to elect representatives to assemble before him in Westminster in 1376, they refused, claiming that 'according to the liberties, privileges, rights, laws and customs of … Ireland since the conquest' they were not obliged to attend the king in England.[15]

The Lordship was a more diverse community than has generally been appreciated and scholars have underestimated the level of Gaelic engagement there and in parliament. Despite Sir John Davies' assertion in his acceptance speech as speaker in 1613, that before 1541 'we do not find any to have had place in Parliament but the English of blood, or English of birth', both houses included Irishmen, albeit presumably in relatively small numbers.[16] Many Irish received the benefit of English laws by denization or other means from the early days of the Lordship and were resident and engaged in the public life of Irish shires and towns and eligible to act as electors and MPs.[17] The writ summoning the Justiciar of Ireland, Edmund le Botiller, to the 1316 parliament also contained the names of many Irish chieftains including O'Donnell, O'Neill, O'Reilly, O'Cahan, O'Ferrall, O'Connor, O'Brien, MacCarthy, O'Toole and Murtagh O'Brien.[18] The allegation that James Butler, fourth earl of Ormond, arranged for 'groomes and pages of his household' of Gaelic origin to be elected as knights of the shire in 1441, which may not have been a unique occurrence, demonstrates the presence of Irishmen as electors and candidates, although the objections might have been as much economic and social as legal, political or ethnic.[19]

Many bishops, abbots and proctors were of Gaelic origin and some at least took their parliamentary roles seriously. Bishop Tomás Ó Cormacáin of Killaloe petitioned the 1359 parliament and in 1408–9 Rísdéard Ó hÉidigheáin, archbishop

15 NAI, MS RC 8/27, pp 446–7; Peter Crooks, 'Representation and dissent: "Parliamentarianism" and the structure of politics in colonial Ireland', *EHR*, 125:512 (Feb., 2010), 1–34; NAI, MS RCH 262/31, quoted in Cosgrove, 'Parliament and the Anglo-Irish community'.

16 Seán Duffy (ed.), *Medieval Ireland: an encyclopaedia* (London, 2005), pp 365–6; F.X. Martin, 'The coming of parliament' in Farrell (ed.), *Irish parliamentary tradition*, pp 37–56; John Davies, *Historical tracts* (Dublin, 1787), p. 301. Davies' assertion also ignores the presence of Welsh in the Irish parliament, e.g., Thomas Williams and Rice Ap Hugh for Mayo and Carlingford, respectively, in 1585. W.J. Johnston, 'The parliament of the Pale', *Law Quarterly Review*, 34:135 (July, 1918), 291–303.

17 John Davies, *A discoverie of the true causes why Ireland was never entirely subdued, nor brought under obedience of the crowne of England untill the beginning of his majesties happy raigne* (London, 1612), pp 103–13; Stephen Hewer, 'Free Gaelic people in English Ireland, *c.*1250–*c.*1327', *History Ireland*, 23:6 (Nov.–Dec., 2015), 14–17; Ellis, 'Citizenship'; Bríd McGrath, '"Mere Irish" in parliaments and towns, 1316–1659' in Simon Egan (ed.), *Beyond the Pale and Highland line* (Manchester, forthcoming); LPL, Carew MS 603: Henry and Conn O'Neill were made denizens and 'Englishe to all purposes' by an act of parliament during the reign of Edward IV. See Memorandum of the denization of Harry O'Neill and his son Conn, TNA, SP 63/5, fo. 214.

18 Ronan Mackay, 'Butler (le Botiller), Edmund', *DIB*.

19 Crooks, 'Representation and dissent'; Dennehy, 'Representation in later medieval and early modern Ireland'; Richardson and Sayles, *Irish parliament in the Middle Ages*, pp 181–2; David Beresford, 'Butler, James, 4th earl of Ormond', *DIB*.

of Cashel, had a French language copy of the *Modus tenendi parliamentum* that contained the provision that it should be held by the archbishop of Cashel for the people of Ireland 'since [Cashel] is in the middle of the land.'[20] A close ally of the fourth earl of Ormond, Rísdéard attended at least the 1408 and 1421 parliaments and presumably others; on the latter occasion John Geese, bishop of Waterford and Lismore accused him of favouring Gaelic clergy over English and presenting his concubine with a ring with an image of St Patrick given him by the seventh earl of Desmond, James FitzGerald, underlining his close links with Norman magnates and prominence in the political community, but also the probability that Cashel's clerical proctors were Gaelic.[21] Finally, the high level of intermarriage between the two communities reduced cultural and ethnic differences and many with English or Norman names had Gaelic kin.

Because the Lordship accepted English law and parliament periodically incorporated English statutes *en bloc*, its legislative business was limited to largely local matters. This did not mean that the English parliament had the right to legislate for Ireland and the Irish parliament continued to enact laws, but Irish statutes were designed 'not to provide the groundwork of the law, but to meet specific local requirements.'[22] As a result, its judicial function was more important than its legislative role and helped compensate for deficiencies in the courts system caused by the contraction of the Lordship. Parliament's decisions had a greater effect on individual lives by resolving local grievances and tensions and it played a larger role in government because of the sheer quantity of administrative and judicial matters with which it dealt. Its remit was to a wider political community than the Lordship: only 155 (roughly 20%) of the 809 recorded acts passed in the years 1462–81 concerned the whole Lordship; the other 80% concerned individuals, with 12.5% relating to communities outside the Pale. Parliament's major work was as a court, dealing with local issues, identifying grievances to be presented to the sovereign, and lastly legislation.[23] Poynings' Law limited the passage of private acts that had been used to resolve local difficulties.

Clerical proctors, representatives of the lower diocesan clergy, attended parliament from 1371. Proctors in England, who were frequently not clergy, sat in Convocation's lower house, whereas proctors in Ireland, who were apparently all clerics, sat in parliament, where they operated in the same way as judges in the seventeenth century, providing advice, but without votes. Unlike judges whose contribution was limited to legal advice to the Lords and acting as their high-class messengers to the Commons, proctors brought an ethos of representing the whole

20 Emmett O'Byrne, 'Ó hÉidigheáin, Rísdéard', *DIB*.

21 Ellis, 'Parliament and community'; BL, Add. MS 4,797, fos. 109v–10; Duffy (ed.), *Medieval Ireland*, pp 365–6; Richardson, 'Irish parliament rolls'; Close roll 32, Edward III, 24 Jan. 1359, Petition of Tomás Ó Cormacáin, bishop of Killaloe in the present parliament, NAI, MS RC 8/27, pp 379–87; Crooks, 'Representation and dissent'; David Beresford, 'FitzGerald, James, fitz Gerald, 7th earl of Desmond', *DIB*.

22 Richardson, 'Irish parliament rolls'.

23 Ellis, 'Parliament and community'; Bradshaw, 'Beginnings'; Richardson, 'Irish parliament rolls'.

community, rather than individual interests. It is frequently asserted that Irish proctors sat in parliament for much longer than their English counterparts who were expelled in 1536, but in fact they were removed just one year later. Despite their small numbers, the loss of proctors probably had a greater impact in Ireland than England.[24]

While the English and Irish parliaments' composition was ostensibly identical – an upper house of temporal and spiritual peers and a lower house of MPs – both had some unique types of constituencies and the means by which they were created was constitutionally different, a distinction that has hitherto been overlooked. English counties were largely formed before the Norman Conquest and Wales was shired by legislation between 1535 and 1542, when that country was first represented at Westminster. All Welsh constituencies, including groups of boroughs, had a single member.[25] There was no Irish equivalent of the Cinque Ports, whose members were called 'barons' and whose returns were managed by the warden of the ports, rather than a sheriff, or of the combined boroughs of Weymouth and Melcombe Regis, which had four seats each and the single seat constituencies of Abingdon, Banbury, Bewdley, Higham Ferrers and Monmouth.[26]

Until 1569 Irish counties could only be created by legislation and thus the local government system of sheriffs, county courts and parliamentary representation could only be extended outside the historical Lordship by statute. Westmeath was created in 1542 and King's and Queen's counties (modern-day Offaly and Laois) in 1556. Shiring proceeded rapidly after the passage of An Act for turning of Countries that be not Shire Grounds into Shire Grounds (11 Eliz. I, c. 19) in 1569 and MPs from new counties appeared in the 1585 and 1613 parliaments and possibly, with dubious legality, in the parliament of 1569. In addition to knights of the shire, the Irish parliament included representatives from two categories unknown in England: liberties and cross counties, which comprised the counties' ancient church lands and were similar to Cromarty in Scotland, which was distributed through Ross-shire. The liberties of Kilkenny, Wexford, Trim and Ulster were represented in 1307; Wexford's liberty continued until it was

24 For example, Dennehy, *Parliament*, p. 3; Duffy (ed.), *Medieval Ireland*, pp 365–6; Richardson and Sayles, *Irish parliament in the Middle Ages*, pp 76–80, 183–6; An Act against proctors to be any member of the Parliament, 28 Hen. VIII, c. 19; Richardson, 'Irish parliament rolls'; Bradshaw, 'Opposition'; James Murray, *Enforcing the English reformation in Ireland: clerical resistance and political opposition in the diocese of Dublin, 1534–1590* (Cambridge, 2011), pp 88–9; Bradford and McHardy (eds), *Proctors for parliament*; Gerald Bray (ed.), *Records of convocation: Ireland, 1101–1690* (Woodbridge, 2006), p. 19 notes the closeness of the dates.

25 Lloyd Bowen, 'Wales at Westminster: parliament, principality and pressure groups, 1542–1601', *Parl. Hist.*, 22:2 (2003), 107–20.

26 Alasdair D. Hawkyard, 'Calais', at https://www.historyofparliamentonline.org/volume/1509-1558/constituencies/calais [accessed 1 Aug. 2019]. One of Calais' 1555 MPs, John Chaloner, represented Dungarvan in 1560. Norah M. Fuidge, 'Chaloner, John', at https://www.historyofparliamentonline.org/volume/1509-1558/member/chaloner-john-ii-1526-81 [accessed 1 Aug. 2019]; P.W. Hasler, 'Cinque ports', at https://www.historyofparliamentonline.org/volume/1558-1603/constituencies/cinque-ports [accessed 4 Feb. 2019]; Hawkyard, *Commons*, pp 33, 63–4; Smith, *Stuart*, pp 22–4.

amalgamated with Cross Wexford into County Wexford in 1537. However, 11 Eliz. I, c. 19 did not empower the crown to eliminate counties but Wentworth amalgamated both Tipperaries by an act of state in or after 1635, finally fully replicating the English shire system in Ireland.[27]

The expansion of urban constituencies raised a different constitutional problem. Promoting urban settlements was a key element of state policy in anglicizing Ireland. Towns were regarded as a positive influence, which promoted 'civilitie' and trade, provided a defence against the rebellious Irish and amenities for social interaction, economic development and good government. In 1590 the chief justice of queen's bench, Sir Robert Gardener and the under-treasurer of Ireland, Sir Henry Wallop, reported that the lack of towns made governing Ulster much more difficult; six years later, the poet, minor official and undertaker in the Munster Plantation, Edmund Spenser proposed that garrisoned forts should be established in strategic places, but in addition 'the state of a towne [should be] layde forth, and incompassed where merchants, artificers and husbandmen of all sorts from England should be placed and to whom charters of incorporation should be granted.'[28]

While 11 Eliz. I, c. 19 had empowered the state to create counties, it did not resolve the constitutional difference between the two islands in creating parliamentary boroughs. Irish boroughs' representation was by prescription (tradition and custom). Most English boroughs were also represented by prescription but the crown also had the uncontested right to create new English and Welsh boroughs; the frequency with which it did so explains the dramatically increased size of the Tudor Commons, but also created an acceptance that the possession of a royal charter conferred representation *ipso facto*, whether or not it was specifically stated in that grant.[29] In medieval Ireland 'the make-up of any

27 Caesar Litton Falkiner, 'The counties of Ireland: an historical sketch of their origin, constitution and gradual delimitation', *Proc. RIA*, 24C (1902–4), 169–94; Act for turning of counties that be not yet shire grounds into shire grounds, 11 Eliz. I, c. 19; 28 Hen. VIII, c. 3 (Wexford); 34 Hen. VIII, c.1 (Westmeath); 3–4 Philip & Mary, c. 2 (King's and Queen's); Christopher Maginn, 'Elizabethan Cavan: the institutions of Tudor government in an Irish county' in Brendan Scott (ed.), *Culture and society in early modern Breifne/Cavan* (Dublin, 2009), pp 69–84; Bradshaw, 'Beginnings'. For Sidney's role in shiring in the sixteenth century, see John Patrick Montano, *The roots of English colonialism in Ireland* (Cambridge, 2011), pp 187–95. John R. Young, 'Representation in the Scottish parliament to 1707 and Scottish representation in the parliament of Great Britain to the 1832 Reform Act' in Joaquim Albareda and Manuel Herrero Sánchez (eds), *Political representation in the Ancien Régime* (Abingdon, 2019), pp 123–40, figure 8.1; Bodl. Lib., Carte MS 59, fos. 80r–1v. I am grateful to Coleman Dennehy for a valuable discussion on Cross Tipperary's disfranchisement.

28 A device for the reformation of Ulster by Justice Robert Gardener and Sir Henry Wallop, 10 May 1590, TNA, SP 63/152, fos. 129r–34r; W.L. Renwick (ed.), *A view of the present state of Ireland by Edmund Spenser* (London, 1934), pp 165–6; F.E. Ball, *The judges in Ireland, 1221–1921*, 2 vols (London, 1926), i, pp 222–3; Terry Clavin, 'Wallop, Sir Henry', *DIB*; Patricia Coughlan, 'Spenser, Edmund', *DIB*.

29 Alasdair D. Hawkyard, 'The enfranchisement of constituencies, 1509–1558', *Parl. Hist.*, 10 (1991), 1–25; Norman Ball, 'Representation in the English House of Commons: the new boroughs, 1585–1640', *PER*, 15:1 (1995), 117–24; Hawkyard, *Commons*, p. 31 notes that charters

single parliament depended on the precise nature of the business to be discussed and the justiciar would therefore tailor the summonses to parliament to meet the specific purposes', i.e., those who would be affected by parliament's business and whose consent was necessary were summoned.[30] Most towns, many of which had been established by local magnates rather than by royal charter, had no, or possibly occasional or intermittent, representation in medieval Irish parliaments and those that had reflected Norman settlement patterns and the crown's limited control in Ireland.[31] As a result, Irish sheriffs traditionally had discretion in deciding to which towns they issued mandates for election, originally depending on whether matters to be discussed affected them or required their consent. While the crown could issue charters as it pleased, as in Scotland, its constitutional power to create boroughs was at best unclear; as one Irish lawyer noted in 1613 'the king can make a Corporation, yet cannot he make a Burrough at this day.' It was not that new boroughs could not be created, but it was unclear how this might be done. This was not a problem for the medieval parliament but it presented a difficulty in extending representation to all the kingdom's subjects as few towns operated outside Leinster and Munster, and boroughs' chief magistrates (mayors, sovereigns or portreeves) were their returning officers. New towns' representation in parliament transgressed the principle of prescriptive rights and the presence of burgesses from towns without prescription was objected to in every single parliament between 1560 and 1641. While Lord Lieutenant Thomas Radcliffe, third earl of Sussex and viceroy of Ireland from 1556 through to 1563, was advised to create boroughs secretly in 1560; if he did so, MPs' successfully objected to them.[32] The presence of burgesses from some unaccustomed towns in Sidney's 1569 parliament provoked protests. The plantations of Leix and Offaly created Queen's and King's Counties with county towns at Maryborough and Philipstown, the only new towns established under the Tudors that had parliamentary representation and while the question of creating boroughs was resolved under the Stuarts, it involved constitutional innovation and provoked fierce resistance inside and outside parliament.

In promoting urban development, the early Stuart administration in Ireland was implementing a policy cherished by the monarch and establishing towns was

granting parliamentary franchise in England were issued between 1439 and 1468, and again from 1553, but most boroughs returned MPs by prescription. For the 15 English boroughs readmitted to the English Commons between 1621 and 1641 on the basis of earlier representation, see Smith, *Stuart*, p. 23. I am grateful to Stephen Roberts for a useful discussion on prescription.

30 Duffy (ed.), *Medieval Ireland*, p. 365. For the variable nature of representation in Scotland, see Alan R. MacDonald, *The burghs and parliament in Scotland,* c.*1550–1651* (Aldershot, 2007), pp 11ff.

31 G. Martin, 'Plantation boroughs in medieval Ireland, with a handlist of boroughs to *c.*1500' in David Harkness and Mary O'Dowd (eds), *Historical Studies XIII: the town in Ireland* (Belfast, 1981), pp 23–55.

32 Proposals for acts to be passed through parliament and other measures to be taken in Ireland, in David Heffernan (ed.), *'Reform' treatises on Tudor Ireland, 1537–1599* (Dublin, 2016), pp 43, 45; Ciaran Brady, 'Radcliffe, Thomas, 3rd earl of Sussex', *DIB*.

an integral requirement for all planters in Ulster and Wexford. James I's personal role in the creation of Irish boroughs and of transforming older towns and cities has been overlooked. Apart from the need for a compliant parliament, James was personally favourably disposed to urban development and created more burghs than any other Scottish monarch. He displayed 'utter contempt … for Gaelic society and culture' and was anxious to 'civilize' the Highlands, including establishing towns and sending Lowland Scots to settle in Lewis, prefiguring the Plantation of Ulster.[33] Having granted new charters with enhanced privileges to many old established Irish towns between 1608 and 1612, James proceeded to issue charters which specifically bestowed parliamentary representation, a move of very dubious legality, starting with Cavan in 1610, followed rapidly by dozens of others.[34] By contrast, Scottish burghs' parliamentary representation followed their enhanced economic standing, unlike the situation created by James in Ireland, where it preceded it (if it ever happened). As Alan MacDonald noted, there were no pocket boroughs in Scotland at this time, although outsiders were sometimes elected; but following his father's innovation in Ireland Charles I issued the first Scottish charter granting parliamentary representation in 1625.[35]

For all practical purposes, Ireland before and for some time after the Act for the Kingly Title was less a Lordship than a collection of disparate lordships and parliament played a key, but changing, role in transforming them into one kingdom with English law and judicial systems, local government structures, land-holding practices and political representation. Under deputy Anthony St Leger, the 1541–3 parliament was the mechanism and location for opening a new relationship between the crown and the Irish people as the national institution and forum, encouraging and increasing Gaelic membership and attendance. He was assisted by its speaker, the Old English lawyer Sir Thomas Cusack, who 'tenaciously pursued his long-term goal of peacefully reconciling a very traditional Irish society with a modernizing and centralizing renaissance state' following a policy of assimilation of Gaelic and Gaelicized into the political community.[36] In theory, the 1541 act established two separate and equal kingdoms with similar structures and systems under the English monarch and marked a serious attempt to create a more

33 Steven G. Ellis and Christopher Maginn, *The making of the British Isles: the state of Britain and Ireland, 1450–1660* (London, 2014), p. 80; Alison Cathcart, 'Scots and Ulster: the late medieval context' in William P. Kelly and John R. Young (eds), *Scotland and the Ulster plantation* (Dublin, 2009), pp 62–77.

34 Bríd McGrath, 'Kick-starting New Ross' renewal: its charter negotiations 1609–12 and subsequent economic development', *Ossory, Laois and Leinster*, 9 (forthcoming); *idem*, 'Unconstitutional acts, violence, intimidation, vote-rigging, fraud and resistance: Cavan's parliamentary elections, 1613', *Breifne*, 15:56 (2021), 4–23; *idem*, 'Electoral strategy'. Athlone and Gowran's charters in 1606 and 1608 included no such provision.

35 MacDonald, *Burghs and parliament*, pp 12, 18–19; Allan Kennedy, 'Representing the periphery: Highland commissioners in the seventeenth-century Scottish parliament, *c.*1612–1702', *PER*, 36:1 (2016), 14–34.

36 Quote from Terry Clavin, 'Cusack, Thomas', *DIB*; Falkiner, *Essays*, pp 225–8; Bradshaw, *Irish constitutional revolution*, pp 240–1.

inclusive state with common liberties and privileges, including parliamentary representation and access to a legal system based on a universally applicable known law for all subjects. In practice, Poynings' legislation had established the English government's primacy over the Irish parliament and, despite the new legislation, very different polities, political communities and legal and judicial systems were created which increasingly advantaged English and later Scottish migrants at the expense of the native population.

Brian MacGillapatrick was created first baron of Upper Ossory immediately before parliament met, the first man of ethnic Irish origin to be ennobled.[37] St Leger persuaded Gaelic chiefs to attend and James Butler, ninth earl of Ormond, known as Séamus Bacach, translated Cusack's acceptance speech as speaker into Irish for 'those lords who could not understand English' 'to their great contentation.'[38] The Act of Kingly Title was read in English and Irish and its formal enactment was observed by 'Donough O'Brien, and the Doctor O'Nolan and a bishop, deputies assigned by the great O'Brien to be for him in the parliament, the great O'Reilly [and] many other Irish captains.'[39] This parliament also repealed legislation that had confined its meeting to Dublin and Drogheda, allowing it to hold sessions closer to the newly welcome Gaelic subjects.[40] One three-week session at Limerick in February and March 1542 (attended by the O'Briens of Thomond and the MacWilliam Burkes of Connacht) was followed by one week at Trim, to which 'most of the Leinster Irish' came. Conn and Phelim Roe O'Neill submitted there, as did Manus O'Donnell, promising that he 'will appear in the next parliament in Ireland, or send to the same some discreet and trust[ed] person authorized by his writing sealed with his seal.'[41] These submissions were followed by Conn's elevation as earl of Tyrone and in the next year Murcadh O'Brien and his nephew were created earl of Thomond and Baron Ibrackan respectively.[42] These creations involved constitutional innovation as some were life peerages, unknown in England. Nevertheless, it appears that the majority of the Gaelic Irish in that parliament were bishops and the recently ennobled lords, rather than MPs.[43]

37 Emmett O'Byrne, 'MacGillapatrick, Brian', *DIB*.
38 David Beresford, 'Butler, James', *DIB*.
39 St Leger to Henry VIII, 26 June 1541, in Constantia Maxwell, *Irish history from contemporary sources (1509–1610)* (London, 1923), pp 102–3.
40 33 Hen. VIII, c. 8.
41 Maxwell, *Irish history from contemporary sources*, pp 102–3; Bradshaw, *Irish constitutional revolution*, pp 240–1; *idem*, *'And so began the Irish nation': nationality, national consciousness and nationalism in pre-modern Ireland* (Farnham, 2015), p. 150.
42 Emmett O'Byrne, 'O'Neill (Ó Néill), Conn "Bacach"', *DIB*; *idem*, 'O'Brien (Ó Briain), Murchadh', *DIB*.
43 Christopher Maginn, 'The Gaelic peers, the Tudor sovereigns and English multiple monarchy', *The Journal of British Studies*, 50:3 (July, 2011), 566–86. Dónal MacCarthy mór was created earl of Clancare (Clancarty) in 1565. Peers attending the 1569–70 parliament included, apart from bishops of Gaelic origin, Clancarty, Dungannon, Ibrackan, Thomond, Tyrone and Upper Ossory. Caesar Litton Falkiner, 'The parliament of Ireland under the Tudor sovereigns: supplementary paper', *Proc. RIA*, 25C (1904), 553–66.

However, the 1541 parliament's appeal was intended to be wider than to the Gaelic Irish: Old English lords from Munster and Connacht who had not recently attended were also persuaded to appear, including Desmond, Barry, Roche, Fitzmaurice and Athenry.[44] As St Leger advised Henry VIII:

> The assembly [in Limerick] shall not only do great good to confirm the obedience of the earl of Desmond and many others in those parts ... but also be an entry to bring that quarter to much civility and quiet, both by the sight of the honourable assembly and the determination of variances, strifes, and debates among inhabitants of those parts, which be now great, in default of the administration of justice.[45]

It is unclear how actively the early Tudor Irish parliament exercised its judicial function, but the Gaelic Irish who came for arbitration and justice at the Dublin, Limerick and Trim sessions were served 'by the consent of all the lords, Irish and English.' The management of this parliament changed it from a small, local body to a more nationally representative one, albeit still without members from most of the country, especially Connacht and Ulster, with a renewed emphasis on parliament's deliberative and judicial functions, 'which in England had been detached almost completely, and separately institutionalized, leaving [that] parliament a supremely legislative body.'[46]

The engagement necessary to create a new-style kingdom was a two-way process that required a significant shift in the attitudes of the monarch and Ireland's inhabitants. The process, implemented at national and local level, was ostensibly successful in creating an Anglicized society that facilitated the expanded political community's wider participation in governing their communities and engaging in decision-making at local and national level. The crown recognized the Irish as equal subjects with a role as local government officers and members of both houses of parliament. Gaelic chieftains accepted the monarchy and English norms of representation, law and justice, geographical boundaries, landholding, primogeniture, central and local government structures and systems and they served as sheriffs and justices and in parliament. These changes transformed the native population's mentality from a purely clan-centric outlook to a greater consciousness of a local, county and Irish national identity, accepting the monarchy and an ethos of representation. This was reinforced by their increasing experience in continental Europe, through growing international trade, their presence at European courts, universities and Irish colleges and the effects of their education in Counter-Reformation Europe, as well as Pope Paul IV's issuing of a Papal bull

44 Maxwell, *Irish history from contemporary sources*, p. 110; Bradshaw, *Irish constitutional revolution*, p. 241.
45 St Leger to Henry, quoted in Steven G. Ellis, *Ireland in the age of the Tudors, 1447–1603: English expansion and the end of Gaelic rule* (London, 2014), pp 153–4.
46 Bradshaw, *Irish constitutional revolution*, pp 240ff.

recognizing Ireland as a kingdom in 1555.[47] Murchadh O'Brien's offer of the Irish throne to the king of Scotland and Hugh O'Neill, second earl of Tyrone's similar offers to Spain demonstrate a growing recognition of the potential of a monarchy among the Gaelic Irish, although curiously they did not seek this role for themselves.[48]

The 1536–7 and 1541–3 parliaments were highly successful in moving the Lordship of Ireland towards a modern, reformed kingdom, increasingly accepted by the formerly excluded Gaelic community. A reform treatise of the mid-1550s recommended building on St Leger's policy and emphasized parliament's role in creating a unified, orderly kingdom of Ireland:

> let their heads [of the Gaelic clans] with the rest of the lords of the realm be persuaded to assemble all in one place, to the intent that there in open parliament not only those statutes which heretofore divided them asunder may be quite abrogated. But also that henceforth that both Irish and English may be joined in one [?regiment] of true and faithful subjects.

Laws agreed in parliament would be applied equally to all subjects 'as an indifferent arbiter throughout the whole realm, to decide forever the controversies and variances depending between them for land and otherwise.' Parliamentary subsidies with additional revenues of wardship, customs, escheats, reliefs and other sources would cover all the costs of administering the entire reformed country, shiring it and running provincial presidencies.[49] After Henry VIII's reign, it was initially intended that there would be sessions held in Limerick, Athlone and either Armagh or Dundalk during Mary's 1556–7 parliament, as local leaders were to participate in devising a system of government for the regions tailored to local conditions and assimilated to central administration. However, it only met briefly in Dublin, recognized Mary as queen, repealed some Reformation legislation, amended Poynings' Law to enable bills to be transmitted during parliament, removed the English privy council from the process of certifying bills and confiscated some additional lands of the Gaelic Irish in Laois and Offaly. Only then was parliament prorogued to Limerick and Drogheda where it sat for a single day in each place and apparently conducted no business.[50]

St Leger's successors relied on New English officials, unsympathetic or inimical to Old English and especially Gaelic interests and under Elizabeth, policy changed from assimilating the Gaelic Irish into the political community and

47 I am grateful to John McCafferty for drawing this bull to my attention.

48 Alison Cathcart, 'James V, king of Scotland – and Ireland?' in Seán Duffy (ed.), *The world of the galloglass* (Dublin, 2007), pp 144–68; Christopher Maginn, 'Contesting the sovereignty of early modern Ireland', *History Ireland*, 15:6 (Nov.–Dec., 2007), 20–5; Hiram Morgan, 'O'Neill, Hugh, 2nd earl of Tyrone', *DIB*.

49 Bradshaw (ed.), 'Treatise for the reformation of Ireland'.

50 John Gibney, *A short history of Ireland, 1500–2000* (London, 2018), pp 55–7; Bradshaw, *Irish constitutional revolution*, pp 274–5; 3 & 4 Philip and Mary, c. 4.

parliament to an increasingly coercive approach, replacing them and the Old English with crown loyalists, a growing number of whom were of English birth. The religious wars of the sixteenth century left Ireland as a possible entry point for French or Spanish invasions of England and governors Sussex, Sir Henry Sidney (1566–71, 1575–8) and Sir John Perrot (1584–8) who had overseas experience were well aware of the danger.[51] Equally importantly, Sidney and Perrot had experience of government in Wales at a time when that principality was being integrated into the English state.[52] Their experience there had a formative influence on their Irish reform agenda, but its implementation was entirely different. Unlike Wales, where the local gentry accepted the Reformation and whose incorporation into the English state provided them with a role and opportunities for advancement, the transformation was effected in Ireland by replacing local Irish elites with English officials, while simultaneously extending English political, social and administrative systems into Gaelic areas.[53]

Unfortunately, from the crown's perspective, the new political community remained stubbornly Catholic and this fed the administration's mistrust, causing them to conflate Catholicism with disloyalty and to treat them with suspicion and hostility. Assimilation was abandoned and coercion was ruthlessly displayed in Elizabeth's Irish parliaments. In his speech on the prorogation in December 1570, Sidney displayed contempt and mistrust for the Gaelic Irish and warned the Old English that they were their common enemies, contrasting the two and attempting to drive a wedge between them in what Bradshaw describes as a 'jingoistic tirade':

> you … a nation derived from our auncestours, ingraffed and incorporate into one body with us, disturbed with a sort of barbarous people odious to God and man, that lapp your bloud as greedily as ours … Your foes lie in the bosome of your Countreyes; more in number, richer of ground, desperate theeves, ever at an inch, unpossible to be severed from you without any fence beside your own valiantnes and the helpe of our Souldiours … Were there such a Sea betwixt you and the Irish, or were they shut up in an odde end of the land, … but you are beset round, your townes be feeble, the land empty, the commons bare, every county by it selfe cannot save it selfe.[54]

The provincial governor of Connacht from the mid-1580s into the 1590s, Sir Richard Bingham's determination to exclude Gaelic Irish MPs for Connacht in 1585 meant that the inhabitants of those areas had no opportunity to develop a parliamentary tradition, although that changed in 1613.[55]

51 Canny, *Elizabethan conquest of Ireland*, p. 30.

52 Ciaran Brady, 'Perrot, Sir John', *DIB*; *idem*, 'Sidney, Sir Henry', *DIB*.

53 Brendan Bradshaw, 'The Tudor reformation and revolutions in Wales and Ireland: the origins of the British problem' in Bradshaw, *'And so began the Irish nation'*, pp 117–40.

54 Bradshaw, 'Beginnings'; Edmund Campion, *A historie of Ireland written in the yeare 1571* (Dublin, 1809), pp 200–2.

55 Richard Hawkins, 'Bingham, Sir Richard', *DIB*.

For Tudor officials, many of whom had English parliamentary experience, English society, structures and institutions were the norm. They had little sympathy with or long-term interest in Ireland or its people, as Sussex's comment, 'I am forced by duty to give advice … not for the care I have of Ireland, which I have often wished to be sunk in the sea', demonstrates. Their main concern was to preserve their reputations in England where they hoped for advancement after their stint in Dublin although the experience of many was the reverse, partly because they were frequently undermined by rivals at court.[56] The means by which they achieved the objectives set out in their letters of instruction was of little interest in England and lack of oversight from London and a high tolerance of official corruption freed them to act in ways that would never have been accepted there.[57] Summoning and managing parliament was not high on their list of priorities and they had in any case little freedom to do so unless they were authorized in their commissions as chief governor. Some were by nature high-handed – Brady suggests that Sussex possessed 'exceptional ambition, a keen sense of *amour propre*, acute sensitivity to criticism, irascibility, a chronic suspicion of being secretly undermined and a highly autocratic approach to government', although he seemed to mellow towards the Irish as he aged.[58] Their highly partisan accounts of their faithful and successful endeavours, despite constant resistance from a disloyal, recalcitrant and uncivilized native population, became the self-fulfilling dominant narrative which coloured attitudes to the Irish in both kingdoms. With the spoils of plantation and control of all official posts, initially under the Tudors, and even more so under the Stuarts, Ireland became a source of immense potential wealth for English immigrants whose personal fortunes were tied to the execution of their roles as crown servants. They were less concerned with local needs and Irish traditions, including the law and their self-interest influenced the conduct of affairs and their management of parliament.

Parliament's moral and practical authority was based on its representing the whole community, with members having '*plena potestas*' (full power) to conclude all business binding their communities. Ireland's larger and more diverse political community required wider parliamentary representation but this presented challenges that required careful management, specifically the tension between achieving genuine representation and parliamentary success. The principle of popular consent would be fatally undermined if areas previously unrepresented were not able to send burgesses to parliament and many areas, especially Ulster and Connacht, with only two boroughs each in 1585 compared to Leinster and

56 Quoted in Canny, *Elizabethan conquest of Ireland*, p. 30. Leonard Grey, deputy in 1536, was executed in 1541. Perrot was accused of treason and died in the Tower of London in 1592. Thomas Wentworth was executed after a trial based on his service in Ireland.

57 David Heffernan, 'Corruption and crown government in late Elizabethan Ireland', *Proc. RIA*, 122C (2022), 1–25.

58 Ciaran Brady, 'A viceregal nervous breakdown? The collapse of the earl of Sussex in 1563' in Terence Dooley, Mary-Ann Lyons and Salvador Ryan (eds), *The historian as detective – uncovering Irish pasts: essays in honour of Raymond Gillespie* (Dublin, 2021), pp 69–73.

Munster's 21 and 11, would have little representation apart from county members.[59] However, as parliament was an instrument for Anglicization, and especially given the constraints imposed by Poynings' Law, it was necessary to control parliament and this required active management of elections and constituencies. Poynings' Law removed the freedom of the king in council to propose an Irish parliament or any legislation, the deputy and Irish council's power to summon parliament at will and MPs' and peers' rights to vote on any bills not pre-approved by the king and Irish council; it was, however, silent on parliamentarians' right to propose or discuss any bills.[60] It also created an enormous administrative burden in both Ireland and England.[61] What has been less appreciated is that the inability to amend legislation precluded the possibility of negotiating on contentious or badly drafted bills unless Poynings' Law was suspended. The position was somewhat ameliorated by An Act declaring how Poynings shall be expounded and taken (3 & 4 Philip and Mary, c. 4), which allowed bills, including amended ones, to be transmitted during parliament. However, Poynings' Law's overall effect was to impel the administration to use any means to ensure unpopular bills' passage. Especially in the absence of consultation about planned bills, and apart from 1536, when Poynings' Law was suspended and the crown negotiated about unpopular legislation, and the carefully managed 1541 assembly, friction was inevitable and parliament functioned as a 'point of conflict' between crown and community, not, as in England, as a 'point of contact'.[62]

The Commons' membership expanded dramatically in the century after 1541. The 1560 parliament's membership of 76 was undoubtedly larger than at any time since the fourteenth century and the number increased steadily thereafter – but the nature of MPs changed and electioneering became increasingly aggressive.[63] Bradshaw was able to claim for the 1536–7 parliament that 'the commons was the group in parliament which most closely reflected the attitude of the colony at large', but that was no longer the position in 1613.[64] At the beginning of Elizabeth's reign, the geographical extent of parliamentary representation was limited to less than one-third of the island, but the vast majority of members were elected by their communities and any non-resident members were objected to, because non-residence infringed the law and violated the principle of representation which the Old English held dear.[65]

59 McGrath, 'Membership', p. 18.

60 Susan A. Lentz, 'The Irish parliament during rebellion and civil war, 1641–1648' (MA, University of Wisconsin, 1974), p. 2.

61 Bradshaw, *Irish constitutional revolution*, p. 30; Clarke, 'History of Poynings' Law'.

62 Bradshaw, 'Tudor reformation and revolutions in Wales and Ireland'.

63 49 constituencies are listed but no MPs' names were provided for ten of them. Irish Archaeological Society, *Tracts relating to Ireland*, 2 vols (Dublin, 1841–3), ii, pp 136–8.

64 Bradshaw, 'Opposition'.

65 Bríd McGrath, 'Electoral law in Ireland before 1641' in Coleman A. Dennehy (ed.), *Law and revolution in Ireland: law and lawyers before, during and after the Cromwellian interregnum* (Dublin, 2019), pp 1–21.

There were no recorded objections to shirings or to abolishing liberties and cross counties but boroughs presented a separate problem. As mayors were returning officers, only existing towns, which were largely in the east and south of Ireland and controlled by Catholics, could conduct elections, but creating new boroughs was fraught with constitutional and political difficulties and needed to be carefully handled. Instead it was executed covertly to rig elections, causing resentment and alarm. Before 1560, Sussex was advised to create new shires and county towns using 'An Act or commission (the commission is secreter) to … enfranchise [the] towns of Wicklow, Arklow … Enniscorthy, a town in Leix and another in Offaly, with the liberties as Wexford.' Sidney invited many towns for the first time in 1569, but all must have had existing town or manor administrations for elections to have taken place.[66]

While the crown regularly influenced English elections, those divisions were along local fault lines, especially since Catholics were debarred from membership, but in Ireland, electoral contests were imbued with both religious and ethnic dimensions, as the administration sought the return of its own placemen, breaching both the principle of representation and the law requiring MPs to be resident in their constituencies.[67] The crown's strategy to secure amenable parliaments in both kingdoms included selecting conformable returning officers, privy councillors and magnates exerting local influence, intimations of future official favour, nominating favoured, and excluding opposition, candidates, creating constituencies and the widespread use of blank returns.[68] Electoral law and practice was common to both kingdoms but its implementation varied between them; MPs' obligation to be resident in their communities was often ignored in England but cherished in Ireland and while sheriffs and mayors were excluded from membership, this provision was often breached, most obviously in 1560 and 1613.[69]

Given the crown's view of the Old English and Gaelic communities' unreliability and as New English settlers formed a small minority of the population, it could only achieve the necessary parliamentary majority by deception, aggression and disregarding electoral law and practice. The crown expanded and changed the Irish parliament's membership, engaged in aggressive electioneering in favour of its own candidates and, when these measures failed, broke the law. It appointed English sheriffs, who lacked basic qualifications such as freeholds in the county, on whom it relied to influence returns of government supporters, especially Englishmen. Sheriffs and privy councillors held secret or poorly publicized elections, conducted repeated elections and overturned legal

66 Heffernan (ed.), *'Reform' treatises*, pp 43, 45; Henry A. Jefferies, 'The Irish parliament of 1560: the Anglican reforms authorized', *IHS*, 26:102 (Nov., 1988), 128–41; Treadwell, 'Irish parliament of 1569–71'.

67 11 Hen. IV, c. 1; 18 Edw. IV, c. 5; 33 Hen. VIII, c. 1.

68 For the Tudors' heavy-handed approach to returns in England, see Hawkyard, *Commons*, pp 87–91, 98–102. See also chapter 5 on electoral strategy.

69 McGrath, 'Electoral law in Ireland'.

ones and used intimidation and violence to achieve the return of crown dependents and supporters.[70]

In 1560, Sussex was required to ensure the passing of the Acts of Supremacy and Uniformity, a seemingly impossible task in a country that remained overwhelmingly Catholic. He engineered the return of at least 15 English privy councillors and officials, most by clearly illegal means. The constituencies for which they sat were so improbable that considerable chicanery, at best, was involved in their returns: none was resident in his constituency and at least three were serving sheriffs, albeit not in the counties for which they were returned and Bradshaw noted the 'ominous indications of intimidation and of gross abuse of parliamentary management to overcome local resistance.'[71] Seeing the fierce opposition to the bills, they adjourned parliament for several days to enable MPs to celebrate religious feasts and, with speaker James Stanihurst's active connivance, 'seven or eight foreigners, co-opted on I know not what basis into the number of members of parliament' assembled before the agreed time to pass the remaining stages of the bill before the majority of the house returned.[72] The custom of the Lords voting by whispering into the chancellor's ear rather than openly may have been another constitutional innovation employed to achieve the passing of those bills.[73] The sleight of hand used to pass these acts had long-term consequences quite apart from the continuing grave disadvantages to the Catholic community. The crown's manipulation of parliamentary business strained its relationship with the political community and each successive breach of the law and underhand practice further exacerbated ethnic and religious tensions and created deep divisions between the Catholic Old English and the administration. In 1569 the Old English objected to the presence of Englishmen as MPs; by 1614 this same group was described as 'foreigners.'[74]

The folk memory of that deception was still live in the early seventeenth century and a potent reminder of the administration's disregard for legality and the norms of political decency, but more immediately it coloured proceedings in subsequent Elizabethan parliaments. Following Sidney's very aggressive and equally illegal electioneering and remembering Sussex's want of principle, the Catholic opposition in 1569 refused to accept the returns of the very many English MPs and strongly contested Stanihurst's re-election as speaker. Even after some illegally returned MPs were excluded, 50 Englishmen, however that term was defined, remained, a dramatic increase on the 15 returned in 1560. MPs came from towns not previously represented and probably from counties yet to be legally

70 Hawkyard, *Commons*, pp 11–13; McGrath, 'Electoral strategy'.

71 Bradshaw, *Irish constitutional revolution*, p. 274.

72 On James Stanihurst, see Colm Lennon, 'Recusancy and the Dublin Stanyhursts', *Archivium Hibernicum*, 33 (1975), 101–10.

73 Moynes (ed.), *Annual letters*, ii, pp 401–4; Jefferies, 'The Irish parliament of 1560'; Archbishop Thomas Jones to Salisbury, 25 Feb. 1612, TNA, SP 63/232, fo. 28r.

74 *Cal. S.P. Ire., 1509–73*, p. 402; Moynes (ed.), *Annual letters*, ii, pp 401–4.

created: Edmund Fitz Alexander was appointed sheriff for Roscommon on 12 November 1568 before the act permitting new counties was passed, but in time to conduct elections and he may not have been the only such instance.[75] Defeated on the speakership and outnumbered by government supporters whose returns they questioned, the Old English opposition refused to allow the suspension of Poynings' Law, fearful of what the unscrupulous government would do with the freedom this would have provided. As Bradshaw noted, the administration's tactics in 1560 and 1569 resulted in

> increasingly effective filibustering on the part of the dissenting majority, and incrementally ruthless intimidation and carpet-bagging on the part of government over half a century, reached due consummation in the addled parliament of Lord Deputy Perrott, 1585–86 which brought the legislative process to a virtual standstill.[76]

The 1585 parliament provided another object lesson in the government's abuse of electoral law and the contradictions implicit in its attitude to the Gaelic Irish. While Perrot stated that he would treat English and Irish subjects equally, for the first time MPs and Gaelic chieftains attending parliament were obliged to wear English clothing.[77] Connacht's returns, managed by the murderous provincial president Richard Bingham, included eight government officials, presumably through both the exploitation of the lack of freeholders in the province and covert and/or aggressive elections. Insult would have been added to injury had the province's inhabitants been levied to pay for their wages, as is highly likely. This was a pyrrhic victory as the local native community fought back. Athenry was no longer prepared to accept crown nominees and five of these Connacht officials and MPs were commissioners for the Composition of Connacht, under which the Irish agreed to accept English land tenures, which they used to create freeholds that guaranteed Catholic MPs in the following parliaments. The Composition might have faced greater resistance had the 1585 election returns been different and the creation of a cohesive, organized Catholic electorate was as lasting, if unintended and, from the crown's perspective, unwelcome a result as the new land settlement. The MPs of Gaelic origin who attended the 1585 parliament obediently followed the lead of the experienced Old English politicians in opposition to Perrot's legislative programme and this pattern of co-operation between Old English and Gaelic MPs continued until the outbreak of the 1641 rebellion.[78] However, the Composition had other political consequences, including promoting two local Gaelic chiefdoms, the O'Briens as earls of Thomond and the Gaelicized Burkes as earls of Clanricard, and creating the insecure land titles that Elizabeth had claimed

75 *Deputy Keeper's Report*, viii, p. 183.
76 Bradshaw, 'Tudor reformation and revolutions in Wales and Ireland'.
77 Maxwell, *Irish history from contemporary sources*, pp 350–1.
78 Treadwell, 'Sir John Perrott'.

the Composition had been instituted to avoid. While locals assumed that they were acquiring clear personal titles to what had been clan lands, the position was exploited by unscrupulous English officials like John Crofton, MP for Sligo in 1585 and Richard Boyle, later first earl of Cork, to grab land in the province, and by wealthy Galway merchants to buy estates there.[79] The question of insecure titles throughout Ireland but specifically in Connacht was a major political problem and one of the reasons for the increase in the number of Irishmen studying law in the inns of court, especially talented Galwegians like Patrick Darcy (*plate 9*) and Richard Martin, sponsored by Clanricard; these and other Galway lawyers formed the backbone of opposition to the plantation of Connacht in the 1630s and in parliament from early 1641. The 1640 parliament's inability to achieve resolution of the issue of insecure land titles was one of the causes of the 1641 rebellion.[80]

However, Poynings' Law had other consequences. Parliament's infrequency and the stiff opposition the crown encountered there led to the Tudor privy council, Great Council and chancery taking on many of its functions, including legislation and justice. The Great Council, a flexible institution unfortunately undefined in Poynings' Law, but in Tudor times comprising the privy council, peers and a range of other invitees including gentry and military captains, was summoned to elect a new chief governor when necessary, declare war, participate in the swearing in of a new deputy and to observe the delivery of new seals at the accession of a new monarch. It also agreed to taxation in the form of the levy of a cess and to other acts of government through another constitutional innovation, Acts of State – law made by proclamation – and provided a forum for consultation between the administration and the political community, in effect, the roles performed by parliaments, especially in England. Sidney implicitly accepted the council's right to act as some sort of modified legislature and it could have played a similar role to the Scottish Convention of Estates, a scaled-down version of the full Estates, but it failed to develop that function. However, the ambiguity in its composition and role made it reasonable for the Catholic lords to claim that as members of the Great Council, they should be consulted on legislation for the

79 Gerard Hayes-McCoy, 'The completion of the Tudor conquest and the advance of the Counter-Reformation, 1571–1603' in T.W. Moody, et al. (eds), *A new history of Ireland*, 9 vols (Oxford, 1977–2005), iii, pp 94–141; David Edwards, 'From land-thief to planter: Kerry transactions and the rise of Richard Boyle, first earl of Cork' in Maurice J. Bric (ed.), *Kerry: history and society* (Dublin, 2020), pp 141–63; Breandán Ó Bric, 'Galway townsmen as the owners of land in Connaught, 1585–1641' (MA, University College Galway, 1974); Nicholas Canny, 'Boyle, Richard, 1st earl of Cork', *DIB*; Henry Thomas Crofton, *Crofton memoirs: an account of John Crofton, of Ballymurry, Co. Roscommon, Queen Elizabeth's escheator-general of Ireland, and of his ancestors and descendants* (York, 1911).

80 Bernadette Cunningham, 'Natives and newcomers in Mayo, 1560–1603' in Raymond Gillespie and Gerard Moran (eds), *'A various country': essays in Mayo history, 1500–1900* (Westport, 1987), pp 11–23; Bríd McGrath, 'Ireland and the third university: attendance at the Inns of Court, 1603–1649' in David Edwards (ed.), *Regions and rulers in Ireland, 1100–1650: essays for Kenneth Nicholls* (Dublin, 2004), pp 217–36. Extensive details on Darcy and Martin are provided in Appendix 3.

1613 parliament.[81] The 1542 Act for the election of the lord justice (33 Hen. VIII, c. 2 or 3), which specified that the chief governor should be an 'Englishman and born within the realm of England', merely affirmed the position since 1534. It also gave the council a mediating role in reconciling local interests, but the gradual replacement of Old English councillors with New English removed this function and instead it became solely an instrument of executive government.[82] Given the slow extension of shiring and the common law courts outside the old Lordship, it was reasonable for the privy council to sit as a court and Sidney's establishment of the Court of Castle Chamber, the Irish equivalent of the English Star Chamber and presidencies in Munster and Connacht with their own courts provided substitute judicial services which could sit outside law terms, allowing for speedy justice. However, these courts continued in place after the creation of a system of courts at local and national level and later provided arbitrary justice and used judge-made law to change the common law.

The common and statute law systems administered in local assizes and courts, touted as a universal benefit for all subjects, did not produce the advantages the state claimed for the native population and the increasingly English judiciary, while loudly proclaiming the theoretical benefits of a universally accepted known law over the 'arbitrary' justice of Gaelic courts, developed a system of judge-made law, which routinely disadvantaged Irishmen to fill what they saw as gaps in the common law.[83] Parliament, as a forum for presenting grievances for redress, as well as its legislative role, was the primary, if infrequent, mechanism for their protection. Moreover, as Bradshaw has shown, it was less a legislative than a consultative forum, but the disinclination of the crown to consult and its determination to have a compliant parliament, partly because Poynings' Law removed its ability to negotiate on unpopular bills, and the rise of highly effective Old English parliamentarians, created inevitable conflict between the administration and the political community.[84]

As the level of coercion and constitutional innovation increased, the Old English and Gaelic Irish were progressively excluded from positions of power, but expected to pay, through parliamentary taxation and fines for not attending church, as was imposed by An Act for the Uniformity of Common Prayer and Service in the Church (2 Eliz. I, c. 2), for the changes which benefitted the minority settler community. Such seismic changes inevitably created and reinforced mutual mistrust between them and the administration and provoked resistance and opposition, inside and outside parliament. The government's response, involving

81 Crawford, *Anglicizing*, pp 32–3, 61–9; W.N. Osborough, 'Eighteenth-century Ireland's legislative deficit' in Michael Brown and Seán Patrick Donlan (eds), *The laws and other legalities of Ireland, 1689–1850* (London, 2016), pp 75–96; Jenny Wormald, *Court, kirk and community: Scotland 1470–1625* (London, 1981), pp 20ff; *Cal. S.P. Ire., 1611–14*, p. 342.

82 *Statutes*, i, pp 207–8. The act is variously given as c. 2 or c. 3. A bill to amend it in 1560 was not passed. *Cal. S.P. Ire., 1509–73*, p. 159.

83 Crawford, *Anglicizing*, pp 245–6.

84 Bradshaw, 'Beginnings'.

disregard for the law and the norms of political discourse and procedure, dramatically worsened the situation. While Catholics were not excluded from parliament, their religious allegiance became a litmus test for their loyalty and many, including MPs, conformed to protect their economic and social standing. The membership of the House of Lords was transformed also. The Reformation settlement excluded abbots and priors and empowered the monarch to make appointments to Irish bishoprics and increasing numbers of Englishmen were chosen, changing the church leaders' backgrounds and attitudes, giving them personal landed estates in Ireland and families to provide for, but also political patronage in elections and therefore close relatives in the Commons.

Two other differences between early modern English and Irish parliaments were the requirement to take the oath of supremacy in England, which, while threatened in Ireland, was not introduced, with doubtful legality, until 1642 and had no statutory basis until 1691, when an English act resolved the matter, and how members' resignations were handled.[85] The English Commons repeatedly refused to allow members to resign (except if appointed to a crown office, such as attorney general) and on 2 March 1624 agreed that 'a Man, after he is duly chosen, cannot relinquish.'[86] In Ireland there were many resignations and no instance of one being refused by the Commons, although Hugh Montgomery's request to resign his seat on 12 October 1640 was referred to a committee.[87] There were at least nine resignations in 1634 and a minimum of 21 resignations in 1640–1, all but one by Protestant MPs; this is however, certainly an under-estimate. In addition, some Irish MPs were replaced for non-attendance.[88] In the eighteenth century, the English mechanism of applying for the stewardship of the Chiltern Hundreds, or other equivalent notional offices of profit under the crown, was matched in Ireland by the escheatorships of Munster and Ulster, but they were unknown in Stuart Ireland.[89]

Membership of the medieval Irish, English and Scottish parliaments, which had varied depending on political and military circumstances, was formalized in the early modern period.[90] The history of the crown's bad faith, secrecy about its

85 Bodl. Lib., Rawlinson MS D 922, fos. 49r–54r.

86 Paul Seaward, 'Resignation', The History of Parliament Trust Blog, 4 Dec. 2018, at https://historyofparliamentblog.wordpress.com/2018/12/04/resignation/ [accessed 25 Feb. 2019]. English Tudor parliaments had facilitated resignations. Hawkyard, *Commons*, pp 96–8, 102–5.

87 Terry Clavin, 'Montgomery, Hugh, 3rd Viscount Montgomery', *DIB*.

88 Arthur Bassett, Thomas Bettsworth, Henry Bingham, Chichester Fortescue, William Kingsmill, Thomas Leake, Henry Lynch, Maltravers and Lott Peere resigned. Barnaby Bryan and Valentine Blake agreed to writs for their replacement if they did not appear in the House. Arthur Chichester, Henry Tichbourne, Philip Lisle and Laurence Crawford were replaced for non-attendance: McGrath, 'Irish elections of 1640–1641'; *Commons' Jn. Ire.*, 9 April 1644.

89 McGrath, 'Irish elections of 1640–1641'; W.E.H. Lecky, *A history of Ireland in the eighteenth century*, 8 vols (London, 1898), v, p. 283; Michael Brown, et al. (eds), *The Irish Act of Union 1801: bicentennial essays* (Dublin, 2003), pp 139–41.

90 Henry Elsynge, *The ancient method and manner of holding parliaments in England* (3rd ed., London, 1675), pp 30–1. For the variable nature of the seventeenth-century Scottish Estates' membership, see Kennedy, 'Representing the periphery'.

legislative programme, aggressive and illegal electioneering, suspicion of the native Irish political community and determination to use the same tactics to engineer a parliamentary majority under the Stuarts formed the background to the summoning of the 1613 parliament and its successors. The Catholics' understandable defensiveness and fears for their own position fuelled their determination to preserve their interests and press for the redress of grievances. Parliament was the forum for this contest, played out by a changing and divided political community, which nevertheless shared many characteristics and concerns because of its common social class, education and economic interests. As a result, elections were very fiercely fought and parliament's developing role was influenced by an administration prepared to act dishonestly and illegally and a cohesive opposition determined to defend its own interests.

CHAPTER TWO

Records of parliament

AS IMPORTANT, IF OCCASIONAL, INSTITUTIONS, a wide range of documents were produced relating to Irish parliaments' role, membership, work, proceedings and practice and to attitudes towards the institution.[1] There are many references to the lack of sources for Irish history in general, and early modern parliaments in particular, and it is certainly true that much material was lost over the years through natural wastage, insecure and unsuitable storage, the disastrous fire in the Public Record Office in 1922 and doubtless contemporary self-censorship.[2] Sources from official or Protestant sources were more likely to survive than those from the native Irish political community, especially since before 1643 the crown controlled the only printing press in Ireland. Lords deputies' self-interested accounts of their engagement with parliament have survived, whereas few documents providing the opposition point of view remain, especially after 1615 and this has necessarily coloured historians' interpretation of parliament and its work. A further difficulty is presented by the use of calendars or abstracts of surviving records that often omit valuable details. Few Gaelic sources refer to parliament, and those that do, such as annals, poems, which reference MPs' activities outside parliament, or prose works, such as *Páirlement Chloinne Tomáis* are satirical accounts of fictional assemblies and provide almost no detail about the actual parliaments of the time. Interestingly, letters written by Catholics about the 1613–15 parliament were published in Spanish for an Iberian audience or written in Latin for reception in Rome.[3]

Despite this, much material has survived in original manuscripts, transcripts and print, although it is difficult to source because it is scattered throughout collections in Ireland, England and America and frequently poorly indexed; the very survival of so many documents attests to parliament's importance and the widespread interest in the institution and its work. Surviving sources comprise original documents and copies; they were created by parliament itself, administrators in their work for parliament, MPs, their constituents and other interested observers. Both houses produced their own journals and orders, correspondence and committee reports. Declarations and remonstrances were agreed by both houses. Very few letters and reports survive. Administrators created

1 This chapter provides a brief overview of surviving sources. Detailed references to documents are provided in the other chapters of this book.
2 For a recent example, see Dennehy, 'Irish parliament after the rebellion'.
3 Marc Caball, '*Pairlement Chloinne Tomáis I*: a reassessment', *Éigse*, 27 (1993), 47–57; Benjamin Hazard, *Faith and patronage: the political career of Flaithrí Ó Maolchonaire, c.1560–1629* (Dublin, 2009), pp 77ff; Thomas White, *Aviso del estado en que al presente estan las cosas de los Catholicos en el Reyno de Irlanda* (Salamanca, 1611). I am grateful to Hiram Morgan for drawing this reference to my attention and to Ricard Torra-Prat for translating it for me.

records relating to parliament's summoning, elections, membership, wages, operations and legislation. MPs produced speeches, petitions and letters. Constituents submitted petitions, letters, draft bills, lists of grievances and proposals for legislation; borough records provide unique sources for elections and wages and maps of towns provide key information about their size, facilities and potential electorates. Very few contemporary petitions have survived, apart from those included in the clerk's rough journal for 1613–15 and two copies from February 1641.[4] Sermons preached before parliament were written and delivered by bishops who were members of the upper house. Similar documents were produced in all countries, but the vast majority of material remains in manuscript form, especially for Ireland. Documents frequently found in other countries, especially diaries, manuals of practice, printed petitions, pamphlets and images of parliament are completely absent for Ireland and other sources, such as transcripts of speeches and committee reports are also very rare. Parliament's inability to initiate legislation explains the lack of corporate petitions and lobbying material found in England, as the route to legislative success was through the lord deputy and privy councillors.

Official records include commissions for summoning and proroguing parliament, mandates for election, writs of return, parliamentary journals and orders, legislation, formal statements such as remonstrances, declarations and proclamations, working papers (e.g., committee reports), documents addressed to either house, such as petitions, letters, lists of grievances, sermons and administrative records (e.g., lists of members and wages). Unofficial documents include speeches and debates, a very small number of which were printed more-or-less contemporaneously. Material about parliament consists of objections to returns, pamphlets, comments in letters, reports and other documents.

Greatest attention is paid here to parliament's most important records: those produced by parliament itself, its journals, legislation, orders and declarations. They are also those which have survived in the greatest number, fullest state and best condition. Irish parliamentary records were extremely poorly managed in the medieval and early modern period. The master of the rolls was responsible for parliamentary rolls and statutes, which were held very insecurely in unsuitable premises in chancery – payments were repeatedly made to make the location waterproof – and under the Tudors there were examples of theft, interference and deliberate damage to the rolls. Bradshaw notes the only surviving roll for 1536–7.[5] A Dublin-based English official wrote *c.*1600 that

4 Copy of petition to the House of Commons of the gentlemen and inhabitants residing and dwelling in the King's and Queen's counties, on the behalf of themselves and the rest of the natives of this kingdom, Feb. 1641, TNA, SP 63/274, fo. 1; *Commons' Jn. Ire.*, 22 Feb. 1641. TNA, SP 63/274, fo. 5 is a similar document, but with the addition of the inhabitants of counties Longford and Leitrim, of which there is no mention in the journals.

5 Connolly (ed.), *Statute rolls*, pp xix–xx, 343–4; McGrath, 'Electoral law in Ireland before 1641'; Bradshaw, 'Opposition'.

> such hath been the former remissnes of Officers, that there is noe Parliament records there but a fewe and those sithence the time of H.6 remayning in the Master of the Rolls Office here and not else to be found saveing for other records remayning with the chiefe Remembrancer, the Auditor and Surveyor concearning her Majesty's revenues and casualties only, and some fewe in the Office of chiefe place there called the Queenes Bench concerning matters of Attainder and a fewe in the common place concerning some late Utlagaries (outlawries).

Even material that did survive was not necessarily available: the same official noted how many records, which were widely regarded as the property of individual officers, were brought to England when those administrators left Ireland: 'Sir William Gerrard late Lord Chancellor here, who they say tooke the chiefe records into England with him and cannot nowe be had.'[6] It is especially surprising that the 1585 Commons' journals could not be located in 1613, as its speaker Nicholas Walsh was still alive and Arthur Chichester, who married John Perrot's daughter, might have been assumed to have access to his papers.[7]

Records were better managed in the early Stuart period. Thomas Chetham, clerk of parliament between 1595 and 1624, sought to remedy deficiencies, copying any records he could trace.[8] However, officials keeping material in their own possession continued and was explicitly referenced in the letter of both houses in response to King Charles' letter in May 1641:

> the few ancient Records which are left here were and are as yet at the Command of the said Lord Chancellor and Lord Chief Justice who even since theire Impeachment had the custody of the Parliament Rolls in their private studies.[9]

Copies of commissions for summoning and proroguing parliament survive for all early Stuart parliaments, as does Chichester's formal justification for calling the 1613 assembly.[10] A template for sheriff's mandates for election is included in the preliminaries to the 1613 printed Commons' journals, but only two originals are known to have survived.[11] Three transcripts of boroughs' returns survive for 1634, 1640 and 1642.[12] Surviving accounts of individual elections are described in

6 Advice and directions for summoning a parliament in Ireland, *c.*1600, Bodl. Lib., Rawlinson MS D. 922, fos. 49r–54. Gerard died in 1581.
7 Terry Clavin, 'Walsh, Sir Nicholas', *DIB*.
8 See chapter nine on personnel.
9 TCD, MS 1180, p. 4.
10 Details and references are given in chapter five. Chichester to King James, 15 Oct. 1611, TNA, SP 63/231, fo. 252.
11 Caulfield (ed.), *Youghal*, p. 181; KCA, MS CR/K/56. I am grateful to David Edwards for drawing this reference to my attention.
12 McGrath, 'Athboy's election returns 1640 and 1641'. An abstract for Ennis in 1634 is in Lodge's parliamentary register, *Liber Mun. Pub. Hib.*, i, pp 1–46. TNA, MS C219/44 are the returns from

chapter five. The original indentures of return, which were stored in chancery, were destroyed in 1922. The clerk's lists of official returns for 1613 and 1640 both survive, but there never seems to have been an authoritative return for 1634 and the returns for 1642–8 were poorly managed, even at the time.[13] By contrast, from 1628, and most especially after 1640, English clerks had regular printed editions of lists of members of the upper and lower houses, notably the London publisher, Thomas Walkley's *A catalogve of the names of the knights for the counties, citizens, burgesses for the boroughs and barons for the ports for the House of Commons for this parliament, begune at Westminster the 17 of March 1627* (London, 1628).[14] While useful for clerks, their handy size made them very beneficial for those wishing to lobby parliamentarians.[15]

Journals succeeded medieval parliament rolls as the formal record of parliament's decisions. Earlier rolls provided full records of parliament's business, but in England from 1484 they contained little more than lists of acts passed; from the sixteenth century English parliamentary clerks also produced journals of parliament's proceedings and decisions, as a tool to keep on top of parliamentary business – manuscript versions include some *aides-memoire* – and as an indispensable source for precedents.[16] Irish journals were also used for precedents – for example whether MPs should wear gowns in 1613 and which constituencies should be represented. Where journals failed to provide guidance, recourse was had to parliament rolls, for example on the question of whether judges might be MPs and what MPs' wages should be.[17]

Hawkyard provides a forensic account of the development of English journals, which survive from 1510 and 1547 respectively for the Lords and Commons.[18] English journals record decisions, orders and letters issued and received and acts passed, with little account of debates, and so present a misleading impression of harmony and accord, which are contradicted by accounts of speeches, personal

1654 which were held in London because they were for the Commonwealth Parliament. I am grateful to David Brown for drawing them to my attention.

13 TNA, MS PRO 30/5/3, fos. 2–10; RIA, MS 24/Q/5, no. 41; McGrath, 'Electoral strategy'; McGrath, 'Recruiter returns'.

14 Henry R. Plomer, *A dictionary of the booksellers and printers who were at work in England, Scotland and Ireland from 1641 to 1667* (London, 1907), p. 187.

15 Despite the title, this small volume included all the English, Scottish and Irish peers, English baronets and the knights of the Bath. Under the heading 'Officers of the House of Commons' it lists the 'Clarkes of the Parliament' and 'Serieante at Armes', but the speaker is the first in the list of MPs. For later editions, see Thomas Walkley, *A catalogue of the dukes, marquesses, earles, viscounts …* (London, 1642).

16 Martyn Atkins, 'Persuading the House: the use of the Commons' journals as a source of precedent' in Paul Evans (ed.), *Essays on the history of parliamentary procedure, in honour of Thomas Erskine May* (London, 2017), pp 69–86.

17 *Commons' Jn. Ire.*, 15, 29 Oct. 1614, 16 May 1615.

18 Alasdair D. Hawkyard, 'The journals, the clerks of the parliaments and the under-clerks, 1485–1601', *Parl. Hist.*, 33:3 (2014), 389–421 also provides a list of English manuscript journals for the period. Chris R. Kyle, 'Parliament and the theater of state: the construction of texts', *Shakespeare Studies*, 30 (2002), 31–7.

diaries and journals. From the 1620s, the English clerk, Henry Elsynge, began to produce fuller records of proceedings in rolls, but the level of detail, especially of contributions to debates, varied, depending on individual clerks and the political exigencies of the day, while also privileging national, rather than local, matters.[19] English MPs were increasingly defensive about having their contributions recorded; in 1610, 1614 and 1621 they ordered reviews of the clerk's books and decisions were made in 1624 to exclude MPs' names from records and in April 1640 to restrict the clerk's record.[20] Moreover, journals only record speech and not responses such as silence, laughter or other commotions, which would have been very telling and which might have been described in diaries, had any survived.[21]

It is unclear when Irish parliamentary journals started, but the earliest survivor is a partial one from the Lords in 1586, suggesting that the Commons were also maintaining journals by that date and probably rather earlier. The 1613–15 Lords' journal, which has not survived, was clearly a substantial record of that house's work as its index detailed records from over 44 folios. It is unclear how many copies were originally made, apart from the official file copy, which was destroyed in 1922, but Chetham was a diligent clerk and it is likely that Chichester, the Commons' Speaker John Davies and the Lord Chancellor Thomas Jones (speaker of the Lords) at least would also have had copies.[22] The seventeenth-century antiquarian and MP for the University of Dublin in 1634 and 1640, Sir James Ware (*plate 18*), acquired the index, but apparently not the actual Lords' journal.[23] Original manuscript versions of the 1634–5 and part of the 1640 journals do survive.[24] A list of the known manuscript versions of the journals is provided in Appendix no. 1.

John Hooker, MP for Athenry, kept a personal diary for the first session of the 1569 Irish Commons, but the first official Irish Commons' journal dates from 1613 and no earlier ones survived into the seventeenth century; however, an order in the Commons on 17 October 1614 that 'the rolls and books of the last parliament shall be brought before the said committees' demonstrates that at least some sources

19 Smith, *Stuart*, p. 12; Alan R. MacDonald, '"Tedious to rehers?" Parliament and locality in Scotland, *c.*1500–1651: the burghs of north-east Fife', *PER*, 20:1 (2000), 31–58; J.C. Sainty, 'Elsynge [Elsyng], Henry', *Oxford DNB*.

20 Jason Peacey, '"Rushworth shall not take any notes here": journals, debates and the public, 1640–60', *Parl. Hist.*, 33:3 (2014), 422–37; Keith A.T. Stapylton, 'The parliamentary privilege of freedom from arrest, 1603–29' (PhD, University College London, 2016), pp 32–3; Andrew Thrush, 'The speaker', at https://www.historyofparliamentonline.org/volume/1604-1629/survey/viii-officers-and-servants-house [accessed 10 May 2019].

21 Patrick Little, 'Silence and laughter in the Cromwellian House of Commons', at https://thehistoryofparliament.wordpress.com/2022/02/08/silence-and-laughter-in-the-cromwellian-house-of-commons/ [accessed 11 Feb. 2022].

22 Judy Barry, 'Jones, Thomas', *DIB*.

23 William O'Sullivan, 'Ware, Sir James', *DIB*.

24 Routledge, 'Journal'; Victor Treadwell, 'The House of Lords in the Irish parliament of 1613–1615', *EHR*, 80:314 (1965), 92–107; TCD, MSS 613–15; NLI, MS 9,607. Treadwell was apparently unaware of the surviving manuscript copies of the Lords' and Commons' journals. William O'Sullivan, 'A finding list of Sir James Ware's manuscripts', *Proc. RIA*, 97C (1997), 69–99.

were available.[25] One rough and three fair copies of the 1613 Irish Commons' journals survive and these and all subsequent Commons' journals, and the Lords' journals from 1634, were published in several editions from 1752.[26] Convocation also kept journals of its proceedings.[27]

Early Stuart Irish Commons' journals follow the English format, commencing with the day's date in Latin. Thereafter entries are in English, unless quoting Latin speech.[28] Journals served as minutes, recording decisions – stages of bills, acts passed, motions, committee formation and membership, orders, resolutions and censures of members or outsiders – rather than reports of debates. As such they supply relatively little detail on debates, speeches, committee proceedings and reports, especially after 1615.[29] All are partial and incomplete records of the House's activity, being compiled in an individual fashion by different clerks, William Bradley and Edmund Medhop in 1613–15 and Philip Fernesly from 1628.[30] The difference between the detail in the 1613–15 and the 1634 and 1640 journals probably stems from individual clerks' approach; the 1613 journals record more details of contributors and speeches, although in the absence of Fernesly's original journals, precise differences between the manuscript and printed journals cannot accurately be established. Institutionalized favouritism towards the New English is evident in omissions of some Catholic contributions in 1613–15, as well as Medhop's listing New English MPs' titles and status, but not Catholics'.[31]

25 Hooker's diary is published in Falkiner, *Essays*, pp 237ff; S. Mendyk, 'Hooker [Vowell], John', *Oxford DNB*. For the lack of pre-1613 Irish journals, see William Molyneux's abstracts from Irish Commons' journals, 1613–66, TCD, MS 622. Molyneux was using originals which no longer survive as he provides folio numbers for all extracts, which are very close to the printed journals, but do not correspond to the foliation of Medhop's fair copies.

26 TNA, MS PRO 30/5/3, fos. 23–144; King's Inns, MS N3/2/1/7; NLI, MS 836; ARL, MS KH.II.7; H.D. Gribbon, 'Journals of the Irish House of Commons', *An Leabharlann*, 2nd series, 2:2 (1985), 51–6; Dermott Englefield, *The printed records of the parliament of Ireland, 1613–1800* (London, 1978), pp 8–10; *idem*, 'Printing the journal of the Irish House of Commons' in Harry Cobb (ed.), *Parliamentary history, libraries and records* (London, 1981), pp 33–43. The process of compilation is traced in Bríd McGrath, 'The compilation of the Irish House of Commons' journals, 1613–15', Paper presented to Tudor and Stuart Ireland Annual Conference, Dublin, 2022, at https://soundcloud.com/history-hub/brid-mcgrath-journals-of-the-Irish-house-of-commons [accessed 19 Nov. 2022]. The proceedings of the 1585 Catalan Corts were edited in the early twenty-first century in the collection *Textos Jurídics Catalans*, published by the Catalan Government and the Catalan Parliament (volumes 18–22). I am grateful to Josep Capdeferro for drawing this reference to my attention.

27 Garstin's transcriptions of Convocation records, No. 8, 1639–41, ARL, MS KE.I.7. For a comprehensive list of Irish Convocation records, see Gerald Bray (ed.), *Records of convocation: Ireland, 1101–1690*; *idem*, *Records of convocation: Ireland 1690–1869, Part 1* (Woodbridge, 2006).

28 Hawkyard, *Commons*, p. 221; Smith, *Stuart*, pp 12–13.

29 The early 1634 Lords' journals provide attendance lists, some speeches, committee proceedings and judicial decisions, TCD, MSS 613–14; Englefield, *Printed records*, p. 19; Coleman A. Dennehy, 'Some manuscript alternatives to the printed Irish parliamentary journals', *PER*, 30:2 (2010), 129–42.

30 Mathew Davies acted as clerk for four days in Nov. 1614.

31 TNA, MS PRO 30/5/3; NLI, MS 836, unpaginated end papers; ARL, MS KH.II.7, unpaginated end papers. This is not included in King's Inns, MS N3/2/1/7.

Chetham and Medhop in particular improved existing records' management and expanded the journals' contents from those of the Lords in 1585, which merely recorded the processing of bills, prorogations, royal assent, committee formation and a petition from the serjeant-at-arms about his conditions, to provide much greater detail about activities in parliament, including attendance, orders, contact between the houses, judicial cases, petitions, disciplining of individuals, presenting grievances to the deputy and even an index.

There were three stages of journal production. First, clerks made rough notes during each sitting day on loose sheets of paper, which they soon after transcribed into the rough draft journal. The clerk in England was issued with two 'fair' bound volumes, presumably for his first and second stage journals, but one, Ralph Ewens kept seven books of his own notes, and the final journals were supplemented by other material, such as petitions and reports from committees.[32] Philip Percival, clerk of the Lords in Ireland, was issued with at least three bound blank volumes in 1634–5, two of which he used in that parliament and one in the following one.[33] The rough and fair copies of the 1640–8 Lords' journals disappeared at some time after 1693 when the extracts in Marsh's Library, MS Z.3.2.5 and NLI, MS 9,607 were made and preparations for printing them, a project undertaken in the following century. These manuscripts provide considerable additional information on contributions and decisions compared to TCD, MSS 613–14, although the latter align very closely with the published Lords' journals.[34]

In 1615 Medhop bound Bradley's and his own rough notes with other documents relating to the Commons' membership, the opening session and details of work such as petitions into one volume, from which he made at least five manuscript fair copies between October 1615 and 1621: the official copy which perished in 1922, three others now held in the King's Inns, the National Library of Ireland and Armagh Robinson Library and one formerly owned by James Ware, the whereabouts of which is unknown. If another copy was made for the speaker John Davies, as is likely, it is not known to have survived.[35] All of these versions are on paper, but, following English practice, the file copy may have been on parchment.[36] An under-clerk wrote the King's Inns copy almost immediately after the dissolution in October 1615 (unless this is a copy of the missing original) and Medhop checked and endorsed two entries as *Clericus Parliamentis* with the year 1615. The entries are clear and close to the draft, albeit sometimes differently

32 Andrew Thrush, 'The speaker', at https://www.historyofparliamentonline.org/volume/1604-1629/survey/viii-officers-and-servants-house [accessed 10 May 2019].

33 TCD, MSS 613–15. All have identical watermarks and binding. Terry Clavin, 'Percival (Perceval), Sir Phillip', *DIB*.

34 Marsh's Library, MS Z3.2.5, pp 29–77. Each extract was endorsed by the clerk, Gerard Bor, as follows: 'This for so much agreeth with the Journall of the House of Lords'. Dennehy, *Parliament*, pp 8–11.

35 TNA, MS PRO 30/5/3, fos. 23r–144; King's Inns, MS N3/2/1/7; NLI, MS 836; ARL, MS KH.II.7. All three fair copies were written on paper with different watermarks.

36 Foster, 'Painful labour'.

phrased.[37] The NLI copy was made *c.*1618 and the Armagh copy between 1619 and 1621.[38] Ware's copy was 'in fol' (unbound), which demonstrates that it was neither the rough notes nor one of Medhop's fair copies, all of which were bound.[39] The Armagh copy was made for Chichester and the NLI copy was probably transcribed for either Francis Annesley, later Lord Mountnorris (*plate 1*), or Sir James Hamilton, later Lord Claneboy (*plate 2*), Medhop's brothers-in-law, whose family trees linking them to Chichester and himself are provided in the front of both of these copies.[40] Many contemporary extracts from the journals also survive, although it is frequently unclear from which original they were copied. The folio numbers cited in Bodleian Library, Carte MS 64, fo. 149r, for instance, do not match any of Medhop's versions.[41] There are also at least two eighteenth-century copies, written in the same hand on paper with identical watermarks.[42]

When writing up the 'fair' version, some changes were made and details lost: Medhop arranged committee members' names in order of their social status, rather than their nomination, which gave greater prominence to the New English who were more likely to be privy councillors and knighted. He also omitted contributions of which he had made notes. Other business was simply not recorded, such as the question of the leases of the bishop of Kilmacduagh and there is no mention in the journals of debate on the Covenant on 18 April 1644, which was so intense that the House was prorogued.[43] Even conscientious clerks like Percival miss some entries and some journals which appear to provide full accounts of business have many omissions: both TCD, MSS 613–14, omit the entry for 16 July 1634, although it appears in the published version; TCD, MS 808, fo. 147v. is an order of the committee of grievances concerning an otherwise unrecorded petition and TCD, MS 672, fo. 239r provides a list of corporations MPs asked to justify their rights to representation on 24 July 1634, of which there is no mention in the journals. On 17 June 1641, the speaker received a letter from the Committee in England during a parliamentary sitting and 'I acquainted the house with the said letters which being severall tymes reade and diligently perused the House after serious debate and deliberate advisement therein had comaunded

37 King's Inns, MS N3/2/1/7, fos. 26r, 54v. This journal is not in Medhop's hand.
38 These datings are based on the birth dates of the children of Francis Annesley and James Hamilton given on the family tree included at the front of both volumes.
39 O'Sullivan, 'Finding list'. Mark Empey (personal communication) suggests that Ware may have obtained this from the Barnewalls of Dunbroe, but it seems more likely that he had it from his father, who was a member of the 1613 Commons, or arranged to have a copy made for himself, especially as he also had a copy of the Lords' journal. Gilbert Library, MS 173. Gilbert's transcription of Ware's extracts from those journals only notes the opening procession on 18 May 1613.
40 Robert Armstrong, 'Annesley, Francis', *DIB*; Terry Clavin, 'Hamilton, James', *DIB*.
41 BL, Harleian MS 4,892, Bodl. Lib., Laud MS Misc. 612.
42 TCD, MS 1,444; FSL, MS W.b.510.
43 E.g., TNA, MS PRO 30/5/3, fo. 24r includes added detail of Sir John Everard's speech, and fo. 32 for 15 Oct. also provides greater detail than in Medhop's fair versions. NAI, MS Chancery Q 2, taken from Ken Nicholls' calendar of chancery documents. *Cal. S.P. Ire., 1625–32*, p. 547; Borlase, *History*, p. 118.

mee to returne vnto you this answearr.' The journals include no mention of this, although they record a series of orders on subjects of apparently less importance.[44] 'The humble petition and declaration of the lords spiritual and temporal and Commons in parliament assembled', 23 June 1642, was clearly agreed between the two houses and the Commons' journals refers to the conference committee and drafts from both houses, but makes no mention of agreement or the text of the petition and declaration.[45] 'The address of the Lords and Commons in parliament assembled made to the Marquis of Ormond the 17 March 1647' is the only record that parliament was sitting in the days around 18 March 1647.[46]

Bradley and Medhop's notes are all on paper with the same watermark, while material from other sources, such as the list of members and petitions, are on paper with at least five different watermarks.[47] Inevitably, given the use of loose sheets, some records were lost. Examples include the four or five days following 18 May 1613, although both houses continued in session into June, debating bills and petitions, and 11 and 12 October 1614, later found by Medhop and included in his fair copies.[48] The fair copy was compiled as the official record after parliament's conclusion; at that point, members would have been unable to check or correct the record, or even ensure that a fair copy was made. The English parliament blamed its clerk Ewens for not having made fair copies of the journal and the 1634–5 Irish Lords ordered that their Committee of Privileges

> shall have power for six days after the end of this present session of Parliament to peruse the Journal-book to the end that all passages, order, speeches and protestations touching any difference between both Houses of Parliament may be cancelled or obliterated.

This implies an expectation that the clerk would make his fair copy very quickly after parliament's end.[49]

No known original notes, drafts or Fernesly's fair copies of the 1634 or 1640–8 Commons' journals survive, although he clearly made at least one fair copy of each,

44 Speaker Maurice Eustace to the Committee in England, 22 June 1641, ARL, Parliamentary Papers, unpaginated.

45 To the Rt. Hon. the Lords Justices & Counsell; The humble petition and declaration of the lords spiritual and temporal and Commons in parliament assembled, 23 June 1644 (recte 1642), TCD, MS 1,178, no. 4, endorsed '*copia vera*', but without a signature.

46 Bodl. Lib., Carte MS 176, fo. 210.

47 TNA, MS PRO 30/5/3; Order in favour of Henry Piers MP, 29 Nov. 1614, Bodl. Lib., Carte MS 61 fo. 33. This is signed by Bradley and has the same watermark.

48 William Farmer, 'A chronicle of Lord Chichester's government of Ireland' in Lodge, *Desiderata Curiosa*, i, pp 205–7; Treadwell, 'House of Lords'; Bodl. Lib., Carte MS 64, fo. 149r includes entries from 22 Oct. 1614. These extracts were not taken from Medhop's fair copies, as they cite folio numbers which do not match those manuscripts or TNA, MS PRO 30/5/3.

49 Andrew Thrush, 'The speaker', at https://www.historyofparliamentonline.org/volume/1604-1629/survey/viii-officers-and-servants-house [accessed 10 May 2019]; *LJI*, 17 April 1635. The work involved in creating the finished journals is comprehensively discussed in Foster, 'Painful labour'.

which the late seventeenth-century political theorist and scientist, William Molyneux, used to make abstracts from all the journals between 1613 and 1641 and 1661–6.[50] Apparently accurate, but incomplete extracts from the 1634 and 1640–1 fair journals were made in the eighteenth century.[51] There are also extracts in Bodleian Library, Carte MS 64, fo. 149r, British Library, Egerton MS 2,541 and British Library, Harleian MS 4,892. The Commons' journals for 16 November 1641 to 26 March 1647 were already missing in the 1680s as Molyneux did not use them, but having been subsequently discovered by Michael Duggan (who was paid £200 for the manuscript) they were produced as an appendix in the 1765 printed edition and incorporated into the third edition in 1782.[52] All of the official journals from 1613 were carefully kept in Dublin Castle until transferred to the Public Records Office where they were part of the 149 volumes of luxuriously bound manuscript fair copies of the pre-1800 Irish parliamentary journals which perished in 1922.[53]

Clerks swore to 'make true entry of all such orders and rules as should be conceived in the said house and for the faithful keeping of the secrets of the said house.' Accuracy was ensured by members' oversight, with frequent references to the Houses' checking and correcting the records. Both crown and parliamentarians understood the journals' importance as parliament's formal record and were prepared to change it either to guarantee accuracy or to alter the record. On 7 July 1641 six lawyer members, three Protestant and three Catholic, were appointed to sit in rotation every day to 'view and peruse the orders, conceived in this house, and to amend, alter, correct, fit, and prepare them according to the sense of this house'; this suggests considerable mistrust of either the speaker or the clerk among MPs.[54]

In 1621 King James I ripped out entries in the English Commons' journals and on 17 November 1640 Lord Deputy Christopher Wandesford (*plate 26*) tore out the Irish Commons' entries for 20 October and 11 November 1640, which were orders about the levying of subsidies agreed in the House, based on the committee's report on that subject.[55] The latter were ordered to be restored, after protests by parliament's agents in England, but do not appear in the printed

50 Patrick H. Kelly, 'Molyneux (Molyneaux), William', *DIB*.

51 TCD, MS 622. Molyneux was born in 1656 and was an MP for Trinity College in 1692. The date of transcription is unclear, but presumably it was undertaken sometime in the 1680s as they would otherwise have included extracts from that parliament. J.G. Simms and P.H. Kelly (eds), *William Molyneux of Dublin* (Dublin, 1982), pp 91ff; King's Inns, MS N3/2/1/8 comprises an accurate but partial eighteenth-century transcript of some extracts from 20 March 1635 to its dissolution and for the Commons between March 1640 and 15 July 1641 with references apparently to the folios of the original journal.

52 R. Mountmorres, *The history of the principal transactions of the Irish parliament from the year 1634 to 1666*, 2 vols (London, 1792), i, p. xiii; Englefield, *Printed records*, pp 8–10; *idem*, 'Printing the journal'.

53 Maurice Craig, *Irish bookbindings, 1600–1800* (London, 1954), pp 3–11 and plates 1–17.

54 E.g., *Commons' Jn. Ire.*, 25 Nov. 1614, 18 April 1615, 17 April 1635; *LJI*, 18 July 1634.

55 Terry Clavin, 'Wandesford, Christopher', *DIB*.

journals and presumably therefore also not in Fernesly's fair copies.[56] The Marquis of Ormond, James Butler's agreement with the Confederates specified that the king

> is gratiously pleased that the Journall bookes of both Howses of Parliament be perused, and that all Acts Ordinances and Orders which shalbe found to have binn made since the 7th of August 1641 to the blemish, dishonor or prejudice of his Majesty's Catholique Roman (sic) subjects of this Kingdom, or any of them who are to receive the benefit of this Treaty shalbe vacated and all other exemplifications and other Acts which may continue the memory of them be made voide by Act of Parliament.[57]

MPs were conscious of the balance between accuracy, full reporting of proceedings and their own safety. Full records could be used against MPs, limiting their parliamentary liberty of freedom of speech. Speeches that led to expulsions or which were instanced during Strafford's trial as evidence of official intimidation in the 1634–5 Commons are not recorded in the journals, but Wentworth had sufficient information on these contributions without recourse to the journals. There are differences between the manuscript and published journals. Editorial decisions about their contents and layout were taken when they were prepared for publication in the eighteenth century, when the clerk Edward Sterling was ordered to undertake the editorial work, for which he was to be paid £300 (later increased to £1000). The speaker chose the journal's type and style. Sterling

> did not consider himself at liberty to determine what part of the proceedings of parliament he was at liberty to reject and that he thought it safer to have even some unnecessary matter inserted than run the charge of omitting anything that was necessary.

The printed journals largely reflect that conservative editorial line, except that they omit Bradley's account of the undignified and divisive choice of a Speaker and Davies' speech on the prorogation on 16 May 1615. The 1796 edition also cut most committee members' names.[58] John McCavitt ascribed the omission of the account of the contested speakership to contemporary censorship, but in fact the Catholics insisted that the violence of the opening session

56 Stapylton, 'Parliamentary privilege', pp 32–3. An image of the mutilated page is plate 4 in M.F. Bond, *A short guide to the records of parliament* (London, 1973). The order of 20 Oct. was the committee's report which is provided in Carte MS 118, fo. 3. There is another copy of this committee report and order in Bodl. Lib., Carte MS 30, fo. 285.

57 Bodl. Lib., Carte MS 63, fo. 3r.

58 Englefield, *Printed records*, pp 8–10; *idem*, 'Printing the journal'; Davies' speech is included in NLI, MS 836, fos. 165–71; King's Inns, MS N3/2/1/7, fos. 50v–2r; Armagh Public Library, MS KH.II.7, fos. 109r–13v.

> might not bee Concealed from after posteritie, after what sorte every thinge was donn a solemne protestatione of the Catholiques should bee recorded in the publique actes, and in the handwritten booke of the parlament, which for an everlastinge memoriall of the same, should remayne extante.

Bradley included it in his notes, as Medhop did in an edited form in the King's Inns and National Library of Ireland copies; however, he omitted it from the journal prepared for Chichester, presumably because it reflected badly on him.[59] Sterling's motive for excluding it from the published journals is unclear. Sterling's other changes included moving the account of the 1634 opening procession from the back of the manuscript to the front in the published journal, and shortened versions of a decision on the Munster planter, Vincent Gookin, who had become mired in controversy for his criticism of the New English community in Ireland shortly before the parliament convened.[60] William Molyneux recorded that the 'last leafe in the [1640] journall' noted the 13 February 1641 safe conduct issued to 'Henry Parry Gent. having speciall occasions to make his speedy repaire unto the Committee or Agents in England', which is not in the printed journals. He also observed 'this journal has neither the list of the names of the members nor any index', which he clearly regarded as intrinsic elements of journals.[61] Medhop devised indexes for at least three of his fair copies, providing ready references for precedents and suggesting that he and Chetham agreed on the best form of records. Fernesly clearly provided a membership list (although it is not included in the published version) and index in 1634, but neglected to do so in 1640, despite having ample time to compile indexes between the end of the Rump Parliament in 1648 and the opening of the Restoration one in 1661. In summary, journals provide a crucial, but partial, account of parliament's work.

Parliamentary orders recorded decisions taken by either house on readings of bills, petitions, committees and any other matter. Each was entered in a 'book of orders' (sadly no such book has survived); copies were signed by the clerk, to guarantee their authenticity, and are found in many different collections.[62] Bills

59 John McCavitt, 'An unspeakable parliamentary fracas: the Irish House of Commons, 1613', *Anal. Hib.*, 37 (1998), 223–35; David Rothe's *Analecta*, NLI, MS 643, fo. 26v. I am grateful to Stephen Hand for providing me with a transcript of this manuscript. Moynes (ed.), *Annual letters*, i, p. 414. This wording echoes St Ignatius Loyola's description of the written word as a 'perpetual witness'. Vera Moynes, '"The written word remains as a perpetual witness …": letter-writing against all odds – the epistolary legacy of the early Irish Jesuits', unpublished paper presented at the Irish Catholic History Society's conference, 14 Sept. 2019; TNA, MS PRO 30/5/3, fos. 11–14; King's Inns, MS N3/2/1/7, fo. 6; NLI, MS 836, pp 18–19.

60 TCD, MS 622, fos. 57–8; Patricia Coughlan, 'Gookin, Sir Vincent', *DIB*.

61 Treadwell, 'House of Lords'; TCD, MS 622, fos. 57r, 61v, 90v; King's Inns, MS N3/2/1/7, fo. 55r; ARL, MS KH.II.7 have rudimentary indexes.

62 E.g., *Commons' Jn. Ire.*, 17 Oct. 1614, 29 April 1615, 2 Aug. 1634, 20 March 1635, 17 April 1635, 11 Nov. 1640; Order for Henry Piers MP against Sir Richard Masterson, 29 Nov. 1614, Bodl. Lib., Carte MS 62, fo. 33; *Commons' Jn. Ire.*, 29 Nov. 1614; Marsh's Library, MS Z3.2.5, p. 29; Copies of orders certified by Val Savage, deputy clerk of parliament, MS Z3.1.1, nos 62–3, 20 April 1643, 24 Feb. 1645–6.

survive in drafts, including those transmitted to England and the English lawyers' reviews thereof.[63] Draft public bills were written on paper by administration lawyers or judges and private bills by lawyers instructed by those promoting the bills. After the third reading, bills were transcribed on parchment; when passed by both houses and given the royal assent, they were sealed and stored on parchment as the official record. In England statutes were increasingly printed in the early modern period. Public statutes were published immediately after the English parliament ended and distributed throughout the country, with print-runs of 500; only 50 copies of 'quasi-public' laws were printed.[64] The English printer Richard Tottell issued a volume of Irish laws in 1572 and public statutes enacted in 1585–6 were published in London. The first major collection of Irish statutes was published by the solicitor general, Sir Richard Bolton (*plate 3*) in 1621.[65] The Connacht-born barrister John Merick published popular versions in 1617 and 1625.[66] Individual Irish acts were often issued as broadsheets for pasting in public places.[67] To facilitate collection, subsidies acts were printed for circulation for each early Stuart parliament, the 1640 one with its accompanying declaration. All the public acts passed in 1634–5 and two private ones sponsored by the archbishop of Armagh James Ussher and the bishop of Derry John Bramhall in the House of Lords were published shortly after parliament's dissolution.[68] Private acts were not part of the public law that lawyers, judges and justices of the peace worked with and it was not necessary to print them, but Bramhall and Ussher's bill had a wider application throughout the Church of Ireland and so their insistence on publication is natural. Four other private acts of naturalization were subsequently published, but other private legislation survives in manuscript form for that parliament.[69] However, there were no equivalent collective publications for the

63 E.g., Clergy subsidies bill, 1615, TCD, MS 1,062, pp 351–5; TNA, MS C. 86/1 (1634 bills); Bodl. Lib., Bankes MSS 65–9.

64 Chris R. Kyle, *Theater of state: parliament and political culture in early Stuart England* (Stanford, 2012), p. 147.

65 Aidan Clarke, 'Bolton, Sir Richard', *DIB*.

66 *In this volume are contained all the Statutes from the tenthe yere of King Henrie the sixt, to the xiii yere of our moste gravious and souereaygne lady Queene Elyzabeth, made and established in her highnes Realme of Irelande* (London, 1572); Quinn, 'Government printing'; Richard Bolton, *The statutes of Ireland, beginning the third yere of K. Edward the second, and continuing vntill the end of the Parliament, begunne in the eleuenth yeare of the reign of our most gratious soueraigne lord King Iames, and ended in the thirteenth yeare of his raigne of England, Fraunce, and Ireland: Newly perused and examined with the Parliament rolls; and diuerse statutes imprinted in this booke, which were not formerly printed in the olde booke. Anno Dom. MDCXXI* (Dublin, 1621); Merick, *Compendious collection*; John Merick, *A briefe abstract of all the English statutes which are in force with in the realme of Ireland: and is verie usefull for sheriffes, iustices of the peace, escheators, coroners, and other officers in particular, as all other His Maiesties subiectes in generall* (Dublin, 1625).

67 *Act for the Kings Majesties most gracious, generall, and free pardon* (Dublin, 1635). See also Quinn, 'Bills and statutes', which includes later material, esp. pp 76–7.

68 John McCafferty, 'Ussher, James', *DIB*; *idem*, 'Bramhall, John', *DIB*.

69 *Anno regni Caroli Regis, Angliae … decimo & undecimo, at the Parliament begun and holden at Dublin, the 14 day of July [1634] and there continued untill the 18 day of Aprill 1635* (Dublin, 1635); Shaw (ed.), *Letters of denization*, pp 49–52; TNA, MS C. 86/1.

other parliaments, although on 17 March 1645 at the chancellor's request, the Lords ordered that their clerk should gather all the public acts passed in that parliament and deliver them to the clerk of the rolls so that they could be printed. The administration issued proclamations relating to parliament as broadsheets, including announcing the summoning of the 1613, 1634 and 1640 parliaments, prorogations in June and October 1613 and October 1641, and Falkland's announcement of the deferral of the 1628 parliament.[70]

It was rare for parliaments to issue their own statements, as they were, with the monarch, part of the operations of the state. But the divisions between the crown and parliament, or in Ireland between the crown's Irish administration and parliament, prompted their formal statements in the 1640s, although the 1640 Subsidies Act had included a declaration by parliament. The English parliament's declarations were printed in increasingly large print-runs from 1640 onwards – up to 12,000 copies, a ten-fold increase on their earlier runs.[71] The crown's control of the printing press constrained the Irish parliament's potential as a publisher and *The humble and just remonstrance of the knights, citizens, and burgesses, in parliament assembled in Ireland* (London, 1641) was published in England. The first Irish publications from the parliament itself were on 16 November 1641, appointing commissioners to treat with the rebels, ordering a levy of troops and money and a Protestation and Declaration.[72] After January 1642, the 'rump' Irish parliament represented only the minority Protestant interest, and 'The humble petition and declaration of the lords spiritual and temporal and Commons in parliament assembled, 23 June 1642' was agreed between the two houses. The Commons' journals refer to the conference committee and drafts from both houses, but make no mention of agreement or the text of the petition and declaration.[73]

The Scottish Estates met frequently and also prompted or produced its own range of publications. During the political upheavals after 1633, a large number of publications emanated from or about the Scottish Estates.[74] The records were so well maintained that the Scottish pamphleteer, journalist and parliamentary theorist George Ridpath was able to compile *An historical account of the antient rights and power of the parliament of Scotland humbly offer'd to the consideration of the estates, when they come to settle limitations for the next successor* ([Edinburgh],

70 An image of posted proclamations is provided in James Cranford, *The teares of Ireland* (London, 1642), opposite p. 78. I am grateful to Alan Marshall for drawing this reference to my attention.

71 Jason Peacey, 'The print culture of parliament, 1600–1800', *Parl. Hist.*, 26:1 (2007), 1–16.

72 Sheila Lambert, 'The beginning of printing for the House of Commons, 1640–42', *The Library*, 6:1 (1981), 43–61; Sheila Lambert (ed.), *Printing for parliament, 1641–1700: List and Index Society special series* (London, 1984); Robert Steele (ed.), *Bibliotheca Lindesiana: bibliography of royal proclamations, Vol. II, part 1, Ireland* (Oxford, 1910), nos 206a–212, 216, 281, 303, 333, 341, 349–52.

73 To the Rt. Hon. the Lords Justices and counsel: the humble petition and declaration of the lords spiritual and temporal and Commons in parliament assembled, 23 June 1644, TCD, MS 1,178, no. 4, endorsed '*copia vera*', but no signature. Not the formal copy. Dated 1644, but clearly 1642, as it refers to the rebellion in October last.

74 John Spottswood, *The history of the church and state of Scotland* (London, 1677).

1703).[75] Sermons preached before the English parliament in the 1620s were regularly published, but only one Irish one, the archbishop of Armagh, Christopher Hampton's on the opening of parliament in 1613, was printed, and that belatedly. Ussher's sermons in 1634 and 1640 and the bishop of Kilmore and Ardagh, William Bedell's in 1634 remained unpublished.[76] Finally, administration records include the clerk's list of members and, for 1613, of their wages. In addition, MPs and lords provided certificates of privilege to their servants and agents, few of which have survived.

Many English MPs took personal notes of proceedings and speeches, a significant number of which survive for the early seventeenth-century parliaments, although they were not published at the time.[77] Only a very few survive for Ireland, with some snippets or phrases; the 1613–15 Commons' journals include some details of contributions but the 1634 and 1640 volumes rarely do. A number of lords deputies' speeches in plenary sessions and speakers' orations accepting their appointments or reporting on parliaments' achievements at prorogations or dissolutions survive. Chichester's speech on the resumption of parliament in October 1614 survives in summary, as do many copies of Strafford's opening speech in 1634, although he pointedly refused to provide it to the Lords, claiming he had no copy.[78] Wandesford's speech to the Commons as lord deputy on 15 October 1640 also survives as do at least two copies of Ormond's response to both Houses' declaration of March 1647, one of which is marked as being more accurate than the other.[79]

Three of James Stanihurst's orations to Sussex and Sidney were still available in his son Richard's time. His 'disabling' speech on being chosen speaker was printed in Holinshed and that on the prorogation, with Sidney's reply, was published by the Oxford scholar and later Jesuit martyr, Edmund Campion, who

75 G.A. Aitkin and John R. Young, 'Ridpath, George', *Oxford DNB*.

76 Christopher Hampton, *An inquisition of the true church, and those that revolt from it: being a sermon pronounced at the second session of the Parliament* (Dublin, [1622]); Chris R. Kyle, 'Parliament and the palace of Westminster: an exploration of public space in the early seventeenth century', *Parl. Hist.*, 21:1 (2002), 85–98. Also, see chapter six of this book. Judy Barry, 'Hampton, Christopher', *DIB*; Aidan Clarke, 'Bedell, William', *DIB*.

77 A list for the period 1621–9 is given in Conrad Russell, *Parliaments and English politics, 1621–1629* (Oxford, 1979), pp xii–xv. Later examples are included in Wilson H. Coates, et al. (eds), *The private journals of the Long Parliament*, 3 vols (New Haven, 1982–92).

78 Davies to Somerset, 31 Oct. 1614, TNA, SP 63/232, fo. 201; Knowler (ed.), *Letters and dispatches*, i, pp 286–9. Contemporary manuscript copies include Inner Temple Library, MS 538/51, fo. 152; BL, Add. MS 30,383; Bodl. Lib., Tanner MS 70, fos. 18r–28r; HMC, *Third Report of the Royal Commission on Historical Manuscripts* (London, 1872), p. 185; HMC, *Fourth Report of the Royal Commission on Historical Manuscripts: Part I, Report and Appendix* (London, 1874), p. 374; *LJI*, 23 July 1634. At his trial he claimed that there was a copy in Ireland. Rushworth (ed.), *Tryal*, p. 166, but the copy that he had sent to his brother-in-law Sir Gervase Clifton was in Nottinghamshire. See Nottingham University Library, MS Cl LP 47. I am grateful to Simon Lewis for his help in establishing this reference.

79 Clarke, *Old English*, p. 133; Bodl. Lib., Carte MS 20, fos. 473–5 notes 'this speech taken by the House of Commons is more perfect then this' (fo. 475). Another copy of this document is found on fos. 539–40 of the same manuscript.

heard the speeches during his sojourn in Dublin in the early 1570s.[80] Walsh's speech at the dissolution of the 1585 parliament was also recorded.[81] Medhop included Davies' two speeches on 21 May 1613 in two of his fair copies of the journal and James Ware also possessed a copy. Nathaniel Catlin's speech accepting the speakership in 1634 does not survive, despite the Lords asking for it so that it could be included in their journal, but Sir Maurice Eustace's speech in the following parliament does.[82] Davies' speech summarizing the Commons' work during the sessions to 16 May 1615 was transcribed by Medhop, but omitted from the published journals; presumably Catlin's unrecorded 'short and pithy oration' at the prorogation after the first session in 1634 also gave an account of the lower house's work.[83]

Contributions from MPs are rarely noted in the journals and almost never in full. Medhop does not record the many contributions the chirurgeon and chronicler, William Farmer provided in his account of the opening of the 1613 parliament, nor the substantial speeches written by the Papal vicar for the archdiocese of Armagh, David Rothe for the Old English candidate for the speakership Sir John Everard and other Catholic MPs, although they were endorsed as 'for the most part moved in the parliament house, although not verbatim as written here' and reported on to English statesmen.[84] One Catholic MP's response to a proposal for two feast days – 'We are prepared to ordain fair days or so-called holidays, as many of them as you wish. But not feast days, because usually we purchase those too dearly' – is also not recorded in the journals.[85] While publishing speeches was controversial because it breached the principle of the secrecy of parliament, it happened increasingly, officially and unofficially, throughout the 1640s. Speeches made in 1641 by the Connacht lawyer and MP for Galway, Sir Richard Blake and the Ulster planter and MP for Tyrone, Audley

80 Terry Clavin and Anthony McCormack, 'Campion, Edmund', *DIB*.

81 Raphael Holinshed, *The chronicles of England, Scotland and Ireland* (London, 1587), pp 119–22; Edmund Campion, *A historie of Ireland written in the yeare 1571* (Dublin, 1809), pp 194–204; Tony Crowley (ed.), *The politics of language in Ireland, 1366–1922: a sourcebook* (Abingdon, 2002), pp 28–9; Falkiner, *Essays*, pp 223, 230; TNA, SP 63/124/24; Bradshaw, 'Beginnings', describes the summary in *Cal. S.P. Ire., 1586–8*, pp 55–8 as 'inadequate'.

82 ARL, MS MS KH.II.7, fos. 15r–25v; NLI, MS 836, pp 20–3. The second speech is printed in Henry Morley (ed.), *Ireland under Elizabeth and James the First* (London, 1890), pp 391–409. Another copy is in Lodge, *Desiderata Curiosa*, i, pp 170ff. There is a copy also in Bodl. Lib., Carte MS 63, fos. 5ff; *Commons' Jn. Ire.*, 16 July 1634; Eustace's speech is given in *Commons' Jn. Ire.* for 1640; TCD, MS 615; King's Inns, MS N3/2/1/8, unpaginated. See also BL, Lansdowne MS 1,208; TCD, MS 646, fos. 90r–2; O'Sullivan, 'Finding list'; Terry Clavin, 'Eustace, Sir Maurice', *DIB*. On Catlin, see Appendix 3.

83 TCD, MS 836, pp 165–71; King's Inns, MS N3/2/1/7, fos. 50v–2r; ARL, MS KH.II.7, fos. 109r–12v, but not included in TCD, MS 1,444; *LJI*, 2 Aug. 1634.

84 Lodge, *Desiderata Curiosa*, i, pp 405ff; HMC, *Report on Franciscan manuscripts preserved at the Convent, Merchants Quay, Dublin* (Dublin, 1906), pp 61–9; Oliver St John to Ralph Winwood, 28 Nov. 1614, Francis Blundell to Winwood, 17 Dec. 1614, *Cal. S.P. Ire., 1611–14*, pp 527, 533; Thomas O'Connor, 'Rothe, David', *DIB*; Bríd McGrath, 'Everard, Sir John', *DIB*.

85 Moynes (ed.), *Annual letters*, i, p. 482. The reference was to the fines imposed through 2 Eliz. I, c. 2 on Catholics for not attending church services.

Mervyn were published in England, though the lawyer and Old English political leader, Patrick Darcy's *Argument* was not published by the House of Commons, but by the Confederation in Waterford in 1643.[86]

In contrast to the 120 surviving English parliamentary diaries, described as 'a standard source for [English] historians', Hooker's 1569 diary is the only known Irish one, albeit two years older than the earliest English example. Brief comments in James Ware's and Lord Cork's diaries provide no details of parliament, but Richard Bellings' account of the Confederation of Kilkenny, which drew on his brief experience as an MP to justify the Catholics' proceedings after 1642, was a quasi-diary.[87]

Copies of a series of letters between the Irish parliament and its committee in England survive.[88] Other letters refer to parliament, a few of which describe proceedings or speeches; many were from Wentworth, but as his statements were invariably self-serving and frequently mendacious, they should be treated with caution.[89] The 1612–14 Jesuit annual letters that the order sent to Rome to brief other congregations about its mission in Ireland are highly informative for the 1560 and 1613 parliaments, but no similar documents survive for Wentworth's parliaments.[90] Letters from the attorney general Sir Thomas Tempest to England

86 Richard Blake, *Sir Richard Blake his speech in the House of Commons at a Grand Committee for the bill against paper petitions: Master Brereton sitting in the chaire Iune XXVIII 1641* (London, 1641); Audley Mervyn, *Captaine Audley Mervin's speech delivered in the upper house to the Lords in Parliament May 24, 1641: concerning the judicature of the high court of Parliament* (London, 1641); *idem*, *Sixteene queres propounded by the Parliament of Ireland to the judges of the said kingdome: as also, another speech, made by Captaine Audley Mervin, to the House of Commons, concerning their priviledges, and their exorbitant grievances in that kingdome*; *idem*, *A speech made by Captaine Audley Mervin to the Vpper House of Parliament in Ireland, March 4 1640: together with certaine articles (of high treason) against Sir Richard Bolton Lord Chancellor, John Lord Bishop of Derrie, Sir Gerard Lowther, Lord chiefe Justice of the Common-Pleas, and Sir George Radcliffe Knight. unto which is added an humble and just remonstrance of the Parliament. by Audley Mervyn* ([London], 1641); Patrick Darcy, *An argument delivered by Patricke Darcy, esquire, by the expresse order of the House of Commons in the Parliament of Ireland, 9 Junii, 1641* (Waterford, 1643, repr. Dublin 1764); Micheál Ó Siochrú, 'Blake, Richard', *DIB*; Aidan Clarke, 'Mervyn, Sir Audley', *DIB*; *idem*, 'Darcy, Patrick', *DIB*.

87 Phillip Baker, '"But private notes for my own memory"? Parliamentary diaries, parliamentary history and the politics of information in early Stuart England', *Parl. Hist.*, 39:3 (2020), 405–22; Falkiner, *Essays*, pp 237ff; Mark Empey (ed.), 'The diary of Sir James Ware', *Anal. Hib.*, 45 (2014), 53–146; Grosart (ed.), *Lismore Papers*, iv, p. 37; Richard Bellings and J.T. Gilbert (eds), *History of the Irish Confederation and the war in Ireland, 1641*, 7 vols (Dublin, 1882–91), i; Micheál Ó Siochrú, 'Bellings, Richard', *DIB*.

88 ARL, MS Parliamentary Papers, unpaginated.

89 Bodl. Lib., Rawlinson MS D 922, fos. 49–54; Chichester to the English privy council, 21 May 1613, in Edwards (ed.), 'Chichester', no. 55; Rothe, *Analecta*, NLI, MS 643, fo. 26v; Farmer, 'Chronicle', pp 155ff; Jackson (ed.), 'Document'; Thomas Bagot to Walter Bagot, 30 April 1614, FSL, MS L.a.91; Guildford Slingsby to Sir Henry Slingsby, 22 June 1634, FSL, MS X.d.428(185). For example, Bramhall to Laud, 4 Nov. 1640, HL, HP, Box 7(66), MS 14,061. Aidan Clarke, '28 November 1634: a detail of Strafford's administration', *JRSAI*, 93:2 (1963), 161–7; Charles Seagrave to Ferdinando Lord Hastings, 12 Nov. 1633 (this date is clearly incorrect), 13 Nov. 1640, in Francis Bickley (ed.), *Report on the manuscripts of the late Reginald Rawdon Hastings, Volume II* (London, 1930), pp 102, 109.

in 1640–1 are sadly rare examples of documents which must have been common at the time and William Ussher's letter from 1644 is a rare instance from the 'rump' Irish parliament.[91]

The *Modus tenendi parliamentum* specified the formal, legal basis for summoning and managing parliaments. G.O. Sayles has convincingly argued that it was first compiled in Ireland *c.*1382 and that the English version was derived from the Irish. Whatever its origins, the Butlers and Prestons owned Latin copies in the first decade of the fifteenth century and Rísdéard Ó hÉidigheáin, archbishop of Cashel, had a French version.[92] The *Modus* was created before parliament increased in size and complexity and each of its 26 'chapters' was only about a paragraph long.

Many copies of, or extracts from, the *Modus* circulated in early seventeenth-century Ireland; Chichester was familiar with the provision in the *Modus* requiring writs to be sent out 40 days before the parliament.[93] Archbishop Thomas Jones of Dublin, chancellor and speaker of the upper house, may have owned a copy of the entire *Modus*, but certainly possessed the extracts made by one of his predecessors, the Henrician archbishop of Dublin and chancellor, John Alen, in his *Liber Niger* in 1533, which Jones' successor Lancelot Bulkeley annotated.[94] The Jacobean master of the rolls Sir Francis Aungier had a copy that had been found in the Waterford treasury.[95] At least four, and possibly five, copies were transcribed early in the seventeenth century for or by the long-serving Ulster king of arms (1597–1632) Daniel Molyneux.[96] There is some uncertainty about their production, but they were probably transcribed during Molyneux's visit to London between February and July 1612 'to receyve some instruction for the ordering of a parliament heare' from copies owned by the seventeenth-century English antiquarians, Robert Cotton and William Hakewill.[97] Two were of the English

90 E.g., Moynes (ed.), *Annual letters*, i, pp 324–6, 331, 399ff.

91 A letter from Ireland concerning the proceedings in their parliament, 23 March 1640, Bodl. Lib., Tanner MS 70, pp 122–5; Thomas Tempest to Lord Keeper Littleton, 19 Aug. 1641, Bodl. Lib., Tanner MS 70, pp 127–9; William Ussher to Philip Percival, 23 April 1644, in Sophia Crawford Lomas (ed.), *Report on the manuscripts of the earl of Egmont*, 2 vols (London, 1905–9), i, pp 210–12.

92 G.O. Sayles, '*Modus tenendi parliamentum*: Irish or English?' in James Lydon (ed.), *England and Ireland in the later Middle Ages: essays in honour of Jocelyn Otway-Ruthven* (Dublin, 1981), pp 122–52; David Natzler, 'Manuals before May: from the fourteenth to the seventeenth century' in Paul Evans (ed.), *Essays on the history of parliamentary procedure, in honour of Thomas Erskine May* (London, 2017), pp 87–96; Hawkyard, *House of Commons*, p. 135; Crooks, 'Representation and dissent'. There was also a seventeenth-century Scottish *Modus*. Nicholas Pronay and John Taylor, *Parliamentary texts of the later Middle Ages* (Oxford, 1980), p. 210.

93 Chichester to Davies, 4 Aug. 1612, HL, HP, Box 3 (46).

94 For Alen's copy, see https://www.ireland.anglican.org/news/8930/preview [accessed 6 July 2019]; Richard Hawkins, 'Alen (Allen), John', *DIB*.

95 Richard Hawkins, 'Aungier, Sir Francis', *DIB*.

96 Terry Clavin, 'Molyneux, Daniel', *DIB*.

97 Stuart Handley, 'Cotton, Sir Robert', *Oxford DNB*; Sheila Doyle, 'Hakewill, William', *Oxford DNB*.

versions and the other two or three of the Irish *Modus*.[98] Ware also had a copy, which he may have made for himself.[99] There were others in private hands: Maude Clarke claims that the manuscript now in the Huntington Library in California came from Jenico Preston, fifth Viscount Gormanston, who may have brought it to London in 1613.[100] Gormanston was outspoken and there are many descriptions of the recusant representatives in London. It is highly unlikely that he would have given it to Lord Chancellor Ellesmere, although he might have allowed a certified copy to be made; had so significant a document been forcibly taken from him, this would undoubtedly have been recorded. The Catholic lawyer who described the opening of the 1613 parliament was also familiar with the *Modus*: 'it is nowe parcell in the common lawe in *modo tenendi parliamentum*.'[101]

The first English publication of the *Modus* was by Hooker as *The order and vsage how to keepe a parlement in England in these daies ... and the like used in hir maiesties realme of Ireland*, while the Irish *Modus* was first published by the bishop of Meath Anthony Dopping in 1692 from a manuscript bequeathed him by his uncle Sir William Domville, who was an MP in 1661–6 and also a son of Gilbert Domville, MP in 1613 (unseated) and 1634.[102] Hooker's first parliamentary experience was as MP for Athenry in 1569–70. He claimed that he wrote his *Order and vsage* at Stanihurst's request, after the uproar in that parliament. It was written shortly after his first stint as MP for Exeter in 1571 (which he also represented in 1586) and published in 1572 in two editions, one dedicated to Lord Deputy William Fitzwilliam and the other to Exeter's civil authorities; it was also included in Holinshed's 1577 *Chronicles* and therefore widely available for the 1585 parliament and any subsequent ones. However, the edition dedicated to Fitzwilliam included provisions irrelevant for Ireland, such as the representatives of the Cinque Ports. Despite the *Modus's* almost totemic status, parliament had naturally

98 Thomas Jones to Salisbury, 25 Feb. 1611–12, TNA, SP 63/232, fo. 28; The English privy council to Chichester, 21 July 1612, *Cal. S.P. Ire., 1611–14*, p. 276; TCD, MS 581, fos. 1–3, 10–15. There is an endorsement (fo. 15r) by Molyneux, stating that this is a true copy of the exemplification under the great seal of Ireland remaining in Sir Robert Cotton's hands. While these were true copies by several scribes, they are not in a fair hand. M.V. Clarke, 'The manuscripts of the Irish *Modus tenendi parliamentum*', *EHR*, 48:192 (Oct., 1933), 576–600, suggests that these copies were made 1611–32. Molyneux was a meticulous officer and would have been careful to use the best authority for his work as herald in assigning precedence in the parliament, and as an MP. Another early seventeenth-century copy of the Irish *Modus* is NLI, GO, MS 95. Its provenance is unclear, but as it is included in a volume of material related to heraldry, it may be another copy for Molyneux or his successors as Ulster king of arms, although it is not in the same hands as TCD, MS 581; NLI, MS 999, a collection of various political manuscripts apparently made for Ormond, *c.*1704, includes a copy of the English *Modus*, pp 341–51.

99 O'Sullivan, 'Finding list'; Pronay and Taylor, *Parliamentary texts*, p. 210, identifies this as Bodl. Lib., Rawlinson MS B.484. They were apparently unaware of NLI, MS 999 and NLI, GO, MS 95.

100 Anthony McCormack and Terry Clavin, 'Preston, Jenico (Genico)', *DIB*.

101 Jackson (ed.), 'Document'.

102 Anthony Dopping, *Modus tenendi parliamenta* (Dublin, 1692); James McGuire, 'Dopping, Anthony', *DIB*; Hazel Maynard and Patrick H. Kelly, 'Domvile (Domville), Sir William', *DIB*.

developed since the fourteenth century and many aspects of its work were not covered in that document.[103] Hooker's *Order and vsage* became the standard manual for Ireland. The rules attached to the list of the 1585 members were very brief and covered etiquette and privilege, rather than detailed advice on procedure and were quite possibly drafted in response to the uproar in 1569, although they presumably merely restated traditional conventions.[104] Chichester's associate Farmer was familiar with both Hooker and Holinshed's publications.[105]

Early seventeenth-century English antiquarians, parliamentarians and officials like Robert Cotton, Henry Elsynge, William Hakewill, Walter Ralegh, Henry Scobell and John Selden, created a series of parliamentary manuals based on the *Modus* and using records going back to 1066.[106] Hooker, Cotton, Hakewill, Ralegh and Selden were MPs and in 1621 Selden was employed as a legal researcher by the House of Lords to collaborate with Elsynge on a draft roll of standing orders and on the privileges of the House of Lords.[107] Elsynge worked over many years on his manuals, during his time as clerk of the English parliament.[108] Hakewill's draft was written by 1611, as the latest precedents cited are from that year. These manuscript manuals circulated widely among their acquaintances and were increasingly published from 1640 onwards, although it is unclear how far their contents could be assumed to be valid in Ireland.[109] The compilation of these manuals demonstrates an increasing commitment to institutional history and to a defence of parliament's role in the English body politic.[110]

When the Irish parliament was under greater threat, reflecting on how earlier Irish parliaments were managed was of little interest to Irish administrators and parliamentarians, even John Davies and James Ware. But the administration's policy of aligning the Irish parliament's practices with the English model suggest that they would have found manuals valuable and that MPs, especially those who had sat in English parliaments, or those with a legal training who developed

103 TCD, MS 1,180 pp 7, 13, *c.*1690, reiterates the claim that Henry II sent the *Modus* to Ireland and therefore the Irish parliament had the same powers of judicature as the English.
104 Irish Archaeological Society, *Tracts*, ii, p. 143.
105 Farmer, 'Chronicle' in Lodge, *Desiderata Curiosa*, i, pp 155ff.
106 Kari Palonen, *The politics of parliamentary procedure: the formation of the Westminster as a parliamentary ideal type* (Leverkusen, 2016), pp 36–8.
107 Peter Crooks, 'The background to the arrest of the fifth earl of Kildare and Sir Christopher Preston in 1418: a missing membrane', *Anal. Hib.*, 40 (2007), 1–15; Paul Christianson, 'Selden, John', *Oxford DNB*.
108 Foster, 'Painful labour'.
109 Presentation copy of Elysynge's *Order and vsage*, to Thomas Lord Coventry, Lord Keeper, 1626, HRC, MS 158; Newberry Library, Case MS Folio OJN 593 E7. Both are in the same hand. See also Observations, rules and orders collected out of the Journals of the House of Commons in ye Reigns of K. Edward VI, Q. Mary, Elizabeth, James I, Charles I and Charles II, Newberry Library, MS Case fk 045.64. The provenance of this is Robert, Lord Petre, baron of Writtle. It starts the same as The Nature of the Court of the Commons' house of Parliament with what matters they may meddle and a contra oppisicons and proceedings therein and other observacons therevpon, Newberry Library, MS fk 0452.613.
110 Foster, 'Painful labour'; Baker, '"But private notes"'.

'know-how' manuals for their professional practice, would have acquired copies. An Irish manual would have been especially helpful in 1634, when neither the clerk nor the speaker had any parliamentary experience, although Fernesly benefitted from Chetham's collection of records and Medhop's efficient compiling and management of the 1613–15 documents. Fernesly's training as clerk of the parliament, if any, is unknown, but if it was from his counterpart Elsynge, he would presumably have had access to these manuscript manuals. Davies corresponded with Hakewill, and Jerome Alexander, MP for Lifford in 1634, possessed a copy of Hakewill's section on passing bills as well as manuscripts by Cotton, Camden and Selden.[111] The privy councillor Edward, Viscount Conway, who had been MP for Yarmouth, had an extensive collection of books and over 8,000 manuscripts at Lisnegarvey and may well have had copies of manuals and journals.[112]

Manuals were printed for other representative assemblies elsewhere in Europe. In Catalonia, where parliamentarism was vibrant all throughout the medieval and early modern eras, both the Spanish monarchy and the three Estates accepted the need to establish the Corts' uses and precedents in 1585. Two separate, and rather different, manuals, largely based on the 1585 Corts, were published in 1599 and 1632; the first, by Miquel Sarroviva, lawyer and member for Barcelona in 1585 and 1599, and the second by Lluís de Peguera an outstanding member of the Catalan Council (which was both political council and supreme court for Catalonia).[113] A manual was also published for the French Estates General; although they had not met for 20 years, the crown was able to rely on local knowledge of the process, suggesting an efficient system of records management. A list of members of the Estates was published contemporaneously, as well as details of their activities.[114]

111 Bodl. Lib., Carte MS 1, fos. 309r–10v; William Hakewill to Davies, 13 Feb. 1604, HL, HP, Box 1 (12); TCD MS 858, fos. 2–40, 717; Terry Clavin, 'Alexander, Sir Jerome', *DIB*. For further details on Alexander, see Appendix 3.

112 ARL, Lord Conway's Irish catalogue of printed books, *Tituli catalogi sequentis*, *c.* 1639–41 (no manuscript number allocated); James Knowles, 'Conway, Edward, second Viscount Conway', *Oxford DNB*.

113 Michel Sarrovira, *Ceremonial de Corts: obra compilada de Llochs, Autentichs, Lleys Del Principat De Cathalunya, Antichs y pratichs doctors per micer Michel Sarrovira, doctor en quis cun dret, y Ciutada a Honrat, de Barcelona* (Barcelona, 1599); Lluís de Peguera, *Practica, forma y stil de celebrar Corts Generals en Catalvnya* (Barcelona, 1632). Both men had doctorates in law and both manuals were reprinted in 1701. Josep Capdeferro, 'Promoció, edició i difusió d'obres jurídiques a Catalunya a cavall dels segles XVI i XVII', *Ivs Fvgit*, 15 (Zaragoza, 2009), 537–59, esp. 539–42; Tomàs de Montagut (ed.), *Practica, forma y estil de celebrar Corts Generals en Cathalunya y materias incidents en aquellas* (Madrid, 1998); Eva Serra, 'Butlletí bibliogràfic sobre les Corts Catalanes', *Arxiu de textos Catalans antics*, 26 (2007), 663–738. I am grateful to Josep Capdeferro for drawing these references to my attention and providing a context for their publication.

114 Henri Grelin, *Ordre Observé En La Convocation, & assemblée des Estats generaux de France, tenuz en la Ville de Paris, en l'Annee mil six cens quatorze, auec les Noms, surnoms, & qualitez des Deputez des trois Ordres, selon comme ils marchent aux ceremonies. Ensemble la diuision des Bailliages en douze, gouuernements, pour opiner esdictes Chambres, ainsi qu'il se peut voir par la carte & figure suiuante* (Paris, 1615). See also *L'ordre tenv engarde en l'assemblée des trois estats* (Paris, 1558), which gives the membership of the 1484 Estates at Tours.

In other countries, increasing numbers of publications were produced relating to representative assemblies, including pamphlets, newsletters and petitions, but they have no Irish equivalents.[115] An estimated 5,000 'mazarinades', many of them concerning grievances, were published in France during the meeting of the 1614 French Estates General. Between October 1614 and spring 1615, the *Catalogue de l'histoire de France* lists 104 pamphlets, 16 of which were 24 pages or longer.[116] Between 60–75% were issued by the state, with the remaining 25–40% produced by groups and individuals and the print run was generally between 500 and 1,200 copies. Jeffrey Sawyer observes that with such print-runs, even the most popular pamphlets might have reached the hands of only 1% of France's urban population, albeit the most influential 1%.[117] The 1620s also saw an explosion of pamphlets and petitions to the English parliament. Petitions from groups and individuals, especially the London livery companies, were increasingly printed and circulated to English MPs, and available to other interested observers.[118]

In summary, there is a very wide range of sources for early modern Irish parliaments, mainly surviving in manuscript form, scattered through many collections internationally, with a strong bias towards material from official and New English Protestant sources and much less information from Irish Catholics. The lack of material common in other countries is largely explained by the provisions of Poynings' Law and state control of printing in Ireland before 1643.

115 Chris R. Kyle, 'From broadside to pamphlet: print and parliament in the late 1620s', *Parl. Hist.*, 26:1 (2007), 17–29; Peacey, 'Print culture of parliament'.

116 Kyle, 'Parliament and the palace of Westminster'; Jeffrey K. Sawyer, *Printed poison: pamphlet propaganda, faction politics and the public sphere in early seventeenth-century France* (Berkeley, CA, 1990); Hélène Duccini, *Faire voir, faire croire: l'opinion publique sous Louis XIII* (Paris, 2003), p. 191; S.H. Duvall, 'French political pamphlets collection at the L. Tom Perry Special Collection, Harold B. Lee Library, Brigham Young University', at http://files.lib.byu.edu/collections/french-political-pamphlets/frenchpamphlets.pdf [accessed 29 July 2019].

117 Chartier and Ricet (eds), *Representation & vouloir*, p. 8; Sawyer, *Printed poison*; Duccini *Faire voir*, pp 191–268; *Catalogue de l'Histoire de France*, 9 vols (Paris, 1870–85), p. 191.

118 In 1621 and 1624 English MPs received lobbying documents from very many guilds. See Kyle, 'From broadside to pamphlet'.

CHAPTER THREE

Powers and liberties of parliament

> Parliament abrogateth old Lawes, maketh new, giveth order for things past, and for things hereafter to be followed, changeth right and possessions of private men, legitimateth Bastards, establisheth formes of Religion, altereth Weights and Measures, giveth forth of succession to the Crowne, defineth of doubtfull Rights, whereof is no Law alreadie made, appointeth Subsidies, Tailes, Taxes, and Impositions, giveth most free pardons and absolutions, restoreth in Blood and Name, as the highest Court condemneth or absolveth them whom the Prince will put to triall.[1]

THE IRISH PARLIAMENT HAD four principal functions: to raise money for the crown; to pass laws for public or private benefit; to represent the citizen to the crown to resolve grievances and promote good government; and, as the highest court in the realm, it exercised a judicial function. Exercising these functions often required combining roles and mechanisms: taxation was agreed through legislation and resolving grievances used parliament's judicial and representative roles and could involve proposing or drafting legislation. The Irish parliament had very limited control over its legislative function and little direct consultation with the monarch, but it found creative ways of dealing with these constraints and its revenue-raising, representative and judicial functions became much more important under the early Stuarts.

The English parliament also had a consultative role, where monarchs could solicit their subjects' advice:

> The most common and best means for the preservation and conservation aswell of private as publique tranquillitie and societie used in all ages and by all nations, is by way of lawful assembly and consultation, which wee call parliament, to looke into the necessitie of publique condition and so to foresee seasonable remedie.[2]

While Cotton instanced numerous examples of English parliaments being called to advise the monarch on significant issues such as royal marriages (the 1614 Addled Parliament was summoned because of the negotiations for one), wars and other threats to the nation, the Irish parliament was not summoned to consider

1 Thomas Smith, *The Commonwealth of England* (London, 1640), pp 73–4.
2 *The priviledges and practice of parliaments in England, collected out of the common lawes of this land* ([London], 1622), p. 1.

such matters, even in times of crisis.[3] To be effective, members needed parliamentary privilege and liberties to protect them, power to regulate their own membership and discipline MPs who infringed parliament's rules and some level of confidentiality during their work. All of these functions, privileges and liberties were under threat during Wentworth's viceroyalty.

TAXATION

Only parliament could grant taxation (called subsidies) and it decided their level and how they were assessed and collected. The Commons' role in assessing and collecting subsidies was specified in the Subsidy Act (19–20 Edw. IV, c. 21) by which knights of the shire, burgesses and proctors were responsible for appointing assessors and collectors and 2 Ric. III, c. 17, which specified that they should 'put into the clerk of the Rolls or the clerk of the parliament sufficient collectors' names.'[4] The English Commons claimed the right to advise on how subsidies were spent, something the Irish parliament never attempted and in the extraordinary upheavals of the 1640s and 1650s the English parliament raised 'unprecedented levels of taxation on their own authority', but Poynings' Law prevented the Irish parliament from doing this, although they did levy contributions to cover the cost of sending agents to England in 1641.[5] There was considerable opposition to paying the £120,000 negotiated for the Graces because they had not been voted by parliament.[6] Unlike the 1620 Scottish Estates and the English parliament that repeatedly declined to grant James and Charles money, the early Stuart Irish parliament never refused them. The prospect of financial support was frequently the incentive to call parliament – Sidney and Wentworth instanced it in their arguments and supplying money for Charles in his dispute with the Scots was the primary reason for summoning the 1640 parliament. While the 1585 subsidy produced very little money, the value of Irish subsidies soared under the Stuarts.[7]

The trade-off between the king's business and subjects' concerns, specifically passing legislation, granting subsidies and redressing grievances, was widely accepted. In 1615 John Sutton, MP for Kildare, moved to delay reading the subsidy bill 'till other acts that tended to the common good of the weale publick

3 Robert Cotton, *That the kings of England have been pleased usually to consult with their peers in the Great Council, and Commons in Parliament, of marriage, peace and war* (London, 1672). However, the 1614 parliament did not discuss the proposed marriage between Charles and Christine of France. See Andrew Thrush, 'The French marriage and the origins of the 1614 parliament' in Stephen Clucas and Rosalind Davies (eds), *The crisis of 1614 and the Addled Parliament: literary and historical perspectives* (Aldershot, 2003), pp 25–36.

4 Quinn, 'Irish parliamentary subsidy'.

5 Smith, *Stuart*, p. 49; *Commons' Jn. Ire.*, 18 Feb. 1641.

6 *Cal. S.P. Ire., 1625–32*, pp 277, 468.

7 Quinn, 'Irish parliamentary subsidy'; Moody, 'The Irish parliament under Elizabeth and James I: a general survey', *Proc. RIA*, 45C (1939), 41–81; David Edwards, *The Ormond lordship in county Kilkenny, 1515–1642* (Dublin, 2003), pp 145, 182; Queen Elizabeth to Sidney, 16 Jan. 1567, TNA, SP 63/20, fo. 18; Knowler (ed.), *Letters and dispatches*, i, p. 183.

were first read: alledging that the old saying would else be verified, "Little said, soon amended, a subsidy granted, the Parliament ended"', and Simonds D'Ewes, a parliamentary antiquarian and member himself of the Long Parliament, expressed similar sentiments in the English parliament; Sutton's caution was justified by parliament's prorogation three weeks after the Commons passed the subsidy bill and its dissolution on the first day of the following session.[8] Having ordered the collection of the subsidies promised for the Graces, Cork, as lord justice, advised that 'when the £120,000 is near drawn from the Country in my poor opinion it will be a fit time to call the Parliament and get new Subsidies or other helps.'[9] The move in 1640 to demand the return of the £120,000 paid for the Graces (which was never likely to succeed) was also based on the belief that there was a trade-off between voting subsidies and the redress of grievances:

> To commend to the consideration of the parliament a fitting course to be by them taken and laid down for restitution of all such moneys to the subiects of Ireland as were taken and extracted from any of them under coulour or pretext of the 120000li which by the kingdome was granted, and willingly yealded to be leavyed to his Majesties use towards the payment of his Army, in acknowledgement of the graces, which he vouchsafed that kingdome in the 4th yeare of his Majesties raigne, and were taken upp since the said 120000li was paid, under pretext thereof, after the said 120000li were wholly paid.[10]

In 1641 William Sarsfield, second Viscount Sarsfield of Kilmallock and Nicholas Preston, sixth Viscount Gormanston, objected to Wentworth breaking this connection: 'By proroguing the parliament after your subjects had chearfully supplied your Majestys occasions before their grievances were heard or examined.'[11] Parliamentary subsidies are discussed further in chapter eight.

LEGISLATION

Parliament dealt with public and private legislation for Ireland; as Eustace noted, 'England cannot make laws at this day to bind our estates without our own consent, a very great and high honour' and the 1642 Adventurers' Acts was the first early

8 J.M. Blatchy, 'D'Ewes, Sir Simonds', *Oxford DNB*.

9 Cork to Dorchester, 23 June 1630, in Clarke, McGrath and Edwards (eds), *A lord justice's letterbook*, no. 56.

10 Considerations to be commended to the Parliament touching the restitution of moneys exacted from the subjects of Ireland after the £120,000 was paid, *c.*1640, RIA, MS 24/Q/5, no 4. There is no reference in the Commons' or Lords' journals to this. John Bergin, 'Preston, Nicholas, 6th Viscount Gormanston', *DIB*.

11 *Commons' Jn. Ire.*, 22 April 1615; J.O. Halliwell-Phillipps, *The autobiography and correspondence of Sir Simonds D'Ewes, bart: during the reigns of James I and Charles I*, 2 vols (London, 1845), i, p. 172; Gormanston and Kilmallock's petition to the King, Feb. 1641, TNA, SP 63/258, p. 163.

modern instance of England legislating for Ireland.[12] Statute law was the highest level of law and provided the greatest protection for citizens. Despite the facility of Acts of State, some matters could only be satisfactorily established by legislation, including recognizing James' right to the throne, plantations, attainders and taxation. Public acts covered matters relevant to the entire realm, while private ones settled business that could not otherwise be resolved, such as problematic land titles, tangled property disputes, restitution in blood of relatives and descendants of attainted persons, as well as naturalization of individuals born overseas.[13] As Audley Mervyn (*plate 24*) said of the Graces, 'without a valid and effectual Parliament to confirme them are but *Statu quo prius*.'[14] Restitution in blood and naturalization were important for the individuals concerned; without this, descendants had problems with titles to lands inherited from attainted persons and only subjects were entitled to hold and inherit land or become members of parliament. The failure of David Condon's 1613 bill for restitution caused problems for his family 30 years later, which Cork was happy to exploit in his own case for Condon's lands in south Munster. Thomas Fitzmaurice FitzGerald was in a similar position in his land dispute with George Courtney in Munster also in 1635, as a private bill to lift the attainder of his grandfather Thomas (Cam) Mac Shane FitzGerald had not been transmitted for the 1613–5 parliament. The Lord President of Munster, Sir William St Leger's Dutch-born wife and children's naturalization in 1635 enabled Lady St Leger's jointure, their daughter's marriage agreements (Elizabeth married Lord Inchiquin in October 1635) and son William Jr's inheritance and permitted the latter to become an MP in 1640.[15]

English parliamentarians could propose public or private legislation, but only bills sanctioned by the crown could be introduced into the Irish parliament where they could be passed or rejected, but not amended. An Act declaring how Poynings shall be expounded and taken (3 & 4 Philip & Mary, c. 4) allowed new draft bills to be transmitted to England during parliament, enabling parliament to propose legislation and amendments, although all bills, including amended ones, still had to be re-transmitted for certification and retransmission. Yet this lengthy route was uncertain of success and still had to gain the approval of both the Irish administration and the English privy council.[16] As Poynings' Law left no room for negotiation, Chichester unsuccessfully argued for its suspension for private bills

12 *Commons' Jn. Ire.*, 20 March 1640; 17 Car. I, c. 33–5, 37 (England).

13 Chichester and the Irish council to the English privy council, 30 Dec. 1612, in Edwards (ed.), 'Chichester', no. 39.

14 Mervyn, *Captaine Audley Mervin's speech delivered*, p. 2.

15 Curtis Clayton (ed.), *Council book*, pp 3–4; *Cal. S.P. Ire., 1611–15*, p. 340; Chichester to the English privy council, 11 April 1613, in Edwards (ed.), 'Chichester', no. 52; Lord Deputy and other Commissioners for Confirmation of Defective Titles, 14 May 1635, in HMC, *Report on manuscripts in various collections, volume III* (London, 1904), pp 156–7; Cork to Joshua Boyle, 28 Sept. 1639, Chatsworth House, Cork Papers, Misc. boxes, box 3, p. 393; Shaw (ed.), *Letters of denization*, pp 49–52. John A. Murphy, 'Murrough O'Brien', *DIB*; Elaine Murphy, 'St Leger, Sir William', *DIB*.

16 Treadwell, 'Irish parliament of 1569–71'; Clarke, 'History of Poynings' Law'.

to encourage Catholics to support government legislation, although that would still have needed to comply with 11 Eliz. I, c. 8, which asserted that no bill to repeal or suspend the statute could be transmitted into England 'before the same bill be first agreed on, in a session of a Parliament holden in Ireland.' In early 1642 the Irish privy council proposed suspending Poynings' Law to deal with indicting those in rebellion, including MPs:

> If there shall be a particular bill drawn to attaint every person in particular, who is in this rebellion, it will be *opus infinitatem*, there being so many, nor can we possibly find their names. If many be included in one bill, and the bill must pass for all or none, for there can be no amendment here by reason of Poynings' Act and it may so fall out that there may be evidence to satisfy the house for some and not for others, and by that means there must be a new transmission into England and allowance there, before any thing can be done, and it may be that on the return thereof back again, it may find the like stop.[17]

The Irish parliament could suggest legislation and develop draft acts as heads of bills. On 29 November 1614 the Commons presented Chichester with a 'brief note or remembrance' of grievances or anomalies, which they divided into matters that the deputy and council could deal with through acts of state or otherwise and those 'to be provided for several acts of parliament, to be propounded in the next sessions.' Six days later, Humphrey Farnham, burgess for Enniskillen, proposed that a bill be drafted to make 5 November an annual holiday.[18] On 16 May 1615 the Commons proposed 33 bills for the following session; parliament's dissolution on the first day of the next session precluded any concrete results from these efforts. Lobbying in one session might produce results in a later one, hence James Martin's recruiting Piers Creagh's support for his private naturalization bill and the formal presentation of grievances at prorogations allowed bills to be drafted and committees to sit between sessions to work on parliamentary business.[19]

The administration had little to lose by permitting either or both houses to propose legislation as it could simply refuse to transmit any bills it did not favour to England, but Wentworth took a different view to Chichester and asserted that peers (and by extension MPs) were 'debarred from penning any act, and have power only to move or petition the lord deputy and council for drawing and transmitting into England such acts as they desired.' Any proposal for amending bills might be 'altered or rejected according as the lord deputy and [Irish] council in their wisdom shall judge and hold expedient' and any measure that passed through both councils and was amended by the Irish parliament was to be

17 Chichester and the Irish council to the English privy council, 30 Dec. 1612, in Edwards (ed.), 'Chichester', no. 39; Bodl. Lib., Carte MS 68, fos. 423v–4r; *Commons' Jn. Ire.*, 1, 6 Aug. 1642.
18 Rolf Loeber and Bríd McGrath, 'The legacy of Humphrey Farnham (d. 1624), a Dublin builder and architect', *JRSAI*, 145 (2016), 33–51.
19 RIA, MS 14/C/2, pp 183–5.

transmitted and scrutinized anew by the English council.[20] This interpretation changed Poynings' Law from being a break on the Irish administration to reducing the Irish parliament 'to the subordinate status of a legislative agency giving statutory effect to executive policy' and was unwelcome to many, if not most, inhabitants of Ireland, regardless of their ethnic origin.[21] Charles Lambart, first earl of Cavan, who had sat in the English Commons in 1626 and 1628, declared 'if Poynings' Law be so understood as that parliament can do nothing but pass bills, that is scarce a parliament.'[22] The 1640 parliament reasserted its right to propose legislation and the agents which it sent to negotiate with the king in late 1640 argued that

> The Act of Poynings is so obscurely penned as it admitts much question and doubt how some of the materiall parts of that lawe shalbe understood and whether the same hath beene pursued in the forme and drawinge of Bills, all which difficulties ought to be cleered by a new Act by way of Supplement and addition

But Charles refused to concede the point and rejected the bills the Commons attempted to transmit directly in 1641.[23]

Poynings' Law created an enormous amount of preparatory work for both the governments in Ireland and England and the resulting legislative vacuum was partly filled by acts of state. Wentworth valued the latitude they provided, noting, 'we uphold acts of state here very strongly, and punish the transgressors against them as familiarly and roundly as we do against any statute … and by that means are they as well obeyed.' Acts of state could not be repealed by parliament except through legislation which had gone through all the stages of Poynings' Law. Gormanston and Kilmallock objected to Wentworth's 'equalling acts of state to acts of parliament to the great dishonour & villifying of that Court', most specifically by his issuing as an act of state the gunpowder bill which the Commons had rejected, as the deputy's close associate and legal advisor, Sir George Radcliffe had threatened in the House.[24]

Despite recommendations from his attorney general, William Ryves, and Lord Chancellor Adam Loftus (*plate 4*), Wentworth refused to consult the political

20 Quoted in Dennehy, *Parliament*, p. 67.

21 Aidan Clarke, 'Patrick Darcy and the constitutional relationship between Ireland and Britain' in Jane Ohlmeyer (ed.), *Political thought in seventeenth-century Ireland: kingdom or colony* (Cambridge, 2000), pp 35–55; Jackson (ed.), 'Document'.

22 Terry Clavin, 'Lambart, Charles, 1st earl of Cavan', *DIB*.

23 Dennehy, *Parliament*, p. 92; James Kelly, 'The making of law in eighteenth-century Ireland: the significance and import of Poynings' Law' in N.M. Dawson (ed.), *Reflections on law and society: Irish Legal History Society discourses and other papers, 2000–2005* (Dublin, 2006), pp 259–77; Clarke, 'History of Poynings' Law', pp 219–21; *Cal. S.P. Ire., 1633–47*, pp 317–22; Agents to the king and council in England, 17 May 1641, TNA, SP 63/259, fo. 80.

24 Osborough, 'Eighteenth-century Ireland's legislative deficit'; Rushworth (ed.), *Tryal*, pp 176–7, 184; TNA, SP 63/258, p. 163; Clarke, *Old English*, pp 90–1; Terry Clavin, 'Radcliffe, Sir George', *DIB*.

community about 'what to propound for the good of the people' before summoning parliament.[25] This lack of consultation and the administration's veto on any bills left MPs in a difficult position, as public bills, drafted by people with little sympathy for their positions, were frequently intended to make subjects', especially Catholics', lives more difficult and their economic status less secure. Moreover, the commissions for Wentworth's parliaments specified that parliament would be determined if the subsidies bills were not quickly passed, effectively obliging them to accept penal levels of taxation (especially since they could not be amended) to enable parliament to continue, but with no guarantee that their grievances would even be discussed, let alone resolved and that bills they rejected could still be issued as acts of state.[26] The process of developing, debating, passing and rejecting bills is discussed in chapter seven.

REPRESENTATION

Parliament was the official and accepted forum for expressing grievances and recommending solutions and the traditional liberty of access to the monarch requested by every speaker symbolized this connection and collaboration. No lord deputy disputed parliament's right to present grievances and suggest remedies, although they may not have accepted the proposed solutions. As David Rothe wrote in his *Dutiful remonstrance of the subjects*:

> There be a suitable correspondency between both – the head with influence of royal clemency and pity to ease and relieve the distressed body of the subjects – and they, with the real vapours of their best digested substance, to refresh the head in due proportion.[27]

Subjects and MPs were well able individually or collectively to identify grievances and solutions and to present them to the crown through the administration; parliament had power to summon witnesses and to gather information, as it did in establishing the fees charged by various crown officers, on which to base its recommendations for reform and in defence of its own privileges and liberties.

The list of 22 grievances submitted by Sir William Sarsfield, representative for Cork City in 1634 and later lord Kilmallock, on behalf of the gentlemen of Munster is a unique survival, but may have been only one of many such documents; the matters which they considered should be dealt with legislatively included land titles, sheriff's activities, officials' fees, freeholders' rights, beggars, witchcraft, agriculture and the navigability of rivers. Their penultimate demand was for

25 Wentworth to Coke, 13 May 1634, in Knowler (ed.), *Letters and dispatches*, i, p. 246; Lentz, 'Irish parliament', pp 7–8. On Ryves, see Ball, *Judges in Ireland*, i, pp 336–7.

26 The commissions are printed in the 1613 and 1640 Commons' journals and the 1634 Lords' journals.

27 HMC, *Franciscan manuscripts*, p. 67.

> An Act that all his Majesties subiects and natives of this kingdome may be enabled to sue livery, and be capable of offices notwithstanding the Act of secundo or xjmo of Queen Elizabeth Such subiects respectively first taking the Oath of Alliegance declared in his Majesties Instructions to his majesties, his highness's heires and successors And that his highness's subiects and natives of this kingdome may be deemed, Called and reputed as those of the British nation and not tearmed meere Irish. That they may purchase marry and Concerte one with another notwithstanding any former Act, Acts or restrictions to the Contrary.

While there is no record of the document being presented to the Commons, the House established committees of members to draft bills, based on English examples, to deal with restraining the conversion of arable lands to pasture, weirs on rivers and supply of corn, which were among the demands presented.[28]

Poynings' Law and the administration's hostile attitude limited parliament's capacity for effective action on grievances. Given the lack of success following the 1613–15 and 1634 Commons' presenting lists of grievances to the deputy, the 1640 parliament found more direct ways of dealing with individual and collective problems. The Commons received a torrent of petitions from a wide range of individuals and communities and the committee sent to present the nation's grievances to Charles harkened back to the medieval delegations sent from Ireland to the monarch in England. The Irish Commons collaborated with the English Commons' attack on Strafford, pushing the limits of Poynings' Law in drafting its own legislation for the common good, including a bill to ban the paper petitions used by Wentworth's extra-judicial courts system, reversing Bramhall's innovations in the Church of Ireland and representing their constituents by adjudicating on their petitions. Petitions are considered below under parliament's judicial function and the process by which they were managed is discussed in chapter seven.

JUDICIAL FUNCTION

The description of parliament as the 'high court of parliament' underlined its judicial function, an impression reinforced by each chamber's layout, which was similar to that of a courtroom. The custom of making delinquent members and other offenders stand at the bar, the presence of counsel presenting their clients' cases and the practice of imprisoning delinquents also reflected its judicial role. The Commons also ordered other courts to postpone hearing cases that were the subject of petitions to the lower house. Both Irish houses were courts of record and

28 A note of the propositions of the gentlemen of the province of Mounster against the Parliament, delivered me by Sir William Sarsfield, TCD, MS 672, fos. 235r–8v (see Appendix 2). This document is undated, but is bound with other material from the 1634 parliament. *Commons' Jn. Ire.*, 17 Nov. 1634, 9 March 1635, 13, 15 April 1635.

the attendance of judges to provide legal advice underlined the upper house's role as a court.[29]

The Commons adjudicated on its own membership, disciplined its members and those who breached parliamentary privilege and both houses worked together to exercise parliament's judicial role by passing legislation with judicial elements, such as attainders and restitution in blood, dealing with petitions, investigating grievances such as crown officials' fees and managing impeachments.[30] The Commons called and examined witnesses and presented their cases to the Lords who pronounced judgment. While Dennehy and McCafferty claim that only the upper house could administer oaths, the 1613 parliament took oaths from its clerk and from witnesses. Wentworth mendaciously claimed Francis Annesley, Lord Mountnorris, arrogantly imposed the change to follow the English practice of oaths being administered in the Lords on the Commons through a conference committee 'out of such scraps as he had gotten' as an English MP in 1628, but Fernesly and Sandes had already taken their oaths as clerks in the upper house and the Commons accepted the Lords' demand that witnesses who were to be examined by the Commons should first 'be sworn at the bar of the lords house.' The practice of oaths being administered only in the Lords was adhered to in the future, apart from MPs swearing the oath of supremacy in the Commons in 1642.[31]

The medieval Irish parliament played an active judicial role, partly because of deficiencies in other institutions, including the common law courts whose operations shrank with the decline of the Lordship: 'the importance of the Irish parliament, especially in the later fifteenth century, derived rather from its handling of a large volume of administrative and judicial business' and 'it came nearer to realizing that other misleading claim of medieval parliaments, to be a court.' In their decisions 'the late medieval parliament reflected the interests of the political nation in Anglo-Ireland as a whole, and not merely those of the palesmen.'[32] Parliament rolls provided precedents to prove its right to hear and

29 Hawkyard, *Commons*, p. 246.

30 TCD, MS 672, fo. 239r; *Commons' Jn. Ire.*, 26 July 1641, where Fernesly had noted 'The undernamed Corporations wirr questioned by many of the members of the last parliament by way of petition presented to the howse of Comons the 24th. July 1634.' There is no record of this in the journals. It was no. 16 of the queries and it was decided that 'the right of sending burgesses to the parliament is questionable in parliament only.' The English Commons' right to decide on its own membership had only recently been put beyond question. See Mary Frear Keeler, 'The committee for privileges of the House of Commons, 1604–1610 and 1614', *Parl. Hist.*, 13:2 (1994), 147–69; John McCafferty, '"To follow the late precedents in England": the first Irish impeachment proceedings in 1641' in Desmond Greer and Norma Dawson (eds), *Mysteries and solutions in Irish legal history* (Dublin, 2001), pp 51–72; Dennehy, *Parliament*, p. 67; Paul Seaward, 'Impeachment', at https://historyofparliamentblog.wordpress.com/2017/09/04/impeachment/ [accessed 10 Sept. 2019].

31 Dennehy, *Parliament*, p. 23; McCafferty, '"To follow the late precedents in England"'; *Commons' Jn. Ire.*, 25 Nov. 1614, 18 April 1615, 1, 5, 12 May 1615, 17 July 1634, 15 July 1641, 21 June 1642; Wentworth to Coke, 16 Dec. 1634, in Knowler (ed.), *Letters and dispatches*, i, p. 349; *Commons' Jn. Ire.*, 23 June 1641.

32 Graves, *Parliaments*, p. 49; Ellis, 'Parliament and community'.

adjudge cases such as those of Nicholas Hussey, baron of Galtrim and John Kennock (*c.*1449), Richard Chambers (*c.*1457) and William Wells (1467) and of two successive archbishops of Dublin, Michael Treguy (*c.*1465) and John Walton (*c.*1476).[33] A summary of the Lords' rights claimed that King Henry II sent the *Modus* to Ireland, 'in which record it is said that such things may be examined and corrected in *Pleno parliamento et non alibi*' and in 1355 King Edward III ordained that 'in all cases whatsoever Errors in Judgments in Records and processe in the Courts of Ireland shall be corrected and amended in Parliament in Ireland.' They claimed that because of Henry II's action 'the house of lords in Parliament in Ireland may proceed to hear and determine judicially such matters which shall be brought before them, in the same manner as the lords in England.'[34]

The convoluted requirements of Poynings' Law reduced parliament's frequency to the extent that it was unable to exercise its judicial function, one of its most significant roles before that time and this instigated some constitutional innovation.[35] The Old English lords objected to the administration's proclaiming Tyrone a traitor in 1596, as this should have been done by his peers, not lower status English officials. The Pale lawyer Richard Hadsor supported this reading of the constitutional position. When Edmond Butler, Lord Dunboyne, was found guilty of manslaughter by the Tipperary Grand Jury, Charles ordered Falkland to appoint a nobleman as High Steward to try him, as it had to be done by his peers.[36]

John McCafferty claims that parliament lost its judicial role through Poynings' Law and the English parliament had allowed this function to lapse and only revived it in 1621.[37] While the lack of journals makes it difficult to assess this aspect of the Irish parliament's work under the Tudors, the 1541 parliament adjudicated disputes between Gaelic chiefs at the very least and peers certainly exercised this role in 1613–5, when they dealt with a writ of error for Bartholomew Dillon and cases between Ford and Travis, Fitzmaurice v Fitzmaurice and Sir James Carroll and Daniel Molyneux.[38] Early in the first 1634 session, the judges 'conceaved an adjournment of the house [of lords] every day was necessary, this being a Court of Law the highest in the Kingdome that sends writts of Error to the King's Bench' and the peers proceeded to deal with the cases of the Dublin Alderman Patrick Gough versus Arthur Bagenal of Newry and Richard Bourke versus the MP Sir

33 Marsh's Library, MS Z3.2.5, pp 1–27. The case of the Prior of Lanthony (8 Hen. VI, n. 790) was also recorded in TCD, MS 1,180, pp 12–13; David Beresford, 'Tregury, Michael', *DIB*; *idem*, 'Walton, John', *DIB*.

34 TCD, MS 1,180 p. 7, from Sir Robert Southwell's Papers. See Michael Perceval-Maxwell, 'Southwell, Sir Robert', *DIB*.

35 Bradshaw, 'Beginnings'.

36 Ruth Canning, *The Old English in early modern Ireland: the Palesmen and the Nine Years War, 1594–1603* (Woodbridge, 2019), pp 172–4; Charles to Falkland, 12 May 1628, *Cal. S.P. Ire., 1625–32*, p. 328; Empey (ed.), 'Diary of Sir James Ware'.

37 Elizabeth Read Foster, 'Procedure and the House of Lords in the seventeenth century', *Proceedings of the American Philosophical Society*, 126:3 (June, 1982), pp 183–7; Smith, *Stuart*, p. 13. For Pym's remarks on impeachment then, see McCafferty, '"To follow the late precedents"'.

38 Ibid.; Routledge, 'Journal'; Treadwell, 'House of Lords'.

Henry Bingham. On 13 November 1634 they referred the Gough-Bagenal case to the committee of privileges who were to report

> theire lordshipps' opinions what is fitt to be further proceded in that cause … and that the Lord Chiefe Justice of the Cheife Place, Lord Chiefe Justice of the Common Pleas, Lord Chiefe Baron of the Exchequer and the parties or theire Learned Councell shall attend.

Clandeboy suggested that 'the jurisdiction of the house was in question as well as the forme of proceeding', but the chancellor, supported by Mountnorris, replied that 'this High Court have power to try all causes between party and party.' Four days later, when the Bourke-Bingham case was discussed, Clandeboye argued that 'the house has many pressing issues for the commonwealth and should not admit petitions but such as could not be determined elsewhere', but the bishop of Raphoe, John Leslie, opined that 'A judge must *jus dicere*, but this house may *jus dicere*.'[39]

Wentworth's novel reading of Poynings' Law prevented parliament from impeaching the Munster planter Vincent Gookin in 1634, but he was well aware that he was on shaky ground in restricting its judicial function.[40] After Wentworth's fall from grace, the Irish parliament renewed its judicatory role. The Commons singly, and both houses jointly, explicitly asserted this function, asking the judges to advise on the *Queries*, commissioning Darcy's *Argument*, instituting impeachment proceedings and insisting on petitions being presented on parchment, the material used for high-status legal documents, despite having accepted them on paper in 1613. Audley Mervyn made a strong case in defence of parliament's judicial function in his speech on 24 May 1641 at the impeachment of Bolton, Bramhall, Lowther and Radcliffe (which was intended to prevent Wentworth's supporters testifying in his favour in London) citing many examples and emphatically basing his case on the presumption that the Irish parliament had the same powers as the English, including judicature, describing 'a parliament without Judicature' as 'ill suteable.'[41] More explicitly, both houses issued a Declaration and Protestation on 24 May 1641:

> The court of parliament being the supream and highest court in this realme and the four ordinary courts of justice and all other inferiour courts and all

39 Marsh's Library, MS Z3.2.5, pp 34, 57, 67, 71. These entries are not in the published journals. The latter case was dismissed because Bingham had privilege as an MP John Gibney, 'Leslie, John', *DIB*.

40 Knowler (ed.), *Letters and dispatches*, i, pp 350–1; Clarke, 'History of Poynings' Law'; TCD, MS 1,180, p. 9; Patricia Coughlan, 'Gookin, Sir Vincent', *DIB*.

41 Mervyn, *Captaine Audley Mervin's speech delivered*; A.R. Hart, 'Audley Mervyn: lawyer or politician?' in W.N. Osborough (ed.), *Explorations in law and history: Irish Legal History Society discourses, 1988–1994* (Dublin, 1995), pp 83–105; Dennehy, *Parliament*, pp 21–2, 30; Birr Castle, MS A/1/19; TNA, SP 30/5/3, fo. 100.

> officers and ministers of justice within this realme were are and ought to be guided and directed by the precedents and course of proceedings of the Courts of Parliament of England agreeable to the Common Laws there and in this kingdom, for the avoiding of any doubt or ambiguity which might be moved or stirred against the power of Judicature of the high Court of Parliament of this Realme … a most clear and undoubted and undeniable truth to all posteritie, the lords spiritual and temporall and Commons in Parliament assembled doe hereby declare and protest that the said Court of Parliament of this Kingdom hath alwaies had and ought to have full Power and Authority to heare and determine all Treasons and other offences, crimes, causes and things whatsoever as well Capitall and Criminall as Civill contrived perpetrated done or happened within this Realme and likewise to inflict Condigne punishment upon all offenders and to administer equall justice unto all persons whatsoever in the said Realme according to the antient course and rights of parliament in all times and ages used and exercised in the Realme of England.

Their response to Charles noted that calling parliament's right to judicature into question would raise the same issues for the administration of justice in other Irish courts and the fundamental laws of the kingdom.[42] The precedents set in 1641 held after the Restoration, although in 1693 the archbishop of Armagh, Michael Boyle, along with William Molyneux and the bishops of Clogher and Derry, Richard Tenison and William King, sought precedents from the medieval period to justify the parliament's powers of judicature.[43] However, even when parliament's judicial role was implicitly or explicitly accepted, there was doubt as to how far it extended. The privy council debated this issue in early 1642, in the context of indictments for rebellion:

> If a peer be indicted & that this happen in time of Parliament, and that he do appear of himself or be brought in upon the *capias*, the indictment is to be brought into the parliament, and there he is to be tried by his peers, if the parliament here have power of judicature in capital cases.[44]

42 Declaration of the Irish Parliament on the power and authoritie of the Court of Parliament, 24 May 1641, Marsh's Library, MS Z3.2.5; TCD, MS 1,180, pp 3–4; *Commons' Jn. Ire.*, 24 May 1641; *LJI*, 24 May 1641.

43 Clarke, 'Patrick Darcy and the constitutional relationship'; Dennehy, *Parliament*, pp 30–2; Paul M. Hunneyball, 'The development of parliamentary privilege, 1604–29' in Chris R. Kyle (ed.), *Managing Tudor and Stuart parliaments: essays in memory of Michael Graves* (Chichester, 2015), pp 111–28; H.F. Berry (ed.), *Statute rolls of the parliament of Ireland: King John to Henry V* (Dublin, 1907), pp 406–7; James McGuire, 'Tenison, Richard', *DIB*; Philip O'Regan, 'King, William', *DIB*; John Bergin, 'Tenison, Richard', *DIB*.

44 Bodl. Lib., Carte MS 68, fo. 423r, notes of Lords Justice William Parsons and Dillon and the Irish Council (undated, but sometime between Feb. and June 1642) difficulties which will fall out in the course of the proceedings which is to be held in the attainting of those rebels, who are now in actual rebellion.

Lentz's conclusion that 'the crown did not succeed in denying the Houses' judicature nor did the lords and commons disavow their competence in the matter' is probably the most accurate summation of the situation.[45]

Parliaments dealt with petitions from the public, which could be addressed to either house, as well as to Convocation. Petitions had been preferred to the English parliament under Edward the Confessor; as Elsynge remarked, 'Petitions were exhibited by private persons to the King and his Councel, or to the Commons' and to Irish parliaments since at least the fourteenth century when 'the Prior of the House of St Patrick of Downe, in Ulster by petition to the earl of March, lord lieutenant, and Council in Parliament assembled at Dublin, on Saturday the morrow of All Souls 1380.'[46] Scottish parliaments also dealt with petitions, known there as 'supplications'. Curiously, Irish residents petitioned the English parliament, even when the Irish parliament sat.[47] Petitions to people of influence and to corporate bodies were standard in the early modern period; Wentworth complained to Coke in May 1639 that 'this state is continually pestered with the petitions of such as pretend themselves much weakened, if not ruined in their estates' but parliamentary petitions are different, in that they are presented to a representative body and express problems in the administration by means of individual cases.[48]

Just as Charles had suppressed petitions (known as supplications) in the 1633 Scottish Estates as a threat to his regime, so Wentworth discouraged the 1634 parliament from dealing with petitions, reserving that function to himself:

> honourable and just redemptions of the subject from oppression and wrong, should be the immediate acts of sovereignty, indeed the proper charge and office of kings to provide for, without interposition of any parliament, or

45 Lentz, 'Irish parliament', p. 67.

46 John Lodge, *The usage of holding parliaments and of preparing and passing bills of supply, in Ireland; annotated by C. Lucas, M.D.* (Dublin, 1770), p. 36; Henry Elsynge, *Ancient method and manner of holding parliaments* (London, 1660), p. 22.

47 'Records of the parliaments of Scotland to 1707', at www.rps.ac.uk [accessed 31 March 2021]. For the development of the Scottish Estates' judicial function, see A.M. Godfrey, *Civil justice in renaissance Scotland: the origins of a central court* (Leiden, 2009), pp 13ff; Foster, 'Procedure'; Smith, *Stuart*, p. 13. For Pym's remarks on impeachment then, see McCafferty, '"To follow the late precedents in England"'; Grosart (ed.), *Lismore Papers*, 1st. series, ii, p. 302 under 25 Feb. 1629; Mountnorris, 'Humble petition ... to the ... knights, citizens and burgesses, of the Commons House of Parliament' in T. Cadell and W. Davies (eds), *A collection of scarce and valuable tracts on the most entertaining subjects: reign of King Charles I* (London, 1810), pp 203–5; Petition of Arthur O'Kiefe, 9 Feb. 1641, House of Lords, MS HL/PO/JO/10/1/51; *LJI*, 3 March 1641, which outlines a petition of Teige O'Roddy against the bishop of Ardagh in the English House of Commons. The different sittings of English and Irish parliaments make a direct comparison difficult before 1640, when parliaments were sitting in both kingdoms.

48 Wentworth to Coke, 18 May 1639, Coke to Wentworth, 24 Oct. 1633, Wentworth to Coke, 8 Nov. 1633, all in Knowler (ed.), *Letters and dispatches*, i, p. 152, ii, pp 137, 341; Jon G. Crawford, *A Star Chamber court in Ireland: the Court of Castle Chamber, 1571–1641* (Dublin, 2005), pp 379ff; NAI, MS 2,448; Gifford Charles-Edwards (ed.), 'Calendar of petitions to Ormonde in 1649 and 1650', *IG*, 6 (1980–5), 423–44, 577–600, 724–47.

> other body betwixt their light and the eyes of their people; who discerning whence those blessings are communicated may be justly moved to praise and magnify them for their goodness and protection; nor did I ever intend to interest a parliament therein.[49]

This grandiose statement, appropriating the role of adjudicator of all petitions in line with his monarchical ambitions, was explicitly contradicted by his collusion with Coke in preventing Irish petitions reaching the king. However, it did successfully reduce the number of recorded petitions to the 1634–5 parliament to 12 for the Lords and 19 for the Commons.[50] The small number of petitions in early Stuart Irish parliaments may partly result from deficiencies in the records, as there are many general references to petitions and procedures for dealing with them. There are 28 petitions recorded as having been presented to the 1613–15 Commons, almost all concerned grievances against MPs or MPs' servants and agents claiming privilege; others were from those who had private bills before the House, asking to be admitted to plead their cases, with their counsel. Examples include Piers Lacy's private bill. There were presumably other unrecorded petitions.[51] On 6 May 1615, the Commons named a committee of eight 'to take into consideration the contents of such petitions as are directed to this house by any persons, and to report to the House of their proceedings therein.' It would hardly have been worthwhile to establish a committee to deal with the small number of recorded petitions. It might be anticipated that there would be fewer petitions for redress of grievances in 1640–1, given the short time since the previous parliament but the opposite is the case. The dramatic increase in the number of petitions in 1640–1 is described by McCafferty as a 'torrent', but it follows a similar pattern to the 1638 Scottish Estates.[52]

Considerable attention has been paid to petitions to the English parliament, especially those from women, but much less to those in the Irish Parliament.[53] This

49 Laura A.M. Stewart, 'Petitioning in early seventeenth-century Scotland, 1625–51', *PER*, 38:3 (2018), 307–22; Wentworth to Coke, 13 May 1634, in Knowler (ed.), *Letters and dispatches*, i, p. 245.

50 Dougal Shaw, 'Thomas Wentworth and monarchical ritual in early modern Ireland', *The Historical Journal*, 49:2 (2006), 331–55; Coke to Wentworth, 17 June 1637, in Knowler (ed.), *Letters and dispatches*, ii, p. 82. Coke confirmed he was keeping as many petitions as possible from the king. *Commons' Jn. Ire.*, 20 July 1641; Dennehy, *Parliament*, p. 21. However, gaps in the records makes it possible that there were many others, e.g., that from Athenry. See M.J. Blake (ed.), *Blake family records, 1600–1700* (London, 1905), pp 41–2.

51 *Commons' Jn. Ire.*, 21–2 Oct. 1614.

52 John McCafferty, *The reconstruction of the Church of Ireland: Bishop Bramhall and the Laudian reforms, 1633–1641* (Cambridge, 2007), p. 216; Stewart, 'Petitioning'.

53 E.g., David Dean, 'Public space, private affairs: committees, petitions and lobbies in the early modern English parliament' in Christopher Kyle and Jason Peacey (eds), *Parliament at work: parliamentary committees, political power and public access in early modern England* (Woodbridge, 2002), pp 169–78; Kyle, 'From broadside to pamphlet'; Peacey, 'Print culture of parliament'; Ellen A. M'Arthur, 'Women petitioners and the Long Parliament', *EHR*, 24:96 (Oct., 1909), 698–709; Patricia Higgins, 'The reactions of women, with special reference to women petitioners'

may be partly because from the 1620s many English petitions resulted from collaborative agitation on policy issues and were published to make them available to a wider audience unlike Irish petitions, which almost invariably concerned individual and community grievances (although many were orchestrated by MPs as part of their campaign to change Irish political leadership) and the only printing press in Ireland was controlled by the crown.[54] The majority of petitions were from New English and Scottish settlers attempting to resolve their grievances and maintain their personal positions. Petitions are of especial interest as the only part of parliamentary business, apart from a small number of private bills for property, restoration in blood, or naturalization, which directly concerned females. Of the petitions in 1640–1, 8% came from women.[55]

PRIVILEGE

Members of both houses and their 'necessary or menial' servants or agents enjoyed freedom from arrest, imprisonment and suits and security for themselves and their property during parliament. Officers of the houses, including judges and heralds, and their servants also enjoyed privilege, as did, following recent English precedent, members of Convocation, although the latter had to channel their complaints through the Lords who had staff to police them and access to prisons for confinement.[56] Those summoned to appear before parliament were also covered for their journeys there and back: in 1615, a London merchant breached privilege by arranging the arrest of the sheriff of Wexford who had been ordered to attend the house; on 29 April 1615 the house ordered both to appear, the sheriff to answer his contempt in not appearing and the merchant to answer for arresting him.

The chief justice of common pleas, Edward Coke, defined privilege as applying 'in case of any arrest, or any distress of goods, serving any process, summoning the land of a member, citation or summoning his person, arresting his person, suing him in any court.'[57] Privilege was originally designed in the crown's interest, to ensure MPs' constant attendance and freedom to concentrate on their parliamentary duties without distraction and was exercised by at least 1450, when

in Brian Manning (ed.), *Politics, religion and the English civil war* (New York, 1973), pp 179–222; Ann Marie McEntee, '"The [Un]Civill-Sisterhood of Oranges and Lemons": female petitioners and demonstrators, 1642–53' in James Holstun (ed.), *Pamphlet wars: prose in the English Revolution* (London, 1992), pp 92–7, 99, 108–9; Charlotte F. Otten, *English women's voices, 1540–1700* (Gainesville, FL, 19), pp 85–94; Patricia-Ann Lee, 'Mistress Stagg's petitioners: February 1642', *The Historian*, 60:2 (1990), 241–56.

54 McCafferty, '"To follow the late precedents in England"'.

55 Hakewill, *Modus*, p. 11.

56 8 Hen. VI, c. 1 and 12 Hen. VI, c. 15; TCD, MS 615, Lords' journal (unpaginated), 26 March 1640; *Commons' Jn. Ire.*, 19 May 1641, 10 June 1641, 19 Nov. 1642; Hunneyball, 'Development of parliamentary privilege'. See the protections granted by judges William Hilton and George Shurley and the Athlone Pursuivant, Albon Leverett, in *LJI*, listed after 19 Aug. 1643.

57 Quoted in Stapylton, 'Parliamentary privilege', p. 11.

'Order [was] given for a citizen of Lim[eric]ke to be discharged of an areste in Dublin for that he cam to the parliment' and incorporated into Irish law 13 years later by 3 Ed. IV, c. 1, which specified that all 'ministers' of parliament should 'not be empleaded, vexed nor troubled by no mean [and] … be discharged and quitted of all manner actions had or moved against them' for the duration of parliament and 40 days before and after.[58] The 1585 rules specified that

> Yf during the tyme of parlyament any of this howse, his servantes or goods be sued, arested or vexed, contrary to the auncient customes in souche cases used, the speaker ys, upon information thereof to hym given, to send the sarjent at armes to souche courte, to declare the person so troubled to be of the parlyament, and therupon requiryng the officers thereof to stay in further proceading therin; whiche, being dysobeyed, the part[y] or officer so doyng ys by auctoritie from the speaker, to be sent for, and to be imprysoned and receive punyshment, according the discrecyon of the howse, to be assigned and laid downe.[59]

The Commons re-asserted this rule in 1614, 1615 and 1647.[60] Early modern parliaments met for longer periods than those of 1463–4 and the early Stuart parliaments' lengthy prorogations meant that parliamentary privilege covered much longer timescales. Members of the Confederation's General Assembly claimed similar privilege.[61]

Protection was not absolute, however; members of both houses were subject to discipline by their own house for any misdemeanours and privilege did not apply to those accused of treason or felony. Radcliffe's alleged treason was cited by the Long Parliament in November 1640 as justifying disregarding his privilege. It was possible to waive privilege as Wentworth claimed Cork did in 1634 and it was suggested that MPs George Wentworth and George Carr should do so in their dispute with George FitzGerald, sixteenth earl of Kildare.[62]

Peers were regarded as sufficiently well-known not to need to assert their privilege and they certified their followers' privilege. MPs claimed protection by stating that they were a 'parliament man' and had to obtain warrants for their

58 Abridgement of acts in Irish parliaments, TCD, MS 1,445, fo. 11r; Hunneyball, 'Development of parliamentary privilege'; An Act whereby the Lords and Commons of the parliament hath (sic) privilege for certain days before and after the said Parliament, 3 Edw. IV, c. 1; Bolton, *Statutes*, pp 32–3; Merick, *Compendious collection*, pp 300ff relates to parliaments and lists the relevant statutes; *Commons' Jn. Ire.*, 29 Oct. 1614, 23, 25 Nov. 1614; *LJI*, 26 March 1640; Stapylton, 'Parliamentary privilege', pp 56–8; 11 and 12 Edw. IV, c. 80 also concerned parliamentary privilege.

59 Irish Archaeological Society, *Tracts*, ii, p. 143.

60 Quoted in Dennehy, *Parliament*, p. 171; *Commons' Jn. Ire.*, 25 Nov. 1614, 27 April 1615, 15 May 1647.

61 TCD, MS 829, fos 443r–6v.

62 Knowler (ed.), *Letters and dispatches*, i, p. 347; *LJI*, 20 April 1643; Fiona Pogson (ed.), 'Financial accounts of Thomas Wentworth, earl of Strafford and Sir George Radcliffe, 1639–40', *Anal. Hib.*, 48 (2017), 89–168; Kearney, *Strafford in Ireland*, pp 247–8; Aidan Clarke and Bríd McGrath (eds), *The letterbook of George FitzGerald, 16th earl of Kildare* (Dublin, 2013).

servants and agents, paying the clerk 5*s*. for each, a lucrative perk for the clerk, given the number of hangers-on early modern parliamentarians had – Lord Gormanston brought a retinue of 20 to Dublin when he attended the 1613 parliament, apart from his servants or agents at home – this group could more properly be described in today's terms as 'staff or colleagues.'[63]

Privilege was very useful to MPs and peers and to anyone who could be classed as their servant or agent and became seen in England during this period as a personal benefit. MPs who were short of money, like Thomas Davills and Mathew Ford, or subject to legal proceedings, like Richard Blacknall or John FitzGerald, were safe from their creditors' or litigants' demands during parliament.[64] When old towns were under pressure to elect conforming officers, three Kilkenny MPs were selected as mayor or sheriff (Nicholas Langton, William Murphy and Lucas Shee) in 1614 and 1615, safe in the knowledge that they were protected from prosecution until 40 days after the dissolution of parliament. Limerick and New Ross took the same action in electing James Galway and James Fitzharris respectively in 1614, as did Youghal with Edmond Coppinger in 1615. John Forrest's unsuccessful candidacy for that town's recordership in 1614 may have been based on the same calculation.[65] Privilege was widely claimed and the range of people covered increased in this period. The possibility of whether it extended to tenants was referred to the Grand Committee on 4 and 9 November 1614, although its ruling is not recorded. Nine days later the question of attorneys and legal counsel's privilege was debated and the house agreed that plaintiffs and their attorneys breached privilege in serving writs on MPs, but lawyers were exempt.[66]

Early seventeenth-century English MPs described their privileges as 'ancient' and 'undoubted', but they were based on custom. From the fourteenth century it had been accepted that MPs and their servants should be safe travelling to and from parliament, which the 1433 Act against assaults upon lords and others coming to parliament confirmed.[67] English privilege operated only during and for between 16 or 20 days before and after each individual session, not for the entire course of the parliament and had a more limited statutory basis than Ireland even after 1 Jac. I, c. 13 (England) established it more clearly. Thereafter it was steadily

63 *Commons' Jn. Ire.*, 3 March 1641, 9 Aug. 1642, 20 April 1643, 20 Jan. 1645; Curtis Clayton (ed.), *Council book*, pp 267–8; Dennehy, *Parliament*, p. 138; *Cal. S.P. Ire., 1611–14*, pp 445–6; Stapylton, 'Parliamentary privilege', 58; Hunneyball, 'Development of parliamentary privilege'.

64 For Davills' financial difficulties, see Bodl. Lib., Carte MS 176, fos. 9r, 17r–43, 102r–45. For similar cases in Tudor England, see Hawkyard, *Commons*, pp 241–3; Hunneyball, 'Development of parliamentary privilege'. Ford, who was returned sometime between Aug. and Nov. 1642, was being pursued by Lord Howth for £15 arrears of rent, *LJI*, 12, 16 Aug. 1642.

65 Langton, Murphy and Shee represented Kilkenny City, Inistioge and Kilkenny County respectively. Murphy and Shee were prosecuted in the Court of Castle Chamber after parliament ended. Crawford, *Star Chamber*, p. 525; Caulfield (ed.), *Youghal*, pp 38–9; Maurice Lenihan, *Limerick, its history and antiquities, ecclesiastical, civil and military* (Dublin, 1866), p. 701; McGrath, 'Kick-starting New Ross' renewal'.

66 *Commons' Jn. Ire.*, 18 Nov. 1614.

67 Hawkyard, *Commons*, pp 244ff.

extended and vigorously defended. Both English houses significantly pushed the bounds of privilege as a benefit to members and a facilitator of parliamentary opposition and it was also used to assert the customary distinctions between the houses, e.g., their separate roles in exercising parliament's judicial function, the Lords' right to initiate private bills of honour and the Commons' subsidy bills and who should decide the time, place and etiquette of conference committees (see chapter seven). Both houses were very defensive of their own dignity, including any perceived slight from the other chamber.

The effect of prorogation was one area in which the Irish Commons' and Lords' interpretation of privilege diverged during this period. Whereas they had been in agreement about the provisions of 3 Edw. IV, c. 1 in 1613–15, by 1634 the Lords held that privilege was not provided for prorogations of more than 40 days and in 1643, when Kildare was attempting to recover rent arrears from George Wentworth and Carr, he was left 'to the ordinary course of law', as prorogation was imminent, although other peers' warrants for privilege outside the 40 days were accepted in 1643.[68] It is unclear why the Lords should have taken this course, as it ran counter to the statute and their own interests, but it may have been part of the protection Ormond was extending to Strafford's coterie.[69]

Parliament had gradually acquired a number of traditional liberties as well as privileges: access to the sovereign, freedom of speech for members in the House and pardon for the speaker for errors. Traditional liberties were always requested in Irish speakers' acceptance speeches precisely because, unlike freedom from arrests and suits, they had no statutory basis.[70] These liberties were frequently conflated with privilege and came to be extended also to matters of personal honour, a very important matter in early modern societies and there were many cases of members of both houses objecting to insulting behaviour as infringements of privilege, although such claims had no legal basis. No lord deputy refused to meet a delegation from parliament or respond to requests; however, Wentworth restricted Irish residents' freedom of movement to England, including to the court and Wandesford made strenuous attempts to prevent the committee of Irish MPs from travelling to England to make their case to Charles.[71]

This expansion of rights and the crown's attempts at infringement in the 1620s, explains why the English MP for Colchester, Harbottle Grimston's list of privileges is so much more detailed than Coke's:

1. to speake freely without interruption or contradiction in any debate, dispute, or argument;
2. not to be questioned, for any such free dispute, argument or debate to be taxed or accused for the same, either during the free sitting thereof, or after;

68 *Commons' Jn. Ire.*, 20 April 1643; *LJI*, pp 228–30.
69 McGrath, 'Recruiter returns'.
70 Mary Frear Keeler, 'The emergence of standing committees for privileges and returns', *Parl. Hist.*, 1 (1982), 25–46.
71 Clarke, *Old English*, p. 135.

3. freely to give vote, judgment, or sentence, upon the reading of any Bill to be made law, or any bill, either of Attainder, or other charge against Delinquents and Criminous persons of the state at their trial;
4. to defend and maintain free votes judgments and sentences of the whole house by protestation, Remonstrance or other Declaration;
5. not to be accused of any crime or impeached for treason by any person whatsoever, during the continuance of the parliament for things done in the same, without legall accusation and prosecution of any such member by the whole house;
6. not to be apprehended upon such impeachment, or arrested by any officer, or to have upon such accusation their Chambers, Trunks, and Studies broken open, their bookes and writings seazed upon, without consent or warrant of the whole Parliament.[72]

Wentworth's assaults on parliament's privileges and liberties should be seen in the context of the debates about privilege and parliament's powers in England in the 1620s, when he was an MP. Grimston defended parliament's privileges when they were under pressure; MPs vigorously asserted their rights in the 1628 English parliament that saw some members imprisoned. Two of the imprisoned members were asked to confirm what they had said in parliament; Sir John Eliot, who eventually lost his life for advocating for parliamentary privilege, asserted that

> Whatsoever was said or done in that place, was performed as hee was a publique man, and a member of the House, and that he was and alwaies will bee readie to give an accompt of his sayings and doings in that place when soever hee shall be called unto it by the House, where, he took it, he was only to be questioned.

Sir Miles Hobart, who was no stranger himself to denying royal authority in the face of parliamentary privilege and famously ordered the doors of the Commons closed to prevent the king's messenger entering on a debate surrounding tonnage and poundage in early March 1629,

> desired to knowe by what Authoritie hee was examined to give an Accompt of his Actions in Parliamentt whilst he was a member of that Parliament, and that no Court or Commission could take notice of anie thing done, or said, in Parliament, but a Parliament. Neverthelesse hee would not stick to confess, that it was hee that shutt the Doore. And that hee did soe because the House commaunded it.[73]

72 Harbottle Grimston, *Mr Grimston his speech at the committee sitting in Guildhall on Thuesday the 6. of Ianuary 1641 [–2] concerning the breaches of the priviledges of Parliament by breaking open the chambers, studies, and trunks of the Lord Kimbolton and the rest of the members of the House of Commons* (London, 1642) (unpaginated); M.W. Helms, et al., 'Grimston, Sir Harbottle' in B.D. Henning (ed.), *The history of parliament: the House of Commons, 1660–1690* (London, 1983).

73 HRC, MS 76, fo. 145; Conrad Russell, 'Eliot, Sir John', *Oxford DNB*; L.J. Reeve, 'Hobart, Sir Miles', *Oxford DNB*.

In general, the English Lords drove the expansion of parliamentary privilege there, closely followed by the English Commons and both Irish houses.[74] While privilege was a live issue in the early modern period, disputes seen in England about its origin and extent had no Irish counterparts, presumably because of its statutory basis, although the level of infringement by the crown was comparable in both kingdoms.[75]

Freedom of speech in Ireland was limited by the requirement to be polite and to the point, with the 1585 rules specifying that each MP

> in uttering his mynd to any bill, to use and frame his speache after a quyet and curtyous manner, without any taunts or wordes tendyng to the reproche of any person … as eche person, here assembled, hath graunted unto hym free libertie of speach, in declaryng his mynd and opynion to eche matter proponed.[76]

Each house policed and disciplined its own members and adjudicated on their complaints against the administration, members of either house or outsiders and could investigate cases and order solutions, which the speaker was to enforce.[77] The 1585 rules laid down that 'If any offend or mysbehave hymself in this howse, his punyshment ys to be consdydered of and assygned by the speaker, with thadvise and assent of the residue of the howse.'[78] Miscreants, whether MPs or outsiders, were made to kneel at the bar to confess their faults, apologize and receive their sentence from the speaker on behalf of the house.[79] The Commons could and did censure MPs for insulting or offensive speeches. The furious response to Hooker's speech in which he insulted the Irish – he had to be escorted from the House and an angry Edward Butler declared 'if these words had been spoken in any other place than in this house, there be a great many here that they would rather have died than to have suffered it' – demonstrates the power of privilege. Hooker's punishment is unrecorded, but the principle of freedom of speech was maintained.[80] The limits to freedom of speech were seen in 1614–15: John Fishe, Cavan County's representative, was disciplined for claiming that the Lords 'have no care of the common-wealth' and imprisoned by the serjeant-at-arms, while a committee devised a suitable form of apology. Thomas Crooke was confined by the serjeant-at-arms during the House's pleasure for maligning Catholic members and Thomas Ryves, as registrar of Convocation, was regarded as culpable for the insult to recusants contained in the preamble to the Clergy Subsidy bill and imprisoned by the House for disparaging its members. Gerald Nugent escaped censure for

74 Hunneyball, 'Development of parliamentary privilege'.
75 Stapylton, 'Parliamentary privilege', 43–5; Hunneyball, 'Development of parliamentary privilege'.
76 Irish Archaeological Society, *Tracts*, ii, p. 143.
77 Stapylton, 'Parliamentary privilege', 55; S.A. Ferrall, *An exposition of the law of parliament as it relates to the power and privileges of the Commons House* (London, 1837), p. 168.
78 Irish Archaeological Society, *Tracts*, ii, p. 143.
79 E.g., *Commons' Jn. Ire.*, 8 Nov. 1614, 1 Aug. 1634, 4 Nov. 1634, 14 May 1641.
80 Treadwell, 'Irish parliament of 1569–71'.

insulting the son of the notorious archbishop of Cashel Miler Magrath, by falling into an epileptic fit.[81]

Despite clear legislation and custom, and the houses' repeated assertions of privilege, it was frequently breached and MPs in each parliament petitioned against infringements. The privilege of the MPs who went to England to complain about the course of the 1613 elections was breached by their imprisonment there, but they continued otherwise to benefit from its provisions. On 31 January 1614 Sir William Talbot, a scion of one of the Pale's most prominent families of Old English lawyers and an MP for Kildare, was tried in the Star Chamber for refusing to condemn the views of the Jesuit theologian Francisco Suarez.[82] He was then imprisoned until July 1614 and fined £10,000, but the English privy council upheld his complaint against a relative stealing legal documents about disputed land. James may have classed their opposition as tantamount to treason to intimidate them.[83] While Grimston's list included freedom for MPs to vote as they chose, Wentworth imposed a collective responsibility on privy councillors, stating that 'in parliament noe vote to be made contrary to the vote of this (Council) board being a[n] order in the same matter' and Sir Piers Crosby was expelled from the Irish privy council for transgressing this rule.[84] The Irish agents to Charles asserted parliament's privilege when they declared that privy councillors in both houses should have free votes in parliament and that there should be 'free repaire oute of Ireland'.[85]

Freedom from arrests and suits tended to be the most frequent complaints from both MPs and peers; almost 200 cases were raised by English MPs between 1604 and 1629, steadily increasing from a low base during this period.[86] MPs complained about debts or trespass on their property.[87] In Ireland the penalties could be significant. Sir Francis Rushe complained that his servant, Mr Gibbes, was arrested for debt owed to one Carey. The House then summoned creditor Carey and the officer who served the warrant to appear and ordered him to pay Gibbes £10 for his charges and Rushe £39 10*s*., before releasing him from prison. Similarly, Richard Morgan and Teigue O'Murrey were charged at the bar for distraining William Talbot's goods and were committed to the Marshalsea. Insults to MPs were severely punished: George Lowe, who abused John Warren, burgess for Navan, in Fishamble Street, was ordered to be publicly whipped at the same

81 *Commons' Jn. Ire.*, 8–10, 18 Nov. 1614; 3–4, 16 May 1615; Moynes (ed.), *Annual letters*, i, pp 481–2; Christopher Maginn, 'Magrath, Meiler', *Oxford DNB*.

82 Terry Clavin, 'Talbot, Sir William', *DIB*.

83 Moynes (ed.), *Annual letters*, i, pp 414–15; *Cal. S.P. Ire.*, 1611–15, p. 490.

84 Bolton's abstract of Charles I's letter concerning Strafford's government in Ireland, Marsh's Library, MS Z2.1.1, no. 58; Aidan Clarke, 'Sir Piers Crosby, 1590–1646: Wentworth's "tawney ribbon"', *IHS*, 26:102 (1988), 142–60; Clarke, *Old English*, pp 84–5; Robert Armstrong, 'Crosby, Sir Piers', *DIB*.

85 Hunneyball, 'Development of parliamentary privilege'; Smith, *Stuart*, pp 64–6; RIA, MS 24/Q/4, fo. 46r.

86 Stapylton, 'Parliamentary privilege', 13; Hunneyball, 'Development of parliamentary privilege'.

87 E.g., *Commons' Jn. Ire.*, 7 Aug. 1641.

place. When Laurence Lambert insulted and assaulted the MP Thomas Johnson about a minor debt, the house ordered him to be brought from the Marshalsea to the gibbet at the corn market to confess his fault in public and to pay £100 each to Johnson and the king.[88] These punishments were in line with procedures laid down in 11 Hen. VI, c. 11 for peers, MPs, king's counsel (and presumably judges attending the upper house) and their servants who were subject to assault or affray, which involved magistrates proclaiming on three separate days in 'the most eminent places of the Towne (where such assault or affray is made)' that the offender appear before the king's bench within three months where he would be judged and made to pay damages.

The development of standing committees of privileges in 1613–15 added an efficient means of dealing with complaints and the house confirmed its recommendations. On 17 November 1634 the house ordered that all petitions relating to MPs' privilege had first to be submitted to that committee; 30% of petitions to the Commons in 1641 came from MPs. The Commons vindicated the privilege of members who were being pursued in the Court of Castle Chamber in 1614, 1634 and 1641, but there was a strong bias against Catholics. On 10 June 1634 Sir Daniel O'Brien, MP for Clare, unsuccessfully requested Wentworth to have the case instigated against him by the attorney general dismissed on the grounds of his privilege; the case was not dropped and he was eventually convicted in 1637. On the other hand, the house defended Thomas Tallis, an agent of the earl of Cork's, on 8 November 1634. There is no record of O'Brien appealing to the house at the time although this would have been the obvious course, but in August 1641 he complained to the Commons, who decided that his privilege had been broken and ordered all proceedings to be vacated.[89] However, in 1644 instead of supporting Adam Loftus, who was being pursued in the same court, they objected to the speaker acting as counsel against him.[90]

Not all breaches of privilege came before the house; Sir William Stewart's murderous assault on the Ulster king of arms, Daniel Molyneux in autumn 1613 over a question of precedence between Stewart's wife and daughter-in-law was a clear breach of privilege. Molyneux only survived because his cook appeared and chased Stewart away, brandishing his red-hot roasting spit, with which he stabbed one of the assailants. Parliament was prorogued between June 1613 and October 1614, so Molyneux could not raise the matter in the house, even had his health permitted. Molyneux sued the Scotsman in the courts, but the case was protracted and inconclusive and Stewart went to England and successfully used his influence at court for protection. The seriously wounded Molyneux appealed to the English privy council, who wrote in his favour to Chichester on 8 May 1614. The case was

88 Ibid., 29 Oct. 1614, 3 Nov. 1614, 12 April 1644, 2 May 1646. See also 7 Aug. 1641 for a series of decisions on petitions including the insolent behaviour of Nicholas Patty towards the MP Henry Talbot.

89 Ibid., 7 Aug. 1641; John O'Donoghue, *Historical memoir of the O'Briens* (Dublin, 1860), p. 262.

90 *Commons' Jn. Ire.*, 8, 17–18 Nov. 1614, 8 Nov. 1634, 22 June 1641, 15 July 1641, 17 Feb. 1644.

remitted to Chichester for judgment, who gave a very biased decision in Stewart's favour.[91] The normal remedies through the King's Bench, the committee of privileges and referral to Chichester all failed Molyneux, although fortunately he recovered his health.

The most famous early modern Irish privilege case concerned John FitzGerald whose providential return for Inistioge in 1640 allowed him to defer, and ultimately escape, the ruinous sentence passed on him by the Court of Castle Chamber in the defamation case Lord and Lady Kerry took against him. The administration's main concern was the possibility that he would escape the sentence. The attorney general, Sir Thomas Tempest's legal advice, possibly for Ormond who chaired a committee considering the matter, centred on the speed with which the writ of return was dealt with and FitzGerald's not being resident in Inistioge, a novel concern for the administration. Only English custom and precedents were cited, declaring that the 'Sentence in Castle Chamber being affected by the Prorogation and above 40 dayes before this session, it is out of the tyme of his pretence of priviledge.' It also noted that FitzGerald 'did not offer anything to the Court … to make his priviledge judicially to appear', possibly because he did not know whether his election had been secured. It also noted that in

> so foule a crime against a Peere of the Upper House … Hee is not to be protected against … Upon pretence of priviledge of the Lower House … In cases especially where a Peere of the Realm and the kinge is concerned the Commons are not to be judges of their owne priviledges. And the parliamentary Judicature appertaineth to the Upper House.

FitzGerald's election stood, possibly because the Commons recognized Irish privilege's wider scope and statutory basis but the decision was also a turning point in the administration's control of the House.[92]

Crown servants who claimed privilege included the pursuivant George Bentley and Michael Stanhope, registrar of the Court of High Commission, who used it to avoid giving evidence to the grievances committee about fees and fines in that court, as a 'domesticke servant to my Lord Lieutenant … my lord lieutenant is now engaged in the cause for his privilege.' As MP for Ballyshannon in 1634 and a member of that parliament's committee on grievances, Stanhope, who was by no stretch of the imagination Wentworth's 'domesticke servant', would have been well aware of the extent of parliamentary privilege.[93]

91 Capel Molyneux and T. Phillipps (eds), *An account of the family and descendants of Sir Thomas Molyneux, kt., chancellor of the exchequer in Ireland* (Evesham, 1820), pp 11–17; *APC, 1613–14*, p. 429; Brendan Kane, *The politics and culture of honour in Britain and Ireland, 1541–1641* (Cambridge, 2010), pp 202–4.

92 Bodl. Lib., Carte MS 1, fos. 309r–10r; McGrath, 'Sex, lies and rigged returns'; Bríd McGrath, 'Inistioge's elections in 1640', *Old Kilkenny Review*, 57 (2005), 75–82. Tempest was Christopher Wandesford's cousin.

93 Peacey, '"Rushworth shall not take any notes here"'; *Commons' Jn. Ire.*, 9 Nov. 1614; Bramhall to Laud, 4 Nov. 1640, HL, HP, MS 14,061; *LJI*, 13 Nov. 1643.

Privilege was widely abused by giving protections to people who were not genuinely peers' or MPs' servants, so allowing them to escape court proceedings including recovery of debts, although there is no record in Ireland of the types of corruption endemic in England in the early 1620s.[94] This abuse was remedied in Ireland by 10 Car. I, c. 12, which allowed for writs to be re-issued after parliament's dissolution, so that cases stalled during parliament could resume after its dissolution, enabling debtors to be pursued for repayment.[95] Abuse of the system in Ireland was only identified as a problem after 1641. On 13 May the House of Commons ordered that all protections granted by any MP to anyone other than 'waged and necessary tending servants' were void, although it added the rider that this 'be no precedent to the prejudice of future parliaments.' In 1643 the Lords took action to restrict privilege being issued to people who were not genuinely peers' or MPs' servants and ordered the clerk to keep a record of any protections within ten days of issue, although this order was reversed in the following year. The Catholic peers Dunsany, Fitzwilliam, Kilmallock and Taaffe issued warrants for privilege between 1643 and 1645, even while they were not attending parliament, in Dunsany's case while he was in prison.[96] The Commons, recognizing how many MPs' followers were avoiding paying their debts, made the same order about registering protections within ten days, withdrew privilege for any of them who were six months out of Ireland, voided protections for anyone not a 'waged, menial, or necessary attending servants, really employed by the member' and ordered that MPs would be liable for damages to anyone adversely affected.[97]

Chichester was careful to observe privilege; when instructing Lord Thomond, Lord President of Munster to ensure that all new sheriffs and chief magistrates of towns who were shortly to hold elections were to be conformable and to bind over voters who elected known recusants, he cautioned him to 'have care not to bynde over any member of the house of parliament until the same be disolued.'[98] Wentworth, like the king in England, blatantly disregarded privilege in a series of moves against MPs in 1634–5. These are discussed in further depth below in the section about the Commons disciplining its members.

In 1614 the Commons was accepted as having power to decide on its membership, establishing a long claimed principle (e.g., 1569 and 1585) only established in England in 1604, where it led to the restoration of representation to at least 15 boroughs between 1621 and 1640.[99] This power included which

94 Hunneyball, 'Development of parliamentary privilege'; Dennehy, *Parliament*, p. 169.

95 For the development of privilege in Tudor England, see Hawkyard, *Commons*, pp 232–46; Stapylton, 'Parliamentary privilege', 65; Hunneyball, 'Development of parliamentary privilege'.

96 *LJI*, listed after 19 Aug. 1643.

97 Marsh's Library, MS Z3.1.1, no. 62 (20 April 1643), no. 63 (24 Feb. 1645–6). Copy of orders certified by Val Savage, deputy clerk of parliament, House of Lords; *Commons' Jn. Ire.*, 20 April 1643; *LJI*, 20 April 1643, 12 April 1644.

98 Chichester to the President of Munster, 20 July 1615, in Curtis Clayton (ed.), *Council book*, p. 210.

99 Elizabeth de Villiers, 'Parliamentary boroughs restored by the House of Commons, 1621–1641', *EHR*, 67:263 (April, 1952), 175–202; Keeler, 'Committee for privileges'; Hunneyball, 'Development of parliamentary privilege'.

constituencies should be represented and adjudicating on disputed returns or members' eligibility to sit. However, these powers were constrained by privy councillors' dominance of the Commons, especially under Wentworth and his deployment of *Quo warranto* proceedings against 27 old boroughs to disfranchise them which transferred authority to decide on boroughs' representation to the Court of Exchequer, an infringement and innovation denounced by the Commons in their Remonstrance on 7 November 1640.[100] Every early modern Irish parliament heard Catholics' objections to boroughs' representation and to the return of non-residents; this is discussed in chapters four and five.

In 1634 the Commons decided on disputed returns in Kerry and Carlow, rejected Thomas Bramston's membership as he had returned himself for Belfast and questioned Bryan McPhelim Byrne's election for Wicklow as he had been indicted of treason. In 1641 they pronounced in favour of FitzGerald's return for Inistioge, with Audley Mervyn making a strong case in defence of their right to decide on their own membership, citing old and recent precedents including Sir John Eliot and Charles' response to the Petition of Right in 1628.[101] It later decided to impose an age limit by disqualifying minors from membership.[102]

The House disciplined members for infringing rules or poor behaviour; sanctions included imprisonment, suspension and, from 1634, expulsion. In each case, the culprit was summoned to the bar to answer for his conduct. In 1615, MPs were unsure whether they had the power to expel Paul Sherlock for attempting to bribe the chancellor, with Sir John Everard arguing that 'the country choosing him, we cannot for a contempt dismiss him, unless in case of treason.' English precedents were adduced and the matter referred to the committee on privileges whose decision was unrecorded, but there were no recorded expulsions in that parliament.[103] This cautious approach was in stark contrast to the following parliaments but Wentworth rode roughshod over the Commons' right to discipline its members in 1634–5, setting a pattern for expulsion that was eagerly adoption by the opposition in 1640–1 and the 'rump' parliament in June 1642.

In 1641 Lords Gormanston and Kilmallock, the latter of whom as Sir William Sarsfield sat in the 1634 Commons, petitioned the king stating that 'the right liberties and proceedings of the said court have been violated' by Wentworth in eleven ways, four of which related to privilege and liberties: imprisoning members during parliament; infringing freedom of speech and action by obliging privy councillors to vote with the administration, regardless of their opinions; refusing to allow parliament to exercise its judicial function and tearing out and defacing parliamentary orders.[104]

100 McGrath, 'Electoral strategy'.
101 McGrath, 'Sex, lies and rigged returns'; *Commons' Jn. Ire.*, 19 July 1634, 12 Nov. 1634, 3, 10 Dec. 1634, 26 Jan. 1641, 4, 11, 13, 15, 18, 27 Feb. 1641; ARL, MS Parliamentary Papers, unpaginated; Mervyn, *Sixteene queres*.
102 *Commons' Jn. Ire.*, 24 May 1641.
103 Ibid., 27 April 1615.
104 TNA, SP 63/258, p. 163.

Wentworth violated MPs' liberty of speech when he engineered the expulsion of Sir Robert Talbot, Lucas Netterville and Geoffrey Baron from the 1634–5 parliament for speeches to which he took exception, the contents of which were unfortunately not recorded. We do know that Talbot denied that his remarks were aimed at the lord deputy, but asserted that what he had said needed to be said although he was sorry that it fell to his lot to do it.[105] The cousins Netterville and Talbot were dealt with in swift succession on 30 July and 1 August 1634. Wentworth's intervention was a signal of things to come and his choice of Netterville and Talbot was significant, as both had powerful connections in England, even among Wentworth's own friends. Despite the intervention of Richard Weston, first earl of Portland, the deputy declared his intention to prosecute Netterville in the Castle Chamber for having 'most barbarously and insolently demeaned himself this last session of parliament, expressing upon all occasions wondrous ill affections towards his Majesty's affairs and towards his ministers.'[106]

Wentworth's victimization of Catholic MPs continued during the recess when he intervened to attack Talbot's brother-in-law, Sir John Dongan, MP for Newcastle, County Dublin, using as his excuse a minor spat in the house on 18 July 1634 between Dongan and Wentworth's associate Capt. Charles Price, MP for Belfast. Dongan was claimed to have resented remarks made by Price, an active member of parliament in the 1620s for his native Radnorshire, on the procedural question of whether the House should be purged while the committee of privileges was considering returns. During the recess, Wentworth ordered that both be imprisoned and appointed a committee of the privy council, composed of MPs and justice George Shurley, to investigate the matter, questioning two other MPs, the Munster planter and future regicide Hardress Waller and Nicholas Barnewall.[107] The well-primed committee decided that Dongan had acted egregiously against the king, Price and the Commons, forced him to apologize on his knees at the council table, had him re-imprisoned four days before the next session and on the first day of the second session ordered him to be brought to the House as a prisoner to repeat his apology, kneeling at the bar. The House appointed a committee of privy councillors to entreat Wentworth to remit a further punishment for the offence to the king.[108] Wentworth's next victim, Geoffrey

105 Clarke, '28 November 1634'; *idem*, *Old English*, pp 84–5; *idem*, 'Sir Piers Crosby'.

106 Netterville was connected to Lord Portland, who wrote to Wentworth asking for lenience on 27 Oct. 1634. Wentworth replied that Netterville was 'as well replenished with insolence in himself, and with ill Affections towards the State, as any other.' See Wentworth to Portland, 3 Dec. 1634, in Knowler (ed.), *Letters and dispatches*, i, pp 339–40. Talbot was the son-in-law of George Calvert, Lord Baltimore, whose election for Yorkshire in 1621 Wentworth had engineered. John K. Gruenfelder, 'The electoral patronage of Sir Thomas Wentworth, earl of Strafford, 1614–1640', *The Journal of Modern History*, 49:4 (Dec., 1977), 557–74; Alan Davidson and Ben Coates, 'Weston, Sir Richard' in Thrush and Ferris (eds), *History of parliament*.

107 Patrick Little, 'Waller, Sir Hardress', *DIB*; Richard Hawkins, 'Barnewall, Sir Nicholas', *DIB*. On Shurley, see Ball, *Judges in Ireland*, i, pp 328–9.

108 Lloyd Bowen and Simon Healy, 'Price, Charles' in Thrush and Ferris (eds), *History of*

Baron, MP for Clonmel, expelled on 3 December having been exonerated by the house of an unspecified offence on the previous day, was clearly taken completely by surprise and experienced a physical collapse.[109] Only Talbot is known to have been replaced, reflecting the administration's reluctance to have them succeeded by other Catholics. Unusually, the journals do not record that the Commons pressed for writs to be issued as they did in other cases, demonstrating Wentworth's control over the House and Speaker Nathaniel Catlin's failure to defend the Commons.[110]

Just as Charles arrested several of Buckingham's critics in the English parliament in 1626 and had Edward Montagu, Lord Kimbolton's study sacked and papers seized, Wentworth's henchmen, the MPs Robert Farrar and Philip Mainwaring, broke and entered Piers Crosby's study following the latter's sequestration from the privy council and imprisonment for voting against the administration.[111] Wentworth's involvement in this and the Dongan–Price dispute were indefensible as he abrogated the power to punish MPs for their actions in the house. These clear breaches of privilege of freedom of speech and action and from arrest and seizure of property were aimed solely at Catholics (except Crosby, at that period), and in Crosby's case, any investigation, search of his study and seizure of his papers or punishment should have been undertaken by the Commons alone. While Chichester respected MPs' privilege, Catlin made no recorded attempt to defend the House and its members from Wentworth's attacks on Baron, Crosby, Dongan, Netterville and Talbot, the Castle Chamber case against O'Brien or Radcliffe's intimidation of Barnewall and the east Ulster planter, Sir John Clotworthy (*plate 12*).[112] Wentworth's abuse of parliamentary privilege and liberties was raised at his trial.[113] Dongan was elected to the next parliament and Crosby in a by-election late in 1641, but Baron, Netterville and Talbot's next political involvement was not until the Confederation of Kilkenny.[114]

The opposition cheerfully used the power of expulsion in 1640 as a means of attacking Wentworth's clients and allies such as Joshua Carpenter, Edward Lake, Thomas Little Jr, William Peisley and Thomas Radcliffe, while simultaneously freeing up seats for those useful to the opposition, such as the lawyers Darcy, Richard Martin and James Cusack, and Walter Cruise and Richard Bellings, those

parliament, where he is quoted as stating that the recusants opposed 'our best laws'; *Commons' Jn. Ire.*, 4, 8, 14–15 Nov. 1634.

109 Clarke, '28 November 1634'; *idem*, *Old English*, p. 84; *Commons' Jn. Ire.*, 6 Dec. 1634.

110 It was assumed that Sir William Anderson replaced Netterville but he was already in the house on 21 July 1634 before the expulsion.

111 Smith, *Stuart*, pp 65–6; Clarke, 'Sir Piers Crosby'; *Commons' Jn. Ire.*, 9 July 1641; Ian J. Gentles, 'Montagu, Edward, second earl of Manchester', *Oxford DNB*.

112 Treadwell, 'Sir John Perott'; Clarke, 'Sir Piers Crosby'; *idem*, '28 November 1634'; Raymond Gillespie, 'Clotworthy, Sir John', *DIB*.

113 Rushworth (ed.), *Tryal*, pp 110, 112.

114 Bríd McGrath, 'Parliament men and the confederate association' in Micheál Ó Siochrú (ed.), *Kingdoms in crisis: Ireland in the 1640s; essays in honour of Donal Cregan* (Dublin, 2001), pp 90–105.

victimized by Strafford including Sir William Stewart and Cork's clients Robert Smith and Joshua Boyle. Carpenter was expelled for lying, evading questions and having acted in a criminal matter when dealing with the tobacco monopoly, Lake for subverting the work of the committee dealing with Stanhope's recalcitrance in providing information to the house, Little for refusing to answer the house's questions and Peisley for some reason connected with the tobacco monopoly. Thomas Radcliffe's expulsion (ostensibly for being under age) was clearly a means of getting at his father George. While these were undoubtedly genuine causes, their closeness to Wentworth was the motivation for their expulsions.[115]

The Irish Parliament, now effectively a 'rump' Protestant assembly that continued to sit between 1642 and 1648, brought control of its membership to a new level. The Commons expelled Rory Maguire, Phelim O'Neill (*plate 23*) and Philip Mac Hugh O'Reilly for rebellion in November 1641 and on 22 June 1642 excluded 41 other Catholics for being in open rebellion or indicted of treason. A further six members were deemed to have excluded themselves and the Commons effectively debarred all Catholics by decreeing that all MPs should take the oath of supremacy. Despite the dubious legality of these proceedings (Charles I objected to it as an infringement of his prerogative, on which see chapter eleven), the Commons moved almost immediately to fill many of the vacancies, although genuine elections were rare. As the cohesion of the Protestants crumbled, Lord Philip Lisle and Laurence Crawford were expelled in 1644, although their offence was not noted.[116]

SECRECY OF PARLIAMENT

The 1585 rules specified that

> no knyght, cyttizen or burges disclose the secretes, either spoken or done in this said howse, to any stranger not being of the same house, under payne of souche punyshment, as by the specker, with thassent of the residue of the house, shalbe lymyted

and the clerk took an oath to 'keepe secrett such matters as shall be treated in his said parliament, & not disclose of the same, before they shall be published, but to such as it ought to be disclosed unto'.[117] The emphasis on secrecy related to MPs' freedom of speech; confidentiality enabled them to give their best advice without fear of consequences and protected them, at least in theory, from being threatened

115 *Commons' Jn. Ire.*, 9, 13 Nov. 1640, 24 Feb. 1641.

116 McGrath, 'Recruiter returns'; *Cal. Carew*, v, p. 146; King Charles I to Ormond, 22 Jan. 1644, Bodl. Lib., Carte MS 63, fo. 305.

117 Irish Archaeological Society, *Tracts*, ii, p. 143; *LJI*, 18 July 1634. This is identical to the oath taken by the clerk of the English parliament in 1628. See Yale University, Beinecke Library, Osborn MS FB 158, III6; *Commons' Jn. Ire.*, 25 Nov. 1614, 18 April 1615.

or intimidated. The English Commons ordered in 1589 by 'consent of the House admonition was given to the members of this House that Speeches vsed in this House should not be made table talk nor in notes of writing to any not members of the house.'[118] English MPs were increasingly defensive about having their contributions recorded; in 1610, 1614 and 1621 they ordered reviews of the clerk's books. Decisions were made in 1624 to exclude MPs' names from records and in April 1640 they moved defensively to restrict the recording of contributions to debates in the journals, to protect its members.[119]

When the English clerk of parliament Robert Bowyer left his manuscripts to his nephew, he specified that no copies of any parliamentary journals should be made except for family use, but the clerk's oath makes clear the moratorium was temporary and limited by practicality, as well as by personal and client relationships. While the journals' contents was restricted to prevent reports of contributions to debate, in fact, parliamentary proceedings were 'made public to an unprecedented degree' during this period. The number of surviving copies and contemporary extracts of the 1613–15 Irish Commons' journals demonstrates that confidentiality was to be observed only during the parliament's sittings.[120] John Merick's incorporating the Commons' interpretation of 12 Ric. II, c. 12 on county members' wages into his 1617 breviat of Irish statutes demonstrates the access the public had to the journals after parliament's dissolution.[121] Much business was open to the public; the doors of the Commons' chamber were generally left open, unless ordered to be closed and visitors were admitted to view proceedings unless the house was 'cleared of visitors', as happened with every division.[122] Campion was present for Stanihurst's oration at the dissolution of the 1569 parliament and the royal assent to bills; in the following parliament

> repayred hither as Voluntaries without any Summons Trelagh Leynagh [O'Neill] … and all the Irish Lords of Ireland to see the Order of the Parliament, and were admitted one day to come into the parliament house to see the order thereof, which they much liked without any needling there.[123]

118 The Nature of the Court of the Commons house of Parliament with what matters they may Meddle & a contra Oppisicons & proceedings therein & other Observacons therevpon, 15 Feb. 1588, Newberry Library, MS fk 0452.613, fo. 27.
119 Peacey, '"Rushworth shall not take any notes here"'; Stapylton, 'Parliamentary privilege', 32–3; Andrew Thrush, 'The speaker', at https://www.historyofparliamentonline.org/volume/1604-1629/survey/viii-officers-and-servants-house [accessed 10 May 2019].
120 Foster, 'Painful labour'; Irish Archaeological Society, *Tracts*, ii, p. 143; *LJI*, 18 July 1634; Yale University, Beinecke Library, Osborn MS FB 158, III6; *Commons' Jn. Ire.*, 25 Nov. 1614, 18 April 1615; Peacey, '"Rushworth shall not take any notes here"'. See Appendix 1.
121 Merick, *Compendious collection*, p. 300; *Common' Jn. Ire.*, 10 May 1615.
122 Kyle, *Theater of state*, p. 40; e.g., *LJI*, 27 Feb. 1640–1, when the house was cleared for the impeachment proceedings against Bramhall, Bolton, Loftus and Radcliffe.
123 Campion, *Historie of Ireland*, pp 194–204; Advice and directions for summoning a parliament in Ireland, *c.*1600, Bodl. Lib., Rawlinson MS D 922, fos. 49r–52v.

Michael van Meer attended the opening of the 1614 English parliament and made detailed paintings of James in the Lords' chamber in Westminster.[124] English MPs brought advisors with them (frequently their boroughs' recorders) and in 1585 Clanricard brought four Galway merchants as his advisors to the Irish parliament; his successor intended to appear with a similar retinue if the rumoured parliament met in 1621.[125] In October 1640 a number of Kilkenny men staged a protest from the public gallery in the Commons' chamber.[126] The inclusion of Darcy and Martin, who were not then MPs, to advise their committee on the bill for the Connacht plantations necessarily opened parliamentary business to outsiders.[127]

While there are many references to the importance of parliamentary secrecy, there was no absolute prohibition of discussion of parliament's business, some of which was certainly known beyond its membership before, during and after sessions.[128] Much of parliament's business, specifically its membership, legislation, declarations, proclamations, orders and letters from either house were necessarily publicly known. Chichester's nephew, George Trevelyan, MP for Belfast in 1613, offered to send his father a list of MPs in 1613 (at least three others were his cousins), and the earl of Cork had no difficulty in obtaining a list of the members before the opening of the 1640 parliament, despite being in England.[129] Thomas Walkley issued a series of regularly updated membership lists of the English parliament from 1625, in a handy pocket size for easy portability, which were very useful for lobbying.[130] Administration members and officials, including the clerks of the parliament and judges and learned council who drafted the bills, were well-informed of the legislative programme beforehand. As soon as the royal assent was granted, bills acquired the status of public acts and could not be regarded as confidential. Taxpayers needed to know the substance of the subsidy acts as they would swiftly be required to pay the first instalments of the amounts assessed on them before parliament ended. The subjects of private bills needed notice of their introduction and movement through the House and petitioners had to be informed of the progress of their cases so that they could respond to them and appear in the

124 June Schlueter, 'Michael van Meer's *Album Amicorum*, with illustrations of London, 1614–15', *Huntington Library Quarterly*, 69:2 (June, 2006), 301–14.

125 Kyle, 'Parliament and the Palace of Westminster'; Ó Bric, 'Galway townsmen', p. 147; Clanricard to Sir Henry Lynch, 6 May 1621, in Bernadette Cunningham (ed.), 'Clanricard letters', *The Journal of the Galway Archaeological and Historical Society*, 48 (1996), 162–208, no. 7.

126 Edwards, *Ormond lordship*, p. 303.

127 *Commons' Jn. Ire.*, 8 June 1640.

128 Hawkyard, *Commons*, pp 247–51.

129 George Trevelyan to his father, 25 Nov. 1614, in John Payne Collier, Walter Caverley Trevelyan and Charles Edwards Trevelyan (eds), *Trevelyan Papers: Part III* (London, 1872), p. 132. Cork was a member of the Lords, which Wentworth had prevented him attending. He asked his cousin and agent Joshua Boyle, who was not then an MP, for early information of the names of all those returned as knights and burgesses, Cork to Joshua Boyle, 17 March 1640, Chatsworth House, Cork Papers, Misc. boxes, Box 3, p. 420. Joshua had anticipated the request as his reply, RIA, MS 24/Q/4, was dated 16 March 1640 and does not include last-minute rejigging, such as Sir William Parson's replacement of John Karnes.

130 E.g., Walkley, *Catalogue*.

house if necessary.[131] Tipperary residents appointed an agent to manage their petition against the abuses they claimed Piers Butler committed as sheriff of their county and the deliberations in committee, including voting, were well known locally. Over a hundred King's County freeholders signed a petition on 31 August 1641 in response to a vote in the house on 7 August and presumably much other parliamentary business was equally widely shared.[132]

Trevelyan wrote to his father, 'Our parlyament here continues with good hopes in doing good to this pore land wher in wee leve: ther ar som actes past, but must nott be revayld till albe ended.' He had earlier sent his father an account of the parliament, but, significantly, at the time that he wrote he should not have known about proceedings as he was no longer an MP.[133] Francis Lloyd, the Herberts' agent in Kerry, reported a week before parliament resumed in early 1635 about both proposed and confirmed legislation:

> It is said there is an act to pass this parliament to confirm the estates of heirs and assigns of patentees who renew their patents with the Commissioners of Defective Titles for Plantation Land; their estates shall be good against the King, not withstanding any jeofail in the patent and all pretenders ... There are so many good laws made this parliament for securing men's estates, goods and lives, that persons of all countries will come to live here and land will be dear. There was no act against excessive interest, as £20 and £30 in the hundred yearly, which made the [money men] forbear to deal for land except by mortgage. Now there is an act that above £10 in the hundred must not be taken.[134]

As MPs had *plena potestas* to act on behalf of their communities, they had to report back on parliament's decisions, distinguishing between the need for silence on the discussions and freedom to report their results. As in England, breach of secrecy was generally tolerated and occasionally formally sanctioned and Phillipe Baker has argued that the production of parliamentary diaries was part of a process of opening up parliamentary business to wider scrutiny.[135] Decisions on the extent to which secrecy was maintained were often political and pragmatic, such as the publication of speeches, e.g., Mervyn's speeches on the *Queries* and the impeachment proceedings against Bramhall, Bolton, Lowther and Radcliffe.[136]

131 E.g., Henry Elsynge's note to contact the clerk of the Grocers' Company when a bill for apothecaries appeared. See Foster, 'Painful labour'.
132 Bodl. Lib., Carte MS 42, fo. 462v; Birr Castle, MS A/1/19.
133 George Trevelyan to his father, 19 Sept. 1613, same to same, 25 Nov. 1614, in Collier, Trevelyan and Trevelyan (eds), *Trevelyan Papers*, pp 123, 132.
134 Francis Lloyd to Richard Herbert, 27 Feb. 1635, in W.J. Smith (ed.), *Herbert correspondence* (Dublin, 1963), pp 81–2.
135 Baker, '"But private notes"'.
136 Mervyn, *Captaine Audley Mervin's speech*; *idem*, *Sixteene queres*; *idem*, *Speech made by Captaine Audley Mervin*.

On both sides, the principle of secrecy was more honoured in the breach than the observance. Two senior Irish officials, Francis Blundell and Oliver St John (*plate 7*), kept Sir Ralph Winwood apprised of parliamentary proceedings in 1614.[137] John Davies, who knew parliamentary procedure better than most, wrote detailed accounts of the English parliament to Lord Huntington during its sessions, including of proceedings in the Lords.[138] Bramhall informed the archbishop of Canterbury, William Laud, of the progress of business relating to the church in the 1634 parliament, but maintained silence on Convocation:

> I am glad you made soe good a shift to stay ye Acts in Parliament that would have proved so priudicall to the Church. And for your busyness in Convocacon, since you are tyed by a promise to secrecy, I shalbe very well content to be ignorant, either altogether, or at least till such time as you may speake more freely.[139]

Information for the reports of the proceedings in parliament discussed in both the Jesuit annual letters and the document in St Isadore's could only have come from Catholic MPs and the Dublin merchant William Baggott's harbouring of a priest during 'Parlyament tyme' was condemned on the basis that the priest 'might be ready to advise and consult with or to direct (accordinge to his capacite) such of the Romanistes as were specyally Interested in the publique affairs', implying very little confidentiality in parliamentary affairs. Chichester correctly assumed that Catholic MPs discussed the question of granting subsidies with priests and Jesuits, as Rothe and the Irish Franciscans were sufficiently well-informed to write speeches for MPs and know how faithfully they had been delivered.[140]

Privy councillors who were responsible for managing the government's legislative programme in both houses certainly discussed parliamentary business outside the chamber with the deputy and other councillors who were not parliamentarians.[141] Twelve MPs who were members of the privy council wrote to the English secretary of state, Sir Edward Nicholas, on 23 March 1640 to inform him of the unanimous passage of the subsidies bill in the Commons, with an account of proceedings there.[142] Wentworth could only have known from other MPs about Talbot, Netterville, Dongan and Baron's speeches, Sir John

137 Judy Barry, 'St John, Oliver', *DIB*; M. Greengrass, 'Winwood, Sir Ralph', *Oxford DNB*.

138 Davies to Huntington, 10 April 1624, 21 July 1625, 26 Feb. 1625–6, in Bickley (ed.), *Hastings, Volume II*, pp 65–70.

139 Laud to Bramhall, 1 Oct. 1634, HL, HP, MS 15,155; Anthony Milton, 'Laud, William', *Oxford DNB*.

140 Moynes, '"The written word remains as a perpetual witness"'; Moynes (ed.), *Annual letters*, i, pp 399–416, 481–2; Jackson (ed.), 'Document'; Crawford, *Star Chamber*, p. 330; Chichester to James, 16 Oct. 1614, TNA, SP 63/232, fos. 193–4; *Cal. S.P. Ire., 1611–14*, pp 527, 533; HMC, *Franciscan manuscripts*, pp 61–9.

141 The proceeding of the parliament being this day related to the King at the Councell Boarde by the Counselours of the Lower House of parliament, 4 April 1628, HRC, MS 76, fo. 60.

142 TNA, SP 63/258, fos. 35–6; S.A. Baron, 'Nicholas, Sir Edward', *Oxford DNB*.

Clotworthy's speaking against a bill and Crosby and Waller's voting against the government; Radcliffe acted as Wentworth's eyes and ears in the house, threatening Clotworthy and Nicholas Barnewall.[143] Wentworth showed as little regard for the principle of secrecy in parliament and Convocation as he did to respecting MPs' privilege, demanding that the clerk of the lower house of Convocation provide him with voting lists on one division and attacking George Andrews for a speech he made there.[144] As opposition grew in both England and Ireland through 1640 and 1641, both parliaments shared information in a combined campaign.[145]

CONCLUSION

Despite frequent references to historical precedent, the early Stuart period was a time of considerable development and consolidation of parliamentary powers and capacity, including the power to decide on the Commons' own membership, the expansion of parliamentary privilege, the exercise of judicial powers, the creation of a committee structure for efficient management of parliamentary business and representing parliament in England, as well as the more active involvement in assessing subsidies were all major elements in establishing a more modern parliament. The procedures and structures they developed lasted until until 1800, when the Act of Union abolished the Irish parliament.

Parliament incrementally acquired other privileges and powers and followed recent English precedents, including controlling its own membership by adjudicating on disputed elections, deciding on expulsions and disciplining its members, although these had no statutory basis. The Remonstrance of grievances agreed by the Commons on 8 November 1640 denounced the issuing of *Quo warranto* proceedings against ancient boroughs to justify their parliamentary representation as 'contrary to the laws and the privileges of the House of Parliament; and, if way should be given thereunto, might tend to the subversion of Parliaments, and, by consequence, to the ruin and destruction of the Commonwealth' and regretted that they had 'been deprived of the advice and counsel of many profitable and good members by means thereof.' It also denounced the pressure the administration had put on MPs which deprived parliament 'in its members and actions [of] its natural freedom.' However, after the 1641 rebellion, parliament moved to assert an effective veto over members and arranged speedy replacement of any expelled members as much for political reasons as for any specious behaviour.

143 Clarke, '28 November 1634'; Radcliffe to Wentworth, 28 Oct. 1640, FSL, MS X.c.101(2); Rushworth (ed.), *Tryal*, pp 110–12.

144 Wentworth to the prolocutor of the lower house of convocation, 10 Dec. 1634, Bodl. Lib., Carte MS 64, fos. 281ff; Robert MacCarthy, 'The Church of Ireland in Carlow 1549–2000' in Thomas McGrath (ed.), *Carlow: history and society* (Dublin, 2008), pp 331–54.

145 Dennehy, *Parliament*, p. 170.

As parliament was the forum for addressing grievances, parliamentary privilege afforded MPs some 'protection while they engaged in that task'.[146] While this operated well in 1613–15, Wentworth's disregard for parliament, MPs and privilege, meant that MPs had no protection for undertaking their role, but parliament reasserted their privileges comprehensively in 1640–1. As in England, privilege during this period moved from being a mechanism for ensuring that MPs were able to devote their time and attention to parliament, in the king's interest, to being also a tool for personal protection and advantage.

The crown saw parliaments as bodies to be mistrusted and controlled, rather than as partners in government. In Ireland, a further dimension was added by ethnic, cultural and religious tensions and the administration being overwhelmingly composed of Englishmen with little respect or sympathy for the largely Catholic political nation, Old English and Gaelic Irish. Privy councillors were relied on to limit parliament's freedom of action and restrict its exercise of all of its powers. As a result, Wentworth and his allies repeatedly breached parliamentary privilege and liberties. Despite this, from early 1641 a coalition of New English, Old English and Gaelic Irish parliamentarians combined to resist this control and use parliament as an instrument for genuine representation of the political community and for reform of abuses and preservation of parliament's privileges and liberties. Their ultimate failure was not reflective of their hard work, commitment and expertise.

146 Hunneyball, 'Development of parliamentary privilege'.

CHAPTER FOUR

Attitudes to representation and parliament: government, MPs and their communities

THIS CHAPTER CONSIDERS THE NATURE of representation in Ireland, the interest in and attitudes to parliament among government, MPs and the general public, as well as the advantages and disadvantages of membership and MPs' relationships with their constituencies: 'Parliament was not only an expression of officialdom and state power, but also a body offering the wider political community an institutional forum for interfacing with government and transmitting their concerns and preoccupations from locality to centre.'[1] Representative institutions were regarded internationally as a key element of modern states:

> n'y a Royaume bien ordonné qui ne suyue ceste ancienne & saincte coutume d'assembler les Estats, comme l'on voit à l'Empire où l'on tient les dietes: & d'ailleurs, aux Royaumes d'Espaigne, d'Angleterre, d'Escosse, Danemarch, Suede, Boheme, Hongrie, & par tout ailleurs.'[2]
>
> (There is no well managed kingdom that does not follow this ancient and holy tradition of gathering the estates, as one sees in the Holy Roman Empire where they hold diets, and others in the kingdoms of Spain, England, Scotland, Denmark, Sweden, Bohemia, Hungary and all other places.)

Bradshaw noted that,

> the thrust of a major dynamic of early modern state formation … was the assimilation of peripheral territories by their cores under the impulse provided by Europe's consolidating Renaissance monarchies striving to transmute their disparate feudal patrimonies into centralized unitary realms by abrogating to themselves the absolute sovereignty vested in the Roman emperor

and this centralization of power required careful management, including of the state's relationship with the regions, which they did not necessarily receive. In those cases, parliaments and estates became a focus of, forum for and a mechanism

1 Kennedy, 'Representing the periphery'.
2 Jörg Feuchter and Johannes Helmrath, 'Oratory and representation: the rhetorical culture of political assemblies, 1300–1600', *PER*, 29:1 (2009), 53–66.

for resolving the inevitable tensions, with varying levels of success (see chapter eleven).[3] For individuals and communities, parliament, even when not in session, remained firmly lodged in popular consciousness for its role as the 'ultimate mechanism for helping them.'[4]

This context shaped attitudes to the opportunities and threats parliaments presented to the crown, political community and individuals and created an international interest in all such assemblies. Respect for parliament's moral and practical authority and role prompted both sides to try to control its membership and operations and there was a contradiction between the rhetoric of its importance and unifying role and the mistrust between the state and the parliamentary community, exacerbated in Ireland by ethnic and religious tensions in an aggressively colonizing state. As the Elizabethan statesman and political theorist, Thomas Smith, had stated:

> Every Englishman is intended to be there present, either in person or by procuration and atturny, of what preheminence, state, dignitie or quality soever hee be, from the Prince (be he King or Queen) to the lowest person in England. And the consent of the Parliament is taken to be every mans consent.[5]

Smith's description of the English parliament's representative nature held also for Ireland, although in practice it operated rather differently and the reality of representation changed in the early modern period. Tudor parliaments, despite their infrequency, limited geographical extent and growing numbers of English placemen were largely representative of their communities but under James and especially Charles, they became decreasingly so. The legal requirement that MPs be the monarch's subjects and resident in their constituencies was critical to the ethos and practice of representation, reconfirmed legislatively in 1542 and expressed in the forcefully-put, if unsuccessful demands for the exclusion of non-resident members in every early modern Irish parliament.[6] MPs' election with *plena potestas* to act on behalf of their individual communities, the payment of their salaries and the expectation that they would report back to their electorates marked their position as their communities' paid agents; members' uncertainty that they had the power to expel anyone chosen by their electors demonstrates an acceptance of the primacy of voters' choices.[7] As parliament represented the entire nation, its

3 Bradshaw, *'And so began the Irish nation'*, pp 117–40; W.R.B. Robinson, 'The Tudor revolution in Welsh government', *EHR*, 103 (1989), 1–20; Bowen, 'Wales at Westminster'.

4 Victor Morgan, 'A provincial perspective: the local origins of parliamentary culture in England, *c.*1530–1640', Paper presented to the conference 'Rediscovering Europe's Parliamentary culture, 1500–1700: concepts, methods, approaches', Krakow, 22–4 June 2022.

5 Smith, *Commonwealth*, pp 73–4; Ian W. Archer, 'Smith, Sir Thomas', *Oxford DNB*.

6 Aidan Clarke, 'Colonial constitutional attitudes in Ireland, 1640–60', *Proc. RIA*, 90C (1990), 357–75; McCavitt, 'An unspeakable parliamentary fracas'.

7 *Commons' Jn. Ire.*, 27 April 1615.

decisions, once given royal assent, bound all citizens and the crown. In the medieval period, election writs were issued only to towns whose consent to proposed measures was necessary, confirming the principle that *quod omnes tangit, ab omnibus approbetur* (what concerns everyone should be approved by all). After the creation of the kingdom of Ireland, the entire country, not merely the Lordship, was bound by its decisions.[8] The anomaly that all of Ireland was subject to legislation enacted under the Lordship never seems to have been publicly contested, although resolving this incongruity was cited as a reason for summoning the 1613 parliament.[9] Decisions taken in parliament were not revisited, even if, like Poynings' Law, they passed by an exceptionally small number of MPs drawn from a minority of the island, were dishonestly effected, like the 1560 Reformation legislation or Chichester's underhand electioneering, or simply when tellers made mistakes, as when a vote was lost when Sir James Ware failed to count himself (see chapters five and seven). The outbreak of the 1641 rebellion caused the privy council to question the perception of the validity of acts passed by a very small number of MPs in the 'rump' parliament but the issue was not resolved.[10]

The allegations of electoral fraud Catholics submitted to James reflected their understanding of parliament's powers and the ethos of representation:

> actes of parliament doe binde all Subiectes of the kingdome as thinges done by theire owne consentes, wherby not onely lawes are made or altered, but alsoe the lives, landes and estates of anie person may be taken awaie or otherwyse disposed of thereby: and to the end therfore that the subiectes should Choose those in whom [they] may repose most Confidence the lawes doe provide that the election of knightes of the shires, Cittizenes and Burgesses who doe represent the wholl bodye of the Commons of the Kingdome, should be made openly and freely without force or fraude: And that such men should be chosen as are resident and have estates in the places for which they are elected, to the end that such men (being best acquainted with the Condition and natures of the people may make lawes and statutes most agreeable and expedient for them.[11]

Assertions of its representative nature were generally made by parliament itself and by MPs seeking to defend and retain its official role, rather than the crown. While James Stanihurst's 1570 prorogation speech declared,

> in the behalfe of our selves, and our countryes, whom we represent in this parliament … to the uttermost of our skill we have intended without injury, the Crowne to enrich, treasons to chastise, to better the state, traffique to

8 Dennehy, 'Representation in later medieval and early modern Ireland'.

9 *Cal. Carew*, v, p. 166.

10 Bodl. Lib., Carte MS 68, fos. 422r–4.

11 TNA, SP 63/232, fo. 98, 31 May 1613. Also, see Smith, *Commonwealth*, pp 73–4.

> further, learning to cherish, and in briefe to maintaine with our best advice those benefits, which the Prince hath inferred upon this Realme by you

and Davies in his acceptance speech described parliament as 'a Common Council, wherein all the commons throughout the kingdom are present, and have free voices by their knights and burgesses.' Davies justified James' creation of so many new boroughs 'to give all his free subjects of this kingdom indifferent and equal voices in making of their lawes, so as one half of them should not make laws alone which should bind the other subjects half without their consent.' His oration on the prorogation only referred to its legislative work. Eustace's acceptance speech made no reference to the Commons' representative role other than describing them as '*vox populi*'.[12]

Catholics' belief in parliament's representative role and the institution's importance and robustness provoked outrage at its subversion by the state. Additionally, in a status-obsessed age, the replacement of the community's natural leaders as MPs by absentee lower-caste clerks and 'serving men' diminished parliament's representative nature and standing. They were prepared for 30 new boroughs, but the presence of burgesses from the additional covertly incorporated ones provoked their absolute fury. Catholic observers in 1613–15 stressed parliament's representative character in strikingly similar terms to Thomas Smith during Elizabeth I's reign:

> in parliament, every man is intended to be present, because the voyces are by the election of all and they are your atturnyes ... Now if the king by this colaterall meanes might appoint other atturnyes for you, which is so in effect when he putteth in men that shall out-voyce you, and so leaving you dumbbe you are in a worst cast than you can be in anny other course of trial for your life or estate.[13]

The petition David Rothe framed for recusant members explicitly referenced the 'universal body of the republic represented by us in this honourable House of Commons' and MPs' obligations to represent their communities: 'It resteth ... that we also accomplish some part of our obligation to God, to country and to our consciences ... being employed by our commonwealth to represent her sighs to the ears of our common father', an approach echoed in the 1614 Jesuit annual letter.[14] The Remonstrance agreed on 8 November 1640 denounced the issuing of *Quo warranto* proceedings requiring ancient boroughs to justify their representation as 'contrary to the laws and the privileges of the House of Parliament; and, if way should be given thereunto, might tend to the subversion of Parliaments, and, by consequence, to the ruin and destruction of the

12 Campion, *Historie of Ireland*, p. 194; Morley (ed.), *Ireland under Elizabeth and James the First*, pp 403–5; NLI, MS 835, pp 165–71; *Commons' Jn. Ire.*, 20 March 1640 (new style).

13 Jackson (ed.), 'Document'.

14 HMC, *Franciscan manuscripts*, pp 62, 67; Moynes (ed.), *Annual letters*, i, p. 266.

Commonwealth' and it regretted that it had 'been deprived of the advice and counsel of many profitable and good members by means thereof.' It also denounced the pressure the administration put on MPs, which restricted parliament 'in its members and actions [of] its natural freedom.' Underlining their duty to represent their community, they demanded the right to present their grievances directly to Charles in England if the deputy did not redress them, following the well-worn path of appealing to the king over the Irish administration. While the agents in 1613 had only represented Catholics, in 1615 parliament asked to send a delegation to James which the king initially agreed to and then refused, while the 1640 parliament mandated a delegation to Charles which reported directly to it.[15] While sending a committee to England was an innovation, albeit based on the precedent of agents sent for consultation in 1628, it was an effective means of preventing the administration's blocking its work and ensuring parliament would be able to continue its representative role in the face of threats of prorogation or dissolution.[16]

The concentration on parliaments as representative institutions obscures the reality that early modern communities constantly exercised all its functions at local level, using the same terminology. Lords, gentry and freeholders formed the political community in counties and baronies and were expected to assemble for consultation and collective decision-making; Grand Jury presentments were not merely findings of criminality but also an opportunity to present grievances and it is noteworthy that those who formed the Tipperary Grand Jury in 1641 were much lower down the social scale than justices of the peace or members of parliament.[17] Freemen of towns, referred to as 'the commons', were obliged to participate in decision-making through their common councils and quarterly assemblies (and were fined for non-attendance) at which they elected councils composed of burgesses, appointed officers, agreed rules called 'acts', raised money, managed commerce, organized defence and mandated agents to represent the town. Towns were not democracies in the modern sense – some councillors had more votes than ordinary freemen and in some cities panels of senior freemen formed an inner ring of decision-makers – but participation in and responsibility for collective agreement was an everyday reality for townsmen.[18] The number of electors in old-

15 Moody, 'Irish parliament'; Bodl. Lib., Carte MS 66, fo. 319; Carte MS 67, fos. 53–4.

16 Ibid.; Simon Digby to the Irish Commons, 7 May 1641, Maurice Eustace to the Committee in England, 22 June 1641, ARL, MS Parliamentary Papers (unpaginated); Clarke, *Old English*, pp 44–54.

17 Bríd McGrath, 'Mount Taragh's triumph: commitment and organization in the early stages of the 1641 rebellion in Meath' in Eamon Darcy, et al. (eds), *The 1641 Depositions and the Irish Rebellion* (London, 2012), pp 51–63; Ormond to Sir Thomas Nugent and others in Westmeath, Bodl. Lib., Carte MS 20, fos. 75–8, implicitly accepting their role in representing the county; Morgan, 'A provincial perspective'; Presentation of the Tipperary Grand Jury, 1641, Bodl. Lib., Carte MS 59, fos. 80r–1v.

18 Bríd McGrath, 'The communities of Clonmel, 1608–1649' in Robert Armstrong and Tadhg Ó hAnnracháin (eds), *Community in early modern Ireland* (Dublin, 2006), pp 103–19; McGrath (ed.), *Clonmel*, pp 146, 148; Bríd McGrath, 'The nomination of Kilkenny MPs in 1628', *Old*

established towns was not negligible and certainly much greater than many English and Scottish electorates, although less than the 10% of the population which was eligible to vote in the Polish Sejm (see chapter five for more on electors). Urban and rural elites exercised a judicial role at local assizes, sheriffs' courts, town courts, manor courts and courts of pie powder. Gentry served as justices of the peace, joined by the chief officers of towns whose charters granted *ex-officio* membership of the commissions of the peace.[19] As a result, those involved in local government were used to working collectively to manage their communities, serving as agents and representatives, negotiating charters and other agreements, enacting local laws, assessing and collecting taxes and levies, managing public works and defence and acting as judges. Sheriffs and mayors served as intermediaries between the crown and their communities and MPs who had held those positions had gained valuable experience and contacts.[20] Parliamentary membership involved this assured political community in national decision-making and their experience stood them in good stead, especially in committees where most of the detailed work was done, as well as adjudicating on petitions or impeachments, promoting local bills and petitions and appointing commissioners to assess and collect subsidies. Local democracy made it easier for counties and old-established towns to reject crown nominees, a problem the administration sought to resolve through plantation, issuing new charters and instituting *Quo warranto* proceedings.[21]

These points aside, only those of a certain social or economic standing were represented at local or national level and a majority, most obviously women, children, lease-holders, labourers, servants and apprentices and the poor were excluded. Moreover, many of the small group of councillors who formed the electorate in boroughs created after 1612 (except for Coleraine and Londonderry) had a minor stake in those towns; local power brokers or garrison commanders who nominated them were likely to choose the submissive or malleable, although that could not be guaranteed, as Stephen Butler discovered in Belturbet in Cavan when he became the principal landholder in the region.[22] Parliamentarians' current (or

Kilkenny Review, 55 (2003), 119–25; Colm Lennon, *The lords of Dublin in the age of reformation* (Dublin, 1989), pp 53–5; NLI, MSS 41,667/3, 41,667/7. For a fascinating account of council decision-making in Zurich and Muenster, see Uwe Goppold, 'Norms, symbols and modes of everyday decision-making in early modern cities: the examples of Zurich and Munster' in Rudolf Schlögl, et al. (eds), *Urban elections and decision-making in early modern Europe, 1500–1800* (Newcastle-upon-Tyne, 2020), pp 52–61.

19 Courts of pie powder were held on market days to provide swift decisions in commercial disputes in market towns: Charles Gross, 'The courts of pie powder', *Quarterly Journal of Economics*, 20:2 (Feb., 1906), 231–49.

20 E.g., *Cal. S.P. Ire., 1625–33*, pp 468–9; Mayor of Youghal to Sir William St Leger, 11 Dec. 1628, Cork City Archives, MS YTR1/68; A draft letter from the Mayor to Sir Edward Bolton, 29 May 1640, KCA, MS CR/K/52.

21 Clarke, *Old English*, p. 126.

22 Brendan Scott, 'Belturbet, County Cavan: the development and administration of an Ulster plantation town' in Brendan Scott (ed.), *Society and administration in Ulster's plantation towns* (Dublin, 2019), pp 56–68.

hoped-for) social class and education formed a shared mind-set, common throughout Europe, influenced by the humanist concepts of state and society derived from classical authors. The cooperation of the king and estates in parliament created a balanced state which relied on the political community's participation in its own governance.[23]

Recognition that lords and commons comprised the political community extended beyond local government and parliament. In November 1626, temporal peers summoned by the privy council refused to support the crown financially, claiming they 'were but a parte and had no binding power over the country' and insisted on consulting the commons. Commissions authorized the nobility and 'prime gentlemen' to 'assemble the Country which was to delegate certaine persons (by whome they should be concluded) to send to Dublin the next Sessions sufficiently authorized to treat in their behalf.' When the lords met informally with some gentry who opposed this manner of consultation, Chancellor Loftus replied that 'those Gentleman were not authorized from the Country and soe it was not to be taken as the Countrys answere.' Agents from counties, 'petty corporations' and cities were to assemble as a 'Great Assembly' in Dublin 'in a parliamentary way' fully authorized to 'give their voices', but this was convened as a consultation mechanism to raise money without granting any concessions, not a parliament. Delegates were not MPs and it is unclear which towns were represented.[24] Despite James Ussher's insisting that they had no right to refuse financial support, each province's agents delivered a written refusal. Falkland declared the 'commission was to consent of a way for the plotting and costing of that maintenance and not to summon the Comons whome they had found very refractorie' and angrily told the Lords 'if you have the authority to treat you have the authority to undertake for them.' Yet the peers' and commons' understanding of their roles did not allow them to consent for the wider community without redress of grievances and a parliament.[25]

As the Great Assembly's failure demonstrates, MPs were agents and representatives, rather than delegates, and had an obligation to think for themselves and exercise their own judgment; indeed, this was essential, given that MPs generally were unaware of the legislative agenda until bills were read in parliament. Privy councillors were informed about proposed legislation but they also represented constituencies and should have been free to vote according to their conscience, despite Wentworth's order in council that 'in parliament noe vote to be made contrary to the vote of this (Council) board being a[n] order in the same matter' and his punishment of Piers Crosby for transgressing this order.[26]

23 Richard Butterwick, *The Polish–Lithuanian Commonwealth: light and flame* (New Haven, 2021), pp 19–20.

24 Clonmel had a single representative. McGrath (ed.), *Clonmel*, p. 151.

25 BL, Add. MS 72,414, Trumbull Papers 173, fos. 90r–4v; Diary of the proceedings of the Great Assembly, TNA, SP 63/245, fos. 26v–35v.

26 Bolton's abstract of Charles' letter re. Strafford's government in Ireland, Marsh's Library, MS Z2.1.1, no. 58.

The absorption of all of Ireland into a centralized, Anglicized state required local adjustment and the process by which this was effected and the Irish political community's response changed its relationship with the crown and its sense of whom it represented. The transformation replaced local Irish elites by English officials and the Old English came to see themselves, despite being the loyal 'English by blood',

> as the self-perceived victims of centuries of metropolitan political bullying, economic fleecing, cultural hauteur and, in time of need, indifference and dereliction [which] served to instil a countervailing anti-metropolitan sensibility and with it the consciousness of a distinct colonial identity predicated upon Ireland as the community's historic patria

claiming ancient 'liberties and privileges' of subjects equally with English and thereafter the community they represented changed from being a local elite to a national one, under constant threat.'[27] Clerical proctors' exclusion placed the whole burden of community representation on MPs and the expansion of parliamentary membership across the whole country, the crown's coercive and illegal electoral strategy which returned increasing numbers of non-resident Englishmen and the developing sense of national identity placed an onus on Catholic MPs to co-operate and represent the wider political community, not merely their own constituencies within the Lordship. Parliament was the forum in which they were able to represent their beleaguered community and their developing sense of national identity was reflected in their electoral strategy and demeanour in parliament.

Parliament's consent was necessary to pass legislation and grant subsidies but Poynings' Law left the administration powerless to compromise, even had it been inclined to make concessions. Faced with the impossibility of obtaining consent through genuinely representative parliaments, the administration engineered unrepresentative but pliant ones by subverting electoral law, provoking explicit resistance in parliament, most notably in 1569 and 1613, when Catholics refused to proceed with any business. The secession was a protest against the violation of the principle of representation and electoral law and while both houses continued to sit until 17 June 1613 with 'no business perfected, by reason the recusants of all degrees either absented themselves altogether from the parliament, or else consented not to any conclusion of such questions as were propounded' and excision of those entries from the Commons' journals (although not from the Lords') and acceptance that this was not regarded as the first session was tacit confirmation that only a fully representative Commons could conclude public business. The same question arose in early 1642, given the absence of Catholic MPs.[28]

27 Bradshaw, 'Tudor reformation and revolutions in Wales and Ireland'.
28 Farmer, 'Chronicle' in Lodge, *Desiderata Curiosa*, i, pp 205–7; Treadwell, 'House of Lords',

A key factor in attitudes to parliament was the question of whether Ireland was a colony of England. The regular assertion, as much by officials (for example in Eustace's acceptance speech), as opposition spokesmen like the lawyer Patrick Darcy, that English statutes only applied in Ireland when confirmed by the Irish parliament, underlines a common understanding of the importance of consent by those represented in parliament and of Ireland's political independence from the English parliament which was first breached by the 1642 Adventurers' Acts.[29] To the New English, Ireland was a colony and the Irish a conquered people. As such they perceived its parliament as being subordinate to that of England, except when it suited them to argue otherwise. The July 1641 Declaration that

> the subjects of this his Majesty's kingdom of Ireland are a free people and to be governed only according to the common-law of England, and statutes made and established by parliament in this Kingdom of Ireland and according to the lawful customs used in the same

was an explicit assertion of the Irish parliament's independence based on Darcy's *Argument* that Ireland, while annexed to the English crown, was legislatively autonomous, albeit with the monarch's role in pre-approving legislation introduced in the Irish parliament, as was the 'Declaration how and by what means the statutes of England from time to time came to be of force in Ireland.' That the question was entirely shaped by immediate political needs in England and Ireland and the closeness between the establishment and the highly-conservative Old English position is shown by the difficulty scholars have had in deciding whether the Declaration was written by the New English Lord Chancellor Richard Bolton, or the Catholic lawyer Darcy.[30] Whatever the arguments, the fact that the administration had to summon parliament to pass legislation and grant taxation is itself evidence that the Irish parliament was legislatively independent of its English counterpart and despite the occasional wholesale incorporation of English statute law into Ireland, many English laws were not in force in Ireland.[31]

In England lip service was paid to the importance of local representation, although the civil wars increased the numbers of locals elected; under Queen

records sittings in the upper house between 19 May and 17 June 1613; Undated notes of the Lords Justice Parsons and Dillon and the privy council, *c.*Feb.–June 1642, Bodl. Lib., Carte MS 68, fos. 422r–4.

29 17 Car. I, c. 33, 35, 37 (England). Dennehy notes that the English parliament occasionally legislated for Ireland after 1660. Dennehy, *Parliament*, pp 61–2.

30 Clarke, 'Colonial constitutional attitudes in Ireland'. For a maverick and highly self-interested Old English view of Irish constitutional arrangements, see Linda Levy Peck, 'Beyond the Pale: John Cusack and the language of absolutism in early Stuart Britain', *The Historical Journal*, 41:1 (March, 1998), 121–49.

31 Darcy, *An argument delivered*; Clarke, 'Patrick Darcy and the constitutional relationship'; Bríd McGrath (ed.), 'Additional Patrick Darcy Papers: letters from Anthony Martin, bishop of Meath, 1632 and to John Bramhall, with two legal opinions, 1661–2', *Anal. Hib.*, 48 (2017), 73–88.

Elizabeth, only *c.* 24% of urban MPs were resident in their constituencies.[32] In Ireland, while the practice of electing residents was eroded, the principle was strongly held by Catholics, although Darcy's return for Navan in 1634, John FitzGerald's for Inistioge and Darcy, Richard Martin and Walter Cruise for Ulster constituencies showed their flexibility when circumstances dictated.[33] The fact that non-resident MPs were almost invariably Protestants and supporters of the government was doubly significant. Their presence demonstrated the administration's disregard for the law that the Old English cherished. Instead their focus was on pleasing their patrons in the administration, not representing their constituencies. After 1642 a series of returns for mainly Leinster seats replacing expelled MPs maintained an ostensibly representative parliament which excluded most of the population and whose new members were rarely elected by voters and frequently not based in their constituencies, where they can be identified.[34] By contrast, the Confederate Assembly at Kilkenny in the 1640s relied on the widespread acceptance of the principles of representation and consensus and strengthened its legitimacy by following parliamentary processes as far as possible, although it also included non-resident members.

The crown, parliamentarians and the general public displayed very different attitudes to parliament. While the Old English saw parliament as 'an assembly of men of eminence and estate, working in conjunction with royal power for the greater good', one with a strong element of consultation and which would not be distorted by royal prerogative, the administration saw it very differently.[35] For the crown, as in all Europe's early modern states, assemblies' membership and proceedings were matters to be carefully managed, displaying the unity of the state, achieving as much of its own programme and raising the highest possible taxes while making the fewest concessions. For the Irish administration, parliament was an instrument of policy, a tool to Anglicize Ireland, pass its own legislation and raise much needed money for the crown, not a partner in managing the kingdom. As it paid no attention to the native population's interests and grievances, parliament inevitably served more as a point of conflict than contact and unity. Chichester and Sir William Parsons and Borlase's organizing soldiers around Dublin Castle on 18 May 1613 and November 1641 anticipated negative and possibly violent responses to parliament's meeting.[36]

32 Norm Jones, 'Representative of what? The politics of representative institutions', Paper presented to the conference 'Rediscovering Europe's Parliamentary culture, 1500–1700: concepts, methods, approaches', Krakow, 22–4 June 2022.

33 McGrath, 'Inistioge's elections in 1640'; *idem*, 'Sex, lies and rigged returns'; *idem*, 'Irish elections of 1640–1641'.

34 *Idem*, 'Recruiter returns'.

35 Tadhg Ó hAnnracháin, 'Imagining political representation in seventeenth-century Ireland' in Armstrong and Ó hAnnracháin (eds), *Community in early modern Ireland*, pp 34–50.

36 Jason Peacey, 'The street theatre of state: the ceremonial opening of parliament, 1603–1660' in Kyle (ed.), *Managing Tudor and Stuart parliaments*, pp 155–72; Jackson (ed.), 'Document'; NLI, MS 643, fos. 26v, 31v–2r, 64r; Perceval-Maxwell, *Outbreak*, p. 243; Robert Armstrong, 'Borlase, John', *DIB*.

The administration's prevailing narrative, reflected by many English writers, was that it disinterestedly proposed 'wholesome laws', which untrustworthy and obstructive Irish Catholics unfortunately opposed, against their own best interests. Thomas Haynes judged that the problem of theft could not be 'reformed by Actes of parliament there because yt must be done by the Piers (peers) gent[lemen] ffreeholders and Burgesses of that place, who will never consent to anie acte preiudicial to them selves or theire freindes.' It might be asked why they should? Contradictorily, his suggested solution was through parliament, but by rigging its membership:

> It is to be considered howe the reformation of the Lawes, Customes and Religion maie be wrought, and because yt wilbe harde to alter the Common Lawes there in all pointes and to make newe Statutes repealinge all the former, It were good to redresse onely the abuses of them by Parlyament, Wherein because thje higher house wilbe of necessitie of the Irishe that maie perchaunce be ever headstronge, It must be handled as Kinge Edward did amonges the Lordes of the Cleargy whoe were not to be matched by the Temporall Lordes and therefore sent wryttes amongst the moste woorthie gent[lemen] and made them Barrons of the Parlyament. Whereby theire obstinacy was sufficientlie Curbed.[37]

An official planning the 1613 parliament reflected the same attitude:

> it is to bee dobted that the Irish and such as are discended of English race of whom both the houses of parliament consist, be for the most part popish recusants, will distast and reject such bills as shall be transmitted out of England to bee propounded … although they bee for the benefitt of the crowne and the kingdom, which was observed in the last parliament when the lower house did obstinately refuse to pass divers good bills containing matter of civill government only out of a froward and perverse affection to the state.[38]

Rothe claimed that any proposals Catholics made were repulsed: 'whatsoever the natives had prepared for moderating excesse, for cutting of abuses, for lightining theire burthens, for direction of government … the authoritye of those of the opposite part, with one force defeated, with one resistance discovered.' The solicitor general of Ireland between 1606 and 1618, Sir Robert Jacob also reflected this attitude, although he emphasized recusants' opposition to anti-Catholic bills rather than to legislation in general.[39] The MP Edmund Skory asserted that Catholics chose

37 ARL, MS Haynes, *Certaine principall matters*, fos. 7v, 26r. This work was dedicated to the earl of Nottingham.
38 Bodl. Lib., Carte MS 61, fo. 90r; *Cal. Carew*, v, p. 168.
39 NLI, MS 643, fos. 63v–4r; Jacob to Northampton, 26 May 1613, Bodl. Lib., Carte MS 62, fos. 241r–4v. For biographical details on Jacob and his political views, see Canny, *Making Ireland British*, pp 175–7.

> the most infamous men in every Towne and Countrey for theire knights and Burgesses, in matter of conformity, either in religion, or other civill obedience, and … admitted of none to be of the parlement house that were English … to overthrow your Majestys most pious, and princely purpose of the parlement.

Vincent Gookin averred that the Irish desired a parliament in which 'they ayme not soe much at good lawes to bee made as to gett good lawes repealed', despite the fact that Poynings' Law made that impossible. Wentworth's client Charles Price, MP for Belfast, claimed that the Irish had opposed 'our best laws' in 1634–5, even though opposition was not based on confessional positions.[40]

Chichester respected parliament's role and privileges, while flouting constitutional practice and electoral law to control it, but Wentworth displayed utter contempt for it, its members and for Convocation. Despite impressive opening ceremonies, he accommodated them in 'a mean and ordinary place' within the castle, where he could control them, rather than use the magnificent Kildare Hall. He flouted electoral law, excluded almost all Catholic MPs from the opening processions, refused to provide a copy of his speech to the Lords, violated MPs' privileges and liberties and by-passed parliament by issuing as acts of state bills which it rejected (see chapter seven). He significantly reduced the upper house's prestige by engineering the absence from the 1640 parliament of local peers with a knowledge of and interest in Ireland, preferring to depend on the proxies of absentee English holders of Irish peerages and prorogued parliament in November 1640 to prevent it pursuing its own agenda.[41] However, he did not deny parliament's representative role, providing a detailed (if disappointing) answer to the Commons' remonstrance about the Graces. He also responded to another petition about the export of tallow by suspending the restrictions until further consideration.[42]

MPs' attitudes are revealed by their attendance and productivity. Appearance levels were high and they showed commendable commitment to parliamentary business. Even after 1642, members continued to attend the Commons (see chapter seven). Irish MPs' radically different attitudes depended on which groups they belonged to. There were four main groups in this respect, the Old English, the Gaelic Irish, the New English who had arrived before 1632

40 Bríd McGrath, 'Unmasking "E.S.": the author of "A survey of the present estate of Ireland, anno 1615"', *Archivium Hibernicum*, 71 (2018), 7–33; Gookin to Wentworth, *c.*1633, TNA, SP 63/270, fos. 66v–79r; Lloyd Bowen and Simon Healy, 'Price, Charles' in Thrush and Ferris (eds), *History of parliament*.

41 William Brereton, 'Sir William Brereton's travels in Ireland, 1635' in Caesar Litton Falkiner (ed.), *Illustrations of Irish history and topography* (London, 1904), pp 363–407; Clarke, *Old English*, p. 90; McGrath, 'Irish elections of 1640–1641'.

42 Bodl. Lib., Carte MS 66, fos. 300r–2v; *Commons' Jn. Ire.*, 1 Aug. 1634; Knowler (ed.), *Letters and dispatches*, i, p. 308.

and, finally, Wentworth's clique in the 1630s and early 1640s.[43] The Tudor administration had developed a negative attitude to recalcitrant MPs, initially presumed to be all Catholics, but under Wentworth increasing numbers of Protestants also became suspect. Following their experience in 1634, many of the first three groups coalesced in June 1640 to oppose Strafford.

Parliament was part of the Old English political tradition and they retained a reverence for the institution and a belief in its role in creating good laws and redressing grievances. Their attitudes were also shaped by strong folk memories; Sussex, Sidney and Perrot's inept and contemptuous handling of parliament left a legacy of deep distrust between them and the administration, but also reinforced their sense of its importance and belief that opposition was necessary and likely to be at least partially successful. They were dismayed by the transformation of an ancient and respected body to 'only a shadow or imitation of the real thing' and felt deep disgust at Chichester's administration, which 'neglected the customs of our ancestors [and] neglected the law of the land.' Rothe resented the absence of the usual formalities on dissolving the 1613–15 parliament.[44]

Canny contended that the Old English saw parliament as the primary bulwark of Irish Catholic interests until their experience in 1613–15 proved to them that they had lost dominance there. But this overlooks the reality that only the deputy had the constitutional right to propose a parliament and the monarch power to summon one, that recusants' experience of at least partial success under the Tudors was confirmed under James when they were able to hold their own and that they continually pressed for a parliament between 1627 and 1633. The 1628 and 1634 elections demonstrate that Catholics vigorously contested seats, rejected Wentworth's nominees, achieved greater success than anticipated and selected their own candidate for speaker.[45] The Old English understood that the strongest guarantee of their rights came not from royal promises but statute law; despite deep concerns about how parliament might be manipulated, legislation was the only means of ensuring protection for subjects' rights, hence their secession in 1613 and refusal to engage wholeheartedly with the Great Assembly, whose agents

> generally desired a Parliament that abuses might be certified and by that way some supply and addition might come to helpe his Majesties Revenue … The Lord Deputy replied they would putt propositions to the Kinge but not answeare us. Ffor he promised a Parliament uppon their conclusions of this but they would begin with it.[46]

43 Derek Hirst, *The representative of the people? Voters and voting in England under the early Stuarts* (Cambridge, 1975), p. 2; MacDonald, *Burghs and parliament*, p. 84.

44 Jackson (ed.), 'Document'; Moynes (ed.), *Annual letters*, i, pp 129–36; NLI, MS 643, fo. 25v.

45 McGrath, 'Electoral strategy'.

46 TNA, SP 63/245, fos. 26v–35v.

After Falkland's botched summoning of the 1628 parliament, Ormond, Westmeath, Fingall, Gormanston, Mayo, Meath and Slane, along with members of the gentry, petitioned the lords justices for a parliament; Cork and Loftus were unwilling to risk this and promised to try to resolve their grievances by other means, but their inaction reinforced Catholics' insistence on the need for legislation to guarantee the Graces. Wentworth's management of his first parliament strengthened their understanding of its importance as both a protection and a threat, especially given the wide exclusions to the royal pardon it enacted. His encouraging signals to the Catholic political community in advance of the 1634 parliament engendered what Clarke described as 'a hope born of credulity and weaned on deceit.' Yet their confidence in him, like many Protestants, was tempered by their knowledge of his track record in England and his actions on his arrival in Ireland and they fought hard for every possible seat in that parliament.[47] The late 1630s were a low time for confidence in parliament's powers, but this did not dilute the Irish political community's commitment to the institution and belief in its potential to redress grievances, continued by their pressing for a parliament in 1643.[48]

Gaelic folk memory was as strong, but very different and of much more recent origin. Few mentions are made to parliament in Gaelic sources before 1585 when the Annals of Loch Cé reported

> The men of all Erinn – such of them as were of any account – went to Baile-atha-cliath to an Act of Parliament. The son of O'Maelmhuaidh, and Edmond Dorcha, son of Domhnall, son of Murchadh Mac Suibhne, and several other persons, were hanged at this [1585] Act of Parliament … The nobles of Erinn came safely from that Council of Ath-cliath, without profit … A great tribute was imposed on Connacht by Saxons, i.e., an ounce of gold on every quarter, both ecclesiastical and lay; and the sovereignty of each Gaeidhelic lord was lowered by them.

Gaelic MPs supported the Old English opposition in that parliament and there is no suggestion of their having a separate strategy or voice.[49] The satire *Pairlement Chloinne Thomáis*, which mocks the nouveaux riches who had advanced through the Munster Plantation, including upstart Gaels who took advantage of the upheaval to improve their own financial and social standing by adopting Anglicized

47 Cork to Dorchester, 8 Dec. 1630, in Clarke, McGrath and Edwards (eds), *A lord justice's letterbook*, no. 93; Clarke, *Old English*, p. 77; McGrath, 'Electoral strategy'; Mark Empey, 'Power, prerogative and the politics of Sir Thomas Wentworth in England and Ireland', *Historical Journal*, 65:2 (2022), 275–96; *Act for the Kings Majesties most gracious, generall, and free pardon* (Dublin, 1635); 10–11, Car. I, c. 19.

48 Canny, *Making Ireland British*, p. 407; Clarke, *Old English*, pp 53–61; Cork to Dorchester, 8 Dec. 1630, in Clarke, McGrath and Edwards (eds), *A lord justice's letterbook*, no. 93.

49 William H. Hennessy (ed.), *The Annals of Loch Cé: a chronicle of Irish affairs from AD 1014 to AD 1590*, 2 vols (London, 1871), ii, p. 467; Treadwell, 'Sir John Perrott'.

names and customs, demonstrates continuing Gaelic reservations about the institution. That assembly dissolved into brawls and disorder satirizing the limited competence of the lower orders who took advantage of the changes in land-holding practices imposed in the province, as social advancement was tied to property ownership.[50] If Marc Caball's conclusion that the first half of this poem was written in 1608–11 and aimed specifically at the Mac Crossans/Crosbies is correct, it reflects a memory of Elizabeth's parliaments and anticipates James', implying the next assembly's membership would be debased by the inclusion of members of inferior social standing. It may have been directed as much at social-climbing Gaels like the lawyer Charles Doyne and official George Sexton as at lower class English settlers like Richard Boyle and Roger Rice, and quite possibly at the members of the Seven Septs of Laois that Patrick Crosby, father of Sir Piers, was attempting to transplant to Tarbert in Kerry around this time.[51]

This earlier silence is understandable, because before James' reign, and especially before 1585, only a small part of Ireland had parliamentary representation. Areas which were predominantly Gaelic in society, especially across Connacht and Ulster, had almost none and therefore the majority of Ireland's inhabitants had no opportunity to develop a parliamentary tradition prior to the late sixteenth century. Even in 1541, when St Leger explicitly used parliament as a means to integrate the Gaelic Irish into the new kingdom, most parliamentarians from that community were the recently ennobled lords or bishops, rather than MPs. However, the expansion of representation in Elizabeth's last Irish parliament and especially James' only one slightly changed that, as it was now Englishmen being returned for the western and northern provinces, although Bingham's engineering the return of Englishmen for Connacht counties meant that Gaels from those shires first appeared in parliament in 1613. The appearance of the Gaelic gentry in Dublin in 1585 may be read as their making the point that they, as leaders of their community, should have been in the chambers as members, rather than Englishmen with few if any local connections and no legal right or credibility to represent those counties. Moreover, surviving annals come largely from predominantly Gaelic areas. As such they may not reflect the experience or attitude of the ethnic Irish in culturally diverse parts of the Lordship, including towns, who were electors and paid, assessed and collected subsidies and MPs' wages, who were part of the parliamentary tradition which has been regarded as exclusively Old English.

1613 represented a sea-change in the Gaelic community's interactions with the state as they collectively extended their previous role as electors and spectators to

50 Bernadette Cunningham, 'Native culture and political change in Ireland 1580–1640' in Ciaran Brady and Raymond Gillespie (eds), *Natives and newcomers: essays on the making of Irish colonial society, 1534–1641* (Dublin, 1986), pp 148–70.

51 Caball, '*Pairlement Chloinne Tomáis I*'; Clarke, 'Sir Piers Crosby'; Walter FitzGerald, 'Notes on the family of Patrick Crosbie of Maryborough, by whom the Seven Septs of Leix were transplanted to Tarbert in the County Kerry in 1608–9', *JRSAI*, sixth series, 13:2 (Dec., 1923), 133–50. On Doyne, see Appendix 3.

stand as candidates, even though some had little or no English. They were facilitated in this by Catholic clergy and Old English who made strenuous efforts to involve them in some of the most fiercely fought contests, including Armagh, Fermanagh, King's County and Tyrone. Counties Carlow, Clare, Cork, Kerry, Longford, Monaghan, Sligo and Wicklow returned old Irish MPs, apart from the Gaelicized Bourkes elected for Galway and Mayo and many Anglicized burgesses. This demonstrates their growing acceptance of the crown's authority in all aspects of public life which is also reflected in the number of men of old Irish origin educated abroad and at the London inns of court, and Gaelic intellectuals' movement from using parchment to paper.[52] However, they remained mistrustful and despite or because of the dramatically increased number of constituencies, comprised the same percentage in 1613 (*c.*10%) of parliament's membership as they had in 1585. Stoked by fears for their estates and religious freedom, their increasingly militant religious commitment sparked outrage at Catholic prelates' exclusion and they resisted the administration inside and outside parliament. O'Sullivan Beare reported the opening when 'Lord Buttevant carried the sword before the Deputy to the church, to hear the blind ministers of the devil … the Catholic bishops are excluded, and the heretic usurpers of their titles and sees vote in Parliament in their stead.'[53] Shane Mchilimy O'Donnelly described their fears and response:

> The coming parliament was meant to cozen them and bring them from their religion; but they should stand fast together; an assessment of 4*d.* on every couple was made for the expenses of agents to England and for knights of the shire; they should pay it willingly.[54]

Increasing Gaelic engagement reflected their Welsh and Scottish counterparts' experience; the expansion in the size of the Scottish Estates did not benefit inhabitants of the Gaidhealtachd where there were no burghs and rural dwellers had limited opportunities for involvement as the large sheriffdoms covered both Gaelic and Scots-speaking areas. Peers and bishops were almost invariably Anglophone and no attempt was made formally or otherwise to draw Gaels into the political process, but, as in Ireland and Wales, they were able to use parliament in their own interests to raise very local issues, chiefly through petitioning.[55] Although the Old Irish may not have led debates and, like many non-lawyers, were

52 McGrath, 'Ireland and the third university'; Pádraig Ó Macháin, 'The emergence of the Gaelic paper manuscript: a preliminary investigation' in Pádraig Ó Macháin (ed.), *Paper and the paper manuscript: a context for the transmission of Gaelic literature* (Cork, 2019), pp 21–43.

53 Quoted in Bennett, *Bandon*, pp 28–9.

54 Examination of Shane Mchilimy O'Donnelly, 22 Oct. 1613, in Charles MacNeill (ed.), 'Harris: *Collectanea de Rebus Hibernicis*', *Anal. Hib.*, 6 (Nov., 1934), 248–450 (quote on p. 384).

55 Bowen, 'Wales at Westminster'; Kennedy, 'Representing the periphery'. I am grateful to John Young and Allan Kennedy (email correspondence 18 Oct. 2019) for their observations on this subject.

not well represented on committees, they demonstrated their commitment to the parliamentary process through regular attendance and facilitating their constituents' search for redress. Nevertheless, their emphasis was on local, rather than national affairs. By 1641, however, the rebels in Cavan described the parliament as 'the representative body of this kingdom.'[56] At least 10% of parliamentary petitions recorded in 1640–1 came from people with identifiably Gaelic names, including three women; this is clearly an underestimate, given the routine Anglicization of Gaelic names and petitions from other groups, such as the inhabitants of Courtmacsherry or Carlow, included many Old Irish. Welsh cases about the location of county days which enabled specific groups' control over local matters provide a parallel to the Parsons' attempts to have Birr designated as the county town and may indicate why so many men of Gaelic origin, led by MP John Coughlan, were prepared to support Parsons against the Digbys' interests through petitioning parliament.[57] Perhaps ironically, the greatest evidence of Gaelic 'buy-in' to parliaments as a means of managing the country was the number of Old Irish members of the Confederate General Assemblies.[58]

For Protestants, parliament was a means of resolving personal problems through private acts and achieving social advancement by attracting or retaining patronage; many made very beneficial contacts and received preferment during or shortly after parliament. Their sense of parliament's importance was generally high. Ware owned copies of the *Modus*, the 1613 Commons' journals and the index to the Lords', while Jerome Alexander possessed transcripts of Cotton and Hakewill's writings on parliament. Archbishop Dopping's copy of the *Modus* was inherited from his uncle William Domville, son of the 1634 MP Gilbert Domville and grandson of Archbishop Thomas Jones.[59] Audley Mervyn had a firm belief in parliament's role and potential and worked hard to build bridges between the New English and native populations. His ultimate aim was to create a coalition to pursue common interests against the administration, bringing Darcy and Martin back into the Commons to provide critical legal expertise. He also continued to promote parliament's role even in 1645, offering to ensure the return of 'moderates' through 'legal elections' who would support Ormond's 'peace with the Irish.'[60]

Wentworth's handling of the 1634 parliament reversed Catholics' earlier experiences of successful opposition, but 1640–1 reinforced its value, especially since New English Protestants, whose attitude to parliament had formerly been largely limited to concern for their own personal self-interest, came, through suffering from Wentworth's arbitrary government, to fear his agenda and

56 'Remonstrance from county of Cavan to lords justices and council', 6 Nov. 1641, in J.T. Gilbert (ed.), *A contemporary history of affairs in Ireland from 1641–1652*, 3 vols (Dublin, 1879–80), i, pp 364–5.

57 Bowen, 'Wales at Westminster'; Birr Castle, MS A/1/19.

58 McGrath, 'Parliament men'.

59 O'Sullivan, 'Finding list'.

60 Mervyn to Ormond, 4 Feb. 1645, in HMC, *The manuscripts of the marquis of Ormonde, preserved at the castle, Kilkenny* (London, 1899), i, p. 94.

determined to use parliament to defend their rights. Between 1560 and 1613, and again in 1640, Catholics generally adopted a defensive attitude hoping to limit damage to their community's interests, but the range of their concerns widened. In 1613 they were mainly anxious about anti-Catholic legislation. In 1628 and 1634 they were optimistic that the Graces would be given legislative form, securing their estates and economic and social position. Wentworth's novel reading of Poynings' Law and thuggish tactics made it impossible for Catholics to achieve their objectives, but after that parliament, their primary concerns, increasingly shared by the New English, were security of land titles, punitive taxation, exorbitant fees for officials and an end to arbitrary government.[61] By June 1640 both sides had become acutely aware of their common interests; Irish inhabitants, regardless of their ethnic origin, objected to Wentworth emasculating the Irish parliament 'to the subordinate status of a legislative agency giving statutory effect to executive policy.' This threatened all of their rights and they formed a coalition to oppose Wentworth's regime.[62]

However, many New Englishmen seemed curiously uninterested in electoral patronage. Laurence Parsons, for instance, failed to pursue his 1620 letters patent for two manorial boroughs, apparently seeing little advantage in controlling four seats. He might have felt differently by 1640. Similarly, Ussher and Bramhall's 1635 act that forbade Ulster clergy to grant freeholds of church lands also reduced their potential influence in county elections.[63] Cork was one of the few settlers who pursued political influence through parliamentary patronage, but as lord justice he had been unwilling to summon parliament until the money raised for the Graces ran out; however, after suffering from Wentworth's vindictiveness and needing his own private bill to pass, recalled in 1640 how the previous parliament extracted heavy taxes while providing little or no redress of grievances and advocated a return to the traditional format of addressing complaints before granting subsidies.[64]

Despite, or perhaps because it met so rarely, there was strong public interest in parliament, because its decisions affected everyone through the invariable subsidies and royal pardons, groups or individuals whose difficulties could be resolved by petitions or private acts and anyone rich enough to be liable for subsidies. The strong interest in becoming candidates and the high number of elections attests to public confidence in parliament (see chapter five), as does the level of petitions submitted in 1641, underlining public trust in its ability to resolve individual and collective grievances. Details of what occurred and had been said in the Irish parliament featured regularly in personal correspondence and private and public

61 Baltinglas to Lord Herbert of Cherbury, 5 Feb. 1634; same to same, 15 March 1634; F. Lloyd to Richard Herbert, 27 Feb. 1635, all printed in Smith (ed.), *Herbert correspondence*, pp 78–9, 81–2.

62 See chapter 3. Clarke, 'History of Poynings' Law'.

63 Birr Castle, MS A/5/46, fos. 1r–2r. Parsons died in 1628. An Act for confirmation of leases made by the lord primate, and other bishops in Ulster, 10 Car. I, c. 5 (1634) (Ireland).

64 Cork to Dorchester, 23 June 1630, in Clarke, McGrath and Edwards (eds), *A lord justice's letterbook*, no. 56; Cork to Ormond, 16 March 1640, BL, Add. MS 19,832, fo. 47.

conversations, but the accounts of speeches and debates, which were widely circulated in published and manuscript form in England, were almost entirely absent in Ireland.[65]

Those wishing to promote or at least defend their private interests through parliament did so by ensuring their supporters' returns, through petitions and personal lobbying. Richard Boyle, who became earl of Cork in 1620, promoted his supporters' return in 1613 to enhance his standing with the administration and obstruct John Lancaster, the bishop of Waterford and Lismore's private bill, which threatened his property; when he and the MPs for his boroughs of Clonakilty, Lismore and Tallow were removed from membership, including his close associate and legal advisor Geratt Lowther, Boyle's then-ally but later mortal enemy, Francis Annesley and his cousin and client Laurence Parsons hoped Chichester would 'insert [our] names into some of the new elections … to do [you] service concerning Lismore, wherein the Bishop will do his utmost to get voices.'[66] Clanricard's coterie of Galway lawyers in 1634 and 1640–1 were present to resist the plantation of Connacht which threatened his property. St Ann's Guild's members returned in the summer of 1642 shamelessly used their membership to try to regain control of the fraternity's assets.[67]

However, public interest was ambivalent, recognizing the opportunities for redressing grievances and legislation to improve economic, social and political life, but sensing disquiet about how the administration would handle it and what its other consequences would be for individuals and communities. Parliament presented a welcome opportunity to make money: Dublin's innkeepers, merchants, stationers, tailors and other artisans would have welcomed the additional custom from visitors to the capital. For actors and writers, parliamentary gatherings were an opportunity to stage cultural events, such as the performance of Burnell's *Landgartha* (see chapter six). However, there was concern about anti-Catholic measures and while the 1613–15 parliament worked out better than either side had expected, and although Chichester reported its dissolution on the first day of the new session as an unpopular move, the failure to redress grievances MPs presented provoked general discontent, especially as there was no expectation of another meeting soon.[68] Every assembly failed to redress grievances and while few public comments about the Irish 'rump' parliament have survived, MP Thomas Johnson

65 Thomas Bagot to Walter Bagot, 30 April 1614, FSL, MS L.a.91. Walter lived in Staffordshire and is not to be confused with the Dublin merchant of the same name. Crawford, *Star Chamber*, p. 330. George Trevelyan to his father, 25 Nov. 1614, in Collier, Trevelyan and Trevelyan (eds), *Trevelyan Papers*, iii, p. 132; Guildford Slingsby to Henry Slingsby, 22 June 1634, FSL, MS X.d.428(185); Charles Seagrave to Ferdinando Lord Hastings, 12 Nov. 1633 (this date is clearly incorrect), 13 Nov. 1640, in Bickley (ed.), *Hastings, Volume II*, pp 102, 109; McGrath, 'Recruiter returns'.

66 Laurence Parsons to Richard Boyle, May 1614, Chatsworth House, Cork Papers, vol. 5, no. 43; *Commons' Jn. Ire.*, 25 Oct. 1614; Henry Cotton, *Fasti ecclesiae Hibernicae: the succession of the prelates and members of the cathedral bodies in Ireland*, 6 vols (Dublin, 1847–78), v, p. 128.

67 McGrath, 'Recruiter returns'.

68 Chichester to Winwood, 31 Oct. 1615, *Cal. S.P. Ire., 1615–25*, p. 95; NLI, MS 643, fo. 25v.

claimed in a nasty personal dispute in August 1642, that his assailant asked 'Would this parliament never be at an end?'[69]

Public reverence for parliament reflected on MPs and membership was prestigious, even when debased by blatant rigging of constituencies and returns. Membership provided an opportunity to promote or defend individual and common interests and given the lack of other means of collective engagement was an important, if challenging, role. This explains the hard-fought elections in each early Stuart Irish parliament. Parliamentary privilege provided valuable protection for members and their servants, especially Catholics subject to fines and prosecution for holding local offices without swearing the oath of supremacy and those in legal difficulties. In 1613–15 several towns elected MPs as mayors, bailiffs and recorders because their parliamentary privilege protected them from prosecution until dissolution and the general pardon enacted in the parliament prevented punishment after its determination.[70] However MPs' experience of parliament differed sharply, presenting opportunities for some but danger for others. The same considerations influenced Catholics in all parliaments: membership was vital to defend their interests, demonstrate their loyalty to the king and press for redress of grievances. For Protestants, it presented an opportunity to promote the Anglicization of Ireland, cement their relationships with the regime and promote their economic and social advancement, but their prospects differed depending on whether they were favoured by Wentworth or not.[71]

Protestant clergy relied on parliament to strengthen the Church of Ireland's position: in 1634 Ussher wrote to Samuel Ward, Master of Sidney Sussex College declaring, 'We are to have a parliament to be summoned here very shortlye: upon the good successe whereof the whole settlement of this kingdome dependeth.'[72] Bramhall also noted its importance in his *Serpent Salve* (1643), in which he stated that 'the very name of parliament was music in our ears; at the summons thereof our hearts danced with joy.' This aside, he regarded parliaments as consultative bodies, depending on the king: 'When the great representative body of Parliament are assembled, they are yet but [the king's] great council; not commanders. He calls them, he dissolves them; they do not choose so much as a speaker without his approbation.'[73] While Guildford Slingsby, Roger Lort and Edmund Borlase

69 *Commons' Jn. Ire.*, 9 Aug. 1642.

70 McGrath, 'Sex, lies and rigged returns'; Bríd McGrath, 'Kilkenny merchants and the 1613 parliament' in Jane Fenlon and Sarah Maguire (eds), *Magnates and merchants in early modern Kilkenny* (Dublin, 2023), pp 162–75.

71 McGrath, 'Electoral strategy'; Bríd McGrath, 'Poets and patronage under Falkland and Wentworth: the commendatory verses to Richard Bellings' *Arcadia* (1624) and James Shirley's *The Royal Master* (1638)', *Archivium Hibernicum*, 74 (2021), 7–27.

72 Ussher to Ward, 30 April 1634, in Elizabethanne Boran (ed.), *The correspondence of James Ussher, 1600–1656*, 3 vols (Dublin, 2015), ii, p. 630; Margo Todd, 'Ward, Samuel', *Oxford DNB*.

73 John Bramhall, *The serpent salve* (s.l., 1643), pp 299, 327. For Bramhall's views on parliament, see Jack Cunningham, *James Ussher and John Bramhall: the theology and politics of two Irish ecclesiastics of the seventeenth century* (Aldershot, 2007), pp 134–9.

described membership of the Commons conventionally as an honour, the attitude of Wentworth's clients may best be characterized as indifference and the admittedly limited accounts of proceedings do not suggest their active participation, although Borlase was very young.[74]

In a highly clientelist society, making, developing and nurturing useful connections was key to maintaining and enhancing personal and familial economic and social status; membership of parliament was a prestigious position that provided an opportunity to make or cement important contacts and build credit with the administration, current and potential patrons and local communities. English 'gentlemen began to see the House of Commons as a means of realizing political as well as social objecties' and an opportunity for social climbing. Nevertheless, funeral entries and monuments in both countries show little evidence of MPs making much of their membership. Two possibly unique Irish occurrences were Stephen Rice, MP for Kerry in 1613, whose tombstone in Dingle Churchyard proudly recorded that he was 'late Knight of Parliament' and Thomas Peppard whose funeral entry may have cited his membership only because he died during the course of the 1640 parliament. The family account of Nicholas Langton, Kilkenny's MP in 1613, does not mention his membership.[75] Cork attempted to persuade Richard Parsons to become a member of the Short Parliament in England, arguing that it would be 'tyme spent to very good purpose, for thereby you shall have the opportunity to better your judgment by understanding the state … and make you better knowne to the best sort of people that are in this kingdom', adding that his proposal was 'wholy entended for your advantage.'[76] This was especially true for Protestants, for whom it was an opportunity to impress the administration, from whom appointment to crown offices, awards of profitable wardships or licences and grants of land could flow.

Many Protestant MPs received crown offices or honours shortly after parliament; ten were knighted, while four were ennobled shortly after 1615 and many more in future years. Edward Blayney and Edward Brabazon became members of the council of Munster in 1615, although they had no known connections with the province, and Francis Blundell, Christopher Conway, Humphrey Farnham, Thomas Hibbotts, Nicholas Loftus (*plate 5*), Richard Pemberton, Thomas Ryves, George Trevelyan, James Ware, Walter Weldon and Walter White all received favours. Farnham's future prosperity was based on

74 Guildford Slingsby to Henry Slingsby, 22 June 1634, FSL, MS X.d.428(185); Rushworth (ed.), *Tryal*, p. 184; Borlase, *History*, p. 8; Toby Barnard, 'Borlase, Edmund', *DIB*.

75 M.F. Cusack, *A history of the kingdom of Kerry* (Dublin, 1995), appendix iv, p. xxiii; NLI, GO, MSS 64–79, Funeral Entries, Volumes 6–17; Anonymous, '*Laus Deo. Ad majorem Dei gloriam*', *Journal of the Kilkenny and South-East of Ireland Archaeological Society*, new series, 5:1 (1864), 85–108. I am grateful to Paul Hunneyball for his observations on English MPs (email correspondence 8 Sept. 2021).

76 Cork to Richard Parsons, 14 Jan. 1640, Chatsworth House, Cork Papers, Misc. boxes, Box 3, pp 403–4.

connections he made in parliament.[77] Roger Rice received a grant to sell wine and acquavit in 1615 and Edward Southworth was awarded an army pension.[78] St John, who was very active in parliament, was made lord deputy in 1616; 23 of the 37 laymen invited to attend his inauguration had been fellow MPs, including low status clerks like Henry Andrews, William Crowe, Roger Downton and Anthony Stoughton.[79] Despite being humiliated in parliament in 1614, Fishe was made sheriff of Cavan in 1616.[80]

MPs who came to Ireland with Wentworth flourished through his patronage. Serving as his nominees was only one of the many ways Joshua Carpenter, George Carr, Robert Farrar, John Jackson, Thomas Little Sr, William Peisley, Charles Price, Guildford Slingsby and Michael Stanhope served his and their own interests and they were well-rewarded for their loyalty: 'It hath ever been my rule, that good servants are in degree with me next to good children, and that if God add to my fortunes, to take them along with me and to better them as well as myself.' Wentworth remarked to Laud, 'I am so great a lover myself to see my servants thrive.'[81] His kinsman Slingsby, burgess for Carysfort in 1634, complained to his uncle on his arrival in Ireland of being 'extremely ill-provided of many necessities' and in want of money, but after six years as the deputy's secretary he had invested £6,000 in the soap monopoly, which Wentworth promised to protect.[82] Knighthoods were frequently used as rewards: Farrar was knighted during the 1634 parliament and Catlin at its conclusion, and over the following four years so were Richard Scott, Robert Meredith, William Ussher, Paul Davies, Maurice Williams (*plate 20*), Maurice Eustace and only two Catholics, Dominic Browne and Dominic White, as mayors during Wentworth's visits to Galway and Limerick respectively.[83] While

77 Francis Annesley, Arthur Bassett, John Beare, Barnaby Bryan, William Colley Moses Hill, Beverley Newcomen, George Sexton, John Vaughan, James Ware. Peers created in 1616 were Richard Boyle, Brabazon, Garrett Moore and Ridgeway, and by 1619 Oliver Lambart, Richard Wingfield and James Hamilton. Charles R. Mayes, 'The early Stuarts and the Irish peerage', *EHR*, 73 (1958), 227–51. Medhop's fair copies of the Commons' journals, NLI, MS 836, King's Inns, MS N3/2/1/7 and the copies in ARL include lists of those subsequently knighted at the end of the volumes. McGrath, 'Membership', pp 175–87; Loeber and McGrath, 'Legacy of Humphrey Farnham'; McGrath, 'Poets and patronage'; Robert Armstrong, 'Brabazon, Sir Edward', *DIB*. For discussion of many of these individuals, see Victor Treadwell, *Buckingham and Ireland: 1616–1628: a study in Anglo-Irish politics* (Dublin, 1998), passim.

78 Letters patent from James I to Chichester, grant to Gilbert Rice and Roger Rice, of Askeaton, gents., licence to sell wine from their house or houses, and to Francis and Robert Rice of Askeaton to sell aquavit, 22 March 1615, HL, HP, Box 4(33), MS 15,077; *Cal. S.P. Ire., 1615–25*, p. 12.

79 FSL, MS X.d.607. There were just three Old English peers (Killeen, Roche and Louth) and two clerics (Chancellor Thomas Jones, archbishop of Dublin and James Ussher).

80 *Commons' Jn. Ire.*, 9 Nov. 1614. On Fishe's career more broadly, see R.J. Hunter, *The Ulster plantation in the counties of Armagh and Cavan, 1608–41* (Belfast, 2012), passim.

81 McGrath, 'Electoral strategy'; *idem*, 'Poets and patronage'; *idem*, 'Bio. dict.', i, p. 8. On many of these individuals in Wentworth's circle, see Charlotte Kate Brownhill, 'The personal and professional relationships between Thomas Wentworth, earl of Strafford, and his closest advisors', 2 vols (PhD, University of Sheffield, 2004).

82 Slingsby to Sir Henry Slingsby, 22 June 1634, FSL, MS X.d.428.

83 Colum Kenny, 'Meredith (Meredyth), Robert', *DIB*; Terry Clavin, 'Davies (Davis), Sir Paul', *DIB*; McGrath, 'Bio. dict.', i, pp 290–1. On Eustace, Browne and White, see Appendix 3.

most of Wentworth's associates came with him, Robert Dillon, Maurice Eustace and James Ware's work in parliament, and that of other privy councillors, promoted their relationship with the deputy, and therefore their prosperity in Ireland; many lawyers subsequently became judges (see chapter ten).[84] While other MPs like the Cootes, Mervyn, George Rawdon (*plate 25*) and Sir Hardress Waller, did not necessarily benefit directly from their work as MPs, they made connections and formed networks which supported them throughout the 1640s and 1650s and many were members of the 1660 Convention which facilitated the Restoration from which they again benefitted.[85] Even for those who were not members, parliament offered an opportunity to impress: those able to influence returns could ingratiate themselves with the administration and Cork wrote to his son-in-law Barrymore to advise the attorney general of Munster to appear at parliament 'which will make him knowne and put a good esteame upon him.' He also offered to provide him with board and lodgings in order to facilitate this.[86]

However, membership also incurred disadvantages. Attendance occupied a great deal of time and wages would not compensate for loss of merchants' and lawyers' earnings (see chapter eight). Catholics expected membership would damage their individual and collective interests. Sir Patrick Barnewall anticipated retribution for his intended opposition in the 1613 parliament, noting

> a purpose to withhold some courses, that which will overthrow the states of most men in the kingdom if they take effect, to which if I shall be of that society, it is like among the rest, I will give the best opposition I may, which like enough, in my private, will debar me from the expectation of any good from thence.

The Jesuits and Bishop David Rothe also anticipated a parliament 'full of dangers. For it was there where religion was either abolished or made stronger.' They were relieved that parliament was 'dissolved and dispersed harmlessly, contrary to what everyone had expected' without further damage to the Catholics' position.[87] Recusants faced severe consequences for their opposition; James assured Chichester that the commission to enquire into the elections would be used to punish Catholics and non-conforming lawyers were barred from practicing in court as a direct result of their resistance in parliament.[88] Catholics' role in

84 Aidan Clarke, *Prelude to restoration in Ireland: the end of the Commonwealth, 1659–1660* (Cambridge, 2004), pp 169–242; McGrath, 'Recruiter returns'.

85 *Idem*, 'Bio. dict.', i, pp 252–3; Patrick Little, 'Waller, Sir Hardress', *Oxford DNB*.

86 Cork to Barrymore, 6 June 1634, in Cork's letterbook, 1634–41, Chatsworth House, Cork Papers, Misc. boxes, Box 3, p. 38. The attorney general was probably Henry Fisher. See Establishment of Ireland, 1629, TCD, MS 672, fo. 222; Robert Armstrong, 'Barry, David FitzDavid, 1st earl of Barrymore', *DIB*.

87 Rothe, *Analecta*, NLI, MS 643, fos. 26r, 31v–2r, 63v–4r; Moynes (ed.), *Annual letters*, i, pp 159, 325, 481; Judy Barry, 'Barnewall, Sir Patrick', *DIB*.

88 Barnewall to Christopher Darcy, 16 July 1612, in Farmer, 'Chronicle' in Lodge, *Desiderata Curiosa*, i, p. 164. Barnewall was summoned to England to ensure that he could not be an MP; Colum Kenny, *King's Inns and the kingdom of Ireland: the Irish Inn of Court, 1541–1800* (Dublin,

parliament could count against them even among their own: Rothe's record in 1614, for example, was held against him during discussions on the appointment of the new archbishop of Armagh in 1626.[89]

Actions in parliament and Convocation could draw unwelcome attention, even to Protestants, during Wentworth's government. A false move could bring humiliation as Fishe, Barron, John Dongan, Robert Talbot and Edward Lake found and those who crossed or failed to support Wentworth faced punitive sanctions.[90] Those in power noted opposition for future reference; Laud advised Bramhall during the 1635 parliament and Convocation:

> tis now matter now, since all is well passed what ye Opposition was. It may be, tis better now, then if there had been none, and for my part, I thinke soe. For now you are as certane as you could any way [page torn] been; and yet you know what enemyes you may expect upon like occasions; and perhaps [page torn] know whoe those enemyes are.[91]

Wentworth's instruction to the prolocutor of the lower house of Convocation to 'give me a particular account of how each man gives his vote' would have been understood for the threat it was. George Andrews owed his appointment as bishop of the impoverished sees of Ferns and Leighlin to the deputy's anger at his opposition to the 39 articles proposed there in 1634.[92] Bramhall considered that Ussher's reluctance to advance the career of one of Laud's protegés was because 'the yonge man shewed himself too forward in ye Convocacon and yt makes ye Primate doubt, he will not serve some turne.'[93] Wentworth expressed a similar view regarding Waller who 'compleins with the king [in parliament] but voates against us' and 'may be remembred at leasure' when it came to the plantation of Connacht, where the latter's lands, like all native proprietors and other New English including Cork and Ranelagh's, would have been open to confiscation.[94] MPs who crossed Wentworth, including Baron, Piers Crosby, Darcy, Richard Martin, Luke Netterville and Robert Talbot, faced dire consequences, including imprisonment and it was no coincidence that they all remained outside the 1640 Commons until

1992), pp 70, 102–3; John McCavitt, *Sir Arthur Chichester, lord deputy of Ireland, 1605–16* (Belfast, 1998), pp 118–19.

89 Memorial against the promotion of the bishop of Ossory or the bishop of Meath to Armagh, 1626, in Brendan Jennings (ed.), *Wadding Papers, 1614–38* (Dublin, 1953), p. 166.

90 See, for example, Clarke, 'Sir Piers Crosby'; Darcy to Ormond, 20 Aug. 1636, HMC, *Ormond*, pp 35–6.

91 Laud to Bramhall, 16 Jan. 1635, HL, HP, MS 15,156.

92 Helen Andrews, 'Andrews, George', *DIB*; Bríd McGrath, 'Town and mitre: relations between the episcopal borough of Old Leighlin and its bishops, 1635–1688', *Ossory, Laois and Leinster*, 8 (2022), 73–93.

93 Wentworth to the prolocutor of the lower house of convocation, 10 Dec. 1634, Bodl. Lib., Carte MS 64, fos. 281ff; Laud to Bramhall, 4 March 1635, HL, HP, MS 15,158; McGrath, 'Town and mitre'.

94 Radcliffe to Wentworth, 28 Oct. 1640, and Wentworth's reply of 5 Nov. 1640, FSL, MS X.c.101(2); Micheál Ó Siochrú, 'Sarsfield, Dominick', *DIB*.

after Strafford's downfall, although none of their reputations appear to have suffered in any other way.[95] Intimidation suppressed open dissent, as Kilmallock, who as William Sarsfield had sat in the 1634 Commons, described at Wentworth's trial how members remained silent despite their distress at his describing Ireland

> as a conquered nation and [one which] therefore must expect laws as from a conquerer ... having a great misery on his heart in the speaking: And whereas it is said, none did take notice of them; They did, but they durst not, it wrought inwardly and had they spoken of it, they expected no redress, but a greater addition of calamity to them.[96]

Equally, Cork only felt free to stand against Strafford at his trial and to support the Irish agents in London once his private bill guaranteeing his land settlement with the bishop of Waterford, John Atherton, long delayed by Wentworth's regime, had received the royal assent.[97]

The notion of representation may have taken on a more acute form at times of crisis, or when it seemed possible to achieve something. Thus Darcy and others refused to stand for the 1640 parliament when there was little advantage to be had to them personally or to their communities. When it appeared possible to influence public affairs, either in the 1641 parliament or in the Confederation, they were willing to be active, a situation seen also in the sixteenth-century Scottish Estates.[98]

All outside Wentworth's circle approached the 1640 parliament with trepidation and concern and many who anticipated that opposition in parliament would damage their personal interests, like Piers Crosby, Sir John Clotworthy, Cork, Lambart, Mountnorris and William Stewart, as much as Baron, Darcy, John Dongan, Richard Martin, Netterville and Robert Talbot preferred not to stand, including Cork's nephew Sir Percey Smith.[99] However chary anyone outside Wentworth's clique might have been about the 1640 parliament, including those excluded like Maurice Roche, third Viscount Fermoy and Cork or those who excluded themselves, they could not fail to acknowledge its importance and power over their lives and economic and social interests.[100] Cork asked his cousin and agent for early information about parliament's membership – Joshua Boyle anticipated this request and obtained the list the day before the earl wrote – and urged him to ensure that his private act finally to resolve the issue of his land dispute with the bishop of Waterford and Lismore was drafted and presented to

95 McGrath, 'Irish elections of 1640–1641'; Clarke, 'Sir Piers Crosby'; *idem*, '28 November 1634'; Patrick Darcy to Ormond, 20 Aug. 1636, in HMC, *Ormond*, i, pp 35–6; Darcy to Muskerry, 6 Nov. 1647, Bodl. Lib., Carte MS 21, fo. 517.

96 Rushworth (ed.), *Tryal*, p. 171.

97 Aidan Clarke, 'Atherton, John', *DIB*.

98 MacDonald, '"Tedious to rehers?"'.

99 Raymond Gillespie, 'Clotworthy, Sir John', *DIB*.

100 Micheál Ó Siochrú, 'Roche, Maurice, 3rd Viscount Fermoy', *DIB*.

the privy council.[101] However, after March 1641, public-spiritedness and the need to redress grievances led to a series of by-elections that saw the admission of many of Strafford's opponents to the Commons, underlining parliament's importance as a representational institution for reform.

There was an international and local interest in all representative bodies. Ambassadors reported back to their own countries on ceremonies and proceedings and many descriptions of the English parliament's opening and proceedings come from London-based diplomats and letter-writing circles. Ireland had no ambassadors, but reports of the opening ceremonies were produced by English observers and its business was noted abroad, especially in England, Spain, France, Rome and Venice, to both expatriate Irish and foreigners, although such reports are unfortunately less numerous after 1628. The head of the Irish College in Salamanca, Jesuit Thomas White from Clonmel published *Aviso del estado en que al presente estan las cosas de los Catholicos en el Reyno de Irlanda,* as a newsletter in 1611, alerting a Spanish audience to the trials of Irish Catholics facing a rigged parliament that would worsen their situation. Flaithrí Ó Maolchonaire, Tyrone's representative at the Spanish Court, also wrote for a Hispanic audience condemning O'Neill's 1614 attainder.[102] While the Franciscans' correspondence and annual Jesuit letters to Rome detailed events in 1613–15 and the Franciscan Thomas Strange noted in 1628, 'Aqui tendremos parliamento, que commercará los primeros de Noviembre próximo. Dios lose inspire para lo que fuere de su santo servicio y bien de la iglesia Y república' (here will be held a parliament, which will start the first of November next. God inspire them to do good for his holy service and of the church and commonwealth), they were otherwise silent on subsequent Irish parliaments. Conversely, Wentworth's imprisonment of the sheriff of Dublin for conducting the 1634 city election was reported as far away as Venice and Richard Blake's 1649 speech to the Confederation was published in French.[103]

Relations between MPs and their constituencies are hard to reconstruct. Few letters and no diaries have survived and the government's control of printing, as well as Poynings' Law's prohibition on introducing legislation on the floor of the House, limited the lobbying and public debate that was conducted through print in England and France. Smith's question, 'what did constituents expect from their

101 Fermoy to Mountgarrett, 15 March 1640, TNA, SP 63/258, p. 33; Cork to Joshua Boyle, 17 March 1641, Chatsworth House, Cork Papers, Misc. boxes, Box 3, p. 420. The list Joshua provided for him was dated 16 March 1640. See RIA, MS 24/Q/5.

102 Thomas White, *Aviso del estado en que al presente estan las cosas de los Catholicos en el Reyno de Irlanda* (Salamanca, 1611). I am grateful to Hiram Morgan for drawing this reference to my attention and to Ricard Torra-Prat for translating it for me. Benjamin Hazard, *Faith and patronage: the political career of Flaithrí Ó Maolchonaire, 1560–1629* (Dublin, 2009), pp 77ff; Terry Clavin, 'White, Thomas', *DIB*.

103 Strange to Luke Wadding, 5 Aug. 1628, in Jennings (ed.), *Wadding Papers*, pp 268–9; McGrath, 'Electoral strategy'; *Novvelle extraordinaire, tovchant l'estat present des affaires dv Roy de la Grand' Bretagne. Avec devx harangves eloquentes & Zelees, … l'une prononcee par le Chevalier Richard Blaque de la part de l'Assemblee des trois Estats du party Catholique d'Irlande* (Paris, 1649).

MPs?' is therefore more difficult to answer for Ireland.[104] Nevertheless, MPs understood their representative role and that they were answerable to their communities, however variably this was achieved, presumably taking instructions from and reporting back to their voters, although placemen had few local contacts and little interest in their electors and unlike resident members did not have to implement parliament's decisions locally.

While the French system of local and regional consultation that produced their lists of grievances, the Cahiers de Doléance, was well-established, local meetings were also held in Ireland to prepare for parliament and consider what legislation and redress of grievances local communities wanted. The mechanisms are unclear, although the gatherings to agree county candidates and town councils' meetings to nominate their prospective burgesses were obvious opportunities for these discussions.[105] In 1613, Catholics collectively agreed reforms that they wished to promote in parliament, 'in which many daies and nights the laborious industrie of the frindes of the Comminaltye and loveres of theire Cuntry had painfully labored'.[106] On 4 December 1610, Dublin city council established a high-powered committee of current and former mayors to sit twice-weekly 'to consider what is meet to be provided in parliament for the good of the city, and having agreed, to send propositions to the recorder to draw up acts of parliament to be sent into England.' Edinburgh appointed a similar committee in 1639.[107] Little direct evidence survives of the lobbying which must have occurred. Dublin's representatives would be expected to promote this legislation and account for its progress, especially since its recorder was one of its MPs, as would Meath and Carlingford's MPs on their unsuccessful local bills.[108] The process that produced the list of proposed legislation from Munster delivered by Sarsfield 'against the parliament' was presumably replicated elsewhere and the province's inhabitants would certainly have expected progress reports. Sarsfield would also have been able to point to the committees appointed to draft legislation to deal with a small number of the grievances.[109] Athenry's 1634 MPs Richard Martin and Dominic Browne presumably presented and promoted their petition as did Tipperary's inhabitants who appointed an agent to monitor the progress of their petition against Piers Butler.[110] All MPs for port towns, including the speaker, were

104 Smith, *Stuart*, p. 26.
105 Hayden, *France*, pp 129–30, 174–218.
106 NLI, MS 643, fos. 63v–4r.
107 Lennon, *Lords of Dublin*, p. 46; H.F. Berry (ed.), 'Minute book of the Corporation of Dublin, known as the "Friday book", 1567–1611', *Proc. RIA*, 30C (1913), 477–514. Details of the committee members are included in Lennon, *Lords of Dublin*, pp 229–75; R.K. Hannay and G.P.H. Watson, 'The building of the parliament house', *Book of the Old Edinburgh Club*, 13 (1924), 1–78, at p. 72.
108 Berry (ed.), 'Minute book'; *Commons' Jn. Ire.*, 24 Nov. 1614, 6 May 1615.
109 TCD, MS 672, fos. 235r–8v (see Appendix 2); *Commons' Jn. Ire.*, 17 Nov. 1634, 9 March 1635, 13, 15 April 1635.
110 Blake (ed.), *Blake family records*, pp 41–2; *Commons' Jn. Ire.*, 28 July 1641; Bodl. Lib., Carte MS 64, fo. 463r.

appointed to the committee for the bill limiting the times for loading and landing of merchandise where they could represent their boroughs' interests.[111] Francis Slingsby offered Bandonbridge's Provost 'if there be anything that you would have me to do for the benefit of your corporation. If you give me my instructions, I shall willingly do my best endeavor for your advantage and interest.'[112] On a more personal level, Captain William Parsons, helped by John Coughlan, lobbied freeholders to support his petition over the location of King's County assizes and county town.[113] Limerick's Piers Creagh canvassed for a bill of naturalization for the Clare-based Dutchman James Martin in the summer of 1641; while Creagh as a Catholic had little personal influence, he was able to persuade a fellow MP, lord justice Parsons' son Richard, to promote the issue. Martin might have considered the wealthy, self-confident Limerick merchant a better bet than the O'Brien county members or Ennis' placemen Ralph Leventhorpe or Robert Casey.[114] This ability to use personal connections to represent constituents or others enhanced MPs' local standing.

Despite parliamentary secrecy, local communities were well-informed of proceedings although there is little evidence of the communications mechanisms used in England and Scotland; no formal reports survive for Ireland and the production of parliamentary diaries as a tool for communicating with constituents is unknown. As MacDonald noted, the 'intensification of government' induced Scottish burghs 'collectively and individually, [to seek] protective legislation' and the Convention of Royal Burghs provided a forum for collaboration.[115] The same increasing intrusion of the crown at local level was at work in Ireland, with added ethnic and religious dimensions and local communities wary of this trend expected their representatives to defend their independence and interests: 'Over a wide range of constituencies then, two-way communication took place with their representatives and, predictably, this communication became far more urgent from 1640.'[116] Thomas More as chancellor on the eve of a prorogation said, 'Now, you of the Common House may report in your countries what you have seen and heard' and Rothe wrote for the Catholic MPs in 1614–15,

> we are at our return hence to be accountant to the counties and corporations whose voice and suffrage we were entrusted withal. Wherein, when a true calculation were to be made of what we received in charge, and what we have done, if we should not unfold the [com]plaints … we should but fall from ourselves and frustrate the long conceived hopes of friends for posterity.[117]

111 *Commons' Jn. Ire.*, 9 April 1635.
112 Bennett, *Bandon*, p. 98.
113 Birr Castle, MS A/1/19; RIA, MS 14/C/2, pp 183–5; McGrath, 'Bio. dict.', i, pp 115–16.
114 RIA, MS 14/C/2, pp 183–5; McGrath, 'Bio. dict.', i, pp 116–17.
115 MacDonald, '"Tedious to rehers?"'.
116 Hirst, *Representative of the people?*, pp 178–81.
117 Hawkyard, *Commons*, p. 249; HMC, *Franciscan manuscripts*, pp 67–8.

Resident MPs who returned home after each session could report on their work and receive directions for the following sessions; it is unclear whether placemen took the trouble to communicate with their voters. English knights of the shire wrote to their families and friends at home about parliament, rather than to their county electors although it is likely that their reports were primarily transmitted verbally.[118] Irish knights of the shire presumably communicated through county courts whose justices and jurors were fellow electors, at local assizes and other less formal gatherings. The lines of communication were clearer in towns: aldermen, burgesses and recorders could anticipate queries about parliamentary affairs at town councils, deerhundreds (the quarterly assemblies which decided the town's business) and common councils, and letters to mayors would be read to the inhabitants.[119] Especially under Wentworth, many MPs may have been wary of committing their reports to paper. The fiction of smooth and successful parliaments was maintained in the flowery speech of welcome to Wentworth on his visit to Kilkenny in 1637, which instanced

> the scope of so many wholesome laws and statutes, voted in the last parliament; of so many provisions of state, regulating the disorders of human society, daily issuing from your Solomon-like prescience, in which and by which we, in this your garden of Ireland, smell the gracious flowers of your government.

However, this fulsome tribute has to be seen in the context of invariably flattering reception orations, the climate of fear he engendered and his own self-promoting narrative.[120]

English reports became progressively more focussed on national issues and this was likely to have been the case also in Ireland, especially given the lack of local bills in 1634 and 1640, Wentworth's disinclination to support requests for redress of local problems through parliament and the entirely national nature of the instructions from Munster. However, the torrent of petitions after June 1640 showed the pressing nature of local grievances and involved briefing MPs who were frequently members of the committees considering them and their reporting back, to ensure that replications and queries were answered.[121]

118 For instructions to Scottish MPs, see Kennedy, 'Representing the periphery' and Patrick Little, 'Scottish affairs at Westminster: a letter from the Union parliament of 1654–5', *Scottish Historical Review*, 84:2 (2005), 247–56. For Cupar's representatives' regular reports to the burgh, see MacDonald, '"Tedious to rehers?"'; Baker, '"But private notes"'.

119 McGrath, 'Communities of Clonmel'.

120 *Idem*, 'Recruiter returns'; Charles Vallancey, *Collectanea de rebus Hibernica* (Dublin, 1774), i, pp 413–14.

121 Hirst, *Representative of the people?*, pp 178–81; TCD, MS 672, fos. 235r–8v (see Appendix 2). *Commons' Jn. Ire.*, 15 June 1640, 13 16, 20, 22 Feb. 1641, 4 March 1641, 13 May 1641, 7, 10, 18 June 1641, 1, 15 July 1641; Bodl. Lib., Carte MS 64 fo. 462v.

The closeness of relations depended on MPs' local connections and some were more responsive to their electors than others. Between 1613 and 1640, the number of MPs with local connections decreased significantly, creating a distance between members and the communities they nominally represented, especially during the Irish 'rump' parliament (see chapter eleven). Counties invariably returned residents, except Paul Davies and Darcy in 1641, and towns and cities that returned citizens familiar with their conditions and priorities were better placed to promote their interests, especially lawyers who were more likely to be engaged in the detailed work done in committees. Mullingar's tardy payment of its burgesses' wages and New Ross' inhabitants' appealing the tax assessment apparently raised to pay its MPs' salaries hint at local dissatisfaction with their effectiveness in parliament, but this sanction was not available for unwaged placemen who were immune to financial pressure, although those like Francis Slingsby who lived locally might experience tension from neighbours.[122] Given the fears about anti-Catholic legislation and bills facilitating the plantations of Ormond and Connacht, perhaps the Scottish MP William Thomsone's justification for his own work, that 'to hold off evill is not some tymes the leist service', encapsulates Irish MPs' work in representing their constituencies.[123]

Respect for parliament's role as a representative institution remained high, despite the crown's regarding it as a tool of government, rather than a point of contact or partnership with the Irish political community. The desiderata Sarsfield presented on behalf of the inhabitants of Munster and the lists of grievances devised in 1640 demonstrate the popular understanding that parliament was the forum for presenting grievances agreed locally, as well as individual petitions, for redress.[124] The need for parliament's consent prompted both the crown and opposition to attempt to dominate it, leading to bitter conflict. Yet consent was a double-edged sword for the crown; Poynings' Law left it powerless to compromise, but even when it could not control parliament, it needed MPs' attendance, hence Chichester's reluctance to proceed after the secession. The same issue of parliament's declining authority and prestige was raised as the Long Parliament became increasingly depleted.[125] Tudor and Stuart Irish parliaments were rare because of the crown's inability to control them. In other words, parliaments between 1560 and 1615 fulfilled their representative function by acting in the interests of their community. Chichester's underhand electioneering, while unsuccessful in producing a pliant parliament in 1613, laid the groundwork for Wentworth's dominance of the Commons through returns that did not reflect the

122 BL, Harleian MS 430, pp 2–3, 62 (1637). I am grateful to Aidan Clarke for drawing this reference to my attention. Bríd McGrath, 'A fragment of the minute book of the Corporation of New Ross, 1635', *JRSAI*, 144 (2014–15), 100–12; *idem*, 'Membership', pp 117–23; *idem*, 'Electoral strategy'; *idem*, 'Recruiter returns'.

123 Little, 'Scottish affairs at Westminster'.

124 TCD, MS 672, fos. 235r–8v (see Appendix 2); RIA, MS 24/Q/5.

125 R.N. Kershaw, 'The recruiting of the Long Parliament, 1645–7', *History*, new series, 8:31 (Oct., 1923), 169–79.

nature of the Irish political community, but this paradoxically reinforced its role as a representative institution and a means of resolving collective and individual grievances.[126] However, Wentworth's insistence on painting the opposition as led by Catholics, even though the divisions were not driven by confessional positions, and vindictiveness towards anyone who crossed him or whom he disliked, produced a coalition that worked through parliament to defeat him.

While gentry dominated the House of Commons in England, the Old English and Gaelic exclusion from positions of power, profit and influence left the Irish parliament as the only official forum in which they could represent their communities directly, although the expansion in the size of the Commons designed to guarantee a crown majority reduced their effectiveness, until Wentworth's arbitrary regime concerned many of the New English enough to combine with them to defeat Strafford.[127] The breakdown in representation and consultation and the administration's blocking the redress of grievances by ignoring Charles' instructions and disregarding parliament's decisions, especially in ensuring security of land titles, was a key reason for the rebellion in 1641. It is worth remembering that this was led by three current (Rory Maguire, Phelim O'Neill and Philip Mac Hugh O'Reilly), and one former (Coll MacMahon), Gaelic Irish MPs who discovered that parliamentary representation did not reduce their political isolation.[128] O'Neill's *True demands of the rebells in Ireland* cited the need 'to procure redresse of our manifold grievances and oppressions, wherewith wee have been for a long time together afflicted, and could never yet obtain any remedy of the same, neither by our humble petitions nor otherwise.'[129] The rebellion destroyed any chance of legislation confirming land titles, but parliament retained its importance as the visible sign of the political community and as the body which would have to approve any agreement reached between Ormond and the Confederates. However, as Clarke has shown, the new Protestant elite faced the same problems as the Old English whom they displaced and held the same line on constitutional legislative independence from England.[130]

The changes in representation and the centralizing forces inherent in the Tudors' state-building provide the context for the expansion of parliamentary membership and elections explored in the next chapter on constituencies and elections.

126 McGrath, 'Electoral strategy'.
127 H.G. Koenigsberger, 'Monarchies and parliaments in early modern Europe: *dominium regale* or *dominium politicum et regale*', *Theory and Society*, 5:2 (March, 1978), 191–217.
128 Michael Perceval-Maxwell, 'Ulster 1641 in the context of political developments in the three kingdoms' in Brian Mac Cuarta (ed.), *Ulster 1641: aspects of the rising* (Belfast, 1993), pp 93–107; Micheál Ó Siochrú, 'O'Reilly, Philip MacHugh', *DIB*; *idem*, 'O'Neill, Sir Phelim', *DIB*; Terry Clavin, 'Maguire, Rory', *DIB*.
129 Phelim O'Neill, *The true demands of the rebells in Ireland* (London, 1641), p. 1.
130 Clarke, 'Colonial constitutional attitudes in Ireland'.

CHAPTER FIVE

Summoning parliament, composition, electoral practice and strategy, adjournments, prorogations and dissolutions

THIS CHAPTER DEALS with summoning and dissolving parliament, adjournments, prorogations and dissolutions, parliament's composition, constituencies and their electorates, candidates, the conduct of elections and dealing with electoral abuses.

Summoning and dissolving parliament was the monarch's prerogative; under Poynings' Law, the Irish parliament was summoned by the king's commission (the English parliament had no need for a commission) and ended with a dissolution, again at the monarch's discretion. Parliament could also end by accident, either through the monarch or chief governor's death or because the commission under which it was summoned had lapsed.[1]

A parliamentary session was made up of any number of sitting days and ended by a prorogation. Either house could adjourn itself during sessions and the administration could prorogue parliament, cancelling its sittings until a specified day, if the commission authorized it. Prorogations ended the session, but not the parliament. The two houses generally sat separately, but on important occasions, such as the opening day, presentation of the speaker, prorogations and dissolutions, or when jointly addressed by the chief governor, plenary sessions were held at which peers and members of the Commons attended, generally in the House of Lords but occasionally in the Presence Chamber in Dublin Castle.

Poynings' Law imposed a great deal of preparation and the importance of attention to detail was well-recognized if not always implemented: in 1559 the author of proposals to be passed through parliament reminded the administration 'it was and is deemed the parliament holden before the earl of Sussex was void. Therefor foresee and consider this next parliament be summoned and kept according to the law and the acts penned accordingly.'[2] The 1569 parliament was almost a decade in planning and that of 1613 was in prospect from 1604, although Lord Shrewsbury had anticipated one being held 'shortly' after December 1602, with the detailed preparations taking place from 1610.[3] On 15 August 1628, the

1 This remained the case until the Octennial Act of 1768, 7 George III, c. 3.

2 Proposals for acts to be passed through parliament and other measures to be taken in Ireland, 20 May 1559, in Heffernan (ed.), *'Reform' treatises*, p. 43.

3 Treadwell, 'Irish parliament of 1569–71'; Moody, 'Irish parliament under Elizabeth and James'; Shrewsbury to Ormond, 31 Dec. 1602, HMC, *Ormond*, pp 3–6; Michael Hicks, 'Talbot, Gilbert, seventh earl of Shrewsbury', *Oxford DNB*.

English privy council wrote to Lord Conway that 'the formalities preliminary to calling such a parliament are so long that it could not be called next November.'[4] However, both of Wentworth's parliaments were summoned quickly, despite which they dealt with considerable quantities of business.

Under Poynings' Law, when the lord deputy and council decided that a parliament was required they formally requested the monarch, under the great seal of Ireland, to summon it and transmitted proposed legislation. Having reviewed the request and draft bills, if he accepted the recommendation the monarch issued a commission and returned the transmitted bills he approved, and frequently had amended, under the great seal of England. The monarch had no right directly to propose either a parliament or legislation, but chief governors' appointments often included power to summon parliament, in which case permission was generally a matter of form. Chief governors could announce their intention to call parliament, but were prevented from announcing its summoning or issuing writs for election before receipt of the commission and returned bills; Falkland's breaching these provisions caused the cancellation of the 1628 parliament.[5]

Wentworth listed *in extenso* his reasons for summoning the 1634 parliament, emphasizing the anticipated revenue from subsidies and his determination to make as few concessions as possible to the natives and outlining his intended electoral strategy, but providing no information about his planned legislative agenda.[6] When he needed to summon the 1640 parliament very quickly, he wrote to Radcliffe,

> for the love of God, plie the time, and send us over so much as may give a grounde for issuing the sommons, as soon as possible, for if your Parliament ther begin not by or nere the seconde of Marche, I shall not be back [in London] in time.[7]

The short timescale was underlined by the first transmission containing only 11 bills, three of which were standard for all early modern parliaments (subsidies, general pardon and that parliament should not be determined (ended) by the royal assent to some bills) and one, a private act in favour of the privy councillor Sir Robert Meredith, being sent from Ireland on 20 January, leaving very little time for review and retransmission.[8]

The commission for parliament was directed to a named chief governor and gave him authority to give the royal assent to bills; it might also specify the period for which parliament might sit, include the power of prorogation and other provisions. The 1613 commission provided no time or other constraints and

4 *Cal. S.P. Ire., 1625–32*, pp 378–9.

5 The process is traced in Clarke, 'History of Poynings' Law'.

6 Wentworth to King Charles, with Charles' response, 12 April 1634, in Knowler (ed.), *Letters and dispatches*, i, pp 183–7; McGrath, 'Electoral strategy'.

7 Wentworth to Radcliffe, 10 Dec. 1639, in T.D. Whitaker (ed.), *The life and original correspondence of Sir George Radcliffe* (London, 1810), p. 187.

8 RIA, MS 24/Q/4.

allowed Chichester to prorogue parliament, but the 1634 commission, which also permitted prorogation, specified that parliament would end if two acts, that for subsidies and that parliament should not be determined by the assent to some acts, were not passed within three weeks of its opening. The 1640 commission empowered Wentworth as lord lieutenant, Wandesford as deputy or the lords justices to hold the parliament which should last no longer than nine months and would be determined if the same two acts were not passed within 30 days, but it gave no power to prorogue.[9] Inclusion of power to prorogue in the commission did not affect the king's right to order a prorogation, as the English privy council urged Charles to do in October 1641.[10]

Any change in circumstances required a fresh royal warrant. Both of Wentworth's parliaments received warrants to sit for longer than originally specified and Wandesford's death created a crisis by raising the question of whether parliament could continue.[11] The Irish council agreed that there was

> to be noe determinacon or discontinuance till the 26 January (to which it had been prorogued) notwithstanding the death of the deputy for the Lord Lieutenant might come over in the mean tyme … Poynings Act & the other Lawes are onely for the manner of calling & somoning a parliament & transmitting & retorning of all such bills as are to passe but gives noe [?restraint] concerning the continuance or discontinuance but ye same [illegible] onely to be guided and further directed by the King.

The Commons' journals for 26 January do not record any debate about the legality of its continued sitting but the Lords asked the judges for advice; they were evenly split on the subject and recourse was had to the parliament rolls for precedents.[12] The 4 January commission to enable the new lords justices William Parsons and John Borlase (*plate 10*) to continue parliament did not arrive in Dublin until 6 February and they were sworn on 10 February.[13] Doubts persisted and Charles issued a letter reassuring parliament that it had not been ended and offered that 'our justices and councel there, do forthwith cause a short bill to be transmitted unto us, to supply the defects' and to summon a fresh parliament if the houses

9 Bodl. Lib., Bankes MS 55/65, 27 Jan. 1640, provided that the parliament should sit for nine months only. In the event it sat for eight years.

10 The English privy council to King Charles, 12 Oct. 1641, *Cal. S.P. Ire., 1633–47*, p. 341.

11 The commissions are printed in the 1613 and 1640 Commons' journals and the 1634 Lords' journals; Knowler (ed.), *Letters and dispatches*, ii, p. 394; Charles to Bankes, 27 Feb. 1635, Bodl. Lib., Bankes MS 10/6, authorizing an additional month for that parliament; Warrant to Bankes from Charles, 18 April 1635, Bodl. Lib., Bankes MS 57/8, that the Irish parliament should sit for longer than the original commission specified, and be adjourned rather than dissolved; Charles' warrant to Bankes, 11 Sept. 1640, Bodl. Lib., Bankes MS 10/4, in which the time period is left blank.

12 ARL, MS Richard Bolton's Case Notes, fos. 22ff, undated; Empey (ed.), 'Diary of Sir James Ware', entry for 26 Jan. 1641; *LJI*, 26 Jan. 1641.

13 Terry Clavin, 'Parsons, Sir Williams', *DIB*; Robert Armstrong, 'Borlase, Sir John', *DIB*.

requested it, although all of these suggestions contravened Charles' powers to propose either a parliament or legislation and the administration would certainly not have welcomed fresh elections.[14]

Simple clerical errors in commissions could present difficulties. A mistake in the regnal year in the warrant for the lords justices in April 1643 was circumvented by an act of state, but the commission was directed to the previous justices and the council was worried that parliament would end if a new commission authorizing the lord lieutenant to hold it did not arrive before its next sitting on 13 November. The justices wrote repeatedly to the English privy council to correct this but the issue was only resolved after the desperate administration sent a draft commission to the English council: 'They had no notice taken of it in the answers to their former letters and the neglect of it would be irrecoverable damage to the king and his posterity' as they had no power of prorogation and parliament would have been dissolved. Summoning a new parliament would have created untold political and constitutional difficulties at that point – more Catholics would surely have been elected, quite possibly as a majority – so the Irish administration was desperate to avoid parliament's accidental determination. The corrected commission arrived the day before parliament was to meet, when it sat for a single day, being prorogued until 18 December on Charles' order, despite the Commons' requesting a longer sitting.[15]

ADJOURNMENTS, PROROGATIONS AND DISSOLUTIONS

Adjournments were temporary suspensions of sittings of the house, agreed by the members. Houses could adjourn either to a named day and time or without specifying the date of the next sitting. Prorogations could be short suspensions or last many months. Prorogation was effected by an announcement delivered personally by the lord deputy or lords justices in a joint meeting of both houses in the Lords if parliament was sitting, or by proclamation during recesses. When MPs delayed appearing in the upper house for a prorogation, the peers questioned whether their presence was necessary and threatened to complete the ceremony without them; the Commons appeared promptly.[16] Plenary sessions for prorogations were often also occasions for giving royal assent to bills passed during the session and for the Commons to report on its work and propose additional legislation or present grievances.[17] The speaker remained in office between sessions

14 Warrant from Charles to Bankes for a commission for Parsons and Borlase to hold a parliament in succession to Wentworth and Wandesford, 30 Dec. 1640, Bodl. Lib., Bankes MS 55/113. Letter printed in *Commons' Jn. Ire.*, 22 May 1641.

15 Lords Justice and Council to Secretary Nicholas, 11 May 1643, Bodl. Lib., Carte MS 68, fo. 489v; same to same, 11 July 1643, ibid., fo. 496; same to same, 28 Sept. 1643, ibid., fo. 501v; same to same, 18 Nov. 1643, ibid., fo. 502r.

16 *LJI*, 13 Nov. 1643.

17 E.g., *Commons' Jn. Ire.*, 16 May 1615; *LJI*, 2 Aug. 1634. The content of Catlin's 'short and pity oration' was not recorded. Ibid., 15 Dec. 1634.

and could consult with any MPs he could find if necessary and committees could also continue to meet if the house so decided.[18]

The administration might prorogue parliament for a number of reasons, including displeasure at its actions (these were generally very short suspensions), when there was no business for the house (e.g., if bills had not been transmitted back from England) or if it considered sufficient work had been completed for that session. Sidney issued a prorogation to 'hold the parliament to ransom' and in 1585–6 Perrot repeatedly prorogued parliament after a vote went against him, over suspending Poynings' Law, when bills had not arrived back from England and because Drogheda was unable to accommodate the parliament.[19] Chichester suspended parliament when its opening session resulted in uproar and successive prorogations were issued until 15 July, 5 October, 10 November 1613, 3 May 1614, 4 July and 11 October 1614, when parliament finally met. It then convened until 29 November, when it was initially prorogued to 31 January 1615 and then 18 April.[20] As Cork had anticipated, Wentworth prorogued the 1634 parliament so that it would not sit during the harvests and local assizes.[21]

Parliament could request a prorogation or continued sittings or postponing implementing a warrant for prorogation, but the final decision was always the crown's to make. On 18 November 1614 Everard 'moved, that my lord deputy might be sought unto for a prorogation, and, in the mean time, that the royal assent may be given to the acts or bills already passed … by both the houses.' When the Commons requested that parliament be not prorogued on 1 March 1641, the lords justices agreed to suspend the prorogation till the following Thursday when parliament was prorogued to 11 May 1641. Similar requests were made on 24 May 1641 and in November 1641. The lawyer Thomas Bourke asserted that the lords justices' proclamation in October 1641 proroguing the next session for a week after its intended meeting, was illegal and the lords justices permitted it to sit for two days.[22] In April

18 E.g., *Commons' Jn. Ire.*, 29 Nov. 1614, committee for fees, and 17 June 1640 the committee of grievances to sit between sessions.

19 Treadwell, 'Irish parliament of 1569–71'; *idem*, 'Sir John Perrott'; Routledge, 'Journal'; Falkiner, *Essays*, pp 218–19.

20 Farmer's 'Chronicle' in Lodge, *Desiderata Curiosa*, i, pp 155ff; Chichester to the English privy council, 6 June 1613, same to same, 30 June 1613, 14 Sept. 1613, in Edwards (ed.), 'Chichester', nos 60, 67, 77; Treadwell, 'House of Lords'. Medhop gives the dates of the sessions and the prorogations in NLI, MS 836, p. 1.

21 Mark Empey (ed.), *Early Stuart Irish warrants, 1623–1639: the Falkland and Wentworth administrations* (Dublin, 2015), p. 198; Wentworth's prorogation, 2 Aug. 1634, Bodl. Lib., Carte MS 30, fo. 197r; Wentworth to Charles, with Charles' response, 12 April 1634, in Knowler (ed.), *Letters and dispatches*, i, pp 183–7; Cork to Barrymore, 6 June 1634, Chatsworth House, Cork Papers, Misc. boxes, Box 3, p. 38.

22 Proclamation for 'prorogation of the Parliament. Parsons, John Borlase. Not to appear on 9th. or 16th. of Nov., at the Castle of Dublin, &c. Nevertheless we command them that they personally appear on 24th. next, at H. M. Castle of Dublin, to consult such matters in said Parliament of the Common Councill of the realm, &c. 1641. W. Thyrry, deputy sheriff, County Cork. Proclaimed 10 Nov. 1641, by the Sheriff's direction' in Caulfield (ed.), *Youghal*, p. 214; *Commons' Jn. Ire.*, 16 Nov. 1641.

1643, the Lords requested that Charles' commission for prorogation to 13 November be suspended to allow them to debate a petition from army officers.[23]

When George Radcliffe faced opposition to raising the money originally granted in the subsidies and to the plantation of Connacht, he consulted Wentworth in England:

> I am altogether of opinion to prorogue the parliament if I could gett the Connaught act passed (thoe mee thinckes they doe not nowe much like that lawe) or without it, rather then to keepe them too longe together, onely yor Lordships resolution what wee shall doe concerning the subsidies accept their offer or protest against their order, and what course then to be taken.

Strafford arranged the prorogation from London.[24]

Dissolution was effected by a commission from the crown. When parliament reassembled on 24 October 1615, MPs were summoned to the Lords, where the Commons' journals noted

> certain select commissioners were authorized by commission under the great seal of this realm to dissolve the same, who accordingly this day assembled themselves in the higher house of parliament, and then, and there, by virtue of the same said commission to them directed, finally dissolved the same.

There was no formal dissolution of the 1640 parliament – on 15 June 1648 the Commons adjourned to 27 March 1649 – but it would have been determined by Charles I's execution on 30 January 1649.

Following receipt of the commission, the chief governor of the day issued a warrant to the chancellor to send out writs of summons to sheriffs; Adam Loftus' reinstatement as lord chancellor on 1 August 1628 may have been accelerated to have him in place before the projected parliament.[25] The *Modus* specified that writs were to be sent out 40 days before parliament was to meet.[26] Chichester noted:

> I am glade that his majestie is pleased to putt [parliament] off untyll Februarie, and thoe ther be but 40 dayes for the sommons I wysh that all men might knowe that a parlyament is intended presently, that such as it concearnes maye provide themselves accordingly, who otherwise wyll excuse thir defects for want of tyme.[27]

23 Bolton to Secretary Nicholas, 22 April 1643, Bodl. Lib., Carte MS 5, fos. 111r–12v.

24 Borlase, *History*, p. 9; Empey (ed.), 'Diary of Sir James Ware', entry for 5 March 1641; Radcliffe to Wentworth, 28 Oct. 1640, FSL, MS X.c.101(2); Wentworth to Radcliffe, 6 Nov. 1640, FSL, MS X.c.101(3). Charles' Commission of 4 Jan. 1641 gave the justices authority to continue, prorogue or determine the parliament, as they thought fit and they prorogued it on 5 March.

25 King Charles to Falkland, 1 Aug. 1628, Yale University, Beinecke Library, Osborn MS Folder 3065.

26 Hakewill, *Modus*, p. 2; Smith, *Commonwealth*, p. 76; Martin, 'The coming of parliament'.

27 Dopping, *Modus*, p. 1; Hakewill, *Modus*, p. 2; Chichester to Davies, 4 Aug. 1612, HL, HP, MS Box 3 (46).

This timescale was in sharp contrast to the French Estates General, which in 1614 took more than four months between summoning and meeting, although much of this time was occupied in consultations about the Cahiers de Doléance documenting grievances to be presented to the king.[28] However, no English Tudor or early modern Irish parliament actually met within 40 days and in 1634 and 1640 election writs were illegally issued before the commissions were sent from London.[29]

Table 5.1. Timescale for summoning parliament, 1613–40

Year	*Commission*	*Writ*	*Elections*	*Meeting*	*Timescale*
1613	6 March	Unknown[30]	2 April–25 May	18 May	73 days
1628	No commission	22 Sept.[31]	30 Sept.–10 Oct.[32]	3 Nov.	42 days
1634	23 May	14 May	10 June–? July	14 July	62 days
1640	29 Jan.	2 Feb.	6 Feb.–13 March	16 March	43 days

COMPOSITION OF PARLIAMENT

The Irish parliament consisted of the monarch, represented by the chief governor, spiritual and temporal peers and the Commons. The lower house comprised four types of constituencies: counties, cities and towns, manor and university seats. University seats were one of James' innovations, starting with Cambridge and Oxford in 1604 and Trinity College Dublin in 1613. The only certain manor borough in Ireland at this time was Mullingar, although Downpatrick may also have been one.[33] Each Irish seat returned two members, as did all English constituencies, except London which had four and a small number of single-seat constituencies; all Welsh constituencies, including groups of boroughs, elected single MPs.[34] The Catholic opposition in 1613 instanced the Welsh situation, arguing that the discrepancy between newly incorporated and old-established boroughs would be more equitably managed with a single MP for groups of boroughs in newly planted counties; this solution was unlikely to be accepted by

28 Hayden, *France*, pp 74ff.

29 McGrath, 'Irish elections of 1640–1641'. Wentworth sent the Commission and transmitted acts on 17 Feb. 1640, but the first election was held on 6 Feb. Wentworth to Radcliffe, 17 Feb. 1640, in Whitaker (ed.), *Life and original correspondence*, p. 195. Hawkyard notes that summoning Tudor parliaments invariably took longer than 40 days. Hawkyard, *Commons*, p. 9; Neale, *House*, p. 417.

30 Dates are not included on the copies of writs included in the preliminaries to the printed editions.

31 H.J. Monck Mason, *The life of William Bedell, D.D., lord bishop of Kilmore* (London, 1843), p. 156.

32 Details of known elections in Clonmel, Coleraine, Dublin City, Limerick, Trinity College and Youghal are given in McGrath, 'Electoral strategy'.

33 Marsh's Library, MS Z3.1.1, nos 2–3. The seneschal of Downpatrick issued a token in 1664. See https://www.britishmuseum.org/collection/object/C_1933-0413-345, [accessed 4 Jan. 2021].

34 Calais, which was represented between 1536 and 1558, also had two MPs.

an administration whose impetus in creating boroughs at that time was to achieve a Protestant majority.[35]

Irish county seats were represented by knights of the shire, cities by citizens, and boroughs, manors and universities by burgesses. Differences between constituency types may once have been significant but by this time were confined to their electorates, members' wages and the fees each category paid parliamentary officials. The number and extent of both houses was determined by the crown, which could at will grant peerages, and, since 1569, create and change shires' number and boundaries.[36] However, as has been demonstrated in chapter one, while the crown could issue charters to cities, towns, manors and universities, no Irish charter before 1610 included parliamentary representation and James' creation of new parliamentary boroughs after that date was a dubious constitutional innovation.

The English upper house in 1614 comprised 81 temporal and 26 spiritual peers, reflecting not merely that country's greater size and population, but also its different social structure; however, like the Irish peerage, it grew rapidly thereafter, due to the number of nobles created by James and Charles.[37] The 1603 English and Welsh Commons comprised 90 knights of the shire and 372 burgesses and while the county membership remained the same, the number of burgesses had grown to 417 by 1640.[38] The early modern Scottish Estates grew rapidly, first with the inclusion of lairds from 1560, from some 60–70 in 1585, to over 170 in 1617.[39] The 1639 Scottish Estates expelled prelates, followed three years later by the English and Welsh parliament, but this did not happen in Ireland.

The Irish parliament's membership grew steadily through the sixteenth and early seventeenth centuries and the 1613 parliament was larger than all earlier ones, thanks to the expansion of the Commons. The 1560 and 1585 upper houses contained 43 and 52 members respectively, but only 43 in 1613, its 25 peers and 18 prelates reflecting high rates of pluralism in the 32 bishoprics, although some British peers with interests in Ireland were also summoned by writ, and the sons of peers were also allowed to attend, following English practice.[40] To his discomfiture, Chichester was the only new peer ennobled in 1613 but at least 20

35 Lodge, *Desiderata Curiosa*, i, pp 221–2, 228–9.
36 11 Eliz. I, c. 19; Maginn, 'Elizabethan Cavan'.
37 Smith, *Stuart*, p. 20; Mayes, 'Early Stuarts and the Irish peerage'; Ohlmeyer, *Making Ireland English*, pp 27–51.
38 Smith, *Stuart*, p. 22.
39 See Hawkyard, *Commons*, pp 23–42 on the increase in the English and Welsh Commons. Thomas L. Moir, 'The Addled Parliament of 1614' (PhD, University of Dublin, 1950), p. 126; Julian Goodare, 'The admission of lairds to the Scottish parliament', *EHR*, 116:469 (2001), 1103–33; MacDonald, *Burghs and parliament*, pp 16–20. As Scottish officers of state vacated their elected seats on appointment, they are not included in this figure. C.S. Terry, *The Scottish parliament: its constitution and procedure, 1603–1707* (Glasgow, 1905), pp 1–36.
40 Treadwell, 'House of Lords'; Elizabeth Read Foster, *The House of Lords, 1603–1649: structure, procedures and the nature of its business* (Chapel Hill, 1983), pp 13, 15; Moody, 'Irish parliament under Elizabeth and James I'.

peerages were created in 1628 alone, a very small number being promotions from lower ranks and by 1640 there were 99 temporal peers, 30 of whom were English or Scotsmen resident outside Ireland; of the 69 based in Ireland, 33 were Catholic and 39 Protestant.[41]

The Commons grew rapidly, initially by shiring more of the country, but under James many new boroughs were created with charters granting parliamentary representation to add to the older urban seats represented by prescription. Before this time, only towns with functioning councils and portreeves to act as returning officers could hold elections. Chichester's innovation was to create towns from scratch as parliamentary boroughs (see table 5.2).[42]

Table 5.2. Constituencies in the Irish House of Commons, 1560–1641[43]

Year	*Counties*	*Boroughs*	*Total*
1560	20	29	49
1585	27	36	63
1613a	33	84	116
1613b	33	72	105
1634	33	94	128
1640	32	89	121
1641	32	95	127

The Commons that assembled on 18 May 1613 had 232 members representing 33 counties (the 32 present counties and Cross Tipperary), seven cities (Clogher, Cork, Dublin, Limerick, Kilkenny, Londonderry and Waterford – Cashel attained this status in 1637), 75 boroughs, and Trinity College. Eight urban seats (Carrickfergus, Cork, Drogheda, Dublin, Galway, Kilkenny, Limerick and Waterford) had the status of counties. In 1613, Athenry, Carrickfergus, Drogheda, Dundalk, Galway, Kinsale, New Ross, Wexford and Youghal were described in the members' roll as 'villa' rather than borough, acknowledging their relative importance over smaller boroughs.

In addition to Athlone, Cavan, Gowran and Derry, which were incorporated between 1604 and 1610, and Trinity College, 34 new boroughs were created, and warrants were issued also for charters for Mountjoy, Rathmullan and Tulsk, whose incorporations were not proceeded with. Careful consideration was given to which towns to incorporate, including examining their geographical features, antiquity,

41 Jane Ohlmeyer, 'The Irish peers, political power and parliament, 1640–1641' in Brady and Ohlmeyer (eds), *British interventions in early modern Ireland* (Cambridge, 2005), pp 161–85.

42 McGrath, 'Unconstitutional acts'. I am grateful to Stephen Roberts for a very useful discussion on boroughs by prescription.

43 1613a and 1613b refer respectively to the boroughs which returned MPs for the opening of parliament, including those incorporated after the writs of election were issued, and the boroughs which continued to be represented after Oct. 1614. The 1640 figure does not include the disfranchised boroughs which are included in the 1641 figure.

extent and defence, but after 1610 the overriding consideration was whether they would return Protestant MPs.[44] Existing corporations that were considered as potential new parliamentary boroughs included Loughrea and Arklow; the former was under Clanricard's influence and its addition would be seen as a sop to the earl and Catholics in general. Arklow was an Ormond borough and the major Wicklow and Wexford landholder, Laurence Esmond wrote to the earl on Chichester's behalf suggesting that he name new burgesses for a new charter in anticipation of the parliament; the town was not included, presumably because Gowran's recent royal charter had freed its citizens to shake off Ormond's control and he was reluctant to repeat this experience.[45] While Chichester let it be known that 30 boroughs would be created, instead, as he reported to London on 14 April 1613, he had secretly held back charters for Augher, Belfast, Carlow, Charlemont, Clonakilty, Fethard, Lismore and Tallow, which he covertly issued and arranged their returns using blanks immediately before parliament met; the episcopal seat of Clogher returned burgesses despite receiving no charter. This mass incorporation generated enormous public resentment. Robert Jacob recommended to Henry Howard, Lord Northampton, that parliament be postponed for some years to let the clamour subside, even though the summons had been issued.[46] Davies vigorously defended James' right to create all the boroughs in his acceptance speech as speaker, but tellingly did not address his constitutional innovation.[47] In addition, new charters were issued replacing Athy and Wicklow's councils with conformable men who could be relied upon to return Protestants.

James directed English sheriffs to withhold mandates for elections in 1604 from 'any ancient Borough town within their counties, being so utterly ruined and decayed, that there are not sufficient resiants to choose members.'[48] There is no record of a similar direction in Ireland or of towns being disfranchised before 1635, but Irish sheriffs already exercised discretion although, given Tudor deputies disregard of both electoral law and political norms, they may well have been persuaded to do so by direction from Dublin, rather than exercising their own judgment. The historically unestablished nature of urban representation explains repeated complaints that previously represented towns were excluded and Catholic agents' claimed in 1613 that writs had not been sent to some Westmeath and Wexford boroughs, and that returns from some in Meath and Kildare were not

44 R.J. Hunter, 'Towns in the Ulster Plantation', *Studia Hibernica*, 11 (1971), 40–79; TCD, MS 743; TCD, MS 807, fo. 287v; HL, HP, MS 14,987, for lists of towns. McGrath, 'Membership', pp 32ff; Bodl. Lib., Carte MS 62, fos. 149r, 161r, 163r.

45 *Cal. S.P. Ire., 1611–14*, p. 161; Esmond to Ormond, 14 Aug. 1612, HMC, *Ormond*, p. 10; Adrian Empey, *Gowran, Co. Kilkenny: custom and conflict in a baronial town* (Dublin, 2015); Terry Clavin, 'Esmond, Sir Laurence', *DIB*.

46 Jacob to Northampton, undated, but between 6 March 1613 and 25 March 1613, Bodl. Lib., Laud MS Misc. 612, fos. 138r–40r; Chichester to the English privy council, 14 April 1613, claimed to have erected 40 new boroughs, but the charters for the last nine were dated between 15 April and 25 May 1613. See Edwards (ed.), 'Chichester', no. 53; McGrath, 'Membership', pp 216–17.

47 Morley (ed.), *Ireland under Elizabeth and James the First*, pp 391–409.

48 Quoted in Hawkyard, *Commons*, p. 42.

transmitted to Dublin.[49] It also underlines the importance of the roles of the sheriffs and the *custos rotulorum* who managed the county's records and who were both appointed by the crown.[50] The commission for the 1613 parliament reflected this variable attendance, describing those attending as 'omnes et singulos Dominos spirituales et temporales, Milites Comitatuum, Cives Burgenses Civitatum et Burgorum, *ac alios quosque dicti Regni nostri ad Parliamentum nostrum ibidem venire consuetos*' (emphasis added) (all and every Lords spiritual and temporal, knights of shires, citizens and burgesses of cities and boroughs, and others whom the said kingdom of ours is accustomed to come to our Parliament there).

James decided that the eight covertly incorporated boroughs should not be represented in 1613–15 and on 10 November 1614 the Commons agreed that Clogher, Athlone and Gowran should be excluded as James had adjudged them to have no right of representation by prescription or charter; however, they were represented in all future parliaments.[51] Incorporations continued after 1613: Killybegs, Gorey, Jamestown and St Johnstown received charters in 1615, 1619, 1621 and 1627 respectively and Carysfort and Banagher in 1628, in anticipation of, but in Banagher's case, just too late for, the intended parliament. Clogher's charter was finally passed in 1629.[52]

The ancient boroughs that were claimed to be omitted in 1613 have not previously been identified, but tentative suggestions can be made. Chichester's concern that 'divers persons were like to intrude themselves into the House of Commons, which were not returned, either as knights or Burgesses', presumably related to the unforwarded elections from Westmeath and Wexford complained of by the Catholics who also singled out some Meath and Kildare boroughs as having not received mandates for election.[53] Presumably Fore in Westmeath and Bannow, Clonmines and Tagmon in Wexford, all of which had functioning town governments and therefore returning officers, held elections as they did in 1634. The Confederation of Kilkenny followed all parliamentary practices and burgesses for those boroughs appeared in its General Assembly.

The Meath boroughs were presumably Duleek and Ratoath both of which had functioning town councils and were represented in the Restoration Irish parliament without receiving new charters. Duleek was possibly represented under Edward IV, received a new charter in 1613 and was represented in the General Assembly; Ratoath was, like Fore, described by the Report on Municipal Corporations in Ireland which did a thorough investigation of all historical records,

49 Petition of Gormanston, Dunboyne, Christopher Plunkett, James Gough, William Talbot and Edward Fitzharris, agents, 2 July 1613, HMC, *Franciscan manuscripts*, pp 57–8; *Cal. S.P. Ire., 1611–14*, pp 361–4, 438–43; Jackson (ed.), 'Document'; McGrath, 'Sex, lies and rigged returns'.

50 Falkiner, *Essays*, p. 237; Hawkyard, *Commons*, p. 41. He also suggests (p. 10) that sheriffs kept 'precedent books' and this seems likely also for Ireland, although none is known to have survived.

51 Moody, 'Irish parliament under Elizabeth and James I'; Lodge, *Desiderata Curiosa*, i, pp 324–5.

52 *CPRI*, iii, pp 466–7.

53 McCavitt, 'An unspeakable parliamentary fracas'.

as boroughs by prescription.[54] Kildare's borough may have been Donadea, which was close to the earls of Kildare's castle at Kilkea and may have been represented when the eighth and ninth earls were lords deputy. Sidney established his household there as deputy and given the anomaly Hooker described of the numbers of members of the 1569 parliament may well have been represented then also. As Kilkea was not listed as one of the 'townes as were no corporations' in Kildare in 1608, it was probably a manor borough.[55]

The Commission on Municipal Corporations found no charter for Ardee, Clonmines, Swords, Taghmon or Downpatrick; all but the latter had portreeves and functioning town councils, suggesting that it was a manor borough. Downpatrick's uncertain status may have been because no members' names were given on the 1585 list, suggesting that it may not have sent burgesses to that parliament despite receiving a mandate for election.[56] On 17 October 1614, the Commons agreed an order recommended by the Grand Committee 'that no cities or boroughs that have sent citizens or burgesses to the parliament, holden [in 1586] or in any other parliaments holden before that parliament, shall be questioned withal for their power to send citizens and burgesses', however, they did not list these towns and this order was ignored by Wentworth whose *Quo warranto* proceedings left the Court of Exchequer to decide the issue, a situation which would not have been tolerated in England.

In 1620 patents were passed creating manors with parliamentary franchises in Parsonstown (Birr) and Leighlinbridge for Sir Laurence Parsons, with the seneschal as returning officer and the manors' freeholders comprising their electorate. These creations were never pursued, possibly because Parsons, like other New English landlords, was reluctant to create freeholds, but other constituencies may have shared this legal structure.[57]

54 RIA, MS 24/Q/11, unpaginated; Exemplification of an act of Parliament in King Edward the fourth's reign by which it appears that the Town of Duleek in the County of Meath was then a corporation consisting of a portreeve, burgesses & commonalities, *Cal. Carew*, v, p. 32; Martin Weinbaum, *British borough charters, 1307–1660* (Cambridge, 2010), pp lxiv–v, 208–9; Geraldine Tallon (ed.), *Court of Claims: submissions and evidence, 1663* (Dublin, 2006), pp 45, 362; Great Britain, Commissioners on municipal corporations in Ireland, *Report on municipal corporations in Ireland*, Appendix 1 (London, 1835), Ratoath, p. 256, Fore, p. 176; United Kingdom, Parliament, *Accounts and papers related to representation* (s.l., 1832), pp 37, 121, 134, 140, 145.

55 Falkiner, *Essays*, p. 237; Richard Hawkins, 'Carew, Peter', *DIB*; Account of Robert Holdiche, 1556–9, in HMC, *Report on the manuscripts of Lord De L'Isle and Dudley preserved at Penshurst Place, Volume 1* (London, 1925), p. 372. I am grateful to David Edwards for this observation. Also, see chapter one for the size of the 1569 parliament; *Cal. Carew*, v, p. 23. For the difficulty in establishing categories of seats in Tudor England, see Hawkyard, *Commons*, pp 61–4.

56 The commission is printed at the beginning of volume one of the *Commons' Jn. Ire.* Commissioners on municipal corporations in Ireland. *Report on municipal corporations*, pp 6–7, describes the history of each municipal corporation and their known charters, if any. *Cal. Carew*, v, p. 32; Gilbert Library, MS 35; Robinson collection, unpaginated, also records no trace of charters for Ardfert, Bannow, Clogher, Clonmines, Fore, Kildare, Old Leighlin, Swords or Taghmon. McGrath, 'Town and mitre'; Irish Archaeological Society, *Tracts*, ii, p. 134.

57 Transcript of grants of the creation of manors at Parsonstown (Birr) and Leighlin Bridge (not be confused with its near neighbour, Old Leighlin), to Laurence Parsons, Birr Castle, MS A/5/46,

ELECTORATES

Eligibility to vote varied between types of seats. County electorates were laid down in law, older urban electorates depended on historical practice and could be varied, and newer ones were specified in the town's charter; manor boroughs' voters were their freeholders. Like Cambridge and Oxford, Trinity College's electorate was its provost, fellows and scholars, a limited group of Protestant men.

As in England, Irish county electors were the famous 40 shilling freeholders, 'the inhabitants … present at the election … [able] to dispend and have lands and tenements of estate and freehold within the said counties, at least to the yearly value of fortie shillings over and above all charges' and electors should also have been born and reside in the county.[58] Freeholds were leases for an indeterminate period but lease-holding, which was less secure for tenants but much more profitable for landlords, was the usual Irish form of landholding, and there were frequent complaints about the lack of freeholders in early modern Ireland.

Apart from their role as electors, freeholders were important as the pool from which jurors and assessors and collectors of subsidies were chosen; sheriffs maintained records of freeholders in their counties and could question any voter about the value of his freehold and make him swear to this on the bible.[59] The 40*s.* qualification was established in England in 1430 and by the seventeenth century presented a very low bar. Thomas Smith (d. 1577) equated it to £6 in his lifetime, and it would have been worth less in the seventeenth century, so creating 40*s.* freeholds would not have markedly reduced landlords' incomes, but would limit their control and influence over their tenants. The practice, frequently found in England, of landlords creating freeholds shortly before elections, occurred in Limerick and Down (where it was alleged that freeholds were created after the election) in 1613, in Kerry in 1634 and in Down in 1640, and doubtless many other counties.[60] Irish county electorates were frequently smaller than English but larger than Scottish ones; the 40*s.* freehold qualification was introduced there with shire representation in 1587, but the system of landholding meant that as few as 40–60 men were eligible to vote in the counties.[61]

It is impossible to estimate the size of the shires' electorate, as it was determined by the county's size, number of freeholds, the distance voters had to travel to an election and the publicity the sheriff or canvassers gave to the election's

fos. 1r–2r; Rent roll of Birr Castle, 1620s–1630s, Birr Castle, MS A/4, pp 224ff, shows no evidence of the granting of freeholds. *Report on municipal corporations in Ireland*, Appendix 1, Ratoath, p. 256. Manor boroughs continued to be created and the 1689 parliament included Rathcormuck and Doneraile manors. See Marsh's Library, MS Z3.1.1, nos 2–3.

58 *Commons' Jn. Ire.*, i, prelims; McGrath, 'Electoral law in Ireland'; Hirst, *Representative of the people?*; *A word of advertisement to the Godly party in Scotland* (Edinburgh, 1651). For English electoral law, see Hawkyard, *Commons*, pp 21ff. The English act was incorporated in Ireland through 10 Hen. VII, c. 22.

59 *Priviledges and practice of parliaments.*

60 McGrath, 'Electoral law in Ireland before 1641'.

61 Kennedy, 'Representing the periphery'.

time and location, although the county days should have been well-known. The few surviving figures show considerable variations. In 1591, 281 freeholders were listed in Monaghan.[62] Electorates of 232, 52 and 57 were reported for Down, Tyrone and Armagh respectively in 1613, when 314 freeholders, described as the majority, voted for Limerick's Catholic candidates, but the numbers supporting the Protestant Francis Berkeley and Thomas Browne were not given. Despite reportedly having only one freeholder, Leitrim returned two MPs.[63] While no figures are given for the number of voters in the 1613 Cavan election, they were able to gather in separate areas of a court-room that was full of furniture for the county court, suggesting the numbers were not large but a 1629 petition from the 'inhabitants of Cavan' contained 103 signatures, presumably many, if not most, of the freeholders. Coincidentally, a petition claiming to be from 'the greater parte of the freeholders' of King's County in 1641 also had some 103 signatories, suggesting a maximum electorate of roughly 200, although not all may have voted.[64] The thousand men who gathered for public meetings at Crofty and Tara in 1641 were presumably freeholders, possibly most of Meath's electorate.[65]

Ulster planters were required to grant freeholds, but not to the Irish, which should have reduced the number of Catholic electors in those counties; however, plantation agreements were not well observed and as planters were notoriously reluctant to create freeholds, many British settlers were also excluded from voting. Thomond refused to grant freeholders to New English settlers on his estates, as did Parsons in King's County. The 1635 act for Ulster bishops that prevented them granting freeholds also reduced their electoral patronage. As crown policy was to reduce the number of small freeholds, it is likely that the size of the electorate declined in the early seventeenth century despite inflation reducing the qualification.[66]

Given the lack of new freeholds, the electorate was in many counties largely composed of native Old English and Gaelic, even in planted areas, and Chichester

62 *Inq. cancel. Hib. repert.*, ii, Ultonia, pp xxi–xxxi.

63 *Cal. S.P. Ire., 1611–14*, pp 361–4, 438–43; *Cal. Carew*, v, p. 168; 'Clanricard may nominate who he pleases, for there is no freeholder in [Leitrim] but young O'Rork'.

64 McGrath, 'Unconstitutional acts'; Brendan Scott, 'Petition of the inhabitants of Cavan to the Lord Deputy and council, 8 July 1629', *IHS*, 43:163 (2019), 111–25; Birr Castle, MS A/1/19, 30 Aug. 1641.

65 McGrath, 'Mount Taragh's triumph'.

66 Smith, *Commonwealth*, pp 59–60; Hawkyard, *Commons*, p. 46; Martin Breen, 'The 1626 rental of Thomond property', *North Munster Antiquarian Journal*, 54 (2014), 1–25; Rent-roll of Birr Castle, 1620s–1630s, Birr Castle, MS A/4, pp 224ff; Victor Treadwell (ed.), *The Irish commission of 1622: an investigation of the Irish administration, 1615–1622 and its consequences, 1623–1624* (Dublin, 2006), pp 607–12; Michael MacCarthy-Morrogh, *The Munster plantation: English settlers in southern Ireland, 1583–1641* (Oxford, 1986), pp 181ff; *Cal. S.P. Ire., 1611–14*, pp 222–3; Aidan Clarke, 'The Irish economy, 1600–60' in Moody, et al. (eds), *New history of Ireland*, iii, pp 168–86, at p. 169. For a description of different classes in Irish society and their obligations, see Clodagh Tait, 'Society, 1550–1700' in Jane Ohlmeyer (ed.), *The Cambridge history of Ireland*: Vol. 2: *Early modern Ireland, 1550–1730* (Cambridge, 2018), pp 273–98; 10 Car. I, sess. 3, c. 5; *Cal. S.P. Ire., 1633–47*, p. 322.

noted that there were few Protestant freeholders of sufficient social status to serve as sheriffs. All the freeholders in Kilfenora diocese in 1601 were of Gaelic origin; 15 freeholders on a jury at Tralee in 1622, an area controlled by the New English Denny family, included six with Old English names, nine with Gaelic names and no New English, while the jurors in Ballinrobe in 1623 were overwhelmingly of Gaelic origin. Tipperary's Grand Jury in 1641 comprised eight old Irish, six Old English and a single New Englishman.[67]

Old Irish towns' and cities' electorates had no legislative basis and the limited evidence suggests that they depended on tradition and that different practices operated and evolved over the early modern period. Some allowed the council and freemen to vote, others also the 'commonalty' – inhabitants who were not freemen. Older Irish towns' electorate could be extensive and much larger than English boroughs and Scottish burghs where town councils frequently chose their MPs without reference to the town's inhabitants, but, apart from Coleraine and Londonderry in 1613, this only happened for Irish towns incorporated after 1611, the first to base their privilege on charters, not prescription. The complicated electoral systems employed by some English boroughs were unknown in Ireland. London's aldermen selected two of their number and nominated twelve others to be chosen by a mere 200 members of its common council. Scottish burgh electorates were frequently as few as 20 councillors.[68] The nature of the eight county boroughs' electorates was unclear but presumably included their freemen and any 40*s*. freeholders within their franchises.

The franchise's unestablished nature allowed the council and mayor to decide on or change its extent, which explains Chichester's excluding Catholic magistrates, especially before the 1613 election. Catholic aldermen attempted to restrict the 1613 Dublin city election to freemen, who were overwhelmingly recusants, but its corrupt mayor Sir James Carroll 'marvelling att their great insolencie, and on the Contrary affirming that every Cittizen though they were not a ffreeman had as much authority to ioyne in that election as any other' and held the election at 4 a.m. in the tholsel without giving Catholics notice of the poll.[69] The tholsel was relatively commodious, as Darcy suggested that the Commons could meet there in early 1642, but would not have accommodated the 2,400 electors Ware claimed voted in the city's election in 1628 on Oxmantown Green.[70]

67 Luke McInerney, 'A list of freeholders in Kilfenora diocese in 1601', *Eolas: The Journal of the American Society of Irish Medieval Studies*, 11 (2018), 60–103; Cusack, *History of the kingdom of Kerry*, pp 243–4; John Ainsworth, 'Survey of documents in private keeping: third series', *Anal. Hib.*, 25 (1967), 1–273, at p. 174; Bodl. Lib., Carte MS 56, fo. 80r.

68 Hawkyard, *Commons*, pp 49–52, 57–61; Smith, *Stuart*, p. 245; Kennedy, 'Representing the periphery'.

69 Stephen Carroll, 'The Dublin parliamentary elections, 1613' in William Sheehan and Maura Cronin (eds), *Riotous assemblies: rebels, riots and revolts in Ireland* (Cork, 2011), pp 50–63; McGrath, 'Unmasking "E.S"'.

70 *Commons' Jn. Ire.*, 17 Nov. 1641; Empey (ed.), 'Diary of Sir James Ware'.

1 Francis Annesley, MP for Lismore and Armagh County, 1613, later Baron Mountnorris, 2nd Viscount Valentia. Unknown artist, undated. Image courtesy of the Ulster Museum.

2 Richard Bolton, MP for Dublin City, 1613. Follower of Marcus Gheeraerts, 1620.
Image reproduced with the kind permission of Titian Fine Art. See Appendix 3.

3 Sir James Hamilton, MP for Down County, 1613, later 1st Viscount Claneboye. Unknown artist, 1620. Image courtesy of the National Trust.

4 Adam Loftus, MP for King's County, 1613, later lord chancellor and 1st Viscount Loftus of Ely. Unknown artist, 1619. Image courtesy of the National Gallery of Ireland, NGI.410. See Appendix 3.

5 Nicholas Loftus, MP for Fethard (Wexford), 1613, 1634, Wexford County, 1640. Unknown artist, 1648. Private Collection.

6 Sir Arthur Savage, MP for Ballyshannon, 1613, privy councillor. Unknown artist, after 1616. Image courtesy of Birr Trustee Co. Ltd.

7 Oliver St John, MP for Roscommon County, 1613. Later lord deputy and 1st Viscount Grandison. Cornelius Johnson, 1622. Image reproduced by kind permission of Lydiard House Museum, Swindon.

8 James Barry, MP for Lismore, 1634. Later 1st Baron Barry of Santry. Unknown artist, undated. Image reproduced by kind permission of the Honorable Society of King's Inns. See Appendix 3.

9 Patrick Darcy, MP for Navan, 1634, Tyrone, 1641. Photograph of lost portrait by an unknown artist, 1645. Image courtesy of Adrian Lead. See Appendix 3.

10 John Borlase, MP for Enniskillen, 1634, Belturbet, 1640, lord justice, 1641. Michiel Janszen van Miereveldt, 1625. © National Portrait Gallery, London.

11 John Bysse, MP for Charlemont, 1634, Dublin City, 1640. Thomas Pooley, after 1660. Image courtesy of Viscount Molesworth. See Appendix 3.

12 John Clotworthy, MP for County Antrim, 1634. Later 1st Viscount Massereene.
Unknown artist, after 1648. © National Portrait Gallery, London.

13 Charles Coote sr, MP for Jamestown, 1634, Queen's County, 1640. Privy councillor. Cornelius Johnson, undated. Reproduced with the kind permission of Ballyfin Demesne.

14 Charles Coote jr, MP for Leitrim, 1634, 1640. William Dobson, before 1646. Reproduced with the kind permission of Ballyfin Demesne.

15 James Donnellan, MP for Trinity College Dublin, 1628, 1634. Unknown artist, after 1660. Image courtesy of the Public Record Office of Northern Ireland. See Appendix 3.

16 Donough MacCarthy, MP for Cork County, 1634, 1640, later 2nd Lord Muskerry, 1st earl of Clancarty. Unknown artist, probably after 1660. Image courtesy of the Hunt Museum, Limerick.

17 Roger O'Shaughnessy, MP for Galway County, 1634. Unknown artist, undated. Portrait formerly in the collection at Kilkenny Castle. Reproduced from R.S. Rait, *The story of an Irish property* (Oxford, 1908).

18 Sir James Ware jr, MP for Johnstown, 1634, 1640. Auditor general and scholar. Image from J. Thane, *British autograph.* (London, 1819), vol. 2.

19 Sir William St Leger, MP for Cork County, 1634, 1640. President of Munster. Copy of portrait by an unknown artist, possibly *c.*1628. Image reproduced by kind permission of the Durdin Robertson family, Huntington Castle, Co. Carlow.

20 Maurice Williams, MP for Askeaton, 1634, 1640. Wentworth's physician. Portrait by Francis Cleyn, *c.*1643, with Williams's pupil, John Bankes, eldest son of Sir John Bankes (plate 27). Image reproduced by kind permission of the National Trust.

21 Richard Fanshawe, MP for Ballinakill, 1641. Poet and diplomat. William Dobson, 1644.
Image courtesy of Valence House Museum, London Borough of Barking and Dagenham.

22 Edward Lake, MP for Cavan, 1640. Lawyer and advocate general. Image from J. Thane, *British autography* (London, 1819), vol. 2. See Appendix 3.

23 Phelim O'Neill, MP for Dungannon, 1641. Leader of the 1641 rebellion. Nineteenth-century line engraving after unknown artist. © National Portrait Gallery, London.

24 Audley Mervyn, MP for Tyrone, 1640. Later speaker of the 1661 parliament and prime serjeant. Detail of Thomas Carlton's portrait, undated. Private collection. Photograph © Robert D. Marshall.

25 George Rawdon, MP for Belfast, 1640 and agent of Edward Conway, 2nd Viscount Conway and Killultagh. Robert White, line engraving, *c.*1667. © National Portrait Gallery, London.

26 Christopher Wandesford, MP for Kildare, 1640, master of the rolls, lord deputy, 1639–40. Portrait attributed to George Perfect Harding, after unknown artist, watercolour, early nineteenth century, based on a work of after 1630. © National Portrait Gallery, London.

27 Sir John Bankes, English attorney general who checked and amended Irish bills and issued commissions for the Irish parliament. Possibly after Gilbert Jackson, based on a 1641 portrait. © National Portrait Gallery, London.

It was claimed that only ten of Trim's councillors voted in a covert election in 1613, but the usual meeting place beside the river would have accommodated many more voters than the tholsel, indicating a sizeable electorate. Cavan's electorate included all its adult male inhabitants, as objections to Molmore O'Reilly were based on his not residing in the town.[71] If, as seems likely, townsmen entitled to elect mayors also had votes in parliamentary elections, some urban electorates were large: Carrickfergus' commons elected its mayor and 244 men were entitled to vote for Limerick's mayor in 1632, clearly still only a fraction of the number of freemen. In 1624, Galway's changing its rules to enable freemen, rather than just councillors, to elect its mayor may have changed its parliamentary franchise also.[72] Youghal's MPs were elected by between 120 and 133 votes but as the town's mayor and aldermen had several votes each the actual number of voters was fewer; while other towns also had citizens with multiple votes (e.g., Limerick), these are still much larger electorates than those of more populous English towns. Lifford's request for privileges for its charter in 1612 included that the warden (equivalent of portreeve) should have a 'double vote'.[73] Moreover, it was possible for individuals to have votes in more than one constituency; many men had freeholds in more than one county and townsmen, especially merchants, often held lands in their own or neighbouring counties or were freemen in more than one town to facilitate their commercial activities.[74] Galway's merchants had built up substantial land holdings in Clare, Galway, Mayo and Sligo, entitling them to vote in those county polls, as well as in their city. Dublin's mayor, who had lands in Kilmainham, voted in the 1613 Dublin county election.[75] The electorate was also changing thanks to the influx of English, Welsh and Scottish immigrants who were granted freeholds or freedom of towns. Although it is hard to estimate their numbers, Protestant candidates in Youghal's parliamentary elections made little headway in this period.

Manor boroughs' freeholders, apparently not subject to the 40*s*. qualification, were likely to be very few in number and subject to strong pressure from the lord of the manor either directly or through his seneschal. Trinity College's electorate was the provost, fellows and scholars, a small but fluctuating group, larger than the new boroughs, but much less than the old-established towns.

71 *Cal. S.P. Ire., 1611–14*, pp 363–4, 443.

72 NLI, MS 41,677/3. The 1641 list includes 371 names, but it is unreliable as there were later amendments and additions. See NLI, MS 41,677/7; *Cal. S.P. Ire., 1611–14*, p. 363. An exception was made in Feb. 1622, when councillors voted to replace Carrickfergus' recently deceased mayor 'without the voice of the commons'. PRONI, D 162|1, p. 83; James Hardiman, *History of the town and county of Galway* (Dublin, 1820), p. 21; Bríd McGrath, 'Managing the Windsor of Ireland: Galway town council, 1603–1653', *The Journal of the Galway Archaeological and Historical Society*, 69 (2017), 61–81.

73 McGrath, 'Electoral law in Ireland before 1641'; Hawkyard, *Commons*, pp 50–2. Bodl. Lib., Carte MS 62, fos. 242–3.

74 E.g., McGrath, 'Communities of Clonmel'; *idem*, 'Fraternities and mysteries: early-modern provincial Irish guilds and trade companies', *JRSAI*, 150 (2020), 225–45. For the admission of a Dingle merchant to Tralee in 1624, see ARL, MS Richard Bolton's case notes, fo. 56r.

75 See Farmer's 'Chronicle' in Lodge, *Desiderata Curiosa*, i, pp 155ff; Ó Bric, 'Galway townsmen'; McGrath, 'Managing the Windsor'.

The question of women's franchise was raised in England and Massachusetts, but is not recorded in Ireland and neither of the lists of Limerick's citizens entitled to vote for the city's mayor contains a single woman despite their having freedom of towns and being taxpayers and members of guilds.[76] A number of English boroughs were held by Tudor queens as part of their jointures and it was not unknown for noble English women to canvass in elections and at least one indenture of return was made by an Englishwoman.[77] A small number of women might have been able to exert some influence over elections; had Donadea been represented between 1613 and 1640, the fiercely Catholic and assertive dowager countess of Kildare, whose jointure included the manor, would undoubtedly have attempted to influence its returns.[78]

Candidates were required to be of Irish or English birth, or have acquired denization and to be resident in their constituencies. Men born abroad, including to English or Irish parents, needed to regularize their position by private acts of parliament in either England or Ireland to be able to stand for election. This provision affected the MPs John Ogle, William St Leger Jr (*plate 19*), Theodore Schout and Peter Wybrants.[79] Before 10 Car. I, c. 4, Scots born before 1603 were also obliged to become denizens, as Hugh Montgomery, Robert and William Stewart and others did. Returning officers, judges, clergy and Irish peers were excluded from candidacy, although a number of returning officers returned themselves in 1569, 1613 and 1634. Provost William Temple was elected for Trinity College in 1613 despite being its returning officer but his successor William Bedell declined the position.[80] Judges were returned in 1613 but not thereafter. Attorneys general were debarred from membership of the English Commons from 1614 and the same practice operated in Ireland after 1615.[81] Men convicted of treason could not be MPs.[82] There was no explicit age qualification and minors were returned;

76 NLI, MS 41,477/3, 7; Bríd McGrath, 'Reconstructing an early-modern Irish urban economic community: Clonmel's cess list of 1642', *IESH*, 44:1 (2017), 122–42; *idem*, 'Fraternities and mysteries'.
77 Hawkyard, *Commons*, pp 47, 66–7, 73.
78 McGrath, 'Electoral law in Ireland before 1641'; Clarke and McGrath (eds), *Letterbook*, pp 72–3; Rolf Loeber and Terry Clavin, 'FitzGerald, Elizabeth', *DIB*.
79 Chichester raised this point in proposing a suspension of Poynings' Law in 1612, despite which seven Scots were returned in 1613. Chichester to the English privy council, 30 Dec. 1612, in Edwards (ed.), 'Chichester', no. 39. For Scottish members of the Irish parliament, see McGrath, 'Membership', pp 124–35; *idem*, 'Bio. dict.', ii, pp 67–76; Shaw (ed.), *Letters of denization*, passim, but especially pp 319ff for Irish denizations and 49ff for private Irish acts of naturalization. For Wybrants, see McGrath, 'Recruiter returns'.
80 TCD, MS Particular Book, fo. 100r. Thomas Bramston was displaced for Belfast in 1634 for returning himself. Terry Clavin, 'Temple, Sir William', *DIB*.
81 The question of the attorney general's eligibility rose in England in 1606–7, but was not resolved until 1614. Keeler, 'Committee for privileges'. Robert Heath and Edward Herbert had to resign their memberships when appointed attorney general. Alan Davidson and Ben Coates, 'Heath, Robert', and Simon Healy, 'Herbert, Edward' in Thrush and Ferris (eds), *History of parliament*.
82 Hooker's diary in Falkiner, *Essays*; McGrath, 'Membership', p. 30; 18 Edw. IV, c. 5; TNA, SP 60/6, fo. 4; *Commons' Jn. Ire.*, 27 April 1615, 10 Dec. 1634.

Arthur Jones, the future second Viscount Ranelagh, was only 14 when he became MP for Sligo in 1634.[83] The Commons' declaration on 24 May 1641 that no one under 21 should be a member was aimed at excluding Wentworth's associates Thomas Radcliffe and Thomas Little Jr, rather than a position of principle.

The residency rule specified in 1 Hen. V, c. 1 was routinely breached by administration supporters in Tudor and Stuart parliaments in England and Ireland, as Chichester explicitly stated in 1613: 'they were lawfully chosen, no doubt, according unto the practice of England at least, which admitteth men of qualitie in the same kind, though they be otherwise strangers to the corporation electing them'. A similar decision had been made in 1569 and 1585 to the incredulity of the Old English.[84] Before March 1641, only two Catholics were returned for constituencies with which they had no obvious connection: Patrick Darcy for Navan in 1634 and John FitzGerald for Inistioge. Some MPs were retrospectively admitted to freedom, like Richard Gethings and William Smyth in Clonmel, Andrew Barrett in Cork and Philip Wenman in Belfast in 1640.[85] However, while objections were invariably made at the beginning of each parliament to purge the House of those unduly returned, including non-resident members, to such an extent that Wentworth derided Catholics' 'seething warmly to move for the purging of the House, as they termed it, with an aim doubtless to put out a great company of the protestants upon the point of non-residency', no one was ever excluded for that reason, although, ironically, the administration made an issue of FitzGerald's non-residency (see chapter three).[86] Non-residency remained a bone of contention for Catholics, reflecting the difference between English and Irish practice and the crown's opportunism. While Ormond's agreement with the Confederates specified that 'none be admitted into the Howse of Commons but such as shalbe estated and resident in this kingdome', members who were not resident in their constituencies were elected to the General Assembly.[87]

ELECTORAL PRACTICE

Sheriffs were under pressure to conduct elections in the crown's interest, attested by the conduct of the 1569, 1613 and 1634 elections. The state intervened in elections, although this was illegal 'None of what degree soever he or they be of,

83 For brief details on Arthur Jones, see John Bergin, 'Jones, Richard', *DIB*.

84 Chichester to the English privy council, 6 June 1613, in Edwards (ed.), 'Chichester', no. 61. Similar objections were made in 1569. See Hooker's diary in Falkiner, *Essays*, pp 218–19. Nicholas White to Burghley, 27 May 1585, TNA, SP 63/116, fo. 138.

85 McGrath (ed.), *Clonmel*, p. 268; Caulfield (ed.), *Cork*, p. 197; Robert Magill Young, *The town book of the Corporation of Belfast, 1613–1816* (Belfast, 1892), p. 249.

86 Wentworth to Coke, 18 Aug. 1634, in Knowler (ed.), *Letters and dispatches*, i, p. 277; McGrath, 'Sex, lies and rigged returns'; Bodl. Lib., Carte MS 1, fos. 309r–10v.

87 Bodl. Lib., Carte MS 64, fos. 1–3v.

shall disturbe any free election, by force or threats, on great paines to be inflicted upon the offender'.[88] Under Chichester, all sheriffs were Protestant and towns' chief officers and recorders were dismissed if they did not take the oath of supremacy. As the Jesuit annual Irish letter for 1612 noted:

> those who desire to wipe out our religion leave no stone unturned so that there are elected to parliament only those whom they hope they will have as supporters of their own sect. And they know that in order to fulfil this wish it is most important that they be Protestant magistrates. For that reason, in the counties the sheriffs (who are renewed each year by the king himself) consisted of hardly any other than sectarians. Although it was not permitted to nominate any of these to parliament, because within their own boundaries they hold the position of the king, and they can use a thousand tricks so that popular election is frustrated by their influence. Insofar as pertains to the magistracy of cities and towns they can by royal diploma be established every year by their own citizens and townsmen (this happens around the feast of St Michael). But our adversaries, since they saw that most of these were Catholics and would be opposed in no small degree to their intention, they obtained letters from the king to be addressed here severely prohibiting that in future anybody in any city or town would not be permitted to hold the magistracy who refused to swear to his Ecclesiastical Primacy.[89]

Falkland and Wentworth did not exclude Catholics from these roles, but the latter had other ways of dealing with those who did not implement his wishes. However, as MacCarthy-Morrogh noted, the administration significantly over-estimated sheriffs' ability to influence elections.[90]

The first stage in the electoral process was chancery issuing writs directing sheriffs to hold county elections and to send mandates to boroughs' chief officers to conduct elections for their citizens or burgesses.[91] County boroughs' sheriffs were the returning officers for their towns, rather than the mayors.[92] 7 Hen. IV, c. 14 specified that county elections be held between 8 a.m. and 12 p.m. 'in one of the principal towns of the county'; in practice they were generally conducted between 8 a.m. and 9 a.m. at the first county court after the writ's receipt, a date and location which was widely known in advance. Sheriffs were supposed to ensure that elections were well publicized but had discretion about where to hold the court which they could use to influence returns, as was attempted in Tyrone in 1641. The 1654 writs of election returns specified that notice of the election was to be

88 Westminster 1, c. 5, 3 Edw. I.

89 Moynes (ed.), *Annual letters*, i, p. 266.

90 McGrath, 'Electoral strategy'; MacCarthy-Morrogh, *Munster plantation*, pp 262ff.

91 The warrant for summons to Convocation was issued on the same day in 1634. Empey (ed.), *Early Stuart Irish warrants*, p. 187. For the legal background to Irish elections, see McGrath, 'Electoral law in Ireland'. The various systems for managing elections in Tudor England did not apply in Ireland. Hawkyard, *Commons*, pp 9–10.

92 I am grateful to Hannes Kleineke for this observation.

proclaimed at 'every market town in the county', presumably reflecting earlier practice. The returning officer read out the writ in Latin, and a summary in English and presumably also in Irish.[93]

The means by which elections were to be conducted and results determined was not specified; returning officers used a number of methods, at their discretion. They could judge by the volume of cries for each candidate or pair of candidates, depending on whether seats were filled singly as in 1613 in Roscommon County and Carlingford, or together as Down and Tyrone, or by means of a 'showing' (by the electorate's dividing into two groups, to judge which was the larger). Only when these methods failed to indicate a majority, and not even necessarily then, might a poll be taken and voters' credentials checked. The successful candidates' names were entered in a prepared indenture and the 'chief freeholders, who shall give their voices to the election set their hands thereto.'[94] The Confederation of Kilkenny followed exactly the same procedure for elections, using identical terminology in the writs of return.[95] Concerns seen in England about who was elected first are not recorded for Ireland.[96]

Borough elections followed the same procedure; no specific date was stipulated and their chief officers appointed a convenient day as soon after the receipt of the writ as was practicable. They were also responsible for publicizing its time and location, although it is unclear how conscientiously this was done. Trinity College's provost acted as returning officer there; Dublin city's sheriffs attended the 1613 election, under protest from the College, asserting their responsibility as returning officers for a county borough.[97] There were frequent allegations of returning officers' chicanery in elections' timing and location; when they illegally held an election at 2 p.m. or 4 a.m. this was regarded as unusual, but not in itself as grounds for objection, even by the losing side.[98]

Mayors sent the indentures of return to the sheriff who sewed them together and delivered them to chancery, where they were filed and MPs' names 'certefyed in one Authentique Book' to the clerk of the Commons. English membership lists followed an old order of precedence but the Irish practice giving counties in alphabetical order, with boroughs included under their counties, was more appropriate for an expanding lower house.[99] By-elections caused by death,

93 McGrath, 'Electoral law in Ireland'; *Cal. S.P. Ire., 1611–14*, p. 361; TNA, MS C 219/44.
94 *Commons' Jn. Ire.*, i, prelims; Hawkyard, *Commons*, pp 46–8.
95 Bodl. Lib., Carte MS 204, fos. 69–70, 21 Aug. 1648; McGrath (ed.), *Clonmel*, pp 268, 307, 310, 322, 330.
96 E.g., Knowler (ed.), *Letters and dispatches*, i, pp 8–14, 25–7.
97 TCD, MS MUN/V/1/1, fo. 186v.
98 Carroll, 'Dublin parliamentary elections'; McGrath, 'Unmasking "E.S"'; *idem*, 'Electoral law in Ireland'; Moynes (ed.), *Annual letters*, i, p. 266.
99 The returns template is given in *Commons' Jn. Ire.*, i, prelims; McGrath, 'Athboy's election returns 1640 and 1641'; *Commons' Jn. Ire.*, i, prelims; TNA, MS PRO 30/5/3, fos. 2–10 is Francis Edgeworth's 'Authentique' book for 1613; RIA, MS 24/Q/5, no. 41; NLI, MS 836, p. 8. The inclusion of Welsh MPs in 1541 altered the sequence, but it still differed from the Irish alphabetical listing. Hawkyard, *Commons*, pp 72–3, 93–5.

resignation, expulsion, accession to peerage and double returns were conducted in exactly the same way as initial elections.[100] The English practice of giving a general order at the beginning of parliament authorizing the speaker to give warrants for new writs to replace deceased members is only recorded in Ireland on 3 October 1640; this may demonstrate Wandesford's confidence that he could control the Commons, but after the administration lost the Inistioge election in the following month, MPs had repeatedly to order the speaker to issue warrants to chancery suggesting that Eustace was stalling to preserve the administration's majority.[101]

Elections were held over several weeks, although as county elections were frequently held at the county town, where there was one, that borough's election often happened on the same day, which may have increased turnout; conversely, holding elections in other boroughs on county days may have reduced the number of voters. The spread of election days was an advantage for the crown, as it facilitated men standing for more than one seat, resulting in double returns and more rarely single returns (where boroughs only returned one MP, such as Coleraine in 1634, and Ardee and Fore in 1640), either because they were awaiting a nomination or their intended member was returned elsewhere, and re-jigging results by inserting the names of those who had been unsuccessful elsewhere, or replacements for those returned for other constituencies.[102]

There was considerable interest in elections and no shortage of candidates, at least until 1640, when those who had experienced Wentworth's vindictiveness did not stand.[103] The Irish experience reflects the increased English interest in elections and Kearney's statement that 'elections in the normal sense of the word were few and in most cases were a formal registering of a decision which had been arrived at by less formal means' was clearly wide of the mark, as was MacCarthy-Morrogh's assertion that electioneering was largely confined to county seats.[104]

The gentry met in advance in their respective counties to discuss the county seats; in 1613, in Armagh, Cavan and King's counties the 'gentlemen and freeholders [met] the day before to confer of the election, the Irish supposing, (as they said) that day to be the day of choice.' The Scots in Down combined to ensure the return of Hamilton and Montgomery, despite Chichester's nominating the former army servitor and Wicklow landholder, Sir Richard Wingfield, and the Irish supporting two scions of the Irish septs of east Ulster, Sir Arthur Magennis

100 E.g., Mandate from Sir Cyprian Horsfall, sheriff of Kilkenny, to Piers Keally, Portreeve of Gowran, 7 Nov. 1641, KCA, MS CR/K/56. I am grateful to David Edwards for drawing this reference to my attention.

101 Scobell, *Memorials*, p. 20; *Commons' Jn. Ire.*, 3 Oct. 1640, 4 Feb. 1641, 5 March 1641, 15, 21, 27 May 1641.

102 McGrath, 'Electoral strategy'; McGrath (ed.), *Coleraine*, p. 89.

103 For Darcy's reluctance to stand in 1640, see Darcy to Muskery, 6 Nov. 1647, Bodl. Lib., Carte MS 21, fo. 517; McGrath, 'Electoral strategy'.

104 Hawkyard, *Commons*, p. 47; Kearney, *Strafford in Ireland*, p. 45. See also Smith, *Stuart*, pp 24–6; MacCarthy-Morrogh, *Munster plantation*, p. 263.

and Rowland Savage.[105] At least seven (and apparently more) gentlemen expressed an interest in representing Tipperary in 1634: Richard Butler, Kilcash, Theobald Purcell baron of Loughmoe, Sir Richard Everard, Sir John Morres, Thomas Butler, Kyleconnell

> and many others of the prime gentlemen of the County aimed severally to prevail and to be in the list or leet then prepared for the votes, wherein likewise Mr Piers Butler pressing to have his own name inserted, which was allowed him, but not satisfied therewith, … out of confidence on the petty freeholders of both the Ormonds, Keyllnamanagh, Ellyogourty and Ikerryn, Clanwilliam, [Owney & Arragh], he unadvisedly broke out in the presence of all the gents [sic] that being in the list, he did not doubt of carrying the election in spite of all that would oppose it. This declaration lost his election which else he might have carried.

This created a great deal of local tension, which later surfaced in a petition to the following parliament against Butler's activities as sheriff.[106] Waterford's 1634 county election was acrimonious, suggesting a contest within the Catholic political community which did not subside after the poll.[107] In 1640 in Down, the Scottish Hamiltons and Montgomerys faced opposition from the local English settler families of Trevor, Hill and Bagenal, as well as the Irish Magennises, O'Neills and Savages; the identity of all the candidates is unknown, but the contest was keenly fought and given added edge by the Down planter, Sir Edward Trevor's successful domination of borough returns there in 1634 and by Downpatrick's disfranchisement.[108] The same level of interest was obvious for the 1647 General Assembly, with instances of three men being returned for some seats, although this was an especially fraught period for the Confederation.[109]

Towns also saw contests, with Dublin's especially fiercely contested. Youghal's voters never had fewer than four candidates and Kilkenny city had six candidates in 1628.[110] Wentworth instructed St Leger, who was managing Munster's 1634 elections to

105 George Hill (ed.), *The Montgomery manuscripts, 1603–1706* (Belfast, 1869), p. 86; Terry Clavin, 'Wingfield, Sir Richard', *DIB*.

106 Bodl. Lib., Carte MS 64, fo. 462v; *Commons' Jn. Ire.*, 28 July 1641. Thomas Butler and Purcell were elected for Tipperary and Geoffrey Mockler and Thomas Gough for Cross Tipperary. The named baronies were largely in the north and west of Tipperary. For the petition against Piers, see *Commons' Jn. Ire.*, 20 May 1641 and chapter 3.

107 Empey (ed.), *Early Stuart Irish warrants*, pp 160–1; Grosart (ed.), *Lismore Papers*, iv, p. 37.

108 Hill (ed.), *Montgomery manuscripts*, pp 306–8; McGrath, 'Electoral strategy'; *idem*, 'Bio. dict.', i, pp 286–7.

109 Bellings, 'Fragmenta' in Lodge, *Desiderata Curiosa*, ii, pp 427–8. Interestingly, those elections were allowed to stand.

110 Caulfield (ed.), *Youghal*, pp 22, 146, 181, 197. Youghal also had at least four candidates for its mayoralty each year; for its 1640 election, see Cork City Archives, MS YTR B/1, p. 400; McGrath, 'Nomination of Kilkenny MPs in 1628'.

> keepe the towns under your government from factious and tumultary labouring for places beforehand … and to keep them free without engagement and to send me a list of some twenty of the most leading men in the province which you conceive to be well-affected and fitt to be sent to the meeting as well as your advise how upon recommendations hence to the towns we may gett such others chosen as shall be named unto them.[111]

William Wiseman (agent for Richard Boyle, earl of Cork and MP for Boyle's town, Bandonbridge) noted 'much ado, for I find that the business is already in agitation in the country, though there be a course taken by several letters from [St Leger] to the chief gentlemen, not to stir therein by parading of voices till the day of election.'[112] The inferences are clear: Wentworth was discouraging local candidates in towns, to enable his own nominees to be successful. The local Protestant community was not openly to discuss the likely voters and candidates and their level of support and newly-created freeholders would appear on election-day to vote for Protestant candidates in the counties.

Anyone could propose candidates: town councils, privy councillors and local magnates, as well as aspirant MPs, nominated contenders. Uniquely, Carrickfergus' 1570 charter specified that Sidney's secretary, Edward Waterhouse, who had been instrumental in obtaining the grant, should be the town's next MP and he was duly returned in 1585.[113] A Catholic observer claimed that in 1613 sheriffs were directed to return only those nominated by the administration for the boroughs incorporated after writs for election were issued, but it is far more likely that names were inserted without holding elections at all as their sponsors were all privy councillors or officials and only Lismore had a functioning council; the crown's hopes for its nominees in Athlone and Gowran were clearly disappointed.[114]

As Clyve Jones has pointed out,

> smaller boroughs often stood to gain more by offering their seats to powerful external patrons who might help them in between parliaments, and outsiders

111 Wentworth to St Leger, April 1634, quoted in Kearney, *Strafford in Ireland*, p. 46.

112 Wiseman to Boyle, NLI, MS 13,237/20, quoted in MacCarthy-Morrogh, *Munster plantation*, p. 263; Andrew Hadfield, 'The will of William Wiseman, Edmund Spenser's son-in-law', *Notes and Queries*, 60:1 (2013), 37–40.

113 K.W. Nicholls (ed.), *The Irish fiants of the Tudor sovereigns*, 4 vols (Dublin, 1994), ii, no. 1503; Terry Clavin, 'Waterhouse, Edward', *DIB*. For Tudor English practice, see Hawkyard, *Commons*, pp 17ff.

114 Chichester nominated Wingfield, MP for Downpatrick, for Down; Gosnold was returned for Clonakilty, having failed to be elected in Youghal; for privy councillors' failure to be elected county members, see Jacob to Northampton, 26 May 1613, Bodl. Lib., Carte MS 62, fos. 241–3; TCD, MS 843, pp 489–502. However, as Ballinakill was Ridgeway's own borough, he was unlikely to be paid for his parliamentary attendance. Jackson (ed.), 'Document'. English privy councillors also found it difficult to secure election to county seats. See Gruenfelder, 'Electoral patronage of Sir Thomas Wentworth'; Moynes (ed.), *Annual letters*, i, p. 266.

> were less likely to demand wages in return for service ... That said, the larger towns in particular generally opted for local men who were best qualified to promote their constituencies' interests in the Commons.[115]

Proposing candidates who would serve unpaid was used by patrons to ensure their right of nomination. Where one resident and one outsider were elected, the former was likely to be paid but not the latter, as happened in Athy, Ballinakill, Maryborough and Newry in 1613 and Cork in 1640.

Town councils nominated candidates for the voters in their boroughs to choose from, but these proposals met with mixed success: Dublin invariably returned its former mayor, Alderman Richard Barry, and its recorder, but only after earlier polls which elected Catholics were illegally overturned in 1613 and 1634 at least (and possibly 1628). Youghal and Kilkenny's council nominations already noted were presumably replicated in all older towns; unlike English and Scottish boroughs, whose councillors selected their MPs, these Irish elections were invariably contested until 1640, when the threat of disfranchisement proved too strong for many towns.[116] The City of London nominated Coleraine and Londonderry's 1613 burgesses but after 1623 those towns enjoyed greater autonomy; in 1628 Coleraine returned townsmen but, like Londonderry, under Wentworth always elected a crown nominee and a townsman.[117]

Chichester and Wentworth relied on privy councillors to nominate candidates and manage elections at local level; as in England, councillors found it difficult to secure county seats and faced considerable opposition in older boroughs before Strafford's *Quo warranto* threat removed opposition in many, but not all, of them. Sir William Parsons represented different seats in all three parliaments and only managed to be elected in 1640 after replacing John Karnes for the pocket borough of Augher at the last minute, attesting to his widespread unpopularity.[118] New towns were more amenable, frequently because placemen served unpaid.[119] Henry VII initiated the practice of sending nominating letters to each English constituency; but there is no evidence of such circulars in Ireland before Wentworth's famous 100 letters of nomination in 1634, repeatedly proposing the

115 Clive Jones, *A short history of parliament: England, Great Britain, the United Kingdom* (Woodbridge, 2009), p. 101.

116 Hawkyard, *Commons*, pp 11–17; Empey (ed.), 'Diary of Sir James Ware'; McGrath, 'Nomination of Kilkenny MPs in 1628'; Caulfield (ed.), *Youghal*, pp 22, 146, 181, 197.

117 *Cal. S.P. Ire., 1611–14*, pp 360–4, 438–43; T.W. Moody and J.G. Simms (eds), *The bishopric of Derry and the Irish Society of London, 1602–1705*, 2 vols (Dublin, 1968), i, pp 93–4; McGrath (ed.), *Coleraine*, pp 24, 58, 89.

118 In England this role was standard during the Tudor period. Hawkyard, *Commons*, pp 14–15; Jacob to Northampton, 26 May 1613, Bodl. Lib., Carte MS 62, fo. 241–3; TCD, MS 843, pp 489–502; Gruenfelder, 'Electoral patronage of Sir Thomas Wentworth'; McGrath, 'Electoral strategy'; RIA, MS 24/Q/5, no. 41.

119 McGrath, 'Electoral strategy'. For example, the lords justices' nomination of Francis Slingsby in Bandon. See Bennett, *Bandon*, p. 98. Bennett gives the letter's date as 3 Feb. 1634, but it is clearly from 1640 (new style). Kearney, *Strafford in Ireland*, pp 46–7.

same candidates who found success elusive.[120] Other power-brokers were not necessarily more successful; Ormond was responsible for Henry Frederick Howard, Lord Maltravers and Thomas Wharton's return for Callan in 1634 and 1640.[121] He also engineered the latter's replacement by Richard Bellings, as well as the election of his secretary William Smyth and kinsman Patrick Wemys respectively for Clonmel and Gowran in 1640 and Piers Crosby's for Gowran in a by-election in November 1641. Otherwise Ormond's influence seems to have been very limited, despite which John Barry assumed that the earl's nomination would secure him a seat. Those with the best records of successful nominations were Richard Boyle in 1613 and 1634, Robert Dillon in Donegal in 1634 and Audley Mervyn, through whose interest so many Catholics were returned in by-elections from early 1641.[122]

Blank returns, where electors sent a signed writ of return to a power-broker for them to insert their candidate's names, were used by some boroughs but never for county elections. While some Tudor returns strongly suggest that blanks were used, the first allegation of this practice was in 1613, when the clerk of the crown's list of returns left blank spaces for burgesses from Athlone, Clogher and Gowran and for the eight boroughs which were covertly incorporated at the end of the election period whose members' names were added later, indented and in a different hand. When James adjudicated that boroughs whose charters were issued after the commission for the parliament should not be represented, Laurence Parsons wrote to Boyle that they were both 'cashiered out of the Parliament house. My Lord Deputy must be applied to, [to] insert [our] names into some of the new elections', presumably by blanks.[123]

On 22 June 1634 Cork recorded that his agent 'sent me two blancks under the officers, & townes seals of Tallagh & Lismoor, with power to insert suche 4 Burgesses names as I should think to serv his Majesty in the next parliament.' He demanded the same from Bandon, but assured its electors that 'I doe engage my creddit, that I will nominate two able and sufficient gentlemen, such as shall discharge the duties with creddit, and without any charge to the town.'[124] Inistioge used blanks for its original return in 1640, which was dated on a Sunday. Blanks were used widely by the 'rump' Irish parliament which faced serious problems in

120 For the Tudors' heavy-handed approach to returns in England, see Hawkyard, *Commons*, pp 11–17, 87–91, 98–102; McGrath, 'Electoral strategy'; Grosart (ed.), *Lismore Papers*, iv, p. 30; Kearney, *Strafford in Ireland*, pp 46ff; William Brereton's 'Travels' in Falkiner (ed.), *Illustrations*; Wentworth to Ormonde, 30 May 1634, in HMC, *Ormond*, p. 43.

121 McGrath, 'Bio. dict.', i, pp 308–9; Alan Davidson, 'Howard, Henry Frederick, Lord Maltravers' in Thrush and Ferris (eds), *History of parliament*.

122 McGrath, 'Electoral strategy'; *idem*, 'Irish elections of 1640–1641'.

123 TNA, MS PRO 30/5/3, fos 2–10; Jackson (ed.), 'Document'; Jacob to Northampton, 26 May 1613, Bodl. Lib., Carte MS 62, fos. 241–3. Jacob sat for Carlow and would have known how the returns were made. Laurence Parsons to Boyle, May 1614, Chatsworth House, Cork Papers, vol. 5, no. 43.

124 Boyle to the Provost of Bandon, 31 May 1634, in Bennett, *Bandon*, p. 94.

filling seats, especially in areas outside their control, and by the General Assembly.[125] Blanks were also an efficient way of replacing double returns.

The English act 11 Hen. IV, c. 1 (formerly c. 5) specified serious penalties for returning officers who made mis-returns, with fines of £100 and a year in prison for sheriffs and £40 for mayors, with the same amount payable to the winning candidate who was not returned. Justices at the assizes had power to enquire into false returns and appeals had to be made within three months of the election; Merick seemed doubtful as to whether the justices could give satisfaction: 'it seemeth that [they] … may give judgment thereon.' The English practice of referring disputed returns to the chancellor or privy council was not known in Ireland.[126] Given the number of highly contentious elections – in 1613 Catholics objected to 14 elections which they claimed were illegally conducted – there are curiously few formal recorded objections to returns and no evidence of sheriffs facing any serious consequences for illegality, although the recusants' agents in London in 1613 noted that the penalties due to the crown, 'as well upon the sheriffs and officers, as upon the parties' from the 'diverse false and undue returns' would amount to a large sum.[127] There is no account of a sheriff being fined for mis-returns although this may be due to lack of surviving court records. Indeed, the returning officers who faced consequences were Dublin city's sheriffs in 1613 and 1634 who were imprisoned for returning Catholic MPs, clearly correctly, against the administration's wishes, an explicit breach of electoral law. The Commons overturned the 1634 Carlow and Kerry returns and in 1640 they decided on an objection to John Davies' return for Carrickfergus and confirmed FitzGerald's for Inistioge.[128]

CONCLUSION

After 1640 the English and Irish parliaments shared the same system of rural, urban and university seats. The early modern period saw a dramatic increase in the number of MPs and the administration's influence in elections facilitated by changes in the electorate and constitutional practice. Changes in landholding brought about by formal and informal plantations and legally questionable

125 McGrath, 'Electoral law in Ireland'; Grosart (ed.), *Lismore Papers,* 1st series, iv, p. 33; McGrath, 'Inistiogue's elections in 1640'; *idem*, 'Sex, lies and rigged returns'; *idem*, 'Athboy's election returns'; *idem*, 'Recruiter returns'; Hawkyard, *Commons*, pp 80–4 discusses the use of blanks in Tudor elections in England. For the 1646 Cork City return, conducted when the city was under Protestant control, see Micheál Ó Siochrú, *Confederate Ireland, 1642–1649: a constitutional and political analysis* (Dublin, 1999), p. 208.

126 *Priviledges and practice of parliaments*, pp 11–12; Hawkyard, *Commons*, pp 47–8, 70–1; 6 Hen. VI, c. 4 also applied. Merick, *Compendious collection*, p. 303; 8 Hen. VI, c. 7; 10 Hen. VI, c. 2.

127 *Cal. S.P. Ire., 1611–14*, pp 360–4, 438–43.

128 Farmer's 'Chronicle' in Lodge, *Desiderata Curiosa*, i, p. 229; McGrath, 'Electoral law in Ireland'; *idem*, 'Sex, lies and rigged returns'.

expropriation transformed the county electorate from an overwhelmingly Catholic group of freeholders to a more mixed one. The urban electorate also altered, largely through the creation of new boroughs by introducing the English practice of granting representation in charters to newly established or intended corporations, designed to have an exclusively Protestant electorate, but also by towns' oligarchies' widening their electorates and through an assault on older towns' liberties. These changes, when accompanied by the crown's increasingly intimidatory electioneering, tilted the balance of power within parliament from the Old English and Gaelic Catholic gentry and townspeople towards a majority of Protestant MPs, frequently non-resident administration nominees serving without pay. Despite the administration's illegal and aggressive electioneering, Old English and old Irish communities fiercely resisted this intimidation and unlike in England, most elections were contested in the counties and older boroughs, although the use of *Quo warranto* warrants against recalcitrant older towns after 1635 had a deadening effect on their resistance. Perhaps more curiously, Protestant interests appeared uninterested in expanding their electoral patronage; Laurence Parsons' failure to implement his letters patent for two new manor boroughs was matched by James Ussher and Bramhall's prohibition of Ulster bishops' granting freeholds and consequently creating new electors in their dioceses after 1635.[129]

The coalition of New English, Scottish, Old English and Gaelic forces that engineered Wentworth's downfall used by-elections to ensure the return of selected personnel to represent their interests and strengthen their hands in pressing for the redress of grievances. Beginning with FitzGerald's return for Inistioge, a steady stream of Catholics and New English and Scots opposed to the regime was elected. New English figures including Audley Mervyn ensured the return of non-resident Catholics for pocket boroughs that had formerly returned Protestant placemen. The strategies pursued by the administration, including blank returns and expulsions, were used in a parliamentary campaign against Wentworth's policies in Ireland and the Commons briefly reflected and represented the community more faithfully than at any time since 1585.

129 Smith, *Stuart*, pp 25–6; 10 Car. I, sess. 3, c. 5.

CHAPTER SIX

Culture, ceremony and the social aspects of parliament

PARLIAMENT WAS THE VISIBLE SIGN of the kingdom's four elements working together, 'a major ceremonial occasion capable of demonstrating ethnic, sectional and class harmony amongst subjects, their loyalty towards the state and the state's reliance on their elite participation.'[1] Its culture included the houses' ceremonial, most clearly seen in the opening and closing ceremonies and members' and officers' dress, but also in the daily protocols within and between both houses, its locations and layout and the material culture of its furniture and fittings. As there were no coronations in Ireland and Wentworth made his inauguration a private event, parliament provided the greatest public spectacle and an opportunity to make, cement and develop reputations and connections. In a status-obsessed age, conventions were carefully researched and observed, but could also be modified; questions of precedence were live issues, especially for prelates and peers, but also for the Commons.

The elements of parliamentary culture were familiar to most subjects. Representative assemblies' basic layout changed little over the centuries although their membership grew significantly. There are no contemporary images of the Irish parliament but descriptions match those of the English houses of parliament, the Scottish Estates and French Estates General.[2] The layout of the Commons' chamber, while on a much larger scale, would have been very familiar to any townsman, lawyer or justice of the peace acquainted with tholsels and court houses. The speaker's role as chairman and the clerk's work were similar to the mayor's and town clerk's and the order of business apparently followed a similar pattern; towns' recorders played a similar part to the judges in the House of Lords, providing legal advice.[3] The serjeant-at-arms preceding the speaker bearing the mace was exactly the role the serjeant-at-mace played before the mayor or sovereign in every town. Kathrin Strauss argues that this practice was directly

1 Hiram Morgan, 'An introduction to the study of political ideas in early modern Ireland', Keynote address to 'Ireland 1598: contexts, representations and revolts', organized jointly by the departments of History and English at University College Cork, May 1998, at https://celt.ucc.ie//Ideology.pdf [accessed 3 April 2019].

2 Alasdair D. Hawkyard, 'Inigo Jones, the surveyor of the works and the "Parliament House"', *Parl. Hist.*, 32:1 (2013), 16–59 includes many contemporary images of the English parliament. BL, Cotton MS Caligula E VI, fos. 349v–50r is a drawing of the 1576 French Estates General. Grelin, *Ordre Observé* includes a plate with the layout of the 1614 Estates. I am grateful to Scott Duvall, Brigham Young University, for providing me with a copy of this image. W.D. Cullen, *Parliament House: a short history and guide* (Edinburgh, 1992), p. 3.

3 Goppold, 'Norms, symbols and modes of everyday decision-making', pp 52–61.

adopted from urban ceremonial as part of the process of elevating the speaker's role in parliament from being the Commons' mouthpiece into 'a powerful political player within the house, chosen by the monarch'.[4]

Public interest in parliament and its activities and the social occasions around its meeting created the atmosphere in which its work was accomplished. Even for those without any direct connection, parliament's meeting was a cause for comment; in a letter devoid of almost any other news, Thomas Bagot of Dublin wrote to his English cousins, 'the parlement shall begine at Dublin the 4th of July next'.[5]

CEREMONIAL OF PARLIAMENT

Parliament opened with considerable pageantry and spectacle, designed to stress the state's prestige, the importance of parliament and its business, and its inclusive nature. Its very rarity made parliament's public ceremonial aspects even more compelling. Seating arrangements were laid down in the *Modus* and rituals had developed over centuries. Their core elements of performance, procession, church service, dress and speeches remained constant over time in England, Ireland and Scotland, but the ceremonies were influenced by other considerations, including the extent of the crown's control in Ireland at a given time and the lord deputy's personality.[6] All MPs entered their appearance with the clerk of the crown (1613) or the Commons (1634) on the day specified in the commission for the parliament, unlike in England where different qualities of members made their appearance on successive days, possibly because of the additional logistics contingent on their swearing the oaths, or of sheriffs appearing to verify the indentures of return.[7] Religion played an important part in all public life and parliament's colourful and solemn opening ceremonies began with a church service in one of Dublin's two cathedrals followed by a procession to the parliament house; the formal opening took place in a plenary session in the House of Lords in the presence of the lord deputy and members of the Commons.

The 1541 parliament's opening was designed to be especially impressive, setting the scene for Henry VIII's recognition as King of Ireland; St Leger copied the 1539 English precedent, the first parliament to involve a procession from Whitehall to Westminster Abbey.[8] Parliament opened on 13 June, but the peers

4 Kathrin Strauss, 'The ceremonial mace in the House of Commons and great maces of cities and boroughs in the 16th and early 17th century', *Parl. Hist.*, 41:3 (Oct., 2022), 389–405.

5 Thomas Bagot to Walter Bagot, 30 April 1614, FSL, MS L.a.91.

6 Thomas Duffus Hardy (ed.), *Modus tenendi parliamentum: an ancient treatise on the mode of holding the parliament in England* (London, 1846), p. 36; Peacey, 'Street theatre of state'; Aonghus MacKechnie, 'Housing Scotland's parliament, 1603–1707', *Parl. Hist.*, 21:1 (2002), 99–130; Hawkyard, *Commons*, pp 91–2.

7 Hakewill, *Modus*, p. 10, first day, burgesses to come; third day, the barons of the Cinque Ports, barons and earls. Hawkyard, *Commons*, pp 91–2.

8 Peacey, 'Street theatre of state'.

joined the traditional Dublin Corpus Christi procession on 16 June, possibly the day that the speaker was presented in the Lords: 'Sir antony sellenger Deputie with the kings conyssiall held a parlament at Dublin … with mane Irishe lords and one carpus Christie Daye they rode about with the procession in the parlement robes and the ix Worthies was played.'[9]

Sidney's parliament opened on 17 January 1569; after service in Christ Church, they proceeded to the parliament chambers there and 'the Lord Chancellor made a verie eloquent oration' and requested the Commons to choose a speaker.[10] Perrot's parliament opened on 26 April 1585 with a procession stated to be comparable in splendour only to St Leger's. The lord deputy in his parliament robes was preceded by Turlough Luineach O'Neill, earl of Clanconnell, carrying the sword.[11] 'Delegations' from 42 Irish septs attended, dressed for the occasion in English garb and Perrot boasted 'there never came the fourth man to any parliament of the uriaghts and great lords of Ireland as came in my time.'[12]

Chichester's parliament opened on 18 May 1613 with a procession from the Castle to St Patrick's Cathedral. A number of considerations prompted the move from Christ Church, including the fact that parliament was not to sit there because the noise and tobacco fumes from the tippling den in its basement disrupted services, but the longer route to and from St Patrick's also gave greater prominence to the procession.[13] The church service set the tone for the parliament with the singing of a *Te Deum* and the primate preaching a sermon. Christopher Hampton, consecrated archbishop of Armagh only ten days before and described as 'a Reverend wise Preacher, a good divine and an exceeding honest man', took as his text 'render unto Caesar the things that are Caesars', a useful prompt for the subsidy bills.[14] His text for the opening of the second session, 1 John 2:19, which reads 'They went out from us, but they were not of us, for if they had been of us, they would have continued with us', while ostensibly about the Anti-Christ, was a pointed jibe at Catholics' secession in the previous year. Ussher's opening sermon in 1634 on Genesis 49:10, in which it is stated that 'The scepter shall not depart from Judah, nor a law-giver from between his feet, till Shiloh come and to him shall the gathering of the people be', neatly set the scene for Wentworth's 'thorough' approach to both parliament and Convocation and the text was cited by

9 Alan J. Fletcher, *Drama, performance and polity in pre-Cromwellian Ireland* (Cork, 2000), p. 133. For the Nine Worthies, see Horst Schroeder, *Der Topos der Nine Worthies in literatur und bildender Kunst* (Goettingen, 1971). I am grateful to Ruth M. Karras for drawing this reference to my attention. Also, see Alan J. Fletcher, 'The civic pageantry of Corpus Christi in fifteenth- and sixteenth-century Dublin', *IESH*, 23:1 (1996), 73–96.

10 Falkiner, *Essays*, pp 237ff; Sidney to William Cecil, 12 Nov. 1568, TNA, SP/63/26, pp 378–9; Cecil to Sidney, 5 Jan. 1569, TNA, SP 63/27, p. 304.

11 Ciaran Brady, 'O'Neill, Turlough Luineach', *DIB*.

12 Quoted in Treadwell, 'Sir John Perrott'. For the English peers' procession in 1512, see Bodl. Lib., MS Ash Rolls 45.

13 Edward Seymour, *Christchurch Cathedral: Dublin, 1855–1878* (Dublin, 1878), p. 51.

14 Judy Barry, 'Hampton, Christopher', *DIB*.

Eustace in his acceptance speech as speaker.[15] In 1640 Ussher preached on Deuteronomy 33:4, 5, in which it is said 'And Moses commanded us a Law, even the inheritance of the congregation of Jacob: and he was King in Jeshurun when the heads of the people and the tribes of Israel were gathered together', were described as 'most fit texts for a parliament, so each full of rare and emenent Learning.'[16]

Chichester was attended by bishops and peers 'all on foteclothes, on horseback', MPs and the deputy's servants, preceded by Donough O'Brien, fourth earl of Thomond, and David FitzJames Barry, third Viscount Buttevant, bearing the cap of state and sword respectively, presumably because the aged Thomas Butler, tenth earl of Ormond, was in poor health, and Gerald FitzGerald, fifteenth earl of Kildare, was only two years old.[17] Thomond's heir Henry Bryan bore 'his Lordship's trayne, the steward comptroller and his Secretaryes, rydeing on their foteclothes before his Lordship they being uncovered.'[18] The procession was both splendid and lengthy, with 'four archbishops and other lords &c. to the number of one hundred on horseback and on foote before him by three hundred gentlemen.'[19] Another account noted 'Dr Medcalf in his broad black velvet Cap being Physician to the state.'[20] Not specifically mentioned but certainly present, was the Ulster king of arms, Ireland's chief herald, who played a key role in managing parliament's protocol, especially in the upper house.[21]

The opening ceremony's grandeur increased markedly between Chichester's and Wentworth's parliaments and became more closely aligned to English ritual, but its inclusiveness was significantly reduced. The Earl Marshal, the fourteenth earl of Arundel, Thomas Howard, who supervised English parliamentary ceremonial visited Dublin with his eldest son, Lord Maltravers, for the 1634 parliament, advising Wentworth on ritual. The heralds were also consulted.[22]

15 *Commons' Jn. Ire.*, 20 March 1640; Phil Kilroy, 'Sermon and pamphlet literature in the Irish reformed church, 1613–34', *Archivium Hibernicum*, 33 (1975), 110–21.

16 Jacob to Northampton, 12 April 1613, in Francis Bickley (ed.), *Report on the manuscripts of the late Reginald Rawdon Hastings, Volume IV* (London, 1947), pp 11–12; Nicholas Bernard, *The life & death of the most reverend and learned father of our church, Dr James Ussher* (Dublin, 1656), p. 104; Richard Snoddy, *The soteriology of James Ussher: the act and object of saving faith* (Oxford, 2014), p. 26.

17 Judy Barry, 'O'Brien, Donough, 4th earl of Thomond', *DIB*; *idem*, 'Barry, David Fitz-James de, 3rd Viscount Buttevant', *DIB*; David Edwards, 'Butler, Thomas, 10th earl of Ormond', *DIB*.

18 Lodge, *Desiderata Curiosa*, i, pp 166ff; McCavitt, 'An unspeakable parliamentary fracas'.

19 Gilbert Library, MS 713, no. 3a (Gilbert's transcript), also records that Chichester's train was borne by a viscount and three knights.

20 James Medcalf (d. 17 Jan. 1632?–3), in W. Fitzgerald and Charles T. Lamacraft (eds), *Some funeral entries of Ireland (from a manuscript in the British Museum)* (Dublin, 1910), p. 161; King's Inns, MS N3/2/1/7, fo. 6r.

21 For the establishment of the Ulster king of arms' office and their role, see Bríd McGrath, '*Obedientia Civium Urbis Felicitas*: Sir Henry Sidney's return to Dublin as depicted in Derricke's *Image of Irelande*' in Thomas Herron, Denna J. Iammarino and Maryclaire Moroney (eds), *John Derricke's The Image of Irelande: with a discoverie of Wood Karne: essays on text and context* (Manchester, 2021), pp 65–76.

22 Wentworth to Coke, 29 April 1634, 31 May 1634, in Knowler (ed.), *Letters and dispatches*, i,

These arrangements were similar to the opening of the 1614 and 1626 English parliaments, although with more soldiers and adjusted for the differences between the two countries (e.g., there were no Irish clerks of the signet or privy seal, lord chamberlain or esquires of the body) and MPs were excluded unless they were privy councillors, crown officials, Wentworth's servants, knights or baronets, soldiers in their troops or selected to bear trains or insignia.[23] These changes reflected the incrementally elaborate ceremonial in early seventeenth-century English and Scottish parliaments, although Charles himself increasingly shrank from public appearances, especially for the opening of the Long Parliament following the failure of the Short Parliament after an absence of parliaments since 1628.[24]

Wentworth boasted of the magnificence of the opening ceremonies to the Lord Treasurer of England, Richard Weston, first earl of Portland, and the Secretary of State, Sir John Coke:

> The meeting was, I am persuaded with the greatest Civility and splendor Ireland ever saw, and I assure your Lordship the Aspect of the Nobility, Clergy and Gentry, far above that which I expected, and all this accompanied with a singular Chearfulness towards his Majesty's affairs.[25]

Wentworth's processions to and from parliament were much longer and more stage-managed than Chichester's, presumably both to flatter his own ego and to inspire greater awe and deference. The procession included a foot company followed by two trumpeters and a troop of horse, two messengers, gentlemen and esquires (it is unclear who these were), a clerk of the crown and of the Commons, the clerk of the parliament and another clerk of the crown. These were followed by Wentworth's secretaries, steward and comptroller, the puisne serjeant, masters

pp 240, 259; Shaw, 'Thomas Wentworth and monarchical ritual'. Maltravers was returned, on Ormond's nomination, for Callan, although, with his father, he left for England almost immediately after the parliament first met and resigned his seat. R. Malcolm Smuts, 'Howard, Thomas, fourteenth earl of Arundel', *Oxford DNB*.

23 Inner Temple, MS 538.44, fos. 280r–2v procession of 1627 English parliament, fos. 284r–7r. This volume is almost entirely concerned with precedence, including fos. 47r–58v, Kerry's claims of precedency over Slane which arose in the 1613 parliament and was brought to James who directed a commission under the great seal of England to the lord deputy and council in Ireland to determine it. The council decided on 11 Nov. 1614 that Kerry took precedence unless Slane could produce better evidence than he had already done, fos. 47r–58v; Peacey, 'Street theatre of state'; *Commons' Jn. Ire.*, 14 July 1634; NLI, GO, MS 6, fos. 39–41.

24 Thomas Jones to Salisbury, 25 Feb. 1612, TNA, SP 63/232, fo. 28r; English privy council to Chichester, 21 July 1612, *Cal. S.P. Ire., 1611–14*, p. 276; Wentworth to Coke, 13, 29 April 1634, 31 May 1634, all in Knowler (ed.), *Letters and dispatches*, i, pp 240, 259; Peacey, 'Street theatre of state'; Hannay and Watson, 'Building of the parliament house'.

25 Wentworth to Portland, 19 July 1634, in Knowler (ed.), *Letters and dispatches*, i, p. 274. He wrote in the same vein to Coke on 18 Aug., ibid., i, p. 276. The procession was described in the Commons' journals in the same detail. Brian Quintrell, 'Weston, Richard, first earl of Portland', *Oxford DNB*; Michael B. Young, 'Coke, Sir John', *Oxford DNB*.

in chancery, king's solicitor and attorney general, knights bachelor, judges of the exchequer, chancery, common pleas and king's bench. After them came privy councillors who were not peers, knights and baronets, the principal secretary, master of the ordnance, master of the rolls, chief baron of the exchequer and other officers of state, followed by the barons, viscounts and earls, led by the youngest. The procession was very lengthy, as most went in twos, and each section was separated by either two trumpeters or messengers, or both, and in some places other functionaries, such as the Athlone Pursuivant at Arms, Ireland's second-most-senior herald, Albon Leverett at the time, who, with two trumpeters, marked the distinction between barons and viscounts.[26] Great attention was paid to precedence and some officials, such as the master of the ordnance, treasurer at war and marshal, went by their rank rather than their offices and others, like Cork, took his place as treasurer, rather than as an earl. Ormond and Kildare were not part of the peers' procession, but walked immediately before the lord deputy carrying the sword and cap behind the Ulster king of arms who was flanked by two gentlemen ushers. Ormond was flanked by three serjeants-at-arms. Wentworth himself was accompanied by one of his secretaries, footmen and yeomen of horse. Behind him a gentleman of the horse led a riderless 'horse of estate' followed by the colonel, the guard, two more trumpeters and finally a troop of horse. The list named many New English peers, marked as absent. As most of the afternoon was spent inducting lords and establishing them in their places and announcing the names of the very many absent peers and their proxies, the deputy postponed any other business until the following day. The 1640 procession was very similar, except that fewer troops of soldiers are mentioned, and the six clerks in chancery joined the procession. As the lords justices took Wentworth's place, royal dress had a prominent position:

> Royal Robes, or Mantell, The Capp of Estate togither with the hood and sur-roabe the ermine turned outsward & capp upp somewhat long born by the Earl of Ormond supported on the left hand by 2 bare headed [men] Sir Robert Loftus and Capt [Arthur] Chichester.[27]

Wentworth's notions of decorum were served in 1634 by assigning prominent roles to the premier earl (Kildare) and Ormond, both Protestant natives, but also increased his own prestige by having two earls carrying the insignia. While Thomond's heir had carried Chichester's train, Wentworth's was borne by three MPs (William Brabazon, first earl of Meath, Sir Robert Loftus and Arthur Jones), the eldest sons of New English Protestant peers.[28] On 16 March 1640 Thomas

26 Leverett held the office for over 30 years (1618–50) in succession to his father, William Leverett (1595–1618). See H.F. Berry, 'Notes on a statement dated 1634, regarding St Thomas' Court and St Katherine's Churchyard, Dublin', *JRSAI*, fifth series, 37:4 (Dec., 1907), 393–6.

27 NLI, GO, MS 6, fos. 39–41. Loftus and Chichester were MPs and the heirs of the New English viscounts Ely and Chichester.

28 On Brabazon, see 'Meath' in G.E.C., *Peerage*.

Cromwell, first Viscount Lecale and Henry Power, first Viscount Valentia, bore the sword and cap and Robert Loftus and Captain Chichester the train, marking a move from Old English nobles to the New English ascendancy, but when Strafford entered on 20 March, Thomond and Ormond carried the sword and cap respectively and Wentworth's son Lord Raby, Robert Loftus and Captain Chichester bore his train.[29] All the participants on both occasions were Protestant, but at the prorogation on 17 June 1640 Nicholas Preston, sixth Viscount Gormanston, bore the sword and Christopher Plunkett, second earl of Fingall, the cap and the latter carried the sword on 12 November 1640.[30]

The presence of peers, bishops, heralds and other officials in their colourful gowns, trumpeters and beautifully caparisoned horses added greatly to the magnificence and opulence of parliament's openings, as well as swelling the numbers in the procession. Catholic lords, who were increasingly excluded from other state occasions, would have welcomed the opportunity to participate in parliamentary ceremonial, especially since old-established Irish peers took precedence over newer creations, most of whom were New English Protestants, including in seating arrangements. Only three native peers were invited to St John's inauguration as deputy in 1616 and none was mentioned as being present at Wentworth's.[31] The exclusion of Maurice Roche, third Viscount Fermoy, and others from the 1640 parliament would have rankled for many reasons, including being deprived of one of the few occasions in which their status was still formally recognized.[32] Irish peers' precedence disputes underscore their perception of the importance of place; the 1613 parliament saw bitter contention between Delvin and Killeen, Buttevant and Gormanston, Kerry and Slane, Trimbleston and Dunsany; Barry, Courcy and Fermoy later joined the lists.[33] Prelates also disputed precedency; Hampton pushed hard for his primacy over the archbishop of Dublin in Convocation but was over-ruled by Chichester on the grounds that Jones was chancellor, and 'matters of honour stood otherwise here than in England.' There was subsequently an undignified spat between the prelates at the opening of Convocation. Ussher raised the issue of clerical precedence in both parliament and Convocation in 1634.[34]

29 'Lecale', 'Valentia' in G.E.C., *Peerage*.
30 TCD, MS 615 (unpaginated), entries for 16 and 20 March 1640; John Bergin, 'Preston, Nicholas, 6th Viscount Gormanston', *DIB*; 'Fingall' in G.E.C., *Peerage*.
31 FSL, MS X.d.607; Bríd McGrath, 'An invitation to an early modern Irish funeral or a celebration: Folger MS X.d.607', *Anal. Hib.* (forthcoming); BL, Add. MS 72,414, Trumbull Papers 173, fos. 102ff; Walsingham Gressley, *A letter of newes from Ireland, contayning (among other thinges) the new lord deputies entertainement and taking his place there anno domini, 1633* (London, 1633); McGrath, 'Irish elections of 1640–1641'.
32 Micheál Ó Siochrú, 'Roche, Maurice, 3rd Viscount Fermoy', *DIB*.
33 Kane, *Politics and culture of honour*, pp 200–3.
34 Hampton to Abbott, archbishop of Canterbury, 16 Aug. 1613, TCD, MS 1,062, pp 49–53. For Hampton, see Alan Ford, 'Hampton, Christopher', *Oxford DNB*; Ussher to Laud, 20 Aug. 1634, in Boran (ed.), *Correspondence of James Ussher*, ii p. 648.

Towns and cities were used to impressive, colourful civic functions and pageants, including the annual processions for mayors' election and installation, riding of franchises and civic entries, such as Wentworth's in Galway and Limerick.[35] Urban civic occasions included women, and the 1585 London parliamentary procession included 24 'women and maidens', otherwise described as 'many noblewomen [and] ladies' who rode in single file, each of them out-vying the others in raiment, adornment and horse-trappings and the 1601 procession also included women of the court. Chairs were placed in the English upper house for the queen and Prince of Wales, but Jason Peacey describes 'many great ladies', including Buckingham's wife and mother, viewing the opening procession in 1621 from the windows of houses overlooking the route.[36] Women of the royal family sat with the monarch at the French Estates General and one woodcut of the 1577 estates at Blois included a gallery from which women could view the proceedings. There is no reference to women's presence at the opening of any Irish parliament although they were involved in urban ceremonies.[37]

Wentworth's opening procession was not merely a display of great magnificence – it represented the entire New English administration in all its glory and projected a clear image of the Anglicized, Protestant kingdom of Ireland, excluding most Catholic MPs and downgrading the role of native lords. The power to dub knights was used extensively by lords deputy to promote their family, friends and associates and far more Protestants than Catholics were knighted by Chichester and Wentworth; 65% of the 258 Irish knights created between 1603 and 1629 were Protestant. Immediately after his inauguration, Wentworth dubbed three Yorkshiremen (his brother George, Wandesford's son-in-law Thomas Danby and Thomas Remington, 'a very young Gentleman vnder yeares, who hopes to save his Wardshipp thereby').[38] Gallingly, Wentworth knighted his newly appointed Secretary of State, Philip Mainwaring the day before parliament met to give him a more prestigious position in the procession.[39] Peers and 19 and 15 Catholic knights and baronets respectively were the only Irish Catholics in the 1634 and 1640 processions (Table 6.1). Most Catholic MPs who wished to see the procession were left in the humiliating position of having to queue in the street, possibly behind barriers, or peer from houses with windows overlooking the route.

35 Fletcher, *Drama, performance and polity*, pp 197–205.

36 https://folgerpedia.folger.edu/mediawiki/media/images_pedia_folgerpedia_mw/e/e7/ECDbD_1584.pdf [accessed 26 March 2019]; Kyle, 'Parliament and the palace of Westminster'; Peacey, 'Street theatre of state'.

37 Jonathan Patterson, 'The Estates General of Blois (1588) as represented in Pierre Matthieu's *La Guisiade* (1589)', Unpublished paper given at 'Political assemblies in European historical drama, *c.* 1550–1650', 23–30 June 2021; Bríd McGrath, 'Looking the part: dress and civic status and ethnicity in early-modern Ireland', *JRSAI*, 148 (2018), 101–21.

38 BL, Add. MS 72,414, fo. 106v.

39 Terry Clavin, 'Mainwaring, Philip', *DIB*.

Table 6.1. MPs who were knights or baronets, 1613–40, at opening of parliament[40]

Year	*Protestants*	*Catholics*
1613	40	10
1634	55	19
1640	52	15

Scottish protocol, known as 'the riding of the estates', was different, if changing. Scottish processions included all members of the estates, heralds, pursuivants and trumpeters, although Scottish etiquette and protocol was somewhat different from English and Irish, and the participants' coloured robes were more vibrant.[41] Burgesses and shire commissioners were fined if they did not appear in the prescribed 'futemantillis'; many refused to buy the hugely expensive new gowns and avoided the procession.[42] At the opening of the 1639 Scottish Estates, the burgesses went first in the procession, riding two and two, unlike the Irish MPs in 1613 who were on foot, followed by the commissioners of the shires and lords, in order of their precedence.

English peers did not present their writs of summons until the third day, but Irish lords were admitted to and placed in their assigned seats with elaborate ceremony by the Ulster king of arms before the deputy arrived and asked the chancellor to have the Commons summoned by the gentleman usher (Black Rod). The chancellor declared the reasons for summoning parliament and requested the Commons to return to their house to select their speaker and to present their choice in another plenary session on a specified day. In 1640, the lords justices declared the reasons for summoning parliament, an unexplained deviation from normal practice.[43] The English parliament and French and Scottish Estates' opening session also included statements of the causes of their meeting.[44]

The timescale for choosing the speaker was formalized in the early Stuart period; the 1569 parliament adjourned for three days before the Commons met to elect a speaker, possibly because of strong objections to the eventual speaker James Stanihurst. Under the Stuarts, the Commons went straight from the plenary session to select the speaker. In 1613 the several days between Davies' election and presentation were filled with frantic attempts to persuade the Catholics to accept

40 MPs returned in by-elections are excluded, and religious adherence is based on their positions at the time of their election (e.g., Piers Crosby and Thomas Esmond were classed as Protestant).

41 For the Scottish procession see Hannay and Watson, 'Building of the parliament house'.

42 MacDonald, *Burghs and parliament*, pp 175–9. Footmantel was a full-length cloak, of sumptuous velvet and silk.

43 HRC, MS 158, p. 68. For the usual procedure, see 'Mr Mason's advice to me of my mannor of proceeding in parliament Sir Christopher Hatton, Lord Chancellor', FSL, MS V.b.303, fo. 145. Foster assumes that this note from the clerk of parliament was from 1587. Foster, 'Painful labour'. Elsynge devoted considerable space to the question of who should make this declaration and how the practice had varied over time. See HRC, MS 158, pp 100–6.

44 Alastair Mann, 'House rules: parliamentary procedure' in Keith M. Brown and Alan R. MacDonald (eds), *Parliament in context, 1235–1707* (Edinburgh, 2010), pp 122–56; Hayden, *France*, pp 105ff.

his victory and return to the Commons. In 1634 Nathaniel Catlin was presented the day after being chosen but Eustace's presentation was deferred to 20 March because of Wentworth's delayed arrival in Ireland.

On his election, the prolocutor, as he was described before his confirmation, was placed in the chair by some of his fellow MPs., invariably led by privy councillors and, in Catlin's case, by Robert Dillon, who nominated him, Barnaby Bryan, later earl of Thomond, St Leger, Wandesford 'and diverse others'.[45] Speakers were formally presented to the deputy in a set-piece ceremony in the Lords where they made a formulaic 'disabling' speech expressing their unfitness for the role, which the deputy over-ruled and the speaker gave a formal oration on the importance of parliament and requested the traditional freedoms and liberties; after the deputy's response, the Commons returned to their own house to begin their business. The speeches were invariably described as learned and eloquent but Chichester's speech may not have been impressively delivered, as his nephew Faithful Fortescue who would have heard it described him as 'noe very good orator, but had a singular good Expression with his pen, sublime and succinkt'.[46]

Stanihurst concluded his acceptance speech requesting MPs traditional freedoms: to be free to come and go to the parliament during its sitting, to be able to speak freely on any bill or other matter before the house and that the Commons might have the right to discipline its own members if they transgressed any law or procedure. These differed from the traditional English freedoms, which included that a favourable construction be placed on his speech, and access to the sovereign.[47] Davies asked for the first two freedoms 'and if that in anything not well understood, they should happen to offend, he requesteth leave, as well for himself as for the rest, to have access' to Chichester.[48] Eustace requested all four freedoms, free speech, disciplining members and access to Strafford, and implicitly also a favourable construction on his speech.[49]

Prorogations were held as plenary sessions (chapter five) with considerable ceremony. The speaker and other MPs who wished to accompany him were summoned to the upper house by the Black Rod. Royal assent was given to bills passed in that session and the speaker traditionally summed up the Commons' work and transmitted their request for the redress of identified grievances. On 16 May 1615, Davies justified the Commons' work in that session, presented 33 draft bills intended to redress grievances which he requested be transmitted into England and asked that parliament be continued with a new session.[50] On 2 August

45 The term was used for the speaker in Convocation, and by the Confederation to describe the chairman of their assembly, who had not been approved by the monarch.

46 Faithful Fortescue, *An account of the Rt. Honourable Sir Arthur Chichester, Lord Belfast, lord deputy of Ireland* (London, 1858), p. 19; McGrath, 'Bio. dict.', i, pp 162–3.

47 Campion, *Historie of Ireland*, pp 194–6; Crowley (ed.), *Politics of language*, pp 28–9; Falkiner, *Essays*, p. 202.

48 Morley (ed.), *Ireland under Elizabeth and James the First*, p. 409.

49 TCD, MS 646, fo. 92v.

50 Davies' speech, 16 May 1615, NLI, MS 834, pp 165–71; ARL, MS Commons' journal, fos. 109r–12v; King's Inns, MS N3/2/1/7, fos. 50v–2r, is not included in the printed journals.

1634, Catlin made a 'short and pithy' (sadly unrecorded) oration and royal consent was given to bills. On 15 December 1634, the assent was given to bills and the Commons, presumably through the speaker, asked for grievances relating to excessive official fees and the establishment of a mint to be considered. While MPs were present when the royal assent was given on 18 April 1635 and 12 November 1640, there is no reference to their active participation, but the Commons had presented a lengthy list of grievances to be redressed on the 17 June 1640 prorogation.[51]

Parliament's dissolution was more subdued than its opening, with no procession or church service, but it was still a formal ceremony, held as a plenary session in the Lords; the lord deputy and peers wore their robes and the speaker may have given an oration before the commission for the dissolution was read. Stanihurst and Walsh gave closing orations; the former used his speech to push his own pet project of diocesan schools to Anglicize the Irish and the establishment of a university.[52] However, when parliament was dissolved on the first day of the new session in October 1615, there was no opportunity for the Commons to make requests, or the speaker to rehearse their achievements, as he had done at the end of the previous session. Only sparse details of the dissolution were given in the Commons' journals, and Rothe expressed resentment at 'the accustomed solemnitie, and wonted ceremonye of Conkludinge it beinge omitted', which may refer to the speaker's not contributing to the proceedings or to the lack of royal assent being given, although both had happened at the end of the last session.[53] There is no reference to the Commons' participation on the dissolution on 18 April 1635, but assent was given to legislation and Wentworth knighted Catlin in the presence chamber in appreciation of his work as speaker.[54] There was no concluding ceremony for the 1640 parliament, which was determined by Charles' execution.

Religious services were not confined to parliament's opening. There was no Irish equivalent of the stream of sermons preached to early modern English parliaments, nor did the Irish parliament commission any, nor were Irish ones published as quickly as Laud's sermons at the opening of the 1625, 1626 and 1628 parliaments. Between 1603 and 1640, only 13 sermons or collections of sermons were printed in Ireland.[55] However, other sermons were delivered during

51 All references are to *LJI* on those dates and *Commons' Jn. Ire.*, 17 June 1640. This was illegal as the commission for that parliament had not authorized prorogations.

52 Campion, *Historie of Ireland*, pp 194–6; TNA, SP 63/124, fo. 44.

53 David Rothe, *Analecta*, NLI, MS 643, fo. 25v. I am grateful to Stephen Hand for drawing this reference to my attention and providing me with a transcription.

54 All references are to the Lords' journals on those dates. Grosart (ed.), *Lismore Papers*, 1st series, iv, p. 94.

55 L.A. Ferrell, 'Preaching and English parliaments in the 1620s' in Chris R. Kyle (ed.), *Managing Tudor and Stuart parliaments: essays in memory of Michael Graves: Parliamentary History Yearbook*, 34:1 (Chichester, 2015), pp 142–54; Tom Webster, 'Preaching and parliament, 1640–1659' in Peter McCullough, Hugh Adlington and Emma Rhatigan (eds), *The Oxford handbook of the early modern sermon* (Oxford, 2011), pp 404–20; Raymond Gillespie, 'Preaching the reformation in early modern Ireland' in McCullough, Adlington and Rhatigan (eds), *Oxford handbook of the early*

parliaments. Bedell's before Wentworth in Christchurch in November 1634, on Revelation 18:4, which states 'And I heard another voice from heaven saying: Come out of her my people that yee be not partakers on her sinnes, and that ye receive not of her plagues', was regarded as conciliatory towards Catholics, although presumably none were in the congregation to hear it.[56]

Prayers were said daily in both houses before the start of business.[57] A bishop led prayers in the upper house and recusant lords absented themselves until after prayers in October 1614; the 1634 order fining peers who arrived more than 15 minutes after prayers may have been tactfully intended.[58] A prayer written for the second session in 1634, probably by Bramhall, was especially unsubtle and entirely in the mould of Laud's parliamentary sermons which clearly articulated the view that 'a parliament expresses the will of the king':[59]

> O god which art the fountaine of all goodnesse, by whome Kinges raigne, and Princes decree Justice, to whome the Kingdomes of the earth are but as droppes of morning dewe, by whose providence they are exalted, depressed, formed, deformed, builded, destroyed, wee laud and magnify thy glorious name, for that blessed tranquility which wee enioy, by thine especiall grace, under the government of our dread Soveraigne Lord give us thankefull hartes towards the[e], loyal towards him, loving one towards another. As thou haste given a prosperous beginning to this great assembly of all estates. Soe crowne it with a successful conclusion, that it may answer, and exceed, the expectation of the world, and become a firme foundation of future happinesse to posterity, both in Church and common wealth. O eternall father, suffer noe evill spirit of discord to walke amonge us. But be thou present and Precedent at all our Counsailes and Consultations, that they may tend to the advancement of thy glory, the honor of his sacred Majestie, the restauration of this miserable Church, the reformacon of abuses, the settlement of this Kingdome, and finally the reduceing of all thinges that are out of order to a sweet and perfect harmony.[60]

There is no record of a Commons' chaplain so the speaker, a layman, read the prayers, although their substance is unknown and it is unclear who composed them. For the first week of the October 1614 session, Catholic MPs 'sat still, soberly, during the time of prayer', but then stayed away until after prayers, a

modern sermon, pp 287–302. This paper does not mention Irish parliamentary sermons. There are no recorded Catholic sermons on the parliament. I am grateful to Tadhg Ó hAnnracháin for this point.

56 Bodl. Lib., Tanner MS 70, fos. 33r–40r; Monck Mason, *Life of William Bedell*, pp 258–62.

57 Prayers are not expressly mentioned in the 1634 journals, but the speaker is recorded as conducting prayers at the opening sessions of 11 Oct. 1614, 18 April 1615 and 21 March 1640. The journals do not record who conducted prayers on 1 June 1640 and 1 Oct. 1640.

58 *LJI*, 19 July 1634.

59 Ferrell, 'Preaching and English parliaments'.

60 A prayer for the parliament 1634, HL, HP, Religious Papers, Box 1 (16).

change Davies blamed on priests' influence.[61] The order on 17 November 1642 that members who 'shall not come to attend … before the end of morning prayers, shall pay one shilling to the poor' was probably designed to encourage punctuality in a poorly attended Protestant assembly.

LOCATION AND LAYOUT

Medieval parliaments met wherever the ruler happened to be and their locations varied into the sixteenth century, but were established in the seventeenth. The French Estates General met at Orleans (1560), Pontoise (1561), Blois (1576, 1588) and Paris (1592, 1614) and had formerly sat at Tours. The Scottish Estates met in the Tolbooths (town halls) of Edinburgh, Linlithgow, Perth and Stirling, in Holyrood and St Giles' Cathedral in Edinburgh before Charles constructed a complex of offices in Edinburgh in the 1630s, including the Court of Session, privy council chamber and magnificent parliament house.[62]

The English parliament generally met in Westminster from at least the fourteenth century, either in the Painted Chamber in the palace of Westminster, or Westminster Abbey's rectory, the chapter house, St Stephen's chapel or at Blackfriars monastery. It acquired its first permanent, exclusive home, St Stephen's Chapel, under Edward VI in the mid-sixteenth century. The joint sitting of both houses James assembled on his son Henry's inauguration as Prince of Wales was held 'in the Court of Requests, the Lords sitting on the right hand by themselves and the Commons on the left hand.' Presumably the Court of Requests was large enough to accommodate both houses comfortably.[63] Parliament assembled in Oxford in 1625 and 1665 to avoid the plague, from 1643, when the king and court were based there during the civil war, and in 1681, for political reasons, as the Commons wanted to exclude the duke of York, the king's brother and heir (later James II) from the succession and Charles II thought he could more easily control them in Oxford.[64] In 1625 the Commons met in the Divinity School and the Lords in Convocation House. The same locations were used in the 1640s for the Royalist members and peers; however, in 1665, the Commons met in Convocation House and the Lords in the Geometry Room.[65] These locations were

61 Davies to Somerset, 31 Oct. 1614, TNA, SP 63/232, fo. 201.

62 Jenny Wormald, 'James VI & I', *History Today*, 52:6 (June, 2002), 27–33; MacKechnie, 'Housing Scotland's parliament'; Hannay and Watson, 'Building of the parliament house', esp. p. 7, for the parliament house's location and p. 2 for its internal layout. The parliament house cost £127,000 Scots (£10,583 sterling) to build.

63 Elsynge, *Ancient method and manner*, pp 100–1.

64 Hawkyard, *Commons*, pp 189–95; Alasdair D. Hawkyard, 'From Painted Chamber to St Stephen's Chapel: the meeting places of the House of Commons at Westminster until 1603', *Parl. Hist.*, 21:1 (2002), 62–84; Kyle, 'Parliament and the palace of Westminster'.

65 https://www.bodleian.ox.ac.uk/whatson/whats-on/online/parliament-week/parliament-week-2011/Parliament-in-Oxford [accessed 15 March 2019]. I am grateful to Mike Webb for giving me a tour of these locations.

presumably chosen because they could accommodate all those attending. Convocation House was roughly the same size as the Commons' chamber, a mere 60 feet by 32. In the 1640s, the majority of peers, but only one third of the Commons, sat in Oxford.[66] The Catalan Corts were usually held in Barcelona, but in 1626 the crown tried unsuccessfully to move them to Lleida, as a 'rather inconvenient place' to reduce Barcelona's influence and also the number of 'undesirables' attending.[67]

Irish parliaments had been held in many locations over the centuries, including Ballydoyle, Cashel, Castledermot, Drogheda, Dublin, Kildare, Kilkenny, Limerick, Naas, Trim and Wexford, and had no established or dedicated meeting place in the early modern period, partly because it met so rarely. Consequently, it assembled in buildings designed and used for other purposes.[68] The 1536–7 parliament met in Dublin, Kilkenny, Cashel and Limerick and 33 H VIII, c. 8 renewed the earlier prohibition on parliament meeting outside the capital and Drogheda. However, in 1541–3 parliament sat in Dublin, Limerick and Trim (see chapter 1) and Mary's parliament met at Dublin, Limerick and Drogheda.[69] The 1585 parliament was twice adjourned to Drogheda, the last time it met outside Dublin, although no business was actually conducted as those sessions were immediately prorogued. There was no obvious or ideal location in the capital; the Tudor parliament met in Christ Church Cathedral and possibly Dublin Castle.[70] Parliaments' location depended on their size and logistical needs and what accommodation was available. The two cathedrals presented difficulties: St Patrick's was the venue for Convocation which met in the afternoons, but whose fixed layout would not be practicable to rearrange every day.[71] While sessions generally met outside law terms, court sittings were, like parliament's, in the mornings.

At the most basic level, parliament needed two chambers large enough to accommodate both houses and with good acoustics, lobbies for voting which doubled as spaces for suitors, legal counsel and others waiting to be called into the House, and offices for the speaker and clerks, who needed room to store

66 Kyle, *Theater of state*, p. 34.

67 Elliott, *Revolt of the Catalans*, pp 215–16.

68 Caesar Litton Falkiner, 'The parliament of Ireland under the Tudor sovereigns: with some notices of the speakers of the Irish House of Commons', *Proc. RIA*, 25C (1904), 508–41; 33 Hen. VIII, Session 2, c. 1. 1542; Berry (ed.), *Statute rolls*, p. v, notes that under Henry VI, parliaments and Great Councils were held in Dublin, Naas, Trim, Drogheda and Castledermot: 'When the houses met in the metropolis, the Commons are expressly stated to have sat in the Common House of the Cathedral of the Holy Trinity.' (Christchurch). Also, see Abridgment of proceedings in Parliaments held at Dublin, Trim, Wexford, Drogheda, from 11 Hen. IV (1409–10) to 11 Edw. IV (1471–2), TCD, MS 1,445.

69 Lodge, *Sketches*.

70 Falkiner, 'Parliament of Ireland under the Tudor sovereigns'; Routledge, 'Journal'.

71 Hampton to James, 28 April 1615, *Cal. S.P. Ire., 1615–25*, p. 49; Empey (ed.), *Early Stuart Irish warrants*, p. 187; Hawkyard, 'From Painted Chamber' states that the sixteenth-century English Commons shared the refectory of Westminster Abbey with the monks and that the serjeant-at-arms and his staff rearranged the furniture for the monastic community's lunch after the Commons had finished their morning's work.

parliament's records which unlike their English counterpart had no designated repository.[72] The serjeant-at-arms and his staff needed storage space and accommodation for themselves and those in his custody, although some were imprisoned in the castle, Marshalsea or Newgate.[73] Hawkyard notes that the Commons' chamber should be 'robust', but that was more important in England where parliament was much larger and had a permanent home with a fixed layout and durable furniture and fittings. Finally, there should be toilets; there is no equivalent mention of the English Commons' 'bog house', but privies must have been conveniently located.[74]

The Lords had fewer members than the Commons and even smaller actual attendance. The number of Irish peers increased dramatically as the seventeenth century progressed, but most new creations were absentee Englishmen with no interest in Ireland, whose personal attendance was not required or possibly desired, as their votes were cast by proxy, guaranteeing a permanent majority for the crown. However, as judges and learned counsel attended the peers and parliament's plenary sessions usually took place in the upper house, a larger room was needed to accommodate the deputy, his retinue, and as many members of the Commons as could squeeze in. There was so little space below the bar in the English upper house that MPs hustled to get in and their own chamber could barely accommodate them. The description of Irish MPs 'standing on a heap together below' in 1613 indicates that this was a problem also in Ireland but Wentworth also used the presence chamber for meeting with both houses.[75] This problem disappeared after 1641, when the 'rump' parliament was so small; in March 1647 Ormond responded to the remonstrance of both houses of the Irish parliament in joint session, when the small attendance would have been easily accommodated in the Lords' chamber.[76]

Ideally, parliament's accommodation should be close to the castle and courts, for the convenience of the deputy, privy councillors, judges, members and officials. The location should be convenient for the deputy attending the upper house or meeting members of both houses in the presence chamber.[77] Privy councillors who were members of either house would appreciate being close to the council chamber where they met in the afternoons to conduct their usual business. Judges who sat

72 Thrush, 'House of Lords' records repository'.

73 Before 1613, the Lords voted by whispering into the chancellor's ear, for which no separate lobby was necessary. King's Inns, MS N3/2/1/7, fo. 6, notes that 'chambers' were prepared for voting in 1613. Prisoners were held in the castle and the other prisons on 30–31 Oct. 1614, 8 Nov. 1614, 26 Nov. 1614, 16 May 1615, 31 Oct. 1634 and 11 Jan. 1642. Wattson's plan, reproduced in J.B. Maguire, 'Seventeenth-century plans of Dublin Castle', *JRSAI*, 104 (1974), 5–14, shows the location of the castle prison in 1606.

74 Hawkyard, 'From Painted Chamber'.

75 Neale, *House*, pp 339–40; Keeler, 'Committee for privileges'; King's Inns, MS N3/2/1/7, fo. 6v. This information is not in the printed journals.

76 Address of the Lord and Commons to Ormond, 17 March 1647, Bodl. Lib., Carte MS 176, fo. 210; Bodl. Lib., Carte MS 20, fos. 471–5.

77 *Commons' Jn. Ire.*, 17 April 1635, 12 June 1640, 15 May 1641.

with the Lords in the morning would wish to be near their chambers and, in term time, courtrooms, which were also used for committees and were convenient for counsel who addressed the houses. Bishops would appreciate not having to travel far to attend either the privy council or Convocation in the afternoons.

Parliament's possible location was frequently considered. In 1606 the chief justice of king's bench James Ley inspected the old Blackfriars monastery, on the north side of the river Liffey, where the present Four Courts stands, as a possible site for the courts and parliament. He deemed its buildings suitable for the courts and the rooms in the east and north-west appropriate for both houses of parliament, but the estimate for the renovation was regarded as excessive at 1,600 harps (£1,200 sterling) and Blackfriars was used to develop the King's Inns instead.[78] The King's Inns greatly improved, adapted and extended their accommodation, and James II's 1689 parliament was held there. Chichester recommended Dublin Castle

> as the fittest, wher the lower Hall maye be prepared for the lower house, and the presence and with drawing Chamber beinge made into one Roome by taking down the particion wyll serve for the lords … I can not thinke of anie place about this towne so convenient.

This was the location for each parliament between 1613 and 1648.[79] Parliament was so established in Stuart Dublin that the Confederation felt obliged to justify its General Assembly meeting elsewhere although the capital would not have been an option in any case.[80]

The Commons' larger numbers justified the Castle's use, but there were also security considerations. Both houses were accommodated in the hall, as there are frequent references to their conferences in the room between the houses, and the presence chamber. The hall was 'built after the form of a church, raised upon severall stately pillars' above the gunpowder stores, a source of concern to the Catholics, especially since memories of the great explosion on the quays of Dublin in 1597, which killed 126 people, would have been fresh.[81] Catholics mistrusted Chichester's motives for choosing the castle,

78 Ley and others to Chichester, 18 July 1606, TNA, SP 63/219, fo. 31; Chichester to the English privy council, 29 April 1606, in MacNeill (ed.), '*Collectanea de Rebus Hibernicis*', p. 380; Colum Kenny, 'The Four Courts in Dublin before 1796', *IJ*, new series, 21:1 (Summer, 1986), 107–24; Terry Clavin, 'Ley, James', *DIB*; King's Inns, MS B1/1 contains considerable detail on the refurbishment and adaptation of the King's Inns to meet that society's needs. A transcript is being prepared for publication.

79 Chichester to Davies, 4 Aug. 1612, HL, HP, Irish Box 3 (46); James to Chichester, 26 Sept. 1612, *Cal. S.P. Ire., 1611–14*, p. 285.

80 Bodl. Lib., Carte MS 68, fos. 91ff.

81 *Cal. Carew*, v, p. 265; Colm Lennon, 'Dublin's great explosion of 1597', *History Ireland*, 3:3 (Autumn, 1995), 29–34.

> either to make the King believe there was feare to be conceaved of our loyaltie, … or … to stryke the greater terrour and amazement to the harts and myndes of the rest, … with great numbers of armed soldiours … so as the parliament men found themselves locked in at the pleasure of the deputy, in nature of prisoners.[82]

Chichester was concerned about security (although not about the gunpowder, despite the recent Irish and English experiences), especially given the tension engendered by his packing the parliament, and not averse to using intimidation, although he justified summoning 100 soldiers 'foreseeing that great crowds would resort to the city in Parliament time, and that he might want men to repress any sudden disturbance.'[83]

Falkland considered Kildare Hall in Back Lane, opposite Christ Church, built by the dowager countess of Kildare, Elizabeth FitzGerald, for the Jesuits in 1627, as suitable, 'there being no convenient place in the Castle.' Kildare Hall was close to Dublin Castle, the cathedrals and courts and on a large site, with 26 rooms plus an elegant hall, 75 feet long and 27 feet wide (larger than the English Commons), designed as a church, with a raised dais for the altar which would have been suitable for the chair of estate for the lord deputy and the chancellor's woolsack in the Lords or the speaker's seat in the Commons, and a cloister above with many other chambers. The hall was beautifully decorated, 'galleried above round about with rails and turned ballasters, coloured … all things most fair and graceful, like the Banqueting house at Whitehall.' Kildare Hall was seized by the administration in 1630 and handed over to Trinity College, but Lady Kildare persuaded Wentworth to restore it to her in 1634.[84]

Dublin Castle was in very poor condition despite being altered, restored and developed by every chief governor, especially Sidney, Falkland and Wentworth. The parliament house failed to impress Sir William Brereton, MP for Cheshire in 1628, who described it in 1635 as

> much less and meaner than ours. The Lords' house is now furnished with about sixty or seventy armours for horse, which are my Lord Deputy's: this a room of no great state nor receipt. Herein there sat the first session about

82 Jackson (ed.), 'Document'.

83 Maguire, 'Seventeenth-century plans'. The gunpowder stores were not moved until shortly before the fire which destroyed the building in 1671. *Cal. S.P. Ire., 1611–14*, p. 445.

84 Sir William Beecher to Cork, 22 Feb. 1630, in Clarke, McGrath, and Edwards (eds), *A lord justice's letterbook*, no. 137; George A. Little, 'The Jesuit university of Dublin, *c.*1627', *Dublin Historical Record*, 13:2 (1952), 34–47; Rolf Loeber and Magda Stouthamer-Loeber, 'Kildare Hall, the countess of Kildare's patronage of the Jesuits, and the liturgical setting of Catholic worship in early seventeenth-century Dublin' in Elizabeth FitzPatrick and Raymond Gillespie (eds), *The parish in medieval and early modern Ireland* (Dublin, 2006), pp 242–65 discusses the house and its accommodation and provides a reconstruction of the chapel. I am grateful to Stuart Kinsella for drawing this reference to my attention. Also, see Rolf Loeber and Terry Clavin, 'FitzGerald, Elizabeth, countess of Kildare', *DIB*.

> eighty lords; not so many the latter. The Commons House is but a mean and ordinary place.[85]

Wentworth was greatly interested in elegant architecture and comfortable accommodation and improved Dublin Castle and ensured that the Presence Chamber and privy council chamber were tasteful and commodious, but Brereton's comments suggest that he expended little care on the parliament chambers. Moreover, assigning permanent accommodation demonstrates an expectation of the institution's likely continuity.[86] Given Wentworth's pretensions, his choice of the unimpressive Castle accommodation rather than the elegant and commodious Kildare Hall underlines his contempt for parliament. However, the accommodation might have improved by 1640, as Howell reported on Wentworth's 'most splendid court kept at the castle … Traffic increaseth here wonderfully, with all kind of Bravery and Building', especially since the fittings were all new and the committees made much less use of the courts for meetings (see below).[87]

When the rebellion broke out in 1641, MPs were advised to consider an alternative venue as Dublin Castle was no longer a suitable meeting place. Darcy suggested 'either the four courts, or St Patrick's Church in the convocation room … [which] might be made up with deal bars with little cost.'[88] The Commons met in the tholsel at the top of Nicholas Street, opposite Christ Church, in January 1642, but seems to have been back in the Castle later that year; presumably the exclusion of Catholic MPs reduced security concerns.[89] The 1660 Convention met in the Four Courts and Chichester House, on the site of the later parliament house and currently the Bank of Ireland in College Green, was the venue for the 1661 parliament.[90]

The English parliament's medieval monastic building was unsuitable for its work and the Commons' accommodation was inadequate even when first assigned

85 The lords justices described the castle as 'much decayed & very ruinous, especially in the parts thereof that are used for the Deputy's habitation, the ruins whereof are no sooner repaired in one part, than they become defective in another.' See Cork and Loftus to Wentworth, 27 Feb. 1632, in Clarke, McGrath and Edwards (eds), *A lord justice's letterbook*, no. 178; Maguire, 'Seventeenth-century plans'; Howell to Sir Edward Savage, 3 May 1639, in James Howell, *Epistolae Ho-Elianae: familiar letters domestic and foreign* (London, 1645), p. 274; William Brereton's 'Travels' in Falkiner (ed.), *Illustrations*; Chris Kyle, 'Brereton, Sir William' in Thrush and Ferris (ed.), *History of parliament*.

86 Strauss, 'Ceremonial mace'.

87 Maguire, 'Seventeenth-century plans'; Shaw, 'Thomas Wentworth and monarchical ritual'. Alice Thornton describes a magnificent chamber above the chapel, 'most richly furnished with blacke velvett, imbroidered with flowrs of silke worke in ten stich; all fruit trees and flowers, and slips imbroidered with gold twist.' See Alice Thornton, *The autobiography of Mrs Alice Thornton of East Newton, Co. York* (Durham, 1875), p. 12.

88 *Commons' Jn. Ire.*, 17 Nov. 1641.

89 John Speed's map of Dublin, 1610, at http://www.dublincity.ie/sites/default/files/galleries/01-speed-dublin-1610.jpg [accessed 13 March 2019]; *Commons' Jn. Ire.*, 11 Jan. 1642; McGrath, 'Recruiter returns'.

90 Clarke, *Prelude to restoration*, p. 244; Payments upon *concordatums* granted upon several occasions for the use of the parliament, HMC, *Ormond*, new series, iii, pp 396–7.

in 1540. This was exacerbated by its significantly increased membership. However, in 1621 it had the expertise of the great architect Inigo Jones, MP for New Shoreham.[91] The only Irish MPs with known expertise in buildings or decoration were Humphrey Farnham and Daniel Molyeux in 1613, but Brereton's dismissal of the Irish parliament's accommodation was presumably in comparison to what Jones had effected in Westminster, including establishing green upholstery as a sort of branding for the Commons, hangings, including some valuable and elegant tapestries from the royal collection, curtains, fires and light, privies and a smoking room for MPs. The elegance of the décor and concern for comfort described in England and evident in the Scottish Parliament House are not mentioned in Ireland – Irish journals do not refer to candles, heat, light, curtains, seats, cushions, tapestry, hangings or a clock, although there must have been one – but do help explain why it was thought that Kildare Hall might have been a suitable venue. None of the complaints heard in England about the inadequacy of the Commons chamber's space, layout and facilities are recorded for Ireland, although this may be due both to higher expectations in England and to lack of Irish sources.[92]

The Irish Commons' chamber's layout, like the English, was 'in an amphitheatre where the seats ascend in tiers' but much smaller, and fitted out expressly for, and dismantled after, parliament. The raw materials were one of the serjeant-at-arm's perks, and he would have had a vested interest in ensuring that the best quality components were used (see chapter nine).[93] In 1604–5, the English parliament reorganized its seating arrangements to a 'cock-pit' style with five full rows of seating for MPs, the lowest row below the raised central space and some additional seating in a short sixth row behind the speaker's chair. English privy councillors' seating allowed them to direct the speaker's business, but while there is no direct evidence of that in Ireland, there are references to privy councillors' sitting next to the speaker's chair; Stanihurst's collusion with the council, Catlin's lack of objection to parliamentary privilege being breached by Wentworth and Ormond's close relationship with Eustace all suggest that this was likely.[94] Special seats were allocated for London and York's members and possibly also for other towns.[95] Scotland also used benches, with those for 1639 borrowed from the Auld Kirk, along with 'buirds' (tables).[96] The seating arrangements for the 1576 and 1614 French Estates General followed a similar pattern to the English and Irish parliaments and General Assembly, with benches in rows around the chamber's walls and the presiding officer's chair in the middle of the seats on one wall, with the clerk's table in the centre of the room. Two rows of seating were on the presiding officer's wall, three on the opposite wall and four on each of the other

91 John Newman, 'Jones, Inigo', *Oxford DNB*.
92 Loeber and McGrath, 'Legacy of Humphrey Farnham'; Hawkyard, 'Inigo Jones'.
93 James Conway Davies, *Catalogue of manuscripts in the library of the Honourable Society of the Inner Temple*, 2 vols (Oxford, 1972), ii, pp 761–2.
94 Neale, *House*, p. 352; e.g., *Commons' Jn. Ire.*, 12, 26, 31 Oct. 1614, 1 Aug. 1634.
95 Hawkyard, *Commons*, pp 203–4; *idem*, 'Inigo Jones'.
96 Hannay and Watson, 'Building of the parliament house'.

two walls. Specific seats were allocated to representatives from different parts of France.[97] When the 1627 Great Assembly met, the nobility and clergy were seated on forms on each side of Dublin Castle's hall, with the deputy and council sitting at a long table in the middle for the opening session, but afterward 'the Councell and nobility to sit promiscuously together.'[98]

The Irish speaker's chair was on a raised platform in the centre of the far end of the rectangular chamber; it had a curious boxed-in design, as the Protestants trying to evict Everard had to 'open up the small door of the seat.' Brereton described it as 'no very convenient seat for the speaker.'[99] This chair filled both practical and symbolic functions: the platform gave him prominence and a good view of the whole House, to see who wished to speak and keep order. The speaker's office was denoted by his presence in the chair – his being placed there by fellow members was a demonstration of their power to choose him and underlined his position as the popular choice, at least in theory. In England members bowed three times to the speaker's chair as they entered and left the House:

> No Member in coming into the House or in removing from his place, is to pass between the Speaker and any Member then speaking; nor may cross or go overthwart the House, or pass from one side to the other or pass from one side to the other while the House is sitting.

Irish members presumably followed the same practice, although the 1585 rules merely note that members entering the House should make their 'dutyfull and humble obeisance and after to take his place'.[100]

Forms on the lowest bench on one side of the speaker's chair were used by privy councillors and Catholic leaders sat on the other side as the House ordered that 'a dozen on each side of the chair' should go as delegates to the lord deputy and on another occasion that the Treasurer 'and the whole lower Formround' should go to a conference committee with the Lords.[101] There is no other indication of assignment of seats, but the Catholic Sir John Dongan sat one seat behind the Protestant Charles Price and Hardress Waller was seated close enough to both to hear their conversation.[102] There were more benches stretching down the chamber's long sides to the bar. Darcy's suggestion that it would have been easy to fit up an alternative space with deal boards implies that the benches and bar were usually made of a more expensive wood, presumably by the state's master carpenter.[103]

97 BL, Cotton MS Caligula E VI, fos. 349v–50r; Grelin, *Órdre Observé*.
98 TNA, SP 63/245, fos. 25ff. At this stage the meeting did not include delegates from the country (Commons).
99 Moynes (ed.), *Annual letters*, i, p. 414; Chichester to the English privy council, 21 May 1613, in Edwards (ed.), 'Chichester', no. 55; William Brereton's 'Travels' in Falkiner (ed.), *Illustrations*.
100 Scobell, *Memorials*, pp 6–7; Irish Archaeological Society, *Tracts*, ii, p. 143.
101 *Commons' Jn. Ire.*, 26 Oct. 1614, 7 Nov. 1614.
102 Ibid., 4 Nov. 1634.
103 Moynes (ed.), *Annual letters*, i, p. 413; *Commons' Jn. Ire.*, 17 Nov. 1641; *Lib. Mun. Pub. Hib.*,

The speaker ascended the chair each day after prayers, marking the difference between the temporal and spiritual elements of public service. He left the chair during committees of the whole house and his return symbolized the resumption of normal business. When the House dissolved into a Grand Committee but could not decide on a chairman, Eustace resumed his seat, conducted a vote and the House again dissolved into a committee, as happened with the administration's candidate Brereton and Hugh Rochford concerning impeachment and Carpenter and Little's role in the tobacco monopoly and in 1647 between John Lewis and Allan Cooke.[104]

A bar was set up towards the end of each chamber; its position depended on their shape and number of entrances. The Irish Commons had two entrances although it is unclear where they were located. The bar was reminiscent of parliament's role as a court and played an important part in protocol. The Commons' rules specified, that 'if the bar be down, no member that comes in may open it, but must go about to his place.'[105] Anyone not a member of that house had to stay behind the bar unless invited in and MPs and others stood there to be censured by the house.[106] At plenary sittings, MPs stood behind the Lords' bar. Lords passing the cloth of estate, near the bar, were to make obeisance, and the speaker and MPs entering the Lords made three courtesies and obeisance. Messengers from the Commons to the Lords were met at the bar and handed documents over it.[107] Richard Boyle was 'reprehended' for stepping from the bar to speak to some MPs while his counsel was making submissions on the bishop of Waterford and Lismore's private bill on 25 October 1614. In England tellers gave the results of divisions at the bar, making 'obeysance to the House three times; once at the Bar, again in the middle of the House, and again when they are come to the [clerk's] Table.' Chairmen of committees of the whole house delivered their reports at the bar and reporting votes only made two bows to the speaker's empty chair. Irish practice is unclear but presumably similar.[108]

The Irish Lords' chamber was more formal than the Commons, as it included a dais that accommodated the chair and cloth of estate for the lord deputy.[109] Sidney had 'steps or greeses [stairs] made and covered for the seat of estate, being richly hanged' under the cloth of state and the chancellor and treasurer (Dr Robert

2(2), p. 107, appointment 15 Jan. 1618 of John Bannister as master carpenter, succeeded in 1661 by John Mills. Conway Davies, *Catalogue*, ii, pp 761–2.

104 *Commons' Jn. Ire.*, 23 June 1641, 18 May 1647.

105 Ibid., 24 Oct. 1614.

106 E.g., Ibid., 2, 8 Nov. 1614, 15 Nov. 1634, 1 Dec. 1634; Bramhall to Laud, 4 Nov. 1640, HL, HP, MS 14,061.

107 E.g., *LJI*, 28 July 1634.

108 Scobell, *Memorials*, pp 27, 37–8; *Commons' Jn. Ire.*, 15 Feb. 1641; Hawkyard, 'From Painted Chamber'; Kyle, 'Parliament and the palace' notes the multiple entrances to the English chambers.

109 A compressed image of both English houses is provided in the frontispiece to *An exact collection of all remonstrances, declarations, votes, orders, ordinances, proclamations, petitions, messages, answers and remarkable passages betweene the King's most excellent majesty and his high court of parliament* (London, 1643).

Weston and Ormond) sat on 'seats enrailed about, and hanged with green.'[110] Chichester chose a different colour-scheme for his elaborate mise-en-scene; he was provided with

> One cloth of estate of crimson or purple wrought velvet and Crimson or purple wrought cloth of gold embroidered with [royal] armes in two places thereof garnished with frendges and laces of gold and silke, silken and sewinge silke, lior [sic] of thread and Coppinge and lined with with fustian and buckeram, and for all other necessaries to the same belonginge, and for cotton to bee betweene the folds of the same to keep it from fretting … one chaire, two stooles, one footestoole and two quishions of like stuff backed damaske, buttoned and frendged and laced with gold and silke suteable and sewed with silke and for [illegible] of Cotton and pillowes of fustian filled with downe guilt nailes of all sizes gathered and tack for the same Quishions and stooles, a stair of Iron to back of the said chaire and all other necessaries &c.[111]

The cloth of estate and sword were on display also during the 1627 Great Assembly.[112]

During formal sessions the chancellor stood on the deputy's right and in 1634 the treasurer (Cork) on his left. In 1634 a woolsack was provided for the chancellor, although it was noted that this was a departure from convention, possibly on account of Loftus' 66 years.[113] When the deputy was not present, a woolsack for the chancellor stood in front of the chair of estate and the clerk's table was placed between that and the lawyers' woolsacks. Peers sat on forms in order of precedence defined by the Ulster king of arms, with bishops on one side and lords on the other side and opposite the chair of state. In 1569, the judges sat at a table in the middle of the upper house but under the Stuarts they sat on the inner sides of the woolsacks, with learned counsel on the outer sides facing the bishops and peers.[114]

The English Commons had a carving of the monarch's arms near the speaker's chair and it is likely that similar ornaments were placed in the Irish parliament also.[115] Elizabeth sent over her portrait 'to hang by the cloth of state, especially for the great assembly of the country to the Parliament', presumably the same one Sorley Boy MacDonnell, head of the MacDonnells of Islay and the Route in Antrim, kissed when he submitted in 1588.[116] Charles I gave Wentworth portraits

110 Falkiner, 'Parliament of Ireland under the Tudor sovereigns'.
111 Warrant to pay for robes for parliament for Sir A. Chichester, 12 March 1613, BL, Add. MS 5,754.
112 TNA, SP 63/245, fos. 25ff.
113 *LJI*, 14 July 1634; TCD, MS 613, fo. 2r.
114 Falkiner, *Essays*, pp 209, 233.
115 Hawkyard, 'From Painted Chamber'; Maguire, 'Seventeenth-century plans'. See the images in Hawkyard, 'Inigo Jones' where the arms are sometimes in a panel over the speaker's chair.
116 Geoffrey Fenton to Walsingham, 7 April 1581, *Cal. S.P. Ire., 1574–85*, p. 297; TNA, SP 63/82, fo. 39; Perrot to Elizabeth, 14 Dec. 1588, *Cal. S.P. Ire., 1588–92*, p. 78; TNA, SP 63/139, fo. 14; Judy Barry, 'MacDonnell, Sorley Boy', *DIB*.

of himself and Queen Henrietta Maria by the court painter, the Dutch-born Daniel Mytens, which hung on either side of the chair of estate in the presence chamber; presumably these or other state portraits hung in parliament and it is likely that James' portrait was displayed in 1613.[117]

While the Scottish Parliament House had integral fireplaces there is no evidence of them in any contemporary image of the English chambers and it is probable that braziers were used there and in Ireland as the English House of Lords paid Joanne Shorlake £300 3*s.* 8*d.* for 'Charcoales' between 1 October 1646 and 25 March 1649.[118] The cockpit layout did not allow for a fireplace, and had one been a fixture of the Castle's great hall and been at the opposite end to the speaker's chair, the heat would have been largely benefitting visitors behind the bar.

As a unicameral body, the Scottish Estates needed a room for plenary sessions, for the three estates to meet (two after the bishops were expelled) and a room for the Lords of the Articles who were chosen out of the different estates to manage the Estates' business.[119] Many of the same considerations applied to the choice of accommodation for the Confederate's General Assembly. A separate room was assigned to the peers but the single chamber was big enough to accommodate all members, preserving the Commons' general layout. There were three rows of seats, but specific places were not fixed for peers and commoners:

> Those at the upper end were designed for the lords and prelates, not so particularly as others of the trustees did not frequently sit there with them. The chair of the prolocutor was placed at the side of the room, somewhat nearer that end.

Darcy sat bareheaded on a stool representing the judges; the Confederation may have been unwilling to use woolsacks for their assembly.[120]

Members stood at their seats to speak. When James Gough stepped into the middle of the chamber he was 'willed by the house to go back into his place and there deliver what he had to say.'[121] The repeated English rules urging courtesy underlined the need for regulation:

> While the House is sitting, no man ought to speak or whisper to another, to the end the House may not be interrupted when any are speaking; but everyone is to attend to what is spoken ... While one is speaking, none else is to stand up or interrupt him until he have done speaking and be sate down

117 Shaw, 'Thomas Wentworth and monarchical ritual'; Oliver Millar, 'Strafford and Van Dyck' in Richard Ollard and Pamela Tudor-Craig (eds), *For Veronica Wedgwood these: studies in seventeenth-century history* (London, 1986), pp 109–23; Anne Thackray, 'Mytens, Daniel', *Oxford DNB*.

118 Receipt by Joanne Shorlake, 5 July 1649, HRC, MS 165.

119 MacKechnie, 'Housing Scotland's parliament'; Hannay and Watson, 'Building of the parliament house'.

120 Bellings and Gilbert (eds), *History of the Irish Confederation*, i, pp lxiii, 111.

121 McCavitt, 'An unspeakable parliamentary fracas'.

> but when the Speaker desires to speak he ought to be heard without interruption and anyone else who is standing should sit down ... Whosoever hisseth or disturbeth any man in his speech, shall answer it at the Bar.[122]

In 1604 a 'motion for interupting ye speech of any by hissing &c [was] well allowed' and it was recommended that the

> Speaker & all others of the Houses of the better sort at the riseing of the House depart & goe out of the House in civil sort (for reverencie of the House) turning them about with low Curtesie as they vse at their entry & not to thrust or throng out as now vsually which caution which was very well allowed of by the House.[123]

That no such rules are recorded for Ireland does not necessarily indicate that Irish MPs were better behaved than the English – Hooker's description of the 1569 Commons and the dispute over the speakership in 1613 prove otherwise – but Chichester reported that all the discussions in the house in early October 1614 'passed in orderly and civil fashion'.[124]

The Commons had the use of the lobby (outer room), the 'void room' that the serjeant-at-arms was to take care of, 'in which the under clearks do sit, as also such as be sutors and attendant to that house and which was used for voting.'[125] There was also an 'inner room' for the serjeant-at-arms and apparently another which was used for committees. The Lords too had additional space beside their chamber; the outer ('other' or 'next') room was used for committees, as was the 'little' room, but was also where the yeoman usher and the serjeant-at-arms attending the lord chancellor waited, and the king of arms when he was required to place peers attending the house for the first time. During sitting days, the serjeant-at-arms probably sat, like his counterpart the Black Rod in the House of Lords, inside the chamber 'without the bar, in a corner near the door.'[126]

Irish parliamentary committees sat in a variety of locations in 1613–15 and 1634–5. The choice was influenced by rooms' availability and committees' size, especially large ones like the standing committees of privileges or grievance which often met in the Commons' chamber and others of indeterminate size, such as those any member could join. Committees of the whole house always met in Commons' chamber as they were formed during sittings; their chair 'is to sit in the Clerks place at the Table and to write the votes of the Committee.'[127]

122 Scobell, *Memorials*, pp 6–8.

123 The Nature of the Court of the Commons house of Parliament with what matters they may Meddle & a contra Oppisicons & proceedings therein & other observacons therevpon, Newberry Library, MS fk 0452.613, fo. 27. This undated document was clearly written before 1606.

124 Chichester to James, 16 Oct. 1614, TNA, SP 63/232, fo. 193r.

125 *Commons' Jn. Ire.*, 28 Oct. 1614.

126 Hardy (ed.), *Modus*, pp 36–8; Orders for the House of Lords, *LJI*, 23 July 1634, no. 13; *LJI*, 2 Aug. 1634.

127 Scobell, *Memorials*, p. 37.

Commons' committees met in the chamber or 'the inner room of this house', which was also used for small groups delegated to do particular work and return to the house, clearly as a matter of convenience, and in the courts of exchequer, king's bench, common pleas, chancery and wards, Dublin's tholsel and private houses. In 1634, the master of the rolls' chamber was used for one meeting and the dining room of the Castle was the venue for another in 1641.[128] The reference to the committee on the buggery bill meeting in the Court of Wards is misleading because that court shared accommodation with the court of chief place until it moved to its own space in the King's Inns in 1636.[129] Courts were close to the Castle and suitably furnished with benches and tables. The four courts moved in 1608 from the Castle to a building in a 'warren of streets and alleys lying immediately south-west of Christ Church Cathedral' which they 'shared with shopkeepers and spinners.'[130] 'The Courtes of Justice (the same as in England) are kept in a large stone building … which is built in forme of a crosse, at the foure ends are the foure courts well adorned, the middle is to walk in'.[131] Brereton's description of them as 'conveniently framed and contrived, and these very capacious; the Star-Chamber, the Chancery, the King's Bench and Common Pleas – these rooms as useful as ours in England, but here is not such a stately structure or hall to walk in as Westminster Hall' suggests that committees were better accommodated than the parliament.[132] Committees in the 1640 parliament are not recorded as meeting in the courts except on 28 March 1640, when chancery was used, and the 12 committees appointed on 10 June 1641 who met in each of the four courts, the custom house, the tholsel's upper and lower rooms and the Commons' 'inner room'. It was rare for so many committees to be appointed together so the courts may have been used because the usual venues were already occupied.

Practicality sometimes dictated locations: on 9 May 1615 the committee on repairing Christchurch met in that cathedral and the 1634 committee for the king's debts met in the auditor James Ware's house in Castle Street, where he may have had relevant papers. On 19 July 1634, the Commons ordered that the committee of privileges 'may sit in any of his majesty's courts', although a former order had specified that they meet in chancery. On 19 May 1641, a committee met in Dublin's tholsel and on 10 June 1641 the committee on Trinity College was ordered to meet in the college itself. Unusually, on 15 July 1641 the committee to draw up a bill on tobacco met in Patrick Darcy's house at 6 a.m., possibly because other venues might not have been available that early.

Conference committees were generally held in the 'Middle Room' between the two houses but on 7 November 1614 they met in the privy council chamber. The

128 *Commons' Jn. Ire.*, 22 July 1634; Borlase, *History*, p. 10.
129 *Commons' Jn. Ire.*, 25 July 1634; Kenny, 'Four courts in Dublin'.
130 Ibid.
131 Wattson's 1606 plan of Dublin Castle, NLI, MS 2,656. I am grateful to Rachael Moss for drawing this reference to my attention. Luke Gernon's 'Discourse of Ireland, 1620' in Falkiner (ed.), *Illustrations*, pp 345–62.
132 William Brereton's 'Travels' in Falkiner (ed.), *Illustrations*.

layout of these meetings probably followed the English practice in Westminster's Painted Chamber, which was more convenient for the Lords than the Commons, as it was adjacent to the upper chamber 'a table was placed & double forms round it. Without those forms we all [the MPs] stood bare-headed. The Lords after we had attended some time came in & sate within the forms.'[133] Archbishop Ussher offered his house as a venue for a conference committee to draft a declaration on the subsidies, but was concerned whether 'being a private house, [it] be a fit place, which he conceives not.' Ranelagh and Ormond recommended meeting there 'because in the usual place of meeting, they of the commons must be uncovered, which they will dislike', but were overruled.[134]

MATERIAL CULTURE

Very little information about parliament's material culture and few if any artifacts or representations of them remain, apart from documentation such as the 1613–15 journals, the printed statutes of 1634–5 and contemporary images of some robes; state insignia – the maces, sword of state, cap, cloth and chair of estate – no longer survive. The chambers and lobbies were fitted up expressly for each parliament and all furniture was made up and disassembled after each dissolution. Four chairs believed to have been used by the Confederation of Kilkenny survive, presumably used by clerks or possibly the Supreme Council (*plate 39*).[135]

Clothes and furniture played a major role in state ceremonial and institutions in all early modern states. Dress played an important role in a society obsessed with status, precedence and ethnicity; regulations prescribed what clothes men and women of different social status might wear and on which occasions they should wear them.[136] Perrot insisted on English dress in 1585 – 'none was permitted to goe in Irish attire, as in former time they used) but to sort themselves in such habite after the English manner' – a further move towards Anglicizing the appearance of parliament and its members.[137] Thomas Ryves, MP for Monaghan in 1613, appeared for work as registrar of the 1613 Convocation with 'his rapier by

133 E.g., 23–4 Oct. 1640, 11 Nov. 1640, 16 Nov. 1641; Clyve Jones, 'Accommodation in the Painted Chamber for conferences between the Lords and Commons from 1600 to 1834', *Parl. Hist.*, 33:2 (2014), 342–57; *LJI*, 23 July 1634.

134 *Commons' Jn. Ire.*, 28 Feb. 1635, 15 July 1641. I am grateful to Mark Empey for information about the location of Ware's house. *LJI*, 26 March 1640. Darcy's house was in Bridge Street inside the city walls and opposite the King's Inns, a convenient location for a lawyer. J.T. Gilbert, *A history of the city of Dublin*, 3 vols (Dublin, 1854–9), i, p. 331. I am grateful to Coleman Dennehy for drawing this reference to my attention.

135 Tony Canavan, 'Royal Society of Antiquaries of Ireland library', *History Ireland*, 25:4 (July/Aug., 2017), 54–5.

136 McGrath, 'Looking the part'; Eamon Darcy, 'Social order in the 1641 rebellion' in Eamon Darcy, et al. (eds), *The 1641 Depositions and the Irish rebellion* (London, 2012), pp 97–111; McGrath, '*Obedientia Civium*'.

137 Montano, *Roots of English colonialism*, p. 374.

his side and a pair of white bootes on his legs', provoking Hampton's jibe that 'his years were as unripe as his attire'.[138]

Different robes were worn by the lord deputy, chancellor, temporal and spiritual peers, speaker, knights of the shire and burgesses, and judges and officers attending parliament. Sadly the only surviving images of parliamentary dress are Bolton in his chancellor's gown (*plate 37*), the sixteenth earl of Kildare in his robes and Thomas Jones' scarlet robes, although representations of some judges' dress and that of the Athlone Pursuivant, the junior herald have also survived.[139]

The deputy's parliament robes were similar to those worn by the monarch in England, the protocol being established in the early modern period. Elizabeth wanted Sidney to wear the same robes as St Leger, but there was confusion about their form and, left to choose between a garter robe (he had been granted that honour in 1564) or a parliament one, he appealed to William Cecil, the English Secretary of State, for guidance.[140] Cecil's reply was dated only 11 days before parliament met, so Sidney must have had to decide or improvise very quickly and while it is unclear which he chose, he was 'apparelled in the princely robes of crimson velvet doubled or lined with ermin.'[141] Presumably Perrot's robes were equally luxurious and a beautiful new gown and accessories were ordered for Chichester: 'a parliament robe, whoode and Tippett of Crimson velvet powdered with Ermynes, in such manner and forme as to the same belongeth, with taffetta bordered with buckeram and sewed with silke and for all other necessaries to the same belonging.' As robes were such an important part of ceremonial, care was taken to ensure that they were well-looked after.[142]

Under 10 Hen. VII, c. 16 Irish lords were to wear the same robes as their English counterparts. Possession of robes was an important element of peers' ennoblement as 'neither the writt, nor the Tenure created a Baron but the Investure of roabes only', a point that Shane O'Neill insisted on in his clashes with Elizabeth's government in the late 1550s and 1560s: 'he had required to have his parlement robes sent unto him as earle of Tiron, which title he claimed and

138 TCD, MS 1,062, pp 54–5; J.D. Davies, 'Ryves, Sir Thomas', *Oxford DNB*.

139 Kildare's portrait is in Castletown House and is reproduced in Ohlmeyer, *Making Ireland English*, plate one. Jones' funeral monument in St Patrick's Cathedral shows him in his scarlet robes. Cork's monument in the same cathedral shows his grandfather-in-law Robert Weston in his chancellor's gown. William Leverett's son and successor, Albon's tabard is illustrated in NLI, GO, MS 66, Funeral Entries, Volume 3, 1604–22, fo. 73r. 'Fees of office and order of dignities for the Irish parliament, 1585–1632', at http://catalogue.nli.ie/Record/vtls000529756#page/23/mode/1up [accessed 13/1/2023]. I am grateful to Clodagh Tait for drawing this reference to my attention. For a discussion on these clothes, see McGrath, '*Obedientia Civium*'.

140 Wallace T. MacCaffrey, 'Cecil, William, first Baron Burghley', *Oxford DNB*.

141 Sidney to Cecil, 12 Nov. 1568, TNA, SP/63/26, pp 378–9; Cecil to Sidney, 5 Jan. 1569, TNA, SP 63/27, p. 304; Falkiner, 'Parliament of Ireland under the Tudors'.

142 Sidney to Cecil, 12 Nov. 1568, *Cal. S.P. Ire., 1509–73*, pp 393–4; Warrant to pay for robes for Parliament for Sir A. Chichester and for Will. Lyverett, pursuivant of arms, 12 March 1613, BL, Add. MS 5,754; Shaw, 'Thomas Wentworth and monarchical ritual'; Warrant for James Hardcastle for the keeping of all 'robes, hangings clothes of state' for Wentworth in Empey (ed.), *Early Stuart Irish warrants*, no. 527.

required (which if it were denied him then he required a trial to be made in parlement).'[143] Creation robes were different to parliamentary gowns, which were of rich red velvet with fur and worn only for parliament's opening or closing sessions, including prorogations, or other special occasions.[144] St Leger ensured that English dress and parliament gowns were provided for Gaelic lords in 1541; the earl of Desmond and the baron of Upper Ossory were sent parliament robes costing £25, and St Leger delightedly reported that O'Donnell and O'Reilly were wearing English clothes, recommending parliament robes also for the former, even though he was not a member of either house.[145]

Chichester was concerned that peers might not have their gowns ready but the only new creations since 1585 were Theobald Butler, Viscount Tulleophelim, Chichester himself and the earl of Tyrconnell, Rory O'Donnell, who had died in exile in 1608 and whose heir was a child living on the Continent.[146] Robert Jacob concurred, although his doubts may have related to the bishops, as Jones at least had no scarlet robes, though Hampton and his suffragans had.[147] Those with established titles already had parliamentary robes but newly created peers who had to acquire them were in curiously little hurry to do so. Boyle, created Baron Youghal in 1616 and earl of Cork in 1620, did not order his robes until 1634, even though he might have expected to need them in 1628. Trying, as ever, to bring his sons-in-law up to the mark, he urged the perennially impecunious Barrymore 'the Perliament robes, which must not be wanting, wilbe your greatest care and charg'. It is unclear whether there was any distinction between Irish peers' robes; anxious to avoid having to subvent Barrymore even further, Cork advised him to use his grandfather, the fifth Viscount Buttevant's gown, but added that 'Earls' robes 'must be of scarlett cloth, enriched with such furre as are not here to be gotten for any money' (Boyle got his own robes from London at a cost of £66 7*s*. 4*d*., plus carriage.)[148] Bishops may have required different robes for parliament and Convocation; Jones had no scarlet robe for Convocation but it is unlikely that he had no bishop's gown, although as chancellor he would have worn the very heavy black robe with gold braiding for parliament (see *plate 37* for Bolton's portrait).[149]

143 HRC, MS 158, p. 63; Holinshed, *Chronicles*, p. 114; Montano, *Roots of English colonialism*, p. 328; Ciaran Brady, 'O'Neill, Shane', *DIB*.

144 Sir George Carew's Suggestions about the Parliament, [Oct.] 1611, *Cal. S.P. Ire, 1611–14*, pp 162–4; Elsynge, *Ancient method and manner*, pp 90ff; Cork to Barrymore, 6 June 1634, Chatsworth House, Cork Papers, Misc. boxes, Box 3, pp 37–8; Routledge, 'Journal'.

145 Montano, *Roots of English colonialism*, p. 328; Fletcher, *Drama, performance and polity*, p. 133.

146 Emmett O'Byrne, 'O'Donnell, Ruaidhrí, 1st earl of Tyrconnell', *DIB*. On Lord Tulleophelim, see chapter 5 of Edwards, *Ormond lordship*.

147 Jacob to Northampton, undated, but between 6 and 25 March 1613, Bodl. Lib., Laud MS Misc. 612, fos. 138r–40r; TCD, MS 1,062, pp 52–3.

148 Grosart (ed.), *Lismore Papers*, 1st series, iv, pp 29, 35, 59, 356; Cork to Barrymore, 6 June 1634, Chatsworth House, Cork Papers, Misc. boxes, Box 3, pp 37–8; Robert Armstrong, 'Barry, David Fitz-David, 1st earl of Barrymore', *DIB*.

149 TCD, MS 1,062, pp 52–3; Hampton 'finding my lord chancellor unfurnished thereof for Convocation, I persuaded our suffragans to leave our scarlets at home and to go to Convocation in our Rotches [sic] to cover my lord chancellor his omission.'

English and Scottish peers' robes depended on their rank; a Scottish act of 1455 specified different colours of robes to be worn in the estates, with brown for earls, red for lesser lords and blue for burgesses, but orders from James VI repeatedly changed them. Charles generated considerable ill-feeling by insisting on Scottish peers obtaining completely different and very costly robes for his 1633 coronation, on top of the gowns they had to provide for parliament.[150]

Judges wore scarlet robes, in line with practice in law courts in Ireland, England and further afield, but it is not clear whether they wore them every day in parliament or only when the deputy attended. Special legal status was accorded to judgments pronounced by judges wearing scarlet in the Parlement de Paris and Parlement de Provence.[151] In July 1648, when the king of France required the officers of the Parlement de Paris to attend a *Te Deum* in Notre Dame to celebrate military success 'avec les robes rouges', they had to stop work to find their scarlet robes; on another occasion the six masters of requests were dressed 'en robe de soye noire' (gowns of black silk).[152] Darcy wore similar robes to judges, of red velvet with a fur cape and a small black cap in the General Assembly (*plates 9 and 11*) for Darcy's and Bysse's portraits).

Other officials also had impressive dress. The Ulster king of arms had 'kingly robes' and in 1613 the Athlone Pursuivant-at-arms, William Leverett, was provided with 'One coat of crimson and blew damaske painted and wrought of fair gold in oyle of such length and bredth made up and furnished as other pursyuvants of armes formerly have had', although this is different to the image of Leverett's usual robes as Athlone Pursuivant (see *plate 38* for Leverett's robes). The four messengers (pursuivants) each received a 'coate of red cloth embroidered in the back and [front] with our letters I and R' (James Rex).[153] The Irish speaker's robes were presumably similar to their English counterparts: a heavily-braided black gown with wide fur trimming for ordinary sittings and a scarlet one during plenary sessions in the Lords.[154]

150 Simonds D'Ewes (ed.), *The journals of all the parliaments during the reign of Queen Elizabeth* (London 1682), p. 11; MacDonald, *Burghs and parliament*, pp 175–7; Hannay and Watson, 'Building of the parliament house'.

151 Guillaume du Vair, *Arrest svr qvelqves qvestions notables prononcez en robbe rovge au Parlement de Prouence* (Paris, 1606). A copy especially bound for King Henri IV is held in the Morgan Pierpoint Library.

152 *Journal contenant ce qui s'est fait et passé en la cour de Parlement de Paris toutes les chambres assemblées et autres lieux sur le sujet des affaires du temps présent ès années 1648 et 1649* (Paris, 1649), pp 48, 51, 66–7.

153 *Commons' Jn. Ire.*, 6 May 1615, where it is noted that 'Daniel Mullinax, esq., King at Arms, a member of this House, came in his kingly robes with a message from the Deputy.' For a sense of those robes, see Schlueter, 'Michael van Meer's *Album Amicorum*'.

154 Falkiner, *Essays*, p. 209. There are no known descriptions or images of early modern Irish speakers' robes. Michael van Meer's painting of the 1614 English parliament shows the speaker in a black robe. See Schlueter, 'Michael van Meer's *Album Amicorum*'.

The 1585 rules specified 'that every knyght, cyttizen and burges, dyring the tyme of his abode in the said howse, be apparayled in his gowne, having no armor or weapon about him.' County members wore short gowns and burgesses full-length ones.[155] English MPs received an allowance of £6 13*s*. 4*d*. to buy a scarlet gown. There is no further description of Irish MPs' robes or their receiving similar payments, but this was about one-third of the cost of a scarlet alderman's robe in Ireland and suggests either that the London allowance only partly covered the cost of parliamentary attire, or that MPs' gowns were much less luxurious than those of urban officers.[156] The long gap between parliaments led Everard to question whether gowns were worn, and Sir Christopher Nugent's recollection that 'Mr Harpoll borrowd a short gown the last parliament' was confirmed by James Galway, who sat in both parliaments.[157] Everard was reported to be wearing a gown when he was pulled out of the speaker's seat when Catholics claimed the Protestants had swords (which were forbidden in the Commons) and were prepared to draw them.[158]

Hats were an integral element of dress, which were doffed in the presence of social superiors. MPs entered and left the chamber and moved between seats in the house bareheaded but wore their hats sitting when the speaker was in his chair as a sign of their equality; standing bareheaded was a signal that a member wished to speak and they remained uncovered during their contributions. It was reported that Everard's hat had not been disturbed during the scrum over the speakership.[159] On 12 May 1615, MPs sat bareheaded while the speaker read the King's letter of thanks for the subsidies. 'Being uncovered' created tensions between both houses; on 7 November 1614, the Commons decided not to follow English practice by resolving to sit covered in conference committees but the Lords resisted; however, when the peers tactfully removed their hats, the Commons did likewise. On 11 November 1634, the Commons refused to deliver bills to the upper house, because 'the lords came, with their hats on, to receive them, which the said committee held

155 Irish Archaeological Society, *Tracts*, ii, p. 143; Moynes (ed.), *Annual letters*, i, p. 400. I am grateful to John McCafferty for drawing this reference to my attention. For Tudor England, see Hawkyard, *Commons*, pp 174–5.

156 A.P.M. Wright, 'London', at https://www.historyofparliamentonline.org/volume/1422-1504/constituencies/london [accessed 28 Oct. 2018]; Betty R. Masters (ed.), *Chamber accounts of the sixteenth century* (London, 1984), pp xx, 39–40; *The penny magazine of the Society for the Diffusion of Useful Knowledge, Volume 3* (London, 1834), p. 511; McGrath, 'Looking the part'.

157 *Commons' Jn. Ire.*, 29 Oct. 1614.

158 Bodl. Lib., Laud MS Misc. 612, fo. 261b: 'A true declaration of the procedinge in the Lower House in the parlyament holden at the Castle of Dublyn, the xviiith of May, 1613' (fo. 259 b), cited in Clarke, 'Irish *Modus tenendi parliamenta*', noted that during the kerfuffle at the choosing of a speaker, that when they pulled Everard out of the chair, they tore his gown. Jackson (ed.), 'Document'.

159 Garthine Walker, *Crime, gender and social order in early modern England* (Cambridge, 2003), pp 42–4; J.W. Cairns, 'Advocates hats, Roman law and admission to the Scots Bar, 1580–1812', *Journal of Legal History*, 20:2 (1999), 24–61; Kyle, *Theater*, pp 13–14; Scobell, *Memorials*, pp 6–7; Irish Archaeological Society, *Tracts*, ii, p. 143; Darcy, 'Social order in the 1641 rebellion'; McCavitt, *Arthur Chichester*, p. 183.

very unfitting.' The row continued until Wentworth adjudged on 13 November that they should follow English practice 'although it was insisted to be otherwise here' and that the chancellor and Lords who receive any message at the bar should stand uncovered at that time, as in England. At conferences of both houses, the Commons were to arrive first and wait for the Lords, who were to enter together; the Lords to sit covered, Commons not to sit or be covered 'unless it be some infirm person, and that by Connivance in some corner out of sight, but not covered.'[160] In 1640, the Lords agreed to permit MPs to wear their hats in a conference committee in a private house, but not in parliament.[161]

Wentworth caused the statutes passed in 1634–5 to be printed; while the cover page had striking images of pillars, the booklet itself was not very impressive, being small and printed on fairly flimsy paper (*plate 35*).[162] Perhaps more importantly, it contained only the public statutes actually passed, with two private ones for Bramhall and Ussher, but not the acts of state issued to enact the bills which had not passed.

SOCIAL SIDE OF PARLIAMENT

Parliament was also a social occasion that excited widespread public interest and other spin-off social and cultural events. The English parliament's opening was such a major public event that streets were especially cleaned and roped off and people paid up to £14 to rent a room with a view of the procession.[163] In Ireland one observer commented on the expectation of 'so great a concourse of people as usually frequented' parliament and this was true in England and Scotland also.[164] Presumably a festival atmosphere obtained in Dublin as in France, where towns where the estates were to meet were 'overtaken by exceptional activity … [with] days of entertainment and the foremost citizens prepared their houses to receive the most exalted guests'. In 1588 Loys Papon's poetry was performed in the provincial estates' assembly room in Montbrison.[165] The festivities surrounding the Irish parliament probably did not match Mme de Sévigné's description of those of the 1671 estates of Vitré ('continuous games, never-ending balls, theatre plays three times a week, a grand braderie (fair), that's the estates'), but they were

160 Orders for the House of Lords, *LJI*, 23 July 1634, nos 13, 15.
161 *Commons' Jn. Ire.*, 10–11 May 1615; Wentworth to Coke, 18 Aug. 1634, in Knowler (ed.), *Letters and dispatches*, i, p. 279; *Commons' Jn. Ire.*, 11 Nov. 1634; *LJI*, 26 March 1640.
162 *Anno regni Caroli Regis, Angliae … decimo & undecimo, at the Parliament begun and holden at Dublin, the 14 day of July [1634] and there continued untill the 18 day of Aprill 1635* (Dublin, 1635).
163 Peacey, 'Street theatre of state'.
164 Maguire, 'Seventeenth-century plans'. In 1641 Charles issued a proclamation, *His Majesties proclamation enent the unnecessary confluence of his Highnesse leiges to Edinburgh in the time of this parliament* (Edinburgh, 1641).
165 Marie-Laure Legay, 'Representation: political foundations of the French province, 15th–18th century' in Albareda and Sánchez (eds), *Political representation in the Ancien Régime*, pp 55–71.

still significant.[166] Dublin granted its mayor additional subventions for social occasions during parliament and Cork gave his niece Kate Boyle £10 for a new dress for the parliament season.[167] While there was a long tradition connecting literature, especially poetry, with the medieval English parliament, no such links have been traced for Ireland and the only known poetry related to the 1634 Irish parliament was Davenport's *Dialogue betweene Pollicy and Piety*, dedicated to Bramhall but apparently written in England. However, given the number of poets in and around the Irish parliament, parliament may well have prompted verse in Latin and English from Bellings, Sir Richard Blake, Francis Butler, Drury Cooper, Richard Fanshawe (*plate 21*), John Jackson, Oliver Jones, William Smith and others. Ormond's papers include a selection of verses used at different political assemblies, including one to the 'five principal members of the House of Commons', another 'sett upon the gates of Kilkenny in the time of the Assembly', and another addressed to Richard Blake as chairman of the assembly by 'Mr Dormer'.[168] Cultural events took place; Cork mentions a 'tragedy' being played in the parliament house in January 1636 (clearly a normal venue for plays before the Werburgh St theatre opened in the following year, but also underlining its suitability as a performance space). The Old English playwright, Henry Burnell's play *Landgartha* was staged on 17 March 1640, coinciding with parliament's opening. The play has been interpreted as concerning the Act for the Repealing of the Statute of Bigamy – a subject close to Wentworth's heart, although a more straightforward political reading suggests that Burnell was encouraging Irish Catholic gentry to support Charles against extremist Protestants as a basis for an honourable reconciliation between Ireland and England.[169]

Any large gathering promotes social interaction, business and forging or strengthening connections and enables families to come together. Visitors were interested to see parliament's location, layout and operations and to conduct their own business; the Four Masters recorded that 'A proclamation of Parliament was issued to the men of Ireland, commanding their chiefs to assemble in Dublin

166 Grosart (ed.), *Lismore Papers*, 1st series, iv, p. 147; Allan H. Stevenson, 'James Shirley and the actors at the first Irish theater', *Modern Philology*, 40:2 (Nov., 1942), 147–60; Legay, 'Representation'.

167 Gilbert (ed.), *C.A.R.*, iii, p. 365; Lennon, *Lords of Dublin*, p. 49; Grosart (ed.), *Lismore Papers*, 1st series, iv, pp 34–5, 28 June 1634.

168 Matthew Giancarlo, *Parliament and literature in late medieval England* (Cambridge, 2010); Albert H. Tricomi, '*A dialogue betweene Pollicy and Piety* by Robert Davenport', *English Literary Renaissance*, 21:2 (1991), 190–216; McGrath, 'Poets and patronage'; HMC, *Ormonde* (Dublin, 1895), i, pp 105–17. Dormer was presumably Michael Dormer, a member of the General Assembly, Ó Siochrú, *Confederate Ireland*, p. 257.

169 Fletcher, *Drama, performance and polity*, pp 275–7; Deana Rankin (ed.), *Landgartha: a tragie-comedy by Henry Burnell* (Dublin, 2014), p. 25; Richard Dutton, 'The Werburgh Street Theater, Dublin' in Adam Zucker and Andrew B. Farmer (eds), *Localizing Caroline drama: politics and economics of the early modern English stage, 1625–1642* (Basingstoke, 2006), pp 129–55. For an alternative reading, see Andrew Hadfield, 'Culture and anarchy in mid-seventeenth-century Ireland: the strange case of James Shirley at Werburgh Street', *Literature Compass*, 15:10 (2018), e12493; Helen Andrews, 'Burnell, Henry', *DIB*.

precisely on May-day … and, accordingly, they all at that summons did meet in Dublin face to face.' Perrot showed Gaelic lords around the 1585 parliament and used their visit to make agreements.[170] As the chieftains were not members, their attendance was social. In 1585 when Ulick Burke, third earl of Clanricard, brought Galway merchants William Martin, Anthony Lynch fitz Thomas, Stephen Roe Lynch and Cornelius O'Halloran with him as advisors, he provided them with 'four several cloaks for their livery to serve him as retainers' and his successor planned to have a similar retinue for the parliament that was expected in 1621.[171] When Chancellor Jones sent for the recusant lords who were absenting themselves from parliament on 22 May 1613, the messenger noted that one lord's lodgings was full of people 'in the hall' and that there were several other lords in the peer's chamber, although presumably their presence related as much to political strategy as sociability.[172]

Cork noted the opportunity for business but also the social capital that could be built up by appearing at parliament.[173] The Herbert's agent in Kerry, Francis Lloyd, visited Dublin during the 1634–5 parliament, keeping a watching brief for his employers on proceedings.[174] At least two sheriffs, Robert Walshe of Waterford and Edward Denny of Kerry, were in Dublin for the opening of the 1634 parliament. Denny's son Thomas was born at his grandfather Lord Baltinglass' Dublin residence, Roper's Rest, two days before parliament opened. Denny presumably wished to defend his illegal return in the Kerry County election and his wife would have welcomed her family's support in childbirth. Edward would also have enjoyed seeing Baltinglass at the opening ceremonies and their presence in Dublin allowed other ties to be created; Thomas was the only child born outside Denny's home in Tralee and Edward chose godparents – Sir Charles Coote (*plate 13*) and Lady Tresham – from outside Kerry Protestant circles.[175] Lady Conway hoped that the third Commonwealth Parliament in 1659 would provide a chance for her to see her son-in-law George Rawdon (MP for Down, Antrim and Armagh) and his wife in London and her son Lord Conway anticipated Rawdon's company and advice.[176]

170 John O'Donovan (ed.), *Annals of the kingdom of Ireland by the Four Masters*, 7 vols (Dublin, 1851), *s.a.* 1585; Advice and directions for summoning a parliament in Ireland, Bodl. Lib., Rawlinson MS D. 922, fos. 49r–52v. Treadwell ascribes this text to the long-serving attorney general of Ireland Charles Calthrope. See Terry Clavin and Judy Barry, 'Calthrope, Sir Charles', *DIB*.

171 Ó Bric, 'Galway townsmen', p. 147; Clanricard to Sir Henry Lynch, 6 May 1621, in Cunningham (ed.), 'Clanricard letters', no. 7; Terry Clavin, 'Burke, Ulick, 3rd earl of Clanricard', *DIB*.

172 Bodl. Lib., Rawlinson MS D. 922, fos. 49rff.

173 Cork to Barrymore, 6 June 1634, Chatsworth House, Cork Papers, Misc. boxes, Box 3, pp 37–8.

174 Lloyd to Richard Herbert, 27 Feb. 1635, in Smith (ed.), *Herbert correspondence*, pp 81–2.

175 Grosart (ed.), *Lismore Papers*, 1st series, iv, p. 37; McGrath, 'Sex, lies and rigged returns'. Mary Tresham was the wife of Sir Lewis Tresham, first baronet. McGrath, 'Bio. dict.', i, pp 132–3.

176 Frances Conway to Rawdon, 28 Jan. 1659, HL, HP, MS 14,575; Edward Conway to Rawdon, 10 May 1659, HL, HP, MS 14,366.

The influx of so many members of both houses swelled Dublin's population, but when their families, servants, adherents and general on-lookers were added, the greater numbers heightened security fears and increased the cost of lodgings (see chapter eight on economics). Chichester ordered 100 soldiers from provincial garrisons as reinforcements, but MPs brought relatively few followers to that parliament:

> only Lord Gormanston came to the city with 100 horse (as is confessed) whereof there were not 20 of his own retinue; – the rest were his friends and kinsmen that went out of Dublin to meet him, the rather because his lady came in his company.[177]

Dining together was a favoured means of social interaction and smoothing difficulties. Davies tried to diffuse discord by inviting Catholic MPs to dinner

> and gave them the best entertainment he could, and they accepted his entertainment cheerfully and friendly. So now their disjointed body is joined so well together that the public service proceeds without impediment, and, if they could agree as well in the Church as they did in the Parliament House, the peace of Ireland were established for ever.[178]

Cork pursued the same strategy in trying to reconcile two of his neighbours, working with St Leger, they

> cawsed Mr Olliver Stephenson to make & draw in writing a submission & acknowledgement of the rash attempt made upon Mr Robert Walsh, of Waterford, in Dublin, in Parliament time; whereupon they were made ffrends & both of them supped together with me.

Oliver was presumably in Dublin with his father Richard, MP for Limerick County, while Walshe was sheriff of Waterford and son of that county's MP[179] Bedell dined with Ussher during the 1634 parliament.[180]

Social occasions did not always improve relations but could breed suspicion, gossip and division. Perrot found parliament an opportune occasion to make an example of supposed malefactors:

> The men of all Erinn – such of them as were of any account – went to Baile-

177 *Cal. S.P. Ire., 1611–14*, pp 445–6. For the retinues which attended nobles to the Scottish Estates, see Goodare, 'Admission of lairds'.
178 Davies to Somerset, 31 Oct. 1614, TNA, SP 63/232, fo. 201.
179 Grosart (ed.), *Lismore Papers*, 1st series, iv, p. 37, under 23 July 1634; McGrath, 'Electoral strategy'; McGrath, 'Bio. dict.', i, pp 275–6, 295–6.
180 Bedell to Samuel Ward, 11 Oct. 1635, Bodl. Lib., Tanner MS 70, fo. 74.

> atha-cliath to an Act of Parliament. The son of O'Maelmhuaidh, and Edmond Dorcha, son of Domhnall, son of Murchadh Mac Suibhne, and several other persons, were hanged at this Act of Parliament.[181]

The large social event in Archbishop Jones' Palace of St Sepulchre, presumably part of a charm offensive to ease the passage of the clergy subsidies bill through the Commons, provided the occasion for the MP Gerald Nugent to insult Archbishop Miler Magrath's son James, calling him a 'a paltry fryar's son.'[182] Cork was incensed to hear that one of his local MPs Thomas Elwall was bad-mouthing him to another burgess in parliament and John FitzGerald spread gossip about Lady Honor Kerry's sexual adventures at court sessions and funerals.[183]

CONCLUSION

Parliament was a major political and social event and its ceremonies and activities were of considerable public interest. Irish parliamentary ceremonial and protocols became more established and aligned to English practice in this period and parliament's meeting also provided an opportunity for other business, cultural and social activities. However, the lack of dedicated, elegant and commodious accommodation for the Irish parliament was evidence both of its lesser importance within the three kingdoms and the crown's ambivalence about its future and more practically, because it met more rarely than its Scottish and, except between 1628 and 1640, English counterparts. Wentworth's failure to provide it with an adequate and prestigious home obliged the Commons to make use of many other venues in Dublin, principally for committee meetings.

181 Hennessy (ed.), *Annals of Loch Cé*, *s.a.* 1585.
182 *Commons' Jn. Ire.*, 16 May 1615; Judy Barry, 'Magrath, Miler', *DIB*.
183 Grosart (ed.), *Lismore Papers*, 1st series, iv, p. 80, under 14 March 1635. McGrath, 'Sex, lies and rigged returns'.

CHAPTER SEVEN

How parliament functioned

THIS CHAPTER DISCUSSES parliament's operations, specifically its sitting days, how bills were drafted and processed, the role of committees and their development, how petitions were handled and orders issued, when and how the house voted, members' participation levels and how attendance was encouraged.

Parliamentary procedure was formalized and tightened in England under Elizabeth I. However, while Hooker refers to uncertainty about procedure in 1569, which he bombastically offered to set down for the information of the Irish parliament (despite having no previous parliamentary experience himself, unlike the speaker James Stanihurst who had held the same role in 1560), procedures described by Neale as being settled during this period appear to have been already in place in Ireland.[1] Like all institutions, parliament's procedure changed incrementally and precedents which developed over time were used to guide, facilitate and justify parliamentary practice; the 'sacralization' of custom and precedent, which imbued them with a sacred and unquestionable quality, provided protection for all parliamentarians and officials, especially at politically tense times.[2] The primary sources for procedure available before 1613 were the *Modus tenendi parliamentum* from which Hooker's *Order and vsage* was derived, the 1585 rules, both of which provided only very basic guidance, and the 1586 Lords' journal; Hooker's work was the only one of these to have been published. Whatever its origins, the *Modus* was accepted as specifying the formal, legal basis for summoning and managing parliaments; however, it was created before parliament increased in size and complexity and each of its 26 'chapters' was only about a paragraph long.[3] The upper house established standing orders in 1634, following the English Lords in the 1620s, which had sought reliable historical precedents and established an archive for future reference; Wentworth had consulted Arundel about those orders before the 1634 parliament.[4] No Irish parliamentary archives were established in this period but procedure developed rapidly, greatly enhancing

1 Hooker (or Vowell), *The order and vsage of keeping of the parlements in England* ([London], 1572), preface (unpaginated); Neale, *House*, pp 356ff; Falkiner, *Essays*, pp 237ff; Routledge, 'Journal'.

2 I am grateful to Josep Capdeferro for this observation. Foster, 'Procedure'.

3 Natzler, 'Manuals before May'; Hawkyard, *Commons*, p. 135; Crooks, 'Representation and dissent'; *idem*, 'Background to the arrest'; NLI, GO, MS 95, pp 159–62. For the seventeenth-century Scottish *Modus*, see Pronay and Taylor, *Parliamentary texts*, p. 210; Irish Archaeological Society, *Tracts*, ii, p. 143.

4 Wentworth Woodhouse, Muniments, StrP14/76, StrP8, pp 130–1; Andrew Thrush, 'Introductory survey, 1604–1629' in Thrush and Ferris (eds), *History of parliament*. I am grateful to Paul Seaward for drawing this reference to my attention. Andrew Thrush, 'The origin of the House of Lords' standing orders', at https://archives.blog.parliament.uk/2021/05/18/the-origin-of-the-house-of-lords-standing-orders/ [accessed 21 May 2021].

the houses' efficiency, a necessary step given the dramatic increase in the size of Stuart parliaments compared to their Tudor predecessors and especially to the medieval assemblies, as well as to the significant growth in business with which they were dealing.[5] The Irish parliament was as carefully managed by privy councillors as the English, or the Scottish Estates by the Lords of the Articles, as demonstrated by the influence of Ridgeway in 1613, Radcliffe in 1634 and 1640 and in privy councillors' dominance of committees in each parliament (see below).[6]

SITTING DAYS AND TIMES

Parliaments were usually scheduled to sit outside law terms and the harvest season, freeing judges to attend the Lords, making courtrooms available for committee meetings and enabling gentry to gather all their crops. The 1613 parliament was scheduled to start the first day after Trinity term ended. Wentworth originally stated his intention of holding the 1634 parliament's sessions in Trinity and Michaelmas terms, while this seems less advisable for the reasons given above, the third session was held in Hilary term as was the first session of the 1640 parliament, but on that occasion Wentworth's choice was limited as he needed the Irish parliament to vote subsidies before the English parliament began four weeks later. He prorogued parliament so it would not sit during the 1634 harvest or assizes, a practice so well established that Cork forewarned his son-in-law Barrymore of the likelihood. On 30 July 1634, the Commons suggested early November for the following session.[7] When parliament was adjourned on its opening, for example on the Catholics' withdrawal in 1613, or in anticipation of Wentworth's return from England in March 1640, the next day of full assembly was accounted parliament's first day.[8]

Convocation was summoned in 1613 because Davies mistakenly believed that the English practice of its meeting concurrently with parliament held also in Ireland; it continued to sit despite parliament's repeated prorogations after the Catholics' withdrawal.[9] In 1634 and 1640, Convocation commenced seven days after parliament opened; the later Convocation continued with several adjournments until its last sitting on 11 May 1641 and was formally dissolved by Charles' death in 1649.[10]

5 Foster, 'Painful labour'; Foster, 'Procedure'.

6 Michael Graves, 'The management of the Elizabethan House of Commons: the council's men of business', *Parl. Hist.*, 2 (1983), pp 1–38; Mann, 'House rules'.

7 English Council to Chichester, 7 March 1613, *Cal. S.P. Ire., 1611–14*, pp 328–9; Wentworth's prorogation, 2 Aug. 1634, Empey (ed.), *Early Stuart Irish warrants*, p. 198; Bodl. Lib., Carte MS 30, fo. 197r; Wentworth to Charles, with Charles' response, 12 April 1634, in Knowler (ed.), *Letters and dispatches*, i, pp 183–7; Cork to Barrymore, 6 June 1634, Chatsworth House, Cork Papers, Misc. boxes, Box 3, p. 38.

8 HRC, MS 158, p. 64. This explains the discrepancy noted by Empey (ed.), 'Diary of Sir James Ware', p. 108; Elsynge, *Ancient method and manner*, pp 84–5.

9 HRC, MS 158, pp 87–8; McGrath, 'Membership', pp 6–7; TCD, MS 1,062, p. 56.

10 Bray (ed.), *Records of convocation: Ireland, 1101–1690*, p. 402; TCD, MS 1,062, pp 56, 60–7; Empey (ed.), *Early Stuart Irish warrants*, p. 187.

Parliament's sitting days and times were usually the same as courts: every weekday except church holidays, usually between 8 a.m. and 11 a.m., but it sometimes started and ended later, if required, especially close to the end of sessions when MPs were trying to complete business. Sidney grew suspicious when the 1569 Commons sat until after 2 p.m and a similar lengthy sitting of the English Commons was also regarded as unusual.[11] Morning sittings enabled bishops also to attend Convocation, which sat from 2 p.m. to 4 p.m. or 6 p.m., although on 23 March 1640 it sat from 11 a.m. to 1 p.m.[12] This was a very long day for bishops and for the MP Thomas Ryves, Convocation's registrar in 1613; Ussher, speaker of Convocation's upper house, had 'been almost tyred with continuall attendance on our long continued Parliament and Convocation.'[13] The Scottish Estates met separately between 7 a.m. and 9 a.m., jointly until noon and committees met from 3 a.m. to 6 p.m., but this regular timetable was disturbed in 1641 when the estates and the Kirk's General Assembly met simultaneously. In July it decided that the estates would sit in the afternoons, to enable members who were elders to attend the assembly in the morning, but four years later the arrangement was reversed.[14]

The English parliament did not generally sit on Sunday, Christmas Day, the feasts of All Saints, All Souls and St John the Baptist (1 November, 2 November and 24 June) or when the Court of Star Chamber was sitting; its meetings on Christmas Day, St Stephen's and St John's days in 1549 were 'singular and occasioned by the troublesome business of the Duke of Somerset'. Hooker noted, the house was 'To begin sitting at mid Prime time except on holy days at prime, because the devine service should first be heard.'[15] The 1656 English Commonwealth Parliament sat on Christmas Day, although it was poorly attended.[16]

11 Neale, *House*, pp 354–5; Falkiner, *Essays*, pp 203–4; *Commons' Jn. Ire.*, 11 Oct. 1614, 2 Nov. 1640. For 9 a.m. starts see, for example, 4, 11, 18, 31 Oct. 1614; Holinshed, *Chronicles*, p. 121; J.E. Neale, 'Parliament and the succession question in 1562/3 and 1566', *EHR*, 36:144 (Oct., 1921), 497–520.

12 ARL, Garstin's transcriptions of Convocation records, No. 8, 1639–41. Convocation's lower house sat between 2 and 4 p.m. on 30 March 1640 to choose their speaker.

13 Hooker, *Order and vsage*, unpaginated; ARL, Garstin's transcripts, pp 109–25; Ussher to Samuel Ward, 15 Sept. 1635, Bodl. Lib., Tanner MS 70, fo. 72.

14 Mann, 'House rules'; David Stevenson, *The government of Scotland under the Covenanters, 1637–1651* (Edinburgh, 1982), pp xxxvi–xxxviii. I am grateful to John Young for drawing this reference to my attention.

15 Elsynge, *Ancient method and manner*, pp 108–14; HRC, MS 158, pp 85ff. Elsynge quotes the *Modus* that it should not sit on a Sunday, but gives the instance of the English parliament doing so on 30 September in 23 Eliz. I, the Sunday after St Martin in Hiem., and prorogued to be held on the following 2 Nov., also a Sunday, and gives a series of other Sundays (p. 86), but notes 'none after 4 Edward 3'. St John the Baptist's feast is 24 June and St John the Apostle's is 27 December. Hooker, *Order and vsage*, unpaginated. On Somerset's downfall and associated events in 1549, see Ethan H. Shagan, 'Protector Somerset and the 1549 rebellions: new sources and new perspectives', *EHR*, 114:455 (Feb., 1999), 34–63.

16 Bernard S. Capp, *England's culture wars: Puritan reformation and its enemies in the interregnum, 1649–1660* (Oxford, 2012), p. 22. For the Tudor parliament meeting around, but not on Christmas Day, see Hawkyard, *Commons*, p. 258. 'Christmas Day in the Commons, 1656', at

The English parliament very occasionally sat on Sundays, but not the Irish, although the committee appointed on 26 May 1641 to manage the house's business was 'required, on every Sunday, humbly to move the house, for an account to be given by the several committees of their doings in their respective employments.' Early Stuart Irish parliaments never sat on All Saints' Day, 24 June or Christmas; winter sessions generally did not begin until after 2 November, although parliament met on that date in 1614 and 1640 and it was due to open on 3 November 1628.[17] Parliament was prorogued until 4 November in 1585 and 1634 and was to reconvene on 8 November 1641. Speaker James Stanihurst's manipulating the Commons to pass anti-Catholic laws in 1560 was facilitated by their not usually sitting on a saint's day.[18] The Irish parliament never sat on 5 November during this period and the 1610 English parliament met only briefly on that day before adjourning for commemorative solemnities.[19] The Dublin architect and parliamentarian, Humphrey Farnham's proposal that 5 November should be made a feast day was well received, although an unnamed Catholic member quipped: 'We are prepared to ordain fair days or so-called holidays, as many of them as you wish. But not feast days, because usually we purchase those too dearly', a reference to fines for not attending Protestant services.[20]

The English parliament did not usually sit on Star Chamber days (Wednesday and Fridays under Elizabeth) because the Lords was a judicial court. Peers agreed to change their sittings on 24 April 1620 to accommodate the Star Chamber. Elsynge records one exception, but notes that the court only sat on one day a week and not usually the same day, so that it was easy to avoid clashing. He also noted that 'not many days were omitted' in earlier times. Limited records make it impossible to know how frequently parliament and the Court of Castle Chamber, the Irish equivalent of Star Chamber in England, sat on the same days, although they certainly did so on 18 and 25 November 1614 and on 5 May 1615.[21]

Committees, except conference committees, generally sat in the afternoons but there were exceptions: many committees in 1634 met at 7 a.m. and in 1641 the tobacco committee met at Darcy's house at 6 a.m. In those cases, the houses presumably sat from 9 a.m.[22] MPs also met outside sitting days, on committees between sessions and when summoned by the speaker: the committees for examining officers' fees were to meet during prorogation and on 17 June 1640 the committee of grievances was ordered to sit between sessions, an innovation only introduced by John Pym, the unofficial leader of the opposition to the crown in the Long Parliament, in England in 1641.[23] When Speaker Eustace received a letter

https://thehistoryofparliament.wordpress.com/2014/12/23/christmas-day-in-the-commons-1656/ [accessed 18 Dec. 2019].

17 *Cal. S.P. Ire., 1625–32*, pp 370–1.

18 Moynes (ed.), *Annual letters*, i, p. 403.

19 I am grateful to Paul Hunneyball for this point.

20 Moynes (ed.), *Annual letters*, i, p. 482; Loeber and McGrath, 'Legacy of Humphrey Farnham'.

21 HRC, MS 158, p. 89; Crawford, *Star Chamber*, pp 520–2.

22 *Commons' Jn. Ire.*, 14 Nov. 1614, 28 July 1634, 15 July 1641.

23 Ibid., 29 Nov. 1614; Russell, 'Monarchies'; *idem*, 'Pym, John', *Oxford DNB*.

from the committee in England the day after parliament had been prorogued he called 'as many of the house together as were then in towne … divers and the most principall leading men amongst them being come together to mee' to communicate its substance.[24]

DRAFTING AND PROCESSING LEGISLATION

Long intervals between parliaments inevitably created backlogs and early Stuart assemblies had heavy legislative burdens.[25] Legislation could only be proposed or sanctioned by the Irish privy council; the crown and English privy council had no right to propose legislation for Ireland. The clergy subsidies bills were an exception: they were drafted and passed by Convocation and the privy council then transmitted them to England. They could not be transmitted before parliament met and were therefore introduced in later sessions, even in Wentworth's parliaments.[26] Henry VIII's chief minister and the lord privy seal, Thomas Cromwell, was able to ask the English lord chancellor, Thomas, Lord Audley to draft bills for the 1537 Irish parliament and Henry VIII to ask for additional acts to those that had been transmitted to him because Poynings' Law was to be suspended.[27] In 1641 Charles I was acting outside his powers when he proposed an act to resolve the doubtful continuance of parliament after Wandesford's death.[28] Bills included preambles explaining their rationale as well as the actual legislative provisions; the author of a memorandum planning the 1560 parliament advised the administration to appoint 'a wise and witty pener to pen the considerations in the preambles of the acts of parliament and so the rest for the law.' Preambles such as that for the 1615 clergy subsidies act caused such offence as to prevent that bill's passing (see below).[29]

The Irish administration planned the legislative agenda, as the Lords of Articles prepared the Scottish Estates' programme.[30] Bills providing for general pardons, subsidies and that parliament should not be determined by the granting of royal assent to bills were passed in each early Stuart Irish parliament. Learned counsel drafted public bills sponsored by the Irish administration. In 1585 Perrot gave this responsibility to Adam Loftus, the archbishop of Dublin and 'the judges and Queen's learned counsel', while the chief justice Humphrey Winch prepared

24 Eustace to the Committee in England, 6 March 1641, ARL, MS Parliamentary Papers, unpaginated, 22 June 1641.
25 Dennehy, *Parliament*, p. 72.
26 *Commons' Jn. Ire.*, 20 Feb. 1635, 14 Oct. 1640.
27 Murray, *Enforcing the English reformation in Ireland*, p. 138; Bradshaw, *Irish constitutional revolution*, p. 145; Howard Leithead, 'Cromwell, Thomas, earl of Essex', *Oxford DNB*; L.L. Ford, 'Audley, Thomas, Baron Audley of Warden', *Oxford DNB*.
28 Charles to the Irish parliament, *Commons' Jn. Ire.*, 22 May 1641.
29 Proposals for acts to be passed through parliament and other measures to be taken in Ireland, 20 May 1559, Heffernan (ed.), *'Reform' treatises*, p. 43; *Commons' Jn. Ire.*, 4 May 1615.
30 Hannay and Watson, 'Building of the parliament house'.

those for 1613.[31] The drafters of bills for 1628 are unknown, although a consultative committee included Francis Annesley.[32] Wentworth created a committee of 'some few of us here' to consider the bills planned by Falkland 'such as shall be judged beneficial, to make them ready; such as may be of too much prejudice to the crown, to lay them aside; and to draw up others, which may chance to have been then omitted.' Radcliffe claimed to have helped draft all the bills for Wentworth's Irish parliaments.[33] The initial bills for 1640 were prepared at considerable speed to enable Wentworth to write the necessary letter requesting Charles to summon that parliament, but the total of all draft legislation in the four separate transmissions from England added up to a significant legislative programme.[34] The reason for many individual bills is difficult to identify but some were based on English statutes and the 1622 Commission recommended many to deal with maladministration, inefficiency and corruption.[35] Eustace's letter to the committee in England instructed them

> to inform yourselves of the practise in the exchequer there uppon the Statute of 1. Jac. Cap. 26 concerning homage and the table of Rates therein mentioned and what is the difference betweene Rates if the lands there and as they are bona fide worth and thereof to certify us.[36]

However, other English models were not legislated for in Ireland, most notably that confirming doubtful land titles, which was also resolved in Scotland, just as the Irish act granting nationality to Scots was not enacted in England. Equally, the 1635 Act for the King's most gracious, general and free pardon contained so many exclusions that rendered it far less valuable than that in 1615 and the Committee in England's request that the similar act to be passed in 1641 would be more inclusive was granted apparently without quibble.[37]

In England,

> in the beginning of every Parliament, some persons have been appointed to consider of such Laws as had continuance to the present Session, whether

31 Nicholas White to Burghley, 27 May 1585, TNA, SP 63/116, fo. 138; Chichester to Salisbury, 18 Feb. 1611, TNA, SP 63/231, fo. 32; James Murray, 'Loftus, Adam, Church of Ireland archbishop of Armagh and Dublin', *DIB*; Wilfrid Prest, 'Winch, Sir Humphrey', *Oxford DNB*.
32 *Cal. S.P. Ire., 1625–32*, pp 378–9.
33 Wentworth to Charles, with Charles' response, 12 April 1634, in Knowler (ed.), *Letters and dispatches*, i, pp 183–7; Pogson (ed.), 'Financial accounts'.
34 John Coke to Bankes, 28 Jan. 1640, Bodl. Lib., Bankes MS 65/59. The list of bills included in each transmission is provided at the beginning of the journal for the 1640 parliament.
35 Treadwell (ed.), *Irish commission of 1622*, pp 38, 161, 221, 224, 234, 289, 291–2, 711–13.
36 Eustace to the Committee, 22 June 1641, ARL, MS Parliamentary Papers, unpaginated.
37 Limitation Act, 23 Jac. I, c. 16; Act XII, 1617, Scotland, Regarding prescription of heritable rights, NAS, MS PA2/19, fo. 14. I am grateful to Coleman Dennehy for drawing this reference to my attention. 10 Car. I, c. 4; *Act for the Kings Majesties most gracious, generall, and free pardon* (Dublin, 1635); *Cal. S.P. Ire., 1633–47*, p. 322.

> they were fit to be continued or determined, as also of former Statutes repealed or discontinued, whether fit to be revived, and what are fit to be repealed.[38]

The Irish parliament did this during sessions, rather than at parliament's beginning because the lack of consultation on the legislative agenda prevented its happening earlier. On 26 May 1585 peers agreed to a conference committee with the Commons to decide on possible legislation and each early Stuart parliament proposed legislation and requested MPs to draft bills.[39] In July 1642 the 'rump' Protestant MPs presented their Declaration and a bill they had drafted enforcing MPs to take the oath of supremacy (presumably the same to suspend Poynings' Law 'concerning Acts to be passed to abolish Popery and to attaint the Rebels', about which they consulted the Lords) to the privy council which agreed to transmit it, along with other bills it was preparing. Ormond transmitted two bills concerning the cessation and land tenures in the escheated counties in Ulster in the mid-1640s.[40]

Some public bills were suggested by MPs singly or collectively and drafted by different individuals and groups; on 20 October 1614 an unnamed MP brought in a bill, although the drafter, messenger and subject are all unknown. The Commons also requested individuals and groups to draft proposed bills, e.g., the speaker to make Gunpowder Treason Day (5 November) a holiday and two lawyers were appointed to draft a bill about holding markets on Sundays.[41] Just before the end of the session the Commons ordered the speaker to move Chichester to appoint a committee of seven Protestant and four Catholic lawyers to draw 'up those acts, as are to be transmitted into England, to be propounded in the next session of parliament' and a further series of bills was proposed at the end of the following session.[42] On 10 December 1634 the Commons ordered Radcliffe and Darcy to draw up a petition to Wentworth about establishing a mint in Ireland and on 13 October 1640 the Commons established a committee 'for drawing up of acts.'

Private and local bills were drafted by lawyers, frequently unidentified, commissioned by those sponsoring them. Bills for restitution in blood or rectifying land titles were only accepted after the king had written a supporting letter. The English privy council refused to consider bills for Dame Ellen Power and William Wogan's restitution as they had no such letters. Even when restitution bills were

38 Scobell, *Memorials*, p. 40.

39 E.g., *Commons' Jn. Ire.*, 29 April 1615, 18 Nov. 1634, 1 April 1640.

40 Lords Justice and Council to the Commissioners for Irish Affairs, 8 July 1642, Bodl. Lib., Carte MS 68, fo. 456v; Lentz, 'Irish parliament', pp 112–15; *LJI*, 6, 11 Aug. 1642; Ormonde to ___, 22 April 1645, HMC, *Thirteenth Report of the Royal Commission on Historical Manuscripts, Appendix 1: the manuscripts of his grace, the duke of Portland, preserved at Welbeck Abbey* (London, 1891), p. 220.

41 Routledge, 'Journal'; *Commons' Jn. Ire.*, 19 Nov. 1614. Farnham made the original proposal on 4 Nov.

42 *Commons' Jn. Ire.*, 29 Nov. 1614, 16 May 1615.

transmitted there was no guarantee that they would be certified or enacted, as David Condon, John Heydon and William Nugent discovered. Roger Dalton's bill to resolve his land title was not entertained in the absence of royal correspondence in his favour, but Cork had obtained Charles' letter before commissioning Darcy to draft the bill to end his 30 year land dispute with successive bishops of Waterford and Lismore.[43] Condon's counsel was to draw up a bill for his lands, as Lady Kildare's lawyer had done for her jointure, and when Farnham raised the long-running saga of the late earl of Desmond's daughters' restitution in blood, the Commons decided that their learned counsel should draft the bill to be sent to the Grand Committee for review and if appropriate forwarded to Chichester for transmission to England. Dublin Corporation established a committee of former mayors to consider what acts it would like from the 1613 parliament and ordered its recorder (later MP, Bolton) to draft the bills.[44] MPs drafting private bills was regarded as poor practice in England, as they would be voting on them in the house, but no such scruples were evinced in Ireland.[45] The MP for Cavan, Edward Lake (*plate 22*) drafted the 1640 subsidy bills for Convocation, subsequently introduced as the clergy subsidies bill. He may have been one of the 'best lawyers in the town' who wrote the private act for Christ Church's lands at Simonscourt which was rejected because it encroached on Lord Merrion's property.[46] Less usually, Chichester asked Davies to draft a bill for Nugent's restitution and the privy council ordered the chief justice, chief baron and master of the rolls 'to reform an Act of Parliament penned by Morrishe Fitz Thomas FitzGerald for the restoration of his blood & order that this may be recommended into England.'[47] Counsel appearing in parliament for their clients supporting private bills (such as John Pollexfen, Bolton and Beare) may well have drafted them, but presumably not the bills they argued against.

Local acts were introduced in 1613–15 and 1640–8 but not 1634, although it is not always possible to distinguish between local and private bills; the 1640 bill for Blaris and Lisnegarvy parishes was also described as Lord Conway's act. Indisputable local bills included that for Carlingford vicarage introduced by its MP on 24 November 1614, that which the house ordered for the Boyne on 6 May 1615

43 *Cal. S.P. Ire., 1611–14*, p. 308; Cork to Joshua Boyle, 17 March 1640, Chatsworth House, Cork Papers, Misc. boxes, Box 3, pp 419ff.

44 *Commons' Jn. Ire.*, 17 Nov. 1614; Bodl. Lib., Carte MS 62, fos. 39r–40r; Berry (ed.), 'Minute book'; Lennon, *Lords of Dublin*, pp 46, 229–75.

45 Neale, *House*, p. 377.

46 James Ussher to Bramhall, 7 May 1640, HL, HP, MS 15,958. Lake was MP for Cavan in that parliament. *Commons' Jn. Ire.*, 14 Oct. 1640; *LJI*, 20 Oct. 1640; Gordon Goodwin revised by Sean Kelsey, 'Lake, Sir Edward, baronet', *Oxford DNB*.

47 *Cal. S.P. Ire., 1611–15*, pp 308, 322, 328; Curtis Clayton (ed.), *Council book*, pp 3–4 on the private bill for David Condon's lands for the next parliament. His counsel to draft the bill and have it transmitted to England, 6 May 1613, *Cal. S.P. Ire., 1611–15*, p. 340; Chichester to the English privy council, 11 April 1613, in Edwards (ed.), 'Chichester', no. 52; *Commons' Jn. Ire.*, 17 Nov. 1614; Nugent's bill, Bodl. Lib., Carte MS 62, fo. 231; Lady Kildare's bill, Bodl. Lib., Carte MS 61, fo. 358.

and Dublin City's bills restricting the number of foreign inhabitants, against thatched houses in the city, concerning the River Dodder's watercourse, extending the city's boundaries, punishing offenders and against the act for keepers of ale houses being bound by recognizances. Interestingly, the Munster inhabitants' submission on desired legislation for either 1628 or more probably 1634 contained no local acts.[48] Acts could only be repealed by fresh legislation and all early Stuart Irish parliaments dealt with repeal bills.[49]

Bills were given very careful attention in both Dublin and London, presumably partly because the Irish parliament could not amend them. Having been considered and approved (or at least allowed) by the Irish council, they were engrossed on parchment and transmitted to England for consideration by the privy council and lawyers including serving and former attorneys general, learned counsel, judges and serjeants-at-law such as Humphrey Winch, Robert Heath, Edward Herbert, Ralph Whitfield and John Bankes.[50] Bills were frequently accompanied by 'paper books' explaining their rationale and providing additional background information on their contents and desirability for the English councillors and lawyers, the vast majority of whom had little direct Irish experience or knowledge of Ireland (and less interest).[51] In 1613 the English council 'wished that the paper books which were agreed on there had been sent over, whereby they might have had a more assured ground for their examination.' Laud expressed his 'want of knowledge of that country' as a reason for amending church bills against Bramhall and Ussher's intentions.[52]

Events in England often slowed down consideration of Irish bills. In 1613, both the law terms, when 'the kings learned Councell, whose triall and examination the bills must suffer and abide are so profitablie imployed otherwise', and Elizabeth of Bohemia's wedding to the Elector Palatine of the Rhine, Frederick V, delayed examination of Irish legislation.[53] In 1630 the secretary for Irish affairs at the English privy council noted that 'the multiplicity of other business is the occasion that they do very rarely sit upon the Irish affairs.'[54] Equally, the Commons' committee in England in 1640–1 experienced great difficulty in having bills

48 TCD, MS 672, fos. 235r–8v (see Appendix 2).

49 *Commons' Jn. Ire.*, 5 May 1615, 18 Nov. 1634, 17–19 Feb. 1635, 1 April 1635, 24 Oct. 1640.

50 Winch to Salisbury, 1 Dec. 1611, TNA, SP 63/231, fo. 280; Bodl. Lib., Bankes MSS 10/1, 65/59–71; Paul E. Kopperman, 'Heath, Sir Robert', *Oxford DNB*; Chris R. Kyle, 'Herbert, Sir Edward', *Oxford DNB*; Rosemary Sgroi, 'Whitfield, Ralph' in Thrush and Ferris (eds), *History of parliament*.

51 Joel J. Epstein, *Francis Bacon: a political biography* (Athens, OH, 1977) contains no reference to Ireland, although he did submit a 'little breviatt of the Irish business' to James. See Bacon to James, 2 July 1613, FSL, MS X.d.158. For his speech about Ireland on Sir William Jones' installation as chief justice of the king's bench in Ireland, see FSL, MS V.a.206.

52 The English privy council to Chichester, 7 March 1613, *Cal. S.P. Ire., 1611–14*, p. 328; Laud to Bramhall, 4 March 1635, HL, HP, MS 15,158; same to same, 11 May 1635, HL, HP, MS 15,159.

53 Ronald G. Asch, 'Elizabeth, Princess, queen of Bohemia and electress palatine', *Oxford DNB*.

54 Bradley to Davies, 5 Feb. 1613, Bodl. Lib., Carte MS 62, fo. 235; Beecher to Cork, 24 March 1630, in Clarke, McGrath and Edwards (eds), *A lord justice's letter book*, no. 63.

transmitted between England and Ireland and deliberate stalling by the Irish council occurred at every point.[55]

The review process in England was detailed, with learned counsel carefully checking every line and making many amendments. It is unclear whether English attorneys general played a straightforward legal role in assessing and examining bills or a political one also. Some bills were easily allowed, others amended or 'stayed' for various reasons, including political considerations, because they conflicted with other statutes or were poorly drafted. Some changes were minor, including correcting clerical 'miswrytings'; others were small but important technical edits, ensuring precision in language, e.g., in the 'Act concerning the appearance of Jurors in the *Nisi Prius* &c, in the eighteenth lyne of the second skin to strike out the words (competent) and after the words (Courts) to add (of Record)', though others had more significant amendments.[56]

It was difficult for any bill, but especially private or local ones, to get through the certification process; Sidney transmitted 12 private acts in 1569, but Dublin City faced stiff opposition in 1613 to its bill to confirm its charter from solicitor general Jacob who, not confident of blocking it in Ireland, lobbied Northampton against it.[57] Of 14 bills considered by the English council in one meeting before the 1613 parliament, seven (two public, five private) were refused, four were allowed and three others were agreed, subject to checking some matters. That so many were 'stayed' or rejected in London suggests poor drafting in Dublin, especially since English lawyers had greater experience of writing legislation, but political considerations also played a role.[58] The bill 'against bringing in of Armes' was refused as 'overstrict, for as it is drawen, no man can carry so much as a Pistoll or Peece into Ireland, no nor in his Barque for defence against Pirats.' The council held the 1613 bill for 'Confirmation of all Graunts made to his majesty' and of all letters patent made by the king 'untill more settled tymes', and the bill for two subsidies depending on it was 'consequentlie to be staied' also.[59] Bills that survived scrutiny in England were still likely to be rejected in Ireland because of poor drafting, as Chichester reported: 'some of them are thought defective in words, or forme or both, and if it prove so, it is the fault or omission of those that drewe them'. The Irish privy council retransmitted the subsidy bill in October 1614 'to make the days of counting and rating perfect'.[60]

55 Commons to the committee, 23 April 1641, Simon Digby to the committee, 7 May 1641, Eustace to the committee, 22 June 1641, ARL, MS Parliamentary Papers, unpaginated; Clarke, *Old English*, p. 153.
56 Bodl. Lib., Bankes MS 10/2, 26 Oct. 1634.
57 Bernadette Cunningham (ed.), *Calendar of State Papers Ireland, Tudor period, 1568–1571* (Dublin, 2010), pp 127–9; Jacob to Northampton, 26 May 1613, Bodl. Lib., Carte MS 62, fos. 241r–4v.
58 For poor drafting in 1569 and 1585, see Treadwell, 'Sir John Perrott'.
59 Bodl. Lib., Carte MS 62, fos. 39r–40r.
60 E.g., Chichester to James, 16 Oct. 1614, TNA, SP 63/232, fo. 193; *Commons' Jn. Ire.*, 20 Oct. 1640.

The English lawyers' amendments had to be authorized by the monarch's warrant.[61] Approved bills, including amended or revised ones, were signed off by the attorney general and counsel, certified, engrossed, sealed with the great seal of England and transmitted back to Dublin for introduction, in paper form, in either house. As there was considerable work in drafting, examining and approving bills, they were transmitted in batches as they were ready by a variety of messengers. Davies, Winch, Bradley and Jacob brought the bills for the 1613–15 parliament.[62] In 1634 Philip Mainwaring, Francis Windebank Jr, William Railton and Archbishop Ussher conveyed bills to England.[63] The Irish agents in London in 1640–1 were busy negotiating about bills and arranging for their transport.[64] The bills, on parchment, formed a heavy load to carry.[65] Cork was well aware of the possibility of single acts being lost in the system and ensured that his bill was transmitted with others, to ensure its safety and that it would receive due attention; however he either overestimated Bramhall's support, or under-estimated Wentworth's cunning, as his bill was included in the third transmission and delivered to the Commons on 17 October 1640 having been passed by the Lords at the point at which Cork as a privy councillor in England was engaged in Strafford's trial. It subsequently received its second and third readings on 22 October and received assent on 12 November 1640.[66]

Legislation had to pass both houses and receive royal assent to become law. Parliament could recommend changes to the administration and amended bills had to be certified and transmitted to England for certification. Both houses felt free to recommend amendments.[67] In 1569 Elizabeth commended parliament's recommendations:

> we perceive that our said Court of parliament hath upon treating and debating the said bills (those of the former session) thought meet &

61 E.g., Bodl. Lib., Bankes MS 10/10 (17 Jan. 1635), MS 10/7 (22 March 1640), MS 10/5 (10 June 1640).

62 Davies to Salisbury, 21 Jan. 1611, *Cal. S.P. Ire., 1611–14*, p. 5; James to Chichester, 26 Sept. 1612, *Cal. S.P. Ire., 1611–14*, pp 285–6; Bradley to Davies, 5 Feb. 1613, Bodl. Lib., Carte MS 62, fo. 235; *Commons' Jn. Ire.*, 21 April 1615; Grosart (ed.), *Lismore Papers*, 1st series, iv, pp 25–6, 57; Ussher to Bramhall, 7 May 1640, HL, HP, MS 15,958.

63 Grosart (ed.), *Lismore Papers*, 1st series, iv, pp 25–6, 57; Wandesford to Radcliffe, 7 Aug. 1640, Bodl. Lib., Add. C 286, fo. 33r; Railton to Bankes, 24 Sept. 1640, Bodl. Lib., Bankes MS 65/69; Ussher to Bramhall, 7 May 1640, HL, HP, MS 15,958. Windebank, son and namesake of the English politician, was Wentworth's secretary and MP for Ennis in 1635. See Brian Quintrell, 'Windebank, Sir Francis', *Oxford DNB*. Railton was Wentworth's agent. See Fiona Pogson, 'Public and private service at the early Stuart court: the career of William Raylton, Strafford's agent', *Historical Research*, 84:223 (Feb., 2011), 53–66.

64 Simon Digby to the Irish Commons, 7 May 1641, ARL, MS Parliamentary Papers, unpaginated.

65 E.g., A bundle of bills from 1634, TNA, MS C. 86/1.

66 Cork to Mainwaring, 17 March 1640, Cork to Joshua Boyle, 17 March 1640, Chatsworth House, Cork Papers, Misc. boxes, Box 3, pp 418ff; Patrick Little, 'The earl of Cork and the downfall of the earl of Strafford, 1638–41', *The Historical Journal*, 39:3 (Sept., 1996), 619–35. Also see the Commons' and Lords' journals for those dates.

67 Routledge, 'Journal'; NLI, MS 836, pp 165–71.

> convenient by their wisdoms to make some alteration or change of some part of them, and likewise to certain others of said bills some good and necessary addition, which their doings we do not mislike, but take in very good part.

However, in 1585 the Lords amended the bills authorizing acts and statutes and that restoring Luke Delahoyde to his blood, following the English practice of reading out all of the amendments twice; they passed and received the royal assent apparently without being transmitted back to England.[68] The 1640–1 Commons' committee in England conceived

> that it would stand with the scope and tenor of Poynings Act that such bills as shalbe transmitted from Ireland under the greate seale there may be drawne by the Lord Deputy and Councell of the Realeme with the privitie and assistance of both houses of Parliament after the said Parliament is mett.

Charles agreed to legislation to redress their grievances.[69]

Bills could be initiated in either house, although by convention subsidy bills were introduced in the Commons and bills dealing with honour (i.e., restitution in blood) in the Lords. Oliver St John asserted that only the Commons could initiate subsidy bills for the laity but the 1615 bill was introduced in both houses on 22 April, passed in the Lords two days later and in the Commons on 28 April. This was highly unusual, as bills should not have been handled in both houses at the same time.[70] The convention was observed in 1634 and 1640, when the subsidy bills were introduced in the lower house. Convocation's separate subsidy bill for clergy had to be confirmed by act of parliament. It was presented to Chichester in a plenary parliamentary session on 29 April 1615 and passed by the Lords but stalled in the Commons when Catholics' objected to its offensive preamble; the chancellor demanded an explanation of its lack of progress at the plenary meeting ending that session.[71] The Irish Lords objected to John Heyden's bill being introduced in the Commons; the other restitution bill in that parliament – for Maurice FitzGerald of Belagh – was initiated in the Lords, where it was rejected.[72] In England, 'estate' bills (private legislation dealing with land titles) were introduced in the Lords, but Irish private bills dealing with land titles were all initiated in the Commons, except Bramhall and Ussher's private acts restoring

68 Lodge, *Sketches*, pp 52–3; Routledge, 'Journal'.

69 The committee's undated submission and Charles' response of 31 July 1641, ARL, MS Parliamentary Papers, unpaginated.

70 The issue arose repeatedly in England in this period. See Sheila Lambert, 'Committees, religion and parliamentary encroachment on royal authority in early Stuart England', *EHR*, 105 (Jan., 1990), 60–95.

71 *Commons' Jn. Ire.*, 2 May 1615; NLI, MS 836, pp 170–1.

72 Smith, *Stuart*, p. 39; *Commons' Jn. Ire.*, 8, 9 and 16 May 1615; Treadwell, 'House of Lords'; e.g., James to Lord Deputy Mountjoy, 7 July 1604, Philadelphia Papers, vol. 1, p. 43; same to same, 31 Oct. 1606, J.C. Erck (ed.), *A repertory of the inrolments on the patent rolls of chancery in Ireland, commencing with the reign of James I* (Dublin, 1846–52), pp 102, 163.

impropriations and Cork's bill settling his dispute with the bishop of Waterford. Welsh bills were also usually introduced in the English upper house.[73] Interestingly, bills introduced in the English Lords had a much higher success rate, underlining that house's importance. Irish public bills generally passed easily in the Lords in the early Stuart period thanks to the bishops and absentee English peers' proxies although many were rejected in the Commons.[74]

The English parliament's options for amending, amalgamating, splitting and rewriting bills were not available in Ireland; when the possibility of dividing the bill repealing the Statutes of Kilkenny into two or three separate bills was raised after the committee examining it had reported back to the house, members, almost all of whom were lawyers, engaged in a lengthy debate in the chamber, including considering whether to ask the opinion of judges' and king's counsel on the matter before referring it to a committee entirely composed of lawyers for further deliberation. Any desired amendments (and there were many) resulted in requests to the lord deputy to incorporate the changes in a new bill to be transmitted under the great seal to the monarch, including the bill to repeal the statutes of Kilkenny, the set of laws which had been established for the colonial Lordship in the fourteenth century.[75] Five separate 1640 bills removing benefit of clergy in different circumstances would undoubtedly have been amalgamated in England.

Bills were very carefully examined in parliament, especially because they could not be directly amended; in 1569 Lord Chancellor Robert Weston noted that bills that were generally welcomed were rejected because they were imperfectly drafted and could not be amended and in 1585 Walsh also noted that some of the bills were poorly drafted:

> [one] for the Attainder of the Earl of Desmonde was penned, with so many savings, as if it did so pass the Queene should gain noting thereby. Those and the most part of all the rest were devised either too farr, or too short, as it might be easily judged, that without the Suspending of Poynings Act they could not be amended here.[76]

MPs diligently checked the paper copies with which they were presented against the transmitted parchment copies. On 13 October 1614, a standing committee was appointed to compare all paper bills with those engrossed and transmitted from England and in 1634 a committee was appointed to check any discrepancies

73 *Commons' Jn. Ire.*, 21, 25 Oct. 1614, 4 Nov. 1614, 26 March and 1 June 1640; Bowen, 'Wales at Westminster'.

74 Smith, *Stuart*, pp 42–3. A number was dashed in 1585, Routledge, 'Journal'.

75 Sheila Lambert, 'Procedure in the House of Commons in the early Stuart period', *EHR*, 95 (Oct., 1980), 753–81; *Commons' Jn. Ire.*, 15, 29 Oct. 1614, 29 Nov. 1614, 21 April 1615.

76 Weston to Cecil, 17 Feb. 1569, TNA, SP 63/27, p. 463; White to Burghley, 27 May 1585, TNA, SP 63/116, fo. 138r. For another instance, see Lord Deputy and other Commissioners for Confirmation of Defective Titles, 14 May 1635, HMC, *Various collections, Volume III*, pp 156–7; Terry Clavin and Anthony McCormack, 'Weston, Robert', *DIB*.

between the drafts.[77] Chichester reported that bills received closer scrutiny in the Commons than the Lords, which he ascribed partly to disloyalty, stating, 'they question all matters punctually being composed of many more heads, and some of them hotter than the gravity of the house would admit', but it was probably because so many MPs were lawyers alive to the implications of each word or phrase.[78] The bill for trial of murders, which had already passed its third reading, was recommitted on 20 October 1614 and found to be 'imperfected … to be new drawn or amended by the same committees.' It is unclear whether they wished to amend it or had found clerical errors in the copy from which they were working. On 29 November 1614 members submitted to Chichester a list of grievances that could be resolved by act of state or otherwise, specifically citing the bills that were 'in some points defective and unfit to pass but with certain amendments and additions' and asking for 15 to be amended in consultation with 12 named MPs, nine of whom were lawyers, before being transmitted to England in time for the following session.[79] Some bills were retransmitted despite there being no record of their being debated, which suggests that amendments were proposed, possibly at their first readings; examples are those in 1640 for enlarging Dublin City and County's boundaries, reducing fees and that for the vicarages of Blaris and Lisnegarvey.

The Irish parliament seems not to have used the same flexibility in the number of readings as Elizabeth's English parliaments and the practice of bills receiving three readings and approval in each house before royal assent was well-established by at least 1569.[80] Bills could be rejected after any reading and those passed by one house were delivered to the other for consideration; judges and senior lawyers (e.g., Serjeant Beare, Jacob and the master of the rolls in 1613, and the attorney general and judge William Ryves in 1640) brought bills from the Lords to the Commons, while the lower house chose privy councillors or MPs closely connected to peers to bring their approved bills to the upper house.[81] In England bills that failed to pass, described as 'dashed', were ritually torn. The same terminology was used in Ireland, but there no evidence of tearing rejected bills.[82]

The first reading was performed by the clerk, standing by his table below the speaker's chair. Reading lengthy bills was time-consuming and on 14 October 1614 the Lords agreed that any of their house might have a copy of a bill after the first reading; no such order seems to have been made for the Commons.[83] The public

77 *Commons' Jn. Ire.*, 20 Feb. 1635.
78 Chichester to James I, 16 Oct. 1614, TNA, SP 63/232, fo. 193v.
79 *Commons' Jn. Ire.*, 21 April 1615 (reporting proceedings of 29 Nov. 1614).
80 Falkiner, *Essays*, pp 238–9; Neale, *House*, pp 357ff; Dennehy, *Parliament*, p. 105.
81 E.g., *Commons' Jn. Ire.*, 28 April 1615, 15 Oct. 1640; Wandesford as Mr of the Rolls bringing bills to the Lords, 20 Nov. 1634, Sir William Parsons, 6 Dec. 1634, William St Leger 6 April 1635, Brabazon, 8 April 1635, Lord Robert Dillon, 16 April 1635, Dillon, 8 and 11 June, 24 Oct. 1640, Radcliffe 22 March, 3 June, 15 Oct., Meredith 31 March 1640.
82 Hawkyard, *Commons*, p. 338; e.g., *Commons' Jn. Ire.*, 10 Nov. 1614, 1 July 1641.
83 Hakewill, *Modus*, p. 36; Treadwell, 'House of Lords'; Dennehy, *Parliament*, pp 138–9.

reading was not merely traditional but in 1613 it also helped MPs with limited literacy, such as Roger Rice and Bryan MacMahon and some native Irish with little or no English; there is no reference in the journals to efforts to ensure their understanding, but bilingualism and the generally high standard of Latin in Ireland would have made interpretation easy.[84] The second reading consisted of the speaker's giving a breviate (synopsis) of the bill and the reasons for its introduction followed by a debate on its provisions, after which it was either rejected, agreed to be engrossed and proceeded to its third reading, or referred to a committee for consideration. Relatively few bills were committed, with the Lords more likely to commit than the Commons, again possibly because the peers were less likely to have legal training and relied on judges' advice.[85] The Commons agreed on 22 October 1614 that counsel might be heard for private bills between the second reading and committal. After committees' reports were accepted, bills were engrossed and passed to their third reading, which consisted of a re-reading of the breviate, following which the house decided whether to pass or reject them, or, occasionally to recommit them for further consideration, as happened to the bill to defeat fraudulent conveyances on 2 November 1614. When the Commons voted against engrossing the bill to secure Piers Lacy's estates to Thomas Standish, they also considered whether to re-commit it for further consideration, but decided against.[86] However, being engrossed did not invariably lead to the bill being put to the question, albeit unusually, the bill for the plantation of Connacht was engrossed on 8 June 1640, but never mentioned again.[87] Most bills were passed without votes, but others required a division.

Bills often received their first and second readings on the same day, e.g., that for the trial of murders on 12 October 1614 and 12 bills on 13 February 1635, ten being engrossed and two others referred to a committee. Very rarely, bills received all three readings on the same day; the bill of joyful recognition of James' title to the throne passed in one day, but when the administration attempted to push three readings of the bill for amending highways and chases through the Commons on 3 May 1615, Sir Christopher Plunkett's motion that no bill could receive three readings in one day was approved.[88] Uncontentious bills could pass very quickly, as they did not need lengthy debate or committal; seven bills engrossed on 13 February 1635 received their third reading the following day, six of which were sent to the Lords the next sitting day.

84 For Rice signing with a mark, see TNA, SP 63/144, fo. 231; Bodl. Lib., Carte MS 61, fo. 219.

85 Dennehy, *Parliament*, p. 81. However, these figures include some double-counting and do not include two bills recorded as being committed by the Lords in 1613–15. Treadwell, 'House of Lords'.

86 *Commons' Jn. Ire.*, 10 Nov. 1614.

87 Perceval-Maxwell notes that it did not reappear from the sub-committee, but its engrossment was recorded. See Michael Perceval-Maxwell, 'Protestant faction, the impeachment of Strafford and the origins of the Irish civil war', *The Canadian Journal of History*, 17 (1982), 235–55.

88 *Commons' Jn. Ire.*, 13 Oct. 1614, 18 April 1635; Dennehy, *Parliament*, p. 76.

The 1585 rules specified that MPs might speak only once to a bill, standing uncovered (not wearing their hats) but the journals' limited record of contributions after 1615 prevents any accurate assessment of the extent to which this was observed. The Commons declared on 18 October 1614 that members might speak on either the first or second readings, although the former was 'unusual' and the question of contributing on first readings was referred to the committee of privileges on the following day. The large number of bills rejected before their second readings shows how frequently debate took place at the first reading. Ridgeway's statement that it was 'against all the rules of parliament to speak to a bill at the first reading' was an attempt to stop Catholics' objections to the preamble to the clergy subsidies bill.[89]

Re-transmitting amended bills was a lengthy route and uncertain of success and MPs felt pressurized to pass defective legislation and the crown applied pressure to ensure that they did so. While no objections are recorded, all native Irish MPs, whether Old English or Gaelic, must have been affronted by the anti-Irish language of barbarism included in preambles to at least four 1634 bills.[90] Radcliffe's threat to have rejected bills implemented as acts of state was no loose talk, as Wentworth demonstrated by issuing one to implement the provisions of the Gunpowder Bill they had dashed the previous day, making it plain he would deal with other rejections in the same way as he did with the unsuccessful bill to amalgamate counties Tipperary and Cross Tipperary. Early modern acts of state are poorly recorded, so it is impossible to know how many other rejected bills were dealt with in the same way.[91] The 1640 subsidy act was rapidly passed but MPs subsequently expressed disgust at the self-laudatory preamble Wentworth included to it in their Protestation, echoed by Gormanston and Kilmallock in their petition: 'prefixing glorious preambles to Acts of Parliament, thereby to justify his lordships plans and proceeding and thereby to ascribe that which was done as a [service] to his majesty (as much as in him lay) to himself.'[92]

89 Irish Archaeological Society, *Tracts*, ii, p. 143; *Commons' Jn. Ire.*, 4 May 1615; Neale, *House*, pp 357–8. The 'Bill for the freedom of working of the materials in this kingdom of Ireland into manufactures' was dashed 17 April 1635.

90 10 & 11 Car. I, c. 5 (Keepers of ale-houses to be bound by recognisances), 10 & 11 Car. I, c. 10 (Ploughing by the tail and pulling wool off sheep), 10 & 11 Car. I, c. 16 (Cosherers and idle wanderers), 10 & 11 Car. I, c. 17 (Burning corn in the straw). I am grateful to John McCafferty for his observations on this subject. The numbers of Gaelic Irish members of the Commons is dealt with in chapter nine.

91 Clarke, *Old English*, pp 90–1; *Commons' Jn. Ire.*, 24 March 1635; Bodl. Lib., Carte MS 59, fos. 80r–1v; The Generall grievances of the Peeres and gentry of this kingdom, undated, but 1641, Bodl. Lib., Carte MS 2, fo. 211r, where it is stated 'That upon the first cominge of the said Lord Strafford into this kingdom it was mainly urged that an act of Parliament should passe against munition and armes to be enioyed by any of vs and that haveing failed here they supplied the same by act of Councell in the kingdom thereby to leave vs naked and disinable vs to defend our selves against theire wicked enterprise and resolutions.'

92 *Commons' Jn. Ire.*, 6 May 1615, 17 Feb. 1641; Dennehy, *Parliament*, p. 67; Gormanston and Kilmallock's petition to the King, Feb. 1641, TNA, SP 63/258, p. 163.

MPs devised creative solutions to problematic bills, including acts of state and explanatory acts or letters. Concerned that the bill for Tyrone's attainder could affect innocent people's property rights, on foot of the committee's report on 26 October 1614, and following a precedent set in 1585, the Commons decided that the speaker and 12 members from each side of his chair should request Chichester to issue an act of state to save strangers against the act, which only passed when the act of state had been delivered to the Commons. This was a more effective resolution than the Lords achieved; peers objected to the bill because of concerns about their own title to lands in Cavan and Chichester persuaded them to pass the bill on the understanding that he would ask James to recompense them.[93] In 1635, the Commons requested an act of state to amend the unrealistic timescale in the bill for erecting houses of correction.[94]

Explanatory acts were used to clarify the meaning, intent or effect of an earlier act and resolve problems in the interpretation of acts without needing to repeal them. Thus, 3 & 4 Philip and Mary, c. 4 clarified the procedure to be used under Poynings' Law and allowed bills to be transmitted during the course of parliamentary sessions. The Commons requested an explanatory act for the bill to guarantee letters patent for defective titles.[95] A formal explanatory act was not always necessary and the bill to repeal the Statutes of Kilkenny was accompanied by a letter of explanation from the English privy council to clarify its provisions.[96]

When private bills failed, their sponsors had to find less secure ways of resolving their difficulties. Despite his influential position, Cork struggled for 30 years to try to settle his land dispute with successive bishops of Waterford and Lismore, finally achieving success through mediation brokered by Bramhall in the final years of the earl's life. James Martin obtained a grant of denization which permitted him to own land when his hoped-for private bill of naturalization was scuppered by the outbreak of the 1641 rebellion.[97] Private bills were supposed to be dealt with early in the morning, when the house was 'thin', but this rule was not consistently followed.[98] There is no record of the lobbying that must have taken place to ensure their passage, other than Laurence Parsons' suggestion in 1614 that he be returned in a by-election to 'to do Boyle service concerning Lismore, wherein the Bishop will do his utmost to get voices' and Piers Creagh's promoting James Martin's bill.[99] Naturalization bills were generally uncontentious; all passed

93 Lord Deputy and other Commissioners for Confirmation of Defective Titles, 14 May 1635, HMC, *Various collections, Volume III*, pp 156–7; *Commons' Jn. Ire.*, 26, 28 Oct. 1614. The act of state was included in the journals for 29 Nov. 1614. Similar issues had arisen on Shane O'Neill's attainder in 1569 and Desmond's in 1585. Cunningham (ed.), *Calendar of State Papers*, p. 141; Routledge, 'Journal'.

94 *Commons' Jn. Ire.*, 18 April 1635.

95 Ibid., 31 July 1634.

96 Ibid., 27 April, 1, 5, 8 May 1615.

97 Inquisition post mortem of James Martin, RIA, MS 14/C/2, pp 183–5.

98 E.g., *Commons' Jn. Ire.*, 13 Feb. 1635. The number of private bills dealt with from 1 June 1640 suggests that the House was poorly attended then.

99 Parsons to Boyle, May 1614, Chatsworth House, Cork Papers, vol. 5, no. 43; RIA, MS 14/C/2, pp 183–5.

with no recorded debate or opposition except James Garnier's, which was committed, and Philip Begoe's was the only one not to obtain a first reading.[100]

Authority to give royal assent to named bills was included in the warrant for transmission.[101] Royal assent could be given at any point after acts were passed, but was customarily granted in a formal plenary meeting in the Lords before prorogation or dissolution. Royal assent was another difference between the English and Irish parliaments, where the monarch could reject any bill, especially since they could be drafted, proposed and amended by any member of either house without reference to the monarch or privy council. Automatic assent might be assumed in Ireland, but in 1586 the Act concerning leases to be good for 21 years without the issue of tenants in tail was 'stayed at the royal assent' and Wentworth refused assent to the 1634 Act of several charges imposed on the lands and persons of *Cestui que use* (a type of trust).[102] Ormond received a commission to grant assent to the act for remittal of rents, services, compositions, first fruits, and twentieth parts act transmitted from England in 1644, debated in the parliament in the summer of that year and passed in 1645.[103] Acts were printed, publicized by proclamation and read out at customary places, such as market crosses (see chapter two) in counties' principal market towns.[104]

COMMITTEES

Committees contributed significantly to parliament's efficiency, saving time, reaching consensus on divisive subjects, gaining access to expertise, gathering information, taking evidence to support its judicial function, streamlining administration and representing the nation in England.[105] While Perceval-Maxwell noted that 'as in England, it was through committees that decisions were reached' they were only used when consensus was not achieved quickly.[106] Parliaments had four main types of committees: standing, *ad hoc,* conference committees and committees of the whole house. Some administrative committees were also

100 *Commons' Jn. Ire.*, 24 Oct. 1640. Bankes had raised questions about Begoe's bill: Charles' warrant to Bankes, 11 Sept. 1640, Bodl. Lib., Bankes MS 10/4. Begoe (Bigoe), possibly a Frenchman, was master and owner of a glass-blowing business in Gloaster, King's County. Deposition of Glawde Bonny's, 16 June 1646, TCD, MS 814, fos. 271r–2v.

101 E.g., Bodl. Lib., Bankes MS 10/4, 10/6, 10/8, 10/9; Bodl. Lib., Bankes MS 55/36, 55/65.

102 *Cal. Carew*, ii, p. 425; *LJI*, 15 Dec. 1634. For a discussion of Cestui que use see J. Byrne, 'News not worth relating: the hanging of Walter Evers, 10 June 1642', *Ríocht na Mídhe*, 33 (2022), 85–91.

103 W.H. Black, *Docquets of letters patent and other instruments passed under the great seal of King Charles at Oxford in the years 1642–1646* (London, 1837), p. 244. I am grateful to Patrick Little for drawing this reference to my attention. Dennehy, *Parliament*, pp 16, 59, 92–3.

104 Brian Mac Cuarta, 'A Catholic funeral in county Down, 1617', *Archivium Hibernicum*, 60 (2006–7), 320–5; Raymond Gillespie, 'Political ideas and their social contexts' in Ohlmeyer (ed.), *Political thought*, pp 107–27.

105 Coleman Dennehy, 'Parliamentary committees in seventeenth-century Ireland: a brief introduction', *PER*, 39:3 (2019), 316–27.

106 Perceval-Maxwell, *Outbreak*, p. 73.

appointed and the committee appointed to travel to England to communicate the nation's grievances to Charles was a unique use of the committee system to fulfil parliament's role in representation and consultation and was used by Charles for that purpose, asking the Irish parliament to propose a means of settling his revenue from tobacco.[107]

Committees could only deal with matters referred to them by the house, which specified their membership, what records or witnesses they could demand or summon and who might attend and vote. When there was a question about the powers of the committee in England, the Commons appointed a committee to enlarge their powers and the speaker sent them a copy of the order to that effect.[108] Any MP could attend any committee and on some occasions all those attending, not just committee members, could vote.[109] Committees appear to have conducted their work very efficiently; there are few if any references to the house reminding them to perform their tasks or meet deadlines. The Confederation of Kilkenny operated in a similar manner to parliament, including committees. On 30 October 1642, the General Assembly appointed a committee to 'consider and lay down a form of civil government; and all such lawyers as are of this house are to be of the said committee and have voice in that settlement'.[110]

Valuable parliamentary time was saved by referring matters to smaller groups of members chosen for their professional expertise (like the committee appointed on 9 April 1635 for the bill limiting the times for loading and landing of merchandise which included all burgesses for port towns or that two days later for By-laws to be made by corporations and fraternities, which included members from towns with guilds), local knowledge, such as the many committees dealing with petitions, or to legislative committees because they had contributed to debates on those bills. As committees could sit simultaneously and take evidence or advice from outsiders, and appoint sub-committees, many more subjects could be dealt with than in sittings of the whole house.[111] Contentious or divisive matters were removed from the floor of the house by appointing committees to explore the issues and achieve consensus. The 1615 clergy subsidies' bill, for example, was referred to the Grand Committee to enable Catholic MPs to discuss their objections to its dogmatic Protestant preamble and its amended version was transmitted to England. The 1640 committee on levying subsidies allowed the house radically to change how much money was to be raised. Opposition or

107 Speaker of the Irish Commons to the committee in England, 22 June 1641, ARL, MS Parliamentary Papers, unpaginated.

108 *Commons' Jn. Ire.*, 30 Jan. 1640–1; Eustace to the committee in England, 30 Jan. 1641, ARL, MS Parliamentary Papers, unpaginated.

109 Scobell, *Memorials*, p. 35. For witnesses, see *Commons' Jn. Ire.*, 28 July 1641; Piers Butler's committee, Bodl. Lib., Carte MS 64, fo. 463r; *Commons' Jn. Ire.*, 23 July 1634, 6 Nov. 1634, 28 March 1640.

110 Bodl. Lib., Carte MS 68, fo. 1v, 30 Oct. 1642.

111 Lambert, 'Committees, religion and parliamentary encroachment'; Neale, *House*, pp 358–63; e.g., *Commons' Jn. Ire.*, 1 April 1640.

agreement did not usually break down on religious or ethnic lines and committees provided the forum for wide discussions leading to agreed positions.[112] Committees allowed the house to avail of outsiders' expertise, such as legal advice from Richard Berford, Patrick Darcy and Richard Martin and possibly Dominic Bodkin.[113] The committee appointed on 30 June 1641 to draw up bills relating to tobacco comprised 'all of the Long Robe and merchants of this house … and they to call to their assistance all such merchants of this City, as they shall see fit.' The committee nominated to consider the petition of Patrick Barnewall and matters relating to cloth included ten named MPs, other MPs who chose to attend and 15 men from various towns, presumably searchers and sealers of cloth.[114] It was also possible to include outsiders on committees, as Ussher was for the English parliament in March 1641 and Sir Richard Everard was on Piers Butler's committee in the summer of the same year in Ireland.[115]

Committees gathered information, such as the various committees researching official fees, and supported parliament's judicial function, especially in 1641 by taking evidence in impeachment proceedings and on petitions and other grievances. Finally, committees contributed to the house's smooth running, for example by the grievances committee undertaking initial scrutiny of petitions and the committee appointed on 13 October 1614 to compare paper bills with the originals.

Committee members were usually nominated by their names being called out, but the order in which this happened is unclear:

> Every one of the House that list may call upon the name of any one of the House to be a Committee, and the Clark ought in his journal to write under the title of the Bill the name of every one so called upon, at leastwise of such whose names (in that confusion) he can distinctly hear.

Once 'a convenient number of Committees are named' the speaker then read the names of the committees and the time and place of the committee's meeting.[116] It

112 *Commons' Jn. Ire.*, 6 and 16 May 1615; Perceval-Maxwell, *Outbreak*, p. 81. For a discussion on the role of committees in ensuring consensus, including between different estates, in the Catalan Corts, see Josep Capdeferro, 'Commissioners, ad-hoc committees and negotiators in the *Cortes* of Catalonia, 1701–02', *PER*, 39:3 (2019), 328–39.

113 *Commons' Jn. Ire.*, 5 March 1641; Borlase, *History*, p. 10 states, 'besides some of the active men of the house, Lawyers, Darcy, Martin, Plunkett, Cusack, Brown, Linch, Bodkin, Evers and others, took upon them, with much confidence to declare the law.' The only Bodkin admitted to the inns of court during this period was Dominic Bodkin, but it is unclear whether he was a practicing lawyer and he is not known to have been an MP; Walter Evers, MP for Kells, 1634, Bríd McGrath, 'Meath members of parliament, 1634–1641', *Riocht na Midhe*, 12 (2001), 90–107. Neither was admitted to the King's Inns.

114 *Commons' Jn. Ire.*, 21 June 1641.

115 Unless his election was unreported. The son of Sir John, he had wished to represent Tipperary in 1634. Bodl. Lib., Carte MS 64, fo. 463r.

116 Smith, *Stuart*, p. 72; Hakewill, *Modus*, pp 145ff. 'Committees' was used in two senses – those to whom the matter had been committed and the group of men who formed the committee.

is generally assumed that only men physically present were nominated, although there is no direct evidence of this. It is curious that five MPs whose constituencies were excluded by James' judgments were nominated to a committee on 14 October 1614, although the journals note that they did not sit for long.[117] The lack of the clerk's rough journals for Wentworth's parliaments prevents any reconstruction of their nomination process, but the first named members of committees are apparently listed in order of their nomination in Bradley's rough journal (although those named later may not be in strict chronological order). However, following English practice, Medhop's fair journals listed them by their social status, with privy councillors and judges followed by knights and then untitled MPs, leaving a false impression of how they were nominated and privileging Protestants who were more likely to receive titles. English clerks kept lists of committees in a 'committees book', but none is recorded for Ireland.[118]

The efficiency with which committees dealt with their business suggests that attendance was not generally a problem, unlike in Catalonia, where political pressures led to a decline in committee membership and effectiveness.[119] However, attendance could be affected by scheduling and very active members had to choose between competing obligations and prioritize their time accordingly. On 24 October 1614 the treasurer moved that the Grand Committee might be 'quickened to attend their meetings' which was ordered to meet on 'Monday, Wednesday, and Friday, weekly, whereof the house are to take notice, to prevent absence by being in other inferior committees'. The house set quora for some committees: the 1634 grievances committee had 75 members and a quorum of 24. The Commons clearly worried about attendance, as they ordered that any other MP attending the committee would count towards the quorum. The sub-committees dealing with officials' fees each had a quorum of six.[120]

The English Commons had five standing committees: privileges and elections, religion, grievances, courts of justice and trade. The first three emerged in the sixteenth century and the last two in the 1620s. The first committee specifically to consider both privileges and election returns was in 1593, evidence of the uncertainty in the number of boroughs entitled to representation, but this innovation almost immediately became established practice. The Irish Lords' committee for privileges established in 1613 pre-dated the first English one by eight years, but no such committee was formed in the Scottish Estates before the

117 Beare, Blennerhasset, Boyle, Gosnold and Fitzharris.

118 E.g., *Commons' Jn. Ire.*, 4 Nov. 1614; TNA, PRO 30/5/3, fo. 65; King's Inns, MS N3/2/1/7, fo. 11v. See also 15 Oct. 1614, NLI, MS 836, pp 42–3; Foster, 'Painful labour'.

119 Josep Capdeferro, 'Sessions plenàries versus comissions de treball a les Corts catalanes del segle XVII' in R. Ferrero and L. Guia, *Corts i parlaments de la Corona d'Aragó: unes instituciones emblemàtiques en una monarquia composta* (Valencia, 2008), pp 307–27.

120 Other assemblies faced similar problems. For the session committees in the Scottish Estates, see Stevenson, *Government of Scotland*, pp xxxvi–viii. I am grateful to John Young for drawing this reference to my attention. Lambert, 'Committees, religion and parliamentary encroachment'; *Commons' Jn. Ire.*, 21, 28 July 1634.

Restoration.[121] The first Irish Commons' standing committees, for privileges and comparing bills, were introduced in 1614. During the ructions over the speakership, St John cited the English practice of appointing a committee to deal with disputed returns, but the Catholics refused to accept this mechanism until the house began sitting again in October 1614. At that interval the privileges committee was established to resolve tensions about the disputed elections, which the English privy council described as 'according to the ancient use of parliament', although it was an innovation in Ireland. A sub-committee of the privileges committee, which had a clear Catholic majority, dealt with petitions and other grievances.[122] Committees were appointed early in the first session of the 1614 and 1634 parliaments, but in the second in 1640.[123] There was no separate committee for grievances until 1634.

The committee of privileges examined disputed election returns and alleged breaches of privilege and decided on questions of procedure, an important function in a parliament whose role and operations were evolving but where there was often doubt about the rules because it met rarely and had deficient records; this expanded role followed the recent English developments of that committee's work. It only dealt with matters referred to it by the house, and many issues of privilege were managed without involving the committee.[124] The English committee of privileges checked the clerk's entries, but this was left to *ad hoc* committees in Ireland until 7 July 1641 when what was in effect a standing committee was appointed to perform this task.[125] The committee on privileges took precedence over all other committees. Confusingly, it was also referred to as the Grand Committee, a term also used for committees of the whole house.[126] Because of its role in deciding on precedents, the English committee usually had many members with previous parliamentary experience who would be able to give guidance. However, only four of the 1614 Irish committee (Digby, Lambart, Ridgeway and St John) had previous parliamentary experience, all in England. The seven men who had sat in 1585 were not members. That committee was heavily reliant on earlier records and on its chair (St John) and especially Ridgeway who sat on the 1604 English privileges committee and played a key role, with Everard describing him as having 'been a lanthorn and light to the proceedings of this parliament.'[127] The 1634 committee included many men with previous parliamentary experience in both England and Ireland.

121 Keeler, 'Emergence of standing committees'; Hunneyball, 'Development of parliamentary privilege'; Keeler, 'Committee for privileges'; Treadwell, 'House of Lords'; Smith, *Stuart*, p. 73. The Grand Committees on Courts of Justice and Trade were formed in 1621 and religion in 1624. Lambert, 'Committees, religion and parliamentary encroachment'; Mann, 'House rules'; *Commons' Jn. Ire.*, 9 Nov. 1614.

122 Davies to Somerset, 31 Oct. 1614, TNA, SP 63/232, fo. 201; Treadwell, 'Sir John Perrott'; *Commons' Jn. Ire.*, 20 Oct. 1614, 2, 4, 9 Nov. 1614.

123 Ibid., 17 July 1634, 17 June 1640.

124 Ibid., 17, 19, 29 Oct. 1614; Keeler, 'Committee for privileges'.

125 *Commons' Jn. Ire.*, 25 Nov. 1614, 18 April 1615, 17 April 1635; *LJI*, 18 July 1634.

126 E.g., *Commons' Jn. Ire.*, 22 July 1634.

127 Keeler, 'Committee for privileges'; McGrath, 'Membership', p. 169; *Commons' Jn. Ire.*, 13 May 1615.

It is unclear how MPs were selected for the 1614 privileges committee, but the clerk William Bradley's note that all privy councillors, judges and learned counsel were members did not reflect the original nominations and was not included in the printed journals. While the 1593, 1597 and 1614 English committees included all the privy councillor MPs, that of 1606–7 had none. Paul Hunneyball ascribed the increasing size of the English committee to its conferring a 'personal cachet'; this does not appear to have been the case in Ireland and was more likely to be due to a determination to control the house and Catholics were concerned to have only seven members out of 22 on the 1614 Irish committee. It is unclear how Catholic membership was so low if a simple nomination secured appointment.[128] In 1634 a motion that one member be chosen out of every county was defeated in favour of nominating them 'out of the body of the house.' That committee had fewer privy councillors, but twice as many Protestants as Catholics. The 1640 committee had only eleven privy councillors but an even greater religious imbalance, with 49 Protestant members and 12 Catholics.[129] A very large committee of grievances was appointed on 21 July 1634 and in 1640 the entire house was named as that committee.

Standing committees sat on at least two days each week. The chairmen of standing committees, except in 1614, are unknown. The English parliament objected to Sir Edward Coke's chairing the grievances committee, claiming no privy councillor had previously occupied the role.[130] The committee of agents to represent parliament's grievances in England established on 11 November 1640 was also a standing committee, with clear membership and tasks and unprecedented powers to continue even if parliament was prorogued or dissolved. It reported back regularly to the Irish parliament. While it was an innovation to send a committee to England, although based on the precedent of agents sent for consultation in 1628 (the 1613 delegation represented only Catholics), it was the best means of preventing the administration's blocking its work and was appointed to ensure parliament would be able to continue its representative function in the face of the threat of prorogation or dissolution.[131]

Ad hoc committees were appointed to consider legislation, petitions and other matters, such as assessing and collecting subsidies, officials' fees and members' agreed communications with the crown or administration (see below). As Scobell described, they were 'made occasionally, & dissolved after the Business committed unto them was reported.' They were first recorded in Ireland in 1585, although

128 TNA, PRO 30/5/3, fo. 29r, 14 Oct. 1614; Keeler, 'Emergence of standing committees'; *idem*, 'Committee for privileges'; NLI, MS 643, fo. 26r; Hunneyball, 'Development of parliamentary privilege'.

129 *Commons' Jn. Ire.*, 14 Oct. 1614, 17 July 1634, 21 March 1640.

130 Lambert, 'Committees, religion and parliamentary encroachment'.

131 E.g., Bodl. Lib., Carte MS 67, fos. 53–4; ARL, MS Parliamentary Papers, unpaginated, 7 May 1641, Simon Digby to the Irish Commons, 22 June 1641, Maurice Eustace to the Committee in England; Clarke, *Old English*, pp 44–54.

they may have operated earlier.[132] Conference committees were appointed as and when needed to meet others, most frequently the Lords, but also the deputy, judges or other individual officials for specific business. The convention was that twice as many MPs as lords were nominated to conference committees of both houses, the Commons appointed their own spokesman to lead delegations, but there was no limit to the number of MPs chosen to deliver messages.[133] Conference committees played an important role in reaching agreement between the houses on a wide variety of issues and were especially important in a bi-cameral house; conference committees were more easily arranged in uni-cameral bodies and different proportions of delegates were chosen by each estate. In Catalonia and Scotland, equal numbers of each estate attended and all had equal voting strengths.[134] Conference committees with judges discussed legislation and one was appointed to meet the privy council 'to know whether they have transmitted those bills [drafted by a committee appointed on 13 October] into England … and if they have not to give their reasons.' The Commons appointed a committee to present the Remonstrance to Wandesford; all but one of its members were Protestant and the majority of them were privy councillors.[135]

Irish conference committees' protocol evolved during this period. A search for precedents in 1614 produced no guidance, and the Commons debated whether or not to follow the English precedent where MPs 'in the conference, stand uncovered, the Lords Commissioners sitting covered.' It was decided they should to sit covered, on benches behind the lords and to be seated before the peers arrive, but MPs were uncertain that the lords would accept this.[136]

Committees of the whole house, also known as the 'Grand Committee', were appointed as and when needed and used to prevent the speaker controlling business. Normal rules of procedure did not apply within committees of the whole house: all MPs were members, meetings were held in the Commons' chamber and the speaker was replaced as chairman by another MP who also acted as rapporteur. Grand Committees emerged in the English parliament in 1606–7 and are first recorded in Ireland on 18 July 1634, after which they were frequently used; unlike England, there is no evidence of the Irish parliament using this mechanism when the speaker was absent.[137] The chairman was to 'sit in the Clerks place at the Table and to write the votes of the Committee.' MPs did not leave the chamber to vote, but separated with yeas on one side of the Chamber, noes on the other, with only

132 Scobell, *Memorials*, p. 9; Treadwell, 'Sir John Perrott'; White to Burghley, 27 May 1585, TNA, SP 63/116, fo. 138r. Hooker makes no mention of them.

133 E.g., Grosart (ed.), *Lismore Papers*, 1st series, iv, pp 93–4; *Commons' Jn. Ire.*, 7 Nov. 1614, 16 April 1635; *LJI*, 24 March 1640; TCD, MS 615, fo. 53r; *Commons' Jn. Ire.*, 30 July 1634.

134 Capdeferro, 'Commissioners, ad-hoc committees and negotiators'; Stevenson, *Government of Scotland*, p. xxxviii notes that additional members sat *ex officio*.

135 Perceval-Maxwell, *Outbreak*, pp 83–5; *Commons' Jn. Ire.*, 17 June 1640.

136 Ibid., 7 Nov. 1614.

137 Keeler, 'Committee for privileges'; Lambert, 'Procedure in the House of Commons'; Foster, 'Procedure'; e.g., *Commons' Jn. Ire.*, 22, 24, 28, 30 July 1634, 16 April 1635.

one teller on each side to report the results, 'making only two obeysances' to the empty speaker's chair instead of the usual three. Scobell states that 'when the committee has done its work, the chairman takes the votes and puts the question, that the same be reported to the House.' When that is resolved, he vacates the chair and the speaker resumes his place. Like the speaker, the chair has a casting vote if the numbers are tied, but 'otherwise no vote in the committee.' Unlike other committees, those of the whole house could not adjourn, 'but a question is to be made for reporting to the House, and that leave be asked, that the committee may sit at another time on that business.'[138] Committees of the whole house could appoint sub-committees: on 11 November 1640, Nicholas Plunkett and Richard FitzGerald were asked to 'retire themselves into the inner room of this house, and there state the question now to be put, and to reduce the same into writing, and presently to present it to this house.'

Committees of the whole house allowed for wide-ranging and detailed discussion of policy matters, but their use changed over this period. In 1634, five of the 12 Grand Committees (apart from the grievances committee which was a standing committee of the whole house) dealt with bills and the others with assessing the subsidies, disputes with the Lords and one on promoting trade and manufacturing. From June 1640, however, they were appointed very frequently, in some cases (e.g., July 1641) almost daily, and were formed only once to discuss the administration's legislation (26 March 1640). Instead, they were mainly used by the opposition to debate their own declarations and remonstrances, parliamentary privileges, the work of their agents in England (including solutions to the problem of compensating Charles for loss of revenue from defective titles and the tobacco monopoly), parliamentary privilege (including John FitzGerald's return for Inistioge), conference committees, responses to the lord deputy or lords justices, their own proposed bills against paper petitions and the Queries; in other words they were used to reach consensus on policy and strategy, using a format that allowed members to speak freely and frequently and debate matters in considerable detail, while also facilitating liaison with the committee in England, without speaker Eustace's partial management of the house's business. On the outbreak of the rebellion, Darcy proposed a committee of the whole house to discuss MPs' response to it. After June 1642, the 'rump' parliament used committees of the whole house to debate their remonstrances or declarations, the Remonstrance of the Roman Catholics, financing their agents in England in 1644 and petitions, but frequently, the journals do not record the matters to be dealt with.[139]

Committees sat in a less constrained atmosphere than formal Commons' sessions and gave MPs greater latitude to contribute to discussions and debates. Members could speak as often as they chose and had 'more freedom of speech, and that argument may be used *pro et contra*, committees are appointed for bills; some times to facilitate and agree of great business, either of the whole house, or

138 Scobell, *Memorials*, pp 37–9.
139 E.g., *Commons' Jn. Ire.*, 7–29 May 1647.

of particular committees.'[140] Members of *ad hoc* committees were chosen for their expertise or the geographical location of their constituencies and from those who spoke at bills' second readings; committees' size may reflect the level of interest in the subject. Clanricard's complaint to Ormond of the level of deference to lawyers in the General Assembly's committees presumably reflected the position in parliamentary committees, but also shows the value placed on professional expertise.[141] Greater credence would be given to contributions by those with expertise and local knowledge was valued. In 1635 Catlin was appointed, with other MPs from port towns, to the committee on the bill on restriction of lading goods, a unique instance of a speaker being on a committee. However, the increasing number of placemen meant that many MPs had little knowledge of their constituencies. Malby Brabazon, burgess for Bangor and a grandson of Sir William Brabazon, the Henrician under-treasurer of Ireland and sometime lord justice, was appointed to the same committee, but his expertise would have been very limited as he was based inland at Ballinasloe and was neither a merchant nor associated with the customs farm.[142] On 17 July 1641 a committee with equal numbers of members from each province was appointed to review petitions to the house, presumably because local knowledge would be helpful in assessing a petition's quality, veracity or importance. In the same month, most members of the committee dealing with the petition against Piers Butler, who were based near him in Tipperary, Cork and Waterford, were people with whom he had come into conflict. Given his unprincipled behaviour and apostasy, it is interesting that two local Catholic members, including the chair Patrick Boyton, showed the greatest sympathy towards him, but they were 'over-voted by the others who [wanted] rather to asert their spleen against Piers' high spirits and ambition than to reform abuses.'[143]

The English convention that those who spoke against bills at the second reading were not nominated to the committee dealing with them was not followed in Ireland. It would have been counterproductive if the objective was to reach consensus, as the example of Christopher Verdon, a member of the committee on the bill to take away benefit of clergy in certain cases of felony, shows. Verdon spoke against it on the third reading and the clergy subsidy bill, whose title ('Subsidy from the clergy of the Church of the kingdom of Ireland, to be paid to his majesty, in compensation for the expense he has incurred in suppressing the Antichrist and the progeny of Antichrist, namely the Jesuits and their adherents') so outraged Catholic members that it was referred to the Grand Committee 'lest the unity [so far shown] should be broken.'[144]

140 *LJI*, 23 July 1634.
141 Clanricard to Ormond, 21 Aug. 1645, Bodl. Lib., Carte MS 63, fo. 357.
142 *Commons' Jn. Ire.*, 9 April 1635.
143 Bodl. Lib., Carte MS 64, fo. 462v.
144 Neale, *House*, p. 363; Hakewill, *Modus*, pp 145ff; *Commons' Jn. Ire.*, 15 Oct. 1614, 29 Nov. 1614, 6 May 1615; Moynes (ed.), *Annual letters*, i, pp 481–2.

Chairmen are frequently unidentified and it is unclear how they were chosen. Bills were given to named members of the committee on a number of occasions in October 1614, presumably chairmen who also acted as rapporteurs; for example, Robert Digby delivered in the bill of distresses, with reasons why it should not be engrossed, 29 April 1615.[145] Radcliffe and Robert Dillon's appointment as committee chairmen demonstrates the administration's tight management of the 1634 parliament.[146] Lawyers were disproportionally represented as chairmen, including on committees of the whole house, e.g., Jerome Alexander, Roger Brereton, Allan Cooke, Patrick Darcy, Simon Digby, Oliver Jones, Robert Kennedy, Edward Lake, Hugh Rochford, John Lewis and John Taylor.[147] Non-lawyers Archibald Hamilton and Thomas Johnson and Henry Bringhurst who was admitted to the King's Inns as an attorney, were appointed committee chairmen by the 'rump' parliament only after most lawyers had left the house.[148]

Rapporteurs reported committees' findings to the house, standing by the clerk's table and reading first 'all the strikings out and then all additions' to bills. It was ordered that where one 'mis-reported', other committee members should correct him in the house.[149] Many reports were made orally, but some were written, although few have survived; that of the committee to Consider of the Assessing and leavying of the three subsequent subsidies in 1640 was carefully drafted and closely argued.[150] The house always accepted committees' recommendations, which were often framed as an order of the house.

Committee membership reflected the influence of the various interest groups in the house and how the management of the Commons slipped from Wentworth's grasp into the control of the old-established New English and Scottish settler community on the Protestant side and Old English Catholics on the other.[151] As Table 7.1 shows, in the first session of 1640, Protestant leaders were overwhelmingly privy councillors, four of whom were pro-Strafford, including his closest friends Radcliffe and Wandesford, with one official and a lawyer (although three other councillors had legal training). In the second session, there were still four privy councillors, but none was a Strafford supporter, with one lawyer and the back-bencher Hardress Waller. The administration lost control in the third session when Protestant back-benchers began to play a prominent role in

145 The English position is similarly unclear. Keeler, 'Committee for privileges'.

146 *Commons' Jn. Ire.*, 24 Nov. 1634.

147 Ibid., 28 July 1634 (Alexander), 29 May 1647 (Bringhurst), 23 April 1643, 31 Oct. 1644, 30 Nov. 1644 (Cooke), 2 June 1641 (Darcy), 9 July 1641 (Jones), 30 March 1647 (R. Kennedy), 14 Dec. 1642 (Sylvester Kennedy) 9 Nov. 1640 (Lake), 31 March, 18 May, 11 June 1647 (Lewis), 23 June 1641 (Rochford), 16 Nov. 1641 (Taylor); Blake, *Sir Richard Blake his speech*.

148 Ibid., 19 Nov. 1642, 9, 13, 17 April 1644, 4 June 1644, 21 April 1647; King's Inns, MS B1/1, fo. 9v.

149 *Commons' Jn. Ire.*, 2 Nov. 1614.

150 Bodl. Lib., Carte MS 118, fo. 3; Report of the committee of the whole house, 20 Oct. 1640, Bodl. Lib., Carte MS 30, fo. 285. For records of conference committees, see Bodl. Lib., Carte MS 20, fos. 176, 210, 567; TCD, MS 1,178, no. 4.

151 Perceval-Maxwell, *Outbreak*, pp 86–91.

committees, along with lawyers. In the final session, five of the six Protestant leaders were back-benchers (Coote was the only remaining privy councillor), all either second-generation New English or settled in Ireland for at least 30 years. Catholic leaders in the first two sessions were all lawyers, but in the final session two leaders were from the higher social echelons (MacCarthy and Richard Blake) and only John Walshe was a practicing lawyer, although Blake had some legal training.[152] Over the first three sessions the number of Catholics appointed to committees rose from 27% of their number to 60%.

Table 7.1. Leaders of the 1640 House of Commons[153]

	Session 1	*Session 2*	*Session 3*	*Session 4*	*Session 5*
Protestants					
Privy councillors	6	4	1	0	0
Lawyers	1	1		2	1
Office-holders	1			3	
Other		1	5	7	3
Catholics					
Lawyers	5	2	1	3	2
Non-lawyers			1	9	1

PETITIONS

Hakewill stressed the importance of dealing with grievances, noting especially that:

> Departing of the parliament: Ought to be in such a manner: first it ought to be demanded, yea and publickly proclaimed in the parliament, and within the palace of parliament, whether there be any that hath delivered a petition to the parliament, and hath not received an answer thereto; if there be none such it is to be supposed that every one is satisfied, or else answered to at the least, so far forth as by law he may be … The parliament should not depart so long as any petition made thereunto hangeth undiscussed or undecided, or at the least to which there is not made a determinate answer: the king's majesty being desirous of his grace and favour to give the subject redress or any injury and not to suffer his people to go unsatisfied.[154]

152 On Blake, see McGrath, 'Bio. dict.', i, pp 68–70. On Walshe, see Appendix 3.
153 Perceval-Maxwell, *Outbreak*, pp 74–5, 130–1, 136–7. Perceval-Maxwell's methodology seems inconsistent and he miscalculates the number of lawyers, which are adjusted here. For MPs' educational background, see McGrath, 'Bio. dict.', ii, pp A95–106 and for MPs who were lawyers, see Appendix 3.
154 Hakewill, *Modus*, pp 28, 30.

There is no record of this happening in Ireland and many petitions submitted to parliament clearly had not been resolved by the dissolution; the abrupt ending of the 1613–15 parliament and the outbreak of the rebellion in October 1641 prevented many complaints being settled or concluded.

Petitions could be submitted to either house. In the Commons they were generally dealt with early in the day when the house was 'thin' and legislation was discussed later in the morning, when more MPs were present. Petitions were held by the clerk of the house who provided copies as required. Petitions on Irish matters were also presented to the English parliament.[155] Petitions that were not instantly rejected were dealt with either by ordering the serjeant-at-arms to summon the person complained of to appear before the house to answer the complaint, or by being referred to a committee which could examine the parties and other witnesses. Petitions concerned with privilege for MPs and their servants or agents or parliamentary officials were generally referred to the committee for privileges; other petitions could be referred to the committee of grievances. Select committees could be formed to consider individual petitions, but their role could be expanded to deal collectively with petitions on similar subjects, especially under pressure of business in 1641, e.g., the committees for tobacco causes, ecclesiastical causes or that dealing with complaints against the bishop of Derry, John Bramhall, to which related complaints regarding Lord Kildare's property were also referred.

In 1614 it was ordered that all petitions had to be presented by MPs.[156] Defendants were required to submit their response, called a replication. At this stage they were generally advised by lawyers who could represent them in parliament, including in committees.[157] Committees recommended action and the house either issued an order to give effect to their solution or referred cases requiring judgment to the Lords. Many petitions in 1641 were against Wentworth and his administration's abuses of power and monopolies, but others were used to pursue purely local grievances and power-plays, such as Tuam's petition for the local assizes, some of Tipperary's gentry against Piers Butler and the Parsons-Digby struggle for pre-eminence in King's County, which centred on the designation of the county town. Many combined both appeals against Wentworth's injustices and local grievances, such as the Piggotts against Revd Jonathon Hoyle and Isabel Pont against Bishop John Leslie of Raphoe.[158] The speed with which

155 E.g., Grosart (ed.), *Lismore Papers*, 1st series, ii, pp 302, 304; Petition of Arthur O'Keife, 19 Feb. 1641, The Parliamentary Archives of the United Kingdom, MS HL/PO/JO/10/1/5.

156 *Commons' Jn. Ire.*, 22 Oct. 1614.

157 E.g., Answer of Sir Richard Bolton, chancellor, and George Shurley to the petition of William Smith to parliament, 8 July 1641, NLI, MS 11,044/ 56. There is no other record of this petition. *Commons' Jn. Ire.*, 10 July 1641, where we see Hoyle's lawyers attending and making representations on his behalf.

158 Blake (ed.), *Blake family records*, pp 41–2; Bodl. Lib., Carte MS 64, fos. 458r–65v; Birr Castle, MS A/1/19; McGrath, 'Electoral strategy'. On the background to the Pont dispute with Leslie, see J.S. Reid and W.D. Killen, *A history of the Presbyterian Church in Ireland: comprising the civil history of the province of Ulster from the accession of James the First*, 2 vols (London, 1853), i, chapter five.

petitions were dealt with depended on many factors: the number of petitions before the committee or the house, the urgency of the matter – the prospect of prorogation always caused a flurry of activity on all business, including petitions – and the co-operation or persistence of all parties.

MPs experienced difficulty in managing the number of petitions presented in 1641; on 15 May, the Commons reaffirmed the earlier practice that

> no petition shall be openly read in the House unless it be presented by a Member of this House, or called upon to be read by a Member of the same; and also that no petition against any member of this House shall be read, unless there is first an order in this House conceived for the reading thereof and the party first have notice thereof.

A series of orders were issued between 22 and 26 June 1641 considering a bill against paper petitions, and ordered that bills should take precedence in the order of business over petitions, culminating in an order that

> all petitions hereafter to be exhibited to this House, unless such as shall consist of urgent and great consequence, shall, for the ease of this House, be referred to the consideration either of the Committee of Grievances, or Committee of Privileges, as the case necessarily requireth, and to be there read, and they to send for all such person and persons, by summons, as they shall think fit.

Finally, it ordered

> that all petitions, answers and other pleadings whatsoever, which shall hereafter be exhibited to this House, shall be exhibited in parchment, provided that this order do no prejudice to any petition, answer, or other pleadings exhibited before this time, and the said petitions and pleadings aforesaid to be hereafter preferred, shall be, from time to time, filed by the clerk of this House.[159]

A small number of case studies will illustrate the process for dealing with petitions and the difficulties involved.

Lady Alison Talbot had been in dispute for some years with the Reverend William Vowell(s) or Powell and his predecessor as rector of Maynooth, Mr Hammond, about the vicarage of Larraghbryen, in Kildare. The vicarage was passed to Alison's husband, Sir William Talbot, in recognition of his legal services to the earls of Kildare and she claimed they were worth £40 annually to the vicar, apart from her own profits; shortly after her husband's death in 1634, she asked Kildare to support her claims to the vicarage. Vowell obtained possession of the

159 *Commons' Jn. Ire.*, 26 June 1641, 20 July 1641.

vicarage after petitioning Bramhall, on foot of an extrajudicial privy council decision. Alison petitioned parliament on 2 March 1641 and Vowell was ordered to respond; on 4 June it ordered that a report should be made the next day. In July the case was referred to the Lords, with a recommendation that she should have her lease and tithes and pursue her arrears at common law. Despite these orders, Vowell held onto the lands, though Alison and her son Garrett stole £100 worth of corn from him in the rebellion in retaliation.[160]

Piers Butler of Shanballyduff had created ill-feeling among his neighbours by his arrogant behaviour at the 1634 Tipperary election and further aggravated them by his behaviour as sheriff, JP and clerk of the crown, as well as his involvement in a nasty property dispute and his having turned Protestant. On 20 May 1641 the gentry and freeholders of Tipperary petitioned against him through their agent, Piers' cousin James Sall, for 'several articles of those fellonies and exactions.' The petition was referred to the committee of grievances and Butler was ordered to appear, on bonds of £3,000. He was to answer on 4 July and again on 26 July, when a conference committee with the Lords was arranged; two days later a committee was appointed largely composed of his Munster neighbours, described as 'none of his friends.' On 3 August Tipperary witnesses provided further details and Butler was to be attached. The committee could not agree on a course and Piers was bound over by recognisance to appear personally at the following session to be tried. In the end the process was halted by parliament's prorogation leaving the petitioners dissatisfied.[161]

Isabel Pont, the wife of a highly non-conformist Calvinist rector was proceeded against in the Court of High Commission following a complaint from her husband's bishop and fellow Scot, John Leslie of Raphoe, with Laud's encouragement.[162] This very nasty case involved her neighbour, supporter and possibly father, the soldier, MP and privy councillor Sir William Stewart, against whom old allegations of 'whoredom and bastardy' were raised. Laud suggested removing him from the privy council. Wentworth imprisoned Isabel in Dublin Castle in 1638 and sent William's company to a remote garrison in Connacht. Isabel subsequently petitioned parliament against Leslie on 20 May 1641 and a committee was appointed to investigate. Bryan O'Neill reported its finding on 3 July 1641, that the bishop had 'run into *premunire* for committing of her by his own authority, and laid high treason to her charge for relieving of rebels'. Her case was referred to the Lords and she was released. The process for many, if not most petitions was long and drawn out, as each side made a series of replies to the other's replications, representing a financial bonanza for lawyers and officials. These Fabian tactics made it difficult to get a resolution of the underlying problem and parliament found it hard, if not impossible, to have some of its orders enforced.

160 Alison Talbot to Kildare, 2 May 1634; Clarke and McGrath (eds), *Letterbook*, pp 34, 104–5; Deposition of Revd William Vowells, 25 June 1642, TCD, MS 813, fos. 330r–1v.
161 Bodl. Lib., Carte MS 64, fos. 458r–65v.
162 John Gibney, 'Leslie, John', *DIB*.

ORDERS AND VOTING

Orders recorded decisions taken by either house on petitions, committees, engrossing bills, membership of the house, authorizing by-elections, methods for assessing and collecting subsidies, respecting MPs' privilege or paying their wages, ordering heads of bills or draft bills, disciplining members or acting against those alleged to have infringed privilege, requiring attendance before committees or the house and specifying the fees to be charged by officers of state and any other resolutions.[163] They were entered in a 'book of orders' and many were also included in the journals, although it is impossible to estimate how many were not. Copies of any order, signed by the clerk to guarantee their authenticity, were to be provided to members and others on payment to the clerk of 6*s.* 8*d.*, 'but if it be for the publick no ffee.'[164]

Traditionally Irish lords whispered their votes in the chancellor's ear, a practice instigated by the crown to enable peers to vote for them without their colleagues' knowledge, but which it wished to end in 1613 as being

> derogatory to the dignity and liberty of that honorable house and savors both of timorousnesse & coremption [sic] and is subiect to abuse, and in truth it is merely against the lawe, which requires faire & open dealing in all things, and especially that the opinions of judges should be pronounced openly in all Corts, whereof the Court of parliament is the highest ... We invented this polling to serve our turns for the tyme, & to save their creditts that they should deliver their voices in the L. Chancellors ears onely; which I feare will [now] be returned upon us to our losse. Ffor I think there are divers Bishops here, which durst nott putt their faces openly to oppose against the proceedings of the State, and yet privately in my L. Chancellors eare will nott stick to give us a blowe presuming that we shall never know who hurt us.

Jones wanted to change the practice 'both for myne owne safetie, & for the furtherance of his majestie's service, open & playne dealing in this poynte I assure myself, wilbe found the best ... otherwise [I] may be exposed to after reckonyngs.' The chancellor proposed the change on 19 May 1613, but it met stiff opposition the new practice of open voting was instituted by an act of state on the same day.[165] A remnant of this practice was the lord deputy whispering his contributions in the Lords to the chancellor, who then communicated the substance to the parliament.[166]

163 E.g., *Commons' Jn. Ire.*, 17 Oct. 1614, 29 April 1615, 2 Aug. 1634, 20 March 1635, 17 April 1635, 11 Nov. 1640; Order for Henry Piers MP against Sir Richard Masterson, 29 Nov. 1614, Bodl. Lib., Carte MS 62, fo. 33; *Commons' Jn. Ire.*, 29 Nov. 1614; Bodl. Lib., Carte MS 66, fo. 295; Marsh's Library, MS Z3.2.5, p. 29; Marsh's Library, MS Z3.1.1, no. 62 (20 April 1643), no. 63 (24 Feb. 1646).

164 Bodl. Lib., Carte MS 66, fo. 295.

165 Jacob to Northampton, 12 April 1613, HL, HP, Box 4 (1), fo. 10r; Jones to Salisbury, 25 Feb. 1612, TNA, SP 63/232, fo. 28r; Treadwell, 'House of Lords'.

As in other early modern assemblies, the Irish parliament sought to reach agreement by consensus and debates in committees were a key, and generally successful, mechanism for this; the vast majority of business was handled without ballots but inevitably some questions were voted on and it was accepted that a majority decision bound the whole house as 'a parliament can conclude nothing but by the greatest voyces'.[167] This convention was at the heart of the Protestants' attempts to induce Catholics to vote on the speakership in 1613 and their refusal to implicitly give their consent to the process and the result by participating in proceedings. The same issue arose after the rebellion when the 'rump' parliament was so poorly attended.[168] Formal divisions were an innovation in England from 1523 and were used in Ireland by 1569, when Hooker reported the number of votes on suspending Poynings' Law.[169] It is highly probable that lists were made by both sides calculating likely supporters and opponents of motions, although only one contemporary division list survives for England or Scotland and none for Ireland.[170]

Questions or motions were put by the speaker and MPs voted 'by acclamation', either with a show of hands or shouting 'aye' or 'nay'. The speaker 'ought by his ear to judge which of the voices be the greatest; if that be doubtful, the House ought to be divided touching the matter.' The result was clear for the vast majority of motions, e.g., on 8 May 1615, when a bill was put to the question, 'the yeas were far greater, so it passed' and the clerk was to 'take the notice of the most hands or voyces sounding at once. And therefore if their assent be issuable, the clerke may say *Per maiorem numerum generalis*' (by the greater number of the general).[171] Votes could be affected by how questions were framed: the numbers could not be determined on 28 April 1615, but the issue was resolved by putting a slightly different question, which was carried. Seaward notes one English case where the speaker put the case in the negative – that a bill be rejected – which might have influenced the result.[172] The time of putting the question could affect the result, as happened with the Reformation legislation in 1560. This might also explain the contradiction between the Commons agreeing to a sub-committee with a two-thirds majority of Catholics to Protestants of the committee for the plantation of Connacht, assisted by Richard Martin and Patrick Darcy, who were then not MPs,

166 Dennehy, *Parliament*, pp 87, 114.

167 Butterwick, *Polish–Lithuanian Commonwealth*, p. 21; Jackson (ed.), 'Document'.

168 Notes of the Lords Justice Parsons and Dillon and the privy council, undated, but Feb.–June 1642, Difficulties which will fall out in the course of the proceedings which is to be held in the attainting of those rebels, who are now in actual rebellion, Bodl. Lib., Carte MS 68, fos. 422r–4.

169 Hawkyard, 'From Painted Chamber'; Bradshaw, 'Beginnings'; 'Irish parliamentary antiquities' in Falkiner, *Essays*, pp 193–220. Hooker's account is the same as that described in both McCavitt, 'An unspeakable parliamentary fracas'; Moynes (ed.), *Annual letters*, i, p. 403.

170 Hawkyard, *Commons*, pp 335–6; Paul Seaward, 'Divisions, tellers and management in the 17th-century House of Commons', *Parl. Hist.*, 32:1 (2013), 79–102; Julian Goodare, 'The Scottish parliament of 1621', *The Historical Journal*, 38:1 (1995), 29–51.

171 Hakewill, *Modus*, p. 145; *Priviledges and practice of parliaments*, pp 35–6.

172 Seaward, 'Divisions, tellers and management'.

to attend a privy council committee later that day 'for the amendment of the [bill] if they find cause' and the decision to engross the apparently unamended bill later that day.[173]

Where votes were unclear, MPs divided into groups in the chamber and the clerk or speaker tried to establish which was the greater. Recusants 'rose out of their places gathered themselves together into a clump to the end they might not be numbered' in the 1613 speakership vote.[174] Formal divisions were only conducted if the result was still inconclusive, with tellers appointed to count each side: 'If it be a doubt which cry is bigger, they divide the House, the Speaker saying, as many as doe allow the Bill goe down with the Bill, and as many as doe not, sit still.' On 29 April 1615 when the MP for King's County, Henry Power, made a complaint against John and Thomas Grove, 'It being put to the question, whether the said Grove should be punished or discharged, it could not be discerned whether was the greater of the yeas or noes.' The journals do not record the house's decision on that occasion, nor which Grove was in question, but on 18 April 1644 the house divided 21 against 19. One crucial motion was lost when Sir James Ware failed to count himself, indicating the narrowest of margins; even in a very thinly attended house.[175] No quorum was ever agreed for parliament (although there were some for committees), hence the ability of a handful of MPs to push through the Reformation legislation in 1560.

Normal practice was for those in favour of the motion to go from the chamber into the inner room, which the serjeant-at-arms had cleared of all but MPs and locked the doors to prevent members leaving or 'strangers' being counted by accident (and swelling the numbers in favour of the motion).[176] Two tellers were appointed for each side, although on 17 and 18 July 1634 five were chosen and in the thinly-attended 'rump' parliament after 1642 a single teller was used for each side.[177] The tellers counted the ayes on the way back into the chamber while those for the nays numbered those remaining there; however, on two votes about the chair of the committee of the whole house on 23 June 1641, the yeas left the room on the first vote, but on the second they stayed in the chamber while the nays exited. There was a perception that the nays remaining in the chamber had an advantage.[178]

In England the speaker selected tellers, but it is unclear how Irish ones were chosen. The administration's strenuous attempts to get Catholics to vote on the 1613 speakership led them to suggest that the tellers count both sides, when the tellers for the ayes 'move[d] Sir Christopher Plunkett and Sir Christopher Nugent

173 Moynes (ed.), *Annual letters*, i, p. 403; *Commons' Jn. Ire.*, 8 June 1640.
174 McCavitt, 'An unspeakable parliamentary fracas'.
175 Smith, *Commonwealth*, p. 88; *Commons' Jn. Ire.*, 26, 29 April 1615; Crawford Lomas (ed.), *Egmont*, i, p. 212.
176 Lodge, *Desiderata Curiosa*, i, pp 352–3; *Commons' Jn. Ire.*, 17–18 July 1634; Neale, *House*, pp 353–4.
177 *Commons' Jn. Ire.*, 8, 17 April 1644, 24 Feb. 1646.
178 Seaward, 'Divisions, tellers and management'.

being within the house to join with them in numbering both parties, which they refused … then did Mr Treasurer and Mr Marshall make offer to number them that were in the house.'[179] In that case, the tellers were counted, but this was not invariable, as it is sometimes specified that tellers were numbered and other times not. However, as, apart from 17–18 July 1634, each side had an even number of tellers, this never affected the result. In James' parliament, tellers are only named in the division on the bill to take away clergy on 18 October 1614, when two Protestants (the treasurer and Sir Adam Loftus) counted the ayes and two Catholics (Nugent and Luttrell) the nays. Tellers announced the vote standing by the clerk's table and bowing three times to the speaker. Hakewill described tellers giving the lower number of votes first and then the higher, but this practice had changed by Scobell's time; the Irish practice is unknown.[180] The vote on the speakership was the only one in which the whole house voted, as once appointed, the speaker had only a 'casting' one on tied votes.

Numbers were not usually recorded, generally being given only when tight votes required a tally. On 16 May 1615, 'it not appearing whether the yeas or noes were the greater, the house was divided'; in that case the majority was 88 to 80.[181] In 1614–15 ten divisions were recorded (details provided in Table 7.2), but figures were given for only eight (five concerned bills, two members' behaviour and one a petition), with between 140 and 173 MPs in the house. Tellers (usually two on each side) are not necessarily included, so the actual figures could be somewhat higher (i.e. plus four for each total). Divisions show a healthy attendance of between 67% and 80% of MPs throughout these sessions, a level rarely achieved in later parliaments, but this is a partial picture of members' fluctuating levels of interest in parliament and its business, as they only record numbers of MPs voting, not those attending. On 5 May 1615, 158 MPs were present for the first vote and 145 for the next; on 23 June 1641, 124 MPs voted on the first division and 121 on the second.[182]

The journals only record three formal divisions for 1634–5, with tallies provided for only two (Table 7.3); two votes concerned the procedure for choosing members of the committee on privileges and a procedural issue about whether to purge the house or to deal with business first, key issues about control of the house. The three Protestant tellers were two of Wentworth's associates – Wandesford and Price – and William Wiseman, an official from Cork. The Catholics were the Palesmen Thomas Luttrell and Nicholas Barnewall. Another division was about the bill restraining marriage and the last on Geoffrey Baron's expulsion. Wentworth's accounts of votes are mendacious and should be treated with extreme caution – on 18 July he claimed the majority was only 8, but it was either 22 or 42.

179 McCavitt, 'An unspeakable parliamentary fracas'.

180 Natzler, 'Manuals before May'.

181 E.g., *Commons' Jn. Ire.*, 3 May 1615, 17 July 1634, 4, 16 Aug. 1642, 13 Dec. 1642, 18 Dec. 1643, 9 April 1644, 11 July 1644.

182 232 MPs were returned; eight new boroughs were disallowed by James before the Oct. 1614 session began and a further three boroughs were disallowed by MPs on 17 Nov. 1614.

Table 7.2. Recorded votes in the Commons, 1613–15

Date	*Yeas*	*Noes*	*Plus speaker*	*Total*	*Percentage of house*
18 May 1613	128	98	0	226	97% (232)
18 Oct. 1614	95	78	1	174	80% (216)
4 Nov. 1614	71	93	1	165	76% (216)
10 Nov. 1614	64	82	1	147	68% (216)
29 April 1615	62	77	1	140	67% (210)
3 May 1615	74	83	1	158	75% (210)
3 May 1615	n/a	n/a	n/a	n/a	n/a
5 May 1615	54	90	1	145	69% (210)
5 May 1615	71	99	1	171	81% (210)
8 May 1615	n/a	n/a	n/a	n/a	n/a
16 May 1615	88	80	1	169	80% (210)

In November he urged privy councillors to improve Protestant attendance; his assertion that Catholics thereafter maintained a steady 95 votes but were outvoted, suggested both that at least 192 MPs (75% of the house including the speaker) were attending and that all votes were cast along strictly religious lines. These claims are unsupported by any evidence.[183] The impression of poor attendance was confirmed by the number of times the 1634 parliament was called, but not by the admittedly limited voting records; given Wentworth's issuing rejected bills as acts of state, many MPs may have seen little point in attending.

Table 7.3. Recorded votes in the Commons, 1634

Date	*Yeas*	*Noes*	*Plus speaker*	*Total*	*Percentage N=256*
17 July 1634	n/a	n/a	n/a	n/a	n/a
18 July 1634	107	129	1	237	93%
17 Nov. 1634	69	78	1	148	58%
3 Dec. 1634[184]	?95	?111	1	?207	81%

There were no recorded tallies of votes in the 1640 parliament until 27 May 1641. Perceval-Maxwell ascribes this to consensual operations but it is more likely that formal divisions were not held because numbers were not close. Opposition was muted by the administration's tight control in the first sitting in March and April 1640 and a consequent assumption that little could be done to stall the

183 *Commons' Jn. Ire.*, 17 July 1634, when the vote was carried, but numbers not given. McGrath, 'Electoral strategy'; Clarke, '28 November 1634'.

184 Based on Wentworth's account of Baron's expulsion and therefore to be treated with caution. Ibid.

legislative programme, but the increasing closeness of the New English and Catholics and the absence of many government clients who were either with Wentworth in England or with the new army meant that fewer voices were needed to carry motions.[185] All the recorded divisions occurred when the house's nominal compliment was 256 members, less the 13 MPs sent to England on 11 November 1640. Only ten votes were recorded between 27 May 1641 and February 1646, but the six votes in 1641 were very different to the later ones. The first five were recorded between 27 May and 7 August, when the administration's control had slipped. A series of by-elections largely returned Catholics and fewer Protestants attended; parliament seized the initiative, but attendance apparently slipped below 50% (see Table 7.4), presumably because fewer Protestants were present.[186] At the sixth vote in the hastily summoned meetings in November, after the outbreak of the rebellion, recorded attendance was under 30%.

Four divisions were recorded between 6 August 1642 and February 1646. After the mass expulsion of Catholics in June 1642, despite at least 87 recruiter returns and the continued if intermittent attendance of a minimum of 86 MPs returned before November 1641, the percentage of those attending the house was generally much less than 20%. At least 174 MPs (including the speaker) appeared at some point, yet only between 31 and 56 of that number (18% – 32%) voted (excluding Eustace). As noted, attendance was so low that only one teller was appointed for each side, a picture confirmed by the number of times the house was called.[187]

None of the recorded divisions in Charles' second Irish parliament (detailed in Table 7.4) concerned legislation – they were about issuing a writ to replace William Peisley, how petitions were to be dealt with, who should chair a committee of the whole house, whether the King's County sessions should be held at Philipstown and whether to enter the protestation and declaration in the journals.[188] Except in the case of the King's County assizes, which was a straightforward power struggle between the Digbys and Parsons, the tellers, where named, were of both religions. Mervyn was teamed with Adam Cusack and Richard Barnewall and Tibbot Taaffe with John Chichester, and Taaffe with Nicholas Plunkett against Paul Davies and Patrick Darcy. On the chairmanship of the Grand Committee, Sir William St Leger and James Ware held the government line against Mervyn and Richard Barnewall. The presumably impartial Bysse brothers, John (*plate 11*) and Robert, James Ware and Robert King counted the tied votes on Philipstown.[189]

185 E.g., 20, 22, 23, 28 March 1640; Perceval-Maxwell, *Outbreak*, p. 70; Clarke, *Old English*, pp 131–2; Whitaker (ed.), *Life and original correspondence*, p. 201.
186 McGrath, 'Irish elections of 1640–1641'.
187 McGrath, 'Recruiter returns'; *Commons' Jn. Ire.*, 8, 18 April 1644.
188 See McGrath, 'Bio. dict.', i, pp 238–40 on Peisley.
189 On the Bysse brothers, see Appendix 3. On Robert King, see ibid., i, pp 188–9.

Table 7.4. Recorded votes in the Commons, 1640–8[190]

Date	*Ayes*	*Noes*	*Plus speaker*	*Total*	*Percentage*
27 May 1641	92	83	1	176	72% (243)
9 June 1641	61	65	1	127	52% (243)
23 June 1641	56	67	1	124	51% (243)
23 June 1641	56	64	1	121	50% (243)
7 Aug. 1641	52	52	1	105	43% (243)
17 Nov. 1641	32	42	1	75	29% (256)
6 Aug. 1642	20	14	1	35	14% (256)
8 April 1644	27	29	1	57	22% (256)
17 April 1644	22	20	1	43	17% (256)
24 Feb. 1645–6	17	14	1	32	13% (256)

However, as Perceval-Maxwell demonstrated, while the number of votes and voters were relatively few, the level of engagement evidenced by committees' membership grew dramatically. While only 23% of Catholics and 36% of Protestants were elected to committees in the first session of the 1640 parliament, the proportions grew significantly (apart from a slight dip for Protestants in the second session) to a remarkable 80% and 66% respectively in the fifth session.[191]

The traditional narrative was that Protestants voted for and Catholics against the administration; Hooker reported votes on the suspension of Poynings' Law as '40 Irish nos, 50 English ayes' and 'English Ayes 44, Irish 48 noes', although it is unclear how he used these terms, as it is highly unlikely that there were 50 Englishmen in the Commons.[192] However, most votes were taken on each motion's merits and did not generally break down on ethnic or religious bases as Everard, Clotworthy, Piers Crosby, Darcy, Mervyn and Waller demonstrated and, more specifically, Bolton's opposition to the poundage bill which was against Dublin city's interests.[193] In his opening speech to the 1634 parliament, Wentworth advised them 'divide not between Protestant and Papist; for this meeting is merely Civil, Religion not at all concerned one way or another … Divide not Nationally, betwixt English and Irish', nor did they do so, except on votes on procedure and personnel which affected control of the house and its business, such as the 1613 speakership

190 Votes before 17 Nov. 1641 are based on 243 MPs; from 6 Aug. 1642 on a nominal 256 MPs.

191 Perceval-Maxwell, *Outbreak*, pp 73, 126. As Perceval-Maxwell notes, these figures are approximate, due to the confusion in returns and by-elections. Perceval-Maxwell notes only five divisions, not six and calculates percentages based on 238 MPs, rather than 256.

192 Falkiner, *Essays*, p. 217.

193 Clarke, '28 November 1634'; Perceval-Maxwell, *Outbreak*, pp 70, 127; Waller 'hath some vogue in the House of Commons where he compleins with the king but voates against us' in FSL, MS X.c.101(2); Radcliffe to Wentworth, 28 Oct. 1640, in Rushworth (ed.), *Tryal*, p. 110; *Commons' Jn. Ire.*, 18 Oct. 1614. For the poundage bill's background and importance, see Victor Treadwell, 'The Irish customs administration in the sixteenth century', *IHS*, 20:80 (Sept., 1977), 384–417; Pawlisch, *Sir John Davies*, pp 127–30, 138.

and divisions in every parliament about whether to purge the s mis-returned MPs before taking other business.[194] While Catholics were justifiably concerned about some legislation proposed for 1613 that would have further penalized them for religious non-conformity, they were also determined to show themselves as good subjects and demonstrate loyalty to the crown. Consequently, there were no recorded dissentions from subsidy bills or attainders, other than the implications of Tyrone's attainder for other property rights. MPs, whatever their ethnic origins and confessional positions, shared similar concerns about economics, land-holding and social order and generally voted to promote their shared interests about prosperity and good behaviour. Opposition to the 1640 bills on the plantations of Connacht and Ormond, the administration and reduction of the subsidies and complaints against the Court of High Commission and church officials' fees came from both sides of the house. The petition to the English Commons in November 1640 was signed by at least 32 Protestants.[195] Proof of the non-confessional basis of decisions on legislation is found on 12 December 1642, when the 'rump' Commons rejected three of Wentworth's bills and a fourth one was committed, demonstrating MPs' concerns about its contents.

ATTENDANCE

Attendance was a necessary element of representation and demonstrated MPs' commitment to their role; they were expected to attend daily unless the house, through the speaker, licensed their absence. The speaker also needed permission to be absent during recess as his office continued until dissolution.[196] Unlicenced absence was punishable by loss of wages and/or fines, which could be substantial. On 22 July 1634 the house ordered

> that if any member of this house have any occasion to absent himself for a day or two, he shall obtain Mr Speaker's licence, acquainting the house with the occasion of his absence … the said licence being entered with the clerk of the house

A similar order was made on 18 June 1641. The speaker could issue licences without the house's consent and as the clerk should have recorded all licences, few are given in the journals. On 20 May 1641

> the commons ordered that the committee, formerly appointed to view and peruse the book of orders of this house, shall also take into their perusal any

194 Knowler (ed.), *Letters and dispatches*, i, p. 289.

195 BL, Egerton MS 1,048. These numbers vary from Aidan Clarke's calculations. See Clarke, *Old English*, pp 135–6. It is unclear which of the two Thomas Butlers signed the petition (one was Catholic and the other Protestant) and one signature is illegible.

196 *Commons' Jn. Ire.*, 13 Dec. 1642, licensed Eustace's absence in England during the recess.

> orders concerning the last call of this house, and compare the books of Mr Speaker and of the clerk of this house together touching the said call; and to take especial notice of those that were absent during the whole time of the last session; and report to this house, what in their discretions they shall think fit, concerning the several fines imposed on them.[197]

Lords only represented themselves and could leave their proxy votes with other peers (Netterville and Blayney were allowed to be absent in 1634, as long as they assigned their proxies) and Wentworth controlled their use.[198] The Tudor period seems to have allowed greater flexibility, as 'the Great O'Brien' sent deputies to the enactment of the Act of Kingly Title and Manus O'Donnell's submission to St Leger in August 1541 included a commitment to 'appear in the next parliament in Ireland, or send to the same some discreet and trust[ed] person authorized by his writing sealed with his seal.[199] Peers were unwaged but could still be fined for non-attendance, as bishops were for their absence from the Great Council under Henry VI.[200] They were fined one or two shillings depending on their rank if they did not appear within a quarter of an hour after daily prayers, the money all going into the 'poor mans box'. Daily roll calls were initially taken in the 1634 Lords until Wentworth advised that the English practice was that the house 'was called but on occasion.'[201]

From 1515, England repeatedly legislated to enforce attendance: 6 Hen. VIII, c. 16 permitted departure from the house only with the speaker's licence, the clerk's record and loss of wages. This act did not solve the problem and further measures were introduced in 1547, 1554, 1555, 1558 and 1610.[202] While similar legislation was not passed for Ireland, members absent without good cause or licence were ordered to be fined or to lose their wages in every early Stuart Irish parliament, although these penalties were almost invariably remitted. The problem may have been exacerbated by the fact that English MPs were not permitted to resign (see chapter one) and therefore Irish attendance might be expected to be higher as those who did not want to continue their membership could leave the house.

MPs' attendance cannot be accurately ascertained – no records of attendance and only limited information on licensed absences survive for Ireland, unlike the

197 Ibid., 20 May 1641.

198 Dennehy, *Parliament*, pp 191–2.

199 Maxwell, *Irish history from contemporary sources*, pp 101–3; McGrath, 'Irish elections of 1640–1641'; Ohlmeyer, 'The Irish peers'. There is no information on Irish clerical proctors' proxies, if any, although their English counterparts had regularly used them. Bradford and McHardy (eds), *Proctors for parliament*, ii, p. xii; Murray, *Enforcing the English reformation in Ireland*, pp 88–9.

200 Berry (ed.), *Statute rolls*, pp xxvii, 153; Richardson and Sayles, *Irish parliament in the Middle Ages*, pp 137ff; *LJI*, 26 July 1634, 17 Nov. 1634. The index to the 1613–15 Lords' journal provides some sense of peers' attendance. Treadwell, 'House of Lords'.

201 *LJI*, 23 July 1634.

202 6 Hen. VIII, c. 16; Alasdair D. Hawkyard, 'The wages of members of parliament, 1509–1558', *Parl. Hist.*, 6:2 (Oct., 1987), 302–11; Keeler, 'Committee for privileges'.

Scottish Estates which kept attendance records from 1612 and Medhop's account of MPs' wages is clearly based on when they were elected rather than their actual daily presence (apart from Cavan and Kildare's burgesses).[203] Some evidence survives from journals, letters and diaries, 'calling the house', licences for absence, fines for non-attendance, votes and activity in the house, e.g., committee membership, speeches, presenting petitions, orders and motions, evidence of whether someone was in Dublin or not at the time of parliament's sitting and deaths. Catholics, who were more likely to be paid and had more to fear from the legislative programme, were generally held to be more faithful attenders, although this may also be attributable to their recollections of the crown's sharp practice in 1560 and the fact that unlike placemen they would have to account to their communities for their actions and live with parliament's decisions in the long-term. They might also be responsible for implementing the decisions locally. The evidence does not suggest that county members, who were better paid, were more assiduous. In 1615 fines were imposed for non-attendance on nine Protestant and eight Catholic MPs, nine of whom were knights of the shire. However, the significant increase in placemen serving unpaid in Charles' parliaments and their duties as soldiers or crown officials contributed to a fall in Protestant attendance and the preponderance of those seeking licences for absence and incurring fines after 1615 were Protestant.

Attendance was high at the opening of parliament; all but six of the 232 MPs were present to vote on the 1613 speakership, 127 for Davies and 98 for Everard.[204] Three more subsequently appeared by 21 May as 130 presented Davies at 3 p.m.[205] There was no vote on the speakership in the two following parliaments, but given the level of double returns and the confused nature of the writs in 1634, the number attending was certainly less than the full complement.

On 19 October 1614, only nine MPs were recorded as speaking, but 173 voted in a division. Medhop appears to have been less likely to record Catholic contributions than Protestant in his fair copies of the journals.[206] Fernesly's limited records of contributions make firm estimates of attendance impossible. Adam Cusack was described as 'one of our great speakers in Our Parliament', but while he had been an active committee member in 1634–5 and sat on many committees from May 1641, there is no record of his contributions to debates.[207] The promoters of the petition to the English Commons in November 1640 had no difficulty in recruiting over 80 opposition MPs to sign the document, an indication of their attending the house at that stage. Yet many of these same MPs were not recorded as contributing to proceedings in the house.[208] Some assessment of

203 Hawkyard, *Commons*, pp 251–3; Kennedy, 'Representing the periphery'; TCD, MS 843, pp 489–95; Dennehy, *Parliament*, p. 46; McGrath, 'Unconstitutional acts'.

204 The number voting for Davies does not appear to include himself.

205 King's Inns, MS N3/2/1/7, fo. 6v; McCavitt, 'An unspeakable parliamentary fracas'.

206 E.g., TNA, MS PRO 30/5/3, fos. 48v, 55v, 56r.

207 J.D., *Special newes from Ireland, newly received in a letter from a gentleman of good worth in Dublin to a friend in London* (London, 1643), pp 3–4.

208 BL, Egerton MS 1,048.

attendance may be made from the twelve committees appointed on 10 June 1641, which included 119 names, 51 Catholic and 68 Protestant. It is highly likely that all of these men were regularly attending at that point as it is close to the 120–6 MPs recorded as voting around that time, especially since 65 (27 Catholics and 39 Protestants) were nominated to more than one committee, with Darcy and Mervyn only appointed to one committee each, leaving them free for other parliamentary business. However, a further 43 MPs (13 Catholic, 30 Protestant) appear in the journals between that date and the end of the session. These figures suggest that generally about two-thirds of available MPs were attending, a higher figure than the voting numbers imply and that Catholics were not, at this point, more assiduous attenders, but that many of Wentworth's associates were no longer present.

Attendance was often slow at the beginning of later sessions, with the house frequently being adjourned on the first or second days. Smith has shown that the English Lords' attendance declined towards the end of the sessions as the balance of business shifted from public to private and judicial; it is unclear whether this occurred also in Ireland.[209] Sometimes warnings to attend prompted resignations: on 12 November 1634 the house was ordered to be called (just before Wentworth's response on the Graces) and on the following day the Commons ordered that 'speedy warning be given to those that have been returned burgesses of parliament unto this House, and have willfully refused to appear the last session and this session to shew cause wherefore they have refused.' In the following days Thomas Leake and Lord Maltravers, MPs for Ballyshannon and Callan respectively, requested that writs be issued for their replacement and on 26 November Arthur Chichester (Antrim) and Henry Tichbourne (Tyrone) resigned.[210] On 20 May 1641 a committee was asked to 'take especial notice of those that were absent during the whole time of the last session; and report to this house, what in their discretions they shall think fit, concerning the several fines imposed on them.' Cork's diary noted that Thomas Elwall was in parliament, although not necessarily in the chamber, Thomas Little wrote from York, 31 October 1640, 'God knows when' he would be back in Ireland, and in May 1641, Hardress Waller was in London borrowing and repaying money for Cork.[211] The siege of Captain William Parsons' home, Birr Castle, between October 1641 and 18 January 1643 prevented him from attending.[212] MPs who were judges or heralds, or Thomas Ryves as

209 E.g., *Commons' Jn. Ire.*, 11 Oct. 1614, 18 April 1615, 26 Jan. 1635, 7 Oct. 1640; Smith, *Stuart*, pp 22–3, 37.

210 Richard Hawkins, 'Chichester, Arthur, 1st earl of Donegall', *DIB*; Terry Clavin, 'Tichbourne (Tichborne), Sir Henry', *DIB*.

211 Grosart (ed.), *Lismore Papers*, 1st series, v, p. 177; Letters of William Cadogan, NLI, MS 2,541, no. 1. James Cusack may have been absent for some time after March 1641, as he arranged letters of recommendation to men in England. Irish privy council to Sir Henry Vane for Cusack, who has occasions to travel to England, 3 March 1641, Bodl. Lib., Carte MS 80, fo. 655; Letter of recommendation from the Irish Commons, *Commons' Jn. Ire.*, 1 March 1641.

212 The Diary of Capt. William Parsons, 18 Oct. 1641–18 Jan. 1643, Birr Castle, MS A/9, pp 1–14. He attended on 20 April 1643 and 17 Feb. 1644.

registrar of Convocation, and those acting as legal counsel attending the upper house, such as Darcy, James Barry (*plate 8*) and Maurice Eustace did in 1634, could only give partial attendance at those times. Apart from his work inducting lords into the upper house and his other duties as herald, Daniel Molyneux was imprisoned by the Lords on 28 April 1615 and Wiseman was excused from fines for non-attendance because he was on official business.[213] Wandesford, Borlase, Dillon and Parsons are not recorded as attending the Commons during their periods as deputy or lords justices. The most obvious reason for absence was the 13 members of the committee sent to England in November 1640 until late 1641 to represent the Commons to Charles.[214] Those who were MPs in both England and Ireland (Philip Mainwaring and John Wandesford were returned to the Short Parliament, and George Wentworth to the Long Parliament) could clearly not attend both and this may have been one of the reasons for George's expulsion from the Irish Commons, apart from a general animus against his brother.[215]

More general evidence of attendance levels is found in the number of times the house was 'called' – a roll-call announced in advance developed in England around the middle of the sixteenth century intended to improve the numbers. Calling was frequently used in all early modern Irish parliaments to boost attendance, especially close to the beginning of sessions, before critical decisions and to assess current membership before ordering writs for replacements for dead, resigned or expelled MPs.[216] The Commons was called the day after parliament's reopening in October 1614 to ascertain how many MPs had died and order writs to replace them and the mis-returned burgesses for Cavan and Kildare. The same procedure was followed in subsequent parliaments.[217] However, most calls were intended to increase attendance rather than to assess current membership. The house was called on 12 and 28 October 1614 and 8 May 1615, when 17 MPs were fined for being absent without licence. The 1634–5 Commons was ordered to be called at least eight times, although frequently there is no mention in the journals of this actually happening; all the calls occurred after the first session, lending some credence to Wentworth's assertion that Protestants were not attending. The house was called at least ten times between 12 June 1640 and 23 July 1641, reflecting a clear decline in attendance after Wentworth's departure. Despite much reduced sittings, it was called at least 12 times between 8 August 1642 and 27 May 1647.[218]

213 Treadwell, 'House of Lords'; *Commons' Jn. Ire.*, 7 April 1635; *LJI*, 14, 26, 30 July 1634.

214 *Commons' Jn. Ire.*, 11 Nov. 1640.

215 There is no record of Mainwaring's attendance in the Irish Commons in the 1640–1 journals, despite his private bill being introduced in the house (having been passed in the Lords) on 24 Oct. 1640. John P. Ferris and Simon Healy, 'Wandesford, John' in Thrush and Ferris (eds), *History of parliament*. On George Wentworth, see Brownhill, 'Personal and professional relationships', i, pp 150–2, ii, chapters 8–9.

216 Hawkyard, *Commons*, pp 252ff.

217 *Commons' Jn. Ire.*, 12 Oct. 1614, 13 Nov. 1634, 18 Feb. 1635, 12 June 1640.

218 Ibid., 12, 20, 24 Nov. 1634, 8 Dec. 1634, 18 Feb. 1635, 26 March 1635, 6, 7 April 1635; Clarke, '28 November 1634'; *Commons' Jn. Ire.*, 12 June 1640, 24 Oct. 1640, 16, 20 Feb. 1641, 1 March 1641, 15, 25 May 1641, 11 June 1641, 9, 23 July 1641; 8 Aug. 1642, 6, 9, 17 April 1644, 3 Feb. 1645, 26–7 March 1645, 6, 29 April 1647, 21, 26–7 May 1647.

Speakers frequently licensed absences; sometimes no reason other than MPs' personal affairs was cited, but on other occasions it was for their own or relatives' illness, the need to travel to England or to conduct business as crown officials. All three licences granted in 1614–15 related to illness.[219] Unsurprisingly, most licences were granted to those based outside Dublin, as those from Dublin would be better able to deal with personal matters without affecting their attendance. New English Protestants were more likely than Old English or old Irish to have business in England. Ten of the 13 licences recorded in 1634–5 were for Protestants; six were permitted to go to England and one to Scotland. John Trevor, MP for Carlingford at this time and later for Newtownards in 1641, was allowed to go home to deal with the affairs of the recently deceased MP Edward Kynaston, Richard Blayney to attend the assizes in Monaghan, for which he sat as MP, and David Rothe, Sir Henry Lynch and Sir Valentine Blake because of sickness.[220] With Blake and Lynch's agreement, a writ to replace them was to be issued if they did not appear by the first day of the next session. Personal business was cited by Thomas Tallis, the MP for Killybegs in both 1634 and 1641.[221] Arthur Bassett, Lynch and Lott Peere linked their requests to a desire to resign their seats; their resignations were accepted.[222] Most licences were not time-limited, but some were given for a fortnight, or one or three months. Barnaby Bryan's licence on 2 August 1634 specified that his seat would be declared vacant if he did not return by the first week of the next session (a writ to replace him was ordered on 4 November).[223] There is no evidence that MPs of Gaelic origin were poor attenders, whereas Highland attendance in the Scottish Estates was only 20% up to 1633.[224]

Twenty-four requests for licence, all but one from Protestants, were recorded between the opening of the 1640 parliament and the outbreak of the rebellion: George Radcliffe, Henry Kniveton, Robert Dillon, Adam Loftus, Christopher Roper and Robert Smith requested permission to go to England, John Bellew, John Chichester, Charles Coote Jr (*plate 14*), David Crosby, Simon Digby (twice), John Gifford, James Hamilton, William Parsons, Edward Trevor and William Somers cited 'urgent ocasions' down the country and the latter also instanced his duties in the Connacht Presidency Court on a second occasion. St Leger was granted 'a fortnight for the dispatch of his affairs in the country', Cadogan for his official duties as commissary and Sir William Gilbert, Sir Richard Osborne, William

219 Ibid., 20 Oct. 1614, 28 April 1615. The unrecorded reason for Walter Butler's license on 2 Nov. 1614 was presumably to attend the final illness of his uncle, Thomas Butler, earl of Ormond, whom he succeeded on 22 Nov.

220 On Trevor and Blayney, see McGrath, 'Bio. dict.', i, pp 72, 287.

221 Ibid., i, p. 283.

222 *Commons' Jn. Ire.*, 2 Aug. 1634, 25 Nov. 1634, 6, 11–12 Dec. 1634, 28 Feb. 1635, 4, 14 March 1635.

223 E.g., ibid., 11 May 1641, 13 Dec. 1642, 3 Feb. 1645.

224 Kennedy, 'Representing the periphery'. For an analysis of English MPs' absence, see Vivienne Larminie, 'Going into the country: leave, holidays and political intrigues in the 1640s', at https://thehistoryofparliament.wordpress.com/2020/07/16/going-into-the-country-leave-holidays-and-political-intrigue-in-the-1640s/ [accessed 20 Aug. 2021].

Parsons and Hugh Montgomery cited their sickness; the latter applied to resign his seat.[225] No formal record of James Cusack's licence to go to England was recorded, but the house appointed a committee to recommend him, implicitly permitting him to depart.[226] A different type of request for absence came on 2 July 1641 from two members of the committee in England, Simon Digby and Richard FitzGerald, to be able to return home, the former about his own affairs, the latter to enable him to perform the duties of his offices in Ireland.[227] FitzGerald's return was agreed, Digby's not. Between August 1642 and June 1647, 14 licences were granted, ten for travel to England and ten to deal with personal affairs in the country. Somers was granted three licences and Robert Casey two, both for England, the second one 'by Mr Speaker's order'. It is unclear whether Somers was absent more than most, or merely more conscientious in applying for licences. Being absent without leave was given as the reason for issuing writs to replace Philip Lisle and Laurence Crawford on 9 April 1644.

The legislative basis for fining Irish MPs is unclear, as no known Irish legislation was passed, but it was consistent with fines levied on towns' freemen for not attending their public assemblies, and of town councillors for absence from meetings.[228] On 8 May 1615, nine Protestants and eight Catholics were censured for non-attendance, despite notice being given two days earlier of the house being called; eight fines were for IR£20, one for IR£5 and 15 included loss of either that session's wages or of all wages for the parliament. Many members incurred both fines and loss of wages. Three fines were remitted on the spot, suggesting that the MPs were present to make their excuses; Paul Sherlock was not fined or deprived of his wages because his absence was ordered by the house for disciplinary reasons. The proviso that fines were to be paid in the following session prevented their collection.

On 7 April 1635 eight Protestants and three Catholics received hefty fines, ranging from £50 for Hugh Montgomery, through £20 for Wiseman, Sir James Montgomery, Maurice Eustace and Patrick Sherlock, to £10 each for James Galbraith, Sir William Colley, Thomas Newcomen, Richard Parsons, Richard Martin and Walter Furlong. The reason for the different amounts is unclear, but a number of features of these fines are significant. First, they confirm the impression of more diligent Catholic attendance. Second, all had their fines cancelled over the following week, on condition of their paying fees, as they presented excuses, including other duties on behalf of the crown, their own or their wives' serious illness or their wives' deaths, attendance at assizes or poverty. Eustace, Newcomen and Parsons' excuses are unknown, as they were presented in petitions which have not survived. Finally, none had his wages cancelled,

225 *Commons' Jn. Ire.*, 8 June 1640, 4, 18–19, 23, 27 Feb. 1641, 11, 19 May 1641, 7, 9–11, 21, 30 June 1641, 13, 20, 22–4, July 1641, 2 Aug. 1641.

226 Ibid., 1 March 1641. On these figures, see McGrath, 'Bio. dict.', i, passim.

227 FitzGerald held many offices simultaneously. For details of both figures, see ibid., i, pp 134–5, 159–60.

228 McGrath, 'Communities of Clonmel'.

suggesting that many served without payment. Not all fines were recorded; there is no note of penalties levied on the ten Catholic and six Protestant MPs whose fines were remitted on 1 March 1641 because they were on the house's business and on 27 May 1641 otherwise unrecorded levies on Denny, Travers, John Chichester and Ralph Gore were struck off.

Attendance was clearly poor in the later sessions in 1641; in June two MPs were appointed to detail the fines due on other members and their total amount and five days later the house decided to call itself and dock that session's wages from anyone absent without good reason.[229] Penalties were usually inflicted on named individuals, but attendance of the 'rump' parliament was so poor that general fines were specified on 17 November 1642. On 26 March and 21 May 1647, general fines of 2*s.* 6*d.* and 1*s.* were imposed for absence, with 34 MPs named as absent on the latter occasion. General fines were also imposed on 17 April 1644, although in the latter case graduated fines were imposed on peers' sons, county members and burgesses. Docking wages would have been pointless at that stage, as they were assuredly not being paid. However, given the speed with which the Irish parliament moved to replace expelled Catholic MPs, compared to the English parliament, attendance in Dublin may have been proportionally higher than in Westminster.

CONCLUSION

This period saw the development of parliamentary institutions and procedure, largely in line with recent English changes, but with understandable differences entailed by Poynings' Law. Irish bills were less well drafted than English and private bills became the preserve of Protestants, but the Irish parliament continued to scrutinize legislation very carefully and to propose statutes in each of the three early Stuart parliaments. The use of committees followed rapidly on their development in England and created procedures for the rest of the Irish parliament's existence; they proved invaluable in ensuring the house's efficiency and effectiveness and its ability to represent the political nation. 1614 appears to have been the first occasion on which two standing committees were appointed and many bills and other matters were referred to select or *ad hoc* committees. Committees of the whole house were first recorded in 1634, as well as many select committees. In 1640, all of these mechanisms were used as well as a very high number of *ad hoc* committees and a quasi-standing committee of agents into England. The large number of committees also reflects the enormously increased amount of business the house was trying to deal with, as well as its ability to fulfil its judicial function, 'seize the initative' in politics and provide national representation. The unprecedented number of petitions presented to the house could only have been managed through committees.[230] By the end of the period

229 *Commons' Jn. Ire.*, 18, 23 June 1641.

230 The experience of the 1640 English House of Lords was similar. See Foster, 'Procedure'.

standing, *ad hoc* committees and committees of the whole house were an integral part of the house's operations, adding enormously to its efficiency and effectiveness. Evidence about Irish MPs' attendance is ambiguous and limited, but it generally appears relatively high, especially in comparison with England, until 1642.[231] MPs' attendance was at its highest in 1613–15, slackening in 1634–5, holding up well in 1641 despite the departure of many of Wentworth's cronies and declining catastrophically after October 1641. Most importantly, it is clear that most decisions were not taken on ethnic and religious grounds, but that there was considerable co-operation between all MPs regardless of their background, which reflects their common interests in promoting economic development, ensuring social order and more realistic levels of taxation. However, considerable tensions about insecure land titles and Catholics' eligibility for offices were not resolved.

231 Smith, *Stuart*, pp 23–4.

CHAPTER EIGHT

Economics of parliament

THE ECONOMICS OF PARLIAMENT included costs to the administration, MPs, communities and individuals, the revenue the administration generated through subsidies and the fees to crown servants for whom parliament provided significant additional income. The crown's costs included those for preparation, charges for summoning and managing parliament, fitting up its accommodation, providing robes and civic dress, organizing the opening day, paying officials' wages and fees, supplies of stationery, candles and fuel and printing the statutes. Much of parliament's cost involved capital expenditure, as officials' salaries had to be paid in any case. Supplies of materials represented a significant expense, especially when parliament sat for a long time, or in winter, or was very active in terms of legislation, committee work, petitions and orders of parliament, as happened between 1640 and 1641. At local level, sheriffs' expenses for election returns had to be covered as well as collecting subsidies and county members' wages.

Communities and individuals had to pay the taxes parliament voted, the costs of MPs' wages and officers' fees, entertainment and in some cases petitions to parliament; in addition, peers' tenants were expected to subvent the lords' costs of travelling to parliament and their subsidy assessments. Candidates had to cover the expense of travel to elections and possibly their constituencies, if they were outsiders, and presumably refreshments for voters. MPs' financial commitments included general living costs, especially if they were based outside Dublin, gowns, fees to officers and donations to the poor and communicating with their electorates, if only by letter. In addition, if they were not officials or soldiers, they faced loss of income while attending to parliamentary business, a problem for merchants and especially lawyers, whose attendance at committees occupied them throughout sitting days.

Unfortunately, there are few direct sources of information on the costs of any early modern Irish parliament, other than MPs' wages, officers' fees and the subsidies. It is impossible to estimate the full amount, as costs were not separately accounted for. Furthermore, different departments were responsible for different elements of parliamentary preparation and work and some expenses, such as lawyers' fees, were incurred in England and paid by the crown there. Chichester requested additional subventions in 1613:

> the expenses of that [parliament] and preparations towards it, now in hand is and will be much Extraordinary. Wherefore seeing our wants must of necessitie encrease and our occasions of charge of all, I ... pray your lordships, to cause both the quarters together to be sent unto Us for this

> once, and with somewhat extraordinary also, suteable unto the expectation and solemnity of the time.

Falkland claimed that his predecessor had been given £10,000 'for his extraordinary equipage and portes.'[1] Wentworth's parliaments could hardly have cost less.

Preparations included drafting legislation, transmitting bills to London, learned counsels' advice in Dublin and London and materials such as paper, parchment and wax. Under the early Stuarts, there are no records of the costs of drafting legislation and transmitting bills to London, but those drafted by crown lawyers may have been regarded as part of learned counsel and judges' general duties. Bills were sent to England with whoever was already going, incurring no great additional expenditure other than parchment, wax and the costs of transport. Fitting up parliament incurred a substantial capital sum, but the recurrent costs of salaries and stationery, fuel and other supplies also mounted up.

It is unclear which of the receipts for the administration's supplies of materials necessary for general government and parliament in the 1420s related to the parliament and which to the exchequer, but they are helpful in indicating the range of costs, although they exclude those for drafting legislation which at that time did not need to be transmitted to England. The crown's expenses included parchment, ink, green wax, paper, green cloth for the exchequer receipts, bags to hold parliamentary rolls, thread to sew them, counters and mats for the offices of the exchequer, messengers' wages for carrying writs and summonses, locks and keys, repairs to chests, timber and wooden boards, posts and nails for the bars and seats of parliament and councils, the labour of making them and the carriage of chests, bags and rolls from one house to another, or from one town to another. In 1425, Richard Row, a clerk in chancery, was granted 40*s.* for writing writs of parliament.[2] At that period, forms and chairs were reused when parliament sat in Dublin and only the bars were new, but new furniture was made when it met elsewhere; in 1439–42 a chair of estate and woolsacks were being made and in 1444–6 a 'Cathedra parliamenti' (chair of parliament) was made with nails bought for the purpose.[3]

The £500 Scottish (£41 13*s.* 4*d.* sterling) assigned 'to prepare all things requisite for accommodating the members of Parliament sitting at Stirling' in 1645, covering building repairs, cloths, cushions and other items of this kind represented capital outlay, not the estates' running costs.[4] A very partial account of the costs recorded for both houses of the 1661 Irish parliament amounted to

1 Chichester to the English privy council, 14 April 1613, in Edwards (ed.), 'Chichester', no. 53; Falkland to Charles, 29 July 1628, TNA, SP 63/247, fo. 70; *Cal. S.P. Ire., 1625–33*, pp 370–1.

2 Philomena Connolly (ed.), *Irish exchequer payments, 1270–1446* (Dublin, 1998), p. 554. Costs for 1355–6 are given on p. 477. NAI, MS RCH 240/50.

3 Connolly (ed.), *Irish exchequer payments*, pp 565, 572, 579, 581, 583.

4 John Imrie and John G. Dunbar (eds), *Accounts of the masters of works, for building and repairing royal palaces and castles, volume II: 1616–1649* (Edinburgh, 1982), pp 445–6.

£818 5*s.* 4*d.*, including £330 for arranging for the use of Chichester House, £167 5*s.* 4*d.* for fitting it out, £31 for building a stable for the horse guards attending the parliament, £140 for coals, candles and other necessities, £50 to Dr John Sterne for overseeing printing the acts and declarations, £90 to the houses' doorkeepers and the keeper of the speaker's chambers, and £10 for a clock for the upper house.[5]

Dublin Castle had to be fitted up, making rooms ready for both houses, including committee rooms and lobbies. There are no records of the cost of providing the bars, tables, chairs and forms in both houses, the dais and woolsacks for the chancellor and judges, the chair and cloth of estate, tapestries and portraits of the monarch, hangings and robes for the lord deputy, chancellor, speaker, clerks, heralds, serjeants, ushers, porters and pursuivants, as well as horses for the procession on opening day, and other ornamentation. Yet, they must have come to a considerable sum. Some items, such as a cloth and chair of estate, were already in use by the deputy in the presence chamber, but additional ones, costing up to £500 each, may have been ordered, to save the trouble of bringing them to and fro for the parliament.[6] In both England and Ireland, the serjeant-at-arms was responsible for fitting up the House of Commons, including tables, forms, chairs and the bars. As the wood was one of his perquisites, there were no storage costs between parliaments; presumably had Irish parliaments sat more frequently, they would have come to an agreement about retaining furniture. When Darcy urged the continued sitting of parliament in November 1641, despite the Castle not being available, he suggested that either 'the four courts, or St Patrick's Church in the convocation room … might be made up with deal bars with little cost.' The serjeant-at-arms might not have been in favour of using cheap wood.[7]

The administration also had to pay officials' salaries and deal with the difficulties which might be caused by MPs who held crown appointments and judges and clerks who were in attendance on the houses being obliged to neglect their other duties to perform parliamentary business. Royal pardons reduced income from fines imposed in courts, including on Catholics holding municipal office without swearing the oath of supremacy. The exclusion of Catholic lawyers from pleading in courts as retribution for their political activities in 1613 further reduced income from courts between then and their readmission in 1628 (see chapter ten).[8]

Officials' annual salaries frequently represented only a fraction of their income from their positions, which were made up of additional payments, especially for clerks who were able to charge for each document they prepared. As such, parliament constituted a bonanza for the clerks of parliament and chancery, the

5 Payments upon concordatums granted upon several occasions for the use of the parliament, HMC, new series III (1904) *Ormond*, pp 396–7.

6 Oliver Millar (ed.), *The inventories and valuations of the king's goods, 1649–1651* (Glasgow, 1972), pp 7–9, 18–19, 81–2, 166–7.

7 Conway Davies, *Catalogue*, ii, pp 761–2; *Commons' Jn. Ire.*, 17 Nov. 1641.

8 McGrath, 'Kilkenny merchants'.

heralds and for the serjeant-at-arms and their underlings.[9] The 12*s*. fee to the clerk in chancery for filing each writ of return would have amounted to IR£69 12*s*. in 1613 and IR£76 16*s*. in 1634, excluding by-elections and double returns, a significant additional income for him; as the clerk was also due 8*s*. 2*d*. for writs for replacement MPs, each constituency's return was worth over IR£1 to the clerks, and presumably more if returns were made separately, as in the case of double returns or by-elections.[10] In 1634, the fees to the clerk of the crown in chancery were 2*s*. 6*d*. for any knight, 18*d*. for any citizen or burgess, 5*s*. each for a writ for a new election and for a writ of expense for their wages. The clerk of the Commons was entitled to twice those amounts.[11] The registrar of Convocation had similar fees.[12]

The clerk of the Commons also received 12*d*. for copies of any bill and petition containing 16 lines, 2*s*. 6*d*. for entering every petition, and the same for entering the names of every committee. The explosion in the number of petitions in 1641 would have netted the clerk Philip Fernesly at least £46, but probably a great deal more.[13] He further received 10*s*. for engrossing any private bill

> for every roll of parchment which conteines much about a yard in length and about a quarter and a little above in breadth to be ruled with a large wide line ... ffor every order longer or shorter but if it be for the publick no ffee and 6*s*. 8*d*., ffor every warrant if not for publick use 5*s*.

This was a significant perquisite, as even relatively short bills required many skins of parchment. Finally, he also received 5*s*. for every document asserting parliamentary privilege for MPs' servants and agents, which would have yielded a further substantial sum.[14]

Fees for private acts were payable to officers in both houses but at a much higher rate in the Lords. The clerk of the Commons was due £10 for every private bill and the same for any public bill 'wherein any provisoe or addition concerning the bennefitt of any private person Towne or Corporation conteined' – a provision that should have yielded Fernesly significant money when the bill for the naturalization of all Scots born before 1603 was passed in 1635, as the fee was potentially due from every Scottish person aged over 31 years either living in

9 List of fees allowed by the present Parliament to the King of Armes, the Pursuivant, the Gent. Usher and the Yeoman Usher, 3 Nov. 1634, NLI, GO, MS 2, pp 31–2.

10 Masters (ed.), *Chamber accounts*, pp xx, 39–40. 8*s*. 2*d*. for the chancery writ for electing a replacement for a deceased MP, 12*s*. 'for the clerk of the crown in Chancery for filing the parliament's writ and the return of the same' (Nov. 1584). The same fee was incurred for the writ for Cork City in 1640. See Caulfield (ed.), *Cork*, p. 202.

11 Bodl. Lib., Carte MS 66, fos. 293–5.

12 ARL, MS Acts of Convocation, 1639–41, pp 109–25.

13 Dennehy, *Parliament*, p. 21.

14 Bodl. Lib., Carte MS 66, fo. 295. e.g., An Act for Confirmation of the subsidy granted by the clergy, TCD, MS 1,062, pp 351–5, filled three skins. Bodl. Lib., Bankes MS 10/2–4, refers to the number of skins in draft bills that were being amended. *Commons' Jn. Ire.*, 3 March 1641.

Ireland or who subsequently settled there, along with their spouses and children. While Fernesly's profit would have potentially been enormous, the clerk of the upper house, Philip Percival, was due twice as much.[15] Ussher and Bramhall shared the cost of their bill on church lands in 1635:

> there is 5^{li} demanded of me by Sir Nathanael Catelyn, and $50^{s.}$ by Mr Fernleye, which I conceived always to be the whole fee which could be demanded for the passing of our common Bill … according to the rule which you observe with the officers of the lower howse, you must in a farre higher proportion do the like unto them of the Higher howse of Parliament.[16]

Private bills were cheaper in Scotland's unicameral system.[17] In addition, the Commons ordered occasional contributions to the clerk from every MP, which would have amounted to £161 in 1635, on top of his usual salary and the extra £10 per session when parliament was sitting.[18] The clerk of the 1649 English Commons, John Browne, was said to have received £500 in fees.[19]

Supplies of materials depended on how long parliament sat and how active it was. The clerk started the 1604 English parliament with four reams each of fine and coarse paper, two 'fair journal books', two or three skins of the best parchment, one hundred 'farrells' (fardells) of vellum parchment, a standish and two fair ink horns. Irish clerks were presumably similarly equipped; Percival had at least three bound blank volumes for the Lords' journals in 1634. In 1614, John Barker, the king's printer, paid £4 16*s*. 8*d*. for paper for the English Lords and £2 16*s*. 8*d*. for the Commons, as an initial stock; it is unclear why the Lords should have cost more than the Commons, although the quality of the paper might account for the difference.[20] Necessary stationery included parchment for engrossing documents, paper, both fine and coarse, good quality Turkey (goat's leather) bags with silk strings to hold bills, petitions and orders and bound volumes for journals, two boxes covered with leather with locks and keys to secure bills, a standish, pens, pencils, ink horns and sand. Individually the cost of these items was not large, although it also depended on their quality, quantity and size. Sir Laurence Parsons generally paid 6*d*. for a quire (25 sheets) of paper, but the City of London was paying £5 18*s*. 6*d*. for five reams, 10*s*. for one skin of parchment, 22*s*. for binding a volume for oaths, and inks of various colours.[21] The annual allowance for paper

15 Terry Clavin, 'Percival (Perceval), Sir Philip', *DIB*.
16 Ussher to Bramhall, 25 Feb. 1636, HL, HP, MS 15,954; 10 Car. I, sess. 3, c. 5.
17 MacDonald, '"Tedious to rehers?"'; 10 Car. I, c. 4.
18 E.g., *Commons' Jn. Ire.*, 21 March 1634.
19 Foster, 'Painful labour'; J.C. Sainty, 'Browne, John', *Oxford DNB*.
20 Foster, 'Painful labour'; TCD, MSS 613–15. Two volumes were used for 1634 and MS 615 for 1640, but all have identical paper and binding and were clearly made together.
21 Accounts of Sir Laurence Parsons, 1621, Birr Castle, MS A/8, p. 17; Masters (ed.), *Chamber accounts*, p. 89. Parsons was presumably paying in Irish currency, which was cheaper, but there is no evidence about the quality or size of the paper purchased.

and parchment for the four courts in Ireland in 1629 was £200.[22] Bags cost between 4*d.* and 1*s.* 4*d.* each in 1621 and a standish 2*s.* 6*d.*, although a higher quality one may have cost much more. Sealing wax cost 1*s.* 4*d.* per pound, although London paid 28*s.* for 28 lbs., a year's supply, in 1585 and 3*s.* 4*d.* a gallon for ink.[23] A pen and ink-horn cost 4*d.* and penknives (for sharpening quills and erasing mistakes on parchment) 5*d.* or 6*d.* A new chest cost 15*s.* in 1647, but again the cost, size and quality could vary greatly.[24]

The cost of books and stationery supplies for the English parliament in 1640–2 (paper, pens, ink, wax, parchment, etc.) came to £763 152*s.* 2*d.*[25] The books included bibles, books of common prayer, statutes and abridgements of statutes, almanacs and books of computations (for regnal years, but also useful for estimating subsidies, MPs' wages and officers' fees, an issue which preoccupied all early Stuart Irish parliaments, and for clerks in calculating the fees they would receive for their work). Many of these books were not available for Ireland in 1613, but the position improved dramatically by 1634. The preface to John Merick's *Compendious collection* includes a list of monarch's reigns 'whereby the date of auncient Euidences, Patents and other writings may speedily and easily be computed reckoned and acompted.' The price of many of these items is unknown, but a copy of the English *Statutes at large* cost £2 in 1603 and Merick's *Compendious collection* cost 1*s.* 6*d.*; almanacs were very cheap at 2*d.*[26]

Heat and light represented significant costs, depending on their quantity and quality. Coal and candles are unlikely to have cost the early Stuart Irish parliaments less than the £80 allowed for them in 1661; the King's Inns paid 2*s.* 6*d.* for candles in 1630.[27] The English House of Lords spent £300 3*s.* 8*d.* on 'Charcoales' between 1 October 1646 and 25 March 1649.[28] Supplies accumulated, especially in long parliaments, to a significant sum and as there were two houses and the speaker and chancellor had separate chambers by at least 1661, but assuredly much earlier, several of the same items, like books, standishes, pens, candlesticks and chests would have been required and more candles and fuel. While courtrooms' usual fittings may have been suitable for committees, presumably additional heat and light would have been required during meetings in the afternoons, when courts would not usually have been sitting.

There are no surviving accounts of sheriffs' expenses in managing election returns, collecting county members' salaries and the subsidies, but paper,

22 TCD, MS 672, fo. 222r. This was presumably Irish pounds.
23 Masters (ed.), *Chamber accounts*, pp 36–7.
24 These costs are drawn from J.E. Thorold Rogers, *A history of agriculture and prices in England: from the year after the Oxford parliament (1259) to the commencement of the continental war (1793)* (Cambridge, 2011), pp 745–7.
25 Kyle, *Theater of state*, p. 61.
26 TCD, MS 2,160, fo. 1r. The flyleaf of Merick's book in the Royal Irish Academy Library notes the price as 1*s.* 6*d.*, with the date 1647, Oxon. The original price is unknown. Thorold Rogers, *History of agriculture*, p. 747.
27 King's Inns, MS B1/1, fos. 25v, 27r.
28 Receipt by Joanne Shorlake, 5 July 1649, HRC, MS 165.

parchment and wax would have been required as well as the costs of sending messengers with mandates to boroughs, travel and entertainment for attending county elections and messengers for delivering the returns to chancery. Local communities faced very heavy costs for MPs' wages, where they were paid, and administrative expenses, including clerks' fees for writs, entertainment for the sheriff and the collection of subsidies. The cost of defending incorrect borough returns also fell on towns: while there are no records for Ireland, Warwick paid £6 15*s*. 4*d*. for various administrative work and travel in its disputed 1625 return.[29] Constituencies also incurred expenses in fitting up locations, especially where there was no fixed location for the county court, or the court was moved for the occasion, for either practical or manipulative reasons. In 1639 Belfast paid £6 9*s*. 8*d*. to fit out its hall.[30] Some French communities raising money for deputies' wages after the Estates General included all of their administrative costs in the sum to be collected.[31]

Not all the costs were to the crown or local communities. Dublin city anticipated higher costs for entertainment during parliaments and presumably also had to pay porters' wages, fuel for fires and candles and possibly some refreshments when the tholsel was used for committee meetings. The city's mayor was reckoned to spend £500 during his year in office 'for their viand and diet' offering lavish hospitality and keeping open house. The corporation traditionally granted him an additional allowance for the extra entertaining that incurred during parliaments and in 1605–6 John Brice, anticipating a parliament, demanded a higher mayoral salary, claiming that others had refused the office and suggesting that the cost of being mayor during a parliament was a deterrent. In 1640 the corporation voted £50 to cover the mayor's anticipated additional hospitality, but this is highly unlikely to have covered the actual expenditure.[32] In 1635, the King's Inns paid its staff twice their usual wages for their attendance to support the judges and for additional social events during parliament time and in early 1640 noted the cost of £2 paid for 'fier and Candlelight spent in the parler about the kinges businesse for the acts'.[33]

Individuals and communities seeking redress of grievances by private acts, petitions, parliamentary orders or other means, faced considerable expense, including payments to counsel, officials' fees and *douceurs* to clerks, secretaries and influential people who could facilitate their processing, and materials. Chichester recommended suspending Poynings' Law for private bills because of the

29 FSL, MS X.d.s (26).
30 Young, *Town book of the Corporation of Belfast*, pp 11–12.
31 John Russell Major, 'The payment of deputies to the French national assemblies, 1484–1627', *The Journal of Modern History*, 27 (1955), 217–29.
32 Richard Stanihurst, 'Plain and perfect description of Ireland' in Maxwell, *Irish history from contemporary sources*, p. 359; Gilbert (ed.), *C.A.R.*, iii, p. 365; Lennon, *Lords of Dublin*, p. 49.
33 King's Inns, MS B 1/1, fos. 44r, 46r. The additional payments to the kitchen staff and laundress indicate that it was at least partly for entertainment (fo. 77v).

prohibitive cost of processing them.[34] On 24 October 1614, the Commons had ordered that '£5 be given to the poor for every private bill that passeth', in addition to all the other fees. Communities who petitioned parliament, such as Carlow, Cavan, Cork, Drogheda, Limerick, Naas, King's and Queen's Counties and Tipperary and the parishioners of Clonmuske and of Tallow had to pay substantial fees and agents' costs.

Voters and candidates faced the cost of travel to elections especially if they did not reside there and the latter presumably paid for some type of refreshments for the electorate. These costs would have varied with the size of the constituencies and electorate and the distance voters had to travel, with many freeholders facing long journeys to attend the assizes as voters, litigants, jurors or JPs, or to boroughs of which they were freemen. Sir William St Leger would have had to travel from his home in Donneraile to Tralee for the Kerry county election in 1634.[35] Sir James Ware lived in Dublin and represented Trinity College but was a burgess of Jamestown in Leitrim; unless that return was a blank, he would have incurred the expense of travelling to vote, although he may have combined it with other business. Even those resident in their counties could face long journeys to the election. Laurence Parsons noted the costs of his attending the assizes at Philipstown at around 20*d. per diem* for a journey of 33 miles each way.[36] Tipperary voters regarded the journey to Clonmel on the southern border with Waterford as a hardship and in 1641 proposed Cashel, the old county town of Cross Tipperary, as the best location for elections.[37]

Given these distances, it would have been reasonable for voters to have been supplied with refreshments at least, as happened in England, although there is no record of this for Ireland.[38] It is impossible to estimate this cost as there is little information about the size and distribution of the county electorate and many electors of old boroughs may have lived outside those towns. Meath's electorate may have numbered over 1,000 and Ware estimated that 2,400 men voted in Dublin City in 1628.[39] Keeping such numbers supplied with refreshments and stabling for horses could have amounted to a substantial sum of money. Providing beer or wine and modest refreshments to even 13 voters in the new boroughs could have come to a tidy sum, although making blank returns avoided this expenditure.[40] Outsiders admitted as freemen after their returns, like Richard Gethings and William Smyth, in Clonmel, Andrew Barrett in Cork and Philip

34 Chichester and the Irish privy council to the English privy council, 30 Dec. 1612, in Edwards (ed.), 'Chichester', no. 39.
35 Elaine Murphy, 'St Leger, William', *DIB*.
36 Birr Castle, MS A/8, pp 14, 34.
37 Bodl. Lib., Carte MS 59, fos. 80–1.
38 Neale, *House*, pp 313, 315–18; Hawkyard, *Commons*, pp 46, 48.
39 See chapter five on elections.
40 MP Humphrey Farnham's funeral expenses included 120 cakes costing 10*s*., 16 quarts of Claret for 8*s*., three quarts of sack at 2*s*. 6*d*., and two shillings for sugar, nutmeg and cloves. See Loeber and McGrath, 'Legacy of Humphrey Farnham'; Birr Castle, MS A/8, p. 35 (1622–3). Laurence Parsons paid 1*s*. for a quart of sack when Mr Bennett White and Mr Nick Herbert visited him.

Wenman in Belfast, presumably incurred the usual fines for freedom.[41] Francis Slingsby was presumably not the only placeman to write to his constituency to thank them and offer his support in anything they might wish him to undertake and this would have incurred at least the cost of paper and a messenger.[42]

MPs' expenses included general living costs, especially if they were based outside Dublin, gowns, fees to officers and donations to the poor. There are no records of the cost of Irish MPs' gowns, but the lapse of time between parliaments and the low level of previous parliamentary experience suggests that many would have had to buy robes.[43] MPs who were not crown officials also faced reduced income from the neglect of their own businesses, legal practices or commercial activities. Speakers were given compensation for the losses from their legal practices but it is unlikely to have made up the difference; they received £10 for every private act passed, but as it was impossible after 1613 for Catholics to get private acts passed all this income came from Protestants.[44] James recognized Davies' loss of income during his time as speaker:

> by his imployment in the last parliament hee was putt to extraordinary charges, & suffred no small losse in the course of his profession … wee have heretofore bestowed upon him a booke of ffeefarme whereof he hath yet passed but a third part only or thereabouts, being hindred & diverted by his attendance of the parliament business, & his journeys into England.[45]

Catlin received £500, although he was presumably also paid his MP's wages, but despite receiving some sort of allowance or salary, at least during parliamentary sessions, Eustace found being speaker 'very troublesome and extremely chargeable, both in Cost and Lost.'[46]

Clerks, soldiers and other crown servants continued to be paid during their membership of parliament, but paying deputies to perform their duties may have lost them additional income from these offices; this may have been behind William Sandes' temporary stepping down from the Commons deputy clerkship.[47] Recorders continued to receive their regular salary, although generally not the additional remuneration that would have comprised most of their takings.

41 McGrath (ed.), *Clonmel*, p. 268; Caulfield (ed.), *Cork*, p. 197; Young, *Town book of the Corporation of Belfast*, p. 249.
42 Bennett, *Bandon*, p. 98.
43 Masters (ed.), *Chamber accounts*, pp 39–40. London's MPs received an allowance of £6 132s. 4*d*. each for gowns, boat hire of 12*d*. *per diem* for each of the four burgesses, 8*s*. 2*d*. for the chancery writ for electing a replacement for a deceased MP, 12*s*. 'for the clerk of the crown in Chancery for filing the parliament's writ and the return of the same' (Nov. 1584); *Penny magazine*, p. 511; McGrath, 'Looking the part'.
44 Ussher to Bramhall, 25 Feb. 1636, HL, HP, MS 15,954; 10 Car. I, sess. 3, c. 5.
45 James to Chichester, 17 Oct. 1615, HL, HP, MS 15,076.
46 Bodl. Lib., Carte MS 1, fo. 432; Thomas Tempest to Speaker Lenthall, 31 Aug. 1641, in Charles McNeill (ed.), *The Tanner letters* (Dublin, 1943), p. 129. Tempest notes that both speakers have 'great estates to bear it out.'
47 *Commons' Jn. Ire.*, 7 Nov. 1634.

Recorders' wages were generally low (Henry White's annual wages as Clonmel's recorder were £3, although Damian Pecke persuaded Galway town council to increase his salary to £30, three times what his Catholic predecessor had been paid) and most of their income was made from additional work, which they would have lost during parliamentary sessions. Other lawyers were likely to lose significant income as parliament, like courts, usually sat in the morning, and committees, on which they were disproportionately represented, in the afternoons; their losses would have been less when parliament was held outside law terms (see chapter seven). Those merchants and landowners who were often absent on business for protracted periods and whose wives and agents were used to 'holding the fort' may have experienced fewer losses.

MPs' wages had a statutory basis and were intended to ensure that members could devote their time wholly to public business. This was another example of the practice of communities paying their agents an allowance when on official business. Delegates to the 1627 Great Assembly were reimbursed their expenses and the Irish agents in 1628 in England were paid for their attendance.[48] In 1640 Belfast granted 10*s*. to the two men who attended the county assizes and 6*s*. 8*d*. *per diem* for their Serjeant Phelemy Coshnan's at the quarter sessions. Clonmel's and Cork's agents to Dublin were paid 5*s*. per day.[49] Burgesses ceased to be paid under Charles II, when towns' charters changed and their inhabitants were stripped of their role in returning MPs; it is unclear what happened to Irish county members' wages.[50]

The principle of paying English MPs was established by 1258. In Ireland the *Modus* specified that MPs' expenses were paid and Robert Emeldon was paid 50*s*. for attending parliament at Kilkenny in 1347.[51] Rates were set down in the late fourteenth and fifteenth centuries (12 Ric. II, c. 12 and 23 Hen. VI, c. 11). MPs' wages were intended to cover their travel and subsistence, with one servant and a horse, based on a six-day week during each session and for ten days before and after each session, to allow for travel to and from Dublin. County members were allowed 13*s*. 4*d*., citizens 10*s*. and burgesses 6*s*. 8*d*. *per diem*, or £4, £3 and £2 per week respectively in Irish currency for 1613–15 and 1634–5, and the sterling daily equivalents of 10*s*., 7*s*. 6*d*. and 5*s*. in 1640.[52] This was a very generous rate when originally established and even two centuries later was regarded as sufficient to cover costs, as the rates actually paid were often lower. These rates had originally

48 St Leger to the Mayor of Youghal demanding payment for John Mead as agent to England, 22 Jan. 1629, Cork City Archives, MS YTR 1/47.

49 Young, *Town book of the Corporation of Belfast*, pp 16, 19–20; McGrath (ed.), *Clonmel*, p. 268; Caulfield (ed.), *Cork*, p. 12.

50 23 Hen. VI, c. 11; William Lynch, *The law of election in the ancient cities and towns of Ireland* (London, 1831), p. 68; R.C. Latham, 'The payment of parliamentary wages: the last phase', *EHR*, 66:258 (Jan., 1951), 27–50.

51 Hawkyard, *Commons*, pp 178ff; Hardy (ed.), *Modus*, pp 8–12; TNA, MS E 101/241/13, Close roll, 21 Edward III, 59, https://chancery.tcd.ie/document/Close/21-edward-iii/59 [accessed 9 March 2023].

52 *Commons' Jn. Ire.*, 25 Nov. 1614, 2 Aug. 1634; Bodl. Lib., Carte MS 59, fo. 80v. The Irish pound was worth 15*s*. sterling. Clarke, 'The Irish economy', p. 168; Caulfield (ed.), *Cork*, p. 202.

also applied in England, but from 1327 English wages were set at 4*s*. for county members and 2*s*. for burgesses, the equivalent of 5*s*. and 2*s*. 6*d*. Irish, and by the Elizabethan period there is little evidence of county members being paid.[53] Perott's jibe when proroguing parliament in November 1585, 'you have hitherto spent some time and charged your country to little purpose. I hope you will at the next assembly consider otherwise of the matter and be better advised to do something that may be worth the travail and cost for the public good', confirms the widespread payment of Irish MPs' wages.[54]

Sixteenth-century English boroughs paid higher salaries, presumably to attract better-quality, more attentive burgesses, but also recognizing that the statutory rate did not cover members' actual expenses. English MPs, especially those without houses in London, found their attendance costs excessive: Sir Henry Slingsby spent £731 staying in London in 1640–1. Sir Thomas Barrington paid £254 18*s*. for 17 weeks' lodgings and, as the Long Parliament continued, found it easier to rent a house for £130 annually.[55] Similar complaints were made in Paris during the 1614 Estates General.[56] The high costs in London continued to be a deterrent into the Commonwealth period: William Dobbins, burgess for Askeaton in 1640, considering standing for election for an Irish constituency in 1657, noted that there was less competition for places because of the cost of travelling to and living in England.[57] Irish parliamentary wages were much higher and accommodation cheaper, but the influx of people attending parliament, including members and their families and anyone with business there, such as those preferring petitions, drove up the cost of lodgings. Francis Lloyd, the Herberts' agent in Kerry, who visited Dublin during the 1634 parliament, complained about being charged 20*s*. a week in the Seven Stars, St Nicholas Street 'for diet and chamber … his expense in travelling here is extraordinary. Yet Sir Edward Trevor [MP] and others he diets with can say he is not more expensive than is necessary and fitting.'[58] Lord Conway, planning a visit to Dublin in May 1661, asked his agent and brother-in-law George Rawdon to advise him what furniture would be needed and also send him money, including for lodgings in Dublin, 'where 'tis probable I may stay a good while, and being deferrd the Parliament coming on will make lodgings both scarce, and deare.'[59] Some Irish MPs were able to stay with relatives or associates.

53 Two of London's four burgesses were regarded as knights and received the higher rate, and York also paid 4*s*. Neale, *House*, pp 308ff; Hawkyard, 'Wages'. For earlier practices, see Hannes Kleineke, 'The payment of members of parliament in the fifteenth century', *Parl. Hist.*, 3 (2007), 281–300.

54 Treadwell, 'Sir John Perrott'; Receipt for wages of John Myagh and Thomas Sarsfield, Cork, Nov. 1585, NLI, MS D. 25, 356; Receipt of Helias Shee for his parliamentary wages (stg.) 5*s*. per diem, 31 July 1586, KCA, MS CR/J/17. Shee had been paid most of his wages in advance.

55 Hawkyard, 'Wages'; Conrad Russell, 'The nature of a parliament in early Stuart England' in Howard Tomlinson (ed.), *Before the English civil war* (London, 1983), pp 123–50.

56 Hayden, *France*, p. 163.

57 Dobbins to John Percival, 9 Dec. 1657, in Crawford Lomas (ed.), *Egmont*, i, pp 592–3.

58 Lloyd to Richard Herbert, 27 Feb. 1634–5, in Smith (ed.), *Herbert correspondence*, p. 82.

59 Conway to Rawdon, 25 Dec. 1660, HL, HP, MS 14,368; Toby Barnard, 'Conway, Edward, 3rd Viscount Conway and Kilultagh', *DIB*.

Clients of important men may have been able to stay in their patron's houses, if they were usually based outside Dublin; Robert Smith wrote letters dated from Cork House. Administration officials and lawyers like Darcy, Geoffrey Galway and Nicholas Plunkett who were based in Dublin at least part of the year, had permanent accommodation there, as had some non-lawyers, such as Simon Luttrell and possibly Stephen Dowdall. Others who were frequently in the capital, like Thomas Davills, had long-standing relationships with landlords.[60] Residence in Dublin, including in the Castle, and their crown salaries, made it easier for placemen to waive parliamentary wages to secure election.

Irish MPs' wages amounted to a significant sum: in 1613–15, £99 6*s*. 8*d*., £74 10*s*. and £49 13*s*. 4*d*. were due to county members, citizens and burgesses respectively, or twice that for each constituency.[61] If all MPs were paid at the statutory rate the total cost of wages would have been IR£7,016 16*s*. 8*d*. (£5,262 12*s*. 6*d*. sterling) (IR£3,267 for county members, IR£521 10*s*. for citizens and IR£3,228 6*s*. 8*d*. for burgesses, or £2,450 5*s*., £391 2*s*. 6*d*. and £2,421 5*s*. sterling respectively), an enormous sum for local communities to bear.[62] James cited the cost of wages as one reason for dissolving parliament, even though the Commons reduced their wages for the last session to 6*s*. 8*d*. for knights, 5*s*. for citizens and 3*s*. 4*d*. for burgesses, 'but where there is agreement for more or, to stand at the agreed rate.' Yet Chichester's statement that the dissolution prompted 'a general regret and distaste to this people' does not suggest any resentment at its cost. Bishop David Rothe agreed that 'Verily there was good Cause that it should bee soe, esepecialy in a kingedome noe better monyed, beecome poore with soe many opressions, burthened with late subsidies, by inConveniences of warres soe latly exhausted', but he was more relieved that parliament's dissolution prevented anti-Catholic legislation being passed.[63] Members could obtain a copy of the order for wages from the clerk of the Commons with which they could request a writ *de expensis* from chancery which their constituencies were to pay on sight. This was frequently unnecessary, as constituencies paid without requiring members to go to the expense of paying the clerks of the Commons and chancery 5*s*. for each writ and many MPs received at least part of their wages in advance.[64]

60 Smith to Kildare, 6 Dec. 1632, same to same, 18 Feb. 1633, in Clarke and McGrath (eds), *Letterbook*, pp 59, 68. Darcy's house was in Bridge Street: Gilbert, *History of the city of Dublin*, i, p. 331. I am grateful to Coleman Dennehy for drawing this reference to my attention. Galway's and Luttrell's houses were on Thomas St, Dowdall's on Market Street and Plunkett's on land from the King's Inns. See David Brown and Micheál Ó Siochrú (eds), 'The Cromwellian urban civil surveys, 1653–1659 [with index]', *Archivium Hibernicum*, 69 (2016), 37–150; King's Inns, MS B1/1, fo. 68v. Lawyers who had chambers in the King's Inns were able to stay there overnight, ibid, fo. 112r; John Huggart, 5 May 1637, Bodl. Lib., Carte MS 176, fo. 109r notes that Davills had lodged in his house in Fishamble Street intermittently for four years.

61 TCD, MS 843, pp 489–95.

62 Ibid., pp 489–502. These calculations are based on 149 days sitting.

63 James to Chichester, 22 Aug. 1615, *Cal. S.P. Ire., 1615–25*, p. 87; Chichester to Winwood, 31 Oct. 1615, ibid., p. 95; *Commons' Jn. Ire.*, 15 May 1615; TCD, MS 843, fos. 489–502.

64 *Commons' Jn. Ire.*, 5 May 1615. This follows the English practice as outlined in Hawkyard, 'Wages'.

Sheriffs were to collect and deliver the wages to county members as soon as possible and MPs could sue for non-delivery by *scire facias*.[65] County members' wages were applotted on the county and collected under the sheriffs' direction under the terms of 23 Hen. VI, c. 11; sheriffs were to issue proclamations that 'Coroners and everie chief Constable of the countie, and the Bailifes of every hundred … &c (and all others that will be at the sessing of their wages)' attend at the next county court to assess their said wages on each hundred and towns within the hundred, with substantial penalties for failing to appear or for defaulting in assessing and collecting. In 1613 10*s*. was levied on each of Waterford's 400 ploughlands for its knights' wages.[66] The flat rate imposed a much heavier burden on smaller and poorer counties and towns as it took no account of constituencies' population or prosperity and paid Dublin's MPs the same as those from the country. The Tipperary Grand Jury at Cashel, 31 September 1641 requested the 'continuance of the union of both [Tipperary] counties', noting

> The ffees of the knights of parleament would be very burthensome to the County Cross, if it had held a county of it self, being it conteyneth scarce four score plows or Colpes of land, and that every Colpe of land there must be Charged with 30*s*. vnto them for every three months sitting of the Parleament, which charge being accompanied with the payment of Subsidies must light very heavy vpon that small County.

This assessment amounted to £40 sterling per month, significantly more than the levy on Waterford in 1613, even allowing for the abolition of the separate Irish currency in 1637.[67]

There was considerable debate in the 1613 and 1634 parliaments as to whether peers (temporal and spiritual) were liable to contribute to county members' wages and burgesses' salaries if they had residences in towns.[68] The Lords claimed exemption under 12 Ric. II, c. 12, as they had to pay their own charges and received no allowance, but the Commons, while conceding this, held that, according to that act, any lands, including dissolved monasteries, acquired since their ennoblement were chargeable, even if they were not in the peers' possession at the time (e.g., leased out, or possessed by dowager peeresses as part of their jointure).[69] The act stated that

65 Merick, *Compendious collection*, pp 304–5.

66 *Commons' Jn. Ire.*, 1 May 1615.

67 Bodl. Lib., Carte MS 59, fo. 80v. This calculation implies a daily rate of IR 10*s*., which would be the sterling equivalent of 13*s*. 4*d*. Irish. The Irish pound, known as a 'harpe', was worth 15 shillings sterling and circulated with sterling in Ireland until abolished by proclamation by Wentworth in 1637. Before that date contemporary documents were careful to specify which currency was intended to be used. Michael Dolley, 'The Irish coinage, 1534–1691' in Moody, et al. (eds), *New history of Ireland*, iii, pp 408–19.

68 None of the anomalies for payment of knights in English counties outlined in Hawkyard, 'Wages' is recorded for early Stuart Ireland.

69 *Commons' Jn. Ire.*, 5–6 May 1615.

> Expences of Knightes of the Parliament shall be levied as hath auunciently bine used, added to the same, that if any Lord or other man, spirituall or temporall, have purchased any lands &c., that before the said purchase did contribute toward such Expences such lands &c should neuerthelesse be contributory to the said expences as formerly they were.[70]

In 1615, peers were holding up the collection and distribution of knights' wages by forbidding sheriffs to collect money from their lands, although Boyle had paid part of his liability for County Cork by that time.[71] On 6 May 1615 the Commons' Grand Committee issued an order for payment, including on lands acquired by peers and on 10 May 1615 both houses met in a conference committee to discuss 'what lands are chargeable with the payment of the wages of the knights citizens and burgesses.' The issue was raised again in 1634–5, when Lord Westmeath complained that sheriffs were taking distresses from peers for county members' wages; the judgment that ancestral lands were not liable, nor any tenants on those lands, significantly advantaged recently created New English peers over the established Catholic ones.[72] However, it also clarified that inhabitants of parliamentary boroughs were also not chargeable because they paid burgesses' wages.[73] These debates confirm that, unlike England, Irish county members were invariably paid, although possibly not at the statutory rate as the Commons ordered

> that the clerk of the Hanaper shall forthwith issue out his majesty's writ for the wages of Sir Robert Talbott, baronet, for so long a time as he continued a member of this house; so as he hath made no former agreement with the county.[74]

Parliaments' uncertain length made it impossible to anticipate the cost of wages, and an estimated sum was collected so that MPs would not have to wait until parliament ended for all their wages; any surplus was to be returned to the contributors.[75] John Berrie wrote to Sir Richard Boyle, from Tralee, on 23 January 1615, that he had 'received His Majesty's writ for raising £190 for the Knights of the Shire, which has been levied on the lands of the undertakers without difficulty.' Boyle himself paid William Bodleigh, sheriff of Cork, £5 in part payment for wages and on 21 February 1615, Lady Honora FitzGerald wrote from Ballymoller that Boyle's 'servant came yesterday with a warrant to levy the Knights fee charges. Sent him to her son for the money.'[76] Coleraine county levied £114 on its

70 12 Ric. II, c. 12; Merick, *Compendious collection*, p. 300; 23 Hen. VI, c. 11.
71 Grosart (ed.), *Lismore Papers*, 1st series, i, p. 69.
72 Micheál Ó Siochrú, 'Nugent, Richard, 1st earl of Westmeath', *DIB*.
73 *Commons' Jn. Ire.*, 3 March 1635; Dennehy, 'Representation in later medieval and early modern Ireland'.
74 *Commons' Jn. Ire.*, 23 Feb. 1635.
75 E.g., County Mayo. Ibid., 19 Nov. 1614.
76 Grosart (ed.), *Lismore Papers*, 1st series, i, p. 68, under 7 April 1615; *Calendar of the Lismore*

inhabitants to pay John Rowley and John Baker £57 each, much less than the £99 6*s.* 8*d.* they were due, although this was probably to supplement an earlier collection.[77] When Sir Tibbott Bourke was fined £20 and deprived of all of his wages for non-attendance on 8 May 1615, he was ordered to repay all the moneys he had already received; Medhop's list of MPs' wages does not record him as being due any payment.[78]

Boroughs used their usual practice of levying their wealthier inhabitants in proportion to their assessed means, with defaulters having their goods distrained.[79] Money was gathered by the usual collectors and given to the towns' financial officer or sheriffs or bailiffs, who disbursed the money to the MPs. Humphrey Farnham's claim that in the boroughs 'there is no indifferent assessment [for wages] but that the poor pay as much as the rich', presumably based on his own experience in Enniskillen, was referred to the committee examining sheriffs' abuses.[80] Wages were collected and paid in instalments. The agitation about payment confirms that county wages were invariably paid and that MPs expected to be paid before or during parliament, often as cash advances and in instalments, unlike in France, where salaries were paid only after the Estates General ended.[81] Kilkenny paid its 1585 MPs in advance and in 1634 paid £20 sterling before parliament met, 'to furnish them for ther Jorney' at 10*s.* Irish each and required them 'to be accountable' for the money. The £12 Youghal advanced to cover its MPs' costs was returned when the 1628 parliament did not meet and Belfast's sovereign John Bramston was ordered to return the £16 advanced for his wages, when he was unseated for having returned himself.[82]

Boroughs had greater control than counties about whether to pay wages and/or at what rate. Placemen were not paid and towns consulted each other about their burgesses' pay. Cork matched Limerick's rate in 1613 and 1640, and in 1628 Clonmel and Kilkenny both paid 5*s.*, which disadvantaged Kilkenny's citizens more, as their statutory daily rate was 10*s.* compared to Clonmel's 6*s.* 8*d.*[83] Cork's

manuscripts with index of matters, 1396–1774, 16 vols (Privately printed, n.d.), i, pp 130–1 and p. 94, the cost of subsidies voted by parliament. Ibid., p. 140.

77 Common Council, London, *Order of the common council made on consideration of the instructions to Mr Proby and Mr Springham, and their report. 1 October 1616, in the court of appeal in Ireland on appeal from her majesty's rolls court in Ireland, the attorney-general (for Ireland) and others and the Irish Society and others*, Appendix: vol. 1, Documents, Appendix, no. 84, pp 421–43, no. 24, pp 438–9. Medhop's list included the full wages for each of them. TCD, MS 843, pp 489–502.

78 *Commons' Jn. Ire.*, 8 May 1615; TCD, MS 843, pp 489–502; Robert Armstrong, 'Bourke (Burke), Theobald (Teabóid na Long, Tibbott-na-Long), 1st Viscount Mayo', *DIB*.

79 McGrath, 'Reconstructing an early-modern Irish urban economic community'; Caulfield (ed.), *Youghal*, p. 26; McGrath, 'Town and mitre.'

80 *Commons' Jn. Ire.*, 8 May 1615; TCD, MS 843, p. 493.

81 McGrath (ed.), *Clonmel*, pp 162, 198–9; McGrath (ed.), *Coleraine*, pp 61–2, 91, 95; Caulfield (ed.), *Cork*, p. 202; Major, 'Payment of deputies'.

82 *Commons' Jn. Ire.*, 1 May 1615; William Gough and William Bluett for their wages, 1628, Cork City Archives, MS YTR/B/1, p. 353; Caulfield (ed.), *Youghal*, p. 147; KCA, MS CR/J/39, 4 July 1634; *Commons' Jn. Ire.*, 19 July 1634.

83 McGrath, 'Nomination of Kilkenny MPs in 1628'; McGrath (ed.), *Clonmel*, p. 162.

representatives to the 1627 Great Assembly were paid at the same rate as 'the agents of Waterford, Limerick, or any other city of this kingdom.' Local arrangements for wages below the statutory rate were common: in 1613 and 1628, Youghal paid its MPs 5*s*. *per diem*, below the statutory rate of 6*s*. 8*d*. and Mullingar's burgesses accepted the equivalent sum of 3*s*. 4*d*. sterling in 1634. Clonmel may have reduced the daily pay to 4*s*. for later sessions and no provision was made in 1640, when Richard Gethings and William Smyth served unpaid.[84] Cork paid alderman Dominic Roche the statutory wage of 7*s*. 6*d*. sterling *per diem* in 1640 but Andrew Barrett, the city's first Protestant MP, went unpaid. Roche's wages for three sessions came to £87, plus 12*s*. for the writ.[85]

Towns were also able to negotiate about travelling time, as it would not necessarily have taken ten days to reach Dublin. In England it was assumed that MPs could travel 26 miles a day in winter and 30 in summer.[86] Having confirmed the statutory rates on 14 April 1635, the Commons ordered: 'Provided, nevertheless, that the ten days preceding the first day of this last session shall not be reckoned among the days allowed for this session, any former order made to the contrary notwithstanding.' In 1613, Youghal only allowed its MPs four days travel each way and Kilkenny's 1634 citizens were granted only four days for travelling to Dublin and two days for returning.[87] In 1628, Clonmel allowed 5*s*. *per diem* 'from the tyme of their departure towards Dublin untill their returne' without specifying the anticipated travel time.[88]

The cost was even higher when parliament sent agents to England 1613–15 and 1640–1. Despite Chichester's ruling against collecting contributions, Youghal levied £30 on its inhabitants to pay Edmund Coppinger and Cork allocated £18 in advance for 36 days for David Tyrry fitz Stephen 'being 10*s*. per diem during his being in England lately as one of the Burgesses of this City, at or before 20 October next', although it added a rider that it would only match what Limerick's burgess, James Galway, was paid.[89] In 1641 the money for the agents in England was levied by order of the Commons on all counties and collected by current and former MPs; Cork City's initial liability was £120 18*s*. 4*d*., but a further £40 was later demanded, the same as Limerick.[90]

84 Caulfield (ed.), *Youghal*, p. 38; William Gough and William Bluett's wages, 1628, Cork City Archives, MS YTR/B/1, p. 353; BL, Harleian MS 430, pp 2–3, 62. Their claim for 3*s*. 4*d*. daily wages was pursued in 1637 by which time the Irish currency had been abolished. I am grateful to Aidan Clarke for drawing this reference to my attention. McGrath (ed.), *Clonmel*, pp 162, 198–9, 319. The entry for the 1634 rate is ambiguous. On Gethings and Smith, see McGrath, 'Bio. dict.', i, pp 166–7, 271–2.

85 Caulfield (ed.), *Cork*, p. 202; MacCarthy-Morrogh, *Munster plantation*, p. 265; McGrath, 'Bio. dict.', i, pp 58–9, 255.

86 Hooker, *Order and vsage*, in Holinshed, *Chronicles*, p. 122.

87 Caulfield (ed.), *Youghal*, p. 38; KCA, MS CR/J/39, 4 July 1634.

88 McGrath (ed.), *Clonmel*, pp 162, 198–9, 319.

89 Caulfield (ed.), *Youghal*, p. 26; Curtis Clayton (ed.), *Council book*, pp 448–9; Caulfield (ed.), *Cork*, p. 4.

90 *Commons' Jn. Ire.*, 5 Aug. 1641; Caulfield (ed.), *Cork*, pp 68, 130, 199–201, 7 Aug. 1641.

Unsurprisingly, many towns, even well-established and prosperous ones, found it difficult to pay wages; for newly established ones, it was nearly impossible. In 1613, Athy, Downpatrick, Maryborough and the new towns of Monaghan, Newry, Sligo and Strabane paid only one of their burgesses, generally the locally based one, although Molyneux was paid by Strabane, despite being the outsider. Enniskillen apparently paid both its burgesses.[91] Dungarvan's sovereign stated frankly that there 'is no revenue to bear the charge of their burgesses in Parliament', although as this statement was made after parliament had ended, the burgesses may already have received at least partial payment, even if they had to wait for their final instalments.[92] Cork had form in using desperate measures to cover its members' salaries: in 1585 it issued a bond for £28 11*s*. 8*d*. due for the diet of soldiers to be cashed at Dublin for £18 sterling to pay Thomas Sarsfield and John Myagh and in 1613 it extracted money from ambitious locals in return for positions in the city's government, auctioned off some Gascon wine and granted the Company of English Taylors special privileges in return for substantial cash payments to pay its MPs' wages.[93] A significant proportion of New Ross' tax-payers appealed against their assessments for an extraordinary levy in 1635, probably for their burgesses' wages. Mullingar's MPs had to resort to petitioning for their payment through Wentworth's small claims court two years after parliament ended.[94] London disbursed £95 to pay Londonderry and Colerane's MPs in 1613, but the money was not allocated equally, with £30 going to Thomas Crewe, £20 to George Carey, £25 to Barnaby Bryan and £20 to John Wilkinson; Coleraine added £27 to Wilkinson's allowance.[95] By 1634 Coleraine was paying its own members, and in 1640 they agreed to assessments of £18 10*s*. and £27 5*s*. to raise the money.[96]

The growing number of placemen with no local connections with their boroughs significantly reduced the cost of wages but also put pressure on locals, especially Catholic merchants, to serve at lower rates or to forgo their salaries. In 1634 Cork city's Catholic MPs, Sir William Sarsfield and the recorder Dominic Coppinger, agreed to serve unpaid. This was a very noble offer as they would have been seriously out of pocket, and their going without wages may have been crucial in enabling the perennially hard-up city to resist official nominees.[97]

Hooker's statement that Irish wages were the same as English suggests that Athenry did not pay him, although when he represented his home town of Exeter

91 TCD, MS 843, pp 489–502.

92 James Hore to Boyle, 18 June 1615, Chatsworth House, Cork Papers, vol. 6, no. 37.

93 Caulfield (ed.), *Cork*, p. 42; Receipt for wages of John Myagh and Thomas Sarsfield, Cork, Nov. 1585, NLI, MS D. 25, 356,

94 McGrath, 'Fragment of the minute book'; BL, Harleian MS 430, pp 2–3, 62 (1637).

95 Common Council, London, *Order of the common council made on consideration of the instructions to Mr Proby and Mr Springham, and their report. 1 October 1616*, Appendix: vol. 1, Documents, Appendix, no. 84, pp 421–43, no. 24, pp 438–9.

96 McGrath (ed.), *Coleraine*, pp 61–2, 91, 95.

97 Caulfield (ed.), *Cork*, pp 174–5; McGrath, 'Sex, lies and rigged returns'.

in 1571 he claimed for an additional day and, as chamberlain, was responsible for collecting the money for his own wages.[98] The number of English cases for mis-returns that failed because they claimed incorrect damages for wages suggests strong competition for seats and widespread non-payment.[99] English MPs were apparently increasingly likely to receive wages, especially as the Long Parliament continued, even for towns which had previously not paid.[100] Some boroughs developed intriguing local practices to attract suitable representatives, such as London's payment of ferries to bring its members from their homes in the city to Blackfriars or Westminster and allowance for their and their servants clothes or Great Yarmouth giving its merchant MPs a quantity of fish to compensate them for their loss of profit during the herring season. There are no known Irish equivalents of these allowances.[101]

Scottish burgh commissioners (burgesses) were invariably paid, partly because they adhered rigidly to the residence requirements and 'a delegate theory of representation'. However, there was no single rate for payment or method of collection; they were frequently paid in advance, with any over-or under-payment rectified at the end of the session.[102] The 1587 Scottish act establishing shire representation provided that representatives should be paid, but no rate was specified until 1633, when the privy council set a flat fee of 300 merks (S£200) and the average cost was about S£50. After 1639 longer sessions made this inadequate and a daily rate of S£5 was established; this was less generous than it appears, as £1 sterling was worth 12 Scottish pounds and there were many complaints about the inadequacy of the payments.[103]

The French Estates General had complicated systems for raising the money for their members, with a different source of money for each of the three estates. On 25 March 1615, the king issued an order for deputies' wages, and meetings were held to organize the assessment and collection of the wages, so members had lengthy waits for payment, but significantly, all three estates were paid and the assessment system in at least some areas also levied the common costs of elections, including payments for clerks and messengers, on all the estates in an area. All sections of society contributed, from clergy, princes of the blood, widows and spinsters and inhabitants of rural areas without suffrage rights.[104]

98 Hooker, *Order and vsage*, in Holinshed, *Chronicles*, p. 122; N.M. Fuidge, 'Hooker, alias Vowell, John' in Hasler (ed.), *History of parliament*. Athenry was then open to outside nominations: in 1560 it had returned Thomas Cusack, who had no connection with the borough, but from 1585 it only returned its own citizens.

99 Hawkyard, *Commons*, pp 85–7.

100 Latham, 'Payment of parliamentary wages'.

101 Neale, *House*, pp 309–13; Hawkyard, 'Wages'; *idem*, *House of Commons*, pp 174–85.

102 MacDonald, *Burghs and parliament*, pp 83ff.

103 Hannay, and Watson, 'Building of the parliament house'; Kennedy, 'Representing the periphery'; MacDonald, '"Tedious to rehers?"'. For the bullion content of Scottish currency and its exchange rate with sterling, see A.J.S. Gibson and T.C. Smout, *Prices, food and wages in Scotland, 1500–1780* (Cambridge, 2007), pp 5–6.

104 Major, 'Payment of deputies'.

The Confederate's General Assembly set a daily rate of 10*s*. for knights of the shire and 5*s*. for burgesses, with no separate rate for citizens, with a travel allowance for 10 days before and after sessions. Micheál Ó Siochrú estimates the cost for the first assembly at over £3,500, had they all been paid. Clonmel levied money in October 1642 to pay its burgesses, but it would have been difficult for constituencies in Protestant hands for at least part of the period to raise money and all sections were under considerable financial pressure due to the war. Gilbert suggested some were remunerated in land or leases and some may have been paid out of central funds.[105]

Despite the established systems for collecting wages, some MPs found it difficult to get paid. In 1613–15 MPs for Cross Tipperary, Dublin, Louth, Mayo and Waterford faced protracted difficulties; in some cases only one county member was paid and the other was looking to parliament for support in extracting payment.[106] Despite Waterford's assessment raising £200, just over the actual amount due, parliament had to order the sheriff to make a recognisance for payment and provide an account of the monies received to the justices of the peace at the next quarter sessions.[107] The Grand Committee recommended an order, agreed on 5 May 1615, that sheriffs and mayors were to pay wages within two months of being shown a writ from the clerk of the Commons, on pain of being required to appear before the house to be censured, and, for sheriffs, a fine of £30, specified in 23 Hen. VI, c. 11, but there was no statutory provision for penalties for boroughs' officers. The Lord President of Munster's threat to billet soldiers on Youghal if the corporation did not pay the £12 10*s*. arrears for the agents in England in 1628 confirms that some money was paid in advance.[108] Waterford's rate for 1640 is unclear, but one of its MPs, Richard Butler, obtained an order against the city's sheriffs for payment of £27 15*s*. due to him.[109]

MPs could be censured for non-attendance without permission, the penalties including loss of wages and a fine, or both, in a system dating back to at least 1312.[110] Fines were a deterrent to absenteeism, especially for those serving unpaid. 17 members were fined and/or ordered to lose their wages on 8 May 1615. Fines varied between £5 and £20 and were generally remitted if MPs had a reasonable excuse, such as sickness, anticipated or actual death of relatives or being on crown business. On 7 April 1635, 11 MPs were fined between £10 and £50 for non-attendance, but no order was made about their wages, perhaps because several were

105 McGrath (ed.), *Clonmel*, p. 339; Bodl. Lib., Carte MS 68, fo. 4r; Ó Siochrú, *Confederate Ireland*, pp 53–4; Bellings and Gilbert (eds), *History of the Irish Confederation*, ii, p. 89.

106 All references from the *Commons' Jn. Ire.*, Cross Tipperary (6 May 1615), Dublin (1 May 1615), Louth (27 April 1615), Mayo (19 Nov. 1614) and Waterford (1–6 May 1615). Cantwell, sheriff of Waterford, paid £46 to one county member before May 1615.

107 Ibid., 6 May 1615.

108 Caulfield (ed.), *Cork*, p. 130; St Leger to the Mayor of Youghal, 22 Jan. 1629, Cork City Archives, MS YTR 1/47.

109 *Commons' Jn. Ire.*, 15 Feb. 1641. On Butler, see Appendix 3.

110 E.g., NAI, MS RC 8/7, pp 4, 7; ibid., C 59/14; ibid., M 10/16.

unpaid; the level of fines may have been related to the extent of their absences.[111] Six Catholic MPs who failed to attend the house in the summer of 1642 were expelled and ordered to lose their wages for that session and the previous one, although it is highly unlikely that wages were being paid at that point.[112] MPs could appeal their fines, but there was a fee for so doing.[113] Peers were fined one or two shillings depending on their rank if they did not appear within a quarter of an hour after prayers, the money all going to the poor (see chapter seven).[114]

SUBSIDIES

The taxation needed to meet the state's essential expenditure on defence and administration was traditionally linked to military obligations and land values and took no account of the rising incomes of groups such as merchants and lawyers. Customary practices produced inadequate amounts for early modern European states and were slow to change; resolving the rising demand for revenues and finding a balance between regular income for current expenditure and extraordinary taxes for emergencies or exigencies was a constant preoccupation of all contemporary states. Crown revenue was divided into ordinary and extraordinary, the former being what the monarch was entitled to by prerogative and the latter whatever could be raised by other means, including subsidies. Ordinary revenue was divided into certain income – crown rents, composition payments – and casual, such as fees for exports, profits from the Court of Wards, fines in courts including the Castle Chamber, payments for writs and especially customs.[115] Of course, some legislation also produced income for the state, such as fines in court for infringement and acts reforming customs and poundage. Some traditional events, such as the monarch's eldest daughter's marriage and eldest son's knighthood were accepted occasions for levies, but states used an increasing variety of new mechanisms to raise revenue, including general taxation. The incremental increase in the number and cost of all these impositions, and the obvious opportunities for profiteering led to great popular discontent.[116] James I resorted to many ways of increasing revenue, including instituting the order of baronets, selling peerages and granting monopolies. Charles I increased ship money, tunnage and poundage, monopolies and forced loans, as well as instituting a hard-line campaign to oblige men to take out knighthoods.[117]

111 *Commons' Jn. Ire.*, 7 April 1635.
112 These were the Catholics who were not known to be in rebellion and had therefore not already been expelled. Ibid., 9 Aug. 1642.
113 Ibid., 8, 11 April 1635.
114 *LJI*, 23 July 1634.
115 George O'Brien, *The economic history of Ireland in the seventeenth century* (Dublin, 1919).
116 McGrath (ed.), *Clonmel*, pp 109, 116; *Cal. S.P. Ire., 1625–32*, p. 244.
117 Mayes, 'Early Stuarts and the Irish peerage'; Charles I, *A proclamation for the ease of the subiects in making their compositions for not receiving the order of knighthood, according to the law* (London, 1630), dated 6 July 1630. For the knighthoods, which it was suggested should be extended to

Subsidies were the only taxes voted by parliament and subject to a popular, communal decision. They have received very little attention from scholars: even Michael Braddick's seminal work on financing the early modern English state devotes only four pages to parliamentary taxes before 1640, although, as he demonstrates, it represented a small and declining part of early seventeenth-century English state revenues and included tenths and fifteenths, property taxes no longer levied in Ireland, as well as subsidies.[118] Subsidies introduced in sixteenth-century England were assessed locally by the gentry, who habitually under-assessed themselves and their neighbours. Their value there consequently declined significantly from £130,000 in the middle of Elizabeth's reign to £55,000 by 1628.[119] Between 1640 and 1642, the inadequacy (from the administration's perspective) in the collection of the subsidy led to two new experiments: a poll tax and a quota tax.[120] By contrast, the value of Irish subsidies soared during this period (see below).

Non-parliamentary revenue-raising strategies included voluntary contributions, like those paid in Ireland in 1628–32 in the expectation of the Graces, fines on Catholics for not attending church, levies, customs and monopolies on commodities such as tobacco, wine, ale and brandy which were farmed out to individuals and syndicates who raked off considerable amounts of the proceeds to line their own pockets. In addition, there were local taxes in towns and counties, parish cess and tithes paid to the Church of Ireland and constant pressure to support the standing army by military cess and by having soldiers billeted directly on individuals and communities.[121] The growing numbers of obligations placed on counties and towns to construct, maintain and manage poor houses, court or session houses, tholsels, market houses, schools, bridges, gaols and houses of correction, along with maintaining highways and local courts, also represented a significant incremental cost to individuals and communities. In 1640, after a series

Ireland, 'The business of the fining of such as should at the coronation have tendered themselves to be knighted goes on very successfully with a general submission to it above expectation, which will cause some other designs for the king's profit to go on more cheerfully. I do believe that your lordship in time will hear of something of that nature for Ireland.' See Beecher to Cork, 28 April 1630, in Clarke, McGrath and Edwards (eds), *A lord justice's letterbook*, no. 68.

118 Michael J. Braddick, *The nerves of state: taxation and the financing of the English state, 1558–1714* (Manchester, 1996), pp 11–12, 91–5; Graves, *Parliaments*, p. 79. Fifteenths were levied in Ireland in 1320, NAI, MS EX 1/2; ibid., M 31, and tenths in 1339, NAI, MS RC 8/21, p. 354. Tenths were levied on ecclesiastical benefices in 1354–5, NAI, MS RC 8/26, pp 528, 687–8; Smith, *Stuart*, pp 50–1.

119 Ibid., pp 49–50. For the development of subsidies in England, see Maureen Jurkowski, Carrie L. Smith and David Crook, *Lay taxes in England and Wales, 1188–1688* (London, 1998), pp xli–xlv.

120 Michael J. Braddick, *Parliamentary taxation in seventeenth-century England: local administration and response* (Woodbridge, 1994), p. 127; J.V. Beckett and M.W. Barley's introduction to W.F. Webster (ed.), *Nottinghamshire hearth tax, 1664, 1674* (Nottingham, 1988).

121 For urban taxes, see McGrath, 'Reconstructing an early-modern Irish urban economic community'; *idem*, 'Fragment of the minute book'. For parish cess see Raymond Gillespie (ed.), *The vestry records of the parish of St John the Evangelist, Dublin, 1595–1658* (Dublin, 2002), pp 14–15.

of very poor harvests since 1637, a petition was drawn up in Ulster 'to stay the building of houses of correction in those parts till the subsidies be paid ... to forbid even good works as building of bridges except in places of great use duringe these necessitous times.'[122]

There was a growing resistance to all forms of revenue-raising by the administration, not merely among Catholics, although they were the hardest hit. Increasingly, Irish Catholics were excluded from benefiting from crown offices and opportunities for profit, but obliged to pay ever larger amounts of money to the crown. In 1627, Charles increased export duties and in the following year direct taxes were imposed by proclamation, a move that was both oppressive and illegal. Local communities had expressed dissatisfaction as far back as 1628 at the burden of the contributions, on top of the billeting of soldiers on individuals and communities. The mayor of Youghal wrote to the Lord President of Munster stating that the town could not pay any more military cess, being impoverished by the troops they were already hosting.[123] Richard Cheevers, mayor of Wexford and subsequently MP in 1634, complained to Falkland that the townsmen could not pay the billet for soldiers cessed upon them:

> the inhabitants of our said town do generally complain that they are, and have been very much overcharged in the disequality of the proportion of the intended subsidies that was granted by Parliament, amounting to 28 thousand and five hundred pounds ster., the province of Ulster being then exempted, the charge allotted upon our town of Wexford was no more than £100 ster., and now of three subsidies intended upon the whole kingdom to be paid in three years amounting in all unto 120 thousand pounds ster., this poor corporation hath hitherto been charged with two thousand and five pounds ster. *per annum* for soldiers intertainment, although we do not enjoy the benefit of his Majesty's grace, besides the charge.[124]

Cheevers was not alone in complaining loudly about the extortion of money at local level; in the same year the community of Cavan wrote to Falkland following a demand for £334 5*s*. 6*d*., stating that if

> the countrie shall refuse the soldiers to bee laide upon the countrie, either of which wilbee the utter ruine of the whole countrie which is brought to that povertie by payinge these heavie burdens for these three yeares and upward that is nowe come to passe that the dead burie the dead for hee that burieth the dead this day lyeth dead in the fields himselfe for want of foode as by the late peticon of the Graund Jury deliverd uppon oath and sent unto your

122 Bramhall to Wentworth, 16 April 1640, HL, HP, MS 14,059; *Commons' Jn. Ire.*, 17 June 1640.

123 The Mayor of Youghal to St Leger, 11 Dec. 1628, Cork City Archive, MS YTR1/68; RIA, MS 24/Q/5, no. 36, gives an account of these levies in Munster.

124 Cheevers to Falkland, 21 July 1629, in Philip Herbert Hore, *History of the town and county of Wexford*, 6 vols (London, 1900–11), v, p. 243.

> honors more at large doth appeare this is no fayned thing for if your lordships look but uppon the face of the whole kingdome they doe all for the most parte looke like the very pictures of death and doe daylie dye at [their] doores for want of foode where the best reliefe is to bee had more like doggs then Christians.[125]

The administration encountered serious opposition as the £120,000 given to Charles for the Graces was running out in 1632. The sheriff of Fermanagh, Edward Archdall, and the inhabitants of the county wrote separately to the lords justices, Lord Cork and Viscount Loftus, refusing to pay the £110 11*s*. 11*d*. levied to support the army for three months; the sheriff reported,

> they absolutely refused to give any assistance complaining grievously of the poverty that this poor county is already reduced unto occasioned chiefly by the great payment that they have formerly yielded unto in this kind. Neither they say will they consent or give way to the collection of any further sums of money towards the payment of the Army upon the plots and proffers of the Recusants as they suppose. But do humbly desire that if [Catholics] have made proffers to his Majesty for the payment of the Army for a year that they may bear the burden thereof themselves who are to receive far greater benefit thereby if the Presentments against the Recusants be suppressed.

The signatories, who were overwhelmingly Scottish, included Lord Balfour and Bishop James Heygate of Kilfenora and his son-in-law, the future MP Henry Manning, maintained that 'by the laws of this Realm, or by any consent of our own, we are not bound.' The lords justices forwarded this letter to the English privy council, describing the signatories as 'knights and gentry', although most were of low social status.[126] A document was prepared for consideration by either the 1634 or 1640 parliament seeking restitution for money exacted after the £120,000 was fully paid, although there is no record of its having been debated.[127]

European representative assemblies' power of granting subsidies gave them a bargaining tool with the crown: 'it was important for a Parliament to establish the principle of redress of grievances before supply.'[128] The English parliament refused to grant subsidies in 1604, 1610 and 1614, and James only summoned the 1621 Scottish Estates after failing to secure a voluntary 'benevolence' the previous year.[129]

125 Scott, 'Petition of the inhabitants of Cavan'.

126 Edward Archdall, sheriff of Fermanagh, to the Lords Justice, 26 Feb. 1633, The nobility and gentry of Fermanagh to the Lords Justice, 27 Feb. 1633, Cork to Beecher, 2 April 1633, all in Clarke, McGrath and Edwards (eds), *A lord justice's letterbook*, nos 233–5. Heygate held lands in Fermanagh.

127 Considerations to be commended to the Parliament touching the restitution of moneys exacted from the Subiects of Ireland after the 120000li was paid, RIA, MS 24/Q/5, no. 4.

128 Koenigsberger, quoted in Smith, *Stuart*, p. 51.

129 John Cramsie, 'Crown finance and reform: the legacy of the Addled Parliament' in Clucas and Davies (eds), *The crisis of 1614 and the Addled Parliament*, pp 37–48.

French kings did not summon the Estates General between 1615 and 1789, although local estates continued to meet and were the usual mechanism for taxation in the reducing number of provinces where they met.[130] In Castile, a bewildering array of local systems was used for raising any taxes agreed in the Corts.[131]

The first subsidy request in an Irish parliament was in 1300, but in general, apart from William Windsor's extortionate revenue-raising in the 1370s, Irish subsidies yielded disappointingly little for the state before 1613.[132] They were worth *c.*£300 before 1476, and although they increased up to 1540, they declined thereafter and were no inducement for the administration to summon parliaments, although Sidney advanced them as one reason for summoning the 1569 parliament. His was the only one of Elizabeth's Irish parliaments to vote subsidies (for ten years as from 1566), and as they were charged only on the Pale and intermittently in Kilkenny, they brought in very little money – on average only £311 7*s*. 5*d*. in the early years of Elizabeth's reign and a mere £200 in 1574–5.[133] The old system of subsidies was unsatisfactory, as it had developed when only part of the country was under crown control, it distinguished between tilled and untilled land, and the measure used, the ploughland, was variable.[134]

The shortfall in Ireland's revenue was made up by heavy transfers of money from England and military cess, which was announced by way of proclamation, rather than act of parliament and its inequitable application caused great resentment. Even a hostile English observer, Edmund Skory, MP for Augher in 1613, acknowledged its unfairness, especially compared to subsidies:

> There must be no Cess vpon in [sic] the Country in tyme of peace, for it is so vncerteine that it comes nowe and then vpon one man twice in a moneth, and vpon his next neighbour not once in 5 yeres. But subsedies, tenths, and fifteenes must be graunted to your Majesty which will fall out equally.[135]

The Irish situation changed dramatically after Kinsale, when the whole island came under crown control, significantly increasing the need for finance to administer the state and to support the standing army, but opening up the possibility of raising tax from the entire country. State revenues increased dramatically after 1611–12, due largely to rents and compositions from Ulster, but a significant shortfall

130 Graves, *Parliaments*, p. 118.

131 Charles Jago, 'Habsburg absolutism and the *Cortes* of Castile', *American Historical Review*, 86:2 (April, 1981), 307–26.

132 Emmett O'Byrne, 'Windsor, William, Baron Windsor', *DIB*.

133 Richardson and Sayles, *Irish parliament in the Middle Ages*, p. 67; Crooks, 'Representation and dissent'; Ellis, 'Parliament and community'; Elizabeth to Sidney, 16 Jan. 1567, TNA, SP 63/20, fo. 18; Quinn, 'Irish parliamentary subsidy'; Moody, 'Irish parliament under Elizabeth and James I'; Edwards, *Ormond lordship*, pp 145, 182.

134 Chichester to Salisbury, 23 Feb. 1612, *Cal. S.P. Ire., 1611–14*, p. 248.

135 McGrath, 'Unmasking "E.S."'. For tenths and fifteenths, see Braddick, *Nerves of state*, pp 91–5.

remained, as James' financial problems in England and Scotland reduced subventions from England.[136]

The preamble to the 1613 subsidy act underlined this change; for the first time, no mention was made of the need for defence, but linked the grants to James' peaceful government of Ireland and concern for his servants, while begging him to accept the subsidy 'as the first fruits of this your poore kingdome of Ireland'.[137] On Davies' advice, Chichester's parliament changed the old system of 13*s.* 4*d.* per ploughland to the English system of 2*s.* 8*d.* per pound on personal goods and 4*s.* in the pound on property throughout the country, payable in two equal amounts on 1 September 1615 and six months later. Aliens paid double those amounts; clergy also paid 4*s.* in the pound on 'their promotions spiritual' in 1613, as well as voting a single subsidy in Convocation, although the bill enacting this was stalled as Catholic MPs objected to its offensive preamble.[138] Ridgeway estimated that the Commons subsidy would raise £30,000 sterling and the assessment on peers and privy councillors £900 sterling. The 1615–16 subsidy probably came to £40,000, the sum on which Catholic agents offered the equivalent of three subsidies for the Graces.[139]

Subsidies' traditional role as a bargaining chip for MPs changed under the Stuarts. Chichester claimed priests and Jesuits persuaded Catholics to hold off granting a subsidy until they saw how parliament went.[140] In 1615 John Sutton proposed 'that in regard it tended to the king's private profit, it might be deferred; alleging, that the old saying would else be verified, "little said soon amended, A subsidy granted, the Parliament ended."' To the administration's amazement, there was no resistance to the 1615 subsidy bill, possibly, McCavitt suggests, because of the threat of the return of O'Neill, despite Sutton's plea that it be deferred until 'other acts that tended to the common good of the weale publick were first read' and the Catholics' proposal to commit it to agree how to assess and collect it was defeated. Chichester sought to make the subsidy more palatable by imposing higher levies on privy councillors, judges and serjeants-at-law.[141] Everard, noting the alacrity with which it had passed,

136 McCavitt, *Arthur Chichester*, pp 37–41; David Edwards, 'Political change and social transformation, 1603–1641' in Ohlmeyer (ed.), *Cambridge history of Ireland*, pp 48–71, esp. pp 51ff.

137 Acte for the grauntinge of one entire subsidie by the temporalitye, 11 Jac. I, c. 5. Convocation voted for a single subsidy from the clergy on 28 April 1615, TCD, MS 1,062, p. 49; *Commons' Jn. Ire.*, 29 April 1615; An Act for Confirmation of the subsidy granted by the clergy, TCD, MS 1,062, pp 351–9; 11–13, Jac. I, c. 10.

138 This rate was originally unsuccessfully proposed in England by Wolsey in 1523 to raise money for the French war. Graves, *Parliaments*, p. 79; Davies, Propositions for the encrease of his majesties revenue, Bodl. Lib., Carte MS 62, fo. 140; Acte for the grauntinge of one entire subsidie by the temporalitye, 11 Jac. I, c. 5. The 1569 Commons voted for a subsidy of 13*s.* 4*d.* on the ploughland: Falkiner, *Essays*, p. 239; Treadwell, 'House of Lords'.

139 Ridgeway to Sir Ralph Winwood, 7 Aug. 1615, TNA, SP 63/233, fo. 89; McCavitt, *Arthur Chichester*, p. 205, estimates IR£33,000. Bray (ed.), *Records of convocation: Ireland, 1101–1690*, pp 376–9.

140 Chichester to James, 16 Oct. 1614, TNA, SP 63/232, fos. 193–4.

141 *Commons' Jn. Ire.*, 25 April 1615; McCavitt, *Arthur Chichester*, pp 197–205 provides a very useful reconstruction of the politics of the grant of the subsidy. BL, Add. MS 29,314, fos. 153–4.

> upon the knees of his heart, in the behalf of his country, he humbly prayeth, that the statutes of the second year of the reign of Queen Elizabeth may be something moderated for a time, which being granted, he doubteth not, but if the king be willing to demand hereafter, two, three, or four, subsidies, as hath been willing to condescend to this, so he doubteth not of any denial hereafter.

He repeated this request on 13 May 1615.[142] The Catholic agents' offer of £120,000 to Charles in 1628 reduced their bargaining position, as the crown had already received any taxation it might have expected from parliament without granting any concessions; in addition, Falkland planned a subsidy bill in 1629, which would have doubled the Irish contribution to the crown, unless it took account of what had already been paid.[143]

Chichester introduced the subsidy bill in what transpired to be the last session of parliament after other legislation had been dealt with, partly because of delays in transmitting the bill back to Ireland, but Wentworth eliminated MPs' negotiating power by the commissions' specifying that parliament would end unless the subsidies bills were passed within 21 or 30 days.[144] Kilmallock and Gormanston complained that Wentworth had subverted the normal order of business 'by proroguing the parliament after your subjects had chearfully supplied your Majestys occasions before their grievances were heard or examined which they were by his lordship promised.'[145] Cork reflected this sense of balance between legislation and redress of grievances in a letter to Ormonde at the opening of the 1640 parliament, which he did not attend:

> I presume that after good lawes are enacted, a following subsedie will be demanded, unto which (although the late Subsedyes were very heavy, and burthensome, and remayne yet fresh in memory, Yet considering how good, and gratious a king wee live peaceably vnder, And his present occasions in the raysing, and mayntenance of an Army, I shalbe as forward as any may to yeild him Subsedyes, soe as wee may be now proportionably rated according the former & accustomed taxations in Parlyament of the nobility in England, with due respect and difference between theire estates, and ours. But to be charged by future Subsedyes in landes, as I was the last Parlyament at £3000 per annum, and to pay £3600 as I did, being neere (if not altogether as much) as all the lords of the privy Councell in England payd at the last Parlyament before, I know if seasonably propounded by your Lordship, [Wentworth] will take into his serious and Judicious consideration, and ease me of the like now. I beseech your lordship [to] interpose your persuasions for a moderate assesment when the opportunitie and tyme wilbe fitting.

142 *Commons' Jn. Ire*, 27 April 1615.
143 Falkland's list of bills for parliament, 1629, Chatsworth House, Cork Papers, vol. 16, no. 163.
144 See chapter five.
145 Gormanston and Kilmallock's petition to the King, Feb. 1641, TNA, SP 63/258, p. 163.

Ormond claimed Cork's letter had arrived too late for him to act, 'so that I have [not] the happiness to serve you by tymely offering those good reasons for your ease in the subsedyes, which is already aportioned on the nobility.'[146] Cork had complained in almost identical terms to Lord Bristol in 1636 about the heavy and unfair burden of the subsidy. As the cost of subsidies on land (as opposed to goods) was passed on as far as possible onto tenants, Wentworth declared that Cork's tenants paid his £3,600, rather than the earl himself, although this was unlikely, as Cork generally granted leases which could not easily be changed; he had paid all his assessment by 1638.[147]

While the income from subsidies was welcome, they were granted for a limited period, after which the state had either to call another parliament to grant more, or find alternative ways of raising money. Given the work involved in summoning parliament and the English and Scottish parliaments' refusal to grant money, it is unsurprising that alternative sources were first investigated. Falkland summoned the Great Assembly of peers in April 1627 to raise a voluntary contribution to support the army; however, the crown had few inducements to persuade the agents to vote money and the gentry 'cried out for a parliament to rectify abuses.' When Lord Westmeath replied that they had no authority to grant money from their communities, Falkland angrily retorted 'if their Lords could claim to represent the country on such a matter, they could undertake for it'. Despite a heavy-hitting speech by Ussher ('you must give me leave (as a Devine) to tell you plainely, that supplie the king with meanes for the necessary defence of the the Countrey, is not a thing left to your discretion, either to doe or not doe; but a matter of Duety, which in Conscience you stand bound to performe. [Refusing to supply Charles] can be accounted Robbinge him of that which is his due') the agents refused to provide money.[148]

Ensuring adequate revenue for the state was one of Wentworth's priorities and he used parliament to effect it. Borlase cited only financial reasons for summoning the 1634 parliament. First, there was a need to raise money, as the contribution towards the army ended in December 1634. Additionally, the current revenues left an annual shortfall of £20,000 and the crown had debts of £80,000. Borlase also stated that no subsidies had been granted for almost 20 years, although this was true only insofar as parliament had not met to authorize taxation, as the £120,000 contribution was always described as subsidies and the original intention of the

146 Cork to Ormond, 16 March 1640, Ormond to Cork, 23 April 1640, BL, Add. MS 19,832, fos. 47, 49. For the assessment of peers, see TNA, MS E179/70/145A, and for an order that Irish peers resident in England be required to pay Irish subsidies, see Bodl. Lib., Bankes MS 10/1, 9 June 1640.

147 Cork to Bristol, 29 May 1635, Chatsworth House, Cork Papers, Misc. boxes, Box 3, p. 125. I am grateful to Aidan Clarke for drawing this reference to my attention. Wentworth to Sir John Coke, 7 April 1635, in Knowler (ed.), *Letters and dispatches*, i, p. 407; Ohlmeyer, *Making Ireland English*, p. 404; Cork to Wentworth, 11 June 1638, RIA, MS 24/Q/5, no. 26.

148 *Cal. S.P. Ire., 1625–32*, pp 244–6; Raymond Gillespie, *Seventeenth-century Ireland* (Dublin, 2006), pp 74–7. For Ussher's speech, see BL, Add. MS 72,414, fos. 90–4.

Old English in agreeing to pay the first instalment in advance of the summoning of the parliament intended for 1628 had been that they were *de facto* popularly agreed and would be confirmed by legislation.[149]

There was a general acceptance that subsidies were fairer than other forms of revenue-raising and Chichester's subsidy was assessed proportionately.[150] However, apart from inserting into the commissions for both of his parliaments a proviso that parliament would be dissolved if the subsidy bills were not passed within a few weeks of its meeting, Wentworth used strong-arm tactics to raise their value and the assessment process was not impartial. He threatened the maximum possible rating to pressurize MPs into agreeing a fixed sum for each county, with a further £6,000 from peers and £3,000 from clergy. As a result, assessors in each county had to rate individuals and organizations to bring in the sum allocated on the shire rather than objectively rating each taxpayer's actual assets, although it was possible to appeal assessments. The first four subsidies voted in 1634 came to £40,000 each and the final two to £45,000 each, a total of £250,000. The justification for the higher final subsidies was that only one was paid per year.[151] This was a massive imposition, especially compared to England where the 1626–7 forced loan had raised £243,000, the equivalent of four subsidies there; in addition, the 1634 parliament passed an act whereby clergy were subject to eight subsidies. However, a bill extending the custom of poundage to imports into Dublin, Drogheda, Galway and Waterford, which had formerly been exempt, failed to pass.[152] In January 1640, the English privy council transmitted two subsidies bills for the Commons, one for four subsidies and the other for six; four were immediately agreed, with a declaration of willingness to provide more, but Wentworth had originally planned for six over three years, a very heavy burden for the country, especially since military cess and other fines and contributions continued to be imposed, despite the dramatic increase in the number and value of the subsidies.[153] Using the 1634 system, four subsidies would have yielded £160,000, but political opposition reduced this to £81,000, of which less than £68,000 was paid, including the peers' and clergy's contributions to the first subsidy, and therefore less from the temporality.[154] The remonstrance of the Commons on 7 November 1640 cited, in addition to the burden of the 1634 subsidies, the decline in trade as a result of new impositions on native commodities, monopolies, fees in courts and other grievances. Subsidies voted in Convocation (confirmed by acts of parliament) also

149 Borlase, *History*, p. 3; Clarke, *Old English*, pp 53–6.

150 Braddick, *Nerves of state*, pp 93–5; A remonstrance humbly presented to the honourable council of state for the speedy raising of money in the ancient way by subsidy, n.d., Birr Castle, MS A/5/72.

151 Wentworth to Sir John Coke, 7 April 1635, in Knowler (ed.), *Letters and dispatches*, i, pp 400–4.

152 Bray (ed.), *Records of convocation: Ireland, 1101–1690*, p. 398.

153 Bodl. Lib., Bankes MS 65/59, 28 Jan. 1639–40; Clarke, *Old English*, p. 127; Wentworth to Radcliffe, 10 Dec. 1639, in Whitaker (ed.), *Life and original correspondence*, p. 188.

154 *Commons' Jn. Ire.*, 10 March 1635; Perceval-Maxwell, *Outbreak*, p. 72; The produce of the revenue for 1640 and 1641, Gilbert Library, MS 205, fo. 1r.

increased to eight in 1634 (running from 1635 to 1642) three of which were unpaid in 1640, to six, payable over three years, in 1640.[155]

Table 8.1. Subsidies from the Commons, 1613–41

Parliament	*No. of subsidies*	*Payable*	*Total amount*
1613–15	1	1615–16	IR£30,000–IR£40,000
1634–5	6	1634 to 1638	£250,000
1640–1	4	1 June 1640 to Dec. 1641	£180,000
1640 Reduction			Reduced to £12,000 per subsidy for the last three subsidies[156]

Similar staggering increases in taxation took place in Scotland in the first half of the seventeenth century. Apart from the traditional aids, including S£240,000 in four annual instalments for Elizabeth of Bohemia's marriage, Prince Henry's knighthood and war, James' requests for money included a further S£200,000 on his visit to Scotland in 1617, and a further request for a voluntary contribution in 1620 to defend James' son-in-law's territories in the Palatinate. A new system of taxation was also introduced there; by the late sixteenth century, benefice-holders (those who held old church lands, including dissolved abbeys), paid 50% of parliamentary taxes, burghs, barons and freeholders 33% and boroughs 17%.[157] Scottish tax was not broken down by estates and there was no separate assessment for nobles; under the new system, the burden fell far more heavily on the burghs, 'each of which raised its share by internal assessment.' In 1625, the Convention of Estates offered an 'ordinary' tax of S£400,000 payable annually until 1628 with an additional extraordinary tax on rents, which was renewed by the 1630 Convention of Estates until 1633 at the same rate. In that year, when Charles was crowned in Edinburgh, parliament granted the same 'ordinary tax' for six years and the extraordinary tax on rents, raised from a 20th penny to 16*d*., for the same period.[158] Hannay and Watson demonstrate that Charles' incessant demands for money, by taxation and for the construction of the parliament house, were significant contributors, along with liturgical changes, in the outbreak of trouble between Charles and his Scottish subjects.[159]

Anyone with property or valuable goods, except minors and heralds, was liable to pay subsidies, including widows and presumably spinsters with assets; in 1615

155 TCD, MS 1,062, pp 49, 61, 64–6, 351–69; 11–13 Jac. I, c. 10; 10 Car. I, c. 23; Smith, *Stuart*, p. 50; Bray (ed.), *Records of convocation: Ireland, 1101–1690*, p. 398.

156 Borlase, *History*, p. 7; Clarke, *Old English*, p. 132.

157 Hannay and Watson, 'Building of the parliament house'.

158 Julian Goodare, 'Parliamentary taxation in Scotland, 1560–1603', *Scottish Historical Review*, 63:1 (April, 1989), 23–52; MacDonald, *Burghs and parliament*, pp 94–8.

159 Hannay and Watson, 'Building of the parliament house'.

all the dowager peeresses were assessed, with Lady Ormonde being rated at £200, and all the others at between £30 and £50.[160] The system of separate payments by all three estates operated also in England and France.[161] Clergy were liable for subsidies on their secular lands, and Bramhall was given an estimate of £65 12*s*. 6*d*. for the first lay subsidy on his Meath property in 1640.[162] Corporate bodies, like the Guild of St Anne's and the College in Youghal were also liable for subsidies, but Trinity College Dublin was exempt and there is no mention of subsidy payments in the King's Inns' accounts.[163]

Peers resenting that the proxies of absentee Englishmen with Irish peerages were used to vote on subsidies which they did not have to pay petitioned Wentworth that men with Irish peerages should have to purchase Irish lands to the value of £200–£300 (depending on rank) and a bill was drafted to that effect; Wentworth refused, on the grounds of Poynings' Law, although an act was passed in the third session 'whereby certain of the nobility of this kingdom of Ireland dwelling within England or elsewhere out of this realm are made liable unto certain charges within this kingdom', but this would only apply to those with property in Ireland.[164] However, on 9 June 1640, Charles asked the attorney general John Bankes to 'direct a Course for certifying into th'Exchequer here, and afterwards for Levying to his Majestys use, such Sommes of money as are, or shalbe assessed upon the Irish Nobility residing here in England.'[165]

Under 19–20 Edw. IV, c. 21, MPs were responsible for appointing assessors and collectors, and under 2 Ric. III, c. 17, also for recommending sufficient collectors' names. 18 Hen. VI, c. 5 specified that collectors from corporate towns had to be able to dispend £100 annually 'above all reprizals within the same Countie.'[166]

160 Nobility of Ireland rated to the subsidie by the Right Honorable Sir Arthur Chichester knight ... with the advise of such as are Authorised thereunto by the Statute, 8 July 1615, BL, Add. MS 29,314, fos. 152ff; NLI, GO, MS 14, pp 19–23, 43–4, exempting Thomas Preston and Albon Leverett. Heralds were also exempt in Scotland. Goodare, 'Parliamentary taxation in Scotland'; Representative Church Body Library, MS 23, p. 111, Subsidy rolls for Shankill Parish, Armagh, includes Alice Smith, widow, at £3; Subsidy Rolls, Dublin City, 1637, NAI, MS M. 2,469, unpaginated, includes Grace Keyser, Grace Southwell, Judith Jacob, Mrs Mary Chetams, and Margaret Hayes, all widows. The subsidy rolls for St Catherine's Parish Dublin, 1637, included Joane Keysar, Joane Southwell, and Judith Jacob, who also appears in the previous list. Herbert Wood (ed.), *Registers of the parish of St Catherine, Dublin, 1636–1715* (Dublin, 2003), pp 233–5.

161 Major, 'Payment of deputies'; Bray (ed.), *Records of convocation: Ireland, 1101–1690*, pp 397–8, 401.

162 HL, HP, MS 14,058.

163 Account book of St Anne's Guild, RIA, MS 12/D/1, p. 144, where under disbursements of the clerk of the guild, 1639–40, it is noted, 'Mr John Ashe subcollector of the subsidies for subsidie imposed on the lands of St Anns guilde (viz) for the first paiement of the 4 intire subsidies as per Receipt apeereth £2'; Grosart (ed.), *Lismore Papers*, 1st series, i, p. 124, where under 26 Aug. 1616 Boyle noted, 'I paid Mr Davids the deputy Register 29 nobles ster: for the last payment of his majesty subsidy taxed on the colledg of yoghall.' The King's Inns' accounts for Feb. to May 1636 do not mention payments of subsidies. King's Inns, MS B1/1, fos. 60v–1r, nor Particular book, TCD, MS MUN. 1/1; NLI, MS 643, fo. 15r.

164 Kearney, *Strafford in Ireland*, pp 51ff; Ohlmeyer, *Making Ireland English*, pp 367–70.

165 Windebank to Bankes, 9 June 1640, Bodl. Lib., Bankes MS 10/1.

166 Quinn, 'Irish parliamentary subsidy'; Merick, *Compendious collection*, p. 86.

In 1615, the county members and two burgesses from each shire nominated commissioners for levying subsidies, and assessors and collectors were nominated and appointed by warrants issued by the clerk of the petty bag in the exchequer to sheriffs.[167] The administration's attempt to take control of the assessment and collection of the subsidies was reversed by the Commons in the second session of the 1640 parliament.[168] This again represented a difference with the English parliament, which only appointed its own commissioners for collection in the first subsidy act of 1641. Earlier commissioners were appointed under the great seal and collection was through justices of the peace.[169]

In 1615, warrants were issued to commissioners for each county, together with detailed instructions and '7 to 8 subsidy books' and, presumably, the printed subsidy act. Time was tight, as the act specified that the first payment from the laity was to be on 1 September, but the process was well under way by 7 August, although the collection in Munster was very slow.[170] The first payments demanded from the clergy in November 1615 and March 1616 must have been for their temporal lands.[171] The Commons retained control of the method of collection and in 1635 a committee composed of nine Catholics and 11 Protestants drafted the instructions for the commissioners and also restricted their number to six in each county.[172] For those with property in more than one county, the Commons ordered

> that every man, that is chargeable with the subsidy, shall be charged within the place of his residence, both for the estate which he hath in the county, and for that which he hath in other counties; of which estate in other counties the commissioners of whose counties are to make certificate to the commissioners, where he is resident, what estate he hath within their several counties in lands and goods; and upon that certificate the commissioners, where he is resident, are to assess him according either to his lands or goods; and the several commissioners, which shall make the certificate, shall be discharged of so much as they shall certify.[173]

In St Catherine's Parish, Dublin, property outside the area was noted in the 1637 assessment and Bramhall's Meath assessment was certified to the Londonderry collectors in 1640.[174]

167 TCD, MS 647, fo. 89v. I am grateful to Jacqueline van den Bergh and Joel Herman for drawing this reference to my attention.
168 Clarke, *Old English*, pp 132–3.
169 16 Car. I, c. 1; Russell, 'Monarchies'.
170 Ridgeway to Winwood, 7 Aug. 1615, TNA, SP 63/233, fo. 89; Curtis Clayton (ed.), *Council book*, p. 76; Empey (ed.), *Early Stuart Irish warrants*, pp 209, 216–17.
171 TCD, MS 1,062, p. 354; Bishop of Cork to Richard Boyle, 19 Oct. 1615, Chatsworth House, Cork Papers, vol. 6, no. 73; Bray (ed.), *Records of convocation: Ireland, 1101–1690*, pp 376–9.
172 *Commons' Jn. Ire.*, 19–20 March 1635, 14, 17 April 1635.
173 Ibid., 16 March 1635.
174 Wood (ed.), *Registers*, pp 233–5; HL, HP, MS 14,058.

Collecting subsidies throughout the country was a huge operation, involving men at every level and, given that 1615 was the first all-Ireland subsidy, its collection was very efficiently implemented. Ridgeway estimated the number of assessors at between 400 and 500 for the whole country. Assessments started with the commissioners and assessors rating themselves, and Ridgeway noted that their assessments were above the English levels. The second subsidy collected in Cork in April 1616, was managed through the quarter sessions.[175] In Dublin and Armagh in the 1630s the collection was made at parish level and the collectors in the capital included the mayor and recorder, at least two aldermen and two administration officials. In Shankill Parish, Armagh, in 1634, the subsidy roll assessment for goods, not land, contained 38 names, including 25 yeomen, seven gentlemen, two tanners, two 'webtters' (sic), one merchant and a single widow, cessed at between £3 and £10 each (a gentleman and a yeoman paid the highest rate), a total of £160.[176] The £61 4*s*. 9*d*. collected in Bandon in 1636 for the 'three rates made on the town' were presumably for three subsidies and in 1637 St Catherine's Parish, Dublin recorded £124 0*s*. 4*d*., plus £17 16*s*. 6*d*. 'intimated' from other areas; most of this money was assessed on goods, rather than land.[177] In 1637, Robert Tinte Jr, under-collector for Cork, took action against 19 named collectors for defaulting on their responsibilities, indicating the scale of the effort and personnel involved in bringing in the subsidies.[178]

As collection was managed locally, under the aegis of the exchequer, problems were referred to the Court of Exchequer, but also occasionally to the Court of Castle Chamber. Cork's commissioners for the second subsidy in 1616 were threatened with fines of £100 if they did not speedily collect the money; soldiers were used to try to force payment in Cork and Limerick.[179] In 1615, problems related to the shortage of coinage and the unmonetized state of many old Gaelic areas, the economies of which were often not based on currency. This had been foreseen by the MP John Moore, who suggested that in 'places, where money is not to be spared, there cattle, corn, etc., might be taken', a proposal MPs had already made to Chichester in October 1614, a time of acute currency shortages.[180] In 1617, William Harrison, collector in Sligo, seized mares and garrans from Sir Thomas Bourke for his subsidy payments and refused to restore them despite a former order:

175 *Commons' Jn. Ire.*, 26 April 1615; Ridgeway to Winwood, 7 Aug. 1615, TNA, SP 63/233, fo. 89; Richard Aldworth to Richard Boyle, 12 April 1616, Chatsworth House, Cork Papers, vol. 7, no. 15; Thomond to Serjeant Robert Flower, Sept. 1616, Chatsworth House, Cork Papers, vol. 7, no. 114; Dominic Tyrry to Boyle, Dec. 1616, Chatsworth House, Cork Papers, vol. 7, no. 200.
176 Representative Church Body Library, MS 23, p. 111; Wood (ed.), *Registers*, p. 235.
177 Bennett, *Bandon*, p. 96.
178 NAI, Ferguson MS 12, pp 350–1.
179 Lords Justice to the Commissioners in Cork, 17 July 1616, Chatsworth House, Cork Papers, vol. 7, no. 64.
180 Chichester to James, 16 Oct. 1614, TNA, SP 63/232, fos. 193v–4r. I am grateful to Gerard Farrell for a useful discussion on the un-monetized nature of Gaelic society. *Commons' Jn. Ire.*, 26 April 1615. See also McGrath, 'Unmasking "E.S."'; Keith Pluymers, 'Cow trials, climate change and the causes of violence', *Environmental History*, 25:2 (2020), 287–309.

> Feeagh Bourke McDavid of Downanmane, Galway, being sessed & taxed in subsidy in £4 St for 2 payments being also cessed in Co. Roscommon, where he is not resident at 40*s.* 6*d.*, Michael Pynnock high collector distrained garrans to the value of £4 contrary to statute.[181]

They were ordered to be restored. In 1618, the Court of Castle Chamber censured, fined and imprisoned the collectors in Ballinacor Barony, Wicklow, for taking the second subsidy payment in sterling, rather than Irish money as their instructions specified and they were ordered to make restitution.[182]

Collecting the six subsidies granted in 1634 represented a significant administrative and financial burden; dissatisfaction was muted but evident. Three of the clerical subsidies remained unpaid by 1640, a significant proportion of New Ross' taxpayers resisted their local assessments, and the sub-collectors of Kilkenny city were in arrears in February 1639.[183] Moreover, the assessments were far from impartial. In St Catherine's Parish, Wentworth's associates (all MPs) were assessed at improbably low rates: Robert Ferrar at £20, Wandesford at £30, Sir William Anderson £18, Thomas Little £25 and Lord Robert Dillon £13, despite his extensive property outside Dublin.[184] Cork complained bitterly about his heavy assessment of £3,600, Mountnorris also objected to being assessed at £1,000, claiming that 'men of farre greater visible and knowne estates are not charged with halfe that proportion.' Their resentment was justified, as peers collectively paid only £6,000.[185] In 1637, the merchant James French, collector for Sligo, took action against the commissioners for that county.[186] There were also cases in Tipperary, Longford and Carlow in 1637, although the substance of each case was not recorded, they included overcharging and double-charging, presumably on those holding land in more than one area.[187] It is also unclear how many other New

181 Equity exchequer orders, 1604–18, NAI, Ferguson MS 11, pp 216–17.

182 Crawford, *Star Chamber*, p. 331.

183 McGrath, 'Fragment of the minute book'; Copy of an order concerning the payment of £25 arrears for the second payment of four entire subsidies, 1 Feb. 1639, KCA, MS CR/K/40. Michael Langton and Peter Archer, sub-collectors of the city under the high collector, Walter Cantwell, were being pursued for the full amount. Their affidavit explained why they could not levy £10 7*s.* 6*d.* and they were given time to pay.

184 Dublin Subsidy Roll, 1637, NAI, M 2,469.

185 Cork to Bristol, 29 May 1635, Chatsworth House, Cork Papers, Misc. boxes, Box 3, p. 125; Receipts for £1200, Chatsworth House, Cork Papers, vol. 18, no. 111, 151–2, vol. 19, no. 51; Demand from Wentworth for £1200, 11 April 1636, Chatsworth House, Cork Papers, vol. 18, no. 130. Mountnorris, 'Humble petition … to the … Knights, Citizens and Burgesses, of the Commons House of Parliament' in T. Cadell and W. Davies (eds), *A collection of scarce and valuable tracts on the most entertaining subjects: reign of King Charles I* (London, 1810), pp 203–5. Lord Huntington was assessed at only £40 for each of the subsidies agreed in 1625. See Bickley (ed.), *Hastings, Volume II*, pp 68, 70.

186 Mary O'Dowd, *Power, politics and land: early modern Sligo, 1568–1688* (Belfast, 1991), p. 59. Abstract of equity exchequer orders, NAI, Ferguson MS 11, pp 216–17; NAI, Ferguson MS 12, pp 352, 355.

187 NAI, Ferguson MS 12, pp 348–52. Daniel Ryan was sub-collector in Tipperary.

English benefitted, as Philip Percival did, from grants of land which included special exemptions from parliamentary and other taxes.[188] The identity of all the commissioners and collectors is unknown, but it is clear that in many cases Catholics were appointed to ensure compliance and take the opprobrium for assessments. In 1634, Sligo's commissioners included MPs Farrell O'Gara and Teige O'Connor, and Bryan McDonogh, Ross Owan McDermott, Teige O'Higgin and Tybbott Taaffe, but only three Protestants, the former sheriff Jasper Brett and William and Thomas Crofton.[189]

In Scotland, the Convention of Royal Burghs kept a close eye on how their taxes were gathered and apportioned between burghs. In France, collection costs could amount to 33% of the total. As Major noted, early modern France was not under-taxed, but very little of what was collected reached the crown. Wentworth insisted the collection charge be limited to 6*d.* in the pound in 1635, but Anthony Stowell claimed that 'More is collected than ever goes into the Exchequer.'[190]

Under Wentworth, the burden of ever-higher subsidies on top of all of these other payments was deeply felt, especially as land titles were insecure and plantations in Connacht and Ormond threatened to take up to 87% of the old proprietors' lands. The grant of four subsidies in March 1640 marked the high point of Wentworth's government of Ireland and he left immediately, to attempt the same feat in England in the following month. However, despite both houses vying to appear most enthusiastic in their support for Charles, resistance to paying the subsidies began to appear almost immediately. A petition from divers knights and gentry of Dublin, Meath, Louth and Westmeath objected to the detail in the preamble to the bill on applotting the new subsidies and claimed that 'the raising of the last subsidies to a certainty pilled the poor and disabled the rich, brought down rents, wasted lands and drew the spunge of the Commonwealth dry.'[191] It also noted the crushing weight of the subsidies so soon after the previous ones and objected to the privy council's infringing parliament's right to manage the subsidies' assessment and collection. The collection of the first subsidy started before the necessary order was issued, prompting an immediate appeal to parliament by 'divers knights and gentry' of Leinster.[192] Moreover, the unfairness in the assessments in 1634 was reproduced for the first assessments in 1640 – Cork's agent was surprised to receive demands for both the earl and his son Lewis

188 Leslie Stephen and Sidney Lee (eds), *The dictionary of national biography*, 66 vols (London, 1885–1901), xliv, p. 373.

189 O'Dowd, *Power, politics and land*, p. 59; NAI, Ferguson MS 11, pp 216–17; NAI, Ferguson MS 12, pp 352, 355.

190 Goodare, 'Parliamentary taxation in Scotland', quoting J.H.M. Salmon, *Society in crisis: France in the sixteenth century* (London, 1975), p. 76. Major, 'Payment of deputies'; John Russell Major, 'Bellievre, Sully and the Assembly of Notables of 1596', *Transactions of the American Philosophical Society*, 64:2 (1974), 1–34; Wentworth to John Coke, 7 April 1635, in Knowler (ed.), *Letters and dispatches*, i, pp 400–1; Anthony Stowell to Cork, 22 Feb. 1641, Chatsworth House, Cork Papers, vol. 21, no. 91.

191 *Cal. S.P. Ire., 1633–47*, p. 240.

192 TNA, SP 63/258, fo. 65.

Boyle, Viscount Kinalmeaky, who was a minor with no property, and wrote that 'the subsidies press hard upon men' – adding to the resentment of the administration's encroachment on parliament's powers of assessment and collection.[193]

The poor state of the Irish economy after bad harvests between 1637 and 1640 and the removal of Wentworth's tyrannical hand led to an immediate reduction in the amount of subsidy being paid. Discontent was widespread and collection of the subsidies was inefficient. The time given for collection was very tight and the £275 levied on Kilkenny city was £30 more than the previous assessment, the number of appeals was high and the commissioners who were to administer oaths to those appealing their assessments had left the city 'the inhabitants are generally poore, and nowe much decyayed from that they have bene at the payments of the last subsidies (as in truth they are).'[194]

On 9 June 1640 the Commons raised issues about how subsidies were collected and the following day ordered that the last three subsidies would be levied 'in a parliamentary way' (i.e. by assessment on wealth, rather than a fixed sum on each county). Wandesford was deferring replying to the Commons until the subsidies came in, but on 13 June the house issued a declaration effectually reducing the value of the subsidies, which were 'to be proceeded in, assessed, and levied for ever hereafter in a moderate parliamentary way, and an easy and equal rate of each man his estate, without relation to any former certainty.' On 21 June Wandesford wrote to Radcliffe of the lack of support in the privy council

> in that debayte which was often handled att the Boarde concerning this layte declaration their was not above 3 of those Gentlemen which stode to the Deputye … the assistance I have had from my Lord Dillon hath been performed with all Constancye and with singular advantage to his Majesty, for had he not struggled dextiously in the house (after you weare gone) for the kings honor we had lost so much of that or all the subsidyes.

Resistance continued to grow. On 24 June 1640 Clonmel corporation appointed former MPs (not the current ones, who were Protestant placemen) to draft a petition, objecting to the manner in which the subsidies were being cessed on the town.[195] Wandesford wrote to Radcliffe, 'You will hear what the vice-treasurer speakes of the slowness of cumming in of moneys. I think the care he hath of the revennewe makes him full as apprehensive of the matter as there is cause', and reported to Ormond

193 Walley to Cork, 30 April 1640, Chatsworth House, Cork Papers, vol. 21, no. 10. Lewis Boyle Lord Kinalmeakey was very close to being of age, being born on 23 May 1619. Grosart (ed.), *Lismore Papers*, ii, p. 110. He was assessed at £25 on the basis of assets of £125 for subsequent subsidies, *Cal. S.P. Ire., 1633–47*, p. 337.

194 Draft letter from the Mayor to Sir Edward Bolton, 29 May 1640, KCA, MS CR/K/52; Letter to Edward Bolton from the local commissioners of the subsidy, 12 June 1640, KCA, MS CR/K/53.

195 McGrath (ed.), *Clonmel*, p. 272.

> there is not 300[li] come in hitherto from the commons, by which your lordship may se (which us all here beleve) that it was resolved by the whole Kingdome that no monyes shoulde be leuyed untill the Parlament had satisfaction concerning there declaration, which nowe giuen them, we may hope for the monyes.[196]

In July, the council wrote to Wentworth explaining that they could not send him money, because the subsidies were not being paid:

> all possible diligence hath been used to quicken the paymente expected of the subsidies, and yet all that could be gotten in of his Majesty's moneyes and all that was in Mr Vice-treasurers hands beside, was but little more than sufficient to pay the Captaines and Soldiers of the eight thousand foote now at Carregfergus to the 28th of August.[197]

Radcliffe was in no hurry to pay his share, as he only paid the £57 5*s*. 8*d*. due from his Sligo lands for the first subsidy on 13 August; Dillon's commitment to raising the subsidies would have been prompted by his paying such negligible amounts himself, in contrast to others.[198]

Parliament was prorogued on 17 June, but on its resumption in October, a committee of the whole house considered the levying of the second, third and fourth subsidies, and reported its opinion that anyone other than aliens chargeable for payment with 'lands or other profits of £30 annually shall be set down in the subsidy book at £3, and shall pay 4*s*. in the pound, or 12*s*. in all' and *pro rata* for higher incomes. Persons having goods and chattels of £30, be rated at £3, and pay eight groats (2*s*. 8*d*.) in the £1, and that anyone having lands of profits between £5 and £29 annually was to be combined with others in the same position, and be jointly liable for payment at those rates. The same system was specified for those with goods and chattels worth between £10 and £29. Aliens were to pay twice these rates. The committee also recommended that the second and third subsidies should be collected together. Radcliffe wrote to Wentworth for advice, 'what wee shall doe concerning the subsidies accept their offer or protest against their order, and what course then to be taken.' Wentworth's response was clear. He wrote to London for a commission to prorogue parliament and rejected compromise:

> The subsidies are not to be accepted, as they offer them, there order is to be protested against by my Lord Deputy at the concludinge of this cession and to be vacated and torne out the the booke as beinge that, which nether they can iustifie, nor is in there power soe to limit. The first in respecte of

196 Whitaker (ed.), *Life and original correspondence*, pp 250–6; Wandesford to Ormond, undated but *c.* 29 June 1640, Bodl. Lib., Carte MS 1, fo. 211.
197 Bodl. Lib., MS Add. C. 286, fos. 31r–2v; Bodl. Lib., Carte MS 63, fos. 108–9.
198 Pogson (ed.), 'Financial accounts'.

> Poynings act, the second, because against the acts of parliament for the subsidies.

On 19 November, the order was torn out of the Commons' journals, although subsequently restored.[199]

Even after the reduction of the subsidies, there were problems in collection; the second subsidy brought in a mere £9,922 10*s.* 8*d.*, a drop of almost 80% on the intended £45,000, and still 16% below the new figure.[200] There were claims of corruption in the collecting. Stowell reported from Clonakilty that men 'Are very much burdened with the payment of 7 subsidies' and claimed that 'More is collected than ever goes into the Exchequer', urging that commissioners examine the collection process.[201] Cork representatives asserted that the county had been over-charged by £1,400 or £1,500 on the first subsidy and demanded to see the books of subsidy and Cork's agent complained of difficulty in getting rents paid, due to the subsidies. It was claimed that St Leger collected £40 in subsidies but claimed only 10*s.* 9*d.*[202] On 27 March 1641 the five merchants appointed assessors for the second and third subsidies within Clonmel were directed to appear before the commissioners at Cashel 29 March 1641, well after the payment date of the second subsidy, presumably to assert the town's continued resistance.[203] On 21, 24 and 25 May 1641 the Commons dissolved into a Grand Committee to discuss the subsidies and other matters and on 15 July formed a committee to draft an order concerning the collectors who were not handing over the moneys collected to the exchequer. On 26 July 1641 Eustace wrote to Ormond concerned that his allowance as speaker would not be paid because too little money was coming in from the subsidies.[204] In the summer collectors were accused of gathering more than was aplotted and retaining it in their own hands, and the Commons ordered that justices of the peace 'and other prime gentlemen' summon collectors to account for their collections at the assizes and to certify to the Commons within 2 months of the assizes; another order of 5 August 1641 required sheriffs and head collectors to pay the moneys to Sir William Ussher, Valerian Weasley and William Plunkett within ten days, or a summons would be issued to the serjeant-at-arms.[205]

199 Bodl. Lib., Carte MS 118, fo. 3; Bodl. Lib., Carte MS 30, fo. 285, 20 Oct. 1640; *Cal. S.P. Ire., 1633–47*, p. 251; *Commons' Jn. Ire.*, 17 Nov. 1640; Radcliffe to Wentworth, 28 Oct. 1640, Wentworth's reply, 5 Nov. 1640, FSL, MS X.c.101(2–3); Clarke, *Old English*, p. 137.

200 Perceval-Maxwell, *Outbreak*, p. 78.

201 Stowell to Cork, 22 Feb. 1641, Chatsworth House, Cork Papers, vol. 21, no. 91; Further complaints from the towns, Walley to Cork, 25 March 1641, Chatsworth House, Cork Papers, vol. 21, no. 96.

202 Representation of the grievances of the inhabitants of Cork, 24 March 1641, Chatsworth House, Cork Papers, vol. 21, no. 96; Walley to Cork, 14 April 1641, Chatsworth House, Cork Papers, vol. 22, no. 6; Thomas Badnedge to Cork, 27 May 1641, Chatsworth House, Cork Papers, vol. 22, no. 23.

203 McGrath (ed.), *Clonmel*, p. 278.

204 Bodl. Lib., Carte MS 1, fo. 432.

205 Caulfield (ed.), *Cork*, pp 200–1.

While subsidies yielded £49,916 8*s*. 4½*d*. in 1640 (including the peers and clergy), in 1641 only £17,660 19*s*. 11*d*. was received.[206] The parliamentary agents agreed on 16 July to two further subsidies in exchange for concessions; the Irish administration adjourned parliament but failed to transmit the subsidy bills in time for its meeting on November 7, moves which significantly contributed to the lack of trust between the Old English and the administration and facilitated the spread of the rebellion.[207] After the outbreak of the rebellion in October 1641, there is no further reference to the subsidies in the Commons' journals and Cork, at least, was refusing to pay subsidies in December 1641; the fourth subsidy presumably remained unpaid, along with much of the second and third.[208]

The Confederation also raised money to support its work. On 13 November 1642, the Assembly

> Ordered that the summ of 30,000li in money be aplotted and levied forth, within and upon the several counties within the province of Leinster towards the furtherance of the publick service and that warrants subscribed with the hand of Mr Nicholas Plunkett for the levying of the same shall issue forth.

This was a much higher exaction than the subsidies on a single province. Despite this heavy demand, contributions were widely paid. On 15 November 1642 the assembly ordered £4,000 in coins to be minted.[209]

CONCLUSION

The economics of parliament were different for the crown and general population. The crown's expenses for administration, wages and physical infrastructure were more than compensated for by the significant subsidies invariably voted by early Stuart Irish parliaments, in stark contrast to their English and Scottish counterparts who were reluctant to vote realistic subsidies to the crown. However, the costs to individuals and communities in Ireland were very burdensome, not merely for subsidies and MPs' wages, but also through the many other contributions, taxes, levies, impositions, customs and monopolies. As in Scotland, the taxes placed too heavy a burden on the economy and communities and the unfairness of the assessments and abuses in the collection process provoked discontent which, combined with the lack of redress of grievances, resulted in resistance and eventually rebellion.

206 The produce of the revenue for 1640 and 1641, Gilbert Library, MS 205.
207 Clarke, *Old English*, pp 149–53.
208 St Leger to Cork, 17 Dec. 1641, Chatsworth House, Cork Papers, vol. 22, no. 106.
209 Bodl. Lib., Carte MS 68, fos. 2r–3r.; Bodl. Lib., Carte MS 64, fo. 460v.

CHAPTER NINE

The personnel of the Commons

THE COMMONS' PERSONNEL comprised MPs, its speaker and clerk and other functionaries who attended the house, including the serjeant-at-arms, gentleman usher, heralds, pursuivants, judges and porters of the rooms in which MPs met.[1] Both houses had a number of officials, but the only two appointed directly were the speaker and the clerk; the latter was the older office, as the *Modus* refers to clerks but not the speaker. MPs chose their own speaker, termed 'prolocutor' until he was approved by the lord deputy. Both speakers held their office only during parliaments. The clerk of parliament was keeper of the records and clerk to the upper house and another clerk was appointed to the Commons; their role was to manage the house's administration and record its decisions. These were permanent appointments, as the clerks' work managing records continued between parliaments.[2] The speaker and clerks' qualifications, experience and personal relationships were critical to parliament's effective operations and their physical positions in the house reflected their need to cooperate: 'the Speaker sits in a Chair, placed somewhat high to be seen and heard the better of all; the Clarks of the House sit before him in a lower seat.'[3]

Convocation's equivalent officers were its prolocutor and registrar. In 1613 chancellor Thomas Jones presided in both the Lords and Convocation's upper house and Chichester's chaplain, Randolph Barlow, archdeacon of Meath, was prolocutor of the lower house, with the MP Thomas Ryves appointed registrar by royal writ.[4] Jones had the helpful experience of having sat in the 1585 parliament and so was familiar with procedures there. Archbishop Hampton objected to Ryves as he was not a notary public (he subsequently qualified), although he was a doctor of civil law: 'A strange convocation that shall be held without a publick notarie.'[5] In 1634, James Ussher was speaker of the upper house and Dean Henry Leslie of Down prolocutor of the lower, with John Forth as clerk of the upper house and John Peire of the lower. In 1640, James Margetson, a Yorkshireman and dean of Christ Church, was prolocutor and John Sharpe, a notary public, registrar.[6]

1 TCD, MS 647, fos. 89r–90r. Judges are dealt with in chapter ten on lawyers in and around the house. The following who dealt with Commons' officers and members are not considered in this chapter: officials in chancery, headed by the chancellor who was *ex officio* the speaker of the Lords, the clerk of the hanaper who issued writs of election and the clerk of the petty bag who sent out those writs and collated information for nominating collectors and assessors for subsidies.

2 A.F. Pollard, 'The clerical organization of parliament', *EHR*, 57:225 (1942), 31–58; Foster, 'Painful labour'.

3 Hakewill, *Modus*, p. 36. Hakewill's edition contained many additions to the original *Modus*.

4 Robert Armstrong, 'Barlow, Randolph (Randal)', *DIB*.

5 TCD, MS 1,062, pp 54–5. Ryves certified Hampton's letter to James reporting on Convocation's subsidy on 28 April 1615 as a notary public. See *Cal. S.P. Ire., 1615–25*, p. 49.

6 Bodl. Lib., Carte MS 64, fos. 281r, 287v; TCD, MS 1,062, pp 49, 54–5, 61; ARL, MS Acts of

THE SPEAKER

Cotton described the English speaker as '*vice totius Comunitatis* as Speaker or Proctor of the Commons.'[7] His role was to manage the house's business, chair sittings, encourage MPs' attendance and good behaviour, discipline poor conduct and infringement of procedures as determined by the house, to be its spokesman and to defend MPs and their privileges. Speakers needed to be experienced, with good judgment and standing: 'a man for gravitie, wisedome, experience, and learning … [able] to direct and guide that house in good order; and to see the ordinances, usages, and customs of the same to be firmlie kept and observed.'[8] When the English secretary of state, John Herbert, nominated Sir Edward Phelips as speaker in England in 1604, he referred to his 'knowledge of the laws, the gift of Utterance, his long experience and practice in Parliament.'[9] Knowledge of the law and parliamentary procedures were essential and speakers would be expected to have good organizational and communications skills, a commanding presence and gravitas, while also inspiring MPs' respect. As his role was to keep MPs' speeches on the business in hand, he had to act impartially and possess confidence and tact to defend the house and its members and a good memory to remember their names.[10] He should also be in good health; the English parliament sat as a committee of the whole house during its speaker's indisposition, but the 1634 Irish parliament suspended all business when Catlin was ill.[11]

Sir John Davies described the role's requirements:

> for he that must be the tongue and voice of so many eloquent men, he that must deliver the knowledge of so many learned men, he that must pronounce the judgments of so many grave and wise men had need have the quintessence of spiritts of all their gifts and perfections to qualify him, and to make him sufficient for such an employment. For it is not enough for him to be meanly enabled, to be tollerable and reasonably well, but he had need be passing well furnished, he had need be accomplished singularly well with

Convocation, 1639–41, pp 109–25; Terry Clavin, 'Margetson, James', *DIB*; Alan Ford, 'Leslie, Henry', *DIB*.

7 Robert Cotton, A relation to prove that the Howse of Commons had equall power with the Peeres in point of Judicature, 1621, Yale University, Beinecke Library, Osborn MS b22, fo. 184v; 'Speakers of the House of Commons (1376–2015)', at https://doi.org/10.1093/ref:odnb/92975 [accessed 23 Feb. 2019].

8 Coleman A. Dennehy, 'Speakers in the 17th-century Irish parliament' in Paul Seaward (ed.), *Speakers and the speakership: presiding officers and the management of business from the Middle Ages to the 21st century: a special issue of Parliamentary History*, 29:1 (Chichester, 2010), pp 62–74; Holinshed, *Chronicles*, p. 125.

9 T.G. Watkin, 'Herbert, Sir John', *Oxford DNB*; Rebecca S. More, 'Phelips, Sir Edward', *Oxford DNB*.

10 Scobell, *Memorials*, pp 4, 6–7. For the speaker's role in keeping members on the subject, see pp 32–4.

11 E.g., *Commons' Jn. Ire.*, 18–19 March 1635. The issue arose in the 1606–7 English session when the speaker was ill for a week. The committee on privileges was asked to search for precedents and recommended that 'if Mr Speaker was absent, the whole house might be a committee.' Keeler, 'Committee for privileges'.

> all gifts and graces, with all the abilities and ornaments that are required in an excellent speaker. He had need have a quick conceipt [sic] and apprehension, large and faithful memory, a deep [blank] and a sound judgment and a long practice and experience in all the affairs of the Commonwealth and with all, and above all, he ought to have a singular facility and elegancy of speech, whereby he may be able on all occasions to speak readily, roundly, plentifully, properly, judiciously and wisely of all matters that shall arise, matters of state, matters of law, matters of the church and of the crown, the causes or cases of particular men, and the general state of the Commonwealth. In a word, whereas every other perfection hath a particular science, sufficient to enable the possessor thereof, itt is the perfection of a perfect speaker to be skillful in every man's profession, for there is no state, or condition of men, no action, no accident but may happen to be a subject for him to speak of so as it is not sufficient for such a speaker to have a volubility of tongue only, or a Current or stream of words, but he should have a fountain of knowledge in him, out of which his speech should spring, result and flow plentifully. He should have with all a clear understanding of things to make his speech lively, quick and significant, for it is the clearnest of a man's Conceipt that doth give life and spirit unto his words. I omitt to speake of the Continuall use and practise that he ought to have both of his tongue and stile, the singular care and diligence that he ought to have to be thoroughly instructed in every cause that he undertakes to speak in, the clearness and sweetness of his voice, the comelyness of his gesture, the assuredness of his Countenance, and the life and spirit of his pronunciation, these and many other like gifts and abilities are needful and requisite in a perfect speaker.[12]

As this was his 'disabling speech', Davies did not suggest that he possessed those qualities and certainly he was not known for the 'comelyness of his gesture', being overweight and ungainly. A fellow law student described him 'waddling with his arse out behind as though he were about to make everyone that he meets a wall to piss against … He never walks but he carries a cloakbag behind him, his arse sticks out so far' and Tyrone described him as 'more fit to be a stage-player than a counsellor to the king.' He had been the butt of cruel jokes and satires from John Donne and Ben Jonson and was ridiculed in the 1598 Middle Temple Candlemas revels which were directed by his friend Richard Martin (not the Irish lawyer). Hurt by this, he attacked Martin in the Middle Temple hall and was expelled from the Inn.[13] Nor was he well regarded by many of his fellow MPs, being described by a Catholic lawyer, admittedly in the heat of the controversy about the elections and the contest for the speakership, as 'the cancred, mortall and known enemye of this kingdome'; the Catholic agents in England continued strenuously to object to

12 Bodl. Lib., Carte MS 63, fos. 5–6; NLI, MS 836, pp 20–3.
13 Quoted in Ben Coates, 'Davies, Sir John' in Thrush and Ferris (eds), *History of parliament*.

Davies as speaker. Once parliament resumed, Davies made considerable efforts to improve relations with Catholic MPs.[14]

While it was not a formal requirement, speakers were invariably lawyers – Scobell described them as 'some person of fitness and ability for that service and dignity; which usually hath been one of the long robe.'[15] This included the first known Irish holder of the office, John Cheevers (Table 9.1). This originated in their role in 'expounding to the House of Commons the purport of the measures laid before it and the consequent desirability of some legal training.'[16] The position was different in the Lords; the chancellor was not always a lawyer (for example, Jones), but peers had access to legal advice through the judges who attended the upper house. However, lawyers were generally chosen when a substitute for the chancellor was needed, as Chief Justice James Ley in 1621 in England until a new lord keeper (or chancellor) was sworn and William Ryves, MP for Belturbet in 1634, during Bolton's impeachment in 1641.[17]

Table 9.1. Identified speakers of the Irish Commons and their backgrounds

Parliament	*Speaker*	*Other role*	*Previous parliamentary experience*
1450	John Cheevers	Master of the Rolls	not known
1541–3	Thomas Cusack	Chief Justice of Common Pleas (1535) and Chancellor of the Exchequer	1536–7
1557, 1560, 1569	James Stanihurst	Recorder of Dublin, Clerk of Parliament	None known before 1557
1585	Nicholas Walsh	Recorder of Waterford, Chief Justice of Munster (1577), Second Justice of Queen's Bench (1585)	none
1613	John Davies	Solicitor General (1603), Attorney General (1606), Serjeant-at-Law (1616)	England, 1597, 1601
1634	Nathaniel Catlin	Recorder of Dublin, Second Serjeant-at-Law	none
1640	Maurice Eustace	Lawyer, Prime Serjeant (1634)	1634

14 Jackson (ed.), 'Document'; John Throckmorton to William Trumbull, 19 July 1613, in E.K. Purnell and A.B. Hinds (eds), *Report on the manuscripts of the marquess of Downshire*, 4 vols (London, 1924–40), iv, p. 168; Davies to Somerset, 31 Oct. 1614, TNA, SP 63/232, fo. 201.

15 Falkiner, *Essays*, pp 221–32; Berry (ed.), *Statute rolls*, Hen. VI, pp vi–vii on speakers, on Cheevers, pp 111ff, 179, his protest and request, 1449–50; Richardson and Sayles, *Irish parliament in the Middle Ages*, pp 318–20. Richardson and Sayles also note Maurice Stafford, Robert Plunkett and James Alleyn as speakers of Great Councils in 1414–15, 1442 and 1444: ibid., pp 159–60, 185, 189, 350–1, 354; Scobell, *Memorials*, p. 3.

16 Falkiner, *Essays*, pp 221ff.

17 Foster, 'Painful labour'. The lord keeper of the great seal was a senior royal official and in this period holders of the office were generally raised to the chancellorship. Wilfrid Prest, 'Ley, James, first earl of Marlborough', *Oxford DNB*.

Speakers in the English parliament were nominated by the crown and the Commons acquiesced, although not necessarily willingly; they were so much the creature of the crown that Heneage Finch, designated speaker in 1626, was asked to submit his speech to the government beforehand.[18] As serjeants-at-law and therefore crown lawyers, Davies, Catlin and Eustace would not have been permitted to be MPs, let alone speakers, in England. It was presumed that English speakers would be county members (as Davies, Everard and Eustace were), their possession of senior seats a reflection of their higher status, but Stanihurst, Catlin and Walsh represented Dublin and Waterford cities.[19]

The Irish Commons' sense of independence and determination to nominate a speaker was in stark contrast to England and there was always a contest between 1569 and 1613. In 1560, the administration considered Cusack and Stanihurst; the latter was apparently unopposed, but his chicanery in rigging the passing of anti-Catholic legislation reduced his stock and he faced a contest against Christopher Barnewall in 1569, which he won to loud complaints.[20] Bolton, recorder of Dublin and subsequently a judge and chancellor, might have been considered in 1613, but James regarded parliamentary experience as a telling advantage and was happy to act on Chichester's recommendation of Davies 'by reason he has seen the form of the Parliaments here in England, and has been chiefly employed in the preparation of this Parliament now to be held in Ireland.'[21]

The infrequency of Irish parliaments limited the range of Irish candidates for the speakership in 1613, when James Galway was the only Irish lawyer who had also sat in 1585. Apart from his lack of parliamentary experience, Everard was as well qualified as Davies and would have been a more popular choice as he was widely respected, an eminent judge and personally well regarded on all sides. Sir William Talbot, former recorder of Dublin, and Sir James Gough would also have been suitable, although the latter might not have shown the same sound judgment as Everard or Talbot.[22] The unseemly tussle in 1613 was the last such contest, because Wentworth, having heard that the Catholics intended to nominate a candidate in 1634, made it plain that he would veto anyone except Catlin:

18 Kyle, *Theatre of state*, p. 16; Andrew Thrush, 'Finch, Sir Heneage', *Oxford DNB*.

19 Alasdair D. Hawkyard, 'The Tudor speakers, 1485–1601: choosing, status, work', *Parl. Hist.*, 29:1 (Feb., 2010), 22–48.

20 Moody, 'Irish parliament under Elizabeth and James I'; Jefferies, 'The Irish parliament of 1560'; C.J. Wood, 'Barnewall, Sir Christopher', *DIB*; Moynes (ed.), *Annual letters*, i, pp 129–31, which, intriguingly, describes Stanihurst as having been born in a foreign country. Daniel Molyneux, Visitation of Dublin, 1610, NLI, GO, MS 48, p. 91, gives James as the eldest son of Nicholas Stanihurst and grandson of Henry 'which Henry is thoughte to be the firste of his name that came into Ireland.' But this is clearly incorrect as a Henry was in Ireland in 1404. 'Patent Roll 5 Henry IV', at https://chancery.tcd.ie/document/patent/5-henry-iv/103 [accessed 16 June 2021].

21 Chichester to Salisbury, 23 Feb. 1612, *Cal. S.P. Ire., 1611–14*, p. 248; James to Chichester, 26 Sept. 1612, *Cal. S.P. Ire., 1611–14*, p. 285. Davies' background is given in Paul Brand, 'Sir John Davies: law reporter or self-publicist?', *IJ*, new series, 43 (2008), 1–20.

22 For Gough's behaviour, see *Cal. S.P. Ire., 1611–14*, p. 456. On Talbot, see Terry Clavin, 'Talbot, Sir William', *DIB*.

> it was not worth their contention, considering the power of allowance was undeniably in the King, and that if he rejected, they were still to chuse another, and another, till his Majesty approved thereof; and that it would be taken as an ill presage of some way-wardness or forwardness of Mind reigning in them, if they should go about to deny such for their speaker as should be recommended by his Majesty's privy council.[23]

Possible candidates included the experienced lawyers Dr John Haly, chancellor of the Liberty of Tipperary and MP for Cashel in 1613 and 1634, Sir Geoffrey Galway and Sir Thomas Gough, although there were many other options, as lawyers formed a significant element of the Catholic membership of each parliament; Haly's previous parliamentary experience might have given him the edge over other candidates.[24]

As a lawyer, author and poet, Davies' communication skills were excellent and Eustace's high standard of education stood him in good stead. His advice to his nephew and namesake, 'when you write studdy a Laconian brevity & to be sententious, rather than a Ciceronian style', gives a sense of what he thought important in terms of delivery. Catlin's communications skills are unclear, as his speech has not survived. He had a strong legal background and administrative skills, but shared Davies' history of violence in English legal circles through his involvement in the riotous kidnapping of an elderly member of Staple Inn in 1622, which may have prompted his arrival in Ireland in the following year.[25]

Privy councillors nominating speakers underlined their status as official candidates. Sir Thomas Ridgeway nominated Davies, Lord Robert Dillon and Barnaby Bryan proposed Catlin and St Leger named Eustace. Significantly, Dillon and Bryan were prominent Protestant members of old native families and later, respectively, earls of Roscommon and Thomond. St Leger, while a prominent member of the administration, was also a third-generation settler.[26] Wentworth may have wished to give an impression of his respect for the native community, but the suggestion that he chose speakers who might be thought more acceptable to Catholics (Catlin through his defence of Dublin's privileges and Eustace as he shared Catholic MPs' cultural background, if not their religion, but he

23 Knowler (ed.), *Letters and dispatches*, i, pp 276–92.

24 For details on Haly, Galway and Gough, see Appendix 3.

25 Jean R. Brink, 'Sir John Davies: lawyer and poet' in Thomas Herron and Michael Potterton (eds), *Ireland in the Renaissance*, c.*1540–1660* (Dublin, 2007), pp 88–104; Eustace to Maurice Eustace, 11 May 1659, in F.W.X. Fincham (ed.), 'Letters concerning Sir Maurice Eustace, lord chancellor of Ireland', *EHR*, 35:138 (April, 1920), 251–9. Both Wentworth and Catlin refused to provide copies of their speeches to the Lords in 1634. *LJI*, 23 July 1634, 2 Aug. 1634; J.H. Baker, *The Inns of Chancery, 1340–1640: with an edition of the surviving statutes and orders: Selden Society Supplementary Series, Volume 19* (London, 2017), pp 214–18.

26 Terry Clavin, 'Dillon, Robert, 2nd earl of Roscommon', *DIB*; Bernadette Cunningham, 'O'Brien, Barnabas (Bryan, Barnaby), 6th earl of Thomond', *DIB*; Elaine Murphy, 'St Leger, Sir William', *DIB*.

nevertheless threw in his lot so thoroughly with the administration that he was described as 'the second [George] Radcliffe') is unsupported.[27]

Speakers in England could rely on experienced and knowledgeable clerks for advice, but the Irish clerks in 1613–15 and 1634–5 had no previous experience of parliamentary business, placing a greater burden on the speaker. Davies had a good grasp of procedure from the English Commons and corresponded with William Hakewill, who researched parliamentary procedure.[28] Catlin had no parliamentary experience nor had his clerk, Fernesly, although he should have been familiar with the records. Catlin spent at least two weeks preparing for his role as speaker, presumably reading up on procedure and the legislative agenda.[29] The 1640 speaker-clerk team was the most experienced since Stanihurst's time, as Eustace was a lawyer who had been an MP and Fernesly had a track-record as its clerk.

THE SPEAKER'S ROLE

The speaker's role as spokesman was taken so seriously in earlier times that Elsynge noted 'diverse parliament Rolls R[ichard] 2 wherein the Speaker is not once named at all.' The speaker was seen to have no constituency but the house: in Walkley's 1628 directory of the English parliament, the speaker's name precedes all other MPs', with no mention of his constituency. On 7 November 1614, the Commons decided that the speaker should be sent as their messenger only to the king (i.e., lord deputy). Letters to the Commons were delivered to and read by the speaker and all correspondence from the Commons was written by the clerk and signed by the speaker.[30] The remonstrance of both houses, detailing the grievances of the subjects of Ireland, was 'publikely Reade by the Speaker unto the Lord Deputy in the Presence Chamber, 9 November 1640.'[31] Joint communications of both houses were signed by both speakers and certified by their clerks.[32] At the end of the sessions the speaker requested, on the Commons' behalf, redress of specific grievances and raised any other matter they considered important and gave his own account of their work.[33]

27 C.V. Wedgwood, *Thomas Wentworth, first earl of Strafford, 1593–1641: a re-evaluation* (London, 1962), p. 150; *The plot and progresse of the Irish rebellion* (London, 1644), p. 9.

28 Hakewill to Davies, 13 Feb. 1604, HL, HP, Box 1 (12), expressing his love and continued correspondence. Andrew Thrush, 'Hakewill, William' in Thrush and Ferris (eds), *History of parliament*; Sheila Doyle, 'Hakewill, William', *Oxford DNB*.

29 Grosart (ed.), *Lismore Papers*, 1st series, iv, p. 35, under 2 July 1634. Parliament opened on 14 July.

30 E.g., *Commons' Jn. Ire.*, 17 June 1640, 6 Oct. 1640, 24 Feb. 1641, 9 July 1641, 18 April 1644. Transcripts of Maurice Eustace's letters as speaker to the committee in England, ARL, MS Parliamentary Papers, 1640–1, unpaginated.

31 RIA, MS 24/Q/5, no. 45.

32 E.g., 18 April 1644. Address of the Lords and Commons, 17 March 1647, Bodl. Lib., Carte MS 176, fo. 210.

33 Tony Crowley (ed.), *The politics of language in Ireland, 1366–1922: a sourcebook* (Abingdon, 2002), pp 28–9. Davies' speech at the end of the second session, NLI, MS 836, fos. 165ff (not in the published journals); *Commons' Jn. Ire.*, 17 June 1640.

As spokesman, a speaker could mediate between MPs and between the house and the administration. MPs objected to Nicholas Walsh in 1585 precisely because he had been recommended by Perrot, but he acted in a conciliatory manner, especially over the suspension of Poynings' Law, mediating between Perrot and the Commons and initially refrained, on the advice of some privy councillors, from putting the proposed suspension of Poynings' Law to a vote. His closing speech, unusually, chided both the Commons for refusing to vote the taxes needed by the crown and the administration for undermining Irish autonomy and liberty.[34] Davies exercised tact and used social occasions to ease tensions with MPs. and when Theodore Schout and William Plunkett were at odds in the house, Eustace reconciled them from the chair.[35]

Speakers had a leadership role, and Eustace's name is first on the list of MPs swearing the oath of supremacy in the house on 21 June 1642.[36] While the speaker's position was supposedly neutral, the administration's determination to ensure the election of its candidate demonstrates the chair's powerful role in managing parliament's work. In 1559 the author of proposals to be passed through Parliament, possibly James Barnewall, advised the administration 'to foresee a chosen speaker and a trusty clerk of the parliament house.'[37] While Stanihurst's personal religious position was ambiguous – he steered both the Marian and Elizabethan religious settlements through the Commons – his underhand actions in the latter case raised questions about his 'sufficiency' and the folk memory of his double-dealing was one reason that Catholics so strongly supported Everard in 1613, 'the Catholics, knowing well enough how very important it is to be sure of the speaker's integrity.'[38]

Wentworth had no interest in having a neutral speaker and selected men who would further his policies; Catlin followed Wentworth in refusing the Lords a copy of his speech for their journals and his failure to protect MPs from assaults on parliamentary privilege and liberties, while his intimidatory behaviour demonstrates his subservience to the viceroy, confirmed and rewarded by his subsequent role as crown counsel in finding the king's title to lands in Connacht.[39] Speakers could influence the course of events in parliament by selecting bills and putting motions when the house was thin, as Stanihurst did, or by the way that they phrased motions.[40] Strafford's order for 'the Act for Connaught to be passed

34 Nicholas Walsh to Burghley, 27 May 1585, TNA, SP 63/116, fo. 138; Terry Clavin, 'Walsh, Sir Nicholas', *DIB*.

35 *Commons' Jn. Ire.*, 11 June 1647.

36 HRC, MS 158; Henry Elsynge, *Modus tenendi parliamentum* (London, 1630), p. 116; Walkley, *Catalogue*, sig. A2.

37 Proposals for acts to be passed through parliament and other measures to be taken in Ireland, 20 May 1559, in Heffernan (ed.), *'Reform' treatises*, p. 43.

38 Petition of Edward Waterhouse on behalf of Sidney, March 1569, in Cunningham (ed.), *Calendar of State Papers*, p. 147; Moynes (ed.), *Annual letters*, i, p. 138.

39 Clarke, *Old English*, p. 93.

40 Seaward, 'Divisions, tellers and management' notes one case where the speaker put the case in the negative – that the bill be rejected, which might have influenced the result.

if possible may be and the House of Commons there, to be kept to consider onely of the lawes transmitted, without admitting them any newe discourse of other matters' suggests the level of control he expected Eustace to exert over the house.[41] Wentworth took a similar approach to the prolocutor of Convocation's lower house:

> I send you here inclosed the forme of a Cannon to be passed by the votes of the lower house of Convocation, which I require you to put to the question for their consents, without admitting any debate or other discourse … therefore I require from you to take only the voices consenting or dissenting and to give me a particular account of how each man gives his vote.

This demand breached Convention's rule on secrecy.[42]

In 1637 Wentworth wrote approvingly of Eustace: 'I am very confident that [he] is as well provided with all the necessaries requisite [for a judge] to wit, with learning and integrity' and in December 1640 praised his ability and loyalty: 'he hath noe friend more ready to serve him on all occasions, nor am I yet out of hope to be able to give him a better proofe of it then nowe I can doe, for I must never forget his faithful service to the King.'[43] The Commons' repeated orders to Eustace to issue warrants for by-elections after November 1640 suggests that he was stalling to maintain the administration's dominance, as does the letter 84 MPs sent to the English speaker that he was resisting sending that communication.[44] His repeatedly rephrasing the motion for voting on whether the administration's candidate Roger Brereton or the opposition's Hugh Rochford should chair the committee of the whole house discussing the lords justices' response to impeachment suggests that he was not acting impartially.[45] Speakers usually presented the case for impeachment to the Lords, so the Commons' choice of Mervyn demonstrates their determination to by-pass Eustace in favour of a spokesman whom they could trust.[46]

The speaker decided the order in which bills were to be taken, unless the house objected, ensured the accuracy of the clerk's records of proceedings, orders, and

41 Borlase, *History*, p. 9; Empey (ed.), 'Diary of Sir James Ware', entry under 5 March 1641; Wentworth to Radcliffe, 6 Nov. 1640, FSL, MS X.c.101(3).

42 Wentworth to the prolocutor of the lower house, 10 Dec. 1634, Bodl. Lib., Carte MS 64, fo. 281r.

43 Chancellor Loftus to Wentworth, 13 April 1637, Wentworth to Loftus, 14 April 1637, Wentworth to Loftus, 15 April 1637, all in Knowler (ed.), *Letters and dispatches*, ii, pp 67–9; Wentworth to Ormond, 17 Dec. 1640, Bodl. Lib., Carte MS 1, fo. 294r.

44 Clarke, *Old English*, pp 135–6; BL, Egerton MS 1,048, fo. 12. There is no record of a division on the matter and while theoretically 120 MPs would have been needed for a majority, the absence of many administration clients and the 11 agents in England would have reduced that number significantly.

45 On Brereton and Rochford, see Appendix 3.

46 *Commons' Jn. Ire.*, 3 Oct. 1640, 4 Feb. 1641, 5 March 1641, 15, 21, 27 May 1641, 23 June 1641; Catherine Strateman Sims, '"The moderne forme of the parliaments of England"', *American Historical Review*, 53:2 (Jan., 1948), 288–305.

faithful transcriptions of amendments to bills, or when engrossing them; this required planning the house's agenda before each sitting day and checking the record afterwards.[47] The order of bills was determined by which were available for processing and the administration's priorities, but also required liaison between the speaker and chancellor and their clerks, as bills were not supposed to be deliberated on in both houses at the same time. After the clerk read any bill for the first time, the speaker explained its contents, intent and implications. All debates and discussions in the house were addressed to and through the speaker, who decided in which order MPs should speak and ensured that anyone wishing to speak could do so.[48] They maintained order in the house and the 1585 rules note that 'if any offend or mysbehave himself in this howse, his punishment ys to be considered of, and assigned by the speaker, with thadvise and assent of the residue of the howse' and if any MP disclosed the secrets of the house, the speaker was to punish him.[49] During the uproar in the 1569 parliament over a very wide range of matters, Sidney charged the speaker 'to have regarde bothe to the chardge comitted vnto him as also to see punyshment to be donne vpon such as dyd disorder them selffes yn the house.'[50]

The speaker had no voice and no vote, except on the speakership and a casting one on tied divisions and in committees.[51] During 'the time of the parliament [he was expected to] sequester himself from dealing or intermingling in anie publique or privat affaires, and dedicat and bend himselfe wholie to serve his office and function.'[52] As a result, speakers generally had no role in committees, except those of the whole house which they did not chair and in which they could speak and vote, although they might have attended those committees which invited any member who or chose to attend or more specifically those 'of the long robe', to join their deliberations. However, when Commons appointed a committee to consider the bill for limiting the times for loading and landing of merchandise on 9 April 1635, every MP for the port towns, including Catlin, was 'to sit and have voices with them.' On 3 February 1645, Eustace, with the MP Robert Parke, proposed that the serjeant-at-arms should have 2*s.* 6*d.* for 'every protection' (for parliamentary privilege), which, strictly speaking, he should not have done. If the chancellor wished to speak for himself in the Lords, he was to 'go to his own place as a peer.' As Bolton and Ryves were not peers they consequently had no vote.[53]

47 While Poynings' Law forbade amendments, there are references to them, e.g., *Commons' Jn. Ire.*, 29, 31 Oct. 1614, 2 Nov. 1614, 28 July 1634, 15 Nov. 1634, 8 June 1640.
48 Holinshed, *Chronicles*, p. 125.
49 Irish Archaeological Society, *Tracts*, ii, p. 143.
50 Falkiner, *Essays*, p. 238.
51 The only recorded tied vote during this period was on 7 Aug. 1641. In this instance Eustace did not exercise his casting vote but asked for the matter to be deferred.
52 Holinshed, *Chronicles*, p. 125.
53 On 16 Nov. 1641 Eustace proposed a select committee be appointed. Ibid.; Scobell, *Memorials*, p. 27; *LJI*, 23 July 1634.

Speakers were well rewarded for their work: Walsh was granted £40 in lands for his service, although not knighted until 1597. Davies and Eustace were already knights at the time of their appointment, but Catlin was dubbed immediately after the dissolution.[54] Davies received £100 in lands in recognition of his work in preparing for parliament and his anticipated service and was granted more lands and his travelling expenses to England after the dissolution.[55] Catlin was awarded £500 in compensation for loss of income during his speakership (later raised to £1,600) and Wentworth commended his service: '[he] deserveth passing well, having discharged the place not only with good affections, but with good abilities also'.[56]

In the Confederation government, Patrick Darcy as chancellor and Nicholas Plunkett as chairman of the General Assembly, had a similar role to the presiding officer of the Scottish Estates; however, unlike with the Irish parliament, business did not cease if the prolocutor was unavailable, as Sir Richard Blake substituted for Plunkett as chair in 1646.[57]

CLERKS OF THE PARLIAMENT

The clerk of the parliament was clerk of the upper house and superior in status to the clerk of the Commons, although the latter also signed themselves 'clericus parl:.' Their warrants of appointment allowed them to appoint deputies. Clerks' management of their respective houses' administration was central to parliament's effectiveness and efficiency. The clerk's work was summed up in his oath, to 'make true entry of all such orders and rules as should be conceived in the said house and for the faithful keeping of the secrets of the said house.'[58] Henry Elsynge, clerk of the English Commons, 1639–48, was described as 'clerk, communication center, administrative officer and dispatcher. He even distributed alms for the House.' Elizabeth Read Foster's careful reconstruction of his role held true for Irish clerks also and demonstrates their importance in parliament's smooth operations.[59]

54 Grosart (ed.), *Lismore Papers*, 1st series, iv, p. 94; Empey (ed.), 'Diary of Sir James Ware', entry for 18 April 1634.

55 *Irish patent rolls of James I: facsimile of the Irish record commissioners calendar prepared prior to 1830*, Foreword by M.C. Griffith (Dublin, 1966), p. 250; James to Chichester in favour of Davies, 17 Oct. 1615, HL, HP, MS 15,076.

56 Falkiner, *Essays*, p. 231; Wentworth to Coke, 7 April 1635, in Knowler (ed.), *Letters and dispatches*, i, p. 404; Dennehy, *Parliament*, pp 34, 121.

57 Ó Siochrú, *Confederate Ireland*, pp 44–6, 191; Alan R. MacDonald, 'Chancellors, presidents and speakers: presiding officers in the Scottish parliament before the restoration', *Parl. Hist.*, 29:1 (Feb., 2010), 49–61; Micheál Ó Siochrú, 'Plunkett, Nicholas', *DIB*.

58 *Commons' Jn. Ire.*, 18 April 1615. A slight variant is recorded on 25 Nov. 1614. The oath of the clerk of the upper house given in *LJI*, 18 July 1634 is identical to that for the English clerk in 1628, Yale University, Beinecke Library, Osborn MS FB 158, III6; 'The speaker', at https://www.historyofparliamentonline.org/volume/1604-1629/survey/viii-officers-and-servants-house [accessed 10 May 2019]; *Commons' Jn. Ire.*, 25 Nov. 1614, 18 April 1615, 17 July 1634.

59 Foster, 'Painful labour'.

The clerk's role was to minute the house's decisions and, where necessary, also its committees through accurate recordings in the journals and book of orders, giving the first reading of bills, announcing results of votes, maintaining lists of the house's membership and their attendance, ordering writs of return to be issued by the clerk in chancery, managing copies of bills, petitions, the names of MPs' servants or agents who were entitled to protection under parliamentary privilege and any other relevant documents or administrative material. In the 1570s, John Hooker summarized the role:

> his office is to sit next before the speaker at a table, upon which he writeth & laieth his books. He must make true entry of the records and bills of the house, as also of all the orders thereof. The bills appointed unto him by the speaker to be read; he must read plainly and sensibly. The bills which are to be ingrossed, he must do it. If any of the house ask the sight of any bill, there, or of the book of the orders of the house, he hath to deliver the same unto them. If any desire to have a copy of any bill, he ought to give it to him, receiving for his pains after ten lines a penny. He may not be absent at any time of sitting without special licence.[60]

Clerks were involved in parliament's planning and preparation and responsible for managing its archive, including journals, books of orders and copies of acts. The clerk had an important role in contests for the speakership:

> one of the members standing in his place, doth by direction or leave of the House, put a Question for determining the same … the House … directed the Clerk, sitting at the Board (as the order is before the speaker be chosen, so it is entred in the Journal of that Session) to make the Question upon his name.[61]

Managing bills' administration included recording their stages, engrossing (transcribing) them on parchment after the second reading and when passed, noting amendments, committees' reports and votes to pass or reject them and supplying copies for printing.[62] They also recorded any other decisions, parliamentary orders, declarations and remonstrances, managed correspondence, noted any other votes, details of discipline, censuring of members or cases of breach of privilege, while also providing copies of any document to MPs or others, such as rules of the house, orders and certificates of wages.[63] Documents were lodged with the clerk for safekeeping, including those the house requested from outside parties and they managed money on behalf of the Commons, including

60 E.g., *Commons' Jn. Ire.*, 21 July 1634; Hooker in Holinshed, *Chronicles*, p. 125.
61 Scobell, *Memorials*, p. 4.
62 *Commons' Jn. Ire.*, 29 Oct. 1614; *LJI*, 17 March 1645.
63 *Commons' Jn. Ire.*, 1 June 1640, 13 Oct. 1640; Scobell, *Memorials*, p. 27 says it is the speaker (see section on voting) but the clerk is to 'enter the vote "resolved"'.

fines, securities, contributions to the poor or for other officers.[64] After parliament concluded, they organized its results. This activity included recording of acts, including private acts, which were usually not printed, and copies of orders, as well as compiling fair copies of the journals and certifying wages for payment, if that had not already happened.

The clerkship was a full-time position during parliamentary sessions, but part-time when they were not sitting and was invariably held by men who held other crown clerkships. Unlike their English counterparts, Irish clerks were not provided with official lodgings close to their records and their salary was much lower.[65] Stanihurst had combined his position as recorder of Dublin and clerkship of parliament with the offices of speaker, presumably employing a deputy during parliamentary sittings.[66] He was succeeded as clerk of parliament in 1595 by Thomas Chetham, keeper of records in the Bermingham Tower of Dublin Castle. A conscientious and painstaking officer, Chetham worked hard to develop the scanty collection of records he inherited, making copies of many missing records: 'he is carefull and diligent in his place, and the fee small and the office of good use. And this is noted in the last Establishment to cease upon Death, which notwithstanding wee thinke meete the office should be continued.'[67] Good archival management was essential, as records might be needed at any time, but especially during preparations for parliament and Chetham made copies of acts in anticipation of parliament's being summoned.[68] An Englishman, he was well-connected, as the son-in-law of alderman Christopher Forster of Dublin and brother-in-law of Sir John Eliot, baron of the exchequer; his only child married the MP Nicholas Loftus.[69] Chetham was well rewarded for his work, receiving grants of lands from the crown.[70]

Chetham died in 1624 and his successor was Philip Percival. While it is stated that his father had trained him in the mechanics of the operations of the Court of Wards of which he was the first clerk, Philip, who succeeded to that post also, was only 15 at his father's death and very young to be appointed to such responsible

64 E.g., *Commons' Jn. Ire.*, 28 July 1634, 1 Aug. 1634, 12 Oct. 1640, 30 Jan. 1641. e.g., ibid., 27 April 1615, 13, 15 June 1640, 7 Nov. 1640, 17, 18 July 1634, 30 Jan. 1641, 2 Aug. 1634; 22 July 1634, 10 Oct. 1640. For fines, see 27 April 1615, contributions to the poor, 27 April 1615, bail, 13, 20 Feb. 1641.

65 Thrush, 'House of Lords' records repository'.

66 Lascelles, *Liber Mun. Pub. Hib.*, ii, part 2, p. 94; Falkiner, *Essays*, pp 229–30.

67 William Nicholson, *The English, Scotch and Irish historical libraries* (London, 1776), p. 54; BL, Add. MS 4,756, fo. 6r.

68 BL, Add. MS 4,790; BL, Add. MS 4,801, which contain abridged statutes in Chetham's hand. I am grateful to Peter Crooks for drawing these references to my attention. Extracts of acts made by Chetham on customs, tolls &c. in Ireland, 1461–1583, HL, HP, Box 1 (1), is clearly a working document for planning legislation on poundage. For the context to this bill, see Carroll, 'Dublin parliamentary elections'.

69 On Elliott, see the entry in Ball, *Judges in Ireland*, i. p. 223.

70 NLI, GO, MS 66, Funeral Entries Ireland Volume 3, 1604–22, fo. 40r; *Irish patent rolls of James I*, pp 17, 118.

positions.[71] He shortly afterward became joint clerk with the MPs Henry Andrews and Edward Bagshaw of the courts of king's bench and common pleas and customer of Dublin. Such a range of roles could only be fulfilled by employing deputies and his underlings as clerk of parliament included Edmund Smith in 1634 and Valentine Savage in 1647.[72]

The clerks of the Commons during this period were William Bradley, Edmund Medhop and Philip Fernesly. Bradley was keeper of the writs in the Court of Common Pleas from 1607, chirographer and clerk of the crown in Leinster; he already had a close working relationship with the speaker, who was familiar with his organizational and administrative skills as agent for Davies' Tyrone estates.[73] Medhop was also clerk of the common pleas in the exchequer and chirographer and worked as an attorney in the Court of Castle Chamber. Fernesly was remembrancer in the exchequer from 1635, as was his deputy, William Sandes. Sandes, who was unique among clerks of this period in actually becoming an Irish MP (Percival was briefly MP for Newport in Cornwall in 1647), temporarily resigned his deputy clerkship as he claimed it left too little time for his other work as remembrancer and was replaced as deputy clerk by Walter Heighter, about whom nothing further is known. Sandes presumably owed his position as deputy clerk to Fernesly; the connection may have gone back to Philip's father-in-law as Sandes had formed part of Sir John Blennerhassett's funeral procession in 1624.[74] These additional offices would have facilitated the clerks' work in parliament, as they understood the operations of the other departments and had close working relationships with officials whose cooperation was needed for the house's work, e.g., in issuing writs or ensuring that courtrooms and other accommodation was available for committees as necessary.

Bradley was replaced temporarily during his illness by Mathew Davies, presumably a relative of the speaker, but not his brother of the same name, and for the following session by Medhop, who was granted the office permanently in November 1615.[75] If Bradley was appointed because he was trusted by Davies, Medhop had a good legal education, administrative experience and important

71 Terry Clavin, 'Percival (Perceval), Sir Philip', *DIB*; Simon Healy, 'Percival (Percyvall, Perceval), Richard' in Thrush and Ferris (eds), *History of parliament*; Canny, *Making Ireland British*, pp 328–9.

72 *CPRI*, iii, p. 31,23 June 1625. For Percival's deputies see *LJI*, 18 July 1634 (Edmund Smith); Address of the Lords and Commons in parliament assembled made to the Marquis of Ormond, 17 March 1647, Bodl. Lib., Carte MS 176, fo. 210 (Val Savage).

73 Deed dated 30 Sept. 1611, between Sir George Tuchet, Lord Audley and his son Sir Mervyn, sale of lands in Carlow, witnesses John Davies, Edward Blount and William Bradley, HL, HP, D 3517; *Cal. S.P. Ire., 1611–14*, p. 125.

74 McGrath, 'Recruiter returns'; Marsh's Library, MS Z2.1.1, no. 53; *Commons' Jn. Ire.*, 7, 10 Nov. 1634; NLI, GO, MS 79, pp 124–5, available at https://catalogue.nli.ie/Record/vtls000529291#page/124/mode/1up [accessed 30 July 2022].

75 *Commons' Jn. Ire.*, 25 Nov. 1614, 18 April 1615. Bradley died between 24 May 1615 and 12 Nov. 1615, Bodl. Lib., Carte MS 62, fo. 326; Chichester's warrant, to draw up a fiant for the granting of the office of clerk of the lower house to Medhop, ibid., fo. 364; NLI, GO, MS 44, fo. 45v.

political connections. Claiming descent from King Edward III, he was the son of Thomas Medhop and Helen Dickinson, attended Trinity College Cambridge and Lincoln's Inn and married Elizabeth, daughter of Sir John Philips, Picton, and Anne, daughter of Sir John Perrot, and therefore niece of Chichester's wife Lettice Perrot. Elizabeth's sisters Dorothy and Jane respectively married Sir Francis Annesley and Sir James Hamilton, both later privy councillors ennobled as Lords Mountnorris and Clandeboy.[76] Medhop's son and heir Francis, possibly named after Mountnorris, married Margery, daughter of the privy councillor, Sir Edward Trevor.[77] Medhop died in 1621, but Fernesly was not appointed until 4 August 1628 in anticipation of the parliament 'during good behaviour by himself of his sufficient deputy, in as ample a manner as Edmond Medhop held that office.'[78]

Fernesly also had both administrative experience and influential connections. His wife Anne was a daughter of Sir John Blenerhassett, chief baron of the Court of Exchequer and MP for Belfast in 1613, and Ursula Duke. The marriage made him brother-in-law of Charles Moncke, surveyor general of the customs and MP for Coleraine, and cousin of Robert Blennerhassett, MP.[79] Sandes and Fernesly were both admitted to the King's Inns, the former for the usual attorneys' 10*s.* fine, but the latter for the unusually high £3 13*s.* 4*d.*[80] While Bradley clearly worked well under supervision, Medhop took a much more pro-active and managerial approach to his work. His detailed records, excellent organizational and archival skills and diligent production of the journals suggest that he was well able to take responsibility for his role and had a greater sense of autonomy and of the prestige of his office than Bradley, presumably partly due to his higher social status and prestigious connections. Fernesly was also of a more elevated rank than Bradley, but had a more restricted sense of his role as clerk of the Commons and provided more limited and less well organized records, despite working in a much more active parliament than Medhop or Bradley. Fernesly's relations with Falkland and Wentworth are not known, but Percival was very close to Strafford and his associates and was knighted in 1638. Ormond's client George Lane replaced him

76 Robert Armstrong, 'Annesley, Francis, Baron Mountnorris', *DIB*; Terry Clavin, 'Hamilton, James, 1st Viscount Clandeboye', *DIB*.

77 Medhop provided this pedigree in the front of the Commons' journals, NLI, MS 836; ARL, MS Irish Commons' journals, but not King's Inns, MS N3/2/1/7. NLI, GO, MS 66, Funeral Entries, Volume 3, 1604–22, p. 109; *Inq. cancel. Hib. repert.*, King's County, Jac. I (17); *Commons' Jn. Ire.*, 27 April 1615.

78 *CPRI*, iii, p. 328; *Liber Mun. Pub. Hib.*, ii, part 2, p. 94.

79 Linde Lunney, 'Blennerhassett, Sir John', *DIB*; Ball, *Judges in Ireland*, i, pp 242–3. Ursula Blenerhassett died in 1638 and in her will left land to Fernesly: Dame Ursula Blenerhassett vs. Philip Fernesly and Ann (Blenerhassett) his wife (taken from Kenneth Nicholls' calendar of chancery documents), NAI, Chancery G353. On Charles Moncke, see McGrath, 'Bio. dict.', i, pp 216–17.

80 King's Inns, MS B1/1, fo. 16r (Sandes, 1627). Other admissions at this higher rate were the attorney general, Richard Osbaldeston, Philip Percival, George Carleton, Ralph Leventhorpe and William Plunkett: ibid., fos. 65, 66r; Kenny, *King's Inns*, pp 280–1. It is possible that this fine was linked to the use of a chamber in the Inns. I am grateful to Colum Kenny for this observation. For Carleton, Leventhorpe and Plunkett see McGrath, 'Bio. dict.'.

after his death in 1647; as an MP from 1644 he would presumably have employed a deputy during sittings, but there is no record of the Lords meeting and the Commons only sat briefly on 15 June 1648 and immediately adjourned.[81]

The Commons kept a close eye on the clerk's record-keeping, frequently making orders to check the journals. There are no instances of finding them defective, although the entry of 2 August 1634 suggests a problem:

> It is ordered by the house, that, for the better regulating of the house the next parliament, the persons undernamed shall, at some convenient time this vacation, collect and gather together such orders of the house as are extant; and also to add thereunto such other orders of the house, as their own memories can inform them of, that the next sessions they may be published and entred with the clerk of this house, that every member thereof may take notice of them.[82]

The clerk was paid £10 per session in addition to his usual salary, but he also had income from copies of documents, for submitting petitions and their replications, for every private bill passed and contributions from MPs (all of which are explored in chapter eight), as well as from his other offices.

Chichester was concerned about parliament's smooth operations because of the long gap since the previous parliament, lack of records of the Irish Commons and their procedures (see chapter two) and the clerk's lack of experience – Bradley claimed that he had been able to do some research in Dublin 'though but suddenly and rawley.' Parliament had developed considerably since the Irish *Modus* had been drawn up and the single page on procedure surviving from the 1585 Irish Commons provided very little detail. Carew suggested that 'extracts from the books kept by the Clerks of the Parliament House should be sent over for [Bradley's] instruction.'[83] This may have happened but Chichester dispatched Bradley to London to learn from Ralph Ewens, clerk of the English Commons,

> considering with my self, that he hath yet had no actuall experience in these affairs, (though he be otherwise verie capable & sufficient, nor hath he anie bookes of orders or presidens to directe him, it is thought expedient & necessarie that he presently repaire thither, before hande, to instructe himself in the due course to be therein observed, by conference with the Clercke of the Lower house there. In accomplishment whereof, it maie please yor good lordship to give order to Mr Ewens that it maie be lawfull for him to peruse & consider of the manner of proceedinges there, & besides private documents, to take notes of the orders, presidents & entries which have bin

81 John Cronin and Terry Clavin, 'Lane, George, 1st Viscount Lanesborough', *DIB*.

82 E.g., *Commons' Jn. Ire.*, 22 April 1615, 2 Aug. 1634, 13 June 1640, 26 Jan. 1641, 23 Feb. 1641, 2 Aug. 1634. For the English Commons' checking on Ewens, see Sheila Lambert, 'The clerks and records of the House of Commons, 1600–1640', *Historical Research*, 43:108 (1970), 215–31.

83 *Cal. S.P. Ire., 1611–14*, p. xxxviii.

> there made, to the pointes for some times past, to the end wee maie avoide confusion & disorders in the passinge of Actes & other proceedinges of that house; and this I recommend to yor lordship the rather, because there are, now, few men of observation & good note living, who were members of the last parliament here it being 25 years past or thereabouts.[84]

Ewens would have empathized with Bradley's inexperience as he had little training before he took up his role in 1603, although he had attended Gray's Inn and been MP in 1597 and 1601. It is speculated that 'the dispersal of his estate through the lack of an heir may have been the reason for the loss of the fair copy of the Commons' journals for 1584–1601'.[85] In addition, the Irish administration was attempting to draw Irish procedures and practices into line with English ones and the English parliament's role and procedure had also developed since the sixteenth century, so Bradley's visit was a sensible move, with the added advantage that he was able to carry some bills and commissions to England.

Bradley was an efficient and organized man and the list which he drew up for guidance was clear, structured and comprehensive:

1. Of the calling of a Parliament.
2. Of the choice of a Speaker.
3. Of the place and duty belonging to a Speaker.
4. Of the proceedings in reading and passing of bills.
5. Of the orders in speaking to a bill.
6. Of the proceedings of committees for bills or other causes.
7. Of the examinations of elections of members to serve in the House of Parliament.
8. Of the punishing of such as break the privileges and orders of the House.
9. What is to be done by the clerk of the Parliament, and what is due unto him.
10. What course is to be held in messages, meetings, and at conferences betwixt the higher house and Commons House of Parliament and their committees.
11. The difference betwixt a prorogation and an adjournment.
12. What makes and concludes a session of Parliament.
13. With some other rules and orders necessary to be observed and used in Parliament.[86]

Bradley's training with Ewens paid off, as he was clearly well-briefed and able to answer English privy councillors' questions about Poynings' Law and some draft bills.[87]

84 Chichester to Salisbury, 17 Feb. 1611, TNA, SP 63/231, fo. 30.
85 Atkins, 'Persuading the House'; R.C.G., 'Ewens, Ralph' in Hasler (ed.), *History of parliament*.
86 *Cal. S.P. Ire., 1611–14*, p. 18.
87 Bradley to Davies, 5 Feb. 1613, Bodl. Lib., Carte MS 62, fo. 235.

Clerks required excellent administrative skills, a thorough knowledge of parliamentary procedure and understanding of legislation, clear written and oral communication skills, some accounting and mathematical competence (to manage money and records of MPs' wages), good Latin and preferably legal French, which was still the language used in court reports and judgments and of the Irish parliament until 1494. In addition, they needed to have an excellent working relationship with the speaker and other officials, especially the clerk of the parliament, those in chancery, serjeants-at-arms and pursuivants.

English clerks had built up core libraries to support their work and it is likely that Irish clerks created similar collections, allowing for the differences between the two countries. English clerks' libraries included printed statutes, the bible, *Book of Common Prayer*, almanacs, books of computations, apparently for regnal years, but possibly also for calculating the costs, value and distribution of subsidies and parliamentary wages and MPs' contributions to officers. Given the Irish Commons' interest in officials' fees, these books of computation were presumably also for estimating those.[88] There was no published edition of the Irish *Modus* other than Hooker's version of the *Order and vsage* which was also included in Holinshed, nor any known *vademecum* (pocket reference book) for clerks like those available in manuscript in England.[89] In 1613 Bradley would have had the bible, possibly the 1611 King James Bible, and the *Book of Common Prayer*.[90] Editions of statutes were published in 1572 (10 Hen. VI to 14 Eliz. I) and for the 1585–6 parliament, and individual acts had been issued so that when a query arose about legislation on 10 May 1615, 'the statute book being brought, the statutes of 12 Ric. 2 and 23 H. 6 were read.'[91] Available resources improved after 1615. Merick published his *Compendious collection and breefe abstract of all the auncient English statutes* in 1617, and four years later Bolton's *Statutes of Ireland* (1621) appeared.[92] By 1640, the 1634–5 Irish public acts were in print, as well as Bolton's *A justice of the peace for Ireland* (1638).[93]

Philip Kearney held a similar role to the clerks of parliament as clerk of the General Assembly of Kilkenny, although it was closer to that of the Scottish Estates, which was also a unicameral body and had a chief clerk, called the 'Clerk Register' and deputy clerks. Kearney had at least one deputy, Jerome Greene, a New Englishman settled in Kilkenny.[94] Kearney came from a very literate and

88 Foster, 'Painful labour'.

89 Holinshed, *Chronicles*, pp 119–29; Clarke, 'Irish *Modus tenendi parliamenta*'. Clarke dates this transcription to between 1610 and 1632, when Molyneux died. It is probable that it was made in 1612. This manuscript was finally published by Bishop Anthony Dopping, *Modus*. Natzler, 'Manuals before May'.

90 Marc Caball, 'The Bible in early modern Ireland: tradition, collaboration and alienation' in Kevin Killeen, Helen Smith and Rachel Willie (eds), *The Oxford handbook of the Bible in early modern England,* c.*1530–1700* (Oxford, 2015), pp 332–49.

91 Quinn, 'Government printing'; King's Inns, MS N3/2/1/7, fo. 43. This reference is not in the published journals for 10 May 1615.

92 Merick, *Compendious collection*; Bolton, *Statutes.*

93 *Anno regni Caroli Regis, Angliae*; Richard Bolton, *A justice of the peace for Ireland* (Dublin, 1638).

94 Alastair Mann, 'A brief history of an ancient institution: the Scottish parliament', *Scottish*

cultivated family (they were custodians of St Patrick's Crozier). His father Michael, burgess and repeatedly sovereign of Fethard, was a noted Gaelic scholar, the first translator of Geoffrey Keating's *Foras Feasa*. Philip was the nephew of the poet Padraigín Haicéad and Bishop Patrick Comerford of Waterford and Lismore. Despite lacking a library of precedents and guidance, Kearney's work was very efficient and highly organized although the presence of so many former MPs as members of the Assembly would have helped him.[95] Kearney's background for this role has not been established but he was a skilled clerk, who spoke Irish and presumably Latin and he may well have been a notary public or town clerk in Leinster or Munster; the ease with which the Confederation was able to locate someone of his skill attests to the widespread presence of experienced clerks in Ireland. Interestingly, just as parliament's clerk and speaker were administration figures, Kearney was described as 'ar thaobh Ormond' (on Ormond's side), although this might be a mis-reading – his family had been close to Walter Ormond. Bellings, as secretary of the Confederation, and Richard Shee, as clerk to the Supreme Council, the counterparts of Secretary Philip Mainwaring and Paul Davies, were also connected with the earl, which presumably helps to explain their appointments, given how hard the Jesuit Matthew O'Hartegan, correspondent of Fr. Luke Wadding, pressed for Geoffrey Baron (nephew to both of them) to be appointed secretary.[96]

THE SERJEANT-AT-ARMS

Other officers who served parliament as part of their wider duties included the serjeant-at-arms, heralds, pursuivants and porters. The serjeant-at-arms, the equivalent of the Black Rod (Gentleman Usher) in the House of Lords, was a

Parliamentary Review, 1:1 (2013), 1–50; Declaration of the Lords, Gentry & others of the Province of Leinster & Munster and of their intention towards the English and Scotts, 10 May 1644, signed by Hiorom Greene, Cle[ricus]: Con[ci]ll[ium Kilk[enniensis], HL, HP, MS 15,000; NAI, MS 999/670, 20 Nov. 1645. I am grateful to David Edwards for identifying Greene.

95 Bodl. Lib., Carte MS 68, fos. 1rff; McGrath, 'Parliament men and the confederate association'.

96 NLI, GO, MS 71, Funeral Entries, Volume 8, pp 365–7, at http://catalogue.nli.ie/Record/vtls000529247#page/101/mode/1up [accessed 1 Sept. 2021]; Máire Ní Cheallacháin (ed.), *Filíocht Phádraigín Haicéad* (Baile Átha Cliath, 1962), p. xvii, based on Richard O'Ferrall and Robert O'Connell, *Commentarius Rinuccinianus, de sedis apostolicae legatione ad foederatos Hiberniae catholicos per anos 1645–9*, ed. Stanislaus Kavanagh, 6 vols (Dublin, 1932–49), v, pp 76–80; Bernadette Cunningham, *The world of Geoffrey Keating: history, myth and religion in seventeenth-century Ireland* (Dublin, 2000), pp 24, 175–7, which notes their links with Lords Dunboyne. I am grateful to Michelle O'Riordan for information on Kearney and his background, Michelle O'Riordan, *The Gaelic mind and the collapse of the Gaelic world* (Cork, 1990), pp 242–3. Also, see Joseph Francis Kukhta, 'Sources for further research, Michael Kearney: a missing link to the mysterious Geoffrey Keating', *The Canadian Journal of Irish Studies*, 31:2 (Fall, 2005), 50–3; Robert Armstrong, 'Comerford, Patrick', *DIB*. For O'Hartegan's championing Baron's appointment, see O'Hartegan to Wadding, 8 Aug. 1642, 22 Aug. 1642, HMC, *Franciscan manuscripts*, pp 172, 178; same to same, 19 Aug. 1643, UCD Archives, Luke Wadding Papers, UCD-OFM, D.01, vol. 2, pp 349–50.

permanent officer of the crown who had specific additional duties when parliament was sitting, being responsible for the Commons' buildings, services and security. This position was only clarified in 1586 when the then serjeant petitioned the House of Lords for his fees; peers 'ordered that serjant at armes ought not to attend upon that howse at all, but upon the Speaker of the Lower howse, and there to have his fee or reward.'[97] The serjeants in position during these parliaments were Morgan Mathews, chief serjeant-at-arms from 31 March 1612; a second serjeant, Edward Davies, possibly John's brother, was appointed for life because of the additional work caused by parliament, on 26 September 1612.[98] William and George Peisley were appointed on 23 August 1628 for life and there were at least three serjeants-at-arms in parliament's opening procession in 1634 and they also had deputies, 'Mr Sheppard and others under him.' Peter Hill and William Hill junior succeeded after the Peisleys' surrender on 19 December 1635 and Thomas Dee and George Starky were deputy serjeants-at-arms in 1641.[99] While this might seem a rather menial position, all were described as 'gentlemen' or 'esquire' and Peisley, MP for Augher in 1640 and King's County in 1645, was son-in-law of George Calvert, Lord Baltimore.[100] Black Rod Drury Cooper came from a Nottinghamshire gentry family, attended Gray's Inn, was part of the Dublin Castle intelligentsia under Wentworth and contributed a dedicatory verse to James Shirley's *His Royal Master* for the Werburg Street theatre.[101]

The serjeant managed the chamber's physical space and its environs, ensured necessary supplies, delivered messages, admitted visitors to the house, and took offenders into his custody.[102] On 8 October 1614, the Commons decided that 'it was given in charge to the serjeant at arms, to take care of the void room' and on 15 February 1641

> that the serjeant at arms attending this house from henceforth shall not permit or suffer any one, that is a stranger to the house, to listen or hearken within the two doors of the commons house, or in his inner room, or otherwise to understand the secrets of this house; and if the said serjeant shall find anyone to offend contrary to the intent of this order, he shall immediately bring him his prisoner into this house, to abide the censure of this house.

Hooker described the serjeant's role:

97 Entry for 6 May 1586, Routledge, 'Journal'. See also TCD, MS 647, fo. 91v.

98 James to Chichester, 26 Sept. 1612, *Cal. S.P. Ire., 1611–14*, p. 285; NLI, GO, MS 44, fo. 45v.

99 *Commons' Jn. Ire.*, 18 April 1635; *Liber Mun. Pub. Hib.*; *Commons' Jn. Ire.*, 22 June 1641, 17 July 1641, 7 Aug. 1641.

100 McGrath, 'Bio. dict.', i, pp 238–40; Robert Armstrong, 'Calvert, George, 1st Baron Baltimore', *DIB*.

101 McGrath, 'Poets and patronage'; Bramhall to the Lords Justices cancelling his Recognizance for delivering up himself to the Black Rod, 4 May 1641, Marsh's Library, MS Z3.1.1., no. 56.

102 E.g., *Commons' Jn. Ire.*, 19 Oct. 1614, 30 Oct. 1614, 28 July 1634, Nov. 1634, 3 Dec. 1634, 30 March 1640.

> to keep the doors of the house, and for the same he has others under him. He himself keepeth the doore of the inner house, where the commons sit, and seeth the same to be clean. He maie not suffer any to enter the house during the time of the sitting there, unless they be members, sent from the king or the lords, or having business there [or] otherwise licenced to come in. He admits them, preceding them, with his mace upon his shoulder. Anyone committed to his ward he is to take charge of them and keep them safely. If he is sent for anyone or on any message, he is to appoint a substitute to keep the doors.[103]

The serjeant-at-arms assisted in enforcing privilege and any orders of the house.[104] On 7 November 1614 he was ordered to bring in sheriffs who were in Dublin who had received money for county members' wages, but not given it to the MPs. and further orders were issued to the serjeant in connection with this on 20 and 26 April 1615 for the sheriffs of Wexford and Mayo respectively. Those the serjeant took into custody for breaching parliamentary privilege included MPs John Fishe, Robert Talbot, Edward Fitzharris, Geoffrey Baron, Edward Southworth and Edward Lake.[105] When FitzGerald was adjudged duly elected for Inistioge, the serjeant-at-arms brought him from the Marshalsea prison and accompanied him to the Commons for admission as an MP.[106]

Outside parliamentary sessions, MPs might meet the serjeant-at-arms doing his ordinary duties of attaching prisoners. The aggrieved Edmond Warren threatened the MP Thomas Davills with this in an attempt to get him to pay his debts:

> seeing you take noe Course to pay me I am driven to take as many wayes as I can to prosecute you. First you know you are outlaw=d (sic) and now I shall follow you to the Sergent at Armes if you prevent it not. You promised to pay Cisly Butlers debt a long time agoe & to give me £100 as you have not done neither, and therefore assure yourself I will send presently the sergent at arms for her and though I must confess the Charges wilbe wonderful much, yet before I loose my due, I must not spare her nor noe body else, when with fayrer means they doe not pay me. You shall receive the copy of the Command in closed.

Davills had been in the custody of the serjeant-at-arms two years earlier, when he was charged £8 for two months including 'house fees', attendance, serving orders and travel expenses.[107]

103 Holinshed, *Chronicles*, pp 125–6; *Commons' Jn. Ire.*, 28 July 1634, 18 April 1635, 30 March 1640.
104 Irish Archaeological Society, *Tracts*, ii, p. 143.
105 *Commons' Jn. Ire.*, 1 Aug. 1634, 1, 6, 12 Dec. 1634, 16 June 1640. For other examples of enforcing privilege, see 29 Oct. 1614, 4 Nov. 1614, 17, 25 Nov. 1614, 6 May 1615, 8, 10 Nov. 1634, 9 April 1635.
106 Ibid., 18 Feb. 1641.
107 Warren to Davills, 29 June 1640, Bodl. Lib., Carte MS 176, fo. 115; Bills to Mr Davills, Bodl.

Hooker noted the serjeant's daily allowance of 12*d*. during parliament in addition to his usual salary, and he also had a contribution from the members, which rose from 2*s*. 6*d*. from every knight and citizen, and 2*s*. from every burgess, to 10*s*. from knights of the shire and 5*s*. for citizens and burgesses during this period. He also received 20*s*. for any private act that passed and 6*s*. 8*d*. *per diem* from anyone in his custody.[108] Despite his salary, the profits of his office and MPs' contributions, Peter Hill was agitating for money and on 26 February 1641 the Commons ordered that

> report shall be made by the committee, that had formerly debated touching the serjeant at arms attending this house his fees, on Monday morning next; and that, after the said report, the said serjeant may produce his council to this house, to speak in his behalf touching his said fees.[109]

His application was supported by his English counterpart John Hunt, who certified his duties and fees: 'Upon the summons of a parliament, I am to provide all things necessary for the said House of Commons from the [blank], only the tables, forms and other wooden work … and at the end of Parliament they are all fees to the serjeant.' On 3 March 1641 the Commons decided on Hill's petition, basing it on Hunt's document with adjustments for Irish circumstances, such as omitting the money paid to the English serjeant on the first day of the parliament and the 10*s*. English serjeants received from any subject of a private naturalization bill on his taking the oath of allegiance before the speaker, which was not recorded as happening in Ireland.[110]

HERALDS

Heralds played an important role in devising and managing formal events, such as the opening of parliament and answering questions of precedence in the Lords; they received substantial fees from both temporal and spiritual peers for their induction into the house. Their role had developed since Nicholas Narbonne's appointment as first Ulster king of arms in 1552.[111] Ulsters attending early Stuart Irish parliaments were Daniel Molyneux, Thomas Preston and William Roberts. While a number of heralds sat in the English Commons, Molyneux was the only

Lib., Carte MS 176, slip of paper between fo. 114 and fo. 115, and fo. 144v. Davills had many money worries, but should have been covered by parliamentary privilege.

108 Holinshed, *Chronicles*, pp 125–6; *Commons' Jn. Ire.*, 28 July 1634, 18 April 1635, 30 March 1640.

109 Ibid., 1 March 1641.

110 Conway Davies, *Catalogue*, ii, pp 761–2; *Commons' Jn. Ire.*, 3 March 1641.

111 The development of the herald's role is discussed in McGrath, '*Obedientia Civium*'; David Edwards, 'Fashioning service in a renaissance state: the official journals of the Elizabethan viceroys in Ireland' in Brendan Dooley (ed.), *Renaissance now: the value of the Renaissance past in contemporary culture* (Oxford, 2014), pp 139–64.

one to do so in Ireland in this period.[112] MP for Strabane and 'a gent of good knowledge and sufficiency, and of verie honest reputation', Molyneux visited England in 1612 to research parliamentary protocols.[113] On 16 May 1615, 'Daniel Mulllinax, esq., King of Arms, a member of this House, came in his kingly robes' with a message from Lord Deputy Chichester. The Athlone Pursuivant (junior herald) Albon Leverett also took part in the procession at the opening of parliament. Molyneux and William Leverett (Albon's father) were paid £35 11*s.* 1¼*d.* and £13 6*s.* 8*d.* annually in 1611, although their salaries were greatly augmented by fees for their services.[114] Preston was an energetic officer, especially in collecting his fees and avoiding taxes. Roberts, herald from 1639, was a doctor of law and an assiduous officer, who endured vilification and assault when proclaiming the peace in Limerick in 1646.[115]

ROYAL MESSENGERS

Royal messengers called pursuivants-at-arms were easily identified by their red coats with the monarch's arms or monogram; new coats embellished with the king's initials were ordered in advance of the 1613 and 1634 parliaments.[116] Three pursuivants were employed 'for carrying Letters and Dispatches for his Majesty's Service'; pursuivants during this period included Gyles Stanley, William Bell and Nicholas Bennett, who were each paid £18 5*s.* annually in 1611.[117] More were appointed from 1612, possibly because of the parliament: Robert Madden (1612–16), Mathew Bentley (1616 and from 1627 jointly with his son George) and Joseph Savill (1630), later with Robert Savill. The Bentleys were dead by 1660 when George Wakefield was appointed.[118] Like the serjeant-at-arms, while this appears a menial office, pursuivants were described as 'gentlemen' and were well off, possibly as a result of holding this office. Mathew

112 I am grateful to Paul Hunneyball for information on the English heralds. See Alan Davidson and Andrew Thrush, 'Borough (Burgh, Burroughes), John' in Thrush and Ferris (eds), *History of parliament*; Peter Lefevre and Andrew Thrush, 'Philipot, John' in ibid.; J.S. Crossette, 'Bysshe, Edward' in Henning (ed.), *History of parliament*.

113 Thomas Jones to Salisbury, 25 Feb. 1612, TNA, SP 63/232, fo. 28r; English privy council to Chichester, 21 July 1612, *Cal. S.P. Ire., 1611–14*, p. 276; Moody, 'Irish parliament under Elizabeth and James I'; Terry Clavin, 'Molyneux, Daniel', *DIB*.

114 LPL, Carew MS 629, p. 105. The single penny and farthing in Molyneux's salary are curious.

115 List of persons who have not paid their dues in respect of funeral certificates, 1633, NLI, GO, MS 2, p. 8; Statement as to exemption of taxes, Thomas Preston, NLI, GO, MS 4, pp 19–23; Letters patent appointing Roberts, 15 April 1639, NLI, GO, MS 4, pp 55–8; Thomas Preston, Note of fees for parliament, 28 Nov. 1634, Bodl. Lib., Carte MS 66, fo. 292; Petition of Thomas Preston to be exempt from subsidies and taxation, 1636, NLI, GO, MS 14, pp 119–200; McGrath, 'Looking the part'. The source of Roberts' degree is unknown but it was not from Dublin, Cambridge or Oxford.

116 McGrath, '*Obedientia Civium*'; BL, Add. MS 5,754; Knowler (ed.), *Letters and dispatches*, i, p. 68.

117 LPL, Carew MS 629, p. 105.

118 *Liber Mun. Pub. Hib.*; *CPRI*, iii, p. 569.

Bentley was a founding burgess of Banagher and claimed losses of £2,570 in the rebellion. Peter Kay, like others appointed under Wentworth, although originally from Kent, had Yorkshire connections and merited a funeral entry, a clear sign of social status.[119] During parliament, the porters or janitors of Dublin Castle and the Four Courts were in attendance to open and keep the doors of the chambers and committee rooms.[120]

MEMBERS OF PARLIAMENT

The hopelessly confused state of returns especially in 1634 and after 1642 makes it impossible to establish the full Commons' membership, a situation that also obtained in early Tudor England.[121] However, some conclusions can be drawn, albeit with some caveats, about their ethnic background, occupations and social status. Unlike English and Scottish assemblies, parliaments in Ireland were ethnically mixed. While the number of English and Welsh MPs was small, if growing, in Tudor parliaments in Ireland, they increased rapidly under the Stuarts and were joined by Scots. Protestant MPs were overwhelmingly of British origin and Catholics were almost entirely of Old English and Gaelic stock, although ten Protestant MPs in 1634 were Old English and seven were of Gaelic origin. Conversely, George Bagenal, Valentine Browne and Oliver Stephenson were New English Catholics.

Almost equal numbers of 1613–15 members were Old English and New English, 9% were Gaelic, 3% Scottish and the same number Welsh. The Molyneux brothers, whose father was originally from Calais, made up slightly less than 1%. However, this analysis based on surnames ignores the many who were of mixed origin.[122]

Table 9.2. MPs' ethnic origins, 1613–15

New English 44%	Scottish 3%
Old English %	Welsh 3%
Gaelic 9%	Other 1%

In 1634, 47 Protestant MPs were second-generation settlers and 85 in 1640. The disconnection between Protestant members and their constituencies in Wentworth's parliaments is shown both by the number who were recently arrived – in 1634 at least 16 MPs came to Ireland within the previous 10 months and 42% of the 151 Protestant MPs were non-resident in their constituencies.[123] In 1640,

119 Ibid., iii, pp 360–5; Aidan Clarke (ed.), *1641 Depositions, Volume IV: Dublin* (Dublin, 2017), p. 309; NLI, GO, MS 72, Funeral Entries, Volume 9, 1640–63, p. 254.
120 *Liber Mun. Pub. Hib.*; *Commons' Jn. Ire.*, 19 Oct. 1614.
121 Hawkyard, *Commons*, p. 108.
122 McGrath, 'Membership', pp 124–37.
123 McGrath, 'Electoral strategy'.

roughly half of all Protestant MPs were second-generation settlers, although this includes a number whose arrival in Ireland was of very recent origin, including Edmund Borlase, Little Jr, Thomas Radcliffe and the Wandesfords. Eleven were of Old English origin, eight each of Gaelic and Scottish origin and four Welsh. 40% of the Old English and 25% of the Gaelic Protestants were county members.[124] This compares to the Scottish Estates, where roughly 16% of the members were from the Highlands. Interestingly, Scottish historians make no distinction between Gaelic Highland clans and Lowland Scots in discussing parliamentary membership and engagement.[125] Three other MPs were from European families – Matthew de Renzy, whose father was German and the Dutchman Theodore Schout, who would later be joined by Peter Wybrants.[126] In addition, John Ogle and St Leger Jr had been born in the Low Countries and Peregrine Bannister had spent his youth there.[127]

The character of the MPs returned after 1642 showed a different ethnic balance: 62% were New English, less than one-fifth (17%) were Old English; 8% were of Gaelic origin (including the highly Anglicized Kennedys), 2% were Dutch and 1% each were Scottish and Welsh. The ethnic origins of nine (10%) are unknown. These figures do not distinguish between those New English whose families had been based in Ireland for some decades and the recently arrived, but the balance was overwhelmingly in favour of those settled for at least two generations.[128]

50% of MPs in the English parliament were gentry, 8–9% were peers' sons, 14–15% were lawyers and roughly 10% merchants and tradesmen were also represented. Given the far greater number of boroughs than county seats, this demonstrates a significant level of under representation for merchants, although the lawyers included recorders from the towns who returned them. Nearly all county members were locally resident, but only 23% of borough members lived in those towns, a significant drop from the Elizabethan period. However, while the number of non-residents rose, there was also an increasing disinclination to return those with no local connections, who would be less well able to represent their constituents and lobby on their behalf.[129]

It is difficult to make exact comparisons with the Irish parliament, as social status was even more complicated in Ireland than in England or Wales.[130] English social structures took no account of Irish norms. MPs who held unique Irish titles

124 1640 MPs' ethnic backgrounds are discussed in McGrath, 'Bio. dict.', ii, pp 67–76.

125 Kennedy, 'Representing the periphery'.

126 Brian Mac Cuarta, 'De Renzy, Sir Matthew', *DIB*; Rolf Loeber, 'English and Irish sources for the history of Dutch economic activity in Ireland, 1600–89', *IESH*, 8:1 (1981), 70–85.

127 On Bannister and Ogle, see McGrath, 'Bio. dict.', i, pp 51–2, 227–8. For more on Bannister, see David Edwards, 'Richard Boyle's private army: the creation of a colonial security force in early Stuart Munster' in David Edwards and Colin Rynne (eds), *The colonial world of Richard Boyle, first earl of Cork* (Dublin, 2018), pp 223–44, esp. pp 235–6.

128 McGrath, 'Recruiter returns'.

129 Smith, *Stuart*, pp 27–9; Hawkyard, *Commons*, pp 145–9.

130 Robinson, 'Tudor revolution in Welsh government'.

such as barons by warrant (e.g., Galtrim, Loughmoe or Navan) or hereditary knighthoods such as the Knight of Kerry, were described as 'Mr' or esquire.[131] There was no clear way of reconciling the explicit hierarchy of English peers and gentry who succeeded to their titles and estates through primogeniture and Gaelic families whose estates were held by the clan and whose chieftainship was not designated by birth order. While 'surrender and regrant', the Composition of Connacht and plantation imposed the English system and a few Gaelic chiefs were ennobled, by the seventeenth century, fewer Irish were knighted or received baronetcies and as many lost their lands in the plantations, the link between hereditary elites and property was weakened for Gaelic and Old English families and strengthened for the New English settlers.

Oliver St John, Falkland and Wentworth implemented a programme of reconstructing the Irish 'social pyramid', replacing the native elites with recent English arrivals.[132] Only those whose prospects of advancement were limited in England would choose to come to Ireland, but when they did, their social and economic status was consistently promoted at the expense of the native community. There is clear evidence of bias in the way that social status was recorded in official documents: the consistent practice of elevating Protestants' status and diminishing that of Catholics makes official descriptions unreliable, but also underlines the newcomers' inferior origins.[133] English settlers were described as 'armiger' (esquire), whether they had coats of arms or not, and were far more likely to be knighted or granted baronetcies than Catholics. Robert Nettleton is described as armiger in the list of returns and his younger brother George as 'generosus', although their father was described as 'gent.' in his will.[134] The variability around the use of titles was exemplified by Edward Tarleton and Cosny Molloy, described as 'generosus' on joining the King's Inns (thus liable for lower admission fees), but as 'esquire' as MPs.[135]

Establishing status was further complicated by using men's highest titles, so merchants who were also aldermen or entitled to be called 'Mr', having served as mayor, were listed as alderman or 'generosus' (gentleman) rather than by their occupation. Military rank superseded civil titles other than knighthood or higher. As MacCarthy-Morrogh noted, gentlemen in plantation Munster were self-appointed and men 'might get away with a social claim that would be ridiculed in England.' Sir John Leek's dilemma contemplating his daughter's marriage to

131 A number of Irishmen held titles which allowed them to be styled baron, but which did not entitle them to sit in the House of Lords, including Patrick Hussey of Galtrim, Theobald Purcell of Loughmoe, Thomas Nangle of the Navan, MPs for Meath in 1613 and 1634, Cross Tipperary in 1634 and Navan 1640 respectively. The three hereditary knights, of Kerry (John FitzGerald, MP for in Kerry 1634 and Inistiogue in 1640), Glin and the Valley, had no English equivalent.

132 Treadwell, *Buckingham and Ireland*, pp 103ff.

133 See NLI, GO, MS 44, 1607, a who's who of administration officials in Ireland and MS 58, grants of arms.

134 William Brown (ed.), *Yorkshire deeds*, 10 vols (Leeds, 1909–55), i, p. 167.

135 King's Inns, MS B1/1, fos. 18v, 75r.

another settler whose age and fortune were suitable but not his low social status encapsulates the issue; if the marriage went ahead, 'her place must be in the arse of all the country ... for we stand here more upon place than in England; here are many [upstarts] that wealth doth advance from baseness to preferment.'[136]

As the route to social advancement was through military service and crown office from which the native community was increasingly excluded, the two communities' social and economic position diverged markedly through this period, causing understandable resentment:

> men of meen birth who aimed to raise estates by the ruine of innocents, so that Sir William Parsons and the late Earl of Corke who within this 60 years past coming as naked lads here without either friends, means or learning other than an ordinary faculty of reading and writing in English ... learned those tricks of acquiring by hook and crook lands, offices and livings [so] that they were shortly the ablest men for riches in the kingdom ... rather by cunning and the suppression of many other families of good esteem than any direct or honest industry.[137]

Relatively few sons of long-established Irish peers sat in the Commons; Bryan, Walter Ormond, David and Theobald Burke of Mayo, Donough MacCarthy (*plate 16*), Nicholas Plunkett, Taaffe, Redmond Roche, Robert Dillon and his son James, and members of the Dunboyne and Ikerrin families were rare exceptions. Thomas Burke was a cousin of Clanricard, but his return was due to his role as the earl's lawyer and Daniel O'Brien was Thomond's brother.[138] A larger number of Protestants were peers' sons largely because so many settlers acquired titles including the Chichesters, Hamiltons, Loftuses, Montgomerys and Moores but also Caulfield, Dungarvan, Simon Digby, Arthur Jones and Christopher Roper. Thomas Esmond and William Sarsfield (Kilmallock) were unusual in being sons of recently ennobled Old English Protestants. Kilmallock consistently, and Esmond after the 1641 rebellion, were Catholics.[139] Maltravers, Philip Lisle and Philip Wenman were descended from lords in England, and Robert Byron and Wharton were brothers of English peers. Some Protestants, Roger Jones (later Lord Ranelagh, not the MP for Sligo in 1634), Robert and Thomas Meredith, Roger Moynes, Philip Pillsworth, Henry Spottiswood and Marcus Ussher were bishops' sons.[140] Others were peers' sons- or brothers-in-law.

136 Quoted in MacCarthy-Morrogh, *Munster plantation*, p. 208.
137 Bodl. Lib., Carte MS 64, fos. 459v–60r.
138 Clanricard to Ormond, 11 March 1643, Bodl. Lib., Carte MS 4, fo. 458, wherein is noted 'the sad newes of my Nephew Tho: Burkes death which doth much perplex me being one I had occasion to vallue and in present his imployment doth make his Loss very considerable in many respects.'
139 On many of these figures, see Ohlmeyer, *Making Ireland English*, passim.
140 For connections between MPs in 1613 and the House of Lords, see McGrath, 'Membership', pp 188–95.

MPs included a wide range of occupations, including gentry, merchants, soldiers, lawyers, crown officials and doctors, but only one, the wealthy, self-confident tanner Thomas Elwall, was a tradesman and Richard Blacknall and John Ingersoll worked in the iron industry; all were Protestant settlers.[141] Maurice Williams was the only medical doctor. These categories conceal large differences between the groups as well as some overlap, as some soldiers and lawyers also held other crown office and prosperous merchants were in the process of gentrification.

Irish gentry who had dominated the Tudor Commons were decreasingly represented in the Irish Commons because of the crown's determination to return Protestants, especially newly arrived ones. Opposition was anticipated from Catholic gentry, merchants and lawyers (all of whom stemmed from gentry and merchant families). As votes did not break down on confessional grounds, the crown experienced opposition also from Protestant gentry. While some Catholic gentry, merchants and lawyers acquired knighthoods or baronetcies, there are striking differences between Protestant and Catholic MPs' status (Table 9.3).

Table 9.3. MPs who were knights or baronets, 1613–48

Parliament	*Protestants*	*Catholics*
1613	39	10
1634	55	19
1640	52	15
1642–8 Additional MPs	9	–

Merchants were overwhelmingly Catholic from the old towns in Leinster and Munster and Galway and formed a solid block of MPs (Table 9.4). They were elected in Clonmel, Coleraine, Limerick, Youghal and possibly Dublin and Kilkenny in 1628. The strategy of returning as many placemen as possible largely excluded Protestant merchants in new boroughs until 1642, but after 1635 also barred Catholics in disfranchised boroughs like Clonmel. In 1640, 25 Catholics and five Protestants were merchants, although several were not working in that capacity and a further number came from merchant families, including many lawyers. Catholic merchants were returned for the towns in which they lived and traded, but not the gentrified Arthur Champion and John and William Wandesford and, after 1642, six Dublin merchants were returned, all non-residents in their constituencies.[142]

141 On Blacknall and his ironworking activities, see Paul Rondelez, 'The metallurgical enterprises of Richard Boyle, first earl of Cork' in Edwards and Rynne (eds), *Colonial world*, pp 112–20.

142 McGrath, 'Recruiter returns'; Raymond Gillespie, 'The murder of Arthur Champion and the 1641 rising in Fermanagh', *Clogher Record*, 14:3 (1993), 52–66.

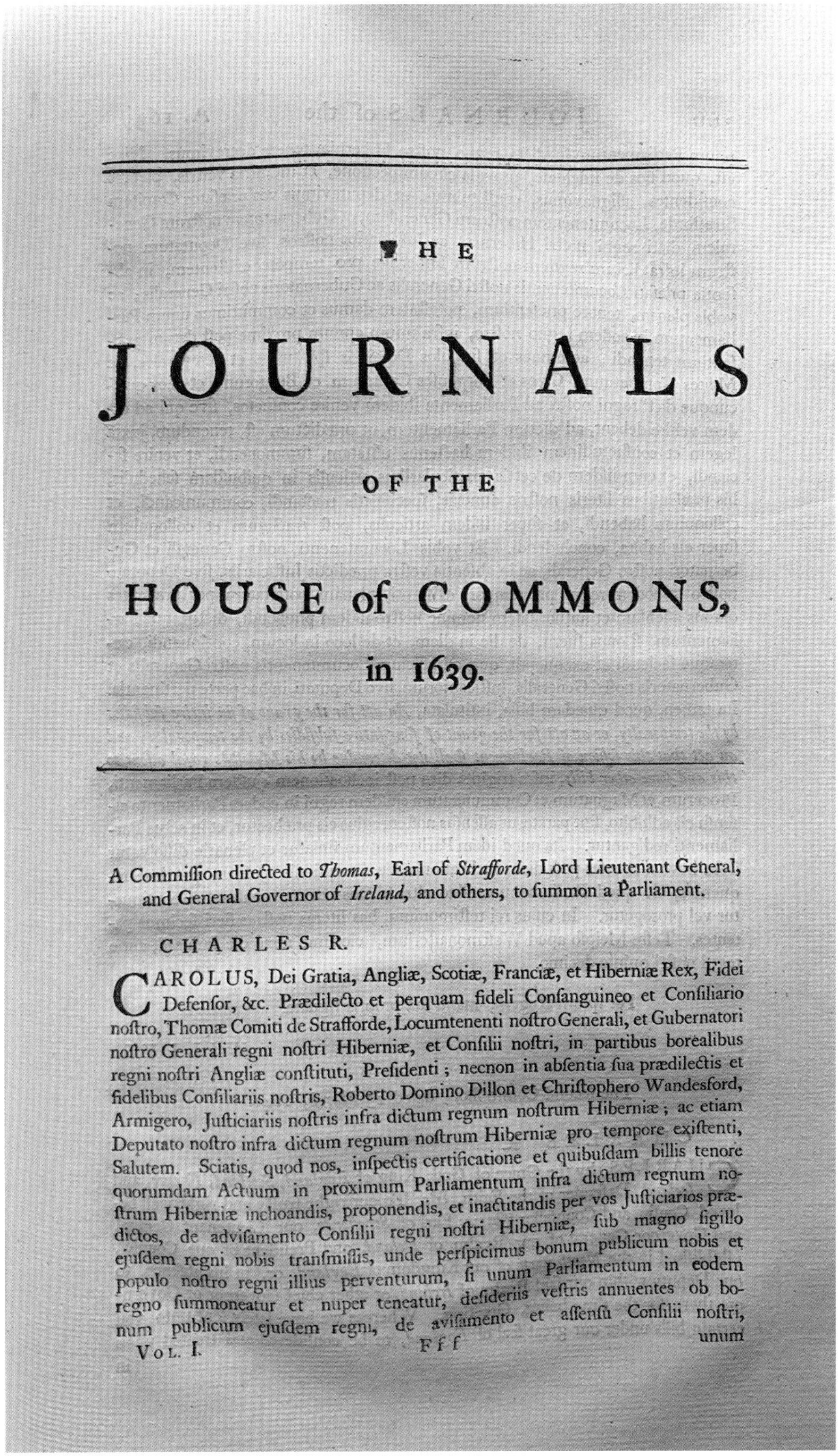

THE

JOURNALS

OF THE

HOUSE of COMMONS,

in 1639.

A Commiſſion directed to *Thomas*, Earl of *Straffordе*, Lord Lieutenant General, and General Governor of *Ireland*, and others, to ſummon a Parliament.

CHARLES R.

CAROLUS, Dei Gratia, Angliæ, Scotiæ, Franciæ, et Hiberniæ Rex, Fidei Defenſor, &c. Prædilecto et perquam fideli Conſanguineo et Conſiliario noſtro, Thomæ Comiti de Strafforde, Locumtenenti noſtro Generali, et Gubernatori noſtro Generali regni noſtri Hiberniæ, et Conſilii noſtri, in partibus borealibus regni noſtri Angliæ conſtituti, Preſidenti; necnon in abſentia ſua prædilectis et fidelibus Conſiliariis noſtris, Roberto Domino Dillon et Chriſtophero Wandesford, Armigero, Juſticiariis noſtris infra dictum regnum noſtrum Hiberniæ; ac etiam Deputato noſtro infra dictum regnum noſtrum Hiberniæ pro tempore exiſtenti, Salutem. Sciatis, quod nos, inſpectis certificatione et quibuſdam billis tenore quorumdam Actuum in proximum Parliamentum infra dictum regnum noſtrum Hiberniæ inchoandis, proponendis, et inactitandis per vos Juſticiarios prædictos, de adviſamento Conſilii regni noſtri Hiberniæ, ſub magno ſigillo ejuſdem regni nobis tranſmiſſis, unde perſpicimus bonum publicum nobis et populo noſtro regni illius perventurum, ſi unum Parliamentum in eodem regno ſummoneatur et nuper teneatur, deſideriis veſtris annuentes ob bonum publicum ejuſdem regni, de adviſamento et aſſenſu Conſilii noſtri, unum

VOL. I. Fff

28 Detail of the 1640 commission for summoning parliament. *Journals of the House of Commons of the kingdom of Ireland* (Dublin, 1753), 8 vols, I, p. 205.

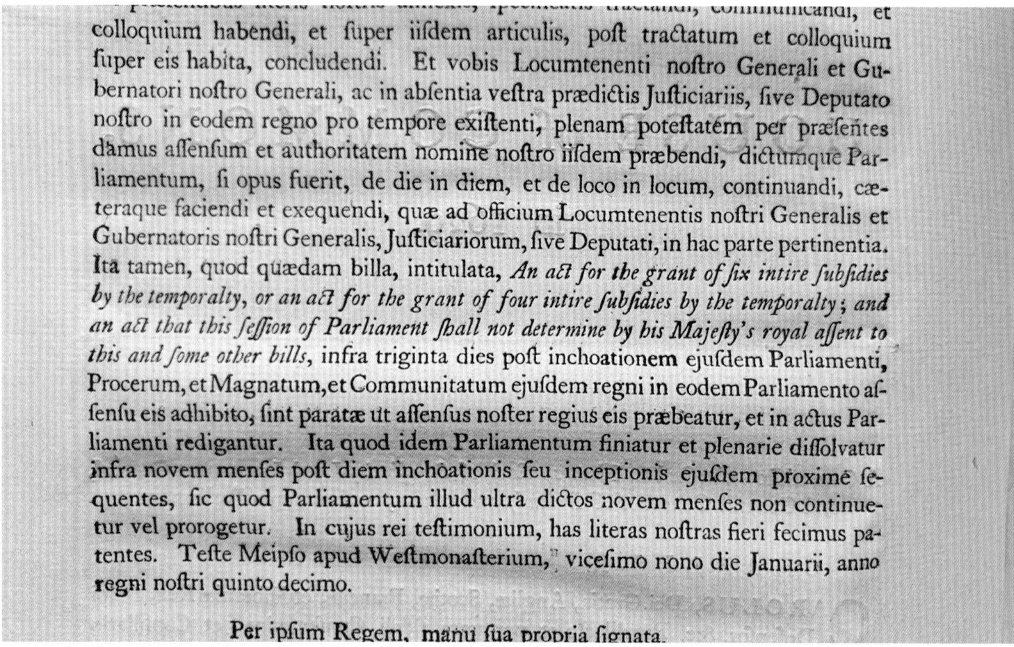
colloquium habendi, et ſuper iiſdem articulis, poſt tractatum et colloquium ſuper eis habita, concludendi. Et vobis Locumtenenti noſtro Generali et Gubernatori noſtro Generali, ac in abſentia veſtra prædictis Juſticiariis, ſive Deputato noſtro in eodem regno pro tempore exiſtenti, plenam poteſtatem per præſentes damus aſſenſum et authoritatem nomine noſtro iiſdem præbendi, dictumque Parliamentum, ſi opus fuerit, de die in diem, et de loco in locum, continuandi, cæteraque faciendi et exequendi, quæ ad officium Locumtenentis noſtri Generalis et Gubernatoris noſtri Generalis, Juſticiariorum, ſive Deputati, in hac parte pertinentia. Ita tamen, quod quædam billa, intitulata, *An act for the grant of ſix intire ſubſidies by the temporalty, or an act for the grant of four intire ſubſidies by the temporalty; and an act that this ſeſſion of Parliament ſhall not determine by his Majeſty's royal aſſent to this and ſome other bills*, infra triginta dies poſt inchoationem ejuſdem Parliamenti, Procerum, et Magnatum, et Communitatum ejuſdem regni in eodem Parliamento aſſenſu eis adhibito, ſint paratæ ut aſſenſus noſter regius eis præbeatur, et in actus Parliamenti redigantur. Ita quod idem Parliamentum finiatur et plenarie diſſolvatur infra novem menſes poſt diem inchoationis ſeu inceptionis ejuſdem proxime ſequentes, ſic quod Parliamentum illud ultra dictos novem menſes non continuetur vel prorogetur. In cujus rei teſtimonium, has literas noſtras fieri fecimus patentes. Teſte Meipſo apud Weſtmonaſterium, viceſimo nono die Januarii, anno regni noſtri quinto decimo.

Per ipſum Regem, manu ſua propria ſignata.

29 Detail of the 1640 commission for summoning parliament. *Journals of the House of Commons of the kingdom of Ireland* (Dublin, 1753), 8 vols, I, p. 206.

30 *(opposite)* Cork county sheriff's mandate and election, Youghal, 1634. Cork City and County Archives, MS YTR/B/1, p. 426. Reproduced courtesy of Cork City and County Archives.

The copie of the mandatt from ye Shireffe.

Com Cork.

Edmond fitz Gerald esquier high shireffe of the Countie of Cork to the maior of the towne of youghall greeting by vertue of his mat[ies] writt of eligendo militibus et burgensibus parliament[i] directed unto me from the lord deputie generall of Ireland bearing date in Dublin the ninth day of May anno regni Caroli 10o — These are therefore to will and require you jointly upon receipt hereof with the consent and assent of your aldermen and comminaltie of the towne aforesaid to elect and make choice by way of election of 2 sufficient burgesses of your towne of youghall men of good understanding witt knowledge and discretion for the causes concerning the weale publique of this realme of Ireland and them haveing so elected and chosen to come and to commaund them and every of them to appeare in his maties high Court of parliament to be houlden at his highnes citie of Dublin the 14th day of July next whereof you may not faile and also to make returne of this mandat or precept under your comminaltye seale there unto annexed unto me or my subsheriffe within 12 dayes after receipt hereof at your perills And for your so doing this shall be your sufficient warrant Given under my hand and seale of office the 11th day of June 1634.

Whereupon and by vertue of the said mandatt the maior Bayliefs burgesses and comminaltie after theire severall summons to that effect made according to theire auntient custome in such cases of election have proceeded to their election as followeth.

Christmas Harford ald	Are named	5	Suffragia
Edward Gough alder		59	
Edward Stoute alder		21	
Theobald Ronane ald		41	

So that by election and pluralitie of voices Edward Gough and Theobald Ronane were chosen and appointed burgesses for this present parliament.

10 die Decembris 1628.

Memorandum that the maior Balives burgesses & commons of Youghull aforesaid have acquitted discharged and exonerated william Blwett of Youghull alderman and Edward Coyge of the same alderman late elected burgesses of Parliament of & concerning the 12li sterl which they received towards their charge having delivered [illegible] sterl to the use of the corporation, and being allowed the remainder to them selves towards their charge & labor allreadie sustayned witnes

Wm Gough

Ed Chudleton

32 Replication of freeholders of King's County, to the Irish House of Commons, 1641. Birr Castle, MS A/1/19. Reproduced courtesy of Birr Castle Archives.

31 (*left*) Payment of wages for Youghal MPs William Gough and William Bluett, 1628. Cork City and County Archives, MS YTR/B/1, p. 353. Reproduced courtesy of Cork City and County Archives.

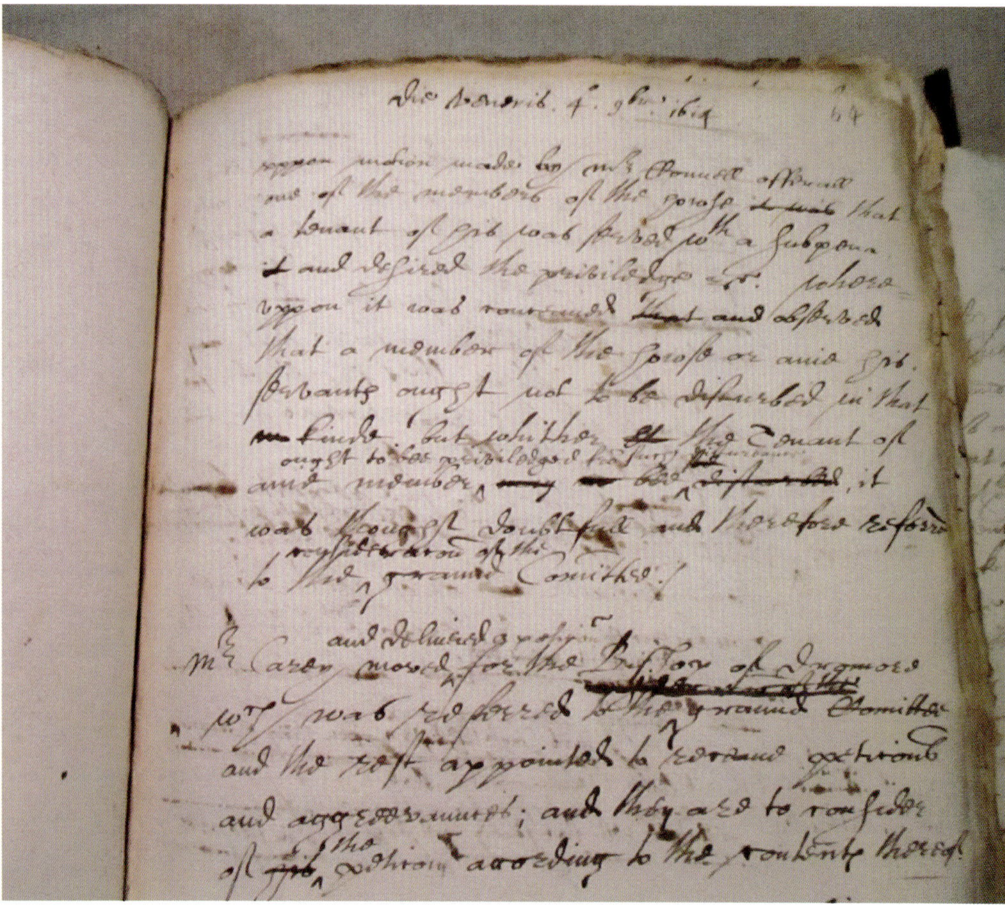

33 Clerk's rough journal notes, 1614. TNA, MS PRO SP 30/5/3, f. 64. Reproduced courtesy of The National Archives, UK.

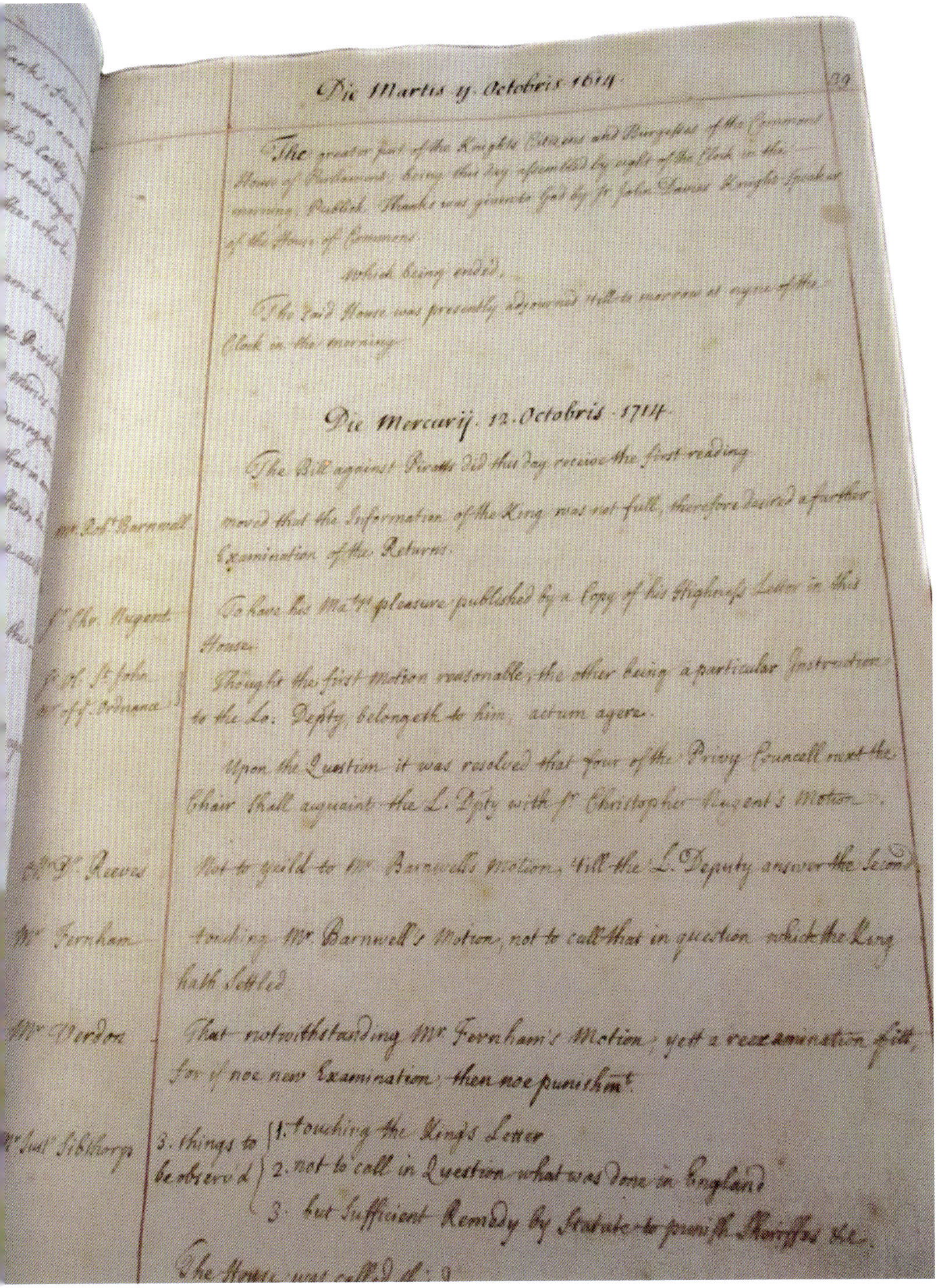

34 Page from fair copy of the Commons' journals, 1614. NLI, MS 836, p. 39.
Reproduced courtesy of the National Library of Ireland.

35 Published 1634 statutes. *Anno regni Caroli Regis, Angliae … decimo & undecimo, at the parliament begun and holden at Dublin, the 14 day of July [1634] and there continued untill the 18 day of Aprill 1635* (Dublin, 1635). Reproduced courtesy of Archbishop Marsh's Library, Dublin.

BEATI PACIFI[C]I

C R

ANNO REGI[NI]

CARO[LI]

REGIS, AN[G]LIÆ,

SCOTIÆ, FRANCIÆ,

ET HIBERNIÆ,

Decimo & Vndec[imo].

At the Parliament begun [a]nd holden at

Dublin, *the* [illegible] *day of Iu[ly], in the tenth*

yeare of the Raigne of o[u]r most graci-

ous Sov[e]raigne Lord, CHARLES

by the [grace] of God, [of] England,

Scotlan[d], France, an[d Ir]eland

King, Defender [of] the

Faith &c.

And there continued untill the

18. day of Aprill, 1635.

To the high pleasure of Almighty God, and to the

Weale publique of this Realme, were ena-

cted as followeth.

Imprinted at DUBLIN

by the Society of Stationers,

Printers [to] the Kings most

excellent Majesty.

Anno Dom. M. DC. XXXV.

by

SILVANUS GLEG ... RI: MORTON FECIT

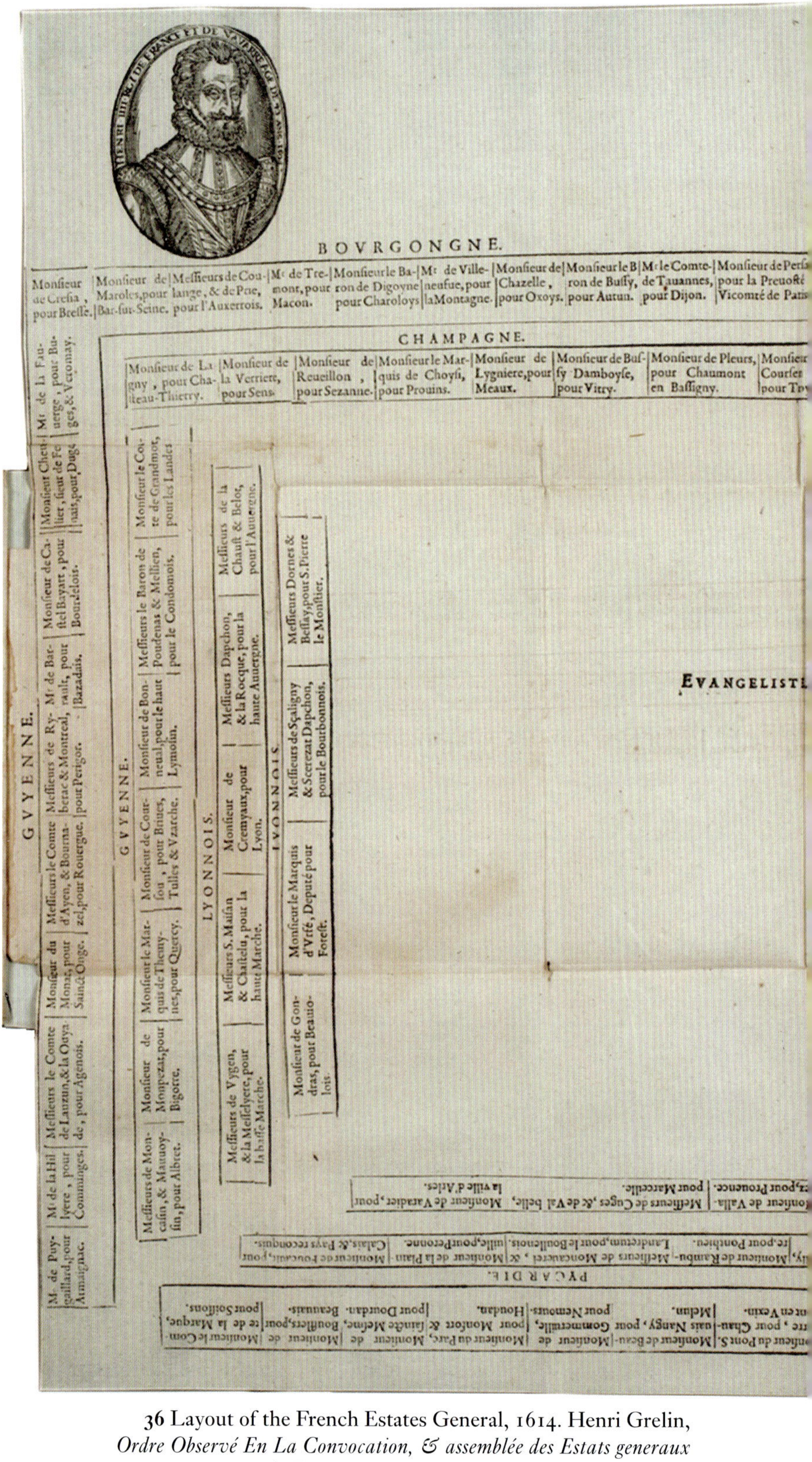

36 Layout of the French Estates General, 1614. Henri Grelin, *Ordre Observé En La Convocation, & assemblée des Estats generaux de France, tenuz en la Ville de Paris* (Paris, 1615).

NORMANDIE.

Monsieur de la Mailleraye, pour le Bailliage de Roüen.	Monsieur de Longaunay, pour Caen.	Monsieur de sainct Cere, pour le Bailliage de Cault.	Monsieur de sainct Vast, pour Costantin.	Monsieur de Breauté, pour Eureux.	Monsieur de Flaucour, pour Gisors.	Messieurs de Sassy & Fontenelle, pour Allençon.

LANGVEDOC.

Mr de Cornuson, pour Thoulouse.	Messieurs le Marquis de Portes & Chambault, pour Beaucaire & Nymes.	Monsieur le Vicomte de Polygnac, pour le Puy en Vellay.	Messieurs le Murles & S. André, pour Montpellier.	Monsieur le Comte de Ryeux, pour Carcassone.	Messieurs de Ferrail, & S. Rome, pour Louragais.	Monsieur de Castagnac, pour Foys.

BRETAIGNE.

Monsieur le Comte de Brissac, pour la Duché de Bretagne.	Monsieur de Gaymaduc, pour la Duché de Bretagne.	Monsieur de Montmartin, pour la Duché de Bretagne.	Monsieur de Cayduc, pour la Duché de Bretagne.	Mr le Vicomte de la Piguelaye, pour la Duché de Bretagne.	Monsieur de Querholin, pour la Duché de Bretagne.

ORLEANS.

Monsieur de la Salle-rougerie, pour le Perche.	Messieurs de Langeron, & Blanchefort, pour Lyuernois & Donziers.	Monsieur de Loudriere, pour la Rochelle.	Monsieur Dars, pour l'Angoumois.	Monsieur Dimmonuille, pour Estampes.	Monsieur des Radrets, pour le Vandomois.	Monsieur de l'Isle Roüet, pour Chastel-Rodais.

ORLEANS.

Messieurs de Rhodes, & Nançay, pour le Berry.	Monsieur de Maintenon, pour Chartres.	Monsieur du Hallyer, pour Orleans.	Monsieur de Ville-gomblain, pour Bloys.	Monsieur de Couberon, pour Gian.	Monsieur des Hayes, pour Montargis.

ORLEANS.

Messieurs de la Chastaigneraye, & de la Noue, pour Poictou.	Monsieur du Bellay, pour Anjou.	Messieurs de Boullay & Rocheux, pour le Mayne.	Monsieur de Pons, pour la Tourayne.

Moncasin, pour ret:	EVANGELISTE.
e de la esse.	

PROVE

Monsieur le Marquis de Zaics, pour Prouence.	Monsieur le Comte de Boulbon, pour Prouence.	Monsieur de Monmeian, pour Prouence.	Monsieur de Vinces, pour Proence.	Mon dicte

DAVPHINE.

Monsieur de Murynes, pour Dauphiné.	Monsieur Duquais, pour Dauphiné.	Monsieur de Monbrun, pour Dauphiné.	Monsieur le Comte de Tonnerre, pour le Dauphiné.

L'ISLE DE F

Monsieur le Vicomte Dauchy, pour Vermandois.	Monsieur de Clermont Dantrague, pour Dreux.	Monsieur de Bleru, pour Mantes & Meulan.	Mr le Vidasme de Chartres, pour Chasteauneuf en Thymerais.	Monsieur de Bouteville Mõmorancy, pour Senlis.	Mr le Cmte de Tresme pour Crespy en Valloys.	Monsieur court, en Bea

37 Richard Bolton in his robes as chancellor and speaker of the House of Lords, unknown artist, 1639. Image courtesy of Whyte and sons, Dublin.

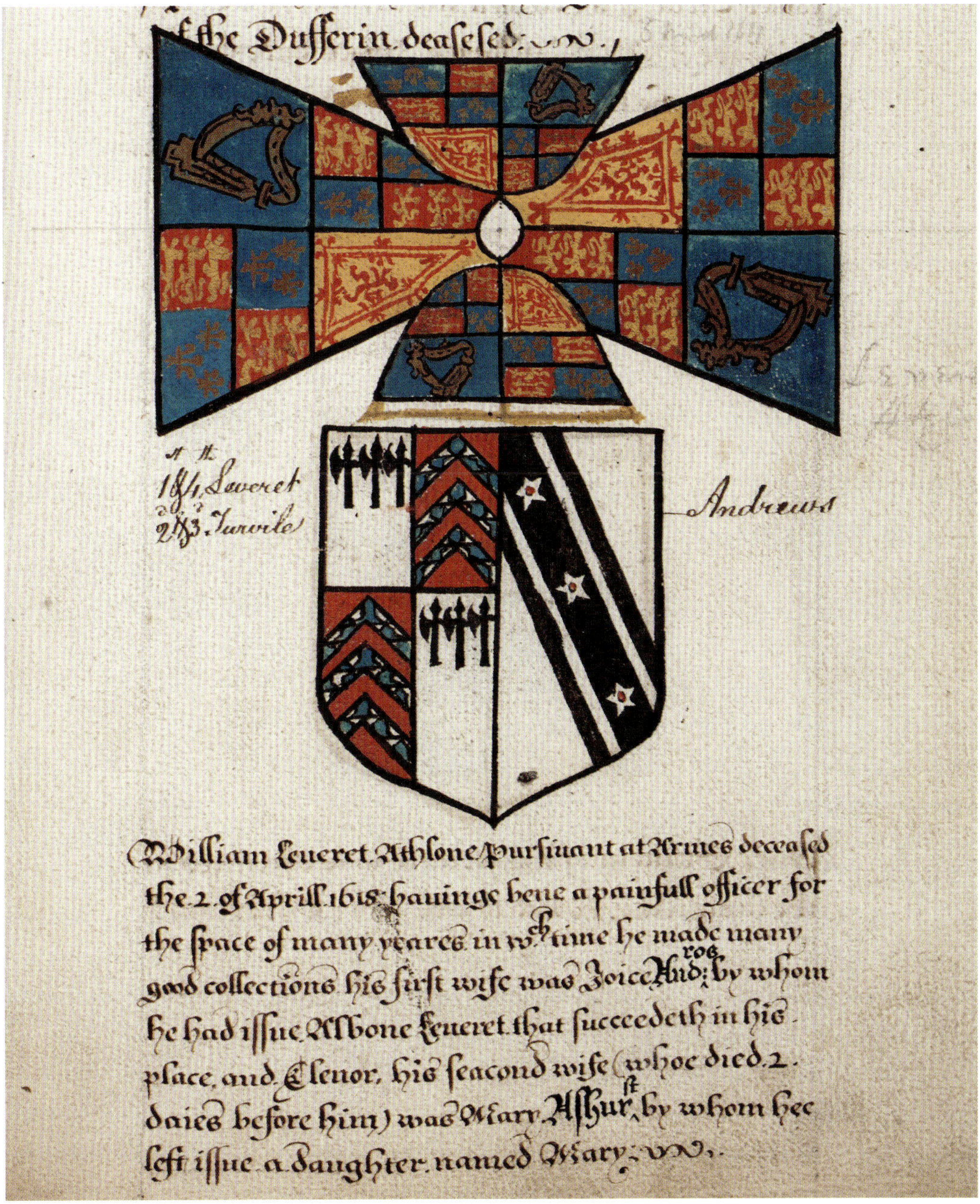

38 William Leveret's robes as Athlone Pursuivant. NLI, GO MS 66, Funeral Entries, vol. 3, 1604–22, f. 73r. Image reproduced courtesy of the National Library of Ireland.

39 Chair reputed to have been used at the Confederation of Kilkenny. Collection of the Royal Society of Antiquaries of Ireland. Photograph © Robert D. Marshall.

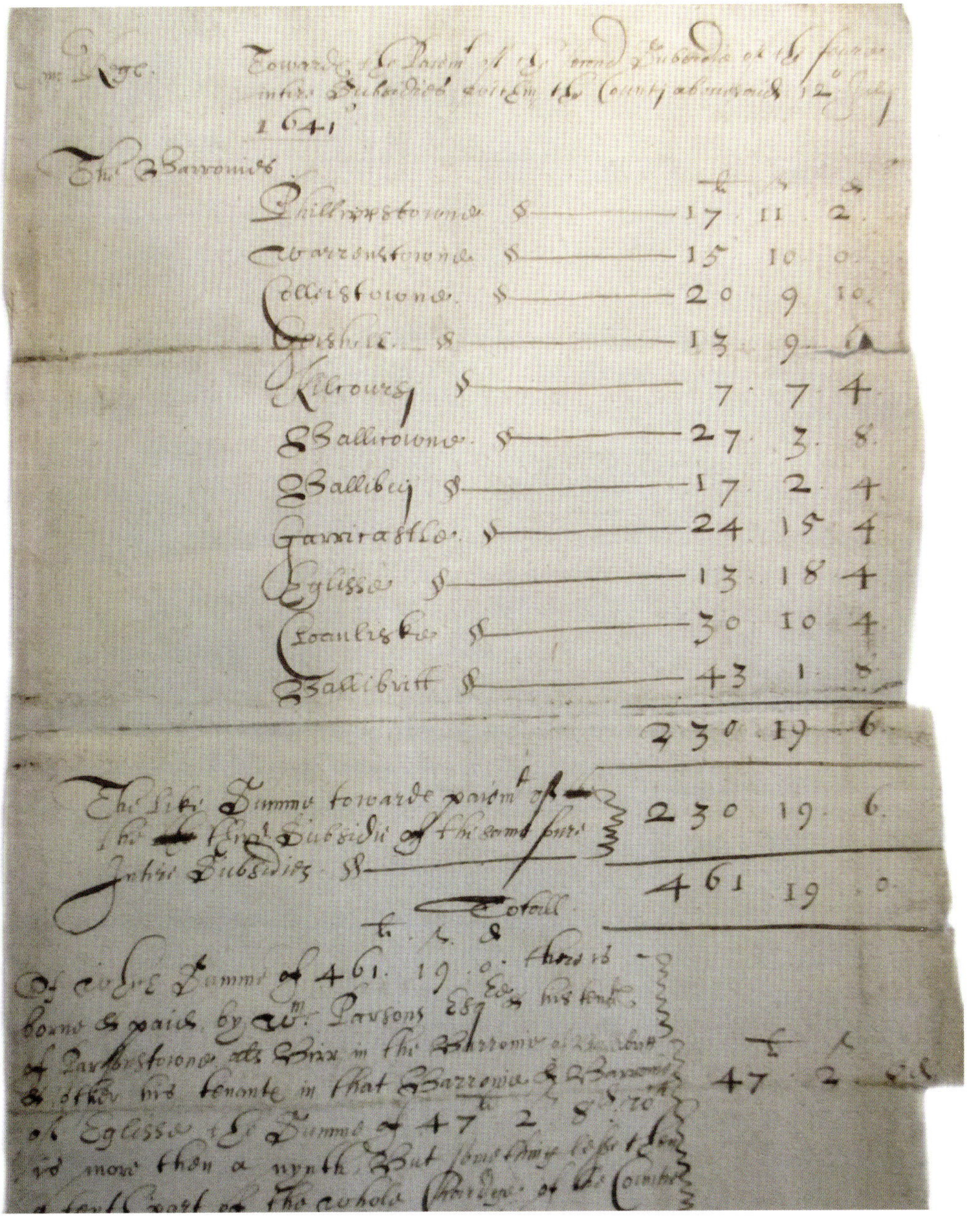

40 Notes on the collection of the 1641 subsidy in King's County. Birr Castle, MS A/5/43. Reproduced courtesy of Birr Castle Archives.

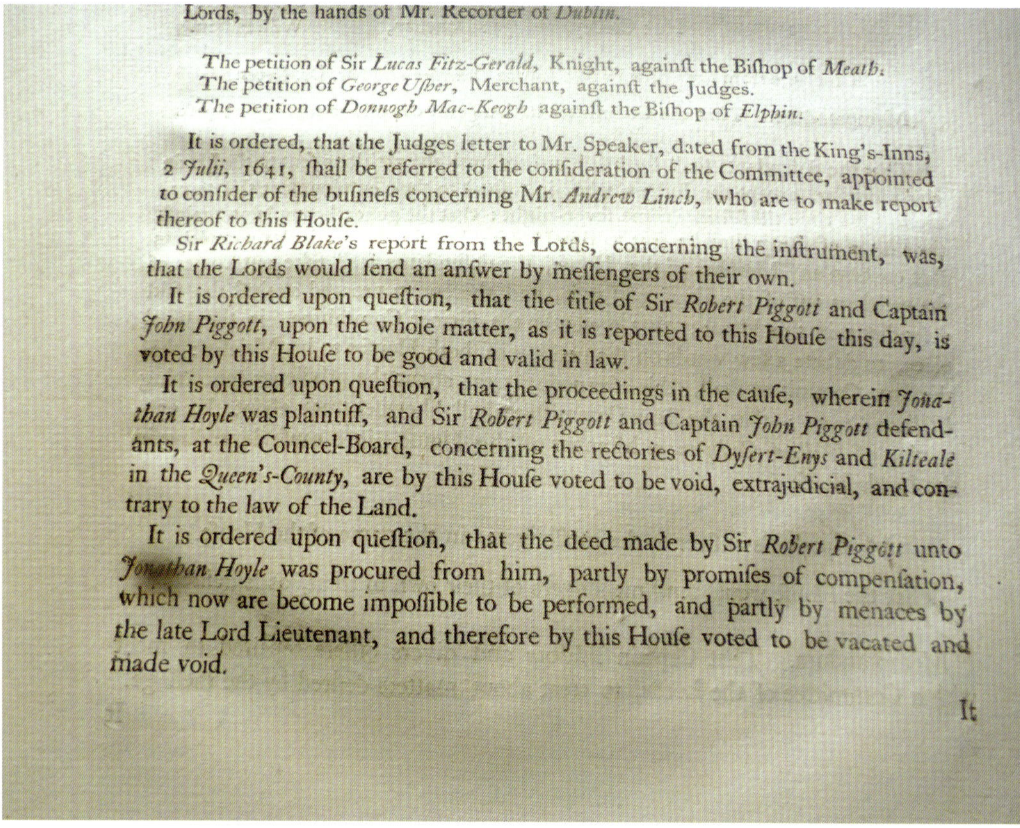

Lords, by the hands of Mr. Recorder of *Dublin*.

The petition of Sir *Lucas Fitz-Gerald*, Knight, againſt the Biſhop of *Meath*.
The petition of *George Uſher*, Merchant, againſt the Judges.
The petition of *Donnogh Mac-Keogh* againſt the Biſhop of *Elphin*.

It is ordered, that the Judges letter to Mr. Speaker, dated from the King's-Inns, 2 *Julii*, 1641, ſhall be referred to the conſideration of the Committee, appointed to conſider of the buſineſs concerning Mr. *Andrew Linch*, who are to make report thereof to this Houſe.

Sir *Richard Blake*'s report from the Lords, concerning the inſtrument, was, that the Lords would ſend an anſwer by meſſengers of their own.

It is ordered upon queſtion, that the title of Sir *Robert Piggott* and Captain *John Piggott*, upon the whole matter, as it is reported to this Houſe this day, is voted by this Houſe to be good and valid in law.

It is ordered upon queſtion, that the proceedings in the cauſe, wherein *Jonathan Hoyle* was plaintiff, and Sir *Robert Piggott* and Captain *John Piggott* defendants, at the Councel-Board, concerning the rectories of *Dyſert-Enys* and *Kilteale* in the *Queen's-County*, are by this Houſe voted to be void, extrajudicial, and contrary to the law of the Land.

It is ordered upon queſtion, that the deed made by Sir *Robert Piggott* unto *Jonathan Hoyle* was procured from him, partly by promiſes of compenſation, which now are become impoſſible to be performed, and partly by menaces by the late Lord Lieutenant, and therefore by this Houſe voted to be vacated and made void.

It

41 Parliamentary orders, 9 July 1641, *Journals of the House of Commons of the kingdom of Ireland* (Dublin, 1753), 8 vols, I, p. 463.

Table 9.4. Merchants in the Commons, 1613–47

Parliament	*Catholic merchants*	*Protestant merchants*
1613–15	52	2
1634–5	38	3[143]
1640–1	27	7
1642–7	–	6

Younger sons of gentry families were apprenticed to merchants (e.g., William Lattin's brother Michael and John and William Wandesford) forming close connections between the two groups and wealthy merchants bought property within and outside their towns, so beginning the process of gentrification.[144] The experience of Galway merchants is best documented, but there were many other examples including Henry Archer, Baron, George Blakeney, Edward Fitzharris, John Fitzsimons, Geoffrey Galway, Lucas Shee, Christopher Sherlock and Champion.[145] The prominence of merchants in the Irish parliament is in stark contrast to France where, although the Estates General represented only urban areas (even though 85% of the population lived in the countryside), the majority of the Third Estate was comprised of lesser gentry and lawyers, as in Ireland. In 1614 merchants, who had very low social status in France, were almost entirely absent, even though two men described as 'paysans' (peasants) were returned.[146]

Merchants' influence in parliament can be traced; many of the injustices expressed by the agents to Charles related to trade. Monopolies, specifically those of tobacco and yarn, constituted significant public grievances. Merchants' commercial knowledge was crucial in developing the case against Strafford; they were easily able to compile estimates of his profits and, through their commercial contacts, orchestrated the explosion of petitions presented to the Commons concerning the tobacco monopoly, acquired and managed by Wentworth and his cronies.[147] It was no coincidence that the leading Dublin merchants Patrick Gough and Thady Duff and the Waterford merchant, lawyer and MP John Walshe, were key witnesses at his trial.[148] Merchants' detailed knowledge of fees and customs made them invaluable members of relevant committees and enabled the House to make clear recommendations for the future administration and level of costs, although the Commons covered itself by ordering that any member personally involved in the subject should provide information and clarification in the committee, but be excluded from voting; it subsequently widened the membership of this committee to all members of the House.[149] Although they were a minority

143 Plus Bramston who was unseated for Belfast.
144 William Lattin, MP for Naas, 1613. For his brother, see *Irish patent rolls of James I*, p. 140.
145 Ó Bric, 'Galway townsmen'.
146 Grelin, *Ordre Observé*.
147 Harold G. Fox, 'The earl of Strafford and monopolies in Ireland' in Harold G. Fox, *Monopolies and patents: a study of the history and future of the patent monopoly* (Toronto, 1947), pp 146–50.
148 Rushworth (ed.), *Tryal*, pp 244–5, 404–5, 420.
149 *Commons' Jn. Ire.*, 10 Feb. 1641.

in the House, the records suggest that Catholics were better attenders and therefore merchants formed a more sizeable block within the active Commons than their numbers might initially suggest. 15% of the petitions to the Commons in 1641 came from merchants, but this figure excludes the 30% of the petitions that were preferred by MPs, many of them merchants. The presence of merchants and town officials in the Commons would have smoothed access to premises connected with trade and the municipality for the parliament's business, such as the use of the inner and upper rooms of the tholsel and the custom house for committee meetings.

Soldiers were almost invariably New English settlers in the king's army, and like the officials all depended on the state for their position and advancement and some Protestant lawyers worked also for the crown. Wentworth's electoral strategy of ensuring the return of crown servants and soldiers had a strong logical base and was further expanded in 1640 when much larger numbers of both groups were returned.[150] While there were many career soldiers in the Commons, especially the New English who arrived in Ireland in that capacity, it was not unusual for gentry to spend some time in military service. For Catholic Irish, or those with equivocal religious positions, who had served in the Nine Years War (including Morgan Cavanagh, Walter Butler, Daniel O'Sullivan, Bryan MacMahon and several unsuccessful candidates in 1613 like Richard Tyrell who were not serving soldiers by that time) who were not recruited to the Irish army before 1640, that entailed service in continental armies. The same applied for Piers Crosby, Thomas Esmond, Sir James Dillon, Oliver Eustace, Richard Haly, Philip Mac Hugh O'Reilly and Nicholas Whyte and possibly Walter Evers and James Dulan (Inistioge 1634).[151] However, many Protestants including Laurence Crawford, Sir James Erskine, George Montgomery, Bryan O'Neill, John Ogle, Sir William St Leger and Robert Stewart had also served on the continent.

At least 44 career soldiers, all Protestants, were returned in 1613, 33 in 1634 and 44 in 1640; on the formation of the new Irish army in spring 1640, Catholics were permitted to join and James Dillon, Lucas and Maurice FitzGerald, Rory Maguire, Dermot O'Brien and Theobald Taaffe were all appointed captains, as were other Protestant MPs who had not previously been soldiers, including James Dillon Jr, Arthur Chichester and Mervyn (these are not included in the statistics in Table 9.5). Carpenter and Tallis were involved as administrators arranging supplies. After October 1641, at least 30 more Protestants took on a military role and 25 recruiter MPs served as soldiers, including many who would not have done so in normal times such as Schout and the lawyer Michael Jones. Equally, Catholics like John Bellew, William Browne, Walter Cruise, Lucas and Maurice FitzGerald, Rochford and Walter Walshe, who were not active in the military before 1640, subsequently served in the Confederation's forces.

150 McGrath, 'Electoral strategy'.

151 *Idem*, 'Membership', pp 172–4; Clarke, *Old English*, p. 120.

Table 9.5. Soldiers in the Commons, 1613–47

Parliament	*Catholic soldiers*	*Protestant soldiers*
1613–15	–	44
1634–5	0	33
1640–1	6	40
1642–7	0	25

Very many Protestant MPs held crown office or worked for the lord deputy as secretary, steward or controller of his household. No Catholic held crown office during this period, but James Cusack who conformed is included in these figures as a Protestant. Many others like Humphrey Farnham were rewarded with offices after their time in parliament and, again, these are not included in the figures presented in Table 9.6, nor are privy councillors like Coote, Robert Forth, Radcliffe, Trevor or George Wentworth who held no other civil offices.

Table 9.6. Crown officials in the Commons, 1613–47

Parliament	*Catholics*	*Protestants*
1613–15	0	82 (34%)
1634–5	0	31
1640–1	0	59
1642–7	–	19

While Hooker characterizes Irish MPs as 'rude rustics', in fact they were educated, talented and sophisticated thinkers, well aware of humanist thinking and capable of devising and enunciating a clear constitutional position for Ireland.[152] The Papal nuncio to the Confederate Catholic government in Ireland in the 1640s, Archbishop GianBattista Rinuccini, described Baron, whom he met at La Rochelle on his way to Paris, as a 'gentleman [with] a fine appearance, very polished manners.'[153] MPs' educational level and cultural interests, where they can be established, varied widely. A few were poets and writers, such as Ralph Birchenshaw, Francis Butler, John Davies, Richard Fanshawe, John Jackson, Roger Lort, Edmund Skory, William Smyth and Bellings, who was also a linguist and later a historian; others, such as Bolton, Darcy, Davies, Thomas Ryves and Wilkinson, wrote legal and political works.[154] At the other end of the scale, neither Roger Rice nor Bryan MacMahon could sign their names.[155]

152 Bradshaw, 'Beginnings'.

153 Rinuccini to Pamphili, 5 Oct. 1645, quoted in William Burke, *History of Clonmel* (Waterford, 1906), p. 476; Tadhg Ó hAnnracháin, 'Rinuccini, GianBattista', *DIB*.

154 Andrew Hadfield, 'War poetry and counsel in early modern Ireland' in Brendan Kane and Valerie McGowan-Doyle, *Elizabeth I and Ireland* (Cambridge, 2011), pp 239–60.

155 For a discussion of English Tudor MPs, see Hawkyard, *Commons*, pp 120–32.

CONCLUSION

The Commons' personnel included most obviously its members and the officials who served the house. Only the clerk was a permanent appointment and the speaker was chosen by the members, although, in a break with Irish custom, under Wentworth, they merely assented to his nomination. MPs, apart from Richard Blacknall, Thomas Elwall and John Ingersoll, were invariably above the artisan class, with all Catholics being gentry, merchants or lawyers. Catholics were well aware that the number and calibre of their MPs was essential to achieving their aims in parliament, unlike the administration which was content with lobby-fodder. Many Protestants were the sons of settlers who had used their roles as soldiers or officials to enrich themselves and establish themselves as gentry (e.g., Charles Coote Jr, John Edgeworth, Robert Forth, John Hoey, and the Hamiltons, and Montgomeries and Parsons). As such, they brought a wide range of professional and life experience to their role, and provided valuable expertise to the Commons. They were united by an educational experience, Christian background and almost entirely middle-class status, which provided a common world-view, regardless of their ethnic origin and confessional status, explaining why they shared so many concerns about property, social organization, public order, finance and administration. As a result, they co-operated in parliamentary business and parliamentary opposition did not generally break down on religious or ethnic lines.

CHAPTER TEN

Lawyers in and around parliament

LAWYERS PLAYED AN IMPORTANT ROLE in parliament's preparation and proceedings, providing essential professional expertise in both houses and especially as members of the Commons, all of whose speakers were lawyers, as was the unsuccessful candidate, John Everard, in 1613. The relationship between lawyers and parliament was symbiotic; lawyers who were MPs pleaded cases in the courts (and in parliament while it was in session) and these cases were heard by judges who provided legal advice in the Lords. Lawyers in Ireland, including judges, drafted legislation and senior legal officers in England reviewed the Irish bills. In England some MPs brought aldermen and recorders of their towns to parliament as advisors and while there is no evidence for this in Ireland, it may well have happened.

Lawyers' skills – mastering briefs, dealing with legal minutiae, presenting cases, drafting reports and mediating – were valuable in parliament, especially in committees. There was considerable respect for, or at least deference towards, lawyers: they were described in the 1613 list of members as '*in legibus eruditis*' (learned in the law) and Medhop listed them separately in his fair journals, noting which were judges, civil or common lawyers and recorders. Additionally, their appointments to and chairmanship of committees demonstrates the value placed on their professional expertise, as does the use of lawyers who were not MPs to advise committees.[1] Darcy's return for Navan in 1634 indicates a determination to have him in the house, as well as the other Galway lawyers, Henry Lynch and Martin, and many of those returned in by-elections in 1641, including Darcy and Martin, Garrett Cheevers, Matthew de Renzy and Richard Haly were lawyers.[2] Nor did the Commons confine itself to legal advice from its own members; on 29 May 1641 it ordered that

> Mr Richard Berford, Mr Richard Martin, Mr Thomas Tirrell, Mr William Brent, Mr Patrick Kirovan, and such other gentlemen of the long robe as are in town, and not of this house, shall immediately have copies of the *Queries*, and the said, called, *An answer of the judges*, sent unto them, who are hereby required to deliver their opinions and their authorities in writing, unto the said Mr Patrick Darcey.

1 *Commons' Jn. Ire.*, 5 March 1641; Borlase, *History*, p. 8; TNA, MS PRO 30/5/3, fos. 2–10; NLI, MS 836, p. 175; Clanricard to Ormond, 21 Aug. 1645, Bodl. Lib., Carte MS 63, fo. 357.

2 For biographical details of each of these, see Appendix 3.

All were Catholics, although Brent was an Englishman, educated at Douai and Gray's Inn and admitted to the King's Inns in 1639.[3] On the other hand, the minor officials and clerks who were increasingly returned as placemen, many of whom were admitted to the King's Inns, were used to taking orders rather than negotiating and their contribution to parliamentary business was less significant than their intended and actual role as lobby fodder.[4]

The vast expansion in legal work after the end of the Nine Years War facilitated the development of the profession and created a greater demand for lawyers trained at the inns of court in London.[5] While the obvious causes are the Anglicization of Ireland, the opening up of the inns of court to Irish students, the extension of English common law and legal systems throughout the island and the increasing urbanization of early modern Ireland (creating a demand for recorders and establishing town courts), this is a partial and overly benign reading of this growth in the profession. The development of judge-made law under Davies and his contemporaries meant that the supposed benefits of a known, universally and impartially applied and accepted body of law to all Irish inhabitants overwhelmingly discriminated in favour of New English settlers and against the native, especially Catholic, community.[6] The overthrowing of existing land titles created a demand for lawyers to defend the Old English and Gaelic community's estates and under Wentworth also those of New English settlers and an incentive for Irishmen to acquire at least a basic understanding of law: spikes in enrolment of Irishmen at the London inns coincided with the readmission in Ireland of Catholics to plead in court in 1628 and the 1637 publication of the *Case of tenures upon the Commission of Defective Titles* by the MP and lawyer James Barry.[7]

Respect for lawyers was not impartial: preferential treatment given to English lawyers encouraged their migration into Ireland, where they prospered, but Catholic lawyers were 'anathema' to the crown. Chancellor Thomas Jones attempted to have Catholic lawyers and attorneys barred from practice as 'ringleaders of the people in their recusancy'.[8] From 1611, Catholic mayors and recorders were deposed and replaced by Protestants to prevent the former acting as returning officers and depriving the latter of a position that James I mistakenly believed enhanced their chance of being elected as MPs; Youghal's recorder and

3 Kenny, *King's Inns*, p. 81; Antony A. Wood, *Athenae Oxonensis: an exact history of all the writers and bishops who have had their education in the University of Oxford* (London, 1817), iii, col. 517.

4 McGrath, 'Electoral strategy'.

5 A.R. Hart, *A history of the king's serjeants at law in Ireland: honour rather than advantage?* (Dublin, 2000), pp 48–51 traces these changes. Donal F. Cregan, 'Irish recusant lawyers in politics in the reign of James I', *IJ*, new series, 95 (1970), 306–20; McGrath, 'Ireland and the third university'.

6 Brand, 'Sir John Davies'.

7 McGrath, 'Ireland and the third university'; Donal F. Cregan, 'Irish Catholic admissions to the Inns of Court, 1558–1625', *IJ*, new series, 95 (1970), 95–114; Jane Ohlmeyer, 'Irish recusant lawyers during the reign of Charles I' in Micheál Ó Siochrú (ed.), *Kingdoms in crisis: Ireland in the 1640s* (Dublin, 2001), pp 63–89; Colum Kenny, 'Badge of servitude? The Irish at England's inns of court', *Proc. RIA*, 119C (2019), 199–227; Kenny, *King's Inns*, p. 96; James Barry, *Case of tenures upon the Commission of Defective Titles, argued by all the Judges of Ireland* (Dublin, 1637).

8 Kenny, *King's Inns*, p. 91.

MP Edmund Coppinger was successively replaced by Protestant MPs Edward Harris, Henry Gosnold and Laurence Parsons and Damian Pecke was installed in Galway.[9] In Clonmel Thomas Gough, later MP, was replaced by the conforming but unqualified local men Edmund Bray and John Prendergast, a situation which was presumably widely replicated.[10] However, Catholic-dominated towns did not always elect their Protestant recorders as MPs: Pecke and Gosnold, were returned for Tuam and Clonakilty in 1613 and Drogheda refused to choose its recorder Robert Bysse as its MP in 1640. Dublin invariably returned its recorder, but only after earlier elections that returned Catholics in 1613, 1634 and possibly 1628, were illegally overturned.

Catholic lawyers were heavily involved in developing the opposition's electoral strategy, selecting candidates, informing their co-religionists about electoral law and procedure and their tactics after the elections. Jacob claimed they were more influential than the priests in directing the elections:

> The popish priests which swarme in all parts of the Realme, and the Irish Lawyers which doe more harme then the priests and those Recusants that have druncke of the cuppe of Spaine, Cease not night and daye to sollicite & perswade by large promises, to terrifye by threatts and suggestions of imminent dangers, to Compell by Curses & excommunications, to bynde by oathes of Association, and by all the practises and pollicies the witt of man can devise, to Circumvent all manner of persons that shall have any stroke in this election, that they shall chuse none to be knights or Burgesses for this parlament, but Certaine pickd men long since agreed vpon & appointed by the priests for those places, which indeed are for the most part the very firebrands of sedition, the most open and apparent [enemies] to the state, and the principall opposers against the present government. They had plotted it.[11]

Chichester noted 'the contrary faction are now in consultation dayly, with their lawyers, Jesuits and Seminary Priests, how to make their party strong and to give impediment unto the designs in hand.'[12] Concerned that some who were not returned as MPs would 'intrude themselves' into the parliament house, Chichester caused 'proclamation to be made in the King's Courts that all those returned should present themselves before the deputy and council in Dublin Castle', aware that lawyers were the best conduit for this message.[13]

9 On the Coppingers broadly, see Walter Arthur Copinger, *History of the Copingers or Coppingers of the county of Cork, Ireland, and the counties of Suffolk and Kent, England* (Manchester, 1884). For Gosnold, see Appendix 3.

10 Caulfield (ed.), *Youghal*, p. 39, Peter Marks, apparently unqualified, was also sworn in as recorder, 1614, p. 27; Mary Josephine Donovan O'Sullivan, *Old Galway: the history of a Norman colony in Ireland* (Galway, 1942), pp 365–6; McGrath (ed.), *Clonmel*, pp 37, 63, 66.

11 Jacob to Northampton, 26 May 1613, Bodl. Lib., Carte MS 62, fos. 241r–4v.

12 Chichester to the English privy council, 14 April 1613, in Edwards (ed.), 'Chichester', no. 53.

13 McCavitt, 'An unspeakable parliamentary fracas'.

Jacob also named lawyers as among those who led opposition to the government in 1613:

> The most violent and seditious Ringleaders of this Mutyny that showe themselves in the lower House are Sir William Bourk, Sir John Everarde, Sir Christopher Nugent, Sir James Goghe, Sir Christopher Plunkett, Sutton, called the Baron of Galtrym, Tho: Lutterell, and William Talbott, Robert Barnwall, Richard Wadding and [Christopher] Verdon the Lawyers. Howbeitt, it appeares to vs by their often meetinges & Consultations, that Sir Patrick Barnwell & olde Burnell, though they are not of the house, are underhand the principall Contrivers of those Conspiracies.[14]

Barnewall was imprisoned in London to prevent his being elected and Henry Burnell, one of the ringleaders of the opposition in 1585 advised them to follow the strategy used in Perrot's parliament to appeal directly and publicly to James as loyal subjects.[15]

Catholics' electoral success and refusal to accept Davies as speaker infuriated the administration, who retaliated in late 1613 by issuing an order preventing Catholic lawyers from practicing in the courts, as a clear warning and punishment to them for their leading role in defying the administration, but also to intimidate them during the negotiations in London and later in parliament.[16] This illegal exclusion – 33 Hen. VIII, c. 5, revived by 11 Eliz. I, c. 5, required anyone pleading in courts to have spent at least five years at the inns of court in London, but 'there is no law in force in this Kingdome, that enjoyneth the administring of that Oath to the practisers of Law, or to any other Trade or profession' – was implemented by royal prerogative.[17] An exception was made for Everard, who was readmitted to the King's Inns at Chichester's express request in November 1614 after a 'verye good and Constant report of his late demeanor in this present Parlament and that towards his Majesties service and other like obiectes.' It is unclear what use he made of his membership, even though Chichester requested the inns to assign him 'a Conveynient lodging with in the howse and to permitt him all other benefytts with in the same according to his wourth and the good abeiring he haieth geven of him selfe in euerye thing saving his oppinion in some matters of Religion', but it must have been a very lonely experience as the only Catholic member until his death in 1624.[18]

14 Jacob to Northampton, 26 May 1613, Bodl. Lib., Carte MS 62, fos. 241r–4v; Cregan, 'Irish recusant lawyers'. Patrick Hussey was the baron of Galtrim, not John Sutton.

15 Nessa Malone, 'Henry Burnell and Richard Netterville: lawyers in civic life in the English Pale, *c.*1562–1615' in Salvador Ryan and Clodagh Tait (eds), *Religion and politics in urban Ireland,* c.*1500–*c.*1750: essays in honour of Colm Lennon* (Dublin, 2016), pp 89–107; Terry Clavin and Judy Barry, 'Burnell, Henry', *DIB*; Judy Barry, 'Barnewall, Sir Patrick', *DIB*.

16 Edmond Sexton's diary, NLI, MS 16,085, p. 64, entry for between Oct. and Nov. 1613, 'the recusant lawyers put from practice this tearme'. Kenny, *King's Inns*, pp 91–2.

17 The Irish privy council to James, 15 June 1621, BL, Add. MS 4,756, fos. 63v, 69r; Cregan, 'Irish recusant lawyers'.

Catholic lawyers were obliged to find other ways of earning fees and their clients alternative means of resolving their legal difficulties. Prominent Catholic Munster lawyers ran the Ormond Liberty whose palatinate courts and administration were staffed by legal experts like MPs Patrick Archer, Everard, James Gough and John Haly.[19] Recusant lawyers still pleaded in the presidency courts and in some areas where 'lawyers conformable were lacking' and continued to advise clients, as Richard Butler and Richard Wadding did Waterford Corporation and Darcy, Henry Lynch and William Talbot the earls of Clanricard, Ormond and Kildare.[20] Experienced Catholic lawyers worked as deputy recorders, with the salary going to Protestant office-holders and presumably some agreement about the other profits of the offices. Old English and Gaelic gentry were excluded from the commissions of the peace and so Catholics, with good reason, did not trust the Protestant-run courts; as a result, mediation services thrived. The trebling of Pecke's salary as recorder of Galway suggests not merely greed but also an acknowledgement that he would not attract the additional income incumbents usually enjoyed.[21] These exclusions created such problems that the privy council in 1621 requested that Catholic justices of the peace be appointed and lawyers readmitted to plead:

> since neither gentlemen recusants should be admitted justices of the peace, nor Recusant Lawyer suffered to plead at the Barr, supposeing thereby to draw them to Conformitie in Religion, … yet we observe by experience, that since that direction was put in execution, the Courts of Justice have been left in a manner naked, ffor many of the Causes which were then usually handled are now privately handled in the country by the said Lawyers. Whereby your Majestie doth lose much in your Casual Revenue. Besides, whereas when they did practice heretofore, they were so careful of their Reputacon that they were very warie in their Carriages and so fearefull to offend as they would give no advice at all, or very privately in such thinges as were prejudiciall to the Crowne, least they should loose the Creditts with the State and with their Creditts, their profitts. But since this Course was taken with them, they are most malicious advisors and perverse practizers against your Majestie's title to Lands, Wardshipps and the present Government. And the people being led by them in all their Courses, are by them much seduced. We doe therefore most humbly present it to your Majestie to be considered of, in your High Wisdome, whether for these Reasons it were not more convenient for your Service, and the good of the Kingdome, that some such eminent men in every County, though Recusants will take the Oath of Allegiance, should be made justices and the Recusant lawyers to be admitted againe to

18 King's Inns, MS B1/1, fo. 173r.

19 Edwards, *Ormond lordship*, p. 57.

20 The Irish privy council to James, 15 June 1621, BL, Add. MS 4,756, fos. 63v, 69r; Crawford, *Star Chamber*, pp 328–9.

21 McGrath, 'Managing the Windsor'.

their practice in the Courts of Justice, [n]or be restrained from pleading, as now they are.[22]

This appeal initially fell on deaf ears, but gradually in the 1620s Catholics were again appointed recorders, including Sir John Meade in Cork, Patrick Sarsfield in Limerick and the MPs Henry Lynch in Galway and Henry White in Clonmel. Catholics' readmission to plead in courts and to membership of the King's Inns in June 1628 was intended to create a more positive atmosphere in anticipation of the parliamentary elections some months later.

MPs and parliamentary officials had different levels of legal knowledge and a minority had professional training in common or civil law. MPs and clerks working in the courts and chancery had a basic knowledge of legal matters in those areas and many MPs including gentry and mayors who were *ex officio* justices of the peace exercised a judicial function within their own communities at the county assizes, sheriffs' turn courts and town courts and as jurors. Men with a practically derived knowledge of the law could make a living locally as attorneys in town courts. Some had the required three years of attendance at the chancery inns or inns of court in London, but others had no formal training and had learned 'on the job'.[23] Privy councillors who were judges in Castle Chamber cases– senior judges were *ex officio* privy councillors – may not have had legal training despite exercising a judicial function there and at the privy council. Sheriffs acted as judges in minor cases of small value in their local turn courts.[24] This expansion of the legal system into everyday life created a demand for law books for laymen, filled by Merick's *Compendious collection* and by works from two MPs, Bolton's *Statutes* and *Justice of the peace for Ireland* and John Wilkinson's popular manuals on local government, *A treatise collected out of the statutes of this kingdom concerning the office and authority of coroners and sheriffs* and *An easie and plain method for the keeping of a court leet*.[25]

MPs were drawn from common and civil lawyers and attorneys, although most had no legal education. Those who qualified as barristers through at least five, but frequently seven, years study of common law at the inns of court worked as counsellors; any time spent at the chancery inns before transferring to the inns of court counted towards the required time. Men trained in civil law took degrees at universities in England, Ireland (Charles Doyne, MP for Trinity College 1613 was

22 The Irish privy council to James, 15 June 1621, BL, Add. MS 4,756, fos. 63v, 69r.

23 For the appointment of untrained men as attorneys in town courts, see McGrath (ed.), *Coleraine*, pp 24, 37, 43, 56, 66, 94, 121, 182; Caulfield (ed.), *Youghal*, pp 96, 148.

24 Neal Garnham, *The courts, crime and the criminal law in Ireland, 1692–1760* (Dublin, 1996), p. 95; Matthew Dutton, *The office and authority of sheriffs, under-sheriffs, deputies, county-clerks, and coroners, in Ireland* (Dublin, 1721), p. 586.

25 John Wilkinson, *An easie and plain method for the keeping of a court leet* (London, 1618); *idem*, *A treatise collected out of the statutes of this kingdom concerning the office and authority of coroners and sheriffs* (London, 1618). The *Treatise* was frequently reprinted. For Wilkinson's career, see Bríd McGrath, 'Starting from scratch: the first 30 years of Coleraine's development' in Scott (ed.), *Society and administration*, pp 36–55 and Appendix 3.

the first to be conferred with a doctorate in law from that institution) or more usually on the Continent. Scottish lawyers were admitted to the Faculty of Advocates after studying civil law at a continental university, historically in France, although as Protestants they avoided that country between the St Bartholomew's Day Massacre in 1572 and the Edict of Nantes in 1598, but also in Germany, Italy and the Low Countries. More rarely, some were admitted after years of practice under a Scottish advocate.[26] Recorders might be either civil or common lawyers, or unqualified. A number of unqualified MPs worked as attorneys, e.g., Edmond Cossens (Coleraine), Patrick Tallant (Kells) and Edmund Tarleton (Lifford).

Despite their prominence, it is not always easy to identify lawyers in early modern Ireland and therefore to estimate the numbers in the Commons. Attendance at the inns of court, chancery inns, admission to the King's Inns, whose records are in any case defective, for common lawyers or appointment as recorder do not of themselves prove qualification as a lawyer.[27] The easiest group to identify were the civil lawyers: Medhop noted Humphrey Dethick, Doyne, John Haly, Thomas Ryves and William Temple in this category, although there is no evidence that Dethick was a lawyer. Wentworth's parliaments included the Protestant civil lawyers Allan Cooke, Edward Lake and Robert Travers and the Catholic John Haly and Dominic White. Medhop listed as common lawyers Catholics Andrew Barrett, Robert Barnewall, James Galway, Edmund Nugent, John Sutton, William Talbot, Christopher Verdon and Richard Wadding and Protestants Thomas Crewe and Thomas Crooke, but this excluded anyone with another role, like recorders, crown officials or judges including Davies, Jacob, Beare and Sibthorpe.[28] There was no accurate list of members for 1634 but in 1640 Fernesly listed Cooke, Lake and Dominic White as having doctorates in civil law and John Bysse as recorder of Dublin, ignoring his brother Robert who was recorder of Drogheda (presumably because he did not sit for that town) and the Catholics Richard Butler, Dormer and Richard Haly; Fernesly did not note other lawyers separately.[29]

While many recorders were qualified, others were not, like MPs Thomas Hibbotts in Carrickfergus, Cossens in Coleraine and Tarleton in Lifford. Equally, some crown officials holding legal positions had not qualified as lawyers, notably Wandesford and John Temple as Masters of the Rolls although both had spent some time at the inns of court.[30] Archbishop William Daniel of Tuam unsuccessfully pressed for his brother-in-law Henry Bringhurst, escheator of Connacht from 1617 and MP for Tuam in 1640, to be appointed attorney general of the province in 1626 despite his admission to the King's Inns as an attorney.[31]

26 I am indebted to John Cairns for this information. John W. Cairns, 'Advocates hats, Roman law and admission to the Scots Bar, 1580–1812', *Journal of Legal History*, 20:2 (1999), 24–61.

27 Kenny, *King's Inns*, p. 112.

28 NLI, MS 836, fo. 175.

29 Robert Armstrong, 'Bysse (Bisse), John', *DIB*.

30 Aidan Clarke, 'Temple, Sir John', *DIB*.

31 Daniel to Falkland, 27 Feb. 1626, BL, Sloane MS 3,827, fo. 69; Terry Clavin and Judy Barry, 'Daniel (Ó Domhnuill, O'Donmell), William', *DIB*; McGrath, 'Bio. dict.', i, pp 78–9.

Many MPs had attended the inns of court, but by the early seventeenth century this was as much a social and cultural experience as a form of professional training. Only a minority remained for five years or more and most of the records that would help to establish this have not survived and those that have are incomplete. Chancery inns' registers are largely unpublished.[32] The inns of court admissions registers have been published, although there appear to be at least some omissions. Christopher Plunkett, John Sutton and Richard Wadding were recognized as lawyers. However, others such as Oliver Jones and Audley Mervyn, were described as such and clearly had a legal education, although there is no record of their having attended the inns, and the latter finally entered the King's Inns in 1658.[33] The registers, especially those of the largest, Gray's Inn, provide no clear information on the length of time students remained there unless they were called to the bar, which Catholic students avoided because this required them to take the oath of supremacy. James Cusack, who is only known to have spent four months at the Middle Temple (although he may also have attended a chancery inn), was described by Cregan as an 'eminent lawyer', admitted a counsellor at Wentworth's express request, appointed as the Confederation's attorney general 'as one of his majesty's learned councell in law' and judge of the admiralty. It is inconceivable that he would have received these appointments without appropriate qualifications.[34] Unusually, Robert Goodwin, MP for Londonderry in1634, was admitted to the Middle Temple in August 1612 'because of the transmigration of the said Robert to Ireland on account of the Plantation there by the citizens of London.' This detail is not provided in the published admissions but as Goodwin arrived in Londonderry as its town clerk in spring 1613, just after his admission to the Drapers' Company, he had at most only a few months possible legal education.[35]

King's Inns in Dublin was re-established in 1607, but provided no legal education and functioned as much as a social club as a professional body and many unqualified men, including Fernesly, Sandes and other clerks holding crown posts, some of whom became MPs, joined for networking purposes. Especially in its early days, King's Inns admitted as honorary members many privy councillors and peers with little or no legal training (Thomas Ashe, Richard Boyle, Edward Fisher, Garrett Moore, Richard Moryson, Christopher Nugent and Henry Piers). More critically, before the expulsion of Catholic lawyers in 1614, they were in constant contact with each other and Protestant lawyers as their chambers were very close

32 McGrath, 'Ireland and the third university'; *idem*, 'Poets and patronage'; C.W. Brooks (ed.), *The admissions registers of Barnard's Inn, 1620–1869* (London, 1995); New Inns' admissions records from 1601 are unpublished. See 'New Inn – Middle Temple's lost inn of chancery', at https://www.middletemple.org.uk/archive-history/archive-month/january-2020-new-inn-middle-temple%E2%80%99s-lost-inn-chancery [accessed 22 July 2021].

33 Aidan Clarke, 'Mervyn, Sir Audley', *DIB*; Cregan, 'Irish recusant lawyers'; King's Inns, MS B1/1, fo. 158r; Hart, 'Audley Mervyn'.

34 Donal F. Cregan, 'Some members of the Confederation of Kilkenny' in Sylvester O'Brien (ed.), *Measgra i gCuimhne Michíl Uí Chléirigh* (Dublin, 1944), pp 34–44; Bodl. Lib., Carte MS 68, fo. 3v.

35 G.O. Bellewes, 'Robert Goodwin of Derry', *JRSAI*, 5th series, 36:4 (Dec., 1906), 422–3.

to each other within the inns.[36] As King's Inns' admission fees before 1636 were based on social status – judges paid between £2 and £3 2*s*. 6*d*., knights and esquires £1 and gentlemen 10*s*. – it is not possible to link fees and qualifications, although generally esquires had attended the inns of court, but not necessarily long enough to qualify as a barrister and gentlemen were attorneys or clerks. Many who were described as lawyers, such as Bellings, had slender training.[37] Conversely, many, including civil lawyers, 36 of the 104 barristers pleading in chancery in the early 1630s and several recorders including Edmund Coppinger of Youghal, Nicholas Dormer of New Ross, Henry White and John Wilkinson of Coleraine did not join King's Inns. However, King's Inns made an order on 20 November 1634 that

> none shalbe allowed to practice as a counsellor at lawe, but such as shalbe first admitted of this societie, and that euerie one soe admitted shall pay to the Theasurer of the house for the tyme beinge the somme of foure markes sterling to the use of the house for his admittance.

This still left lawyers free to work as recorders, in local courts and as legal advisors.[38]

The very limited surviving court records provide little additional evidence. The best are from chancery and little evidence remains from the king's bench, common pleas and exchequer, presidency and town or manor courts.[39] Lawyers like Patrick Boyton and Matthew de Renzy may have been predominantly landowners with a local legal practice or worked in courts whose few surviving records are very limited (e.g., local assizes, town courts, presidency courts, Court of High Commission). Oliver Jones presumably practiced in the Connacht presidency court, based in his constituency at Athlone, although there is no evidence for this. Others who were qualified and accepted as common lawyers by Medhop, such as Thomas Crooke, may not have practiced at all in Ireland. Other qualified lawyers worked in other roles, e.g., Radcliffe as administrator or governors for the crown and William Swanton as Sir Henry Wallop's agent in Wexford.[40] Irish and English lawyers, including students, provided legal services in London for Irish clients. Christopher Darcy worked in London for Ormond.[41] Talbot, Martin and Darcy advised clients even while disbarred or imprisoned and others like John Walshe seem only to have acted as advisors and did not plead in court.[42]

36 King's Inns, MS B1/1, fos. 108v–10r.
37 McGrath, 'Poets and patronage'.
38 Toby C. Barnard, 'Lawyers and the law in later seventeenth-century Ireland', *IHS*, 28:111 (May, 1993), 256–82; King's Inns, MS B1/1, fo. 182r.
39 Jane Ohlmeyer, 'Records of the Irish Court of Chancery: a preliminary report for 1627–1634' in Desmond Greer and Norma Dawson (eds), *Mysteries and solutions in Irish legal history* (Dublin, 2001), pp 15–49.
40 On Swanton, see McGrath, 'Bio. dict.', i, p. 279.
41 Edward Comerford to Ormond, 2 April 1636, Christopher Darcy to Ormond, 7 July 1637, NLI, MS 2,305, pp 23, 303; Grosart (ed.), *Lismore Papers*, 1st series, iv, pp 144, 149.

Finally, some MPs were admitted after their elections as MPs. None of them qualified as lawyers, but they did have some legal experience, except Barnaby Bryan whose entry to Lincoln's Inn in June 1613 was clearly an honorary admission. James Montgomery was admitted to Gray's Inn in 1621, after his return to the 1613 parliament and is included in the figures for 1634 and 1640. Richard Barnewall was admitted to Gray's Inn in February 1635, during his time as MP for Swords and Arthur Jones, also to Gray's Inn in 1637, after his stint as MP in Ireland but before his English experience.[43] Barnewall and Jones are excluded from the calculations as being admitted after their elections. Honorary admissions to King's Inns listed above, have been excluded, except for Richard Boyle, who attended the Middle Temple. Thomas Radcliffe, who entered Gray's Inn aged nine before coming to Ireland with his father, has also been excluded. However, as none was qualified, they do not influence the number of lawyer MPs. MPs whose religious positions shifted during the period, e.g., James Cusack, have been classified by their confessional position at the time of their election. Finally, I have accepted anyone identified as a lawyer by Medhop and Cregan and included them in the calculations, except Dethick. Overall, 87 Irish MPs were lawyers in the early Stuart Irish parliaments.[44] MPs who were members of more than one parliament are listed under each house in which they sat. Biographies of men identified as lawyers are provided in Appendix 3.

Based on these criteria, eight members of the 1613 Commons were or had been recorders, apart from Hibbotts: Catholics, Barrett, Edmund Coppinger, John Haly and William Talbot and Protestants, Bolton, George Carey, Pecke and Wilkinson. It is highly likely that Hibbotts accepted the profits of the recordership while the work was undertaken by a deputy, as he was also Chichester's steward and clerk of the casualties from 1603. Ten MPs in 1634 were or had been recorders: Protestants John Bysse, Carey and Catlin (as well as Hibbotts) and Catholics Dominic Coppinger, Dormer, William Galway, Thomas Gough, John Haly, Henry Lynch and Henry White and six in 1640: Catholics Richard Butler, Dormer, Richard Haly and Protestants John and Robert Bysse and William Sambach (as well as Cossens and Tarleton). Very few corporation records have survived for this period so the number of MPs identified as recorders is certainly an underestimate. In addition, a number of MPs, all but two Protestant, were appointed recorders after their time in parliament including Joshua Boyle in Youghal, Roger Brereton in Drogheda, Dominic White in Limerick and Rochford in Wexford.[45]

42 Biographical details on Boyton, de Renzy, Jones, Crooke, Darcy, Talbot, Martin, the Bysse brothers, Walshe and others are provided in Appendix 3.

43 See the stub article on Arthur in John Bergin, 'Jones, Richard, 1st earl of Ranelagh', *DIB*.

44 It is possible that William Disney, MP for Lifford in 1613, was the man of that name who attended Gray's Inn, but there is no evidence that he practiced law in Ireland.

45 Boyle was described as a doctor of laws in 1661, although he does not appear in the lists of Alumni of Oxford, Cambridge or Dublin. HMC, *Ormond*, iii, p. 390; Julian C. Walton, 'The subsidy roll of County Waterford, 1662', *Anal. Hib.*, 30 (1982), 47–96.

In 1613, 48 MPs (28 Protestants and 19 Catholics) had some legal training. 35 were qualified lawyers, 19 Protestants and 16 Catholics, but seven barristers (Beare, John Blenerhassett, Gosnold, Harris, Jacob, Geratt Lowther and Laurence Parsons) were unseated, leaving 28 qualified lawyers in the Commons, with Catholics outnumbering the Protestants. The remaining 12 Protestants were Bolton, Davies, Doyne who was a master in chancery, Adam Loftus, the future chancellor, the judge Christopher Sibthorpe, Carey, Pecke and Wilkinson, and Crewe, Crooke, Thomas Ryves and William Temple, who initially studied law but seems never to have practiced. Medhop also listed Dethick. There is no evidence of his legal training and he appears to have been a merchant and served as collector of imposts in Tralee and Dingle.[46] The 16 Catholics were Patrick Archer, Robert Barnewall, Barrett, Edmund Coppinger, Everard, James Galway, James Gough, John Haly, Luttrell, Christopher and Edmund Nugent, Christopher Plunkett, John Sutton, William Talbot, Verdon and Richard Wadding.[47]

Three other Catholics (William Blakeney, Walter Synnott and Thomas Wadding) and ten Protestants had a legal education of some sort; these included the soldier Edward Southworth who held a BCL from Oxford but is not known to have worked as a lawyer, although he joined the King's Inns and Wentworth noted 'as with many great learned men his hand is not of the best'.[48] The other protestants were Richard Boyle, Humphrey Farnham, three clerks (Henry Andrews, William Crowe and William Marward) who joined the King's Inns and the sons of important officials, Roger Jones (later Lord Ranelagh, son of Chancellor Thomas Jones), Robert Meredith, Edward Moore and Beverley Newcomen.[49] Meredith is known only to have spent 11 months at Lincoln's Inn and there is no evidence that he practiced law, but while there is no record of his admission to the King's Inns, he was heavily involved in its administration from the 1650s, which suggests a greater knowledge of the law than his time at the inns of court indicates.[50]

In 1634, 82 MPs had a legal training of some sort, 34 (19 Catholics and 14 Protestants) of whom were qualified lawyers. Qualified Catholics were the recorders Dominic Coppinger, Dormer, John Haly, Henry Lynch and Henry White, the gentry Mark Cheevers, Peter Clinton, Thomas Gough, Luttrell, Nicholas Plunkett, James Walshe, and the townsmen Patrick Darcy, William Dobbins, Edward Fitzharris, Geoffrey Galway, William Galway, Richard Martin, David Rothe and Dominic White. Qualified Protestants were the recorders John Bysse, Carey and Catlin, Jerome Alexander, Edward Ayscough, James Barry, Allan Cooke, James Cusack, James Donnellan (*plate 15*), Maurice Eustace, William

46 Examination of Humphrey Dethick, May 1602, TNA, SP 52/68, fo. 44; Hugh F. Kearney, 'The Irish wine trade, 1614–15', *IHS*, 9:36 (Sept., 1955), 400–42.

47 On all these members of the 1613 parliament with legal training, see McGrath, 'Membership', passim.

48 King's Inns MS. B1/1, fo. 311v; Bodl. Add. MS C. 286, fo. 15r.

49 John Forrest, MP for Youghal, was an unsuccessful candidate for that town's recordership in 1614, but there is no evidence that he had any legal education.

50 Colum Kenny, 'The Black Book of King's Inns, Dublin, 1649–63: an annotated, chronological and contextualized transcription' in Dennehy (ed.), *Law and revolution*, pp 128–214.

Hilton, George Radcliffe, William Ryves and Robert Travers. Hilton's career was atypical, as he was admitted to King's Inns as an attorney in the Court of Common Pleas in 1608 and pursued a legal career after subsequently attending Gray's Inn. Of the 14 Catholics with some legal training, William Archbold, Nicholas Barnewall, Oliver Cashell, Lucas Dillon, John Dongan, William Esmond, Lucas FitzGerald, Edward Pettit, Theobald Purcell and Richard Strange were gentry and Baron, John Hore and Richard and Valentine Blake came from wealthy merchant families in Clonmel, Dungarvan and Galway respectively.

The 34 Protestants with some legal education or affiliation were the crown officials Edward Bagshaw, Edmund Beaghan, Robert Dillon, Richard FitzGerald, Adam Loftus Jr, Philip Mainwaring, Robert Meredith, Charles Moncke, Southworth, William Ussher, Christopher Wandesford and William Wiseman, or New English settlers who had spent some time at the inns but then pursued other careers, such as the soldiers John Borlase, Thomas Cave, Thomas Meredith, Beverley Newcomen, Henry Tichbourne and Arthur Tyrringham. Others, like Tristram Beresford, Thomas Bettsworth, William Fenton, Chichester Fortescue, John Hoey, James Montgomery, Arthur and Thomas Newcomen, Richard Parsons, Brockhall Taylor and John Trevor were New English settlers. Edward Deane, Richard Scott, George Wentworth and Francis Windebank were Wentworth associates, while Roger Lort was Lord Mountnorris' son-in-law.

The 18 qualified Catholic lawyers in 1640 were again either from a gentry or merchant background, including the gentry Patrick Boyton, Thomas Bourke, Garrett Cheevers, Nicholas Plunkett, Hugh Rochford, John Taylor (described as so 'wholly addicted to the law' that his nickname was 'Magna Charta') and John Walshe, and the townsmen, Geoffrey Browne, Richard Butler, Darcy, Dormer, Fitzharris, Richard Haly, Roebuck Lynch, Martin, Plunkett, Pierce Rothe and Dominic White, as were the other twelve with some legal knowledge, gentry Nicholas Barnewall, John Bellew, Piers Butler, Oliver Cashell, Dongan, Lucas FitzGerald, Phelim O'Neill and the townsmen Richard Blake, Valentine Blake, Hore, Edward Pettit and Philip Roche.

The 13 qualified Protestant lawyers in 1640 were Roger Brereton, John and Robert Bysse, Cooke, James Cusack, de Renzy, Maurice Eustace, Oliver Jones, Edward Lake, George Radcliffe, Sambach, Swanton and Travers. 32 (presumably plus Mervyn) had studied at the London inns, including Bellings, Borlase and his son Edmund, George Carleton, Toby Caulfield, Robert Cusack, Simon Digby, Robert Dillon, William Dobbins,[51] Richard Fanshawe, Chichester Fortescue, John Hoey, Adam Loftus Jr, Walter Loftus, Philip Mainwaring, Robert Meredith, Charles Moncke, James Montgomery, Robert Nettleton, Richard Osbourne, Richard and William Parsons, Toby Poyntz, Anthony Stoughton, John and Mark Trevor, John and William Ussher, Christopher and John Wandesford (who later acquired a D.C.L.), George Wentworth and Thomas Wharton. In addition, nine

51 Confusingly, there were two William Dobbins, the Catholic MP for Waterford in 1634 and the Protestant MP for Askeaton in 1640, both of whom had attended the inns of court.

clerks were members of the King's Inns: Bringhurst, Carr, Dopping, Richard FitzGerald, Thomas Johnson, Ralph Leventhorpe, William Plunkett, Stephen Stephens and Tarleton.[52]

Many Protestants with some legal education came from less elevated social backgrounds than their Catholic counterparts. Some were crown officials or New English settlers who had spent some time at the inns but then pursued other careers. Others like Hoey, Montgomery, Richard Parsons and John and Mark Trevor were second-generation settlers in the process of establishing their families as gentry. Receiving a liberal education was part of that process.[53] The influx of Protestant members after 1642 included four qualified lawyers: the Welshman John Lewis, the master in chancery Dr Dudley Loftus, Michael Jones who subsequently pursued a military career and Richard Kennedy. Other recruiter MPs who had spent time at the London inns were William Ball, Robert and Sylvester Kennedy, John Newman, Charles Ryves, master of the rolls John Temple and Arthur White. Edmund Keating, Cosny Molloy, Sandes and Henry Warren were clerks admitted to the King's Inns.

Men of Gaelic origin who had traditionally not attended the inns of court began to do so in increasing numbers in the early seventeenth century, especially if, like Phelim O'Neill, they were sent as part of their Anglicizing education. Doyne and Donnellan were part of a more general trend of men of Gaelic origin studying civil and common law; it is unclear on what basis Froude described Philip MacHugh O'Reilly as a lawyer.[54] Montgomery was the only Irish MP of Scottish origin listed as having studied at the inns of court and none was admitted to the Faculty of Advocates in Edinburgh. Of the MPs of Welsh origin, John and Mark Trevor, sons of the privy councillor Sir Edward Trevor, and John Lewis (Lewes) attended the inns of court, but only the latter was a practicing lawyer. The delegation of Irish agents sent to England after the botched opening of the 1613 parliament was top-heavy with lawyers. Gormanston, Dunboyne, Sir Christopher Plunkett and three lawyers, Sir James Gough, William Talbot and Edward Fitzharris, the unsuccessful candidate for Limerick and future MP for the city. They were later joined by Barrett, Patrick Barnewall, Everard, Thomas Luttrell and Christopher Nugent, forming what Cregan described as 'a galaxy of brilliant lawyers' and subsequently by Edmund Coppinger, James Galway and Richard Wadding and five other non-lawyer MPs.[55]

The English chancellor Ellesmere was anxious to ensure the presence of crown lawyers able to counter Catholic agents' submissions:

52 On all these Catholic and Protestant members of the 1640 parliament, see McGrath, 'Bio. dict.', i, passim.

53 There is some overlap between the categories. Other Protestants who had spent time at the London inns or joined King's Inns included Lord Robert Dillon, Thomas Bettsworth, Edward Deane, Roger Lort, Richard Scott, Brockhall Taylor, George Wentworth and Francis Windebank.

54 James Anthony Froude, *The English in Ireland in the eighteenth century*, 2 vols (London, 1873), i, p. 96.

55 Ellesmere to John Davies, 31 May 1613, Bodl Lib., Carte MS 62, fo. 566; Cregan, 'Irish recusant lawyers'; *Cal. S.P. Ire., 1611–14*, p. 464.

> In the number of those of the lower house (I mean the dutifull and well affected) that are to be sent hither, this Consideration is to be hadd, that (if your self [Davies] be not one of them) that speciall choice be made of some that be learned in the lawe) and doe well understand and be able to answere the Cavills and objections made by the adverse partie, as well in point of Lawe as in matter of facte, so yt will not stande onely in discourse of reason, but must be allso supported by warr[an]t of lawe and the Customes and *vsage of the Parliament in England*.' (my emphasis)

Chief Justice Sir John Denham was sent with Thomond and Oliver St John.[56]

Lawyers' practices created strong connections between individual counsellors and their clients in both houses, which facilitated co-operation within and between the houses. Some lawyers had very close contacts especially with urban constituencies, most obviously as recorders, but also as those in Galway who were made members of the town council, providing a range of legal expertise to the city.[57] Clanricard had sponsored the legal education of a number of young Galwegians and they served him as advisors in London and Dublin. Cork paid retainers to a number of lawyers including Alexander, Cooke, Darcy, Donnellan, Martin and Sambach. Darcy stressed his long service as counsel to Ormond when he asked the earl to take care of his house and possessions when he left Dublin in early 1642.[58]

Lawyers formed an important block within the Commons, being heavily represented on committees both as members and chairmen; they drafted bills as part of the administration's legislative programme or at the request of the house and private bills for clients, although the quality of some of their work was questionable. Beare, Bolton, Brereton, Darcy and Eustace also acted as counsel in parliament in precedency cases, private bills or petitions. Non-members were also involved as counsel (e.g., John Pollexfen) and in a few instances as members of committees, as Darcy and Martin were before their returns in by-elections in early 1641.[59] Frequently all those of the 'long robe' were added to committees (although it is not clear whether this included civil or only common lawyers) and in 1614 all the privy councillors and 'the judges and king's learned counsell being also members of this house' were added to the Grand Committee. Bradley noted all the Protestant lawyers who were members of the committee on the bill on pirates, but not Everard.[60]

Curiously, only 15 out of 87 (13%) lawyer MPs were members of more than one parliament and the number would have been even fewer had Darcy and

56 Terry Clavin, 'Denham, Sir John', *DIB*.
57 Kyle, 'Parliament and Westminster'; McGrath, 'Managing the Windsor'.
58 McGrath, 'Ireland and the third university'; Grosart (ed.), *Lismore Papers*, 1st series, iv, pp 56, 68–9; Darcy to Ormond, 6 Jan. 1642, Bodl. Lib., Carte MS 2, fo. 266.
59 *LJI*, 14, 26, 29–31 July 1634, 1 Aug. 1634, 26 Nov. 1634.
60 E.g., *Commons' Jn. Ire.*, 18, 25, 27, 30 May 1641; TNA, MS PRO 30/5/3, fos. 24v–5. This entry in Bradley's notes is not included in the published journals.

Martin not been returned in by-elections in 1641.[61] They and Alexander remained aloof from the 1640 elections and Henry White was excluded as Clonmel bowed to pressure to return Protestants rather than lose its charter through *Quo warranto* proceedings. The length of time between the 1613 and 1634 parliaments and general mortality removed some, but others, like Gosnold, lived into old age and the general failure of lawyers to sit more than once remains intriguing.

Judges' presence in parliament was so important that Wentworth cited the need to have justices available for the assizes as a reason for proroguing parliament in 1634, as did the lords justices in March 1641.[62] They provided legal advice to the Lords, a valuable facility as few peers were lawyers, – Dominic Sarsfield and Chancellor Adam Loftus were exceptions – but could only advise when requested to do so and had no vote on any matter.[63] In 1569, their advice was sought on the legality of returns to the Commons.[64] Eustace's acceptance speech noted 'with joy the chief Judges of the land, attended by his Majesty's learned Counsel, and ready to untie any Gordian knot which shall be proposed to them.'[65] They had a key role in parliament's ceremonial, forming part of the opening procession and adding colour to plenary sessions and served as messengers from the upper to the lower house. Catholics were not members of the judiciary after 1607 and experienced Protestant lawyers were promoted to be serjeants-at-law and judges with preference generally being given to Englishmen. Like their English counterparts, Irish MPs often became judges, e.g., Barry, Donnellan, Hilton, Oliver Jones and William Ryves, and constituted 62.5% of the 16 judges of the four courts and senior law officers in early Restoration Ireland: Chancellor Maurice Eustace, the master of the rolls John Temple, master in chancery Dudley Loftus, James Barry, Donnellan, Alexander, John Bysse, Richard Kennedy and Mervyn. However, unlike in England, great officers of state in Ireland had not generally served as recorders of towns.[66]

Judges were barred from membership of the Commons because of the conflict of interest in legislators judging cases and as a Catholic lawyer noted, 'theire office onely being to attend in the Upper house for moving or resolving matters in Lawe.' He further objected to serjeants-at-law who provided legal services to the crown and acted as supernumerary judges:

> And the reason of excluding them from voyce in parliament may be well drawen out of that which forbiddeth they should be of anny Juries, the

61 These figures exclude those elected in 1628, e.g., Donnellan and Henry White and possibly James Barry and Catlin.

62 NLI, MS 9,607, p. 130.

63 Orders for the House of Lords, *LJI*, 23 July 1634.

64 *Commons' Jn. Ire.*, 13, 17 Oct. 1614; Falkiner, *Essays*, pp 211, 238.

65 Empey (ed.), *Early Stuart Irish warrants*, p. 198; *Commons' Jn. Ire.*, 20 March 1640.

66 Coleman A. Dennehy, 'Appointments to the bench in early Restoration Ireland' in Dennehy (ed.), *Law and revolution*, pp 265–88; Catherine F. Patterson, *Urban government and the early Stuart state: provincial towns, corporate liberties and royal authority in England, 1603–1640* (Woodbridge, 2022), p. 26.

> parliament being the grand and petite jurie for triall of the lives and estates of all the subjects.

This was a clear dig at both Beare and Davies, whose elections Catholics claimed were illegal.[67]

Despite this, judges were returned to the 1613 Commons, but the question was raised on 17 October 1614, quite possibly because the committee for the bill on pirates, appointed three days earlier, included serjeant Beare and justices Gosnold and Harris, who should not have been sitting as their boroughs were disfranchised; the parliamentary rolls were searched for precedents.[68] Presumably the records advised against and no judges sat as MPs thereafter, although Sibthorpe, MP for Limavady, continued to sit in that parliament.[69] However, serjeants sat in the English Commons and in Ireland, including all the speakers in this period and Barry and Donnellan in 1634 and Sambach in 1640.

Not all MPs who were lawyers were above reproach; at least five, all Protestant – Alexander, Beare, Catlin, Davies and Wilkinson – were either disbarred or expelled from their inns for misdemeanours. Davies was imprisoned and expelled from the Middle Temple in 1598 for a serious assault on a colleague and had to press hard for readmission three years later. His highly questionable development of 'judge-made law' in Ireland created a very damaging precedent and his publication of selective law reports, including one which was 'straight government anti-Catholic propaganda', have been described as 'essentially the work of a 'self-publicist'.[70] Beare was appointed serjeant-at-law in Ireland in 1609 following his disbarment in England. Wilkinson was expelled from Barnard's Inn in 1615 for being found

> with a lewd woman in bed about midnight, whereupon his chamber door was broken open and he and the said queane and concubine found together in bed, to the great dishonor of God and scandal of [the] society, if the same should not be made an example according to the Rules of the House, whereupon he was fined 20s. and expelled the society.[71]

Catlin's involvement in a serious riot and kidnapping at Staple Inn in 1622 perhaps prompted him to abandon his planned career in the church and migrate to Ireland.[72] Bolton came to Ireland to avoid a sentence in the Court of Star Chamber and Alexander having been disbarred in England for falsifying legal documents,

67 Jackson (ed.), 'Document'.
68 Ibid.
69 Lord Chancellor Loftus to Wentworth, 13 April 1637, in Knowler (ed.), *Letters and dispatches*, ii, pp 67ff; Wentworth to Loftus, 14 April 1637, Loftus to Wentworth, Wentworth to Loftus, 15 April 1637, ibid., pp 68–9; Terry Clavin, 'Sibthorpe, Sir Christopher', *DIB*.
70 Brand, 'Sir John Davies'.
71 Baker, *Inns of Chancery*, pp 214–18, 288.
72 McGrath, 'Membership', p. 45; Baker, *Inns of Chancery*, pp 214–18; Hart, *History of the king's serjeants at law*, pp 53–7, 166.

but these disbarments were no hindrance to their advancement in Ireland.[73] Pym regarded Radcliffe as more culpable than Wentworth because, as a trained lawyer, he was fully aware of the enormity of his illegal actions in Ireland, a view echoed by Mervyn who described him as 'little inferior in wickedness' to Strafford, accusing him of abusing his position as a lawyer by publishing 'false opinions, unjust judgments and sentences, in extra judicial manner against law.'[74] The Chancellor Adam Loftus, Laurence Parsons and Robert Travers were notoriously corrupt in their operations as judges of the Munster Admiralty Court.[75] Nor were those with a more limited legal education necessarily patterns of probity; Oliver St John had to abandon his legal studies having killed a man in a duel and Richard Boyle was imprisoned for his underhand land dealings in Ireland.[76] Barnard regards Alexander's success after disgrace at home as 'exceptional', but these examples demonstrate that he was far from unique in prospering in Ireland despite earlier transgressions.[77]

THE CONFEDERATION

Lawyers provided strong leadership in all aspects of the Confederation; 112 known members of General Assemblies had some legal training, 25 of whom were qualified lawyers. Its most prominent officers were Darcy and Plunkett, judges James Cusack and Richard Martin and one third of its negotiating team in May 1643 (Geoffrey Browne, Nicholas Plunkett and John Walshe) were lawyers. Many of those who served most frequently in its General Assemblies were lawyers or had some legal education, including MPs the Blakes, Geoffrey Browne, Richard Butler, Marcus Cheevers, Peter Clinton, Darcy, Richard Haly, Roebuck Lynch, Richard

73 Aidan Clarke, 'Bolton, Richard', *DIB*; [Jerome Alexander], *A breviate of a sentence given against J.A. ... In the Court of Star Chamber* (London, 1644); *The case between Sir Jerom Alexander Knight, second justice of his majesties Court of Common Pleas in Ireland: and Sir William Ashton Knight, second justice of his majesties Court of King's Bench in Ireland concerning precedency* (s.l., 1661); Charles Rogers, 'Notes in the history of Sir Jerome Alexander, second justice of the Court of Common Pleas, and founder of the Alexander Library, Trinity College, Dublin', *Transactions of the Royal Historical Society*, 2 (1873), 94–116; J.P. Prendergast, 'Further notes in the history of Sir Jerome Alexander', *Transactions of the Royal Historical Society*, 2 (1873), 117–41; Terry Clavin, 'Alexander, Sir Jerome', *DIB*.

74 Audley Mervyn, *Ireland's complaint against Sir George Ratcliffe knight, now prisoner in the gate-house at Westminster, delivered in parliament there by captaine Audley Mervin. VVherein is declared the grievances of that kingdome, occasioned by him, and the late earle of Strafford, the principall cause, why these late troubles are fallen upon them, whereunto is annexed the depositions and articles exhibited against him in parliament* (London, 1641), sig. A1v–A2v; Fiona Pogson, 'Strafford's "spirit" at the royalist court: Sir George Radcliffe and Irish affairs, 1643–5', *IHS*, 43:164 (2019), 175–93.

75 Costello, *Court of Admiralty*, pp 4–19.

76 Judy Barry, 'St John, Oliver, Viscount Grandison and Tregoz', *DIB*; A.M. Mimardière and P.W. Hasler, 'St John, Oliver' in Hasler (ed.), *History of parliament*; Edwards, 'From land-thief to planter'; David Edwards (ed.), 'Interrogating Richard Boyle: the Savoy House proceedings of 1599', *Anal. Hib.*, 49 (2018), 79–115.

77 Barnard, 'Lawyers and the law'.

Martin, Nicholas Plunkett, Rochford, Peter Rothe, John Walshe and Dominick White.[78]

Confederation judges played a similar role as in parliament, including bringing messages to and from the peers when they met separately:

> Mr Patrick Darcy, bare-headed upon a stool, representing all or some of the judges and masters of chancery that used to sit in parliament upon woolsacks … The lords had an upper room, which served them as a place of recess, for private consultation, and when they had taken their resolutions, the same were delivered to the commons by Mr Darcy.[79]

As the Confederation's judiciary expanded, the task may not have devolved solely upon Darcy.

Many MPs with legal training continued to play a key role in Irish public life throughout the 1640s, 1650s and after the Restoration, including Alexander, James Barry, John Bysse, Donnellan, Eustace, Hilton, Michael and Oliver Jones, Mervyn and Temple and the Catholics Darcy, Plunkett and John Walshe. Judges who held their positions through 'thick and thin' (Barry, Donnellan and Temple), had been MPs.[80] At a less elevated level, Brereton and Lewis were the most active barristers practicing in chancery in the 1650s.[81]

Lawyers formed a minority of MPs, but their professional experience and wide range of contacts enabled them to play a more dominant role in parliament than their numbers otherwise warranted, especially in committees that performed the most detailed work and where problems were debated and consensus reached. In 1613 especially, the government's thin majority and the larger number of experienced Catholic lawyers enabled them to have a greater influence on the house's proceedings and play a constructive role in its success.

78 Ó Siochrú, *Confederate Ireland*, pp 257–8.
79 Vallancey, *Collectanea de rebus Hibernica*, p. 416.
80 Colum Kenny, 'Not every judge a phoenix: King's Inns under Cromwell' in Dennehy (ed.), *Law and revolution*, pp 104–27.
81 Barnard, 'Lawyers and the law'.

CHAPTER ELEVEN

Parliaments and crises

THIS CHAPTER DISCUSSES how the Irish parliament responded to the crises of the early Stuart monarchies. It examines the mechanisms and innovations it used to fulfil its representative, legislative, financial and judicial roles, the results of its actions and its successes and failures. The crises caused by the crown's increasingly autocratic government which erupted in the three kingdoms in the 1630s and 1640s had been incubating for many years and the tensions in each country and its parliament were influenced by events in the others. The highly partisan Borlase later reflected:

> I wonder that they did not expect and provide for a Rebellion in Ireland as soon as they began to quarrel with the King in England; for was there any body so ignorant as not to know that the Irish papists did long for a Change of Religion there, as well as the Presbyterians in England? Or that in general the Irish Nation did hate the name of Subjection to England, or would longer be quiet than they feared an Army out of England to chastize them? What better time, then, could they take for their Rebellion than this, wherein they were encouraged, not only by our weakness caused by this Division between the King and his Parliament, but also by the Example of the Presbyterians, both of the Scotch and English nation?[1]

Crises were not confined to the Stuart realms: similar political tensions erupted in states across Europe during the mid-seventeenth century and their representative assemblies were either unable to resolve them or not permitted to do so.

Public acceptance of parliament's role in ensuring a positive relationship between the crown and its subjects, contributing to good governance and resolving tensions, was not shared by monarchs and their administrations. Lord Deputy Falkland only called parliament in 1628 after the Great Assembly failed, but its botched summoning created another crisis, although there is no guarantee that its results would have been acceptable to either side had it actually met. This created expectations for Wentworth's first parliament which, like the Scottish Estates in the previous year, worked only to the crown's advantage – even the general pardon was much more limited than Chichester's act – and set the scene for the 1640 parliament, which was summoned in direct response to the overt crisis in Scotland and England, not to the situation in Ireland.

Strafford's subversion of normal systems earned him the enmity of all groups outside his own circle. Arbitrary justice dispensed in the Court of Castle Chamber

1 Borlase, *History*, pp 106–7.

and at the privy council undermined the rule of law and assaults on property rights threatened all landowners, whether through the Commission of Defective Titles, intended plantations in Connacht and Ormond or the refusal to guarantee insecure land titles including those whose owners had repeatedly paid to have them regularized.[2] His reconstruction of the Church of Ireland, including the operations of the Court of High Commission, alienated much of the new settler community, especially Scottish Presbyterians. Restrictions on trade and *Quo warranto* proceedings alarmed urban communities, especially merchants. Crown officials' exorbitant fees had been a continual grievance in early Stuart Ireland and monopolies such as that on tobacco and the operations of the customs farm oppressed ordinary subjects and enriched Wentworth and his clients and associates. His assault on St Ann's Guild's assets threatened that wealthy foundation's members. All of these grievances were raised in hundreds of petitions to parliament and in MPs' direct negotiations with Charles in 1640–1. In addition, the New English and Scots present before Wentworth's arrival, like the Catholic Irish, were increasingly excluded from opportunities for enrichment (and corruption) as the deputy promoted and enriched his own clients. Based on his record as president of the Council of the North in York, Irish observers had anticipated this arbitrary and oppressive regime at his appointment and saw no prospect of his slackening pace in reconstructing Irish society and government.[3] Strafford ignored the building resentment:

> The Bishop of Rapho tells me your Majesty was told all this Kingdom was disposed to trouble. It is wonderful how men are inclined nowadays to report all wherein I am concerned to the worst possible source. For...there hath not been all this while the least appearance or complexion to any such thing, nor is there yett, or any likely to be, for any thing I can see. Nay Sir, after all their gaping upon me and after me, it will be found I have Estimation and Affection in the Places where I serve you.[4]

The need to transmit bills swiftly to England to justify summoning parliament left little time for drafting a legislative programme and following Strafford's usual practice, public grievances were not considered. George Radcliffe's electoral strategy consisted of a very restricted timescale for returns, reducing the size of both houses by excluding peers like Cork and Fermoy and burgesses from some boroughs. He also engaged in widespread intimidation, repeated elections for the same seats and used blanks extensively. However, the compliant parliament this produced was decreasingly representative of the political community and the administration's majority depended on crown officials and soldiers, many of whom were unable to attend because of their duties in the new army. Wentworth's

2 Perceval-Maxwell, *Outbreak*, pp 284–5.
3 Empey, 'Power, prerogative and the politics of Sir Thomas Wentworth'.
4 Wentworth to Charles, 6 Aug. 1639, quoted in McGrath, 'Irish elections of 1640–1641'.

associates, including some MPs, left with him for England in April 1640 and the administration's loss of control of the situation reduced its capacity to reward its adherents, leading to further weakness in parliament.[5]

Parliaments or estates were already sitting in all three kingdoms as the crisis prompted by the Scottish situation spread throughout England and Ireland. Each responded by taking control of its membership, agenda and operations and co-operated, especially initially, in their attempts to reform the government. They also used the opportunities created by events in the other nations to further their own local agendas. Just as Scots had used petitions extensively in the campaign against the prayer book in 1637 and in the estates, both the Irish and English parliaments exploited them to promote their reform agendas. As Stewart notes, 'petitioning made a major contribution to the collapse of royal government in all three kingdoms.'[6] It is significant that the first opposition shown in the Irish parliament came after Charles' failure to obtain support from the Short Parliament, but contact between the three parliaments was not new. Scottish planters in Ulster successfully petitioned the 1630 estates 'to recommend to his majesty their naturalization and confirmation of their estates and the case of *postnati* in the next parliament to be held in the said kingdom of Ireland.'[7] The estates called on the English parliament to guarantee their position against the threat of the new army raised in Ireland, Irish MPs petitioned the English Commons to help present their grievances to Charles and 17 of the 28 articles introduced in the English parliament against Strafford directly related to his government of Ireland.[8] Information travelled between the parliaments, facilitated by MPs' connections and relatives, like English MPs Arthur Ingram and John Pym, and William Jephson, Henry Wallop and his son Robert who were based in England but had large estates in Ireland. Wallop's agent William Swanton, MP for Wallop's town of Enniscorthy, was also a tenant of Sir Charles Berkeley, MP for Bath in the Short Parliament.[9] Lord Hastings' Irish agent briefing him on proceedings in the Irish parliament noted 'the parliament in England will make all things quicker or slower here.'[10] Irish lawyers could draw on networks formed through their membership of the inns of court. Strafford's Irish opponents built on old connections and infiltrated the English Commons to facilitate their joint efforts to engineer his downfall. Cork offered to procure 'a burgess place' in the Short Parliament for Sir William Parsons' son Richard and accommodate him in his London home. His

5 Ibid.; Clarke, *Old English*, p. 131.

6 Stewart, 'Petitioning'.

7 Instructions given for the kingdom of Scotland authorised by warrant under the great seal to treat with the commissioners for the kingdom of England, 12 Nov. 1630, 'Records of the parliament of Scotland to 1707', at https://rps.ac.uk/ [accessed 21 March 2022]. Postnati were Scots born after James' accession to the English throne in 1603.

8 Rushworth (ed.), *Tryal*, pp 61, 75; Robert Armstrong, *Protestant war: the 'British' of Ireland and the wars of the three kingdoms* (Manchester, 2005), p. 10.

9 TNA, PROB 11/189/205.

10 Seagrave to Ferdinando Lord Hastings, 13 Nov. 1640, in Bickley (ed.), *Hastings, Volume II*, pp 81–2.

heir Dungarvan was returned for Appleby in the Short and Long Parliaments, through Lady Dungarvan's family's interest there, joined in the latter by his brother-in-law Sir Arthur Jones, son of Lord Ranelagh, for Weobly (a seat controlled by Cork's Tomkins relatives) and Arthur's other brother-in-law Sir John Clotworthy for Maldon and Bossiney (through the interest of Lords Warwick and Robartes respectively, the latter through Lord Charles Lambart).[11] Cork may well have tried to influence other returns, while Clotworthy, a Presbyterian, also had many contacts in Scotland.[12] Wentworth clients returned to the Short Parliament included Philip Mainwaring, John Wandesford and George Wentworth and the latter and Charles Price to the Long Parliament.

In 1638 the Church of Scotland's General Assembly abolished the kirk's episcopal structure and demanded ratification of this decision in the estates which met in the following year and which no bishops attended, removing a block vote for the crown. In the light of Charles' manipulation of the 1633 estates, Scotland also demanded regular parliaments that would have a role in selecting ministers (reverting to the former position) including the Lords of the Articles who managed the estates' business, because the monarch's absence 'hindered the airing of native complaints and grievances and the prevention of the 'disorders committed by corrupt councillors.' The estates met without Charles' approval in June 1640 and continued in session as either the full estates or Convention of Estates until 1651.[13]

In 1641 the English Long Parliament passed the Triennial Act that required parliament to sit for a 50-day session at least once every three years and forbade its dissolution without its own consent; in the following year it expelled bishops from the House of Lords.[14] In 1644 Charles summoned English parliamentarians to Oxford where they sat until the following year, with Sampson Eure as speaker.[15] The Long Parliament continued to meet in Westminster under speaker Lenthall and responded to the Oxford parliamentarians by decreeing that no member of either house who had opposed parliament might resume his seat without the consent of both houses. It proceeded to recruit replacements in 1645.[16] Setting its own agenda, it legislated and raised its own army and finance. On 6 December 1648 Colonel Thomas Pride, Hardress Waller and others purged the Long Parliament of those members who were unwilling to put the king on trial; the

11 I am grateful to Patrick Little for his advice on this subject. Cork to Richard Parsons, 14 Jan. 1640, Cork to Wentworth, 16 March 1640, Chatsworth House, Cork Papers, Misc. boxes, Box 3, pp 403–4, 421; Grosart (ed.), *Lismore Papers*, 1st series, v, p. 108, under 19 Sept. 1639: Armstrong, *Protestant war*, pp 1–2.

12 Patrick Walsh and T.G. Doyle, 'Boyle, Richard, 2nd earl of Cork and 1st earl of Burlington', *DIB*; Raymond Gillespie, 'Clotworthy, Sir John, 1st Viscount Massereene', *DIB*.

13 Young, *The Scottish parliament*, pp 1–14, 331; Goodare, 'Scottish parliament of 1621' discusses the shifting nature of the composition of the Scottish Estates. Also, see Smith, *Stuart*, p. 20.

14 16 Car. I, c. 1, England. This act was repealed following the restoration of the monarchy.

15 Stephen K. Roberts, 'Eure, Sir Sampson', *Oxford DNB*.

16 R.N. Kershaw, 'The recruiting of the Long Parliament, 1645–7', *History*, new series, 8:31 (Oct., 1923), 169–79.

remaining members constituted what became known as the Rump Parliament, which tried the king.[17] It was abolished by Cromwell in April 1653, but restored in 1659; in early 1660 the 'secluded members' (those expelled in 1648) were briefly restored, thereby ending the Rump Parliament.

These options were not open to the Irish parliament: its legislative and revenue-raising capacity was constrained by Poynings' Law and bishops remained in the Lords. However, the Commons took control of its membership, defeated the government on subsidies, proposed and drafted bills, used its judicial function and especially petitions to resolve grievances and greatly expanded its representative function within both Ireland and England, negotiating directly with Charles to achieve reform and press for changes in Ireland's constitutional position. In June 1642 the Irish parliament expelled MPs it held to be in rebellion or who refused the oath of supremacy and it continued to sit until 1648, three years longer than the Oxford parliamentarians, with generally low attendance despite the addition of at least 87 new recruits.[18] The Scottish Estates had no local rival, but Irish Catholics, like the Long Parliament at Westminster, established an alternative system of government as the Confederation of Kilkenny in late 1642, operating as a counter-state, with a General Assembly, secretariat, army and navy, diplomatic representation, courts, coinage and printing press.[19]

The opening of the first session of the Irish parliament in March 1640 agreed substantial subsidies to support Charles' military campaign against the Scots, but MPs also took the initiative, establishing committees to examine the long-festering complaints about officials' fees and to sit during the recess to draft legislation to deal with grievances before it met again in June. The administration lost nothing by permitting this since the committee included such government heavyweights as Radcliffe, Sir William Parsons, Paul Davies, James Ware, William Sambach, Robert Meredith and advocate general Edward Lake and it could always refuse or fail to transmit bills to England. While ostensibly willingly granted, however, the onerous subsidies were a source of apprehension, especially given the unfair assessments in 1634–5 (see chapter eight) and the poor economic conditions of the late 1630s. Clarke's assertion that that some Protestants found common ground with Catholics in this vacation committee is supported by the fact that its membership included John Bysse, Audley Mervyn and Hardress Waller who were to become prominent in opposition. Equally interesting is that all four MPs for Limerick City and County and many townsmen were nominated – eight Catholics Richard Blake, Geoffrey Browne, Piers Creagh, Nicholas Dormer, Roebuck Lynch, Thomas Peppard, John Taylor and Dominic White and Protestants Richard Barry, John Brice and, of course, Bysse – whose presence presumably accounts for the emphasis on trade and economic issues in the lists of grievances, especially since, as their towns paid their wages, they were answerable to their

17 Ian J. Gentles, 'Pride, Thomas', *Oxford DNB*.
18 McGrath, 'Recruiter returns'.
19 Ó Siochrú, *Confederate Ireland*.

voters.[20] Emboldened by the failure of the Short Parliament, opposition surfaced early in June when MPs reversed the administration's usurpation of parliament's role in assessing and collecting subsidies and markedly reduced their value. The bill for the Connacht plantation also disappeared into a committee never to reappear, despite Radcliffe, Robert Dillon, Meredith, Sambach and Parsons being members. The Commons used committees of the whole house consistently to be able to discuss policy and strategy, engage in detailed debate and reduce the speaker's control of business. The first petitions, including complaints against officials' fees and the Court of High Commission, Bishop Atherton of Waterford and Lismore and Lake were received and the Commons ordered writs to be issued for elections in disfranchised boroughs. On its illegal prorogation on 17 June, the house presented Lord Deputy Wandesford with a Petition of Remonstrance, outlining complaints against clergy which they wished redressed and mandated the committee of grievances to consider the 'complaints of the country' before its next session.[21]

The Commons adopted a more militant tone on the opening of the second session in October, angered by the lack of progress on grievances identified in the Petition of Remonstrance. They successfully demanded that burgesses be elected from disfranchised boroughs and expelled Lake. Additionally, before its prorogation on 12 November, the opposition had been strengthened by new members from Ardee, Naas and Newcastle at least and John FitzGerald for Inistioge.[22] Faced with solid resistance, Wentworth tried to restrict parliament's work, but the delay in procuring a commission of prorogation allowed the house to continue to sit and defy the administration; their lesson learnt, the lords justices ensured that the next commission of January 1641 gave them authority to prorogue. Seeing little progress in redress of the grievances identified in the Petition of Remonstrance in June, MPs defied repeated summonses to the closing ceremony, refused to agree to send a conference committee to the privy council 'to treat of the matters proposed by [Wandesford] in regard they were formerly voted in the house for grievances' and took the radical step of appointing agents to negotiate directly with the king in London, writing to the English Commons urging support for this delegation.

> This last session of parliament the lower house hath showed much stoutness in presenting a petition to the Lord Deputy of many grievances and monopolies in this commonwealth which only tend to the enriching of some particulars, and to the overthrow of merchandise and to the general impoverishment of this kingdom. The House not receiving an answer to their contentment chose out a committee of thirteen to go for England (whereof

20 Clarke, *Old English*, p. 129.
21 *Commons' Jn. Ire.*, 11–17 June 1640.
22 McGrath, 'Irish elections of 1640–1641'; BL, Egerton MS 1,048; *Commons' Jn. Ire.*, 9–10 Nov. 1640; McGrath, 'Sex, lies and rigged returns'.

> Sir William Cole was one) to present their Remonstrance to the King. The next day the Deputy prorogued the House till the 25th of February and sent for the lower house to come to the higher house. They being busy in voting something caused the door to be locked and the key to be laid upon the table made the Deputy to stay three hours notwithstanding the Serjeant at Arms, the King of Arms and the Black Rod was sent.[23]

The agents – seven Old English including four lawyers, five New English settlers and a Scot, all active in parliamentary committees – were very carefully selected, as much for their influential connections in the English court or parliament as their expertise.[24] Three were chosen from each province, except for Leinster which had four. The lawyers Thomas Bourke and Geoffrey Browne were close connections of Clanricard, as was Roebuck Lynch and Nicholas Plunkett was Fingall's brother.[25] Donough MacCarthy was Lord Muskerry's heir, Nicholas Barnewall an experienced parliamentarian and John Walshe a respected Waterford lawyer and merchant.[26] In addition, because he had spent his professional life in London, Bourke had local knowledge and connections that would be useful to the delegation. James Montgomery, Cole and Edward Rowley, were Ulster settlers; Rowley was Clotworthy's brother-in-law but also able to represent the Londonderry planters and Cole, Montgomery's father-in-law, married Sir William Parsons' niece. Hardress Waller and Simon Digby, cousins respectively of the English MP William Waller and the earl of Bristol, were both close connections of Cork's and Richard FitzGerald was a client of Philip Percival.[27] The Lords also authorized three peers, including Cormac Óg MacCarthy, Lord Muskerry, to attend the king with their own list of grievances.[28]

Wandesford's loss of control allowed parliament to resume its representative role and air a wide range of complaints in the house; it also reduced the administration's power to protect and reward its supporters, further weakening its hand. The diminution in the value of the subsidies and failure of the plantation bills deprived the administration of money and the lands in Connacht and Ormond which Wentworth had intended to distribute to reward his associates and recompense some like the Piggotts who had been the victims of his arbitrary justice.[29] In addition, the administration was unable to protect its officials and

23 BL, Egerton MS 1,048; *Commons' Jn. Ire.*, 12 Nov. 1640; Charles Seagrave, agent, to Ferdinando Lord Hastings, 13 Nov. 1640, in Bickley (ed.), *Hastings, Volume II*, pp 81–2. Hastings' estates were close to Cole's base in Enniskillen.

24 Clarke, *Old English*, p. 135; Perceval-Maxwell, *Outbreak*, p. 90; BL, Egerton MS 1,048.

25 Micheál Ó Siochrú, 'Lynch, Roebuck (Robert)', *DIB*.

26 *Idem*, 'MacCarthy, Donough, 2nd Viscount Muskerry', *DIB*; *idem*, 'Walshe, Sir John', *DIB*.

27 FitzGerald was of lower social status than the others and worked in a clerical capacity; it is unclear whether he was included partly in an administrative capacity.

28 G.E.C., *Peerage*.

29 Drury Cooper to Gervase Clifton, 1 Sept. 1635, same to same, 1639?, Nottingham University Library, MS C1 C, 135–6. I am grateful to David Heffernan for his assistance in dating this letter. *Commons' Jn. Ire.*, 9 July 1641.

institutions like the Courts of High Commission and Castle Chamber from complaints in the Commons.[30]

Borlase traced a link between the lack of leadership and the rebellion:

> the present rebellion was begun when there was no lieutenant there, and when the power (which had been formerly us'd in that Kingdom) was question'd and disgrac'd, when those in the parliament there (by whom that rebellion was hatch'd) were countenanc'd in their complaints and prosecution.[31]

Cork, Loftus, Parsons, Waller and their associates used the Irish parliament to destroy Wentworth and his regime, intending to divide the spoils of government between themselves, as before, but at the point of their victory in November 1640, the nature of the Irish opposition changed, a position reinforced by Wandesford's death, as Protestants and Catholics' aim moved from a desire to change one man's regime to a determination to alter the whole structure of government, one which Parsons and others had every interest in maintaining. Parsons especially, as the supreme land-grabber, was threatened by any legislation securing land titles, a subject addressed in the Graces but still not resolved, despite Charles' promises: 'To rid themselves of Strafford, Parsons and his friends had opened the Pandora's box of parliamentary opposition. When they attempted to close it, they reaped the whirlwinds of rebellion and civil war'.[32]

Events moved quickly in all three kingdoms and the Irish parliament's attention to its counterparts' proceedings was not passive. Strafford's absence in England, especially after his arrest on 11 November and Wandesford's death on 3 December 1640 raised the question of whether parliament could continue, as its commission empowered either man or the lords justices to hold the parliament, but no justices had been appointed (see chapter 5).[33] Charles issued a letter declaring that parliament had not been determined and offered a bill to secure the position legally and new elections, should parliament think it necessary, and an act to that effect was included in the fourth transmission.[34] New elections would have further weakened the administration's position, but the opposition might also have been chary of a promise of a fresh parliament given the experience of 1628 and because a dissolution would have ended its agents' mandate to negotiate with the king.

30 E.g., *Commons' Jn. Ire.*, 15, 17 June 1640, 22 Oct. 1640.
31 Borlase, *History*, p. 3.
32 Bodl. Lib., Carte MS 64, fos. 459v–60r; Perceval-Maxwell, 'Protestant faction', p. 256; Little, 'Cork and the downfall of the earl of Strafford', unconvincingly argues that Cork was slow to act in opposition to Wentworth.
33 Charles to Sir John Bankes, attorney general of England, to summon parliament, 27 Jan. 1640, Bodl. Lib., Bankes MS 55/65.
34 Warrant from Charles to Bankes for a commission for Parsons and Borlase to hold the parliament in succession to Wentworth and Wandesford, 30 Dec. 1640, Bodl. Lib., Bankes MS 55/113. Charles' letter, *Commons' Jn. Ire.*, 22 May 1641; transmitted acts are listed in the preliminaries to the journals for 1640.

There is no record of the transmitted bill declaring the assembly's validity being debated and parliament continued in session with all sides ignoring its dubious legal status. The opposition was gradually strengthening its position as a series of by-elections from other disfranchised boroughs and replacing deceased members generally returned non-governmental candidates, although Edward Trevor managed to secure seats in Downpatrick for his son Mark and William Billingsley and Richard Fanshawe was returned for Ballinakill. The Commons exercised their powers to the full, including those which Wentworth had refused to permit them to use. MPs stoutly defended John FitzGerald's election against objections from the peers and the administration. On 30 January 1641 MPs took a series of decisions that greatly strengthened the opposition's hand: it named 21 new members, at least 15 of them Catholic, to the standing committee of grievances, and issued additional instructions to its agents in London, again adding 33 new members (slightly more Protestants than Catholics) to the committee, considerably extending the agents' powers and giving it authority to appoint subcommittees to draft legislation. The enlarged committee of grievances was asked to consider whether minors should be permitted to be MPs and on 24 May the Commons issued an order disabling men under 20 from membership of the house and another to expel Thomas Radcliffe.[35]

A small number of fairly routine petitions were submitted to the Commons in 1640, but from January 1641 the stream became a torrent. As few have survived, their precise contents are unknown, but they demanded the redress of individual and collective grievances inflicted by churchmen, officials of the Court of High Commission or those administering the tobacco monopoly, challenged officials' fees, decisions at Wentworth's council board and the Court of Castle Chamber, as well the payment of debts and restoration of property. Parliament attempted to address all the petitions, but also used them to press for policy changes including on monopolies. Two early petitions from the native Irish inhabitants of Leitrim, Longford and King's and Queen's counties requested an end to the racial discrimination that prevented them from buying or leasing additional lands there under the plantation settlements; they attached a bill to that effect, which they asked to be transmitted and recommended 'against the next session of this parliament.'[36] The Commons questioned why the lords justices had not transmitted the bills they had proposed and impeached Wentworth's supporters, Bramhall, Bolton, Lowther and Radcliffe. Both houses issued a series of declarations and statements on parliament's powers including the Queries, Darcy's *Argument* and the Declaration and Humble Supplication, focusing on constitutional questions.[37]

35 Ibid., 4 Feb. 1641, 24 May 1641.

36 TNA, SP 63/274, fos. 1–5, Feb. 1641; *Commons' Jn. Ire.*, 22 Feb. 1641. Sadly, the bill has not survived. One of the signatories, Barnaby Dempsey, may have been returned in 1641 for Ballinakill to promote the bill. An end to distinctions between the different ethnic groups had been requested in the petition of Munster inhabitants to the 1634 parliament: TCD, MS 672, fos. 235r–8v (see Appendix 2).

Parliament's potential for resolving grievances was manifest and many of Wentworth's victims who refused to stand in the 1640 election were subsequently returned in by-elections or became active in the upper house. Wentworth's associates, including his brother George, secretary Thomas Little and Little's son and namesake, George Radcliffe and Philip Mainwaring, Thomas Wharton, John Jackson, Joshua Carpenter and physician Maurice Williams, were removed from the house immediately before the prorogation on 5 March and replaced before the fourth session on 11 May, largely with new members opposed to the administration, including William Stewart and the lawyers Adam Cusack, Richard Martin and Patrick Darcy.[38] Generally the old political community reasserted itself, as in Patrick Casey's replacing Radcliffe for Sligo County and the administration's successes, like William Dobbins replacing Williams for Askeaton, Robert Casey in Ennis and Johnson in Carrickdrumruske, depended on new boroughs, but the ease with which these could be influenced posed unforeseen problems when local magnates like Mervyn arranged the return of Catholics for these corporations.[39]

Parliament responded to the administration's resistance to redressing grievances by demanding constitutional change to reduce crown officials' influence and future abuses. The agents' instructions were to request the Commons' right to draft and transmit bills, the removal of an act of state that facilitated oppressive billeting of soldiers on citizens and four pieces of legislation: an explanatory act clarifying Poynings' Law, reforming the customs' administration, reversing the prohibition of exporting commodities and preventing privy councillors' profiting from export licences and enshrining in law existing rules for the operations of courts of justice. They asserted that Poynings' Law's purpose was that the monarch would have prior knowledge of Irish legislation rather than to 'exclude the subject from the knowledge and advice of drawing the said bills' and that it

> is so obscurely penned as it admitts much question and doubt how some of the materiall parts of that lawe shalbe understood and whether the same hath beene pursued in the forme and drawinge of Bills, all which difficulties ought to be cleered by a new Act by way of Supplement and addition.

The Commons demanded a reversion to the old system of consulting the political community about legislation before parliament met and that acts transmitted during parliament should be jointly drafted by it and the council, which they justified by claiming that over 40 bills had been rejected 'because they had been so modified as to serve some private end and that this was the reason why not a single bill passed there last season.'[40]

37 *Commons' Jn. Ire.*, 30 Jan. 1641, 25 Feb. 1641; Perceval-Maxwell, *Outbreak*, pp 147ff.
38 Robert Armstrong, 'Cusack, Adam', *DIB*.
39 McGrath, 'Inistiogue's elections in 1640'; *idem*, 'Irish elections of 1640–1641'.
40 Agents to the king and council in England, 17 May 1641, TNA, SP 63/259, fo. 80.

The crisis raised the question of the English parliament's relationship with Ireland. The Irish parliament's legislative independence was unquestioned: Davies stated in the 1621 English Commons that that body could not make laws for Ireland, because 'Ireland is a member of the crown of England' and 'they have there a parliament of their own', a position reiterated by Eustace in his acceptance speech as speaker. Bolton's *Statutes* included two fifteenth-century declaratory acts to that effect and the 1622 Commission's recommending enacting similar statutes to English ones in Ireland, as Wentworth's legislative programme did, are clear evidence that the parliament of England had no power to legislate for Ireland. The tone of Irish MPs' November 1640 petition to the English Commons requesting their help in presenting their remonstrance to the king is notably friendly and self-confident and expresses a sense of equality and partnership. Darcy's *Argument* against 'the late introduction of an arbitrary government' relied on English precedents, including the 1628 Petition of Right, because they constituted stronger justification for his position than Irish ones, but he did not restate Ireland's legislative independence as it was not in question. Darcy 'assumed that both Ireland's status as a dependency of the crown and its legislative independence were uncontroversial and incontrovertible', a constitutional position based on the creation of the kingdom in 1541 'subject to the same crown as England, but distinct from it', harking back to the position before 1633 and similar to other states in composite monarchies. An intervention in the English parliament in April 1641 claiming that the English parliament had the right to legislate for Ireland as a preliminary to using examples from Wentworth's Irish administration to convict him was dismissed and ignored.[41]

Borlase described the sittings between May and August 1641:

> MPs made ready for the Business, passing that session of Parliament … for the most part away in protestations, declarations, votes upon the queries, the stay of souldiers from going over seas, and private petitions, little to the good of the Common Wealth or advancement of his Majesty's service.[42]

This was unfair; the Commons were waiting for the result of their agents' negotiations which were not concluded until 16 July and the delegation did not leave London before parliament was adjourned until after the harvest. In the meantime, MPs concentrated on their legislative, representative and judicial functions; bills were dealt with, more drafted and members harried the administration about the transmission of others, made judicial orders declaring judgments void in law, annulling judgments in the Court of Castle Chamber, voiding the commission for the Court of High Commission and ordered the exchequer to stop hearing a case until parliament had heard and determined the

41 Clarke, 'Patrick Darcy and the constitutional relationship'; Darcy, *Argument*, p. 46; Treadwell (ed.), *Irish commission of 1622*, pp 38, 161, 221, 224, 234, 289, 291–2, 711–13.

42 Borlase, *History*, p. 12.

cause.[43] The administration's tardiness or failure to act on their grievances and the solutions and legislation authorized by the king provoked their wrath and in the meantime by-elections returned new members, including Richard Bellings.[44]

The London negotiations concluded with 20 of the 37 grievances fully conceded, seven partly granted (and the agents achieved some amelioration on these), two rejected and Charles temporized on eight, either referring them to the English privy council, the future lord lieutenant, or promising legislation in the Irish parliament. Clarke noted,

> it is easy to underestimate the extent of the committee's success, for none of the constitutional advances upon which attention had lately been concentrated had been secured [but] the fundamental aims of old English political action had been achieved and the government had been greatly enfeebled.

Henceforth, Catholics' priority was to uphold royal authority, which could protect them from Protestants' avarice, connive at their religious non-conformity and stall claims to their property; the return in late August of the bills transmitted in April limiting the king's title and securing lands in Connacht, Clare, Limerick and Tipperary supported this assessment.[45] The resolution to 12 grievances involved parliament but still required the council to draft and transmit legislation and most grievances remained unresolved. Borlase claimed that

> The Lords Justices and Councell … sate daily composing of Acts, to be passed the next sessions of parliament, for the benefit of his Majesty and the good of his subjects … the Lords Justices forthwith sending briefs to all the ports in the Kingdom of the Graces concerning customs, commanding the officers punctually to obey those his Majesty's Directions, particularly whatever concern'd Wool, Tobacco, as all other things of that nature.

However, the administration failed to transmit in time subsidy bills compensating the crown for the loss of revenue incurred by its concessions that were to pass before those securing land titles and the English government's request to the Westminster parliament to consider the questions of Poynings' Law and the *Queries* before the Irish parliament should meet (a move which Armstrong describes as showing 'a sense not of inferiority but of partnership', recruiting the English parliament as another 'guarantor of Irish laws and liberties') caused Charles to resolve to defer the next session of parliament until the following February. Moreover, the Irish administration had persuaded Charles to resile from his commitments to the agents. Catholics, unaware of Charles' changed position

43 Lentz, 'Irish parliament', p. 43.
44 Micheál Ó Siochrú, 'Bellings, Richard', *DIB*.
45 *Cal. S.P. Ire., 1633–47*, pp 317–22; Clarke, *Old English*, pp 149–50; *Commons' Jn. Ire.*, 6 Aug. 1641; Clarke, 'Patrick Darcy and the constitutional relationship'.

(his letter proroguing parliament did not arrive until mid-November) anticipated desired legislation would be passed and its other work continue when parliament reassembled in November.[46]

Before that Ulster Catholics made a pre-emptive strike to defend their property and religion, rising in rebellion, citing the difficulty of achieving redress of grievances, notably the security of land titles:

> All their heavy and insufferable pressures prosecuted and laboured by the natives of this Kingdom, with much suit, expense, and importunity, both in Parliament here, and in England before his Majesty, to be redressed, yet could never be brought to any happy conclusions, or as much as hope of contentment, but always eluded with delays.[47]

The rebellion removed any chance of resolving problems, whether universal, local or individual grievances, and especially constitutional change through parliament. The crisis triggered a change in the constitutional relationship between the Irish and English legislatures.

Graves' statement that the Irish parliament could 'play no part in the bloody rebellion of both Irish and Anglo-Irish' is inaccurate; both rebels and MPs hoped that it would be able to intervene in the rebellion and resolve outstanding grievances, but the biggest barrier was the administration's reluctance or refusal to allow it to meet and play that role. Members forced the lords justices to allow parliament to convene, asserting that its prorogation would be illegal and it reluctantly agreed to let it sit for three days.[48] Ulster Catholics presented a remonstrance to the justices,

> to be considered and redressed by Parliament here, which was shortly after to sit, where we doubted not such a fit course would be taken, as should give us content, secure the kingdom and take away the occasion of our taking arms, yet your justices, on first notice of our taking arms to prevent this so general a good, prorogued our parliament by proclamation.

Their propositions for settling the situation recommended:

> The first thing that is fitt to be done, that the nobilitye should apoint a tyme, and place as soone as possible may be for to conferre and consult of those matters taken in hand, and call also two out of every cheefe Citty, and out of

46 Armstrong, *Protestant war*, p. 7; Borlase, *History*, pp 12–13; Clarke, *Old English*, p. 153; Clarke, 'Patrick Darcy and the constitutional relationship'; *Cal. S.P. Ire., 1633–47*, pp 339–44.

47 Perceval-Maxwell, 'Ulster 1641'; Clarke, 'Patrick Darcy and the constitutional relationship'; The heads of the causes which moved the Northern Irish and Catholicks of Ireland to take arms, anno 1641, in Lodge, *Desiderata Curiosa*, ii, p. 80.

48 Graves, *Parliaments*, p. 142. The Lords sat on 9 Nov. and both houses on 16–17. Dennehy, 'Irish parliament after the rebellion'.

> every county, espetially that are neere, or may soone appeare in which consultation ... what covenants, greevances and causes they should propound to his majesty [including] a free parliament without dependency of the parliament or state of England, restoration of lands taken unjustly in plantation, the judgment whereof to be in the definition of the parliament heere.[49]

While Armstrong describes the Commons that met on 16 November 1641 as having 'a large Catholic presence', in fact more Protestants were named in the journals but the sitting was poorly advertised and many members would have been fearful of travelling or unable to leave their posts or homes. The privy council's failure to communicate with St Leger was presumably not unique; he remained in Munster 'although I have a very good mind to be at the beginning of the sitting of the parliament (if it hold) to see if my friend D[arcy] will hold up his nose as confidently as he was wont to do.' Four days later he wrote,

> we hear at random that both the [law] term and meeting in Parliament is put off until the 12 of February, but whether it be or no, I must not stir until I receive the Justices' commands, but I beseech you to let me know, if I should be commanded to stay here and the Parliament set.

Ikerrin wrote to Ormond to ask whether parliament was sitting.[50]

The prorogation until 21 January led to a rapid decline of trust on both sides. By the end of December Darcy concluded that remaining in Dublin was futile. Once more concerned that proroguing parliament without its meeting might determine it, the justices allowed it to sit for a single day, preventing it acting to resolve an increasingly polarized situation in which St Leger and Sir Charles Coote sr's murderous attacks on innocent Catholics pushed many into rebellion. Mountgarrett described himself as forced

> by the example of some as innocent and free from infringing his Majesty's laws as my self ... It is not my cause alone, it is the case of the whole kingdome and it hath been a principall observation of the best historians, that a whole nation, how contemptible soever should not be incensed by any Prince or state how powerful soever as to be driven to take desperate courses, the event whereof is uncertaine, and resteth only in the All guidinge power of the omnipotent, this hath beene most lively represented by the french Cronicler Philip de Commines in the passages betwene the Duke of Burgundy and the Swazers.[51]

49 Bodl. Lib., Carte MS 2, fo. 209, undated, but late 1641/early 1642.

50 Armstrong, *Protestant war*, p. 25; St Leger to Philip Percival, 1, 5 Nov. 1641, in Crawford Lomas (ed.), *Egmont*, i, pp 143ff; Ikerrin to Ormond, 8 Nov. 1641, Bodl. Lib., Carte MS 2, fo. 60.

51 Mountgarrett presumably to Ormond, 25 March 1642, Bodl. Lib., Carte MS 3, fo. 12r.

Catholics' absence from parliament, voluntarily in January but cemented by their increasing involvement in the rebellion and expulsion in June 1642, ensured that grievances would remain unresolved; officials named in petitions were free from further investigation and left the 'rump' of the parliament free to pursue Protestant members' interests, like St Ann's Guild's campaign to restore its property. The refusal to allow parliament to sit for more than one day between November and June also betrayed the Irish administration, crown and English parliament's perception of its being an 'undependable factor in Irish affairs, as a possible threat or even a danger', but it was also questionable whether its dissolution would be advantageous.[52] The administration faced considerable military, political and legal difficulties, specifically how to deal with Catholic members of both houses who were in rebellion, whether parliament should continue in session and, if so, what validity an unrepresentative parliament would have:

> A great part of both houses is in actual rebellion, and whether these may be debarred from coming to the house, or how they shall be debarred is very considerable for if they may come to the house, and cannot be excluded but by the vote of the house, they may fall out to be the major part, and so nothing can be done. Many of his majesty's good subjects who are members of both houses cannot with safety appear, from whence, and the exclusion of such as are in rebellion, may grow this doubt. What number will be requisite by the Courts of Parliament to continue the parliament and whether the number being so few, as it is feared it will be, the acts which shall be passed next session, if any be, will be valid: and if they be shot, whether the passing of bills in this manner, with so few, and such bills are like to trench upon the lives and estates of the other party, being so numerous as they are, may not raise such a clamour in foreign parts, and scruples in succeeding times, as may produce dangerous effects.
>
> Whether it be fit to continue this present parliament, or dissolve it [and] make way for another parliament, which may be better composed, when the kingdom is replenished with better subjects. If the resolution be to continue the present parliament, then the way to proceed with the least difficulty is to prepare a bill which may give power to the parliament to pass acts for the attainting of those who are or shall be in this present rebellion without transmitting them into England and notwithstanding Poynings Act, or any other act of parliament to the contrary, and this will before the transmitting of it is to be agreed upon by the greater number of Lords and Commons in a session of parliament holden in this realm; which may be done upon the first sitting next session, and this is required by the Statute 11 Elizabeth cap. 8.[53]

52 Lentz, 'Irish parliament', p. 107.

53 Notes of lords justices and privy council, undated, Feb.–June 1642. Difficulties which will fall out in the course of the proceedings which is to be held in the attainting of those rebels, who are now in actual rebellion, Bodl. Lib., Carte MS 68, fos. 422r–4.

Despite its unrepresentative nature and dubious validity, the state had reasons to retain this much reduced parliament: it was the only body able to enact legislation or vote taxes and ratify any settlement between Catholics and the king. Elections would be impossible while sheriffs and freeholders were not able to operate as a political community and even if fresh elections could be held, there was no guarantee that a new parliament would have a Protestant majority. The establishment of the Confederation's General Assembly in October 1642 made the Irish parliament's continuation imperative, so that it could retain some legitimacy as the official assembly, no matter how small and unrepresentative its membership, skeleton its form and trivial its work. The question of the size of the lower house was addressed by recruiting replacements for expelled or deceased MPs, but by very dubious means which did little to enhance its reputation or position even in Protestant eyes, as Mervyn's later advocating 'genuine' elections underlined.[54]

While the Irish parliament was adjourned between January and June 1642, its English counterpart passed the Adventurers' Act, raising £300,000 to fight the rebellion secured on lands to be confiscated in Ireland. The acts resolved English MPs' financial barriers to suppressing the rebellion but without considering its Irish counterpart's position and in legislating for Ireland it created constitutional difficulties for Irish parliamentarians regardless of their ethnic origins or religious persuasion. After Charles assented to the Act in March 1642 'Irish Protestants were left with little hope of succor and the rebels left with nothing to lose'.[55] This changed position on Irish legislative independence was always strongly resisted in Ireland and the English parliament used this power very rarely, pragmatically, generally when the Irish parliament was not sitting and, with only one exception, entirely in England's interests. Most significantly in March 1649, it established the Commonwealth.[56]

Irish Protestants were chary of admitting the English parliament's legislative power over Ireland for both practical and legal reasons; the Irish parliament would lose what little prestige and authority it retained and allocating land to English people with no experience of Ireland would alter the balance of power in Ireland to their disadvantage. Peers rejected both the bill to suspend Poynings' Law to attaint rebels in August 1642 because it would admit the influence of the English parliament in Ireland and in the following year a petition from Lord Kildare lest it 'be a precedent that acts of Parliament in England will bind the lands here.'[57] In April 1644, the Lords asked the Commons' opinion on the anonymous *Declaration how and by what means the laws and statutes of England came to be of force in Ireland*, which supported the case for legislative independence, but parliament was almost evenly split on whether to approve it:

54 McGrath, 'Recruiter returns'.

55 Clarke, *Prelude to restoration*, p. 4; Lentz, 'Irish parliament', pp 92ff, 105–9.

56 Clarke, 'Patrick Darcy and the constitutional relationship'. The other examples are the Navigation Acts between 1651 and 1681, Cattle Acts of the 1660s and one to secure Ormond's estates before the Irish Restoration parliament met. Dennehy, 'Irish parliament after the rebellion'.

57 Ibid.; *Commons' Jn. Ire.*, 20 April 1643.

> It might well be wondered at wherewithal the time would be taken up, but it is (to speak freely) to hasten our own ruin, as if it came not on fast enough before. We are now doing that which the Irish would do in that which they call a free parliament. It is by all means laboured that this kingdom may be declared independent unto England: that the act for the Adventurers having entrenched on the honour and independency of this kingdom may be protested against, than which what can be more pernicious and destructive to this poor state in our growing miseries. Easy it is to fathom the bottom of this design. The well-affected among us have interposed, as far as it stood with their [safety]. It is strange to find, in so thin a house as ours must be, so many of the Irish faction.

Blaming shortness of time, MPs referred the question to the next sitting. In September 1645 Bolton agreed that Ireland was not bound by English laws and asserted that a declaratory act to that effect was unnecessary, untimely and futile.[58] The 1660 Convention specifically rejected any claim of English jurisdiction over the Irish parliament but while 'New English collaborators and recent army settlers' were anxious to restore the Irish parliament to secure their lands acquired before or during the Cromwellian settlement and demanded a new parliament with entirely Protestant membership, they fudged the issue, as they were unclear from which parliament it would be more expedient to have the land settlement confirmed.[59]

Catholics, too, resisted any infringement on the Irish parliament's legislative independence. The 1642 manifesto of the Irish Catholic party included demands for the 'emancipation of the Irish parliament from English control, the repeal of Poynings' Act, the Irish parliament to be made sexennial and the repeal of specified statutes against Catholics' and the regular summoning of parliament. These were constant demands in their negotiations.[60] In 1649, Confederates demanded a declaratory act of legislative independence, although this would have little practical effect, since it could not bind the English parliament.[61]

The Irish 'rump' parliament's impotence caused by structural issues like Poynings' Law, which prevented its taking the initiative, was exacerbated by the infrequency and shortness of its meetings, internal divisions and political events in England. Both Charles and the administration kept it in existence just in case it was needed, permitting it to meet infrequently for very short periods during which it could transact little business and was generally only able to react to events. The lords justices were reluctant to let parliament meet in November 1642, but while it debated some legislation, the sitting was inconclusive and almost all the few

58 The authorship of the Declaration has not been established, but Clarke argues persuasively against its being Bolton. See Aidan Clarke, 'Bolton, Richard', *DIB*; Ussher to Sir Philip Percival, 23 April 1644, in Crawford Lomas (ed.), *Egmont*, i, pp 210–11; *Commons' Jn. Ire.*, 18 April 1644.
59 Clarke, 'Patrick Darcy and the constitutional relationship'.
60 HMC, *Franciscan manuscripts*, p. 112.
61 Clarke, 'Patrick Darcy and the constitutional relationship'.

meetings between 4 December 1642 and March 1647, apart from that in April 1644, were single day sittings in which it was unable to accomplish anything constructive and given little legislation to process. The administration also prevented parliament's sitting if it appeared likely to be inconvenient: in a debate on the Covenant, Borlase reported 'the business growing hot, the house was prorogued.' In November 1646 Ormond prorogued it, despite its wish to stay in session 'that they might give their assistance for settling the distempers', because it was likely to agree to deal with the commissioners from the English parliament against his will.[62] It was allowed to be more active in 1647; in February five MPs were sent to the English Commons accepting the terms their commissioners offered, which Ormond had refused because he had no instructions from Charles to surrender the sword of state. In March Robert Bailey and Dr Dudley Loftus were sent with a 'dispatch' on which they were empowered to negotiate.[63]

MPs were as divided as their communities and despite excluding alternative voices were unable to reach agreement; parliament's rare sittings saw disunity and acrimony which prevented its adopting a consistent position, leading to stasis. Borlase noted that

> the People of Ireland (who took a liberty at the uncertainty of Affairs) were strangely divided, whether the Cessation should be concluded or no. Some (who were sensibly touch'd with the Injuries and Cruelties of the Rebels) could not brook it; others (hoping for their advantage by the Change) daily expected it, whilst the City (in general) being burthen'd with Taxes, quartering of Souldiers &c., having no hopes of Relief from abroad, willingly hearkned to their Freedom: so as now the strong Affections which had been commonly born against the Rebels, began to wither into an indifferency, and the course which had been then took to weather out the resolute, either for despair or terrour humbled many, and as Interest lay, several resolv'd what party to take in England, upon the conclusion of the Cessation … the Consequences of dissolving the Parliament were not in the least in consideration at the Council Board, nor was there anything more desired by the Rebels, who thereby hoped to be reseated in a new Parliament, which they questioned not to manage to their own ends and advantage.

The Judges who were consulted declared for its continuance, cited the same concerns as the privy council in early 1642.[64]

The issue of how any Protestant 'rump' Irish parliament could ratify an agreement was never resolved. For Catholics, any settlement would need to guarantee religious tolerance, their property and existing constitutional arrangements, specifically legislative independence; only a new parliament with

62 Borlase, *History*, p. 118; Val Savage to Philip Percival, 21 Nov. 1646, in Crawford Lomas (ed.), *Egmont*, i, p. 335.

63 Lentz, 'Irish parliament', pp 131–5, 159, 162, 194; *Commons' Jn. Ire.*, 31 March 1647.

64 Borlase, *History*, pp 129, 131.

fresh elections which they hoped would return a Catholic majority could guarantee this and they also sought the suspension of Poynings' Law. Irish Protestant agents to Charles in spring 1644 opposed both of these and sought extreme repression of the Catholic religion in Ireland. Any settlement also depended on the king winning his war with parliament and English parliamentary competence being restricted to England, as happened at the Restoration, but while negotiations took place between Confederates and the crown in the 1640s, the possibility of any agreement being ratified by the 'rump' of the Irish parliament was as remote as the likelihood of the English privy council's being able to fulfil Poynings' Law's provisions in summoning it. The 1646 treaty which agreed a new parliament could not be implemented as the great seal of England had been defaced and broken after the English parliamentary forces had captured it, and could not be used to certify bills for transmission.[65]

The Irish parliament remained side-lined and contemporaries largely ignored its existence; Irish Franciscans and Jesuits keeping a close eye on developments in England and Ireland, mentioned the English parliament but not the Irish.[66] Irish Protestant agents to Charles in spring 1644 were not chosen by parliament and when Charles queried how representative they were, Ormond replied there was no assembled body which could reasonably claim to declare 'any sence binding to the whole', a rank dismissal of the Irish 'rump' parliament. Much of its time was taken up with parliamentarians' own business, like the case of St Ann's Guild in which MPs' clear conflicts of interest were ignored. Parliamentary privilege remained an important protection during the 1640s; peers, judges and officers of the houses issued over 100 warrants between 6 January 1642 and 29 November 1645, including the Catholic Lords Dunsany, Fitzwilliam, Kilmallock and Taaffe.[67]

The Irish parliament responded well to crises and had many successes in 1640–1; it reasserted its role and exercised its functions despite having been rendered impotent by Wentworth and was especially successful in representing the wider Irish political community, finding common ground among men of different ethnic and religious backgrounds but similar social class and aspirations. It resisted the administration's usurpation of its role in assessing and collecting subsidies and radically reduced their value, reasserted control of its membership, conducted effective negotiations with the king to resolve pressing grievances and re-established parliament's judicial role. The value of its work is demonstrated by the recognition of its precedents, such as the Confederation's acceptance of parliamentary systems and in the 1690s, Chancellor Michael Boyle used the parliamentary orders issued in 1641 in response to petitions as evidence of its judicial function.[68]

65 Lentz, 'Irish parliament', pp 131–5, 153–5.
66 HMC, *Franciscan manuscripts*, p. 112.
67 McGrath, 'Recruiter returns'; *LJI*, pp 228–30; *Commons' Jn. Ire.*, 1 Aug. 1642, 20 April 1643, 6 April 1644, 6 May 1644, 4 June 1644, 30 Nov. 1644.
68 Marsh's Library, MS Z3.2.5 'extracted from the Records of Ireland to prove the jurisdiction of the Parliament of this Kingdom to hear and adjuge all Causes'; James McGuire, 'Boyle, Michael', *DIB*.

MPs' agenda was conservative, generally seeking a return to the position before 1633, including pre-parliamentary consultation about legislation. It pursued its reform agenda less through innovation than by utilizing its current powers to the full and resuming the exercise of those which Wentworth had restricted, notably its insistence on traditional methods of assessing and collecting subsidies, its judicial function, including the use of petitions to overturn judgments in the courts of High Commission and Castle Chamber and at the council board, and to redress grievances. It drew on existing practice by drafting heads of bills, controlling its membership and a massive expansion of the existing committee system to deal with the stream of petitions. Opposition evolved from a coalition to replace Wentworth's regime to a consideration of the constitutional position of the relationship between the English and Irish parliaments. As its scope for innovation was limited by Poynings' Law, the Irish opposition came to see that adapting that statute, while carefully preserving royal prerogative, was a route to reform and a more representative form of parliament.

MPs appealing to the king over the head of the Irish administration was not new but the appointment of agents for the entire parliament was a radical innovation. Eustace's partiality would have made his position as the Irish Commons' mouthpiece unconvincing – it is significant that the petition to the English Commons was signed by individual MPs, not the speaker – but equally importantly his absence would have prevented parliament's sitting in Dublin. Appointing agents allowed an assembly remote from the monarch to by-pass the Irish administration and ensure parliament's work continued despite the imminent prorogation. The English parliament could address the king only through declarations and remonstrances (Pym's attempt to by-pass the speaker by creating or authorizing a body to speak to the king on behalf of the Commons failed) and certainly could not negotiate with him, as Irish agents did, followed by the Confederation in 1643. The agents successfully negotiated the redress of long-standing grievances to achieve better government, but Charles' reneging on his promises and the Irish administration's rear-guard actions to defeat them induced the Confederates' proposal that a permanent delegation of agents be 'chosen in Parliament, or otherwise, as thought meet to attend continually his Majesty, to represent the grievances of this nation that they may be removable by such as did elect them.'[69] Irish Protestant agents to Charles in 1644 were not a parliamentary delegation nor were those the Catholics wished to send to the Commissioners of Parliament in 1651 because no representative assembly existed at the time.[70]

69 Armstrong, *Protestant war*, pp 100–1, 117; John Temple, *The Irish rebellion: or, An history of the beginnings and first progresse of the general rebellion raised within the kingdom of Ireland* (London, 1646), pp 144ff.

70 *A letter, or paper, signed by Garald Fitz-gerald in behalf of an assembly of the Irish at Glanmaliroe in the province of Leinster in Ireland, to the commissioners of Parliament delivered the 11 of March 1652 also a declaration thereupon made by the said commissioners of Parliament, March 12 1652* (Dublin, 1651); Russell, 'Monarchies'.

Parliament's failure to achieve the constitutional change that adjusting Poynings' Law would have produced meant that its achievements were frustrated by the Dublin administration's deliberate tardiness in processing legislation and the outbreak of the 1641 rebellion, itself caused by the grievances parliament had failed to resolve, despite MPs' hard work and determination. Parliament succeeded in having its role recognized, albeit reluctantly, on the outbreak of rebellion, but its work was rapidly overtaken by events. Despite this, MPs continued to work to represent their communities separately in the 'rump' parliament and more successfully in the General Assembly which had none of the constraints of the Irish parliament and could fulfil all that body's representative, revenue-raising, legislative and judicial functions, while also negotiating directly with the crown, like the parliamentary agents.

Irish, Scottish and English representative institutions could radically adapt their structures, powers and systems because they were already in session at the time of crisis and took control of affairs without reference to, or in defiance of, the monarch and were able to deal with local matters in a highly effective manner. From 1638, the volume of both public and private legislation soared, as the Scottish Estates became the focal point of authority.[71] Petitions were used by the Irish parliament to redress grievances and argue for policy change because it could not introduce legislation; this continued after 1642 because the courts system could not operate although the 'rump's' infrequent sittings and unrepresentative composition severely reduced its effectiveness.[72]

In France, England, Ireland and Scotland, the estates, parliament and Confederation all demanded that they be able to meet in regular sessions and when they were obliged to take government into their own hands, all except France ensured that their representative institutions sat frequently through the 1640s. The English and Scottish parliaments met regularly after the Restoration, but Ireland's was summoned infrequently. Poynings' Law also continued to limit its legislative function and left little scope for MPs to exercise initiative; the effective exclusion of Catholics, who formed the great majority of the population, from the lower house greatly restricted its representative character.

Hayden noted,

> the [French] deputies of 1614 … defined in their cahiers the reforms that France needed: abolition of clerical abuses, restrictions on the unfounded claims of the nobility, rejection of the veniality of office, reduction in the number of officials, close scrutiny of the remaining officials and tax reduction. The deputies pinpointed the major areas of concern for a developing strong government: disloyal elements within the state, a poorly organized system of administration, lack of free trade within France, and a confused policy on foreign trade. They produced an excellent program of

71 MacDonald, '"Tedious to rehers?"'
72 Lentz, 'Irish parliament', pp 67–79.

> reform but the government ... [and] the important provincials did not listen ... The estates general of 1614 failed because it had no means of imposing its will upon the government and because the unity of its cahiers frightened the upper echelon bureaucrats. For the first time, sensible men from the provinces had united and shown the way to reform, but the reform seemed too dangerous.

Graves attributes their failure to the inability of the estates to work together and they were not summoned again until 1789. When Louis XIV refused to summon the Estates General during the Fronde crisis between 1648 and 1653, the Parlement de Paris moved from its judicial role to act as a representative, if not elected, institution and played a key role in national politics. In its Remonstrance, the Parlement de Paris claimed to represent the people and by refusing to register Edicts deprived them of the force of law.[73]

The 1640–1 Irish Parliament had the same role, an agreed and similar reform agenda and suffered the same fate as the 1614 Estates General; the reform agenda was too dangerous for the pre-Wentworth regime of Cork, Loftus, Parsons and Ranelagh and for Charles, especially as the sessions wore on and constitutional questions were raised. Neither assembly behaved in the way the crown wanted, but each genuinely tried to represent its country and reform their states' inadequacies and abuses. Unsuccessful in achieving reform, they nevertheless provided genuine representation of their communities. Hayden's assessment of the 1614 Estates holds true also for the men of the 1640 Irish parliament and the Confederation: 'limited by their past, they were limited by their assigned role and they were limited by lack of effective support from the important inhabitants of the provinces. But within their limitations they performed magnificently.'[74]

Irish, Scottish and Catalan representative institutions' experience converged during the political crises in the 1640s. Existing government structures oppressed and marginalized the majority of those countries' population and in the Confederation of Kilkenny, Scottish Commissioners of the Estates and Catalonia's Kingless Corts, their citizens, while continually protesting their loyalty to the crown, took hold of a representative and governmental role from which their monarchs had excluded them. All sought to manage their own affairs through institutions that provided parallel governments for the three estates in each country. They met without royal summons, decided on their own membership and created parallel institutions for administration and representation as they maintained a voice for the people against a state which did not serve their interests. The Confederation established a radically different and powerful representative institution in the name of, but without, the king, borrowing its structures and operations from the Scottish and French Estates, with an especially strong role for the merchant community.

73 Hayden, *France*, p. 217; Graves, *Parliaments*, p. 133; *Journal contenant*.
74 Hayden, *France*, p. 218.

Early modern political crises had long-term effects on representative institutions; most were weakened or no longer called. Only the English and Polish-Lithuanian parliaments, along with the Landtage in Saxony and Wuerttemberg, enhanced their positions through the 1640s and 1650s. Gustav Adolf worked well with the Swedish Riksdag but his death in 1632 introduced an era of greater difficulty. French monarchs found it easier to negotiate with the shrinking number of provincial estates and the Estates General, like the Aragonese, Castilian and Catalan Corts, were put in abeyance for long periods. The Valencian Corts, Danish Rigsdag, and estates in Naples, Sardinia, Bohemia, Austria and the Spanish Netherlands never met again. Other states were better placed to weather the storm, such as those in the United Provinces, where the provincial estates provided both finance for costly wars and a balance to the central assembly.[75]

The Restoration Irish parliament's position was rather more ambiguous: the Commonwealth Parliament clearly demonstrated to the Protestant community the necessity of having an Irish parliament and its role was recognized and it continued to meet, albeit with a long gap between 1666 and 1689, using the forms and procedures established between 1613 and 1648. However, its powers continued to be circumscribed and the community it represented was much more limited. While ostensibly a national body, it was again representative only of a minority of the population, lacking the powers to take the initiative and any interest in the wider Irish population.

75 Graves, *Parliaments*, pp 115–55. The quotation is on p. 122. Butterwick, *Polish–Lithuanian Commonwealth*, pp 18ff.

Conclusion

EARLY STUART PARLIAMENTS in Ireland built on patterns established in Tudor assemblies, showing both continuity and change. Their composition, operations and business were strongly influenced by the political community's experience of those gatherings. Despite being constrained by Poynings' Law, parliament retained its legislative, revenue-raising, representative and judicial functions throughout the period because statute law retained its primacy and the state needed ever greater levels of income, although the use of acts of state encroached on its legislative function, especially after 1635.

During this period the Irish Commons' composition was formalized and its operations more aligned with English norms, but with important remaining differences. Many aspects of its form, powers and management fluctuated between continuity and change. The most obvious remaining differences between the English and Irish parliaments were the constraints placed by Poynings' Law and the commissions authorizing the summoning of parliament; the Irish Commons' control over the assessment and collection of subsidies; the wider scope and legislative protection provided by Irish parliamentary privilege, the payment of higher wages to Irish MPs, Catholics' continued eligibility for membership and MPs' ability to resign. The constitutionality of the monarch's incorporating parliamentary boroughs remained in question.

All aspects of parliament's documentation, powers, ceremonial, operations, economics, personnel, composition, membership and electorates and attitudes to the parliament demonstrate both continuity and change, evolving to meet new conditions and needs, becoming formalized and accepted. Despite the immense changes in Irish society over the seventeenth century, the legacy of its evolution under James I and Charles I set the mould for the Irish parliament until the Act of Union in 1800. Continuity also involved change, often incremental, like the evolution of parliament's operations to increase its efficiency or changes in its urban electorates, and some were dictated by the administration, such as its changed opening ceremonies, the alteration in the Lords' voting practice or the abolition of Cross counties.

Many of the administration's problems with parliament were caused by its own attitudes and ineptitude; deputies refused to consult on legislation before parliament met, with the privy council deciding on bills without reference to the political community – the projected 1628 parliament was the only one that involved wider consultation about its legislative programme in the agreement to enact the Graces. Under Wentworth, the only consultations were on private bills that exclusively benefitted Protestants and through Convocation's drafting its own subsidies bills which were then transmitted to England, although his control of that body also considerably reduced its freedom of action. Bills were repeatedly rejected because of poor drafting or offensive preambles – compounded by an inability to amend legislation or to negotiate concessions, or a determination not to do so. Initially, Old English and Gaelic MPs and peers and increasingly New English members persistently held the administration to account, but always in an atmosphere of co-operation which was not recognized, appreciated or reciprocated by the administration and certainly played down in their official correspondence. The administration's refusal to regard parliament as a partner in the government of the state created an adversarial atmosphere which made it difficult to achieve success and the prevailing narrative presented by the administration was of a recalcitrant assembly, which voted on confessional grounds, although that was far from being the case.

Wentworth's first parliament was atypical, as the deputy's iron control of the assembly and disregard for legality and political norms temporarily changed the way the institution worked, denying some of its core functions, disregarding protections for MPs and issuing rejected bills as acts of state. Wentworth used the royal commissions authorizing parliaments' summoning to further control their work, specifying their intended length and that they would be determined if the subsidy acts were not passed within three or four weeks after their opening, which obliged MPs to agree to penal taxation before any grievances were debated, much less resolved. His novel reading of Poynings' Law further restricted parliament's functions and revealed ambiguities and uncertainties in the statute's provisions, exacerbated by the lack of any means of appealing the deputy's interpretation. After June 1640, members of both houses reasserted themselves, reclaiming their customary powers and protections and largely reversing his restrictive management of the assembly and its legislative, revenue-raising, representative and judicial functions, vindicating their privileges and liberties and arguing for constitutional reform. The opposition's constitutional agenda in 1640–1 was conservative, seeking to re-establish procedures and powers which operated under Chichester but which Wentworth had restricted or quashed. Wentworth's reading of Poynings' Law was not accepted as the 'default model' (the Irish parliament resumed its judicial function), but it was a useful tool for the crown and anyone trying to revert to earlier practice or have it defined or revised had to be able to counter this interpretation. The Irish parliament's agents in England's strenuous efforts to have it clarified or amended in 1641 were unsuccessful and its interpretation remained open to question and abuse.

The continued appointment of English men to pivotal positions in government was equally important; they had no long-term interest in or sympathy for Ireland and their main concern, other than enriching themselves and their clients, was to preserve their reputations in England where they hoped for advancement on their return. Their reports home all presented their unrelenting but largely successful struggles against a recalcitrant, disloyal and uncivilized native (Catholic) population, further lowering the reputation of Irishmen in general in the English council, although only Wentworth also pointed the finger at the corrupt and self-serving New English. Both Poynings' Law and lords deputies' need to maintain their reputations at home meant that they were pressured to ensure delivery of crown policy despite having no leeway in negotiating or amending unpopular or poorly drafted bills in parliament and they responded to this pressure by illegal electioneering in an even more extreme manner than their Tudor predecessors or, in Wentworth's case, by oppressive behaviour towards MPs and by issuing rejected bills as Acts of State.

While Wentworth was careful to delay the implementation of policies that would 'put the planters to a very great charge and consequently drain their purses and breed a grudging in their minds which would be a ill preparative to that meeting' before the 1634 parliament, as he intended to 'bow and govern the native by the planter and the planter by the native' there, once he had achieved his aims from that parliament he subjected all elements of Irish society to his arbitrary government.[1] Apart from exacerbating the mistrust between his administration and the native political community, increasingly excluded from positions of local and national influence or economic benefit by settlers they regarded as their inferiors, Crosby and Clotworthy's opposition in 1634 and Waller in 1640 should have alerted him to the danger of a wider negative reaction to his government; as a result, he either misjudged the New English response to policies, such as the proposed plantations of Connacht and Ormond and the penal taxation, or he simply did not consider that their views mattered, especially as he had no expectation of needing to summon another parliament. Wentworth's reputation broke down in the face of the arbitrary government he imposed on all inhabitants of Ireland and he failed to recognize that class was a more potent adhesive than religion or ethnicity, as the coalition which formed the parliamentary opposition in mid-1640 demonstrated. However, many problems in all early Stuart parliaments could have been avoided simply by consultation, negotiation and more skilful drafting of bills.

Parliamentarians' appeals to the monarch in 1613 and 1640–7 remained a constant; outside of parliament, the political community negotiated with the crown in 1625–8 and Darcy's freelance mission to London in 1635 was an informal attempt to appeal to Charles about the proposed plantation of Connacht. Wentworth was aware of how all of his predecessors had been undermined in England by negative reports from Ireland, when local supporters at court like Clanricard interceded to provide balance to the picture. Clarke's portrait of Piers Crosby at court as a worldly sophisticate in contrast to the less polished Strafford is a valuable corrective to the usual narrative.[2] Wentworth's solution was to prevent anyone leaving Ireland without his licence, which made it difficult for them to appeal to England for redress and provided justification for Wandesford's refusal to allow parliament's agents to travel, although they defied him.

1 Wentworth to Coke, 12 April 1634, in Knowler (ed.), *Letters and dispatches*, i, p. 199.
2 Clarke, 'Sir Piers Crosby'.

Finally, two linked continuities were the low priority given to Ireland by the monarch and his council in England, which meant that Irish business was given little, limited and frequently very tardy attention, and the Dublin administration's ability to stall and block progress, even when directed by the monarch, a tactic connived at by the English Council at least.[3]

Despite the lack of information about parliament's earlier documents, it is clear that the records, especially the journals, were formalized and that their management improved dramatically during this period, largely due to the appointment of conscientious clerks. Chetham and Medhop in particular improved existing records' management and expanded the journals' contents to provide much greater detail about activities in parliament. While their journals followed the format of the 1585 Lords' journal and those of the English parliament, their contents were more detailed, including attendance, orders, contact between the houses, judicial cases, petitions, disciplining of individuals, presenting grievances to the deputy, contributions from MPs and an index. They were better preserved and more widely distributed. Likewise, legislation was widely published in broadsheet and book forms.

The Irish parliament retained all its existing powers and authority to discipline its members, but it also acquired or gained acceptance of others, although all were threatened and restricted by Wentworth. No attempt was made to restrict Irish parliamentary privilege's statutory base but Wentworth and his privy councillors repeatedly violated MPs' privileges and liberties in 1634–5, although there were no recorded transgressions in 1640–8, following Wentworth's departure. The lower house's power to control its own members, including disciplining MPs for poor behaviour, unlicenced absence or infringing the rules, had long been recognized, but after 1613 wider competencies were accepted, including adjudicating on disputed returns and which boroughs should be represented. From 1634 onwards it could also instigate expulsions, a facility triumphantly used by the opposition in 1640–1 and by the 'rump' parliament in June 1642 and afterwards.

This period saw continuity through the formalization of existing procedures including parliamentary privilege and the systems to assess and collect subsidies established by statute in medieval and Tudor Irish parliaments. It also saw change through the incremental development of the committee system, specifically standing committees and, from 1634, committees of the whole house. These developments increased the house's efficiency, especially in a much larger parliament dealing with a greater level of business, but committees of the whole house also enabled MPs to limit the speaker's control of proceedings and to facilitate open debate on policy and strategy, especially in and after 1640.

Wentworth coerced the 1634 Commons into changing the way subsidies were assessed but his administration's attempts to interfere with the assessment and collection in 1640 were firmly reversed. Wentworth refused to allow parliament to exercise its judicial function in 1634–5, but it reasserted its rights in 1640–1. The

3 Henry Vane to the Lords Justices, 6 Aug. 1641, *Cal. S.P. Ire., 1633–47*, p. 340.

Commons expanded its representative role through petitions and its close liaison with the English parliament in 1640 and appointment of agents to England in 1640 and 1647 were innovations intended to support all its functions. The dramatic innovation of mandating a committee to negotiate directly with the king in England was necessary to by-pass the Dublin administration that was blocking parliament's work. While this liaison and the agents were successful in 1640–1, following the outbreak of the rebellion the English parliament legislated for Ireland for the first time; while this occurred rarely and very selectively, it provoked a constitutional stand-off in the 1640s. Apart from the Adventurer's Acts, the English parliament's most consequential legislation for Ireland came outside this period in 1691 when 3 William and Mary, c. 2 abrogated the oath of supremacy in Ireland and substituted other oaths which were deeply offensive to Catholics but acceptable to Protestant dissenters.[4]

Parliament's resumption of its judicial function involved the use of petitions to redress grievances, with the Commons investigating cases and the Lords pronouncing judgment. The enunciation of the Irish parliament's constitutional role built on earlier parliaments' form and work and were part of the campaign to roll back Wentworth's incursions into parliament's functions and operations. But, like the other operations, they were facilitated by the clerks' better management of records, which enabled the location of precedents for guidance. Parliament's general operations, including its representative function, was assisted by the length of the 1640–1 sessions that enabled MPs to get to know each other and facilitated the formation of the coalition between the New English, Old English and Gaelic; they were able to use these new connections to enhance cooperation within the house and to help them and their constituents.

Irish parliamentarians could not initiate legislation but MPs and lords commonly proposed legislation to the crown directly in parliament, though the administration was reluctant to act on these suggestions, even when supported by directions from the crown. MPs' agents in England were more successful in negotiating directly with the king, but the Dublin administration's stalling nullified their achievements. MPs were also very creative at using the systems effectively to manage and amend flaws in legislation, such as demanding an act of state to protect others who would have been inadvertently damaged by Tyrone's attainder. This aspect of parliament's work relied heavily on lawyer MPs, but was especially necessary given the administration's inept drafting of legislation; even the Irish 'rump' parliament understood the importance of scrutinizing legislation and rejected all but one of the bills presented to it. Convocation's drafting separate subsidy bills for the clergy was an innovation in 1613–15 which was carried

4 J.C. Beckett, *Protestant dissent in Ireland, 1687–1780* (London, 1948), p. 29 and passim; J.G. Simms, 'The establishment of Protestant ascendancy, 1691–1714' in Moody, et al. (eds), *New history of Ireland*, iv, pp 1–30, at p. 24. I am grateful to James McGuire for a useful discussion on this subject and drawing these references to my attention. *idem*, 'The case of Ireland stated' in Farrell (ed.), *Irish parliamentary tradition*, pp 128–38.

through into Wentworth's parliaments; Wentworth ensured that those bills passed, unlike in Chichester's assembly, although as they had to go through the process of certification specified by Poynings' Law, they were not included in the timescale laid down for subsidies bills in the commissions for those parliaments.

St Leger, Sidney and Perrot arranged magnificent and colourful openings of parliament and official robes for themselves and Chichester built on their precedents for his impressive opening ceremonies and robes, but his efforts were eclipsed by Wentworth's enhanced pomp. We know too little of the ceremonial within the houses before 1613, other than that peers' and MPs wore parliamentary robes and the practice of bowing to the speaker's chair remained unchanged, but deputies' ceremonial dress was far more magnificent and the heralds played a more prominent role in establishing precedence and ceremonial under the Stuarts, albeit assisted in 1634 by Arundel. However, while MPs formed part of the opening procession in 1613, they, especially Catholic members, were largely excluded in 1634. Unlike Scotland and England, the Irish parliament still had no designated accommodation and what was provided was of poor quality. This contrast with the other Stuart kingdoms indicates the crown's perception of the Irish parliament as inferior to the others and also its ambivalence about its future continuity.

The economics of parliament showed considerable continuity but also significant changes. MPs' pay remained at the statutory amount, albeit subject to locally agreed lower rates; the Commons' larger membership suggests that the overall cost of salaries should have been higher, but the increasing number of placemen meant that fewer burgesses were waged. Conversely, knights of the shire invariably were paid until November 1641, after which any wages were unlikely to be forthcoming. While there are no clear costs for parliament's operations, it appears that the crown incurred increasing expenses, especially given Wentworth's ostentatious ceremonial and the length of sessions. Unlike England and Scotland, the early Stuart Irish parliament never refused to grant subsidies and their value rose substantially, especially compared to Tudor parliaments, both in the amounts voted and through liability being extended throughout the country. While Chichester was delighted to have effected the increase in the subsidy voted in 1615, this was dwarfed by the oppressive levels of taxation agreed in Wentworth's parliaments, which contributed greatly to his efficient government, although the value of the second and subsequent subsidies was slashed in 1640 and they remained largely unpaid. The Commons also successfully resisted the administration's encroachment on its role in assessing and gathering subsidies, a function the English parliament did not have. Moreover, while the assessments under Chichester appear to have been generally fair, some in 1634 were patently not and this is likely to have held for the first subsidy assessments in 1640, adding to the resentment of the administration's encroachment on parliament's powers of assessment and collection. The establishment of systems for assessment and collection in hitherto unrepresented areas was a major achievement and substantially contributed to the monetization of Irish society. Finally, the subsidiary income received by parliaments' officers – clerks, herald and serjeants-at-arms – also soared during this period as did lawyers' fees for dealing with petitions.

Early modern Ireland saw the extension of parliamentary representation and the creation of a parliamentary culture across the entire island; in addition, there were many changes in constituencies and the means by which they were created or refused representation. Before 1569 counties could only be created by legislation, but this legislation did not allow the crown to abolish or amalgamate them. The unification of both Tipperary counties in 1635 brought an end to Cross counties, but only by an act of state after the bill failed to get through parliament. There was no clear constitutional means to enfranchise urban constituencies which were unestablished but created by prescription. James' unconstitutional creation of parliamentary boroughs by royal charter was strongly resisted in every parliament up to 1641, as was the illegal suppression of others through *Quo warranto* proceedings and refusals to summon them or forward their returns, although there are no recorded objections to his creation of university seats. The exclusion of old boroughs was reversed in 1640 but James' innovation stood and was followed by Charles in Scotland, again as a precedent in 1625. After 1648, the crown's right to grant parliamentary representation by charter was uncontested and nine new constituencies appeared in 1661, only two of which (Duleek and Ratoath) had previously expressed any pretentions to inclusion, although as two-thirds of those new constituencies were in Leinster, this did not improve the nationwide balance of popular representation. James II's issuing of new charters in 1688 naming Catholic councillors for old parliamentary boroughs continued the practice initiated by his grandfather to influence elections, but this time in favour of Catholics.[5]

While MPs successfully resisted the inclusion of judges and attorneys general as members of the Commons, serjeants-at-law were still returned, despite objections in 1613 and the speakers in 1634 and 1640 were both in that category.[6] However, every early Stuart parliament saw a lowering of the membership's social quality with many clerks and minor officials as MPs. This started with Chichester's parliament and the trend accelerated through Wentworth's assemblies and the recruiter returns to the 'rump' parliament. The administration's need for a Protestant parliamentary majority achieved by illegal or questionable electioneering and gerrymandering resulted in increasing numbers of placemen with no connection to their constituencies who were less representative of their constituencies; increasingly English and Welshmen, who had been present in small numbers in Tudor parliaments, were joined by Scots and Dutchmen, providing an ethnic mix unknown in the English or Scottish parliaments. While the extension of representation into Connacht and Ulster created a parliamentary tradition there including among the Old Irish, it is not clear that the proportion of Gaelic Irish

5 McGrath, 'Town and mitre'.
6 Hart, *History of the king's serjeants at law*, pp 50–8.

in Stuart parliaments was higher than in medieval and Tudor ones as Gaelic engagement in those periods has been significantly under-stated and ignores the increasingly hybrid nature of Irish society. Curiously, the level of repeated membership was relatively low, even in 1640, so a cadre of experienced parliamentarians was not built up. The continued ability of Irish MPs to resign their seats increased the likelihood of by-elections which were frequent in this period. Following the part played by lawyers in Tudor assemblies, including Thomas Cusack, but also those from the Pale like Henry Burnell who formed the backbone of the opposition in 1585, counsellors continued to play a prominent role in parliament, and in planning them and drafting legislation. The Irish 'rump' parliament excluded virtually all Catholics, although Simon Luttrell and Terence (Tirlagh) Magrath ducked and weaved around the issue to avoid expulsion. The number of officers working for and around parliament remained largely the same (except for greater numbers of serjeants-at-arms) although they increasingly tended to be of English birth, apart from Maurice Eustace, Daniel Molyneux and Philip Percival.

Some changes are harder to discern but there is evidence of alterations in the number and qualification of voters in urban seats which, unlike the county electorate, were not specified by legislation; Dublin and Galway increased the number of their voters, as others may have done. While the expansion of parliamentary representation throughout Ireland and into many new or newly-established corporations ostensibly increased political participation, in fact the early Stuart period saw progressive marginalization or exclusion of sections of the population, including in parliament. Catholics, and also Scots, were excluded from many state positions, both paid and honorary, including the judiciary, but also from other civic offices for a period. Catholic sheriffs were often appointed to take the opprobrium in collecting taxes, which Protestants often refused to pay. Almost all of the new boroughs had very limited electorates, both in terms of numbers of voters and their nature, excluding virtually all Old English or Gaelic Irish, other local residents and disfranchising others through *Quo warranto* proceedings, while temporary, excluded old boroughs from parliament. Towns that were able to retain their charters by agreeing to return placemen were effectively disfranchised, while ostensibly retaining their parliamentary representation.

The political community's reverence for the early modern parliament was certainly much higher than it had been towards its medieval predecessors where disengagement was high and attendance very low. Under Elizabeth and the Stuarts, parliament's summoning prompted both optimism and apprehension and its continued importance is demonstrated by both sides' efforts to control its membership and to achieve victories when it met. St Leger encouraged greater interest and attendance, but it was the threat to their position that caused the native Irish community to become involved in parliament's work and use it to protect their own and their community's interests. Lords deputy came to anticipate strong and informed opposition and developed reservations about parliament's proceedings despite increasing the associated ceremonial. While Chichester attempted to manage proceedings (apart from the elections) to minimize opposition, Wentworth's scorn for the institution, its operations, privileges and members was palpable. His disregard for parliamentary privilege and liberties and his much more restrictive act for royal pardon diminished the advantages of membership for all MPs. His issuing rejected bills as acts of state undermined parliamentary powers and the norms of political processes and demonstrated his contempt for parliament and parliamentarians. Given Wentworth's iron grip on its business and despite the disengagement of parliamentarians who had fallen foul of him, as well as, from the opposition's point of view, the discouraging results of the first two weeks of the first 1640 session, MPs showed an exceptional commitment to using parliament to reverse Wentworth's reforms, demonstrating their faith in the institution and building coalitions to effect this. They achieved the reversal of the oppressive level of subsidies and boroughs' disfranchisement, although not Cross Tipperary, as there was no way to force the cancellation of an act of state. The willingness of the wider community to raise money to support the agents in England and the range of petitions from all sections of the population, though predominantly from New English and Scots who had come to see parliament as their protector, just as the Old English had under Elizabeth, all demonstrate a widespread respect for and belief in its role among the political community. The 'rump' parliament generated little respect, apart from Mervyn's perennial optimism that the institution could be effective, but its continued existence attests to its importance as a national body and a critical if undervalued element of the state.

In 1613, the recusants' campaign against illegal electioneering and especially the unconstitutionality of the incorporation of new parliamentary boroughs reduced the administration's contrived majority to a minimum. Parliament accepted conditionally most of the new boroughs on the basis that their sitting in that parliament did not establish their right to representation thereafter, leaving the question open for the future. The recusants achieved their goal of preventing further anti-Catholic legislation but not the redress of grievances such as extortionate officials' fees and at the cost of lawyers being excluded from practice in courts. Catholic MPs were able to use their privilege and the royal pardon to protect themselves and their towns' civic autonomy.

By 1634, the situation had changed significantly and parliament's membership closely tracked other social transformations in Ireland; expansion of the privy council (the chamber accommodated 80 councillors, although there were rarely so many present, judges sat *ex officio* and many councillors sat in the upper house) largely through New English office-holders facilitated the development of a legislative agenda whose reference point was English statutes, processes and society. The recently arrived attorney general Thomas Tempest's consideration only of English norms of parliamentary privilege on FitzGerald's election for Inistioge, disregarding Irish privilege's statutory protection, was a case in point.

The incremental transfer of Irish land to English, Scottish and Welsh settlers, through formal and informal settlement, increased the numbers of British MPs. Equally, the appointment of English, Scottish and Welsh prelates and the granting of many new peerages to settlers and absentee Englishmen transformed the House of Lords. The importance of achieving security of land titles became increasingly urgent due to the transfer of property through plantation, dodgy methods of acquisition and rank profiteering of Protestant officials and others from titles described as 'defective' and through the coercive Court of Wards, already addressed in the Graces and in the list of desiderata for the inhabitants of Munster in 1634 and parliament's agents in England in 1640–1. These took a more sinister form under Wentworth, with his refusal to enact the Graces followed by reconstitution of the Commission of Defective Titles in 1634, the illegal and intimidatory finding of the king's title to lands in Connacht and the issuing of the Case of Defective Titles in 1637. Catholics increasingly avoided the Commission, as they mistrusted the administration's good faith, but New English estates were also threatened. These subjects were still outstanding, and more urgent, in 1641 despite legislation to deal with land titles having been introduced in England and Scotland.

Despite the administration's increasingly illegal and intimidatory electioneering, Tudor parliaments had been largely representative of their communities, albeit of only a part, if an increasing one, of the island. However, hardening administration attitudes towards the native population, the need to fulfil successive instructions from the crown and the inability to negotiate or compromise on legislation prompted the administration to use underhand means to achieve any legislative successes, such as the dishonesty used to pass the 1560 anti-Catholic legislation by as few as eight MPs, getting the lords to cast their votes secretly by whispering into the chancellor's ear, and illegal electioneering to engineer a Protestant majority. The Old English and old Irish communities fought back, presenting a united front and helped by the quality of their representatives, including the gentry of the Pale and lawyers. Eventually the mistrust between Wentworth's regime and the political community led to a coalition between the natives and settlers and to a review of the constitutional relationship between England and Ireland and their parliaments, along with a campaign to amend Poynings' Law. The seeds of mistrust were sown in the Tudor parliaments, nourished under Chichester and Falkland, but dramatically exacerbated by Wentworth, when settlers faced the same arbitrary government, self-serving judicial processes, oppressive fees, economic disadvantage, exclusion from office and contrived insecurity of land titles as the native Old English and old Irish.

In its quest for legislative success, the administration learnt the value of having a collusive speaker and a Protestant majority in both houses, by any means, legal or otherwise; curiously or perhaps arrogantly, despite the advice before the 1560 parliament and repeated defeats, it did not learn the importance of consultation, careful drafting of legislation, building consensus and following established procedure, preferring high-handedness, intimidation and illegality. Coming from a tradition of promoting self-interest, they based most of their strategy on the presumption that Protestants would be 'loyal' and Catholics 'disloyal', overlooking the fact that class is a more powerful social glue than religion or ethnicity and that voting did not generally break down on confessional lines, except on questions of the speakership, examining invalid returns or, in the Tudor period, the suspension of Poynings' Law.

Conversely, the native political community learned the importance of effective, united opposition, a Catholic speaker, the need to select local candidates of quality, vigorously contest each seat, ensure that their community was united behind their strategy, propose creative solutions to political, constitutional and legislative questions and, as ever, to appeal to the monarch in times of crisis. Old English and Irish experience under the Stuarts reinforced their mistrust of the administration, their cohesion as an opposition and the need to have experienced, quality representatives able to represent their communities, including talented lawyers, self-confident gentry and merchants, who were consistent in their attendance, and able to negotiate skilfully and construct alliances.

After an exceptionally difficult start, the 1613 parliament functioned very well. That of 1634 was fatally undermined by Wentworth's thuggish management and disregard for the law in both elections and parliamentary operations and privilege. The 1640 parliament saw a much reduced Catholic membership and a subservient beginning, but it quickly reasserted its powers and independence, winning many battles such as its role in assessing and collecting subsidies, deciding on its own membership, reversing the disfranchisement of boroughs, exercising its judicial function and managing its own business, as well as representing its community in the Commons chamber, in meetings with Wandesford in Dublin and through its agents in London. On the outbreak of the rebellion, it insisted on meeting and tried to play a role in resolving tensions and quieting the rising; however, events overtook it and what became a 'rump' parliament failed to fulfil its legislative, judicial, revenue-raising and representative functions, being kept on life-support in case it was needed, but unable to meet often enough to play a useful role in war-ravaged Ireland. In a sense, the Confederates' General Assembly, although a strictly Catholic body, because it was freed from both Poynings' Law and a partisan, mis-trusted and entirely self-interested crown administration, formed the apogee of representative government as a counter-state in Ireland. In professing loyalty to the crown, holding closely to all parliamentary procedures and operations and including so many more Gaelic Irish than there had been in the Commons, it demonstrated the transformation of the kingdom of Ireland as envisaged by St Leger, which his successor prevented from coming into being, and the creation of a *de facto* modern European monarchical state with an effective and accepted representative assembly, albeit briefly. That it was able to operate so effectively was a tribute to the durability of the parliamentary culture which had been extended throughout Ireland, acceptance of the importance of popular assent to policy and a national government which had been embodied in the members of the early modern Irish parliaments.

Parliamentary traditions and culture had extended throughout the entire island and as the proportion of the population able to vote for Irish MPs was higher, its parliament was in that sense more representative than its English, French or Scottish counterparts. The county electorate was defined by statute and the new boroughs and university by their charters, but the old urban seats had variable criteria for voters. As a result, county membership remained almost exclusively the preserve of gentry who held lands there (Patrick Darcy's return for Tyrone was an exception), but the nature of this community changed as land was confiscated from the native elites in the plantations of Ulster, Wexford, Leitrim and Longford and transferred to New English, Scottish and Welsh settlers. This built on the Tudor plantations of King's and Queen's counties and Munster and the longstanding and deliberate policy of ensuring that land titles throughout Ireland were classed as 'defective'. It was, however, inevitable, that as settlers acquired more property, they would be as threatened as the native population were by attacks on land titles and be prepared to use their considerable power to oppose these attacks in parliament. Yet their reluctance (or refusal) to grant freeholds meant that many Gaelic electors remained in planted and unplanted counties and knights of the shire had to take account of their views. While the new boroughs were manifestly less representative in their government and electorate than established ones, older towns' electorates were widened in the early Stuart parliaments, but the reverse was true after the Restoration. In 1585 and 1613, most MPs had local connections with their constituencies, but those links were steadily weakened or completely severed by 1640 (if somewhat reversed in 1641), and even more so by 1648 and 1661, continuing the increasing trend of official nominees or placemen being returned to the Commons. The much higher level of old Irish membership of the Confederation of Kilkenny's General Assembly demonstrates that many who would have wished to serve were excluded by rigged elections and severely restricted Protestant electorates.

Much of the agenda of the 1640–1 opposition was essentially conservative, seeking to return to the position before 1613 and more especially before Wentworth's arrival. On some levels they were very effective. They fought back successfully against his disfranchising boroughs and reasserted their right to decide the membership of the house, although they were not able to reverse granting parliamentary representation by charter. MPs rejected the crown's opposition to FitzGerald's election, which was based exclusively on English precedents, not Irish law. They rescinded Wandesford's innovations in the assessment, collection and value of subsidies and the concessions their agents negotiated in London guaranteeing security of titles and limiting monopolies were achieved on the basis of parliament formulating means of making up the short-fall these would cause in the crown's income, a unique occurrence of the crown consulting the Irish parliament.

Notwithstanding what Chichester described as its 'knotty beginning', the 1613–15 parliament was highly effective, especially in contrast with the 1614 'Addled' assembly in England; despite the administration's mistrust, the Catholic opposition was determined to make it work.[7] It was much harder for Catholics in 1634 and initially in 1640, both because they were fewer in number and because Wentworth was less open to their suggestions than Chichester had been. 1634–5 was an exception in which Wentworth restricted parliament's powers, but his incursions on its functions, privileges and liberties were reversed after June 1640 and especially after March 1641 when the influx of new MPs, including Darcy and Martin with others like Mervyn, were determined to make it work. Its earlier freedoms were not questioned thereafter. However, their concern to have an effective parliament that would redress the country's grievances worked against the polarizing English and New English administrations who were largely motivated by self-interest and, in the latter's case, prepared not to implement Charles' orders.

The early Stuart Irish parliaments saw the development of the form and operations of the Commons that was to last until the Act of Union in 1800. Unlike many other European representative assemblies, the Irish parliament continued to exist. Their experience of the Commonwealth Parliament convinced the Irish Protestant community of its own parliament's vital role in governing Ireland. However, because Poynings' Law remained unamended and open to opportunistic interpretation, the Irish parliament remained in the unsatisfactory position of being an assembly in an inferior satellite kingdom in a composite monarchy that never received much of the sovereign's attention. It was therefore unable to realize its constitutional position as an equal of English or Scottish parliaments as a partner in managing the state.

By 1648 and more obviously 1661, the House of Commons was more firmly established but a less representative and useful body, not merely because the vast majority of the population was effectively excluded from voting or membership, but also because of its less diverse membership. Electorates were greatly reduced and it did not have the breadth of membership of earlier Irish parliaments which had contributed to their quality and success. Many MPs returned in 1661 were very recently arrived in Ireland and knew less about the country than their confreres in 1634 and 1640–1, even allowing for the significant cadre of Wentworth clients who were newcomers; native-born MPs., especially of Old English or old Irish origin, were very few (only 14 Old English MPs were elected in 1661 and only Daniel O'Neill and James Shane had Gaelic surnames, although these figures do not take account of those of mixed ethnicity like Murrough Boyle).[8] While there was no legal exclusion of Catholics, Geoffrey Browne's return for Tuam was overturned by the Commons.[9] The very small number of merchants or soldiers

7 *Cal. S.P. Ire., 1611–14*, p. 357.

8 T.G. Doyle, 'Boyle, Murrough, 1st Viscount Blessington', *DIB*.

9 Dennehy, *Parliament*, pp 203–4. Browne was returned with Thomas Bramhall, son of John. Dennehy is puzzled that an 'anabaptist' could be returned for a borough in which he assumed

was in sharp contrast to early Stuart parliaments and this assembly was unable to benefit from their commercial and military expertise and wider professional knowledge. Not one MP in 1661 was described as a merchant and three of the four who were listed as aldermen did not sit for the cities in which they held that position. However, that parliament was able to work effectively both because so many (at least 50) MPs had previous parliamentary experience and were anxious to reassert its role and importance in protecting the 'Protestant interest' in Ireland and the administration was consequently more open to recommendations for bills from the entirely Protestant 1661–6 Commons.[10]

Despite this, the Irish parliament did not meet for more than 20 years after that assembly's dissolution. When James II's parliament did convene, Lord Deputy Richard Talbot deployed exactly the same tactics as his early Stuart predecessors, but even more successfully, to engineer a Catholic membership of 224 to a mere six Protestants. He did so using *Quo warranto* proceedings in the Court of Exchequer, the only court from which there was no recourse to writs of error in England, as well as issuing new charters with majority Catholic councillors, appointing Catholic sheriffs to rig elections and nominating candidates and excluding others. Notably, he faced the same challenges as Chichester in having his bills approved in England.[11]

The waves of New English settlers who stayed and established families, the second and third generation of which sat in the Irish parliament, came to appreciate that their interests were not the same as England's and they created a new colonial parliamentary tradition that rejected the English parliament's attempts to legislate for Ireland to preserve their own positions and came to see parliament as their own institution.[12] While not seeing themselves as Irish, they established their own identity and pursued their own interests through an initial coalition against Wentworth in 1640–1 and then in the 'rump' and Restoration parliaments. They had mixed feelings about the 1691 English act excluding Catholics, although they were happy with its effect. They insisted on the procedures used before November 1641 to strengthen parliament's legitimacy by harking back to its long institutional history, despite its very different composition to the exclusively Protestant and largely New English Williamite parliament. Their efforts included Dopping's publication of the Irish *Modus*, Chancellor Michael Boyle's researching the Commons' orders to establish beyond question parliament's rights to judicature and Molyneux's combing of the Irish Commons' journals for precedents.

The substantial changes in the House of Lords are outside the scope of this book. The most obvious was the great increase in numbers, especially absentee

the local prelate would have influence, but the archbishop at that time, Samuel Pullen, was Thomas' uncle.

10 Ibid., p. 93.

11 Padraig Lenihan, *The last cavalier: Richard Talbot, 1631–1691* (Dublin, 2014), pp 113–17.

12 Karl S. Bottigheimer, 'The Restoration land settlement in Ireland: a structural view', *IHS*, 18:69 (March, 1972), 1–21.

Englishmen with Irish peerages who created an in-built majority through their proxy votes, although the ending of so many pluralities and lengthy vacancies also increased the number of spiritual peers. 20 prelates attended the 1560 parliament, many of whose commitment to the reformed religion was limited and 26 were summoned in 1585, although fewer attended. Chichester reported that there were only 19 bishops in 1611, increased marginally to 20 by 1613 by dint of consecrating seven new ones in early 1613, four of them in May alone. Their attendance however was patchy, with five sending proxies and two others absent for at least part of the time.[13] By 1634 however, the creation of so many English peers removed the administration's dependence on bishops, only 24 of whom appeared in parliament, compared to the 35 absentee lords whose proxies were recorded in a single day.[14]

These changes resulted in weaker networks between MPs and the House of Lords in general, but possibly strengthened those between Old English or Gaelic peers and parliamentarians. Curiously, prelates seemed uninterested in electoral patronage, which was stronger under Chichester than Wentworth; in 1613, eight MPs were sons, sons-in-law, brothers or nephews of bishops but the numbers were smaller after that date. The change in voting procedure, ending the practice of whispering in the chancellor's ear, forced peers to be more open in their political choices but may also have reduced attendance.

While there are many gaps in the records, the quantity, quality and range of sources available for this book confirms Bradshaw's belief that sufficient material remains to write the story of early modern Irish parliaments and, by extension, many other as yet unexplored areas of early seventeenth-century Irish life.

13 Irish Archaeological Society, *Tracts*, ii, pp 135–40; Routledge, 'Journal'; Treadwell, 'House of Lords'; *Cal. S.P. Ire., 1611–14*, p. 163.

14 *LJI*, 17–18, 30 July 1634.

APPENDIX ONE

Manuscript copies of Irish Parliamentary Journals, 1585–1648

Date	*Reference*	*Notes*	*Watermark*
1569	Hooker, *Order and Vsage*	Printed in Holinshed, *Chronicles* and Falkiner, *Essays*	
1585	Bodl. Lib., Carte MS 61, fos. 1–7	House of Lord's Journal, printed in Routledge, 'Journal'	
1613	TNA, SP 30/5/3, fos. 23r–144	Clerk's original notes (William Bradley and Edmund Medhop)	6 different watermarks
1613	King's Inns, MS N3/2/1/7	Original copy; not in Medhop's hand, but endorsed by him 1615	clear fleur de lys with crown, counter mark Hb
1613	NLI, MS 836	Same as King's Inns and Armagh Robinson Library copies. Medhop's copy, *c.*1618	watermark, a fleur de lys, countermark IA
1613	Armagh Robinson Library	Medhop's copy; for Chichester; includes Davies' speeches, 1619–21; excludes account of the opening on 18 May 1613	Watermark, Pot, MV, no countermark.
1613	TCD, MS 1,444	Fair copy; no account of the May 1613 opening; eighteenth-century copy. Notes last p. ex. p. Edm Medhop Cler Parliament, but not his signature. No indication of those who sat only at the beginning of the session; later binding. No provenance info. Seems same hand as FSL, W.b.510.	Pro Patria watermark
1613	Bodl. Lib., Carte MS 64 (10,510), fos. 149ff	Microfilm copy in NLI (n.746, p. 663)	

* Unless otherwise noted under 'Notes', the following refer to journals of the House of Commons

Date	*Reference*	*Notes*	*Watermark*
1613	FSL, W.b.510	Seems complete but only occupies first part of the volume. Rest of volume blank. Eighteenth-century copy? Spine of volume reads, 'Orders of ye House of Commons'. Catalogue does not suggest that it is a full copy, but it seems so. Looks to be same hand as TCD, MS 1,444. Identical with the original fair copy, but no account of the May 1613 opening.	Watermark, Pro patria, lion on throne, crowned, holding quiver of arrows, countermark LVC or LUG; https://nga.gov.au/whistler/details/Patria.cfm18th. century copy
1613	James Ware's copy	William O'Sullivan, 'A finding list of Sir James Ware's manuscripts', *Proc. RIA*, 97C (1997), 69–99. No evidence that it has survived. Unbound, so not identical with any other known Medhop copy.	
1613	BL, Harleian MS 4,892	Draft extracts, 1613–62	
1613	TCD, MS 622	Abridgement and index of the Commons' journals, 1613–92, clearly taken from original MS by William Molyneux, after 1666; includes folio number of original MS	Fleur de lys, countermark C.D.
1613	BL, Add. MS 4,792	Index to the 1613 Lords' journal. Published in Victor Treadwell, 'The House of Lords in the Irish parliament of 1613–1615', *EHR*, 80:314 (1965), 92–107, at pp 99–105.	
1634	Bodl. Lib., Carte MS 64, fo. 149r	Microfilm copy in NLI (n.746, p. 663)	
1634	King's Inns, MS N3/2/1/8	Irish Commons' journals extracts from 20 March 1635 to the dissolution. Eighteenth-century copy.	Pro Patria countermark RWS with a crown
1634	TCD, MS 622	Abridgement and index of the Commons' journals, 1613–66. Clearly taken from original MS by William Molyneux, after 1666. Includes folio numbers of original MS	Fleur de lys, counter mark C.D.

Date	*Reference*	*Notes*	*Watermark*
1634	TCD, MS 613	Fair copy of the Lords' journal; includes (upside-down) copies of grants of Irish peerages, Loftus, etc. From the Sterne collection	Fleur de lys in a shield, crown on top, query WR below; no counter mark
1634	TCD, MS 614	The Lords' journal. Clearly the clerk's rough copy. From the Sterne collection.	Fleur de lys in a shield, crown on top, looks like WR below Counter mark AB only in front pages, not in body of text.
1640	TCD, MS 622	Abridgement and index of the Commons' journals, 1613–66. Clearly taken from original MS by William Molyneux, after 1666. Includes folio number of original source.	Fleur de lys, counter mark C.D.
1640	King's Inns, MS N3/2/1/8	Irish Commons' journals, extracts March 1640 to 16 July 1641	Pro Patria countermark RWS with a crown. 18th. century copy
1640	BL, Egerton MS 2,541 (Extracts)	Feb. 1640–Aug. 1641. Microfilm copy in NLI (n. 869; p. 751)	
1640	TCD, MS 615	House of Lords' journal, 16 March 1639/40–4 March 1641, 1 Aug. 1642–1646. Clearly a copy from another as entry for 9 Aug. 1642 ends [blank page]; ditto 12 Aug., 22 Nov. Also notes [space] – was this the editorial judgments of the clerk in the 1750s?	Fleur de lys in a shield, crown on top, query WR below. No countermark visible
1640–1	Bodl. Lib., Carte MS 64 (10,510)	Microfilm copy in NLI (n.746, p. 663)	
1640–1	NLI, MS 9,607	House of Lords' journal, 1640–1	
1642–7	Bodl. Lib., Carte MS 64 (10,510)	Microfilm copy in NLI (n.746, p. 663)	

APPENDIX TWO

TCD, MS 672, fos. 235r–8v, endorsed as 'A Note of the propositions of the gentlemen of the Province of Mounster against the Parliament, delivered me by Sir William Sarsfield' (1634)

1. We desire that there may be an Act confirming the last Indentures of the Composicon in every point agreeing virbatim with the substance of the said Indentures – as well in the behalfe of his Majestie as of his Subiectes of this Kingdome.
2. An Act that no Souldiers, foote Companies, or Troopes of horse or any of them be hereafter appointed or authorised by any Governor or Governors to Levie the Kings rents under pretence of any assignement whatsoever; nor any authoritie given them to Levie any Moneyes whatsoever, either Subsidies, Loanes, Taxes or otherwise, or the arreare or arreares of any part of any such rent or moneyes whatsoever, and that power be given by the said Statute to the Justices of the peace to proceede with any such souldiors soe Delinquent uppon the Statute of Coyne and Livery.
3. An Act Confirming all Letters Patents past by his Majestie, or his ffather or other predicessors against his Majesty his heires and successors. And that the Tenures of all lands conteined in such Pattents be confirmed by the said Act, and no Exceptions to be taken to any flawes found in them, in any point or Clause graunted by the said Pattents or the Letter or Letters guiding the said Pattent.
4. An act that no Sherrifs shall retourne any freehoulder to Assizes or Sessions but such whose Estates are yearely worth five pownds ultra all Compositions Contry charges and chiefe rents upon paine of Twentie pownds sterling to be forfeited to his Majestie by every such Sherriff for every time, and that hee likewise beare the poore mans charges so retourned, as the Justices of Assizes or of the peace shall thinke in their discretions fitt and Competent.
5. An Act that his majesties Subiectes of this Kingdome, that owe Homadg to his Majestie may tender their Homadge in person to the Lord Deputie or other chiefe governour, or to the Lord Chancellor or cheife Barron of this Kingdome and that their said Tender be accepted as done to his [235v] Majestie whereby the Subiect may be eased of the respitt of Homadg which

they cannot performe in person to his Majestie by the reason of the Danger of the Sea, the poverty of the people, and the Length of the Jorney. The Charge of the said respitt proving now very chargeable and grievous to the Countrie &c.

6. An Act that no heir or purchasors be enquired off or questioned in the Court of Wards, or any Wardshipp of their bodies, Intrusion, or meane Rates for Landes, unlesse their Estate Exceed twentie nobles Sterling per annum ultra all Compositions, chiefe rents, Impositions, or Country charges whatsoever.

7. An Act that all dormant Conveiances that appeare not or are produced in 21 yeares may Ever after be suppressed and of no force against the ffreehoulder or purchaser Inioying any land conteined within the said deeds in the space of the said 21 yeares.

8. An Act that no officer shall distreyne for the Composition or any part thereof, but upon the very parcell where the same is due and upon no other, and that only so much of the said Composition as the said parcell is Charged with.

9. An Act that the acquittances of the Sherriff and his officers for any monies Levied or to be receaved by them upon the green wax, be receaved and accepted as payment in the Exchequer, soe as the subiect be not againe charged therewith, notwithstanding it be not accompted for by the said Sherriff uppon his Accomptes, but that uppon sight of the said acquittance the same be charged upon the said Sherriff who is to be sued uppon his Bondes.

10. An Act for the reducement and settling of the fees of ministeriall officers with a proviso that any taking, exacting or requiring more, may be questionned and punished as an Extortioner and to forfeict his place, and to be ever after incapable of the same or anie such office, and to pay trebble damages to the party grieved.

11. An Act that no Alienations not Exceeding twentie pownds shalbe questioned, and all Alienations above [236r] pay only at the rate of twentie nobles per hundred pownd and soe ratably, and to be freed by order of Court uppon payment of the said summe without any further Chardge.

12. An Act that all straglers and sturdie beggars be banished out of the Countrie. And all parishes be hereafter Commanded to relieve their owne poore and to be allowed by the next adioyning Justices of the peace, who is to give every such a testimoniall incerting his impotencie and infirmitie and that no other be admitted to begg within the said parish. And that the Church wardens doe quarterly bring in a list of all ympotent, aged and decayed people to the next adioyning Justice of the peace, who shall give such Certificate as afore said, and in that incerting the birth of any fatherless Children or death of any such poore since his last list.

13. An Act to make witchcraft (being prooved) fellony notwithstanding the parties bewitched be not deprived of life, and though it be the first offence of that nature Comitted by the offendor. And if it take effect whereby any

subiect be deprived of his life, that then the offendor be punished in all respects as in the Statute for wilful murder.

14. An Act that where the Countrie is much ympoverished through the dearth of Corne and the Excessive price thereof occasioned (as is generally conceived) through the want of Tilladge most men ymploying their lands to grasing and stocking the same with sheepe which now is growen the generall husbandrie of this Countrie, whereby the Countrie is much prejudiced, It might therefore be heereafter Enacted that every such grasier or gent stocking his land with Sheep, be compelled to plough yearely in every ploughland twelf Irish acres att least, whereby the marketts may be fully served, and the poore subiect contentedly supplied.

15. [1]An Act that the Testimonie or Evidence of any Rebell or tainted or Convicted person who for the safetie of his life, will promise service upon others be not accepted or received for any good or lawfull allegation or information sufficient to take away the life of any subiect, without the accession of some others testimonie. [236v]

16. An Act that where severall of the noblemen and Gentrey of this Countrie and others pass land uppon Letters of Concealements or graunts, and that the said lands passed are commonly distreyned for the rent reserved uppon the said graunt, notwithstanding his Majestie be not intituled thereunto by any office, that it be hereafter provided, for that the partie so passing the said lands and his possessions be only chardged with the said rent or arreare thereof, and no distresses to be taken of the lands so passed before his Majestie bee intituled thereunto by office, and recovered by Course of Lawe.

17. An Act to restreyne any Enquirie or graunt of lands uppon any hidden pretended attaindor, where the same hath been possessed and enioyed to the Contrary for the space of fortie yeares last past, if it appeare not by office that his Majestie hath bin intituled thereunto before or since the last Parlyament by an office as aforesaid of Record. And that all other of that nature be meerely voide if it hath bin concealed during the tyme aforesaid

18. An Act that none of his Majesties subiects their Executors, Administrators nor Assignes be questioned in any Court or Courts for any marriadges Christnings or burialls, hee or they having paid his or their duties for such marriadges, Christnings or Burialls, to the parson, and viccar or their proctors in the parishes where such marriadges, Christnings or Burialls respectively are properly and rightfully due.

19. An Act where great summs of money are due and payable to his Majestie by Composition made by his Highness deere ffather Kinge James of blessed memorie, by his highnes subiectes and that the Collectors of the same besides other Extortions will not receive the same Composition, if they may not have xii^{d} of the pound and 2$^{s.}$ for every pownd if the said Collectors distreyne, that henceforth if the said inhabitantes bringe their money, that they only pay for

1 Given as 14 in the margin, but the following item is listed as 16.

the acquittance 6[d.] sterling. And if the Collectors be forced to distreyne that he have only xij[d.] for the pownd, and that such Collectors and [237r] their Deputies shall beare their owne chardge, and lye uppon the Country uppon any such occasion.

20. An Act, where it is usuall that uppon all chardges, taxes [and] Impositions upon the inhabitants of this Kingdome, the same is taxed and allotted to land, not respecting the value or goodness of such lands, by which occasion his Majesties subiects dwelling upon barren land are forced to foresake their habitacons and begg in other Countries. That indifferent Commissioners be appointed to value and survey the landes of the severall Counties, and according to the value and quallitie of the one and the others, so the chardge to be borne.

21. An Act that all his Majesties Subiectes and natives of this Kingdome, may be enabled to sue Livery, and be capable of offices notwithstanding the Act of secundo or xj[mo] of Queen Elizabeth Such subiects respectively first taking the last oath of Alliegance declared in his Majesties Instructions to his Majesties, his highnes heires and successors And that his highnes subiects and natives of this Kingdome may be deemed, Called and reputed as those of the Brittish nation, and not tearmed meere Irish. That they may purchase marry and Concerte one with another notwithstanding any former Act, Acts or restrictions to the Contrary.

22. An Act that all the auncient weares by graunt from his Majesties Progenitors upon the Rivers of this Kingdome, as [blank] to his Majesties subiects of the same be limitted to make fflood gates, soe as Cotts and small boats may att all tymes passe. And that all other weares not warranted by graunt appart from his Majestie uppon the said rivers be pulled downe.

APPENDIX THREE

Biographical dictionary of lawyers in parliament

THESE BIOGRAPHICAL SKETCHES are drawn from Bríd McGrath, 'The membership of the Irish House of Commons, 1613–15' (MLitt, University of Dublin, 1987) and Bríd McGrath, 'A biographical dictionary of the Irish House of Commons, 1640–1641', 2 vols (PhD, University of Dublin, 1998), with additional material from a wide range of sources. As many of these sources relate to local and family history, but are not germane to the actual text of the book, they have not been included in the bibliography. Works that are given in abbreviated form here on first citation are cited in the main text as well and are also listed in the bibliography. Lawyers that are mentioned throughout the text for whom another entry is provided elsewhere in the appendix are indicated with an asterisk (*). Biographical details of MPs for the 1613 parliament who were not lawyers are available in McGrath, 'Membership of the Irish House of Commons, 1613–15'. Biographies of all of the MPs who originally sat in 1640–1 are given in volume 1 of McGrath, 'Biographical dictionary', while the chapter entitled 'Constituency profiles' in volume 2 of the thesis gives further details of the 1634 MPs. Finally, additional details of new MPs recruited to the 'rump' parliament in the course of the 1640s are found in Bríd McGrath, 'The recruiter returns to the Irish parliament, 1642–1648' in Patrick Little (ed.), *Ireland in crisis: war, politics and religion 1641–50* (Manchester, 2019), pp 119–37.

ABBREVIATIONS USED

b.	born
d.	died
o.v.p.	*obiit sine prole* (died without children)
+	(usually with date) after
-	(usually with date) before
m.	married
rem.	remarried
unm.	unmarried
s.	son of
e.s.	eldest son
s.s.	surviving son
e.s.s.	eldest surviving son
y.s.	younger son

o.s.	only son
2.s	2nd son, etc. or had 2 sons
da.	daughter of
e.da	eldest daughter
y.da	younger daughter
2.da.	2nd daughter, etc., or had 2 daughters
w.	widow
coh.	co-heir(ess)
ed.	educated
knt.	knight
Kt.	knighted
Bur.	buried
exc.	executor
decd.	deceased
c.	*circa*
Ald.	alderman
____	indicates that the name of a parent, etc. is unknown
u.c.	unknown constituency
BCL	Bachelor of Civil Law
DCL	Doctor of Civil Law
LLB	Bachelor of Laws
LLD	Doctor of Laws

JEROME ALEXANDER (1594 – 1670) **Lifford, 1634**
Belfast, 1660 Convention

s. Jerome Alexander, Thorplands, Norfolk; m. 1623, Elizabeth (d. 1667), da. John Havers, London; 16 children, sons Jerome, William and John christened St John's, Dublin, 13 June 1630, 10 January 1632 and 11 March 1633;[1] but survived by only three daughters, including his heiress Elizabeth.
ed. Aylsham, Caius Cambridge, 1609; Furnivall's Inn, 1608; Lincoln's Inn, 1609; Bar, 1623; King's Inns, 1628.[2]
Kt. 1660.
Bur. St Patrick's Cathedral, Dublin.

Alexander was Arundel's steward and became clerk of the Star Chamber and bailiff of Eynsford, Kent, in 1620. Convicted in the Star Chamber for falsifying legal documents, fined £500 (paid by his father-in-law), expelled from Lincoln's Inn in November 1626, disbarred and had to flee England;[3] he remained disbarred in England even after his pardon. Arundel procured his release and he travelled to

1 John Mills (ed.), *The registers of St John the Evangelist, Dublin, 1619 to 1699* (Dublin, 1906), pp 18, 20, 22. On p. 264 it is noted that there were unspecified fees for the burial of two of his children between Easter 1634 and 1635, and another child in the following 12 months. Terry Clavin, 'Alexander, Sir Jerome', *DIB*; Prendergast, 'Further notes in the history of Sir Jerome Alexander'.
2 *The case between Sir Jerom Alexander*, p. 4.
3 [Alexander], *Breviate of a sentence*; Ball, *Judges in Ireland*, ii, pp 348–9; NLI, MS 2,304, p. 249.

Ireland, armed with the earl's letter of recommendation to Chancellor Loftus and was involved in the collection of the impost of wines.[4] He blamed Richard FitzGerald for spreading news of his disgrace in Ireland, but this did not adversely affect his Irish career. With Loftus' support he established a lucrative legal practice including in chancery cases and acted for Lords Baltinglass, Conway, Cork, Hastings and Arundel (who was claiming lands in Ireland) and George Downham, bishop of Derry by 1633.[5] With others, including Donnellan*, he witnessed a church deed in Dublin in April 1633. He formed part of the procession at Lord Aungier's funeral in 1632. He was in England on Arundel's business in 1634, returning to Ireland that September, in time for the next session of parliament, and inherited £10 from Sir Matthew de Renzy.[6] He lent £6,100 on the Dublin Staple between November 1634 and March 1635 much of it in acquiring an interest in the Magennis (Iveagh) lands in County Down by mortgages,[7] leased lands from Lord Kingsland and was granted the Abbey of Kilcooley, Tipperary, by Ormond in 1636, with 2,130 acres, worth £94 annually; he also held 210 acres in Kilkenny.[8] He lived in Ship Street, Dublin and also near Kells, Meath.[9]

Ely recommended him to Wentworth as Catlin's successor and issued a commission to Sir Geratt Lowther* and Alexander to conduct the assizes in Meath. However, Wentworth rejected this in favour of Maurice Eustace* as being king's serjeant, which 'enables him, or at least qualifies him, to be trusted as a judge of assize before the other; and know I do too, that to those who know them both, the Serjeant is held as able in his own profession, Besides (but that I am not apt unnecessarily to touch personally upon any) something I could have mentioned in Mr Alexander's particular, which doth not render him altogether fit for such an imployment', presumably a reference to his disbarral in England.[10] Alexander fell foul of Wentworth by promoting Arundel's claims to Irish lands and claiming that Wentworth had opportunistically grabbed land near Naas after Alexander discovered that the occupiers had no title to it. Fearing vengeance, Alexander went to London in autumn 1637 on Arundel's business without licence and was

4 Brian Mac Cuarta, 'A planter's funeral, legacies and inventory: Sir Matthew de Renzy (1577–1634)', *JRSAI*, 127 (1997), 18–33.

5 NLI, Report on Private Collections no. 133, Montgomery Papers, 2 July 1633, Bond of Thomas Lord Baltinglass to Ald. Robert Parkehurst, London, for £6,000; HL, HP, Box 76 (4); HL, Hastings Legal Papers, Box 5 (5); Ohlmeyer, 'Records'; Grosart, *Lismore Papers*, 1st series, iv, p. 68 under 29 January 1635.

6 Michael Joseph McEnery and Raymond Refausé (eds), *Christ Church deeds* (Dublin, 2002), p. 312; Fitzgerald and Lamacraft (eds), *Some funeral entries of Ireland*; BL, Harleian MS 4,820, fo. 241; Joseph Forster, *Funeral certificates of the nobility and gentry of Ireland* (Dublin, 1882), pp 6–7; Left money by Sir Matthew de Renzy: Mac Cuarta, 'Planter's funeral'.

7 Jane Ohlmeyer and Éamonn Ó Ciardha (eds), *The Irish statute staple books, 1596–1687* (Dublin, 1998), pp 56, 256.

8 William Healy, *History and antiquities of Kilkenny* (Kilkenny, 1893), appendix, p. 74.

9 Ball, *Judges in Ireland*, i, p. 348.

10 Chancellor Loftus to Wentworth, 13 April 1637, Wentworth to Loftus, 14 April 1637, Loftus to Wentworth, same date, Wentworth to Loftus, 15 April 1637, all in Knowler (ed.), *Letters and dispatches*, ii, pp 67–9.

imprisoned in the Fleet. In his absence Wentworth dispossessed him of Kilcooly.[11] He fled to the Continent but returned to London in 1640 to provide evidence for Wentworth's trial.

A member of the Committee for Compounding, he received grants of Adventurers' Lands in Waterford in 1643 and was active in taking details of compositions in Yorkshire in the 1640s, but was removed from that role in February 1647.[12] He was on the Continent in the early 1650s, financing royalist refugees, including the duke of York, but was back in Ireland by 1655, serving as clerk of the peace in Longford, while still acting as a legal advisor to the Committee of Adventurers in England. Despite this he was in financial difficulties and appealed to the government for help. He was living in Hoye's Alley off Werburgh Street in Dublin in 1660 and was a commissioner of the Poll Money Ordnance in Dublin City and County and Meath in 1660 and 1661, and for Kells also in 1660.

He was second justice of the common pleas from 1661 until his death, at an annual salary of £300. He was described approvingly by Bishop Wild as 'acute and episcopal' and 'a resolute anti-presbyter judge.' He kept chambers at the King's Inns in 1661–2.[13] In 1661 he took a case against his fellow judge, Sir William Ashton, claiming precedency over him on the basis of his having been called to the bar before Ashton. Curiously, the issue of his disbarral and expulsion from Lincoln's Inn was not raised during the case.[14] His estate was left to his daughter on condition that she did not marry a Catholic or a man of Irish birth or with any Irish blood, regardless of their social rank. He had an extensive library of books and manuscripts, including tracts by Robert Cotton and John Selden and a copy of Hakewill's writings on passing bills; his books were left to Trinity College Dublin.[15]

PATRICK ARCHER (c.1566 – 1632) **Kilkenny, 1613**

s. Edward Archer, Kilkenny; m. by 1587, Joan, da. Thomas Archer FitzWalter, Kilkenny; 2s., 3 da.[16]
ed. Gray's Inn, 22 November 1581; King's Inns 1607.

Archer was a member of one of the most prominent merchant families in Kilkenny and was closely linked to his fellow MPs. His son Thomas married Helena, daughter of Lucas Shee and his daughters Margaret and Nicola married Patrick Rothe and Nicholas Langton respectively. Patrick was one of the overseers of his

11 *Cal. S.P. Ire., 1647–60*, p. 345; NLI, MS 2,306, p. 65; Ball, *Judges in Ireland*, i, p. 348.
12 Mary Ann E. Green, *Calendar of the committee for compounding, 1643–1647* (London, 1889), pp 8, 56–7.
13 *The case between Sir Jerom Alexander*, p. 12.
14 Ibid., p. 4, claims that he was admitted to Furnival's Inn in July 1609, staying there three or four years before proceeding to Lincoln's Inn, and being called to the bar before seven years of study, i.e. presumably before 1616.
15 TCD, MSS 717, 858, fos. 2–40; V. Teehan, 'The Alexander collection in the library of Trinity College Dublin, with special reference to the law books' (MPhil, University of Dublin, 1991).
16 G.D. Burtchaell, *Genealogical memoirs of the members of parliament for the county and city of Kilkenny* (Dublin, 1888), p. 23; '*Laus Deo. Ad majorem Dei gloriam*'.

uncle Sir Richard Shee's will in 1603, in which he was also left 20 shillings 'for a signet.'[17] He was also executor of his brother Thomas' will, which resulted in a Chancery case against Sir Daniel O'Brien.[18] His son Thomas entered Gray's Inn in 1619.

An eminent lawyer, he shared chambers in King's Inns next to those of John Everard* with the Waterford lawyer James Bryver and was pensioner of King's Inns in 1609 (he collected the members' subscriptions). He frequently acted with Everard as a lawyer for the Ormonds; he was appointed attorney of the Liberty of Tipperary from 1608 and acted for both Kilkenny City and for the earl of Ormond, and signed a number of Ormond deeds from 1586, as well as being appointed overseer of Thomas Ormond's will.[19] In June 1608 he was appointed to enquire into a dispute between Ormond and George Stafford of Wexford, about the prisage of wines in New Ross and Wexford. In the following year he and Lord Dunboyne were arbitrators in a land dispute between the O'Hennessys in Tipperary.[20] He was heavily involved in local government in the city and county, serving as sovereign in 1601–2, JP from 1606, alderman from 1609 and mayor in 1611. The aldermen nominated him as a candidate in the 1628 parliamentary election and he was a commissioner for Kilkenny City managing the export of corn to England in 1631.[21]

His property in Kilkenny included a house and garden in Castle St and half of the tithes of Quarryboy. He also rented a cellar under Kilbryes Tower from Kilkenny Corporation for a minimum of 8*d.* annually between 1596 and 1600.[22] He paid a fine of £26 13*s.* 4*d.* on a grant passed on the Commission of Defective Titles in 1608 and was a grantee of lands in County Kilkenny in 1609 to the use of Sir Nicholas Walsh, the chief justice.[23] He signed the petition of recusant MPs to James, supporting the sending of agents to the king and was an active MP sitting on committees.[24]

17 John Ainsworth and Edward MacLysaght (eds), 'Power O'Shee Papers', *Anal. Hib.*, 20 (1958), 226ff.

18 NAI, Chancery MS I12, Patrick Archer, exr. of his brother Thomas Archer, decd., v. Sir Daniell O Brien, knt., re debt (undated, after 1604).

19 King's Inns, MS B1/1, fo. 109v; Kenny, *King's Inns*, pp 84, 275; NLI, MSS D. 3,365 (11 Dec. 1608); D. 3,513 (10 July 1612); D. 3,536 (27 Oct. 1613); D. 3,553; Patrick Archer's account for drawing up an answer to the complaint of the Portrieve of Irishtown against the Sovereign and Corporation of Kilkenny', April 1597, KCA, MS CR/J/22. This arbitration was conducted jointly with Sir John Everard* on 24 Sept. 1594. Edmund Curtis (ed.), *Calendar of Ormond deeds, Volume VI, 1584–1603* (Dublin, 1970), pp 25–6, 73–6 (Ormond's will), 84, 97–9, 113–14, 184–6.

20 NLI, MSS D. 3,429–3,429a (7 Dec. 1607 and June 1608); D. 3,455 (4 Aug. 1609).

21 Warrant and accounts from Patrick Archer, sovereign, 23 Feb. 1602 and Aug. 1602, KCA, MS CR/J/32–3; NLI, MS 11,048(7); McGrath, 'Nomination of Kilkenny MPs in 1628'; Caulfield (ed.), *Youghal*, p. 161.

22 Curtis (ed.), *Calendar of Ormond deeds, Volume VI*, p. 181.

23 *Cal. S.P. Ire., 1611–14*, p. 104; NLI, MSS D. 3,470–1.

24 *Cal. S.P. Ire., 1611–14*, pp 356, 360.

EDWARD AYSCOUGH (Ascough, Askoe, Askewe) (*c.*1592 – 1647+) Clogher, 1634

6 s. Sir Edward Aysough (d. *c.*1612), South Kelsey, Lincolnshire, and Esther, da. Thomas Grantham; unm.[25]

ed. Lincoln's Inns, 1608; Bar, 1615; King's Inns, 1629.

Ayscough inherited £800 from his father in 1612.[26] He was licenced to travel for three years with one servant in October 1615 and may have come to Ireland after his presumed relative, John Ayscough, customer in Galway by 1622, who was a connection of the Loftus family which may have assisted his advancement; he was active as a lawyer in chancery cases.[27] He proposed to raise money for the king by the sale of soap in England and Ireland, 1625.[28] He carried a banner at Lord Aungier's funeral in 1632.[29] In February 1638 he succeeded William Hilton* as attorney general of Connacht and held that office until 1647.[30] He had no known connections with his constituency at the time of his return; he served on a number of parliamentary committees. Edward should not be confused with his nephew and namesake, MP for Lincolnshire in the Long Parliament.[31]

ROBERT BARNEWALL (*c.*1580 – 3 July 1617) Meath Co., 1613

y.s. Alexander Barnewall of Robertstown and Alison Netterville, da. ____; m. Ellice, da. Michael Fitzwilliams (second brother of the house of Merrion); da. Ales.[32]

ed. Gray's Inn, 1596; King's Inns, 1607.

The Robertstown Barnewalls were not the most important branch of that family and Robert's return was due to his eminence as a lawyer; he shared chambers in the cloisters of the King's Inns.[33] He acted for Dublin Corporation in its defence of its charter in 1605 and represented clients in cases on defective titles in 1611.[34]

25 Pedigree, Lincolnshire Archives, Misc. Dep. 16/11; F.L., Deeds 1,373–4.

26 A.R. Maddison, *Lincolnshire wills, 2nd series, 1600–1617* (Lincoln, 1891), pp 84–5. Inventory of Sir Edward's effects, 1612, by Thomas Grantham, Lincolnshire Archives, Inv. 112B/437; Sir Edward wrote *A Historie contayning the warres, treaties, marriages and other occurrents betweene England and Scotland ... until the happy Vnion of them both in our Gratious King Iames* (London, 1607).

27 *APC, 1615–16*, p. 302; John Ayscough, son of Henry Ayscough of Kemptine, Yorkshire, and Sarah Loftus, Swineshead, Yorkshire, died in Ireland, 12 June 1624. BL, Harleian MS 4,820, fo. 168; TCD, MS 1,216, fo. 29r; Forster, *Funeral certificates*, p. 5; Ohlmeyer, 'Records'.

28 *Cal. S.P. Dom., 1625*, p. 128.

29 BL, Harleian MS 4,820, fo. 241; Forster, *Funeral certificates*, pp 6–7.

30 Warrant of appointment, 27 Feb. 1638, Marsh's Library, MS Z3.2.6, no. 109; Empey (ed.), *Early Stuart Irish warrants*, no. 26.

31 Unclear which is the Edward Ayscough of Lincoln's Inn who was selling lands in Lincolnshire for £744 in 1630 (Lincolnshire Archives, F.L., Deed 1,373) and buying other property in the same year (ibid., F.L., Deed 1,374); Deed of Edward Ayscough of the parish of St Martin in the Fields, 22 Jac. I, Lincolnshire Archives, A.H. 1/10/1/4/1/, purchase of other lands.

32 NLI, GO, MS 66, Funeral Entries, Volume 3, 1604–22, p. 66; Joseph Forster, *Collectanea genealogica* (London, 1881), iv, p. 32; Stephen B. Barnwell, 'The Barnewall family during the 16th and 17th centuries, part II', *IG*, 3:6 (1961), 198–209; Lodge, *Peerage*, iv, p. 207.

33 King's Inns, MS B1/1, fos. 6v, 109v.

34 Berry, 'Minute book of the Corporation of Dublin'; List of warrants made by virtue of letters out of England, 1603–11, HL, HP, Box 3 (40); Bartholomew Thomas Duhigg, *History of the King's Inns* (Dublin, 1806), p. 78.

Robert was one of the most active members of the 1613 Commons. His daughter Ales (Alison) inherited his extensive property and married Sir Thomas Nugent, son of Sir Christopher*.[35]

ANDREW BARRETT (*c.*1565 – 1615–24) **Cork Co., 1613**

s. ____ Barrett; m. by 1594, Katherine, da. ____; 7 sons, 2 da.
ed. Clifford's Inn, Inner Temple, 1582.

Barrett returned from England by 1591 when Edmund Barrett of Ballencoly, Cork, accused him of breaking and entering Edmund's castle, for which he was fined £12 in the Court of Castle Chamber. In 1594 he witnessed deeds for Sir Thomas Norris, Mallow. Andrew signed bond of recognizance for Teague Mac Dermody Charty to appear before the lord president of Munster in 1602. He was agent for Cork corporation to the lord deputy in May 1603 and was elected recorder in 1609.[36] His marriage brought him extensive lands at Ballincollig and elsewhere in County Cork. In anticipation of travelling to England as an agent for the recusants, he drew up his will in Dublin 9 July 1613 and made a settlement of his estates with Patrick Roche fitz Maurice as trustee, but he was back in Cork in January 1614, taking inquisitions post mortem in the city; he was also taking inquisitions on 13 October 1614, two days after parliament resumed sitting and continued doing so on 29 October.[37] However, he was in attendance in the following session, sitting on the committee on the act for the avoiding of privy and secret outlawries.

JAMES BARRY (1603[38] – February 1673) **Lismore, 1634**
Dublin Co., 1660 Convention

e.s. Richard and Anne, da. & coh. James Cusack, Rathgar; m. 1) by May 1635, Catherine, da. Sir William Parsons, Dublin, and Elizabeth, da. Ald. John Lany, Dublin; 4 sons, including James, 5 das. including Elizabeth, Katheren.[39]
ed. TCD, BA 27 April 1621; MA, June 1624; incorp. Cambridge and Oxford, 1627; Lincoln's Inns, 11 July 1621; Bar, 1628; King's Inns, 15 April 1630.
Kt. August 1640; Baron Barry of Santry, 1661.
Bur. St Mary's Chapel, Christ Church, Dublin, 14 February 1673.[40]

Barry (*plate 8*) was from an Old English Dublin merchant family with strong connections through the Cusacks to the network of Meath gentry, but his father's

35 Tallon (ed.), *Court of Claims*, p. 30.
36 Crawford, *Star Chamber*, pp 149, 266, 270, 473, 477–8; John Ainsworth and Edward MacLysaght (eds), 'Doneraile Papers', *Anal. Hib.*, 20 (1958), 55–90; Curtis Clayton (ed.), *Council book*, p. 107; Caulfield (ed.), *Cork*, pp xix, 11.
37 The pedigree from old Andrew Barrett, https://ota.bodleian.ox.ac.uk/repository/xmlui/bitstream/handle/20.500.12024/A90356/A90356.html?sequence=5&isAllowed=y#index.xml-body.1_div.4, [accessed 7 April 2022]; RIA, MSS OS EI 20, Inquisitions post mortem, Cork, vol. 3, pp 78–80, 279–91; OS EI 18, Inquisitions post mortem, Cork, vol. 1, pp 253–66.
38 Visitation of Dublin, 1607, NLI, GO, MS 48, p. 38.
39 da. Elizabeth, Katherine, bapt. St Michan's on 16 Feb. 1638, 7 May 1639, wife's name given as Katherine. Son James bapt. 10 June 1640. H.F. Berry (ed.), *The registers of the church of St Michan, Dublin, 1636 to 1685* (Dublin, 1907), pp 2–4.
40 G.E.C., *Peerage*; Robert Armstrong, 'Barry, James, 1st Baron Barry of Santry', *DIB*.

religious conformity meant that James' own close connections were with the New English, especially with administration families like the Parsons and Wares. He was brother-in-law of another conforming Irish lawyer James Donnellan*, as well as Paul Davies, John Hoey, Arthur Hill, William Ussher and Richard Parsons, while his wife connected him also to the Boyle, Loftus and Dillon networks. Despite his youth, he received money and a lease of lands during his father's mayoralty in 1610 and later held 360 acres in Skreen Barony, Meath. He inherited tithes worth £30 there from his father. His mother or his wife may have been the Mrs. Barry who was left £1 by Humphrey Farnham in 1624.[41]

James was educated at the most Puritan Inn of Court, Lincoln's Inn, and was part of a tight-knit group of Irish Protestants who acted as manucaptors for each other, reinforcing their already strong connections; Eustace* and Donnellan* were James' manucaptors and he acted in that capacity for John Bysse*, Hoey and Richard Parsons among others.[42] As a highly educated lawyer, James was well-qualified for the posts he held as recorder of Dublin from the early 1620s to 1626: prime serjeant in 1629 and second baron (judge) of the exchequer in 1634. He was fortunate to be appointed serjeant, as Charles wished to appoint Maurice Eustace*, and Barry was described as 'young and incompetent.' Falkland was anxious to have him as his counsel in a case in the Star Chamber against Sir Arthur Savage (*plate 6*) in early 1630.[43] Barry was involved in the King's Inns as treasurer, council member and as one of five trustees appointed in 1638 and as treasurer again on the Restoration, but Kenny also suggests that he may have destroyed some embarrassing records (such as the admissions of Radcliffe*, Wentworth and Henry Cromwell). The Inns holds a portrait of him.[44]

James was a supporter of Wentworth (although Cork was clearly responsible for his return for Lismore) and sat on the important grievances and privileges committees as well as those on bills concerning bigamy, ease of pleading actions, and those to present the petition on the Graces to Wentworth and to advise on desirable legislation. In 1637 he was responsible for the publication entitled *The case of tenures* (which he dedicated to Wentworth), a report of the Irish judges' opinion on a test case that left the way clear for the plantation of Connacht.[45] In the following year, Wentworth asked Barry to report on a dispute between George and James Plunkett.[46] Barry defended Strafford in parliament in 1640 and acted against the impeachment of Bolton* and others. He was also one of the judges who answered the *Queries* in parliament in 1641.

41 Ball, *Judges in Ireland*, i, pp 335–6; R.C. Simington (ed.), *The Civil Survey*, 10 vols (Dublin, 1931–61), Meath, pp 60–1, 389; Loeber and McGrath, 'Legacy of Humphrey Farnham'.

42 Lincoln's Inn, Admissions registers, 1616–27, fos. 59r, 83v, 93v, 128v.

43 Quoted in Hart, *History of the king's serjeants at law*, pp 57–8; Falkland to Barry, 23 Feb. 1630, NAI, MS 2,445, p. 59.

44 Kenny, *King's Inns*, pp 105–6, 112–13, 139–42, 197. The portrait is reproduced as the frontispiece. Ainsworth (ed.), 'Survey of documents in private keeping: third series', p. 3.

45 Barry, *Case of tenures.*

46 NAI, MS M. 2,448, p. 218.

Barry and Charles Coote sr were summoned by the English Commons to answer charges of delinquency in the case of Edward Faes, March 1641, although he was supported by the Irish council. He was in Ireland in 1643 when he signed certificates for Thomas Reynolds and Thomas Magner. In June 1646 he was granted £90 by the English parliament and four years later received a special grant of £300, later raised to £500, for special services in Ireland, having been a commissioner with his father-in-law, Robert Meredith, Paul Davies and others to raise £50,000 for Ireland.[47] He was removed from the bench under the Commonwealth but continued to work as a barrister and in other legal capacities.[48] In December 1653 he had argued for Lady Ormond's claim to her parents' estates before Lord Lowther and the attorney general. Fleetwood and Richard Pepys proposed him as a judge in 1654 and he acted as a judge of assize in the following year at least, when he reported on Strafford's alteration of land titles in Connacht and in 1656 on a case of murder by witchcraft in Carrickfergus. He also represented Leinster Catholics in their attempts to avoid transplantation (they were not allowed Catholic lawyers apart from Darcy*), although it is unclear how diligently he performed this role.[49]

He was living in St Michan's Parish, Dublin, in 1659 and was commissioner for the Poll Money Ordnance in Dublin City and County in 1660. He chaired the Committee of Safety and was engaged with Coote jr, Paul Davies and others in plotting the Restoration and represented Dublin County and chaired the Convention which achieved this. Many of his family connections were also members and his cousin was clerk.[50] On the Restoration, he was created a privy councillor, chief justice of the king's bench and a peer and was proposed as successor to Eustace* as chancellor. Ormond supported this unsuccessful move, noting that 'although Santry was indolent and wilful, it was of less consequence as he was generally in the right.'[51] He received a grant of £31 10*s*. for the purchase and storage of three tuns of French wine in his house in 1661.[52]

JOHN BEARE (Beere) (*c*.1573 – 8 May 1617)[53] **Carlow, 1613**

s. Revd ____ Beare, Minster, Isle of Thanet, Kent, and ____; m. 1) by 1590, ____; s. Thomas admitted to Gray's Inn, 1607, King's Inns, 1614.[54]
ed. Gray's Inn, 9 June 1589; Bar, 1596; King's Inns, 1609.

47 Bodl. Lib., Carte MS 67, fo. 109r; Green, *Calendar of the committee for compounding*, p. 362.
48 Kenny, 'Not every judge a phoenix'; *idem*, 'Black Book of King's Inns'.
49 W. Dunn Macray (ed.), *Calendar of the Clarendon States Papers, Volume II* (Oxford, 1869), p. 297; *DIB*; Toby Barnard, *Cromwellian Ireland: English government and reform in Ireland, 1649–1660* (Oxford, 2000), pp 181–2; Clarke, *Prelude to restoration*, pp 146–7 (where his name is incorrectly given as 'John'), 199–200; John Cunningham, *Conquest and land in Ireland: the transplantation to Connacht, 1649–1680* (Woodbridge, 2011), pp 71, 91.
50 Kenny, *King's Inns*, p. 138; Clarke, *Prelude to restoration*, pp 146–7, 199–200, 239–40, 247–8, 254, 284, 289, 299–300, 304, 309, 312.
51 Robert Armstrong, 'Barry, James, 1st Baron Barry of Santry', *DIB*.
52 HMC, *Ormond Papers*, new series, iii, p. 404.
53 NLI, GO, MS 66, Funeral Entries, Volume 3, 1604–22, p. 64.
54 Kenny, *King's Inns*, pp 276–7.

Kt. 19 August 1615.
Bur. Christ Church Cathedral, Dublin.[55]

Beare only sat for the first session, as Carlow's representation was deemed unlawful, despite which he was nominated to the Committee on the bill for pirates. He came to Ireland as prime serjeant in 1609, having been debarred in England. His salary was £50 in 1616 and he was occupied with the crown's general legal business.[56] In 1610 he became commissioner of the Court of Wards.[57] As serjeant he was justice of assize in circuits throughout Ireland, acting as judge at gaol delivery sessions in Monaghan and Armagh in March 1616. He was involved in planning plantations; he was a commissioner for the plantation of Wexford and active in arranging that of Longford where his son benefitted from a grant of 500 acres.[58] In 1616 the archbishop of Canterbury, George Abbott, and Sir Thomas Lake recommended Beare 'and some other mean men' to replace Davies as attorney general in Ireland; Francis Bacon opposed this, recommending Edward Wrythington.[59] Beare was reported to have spread rumours to the discredit of Bishop George Downham of Derry shortly before his death.[60] As one of the lawyers heavily involved in the King's Inns he was named in a lease from Sir John Davies of lands in Oxmanstown, for the Inns' 'Common Hall.'[61]

JOHN BLENNERHASSETT (1563 – 14 November 1624) **Belfast, 1613**

s. ____ Blenerhassett, Norfolk; m. 1) by 1596, Ursula (d. 20 April 1638), da. Edward Duke, Binhall, Suffolk; 3 s. Henry (drowned in the Amazon, 1632), Ambrose (d. unwed.), Edward (d. unwed), 3 da. Dorothy m. Francis Sacheverell, Elizabeth m. Charles Moncke and Anne m. Philip Fernesly.[62]
ed. Furnival's Inn, Lincoln's Inn, 1583; Bar, 1591.
Bencher, Lincoln's Inn, 1609; Baron of the exchequer, Ireland, 1609; King's Inns, 9 November 1609; Treasurer of King's Inns, 1611; Chief baron of the exchequer, 1621.
Kt. 3 October 1609.
Bur. St Patrick's Cathedral, Dublin, 18 November 1624.[63]

55 Raymond Refaussé and Colm Lennon (eds), *The registers of Christ Church Cathedral, Dublin* (Dublin, 1998), p. 90.
56 *Cal. S.P. Ire., 1610–14*, p. 197; HL, HP, MS 15,729, 30 Dec. 1616; *Cal. S.P. Ire., 1615–25*, pp 239–40; Bodl. Lib., Carte MS 59, fos. 232–3.
57 Hughes, *Patentee Officers*; *Rot. Pac. Jac.*, pp 149, 313; M.C. Griffith (ed.), *Calendar of inquisitions formerly in the office of the chief remembrancer of the exchequer* (Dublin, 1991), A21; Brian Mac Cuarta, 'Newcomers in the Irish midlands, 1540–1641' (MA, University College Galway, 1980), p. 101.
58 *Cal. S.P. Ire., 1610–14*, p. 450; *Rot. Pac. Jac.*, p. 467; Crawford, *Star Chamber*, pp 509–10, 514, 521–2; John McCavitt, '"Good planets in their several spheres": the establishment of the assize circuits in early seventeenth-century Ireland', *IJ*, 24:2 (1989), 248–78; James F. Ferguson, 'The Ulster roll of gaol delivery, continued', *Ulster Journal of Archaeology*, 1st series, 2 (1854), 25–8.
59 Bacon to Sir George Villers, 2 July 1616, in James Spedding (ed.), *The letters and the life of Francis Bacon, Volume V* (London, 1869), p. 377.
60 John Richardson to Downham, 6 May 1617, in Moody and Simms (eds), *Bishopric of Derry*, i, p. 123.
61 Kenny, *King's Inns*, pp 288–9.
62 Ball, *Judges in Ireland*, i, p. 323; Forster (ed.), *Collectanea genealogica*, p. 36.
63 TCD, MS 1,216, fo. 29v; NLI, GO, MS 79, pp 124–5, https://catalogue.nli.ie/Record/vtls000529291#page/124/mode/1up, [accessed 30 July 2022].

Blennerhasset came to Ireland as a judge in the Exchequer Court in 1609 and was also a regular judge of assize throughout the country and referred many cases to the Court of Castle Chamber from local courts. With Beare* he undertook preparatory work for the plantation of Longford and was a commissioner for the plantation of Wexford in 1615. He was a commissioner of the Court of Wards in 1613 and became a privy councillor in 1621. With Lowther* and others he was interrogating Teige O'Lenan and others in May 1615.[64] He negotiated the marriage agreement between Cork's daughter Sarah and Thomas Moore, Lord Drogheda's son in 1617. With other judges he gave evidence to the 1622 commission on problems with the system of administration of justice in Ireland.[65] Fernesly and his wife took a chancery case against Ursula Blennerhassett about Sir John's will.[66] Despite being unseated, he was nominated to the committee of the bill on pirates. He was presumably related to the Fermanagh planters Sir Edward, Francis and Thomas Blennerhassett.[67]

RICHARD BOLTON (1565[68] – November 1648) **Dublin City, 1613**

s. John Bolton, Great Fenton (Fenton Culvart), Staffordshire, and Margaret, da. Richard Ash of Ash, Staffordshire (d. 11 October 1620);[69] m. 1) by 1591, Frances, da. Richard Walter, Stafford; e.s. Edward b. 1592; other sons Richard, John, Thomas, James, Carroll and Benjamin, das. Anne, m. Arthur Hill, Mary, m. Patrick Nangle, baron of the Navan; 2) c.2 April 1646, Margaret (d. 1663+), da. Sir Patrick Barnewall, Turvey, w. of Lucas Netterville.[70]
ed. Clement's Inn, Inner Temple 1602; King's Inns, 1610.
Kt. 24 March 1611.
LIKENESSES *Plates 2 & 37* https://www.proantic.com/en/display.php?id=595441#; https://www.whytes.ie/art/portrait-of-sir-richard-bolton-lord-chancellor-of-ireland/165539/?SearchString=&LotNumSearch=&GuidePrice=&OrderBy=&ArtistID=&ArrangeBy=list&Num PerPage=15 & offset=103 [accessed 9 December 2022]

Bolton entered the Inner Temple unusually late and left it unusually soon for a career lawyer, but there is evidence that he practiced law in England in the 1590s and his time at Clement's Inn would also have counted towards his time as a law student. He came to Ireland to avoid a sentence in the Star Chamber Court and quickly obtained prestigious offices, being made recorder of Dublin on a provisional basis in 1604 and confirmed in that position in 1607, which he retained until he resigned in late 1613. As recorder he defended the city's case on customs at Serjeant's Inns in London in 1608, acting against the crown. He developed a

64 McCavitt, '"Good planets in their several spheres"'; Crawford, *Star Chamber*, pp 110, 117, 327n, 501, 509–10, 525, 532–3, 541–3, 548–9; TCD, MS 672, fo. 83r.
65 Ball, *Judges in Ireland*, i, p. 323; Treadwell (ed.), *Irish commission of 1622*, pp 76, 95–6, 130–3.
66 NAI, MS Chancery G353.
67 George Hill, *An historical account of the Plantation in Ulster at the commencement of the seventeenth century, 1608–1610* (Belfast, 1877), pp 489–91.
68 Portrait of Bolton 1620 by a follower of Marcus Gheeraerts gives his age then as 55, at https://www.proantic.com/en/display.php?id=595441#, [accessed 8 Dec. 2022]. This biography is based on Bolton's *DIB* and *Oxford DNB* entries, with additional information.
69 TCD, MS 1,216, fo. 22v; Visitation of Dublin, 1607, NLI, GO, MS 48, pp 14; MS 66, p. 96.
70 Ball, *Judges in Ireland*, ii, p. 338; Charles K. Bolton, *Bolton families in Ireland with their English and American kindred* (Boston, 1937), pp 4–8.

strong professional practice, acting as counsel in cases of tanistry before the king's bench, and that of the dean and chapter of Ferns before the Court of Common Pleas in 1608; he defended Dublin City's customs income in England in the same year.[71] He also served as a judge of assize in the spring of 1609 and was admitted to the King's Inns in 1610, becoming a member of its council by 1619.[72] In 1613 he was returned to parliament for Dublin in a strongly contested and clearly illegal election. In the second parliamentary session he led the successful opposition to a bill to terminate customs exemptions enjoyed by Dublin, Waterford, and Drogheda. Bolton was knighted in 1618 and succeeded Jacob* as solicitor general on 10 February 1619.[73] In the same year he became justice of the Ormond liberty of Tipperary. He had a lucrative private practice.[74] He continued to acquire prestigious and financially attractive appointments: he became attorney general to the newly established Court of Wards in December 1622, with permission to plead in other courts, and he retained his role in the Court of Wards when he became chief baron of the exchequer and *ex officio* a privy councillor, on 29 June 1625. His son Edward succeeded him as solicitor general in 1623. His various appointments kept him very busy (he also acted as a justice of assize between at least 1616 and 1627). Consequently, when he was appointed treasurer of King's Inns at Michaelmas 1628, he was very unusually, if not uniquely, allowed to appoint a deputy to perform that office.[75] In 1643 with the trustees, Donnellan*, Sir William Parsons, William Ryves* and others he had a lease of a house near King's Inns for 41 years.[76]

Bolton's 1621 publication of the statutes passed by the Irish parliament met an urgent need (his 1620 portrait may have been to commemorate his completing that book) and he followed this in 1638 with a manual for the use of justices of the peace in Ireland. In this he instructed justices of the peace, on pain of substantial fines, to report the names of jurors who refused to find defendants guilty of riot where, in the opinion of the state, the evidence indicated that they should do so. He also promoted the prosecution of clothworkers for producing the wrong size of cloth.[77] He was concerned with preventing sexual violence against women and drafted proposals to that effect which may have influenced the unsuccessful bill in the 1640 parliament.[78]

His associations up to Wentworth's arrival in 1633 were with Cork's faction, but he transferred his allegiance to the new deputy and he played a prominent part

71 John Davies, *Le premier report des cases et matters en ley resolues et adiudges en les courts del roy en Irlande* (London, 1628), fos. 42, 48v, 83v; Ratification of lease by William Talbot* to Alderman Thomas Bishop, Dublin by Richard Bolton, 23 May 1610, NAI, MS D. 5,281; Lennon, *Lords of Dublin*, pp 191, 194.
72 King's Inns, MS B1/1, fos. 3v, 13r.
73 HL, HP, MS 15,755, 6 Feb. 1619.
74 Kearney, 'The Irish wine trade'.
75 Hughes, *Patentee officers*; Crawford, *Star Chamber*, pp 349, 532–3; King's Inns, MS B1/1, fo. 18v.
76 Ainsworth (ed.), 'Survey of documents in private keeping: third series', p. 3.
77 Bolton, *Statutes*; Bolton, *Justice of the peace for Ireland*; Crawford, *Star Chamber*, pp 139–41.
78 Crawford, *Star Chamber*, pp 152–3.

in the proceedings of both the Court of Castle Chamber (on which he sat for 14 years) and the Commission for Defective Titles, both instruments of Wentworth's absolutist policies, in which his role, with others, 'damaged the reputation of the Irish court of Star Chamber' with their 'arbitrary manner and officious meddling of his absolutist style', leading to his impeachment in 1641.[79] Despite having served as a trustee for Adam Loftus*, Lord Ely, in settling family property on his eldest son Robert Loftus in 1627, Bolton co-operated with Wentworth in contriving Loftus' downfall and he succeeded him as chancellor in December 1639, conveniently just in time to serve *ex officio* as speaker of the Lords in the parliament which met the following March. He issued a set of 'Directions to be observed in the court of chancery' and commissioned a portrait of himself in his official robes to mark the occasion (*plate 37*).[80] His valuable case notes are preserved in Armagh Robinson Library.[81]

The Bolton family features largely in the will of Richard's fellow MP Humphrey Farnham in 1624; Bolton was bequeathed £5, his wife £2 and a 'maudlin cupp and cover' and their son Edward, a witness to and executor of the will, £50.[82] His many lucrative offices enabled Bolton to purchase property; William Brereton described his house at Brazeel near Swords as 'a dainty, pleasant, high-built wood house, and much right and brave land about it, this placed on the right hand.'[83] He also managed money and investments for relatives; Capt. Thomas Adderley, based in Cork, asked Bolton to buy lands for him or lend the money at 8% until a suitable purchase appeared. Richard refused to lend it, regarding usury as 'unlawful before God' but advised his 'loveing brother' 'to lett the money ly deade a whyle to expect a purchase, for those that sell land for neede wilbe glad of redy money.'[84] On 27 February 1641 the Commons appointed a committee to draw up charges against Bolton, Bramhall, Geratt Lowther and Radcliffe accusing them of high treason, apparently a tactical move to prevent them from appearing as witnesses in Strafford's defence, but also because they had been closely involved in his arbitrary government of Ireland. They attempted to remove the first three

79 See for example his involvement in a marriage settlement with Sir William Parsons in 1620–1. Griffith (ed.), *Calendar of inquisitions*, A29; Crawford, *Star Chamber*, quotation on p. 589. See also pp 118, 121–2, 330–1, 388, 390, 395, 402–10, 550–1, and 102–3 for a summary of his career and actions in that court.

80 Essex County Records Office, Barrett-Lennard Muniments, MS D/DL T28/13, 2 June 1627, calendared in Brian C. Donovan and David Edwards, *British sources for Irish history, 1485–1641: a guide to manuscripts in local, regional and specialized repositories in England, Scotland and Wales* (Dublin, 1997), p. 65. A portrait of Bolton was on sale in 2018. See https://www.whytes.ie/art/portrait-of-sir-richard-bolton-lord-chancellor-of-ireland/165539/?SearchString=&LotNumSearch=&GuidePrice=&OrderBy=&ArtistID=&ArrangeBy=list&NumPerPage=15&offset=103 reproduced as the frontispiece of Bolton, *Bolton families in Ireland*.

81 ARL, MS Richard Bolton's case book.

82 Loeber and McGrath, 'Legacy of Humphrey Farnham'. For maudlin cups, see Philippa Glanville, *Silver in England* (London, 1987), pp 61–2.

83 Simington (ed.), *Civil Survey*, Meath, p. 65; William Brereton's 'Travels' in Falkiner (ed.), *Illustrations*.

84 Bolton to Adderly, 20 April 1630, Boole Library, University College Cork, Kinsale Manorial Papers, UC/KM/PP/U16, nos 14, 15.

from the House of Lords (especially Bolton as speaker, but Lowther was in attendance as a judge) and Radcliffe from the Commons. Bolton's assertion that Poyning's Law prevented their initiating judicial proceedings offended all sides and he was bound over and on 1 March 1641 declared unfit for office by the upper house and replaced temporarily as speaker by William Ryves*.

Despite this, Bolton remained a privy councillor and in that capacity signed the dispatch to the new lord lieutenant advising him of the start of the rebellion in Ireland on 25 October 1641. On 21 June 1642 the 'rump' Commons expelled Catholic members and ordered that all MPs should take the oath of supremacy, removing many of those who had been pressing for the impeachment of Bolton, Bramhall, Lowther and Radcliffe (although Catholics had not been attending the Commons). On the same day the Commons voted unanimously to abandon the impeachment and Bolton was restored as speaker of the upper house. The following October the Irish privy council wrote to Edward Nicholas recommending Bolton and his aged wife and many children and grandchildren, and requesting payment of £1,000 due on his entertainment as his estate had been seized by rebels and he was 'ready to perish through meer want [as he] had for 26 years faithfully served the king and his father, as solicitor general, as an attorny in the Court of Wards, as cheif baron of the exchequer, and as lord chancellor and discharged his duty in all with great ability and integrity.'[85]

Despite his age, Bolton remained active in affairs in Ireland until his death in 1648, advising Ormond in his negotiations with the Confederates in 1643–4, especially concerning the suspension of Poynings' Law and a bill declaring the Irish parliament's independence from its English counterpart. He also signed the proclamation announcing the peace in 1646. He died in 1648 and his widow survived to petition the viceroy, Ormond, for the arrears due to her late husband in 1663.[86] In the archives at Kilkenny Castle is a petition in which Lady Bolton, widow of Sir Richard Bolton, applied in 1663 to the duke of Ormond, then viceroy, for the arrears due to her late husband.

THOMAS BOURKE (*c.*1609 – early March 1643) **Mayo, 1640**

3 s. Walter Bourke, Turlough and Evelyn? Stephenson, Mayo; m. Lettice (1617–1655) only da. Sir Henry Shirley Bart., Stanton Harold, Leicestershire and Lady Dorothy Devereux, da. Robert Devereux (d. 1601), earl of Essex and Frances, da. Sir Francis Walsingham, w. Sir Philip Sidney; son Ulick.
ed. Middle Temple, 1625.

Thomas of Kiranan (now Castlehill), Mayo, was a nephew of Clanricard and his father possessed considerable property in Mayo; as a younger son, his return was due to his work as Clanricard's counsel in England and his marriage tied him more closely to the earl, but also to very prominent English families. His manucaptors were Richard Martin* and John Blake. He was apparently elected while still based in London. He was an active MP, sitting on a number of important committees in

85 Lords Justices and Council to Nicholas, 26 Oct. 1642, Bodl. Lib., Carte MS 68, fo. 471v.
86 *Oxford DNB*.

the first and third sessions including those to draft the declaration to Charles, and as an agent from the parliament to Charles in late 1640 (when he and Plunkett* were believed to have private access to the king) and to treat with the rebels in November 1641.[87] In May 1641 he had been used as a messenger from Charles to Ormond and Antrim, and the king continued to use him as a messenger even after the outbreak of the rebellion. He argued that the intended prorogation in November 1641 was illegal and was thus instrumental in parliament's meeting briefly that month; he was soliciting in favour of the Irish rebels in London in January 1642. He was one of the original supporters of the Confederation, as a member of the 1642 Connacht provincial council, and representative for Galway County in the General Assembly of that year; he was a member of the committee that drew up the model of civil government for Ireland.[88] He should not be confused with Thomas Bourke of Anbally who died in 1648. Clanricard's reliance on and affection for Thomas are expressed in his response to his death ('the sad newes of my Nephew Tho: Burkes death which doth much perplex me being one I had occasion to vallue and in present his imployment doth make his Loss very considerable in many respects, but wee must submitt to the deuine will who hath soe appointed').[89] Thomas' widow married Thomas' cousin, William Bourke (Liam Buuidhe), seventh earl of Clanricard.[90]

PATRICK BOYTON (*c*.1612 – 1666+) **Cashel, 1640**

e.s. Ald. Edward Boyton, Cashel; m. ____; at least 1 da.
ed. Gray's Inn, 1628; King's Inns, 1639.

The Boytons were a notable Cashel family, having settled there by 1384 and provided local officials from as early as 1463; the family is commemorated in the placename Boytonrath, near Cashel.[91] The Boytons had close connections with the local merchant Kearney and Conway families who represented Cashel in previous parliaments. Patrick lived at Thomastown, Tipperary. He had been given 750 acres there by his father and bought a share in a further 2,100 acres.[92] He presumably also inherited the property at Ballytarsny (Ballyturneyhmacoris) that his father bought from Lord Dunboyne. Boyton was an active committee man and chair of the Commons' committee on his Tipperary neighbour Piers Butler.[93] There is no other evidence of his practicing as a lawyer, but his membership of the King's Inns suggests he may well have had a local practice.

87 Perceval-Maxwell, *Outbreak*, pp 59, 75, 90, 106, 136, 140, 198, 243.
88 Bodl. Lib., Carte MS 68, fo. 1r.
89 Clanricard to Ormond, 11 March 1643, Bodl. Lib., Carte MS 4, fo. 458.
90 G.E.C., *Peerage*. I am grateful to Kenneth Nicholls for information about Thomas' mother and wife, which corrects statements made in McGrath, 'Bio. dict.'.
91 Edmund Curtis (ed.), *Calendar of Ormond deeds, Volume II* (Dublin, 1934), p. 197; *idem*, *Calendar of Ormond deeds, Volume III* (Dublin, 1935), pp 195, 270, 327; *idem*, *Calendar of Ormond deeds, Volume V* (Dublin, 1941), p. 40. A stone, probably dating to the fifteenth century, bearing the Boyton arms, is on display in the museum on the Rock of Cashel.
92 Edward had dealings with Cork about Hore Abbey on the outskirts of Cashel. Edward Boyton to Cork, 23 June 1625, NLI, MS 13,237 (10); Simington (ed.), *Civil Survey*, Tipperary, i, p. 241; ii, p. 21.
93 Bodl. Lib., Carte MS 64, fos. 458–65.

Other members of the family, including Patrick and Paul, sons of Alderman Alex Boyton, and a Piers Boyton, took command of the Irish in Cashel after a number of murders there in the early days of the rebellion. Patrick and Piers escorted the local Protestants to Clonmel, presumably for their safety, but this Patrick Boyton was not expelled from parliament in 1642 and appears to have not taken part in the upheavals of the 1640s.[94] In January 1650 Patrick petitioned Ormond claiming that he was cessed in Cashel with 30 soldiers from Hugh Maguire's regiment for bedding, fire and candlelight, but had nowhere to reside within the town, except to continue billeting his troops on the townspeople who had appealed to the authorities for their removal. This was clearly causing trouble, as the troops had no place to go, no support and were effectively robbing local tenants of food and other goods. He also stated that 'Forasmuch as it is fitter for your petitioner to cesse the said soldiers upon his own tenants, than uppon strangers, being the generall course taken within all Corporations and that by the law of arms, soldiers should not abandon their garrisons' and asked Ormond to let him distribute the soldiers among his tenants and to allow him to billet any soldiers cessed on him in the city of Cashel allowing them out of their rents. Ormond referred the petition to John Walshe* as chief justice of Munster and Peter Bryan to consider and certify their opinion and concurred with their opinion that if the property was not in his possession, he could have soldiers cessed on him.[95]

He was transplanted to 537 acres in Roscommon and was living at Clonfee, Cluncraffe, there in 1659.[96] In December 1660, the former inhabitants of Cashel sent for Boyton, intending to elect him as MP when parliament was summoned, but the town's Protestant freemen who refused to hand over the houses in the town to their former Catholic owners frustrated this plan. In 1664 the Court of Claims decided that he should have a final settlement of his affairs and allowed his claim against Birmingham. He signed the 1666 petition to Charles II.[97]

ROGER BRERETON (*c.*1616 – 1659+) **Old Leighlin, 1640**

5 s. Henry Brereton (d. 1627), Loughtige and Shanemullen, Queen's County, and Margery, da. Robert Bowen, Queen's County; m. ____ Bulkeley.
ed. Lincoln's Inns, 1632; King's Inns, 1638.

The Breretons and Bowens settled in Queen's County in the mid-sixteenth century, and Roger's uncle Arthur represented Ballinakill in 1613. His family connections were wide: he addressed Thomas Piggott as 'worthy cozen'. His wife was a Bulkeley who provided links with the Aungiers and Bishop Spottiswood and his sons married members of his neighbouring settler family of Blount. The extent of his legal practice is unclear, but as a student in Lincoln's Inns he had 'a care of Sir Thomas Butler's business' in London and both he and Eustace were paid for advice on St Anne's Guild's case in parliament in 1643 and 1644, despite the

94 TCD, MS 821, fos. 7, 211v, 221v, 227r, 245r, 259.
95 Bodl. Lib., Carte MS 156, pp 425–8.
96 R.C. Simington (ed.), *The transplantation to Connacht, 1654–58* (Dublin, 1970), pp 261, 272, 275.
97 *Cal. S.P. Ire., 1660–2*, p. 113; Tallon (ed.), *Court of Claims*, p. 435; TNA, SP 63/346, fo. 192.

obvious conflict of interest.[98] He lived in Dublin and Tallaght (where the Bulkeleys also lived), and was resident in Fishamble Street in 1646, where he was one of those estimating the cess for the Parliament; his own assessment was for 10*s*.[99] At this time he was also helping transmit the imprisoned Glamorgan's letters – the earl described him as 'my cousin' – at Thomas Piggott's request. With Culme and Schout, he travelled to England on parliament's business, returning in May 1647. Between 1649 and 1653 he was recorder of Drogheda and he was, with Lewis*, one of the most active lawyers in chancery in the 1650s, when Bramhall paid him £128 for legal services.[100] He was living in Templeogue in 1659. He should not be confused with his cousin and namesake, the parson of Ballinakill.

GEOFFREY BROWNE (-1610 – 14 January 1668) **Athenry, 1640**

e.s. Sir Dominic Browne (d. 1656+), Galway and Carrowbrowne, and Anastasia, da. James Rivagh Darcy and Elizabeth, da. Richard Martin (Elizabeth rem. Sir Henry Lynch*, Galway); m. before 1633, Mary, da. Sir Henry Lynch*, Galway; 5s. (Dominic), 1 da. Julian.
ed. Middle Temple, 1627; King's Inns, 1637.
Bur. St Nicholas', Dublin.

Geoffrey was a member of a prominent Galway family with strong connections with Athenry; his great grandfather Dominick, who had been agent for the town under Elizabeth, had been accused of embezzling much of the land granted to the town, while Geoffrey's father was MP for Athenry in 1634. Apart from his business as a merchant, Dominic Browne had been building up a substantial property portfolio in Galway and Mayo and was Mayor in 1634–5.[101] Geoffrey had close connections with other members of Galway's urban oligarchy, especially the Lynches. He was Henry Lynch's* step-son and son-in-law, Darcy's* nephew and Roebuck Lynch's* cousin and brother-in-law. He also had family links with Martin* and the Blakes and, through his sister Jennet's marriage, with the Dillons of Clonbrock. Richard Martin and Roebuck Lynch were his manucaptors in the Middle Temple, where he studied for seven years, practicing in England until he returned home by 1637 when he joined the King's Inns and developed his legal practice in Ireland, including as a legal advisor to Galway corporation and Richard Burke, earl of Clanricard. Like his father, Geoffrey was an alderman of Galway from 1637 and was described in the list of councillors as one of the 'councell learned in the laws, members of the said Towne Council' between 1643 and 1646 at least. He owned at least two fine houses in Galway town in 1641 and had an interest in a lease of some of Richard Martin's property.[102]

Sir Dominic lived until at least 1656, but after his experience of the 1634 parliament and more especially as a member of the Galway jury that refused to find the king's title to land in Galway, he presumably, like Darcy and Martin,

98 Edward Comerford to Ormond, 2 April 1636, NLI, MS 2,305, p. 23; RIA, MS 12/D/1, pp 162–4.
99 Mills (ed.), *Registers of St John the Evangelist*, p. 276.
100 Barnard, 'Lawyers and the law'; Bramhall to ?, addressed to 'My Lords', *c.*1659, HL, HP, MS 14,068.
101 Ó Bric, 'Galway townsmen', pp 242, 261–2, 271, 442.
102 Brown and Ó Siochrú, 'Cromwellian urban civil surveys'; Tallon (ed.), *Court of Claims*, p. 137.

refused to stand in 1640, leaving his son to take his place. Geoffrey was clearly a man of great ability and both his parliamentary and Confederate careers attest to his talents and the esteem in which he was held by all sides. As an experienced and respected lawyer, he was an active MP, sitting on many committees, including that to draft the declaration of support for the king in the first session. Three lawyers connected with Clanricard (Bourke*, Browne* and Roebuck Lynch*) formed the backbone of the opposition in the first session, with Edward Fitzharris* and Nicholas Plunkett.* All except Fitzharris were members of the committee to England in November 1640. Browne, Plunkett and Fitzharris were members of the subcommittee formed to decide on the fate of the bill for the plantation of Connacht on 8 June 1640. Browne and Simon Digby brought back the king's letter of 3 April 1641, which contained instructions to give effect to the concessions they had negotiated and clearly formed a close bond. In that summer he was engaged in recruiting Irish soldiers for service in Spain.[103]

On the outbreak of the 1641 rising, Browne and Darcy argued persuasively against proroguing parliament, although there is no mention of him as attending the Commons in November.[104] Both returned to Galway and Geoffrey was involved in negotiating for the town with Clanricard in May 1642, and he and John Blake were hostages to the earl for the good behaviour of Galway City. Like so many others, he was a very reluctant rebel, aiming to uphold Charles' authority in Ireland and England.[105] He was elected to the first Confederate supreme council on 11 November 1642 and was a member of consecutive supreme councils until February 1646.

One of the Confederates' principal negotiators with Ormond, he served on all of the negotiating committees between May 1643 and 1648–9 and was resident member for Connacht in 1644; an agent to meet Ormond at Kilcullen and Castlemartin, he brought peace proposals from the General Assembly to Charles in 1643 and signed the Glamorgan peace in Oxford in 1645.[106] He was an important link between the Confederation and Clanricard and, with Darcy*, drew up articles of peace with Ormond in 1646. A prominent member of the 'peace party', like others he had a vested interest in agreeing a peace treaty, hoping to benefit from the patronage of both Ormond (as he subsequently did) and Clanricard.[107] Rinuccini ordered his arrest in Galway for supporting this agreement, but the citizens refused to hand him over to the nuncio 'for he being a gentleman allied to the prime men in the town, and generally dear to all the inhabitants, by reason of the merit of his fair carriage and abilities, they were no way inclined to put his life into the power of his enemies, although they thought

103 Clarke, *Old English*, pp 129–30; Borlase, *History*, p. 10; Perceval-Maxwell, *Outbreak*, pp 75, 90, 136, 142, 185.
104 Clarke, *Old English*, p. 171.
105 Tadhg Ó hAnnracháin, *Catholic reformation in Ireland: the mission of Rinnuccini, 1645–1649* (Cambridge, 2002), pp 74, 81, 128.
106 Thomas de Burgo, *Hibernia Dominicana* (Cologne, 1762), p. 424.
107 Ó hAnnracháin, *Catholic reformation in Ireland*, pp 34, 153.

fit to pay their obedience to the commands of the Council and congregation so far as to restrain him of his liberty.'[108] His fellow citizens' respect for him was widely shared, as his successive appointments as negotiator in Ireland, England and France demonstrate.

With Antrim, he was sent as a Confederate agent to France in November 1647 and they arrived in March 1648 to treat with Henrietta Maria and the Prince of Wales, where they co-operated with Ormond. He was one of the small committee who selected the new supreme council of December 1647, and was named a supernumerary member. Browne and Muskerry, both at this point 'deeply distrusted by Rinucinni', wrote to the Supreme Council giving the final answers from the English and French courts, and expressing their 'faire hopes of settling the Kingdome, if they be wise' and 'complaininge of the E. of Antrim's keeping at a distance from them all the while takeing ways of his own.'[109]

Geoffrey was back in Kilkenny later in 1648 when he was one of the Connacht representatives selected to treat for peace with Ormond and signed the second Ormond peace of 17 January 1649. In June 1649 he was appointed one of the commissioners of trust who took office under that treaty in place of the last Confederate supreme council. He was incorrectly reported dead of the plague at Galway in February 1650 and five months later he and Darcy* were commissioners to advise Ormond on petitions from Galway. On 25 June 1650 he was among the agents Ormond appointed to negotiate with an agent from Charles, duke of Lorraine, who had offered aid against the forces of the English parliament and in the following year Clanricard, as Ormond's deputy, named Browne, Plunkett and Theobald Taaffe as agents to treat further with Lorraine in the Netherlands. He reached Brussels on 12 June 1651 and signed an agreement with Lorraine on 22 July. Clanricard, Charles II and Ormond rejected the treaty with Clanricard accusing Browne and his colleagues of betraying their trust.[110]

Browne returned to Ireland in October 1651. On 12 August 1652 the parliamentarians excepted Geoffrey and Darcy from pardon for life and estate, but their lives were preserved by the articles of surrender of Galway. Browne was heir to his father's extensive lands in counties Galway and Mayo which were partially confiscated in 1653; in May of that year he was in London, pleading for his fellow townsmen to be allowed to remain in Galway and have the benefit of the articles of surrender agreed with Charles Coote. Despite being imprisoned in the Gatehouse at Westminster, Browne continued to press the case until he was deported back to Ireland that November, after which the townsmen appointed Richard Blake as their agent. Geoffrey was the only Catholic returned (for Tuam)

108 John Lowe (ed.), *The letter-book of the earl of Clanricarde, 1643–47* (Dublin, 1983), pp 127–8, 157, 209–10, 246–8, 259, 273, 348–9, 468, 476; Lodge, *Desiderata Curiosa*, ii, pp 384–5.

109 Muskerry and Browne to the Supreme Council, 10 June 1648, Bodl. Lib., Carte MS 59, fo. 473v; Ó hAnnracháin, *Catholic reformation in Ireland*, p. 169.

110 A copie of her Majestie's answer to the Commissioners imployed by the Lord of Clanricard to the duke of Loraine, in HMC, *Fourteenth report of the Royal Commission on Historical Manuscripts: Appendix, Part VII* (London, 1895), p. 99.

to the 1661 parliament, but was unseated in a second election. He resumed his role as agent for Galway's townsmen in seeking the Restoration of their lands.[111] Geoffrey himself had recovered some property by 1655, but, although an order was issued for the Restoration of his family estates in January 1661, with Ormond's support, his family did not receive the property until after his death, when his personal property was estimated at £2,000.

RICHARD BUTLER (*c.*1580 – d.1644+) **Waterford, 1640**

s. Thomas FitzGerald, Waterford; m. by 1640, ____; at least 3 s.
ed. Clifford's Inn, Inner Temple, 1596; King's Inns, 1607.

Richard held lands in Waterford County and City, and lived at Ringogona and Ballykene, Waterford. Like his father he was a freeman of Waterford. He returned to Ireland in 1602 from his legal studies, and, as a nephew of Richard Aylward, was recommended to Carew by Sir George Buckhurst. He was recorder of Waterford, sheriff of the city in 1611 and mayor in 1636; he was a member of the 1624–5 commission of the peace for Waterford County. He shared a chamber in the old friar's hall in the King's Inns with the Kilkenny lawyer Michael Cowley. Richard Wadding* and he were the two 'silenced lawyers' who were imprisoned in Dublin Castle for advising Waterford Corporation in its case against the administration's attack on its charter in 1617.[112] Richard was one of the trustees chosen by John Everard* in a settlement of his estates on his eldest son in 1620.[113] He was a member of the 1624–5 commission of the peace for Waterford County. As agent for the recusants in England in 1628, he also presented a petition concerning Waterford's Charter. In 1634 the 1630 mayor Robert Wise of Credan petitioned Wentworth claiming Richard inflicted 'injuries, wrongs and abuses' against him at the county members' election; the deputy commissioned four local Waterford lawyers including James Walshe* to investigate the claims. The outcome is unclear, but regardless it did not lessen the esteem in which Butler was held by his fellow citizens, as he was elected mayor in 1636 and then MP.[114] In 1642 Richard was active in persuading the city to join the rebellion and with his sons John and Thomas was listed as a rebel. He may have been a member of the 1644 General Assembly. His son, Sir James, was an MP in England in 1685.[115]

JOHN BYSSE (Bisse) (1602 – 28 January 1680) **Charlemont, 1634**
Dublin, 1640; Dublin Co., 1656; Dublin City, 1660 Convention

e.s. Christopher Bysse (d. 1614), Dublin, and Margaret (d. 1641), da. Ald. John Foster, Dublin; m. by 1641, Margaret, da. Francis Edgeworth, w. John King; many children but only Judith survived him.[116]

111 Cunningham, *Conquest and land in Ireland*, pp 59–63, 71, 91, 115, 124–5.
112 King's Inns, MS B1/1, fo. 108v; Crawford, *Star Chamber*, pp 328–9; *APC, 1616–17*, pp 311–14.
113 Jennings (ed.), *Wadding Papers*, p. 239; NAI, MS RC 4/11, pp 457–60, 489, 500–1.
114 TCD, MS 672, fo. 183r; Empey (ed.), *Early Stuart Irish warrants*, pp 160–1.
115 J.S. Crossette, 'Butler, Sir James' in Henning (ed.), *History of parliament*.
116 NLI, GO, MS 72, Funeral Entries, Volume 9, 1640–63, pp 19, 225, 281.

ed. Trinity College, Dublin; Lincoln's Inns, 1624; Bar, 1631; King's Inns, 1632, 1636.[117]
Bur. St Audeon's, Dublin.

John was still a minor when his father, second remembrancer of the exchequer, died and his wardship was granted to Sir Francis Annesley, Lord Mountnorris. He received livery of his father's estate in 1623 and he held 579 acres in Dublin, including Preston's Inns, where he lived, and property at Swords and Philipstown, King's County, as well as some tithes in Dublin and Meath. He was also a tenant on Lord Hastings' estate in Tyrone.[118] He was well-connected with other prominent Dublin families, especially through his mother and his uncle Robert Bysse of Ballyowen, King's County, who married a daughter of the Dublin alderman, John Lany, father-in-law of Sir William Parsons. His marriage linked him to other administration families, as Francis Edgeworth was clerk of the crown in chancery and King was clerk of the hanaper.

John had a large legal practice and succeeded Catlin as recorder of Dublin in 1634 (the year in which he was made freeman), a position he held until 1661; curiously, he is recorded as being admitted twice to the King's Inns.[119] He was a justice of assize in Munster from 1636 and two years later Wentworth referred a petition of Thomas Bramley against Robert Coop to arbitration by Bysse as recorder and James Watson as mayor of Dublin. Around the same time Samuel Smith and his wife Joane complained to the deputy about John but he was judged blameless.[120]

Bysse and his younger brother Robert* were among the most active members of the 1640 parliament and leaders of the opposition, perhaps irritated by the treatment of St Ann's Guild; however, they did not sign the letter of other opposition MPs to the English parliament in November 1640. Their involvement extended to the 'rump' parliament, as part of a tight group of Dublin recruiter MPs with whom they had studied at Lincoln's Inns and with whom they worked to protect the interests of St Ann's Guild.[121] With William Parsons, Adam Loftus*, James Ware, Nicholas Barnewall* and others he was engaged in collecting the first parliamentary subsidies in 1640.[122] John continued to work as a lawyer during the 1640s and 1650s, together with his parliamentary duties in Ireland and England. He was admitted to William Ryves' chambers in the King's Inns in June 1643 and continued to be involved in the Inns as a member of its council.[123] He was reported to be collecting money for Trinity College, Dublin in England in the 1640s and was also working hard to defend Percival's Irish interests in 1647.

117 King's Inns, MS B1/1, fos. 19v, 47r.
118 NAI, MS D 2,346; Rent roll of Hastings' lands, 1638, HL, HP, Box 76 (4).
119 Gilbert, *C. A. R.*, iii, pp 295, 301–2.
120 NAI, MS M. 2,448, pp 256–8, 280–2.
121 Perceval-Maxwell, *Outbreak*, pp 74–5, 80, 88, 128, 130, 133–4, 156, 244; McGrath, 'Recruiter returns'.
122 Empey (ed.), *Early Stuart Irish warrants*, p. 209.
123 King's Inns, MS B1/1, fo. 112r; Kenny, 'Black Book of King's Inns', notes a case in the Connacht Presidency Court involving Bysse and others. Peter Gaunt (ed.), *The correspondence of Henry Cromwell, 1655–1659* (Cambridge, 2008), pp 463–4.

Bysse served on the 1651 Leinster commission of the peace and was collecting the Dublin contributions for the Assessment for Ireland in the last quarter of 1654.[124] Fleetwood proposed him as a judge for Leinster in that year, a suggestion repeated three years later by Richard Pepys who described him as 'a man of learninge and integrity'.[125] Neither proposal, nor Henry Cromwell's recommendation that he be made a puisne judge, was acted on and he worked as an assistant in the courts rather than as a judge, although he seems to have served as a justice of assize in Ulster in 1655. In 1656 he was elected MP for Dublin City, defeating the army officers John Jones and John Hewson. Henry Cromwell scotched attempts to have him excluded. Bysse sat on parliament's Irish committee and was reported to have supported moves to make Oliver Cromwell monarch; he was one of the original trustees of the Erasmus Smith Schools in 1657.[126] Henry Cromwell again recommended him for the bench in 1659. He was living in Castle Street, Dublin, in 1660. Despite his collusion with the Cromwellian regime, he was part of the movement of old office-holders to promote the Restoration through the convention. He was a commissioner for the Poll Money Ordnance in Dublin City and County in 1660 and in the county in the following year.

He was appointed chief baron of the exchequer in 1660 (*plate 11*) and held that position until his death, with Ormond's support despite repeated charges of insufficiency (he also remained on good terms with Bramhall), also serving as justice of assize for Leinster. He was sworn a privy councillor in January 1661 and served on a series of commissions, on the land settlement in the 1660s and on the Irish royal revenue in the 1670s and was reappointed trustee of the Erasmus Smith Schools.[127] His attendance at the funeral of the nonconformist preacher Joseph Teate in 1666 indicates that he retained his Puritan inclinations.

ROBERT BYSSE (Bisse) (1607–11 – 29 August 1643) **Roscommon, 1640**
2.s. Christopher Bysse (d. 1614), Dublin, and Margaret (d. 1641), da. Ald. John Foster, Dublin.[128]
ed. Lincoln's Inns, 1627; King's Inns, 1636.

Robert's father and grandfathers were officials of the exchequer and his parents' connections were firmly among the capital's ruling merchant families and crown officials. Robert's links with other MPs were strong – the Edgeworths provided extensive networks of connections, quite apart from his brother John* and their cousin John Taylor*.[129] He was recorder of Drogheda but clearly that town refused to elect him, and his return for Roscommon was due to his family's links with important local settler families through his sister-in-law Margaret Edgeworth, the widow of John King and his sister Dorothy's marriage to Michael Pinnock of

124 Marsh's Library, MS Z3.1.1, no. 68 (1651).
125 Bodl. Lib., Carte MS 63, fo. 618.
126 Patrick Little, 'Irish representation in the protectorate parliaments', *Parl. Hist.*, 22 (2004), 336–56; BL, Egerton MS 2,651, fo. 232; Robert Armstrong, 'Bysse (Bisse), John', *DIB*.
127 HL, HP, Box 75 (17); HL, HP, MS 14,142.
128 NLI, GO, MS 72, Funeral Entries, Volume 9, 1640–63, p. 281.
129 Account of the rebellion in a letter to his brother John*, 16 Feb. 1642, TCD, MS 840, fos. 7r–10v, refers to his 'uncle Taylor' and John.

Turnich. The Pinnocks also had ties to the Yorkshire network within the administration, as Michael's grandson, Talbot Osbaldstone, who lived with him, was presumably related to the attorney general, Radcliffe's* brother-in-law.[130]

GEORGE CAREY (c.1588 – 22 April 1640) Londonderry City, 1613; Londonderry Co., 1634
2 s. George Carey (d. 1601–2), Clovelly, Devon and his second wife Katharine ____; m. 1) by 1616, Jane, da. Tristram Beresford Sr, Coleraine, and Susannah Brooke, London; 5s. Francis, George, Edward, Robert, Tristram; das. Lettice, Elizabeth, Ann, Mary (plus others that died young).[131]
ed. Middle Temple, 7 February 1606.
Bur. Moville Church, Donegal.

Carey came to Ireland in 1611 as a servant of the Irish Society of London and was appointed founding alderman in Londonderry's charter of 1613 and recorder, a position he retained until his death; he was granted 500 acres at a rent of £5 6*s.* 8*d.* in lieu of a salary.[132] He may have been the man of that name who, with Thomas Cheetham, discovered arrears of rent in Cork in 1611; they were granted half of the sum owing.[133] George was active in local affairs, as commissioner of musters in 1615, collector of fines in Londonderry in 1616 and justice of the peace in 1624–5; three years later he was a commissioner to raise money for the army and commissioner for Londonderry and County Derry for managing the export of corn to England, 1631.[134] As recorder, he was closely involved in the Star Chamber case against the London companies in the 1630s, but he also worked as a lawyer for Lord Chichester in the 1630s.[135] Carey's father-in-law, Tristram Beresford, was the utterly corrupt agent of the Irish Society in Coleraine and Londonderry.[136] He leased church property in Armagh and County Derry and acquired further property in Donegal where he lived at Redcastle on the Inishowen Peninsula. He brought a sword to the 1630 muster on Viscount Chichester's Donegal estate. George had land deals with his fellow planters Beresford, the Rowleys and William Gage.[137]

130 Deposition of Michael Pinnock (Pennock), 19 April 1643, TCD, MS 830, fo. 20r.

131 TNA, MS PROB 11/99/464; TCD, MS 1,216, fo. 65r; NLI, GO, MS 72, Funeral Entries, Volume 9, 1640–63, pp 33, 79, 96; Lodge, *Peerage*, ii, p. 297.

132 *A concise view of the origin, constitution and proceedings of the Honourable Society of the Governor and Assistants of London of the new plantation in Ulster* (London, 1822), pp xx, 47. James Ussher pressed Bramhall to appoint his nephew by marriage, Christopher Elliott, as recorder on George's death. See Ussher to Bramhall, 7 May 1640, HL, HP, MS 15,958.

133 Chichester to H.M. Counsel learned in the laws, 20 Dec. 1611, HL, HP, Box 3 (38).

134 TCD, MS 672, fo. 188r; Caulfield (ed.), *Youghal*, pp 163, 166.

135 Jane Ohlmeyer, 'Strafford, the "Londonderry business" and "New British history"' in J.F. Merritt (ed.), *The political world of Thomas Wentworth, earl of Strafford, 1621–1641* (Cambridge, 1996), pp 216–29; Clarke, McGrath and Edwards (eds), *A lord justice's letter book*, no. 179; Bramhall to Edward, Lord Chichester, 28 Oct. 1634, HL, HP, MS 14,046.

136 McGrath, 'Starting from scratch'.

137 Moody and Simms (eds), *Bishopric of Derry*, i, pp 205–6, 217, 281; Simington (ed.), *Civil Survey*, Donegal, pp 7, 15, 90, 152, 207, 241; L.P. Murray, 'A rent-roll of all the houses and lands belonging to the see of Armagh, 1620', *Archivium Hibernicum*, 8 (1941), 99–120; The Great Parchment Book of the City of Londonderry, fos. 11v–12v, 16v, at https://www.greatparchmentbook.org/ [accessed 27 April 2022]; R.J. Hunter (ed.), *'Men and arms': the Ulster settlers, c.1630* (Belfast, 2012), p. 140; HL, HP, MS 14,047.

Carey was an active member of both parliaments, sitting on the committees for the bills against fraudulent conveyances, for the City and County of Londonderry, Piers Lacy and Eustace's bills, and Tyrone's attainder in 1614. He also contributed regularly to debates, presented a petition on behalf of the bishop of Dromore and was appointed by the house 'to view such acts as are not printed, to desire the lords deputy, that such as be not printed, and fit to be published, should be printed'.[138] In 1634–5 George was a member of very many committees on legislation, including bills against bigamy and buggery, ease of pleading troublesome suits and that to recommend legislation as well as conference committees with the lords.

NATHANIEL CATLIN (Catelin, Catlyn) (c.1589 – 5 April 1637) Dublin, 1634 (Speaker)
2 s. Richard Catelyn (d. 11 March 1601), Wolverston Hall, Suffolk, and Dionysia, da. Thomas Marsh;[139] m. 1) Maria Turner (d. 28 July 1625);[140] 2) Rebecca (d. 1681),[141] da. William Thimbleby, Dublin and Alice da. Richard Clark of Chimpton Hall; she rem. firstly Moncke and later Sir Erasmus Borroughs.
ed. Emmanuel College, Cambridge, 1601; Lincoln's Inns, 1605; King's Inns, 1622.
Kt. 18 April 1635.
Bur. St Nicholas' Church, Dublin, 11 April 1637.[142]

Catlin may have fled to Ireland after taking part in a serious affray in Staple Inn in 1622 and was admitted to the King's Inns that Hilary Term.[143] He was appointed second serjeant-at-law in 1627, with an annual salary of £20. He was upset to have lost Chancellor Loftus' support and received sympathy from Falkland who noted that he was 'to be putt to abide the brunt of a double, and yet powerful malice.' As recorder of Dublin from 1623 to 1634, he was involved in the city's dispute with the lords justices about the billeting of soldiers and despite Falkland's support was removed from the post of serjeant, although he was later restored after Falkland's intercessions to Lord Dorchester. He was a commissioner for Dublin City for managing the export of corn to England in 1631.[144] Catlin had an extensive legal practice, advising Falkland in his Star Chamber case against Sir Arthur Savage in 1630, in chancery cases and as counsel for Cork, for Francis Howard and Nicholas Teott, lessees of Lord Hastings against Sir George Hamilton, at the Irish privy council, 18 February 1632, for the Crown in the privy council's case on Dillon's

138 *Commons' Jn. Ire.*, 6 May 1615.
139 Francis Blomefield, *An essay towards a topographical history of the county of Norfolk: volume 8* at www.british-history.ac.uk/report.aspx?compid=78399, [accessed 27 April 2022].
140 Fitzgerald and Lamacraft (eds), *Some funeral entries of Ireland*, p. 127; TCD, MS 1,216, fo. 30v; Bernard Burke, *The general armory of England, Scotland, Ireland and Wales* (London, 1884), p. 177.
141 *Peerage*, at www.thepeerage.com/p17456.htm, viewed 17 September 2010.
142 John O'Hart, *The Irish and Anglo-Irish landed gentry when Cromwell came* (Dublin, 1892), p. 43.
143 https://theclergydatabase.org.uk/jsp/DisplayOrdination.jsp?CDBOrdRedID=186638 [accessed 15 March 2020]; Baker, *Inns of Chancery*, pp 214–18, 288; King's Inns, MS B1/1, fo. 15r. Unusually, the precise date was not given.
144 Falkland to Catlin, 10 Jan. 1630, NAI, MS 2,445, pp 35–7; same to same, 23 Feb. 1630, ibid., p. 59, same to same, 18 April 1630, ibid., p. 75; Gilbert, *C.A.R.*, iii, pp 153, 155, 296, 300, 302; Caulfield (ed.), *Youghal*, pp 160–7; Hart, *History of the king's serjeants at law*, pp 54–5.

defective titles and was ordered to act for Gifford in the Loftus* case in 1637.[145] Wentworth commended his service as speaker: '[he] deserveth passing well, having discharged the place not only with good affections, but with good abilities also.' As a result, the viceroy knighted him on parliament's dissolution and granted him £500 in compensation for loss of income during his office.[146] Catlin was also a commissioner to find the king's title to lands in Idough in 1635 and the administration's counsel in finding crown title to Roscommon in the same year, for which Wentworth commended him as having 'performed his part also very excellently well'.[147] He lived at Swords and died on circuit at the Cavan assizes.

GARRETT (Gerald) CHEEVERS (*c.*1612 – d. 1642+) **Bannow, 1640**

3 s. Christopher Cheevers (d. 1640),[148] Macetown, Meath, and Anne (or Eleanor) Plunkett (d. 1636), da. Christopher Nugent, Lord Delvin; m. by August 1636, Katherine Anne, da. Hamon Cheevers, Killyan, Wexford, and Elizabeth Masterson.[149]
ed. Middle Temple, 1628; King's Inns, 1635.

The Cheevers were a respected Old English family, based originally in Meath, but a fifteenth-century marriage brought lands in Wexford and the family was thereafter settled in both counties, with considerable contact and inter-marriage between the two branches. Two members of the Wexford branch provided MPs for Wexford in 1634. Garrett's return is explained by his marriage to his cousin, whose family owned extensive lands in Bannow Parish. Through his mother, he was Nugent's* cousin and connected with Dempsey, Forth and Lords Inchiquin and Kildare. As Garrett Cheevers of Ballyhealy, he was indicted for rebellion. His older brother John married Bellings' sister and represented Clonmines in the General Assembly. His brother-in-law Arthur Cheevers was a member of the 1644 General Assembly.[150] Garrett continued to use his membership of the Middle Temple and was being pursued for not paying for his meals in 1639; the amount of the time suggests he was in London for extended periods of time.[151] He was a member of the parliamentary committee which drew up charges of impeachment against Radcliffe* and others; Borlase noted that he and 'many of the active men of the house' supported the proposal to keep Irish soldiers in Ireland rather than send them to Spain.[152]

MARCUS CHEEVERS (1590 – 1653+) **Wexford Co., 1634**

e.s. Christopher Cheevers (d. 29 January 1604), Wexford;[153] m. 1) by 1635, ____.
ed. Lincoln's Inns, 1618; King's Inns, 1628.

145 Falkland to Catlin, 16 May 1630, NAI, MS 2,445, p. 85; HL, HP, Box 5 (4); Ohlmeyer, 'Records'.
146 Wentworth to Coke, 7 April 1635, in Knowler (ed.), *Letters and dispatches*, i, p. 404.
147 Smith (ed.), *Herbert Correspondence*, p. 90; Wentworth to Coke, 14 July 1635, in Knowler (ed.), *Letters and dispatches*, i, pp 442, 444.
148 Christopher's 1623 patent for a baronetcy was never enrolled. Tallon (ed.), *Court of Claims*, p. 63.
149 Fitzgerald and Lamacraft (eds), *Some funeral entries of Ireland*, p. 6.
150 Katherine Cheevers' brother Arthur married Garrett's sister. TCD, MS 819, fo. 4r.
151 McGrath, 'Ireland and the third university'.
152 Borlase, *History*, p. 8.
153 *Inq. cancel. Hib. repert.*, i, Wexford, Jac. I. (48).

Sir William Brereton was entertained by Cheevers during his 1635 tour of Ireland, describing him as 'a well-bred gentleman, an inns-of-court man, who is a counsellor, a gentleman that hath an estate in the country, and was knight of this shire for last Parliament', but was less impressed by 'his wife [also] Irish, in a strange habit, a threadbare short coat with sleeves, made like my green coat of stuff, reaching to her middle; she knew not how to carve, look, entertain, or demean herself. Here was a kind of beer (which I durst not taste) called charter beer, mighty thick, muddy stuff; the meat nothing well cooked or ordered.' Marcus, as mayor of Wexford, with the sheriff, accompanied Brereton and the judge to the church door before attending mass himself.[154] Marcus inherited property in Shelmaiere and Forth baronies and leased church property in the county; with others, he was a defendant in a Chancery case of 1622 about property and was a member of the 1624–5 Wexford commission of the peace. He practiced in chancery from 1628.[155] He was a commissioner for Wexford town and county for managing the export of corn to England in 1631.[156] In 1616 he borrowed £240 on bond on the staple.[157] His comment as attorney for the widow of Wexford ship's captain Robert Esmond who died in 1634, allegedly as a result of being assaulted by Wentworth whose goods he had refused to transport because his ship was already full, that 'it was a greater offence in the Lord Deputy than in a private man' led to his prosecution in the Star Chamber, a personal fine of £1,000 and being required to pay part of the collective damages of £5,000 to Strafford. The deputy's enmity may explain Marcus' absence from the 1640 parliament.[158] An active supporter of the Confederation, he was a judge in Wexford and a member of two General Assemblies and the 1648 provincial council; his brother Nicholas was mayor of Wexford in 1641–2 and a key figure in persuading the town to join the rebellion.[159] Ormond decided in Marcus' favour in his 1649 dispute with Catherine, widow of John Colclough, on behalf of her son Adam about lands he had purchased from John.[160]

PETER CLINTON (Clynton) (c.1598 – 1661+) **Dundalk, 1634**

e.s. Thomas Clinton (d. -1637), Dowdstown (Doodstown, Dardistown); m. by 1617, Margaret Bellew, 3 s., 2 da.[161]

ed. Lincoln's Inns, 1614; King's Inns, 1628.

154 William Brereton's 'Travels' in Falkiner (ed.), *Illustrations*.
155 TCD, MS 672, fo. 178v; Ohlmeyer, 'Records'.
156 Caulfield (ed.), *Youghal*, pp 161, 164.
157 NAI, MS Chancery, BB85; TCD, MS 672, fo. 178v; Ohlmeyer and Ó Ciardha (eds), *Irish statute staple*.
158 Crawford, *Star Chamber*, p. 369; Piers Crosby and Lord Laurence Esmond were fined £4,000 and £3,000 respectively. Clarke, 'Sir Piers Crosby'.
159 TCD, MS 818, fos. 9r–11r, 138–9, 176–8; Ó Siochrú, *Confederate Ireland*, pp 256–7; Bellings and Gilbert (eds), *History of the Irish Confederation*, vi, pp 261–2; de Burgo, *Hibernia Dominicana*, p. 886; O'Ferrall and O'Connell, *Commentarius Rinuccinianus*, iii, pp 127, 452.
160 Bodl. Lib., Carte MS 156, p. 94.
161 NLI, GO, MS 225, p. 77.

A lawyer and member of an Old English family established in Louth since the twelfth century, he was well connected with other Old English gentry and his daughter married Roger Gernon, a member of another important Louth family. Clinton could not be called to the Bar in England because he repeatedly refused to take the oath and was expelled from Lincoln's Inns.[162] He practiced in chancery cases from 1629.[163] Clinton held lands in Louth, chiefly in Ardee Barony, where he owned 869 acres, and Derricanagh, Louth barony; he had land dealings with Lords Iveagh and Mountgarrett in 1630 and with neighbours in the county through the 1620s and 1630s. He was granted his lands under a Commission of Grace, with a fine of £6, on 4 August 1630 and received a grant of his father's lands on 8 May 1637.[164] He was a member of the 1624–5 commission of the peace, a commissioner for the Leinster agents in 1628 and took part in a number of land transactions with his neighbours between 1627 and 1632 in Louth and Down. He borrowed £200 on the Dublin staple in November 1635.[165] His neighbour Peter Dromgoole petitioned Wentworth in 1638, claiming that Clinton was suppressing a bond of £100 or £120 due to Dromgoole's late father.[166]

A prominent member of the opposition and an active committee man in parliament, he was appointed captain when the Louth gentry met at Tullaghesker in November 1641, was indicted for rebellion in the following year and was an active supporter of the Confederation, taking part in the early meetings at Kilkenny as a member of the 1642–3 Assembly and signing the letter to Ormond on 31 July 1642, which enclosed a petition to Charles. He was a member of the 1644 General Assembly and was suggested as a possible judge after the 1646 peace.[167] Revd Edward Lappage of Clonkean, Dublin, claimed a debt of £3 from him in 1643.[168] His lands were confiscated, but as he was enrolled in the decree of innocents they were at least partly restored after 1660. He apparently held £5,200 in deeds in the name of John Brice of Dublin in 1661, but was in want, as the government granted him £15 'for his present relief' in July 1661.[169]

ALLAN COOKE (? – 11 June 1647–1654) **Cavan 1634, 1640**

m. by 1630, Susan, da. Bishop James Heygate (Highgate) of Kilfenora and Anne, da. John Blake,

162 *Black Books of Lincoln's Inn*, p. 220.
163 Ohlmeyer, 'Records'.
164 J.B. Leslie, 'The Clinton family in County Louth', *Journal of the County Louth Archaeological Society*, 2:4 (1911), 398–412.
165 Cregan, 'Some members of the Confederation of Kilkenny'; TCD, MS 672, fo. 176v; *APC, 1627–8*, pp 398–9; Charles MacNeill and A.J. Otway-Ruthven (eds), *Dowdall deeds* (Dublin, 1960), pp 313, 321; *Inq. cancel. Hib. repert.*, i, Louth, Car. I (26, 31), ii, Down, Car. I (13, 85); Tallon (ed.), *Court of Claims*, pp 134–5; Ohlmeyer and Ó Ciardha (eds), *Irish statute staple*.
166 NAI, MS M 2,448, p. 238.
167 TCD, MS 834, fos. 22v, 28r; ibid., MS 840, fo. 57v; MacNeill and Otway-Ruthven (eds), *Dowdall deeds*, p. 330; Cregan, 'Some members of the Confederation of Kilkenny'; Ó Siochrú, *Confederate Ireland*, pp 256–7; Bellings and Gilbert (eds), *History of the Irish Confederation*, ii, pp 50–1, 214, v, p. 311.
168 TCD, MS 810, fo. 240r.
169 HMC, *Ormond*, new series, iii, p. 384.

Upton Hellions, Devonshire; 1 s. Edward.[170]
ed. ?Trinity College Dublin, D.C.L., *c.*1637.[171]

Cooke's origins are unknown, but he may well have been one of the Cookes of West Burton, Sussex.[172] He came to Ireland by 1622 when he requested a letter from James to Falkland ordering the archbishop of Dublin to surrender his patent for the office of prerogative in his province, which was to be reissued to Christopher Hampton; two years later he was Hampton's tenant in Armagh.[173] Cooke became chancellor of Kilmore before 1630. His advancement in the church, although a layman, is partly explained by his marriage: James Heygate held the archdeanery of Clogher *in commendam* with his bishopric and Cooke inherited Manor Heygate in Fermanagh from his father-in-law. He attended the 1630 muster as a townsman of Cavan, without arms. Cooke was a sovereign there in 1633.[174] He had leases from Bramhall in 1639 for 61 years of over 2,000 acres of church lands in Armagh, Donegal and Tyrone and also had lands in Cavan and Dublin; he was to pay 12*s.* rent per Irish acre and expend £500 on fencing and building within ten years.[175] His ecclesiastical career did not flourish under Heygate's successors – Bedell accused him, through the Star Chamber, of preying on the local population through the ecclesiastical courts, describing him as 'my unfriendly chancellor', and claimed that he appeared with other Cavan residents at a meeting in Richard Ashe's house, called by Bedell, to deal with the repairs needed to churches in Kilmore, although not invited, to persuade him to sign a letter to the Lords Justice concerning the new applotment for raising money for the army. Bedell regarded Cooke as having tried by underhand methods to get him to sign the petition and was aggrieved that Cooke had tried to get Bedell's church lands included in the applotment at the midsummer assizes. Allan retaliated by accusing Bedell of improper actions on benefices and denounced him as a pluralist, which was ironic, considering the range of offices Cooke himself held. After a protracted struggle, he was eventually replaced as chancellor by Ashe.[176]

170 NLI, GO, MS 225, p. 164; *Inq. cancel. Hib. repert.*, ii, Fermanagh, Car. II (2).
171 Marsh's Library, MS Z4.2.1, no. 20.
172 The name Allan occurs regularly in that family pedigree, although there is no one who can be positively identified with the MP BL, Harleian MS 6,164, fo. 62r.
173 *Cal. S.P. Ire., 1615–25*, p. 344. ARL, MS Abstracts from the rentals of the Archbishops of Armagh, 1615-1746. https://issuu.com/acdcdesign/docs/_archbishop_s_rentals_small, pp 68, 88, [accessed 1 Dec. 2022].
174 Michael Perceval-Maxwell and R.J. Hunter, 'Cavan muster roll', *Briefne*, 5:18 (1977–8), 206–22; J.B. Leslie, *Clogher clergy and parishes* (Enniskillen, 1929), p. 42; NLI, MS D 20,429; Jonathan Cherry, 'Colonial appropriation of Gaelic space: creating the first Ulster town', *Irish Geography*, 20:2 (2007), 112–27.
175 Rental of the lands of the see of Armagh, 1662, HL, HP, Box 75 (5); Lease dated 21 May 1639, HL, Hastings Deeds, HAD 3,617; Simington (ed.), *Civil Survey*, Tyrone, pp 290, 292, 298; ibid., Londonderry, p. 188; Clarke (ed.), *1641 Depositions, Volume IV: Dublin*, p. 70; Clarke (ed.), *1641 Depositions, Volume II, Cavan and Fermanagh*, pp 196, 298.
176 Bedell to Wentworth, 5 Nov. 1633, in Knowler (ed.), *Letters and dispatches*, i, p. 147. This dispute is traced in Alan Ford, 'The Reformation in Kilmore before 1641' in Raymond Gillespie (ed.), *Cavan: essays on the history of an Irish county* (Dublin, 1995), pp 73–98; Alexander Clogie, *Memoir of the life and episcopate of Dr William Bedell* (London, 1862), pp 53–62, 86; E.S.

Cooke had a wide legal practice – Cork retained his services as a lawyer and he may have worked on chancery cases; he was repeatedly recommended to Wentworth by Coke.[177] He was also acting as a surrogate judge in the Admiralty Court by 1628 and Loftus entrusted most of the admiralty work to him (he was nicknamed 'Alan Pouke'). He became master in chancery in 1636, the year in which he appealed for the position of judge in the vice-admiralty court of Leinster. It was also at this time that he demanded that actions be taken against individuals who had received patents that reduced the crown's profits, including through *Quo warranto* proceedings, and was pursuing the issue in the following year.[178] New rules from England on the operations of the Admiralty Court arrived in Ireland in 1633 and Cooke complained that there was 'no act that I have done, or can do, but is questioned at the council board'. He was fined in 1638 over an irregularity in seizing goods from a shipwreck near Dublin.[179]

Cooke's legal and ecclesiastical experience made him a natural person for Wentworth to nominate, with many others including James Barry*, John Bysse*, Hilton*, Radcliffe*, Ryves*, Sambach* and Ware, as delegates to hear appeals from ecclesiastical courts in 1638.[180] He became vicar general of Dublin, in which role he judged a case between William Tyrry and Philip Percival in March 1641; in the same month, Cooke, Thomas Newcomen and George Carr each guaranteed surety of £6,700 for Bramhall's appearance to answer his impeachment.[181] While he clearly profited from his many offices, Cooke was a man interested in good and effective administration and constitutional issues. In 1638 Wentworth referred a petition of Sir Edward Bagshaw concerning his farm of the tithes of Glassowen from the vicars choral of St Patrick's to Cooke*.[182]

Allan was an active MP in both parliaments and was one of the Protestant leaders in 1641. He sat on over 11 committees in the fourth session and played a constructive role in pressing for a resolution to grievances as a member of a conference committee with the Lords who wrote to the agents in London to urge the processing of the bills clarifying land titles and the compensation to Charles for the resulting loss of income in April 1641. He continued to attend parliament until 11 June 1647.[183] In June 1643 he was taking depositions as a judge in the

Shuckburgh (ed.), *Two biographies of William Bedell, bishop of Kilmore* (Cambridge, 1902), pp 311–16; *Cal. S.P. Ire., 1625–33*, pp 170, 204, 218–19, 564–5.

177 Grosart (ed.), *Lismore Papers*, 1st series, iv, pp 68, 91, 108; Ohlmeyer, 'Records'; Coke to Wentworth, 10 July 1633, same to same, 24 Oct. 1633, Wentworth to Coke, 8 Nov. 1633, all in Knowler (ed.), *Letters and dispatches*, i, pp 92–3, 138, 153; Coke to Wentworth, 22 Jan. 1638, *Cal. S.P. Ire., 1633–47*, pp 178–9.

178 HMC, *Ormond*, new series, ii, pp 290, 338; John C. Appleby (ed.), *A calendar of material relating to Ireland from the High Court of Admiralty examinations, 1536–1641* (Dublin, 1992), p. 282; *Cal. S.P. Ire., 1633–47*, p. 124.

179 Costello, *Court of Admiralty*, pp 10–12, 17–18, 20, 23, 25–6, 38–9, 45.

180 HMC, *Various collections, Volume III*, p. 183; Grosart (ed.), *Lismore Papers*, 1st series, iv, pp 68–9.

181 BL, Add. MS 46,924, fos. 234v–41r; Moody and Simms (eds), *Bishopric of Derry*, i, p. 235.

182 NAI, MS M 2,448, pp 248–9.

183 Perceval-Maxwell, *Outbreak*, pp 25, 129–33, 145, 156, 322n.

Leinster vice-admiralty court and drafting articles for the Archbishop of Dublin against the seditious preacher Doctor Harding.[184] In 1644 he was a commissioner for inquiring and seizing rebels' goods in London and was in that city also in 1646.[185]

DOMINIC COPPINGER (c.1595 – 30 October 1642–24 July 1643) Cork City, 1634

e.s. Sir Walter Coppinger (d. 1639), Coppinger's Court, and Margaret, da. William Sarsfield; m. 1) by 1621, Mary (d. 1679–82), da. David Comyn, merchant, Limerick, and Catherine, da. Sir Nicholas Arthur (MP, Limerick City, 1613); sons James, Walter, daughters Alison, Ellen, Marie, Clara, Victoria, Gennett, and Catherine.
ed. Gray's Inn, 1611; Bar, King's Inns, 1629.
Will, 30 October 1642, proved 27 July 1643.
Bur. Christ Church, Cork.[186]

Dominic was a member of one of the wealthiest Catholic Cork families. Sir Walter had a long-running dispute with Crooke* about the possession of lands in west Cork, which Dominic inherited with other property in Cork city and county; he also inherited property from his brother James who died in 1635. His wealth can be judged by the £3,400 he provided for his daughters' marriage portions.[187] He was sworn a freeman and councillor of Cork on 5 October 1629 and elected recorder on the following day, a position he held until 1640. He was negotiating with Falkland about the offices of gauger, search and packer in Cork in November 1629. Both he and his father were elected councillors of Cork city under its new charter of 1633, which Dominic enrolled and may have negotiated. Dominic and his fellow MP, William Sarsfield, agreed to serve without parliamentary wages.[188] A committed Catholic, he and his wife supported the Capuchins in Cork in the 1630s – Mary was the niece of Revd Robert Comyn who headed their mission in the city.[189] Dominic's eldest son James was under age at Dominic's death and Muskerry wrote to Ormond about his wardship, which his widow Mary Comyn was seeking. James obtained an order restoring him to Dominic's property in 1664.[190]

EDMUND COPPINGER (c.1578 – July 1624+) Youghal, 1613

e.s. Ald. Thomas Coppinger, Youghal; m. 1) by 1602, Ellen (Helena) Ronane; sons Stephen, Thomas, Patrick, daughters Catherine, Ellen, Margaret, Mary.[191]
ed. Furnival's Inn; Lincoln's Inns, 1594; recorder, 1612.

184 Clarke (ed.), *1641 Depositions Volume IV: Dublin*, pp 351–2.
185 HMC, *Egmont*, i, p. 240; Clogie, *Memoir*, p. 155.
186 Charles McCarthy Tenison, 'Cork MPs, 1559–1800', *JCHAS*, 2nd series, 1 (1895), 230–4; family tree (unpaginated), Copinger, *History of the Copingers*.
187 MacCarthy-Morrogh, *Munster plantation*, pp 152–4. In 1627 Dominic's mother donated a silver chalice to the Franciscans in Shandon. J.J. Buckley, 'Supplement: Some Irish altar plate (continued)', *JRSAI*, 7th series, 9:2 (1939), 33–56; Tallon (ed.), *Court of Claims*, pp 47–8.
188 Caulfield (ed.), *Cork*, pp 144–7, 151, 161, 170–9, 192.
189 T.J. Walsh, 'The Capuchins in Cork', *Capuchin Annual*, 21 (1952), 173–203.
190 Ormond to Muskerry, 19 Oct. 1643, in Bellings and Gilbert (eds), *History of the Irish Confederation*, iii, p. 38; Tallon (ed.), *Court of Claims*, pp 47–8.
191 Tenison, 'Cork MPs'.

Will, July 1624.
Bur. St Mary's Church, Youghal.[192]

Edmund is also referred to as Edward in the Youghal Corporation records; assuming this was the same man, he was a householder in Cork in February 1604 with a house and garden worth 12*s*.[193] His father had been Youghal's MP in 1585 and mayor in 1564, 1573, 1582 and 1586. Edmund was a trusted citizen of Youghal, serving as bailiff in 1608–9, as one of those appointed to enquire into offences within the town and as recorder, mayor and agent. He also had clearly been recorder for some time before 1612, as the town was liable for significant arrears of his wages, for which it assigned a bond worth £31. Coppinger was an unsuccessful candidate for mayor in that year. He signed the petition of protest to James about electoral abuses and was one of the Catholic MPs ordered to attend the king in England at the end of January 1614 for which the town levied £30 to cover his expenses. He was a member of the Commons' committees to examine officers' fees.

In 1614 the Grand Jury found that he and others had stopped up the highways leading to Glawnemore and Glawneyadie. He lost his position as recorder to the Protestant Peter Marks, but was acting as his deputy, and then to Henry Gosnold* and Laurence Parsons.* He was elected mayor in September 1615. Edmund was subsequently deposed for refusing the oath, but only after parliament had been dissolved, as he was protected by parliamentary privilege.[194] In 1619, he was Youghal's agent to Cork to speak to Lord Sarsfield about the black rent and was paid £5 to go on the town's business, including travelling to Clonmel on 21 May to clarify issues around the towns' 1609 agreement that their freemen should have reciprocal rights and to Dublin that November.[195] In 1620 he was on the jury for perambulating Youghal's bounds. Three years later the town still owed him arrears of £5 10*s*. Thomas Gough* was appointed overseer of Coppinger's will.[196]

THOMAS CREWE (1570 – 22 July 1616)[197] **Londonderry, 1613**

4 s. James Crewe, London; m. 1) 27 January 1598, St Botolph's, Aldgate, Blanche (1574–16??), da. Edward Darrell, Mitcham, Surrey and Mary____.[198]
ed. Middle Temple, 1595; Bar, 26 November 1602; King's Inns 1612.

Crewe came to Ireland with his older brothers Caleb and Joshua as part of the plantation of Londonderry; Caleb, a freeman of the London Bakers' Company had the contract to supply bread for the London Company in Londonderry and Joshua was a founding burgess of Coleraine.[199] He served as a justice of assize in 1612.[200]

192 Copinger, *History of the Copingers*, pp 242–4.
193 Inquisitions post mortem, Cork, vol. 1, RIA, MS OS EI 18, p. 80.
194 Caulfield (ed.), *Youghal*, pp 22–8, 38; *Cal. S.P. Ire., 1611–14*, p. 464.
195 Caulfield (ed.), *Youghal*, pp 62, 65–6; McGrath (ed.), *Clonmel*, p.68.
196 Copinger, *History of the Copingers*, pp 242–4.
197 NLI, GO, MS 66, Funeral Entries, Volume 3, 1604–22, p. 57.
198 Joseph Foster, *London marriage licences, 1611–1828* (London, 1887), col. 354.
199 Moody and Simms (eds), *Bishopric of Derry*, i, p. 93; *Cal. S.P. Ire., 1611–14*, p. 300.
200 McCavitt, '"Good planets in their several spheres"'.

Thomas was active in the house including on the committees for Tyrone's attainder and for the trial of felonies. He is not to be confused with the English lawyer and MP (1564–1634) who was a member of the 1622 Commission.[201]

THOMAS CROOKE (*c.*1574 – 27 Feb.–7 May 1630)[202] **Baltimore, 1613**

s. Revd Thomas Crooke (1545–98), London, and Samuel (sic) ____; m. 1) by 1609 (probably much earlier), Mary, da. ____, w. of John Jackson, clothier, London; 3 s. 2 da.[203]
ed. Gray's Inn, 1 March 1597; King's Inns, 1628.
Kt. 4 March 1624, Theobalds; 1st Bart., 19 April 1624.

Crooke's admission to Gray's Inn, was at the request of his father, the Inn's Minister of God's word, a prominent nonconformist preacher from whom he inherited £40.[204] Thomas migrated to Ireland *c.*1605 and receiving a grant of lands from Sir Fineen O'Driscoll settled in Baltimore by 1606. In 1608 he received the right to hold markets and fairs there.[205] He paid a fine of £10 on a grant passed on the Commission of Defective Titles in 1607 and in the following year was acquitted of involvement in piracy and received a general pardon.[206] He developed a town at Baltimore, planting it with Englishmen and obtained its charter in 1612, but faced continual harassment from Sir Walter Coppinger and other locals about these lands. Coppinger took an exchequer case against Crooke and also accused him of treason at the Cork assizes, leading to a Castle Chamber case in 1615–16, when Geoffrey Galway* was Coppinger's counsel.[207] In 1624 he took a case against Dingle merchants in Tralee and was a member of the commission of the peace for Cork.[208] Crooke also rented lands at Kinalmeakey from Cork and borrowed money from him on bond.[209] Crooke continued to trade out of Baltimore; merchants from Bayonne sued him in chancery about a cargo bound for Lisbon. In 1628 pilchards worth £1,100, laded in Baltimore in partnership with a London merchant, were seized by pirates from Algiers *en route* to Leghorn; he had insured them on the London Exchange.[210]

201 Alan Davidson and Rosemary Sgroi, 'Crewe, Thomas' in Thrush and Ferris (eds), *History of parliament*.
202 Cokayne, *Baronetage*, i, p. 257.
203 Henry F. Waters, *Genealogical gleanings in England, Volume 1 (part third)* (Boston, MA, 1889), p. 325.
204 Brett Ussher, 'Crooke, Sir Thomas', *Oxford DNB*.
205 *Rot. Pat. Jac.*, pp 107–8.
206 *Cal. S.P. Ire., 1611–14*, pp lxi, 102, 266; Curtis Clayton (ed.), *Council book*, pp 367–8; *Cal. S.P. Ire., 1608–10*, pp 42–3, 100–1; *Cal. S.P. Ire, 1611–14*, p. 104; Chichester, warrant, 18 Jan. 1608, HL, HP, Box 2 (19). Warrant to draw up fiant of general pardon to T.C. of Baltimore esq.
207 Account of Crooke's development of Baltimore, RIA, MS 24/Q/4; Crawford, *Star Chamber*, pp 138, 324–5, 523–4; Exchequer case involving Walter Coppinger and others, 2 Feb. 1612, HL, HP, Box 75 (10).
208 TCD, MS 672, fo. 182; ARL, MS Bolton's cases, MS KI.I.14B, unpaginated.
209 Grosart, *Lismore Papers*, 1st series, ii, pp 100, 144–6, 188, 245, 286, iii, pp 93, 245.
210 NAI, Chancery MS I86; Appleby (ed.), *Calendar*, p. 183.

JAMES CUSACK[211] **(*c.*1603 – d. ?1659)** **Old Leighlin, 1634**
Ballyshannon/Old Leighlin, 1640

3rd, but 2 s.s. Edward Cusack, Lismullen, and Elizabeth Aylmer, Lyons; m. Frances (d. 1688), da. Sir William Talbot*, Carton, and Alison Netterville; 3 s. Thomas, William and Nicholas and daughter Elinor.[212]
ed. Middle Temple, 1619; King's Inns, 28 January 1637.

James owed his position as learned council and clerk of defective titles to his experience and contacts made between 1628 and 1633 while working for the privy council committee for Irish affairs in London; he was recommended to Endymion Porter and by Charles to Wentworth 'as having worked diligently in London on the cases of defective Irish titles, returning home to Ireland, to be a special attorney in the same area in Ireland'.[213] His influence in the sensitive post (in which he was assisted by another MP Walter Cruise) decreased after Percival was made joint clerk in 1636, but he was clearly conforming at the times of his returns as Robert Dillon would never have nominated a Catholic for Ballyshannon. Cusack's wife's dowry was £400 but she also brought him extensive parliamentary connections as the sister of Robert Talbot and John Dongan and Henry Talbot's wives, cousin of Lord Netterville and a connection of Cruise, and uncle of Adam Cusack and Robert Forth.[214]

Cusack was an active parliamentarian, sitting on many committees including that on the Bill for the Plantation of Connacht and helped to formulate the articles of impeachment against Bramhall, Bolton*, Adam Loftus* and Radcliffe*. His position as clerk was not always easy and in March 1641, with Sambach* and attorney general Tempest attempting to restrict the scope of his work, he departed for London to make his case personally to Charles, supported by letters of commendation from the privy council and the House of Commons. Cusack's petition to Charles, describing himself as 'one of your majesties learned Councell in Ireland', claimed that he had served Charles as 'speciall Atturney for the service of defective titles' for eight years without fee or stipend. He also advised changes in the proposed bill to guarantee land titles. More damagingly, he claimed that four times the annual income from defective titles would have been raised had Strafford not excluded half the kingdom from the commission 'without shewing any reason or cause' and that the crown had been deprived of significant revenue by officials including Wentworth, Sir William Parsons, Tempest and Sambach pocketing enormous fees at the expense of landholders passing patents. Sambach and Tempest were counter-lobbying the privy council, claiming that no patent was

211 Cregan, 'Some members of the Confederation of Kilkenny'; Micheál Ó Siochrú, 'Cusack, James', *DIB*.

212 H.D. Gallwey, 'The Cusack family of Counties Meath and Dublin (cont.)', *IG*, 5:6 (Nov., 1979), 673–84.

213 Charles to Wentworth, 6 May 1633, in Knowler (ed.), *Letters and dispatches*, i, pp 83–4, 162–3, 191; same to same, Bodl. Lib., Carte MS 80 (Wharton Papers), fo. 644; Grosart (ed.), *Lismore Papers*, 1st series, ii, p. 309.

214 Stephen Edward Talbot, *Into the lion's den: a biographical history of the Talbots of Malahide* (London, 2012), pp 82, 114, 117–18.

passed to him for his office and that he was encroaching on their offices and fees.[215] Given the privy council's support for Cusack, it is likely that James also transmitted some bills and the Commons' reply about John FitzGerald's election (which would also have damaged Tempest's reputation).

On the outbreak of the rebellion he attempted to mediate but in February 1642 it was reported that he and Nicholas Darcy of Plattin 'were to be sent into ... Westmeath, to make enquiry what persons within the said county of Westmeath would not joyne in giving assistance unto the Lords and gentlemen now in rebellion, to the end thereupon some severe course might be taken with such as refuse.'[216] He signed the letter of 31 July 1642 to Ormond and actively supported the Confederation, serving as a member of the 1642, 1644 and 1646–7 General Assemblies and a Leinster representative on the 1642–3 Supreme Council. Cusack encouraged Clanricard to support its work. His administrative experience was very valuable to the Confederation and he was its attorney general and judge of the Admiralty Court. James was a member of the Committee of the 1648 General Assembly that dealt with points of religion raised during the negotiations on the second Ormond peace. He was proposed to Ormond as a possible chancellor of the exchequer or attorney during the negotiations for the first peace and was retained by Rinuccini as commissioner of public revenue. He supported the truce with Inchiquin. He clearly suffered considerable financial hardship for his adherence to the Confederation – he was granted £24 by the Confederation in December 1646 and Ormond granted him money in 1649.[217] He was excluded from pardon under Cromwell's 1652 ordnance, but apparently survived in Ireland until 1659, although he is not mentioned in the Court of Claims documentation.

PATRICK DARCY (1598–1668) **Navan, 1634, Tyrone, 1641**

7 s., Sir James Darcy, Rivagh (d. 1603) and his second wife, Elizabeth (she rem. Sir Henry Lynch*), da. Richard Martin, Galway; m. 1625, Mary, e. da. Sir Peter French and Catherine

215 *Commons' Jn. Ire.*, 1 March 1641; privy council, Borlase, Parsons, Bolton, etc., to Sir Henry Vane, 3, 9 March 1641, Bodl. Lib., Carte MS 80, fos. 655–8; Bodl. Lib., Bankes MS 50/26; Petition of Tempest and Sambach,* Bodl. Lib., Carte MS 63, fo. 637.

216 [William Parsons and John Borlase], *A relation touching the present state and condition of Ireland* (London, 1641–2), p. 8.

217 Petition to Ormond, 1649, Bodl. Lib., Carte MS 156, pp 277–8, acted as A.G. as appointed by the General Assembly for 6 years & more 'to his little advantage and great trouble' and had a pension of £100 p.a. conferred on him for his better support, being banished from his whole estate and fortune, and likewise being made chief justice of the admiralty, and now being displaced from his roles and having only now the commissionership of the admiralty, which he shares with 6 others – lost £300 of corn this season upon his lands in the enemy quarters; asks for £100 toward his maintenance from his pension and arrears for the maintenance of himself, his wife and children; Ormond orders £100 for him (p. 409). Another petition, notes the £100 from the G.A. for his pains, but also the perquisites of the office. See HL, *Huntington Stowe Nugent Catalogues & Inventories, Box 4*. List of papers in the hands of Mr James Tuite of Cavan, no. 2 Order of the General Assembly, November 1642 in favour of James Cusack*; No.5, May 1646 'James Cusack* wrote a letter of strong sence to Mr Andrew Nugent of Drumour re. lands of Tomand in the possession of Sr ?John McNamara which were the inheritance of James' nephews Adam Cusack in fee simple & should be left to his daughter as his only child.'

Browne, Galway, w. of Peter Blake; 2 s. James, Francis, 2 da. Brigid, Clare.[218]
ed. Middle Temple, 1617; King's Inns, 1628.
Bur. Kilconnell Abbey.

Darcy's family connections were with other Galway families; he was step-son of Henry Lynch*, brother-in-law of both Richard Martin* and of his step-brother Roebuck Lynch*, through whom he was linked also to the Blakes. Things were difficult in the Darcy family when Patrick was a child as he was taken into the home of a local schoolmaster called King who kept and educated him at his own expense and there were bitter disputes about his father's will, which led to cases in chancery. Like other Galway lawyers, Darcy's legal education was sponsored by Clanricard, who had a very high opinion of him, personally and professionally; Darcy's step-father Henry Lynch* was the earl's principal man of business and Patrick started his practice in London in 1622 working as counsel for Clanricard and Ormond. Darcy returned to Ireland and was the first Catholic lawyer admitted to the King's Inns in 1628.[219] He was one of the most able and respected lawyers of his generation, with an extensive and lucrative practice (*plate 1*). While he worked for a wide variety of clients, he performed so much work for his old patron Clanricard, along with Ormond and Cork, that he was a virtual or actual retainer of them all, even before he was able to plead in court. From 1622 he worked as counsel for Walter Ormond in the latter's dispute with Sir Thomas Butler and on many other issues, such as the prize wines on which he was engaged from at least 1631 and Walter's opposition to the proposed plantation of north Tipperary in March 1632.

Patrick rented lands worth £200 annually from Ormond, possibly in part payment for legal fees, and he also had a grant of a third of the profits of Ormond's prize wines in Galway from February 1631. He promised to defend Ormond's interests against any claim or suit from Galway Corporation, a commitment easier to fulfil given his membership of that body from 1630 until 1646 at least.[220] From 1634 Boyle recruited Darcy as counsel, with an annual retainer of £80, a £5 'hansell' and £6 and 20*s*. termly fees; in February 1634 Darcy and John Pollexfen were working on Cork's defence in the Castle Chamber case and in early 1640 he drafted the earl's private bill to resolve his long-standing dispute with the bishop of Waterford and Lismore.[221] Patrick acted for his uncle, Bishop Anthony Martin

218 NLI, GO, MS 162, pp 67–8; William O'Sullivan (ed.), *The Strafford inquisition of County Mayo* (Dublin, 1958), p. 72.

219 McGrath (ed.), 'Additional Patrick Darcy Papers'; NAI, Chancery MSS G255, J82 (cases concerning James Darcy's will taken from Kenneth W. Nicholls' calendar); McGrath, 'Ireland and the third university'; King's Inns, MS B 1/1, fo. 17v.

220 Deed of Thomas Colclough, Tintern and others to George Bagenal, Dunleckney the manor of Ballinamore, Co. Carlow, 20 July 1623, NAI, MS RC 5/1, pp 79–87, fiefing him of this property to the use of Anne Colclough, now wife to Capt. Thomas Butler of Newtown, Co. Carlow. Christopher FitzGerald of the Middle Temple (Tecroghan) and Patrick Darcy* and Richard Martin*; J.P. Prendergast, 'On the projected plantation of Ormond by King Charles I', *Trans. Kilkenny Arch. Soc.*, 1:3 (1851), 390–409; NLI, MS 2,305, pp 109, 235; Darcy to Ormond, 20 August 1636, and 30 May 1637 same to same about prize wines, 1639, NLI, MSS 2,306, p. 275; 11,045/25–6, 52–4; McGrath, 'Managing the Windsor'.

221 Grosart (ed.), *Lismore Papers*, 1st series, iv, pp 56, 68–9; Cork to Joshua Boyle, 17 March 1640,

of Meath, in 1631 and many other clients including Antrim and Lambart and Lords Slane, Folliot, Digby, Blayney and Esmond in their cases for precedency in the Lords against Lord Castle-Stewart.[222]

Darcy was the only Catholic MP in 1634 without an obvious local connection with his constituency (his election for Navan was due to the Meath family of Darcy of Plattin to whom he was not related) and is evidence that his expertise was badly wanted in the house. He was one of the leaders of the recusant faction in that parliament, sitting on a remarkable number and range of committees, including that for privileges, bills concerning bigamy, ease of pleading actions, conference committee with the Lords, that to recommend desirable legislation, to draft a petition on behalf of the Commons to the deputy concerning tallow exports, and, with Martin*, carried most of the responsibility for formulating legislative proposals based on the Graces, which Wentworth rebuffed.

With Sir Roger O'Shaughnessy (*plate 17*)[223] and Martin,* he was one of the most prominent opponents of the proposed plantation of Connacht and in the resistance of the Galway freeholders, for which he and Martin* were disbarred. He fled to London where his activities were not confined to opposing the Galway plantation – he also presented proposals on the operation of the Irish customs to Charles. Darcy complained to Ormond of being victimized by Wentworth and Antrim. Other influential clients repeatedly pressed for his and Martin's readmission to legal practice, which occurred in 1639.[224] Apart from his lucrative legal practice, Darcy had extensive property: he held nearly 2,000 acres in Galway, where he lived at Kiltulla, and other lands in Mayo and Sligo which he purchased (he spent £1,540 on purchases in Mayo alone in 1634) or received as part of his wife's dowry. He also owned houses in Newtown, Galway City and Bridge Street, Dublin.[225]

While he and Martin* decided to withdraw from politics after their experiences with Wentworth, they acted as advisor to the Catholic members of the 1640–1

Chatsworth House, Cork Papers, Misc. boxes, Box 3, pp 419ff. For Pollexfen, see McGrath (ed.), 'Additional Patrick Darcy Papers'.

222 Empey (ed.), *Early Stuart Irish warrants*, p. 67; *LJI*, 14, 30 July, 2 Aug. 1634; NAI, MS RC 6/2; Repertories to Decrees in Chancery, ii, 1624–85, p. 267; Darcy vs Antrim and Archibald Stewart. Petition 30 May 1654. Decree 18 Dec 1654, to recover £1005-13-8. I am grateful to John Cunningham for drawing this reference to my attention and providing his notes; Counsel, with Martin* and Kirwin, for Lord Lambart in his petition concerning his lands in Mayo, *LJI*, 1 March 1641; Perceval-Maxwell, *Outbreak*, p. 123.

223 A prominent Galway landowner, and MP for Galway County in 1634; Declaration of Roger O'Shaghnasse, Patrick Darcie and Richard Martin to the Committee for Irish affairs concerning their title to lands in Galway, 1635, Marsh's Library, MS Z3.2.6, no. 106.

224 Being disbarred did not prevent Darcy acting as a lawyer. He continued to advise Ormond and Cork and presumably many others, e.g., NLI, MS 2,305, p. 109; Boyle reported that 'on Thursday next [Darcy] is to be…admitted to plead openly.' Boyle to Cork, 3 June 1639, same to same, 19 Aug. 1639, NLI, MS 13,237 (23–4); John Walter, 'Crowds and political violence in early modern Ireland: Galway and the 1641 Depositions', *IHS*, 45:168 (2021), 178–202.

225 O'Sullivan (ed.), *Strafford inquisition of County Mayo*, pp 53, 72, 102, 154; NAI, MS D 20,681, 6 Nov. 1656. I am grateful to John Cunningham for drawing this reference to my attention and providing me with a transcript of it. Brown and Ó Siochrú, 'Cromwellian urban civil surveys'; Gilbert, *History of the city of Dublin*, i, p. 331.

Commons and were persuaded back into parliament after his downfall, where both were even more prominent – Borlase named him, Nicholas Plunkett*, Cheevers*, James Cusack*, Geoffrey Browne*, Roebuck Lynch*, Bodkin, Evers and others as 'active men of the House' and apart from Darcy's own active leadership, his son delivered letters from the Commons to the committee in England.[226] Darcy's *Argument*, asserting that the Irish people were free and to be governed only by the common law and statutes passed by the Irish parliament, was the clearest expression of the views of the united opposition to Strafford within the Irish parliament, and subsequently became a key document in the parliamentary and nationalist arguments for Irish legislative independence, used in the 1659 Convention and later by Molyneux and others.[227]

On the outbreak of the rebellion, he, Geoffrey Browne* and Thomas Bourke* prevailed upon a reluctant administration to recall the prorogued parliament and to use the loyalty of the Old English to suppress the rebellion. St Leger anticipated his discomfiture on parliament's reassembling. Darcy stayed in Dublin working to reconcile the rebels and maintain a Catholic presence in the Commons and remaining in contact with Ormond, presumably as a channel to the rest of the administration until, understanding that his continued presence was pointless, he left for Galway on 31 December.[228] The government's reluctance to trust Catholics' loyalty forced him and others into a gradual alliance with their co-religionists and 'Patrick Darcy and Richard Martyn lawyers were the men that first moved the Towne of Galway to Rebellion, both by their letters from Dublin and theire insitatio when they came to Galway'.[229] By March 1642 he and Martin* were involved in Galway's government through the town's emergency executive, the Council of Eight, and, according to an account in an English pamphlet, 'An English Ship is put in at Galway laden with salt, so the Townesmen went out to buy it, but in conclusion took the Ship with 8 peeces of Ordnance, and 6 Barrels of Powder, Mr Darcy and Mr Martin Lawyers were the greatest actors in this treason.'[230]

With the Blakes and Martin*, he was one of the leaders of Galway through the 1640s; he was also one of the resident Connacht members of the Supreme Council. He later claimed that he had not been a member of any council of war or other assembly before Kilkenny and that he had moved to live under Clanricard's

226 Perceval-Maxwell, *Outbreak*, pp 137, 148–9, 156; Borlase, *History*, pp 8, 10. There is no record of Bodkin's being an MP

227 Clarke, 'Patrick Darcy and the constitutional relationship'; Perceval-Maxwell, *Outbreak*, pp 173–7.

228 Ibid., pp 243–5; St Leger to Percival , 1 Nov. 1641, BL, MS Add. 46,925, fo. 165v; Borlase, *History*, p. 32; Darcy to Ormond, 6 Jan. 1642, Bodl. Lib., Carte MS 2, fo. 266.

229 Deposition of Revd William Hanmer, Galway, 14 Aug. 1642, TCD, MS 830, fo. 134v, with further allegations on fo. 142v.

230 *The last joyfull newes from Ireland, being the copies of two severall letters* (London, 1642), sig. A2. This pamphlet was signed 'P.R.' Another pamphlet states that weapons were hidden in the salt. See the anonymous *A treacherous plot* (London, 1641); Walter, 'Crowds and political violence in early modern Ireland'.

protection at Easter 1642.[231] He was one of the most important actors in the Confederation, both as chancellor and as a member of every Supreme Council except the 7th and 9th; with Martin*, Bourke*, Nicholas Plunkett* and others, he devised the Confederation's system of government, based on work he and Martin had earlier conducted. He was a member of the Confederation's negotiating team with Ormond in Dublin in 1643 and in 1645 signed the articles of agreement with Glamorgan. In the following year, he and Plunkett* were agents from the Supreme Council to try to persuade the Catholic Bishops to support the Ormond peace. He followed a consistently moderate political line within the Confederation.[232]

His family connections were also prominent in the Confederation, as were many fellow MPs and clients, and their close personal and working relations contributed to its effectiveness. He was a party to Martin's* daughter Mary's marriage settlement with Sir Thomas Blake in 1649 (Richard had died in the previous year) which was witnessed by Dominic Browne.[233] However, his wider connections were also important in his work for the Confederation, such as with Clanricard and Ormond, the latter of whom sold plate on his behalf in Dublin in March 1642. His addressing of Muskerry as 'My deere lord' indicates their closeness as well.[234]

He was appointed a judge by the 1651 Loughrea Assembly, but resumed work for Ormond on the prize wines and continued to work as a lawyer in the 1650s, as the only Catholic (with James Barry* and John Bysse*) permitted to act for displaced Connacht landowners and advising on Lady Ormond's rights to her property in 1658. This was despite the authorities' efforts in the early 1650s to implicate him in the murders that occurred in Galway in the early stages of the rebellion.[235] He was still described as 'of Galway' in a bond for £300 on the Dublin staple in October 1654, but a decree for his transplantation to 66 acres in Omey, Galway, was issued two years later; Darcy used his connections with ruling Protestants including Coote, Eustace* and Ranelagh to ensure his children's future.[236]

On the Restoration, he continued to work as a lawyer. In 1661, with Richard Blake and others, he presented a petition from the former inhabitants of Galway

231 Examination of Darcy, Dec. 1653, TCD, MS 830, fo. 263r–v.

232 Bodl. Lib., Carte MS 68, fo. 1; Ó Siochrú, *Confederate Ireland*, pp 35–6, 39, 44, 46–9, 75–9, 86, 91, 99, 111–17; Ó hAnnracháin, *Catholic reformation in Ireland*, pp 148–51.

233 NLI, MS 40,889/38(4).

234 Bodl. Lib., Carte MS 68, fo. 1r; Ó Siochrú, *Confederate Ireland*, p. 69; Patrick Darcy, 'The state of the prisewines of Galway until this date', 16 June 1650, NLI, MS 11,045/52; Clanricard to Darcy, 15 April 1646, Bodl. Lib., Carte MS 63, fos. 415r–16v; Darcy to Muskerry, 6 Nov. 1647, Bodl. Lib., Carte MS 21, fo. 517.

235 Aidan Clarke, 'Darcy, Patrick', *DIB*; King's Inns, Prendergast MS 1, p. 331. I am grateful to John Cunningham for drawing this reference to my attention. NLI, MSS 11,045/52–4, 11,051/5; Ó Siochrú, *Confederate Ireland*, p. 33.

236 McGrath (ed.), 'Additional Patrick Darcy Papers'; NLI, MSS 11,045/52–4, 11,051/5; Cunningham, *Conquest and land in Ireland*, pp 91, 94; Ranelagh to Darcy, 6 Nov. 1656, NAI, MS D 20,681; Aidan Clarke (ed.), *1641 Depositions, Volume XII: Connacht, Westmeath & Longford*, p. liv.

and Limerick to the privy council, requesting that they be allowed to resettle in their cities; his assignees were paid £100 by the administration in December of that year. He advised clients including John Bramhall, with whom he formed a professional relationship and warm personal friendship despite having earlier worked to impeach him, and Lord Kildare, who in 1662 granted him parliamentary privilege as one of his servants or agents.[237] The description of him as 'tall corpulent & high complexioned' is supported by his portrait.[238]

JOHN DAVIES (Davys, Davis) (1569 – 8 December 1626)[239] Fermanagh, 1613

3 s. John (Edward) Davies (d. 1580), Chisgrove, Wiltshire and Mary (d. 5 July 1590), da. John Bennet, als. Pitte, Pitt House, Wiltshire;[240] m. 1) March 1609,[241] Eleanor Touchet (d. 1652), da. George, earl of Castlehaven (1551–1617) and Lucy (d. c.1610), da. Sir James Mervyn, Dorset and Amy Clarke; Elinor rem. 1627 Sir Archibald Douglas;[242] 2 sons, *o.v.p.*; 1 da. Lucy (b. 1612), m. July 1623, Ferdinando Hastings, later earl of Huntington.[243]
ed. Winchester 1580; Queen's College, Oxford, 15 October 1585; New Inn, 1587; Middle Temple, 1588; Bar, July 1595; King's Inns, 1607.
MP for Hedon in Holderness/Shaftesbury, 1597; Corfe Castle, 1601; Newcastle-under-Lyme and Hindon, 1621 in England.
Kt. 18 December 1603.
Bur. 9 December 1626, St Martin in the Fields, Westminster.

Davies' father was a prosperous tanner and had some connections with the earls of Pembroke, which assisted John in his career. During his studies Davies visited Leiden and met the Dutch scholar and jurist Paul Merula in 1592. He was in Scotland for the baptism of Prince Henry in 1594; he may also have been there in 1603 on James' accession to the English and Irish thrones, but he certainly attended the new king's progress through England. At the same time, he was building a reputation as a writer, primarily as a poet. Apart from epigrams, his longer and more complex works included *Orchestra, or, A poeme of dancing*, and his 'verse-treatise on immortality', *Nosce teipsum*, published in 1596 and 1599 respectively. Davies' friendship with the antiquarian Sir Robert Cotton stemmed from their sharing chambers in the Middle Temple and facilitated his introduction to the antiquarian William Camden. By 1600 he was engaged in the historical discussions of the Society of Antiquaries, some of his papers being subsequently published in Thomas Hearne's *A collection of curious discourses* (1771). Davies

237 *DIB*; McGrath (ed.), 'Additional Patrick Darcy Papers'; Wentworth FitzGerald, Lord Kildare, to Bramhall, 11 June 1662, HL, HP, Box 15, MS 14,729.
238 TCD, MS 830, fo. 226v. His portrait is reproduced as *plate 9*.
239 Will, TNA, PROB 11/150, fo. 282v.
240 NLI, GO, MS 44, fo. 45v. This biography draws on Robert Armstrong, 'Davies, Sir John', *DIB*; J.J.N. McGurk, 'Davies, Sir John', *Oxford DNB*; Ben Coates, 'Davies, Sir John' in Thrush and Ferris (eds), *History of parliament*.
241 NLI, GO, MS 44, fo. 45v, given as unmarried in 1608, but has correspondence addressed to him from George Audley as 'my very loving good sonne in law Sir John Davys' on 15 Dec. 1609, HL, HP, Box 3 (6).
242 Legal case of Sir Archibald Douglas and Eleanor vs. Ferdinando Hastings, earl of Huntington, re. Eleanor's jointures, HL, HP, Box 2 (12), Box 4 (7).
243 Recognizance for the dowry of Lucy Davies, 16 July 1623, HL, HP, Personal Box 17 (1).

composed *A Contention betwixt a Wife, a Widdow and a Maide* for Sir Robert Cecil's entertaining the queen at his new house in the Strand, London in 1602 and sent Sir Thomas Egerton, by then Lord Chancellor Ellesmere, an account of the state of Ireland in 1607.[244]

Davies' intellectual endeavours served him well in acquiring patronage from the earl of Pembroke, Charles Blount, Lord Mountjoy (who introduced him to court in 1594), and the lawyer Sir Edward Coke who sponsored his elections to parliament in 1597 and 1601. Far from a model citizen, his repeated flouting of his inns' rules led to his expulsion in 1591 although he was readmitted. His humble origins, ungainly appearance and presumably his personality led to his being the butt of cruel jokes and satires by John Donne and Ben Jonson and he was ridiculed at a performance directed by his friend Richard Martin at the Middle Temple Candlemas revels in 1598; deeply wounded, he assaulted Martin for which he was expelled for life, but influential patrons, including Cecil and Egerton, ensured his readmission in 1601. He maintained or resumed friendly relations with many members of the inns and parliament including William Ravenscroft of Lincoln's Inn, who wrote in February 1604 'we shall want you exceedingly this parliament – *in Libera Mens, cui Libera Lingua: liberiorij manus*' (a free mind with free speech and free hands). Another contact was the MP, crown official, lawyer, antiquarian and writer on parliaments, William Hakewill.[245]

Davies' appointment as solicitor general of Ireland on 18 September 1603 was due to the absentee Lord Lieutenant Mountjoy (now earl of Devonshire) 'who first transplanted mee' to Ireland. Davies was promoted to attorney general in 1606, the office with which he is most often associated in Ireland. He was commissioner for dividing Cork into two counties in 1606 and of the Court of Wards 1609–16. In 1604 he received a pardon from the king. He served as a justice of assize throughout Ireland between 1604 and 1617 at least.[246] Admitted to King's Inns, he was a member of its council in 1608 and in the following year was allocated a chamber in the dortor next to the judge John Eliot and lawyers Thomas Gough*, John Meade and Patrick Seagrave, although he resigned those quarters to Sir Francis Aungier some months later. He assigned the land for the judges' accommodation to the inns to the chagrin of Ald. Walter Ussher who claimed the land was his inheritance; however, he appears to have played no other role in that institution.[247]

Davies' reputation has benefitted hugely from his own propaganda; Chichester was the driving force behind the reforms in the Irish administration assisted by Davies as a minor official who was never a privy councillor. None of his successors as attorney general sought to develop and implement their own policies or took

244 John Davies, Account of the affairs of Ireland, 12 Sept. 1607, in John Payne Collier (ed.), 'The Egerton Papers', *The Camden Society*, 12 (1840), pp 410–17.

245 Ravenscroft to Davies, 13 Feb. 1604, Hakewill to same, same date, HL, HP, Box 1 (11–12).

246 General pardon, 1 June 1604, HL, HP, Oversized Box M15/5; HL, HP, MS 15,013; McCavitt, '"Good planets in their several spheres"'; Crawford, *Star Chamber*, pp 49–51.

247 King's Inns, MS B 1/1, fos. 3r, 41r, 109r–v, 171r.

credit for such.[248] Davies firmly believed that the successful government of Ireland could not be achieved through military conquest alone but required the imposition of English common law throughout Ireland, notably in Ulster, but it was Chichester who promoted the creation of shires with their standard structures of common law courts and officers including sheriffs and through replacing Irish land tenures with English ones. From 1606 Davies was occupied managing the work resulting from the newly established Commissions for Defective Titles and arranging crown tenants' surrender and regrant of lands. From the time of his arrival in Ireland, Davies supported complaints from Dublin concerning the powers of the northern Irish lords, including Tyrone and Tyrconnell and determined to limit their powers by replacing Gaelic land tenure with English, promoting crown rights and the autonomy of lesser landholders.[249] In 1606 he accompanied the lord deputy to south Ulster and later drafted an extended report on proceedings in Fermanagh, Monaghan and Cavan where he claimed, Chichester 'hath cut off three heads of that hydra of the North … for these three names of chiefry', Maguire, MacMahon, and O'Reilly, 'with their Irish duties and exactions, shall be utterly abolished.'[250]

The 'flight of the earls' in 1607, followed by Sir Cahir O'Doherty's rising, dramatically changed the situation in Ulster. Tyrone and Tyrconnell's lands were declared forfeit and their absence allowed the policy of supporting lesser lords to lapse and cleared the way for confiscation and plantation. In September Davies sent Cecil a full report of the earls' departure. As attorney, Davies was responsible for indicting the earls of treason and was a leading figure on the commission that established the Ulster plantations.[251] His work developing legal structures required his spending much time outside Dublin, especially in the earlier stages of his Irish career.[252]

Religious reform was a core element in the crown's project of establishing 'civility' in Ireland and Davies was a strong supporter of the firm establishment of the Protestant church. He consistently supported levying penalties on those who refused to attend Protestant services, expelling Catholic priests and excluding Catholics from Dublin City corporation to encourage reform of other Irish towns. In 1607 he also initiated proceedings against Waterford corporation over its control of customs.

Even before the plantation, Davies was acquiring lands throughout Ireland including Armagh, Mayo, Monaghan, Tipperary and Dublin city, some of which he held on to and others he sold.[253] Davies' marriage was exceptional for the

248 Jean R. Brink, 'Sir John Davies: lawyer and poet' in Thomas Herron and Michael Potterton (eds), *Ireland in the Renaissance*, c.*1540–1660* (Dublin, 2007), pp 88–104; McCavitt, '"Good planets in their several spheres"'.
249 *Cal. S.P. Ire., 1603–6*, p. 160.
250 Davies, *Historical tracts*, pp 269–70.
251 *Cal. S.P. Ire., 1606–8*, pp 212–13, 389; *Cal. Carew*, v, pp 13–22, 38–40.
252 McCavitt, '"Good planets in their several spheres"'.
253 Copies of extracts of grants to Davies, 5 Dec. 1609 – 27 Feb. 1617, HL, HP, Personal Box 14 (26); HL, Hastings Deeds 3515, 3573, 3592–3.

younger son of a tanner, especially one of very unprepossessing appearance. Eleanor brought a dowry of £6,000 and prestigious connections; John's father-in-law had served in Ireland and intended to create a large estate there.[254] Davies' appointment as attorney general and his role in planning the plantation of Ulster were advantageous to Audley, who benefitted from the scheme, as did Davies, who obtained 5,500 acres in all, 3,500 in Omagh barony, Co. Tyrone, and at Lisgoole Castle, Co. Fermanagh. However, Davies and Audley were far from conscientious planters. Josias Bodley's survey noted that 'the whole precinct of Omey containing 11,000 acres, undertaken by ye Ld. Audelay, his sons & Sir John Davies, remayneth as yet unfournished of castle, bawnes, or other strengths, required by ye rules of plantation: neither is there any settlement of British families, nor any undertakers granted for colonizing those partes, the Irish inhabitants continueing yet on the same as in former times' and they contravened the conditions of their grants by issuing leaseholds not freeholds, a practice continued by his heirs. However, by late December 1616 he and Castlehaven were stocking their Tyrone estates with cattle, horses and sheep and the estates were gradually developed; by 1629 the Fermanagh and Tyrone estates were yielding annually £534 3*s*. 8*d*. and £234 3*s*. 8*d*. respectively.[255] He also facilitated his father-in-law's property transactions in Carlow and Cork; he and Eleanor were administrators of Castlehaven's Irish estates after his death and in 1619 the earl's widow Elizabeth Noel married Piers Crosby who took a case against John and Eleanor presumably about the estate.[256]

Davies found legal studies tedious and saw a career as a lawyer as a means of advancement and never intended his residence in Ireland to be permanent, spending time in England seeking preferment there, maintaining influential contacts and building up estates. He was also a member of the Virginia Company. In 1609 he was appointed serjeant-at-law in England but James discharged him from these duties intending to employ him in preparing for the Irish parliament; he was restored to his duties on 27 April 1612 and exercised that role during his time in England on Irish parliamentary business.[257] In 1610 he petitioned Salisbury for a new appointment in England citing his record of reform in Ireland, 'the assimilation of the autonomous Gaelic lordships to the crown, the reduction of medieval corporate liberties, the implementation of religious conformity and the

254 Legal case of Sir Archibald Douglas and Eleanor vs. Ferdinando Hastings, earl of Huntington, re. Eleanor's jointure, 1629–32, HL, HP, Box 2 (12), Box 3 (1). These documents claim she had a very great marriage portion; Claim about tapestries, fire irons, &c. which Eleanor's father had had in Ireland, Hastings Legal Box 4 (6).

255 Josiah Bodley's account of the state of the plantations, April 1613, HL, HP, Box 4 (2), calendared *in extenso* in Bickley (ed.), *Hastings, Volume IV*, pp 159–82; HL, Hastings Deeds 3546, 3598, 3600, 3602; HL, Hastings Manorial Papers, Box 76 (2–4).

256 HL, Hastings Deeds, 3517; NAI, Chancery MS I89; HL, HP, Family Papers, Box 16 (11); Pleas and demurrer of P.C. in case between Sir John Davies* and Sir Patrick (recte Piers) Crosby and Dame Elizabeth, his wife, late wife of George Earle of Castlehaven, *c.*1620, HL, Hastings Legal Papers, Box 3 (1).

257 HL, Hastings Deeds 3501, 20 March 1609; Purchase of the manor and tithes of Picton in counties Hertfordshire, Essex, Bedfordshire and Northamptonshire, HL, Hastings Family Papers, Personal Boxes 14 (23), 15 (5), Hastings Oversized Box M8/17.

reinvigoration of the Irish revenues.'[258] Salisbury's death in 1612 frustrated his ambitions and he failed to acquire other influential patrons who could facilitate his return; he used his frequent visits to England where he was still serjeant-at-law and his writings to maintain his profile in the hope of advancement there.

Davies was heavily involved in planning for the parliament of 1613, including legislation and the electoral strategy that included the constitutionally doubtful creation of 40 new boroughs with parliamentary representation to ensure a Protestant majority; his own return for Fermanagh County was regarded as illegal by the Catholic opposition who also argued that as attorney general he was ineligible to stand for election. His nomination as speaker was highly offensive to them; the undignified scuffle on his election as prolocutor led to their secession from parliament. On its resumption in October 1614, aware of the need for co-operation, Davies worked hard to ensure its smooth and successful operation and James commended his work and 'bestowed upon him a booke of ffeefarme' to compensate for his financial loss during the parliament, although as he continued to be paid as attorney general it is unclear what those losses could be. He pleaded to be able to resign his Irish offices but James insisted on his remaining in Ireland for the time being.[259] In February 1619 he received licence to be absent from Ireland for four months and having transferred his allegiance to Buckingham, he was finally replaced as attorney general on 30 October 1619 by William Ryves* and returned to England where he resumed his work as serjeant-at-law and as an assize judge.[260]

As a writer, Davies made two major contributions on Irish politics and law, his *Discoverie of the true causes why Ireland was never entirely subdued, nor brought under obedience of the crowne of England untill the beginning of his majesties happie raigne* (1612) and the first collection of Irish law reports *Le premier report des cases … en les courts del roy en Ireland* (1615). While valuable, they were also vehicles of self-promotion for the crown, but especially for Davies. For Davies, a strong crown, in England and in Ireland, was necessary to enforce the law, the only guarantee of peace, property and prosperity and conquest doctrine continued to serve as a justification for English sovereignty over Ireland; the *Discoverie* presented the crown and common law as framing a commonwealth which benefitted all subjects, abolishing ethnic divisions and Gaelic chiefs' tyranny. This repeatedly reprinted work shaped perceptions of Jacobean Ireland, lauding Chichester's regime's reforms and disregarding the 'self-serving nature of the king's Irish administration' of Davies' own day and 'concealing a history of atrocity and injustice.'[261] Lacking relevant common law precedents, Davies adopted 'divers rules of the civil law and the customary law of France agreeable to our law in this point.' A case in point is the valuable Bann fishery, which Davies' advice secured for the crown,

258 *Oxford DNB*.
259 James to Chichester in favour of Davies, 17 Oct. 1615, HL, HP, MS 15,076.
260 Licence from James for John Davies to be absent from Ireland for four months, 23 Feb. 1619, HL, Hastings Oversized Box M8/16.
261 Pawlisch, *Sir John Davies*, p. 13.

providing an inducement for investors in Ulster. Davies' appropriation of civil law precepts allowed the crown to seize the Bann fishery because the sea flows into rivers. Davies' inventive, self-serving and unscrupulous development of 'judge-made law' was consistently used against the native community and inevitably contributed to increasing Catholic mistrust of the Irish legal system, but it also set the pattern for colonial expansion elsewhere.'[262]

Davies was an active member of the 1621 English parliament, sitting on many committees and contributing to debates on economic issues and on Irish affairs. He defended his own financial interests, the Irish parliament and the royal prerogative, asserting that 'Ireland is a member of the crown of England … [and] that this kingdom here cannot make laws to bind that kingdom, for they have a parliament of their own.' He assured the Commons that the abuses in Ireland instanced by Sir John Jephson were few and should be dealt with by the Irish parliament. Davies also opposed a bill restricting Irish cattle imports, describing Ireland as 'a commonwealth but growing. Stop them in their trade and you kill them in their growth.'[263] Promoted to prime serjeant, he was ineligible for membership of the parliament in 1624 but summoned to support the Lords with legal advice.[264]

In 1622 Davies published a revised edition of his three major poems, *Nosce teipsum*, *Astrea*, and *Orchestra*, and in 1624 he translated the Psalms.[265] His *A perfect abridgement of the eleaven bookes of reports* [*of Sir Edward Coke*] (1651) and *The question concerning impositions* (1656) were published posthumously; the latter, written between 1614 and 1621, possibly at Buckingham's request, addressed one of the most controversial issues of the day and was widely circulated in manuscript.[266]

Davies' home life was not happy; both their sons, one of whom was significantly disabled, predeceased him and Eleanor's religious exuberance was frequently aimed aggressively at her husband, prophesying his demise in 1623 and wearing mourning from that date until his death from apoplexy in December 1626, the day before he was to be installed as chief justice of king's bench in England. In addition, his in-laws enjoyed unsavoury reputations. Davies died before their ultimate disgrace, the execution in 1630 of the second earl of Castlehaven for gross sexual misconduct against his wife and her daughter, his own stepdaughter and sodomy with his servants. Eleanor's pronouncements drew her into quarrels and, from 1633, to fines and imprisonment.[267] Their daughter Lucy was John's heir and

262 This case was revisited in the early twentieth century as 'something of a *cause célèbre* within nationalist circles'. See Pawlisch, *Sir John Davies*, pp 11–12, 84–102.

263 Treadwell, *Buckingham and Ireland*, pp 158, 163.

264 HL, Hastings Oversized Box M8/15.

265 Alexander B. Grosart (ed.), *The complete poems of Sir John Davies, with memorial-introduction and notes*, 2 vols (Edinburgh, 1876).

266 An argument upon the question of impositions in Ireland, with an answer, Cambridge University Library, MS Ff.III.17, calendared in Donovan and Edwards, *British sources for Irish history*, p. 13; Bodl. Lib., Willis MS 57, fos. 123–236.

267 Jacob to Davies, 13 May 1617, HL, HP, MS 15,061; Cynthia B. Herrup, *A house in gross disorder:*

was married aged eleven to Ferdinando Hastings, with a dowry of £6,500.[268] Despite their earlier tensions, John Donne preached Davies' funeral sermon.[269]

MATTHEW DE RENZY (de Renzi, de Rinzi) **(1610–13 – 28 August 1650 – July 1652) u.c., 1641[270]**

2 s. Sir Matthew de Renzy (1577–1634) and Anne (d. 1646+), da. Richard Maypowder, Killinaboy; m. by 1633, Mary, da. Sir John Moore, Croghan, King's County, and Dorothy, da. Archbishop Adam Loftus, Dublin, and Alice Purdon.
ed. Inner Temple, 1628; King's Inns, 20 May 1633.

De Renzy's German father settled in Ireland in 1606, acquiring lands in King's County and living at Clanona (Moostowne or Castlederenzy). His mother came from an English family settled in the Irish midlands in the previous century. Sir Mathew was an energetic planter with a deep suspicion of his neighbours, the Coughlans, who wrote to Falkland to request the post of clerk of the council for himself and his (unnamed) son in January 1630; the request was unsuccessful because the post had already been granted to someone else, but Mathew Jr did conduct some business for the former lord deputy in 1630.[271] Sir Matthew was Irish agent for Oliver St John, James Hay, earl of Carlisle, and Lionel Cranfield, earl of Middlesex. Mathew worked with his father on the latter's account.[272]

Matthew's marriage connected him to the extensive Loftus* and Moore networks (he was Thomas Moore's brother-in-law), and to Forth and Digby. He was also linked to Crofton, a member of whose family married Susan Maypowder. He held lands in King's County, Meath, Monaghan, Kilkenny and 1,000 acres in Wexford; his depositions variously claimed losses of £1,892 from lands and debts, some due from John Coughlan, £2,000 in mortgages, £1,000 in property, and

sex, law, and the 2nd earl of Castlehaven (Oxford, 1999); Case against Lady Eleanor Davies, als. Touchet, als. Douglas, 24 Oct. 1633, HL, Hastings Legal Papers, Box 6 (1), where it is noted that she was 'Fined £3,000 & imprisoned until she enter sufficient bond as security that she would write no more.'

268 Deed of gift from John Davies to his daughter Lucy, 1 Aug. 20: Jac. I, HL, HP, Box 16 (16), 'for her better preferment in marriage the mesuage house wherein I do dwell in St Martin in the Fields, all of the manor of Sambourne lately mortgaged unto me by Sir Richard Gifford, seaven peeces of Arras or Bruxelles hanging in my dining room or chamber in the house in St Martin in the Fields, and the three peeces of Tentstitch hangings in the withdrawing room next the gallery with the canopy of green damask there & all other my hangings, beds, bedsteads, quilts, coverings household stuff & furniture in the said house and my dishes and silver and other silver or guilt plate'; Recognizance for the dowry of Lucy Davies, 16 July 1623, Indenture for Lucy Davies' jointure, 17 July 1623, HL, Hastings Personal Box 17 (1–4).

269 Pawlisch, *Sir John Davies*, p. 33.

270 Matthew was elected by 7 July 1641 for an unidentified constituency.

271 Mathew de Renzy to Falkland, 29 Jan. 1630, BL, Sloane MS 3,827, fo. 170v; Falkland to De Renzy, 18 April 1630, NAI, MS 2,445, p. 75; Sir Matthew is buried in St Mary's Church, Athlone, where a large memorial was erected to him by Matthew Jr.

272 Brian Mac Cuarta, 'A planter's funeral, legacies and inventory: Sir Matthew de Renzy (1577–1634)', *JRSAI*, 127 (1997), 18–33; Roy E. Schreiber, *The first Carlisle: Sir James Hay, first earl of Carlisle as courtier, diplomat and entrepreneur, 1580–1636* (Philadelphia, 1984), 158–62.

£300 in profits from leases.[273] His sale of property to Arthur Blundell led to a dispute with Nicholas Loftus which resulted in petitions to the House of Lords in 1647. He was in London in April 1642 and Chester in August 1650, and his will, drawn up in that month, just before his return to Ireland, gives some indication of his estate in Ireland, which he bequeathed to the pregnant Anne Trelawney alias Middleton of Chester, for life, with remainder to her child if it was a son. De Renzy named Maurice Eustace* and Thomas Piggott as two of his trustees.[274] Like his father, Matthew had on-going disputes with his neighbours the Coughlans, nor was he one of the freeholders supporting Captain William Parsons' attempt to have Parsonstown (Birr) made the county town and it is instructive that he was not known to have been returned for any King's County constituency.[275]

WILLIAM DOBBINS (Dobbyns) (*c*.1594 – 1641) **Waterford, 1634**

s. Peter Dobbins, Waterford and ____; m. 1) by 1618, Ellen Sherlock (d. 1663+), Gracedieu, Waterford; 2); ____; e.s. Peter m. Beale Wadding, 1640; younger sons James, Nicholas, John, Laurence, da. Margaret m. 1639, Piers Aylward, e.s. Sir Peter Aylward, Faithlegg, Waterford.[276]
ed. Lincoln's Inn, 1612; King's Inns, 1628.
Bur. Holy Trinity Cathedral, Waterford.

Dobbins was a prominent figure in Waterford city and county, being admitted a freeman in 1626 when its charter was reissued and becoming mayor in 1629–30. Despite this, he was excluded from Waterford's commission of peace in 1625, although he was a corn commissioner for the city in 1630 and mayor of Waterford's staple in 1639. He inherited property from his uncle Nicholas Dobbins of Waterford, gent., in 1623.[277] William held property in St Peter Street, Wattkins Mill and at Whiges Meadow and other places in the city, but lived nearby at Ballymackill where he held 1,169 acres worth £250, as well as other property in Wexford. His wealth may be judged by the dowry of £1,600 he provided when his daughter Margaret married John Aylward, cousin and heir of Sir Peter of Faithlegg, in May 1639.[278] In April 1627, with Wadding*, he was engaged in a chancery case about a green, ownership of which was disputed between the Abbey of St Johns and the Corporation of Waterford.[279] The extent, if any, of his legal

273 Depositions of Matthew de Renzy, 4 Feb. 1642, TCD, MS 809, fo. 274, and undated, TCD, MS 810, fo. 95v.
274 TNA, PROB 11/224/466.
275 NAI, MS M 2,448, pp 20–1, 80–4, 104–5, 124, 180–2; Birr Castle, MS A/1/19.
276 Simington (ed.), *Civil Survey*, Waterford, p. 152; Tallon (ed.), *Court of Claims*, pp 82, 113–14, 255, 328–9; William Carrigan, 'Old Waterford wills', *JWSEIAS*, 11 (1908), 91–6; NLI, MS 40,889/38(3).
277 TCD, MS 672, fo. 183r; Caulfield (ed.), *Youghal*, p. 162; NAI, RC 5/23, pp 246–58.
278 J.T. Gilbert (ed.), 'Archives of the municipal Corporation of Waterford' in HMC, *Tenth Report of the Royal Commission on Historical Manuscripts, Appendix 5* (London, 1885), p. 278; Julian C. Walton, 'The freemen of Waterford, 1542–1650', *IG*, 5:5 (1978), 560–72; Caulfield (ed.), *Youghal*, p. 162; Niall J. Byrne (ed.), *The Great Parchment Book of Waterford: Liber Antiquissimus Civitatis Waterfordiae* (Dublin, 2007), pp 61, 225; Simington (ed.), *Civil Survey*, Waterford, pp 151ff, 193; Tallon (ed.), *Court of Claims*, pp 328–9.
279 NAI, Chancery MS AA184, taken from Kenneth Nicholls' calendar.

practice is unclear, but his membership of King's Inns suggests that he had a local practice.

JAMES DONNELLAN (1588 – 1665) **Trinity College, Dublin, 1628, 1634**[280]
3 s. Nehemiah Donnellan, bishop of Tuam (1595–1609) and Elizabeth (Isabel), da. Nicholas Daniel (O'Donnell); m. by 1627, 1) Mary (d. 5 April 1635), da. Richard Barry and Anne Cusack; 4 s., James, John, Edmond and Richard, 2 da., Ann and Sarah.[281] 2) by 1645 Sarah da. Bishop Jonas Wheeler, Ossory, w. of Ald. M. Tyrell, Dublin.
ed. Trinity College, Dublin, scholar 1607, BA, 1610, F.TCD, 1612,[282] MA, 1613; Lincoln's Inns, 1616; Bar, 1623; King's Inns, 1623.
Bur. Christ Church.
Likeness: *Plate 15* Public Records Office of Northern Ireland.[283]

Although of Gaelic origin, Donnellan was very well connected, especially through his clerical links, which with his stellar academic career in Trinity College contributed to his welcome at Lincoln's Inns, where he was admitted and sponsored by Sir James Ley, the chief justice of the king's bench.[284] He was granted the rectories of Cloghcarroll and Rooghwania, Limerick, in 1612, presumably because he was at that stage expected to make a career in the church. He became one of the small band of Protestant Irish students who regularly signed in other Irish students – in Donnellan's* case, these included Maurice Eustace*, Bellings and James Barry* (Donnellan's* brother-in-law and fellow MP for TCD in 1634). In the same year that he was called to the Bar and admitted to King's Inns, he was appointed as Clanricard's solicitor to attend to his business in Dublin, at a salary of £20 annually, one of the many men with Galway connections to advise the earl.[285] In the following year he was let into chambers in the King's Inns and described as a 'fellow'. He was retained by Boyle in the 1630s.[286] As Clanricard's 'principal servant and steward' he was a member of the jury impannelled in Galway to judge the king's title to land there, in anticipation of the plantation and he was one of only two jurors to support the king's title.[287] With Alexander* and

280 TCD, Particular Book, fo. 100r.
281 Terry Clavin, 'Donnellan, James', *DIB*; Fitzgerald and Lamacraft (eds), *Some funeral entries of Ireland*, p. 47; sons and daughters christened Oct. 1628, 2 Oct. 1629, 4 Oct. 1630, 29 Nov. 1632, 23 Oct. 1631 and 24 Jan. 1639 respectively, St John's, Dublin. Mills (ed.), *Registers of St John the Evangelist*, pp 16–17, 19–21, 31.
282 TCD, MS 2,160, no. 10.
283 https://artuk.org/discover/artworks/sir-james-donnellan-c-15881665-lord-chief-justice-of-the-common-pleas-168847/search/keyword:james-donnellan--referrer:global-search [accessed 12 July 2023]. I am grateful to Liam Maloney for drawing this portrait to my attention.
284 Lincoln's Inn, Admission Registers, 1605–14, fo. 55r. Donnellan's other signatory was Henry Ley. Ley had played a significant role in the re-establishment of the King's Inns in Dublin and was later to become Chief Justice in England and lord treasurer. Kenny, *King's Inns*, pp 76–8; Ball, *Judges in Ireland*, i, p. 337.
285 NLI, MS 3,117, fo. 51, July 1623, also fos. 72, 81. The connection was through a John Donnellan who worked also for Clanricard, although a recusant. BL, Sloane MS 3,827, fos. 165–6.
286 Grosart (ed.), *Lismore Papers*, 1st series, iii, p. 222, under 20 Dec. 1633, lease of lands in Cross Tipperary to Boyle from O'Brien Arragh, Sarsfield & Comyn of Limerick councell for them, Donnellan* & Goodman for Boyle; Grosart (ed.), *Lismore Papers*, 1st series, iv, pp 68–9.

others, he witnessed a church deed in Dublin in April 1633.[288] He leased lands in Roscommon from Clanricard, had a house in Rathmire, Westmeath, and in 1631 he lent £150 on bond on the Dublin staple.

He was nominated as MP in 1634 by Wentworth and was an active member of parliament, sitting on the important privileges committee, and those on bills concerning buggery, bigamy, ease of pleading suits, erecting houses of correction, about levying subsidies in Connacht, and conference committees with the Lords and with the privy council about desirable legislation. As a judge he was not eligible to be returned in 1640. Donnellan had excellent connections in the administration and the Parliament. He was Richard Barry's son-in-law and, through this marriage, connected also to the Ware, Cusack, Parsons and Loftus families. His second marriage linked him to Wemys.

James was described as a 'fellow of the King's Inns' in 1624 when he was assigned a prestigious chamber there and was one of five trustees of the King's Inns appointed in 1638 (the others were James Barry*, Maurice Eustace*, Sir Adam Loftus, and Robert Meredith), treasurer from 1639 and a member of the council. In 1643 with the trustees, Bolton*, Sir William Parsons, William Ryves* and others he had a lease of a house near King's Inns for 41 years and was assigned the new chambers which had been intended for George Radcliffe*.[289]

He was appointed third justice of Connacht in 1627 and chief justice there in 1634 and third justice of the common pleas (1637–44), holding both offices simultaneously. He was a justice of assize in Ulster, 1637 to 1641.[290] He was one of the judges to answer the Commons' queries on Darcy's* *Argument*. Donnellan was in Connacht on the outbreak of the rebellion and assisted Clanricard in keeping the peace between the townsmen and the crown soldiers. He was back in Dublin as part of Ormond's inner circle attempting to arrange a cessation with the Confederates and liaising between Ormond and Clanricard. He gave an opinion about the Confederation's claims for the customs in 1643 and was in Oxford as an agent to advise Charles on Irish affairs in 1644,[291] the year in which Ormond, doubting his loyalty, removed him from his position as justice of the common pleas. With other lawyers, he was consulted by Ormond on the legal aspects of the practice of Catholic rites in 1645. He was wounded and his son was killed near his house at Barberstown, Dublin, in July 1650 and in December 1652, his eldest son James and nephew William Donnellan were killed near his house at the Furroughs,

287 Wentworth and the Commissioners for the Plantation to Coke, 25 Aug. 1635, in Knowler (ed.), *Letters and dispatches*, i, pp 453, 495.

288 McEnery and Refausé (eds.), *Christ Church deeds*, p. 312.

289 Kenny, *King's Inns*, p. 142; J. Ainsworth (ed.), 'Survey of documents in private keeping: third series', p. 3; King's Inns, MS B1/1, fos. 75r, 76v, 85r, 112r–13v, 178v.

290 HL, HP, MS 14,054.

291 Lords J. & Council to Secretary Nicholas, 18 Nov. 1643, Bodl. Lib., Carte MS 68, fo. 502r, That on 12 November they received the king's commission for holding the parliament and a copy of his majesty's letters of 17 October summoning Lord Kerry, Sir Geratt Lowther, Sir William Stewart, James Donnellan* and Sir Paul Davies* to repair to him in England, but excusing Davies, whose attendance was necessary in Ireland.

north County Dublin. November 1652, his horses disturbed at the Furrows but he came to an arrangement with those disturbing them.[292]

Donnellan continued to work as a judge in the 1650s receiving a commission to be a justice of the peace in Leinster in 1651, was responsible for justice in Louth and Dundalk in August 1652. He was in Cork the following December and taking depositions in Dublin in January 1653 as a member of the High Court of Justice, while he was also president of that court by the May 1653, the year in which he was sent to administer justice in Ulster. In 1654 he was still acting as a judge, with a salary of £300, and a supplement of £100 for his work as advisor to the Court of Claims; that year Fleetwood nominated Donnellan, John Bysse* and James Barry* as judges and Cromwell restored him to the bench of common pleas in the following year.[293] Attempts were made to rescind his appointment because of his Irish birth, but he was defended by Henry Cromwell and he became commissioner of the Prerogative Court in 1656; his willingness to hang fellow-Irishmen may have been encouraged by the doubts about his loyalty. On the other hand, he did support some other natives in their quest for reasonable settlements in the 1650s. Lands in Galway and Roscommon were reserved for him in the transplantation, but by 1658 he was forced to ask his fellow benchers for financial concessions and the right to live in the King's Inns.[294] He was a commissioner of the Poll Money Ordnance in Counties Dublin and Roscommon and in Athlone town in 1660. On the Restoration, he was made a privy councillor and chief justice of the common pleas.

NICHOLAS DORMER (*c.*1580 – d. 1642–3) **New Ross, 1634, 1640**

s. ? George Dormer and ____; m. ____; at least 1 s., 2 da.[295]
ed. Clifford's Inn, Inner Temple, 1596; King's Inns, 1607.

The Dormers were influential in the New Ross area; William Dormer was MP for Ross in 1560 and his son George, possibly Nicholas' father, was a lawyer and sovereign of the town who had negotiated its 1567 charter. Nicholas was a justice of the peace by 1608, possibly *ex officio* as sovereign of New Ross, sheriff of Wexford in 1609, and named as recorder in the town's 1612 charter, although he may have held the position earlier. He continued to work as a lawyer, practicing in chancery cases from 1629.[296] In 1623 he was one of those collecting contributions

292 TCD, MS 810, fos. 357n, 375r, 379r. These may be the same places. Clarke (ed.), *1641 Depositions, Volume IV: Dublin*, pp 377, 385–8, 397–9.

293 Marsh's Library, MS Z3.1.1, no. 68; Kenny, 'Not every judge a phoenix'; *idem*, 'Black Book of King's Inns'; Clarke (ed.), *1641 Depositions, Volume IV*, p. 393.

294 Cunningham, *Conquest and land in Ireland*, pp 102, 109; TCD, MS 811, fos. 231, 233, 235; MS 834, fo. 198r; MS 838, fo. 195r; MS 826, fos. 241r–2v, 267.

295 TCD, MS 1,216, fo. 24r; NLI, GO, MS 72, Funeral Entries, Volume 9, 1640–63, p. 262; Fitzgerald and Lamacraft (eds), *Some funeral entries of Ireland*, pp 50, 103.

296 P.D. Vigors, 'List of the sovereigns of the town of New Ross, County Wexford, from 1584–1841', *Journal of the Royal Historical & Archaeological Association of Ireland*, 4th series, 9 (1889), 312–17; McGrath, 'Kick-starting New Ross' renewal'; NAI, Chancery MS BB183, BB207; Ohlmeyer, 'Records'.

to send agents to England and in 1631 was a commissioner for New Ross for managing the export of corn to England.[297] He lived at Camline and he had other property in New Ross and Bantry barony in which it was situated.[298] He was connected to other local families, including the Butlers and Synnotts and Shees who had provided members of previous parliaments. He sat on many parliamentary committees, mostly concerning local issues and was added to the committee on privileges in January 1641. In the first year of the rebellion he moved from Camline to the Irish quarters in New Ross, where he died.[299]

CHARLES DOYNE (Dunne) (Cathaoir Ó Duinn) **(1561+ – May 1617)**[300]
Trinity College, Dublin, 1613

4 legitimate s. Teige O'Doyne (d. 1606), chief of Hy-Regan and Elizabeth, da. James Mac Thomas FitzGerald, Ballyshannon;[301] unm.
ed. Christ Church, Oxford, BA (1586) MA (1591); FTCD, 1593; TCD, LL.D.

Dunne had an unusual career as a scion of a Gaelic family who made a career as a lawyer in crown service. He was educated in England, from where he asked Burghley to forward his petition to the queen seeking relief and reward for his and his father's good services in Ireland against the rebels in 1597.[302] He spent 17 years in Oxford and returned to Ireland to be a fellow of Trinity College, Dublin, and received its first doctorate in law. He was master in chancery from 20 September 1602 and judge of the archbishop of Dublin's prerogative court by May 1605.[303] He was sued in chancery by Nicholas Toole of Clondalkin when he stood surety in the Liberty Court of St Sepulchre for the absconded who was accused of stealing a horse.[304]

He conducted a lengthy and vicious dispute with his brother Teige Óg about their inheritance from their father in King's County in which Charles attempted to uphold the Irish customs of tanistry and gavelkind that Teige denounced as 'barbarous', presumably because that supported his case. Despite attempted arbitration, Charles was able to prolong the suit to his own advantage by switching venues and courts and filing counter-claims, and the matter moved from the assizes to chancery, involving William Talbot* and finally to the common law courts, without resolution.[305] Charles' will largely benefitted his nephews, especially Barnaby Dunne to whom he had made a feoffment of his estates 31 March 1617

297 *Cal. S.P. Ire., 1615–25*, pp 441–2; Caulfield (ed.), *Youghal*, pp 160–7.
298 *Inq. cancel. Hib. repert.*, i, Wexford, Jac. I (19), Car. I (10, 73); Simington (ed.), *Civil Survey*, Wexford, pp 203–6, 235, 238, 245, 249, 251–2.
299 TCD, MS 818, fo. 279.
300 NLI, GO, MS 66, Funeral Entries, Volume 3, 1604–22, p. 64.
301 Kenneth W. Nicholls (ed.), *The O'Doyne (Ó Duinn) manuscript* (Dublin, 1983), pp ix–x, Table B, pp 170–2.
302 Dunn to Burghley, 1597, BL, Lansdowne MS 85, fos. 110–12.
303 Hayes, *Patentee officers*; McEnery and Refausé (eds), *Christ Church deeds*, p. 296.
304 NAI, MS Chancery G367. See also Memorandum signed by Carolus Duinn on 6 November 1613 concerning Sir John Talbot's will, Bodl. Lib., Talbot MS c. 61/1.
305 Nicholls (ed.), *O'Doyne (Ó Duinn) manuscript*, pp x, 8–9, 51–3, 55–73, 92ff, 102; Crawford, *Star Chamber*, pp 35–6.

to Launcelot Bulkeley, Robert Leicester and Henry Lynch.* He also left money to the poor of Iregaine, £10 to chancellor Thomas Jones for a silver jug or bowl and the same to Trinity College to buy a silver cup with his name and arms thereupon, as well as eleven books, reports and Fitzharbart's *Grand abridgement*, specifying that his name be written in each of them.[306] He was succeeded as master in chancery by Thomas Ryves.*[307]

MAURICE EUSTACE[308] (1595 – 22 June 1665) **Athy, 1634**
Kildare Co., 1640 (Speaker)

e.s. John fitz William Eustace (d. 1623), Harristown (Irishtown), Kildare and Catherine ____;[309] m. after 24 May 1633, Charity (1606–78), da. Sir Robert Dixon and Maud Bee, Dublin;[310] no legitimate children, but son Maurice and da. Mary born in Chester.
ed. Trinity College, Dublin, 1610, BA, 1615, MA, 1618, fellow 1617; Lincoln's Inns, 1619; Bar, 1625; King's Inns, 1627.
Kt. March 1640.
Bur. Castlemartin, Co. Kildare.

The Eustaces were an important Old English family in Kildare and Carlow. Most of the family, including his cousin Oliver Eustace, MP for Carlow County in 1640, remained Catholic, but Maurice's father was a Protestant and held the office of Constable of Naas. Maurice was a protégé of Adam Loftus*, later Lord Ely and was presented to Lackagh and Downey vicarages in Kildare in 1612 in anticipation of his embarking on a career in the church, but although he became a fellow of Trinity College, Dublin, and lectured in Hebrew, he chose to become a lawyer. His entrance to Lincoln's Inns was eased by Lord Deputy Oliver St John who had also attended that institution and by a grant from the crown, on the Irish privy council's recommendation, a unique instance of state support for an Irish law student.[311] Maurice developed an extensive practice, advising Cork about a case taken against him and representing Christopher Wiccombe before the privy council in 1632. Ormond retained his services in 1639 and he acted for his cousin Oliver Eustace in a land deal in the same year and for Bramhall in July 1640; he also worked on chancery cases from at least 1628. The value of his legal practice may be estimated from the grant of £1,000 made in March 1641 as compensation for his loss of earnings, due to his role as speaker; this money remained unpaid in 1644–5, when he was granted the abbey of Cong, Co. Mayo, and other lands at

306 Nicholls (ed.), *O'Doyne (Ó Duinn) manuscript*, pp 170–2; TCD, MSS MUN/V/1/1, fo. 199v, MUN/1/51; *Rot. Pac. Jac.*, pp 65, 302.
307 HL, HP, Box 5 (10); HL, HP, MS 15,743, 18 June 1617.
308 Terry Clavin, 'Eustace, Sir Maurice', *DIB*; Robert Armstrong, 'Eustace, Sir Maurice', *Oxford DNB*; Eustace F. Tickell, 'The Eustace family and their lands in Co. Kildare', *Kildare Arch. Soc. Jn.*, 13 (1946–63), 307–41, 364–413; Ball, *Judges in Ireland*, i, pp 262–4, 269, 271, 272–6, 344–6; Hart, *History of the king's serjeants at law*, pp 57–60.
309 NAI, MS Betham Abstracts, Series I (MFGS 38/3), Vol. 21, p. 30.
310 Charity Eustace's will, Betham Prerogative Will Abstracts, NAI, MS 1/21, 1564–1699.
311 Fincham (ed.), 'Letters concerning Sir Maurice Eustace'; Hart, *History of the king's serjeants at law*, p. 57; Ohlmeyer, 'Records'.

Athy as recompense.[312] Charles issued letters appointing him prime serjeant in 1629, but Falkland had already promised the position to James Barry*. The administration continued to press for his appointment, describing Barry as 'young and incompetent' and urging that 'If there is a parliament in Ireland we shall want able men in part like this.'[313]

Maurice inherited his father's property in Kildare and also received grants of rectories, tithes and other property there and in Carlow, Wexford and Dublin in 1627, and further lands in Dublin in 1635; he leased the lands of Creagh Eustace in Wicklow from Boyle from 1630.[314] He was a party to the 1625 marriage settlement of the children of his Kildare neighbours Sir Arthur Savage and Walter Weldon (both MPs in 1613).[315] He was admitted an honorary freeman of Dublin in April 1632. His marriage reinforced his Dublin and Kildare connections, as his father-in-law was mayor of Dublin in 1633 and neighbour of the Eustaces in Kildare; Maurice was William Dixon and Robert Cusack's brother-in-law and Richard FitzGerald's cousin. His sale of lands at Calverstown to his father-in-law for £800 in May 1633 may have been part of his marriage settlement.[316] In December 1640 he guaranteed a bond of James Welleslie (Weasley) of Narraghmore, Kildare, on the Dublin statute staple. He lived at Skinner's Row in Dublin and in the mansion house he built at Harristown, Kildare. By 1639 he was already well-acquainted with Lord Conway and his agent George Rawdon, MP for Belfast in 1640.[317]

Maurice's education fitted him well for the offices he held under the crown – prime serjeant (1634), escheator of Leinster (1644) and master of the rolls (1645).[318] By 1637, however, Loftus was promoting Jerome Alexander* as Catlin's* successor as justice of assize in Meath, but Wentworth insisted on giving Eustace the role, asserting his confidence 'that Mr Serjeant Eustace is as well provided with all the necessaries requisite … to wit, with learning and integrity.'[319] In the summer of 1640 he pleaded with Wandesford not to be made attorney general.[320] Eustace was involved in the King's Inns as treasurer in 1636 and two years later, with James Barry*, Donnellan*, Sir Adam Loftus* and Robert Meredith, he was appointed

312 NLI, MS 43,288/ 2; Clarke, McGrath and Edwards (eds), *A lord justice's letterbook*, no. 194. He wrote to Ormond on Oliver's behalf concerning a lease between Ormond and Oliver, 14 May 1639, NLI, MS 2,306, pp 205ff; HMC, *Ormond*, new series, i, p. 44; William Bulkeley to Bramhall, 15 July 1640, HL, HP, MS 14,101; Bodl. Lib., Carte MS 68, fos. 125, 128v, quoted in Hart, *History of the king's serjeants at law*, pp 57–8; Bodl. Lib., Carte MS 68, fo. 127v.

313 Hart, *History of the king's serjeants at law*, p. 57.

314 Will of John Eustace of Harristown, 1 June 1623, [proved] 12 Feb. 1624, NAI, Betham Abstracts, Series I (MFGS 38/3), Vol. 21, p. 30; Simington (ed.), *Civil Survey*, Kildare, pp 52–6, 110.

315 NAI, MS RC 5/1, pp 190–206.

316 Gilbert, *C.A.R.*, iii, pp 261, 275; deed dated 24 May 1633, in possession of the author.

317 HL, HP, MS 14,335.

318 Hughes, *Patentee officers*.

319 Loftus to Wentworth, 13 April 1637, Wentworth to Loftus, 14 April 1637, Loftus to Wentworth, same date, Wentworth to Loftus, 15 April 1637, all in Knowler (ed.), *Letters and dispatches*, ii, pp 67–9.

320 Wandesford to Radcliffe, 21 June 1640, Bodl. Lib., MS Add. C. 286, fo. 28r.

trustee of the Inns. In 1643, he, with the other trustees and Bolton*, Sir William Parsons and William Ryves*, had a lease of a house near King's Inns for 41 years.[321]

His acceptance speech as speaker on 20 March lauded Wentworth's government and was widely admired for its Latinisms and classical references. Eustace was knighted some days afterwards. His time as speaker coincided with a constitutional crisis in Ireland and England; the Irish parliament was asserting its rights and trying to limit the Irish administration's arbitrary and self-interested exercise of its powers. As speaker, Eustace followed the administration's line and MPs had to work around his partial exercise of his office, e.g., failing to issue writs for by-elections; the high number of committees of the whole house appointed in 1640–1 was an effective means of neutralizing him. Despite his adherence to the administration, he urged moderation on the outbreak of the 1641 rebellion and advised that it would collapse if the Catholics were pardoned, but his recommendations were ignored by an administration bent on taking a very hard line.

Eustace became increasingly close to Ormond through the 1640s; the earl named him as one of the executors of his will in 1642. In March 1643 he was appointed as a commissioner to negotiate with the Confederates and was with Ormond at his meeting with their agents at Castlemartin and Kilcullen in June 1643. His lack of sympathy for the Catholic cause was well known and he was described as 'the second [George] Radcliffe'* and was one of the lawyers asked by Ormond to advise on the legality of Catholic religious ceremonies in 1645. Gradually, however, he came to display more conciliatory views on recusants.[322] He continued to act as speaker during parliament's intermittent sittings during the 1640s and Charles granted him money and property, yet the state of the crown's finances and lack of control over Ireland prevented these from being realized.

In September 1647, Ormond, who had left Ireland after surrendering Dublin to the English parliamentary forces, asked Eustace to write to him weekly to keep him informed of events in Ireland; however, as a strong royalist with pro-Catholic sympathies, the parliamentary authorities in Dublin arrested him in 1648 and sent him to Chester.[323] He remained in restraint until 1655, although he was free to develop a relationship with a local woman who bore his children, Maurice and Mary. In 1655 Arthur Annesley successfully urged Henry Cromwell to allow Eustace to return to Ireland, as 'it will no wayes conduce to the good of Ireland that such useful instruments as he be discouraged or diverted from going thither.'

321 Kenny, *King's Inns*, p. 142; King's Inns, MS B 1/1, fos. 44v, 66r, 70r, 74r; Ainsworth (ed.), 'Survey of documents in private keeping: third series', p. 3.

322 *Plot and progresse of the Irish rebellion*, p. 9.

323 *A letter from Sir Maurice Eustace Knight, His Maiesties serjeant at law in the kingdome of Ireland, and speaker of the House of Commons, in parliament there: being a perfect relation of the last true newes from Ireland* (London, 1642), sig. A2; Bodl. Lib., Carte MS 59, fos. 75r–6r; Secretary Nicholas to Ormond, 4 March 1644, Bodl. Lib., Carte MS 63, fo. 325r; Ormond to Sir Robert King, 9 April 1646, ibid., fo. 421; Edward Lord Conway to his son Edward, 6 Dec. 1643, HL, HP, MS 14,337; Ormond to Eustace, 21 Sept., 1647, in Thomas Carte (ed.), *A collection of original letters and papers, concerning the affairs of England, from the year 1641 to 1660, found among the duke of Ormonde's Papers*, 2 vols (London, 1739), i, pp 144–6.

Nevertheless, he was carefully watched and imprisoned in the following year for corresponding with the exiled King Charles.[324] Eustace resumed his legal practice, with Lady Ormond and Henry Cromwell among his clients; the latter appointed him to a committee to consider establishing a second college in Ireland.[325]

Eustace continued to amass property; he received a grant of lands in Dublin in 1658 and on the Restoration Charles II regranted him extensive lands in counties Kildare, Dublin, and Mayo. Much of these lands had formerly belonged to his Catholic relatives, to whom he either immediately returned or subsequently bequeathed them. He lived mainly in Dublin, moving from Skinner's Row to a magnificent house in Dame Street, with gardens sloping down to the Liffey; he rebuilt his fine mansion at Harristown, which was burned in 1648, and in the 1660s he built a house in Chapelizod, known as the King's House, replacing the earlier Phoenix House.[326] In 1663 the crown bought land from him for £10,000 at Chapelizod, which had cost him £4,000 shortly before the Restoration, in order to create a site for what would become the Phoenix Park; £7,875 of this was outstanding five years after his death. In 1663 he lost his lands at Cong when the Court of Claims decided it should be restored to its Catholic owners, but he built a church, school, bridge, and market place at Baltinglass, Co. Wicklow, which was created a borough under his patronage.[327]

Eustace retained his Kildare connections, including acting as commissioner of the Poll Money Ordnance in Kildare in 1660. In May 1660 he was included as a commissioner appointed by the Dublin Convention, of which he was not a member, to wait on Charles II and present the convention's 'humble desires'.[328] On his return to Ireland later that year he was made lord chancellor, lord justice (with Charles Coote) and a privy councillor, and was granted an annual pension of £1,500. Lords chancellor were traditionally speakers of the House of Lords, but Orrery objected to Eustace's appointment, 'against whom he had several materiall objections, besides his disability of body, and his being at best a cold friend to ye Declaration' (Eustace suffered from melancholy, which reduced his effectiveness). Bramhall was appointed instead but Eustace presided over the Lords in 1662–3.[329]

Eustace sympathized with the plight of Catholic royalists dispossessed by Cromwell and argued for greater tolerance towards Catholics generally, views which put him at odds with Coote and Orrery, both of whom were determined to uphold the Cromwellian settlement. As chancellor, Maurice prevented the transfer of lands that he believed belonged to loyal Catholics, permitted Catholic lawyers

324 Annesley to Henry Cromwell, 8 May 1655, BL, Lansdowne MS 821, fo. 3v.
325 Barnard, *Cromwellian Ireland*, pp 207–9.
326 For information on his houses, Maurice Craig, *The architecture of Ireland from the earliest times to 1880* (London, 1982), p. 140; *An account of the solemn funeral and interment of the right honourable, the countess of Arran, August 21, 1668* (London, 1668), pp 2–3. Lady Arran was laid out in Maurice's house, although this was after Eustace's death.
327 Tickell, 'The Eustace family'; NAI, MS D17,831; Barnard, *Cromwellian Ireland*, p. 193; PRONI, T707 | 1, p. 142; Lake* to Bramhall, 28 Sept. 1661, HL, HP, MS 15,137.
328 Clarke, *Prelude to restoration*, pp 299–300, 316.
329 BL, Add. MS 37,206, fo. 20r.

to plead before him and appointed Catholics to the commission of the peace; he had some influence over the other appointments to the bench and administration and strongly objected to Robert Meredith's re-appointment to the privy council. In 5 December 1660, Bishop John Leslie petitioned Charles II for the £4,000 worth of lands he was granted for his sufferings; Eustace and Orrery were asked to deal with the matter. In the following year, he refused to sign the warrant for Bramhall's *custodiam* of Chapleizod because it contained legal problems.[330] Throughout 1661 he wrote repeatedly to Ormond in London about his difficulties, but while Ormond and Charles II had some sympathy towards Irish Catholics, both were determined to maintain the crown's Protestant credentials. In October 1661 Ormond rebuked Eustace for associating himself too closely with the Catholics and despite minor successes Coote and Orrery frustrated his efforts to improve the recusants' lot and Maurice was glad to step down as lord justice on Ormond's return to Dublin as lord lieutenant in summer 1662. Eustace was concerned that he was too old for the position of chancellor and sickness, depression and the political isolation resulting from his pro-Catholic views reduced his effectiveness in this role. He had faced criticism from many, including the English Chancellor Clarendon.[331] By 1663 Ormond was coming under pressure from London to remove him, but while embarrassed by Eustace's unimpressive performance, he remained loyal to his old friend and ally.

Eustace was exercised about who would inherit his estates, his nephews or his illegitimate son and despite seeking advice from Bishop Jeremy Taylor of Down in 1663 he continued to vacillate. In the event, his estate, estimated to be worth £80,000, passed to his natural son Maurice and nephews Maurice and John Eustace and his final will, dated 20 June 1665 also established a lectureship in Hebrew in TCD. Unhappily there was an unseemly dispute between his heirs.[332] He may have been buried secretly as a Catholic, which would explain why Ormond arranged a state funeral for him on 5 July at St Patrick's Cathedral, Dublin, using a wax figure in the coffin as proxy for his corpse. The funeral sermon's over-emphasis on his loyalty to the Church of Ireland and Protestantism, prompt doubts about his religious position at the end of his life.[333]

JOHN EVERARD (*c.*1560 – 24 September 1624)[334] **Tipperary Co., 1613**

e.s. Sir Redmond Everard (d. by 1607), Ballyboy and Fethard, Co.Tipperary; m. 1) by 1587, Catherine (d. by 1624[335]), da. Fulke Comerford, Callan and Joanna Walsh, Waterford, sister of Sir Nicholas Walsh (d. 1615); 3 sons, Nicholas (1588–1633)[336] (Inner Temple 1604), Richard

330 HL, HP, MS 15,177; Eustace to Bramhall, 28 May 1661, HL, HP, MS 14,672.
331 Dennehy, 'Appointments to the bench'; Ball, *Judges in Ireland*, i, pp 344–6.
332 Fincham (ed.), 'Letters concerning Sir Maurice Eustace'.
333 W. S. B. D. [William Sheridan], *A sermon preach'd at the funeral of the Right Honorable Sir Maurice Eustace … with a short account of his life and death* (1665).
334 Cokayne, *Baronetage*, i, p. 239; Will, 24 Dec. 1624, proved 18 Nov. following, NLI, GO, MS 225, p. 18; NAI, MS RC 4/11, gives his date of death as 24 Dec. 1624.
335 Catherine was presumably dead by 1624, as she is not mentioned in John's will.
336 d. 4 June 1633; married Katherine da. James Butler, Lord Dunboyne, his children John

(created baronet, 1622), John, Gabriel and da. ____ m. Henry White*, son of Nicholas White fitz Henry of Clonmel, and Barbara ____.
ed. Clifford's Inn, Inner Temple, 28 August 1579; Bar, 1590;[337] King's Inns, 1607.
Kt. 10 February 1605.

John came from a Catholic gentry family in Tipperary – his father owned land at Ballyboy and in Fethard and represented Cross Tipperary in the 1585 parliament; John's brother James was a Jesuit, based in Callan from 1608. His father-in-law was treasurer to the tenth earl of Ormond and MP for Callan in 1585. John's late summons to the Bar, after twelve years studying law rather than the usual seven, was presumably occasioned by his marriage and the birth of his first son. John's family connections were important but local; his brother-in-law Garrett Comerford was attorney general of Connacht, his daughter married Henry White*, son of his fellow MP in 1613 and he was brother-in-law of the speaker of the 1585 Commons, Sir Nicholas Walsh. Everard's personal and business relationships were largely within the clique of Ormond lawyers and agents – Archers, Comerfords, Cowleys, Rothes, Tobins, Walshes and Whites – and in 1597 he was granted the wardship of Edmund Blanchville, son and heir of his father's fellow MP Gerald Blanchville. John's sons' and grandsons' marriages were to members of noble families, including the Lords Dunboyne, Fermoy, and Upper Ossory, demonstrating the social advances Everard had been able to make through his legal work and acquisition of property.[338]

On his return to Ireland he established a legal practice and quickly became important to the Butler peers, acting as attorney to recover the annuity of Theobald, Lord Cahir, in 1595, and serving as a trustee for Thomas Butler, tenth earl of Ormond, in land settlements. He continued to play a significant role as an adviser, agent, trustee and confidant to the Ormonds until his death three decades later. He was rewarded with leases of land, as well as his salary as an official of the Ormond Liberty, for his efforts for the earls and their families.[339] In the 1580s and 1590s he was also engaged in a number of transactions about property in Callan, Tipperary and took a chancery case about property in Waterford City.[340]

Everard was also in demand as an arbitrator, acting with his fellow lawyer Patrick Archer in a 1596 dispute between the 'High Town' and 'Irish Town' of Kilkenny and four years later with Garrett Comerford in a land dispute between the archbishop of Cashel and Derby fitz Philip O'Dwyer, sheriff of the liberty of Ormond. On the latter occasion, the earl described them as 'two gentlemen learned in the law'; in 1609 he and Patrick Archer were arbitrators in a land dispute

(m. Anne Roche, da. David, Lord Fermoy), Redmond, Katherine, Ellis and Cicely. Bur. Fethard Church. Fitzgerald and Lamacraft (eds), *Some funeral entries of Ireland*, p. 163.

337 William Henry Cooke (ed.), *Students admitted to the Inner Temple, 1547–1660* (London, 1878), p. 91.

338 NLI, MS D3260.

339 NLI, Ormond deeds, passim; e.g., NLI, MSS 11,046/51; D. 3260, D. 3305–8, D. 3359, D. 3428, D. 3426–9, D. 3437; D. 3454, D. 3456, D. 3499, D. 3553, D. 3579, D. 3581, D. 3587, D. 3589, D. 3591; *Inq. Cancel. Hib. repert.*, Kilkenny, Car. I (54).

340 NAI, MS Chancery, N. 87; NLI, MSS D. 3148–9, D. 3077–8.

between Ormond and Florence FitzPatrick, Lord of Upper Ossory, and in 1612 between Sir Thomas Ridgeway and Ormond.[341] The earl appointed John justice of the Liberty of Tipperary in April 1601, and the crown made him second justice of the queen's bench on 10 May 1602. He served as justice of the Liberty of Tipperary at a salary of £20 in 1612.[342] He held both offices simultaneously and was serving as justice of assize in Meath and Kilkenny (1603) and in Louth (1606), and in the Court of Castle Chamber; his place on the bench explains his eldest son, Nicholas' favourable terms of admission to the Inner Temple in 1604.[343]

John was knighted on 10 February 1605, but by this time his position on the bench was becoming increasingly difficult; although he was widely liked and respected, despite his ability, integrity and accepted loyalty to the crown, his refusal to conform to the established church was at odds with the increasingly strict crown religious policy. Ignoring hints to conform or resign, he was retained only because there was no suitable Protestant to replace him; in January 1607 he finally resigned, succeeded by the conformist Dominick Sarsfield. Chichester also insisted on his being removed from the Kilkenny circuit of assizes. John petitioned for a pension to compensate for the practice he had lost during his period on the bench and in 1607 was granted an annuity of £66 13*s.* 4*d.* (when he was described as 'an aged and civill Gentleman') on condition he would not act in any case against the king. He continued to be favoured by the state, including in property transactions and in obtaining charters for his home town of Fethard and its almshouses.[344]

He returned to practice and was, with his former colleagues in the administration and the coterie of Ormond's legal advisors and agents (including his cousin Michael Cowley, later recorder of Kilkenny who was nominated as a parliamentary candidate in 1628 and Patrick Archer), a founder member of the revived King's Inns on 21 June 1607; he had chambers there, initially with his son Nicholas, and was a member of its council.[345] He continued to act as justice of the Tipperary palatinate under both Thomas Ormond and his Catholic heir, Sir Walter Butler, John's fellow MP in 1613, with whom he worked closely in the Ormond liberty. In 1608 he was a trustee to secure Ormond's property for his daughter Lady Elizabeth Butler and her husband Lord Tulleophelim.[346]

While pursuing his legal career, John was also maintaining and developing his property around Fethard. He inherited substantial possessions from his father, including over seventy houses in the town, which he surrendered to the crown, receiving a regrant of the same property under English tenure in 1602–3. He paid

341 *Cal. S.P. Ire., 1600*, pp 11, 378; NLI, MSS D. 3437, D. 3516.

342 NLI, MSS 11,044, no. 97, D. 3514, D. 3453; Ball, *Judges in Ireland*, i, pp 227–8.

343 Crawford, *Star Chamber*, pp 32–3, 116, 481.

344 Chichester to John Davies, 13 Feb. 1607, HL, HP, Box 1 (61), warrant to draw up fiants of pardons to number of named men from Limerick & Tipperary, who had been examined by John Everard & Richard Boyle. BL, Add. MS 4,756, fo. 7r; Kenny, *King's Inns*, p. 81; Edwards, *Ormond lordship*, p. 269.

345 NLI, GO, MS 225, pp 18, 28; King's Inns, MS B 1/1, fos. 109r, 171r, 172r.

346 NLI, MSS D. 3426–9, D. 3456.

a fine of £2 on a grant passed on the Commission of Defective Titles in 1607.[347] Everard purchased additional property in Fethard and developed the town, negotiating its new charter in 1608 and three years later another charter for two almshouses, one built by his great-grandfather and the other by himself; he also built a substantial tholsel/market house after 1612 and restored his own mansion house in the centre of the town, laying out the main street and preserving and extending his oak wood. By the time of his death he had eighty-four houses, over 100 gardens, three castles, two watermills, and substantial other land in Fethard, as well as property in Clonmel and Cashel and in counties Tipperary and Waterford.[348]

Everard was opposition candidate for speaker in 1613; an unseemly fracas broke out over the administration's legally questionable electoral strategy and the hotly contested speakership, during which the Catholic MPs, including Walter Butler, put Everard in the speaker's chair, which he only vacated when the corpulent John Davies sat on top of him. The recusants seceded from parliament and John was one of the agents sent to represent the views of the Catholic MPs to the king in London, where he was imprisoned.[349] On the resumption of parliament in October 1614, he led the recusant opposition, serving on many committees, supporting the granting of subsidies and petitioning for Catholic lawyers to be restored to practice and for suspension of the penalties for non-attendance at church.[350] Catholics were barred from the King's Inns in retribution for their behaviour in parliament, but Chichester ensured Everard's readmission as a special case in 1615, which suggests he may also have been able to plead in crown courts. After that date, his public role was significantly limited by his Catholicism, though he continued in private practice, remaining closely associated with the Ormonds, defending their interests and regularly acting as trustee in their property deals and marriage settlements, as well as witnessing and overseeing earl Thomas' will. With Robert Rothe and Walter Lawless, he was summoned to England in November 1615, presumably about Ormond's business.[351] He was closely associated with the earls of Ormond and the administration of their estates and, with their other prominent legal advisor Robert Rothe, refused to obey an order for sequestration of the estate, demanding a proper

347 Inquisition held in Kilshelane, 13 Oct. 1607, NAI, MS RC 4/10, pp 1–22; HL, HP, Box 3 (40); *Cal. S.P. Ire, 1611–14*, p. 104.

348 NAI, MS RC 4/11, pp 457–60, 489, 500–1; Bodl. Lib., Carte MS 61, fo. 399; Bodl. Lib., Carte MS 62, fo. 105; Tadhg O'Keefe, 'William Lawson's "A new orchard and garden" (1618) and an early eighteenth-century depiction of Sir John Everard's mansion in Fethard, Co. Tipperary', *JRSAI*, 141 (2011), 201–4; *idem*, 'Townscape as text: the topography of social interaction in Fethard, County Tipperary, AD 1300–1700', *Irish Geography*, 33:1 (1999), 9–25; *idem*, *Fethard: Irish Historic Towns Atlas, no. 13* (Dublin, 2003); *idem*, 'Medieval towns, modern signs, identity inter-spaces: some reflections in historical archaeology' in Eleanor Conlin Casella and Chris Fowler (eds), *The archaeology of plural and changing identities: beyond identification* (New York, 2005), pp 11–32; Thomas Laffan, 'Fethard, County Tipperary: its charters and corporation records, with some notice of the Fethard Everards', *JRSAI*, 36 (1906), 143–53; NLI, MS 5,857.

349 Purnell and Hinds (eds), *Downshire*, iv, pp 128, 401, 407.

350 Jackson (ed.), 'Document' HMC, *Franciscan manuscripts*, pp 63ff.

351 Will, 16 Jan. 1614, NLI, MS D. 3580; *Cal. S.P. Ire., 1615–25*, pp 34, 95, 118, 236.

legal hearing of the matter for which they were imprisoned without trial in 1620–1 in Dublin and London, to facilitate the forfeiture of the Ormond estates.[352] On his release, he was acting with other judges in taking inquisitions post mortem in Waterford in 1621.[353]

In 1622 he resumed a representative role as one of the peers and gentry who contributed a list of grievances to the team of experts examining the ecclesiastical and temporal state of Ireland (which resulted in the publication of 'His majesty's directions for ordering and settling the courts within his kingdom of Ireland' in August 1622). In that forum, he played a prominent role as a legal expert, arguing against the operations of the presidency courts.[354] On 1 March 1620, Everard granted lands to Richard Wadding*, Sir Peter Aylward, Nicholas Everard, Michael Cowley, Thomas Gough*, Richard Butler, John and Richard Haly* and Richard Everard, Ballyboy, merchant, to the use of his eldest son Nicholas; it is significant that so many of these trustees were his fellow Munster lawyers. With his son Richard, he was defendant in a case in chancery taken by Sir William Fenton concerning lands in Tipperary in 1623.[355] He entertained the earl of Cork at Fethard in the summer of 1624, some months before his death. His will was proved the following November.[356]

EDWARD FITZHARRIS (*c.*1572 – d. 3 March 1641) **Limerick Co., 1634, 1640**

2 s. Matthew Fitzharris (FitzHenry), Moghmaine (Muckmayne), Wexford, and Margaret, da. Sir Walter Browne, Mulrankin, Wexford; m. by 1606 (probably much earlier) Gyles (Julia), only da. and heiress, John Roche, Kilfinane, Limerick; 7 s., 4 da.[357]
ed. Middle Temple, 1588; King's Inns, 1607.
Bart. 1622.
Bur. parish church Kilfinane.

Edward should not be confused with Edward (Fitz) Harris*, MP for Clonakilty in 1613. Fitzharris was a member of a family based at New Ross with a strong parliamentary tradition: his father was MP for Wexford County in 1585 and another Fitzharris represented New Ross in 1613.[358] Edward was William Browne's cousin and was related by marriage to Archer*. His Munster connections came through his wife who also brought him extensive lands at Kilfinane; this marriage

352 Edwards, *Ormond lordship*, pp 123, 282; TCD, MS 10,724; James I to the lord deputy of Ireland, 18 Aug. 1621, HMC, *Fourteenth Report of the Royal Commission on Historical Manuscripts, Appendix, Part VII* (London, 1895), p. 68; NLI, MS 11,046/5; NAI, MS Chancery AA/24.

353 Transcript of inquisition post mortem for Sir John FitzGerald, Deddocy (Dromana), Waterford, taken before Dominic Sarsfield, John Everard and others, 28 Oct. 18 Jac. I, Boole Library, University College Cork, MS 24,600/A/2.

354 Treadwell (ed.), *Irish commission of 1622*, pp 162–5, 190.

355 NAI, MS RC 4/11, pp 457–60, 489, 500–1, Chancery K55.

356 Will, 24 Dec. 1623, proved 18 Nov. 1624, NAI, MS Betham Abstracts, Series I (MFGS 38/3), Vol. 21, p. 31.

357 Cokayne, *Baronetage*, i, p. 246; NLI, GO, MS 72, Funeral Entries, Volume 9, 1640–63, p. 273; MS 225, p. 39; Micheál Ó Siochrú, 'Fitzharris, Edward', *DIB*. He was succeeded by his grandson and namesake, with whom he should not be confused.

358 McGrath, 'Membership', p. 64.

and his standing as a lawyer (he was a founder-member of the King's Inns), provided his qualifications for his unsuccessful candidacy for Limerick County in 1613, when he was one of the recusants' agents to London. A further Munster connection came with his son George's marriage to Joan, a daughter of Lord Kerry, which provided links with John FitzGerald, MacCarthy, Piers Crosby, Mervyn and Lord Fermoy. Apart from his Limerick property which included over 4,000 acres, he continued to hold 360 acres in Wexford and some lands from Sir William Sarsfield of Lucan in Dublin County.[359] Fitzharris was counsel in the 1610 exchequer case of the County Palatine of Waterford and acted as a lawyer for Cork and Thomond in the 1620s and 1630s. He also arbitrated a dispute between Cork and Ormond in 1635 and was appointed a commissioner to take evidence in 1639.[360] With David Roche, Callaghan O Callaghan and others he was sued in chancery about lands at Aghcrosse by Sir Arthur Hyde of Carrigineddy, Co. Cork and Edward himself took a case against father and son Thomas and William Roche concerning lands at Glyananayre.[361]

Fitzharris played an active part in administration and politics, as a member of the 1624–5 Limerick commission for the peace and as an agent to negotiate the Graces in 1628. He was also a prominent MP in 1634, when he was a member of a large number of committees. His impact in that parliament may be judged by his being imprisoned by Wentworth for an unspecified offence in November 1634; his contempt was discharged in the following month. Fitzharris was equally active in the 1640–1 parliament until his sudden death in early March 1641 deprived the opposition of a wise man trusted by all sides.[362]

GEOFFREY GALWAY (Galwey) (*c.*1574 – 2 April 1636)[363] **Limerick City, 1634**
e.s. Ald. James* Galway, Limerick and Kinsale, and Ellen Stritch, m. 1) by 1595, Anne, da. Ald. Nicholas Comyn, Limerick; his e. son John m. Elizabeth Betts, Norfolk, *o.s.p.*, leaving son Sir Geoffrey, 2nd Bart.; Geoffrey Sr's other children, Gabriel, Thomas, Nicholas, Geoffrey, Patrick (Thomas, Nicholas and Geoffrey *o.s.p*) and 5 da., Jennett m. William Galway*, Kinsale, Mary m. Nicholas Stritch, Limerick, Anne m. John Stritch, Limerick, Katherine m. Moriertagh O'Brien, Tuagh, Co. Limerick, Christian unmarried at time of father's death; 2) Mary, da. Morrogh MacSheehy, Ballyallevan, Co. Limerick and ____, 4 da., Margaret, Martha, Grace, Clara, all unm. at his death; 3) More (Jane), da. Moriertagh O'Brien, Tuagh, Co. Limerick; she rem. John Browne, Kilcomen, Kerry, 4 s. Sir Nicholas Browne, Molahiffe, da. Eleanor;[364] his grandson, heir

359 Simington (ed.), *Civil Survey*, Wexford, p. 143, Limerick, pp 230, 239–40, 243–6; *Inq. cancel. Hib. repert.*, Wexford, Car. I (27,124), Dublin, Jac. I (27); NAI, MS RC 5/1, pp 13–28.

360 Davies, *Le premier report*, fo. 67v; Grosart (ed.), *Lismore Papers*, ii, p. 123, iv, pp 125–6; NLI, MS 36,383/2.

361 NAI, MS Chancery I 165, L94 (taken from Kenneth Nicholls' calendar).

362 TCD, MS 672, fo. 183v; *Commons' Jn. Ire.*, 22 Nov. 1634, 11 Dec. 1634; Perceval-Maxwell, *Outbreak*, pp 75–6, 81, 136; Described by William St Leger as 'my good friend', St Leger to Ormond, 27 April 1637, NLI, MS 2,305, p. 199.

363 Cokayne, *Baronetage*, i, p. 258; Will, dated 28 March 1636, proved 12 May 1636, NLI, GO, MS 225, p. 79. Children – Mortagh, William, Patrick, Christian; RIA, MS 14/C/3/2, pp 332–5.

364 NLI, GO, MS 71, Funeral Entries, Volume 8, 1639–41, p. 89; NLI, GO, MS 79, Funeral Entries, Volume 17, p. 215, at http://catalogue.nli.ie/Record/vtls000529291#page/215/mode/1up [accessed 12 June 2020].

and namesake was 19 when Geoffrey died.
ed. Gray's Inn, 1591–7;[365] King's Inns, 1607.
1st Bart., April 1624.
Bur. Kinsale.

Geoffrey's grandfather, John Galway, came to Limerick from Kinsale, where the family still had interests. His father James* was MP for Kinsale in 1585 and Limerick in 1613. Geoffrey was mayor of Limerick in 1600 when he had a dispute with George Carew that resulted in his being fined £400 and being dismissed from the mayoralty, but while the English privy council ostensibly backed Carew, Geoffrey's punishment was moderated, partly through his father's intervention; he was still an alderman in 1632.[366] The year 1600 was one in which many Munster towns elected lawyers as mayor, but Geoffrey had already been involved in anti-English riots and was regarded as a key figure in ensuring that Limerick remained a strong Catholic city: it was reported that he 'spent many years in England studying the common law, and returning to Ireland about 1597 did so pervert the city of Limerick that by his malicious council and perjurious example he withdrew the Mayor, Aldermen and generally the whole city from coming to church.'[367]

His reputation in his community remained high – he was one of the seven members of the Limerick gentry and aristocracy whom John Bath suggested might be encouraged to 'compass a benevolence' in Munster and was an unsuccessful candidate for Limerick County in 1613. A lawyer and one of the founder members of the King's Inns, he had an extensive legal practice. In 1611 he was one of three arbitrators in a land dispute between Thomond and the freeholders of Cnonagh. The following year he successfully represented Walter Coppinger (Dominic's* father) and other Cork freemen in an Exchequer Court case against Crooke* and Catholic landowners in their opposition to the Wexford plantation. In 1634 he was acting for Cork in a case about lands in Cross Tipperary. With Henry Lynch* and Darcy* he was arbitrator between Thomond and Sir Tirlagh O'Brien's sons. His possession of a house in Thomas Street, Dublin is natural, given his legal practice.[368] He was a commissioner for Limerick City for managing the export of corn to England in 1631 and mayor of the Limerick staple in 1635.[369] He was an active member of the 1634–5 Commons, sitting on many committees. Geoffrey lived at Kawloin in Limerick County and Nicholas Street, Limerick, beside the Exchange and St Mary's Cathedral; he held other property in Limerick City and county, Dublin, Clare and Kinsale. Galway left some of his Clare property to Ald.

365 Cokayne, *Baronetage*, i, p. 258.
366 Lenihan, *Limerick*, p. 700; Henry Blackall, 'The Galweys of Munster', *JCHAS*, 71 (1966), 138–58; NLI, MS 41,677/3.
367 Cokayne, *Baronetage*, i, p. 258; Crawford, *Star Chamber*, pp 132, 183.
368 Grosart (ed.), *Lismore Papers*, 1st series, i, pp 76, 183, 186, iii, pp 222–5, iv, p. 11; TCD, MS 829, fos. 47r, 60r, 379, 381r; Luke McInerney, 'A 1640 register of the Thomond Papers at Petworth House', *Archivium Hibernicum*, 74 (2021), 27–126; HL, HP, Box 75 (10); Brown and Ó Siochrú, 'Cromwellian urban civil surveys'.
369 Caulfield (ed.), *Youghal*, p. 162; Edward MacLysaght (ed.), 'Survey of documents in private keeping: first series: Roche Papers', *Anal. Hib.*, 15 (1944), 143–52.

Dominic White and James Fox, burgess of Limerick.[370] His own and his childrens' marriages connected him to the most important Limerick gentry and citizens.

JAMES GALWAY (Galwey) (-1553 – 1616+) **Kinsale, 1585**
Limerick, 1613

s. John Galway, Kinsale and Limerick, and Mary, da. Gerald, Lord Courcy of Kingsale and Ellen da. Cormac MacCarthy; m. 1) by 1573, Ellen Stritch, Limerick; father of Geoffrey Galway.*

James' father moved to Limerick but retained interests in Cork County and acquired others in Clare and Limerick. James' representing first Kinsale and then Limerick demonstrates their dual interests; Galways continued to be buried in St Multose's Church, Kinsale, where they had constructed a chapel. He was described as 'counsillor' and '*in legibus eruditis*', but there is no record of his education. Galway was an alderman of Limerick and mayor in 1581, 1604, 1614 and 1616, when he was deposed for refusing the oath. He had served as the city's agent to London in 1575 when he was negotiating for a new charter and a school and again in 1582 when he treated with William Cecil, Lord Burghley, about £116 that was due to the city, but might not be paid because of the Irish under-treasurer, Sir Henry Wallop's intervention. In 1609 he was one of those named as a founder-member of Limerick's statute staple.

With his father he successfully sued for a pardon for Edmond, son of the Limerick merchant David Haly in 1577. Despite his prominent role in Limerick, he was elected for Kinsale in 1585 and was an active member of the opposition, signing a protest against Desmond's attainder unless the rights of those who had been pardoned were protected (a precedent for the difficulties in Tyrone's attainder in 1614). James visited London again in 1600 to intervene for his son Geoffrey* in George Carew's vendetta against him.[371] James was a trustee of the settlement of William Sarsfield of Sarsfield's Court, had a lease of Kinsale rectory from the crown in 1578 and of the wardship of Michael Walter fitz James in 1591.[372] He made an entail of his estates in Clare, Cork and Limerick in 1602 which his son Geoffrey* inherited.[373] He signed the petition of protest to James about electoral abuses and was one of the Catholic MPs ordered to attend James in England at the end of January 1614; he appears to have died shortly after parliament ended.[374]

370 Bodl. Lib., Carte MS 156, pp 495ff; RIA, MS 14/C/3/2, pp 156, 332–5; Boole Library, University College Cork, Kinsale Manorial Records, MS KM/PP/U20/1, no 1; NAI, MS RC 4/1, p. 267; Simington (ed.), *Civil Survey*, Limerick, pp 181, 300, 354, 357, 407–8; Tallon (ed.), *Court of Claims*, pp 325–7; Brown and Ó Siochrú, 'Cromwellian urban civil surveys'.

371 Lenihan, *Limerick*, pp 700–1, 741; *CPRI*, ii, pp 42–3; Robert Herbert, 'The trade guilds of Limerick', *North Munster Antiquarian Journal*, 2:3 (1941), 121–34; *Commons' Jn. Ire.*, 29 Oct. 1614; Blackall, 'Galweys of Munster'; Crawford, *Star Chamber*, p. 183.

372 Henry Blackall, 'The Galweys of Munster: Galway of Kinsale and Limerick', *JCHAS*, 72 (1967), 122–57; Nicholls (ed.), *Irish fiants*, ii–iii, nos 3008, 3225, 3237, 4187, 5375.

373 RIA, MS 14/C/3/2, pp 332–5; Simington (ed.), *Civil Survey*, Limerick, pp 181, 300, 354, 357, 407–8.

374 *Cal. S.P. Ire., 1611–14*, pp 361–2, 464.

WILLIAM GALWAY (Galwey) (c.1590 – 26 December 1637) **Kinsale, 1634**
e.s. Jeffrey Galway (d. 1608), Kinsale, and Margaret Young; m. before 1620, Jennett, da. Sir Geoffrey Galway* and Anne Comyn.
ed. Gray's Inn, 1 August 1607.

William was a member of the family that was still based in Kinsale. His father was sovereign in 1606, when he was fined £100 for recusancy; he purchased large tracts of land from Gerald, Lord Courcy and made a settlement of his estate in 1604.[375] William was recorder of Kinsale by 1623 and a trustee of Sir John Coppinger's 1627 settlement. He made a settlement of his own estate at Old Court and other property in Kinsale shortly before his death. He was a commissioner to manage the export of corn to England for Limerick City.[376] Curiously, for a lawyer, he is not recorded as sitting on any committee.

HENRY GOSNOLD (Gosnoll, Gosnall) (c.1560 – c.1658) **Clonakilty, 1613**
y. s. Matthew Gosnold (d. by 1592), Hempton, Norfolk;[377] m. 1) by 1610, Wilgeford ____ (d. by October 1627);[378] at least 1 da., born by 1614; 2) by October 1627, ____ Fenton.[379]
ed. Trinity College, Cambridge, 1577; Staple Inn, Gray's Inn, 3 November 1581.

Henry received an excellent education at Cambridge (he wrote good Latin and French) where he became friendly with Anthony and Francis Bacon, and Gray's Inn. He was part of the Bacons' intellectual circle in England, which he missed greatly when he moved to Ireland around 1594. There he was employed as secretary by Lord Deputy William Russell in the mid-1590s and by Essex during his Irish campaign of 1599, but also acted as a spy, sending intelligence back to the Bacons and others in England. Gosnold contributed three poems, one in Latin and two in English to Robert Dallington's *Booke of epitaphes made upon the death of the Right worshipfull Sir William Buttes* (London, 1583). Buttes was another Bacon connection. Another contributor was Francis Aungier, later master of the rolls in Ireland; William Buttes' brother Thomas bequeathed 20*s.* for a ring and a manuscript *Aurum ex stercore*, to Gosnold in 1592.[380] He inherited property in Norfolk from his brother Anthony Gosnold in 1591.[381] The Bacons continued to be influential patrons, recommending him to Essex in 1599 'not only out of a particular affection but upon assurance of his good parts and his six years' experience in Ireland'.[382]

375 Inquisitions post mortem, Cork, Volume 3, RIA, MS OS EI 20, pp 245–6; Blackall, 'Galweys of Munster: Galway of Kinsale and Limerick'.
376 Or possibly earlier. See Grosart (ed.), *Lismore Papers*, 2nd series, i, p. 31, ii, p. 29; Caulfield (ed.), *Youghal*, p. 162.
377 Chauncey R. Burr, *Bures of Suffolk and Burr of Massachusetts Bay colony, New England* (New York, 1926), p. 72.
378 NLI, MS 6,140, p. 82, MS 6,142, p. 29; NLI, M 3273, M 3274.
379 Grosart (ed.), *Lismore Papers*, 1st series, ii, pp 229, 302, 316, 328.
380 Arthur F. Marotti, *Manuscript, print, and the English Renaissance lyric* (London, 1995), p. 17; Burr, *Bures of Suffolk*, p. 72; Donovan and Edwards, *British sources for Irish history*, pp 158, 161.
381 J. Henry Lea, *Gosnold and Bacon: the ancestry of Bartholomew Gosnold – a collection* (Boston, 1904), pp 8–9.
382 Paul E. Hammer, 'The use of scholarship: the secretariat of Robert Devereux, second earl of

On 15 November 1599, he wrote to Essex who was in London:

> The ordinary discourse of this country consists of these two points: your Lordship's suspected restraint, and your intended or at least pretended return. The first of these is by some imputed to your repair thither without special licence; by others to some supposed errors in the course of your proceedings here; and by a third sort, more dismal in their conjectures, to some more secret and heinous charges imposed by such as suppose themselves to hold a wolf by the ear. Wherein this is easily observed, that such as we reckon your Lordship's less dissembling friends do esteem it a penance voluntary and formal; those of a colder and more suspicious temper, a punishment violent and dangerous. The God of mercy and innocency, I doubt not, will shortly make them ashamed of their cowardice. Your return some hold assured, because, as it seems, neither peace nor war will be made here without you; some disputable, because neither the commission or proportion that you must of necessity demand will be easily granted. A third sort think it unpossible, either because that kingdom can hardly forbear men of your quality, or because the custom of this country's Governors is to be a little disgraced; or because this unfortunate kingdom has run his full period, and must of necessity perish. The full cry of our poor remnant of friends is, 'Essex or none; Essex out of hand or all is lost.'[383]

Gosnold was appointed attorney general of Munster in 1596, second justice of Munster and member of the Munster presidency council in 1606 in which capacity he acted as a justice of assize and conducted inquisitions post mortem. By 1600 he was well acquainted with Richard Boyle, witnessing a deed for him in 1607 and leasing the chantry house and garden in Youghal and lands in Inchiquin barony from the future earl in 1610.[384] He resigned his position as recorder of Youghal on 7 November 1615 (there is no record of his selection, which must have been recent) but was appointed again in 1628 for life at £4 *per annum*. He also had an involvement in Boyle's iron business in 1628.[385] Gosnold was the unsuccessful administration candidate for Youghal and was then returned for Boyle's town of

Essex, *c*1585–1601', *EHR*, 149:430 (1994), 26–51; Will Tosh, *Male friendship and testimonies of love in Shakespeare's England* (London, 2016), pp 129–30; Christina Waldman, *Francis Bacon's hidden hand in Shakespeare's 'The Merchant of Venice': a study of law, rhetoric and authorship* (New York, 2018), p. 82. His letters to Anthony Bacon and others, LPL, Bacon MSS (LPL, MSS 647–62), calendared in Donovan and Edwards, *British sources for Irish history*, pp 158, 161; Anthony Bacon to Essex, 1599, calendared in HMC, *Calendar of the manuscripts of the most honourable the marquess of Salisbury, preserved at Hatfield House, Hertfordshire, Volume 14, Addenda* (London, 1923), p. 179.

383 HMC, *Calendar of the manuscripts of the most honourable the marquess of Salisbury, preserved at Hatfield House, Hertfordshire, Volume 9* (London, 1902), p. 74.

384 NLI, MS 43,142(3); NLI, MS 6,140, pp 82, 112; NLI MS 6,142, p. 29. I am grateful to David Edwards for these references.

385 Caulfield (ed.), *Youghal*, pp 39, 143, 201, 238; Grosart (ed.), *Lismore Papers*, 1st series, ii, pp 229, 302.

Clonakilty in 1613, one of the disallowed boroughs whose charters were issued after the commission for parliament. Despite only sitting at the beginning of parliament, he was nominated to the bill on pirates.

He became chief justice of Munster in 1624 and a judge of the Admiralty Court, nominated by Edward Villiers, president of Munster, to his brother the duke of Buckingham in 1626.[386] Despite his lengthy legal career in Ireland, he was not a member of the King's Inns. The chief justice's salary was a mere £100 a year and he had a 'great family' with his second wife, Boyle's cousin. As a result, he agitated for a more lucrative grant to support his family and lifestyle, petitioning his old friend, Secretary John Coke in 1628 for a lease of all the heriots and grants in Ireland for 21 years.[387] In November 1631 he travelled to England to plead for this, armed with letters of support from Cork to Coke and Lord Treasurer Weston, describing him as 'an upright gentleman, so qualified, and in no ways infected in the leaven of Ireland' and noting that 'His labour and travail is great and continual. His certain fee a £100 a year, and his perquisites of little or no value, whereby his own estate is much weakened, which induces me now at his repair to Court humbly to commend him to your lordship's favour and consideration, as a gentlemen that has merited very well in the services of the Crown.' There was little progress on the matter and in the following February Cork wrote again to Coke expressing doubts that Gosnold would receive such a lucrative grant, but 'yet if your Honour writes the letters in favour of him, I will be pleased that he may have some yearly certainty out of [the] casualties, as a means for his better subsistence I conceive it may in some measure prove satisfactory unto him & enable him till upon the intended plantations he may by your mediation be recompensed with some of these lands.'[388] Gosnold persuaded Coke to write to Wentworth commending him (describing him as 'a friend of more than forty years acquaintance' to which he a received a positive response) and Henry directly petitioned the new deputy on the subject.[389] Two years later he was reported to be 'outlawed … is aged and has few friends', but he remained in his posts.[390]

386 HL, HP, Box 1 (46); Curtis Clayton (ed.), *Council book*, pp 72–3, 77–80, 134–8, 140–51, 155–63, 165–8, 196, 214, 241, 263–4, 272, 354, 370, 430, 436, 440–2, 445, 447, 459–60, 466–7; Caulfield (ed.), *Cork*, p. 51; TCD, MS 672, fo. 222; NAI, MS M 7008, bundle 1a, Inquisitions, Limerick, nos 1, 5, 29, James I; second series, nos 1, 6, 62. I am grateful to David Edwards for these references. Appleby (ed.), *Calendar*, pp 133, 252– 3; Costello, *Court of Admiralty*, p. 252; Villiers to Edward Nicholas, 8 Feb. 1626, *Cal. S.P. Ire., 1625–32*, pp 91, 123, 314; *Cal. S.P. Ire., 1633–47*, p. 33; Empey (ed.), *Early Stuart Irish warrants*, pp 64, 69–70.

387 Gosnold to Coke, 11 June 1628, HMC, *Twelfth Report, Appendix, Part II: The manuscripts of the Earl Cowper, K.G., preserved at Melbourne Hall, Derbyshire* (London, 1888), p. 348.

388 Cork to Coke, 1 Nov. 1631, same to Weston, 9 Nov. 1631, Cork to Coke, 12 Feb. 1632, in Clarke, McGrath and Edwards (eds), *A lord justice's letterbook*, nos 152–3, 171; *Cal. S.P. Ire., 1625–32*, p. 646.

389 Copy of petition from Henry Gosnold on the same, 1633, http://www.adam-matthew-publications.co.uk/digital_guides/crown_servants_series_one_thomas_wentworth/Detailed-Listing.aspx [accessed 23 Sept. 2010]; Coke to Wentworth, 24 Oct. 1633, Wentworth to Coke, 8 Nov. 1633, in Knowler (ed.), *Letters and dispatches*, i, pp 138, 153.

390 Francis Lloyd to Richard Herbert, 18 April 1635, in Smith (ed.), *Herbert correspondence*, p. 89.

He may have been the man of the same name who was sued by an Edward Goldsmith of Gray's Inn in the High Court of Chivalry in London in July 1639.[391] He suffered losses during the 1641 rebellion and returned to England at some point before 1646 when the committee of both houses of the English parliament for Irish affairs granted him £150 for his relief.[392]

JAMES GOUGH (Geoghe) (*c.*1574 – 1627–8)[393] **Waterford Co., 1613**

e.s. Sir Edward Gough (d. 1603–4),[394] Clonmel and Waterford, and Mary Woodhouse; m. Ellis ____, da. Elizabeth.
ed. New Inn, Middle Temple, 7 July 1596.
Kt. 29 September 1603.

Gough was the eldest son of the mayor of Waterford in 1600, who had extensive interests there and in Clonmel. James was admitted a freeman of Waterford in 1598 with a fine of two half barge stones valued at 4*s*. 8*d*. In 1607 he borrowed £600 on bond through the staple.[395] Lord Laurence Esmond and his wife challenged Gough's father's will in chancery in 1618.[396] Gough was described by Cregan as a brilliant lawyer, although he did not join the King's Inns, unlike his brother Thomas.* James' father had been a client of Thomas Ormond's and signed many deeds for the earl, so James' appointment as keeper of the rolls of the liberty of Tipperary in 1614 continued a family association.[397] His standing in the native political community is evinced by his nominating Everard as speaker when he pointed to the illegality of many of the returns in a speech described as 'nothing pertinent to the matter then in question', as well as being one of the delegation of Catholic MPs to London whom Cregan described, along with Christopher Plunkett* and William Talbot,* as 'the most combative lawyer-members of the House of Commons.'[398] Portrayed by the administration as 'a giddy-headed fellow' who was 'busy and forward in disturbing parliament by speech and writing', his indiscretion in reporting the substance of James' speech promising religious toleration caused fury in Chichester's government and he was imprisoned.[399] Despite his prominence in the early opposition in the parliament, he is not noted as being active in the house and on 8 May 1615 was ordered to lose his wages for that session as a penalty for his unauthorized absence. Gough had extensive

391 Richard Cust and Andrew Hopper (eds), *Cases in the High Court of Chivalry, 1634–1640* (London, 2006), p. 106; https://www.british-history.ac.uk/no-series/court-of-chivalry/248-goldsmyth-gosnoll, [accessed 29 Dec. 2022].
392 *Cal. S.P. Ire., 1633–47*, p. 445.
393 Will dated 13 March 1624, proved 23 May 1628, NLI, GO, MS 225, p. 77.
394 Will dated 7 Oct. 1603, proved 25 April 1604, ibid., p. 73. Sons – James, Thomas, John, Walter, William, da. Katherine.
395 Byrne (ed.), *Great Parchment Book of Waterford*, p. 186.
396 NAI, Chancery MS AA/30, taken from Kenneth Nicholls' calendar.
397 Curtis (ed.), *Calendar of Ormond deeds, Volume VI*, pp 18, 39, 79–80, 83, 112, 184–9, 192–6; NLI, MS D. 3584.
398 Lodge, *Desiderata Curiosa*, i, p. 406; Cregan, 'Irish recusant lawyers'.
399 Crawford, *Star Chamber*, pp 305–6; TCD, MS 567, pp 27–30, 55; McCavitt, *Arthur Chichester*, pp 184–91; Jacob to Northampton, 30 Nov. 1613, Bodl. Lib., Carte MS 63, fos. 96–7.

property in Waterford and Tipperary that his brother Thomas* inherited and he was a member of the 1624–5 Tipperary commission of the peace.[400]

THOMAS GOUGH (Geoghe) (*c.*1584 – 1635–40) **County Cross Tipperary, 1634**
2. s. Sir Edward Gough (d. 1603–4), Clonmel and Waterford, and Mary Woodhouse; m. 1) Mary ____ (d. 1653+); 1 s. Patrick (d. by 1654).
ed. New Inn, Middle Temple, 6 August 1600; King's Inns, 1607; readmitted, 1628.[401]
Kt. 1627.

Thomas inherited substantial estates in Waterford and Tipperary from his brother James*, including the dissolved abbey of Inisloughnacht near Clonmel; he held 5,301 acres worth £611 13*s.*, mainly good quality arable lands. James' pardon for alienating this land was extended to Thomas, and he received a regrant of the same in 1627. He also had land dealings with Walter Evers, Henry Colley and Nicholas White.[402] Like Baron, he divided his interests between Waterford and Clonmel; he was recorder of Clonmel in 1610 and in 1626 was the second freeman admitted to Waterford after the receipt of its new charter and its mayor in 1633. His address was given as Clonmel when he had land deals with Everard* and as Waterford when he was knighted.[403] He shared a chamber next to John Davies in the old dorter of the King's Inns.[404] He acted in Cork's purchase of Garrett fitz John FitzGerald's lands at Camphire in west Waterford in 1622 and as counsel for the latter when the resulting suit dragged on until 1628.[405] Thomas was one of the trustees chosen by John Everard* in a settlement of his estates on his eldest son in 1620.[406] He was a commissioner for Waterford City for managing the export of corn to England in 1631.[407] His widow Mary was transplanted to 1,000 acres in Dunmore Barony, Galway.[408]

JOHN HALY (Haley, Halye) (15__? – 1637+) **Cashel, 1613, 1634**
s. ? Nicholas Haly, Cashel; m. 1) by 1613, Joan, da. Ald. John White fitz Geoffrey (d. 1614), Clonmel, and Alison, da. ____ White, Clonmel; at least 1 son Nicholas b. by May 1614.
DCL by 1611.[409]

John may have been the son of Nicholas Haly, Chancellor of the Liberty of Tipperary, 1605, whom he succeeded in that office in 1613, which he held until

400 *Rot. Pac. Jac.*, p. 108; *CPRI*, iii, pp 141–4, 285–9; TCD, MS 672, fo. 184v.
401 King's Inns, MS B1/1, fos. 4r, 18v.
402 Simington (ed.), *Civil Survey*, Waterford, pp 89–91, Tipperary, i, pp 307–10; *Inq. cancel. Hib. repert.*, i, Dublin, Car. I (80), Dublin City, Car. I (27), Kildare, Car. I (92), Drogheda, Car. I (9); *CPRI*, iii, pp 285–9; *Cal. S.P. Ire., 1625–32*, pp 270–1.
403 McGrath (ed.), *Clonmel*, p. 37; Byrne (ed.), *Great Parchment Book of Waterford*, p. 223; R. Lincoln, 'A list of the mayors and bailiffs of Waterford from 1365 to 1649', *JRSAI*, 7th series, 5(2) (1935), 313–19.
404 King's Inns, MS B1/1, fo. 108v.
405 Grosart (ed.), *Lismore Papers*, ii, p. 36; *Cal. S.P. Ire., 1647–60*, p. 120.
406 NAI, MS RC 4/11, pp 457–60, 489, 500–1.
407 Caulfield (ed.), *Youghal*, pp 160–7.
408 Simington (ed.), *Transplantation to Connacht*, p. 111.
409 Davies, *Le premier report*, fo. 83v.

1633 at least. Nicholas was a staunch Catholic, whose household included the priest Patrick Young.[410] John was probably the portreeve of Cashel in 1600, when the holder of that office was described as 'the profoundest man of learning for the civil law within the kingdom, and as obstinate as learned.' He was counsel in a case on *Commenda* in the Court of Common Pleas in 1611 with Talbot* and Bolton*.[411] John was one of the trustees chosen by John Everard* in a settlement of his estates on his eldest son in 1620.[412] He was overseer and trustee of his father-in-law's will, under which he inherited lands at Kilnalongqurty and a black silk gown, possibly a burgess' robe. A commissioner for Cashel for managing the export of corn to England in 1631, John was portreeve of Cashel in 1637 and continued as a councillor of the town in its charter of that year.[413]

RICHARD HALY (Haley, Halye) (*c.*1592 – 1644+) **Cashel, 1640**

s. ____ Haly, Cashel.
ed. Clifford's Inn, Inner Temple, 1609.

A member of an important Cashel legal family, four members of whom, including Dr John*, were named councillors in its 1637 charter; two were called Richard, one was appointed mayor and this MP was recorder.[414] He inherited 64 acres of land in Cashel, valued at £3 annually and also leased church lands there. Richard was one of the trustees chosen by John Everard* in a settlement of his estates on his eldest son in 1620 and was described as 'Cozen' in the will of John Everard of Fethard, 9 August 1638, the day after Everard made a lease in trust to Richard of lands at Barretstown and Dromdyle.[415] He was a member of a jury which met at Clonmel in 1634. He supported the Confederation and was a member of the General Assembly on at least two occasions, including 1644.[416] He should not be confused with his namesake, the sheriff of Cork City in 1624.[417]

EDWARD (FITZ) HARRIS (Harrys) (*c.*1575 – 1636) **Clonakilty, 1613**

e.s. Sir Thomas Harris, Cornworthy, Devonshire (1547–1610) and Elizabeth, da. Henry Pomeroy; m. 1) by 1602, Elizabeth (d. by 1627), da. Arthur Fowell, Fowellscombe, Devonshire; 4 s., 4 da.; e.s. Thomas illegally returned for Kerry in 1634; 2) 1627, Jane, da. John Bussy, Haydor, Lincolnshire, w. of Sir Richard Waldron, Farnham, Cavan.[418]

410 NLI, MS D. 3358; Edwards, *Ormond lordship*, p. 57; NLI, MS 11,044/29, 38, 90; Edmund Hogan (ed.), *The description of Ireland and the state thereof as it is at this present, in anno 1598* (Dublin, 1878), p. 289.
411 *Cal. Carew*, iii, p. 493; Davies, *Le premier report*, fo. 83v.
412 NAI, MS RC 4/11, pp 457–60, 489, 500–1.
413 Caulfield (ed.), *Youghal*, pp 160–7; Burke, *History of Clonmel*, pp 343–5; McGrath, 'Looking the part'; NAI, MS RC 3/1.
414 NAI, MS RC 3/1, unpaginated. Described as *juris perit* (someone with a legal training). I am grateful to Jason Harris for the definition of *juris perit*.
415 NAI, MS RC 5/23, pp 35–41.
416 BL, Add. MS 46,920A, fo. 128; Ó Siochrú, *Confederate Ireland*, p. 256.
417 Cork City Archives, Vanderplas Papers, MS V675/9; Caulfield (ed.), *Cork*, p. 111.
418 TCD, MS 1,216, fos. 32, 49; BL, Add. MS 4,820, fo. 53v; NLI, GO, MS 79, Funeral Entries, Volume 17, p. 79. https://catalogue.nli.ie/Record/vtls000529291#page/124/mode/1up [accessed 30 July 2022].

ed. Middle Temple, 1588; Bar, 1599; King's Inns, 1616.
Kt. 1619.
Bur. Kilcredan.

Edward should not be confused with Edward Fitzharris*, MP for Limerick County in 1634 and 1640. Harris' father was an English lawyer, serjeant-at-law and repeatedly MP.[419] He was living in the Middle Temple at the time of his appointment as chief justice of Munster in 1608 and member of the Council of Munster.[420] Elected recorder of Cork on 17 June 1617 (a post he held until 1623 when he was appointed third justice of the king's bench), he was made a member of the city council in the following October.[421] While he was fined for not acting as reader in the Middle Temple in 1616, he received a grant for his 'extraordinary services' in Ireland. He had chambers in King's Inns, was a member of its council by 1621 and treasurer in 1632.[422] Harris was a friend of Cork, who gave him a horse in 1615; ten years later he owed Cork £120.[423] He lived at Cahermoney, County Cork, although after 1623 his legal duties required him to spend terms in Dublin and was frequently a judge of assize there between 1608 and his death; he had land dealings with his Cork neighbour Sir Robert Tinte and Harris' daughter married the local settler William Greatrakes. Their son was the famous 'stroker', Valentine Greatrakes.[424] His second wife brought him lands at Farnham, where he kept a stud and made him Thomas and William Ryves'* stepfather.[425]

WILLIAM HILTON (*c.*1588 – 1651) **Armagh, 1634**

m. 1) by 1609 Anne, da. Arland Ussher, Dublin, and Margaret Stanihurst (d. November 1626); at least 1 da., Margaret (d. 15 November 1639), m. Capt. Andrew Wilson, Wilsonsfort, Donegal.[426]
ed. King's Inns, 1608; Gray's Inn, 13 August 1616.
Bur. St Werburgh's, Dublin, 19 August 1651.[427]

Hilton's origins are unknown and his career was atypical, as he was admitted to the King's Inns as an attorney in the Court of Common Pleas in 1608 and pursued a legal career after subsequently attending Gray's Inn; his career was facilitated by his marriage which connected him to the influential Ussher family. He was immediately involved in deeds relating to the Usshers and Stanihursts, which gave him Luccombe Park, Dublin and in 1614 he bought lands in Portmarnock from Adam Loftus*, future Lord Ely, for £300. In 1619 he was granted the seneschalship

419 M.A.P., 'Harris, Thomas' in Hasler (ed.), *History of parliament*.
420 Curtis Clayton (ed.), *Council book*, pp 67, 72–5, 79, 85, 136–9, 143–68, 171, 196, 205, 213, 216, 221, 230, 242, 261, 310, 358, 391, 442, 444–5, 452; Grosart (ed.), *Lismore Papers*, 1st series, ii, p. 164.
421 Caulfield (ed.), *Cork*, pp 69, 72, 79, 90, 94, 98–9, 102, 106, 171.
422 King's Inns, MS B 1/1, fos. 14r, 31r, 34r, 111v.
423 Grosart (ed.), *Lismore Papers*, 1st series, ii, p. 245.
424 Caufield (ed.), *Youghal*, pp 219–20; Daniel Beaumont, 'Greatrakes, Valentine', *DIB*.
425 Ball, *Judges in Ireland*, i, pp 329–30.
426 Fitzgerald and Lamacraft (eds), *Some funeral entries of Ireland*, p. 132; NLI, GO, MS 71, Funeral Entries, Volume 8, p. 223; Ball, *Judges in Ireland*, i, pp 310–11, 338.
427 *Liber Mun. Pub. Hib.*, ii, p. 51.

of all the manors belonging to the archbishop of Dublin for life.[428] He lent £40 on bond on the Dublin staple in 1632.

His improved career prospects thanks to Anne Ussher's family connections were evidenced by his being granted a chamber in the King's Inns in 1612, a unique instance of an attorney having this privilege. It also presumably prompted Hilton's admission to Gray's Inn and his professional qualification, but he was also a diligent lawyer and later judge. He was working as a lawyer on chancery cases in 1620 and was active in matters relating to church property. In 1627 he was appointed king's attorney in Connacht.[429] His return was due to his brother-in-law, the archbishop of Armagh, and in 1635 James Ussher wrote to Bramhall to thank him for his favours to Hilton and to ask him to deliver another letter recommending William to Wentworth and encouraging Hilton to be proactive in canvassing the chief baron personally for his promotion. Hilton was appointed third baron of the exchequer in January 1639 and became treasurer of the King's Inns in the following year; he was involved in managing that society and a member of its council by at least 1643. He was acting as vice-admiral of Leinster in 1646–7.[430] He was a justice of assize on the northwest circuit in 1641 and was in attendance on the House of Lords in 1641–7. After Bolton's death he was keeper of the great seal.[431]

Hilton was an active MP, sitting on the committee of grievances, five committees on specific bills, another to propose desirable legislation and one to propose amendments to the act for weirs. Hilton was a frequent signatory to clergymen's deeds. He continued to act as a judge until his death and in January 1646 was granted a *custodium* of the spiritualities of the see of Armagh during a vacancy.[432]

ROBERT JACOB (1573 – 1618) **Carlow, 1613**

2 s. Robert Jacob, Bockhampton, Dorset, and Anne, da. Thomas Selden, Lyme; m. 1) by 1603, Mary (Mall) (d. 1622), da. William Lynch, Southampton (but originally of Galway), w. of ____ Targett, sailor, of Southampton; she rem. Christopher Brooke, MP,[433] e.s. Robert b. 1606 and da. Mary, in 1607, 2s. Arthur, Francis, 2nd da. Ann.[434]

428 Carlow Public Library, Burton MSS, unnumbered, deeds of 24 Oct. 1609, 13 Feb. 1612, 15 Dec. 1614, 3 May 1615, 1643; Ainsworth (ed.), 'Survey of documents in private keeping: third series', nos 604–6; Raymond Gillespie (ed.), *The first chapter act book of Christ Church Cathedral, Dublin, 1574–1634* (Dublin, 1997), p. 141.

429 King's Inns, MS B1/1, fo. 110r; NAI, MS AA/59; Marsh's Library, MS Z3.2.6, no. 64; Church of Ireland, exceptions against the act for the confirmation of the Court of Prerogatives and faculties, *c.* 1626, HL, HP, MS 14,189; Empey (ed.), *Early Stuart Irish warrants*, no. 4.

430 Ussher to Bramhall, 23 Nov. 1635, HL, HP, MS 15,951; Ussher to Bramhall, date torn off, HL, HP, MS 15,952; Ussher to Bramhall, undated, HL, HP, MS 15,956; Empey (ed.), *Early Stuart Irish warrants*, no. 43; King's Inns, MS B1/1, fos. 80v, 84v, 112r; Elaine Murphy (ed.), *A calendar of material relating to Ireland from the High Court of Admiralty, 1641–1660* (Dublin, 2011), pp 74–5, 309.

431 Ball, *Judges in Ireland*, i, p. 338.

432 E.g., HL, HP, MS 13,930; HL, HP, MS 14,041; Bodl. Lib., Carte MS 68, fos. 123r–4v.

433 John P. Ferris and Simon Healy, 'Brooke, Christopher' in Thrush and Ferris (eds), *History of parliament*.

ed. Middle Temple, 1587; King's Inns, 1607.
Kt. 5 November 1607.

Jacob came to Ireland as solicitor general in 1606 and became a member of the Council of Munster in 1608 and commissioner of the Court of Wards in 1615.[435] According to Barnaby Rich, Jacob, who had 'never a foote of lande, never a house, nor so much as a bedde of hys owne to lye uppon', arrived in Ireland 'in a poore and needy estat', heavily indebted to various London citizens thanks to his wife's extravagance. Rich went on to accuse him of corruption in Ireland to fund Mall's 'excessyve bravery, hyr pompe, hyr pryde, hyr prodygalyte, hyr roystynge, hyr rampyne, hyr revelynge, hyr feastynge, hyr gamynge and other hyr idell and inordynat expendyng' and that 'Syr Robert Jacob's lusty wife wyll play at a payre of cardes in a peece of a nyght' more than the entire annual revenue of her husband's predecessor Roger Wilbraham.[436] Jacob certainly swiftly acquired lands in Mayo from 1608 and Kildare in 1611, as well as the rectory or parish church of Leixlip which he leased to the Shees of Kilkenny.[437]

Whatever about her extravagance, Mary was an assiduous cultivator of influential figures in England, including Northampton and Buckingham, to advance Jacob's career and that of her third husband, the poet and MP Christopher Brooke. Her interventions in politics were welcomed by English statesmen. Robert also cultivated English statesmen, especially Northampton, writing regularly to him with accounts of proceedings in Ireland and recommendations for policy changes. When James summoned Chichester to London to discuss the situation in Ireland in early 1614, Jacob sent Northampton briefing notes recommending reforms in Ireland for the earl to advise the king. His postscript noted his wife's lobbying on his behalf and requested 'some Mark of James' favor in reward of my long service and losse of tyme here.'[438] He wrote to the archbishop of Canterbury about Irish affairs in 1616 and was in London in the following year, attempting to curry favour with Lord Worcester whom he reported as 'ready to do me all good offices'.[439]

Jacob's attitude to the native community can be judged from his letters to Northampton 'in respect of those natives here which pretend themselves to be Lords of Countries, who, being a Conquered Nation, by nature rebellious, hating the Englishe, spurning & repining at our government, infected wth treasonable plots from beyond the seas, and longyng for a day to regaine their auncient liberty

434 NLI, GO, MS 44, fo. 47r; Abstract of will of William Linche, Joseph Jackson Howard (ed.), *Miscellanea Genealogica et Heraldica, Volume IV* (London, 1884), p. 395.

435 Hughes, *Patentee officers*; Curtis Clayton (ed.), *Council book*, pp 242, 370.

436 Caesar Litton Falkiner, 'Barnaby Rich's "Remembrances of the state of Ireland"', *Proc. RIA*, 26C (1906–7), pp 125–42.

437 *Rot. Pat. Jac.*, pp 92, 120, 188, 388–9; Tallon (ed.), *Court of Claims*, p. 180.

438 E.g., Jacob to Northampton, 30 Nov. 1613, Bodl. Lib., Carte MS 63, fos. 96–7; Jacob to Northampton, 12 April 1613, HL, HP, Box 4 (1); Jacob to Northampton, 28 Feb. 1614, HL, HP, Box 4 (15).

439 Jacob to Abbott, 23 July 1616, Christ Church, Oxford, MS 297, fos. 151r–2; Jacob to Davies, 13 May 1617, HL, HP, MS 15,061.

(as they terme itt) if they could once perceive his Maties forces utterly wthdrawen, will presently growe insolent, and fall a burning and spoiling the kings subiects, and being putt out of their lands (though never so iustly) will draw their loose followers together and seek to get them againe by the throat.'[440]

An assiduous officer, he was a justice of assize in Ulster in 1614 and at the gaol delivery sessions in Armagh on 15 February 1615, as well as pursuing the presentation of recusants in Dublin parishes and the corporate towns, 1615–18.[441] In January 1612 Jacob was allocated chambers in the King's Inns which had previously been held by Sir Humphrey Winch, former chief justice of the king's bench, and 'the voyd Rowme over the ketchen'. After his death Edward Harris* was given that chamber and Jacob's servant Thomas Squybb was repaid some of the money received for that transaction from the Inns' council.[442]

MICHAEL JONES (*c.*1609 – 10 December 1649) u.c., 1642

y. s. Lewis Jones, Bishop of Killaloe, and Mabel, da. Arland Ussher, Dublin; m. 1646-7, Mary Dermot, widow Sir Hugh Culme; o.s.p.[443]
ed. Lincoln's Inns 1631, bar 1638, King's Inns, 9 November 1640.
Bur. Boyle family tomb, St Mary's Collegiate Church, Youghal.

Michael was returned by 3 August 1642, when he took the oath of supremacy in the Commons. Jones was a member of an influential family network including his father, uncle James Ussher, Archbishop of Armagh, brothers Bishop Henry of Clogher and fellow soldier Theophilous. Educated at Lincoln's Inns, he presumably practiced law in England for about two years before returning to Ireland between 13 August when he was manucaptor to John Reynolds in Lincoln's Inns and November 1640 when he was admitted to the King's Inns and began to establish a legal practice. On 19 May 1641 the Commons acceded to his petition to be Bramhall's counsel, but his other legal work in Ireland is unknown. Michael was based in Dublin, though he had lands in Cavan and Monaghan; he claimed to have lost annual rents of £249 by the rebellion.[444]

Michael abandoned the law to join the army on the outbreak of the rebellion, being a captain by his return in August 1642. He had an outstanding military career. The 'rump' parliament made good use of his legal expertise, immediately adding him to the committee drawing up bills and appointing him to those to draft legislation 'against recusants in this kingdom' as a priority and to consider a bill to attaint rebels.[445] He combined his military and parliamentary duties, as a captain of foot under Broghill, fighting at the siege of Lismore; on 10 November 1642 the

440 Jacob to Northampton, 29 Oct. 1612, HL, HP, Box 3 (47).
441 HL, HP, Box 3 (43); Jacob to Northampton, 28 Feb. 1614, HL, HP, Box 4 (15); James F. Ferguson, 'The Ulster Roll of gaol delivery, 1613–1618', *Ulster Journal of Archaeology*, 1st series, 1 (1853), 260–70; Marsh's Library, MS Z3.2.6., no. 54; Jacob to George Abbott, 23 July 1616, Christ Church, Oxford, MS 297, fos. 151r–2.
442 King's Inns, MS B1/1, fos. 109v, 172v, 175r.
443 Patrick Little, 'Jones, Michael', *DIB*.
444 Clarke (ed.), *1641 Depositions, Volume IV: Dublin*, pp 139–40.
445 *Commons' Jn. Ire.*, 3–4 Aug. 1642.

Commons requested Ormond to release him from his obligations in the garrison at Naas to 'attend the publick service of this house.' Ormond clearly acceded, as week later Jones was added to the privileges committee and others on 12, 13 and 14 December 1642.[446] On 20 April 1643 he was a member of the committee drafting a remonstrance to Charles describing the case of distressed Protestants in Ireland and he opposed the cessation in 1643. Jones addressed the privy council arguing against any peace deals with the Confederates. On 17 February 1644, by which time he was a major, he spoke against Terence Magrath's membership of the Commons and defending parliamentary privilege. That is the last record of his engagement in parliamentary business, as he joined the parliamentary army in Cheshire. From May 1646 he was negotiating to raise a regiment for Irish service under another Irish 'rump' MP, Philip Lord Lisle, and in March 1647 was appointed commander of the Leinster forces. The following month he became governor of Dublin, in which capacity he negotiated Ormond's surrender of the capital. He continued to fight in Ireland, at Dungan's Hill, capturing Ballyshannon in Kildare in early 1648 and defeating the Irish royalist forces at Rathmines in 1649, opening a base for Cromwell's invasion. Jones fought with Cromwell at Drogheda, Wexford, Duncannon and Waterford and died at Dungarvan. Broghill arranged for his burial in the Boyle family tomb in Youghal, a signal of his esteem for Jones.[447]

OLIVER JONES (*c.*1610 – 1682) **Athlone, 1640**
Roscommon, 1661

3 s. John Jones (d. *c.* 1611), Athlone, and Jane, da. ____ Misset;[448] m. and had children, but there is no information about his wife and children.
ed. King's Inns, 1638.
Bur. St Patrick's Cathedral, Dublin.

Oliver should not be confused with his namesake, the third son of Bishop Lewis Jones of Killaloe, brother of Michael*. Oliver was the third generation of his family in Athlone, where his grandfather, the Welshman Lieutenant Henry had settled. John Jones had considerable property in the town and Roscommon County which Oliver inherited after the deaths of his older brothers Edward (1625) and Christopher (1638) and the latter's son Edward in 1641. Oliver had property in Mayo, Roscommon, Sligo and Westmeath. While he and his brothers were clearly Protestant, his nieces Mary, Jane and Katharine married Edward Dillon of Consese, Westmeath, esq., William Crean of the Sligo merchant family and

446 Bodl. Lib., Carte MS 4, fo. 35.

447 This account of his military activities is drawn from *DIB* and Padraig Lenihan, *Confederate Catholics at war, 1641–1649* (Cork, 2001), pp 99–104, 107, 113–14, 159–60, 181n, 197–215, 220, 227; Jones to Lord Wharton, 31 May 1648, Bodl. Lib., Carte MS 63, fo. 608, acknowledging his care in providing supplies for the army and encouraging him to 'perfect that work.'

448 Ball, *Judges in Ireland*, i, p. 353; NLI, GO, MS 225, pp 169, 173; NLI, GO, MS 79, Funeral Entries, Volume 17, 1619–1729, p. 22; NLI, GO, MS 71, Funeral Entries, Volume 8, 1639–41, p. 317; Tallon (ed.), *Court of Claims*, pp 56, 146–8, 261–3, 417, 419. This corrects the identification in McGrath, 'Bio. dict.'.

William Devenish of Beaulieu, Louth, respectively. His family's standing and his legal training explain Oliver's return, although his brother Christopher's being sovereign of Athlone and therefore returning officer was presumably no disadvantage.[449] Oliver was married and had children, but no details are known of his wife and their offspring.

Oliver was a lawyer although there is no record of his attending the Inns of Court, unlike his oldest brother who entered the Middle Temple in 1611, when his manucaptor was the London-based Louth lawyer Richard Hadsor. Oliver appears to have had a local practice, possibly largely based in the Connacht presidency court in Athlone. His work as an MP shows that his legal training was valued and he was regarded as a trustworthy delegate on conference committees, rapporteur, drafter of orders and minutes and as a committee member. Perceval-Maxwell describes him as a leader of the house, especially in the fourth session. Like Mervyn he appears to have had a deep concern for constitutional issues and was anxious to work with Catholic MPs to resolve difficulties through parliament. On 1 April 1640 he was appointed to the committee to consider which laws to propose and was repeatedly nominated to committees on bills, for conferences, on petitions and drawing up impeachment charges against Bolton, Bramhall, Lowther and Radcliffe, checking the book of orders of the house and as chair of a committee of the whole house. On 17 July 1641 he was one of a committee appointed to consider petitions from Connacht.[450]

While continuing a member of the Commons, he did not appear after this session, possibly because it was not safe for him to travel from Athlone, and on 8 August 1642 the house appointed a committee to raid his lodgings at Henry King's and seize any papers relating to parliamentary business. Apart from one letter to Ormond from near Mullingar on 6 January 1647 providing details of affairs there, including that the Lord President had two separate orders from the nuncio and council at Kilkenny and reporting 'His Lordship is extreamly afflicted that he was not in the Castle to welcome your excellency to these parts', there is no record of his activities until his appointment as attorney general of the province in 1649; however, the inclusion of some of his poems in Ormond's papers attests to their friendship and his literary bent.[451] Oliver continued as attorney general through the Commonwealth. On the Restoration he served as justice of assize in 1661 and became chief justice of Connacht in 1662, a judge of the common pleas in 1670 and two years later to the king's bench.[452] Essex regarded him as a closet Roman Catholic who raised his children in that religion, although his activities in the 1650s

449 RIA, Upton MS 25(141); Harman Murtagh, *Athlone: history and settlement to 1800* (Athlone, 2000), p. 80.

450 Perceval-Maxwell, *Outbreak*, pp 129, 131, 133, 156; *Commons' Jn. Ire.*, 3–4 June 1640, 4, 10, 12, 16, 19, 25–7 February 1641, 1–5 March 1641, 18–20, 24–6, 29 May 1641, 2, 5, 8–10, 17–18, 21–3, 30 June 1641, 7, 9, 13, 17, 21 July 1641.

451 Oliver Jones to Ormond, 6 Jan. 1647, Bodl. Lib., Carte MS 20, fo. 56; HMC, *Ormonde*, i, pp 105–17.

452 Ball, *Judges in Ireland*, i, p. 353.

belie this and it is likely that this suspicion was prompted by his refusal to discriminate against Catholics in legal cases.

RICHARD KENNEDY (? – January 1685) **Mullingar, 1647**
Wicklow, 1660 Convention

2 s. Sir Robert Kennedy (d. 1668), MP for Kildare, 1643, Newtownmountkennedy and Constance, da. Jonas Silyard, Dublin and Margaret da. Ralph Sankey, Fassaroe, Co Dublin; m. 1) *c.*1650, Anne, da. Christopher Barker, Colnbrook, Buckinghamshire and Sarah, da. Bonham Norton; at least 2 s., Robert and William, das. Elizabeth, Bridget.[453]
ed. Lincoln's Inn, 1638–41; Bar 1645; King's Inns, 1657.
Kt. 1660.
2nd Bart., 1668.

Like Michael Jones*, who had been his manucaptor, he trained as a lawyer but also served as a soldier, in Richard's case in Kynaston's regiment in the late 1640s.[454] He followed his elder brother Sylvester (MP for an unidentified constituency, June 1642) to Lincoln's Inns and was manucaptor for William Crofton of Temple House and William Molyneux, son of Daniel.[455] Richard lived at Nicholas St, Dublin and at Newtownmountkennedy, Co. Wicklow and Ballydowd, Lucan, Co. Dublin and had extensive in property in Carlow and other places. He acted as counsel for Phelim O'Neill in 1652 and voted in the election of Anthony Morgan and William Meredith as MPs for Kildare and Wicklow for the Commonwealth parliament in 1654. His father voted in that election too, as well as those for Dublin City and County.[456] Kennedy was one of the Leinster group of members of the Convention classed by Clarke as from the 'elite office-holding class' closely related by family ties who had retained their 'historic role in government and maintain[ed] their traditional practice of accumulating land and influence outside the capital city.' He was also one of those appointed as a commissioner to attend Charles II in London to present Irish Protestants' views on the 'resettlement of Ireland.'[457] In 1660 he was appointed recorder of Dublin but resigned the place on his promotion to the judiciary, and was appointed joint chief remembrancer in the exchequer, second justice of the exchequer and attorney of the Court of Wards; he also attended the House of Lords as a judge, 1661–2 and he was a member of the council of the King's Inns.[458] Richard was agent for the city of Dublin in London in 1664 and was presented with plate for his services; he was active in the suppression of nonconformity.[459] He unsuccessfully sought the position of chief justice of the common pleas in 1665. Richard was a justice of assize in Ulster to 1680 and resigned from the bench in the following year, due to ill health.[460]

453 Cokayne, *Baronetage*, iv, p. 197.
454 Clarke, *Prelude to restoration*, p. 206.
455 Lincoln's Inn, Admissions registers, 1627–40, fo. 147v, 1640–56, fos. 6v, 18v.
456 TNA, MS C 219/44.
457 Clarke, *Prelude to restoration*, pp 239–40, 299–300.
458 Gilbert, *C.A.R.*, iv, pp 575–6; Kenny, 'Black Book of King's Inns'.
459 Gilbert, *C.A.R.*, iv, p. 320.
460 Ball, *Judges in Ireland*, i, p. 347.

EDWARD LAKE (1596–1600 – 1674) **Cavan, 1640**

e.s. Richard Lake, Irby, Lincolnshire, and Anne Wardell, Keelby; m. Anne (d. 1665–70), da. and coh. Simon Bibye, Buckden, Huntingdonshire; 1 s. Edward (d. young).
ed. Oxford, St Catherine's Hall, Cambridge, BA (1626), BCL (1628), MA (1629), LLB (1636); LLD (1637).
Bart. 1644, 1661.
o.s.p.; Bur. Lincoln Cathedral.[461]
LIKENESS: *Plate 22*, John Thane, *British autography: a collection of fac-similies of the hand writing of royal and illustrious personages* (London, *c.*1788–93).

Lake came from Lincolnshire, but his paternal ancestors were from Yorkshire and, although he may never have visited that county, he retained sufficient affection for it, perhaps strengthened by his connections with Wentworth and Bramhall, to leave money to erect a clock in Normanton.[462] He should not be confused with the Dublin alderman, Edward Lake, constable of the Dublin staple in early 1641, who was originally from Brambly, Staffordshire.[463] Lake's qualifications fitted him well for the office of advocate general, which he attained in 1639 on Laud's recommendation. He remained Bramhall's client into the 1660s.[464] Lake was engaged in a case in the commission for ecclesiastical causes concerning the Limerick merchant John Arthur in 1639.[465] He drafted the clergy subsidies bill in 1640. Ussher appreciated his diligence in this and in detecting flaws in the bill for fees: 'Dr Lake hath deserved well of us as in other things, so in the great care he hath taken both in the drawing up [page torn] the Act for our Subsidyes, … and taking exception against the new draught of the Act for fees wherin though there were diverse things omitted which were not in the former, yet doth there yet much remaine therein which will prove prejudiciall hereafter unto our order Ecclesiasticall.'[466]

He was expelled from the Commons on 9 November 1640 for misusing his position as chairman of a committee of the whole house that was considering a plea of parliamentary privilege by Michael Stanhope, registrar of the Court of High Commission. A writ for his replacement was moved on the following day.[467] Unlike his fellow burgess and civil lawyer, Cooke*, Lake had no Cavan connections and was a placeman. Lake's recently acquired Irish property was at Carnew, Wicklow

461 Cokayne, *Baronetage*, iii, p. 313; Gordon Goodwin, revised by Sean Kelsey, 'Lake, Sir Edward', *Oxford DNB*; A.R. Maddison (ed.), *Lincolnshire pedigrees*, 2 vols (London, 1903), ii, p. 577.

462 His monument in Lincoln Cathedral notes that he was '*ex antiquia familia ejusdem cognomin. Normantoniae juxta Pontefract in Agro Eboracensi.*' Pontefract was a town in which Wentworth took a particular interest, being responsible for its restoration as a parliamentary borough, and George Wentworth represented it in the Long Parliament. John K. Gruenfelder, *Influence in early Stuart elections, 1604–40* (Columbus, OH, 1981), p. 94; Alan J. Fletcher, 'Sir Thomas Wentworth and the restoration of Pontefract as a parliamentary borough', *Northern History*, 6 (1971), 88–97.

463 BL, Add. MS 19,843, fo. 84v; TNA, PROB. 11/205/116.

464 Laud to Wentworth, 17 May 1639, Cambridge University Library, MS Add. 23, fo. 55r; McCafferty, *Reconstruction of the Church of Ireland*, p. 166.

465 Marsh's Library, MS Z4.2.1.

466 Ussher to Bramhall, 7 May 1640, HL, HP, MS 15,958.

467 *Commons' Jn. Ire.*, 22, 26–7 Oct. 1640, 9 Nov. 1640; Bramhall to Laud, 4 Nov. 1640, HL, HP, MS 14,061: 'Doctor Lakes was brought upon his knee for the church at the barre. His crime was saiinge at a committee, "It is not so. It is not so."'

and he relinquished its lease to Strafford. This property and his English estates were lost during the wars. On his return to England he fought for Charles at Edgehill (1642) where he was badly wounded; as a reward for his services he was granted a patent for a baronetcy and the nomination of another. The patent was not activated and he was again granted the title in 1661. By 1644 he had moved to Nottingham; in April 1648 he was included in a list of 149 people in Lincolnshire who had been in delinquency against parliament.[468]

He was in York and London in 1661, dealing with Bramhall's financial affairs and repeatedly petitioning him and his brother-in-law Samuel Pullen, archbishop of Tuam, for support and preferment in Ireland, claiming he had been promised offices by Charles I including the chancellorship of Ossory and the mastership of the Court of Wards or of the rolls; Ormond blocked any Irish appointment for him. However, he became chancellor of the diocese of Lincoln and received a mandate as vicar-general there in June 1664, a role he described as 'indifferent competent, but [I] could be content and think myself happy to taste of his Maties favor & more indeiately to bee in place of service towards him; the place is of small value & the enioying of it uncertaine. Yet I should be glad of so much favor.'[469]

JOHN LEWIS (Lewes) (1610+ – 1656+) **u.c., by November 1644**

s. either James Lewis (d. 1629–30), Cwmowen, Ceredigion and ____, heiress of Edward Morgan, Glascrug, who entered the Inner Temple in 1631; if so he was high sheriff of Ceredigion in 1636 and married Maudlin, da. and heiress of Rhys, third son of Morgan David Lloyd, Glascrug. 1 s.;[470] or son and heir of James Lewis of Giversill, Denbigh, who was admitted to Lincoln's Inn in 1627.

ed. either Lincoln's Inn, 1627, or Inner Temple, 1631; King's Inns, 18 June 1647.

Lewis was a Welshman. The date of his arrival in Ireland is unclear, but the fact that he was the only person admitted to the King's Inns between 1641 and 1647 is an indication of the state of the legal world in Ireland at the time. Lewis was an active lawyer in Chancery after 1650.[471] There is no information about whether he was married or had children.

ADAM LOFTUS Sr (c.1568 – 1643)[472] **King's County, 1613**

2nd, but e.s.s. Robert Loftus (d. 1606), Swineside, Coverham, Yorkshire; m. 1597, Sarah Bathoe (d. 1650), w. Bishop Richard Meredith (d. 1597), Ferns and Leighlin; 4 s., including Robert, Edward; 2 da. including Alice.

468 Edward Lake, *Just apology for his sacred majesty* (London, 1642).

469 Lake to Bramhall, 25 May 1661, 6 Aug. 1661, 28 Sept. 1661, 4 April 1662, in HL, HP, MS 15,134–41; T.P. Langmead (ed.), 'Sir Edward Lake's account of his interviews with Charles I', *Camden Miscellancy*, 4 (London, 1859); Lake to Bramhall, 4 Jan. 1664, HL, HP, MS 15,143; Lincolnshire Record Office, Alvingham MS 23/2, FL Misc. 6/2/2/1.

470 J.R. Philips, *A list of the sheriffs of Cardiganshire, from A.D. 1539 to A.D. 1868* (Carmarthen, 1868), p. 15; S.R. Meyrick, *The history and antiquities of the county of Cardigan* (London, 1808), p. 229.

471 Barnard, 'Lawyers and the law'.

472 Terry Clavin, 'Loftus, Adam, 1st Viscount Loftus of Ely', *DIB*; W.N. Osborough, 'Loftus, Adam, first Viscount Loftus of Ely', *Oxford DNB*; Ball, *Judges in Ireland*, i, pp 326–8; G.E.C., *Peerage*, v, 63–5; Hughes, *Patentee officers*.

ed. Jesus College, Cambridge, BA, 1586, MA, 1589, BCL, 1597; Thavies Inn; Lincoln's Inn, May 1592; King's Inns, 1610.
Kt. 25 December 1604.
Viscount Ely, 1622.
Bur. Coverham, Yorkshire.
LIKENESS: *Plate 4*, Portrait in the National Gallery of Ireland.

Adam's uncle and namesake was archbishop of Dublin and the source of great patronage to his family; he made Adam archdeacon of Glendalough in 1592, while he was still studying in London and despite his being a layman, and he held that office until his death. Having studied both civil and common law, Loftus practiced civil and ecclesiastical law in the Irish courts from 1597. His promotion was rapid. Despite his lack of practical experience he was appointed judge-martial for life almost immediately upon his arrival in Ireland and in the following year became a master in chancery, a position he held until 1619. The judge-martial role was onerous and dangerous during the Nine Years War, but after its end in 1603 it became a sinecure worth £162 annually.

Archbishop Loftus was a judge of the faculties and the prerogative court and lord chancellor from 1578 until he died in 1605; Sir Adam repeatedly deputized for him in those roles and also as his vicar-general, a position to which he was appointed for life in 1604. He became a privy councillor in 1608 and as such a judge in the Court of Castle Chamber, constable of Maryborough Castle and judge of the newly established Admiralty Court the following year. The appointment to the Admiralty Court was potentially extremely lucrative as pirates were becoming more active and Loftus expanded his authority both against the officers of the admiralty in England and Irish towns' admiralty rights.[473] While he joined the King's Inns, he played no discernible role in its operations.

A deeply corrupt man, like his uncle before him, Loftus used his legal expertise and state offices to acquire lands and other wealth dishonestly; his lands at Drimnagh and Portnahinch in Queen's County were certainly fraudulently obtained, although the politically influential fourth earl of Thomond bested him in a dispute about a lease in Carlow, accusing Adam of 'cross-dealings'. By 1613, he held land in Dublin, Kildare (where his main residence was at Monasterevin) and King's and Queen's Counties and by 1621, his property yielded £1,145 annually, apart from his income from public office, lands on long leases and bribes; he also obtained pensions for his services as judge-martial in 1607 and master in chancery in 1608.[474] By 1637, he had also acquired estates in Monaghan.[475] In addition, in the early decades of the seventeenth century, he provided legal advice to his colleagues in the Irish administration that enabled them similarly to acquire significant grants of land. In 1612 Sir Thomas Ridgeway named Loftus and Sir William Parsons as arbitrators in a dispute with Ormond about the boundaries of

473 Crawford, *Star Chamber*, pp 36, 410, 496, 507, 589; Costello *Court of Admiralty*, pp 4–11.
474 Chichester to John Davies, June 1608, HL, HP, Box 2 (33); Crawford, *Star Chamber*, pp 101–2.
475 Essex County Records Office, Barrett-Lennard Muniments, MSS D/DL E87, calendared in Donovan and Edwards, *British sources for Irish history*, p. 55.

their lands at Gallenridgeway; Everard* was Ormond's nominee.[476] His dodgy land dealings counted against him in the 1613 election for King's County and he was only returned by the sheriff's fraudulent conduct of the election, which was unsuccessfully appealed by Catholic MPs.[477]

There were few suitable candidates for the Admiralty Court and Loftus' deficiencies and his overreaching the terms of his office quickly became clear when he 'claimed not only to be judge general of all admiralty causes in Ireland but also to have absolute power from the lord high admiral of England to appoint judge, register and marshal in Munster.'[478] When Buckingham became Lord Admiral in 1619 he replaced Loftus with his client Laurence Parsons* whose own admiralty career was equally undistinguished and corrupt, while Loftus was appointed chancellor after a bribe of £1,000, a significant sum, which he soon came to regret as his financial position was worsened when he was given an annual salary of £300 instead of the traditional income from the chancellorship. His wages as judge-martial were also suspended and the duke made Parsons admiralty judge for Munster with jurisdiction over the most lucrative province for captured or shipwrecked cargoes. Loftus found himself short of money, especially since he had to provide money for his eldest son Robert's marriage to Eleanor, daughter of his fellow MP for King's County, Sir Francis Rushe, in 1621. Concurrently, English reformers reduced spending in Ireland in 1623, including Loftus' pension; his position was ameliorated by accepting bribes and by income from his estates and his wife and son's accepting presents of luxury goods.[479] In 1625 Loftus complained to the privy council that his salary from crown offices was only £300 and claimed that his promised daily allowance of 6*s*. 8*d*. as judge-martial had not been paid. His petition to the English privy council for compensation failed apparently because he demanded too much compensation.[480]

Adam was created Viscount Loftus of Ely in 1622 after a douceur to one of Buckingham's hangers-on and was made lord justice with Richard Wingfield, Viscount Powerscourt, pending Falkland's arrival as lord deputy following Oliver St John's recall. Buckingham was not impressed by him, nor was their relationship improved by Loftus' facilitating an English parliamentary commission sent to Ireland that summer to investigate the state of the Church of Ireland, the planted areas of Ulster and the management of the crown courts that produced the king's directions for the courts, but also revealed the corruption inherent in the way in which Buckingham and his clients governed Ireland.[481] Loftus managed to edge

476 NLI, MS D. 3516.

477 *Cal. S.P. Ire., 1611–14*, pp 361–2, 439–40.

478 William Massam to Cranfield, 29 Aug. 1614, quoted in Treadwell, *Buckingham and Ireland*, p. 98.

479 Thomas Barrett-Lennard, *An account of the families of Lennard and Barrett* (privately printed, 1908), pp 439ff; *Cal. S.P. Ire., 1633–47*, p. 225.

480 HMC, *Ninth Report of the Royal Commission on Historical Manuscripts, Part II* (London, 1884), pp 293–317; Treadwell, *Buckingham and Ireland*, pp 232–3.

481 Geoffrey Hand and Victor Treadwell (eds), 'His Majesty's directions for ordering and setting the courts within his kingdom of Ireland, 1622', *Anal. Hib.*, 26 (1970), 177–235; Treadwell, *Buckingham and Ireland*, pp 55, 187; Treadwell (ed.), *Irish commission of 1622*.

Parsons out of the admiralty, despite Falkland's promoting Robert Travers* as 'sufficiently read in the civil law and already practiced in the manner of proceedings in that Court'. Travers was an admiralty judge in Munster from 1625 and proved as corrupt as Loftus and Parsons. Adam was reappointed in 1628 and held the post despite confirming his reputation as 'a difficult and venal appointee', with most of the work done by Allan Cooke* as surrogate judge.[482]

Loftus earlier avoided conflict with powerful members of the administration, but this began to change. His closeness to Cork in the 1610s did not survive the earl's accusation of bias in a chancery case. In 1624, a bitter disagreement broke out between Loftus and Falkland about the jurisdiction of the courts of Castle Chamber and chancery, which widened into a full-blown row with Loftus refusing to accept Falkland's nominees as justice of assize, justices of the peace or to sign fiants for grants of a distillery and a tannery.[483] The crown tried to mollify Adam by increasing his chancellor's salary, paying his arrears and restoring his pensions, but conflict continued with his colleagues, causing Buckingham serious political embarrassment; the English privy council engineered a compromise between Loftus and Falkland and specified a procedure for resolving future conflicts and Loftus remained in place despite being quarrelsome, over-bearing and corrupt.[484]

When the crown was forced to consider making concessions to Irish Catholics in return for money to maintain the royal army during the Spanish and French wars of the mid-1620s, Loftus, unlike most of his fellow officials in Ireland, was conciliatory and acted as an intermediary between the crown and the Catholic nobility and gentry, who specifically requested in talks in November 1626 that they negotiate with the chancellor. Negotiations collapsed, with Falkland claiming that Loftus encouraged Catholics to refuse to pay for the army, undermined his position and detailing miscarriages of justice in chancery. Loftus was summoned to London in June 1627 to justify his conduct and despite clear evidence of his venality, Charles, having agreed to the Graces, completely exonerated him, restoring him to the chancellorship in time for the 1628 parliament and the office of vice-admiral of Leinster, urging that 'those that have preferred any scandalous and false informations or charges against our Chancellor, for his carriage in the execution of his office, be proceeded against in our High Court of Castle Chamber'.[485]

Having engineered Falkland's dismissal, in 1629 Loftus and his bitter enemy Cork were appointed joint lords justices.[486] They feigned a reconciliation and Loftus agreed not to sit in at chancery proceedings involving Cork, but their enmity continued and when Loftus' most influential supporter, Francis Annesley, Lord Mountnorris, was suspended as vice treasurer after a campaign by Cork,

482 Costello, *Court of Admiralty*, pp 4–11.
483 *Cal. S.P. Ire., 1615–25*, p. 533.
484 Treadwell, *Buckingham and Ireland*, p. 55.
485 Treadwell, *Buckingham and Ireland*, pp 286–7; *Cal. S.P. Ire., 1625–33*, pp 358–63; *CPRI*, iii, p. 464.
486 *Liber Mun. Pub. Hib.*, ii, pp 6–7, 15, 21, 106, 127.

Loftus largely concentrated on his work in chancery rather than the day-to-day administration of Ireland. However, while Cork wished to continue to fine Catholics for not attending Anglican services, Loftus opposed this and won a narrow vote in the council.[487] This suited Wentworth's agenda and on his arrival he dismissed charges against Ely and arranged for him to receive £3,000 of his arrears; in 1635 he supported him in his dispute about the admiralty in England requisitioning cargo seized in Ireland. He also permitted him to pass his office as vice-admiral to his son Robert, writing that 'I have a high opinion of his loyalty, and do not think the Chancellorship (not worth above £400 a year) is as well paid as it should be.'[488] When Wentworth travelled to England in 1636, Loftus and Christopher Wandesford were appointed lords justices. However, Wentworth was to turn on Loftus, using both his conduct in office and in his family, specifically his refusal to fulfil conditions alleged to have been agreed on Ely's eldest son Robert's marriage. Eleanor Rushe brought a dowry of £1,750 and the marriage agreement was asserted to have specified that the couple would live with Sir Adam at his own expense and lands worth £1,500 a year would be settled on her and her children, to provide a jointure of £300. Adam did not fulfil these conditions beyond accommodating them in his house and determined to settle his estate on his other children, especially since Robert's only son was sickly.[489] Eleanor and her family felt very aggrieved and Loftus' problems were compounded by the deputy's very close friendship with Eleanor and Sir George Wentworth's 1636 marriage to Eleanor's sister Anne. In April 1636, Wentworth had privately lamented Loftus' failure to provide Eleanor with an adequate income.

Wentworth's first move against Loftus was a dispute about Catlin's* successors as justice of assize in Leinster in April 1637 and a challenge to his control of chancery.[490] Two months earlier, Eleanor Loftus' half-brother, the MP Sir John Gifford, petitioned the king to require Adam to fulfil the conditions of the marriage settlement and the case was referred to the deputy and Irish privy council; Wentworth was probably behind the petition, motivated as much by his affection for Eleanor as by a desire to humiliate Loftus. It is extraordinary that no reference was made to a written marriage settlement and Robert took no part in these proceedings. After long delays due to Loftus' stalling and Wentworth's other preoccupations, the case was heard by the deputy and council in January 1638 and Adam was ordered to settle an estate worth £1,200 a year upon Robert and his heirs; he refused to accept the verdict and was imprisoned and suspended as

487 Clarke, McGrath and Edwards (eds), *A lord justice's letterbook*, passim.

488 *Cal. S.P. Ire., 1633–47*, p. 72.

489 Essex County Records Office, Barrett-Lennard Muniments, MS D/DL L56/12–13 comprise documents about the Gifford/Loftus case, which are calendared in Donovan and Edwards, *British sources for Irish history*, pp 56–65;

490 Loftus to Wentworth, 13 April 1637, Wentworth to Loftus, 14 April 1637, Loftus to Wentworth, same date, Wentworth to Loftus, 15 April 1637, all in Knowler (ed.), *Letters and dispatches*, ii, pp 67–9.

chancellor. Wentworth described Adam's 'covert carriage and cunning dealing' in the matter, but characteristically justified the outcome of the case with a blatant lie about Eleanor's dowry:

> the decree of the Deputy and Council will appear most just, without that there will be found on the Chancellor's part, neither honour, conscience, nature or common honesty, the question there in effect being no more than, whether a lady nobly descended, that brought her husband an estate better than fifteen thousand pounds, should be provided of three hundred pounds jointure for herself, twelve hundred pounds a year land to be estated on her children, according to the Chancellor's own clear agreement with Sir Francis Rushe.[491]

Wentworth prompted allegations of corruption against Loftus and moved to remove Loftus from his archdeaconry of Glendalough. As both were stubborn, high-handed and corrupt, neither was prepared to back down. Released from prison only in August 1639, Loftus was anxious to appeal to the king in England, but Wentworth allowed him to travel in late 1639 only after he had obeyed the judgment, including paying £3,179 to Robert and Wentworth's cronies Robert Dillon, Philip Mainwaring and Wandesford had been appointed trustees to manage Adam's estates, leaving him very short of money.[492] The deputy produced multiple allegations of corruption against Loftus and Charles refused the appeal and dismissed him from the chancellorship, appointing Bolton* in his stead. Completely vanquished, Loftus returned to Ireland to submit to Wentworth and facing financial, social and political ruin. Eleanor died in May 1639 – Wentworth wrote 'With her are gone the greatest part of my affections to the country, and all that is left of them shall be thankfully, and religiously paid to her excellent memory.' Having paid his debt to Robert, Adam was allowed to receive rents from his much reduced estates again in 1640. Robert died in October 1640 and their only son Henry a month later, leaving an infant daughter to inherit their estates.[493]

Wentworth's fall changed matters dramatically. Strafford's actions in Gifford *v.* Loftus received specific mention in the complaints against him in 1641, Loftus testified against him at his trial and the English House of Lords set aside the decree of February 1638 in May 1642 and ordered the lands be conveyed back to Adam. By this time, however, the 1641 rebellion meant that Loftus had lost property worth more than £10,000 and received no income from his Irish estates. He spent his last months in Yorkshire where he died and was buried.

491 *Cal. S.P. Ire., 1633–47*, p. 180; Knowler (ed.), *Letters and dispatches*, ii, pp 260–1, 299, 340–1; HMC, *Ninth Report*, p. 296; Crawford, *Star Chamber*, p. 413.

492 Essex County Records Office, Barrett-Lennard Muniments, MS D/DL T28/38–40, calendared in Donovan and Edwards, *British sources for Irish history*, p. 68.

493 Wentworth to Lord Conway, in HMC, *Ninth Report*, p. 298.

Dr DUDLEY LOFTUS (1618 – 1695) **Naas, 1642; Kildare and Wicklow, 1658 Jamestown, 1660 Convention; Bannow, 1661 Fethard, Co. Wexford, 1692–3**

2 s. Sir Adam Loftus and Jane, da. Walter Vaughan, Golden Grove, Carmarthen, Wales; m. 1) Frances (d. 1691), da. Patrick Nangle, Navan, and Jane da. Sir Edward Bolton and Isabella Ayloff;[494] sons, Dudley and Adam; das., Mary, Jane, Letitia, Frances and Catherine; 2) 16 April 1693, Lady Catherine Mervyn.[495]
ed. TCD, BA, 1638; University College, Oxford, MA, 1640; D.C.L., TCD.
Bur. St Patrick's Cathedral, Dublin.

As a member of the numerous and influential Loftus family, Dudley had many connections in the administration and parliament. His brothers Arthur and Walter were MPs for Wexford County and Carysfort/Roscommon in 1640 and his brothers-in-law included Sir James Ware and Richard Parsons. Arthur Loftus' marriage to Dorothy, daughter of Richard, first earl of Cork, provided a connection to the wider Boyle family. Dudley's first marriage linked him to an old-established Old English family in Meath as well as Bolton*; all but one of their children died young.

Dudley was an outstanding oriental scholar, knowing up to 20 languages by his twentieth birthday and his education was encouraged by James Ussher; his extensive publications and surviving manuscripts in Archbishop Marsh's Library, King's Inns and the Bodleian, British and Trinity College Libraries attest to the depth and breadth of his scholarship. He also published on legal matters, under both his own name and the pseudonym Philo Britannicus. Stokes suggests, however, that his learning was achieved at the expense of intelligence in other areas of his life, especially that he was lacking in judgment, quoting a contemporary's comment he 'never knew so much learning in the keeping of a fool'. His second marriage was regarded as scandalous, given his advanced age and was reported to have brought him only trouble; Ware regarded it as demonstrating his improvident and foolish nature.[496] These views may have had substance, but Loftus' capacity to survive and profit from the many changes in regimes and politics in very turbulent times indicates adeptness and flexibility and his selection as a parliamentary agent to England in 1647 demonstrates his colleagues' confidence in his capacity to represent them, although their options were admittedly limited.

On his return to Ireland at the outbreak of the Irish rising of 1641, despite his youth and lack of military experience, Dudley was entrusted with the defence of his family home, Rathfarnham Castle, and he ably protected both the castle and the route from Wicklow to Dublin City. In the following year he was returned as MP for Naas in the 'rump' parliament and he remained loyal to Ormond until he left Ireland when Loftus reached an accommodation with the parliamentarians. At some point in the 1640s he qualified as doctor in civil law from Trinity College, Dublin. He prospered throughout the Cromwellian period, being appointed Provost of

494 Bolton, *Bolton families in Ireland*, pp 6–7.
495 Elizabethanne Boran, 'Loftus, Dudley', *Oxford DNB*; *idem*, 'Loftus, Dudley', *DIB*.
496 Ibid., G.T. Stokes, 'Dudley Loftus: a Dublin antiquary of the seventeenth century', *JRSAI*, 1 (1890), 17–30.

Trinity College, Dublin in 1650, and professor of civil law, and with Paul Davies, Eustace*, Ware and others took part in a review of the University of Dublin to assess whether a second college was needed. Dudley created Charles Coote a doctor of civil law in 1655 when Henry Cromwell was installed as chancellor of the university, although there is no evidence of Coote having studied any form of law.[497]

Loftus also received other state offices, being appointed deputy judge advocate general and commissioner of the revenue in 1651 and around the same time was made a commissioner to prove wills and decide on testamentary cases; three years later he became judge of the admiralty and in 1655 he was made a master in chancery and ingrosser of the great roll of the clerk of the pipe and chief ingrosser for life.[498] He continued to play a political role, voting in the 1654 parliamentary elections for both Dublin City and county, managing Dublin City's petition that Henry Cromwell should replace Fleetwood as lord deputy and representing Kildare-Wicklow in the 1658 Commonwealth parliament where he sat on committees for Irish affairs and prepared bills, including an act of union and a bill for the 'settlement of the ministry.'[499] His mastership in chancery was renewed in 1659.[500]

Though he had prospered under the Cromwellians, Loftus was swift to acclimatize to the Restoration; Borlase attributes the decision to call the Convention to Dudley's 'vigilance and excellent contrivance and industry', acting on Bishop Henry Jones' advice. He was returning officer for the Convention in which he sat for Coote's borough of Jamestown and chaired a number of committees, among them the committee on religion.[501] He was appointed vicar general of Ireland, and judge of chancery in 1660 and reappointed master in chancery in 1661; Loftus was also made judge of the prerogative court and faculties.[502] As clear evidence of his commitment to the new dispensation, he wrote to Ormond urging the preservation of 'orthodox protestant clergy' including the episcopacy and 'the use of the liturgy' and he played a role in the pageantry of the restoration of the bishops.[503] At Ormond's request, some time in or after 1661, he drew up 'such queries as wer fit to be resolved' about accounts of the negotiations for the cessation in 1643 and peace of 1646, to set the public record straight.[504]

He borrowed £600 on bond on the Dublin staple in 1669. His political career was disrupted by his imprisonment in 1673 following his strong condemnation of new regulations covering government control of corporations, which Loftus, as judge of the prerogative court, considered illegal. Despite his successful

497 Clarke, *Prelude to restoration*, p. 253.
498 Hughes, *Patentee officers*.
499 Barnard, *Cromwellian Ireland*, pp 209, 259; TNA, MS C219/44; Clarke, *Prelude to restoration*, pp 167, 228.
500 Hughes, *Patentee officers*.
501 Clarke, *Prelude to restoration*, pp 123, 167, 247, 253.
502 Hughes, *Patentee officers*.
503 Clarke, *Prelude to restoration*, p. 310; [Dudley Loftus], *The proceedings observed in order to, and in the consecration of the twelve bishops* (London, 1660).
504 Loftus to Ormond, undated but after March 1661, Morgan Pierpoint Library, MS Rulers of England, Box 07B, Charles I, no. 120.

adaptations to several completely opposing regimes, he kept his head down during James II's reign, remaining in his Dublin house in Exchange Street 'quietly at work upon his Syriac studies' and publications in a range of fields including *An history of the twofold invention of the cross* (Dublin, 1686) and *Anaphora* (Dublin, 1693). He re-emerged into Irish politics as MP for the Loftus borough of Fethard, Co. Wexford in 1692–3.[505] He died two years later.

GERATT[506] (Garrett, Gerard) LOWTHER (*c.*1561 – 14 Oct. 1624) **Tallow, 1613**

4. s. Sir Richard Lowther (1532–1607), lord warden of the western marches, and his wife Frances, daughter of John Middleton of Middleton, Westmorland; m. 1) Grace (1558–94), daughter of Alan Bellingham of Levens, Westmorland, w. Edmund Cliborn (Cleborne), Westmorland; 2) (1598) Anne (d. -1624), daughter and coh. of Sir Ralph Bulmer of Wilton, w. of Anthony Welbury, Castle Eden, Durham (d. 5 November 1596).[507] *o.s.p.*
ed. Lyons Inn, Inner Temple, 1580; Bar, 1590; King's Inns, 7 November 1610.
MP Cumberland, 1601.
Kt. 3 May 1618.
Bur. Christ Church, Dublin, 19 October 1624.

Geratt should not be confused with his nephew and godson, the future chief justice of the common bench.[508] He may have had Puritan tendencies as he was fined in November 1589 for wearing his hat in church.[509] Lowther practiced in England for twenty years before being appointed a justice of the common bench in Ireland on 12 October 1610 with an allowance of an additional £100 above the usual salary; fourth in seniority on that bench in 1611, his salary was £266 13*s.* 4*d.* Walsingham wrote to the Inner Temple concerning his being called to the Bar. His work in England initially followed that of his uncle and namesake, from whom he inherited not merely lands in Penrith but also some of his legal offices, as legal advisor to Lord William Howard, whom he double-crossed about the ownership of the Dacre estates in Westmoreland, when he was steward there. He continued to receive some income from the family's estates in England.

After a stint as MP in England, he concentrated on his legal practice until he moved to Ireland.[510] An active justice of the court until his death, he was justice of

505 Stokes, 'Dudley Loftus'.

506 His signature was 'Ger^{t} Lowther'. King's Inns, MS B 1/1, fo. 10v.

507 Anthony McCormack, 'Lowther, Sir Gerard (Gerrard, Gerald, Garret)', *DIB*; Joseph Foster (ed.), *Pedigrees recorded at the heralds' visitations of the counties of Cumberland and Westmorland : made by Richard St George, Norry, king of arms in 1615, and by William Dugdale, Norry, king of arms in 1666* (Carlisle, 1891), pp 84–5; E.T. Bewley, 'Some notes on the Lowthers who held judicial office in Ireland in the seventeenth century', *Transactions of the Cumberland and Westmorland Antiquarian and Archaeological Society*, new series, ii (1902), 1–10; C.B. Norcliffe, 'Paver's marriage licences (Part IV)', *Yorkshire Archaeological and Topographical Journal*, 10 (1898), 35–50; NLI, GO, MS 79, p. 124, at https://catalogue.nli.ie/Record/vtls000529291#page/124/mode/1up [accessed 30 July 2022].

508 Kenny, 'Not every judge a phoenix', p. 123.

509 Ball, *Judges in Ireland*, ii, pp 323–4.

510 B.D., 'Lowther, Gerard' in Hasler (ed.), *History of parliament*; F.A. Inderwick (ed.), *A calendar of the Inner Temple records, 1505–1603* (London, 1896), pp 359, 368; C.B. Phillips (ed.), *Lowther family estate books, 1617–1675* (Durham, 1979), pp 16–17, 22, 35, 220.

assize in Clonmel 1612–13 and Cork in 1612–13, Limavady 9 August 1614, Armagh 15 February 1615, and Monaghan 2 March 1616. He examined rebels connected with Alexander MacDonnell and Rory Óg O'Cahan's 1615 plot to burn Coleraine, Lifford, and other places in Ulster. The following year he was one of the judges who investigated the royalties of the liberty of Tipperary and found against Ormond's claim to palatinate status there.[511] A close associate of Cork's, he 'winked' at Boyle's counsel from the bench. On his admission to the King's Inns, he was instantly appointed a member of the council and granted a chamber which he had built for himself at considerable expense (although the timescale makes this improbable) and was treasurer in 7 November 1616.[512] He purchased 1,000 acres in both Tyrone and Fermanagh from the original grantees and by 1618 and had property also in Meath and Kildare. Geratt built a house near Lowtherstown (now Irvinestown), Fermanagh, and on 20 February 1619 received a patent to hold a fair there; he appointed his brother Hugh to look after his Ulster interests. In his will of 24 September 1624 he bequeathed his estate among his brothers William, Hugh, and Lancelot, nephew Richard and godson and namesake.

THOMAS LUTTRELL (1574 – 12 November 1634) **Dublin Co., 1613, 1634**

e.s. Simon Luttrell (d. 1596) and Elizabeth, da. Richard Finglass, Waspelston; m. 1) 1596–9, Eleanor (d. 1610), da. John Cheevers, Macetown, and Katherine, da. and coh. Henry Trevers, Monkstown, Co. Dublin; 2 s. Simon and Stephen, 1 da.;[513] 2) by April 1615, Alison (d. 1663+) da. Nicholas St Laurence, Lord Howth and ____; 2 s. Thomas, John, 3 da. Alson, Mary, Margaret; also Martha.[514]

ed. Middle Temple, 31 July 1591.

Bur. 30 November 1634, Clonsilla Church.

Thomas inherited significant property at Luttrellstown, county Dublin, Meath and Kildare from his father; he paid a £100 fine on a grant passed by the Commission of Defective Titles in 1609; this was one of the largest such fines, suggesting that the grant was extensive. He left a very considerable estate of lands, livestock, plate, jewellery and cash to his widow and children.[515] Thomas was involved in the 1605 Mandates crisis and imprisoned in Dublin Castle for refusing

511 Chichester to the A.G. or solicitor general, warrant for a fiant for Gerard Lother esq. place of a justice of the Common pleas in Ireland; salary £100 p.a., 9 Oct. 1610, HL, HP, Box 3 (19); Crawford, *Star Chamber*, pp 515–17; HL, HP, Box 4 (49); Draft gaol delivery book, general sessions, Monaghan; taken by Sir John Davies* & G. Lowther*, lords justices of assize, 12 April 1617, HL, HP, MS 15,013; Ferguson, 'Ulster Roll of gaol delivery, continued'; TCD, MS 672, fo, 83r.

512 King's Inns, MS B 1/1, fos. 171–2, 176r; Ball, *Judges in Ireland*, ii, pp 323–4.

513 Bernard Burke, *Irish Family Records* (5th edition, London, 1976), p. 229; F.E. Ball, *A history of the county Dublin*, 6 vols (Dublin, 1902–20), iv, pp 8–11.

514 Maighréad Ní Mhurchadha, 'Documents concerning the Oath of Supremacy in early seventeenth-century Ireland', *Archivium Hibernicum*, 63 (2010), 264–73; Tallon (ed.), *Court of Claims*, pp 1, 9.

515 *Cal. S.P. Ire, 1611–14*, p. 104; HL, HP, Box 3 (40); *Rot. Pac. Jac.*, pp 3, 82, 146; *Inq. cancel. Hib. repert.*, i, Meath, Car. I (4); Griffith (ed.), *Calendar of inquisitions*, pp 307–8, 314, 349–51; Ball, *History of the county Dublin*, iv, pp 10–11; Maighréad Ní Mhurchadha, *Fingal, 1603–60: contending neighbours in north Dublin* (Dublin, 2005), pp 48, 59, 64, 69–74, 211.

the oath of supremacy. His leadership in this campaign, as well as his family standing and extensive estates were factors in his election as MP in 1613. Luttrell was vocal in his objections to Chichester's illegal incorporation of additional boroughs and Davies' candidacy for the speakership and was one of the second set of Catholic agents sent to England (described by Cregan as a 'galaxy of brilliant lawyers'). There he was imprisoned in the Fleet for eleven weeks. He submitted at least two petitions against Chichester to James and the English privy council, which the deputy answered with a stinging denunciation of Thomas' aggressive and insolent behaviour. On the resumption of parliament, he was an active MP, sitting on the Grand Committee and that for Tyrone's attainder, and remained prominent in campaigns for Catholics' rights after its dissolution.[516] He was one of the Leinster agents sent to London to negotiate the Graces with Charles in 1627.[517] Despite Cregan's encomium, there is no evidence that Luttrell worked as a lawyer. Thomas' eldest son Simon, a recruiter MP for Navan in 1643, married Mary, daughter of Lord Gormanston and his daughters Katherine and Martha married Robert Harpole and Thomas Tuite son and heir Sir Oliver Tuite, respectively.[518] Thomas was involved in a number of chancery cases, as well as a dispute with his nephew Christopher Cheevers which centred on £2,000 borrowed on bond on the Dublin staple in 1601.[519]

HENRY LYNCH (? – 21 February 1635)[520] **Galway, 1634**

e.s. Nicholas Lynch fitz Stephen fitz Arthur, Galway, and ____; m. 1603+, Elizabeth (w. James Darcy, Galway), da. Richard Martin, Galway; sons Roebuck*, Nicholas, Maurice; da. Eleanor m. Sir Valentine Blake.
ed. King's Inns, 1607.
1st. Bart., 8 June 1622; Kt. 1625.
Bur. 6 March 1635, St, Nicholas', Galway.

Henry was a member of one of the most prominent families who had managed Galway for some generations; his father had been mayor and Henry was an alderman and former recorder of the town. Additionally, his own marriage linked him to other important local families. He was Darcy's* step-father, father of Roebuck* and Nicholas, MP for Galway in 1634 and father-in-law of Valentine Blake. While his name is not recorded in the registers of the inns of court, Henry was a respected lawyer, one of the founders of the King's Inns in 1607, at which time he was described as 'learned in the laws', and was involved in the society's administration, although he is not listed as having chambers there. He was counsel in a 1604 exchequer case on proxies reported in Davies' *Premier report* and he presumably worked on cases in all the courts until Catholic lawyers were prevented

516 Ní Mhurchadha, 'Documents concerning the Oath of Supremacy'.

517 Clarke, *Old English*.

518 NLI, GO, MS 79, Funeral Entries, Volume 17, at http://catalogue.nli.ie/Record/vtls000529291#page/195/mode/1up [accessed 28 Feb. 2023].

519 NAI, Chancery MSS AA 153, AA 203, G 174, J/7; Ohlmeyer and Ó Ciardha (eds), *Irish statute staple*.

520 Cokayne, *Baronetage*, i, p. 241.

from pleading in 1614.[521] Henry was also Clanricard's principal man of business from at least 1617 and the two men were personally very close; Henry asked the earl's advice about his sons' education and Clanricard sponsored the education of many Galwegians at the London Inns, including Darcy*, Donnellan* and Martin*.[522]

Lynch was a member of Galway town council from 1622 until his death, had extensive estates in Galway, including old church lands at Clonfert and the Aran Islands and in Mayo; his property disputes with the bishop of Clonfert were decided at the privy council in 1633.[523] He was a member of the 1624–5 Galway commission of the peace, a commissioner to raise money for the army in Galway in 1625 and for Galway City and County for managing the export of corn to England in 1631. He was also one of the agents who negotiated the Graces in England in 1628.[524] The Commons ordered Henry, Robert Talbot, Darcy* and Alexander* to witness the Commons' clerk and his deputy take their oaths of office before the chancellor and he was a member of the standing committees on privileges and grievances, and that to urge Wentworth to implement the Graces. He resigned his seat on the grounds of ill-health in December 1634 and died two months later.[525]

ROEBUCK (Robert) LYNCH (*c.*1606 – 28 August 1667+)[526] **Galway, 1640**

e.s. Sir Henry Lynch* (MP Galway, 1634), and Elizabeth, da. Richard Martin, Galway, w. James Rivagh Darcy; m. *c.* 1629, Ellis, da. Sir Peter French, Galway and Catherine Browne, Galway; sons Henry, Nicholas, Ignatius, Peter, Arthur, das. Wenefrid Lynch, Mary Nolan, Julian, Margaret.
ed. Middle Temple, 1620; Oxford, King's Inns, 1628.[527]
2nd Bart., 1635.
Bur. St Nicholas' Collegiate Church, Galway.

The Lynches were one of the wealthiest and most important Galway families. They had been established there for centuries and, with the Blakes and Brownes, with whom they had many marriage and trade connections, they controlled the commerce of the area and used their wealth to acquire extensive property in Galway and Mayo. In 1636 he was one of the Galway landowners opposed to the intended plantation of Connacht.[528] He and his father had a long-running dispute

521 King's Inns, MS B1/1, fo. 302r; Davies, *Le premier report*, fo. 6v.
522 Cunningham, 'Clanricard letters'; McGrath, 'Ireland and the third university'.
523 *Cal. S.P. Ire., 1608–11*, p. 493; Kenneth W. Nicholls (ed.), 'The Lynch-Blosse Papers', *Anal. Hib.*, 29 (1980), 113–218, at 141–4; NAI, Chancery MS G 361; Knowler (ed.), *Letters and dispatches*, i, p. 172; O'Sullivan (ed.), *Strafford inquisition of County Mayo*, p. 181; NAI, MS M. 2,448, p. 160.
524 TCD, MS 672, fo. 181r; *Cal. S.P. Ire., 1625–35*, p. 253; Caulfield (ed.), *Youghal*, pp 160–7; Clarke, *Old English*, pp 46, 84, 127.
525 *Commons' Jn. Ire.*, 17 July 1634, 2 Aug. 1634, 12 Dec. 1634.
526 Will, 28 Aug. 1667, Nicholls (ed.), 'Lynch–Blosse Papers', pp 144ff; Micheál Ó Siochrú, 'Lynch (Robert) Roebuck', *DIB*.
527 He is recorded as of Gray's Inn on his admission to the King's Inns. King's Inns, MS B1/1, fo. 18r. See *DIB* for his education at Oxford.
528 Nicholls (ed.), 'Lynch–Blosse Papers'.

with Richard and Ulick Bourke about lands.[529] Apart from the position gained by their own wealth and family connections, their close association with the Clanricards increased their local and national influence. Sir Henry Lynch, a former recorder of Galway, was Clanricard's principal man of business and his good friend. Sir Henry asked Clanricard's advice about his children's education and marriages.[530] Roebuck was also Darcy's* step-brother and brother-in-law and Richard Martin's* brother-in-law. Like his father, whose title and estates he inherited, he was active on the town council as burgess from 1636, alderman and mayor of Galway in 1638 and mayor of the staple the following year. He remained a member of Galway Corporation until 1653. The extent of his legal practice is unknown, but he spent time in Dublin during legal terms, suggesting he was engaged there for clients.[531]

He was one of the most active MPs in 1640–1 and a member of numerous committees, including that formed to draft a declaration of loyalty to Charles to be attached to the Subsidies Act, the Commons' impeachment committee and also of the committee sent to present the house's grievances to the king in England.[532] On the outbreak of the rebellion, he was one of the MPs attempting to negotiate with the Ulster rebels to establish their complaints, but in the following year was a member of the Council of Eight which governed Galway in the early years of the rebellion. With Ulick Burke, Valentine Blake and others, he also formed part of the force raised locally by Colonel John Burke to defend Galway in April 1643.[533] Clanricard wrote to Roebuck, Dominic Browne, Darcy* and Richard Martin* in early 1644 to object to the Connacht provincial council's cessing Captain Richard Bourke's company on Longfort barony, near his base at Loughrea, as well as expressing his annoyance at the impositions laid on him.[534] Roebuck was one of the most prominent members of the Confederation, a member of all the Supreme Councils except the first and sixth, and a member of the 1647 General Assembly. Like Darcy*, Richard Blake and Rochford*, he was a member of the peace faction. Lynch was one of the resident Connacht members of the Council and of the Galway provincial council. With Geoffrey Browne* he was an agent from the Assembly to Clanricard in May 1645.[535] Roebuck was on the Continent in 1651, when he made an agreement with the duke of Lorraine on Clanricard's behalf, which included a commitment to send Lynch to the Aran Islands (which he had inherited from his father) with 200 musketeers to protect the entrance to Galway

529 Petition of Richard Bourke and Ulick Bourke to Wentworth, 4 July 1638, NAI, MS M. 2,448, p. 160.
530 Clanricard to Sir Henry Lynch, 12 June 1624, 2 May 1625, 15 July 1627, NLI, MS 3,111. Henry had, however, ignored this advice at least in one respect, in that he sent Roebuck to be educated in Oxford, an unusual step for an Irish Catholic at the time.
531 Nicholls (ed.), 'Lynch–Blosse Papers'.
532 Clarke, *Old English*, pp 127, 135; Perceval-Maxwell, *Outbreak*, pp 71, 75, 90, 136; Borlase, *History*, p. 10.
533 Ó Siochrú, *Confederate Ireland*, p. 25; O'Sullivan, *Old Galway*, p. 258.
534 Lowe (ed.), *The letter-book of the earl of Clanricarde*, pp 42–3, 62–3, 68–70, 74, 85, 122.
535 Ó Siochrú, *Confederate Ireland*, pp 17, 141, 161, 165, 181–2, 213, 223–4, 247, 256–7; Ó hAnnracháin, *Catholic reformation in Ireland*, p. 219.

Bay. He returned to Galway, where, with Clanricard and other prominent citizens of Galway, he negotiated the city's surrender to Ludlow in early 1652. Lynch was granted transplantation lands in Mace, Galway and Castlecana, Mayo.

RICHARD MARTIN (1602 – 1648) **Athenry, 1634; Augher, 1641**

e.s. Oliver Martin (d. 1657), Galway; m. by 1628, Margaret (Maggin), da. Sir Peter French (d. 1631) and Catherine Browne, Galway; sons Oliver, Sebastian (d. 1644), Peter, Stephen (d. 1644), John, Patrick; das. Clara (d. 1640), Mary and Magdalen.[536]

ed. Middle Temple, 1622–9; King's Inns, 1631.

Martin was a member of the small number of wealthy merchant families that had controlled Galway for centuries. The Martins were a wealthy family – Oliver's annual income from lands in Galway alone was estimated at £400 and he had some interest in Thomond's lands – and Richard held substantial lands in Galway (including in Athenry and the Castle at Dun Guaire, Kinvara), as well as acquiring estates in Mayo, Roscommon and Sligo; his wife brought him a house in Lombard Street, Galway, and other property. This extensive property and his daughter's marriage portion of £1,500 in cash when she married Sir Thomas Blake, baronet, in 1649 indicate Richard's own wealth.[537] He was Roebuck Lynch* and Darcy's* step-brother and brother-in-law respectively. Both his father and father-in-law were deprived of their mayoralties (in 1632 and 1616 respectively) for refusing the oath of supremacy. Richard was a member of Galway town council from 1631 to 1646 and was elected alderman and mayor in his absence in 1641. He was mayor of the staple in 1643. Martin's close personal and working relationships with his fellow Galwegians were very important, as they formed a tightly-knit groups of able and respected merchants and lawyers who worked well together in legal practice, finance and politics. His links with Darcy* were especially significant and also those with Clanricard.[538]

One of the most prominent lawyers in Ireland (Wentworth described him as 'very able'), he had an extensive practice, beginning during his studies in London. He was permanently retained by Clanricard and Cork and acted also for Lord Antrim; he practiced in all courts including chancery, privy council, Castle Chamber and parliament. He received leases of land in Carlow from Ormond in recognition of his services. He represented John Kennedy, brother of Richard* in his long-running chancery case about his father's estate, Galway merchants before the privy council in 1637 and Charles Lambart in his petition concerning his lands in Mayo in the House of Lords.[539]

536 Nicholls (ed.), 'Lynch–Blosse Papers', p. 169; NUIG, MS Liber A, fo. 179r, where we see Martin chosen as alderman and mayor 1 Aug. 1642 aged 40 years, in his absence; *DIB*; Tallon (ed.), *Court of Claims*, pp 135–40; Mills (ed.), *Registers of St John the Evangelist*, p. 36; NLI, MS 40,889/38(4).

537 Acquittance for £20 and 20*s*. by Dick and Oliver Martin respectively, Sept. 1629 and Nov. 1630, NLI, MS Thomond 108/; Tallon (ed.), *Court of Claims*, pp 135–40; NLI, MS 40,889/38(4).

538 E.g., Clanricard to Martin, 3 May 1644, in Lowe (ed.), *Letter-book*, pp 79–80.

539 NAI, MS RC 5/1, pp 79–87; Grosart (ed.), *Lismore Papers*, 1st series, iv, pp 68–9, under 4 Feb. 1634–5; Bodl. Lib., Talbot. MS C. 99; Rushworth (ed.), *Tryal*, pp 176–7; *LJI*, 1 March 1641.

With Darcy*, Richard was one of the leaders of the Catholic faction in the 1634 parliament, sitting on a large number of committees, including the standing ones on privileges and grievances and those to present petitions relating to the Graces. His relationship with Wentworth was chequered: his role in parliament and his representing (with Darcy* and Sir Roger O'Shaughnessy) Galway landholders resisting the proposed plantation of Connacht led to the deputy's enmity. In late 1635 he and Darcy travelled to England to protest to the king against the intended plantation. After their mission failed, Martin went into hiding, but was found by the deputy's servant William Railton in Fetter Lane in February 1636, arrested and sent back to Dublin where he and Darcy were imprisoned and disbarred from practice. Influential clients including Antrim persuaded Wentworth to release him (Darcy continued to be imprisoned) in May 1636. Being disbarred did not prevent him and Darcy* from acting as lawyers and they continued to advise clients from prison. They were supported during their disgrace by a number of influential men and Antrim and others repeatedly made the case for their readmission. Martin advised the Clare freeholders who conveniently cleared the way for the planting of their estates by acknowledging Charles' title to their lands before the inquisition; this improved his relationship with Wentworth who acceded to his petition to be restored to practice in October 1637 with the optimistic, if misplaced, hope, that 'he will in truth I think futurely become a new man.'[540] Martin was universally liked and trusted, but Wentworth's more favourable account of him may have been as much to point to a contrast with Darcy than to commend Richard. Martin's links with MPs other than his fellow Catholic lawyers are more difficult to reconstruct, although Richard FitzGerald is recorded as owing him £200 in May 1637.

Like others who had been victimized by Wentworth, Martin refused to stand for election in early 1640, but he and Darcy* acted as advisors to parliament, specifically to the sub-committee on the bill for the plantation of Connacht and Ormond, before their own returns for Tyrone constituencies which can only be ascribed to opposition MPs' desire to strengthen the quality of legal expertise in their ranks. Both men, and Adam Cusack immediately became opposition leaders, sitting on more than 20 committees.[541] On the outbreak of the rebellion, Martin, with other townsmen, sought to preserve Galway from the neighbouring Irish who rebelled and he supported Clanricard's attempts at mediation between the insurgents and the king in early 1642.[542] He wrote to Ormond to ask for arms and ammunition to defend the town, but this request was refused. William Hanmer deposed that it was the 'lawyers that first moved the Towne of Galway to Rebellion, both by their letters from Dublin and theire instigitio (sic) when they came to Galway.' When Martin was chosen mayor in his absence in September 1642 (he

540 Pogson, 'Public and private service'; Petitioned to be restored to practice, 28 Aug. 1637. Wentworth to Coke, 28 Aug. 1637, Coke to Wentworth, 5 Oct. 1637, in Knowler (ed.), *Letters and dispatches*, ii, pp 98, 113; Wentworth to Coke, 27 Nov. 1637, quoted in Clarke, *Old English*, p. 110.

541 Perceval-Maxwell, *Outbreak*, pp 81, 123, 137–9, 148; Borlase, *History*, pp 8, 10.

542 Ó Siochrú, *Confederate Ireland*, pp 30–6.

demurred but was overborn by his fellow townsmen) Hanmer described him as being 'proved as badd or worse than any other rebell and would not releeve nor partake with them of the fort'.[543]

Martin spent much of the 1640s in Galway, where he and Darcy* were leading members of the Council of Eight, established to govern the city. With Darcy he was involved in shaping the political structures of the Confederation, attending the first Confederate General Assembly in Kilkenny in October 1642 as a delegate from Galway, and, together with others including the lawyers Bourke*and Darcy, with Adam Cusack drew up a constitution or 'form of civil government' which was based on work he and Darcy had done earlier that year; however, Martin refused to take the oath of association so as not to 'upset the delicate power balance in Galway.'[544] He sat on the Confederate provincial council in Connacht up to 1645, playing a key role in local administration in Galway City. In 1644 he became more closely involved in central Confederation business, acting with Muskerry as part of a Confederate delegation to the court at Oxford, sitting as a member of the General Assembly and in August accepted an appointment to the Confederate judiciary.[545] Nothing was resolved at the Oxford talks but Richard was one of the Confederate team in negotiations with Ormond in Dublin, although Darcy appears to have replaced him as delegate. Richard concentrated on legal matters as judge until his death in 1648 as part of an effort to separate judicial and political matters within the Confederation.[546]

SIR CHRISTOPHER NUGENT (-1562 – 15 December 1620) **Westmeath Co., 1613**

s. Sir Thomas Nugent, Moyrath, and Mary Nugent, da. Lord Delvin; m. 1) by 1597, Elizabeth, da. Richard Luttrell, Luttrellstown; 5 s. Thomas, James, Francis, Christopher, Edward; 2 da. Bridget, Mary.[547]
ed. Gray's Inn, 1588; King's Inns, 1609.
Kt. 25 December 1604.
Bur. Taghmon Church, near Mullingar.

Christopher's father Thomas was MP for Westmeath in 1560 and his relatives included the important Delvin and Luttrell families. His children married into the locally important Nugent, O'Farrell and Sherlock families. Christopher was part of the first intake of lawyers to the re-established King's Inns in the late 1600s. He seconded Everard as speaker and refused to act as teller for the votes in that contest. Cregan described him, Everard and Luttrell as the most important of the commoners sent as delegates to argue the Catholic case concerning electoral fraud before James in London; he was imprisoned in the Gatehouse during his time there. Nugent was an active MP, sitting on many committees, including that of privileges, and a frequent contributor to debates. Nugent held lands in Cavan, Sligo, Meath,

543 William Hanmer's deposition, TCD, MS 830, fos. 134v, 148v.
544 Bodl. Lib., Carte MS 68, fo. 1r; Ó Siochrú, *Confederate Ireland*, pp 44–7.
545 Ibid., p. 86.
546 Ibid., pp 75, 230, 263.
547 Anonymous, *Historical sketch of the Nugent family* (Ledestown, 1853), p. 15; John Ainsworth and Edward MacLysaght (eds), 'Nugent Papers', *Anal. Hib.*, 20 (1958), 126–215, at p. 139.

Longford and Westmeath and was a member of a Cavan jury in 1606 that decided the case of the deceased Sir John O'Reilly. In 1613 he leased some lands at Lurgan to Richard Lane for 21 years.[548] He was a member of the 1620 Commission for Quiet Settlement of Undertakers and Natives in the Longford plantation.

EDMUND NUGENT **(c.1574 – July 1622)** **Westmeath Co., 1 May 1615**
s. Ald. Piers (Peter) Nugent (d. 1608–9), Drogheda; m. 1) by 1598, Martha, da. Sir Edward Herbert, Durrow, King's Co., and Elizabeth, da. Patrick Finglas of Westpalstown;[549] e.s. John, da. Anne and other children. Martha rem. Charles Mageoghegan, Bealathmiragh, Westmeath.[550]
ed. Staple Inn, Gray's Inn, 1590; King's Inns, 1607.
Bur. Multyfarnham Abbey.

Edmund replaced the deceased Edward Nugent in parliament on 1 May 1615. His father was from the gentry family based at Multifarnham but had become a prosperous merchant in Drogheda; his son Walter (d. 1609), was mayor of Drogheda. They retained their Westmeath connections. Edmund lived at Roconnell and both he and Piers were buried in Multifarnham; he held 'the moytie of Lanargid alias the weir of Coylerand' part of the lands in dispute between the earl of Kildare and Lady Lettice Digby.[551] He also had lands in Longford, as he was prosecuted in the Court of Castle Chamber for refusing to present recusants there in 1614 for which he was fined £40 and imprisoned at Chichester's pleasure. Nugent surrendered and was re-granted 711 acres in the plantation there.[552] Edmund was described as '*in legibus eruditus*' and was executor for both his father and brother Walter; he shared with William Talbot* a chamber in the east end of the old Friar's Hall in the King's Inns.[553] He was mentioned in chancery pleadings of Elinor Nugent and Michael Casey, about castle and lands in Athboy, 20 May 1620. His widow complained to chancery about the executors of Edmund's will, his cousin Andrew Nugent of Donower and the merchant Nicholas Casey of Mullingar.[554]

LAURENCE (Lawrence) PARSONS **(1572+ – 8 September 1628)**[555] **Tallow, 1613**
y.s. James Parsons, Leicestershire, and Catherine, da. Henry Fenton, Nottinghamshire and Cecily, da. John Beaumont, Coleorton, Nottinghamshire; m. 1) by 1612, Ann (d. 1646), da. ____ Maltham, Yorkshire; 3 s., 2 da.
ed. Gray's Inn, 1607; Bar, 5 February 1612;[556] King's Inns, 1612.

548 *Rot. Pac. Jac.*, pp 169, 234; *Inq. cancel. Hib. repert.*, Westmeath, Jac. I (5, 6, 9); Clarke and McGrath (eds), *Letterbook*, p. 124; Tallon (ed.), *Court of Claims*, p. 30; Bodl. Lib., Carte MS 61, fo. 329r; NAI, MS Chancery BB70 (taken from Kenneth Nicholls' calendar); HL, HP, Box 3 (40).
549 TCD, MS 1,216, fo. 34v; Cokayne, *Baronetage*.
550 Griffith (ed.), *Calendar of inquisitions*, pp 238–9, 379; Ainsworth and MacLysaght (eds), 'Nugent Papers', esp. pp 135–40; FitzGerald and Lamacraft (eds), *Some funeral entries of Ireland*, p. 147.
551 Clarke, and McGrath (eds), *Letterbook*, p. 124; *Inq. cancel. Hib. repert.*, i, Westmeath, Jac. I (6, 25, 64); *Rot. Pac. Jac.*, pp 233, 468.
552 Crawford, *Star Chamber*, pp 519–20; TCD, MS 672, fo. 158; Treadwell (ed.), *Irish commission of 1622*, p. 659.
553 King's Inns, MS B1/1, fos. 3v, 108v; ibid., N3/2/1/7, fo. 6r.
554 NAI, MSS Chancery AA/59, Chancery BB 109.
555 TCD, MS 1,216, fo. 33v; Judy Barry, 'Parsons, Sir Lawrence', *DIB*.
556 Reginald James Fletcher (ed.), *The Pension Book of Gray's Inn (Records of the Honourable Society), 1569–1669* (London, 1901), p. 197.

Laurence and his older brothers Sir William and Fenton came to Ireland when their uncle Sir Geoffrey Fenton was secretary of state for Ireland. William and Laurence benefitted greatly from Geoffrey's patronage and his daughter Catherine's marriage to the future first earl of Cork, Richard Boyle, in 1603. This connection benefitted both sides and they had a close working and family relationship, with Laurence becoming Boyle's agent. They were also godfathers to each other's children.[557] In 1604 Boyle granted Laurence a lease of Myrtle Grove, Walter Raleigh's old house in Youghal; the year after Laurence became clerk of the Council of Munster (1605–16) and then escheator and receiver general in Munster (1606, jointly with William).[558] These offices gave him a solid basis on which to develop his career and estates and were presumably exercised through deputies when he entered Gray's Inn relatively late in life and was called to the bar and 'discharged of his vacacons in respect of his intended service in Ireland' where he was immediately appointed attorney general of Munster. He provided legal services for Boyle during his time in London and continued to do so on his return to Ireland.[559]

He was returned for Boyle's town of Tallow, one of the disallowed boroughs, and his assertion that 'I aim at a restitution (to parliament) for no other end, but to do [Boyle] a faithful service touching Lismore' demonstrates the strength of their connection. His position did not affect his service for Boyle or acquiring other offices, succeeding Gosnold as recorder of Youghal in 1615, acquiring other property and developing a legal practice – he was working for Boyle on chancery cases in 1618.[560] From 1619 he also became a client of Buckingham and the duke's patronage resulted in his appointments as judge of the Admiralty Court (1619) and second baron of the exchequer (1624).[561] As might be expected of an associate of Cork, his probity in office was questionable.[562] He continued to be involved in Youghal, where he maintained a house and the town gave him the right to nominate one inhabitant of the poor house. Parsons also acquired property in Cork, where he was sheriff in 1620.[563]

Laurence had chambers in King's Inns consisting of 'Chambers with two Studdys therein, and one Cocklofte and studdy' in 1624 and was treasurer of the Inns in 1626.[564] Laurence benefitted greatly from the Plantation of Ely O'Carroll,

557 Grosart (ed.), *Lismore Papers*, 1st series, ii, passim, pp 72, 93, 110, 118, 126, 158, 244–5, godfather to Boyle's daughter, 1617, Boyle godfather to Parson's son Richard, p. 329.

558 Curtis Clayton (ed.), *Council book*, pp 80, 166, 168, 171–2, 214–5, 231, 258–9, 358; Birr Castle, MS Q/1–3.

559 *Calendar of the Lismore manuscripts*, i, pp 50–1, 87, 109, 119.

560 Caulfield (ed.), *Youghal*, pp 39, 82, 101; RIA, MS OS EI 21, pp 271–9; Cork to Bramhall, 4 Feb. 1640, HL, HP, MS 14,001; NAI, MS AA/28.

561 Hughes, *Patentee officers*; Appleby (ed.), *Calendar*, pp 144 (Dec. 1621), 148; Ball, *Judges in Ireland*, ii, p. 330.

562 John C. Appleby and Mary O'Dowd, 'The Irish admiralty: its organization and development, *c.*1570–1640', *IHS*, 24:95 (1985), 299–326, at 323; *Cal. S.P. Ire., 1625–32*, p. 428.

563 Caulfield (ed.), *Youghal*, p. 101; Birr Castle, MS A/5/69; University College Cork, Kinsale Manorial Records, MS KM/PP/U20/1, nos 3–5.

564 King's Inns, MS B1/1, fos. 178r, 180r; *DIB*.

receiving 1,000 acres around Birr Castle where he built up an estate and developed the town which his descendants tried to have established as the county town of King's County; he was also a member of the 1624–5 commission of the peace in that county.[565] Curiously, he did not pursue the letters patent which granted parliamentary representation to his manors of Birr and Leighlinbridge.[566]

DAMIEN (Daniel) PECKE (*c.*1566 – 1621–September 1625)[567] **Tuam, 1613**

s. ____ Pecke, Calcott, Cambridgeshire, and m. 4 October 1582, St Andrew's, Holborn, Anne (d. 1629+), da. Caesare Adellmare, Tottenham, and Margery (or Margaret) Perient (or Perin);[568] at least one son Richard (*c.*1607), admitted Cambridge 1623 as of London.
ed. Staple Inn; Gray's Inn, 8 February 1582.

Pecke's career was advanced by his marriage to the sister of the English judge Sir Julius Caesar, chancellor of the exchequer, 1610–14, who pressed Chichester hard for Damian's promotion. Pecke suggested himself as recorder of Dublin and Caesar supported his claims to be attorney of Ulster, but the position was not vacant. Chichester exerted himself and Pecke replaced the Catholic recorder of Galway (trebling his salary to £30) in 1610, holding this office until 1618. He was justice of assize for Westmeath and Meath in August 1612 and was appointed attorney general of Connacht in July 1613.[569]

CHRISTOPHER PLUNKETT (*c.*1568 – 30 June 1634–6)[570] **Dublin Co., 1613**

only s. James Plunkett, Dunsoghly and Catherine, da. Thomas Fitzwilliam, Merrion; m. 1) by 1586, Margaret da. Sir Nicholas Bagenal, Newry, and Eleanor Griffith, Penrhyn; e.s. James of Longwood, Co. Meath; other sons James, Ambrose, John, Richard, Christopher, Henry, Francis, Nicholas; da. Clare.
Kt. 15 August 1597, Dunsoghly.

Christopher inherited his grandfather Sir John Plunkett's extensive estates at Dunsoghly in Dublin and Longwood, Meath, in August 1582 when he was described as over 14 and married. John had been a distinguished lawyer and chief justice of the queen's bench in the 1560s. There is no record of Christopher's attendance at the inns of court, or admission to the King's Inns, but he was described as a lawyer at the time and was one of the MPs with legal training that

565 TCD, MS 672, fo. 178r; Terence Reeves-Smith, *Irish gardens and gardening before Cromwell* (Cork, 1999), p. 31.

566 *Rot. Pac. Jac.*, p. 313; Birr Castle, MSS A/5/46, fos. 1r–2r, A/8.

567 Warrant for Walter Archer to be made attorney of Connaught in succession to Damian Pecke, deceased, 27 September 1625, in Empey (ed.), *Early Stuart Irish warrants*, no. 7.

568 Renold Elstrack, 'Caesar, Sir Julius', *Oxford DNB*; Foster, *London marriage licences*, Col. 1038.

569 *Cal. S.P. Ire., 1608–10*, p. 444; *Cal. S.P. Ire., 1611–14*, pp 275, 314, 405, 551; Crawford, *Star Chamber*, pp 513–15; Gilbert (ed.), 'Archives of the municipal Corporation of Galway'; McGrath, 'Managing the Windsor'; McCavitt, *Arthur Chichester*, p. 55; NAI, MS Chancery BB117; Hughes, *Patentee officers*; BL, Lansdowne MS 159, fos. 213, 221, 226; BL, Add. MS 2,496, fo. 140.

570 Micheál Ó Siochrú, 'Plunkett, Sir Christopher', *DIB*; Will, in Griffiths (ed.), *Calendar of inquistions*, pp 456–8

the Commons requested the administration to use to draft the acts they desired.[571] A fervent Catholic, Christopher's son Nicholas studied for the priesthood in Douai. Well-connected with the Pale gentry, his sister-in-law Anne Bagenal's successive marriages to Sir Dudley Loftus and Dominic Sarsfield also provided connections with the administration. Christopher made a number of visits to court and impressed James with his 'modesty, humility, and discretion' and received fresh grants of his estates in Meath.[572]

A leader of the opposition in 1613, he was one of the actors behind the objections to the fraudulent returns, described as 'a chief ringleader and countenancer of the first disobedience'. Plunkett also nominated Everard* as speaker. Sent as an agent from the Catholic MPs to London, he was imprisoned in the Fleet but after apologizing for his conduct returned to Dublin where he was active as an MP, sitting on many committees including the prestigious Grand Committee; he proposed that the act of general pardon be committed, 'to see whether it were general indeed'.[573] For the ten years after parliament's dissolution, Plunkett actively promoted economic and administrative reform, travelling to London in 1620 with Delvin and others to discuss how beer was brewed, births deaths and marriages registered and the ever-contentious issue of ploughing by the tail. Three years later he was part of a delegation proposing the end of restrictions on the export of wool and he was involved in raising money for the army in Ireland from Catholics. He was a commissioner for County Dublin for managing the export of corn to England in 1631.[574]

NICHOLAS PLUNKETT (*c.*1601–80) **Meath, 1634, 1640**

3 s. Christopher Plunkett, 9th Lord Killeen, and Genet (Jane), da. Sir Lucas[575] Dillon, Lord Kilkenny West, sister of James, earl of Roscommon; m. 1) Catherine, da. and coh. Ald. William Turner, Wexford; 2 da.; 2) Mary, da. Christopher Plunkett, the Grange; 3) Catherine, da. James Aylmer, Lyons, and Carrickbrien, Clare.
ed. Gray's Inn, 1622; King's Inns, 1628.
Kt. 1648.[576]
Bur. Killeen.

Nicholas Plunkett of Balrath was a member of one of the most important Old English families of the Pale, that held extensive property and played a prominent role in politics; he was connected with virtually every Old English family in both houses and also many New English. He was a cousin of Lord Robert Dillon and James Dillon, and his brother Lucas was created earl of Fingall. Family marriages

571 Ibid., pp 67, 269–71, 291–2, 315–16, 353, 456–8, 465–6; NAI, MS RC, 5/2, pp 1–61; *Rot. Pac. Jac.*, pp 40, 200; *Inq. cancel. Hib. repert.*, Dublin, Car. I (15, 30, 41, 43, 49); NAI, MS Chancery J236 (taken from Kenneth Nicholls' calendar); HL, HP, Box 3 (40); *DIB*; Cregan, 'Irish recusant lawyers'; *Commons' Jn. Ire.*, 21 April 1615.

572 *Cal. S.P. Ire., 1615–25*, p. 282.

573 *Commons' Jn. Ire.*, 2 May 1615.

574 *Cal. S.P. Ire., 1615–25*, p. 282; Caulfield (ed.), *Youghal*, p. 163.

575 Walter Fitzgerald (ed.), *Association for the preservation of memorials of the dead, Ireland, Volume 8* (Dublin, 1910), pp 407–9, gives Genet's father as James Dillon.

576 Nicholas was knighted by the Pope. See Gilbert Library, MS 169, p. 244.

connected him to members of the O'Donnell, FitzGerald, Brabazon, Bagenal and Preston families. His sisters Joan and Ellice married Richard, earl of Westmeath, and Lord Slane, respectively, and his nephew and niece married into the Barnewall* (Kingsland), and Dowdall families. His brother Patrick was bishop of Ardagh (1647) and Meath (1669).[577] Nicholas should not be confused with the author of the manuscript *History of the Irish Rebellion*.

Plunkett was one of the foremost lawyers of his day. He was retained by Lords Cork (although he also acted for the earl's adversary Richard Blacknall) and Taaffe, was counsel for the Galway jurors who failed to find the king's title to their lands, for Thomas Lord Costello-Gallen in the case of tenures upon the Commission of Defective Titles and Sir John Gifford in his dispute with Lord Chancellor Loftus about the payment of a marriage portion. He also worked on cases in chancery and before the privy council.[578] Plunkett was largely based at Trim and owned extensive lands in Meath and Monaghan and, through his first wife, property in Wexford. However, he also built a house on lands adjacent to the King's Inns in Dublin, 'for his nearer habitation to soe good a societie'.[579] His family background, property and legal expertise all contributed to his elections and he played a prominent role in both parliaments and later in the Confederation.

In 1633–4 he worked closely with Wentworth preparing Catholic proposals for reform. He was a member of the standing committees for privileges to meet with the privy council to discuss desirable legislation for transmission to England and those on bills against bigamy and ease of pleading troublesome suits, but there is no record of his further activity after the first session when Wentworth refused to implement the Graces. Plunkett was one of the Catholic leaders in the first session of the 1640 parliament and among those who built a coalition between the Old English and New English within the Commons; he was also one of the drafters of the declaration of the Commons' willingness to grant subsidies, sat on the committee for the plantation of Connacht and was one of the Commons' agents to the king in November 1640. Plunkett gave evidence at Strafford's trial and he and Nicholas Barnewall negotiated with Charles to prevent the plantation of Connacht. With Geoffrey Browne*, he was suspected of directing the King's Irish policy, through Cottington's agency. Plunkett and his colleagues returned to Ireland, confident they had averted a major crisis and convinced that Irish Catholics' property would be secure under the king's protection.[580]

Nicholas was one of the MPs who attempted to use parliament to resolve the rebellion and drew up the proclamation, issued by the lords justices, admonishing

577 Micheál Ó Siochrú, 'Plunkett, Nicholas', *DIB*.

578 Grosart (ed.), *Lismore Papers*, 1st series, iv, pp 35, 108, 136, 152, 162, 195; Barry, *Case of tenures*; HMC, *Various collections, Volume III*, p. 159; Ó Siochrú, *Confederate Ireland*, pp 45–6; Ohlmeyer, 'Records'.

579 Simington (ed.), *Civil Survey*, Meath, p. 210; *Inq. Cancel. Hib. repert.*, Meath, Car. I (8, 108, 138, 136); Car. II (2, 3), William & Mary (3), Monaghan, Car. I (69, 95, 109, 119); King's Inns, MS B1/1, fos. 68v, 85v.

580 Clarke, *Old English*, pp 84, 102, 127–30, 135–7, 164, 182, 203, 213, 217–19; Perceval-Maxwell, *Outbreak*, pp 75, 79, 106, 136, 198, 312 n. 51; Borlase, *History*, pp 8, 10.

'freeholders, not having their hands in blood, within 10 dayes to submit themselves before any justice of the peace' and was one of the delegation appointed to meet the rebels and hear their demands.[581] However, parliament was prorogued the following day and as the Pale gentry had no political means of action, he attended the meeting of the Meath gentry at Crofty in December 1641. There, with his fellow lawyers Gerald Aylmer and Robert Berford, he was appointed to advise the Meath county council on legal matters.[582]

As a constitutionalist and political moderate, he was uncomfortable in the role of rebel and supported Clanricard's attempts early in 1642 to reach an accommodation with the king. When this initiative failed and the conflict intensified during the summer, his neutral position became increasingly untenable, especially after his home was burned by crown troops and he was expelled from parliament. He joined the Confederation, becoming the General Assembly's first chairman, a position he held until 1648; he sat on all nine Supreme Councils and was central to the Confederation's work, following always a policy of moderation and compromise. He brokered the cessation of 1643 and in the following year attended talks with Charles in Oxford. He worked hard, with others including Geoffrey Browne* and Muskerry to come to terms with Ormond, but religious differences prevented an agreement. In 1645 Plunkett and other Confederate leaders signed a secret agreement with Glamorgan accepting substantial concessions from Charles on religion in return for military assistance. This agreement was put under pressure by the arrival of the papal nuncio Gianbattista Rinuccini and Nicholas was caught between his loyalty as a Catholic and his inclination to support the peace; he and Darcy were sent to Waterford to explain the treaty, but sensing the widespread opposition, they changed sides and opposed it.[583]

After the treaty with Inchiquin in 1648, he travelled to Rome to present the case for that peace, where he was knighted by the Pope. As a commissioner of trust, he was in Galway in February 1651, dealing with the duke of Lorraine's ambassador. In the following month he was drafting an agreement between Clanricard and Lorraine. He left Ireland for Brussels in that April. His lands were declared forfeit and he was transplanted to Galway and Mayo. Like other Old English lawyers with whom he worked, Plunkett was essentially a man of the gown, rather than the sword, and he worked consistently for a peaceful, legal solution to the problems in Ireland. He did not follow Lake's* example in taking to the battlefield. Despite his involvement in the Catholic cause of the 1640s, he survived the 1650s and became the chief spokesman for his co-religionists with Charles II

581 *The false and scandalous remonstrance of the inhumane and bloody rebells of Ireland* (London, 1644), p. 70.

582 McGrath, 'Mount Taragh's triumph'; Ó Siochrú, *Confederate Ireland*, pp 25, 36–8.

583 Lowe (ed.), *Letter-book*, pp 22, 164, 185, 191, 209, 226, 236, 239, 242, 246–8, 252–4, 256, 398, 413–14, 422, 448, 473–4; Ó Siochrú, *Confederate Ireland*, pp 19–20, 49, 70, 81, 86, 91, 104–6, 108, 114–17, 123–7, 130–1, 136, 138, 140–2, 145–6, 152, 155, 161, 163, 165, 168–9, 193–4, 205, 217, 222–3, 230, 243, 246–8, 256–7, 259, 269–71; Ó hAnnracháin, *Catholic reformation in Ireland*, pp 110, 135, 137, 144n, 148–50, 152, 156n, 166, 171–5, 184–6, 189, 192–3, 196–7, 200, 203, 206–9, 215–16, 262–4, 278.

in the 1660s in London and Ireland, especially over the Act of Settlement and before the Court of Claims, where he represented Lord Antrim. With his wife, he was adjudged an innocent papist in November 1662 and recovered much of his property, including in Wexford.[584] He lived in Dublin after 1665, continuing to represent clients.[585]

GEORGE RADCLIFFE[586] (Ratcliffe) (4 April 1594 – 22 May 1657)
Armagh Co., Armagh, Tralee, Sligo Co. 1634;[587] Sligo Co., 1640[588]

e.s.s. Nicholas Radcliffe (d. 1599), Overthorpe, Yorkshire and Margaret, da. and coh. Robert Marsh, Darton, Yorkshire; m.) 21 February 1622, Anne (*c.*1600–59), e.da. Sir Francis Trappes, Harrogate, Yorkshire; son Thomas.[589]
ed. Oldham; University College, Oxford, 1609, BA, 1612, DCL 1643; Gray's Inn, 1612; Bar, 1618; Bencher, 1632; King's Inns, 1634.
MP for Callington, 1628.
Kt. 1633.
d. Sluis.
Bur. Flushing.

George came from a Yorkshire gentry family with good connections but limited wealth; he inherited a mere 400 acres from his father and his mother was able to purchase his wardship for only £12. Radcliffe's father's patrons, the Saviles of Thornhill, were influential in his career: his godfather, Sir George Savile, taught him basic Latin grammar and he became a lawyer 'to make me serviceable to Sir George Savile.' Savile's widow introduced him to her brother, Thomas Wentworth, and he quickly became the latter's legal adviser, confidant and close friend, acting for him, his sister and father-in-law, John Holles, earl of Clare.[590] With Wandesford and others, Radcliffe managed Wentworth's estates from the early 1620s, but he also practiced law in London. His wife was Wentworth's cousin and Lady Radcliffe stood godmother to Wentworth's son Thomas.

Radcliffe showed no interest in politics until 1627 when he refused to pay the Forced Loan and the privy council ordered his imprisonment in the Marshalsea on 24 April, apparently in collusion with Wentworth. He was released shortly after

584 Simington (ed.), *Transplantation to Connacht*, pp 173, 209; Cunningham, *Conquest and land in Ireland*, pp 122, 125, 143; Tallon, *Court of Claims* (ed.), pp 10, 395, 399; Richard Clifton to Thomas Symes, 7 Sept. 1666, HL, HP, MS 14,231; Richard Clifton to George Rawdon, 8 March 1667, HL, HP, MS 14,235; *DIB*.

585 E.g., Legal opinion of Nicholas Plunkett on the way that the nominees should proceed in arguing to get their settlement, 15 Nov. 1676, HL, Stowe Nugent Papers, Legal Box 1 (16).

586 Simon Healy, 'Radcliffe (Ratcliffe), George' in Thrush and Ferris (eds), *History of parliament*; Terry Clavin, 'Radcliffe, Sir George', *DIB*; Fiona Pogson, 'Radcliffe, Sir George', *Oxford DNB*.

587 Wentworth sent out 100 nominations in 1634, many of them to multiple constituencies for the same candidate. That is what happened in Radcliffe's case, as Wentworth was determined to have Radcliffe in parliament in 1634 (some others who were nominated were lobby fodder). As such he was nominated for numerous constituencies, but eventually sat for Sligo: see McGrath, 'Thomas Wentworth's Irish electoral strategy'.

588 He opted for the county seat.

589 He was contracted to marry the only daughter of the lawyer John Finch, Baron Finch of Fordham, but she died in 1621 aged 10: *Oxford DNB*.

590 Whitaker (ed.), *Life and original correspondence*, p. 6.

Christmas and in July unsuccessfully sought the recorderships of Doncaster and Pontefract. Wentworth's appointment as president of the Council of the North benefitted Radcliffe who was appointed king's attorney at York in 1629. He also acquired an eighth share in the Irish customs farm at this time. His behaviour in office foreshadowed his aggressive and threatening tone in his career in Ireland as Sir Thomas Gower complained York lawyers refused to act for him in a case against Radcliffe, fearing that his enmity would prejudice their careers. In 1632, he was appointed bencher of Gray's Inn and one of the king's council learned in the law.

Wentworth's appointment as lord deputy in 1632 also benefitted Radcliffe as Strafford relied heavily on his Yorkshire relatives, clients and hangers-on in his government of Ireland, especially Radcliffe and Christopher Wandesford, and rewarded them accordingly. George preceded Wentworth to Dublin in January 1633 and lords justices Cork and Adam Loftus* were instructed to support him in his unspecified work. On the new deputy's arrival seven months later he was knighted and appointed to the privy council. In the meantime, Cork, wishing to ingratiate himself with Wentworth, had suggested Radcliffe as master of the rolls, but Wandesford took that role and Radcliffe accepted no formal office in Ireland. Nevertheless, he played a key part in the regime and benefitted hugely from his time in Ireland, being paid an annual salary of £500, acquiring a significant property holding of 560 acres in Rathmines, 18,000 acres in Sligo with Wentworth and other lands in Fermanagh and Wicklow, while also amassing huge profits from his share of the customs farm – £2,800 in 1636–7 alone – which he invested in lands. On a visit to England in 1637 he bought 2,000 oz. of silver plate and an interest in the manors of Fairburn and Colton, Yorkshire; the rent for his sequestered English property was £490 in 1648. In November 1640 he guaranteed a bond of the merchant Gerard Baxter of Sligo at the Sligo staple.[591]

Radcliffe was intimately involved in all Wentworth's concerns, personal, legal, financial and political and his influence was universally acknowledged; he also handled Wentworth's friends and political allies' private commercial interests, including acting as Wentworth's proxy in negotiating the marriage settlement of Cork's son Dungarvan to Elizabeth Clifford in 1634.[592] The deputy told his English correspondents that 'there is no minister on this side that knows anything I either write or intend, excepting the master of the Rolls [Wandesford] and Sir George Radcliffe, for whose assistance in this government, and comfort to myself amidst this generation I am not able sufficiently to pour forth my humble acknowledgements to His Majesty. Sure I were the most solitary man without them, that ever served a king in such a place.'[593]

Milton noted that 'none of his servants in Ireland was more important to Wentworth, or more trusted, than Sir George Radcliffe, his legal expert, whose

591 Crawford, *Star Chamber*, p. 412; Pogson (ed.), 'Financial accounts'. Not all his relations with other inhabitants of Sligo were amicable – the lords justices decided a case between Radcliffe and O'Connor Sligo in October 1641: TCD, MS 809, fo. 154r.

592 Clarke, McGrath and Edwards (eds), *A lord justice's letter book*, passim.

593 John Forster, *Eminent British statesmen*, 2 vols (London, 1836), ii, p. 290.

ingenious legal trickery was vital in enabling the crown to regain the political initiative in Ireland.'[594] Kilmallock described him as 'Strafford's echo in parliament' (Radcliffe informed the council of Sir Piers Crosby's opposition to a government bill, prompting his removal from the privy council).[595] When Strafford pointed out that he had not been in Ireland when the alleged intimidation of Nicholas Barnewall took place, Pym observed that 'the Spirit of my lord of Strafford could move in Sir George Radcliffe, whensoever it was spoken.'[596] His influence with Wentworth was widely recognized – he was described during Strafford's trial as 'his bosom friend' and one petitioner to the privy council counselled 'What he wotes the lord Deputy most commonly orders … It's the voice of Sir George Ratcleif that must help more than the advice of the best counsel.'[597]

Radcliffe was an able lawyer and advised Wentworth on his defence for his trial. Pym dismissed George's defence that he was a mere instrument of policy, maintaining that as a lawyer he was more culpable in his actions in Ireland than Strafford. Mervyn described him as 'little inferior in wickedness' to Strafford, accusing him of abusing his position as a lawyer by publishing 'false opinions, unjust judgments and sentences, in extra judicial manner against law', and, less probably, 'cuntenanced Papists and yeelded to the building of Monasterys, to alienate the affections of the Irish from the subjection of England.' Edward Nicholas described him as 'a very busy and meddling person and none of the most secret or the most discreet'.[598]

Radcliffe drafted legislation for the 1634 parliament and was an active MP, serving on many conference committees and others concerned with petitions, but on few relating to bills. Unsurprisingly, he was commended by Wentworth for his activities in the Commons, but his intimidatory behaviour in the house was also raised at Strafford's trial.[599] There is no record of his membership of the King's Inns, yet the suggestion that he was given an honorary admission in 1634 is supported by his appointment as trustee in 1638 and he was allocated chambers in the 'new building', which were assigned to Donnellan* on 13 June 1643 'duringe the absence of the saied Sir George out of this kingdom'.[600] Radcliffe often acted as an unestablished law officer: he presented a case relating to the bishop of Kilfenora to the privy council shortly after his arrival in Dublin, occasionally

594 Anthony Milton, 'Thomas Wentworth and the political thought of the personal rule' in Merritt (ed.), *Political world of Thomas Wentworth*, pp 133–56, p. 140.

595 Samuel March Philips, *State trials, or a collection of the most interesting trials*, 2 vols (London, 1826), i, p. 119.

596 Rushworth (ed.), *Tryal*, p. 112.

597 Rushworth (ed.), *Tryal*, p. 725; Francis Lloyd to Richard Herbert, 18 April 1635, in Smith (ed.), *Herbert correspondence*, p. 189.

598 Mervyn, *Ireland's complaint against Sir George Radcliffe*, sig. A1v–A2v; George F. Warner (ed.), *The Nicholas Papers: correspondence of Sir Edward Nicholas, secretary of state*, 4 vols (London, 1886–1920), i, p. 292.

599 Rushworth (ed.), *Tryal*, pp 110, 112.

600 Kenny, *King's Inns*, pp 111–12, 150, 289; Crawford, *Star Chamber*, p. 41; King's Inns, MS B1/1, fo. 112v.

worked with Irish judges to rule on difficult legal cases, and decided on cases in the Court of Castle Chamber and at council board.[601] In 1636 he was appointed commissioner for ecclesiastical causes and two years later was named as a possible delegate to hear appeals from ecclesiastical courts. He played an active part in the commissions for concealed lands and for plantation of Connacht, from which he and others in Wentworth's retinue expected to benefit substantially.[602]

He and Wandesford managed the crown's electoral strategy in 1640 – his young son Thomas was MP for Sligo, nephews George and Robert Nettleton, cousins the Wandesfords and George Carr were all MPs – and the business of the early stages of the 1640 Irish parliament, but after June 1640 they were unable to control parliament or to deal with the coalition of New English and Irish Catholic MPs who opposed the administration, especially since George joined Wentworth in England that month. He returned to Ireland in October 1640 to try to ensure the passage of the act on the Connacht plantation; he failed in this and the English Commons ordered on 13 November that Radcliffe's membership of the Irish parliament did not protect him against charges of high treason. Subsequently, he was recalled to England to answer the same treason charges as Strafford. He was imprisoned and on 27 February 1641 articles of impeachment against him, Bramhall, Bolton*, and Chief Justice Geratt Lowther were initiated in the Commons, instituted at least partly to prevent their appearing as witnesses for Strafford's defence. The impeachment proceedings were later dropped and after his release from prison in 1642 he joined Charles in Oxford and remained part of the royalist circle throughout that and the following decade. He remained loyal to Strafford's children and clientele, writing to Ormond about Irish affairs and in 1644 in favour of Joshua Carpenter, Stafford's steward.[603]

Radcliffe's Yorkshire estates were sequestered and his Irish estates were in Confederate hands. By 1647 he was in exile in Caen and was found in Rouen in July 1649. He was made a gentleman of the bedchamber to the duke of York in 1646 and a member of his council and remained with him on the Continent, living in Brussels in 1651–2 where he encouraged the duke of Lorraine's interest in Ireland. By 1653 he was in Paris. Radcliffe's scheming, including plans to marry York to Lorraine's daughter, created mistrust and concern among the royalist community abroad, where he had a mixed reputation; he complained to Secretary Edward Nicholas that York no longer consulted him and that the queen spoke disparagingly of him – Nicholas' assessment was that while Radcliffe was right, his 'vanity in blabbing and feare to offend heere is able to spoile all his honest endeavors'. Clarendon regarded him as 'a man very capable of business; and if the prosperity of his former fortunes had not raised in him some fumes of vanity and self-conceitedness, very fit to be advised with, being of a nature constant and sincere.'[604] In September 1656 he left

601 Crawford, *Star Chamber*, pp 390, 410, 583, 589.
602 McGrath, 'Poets and patronage'.
603 Radcliffe to Ormond, 8 March 1644, in Carte (ed.), *Collection*, p. 47.
604 Warner (ed.), *Nicholas Papers*, ii, p. 134; Edward Hyde, earl of Clarendon, *The life of Edward, earl of Clarendon*, 3 vols (Oxford, 1759–61), i, p. 191.

Paris and joined the exiled court in the Low Countries where he died. It was reported that 'all the cavaliers were at his burial, except the chancellor and two more that was at Bruges. They are generally sorry for him; for they say he was the best counsellor their master had', a contrast to other comments about him.[605]

HUGH ROCHFORD (Rochfort) (1607 – *c*.1651–63) **Fethard, 1640**

e.s. James Rochford (d. 1657) and Ales, da. Michael Keating, Baldwinstown, Wexford; m. 1) - 1635, Catherine Williams (d. 1641, Bur. St Michan's, Dublin); 2) after 1641, Elizabeth, da. Patrick Esmond (d. 1637), Clonegallin, Carlow, 1 da. Ellis.[606]
ed. Middle Temple, 1628; King's Inns, 1635.

Hugh was a wealthy man, even during his father's lifetime, as he held lands at Taghmon (Tagunnan), Forth barony, where he lived and his first wife's dowry was £1,500; his second wife was also an heiress, bringing lands in Carlow and Wexford. On 24 August 1641 a commission was issued to Nicholas Loftus, Hugh Rochford* and others to alot to Dame Alice Colclough a moiety of lands and tenements of her late husband Sir Adam Colclough.[607] Hugh was an active MP and a leader of the opposition, sitting on many committees and was present in the November 1641 sitting. He was high sheriff of Wexford in 1641 and continued in that capacity under the Confederation. He was expelled for being in rebellion, joined the Confederate army and was a captain from very early in the rebellion, as a commander at the siege of Duncannon and was with his troops at Tintern Abbey in July 1642. Rochford was also a member of Wexford county council. His brothers Matthew and John fought for the Confederation too, John as a lieutenant colonel. The Confederation used his legal training and he was a judge of assize in Leinster in 1646, recorder of Wexford in 1649 and a commissioner to judge prizes in ports. He was a member of the 1647 General Assembly and the eighth Supreme Council. Hugh was involved in privateering and was engaged in the rebellion under Ormond in October 1647. He was in Wexford in late 1649 and 1650, when, with Geoffrey Baron, he tried to persuade the town to come to an agreement with Cromwell. Rochford is last reported in June 1651, preparing to leave for La Rochelle with Bishop Nicholas French. He died before the Court of Claims adjudicated his daughter's claim. His lands were forfeit to Raphael Le Hunt and later, by act of parliament, to George Moncke, duke of Albemarle.[608]

DAVID ROTHE (Routh) (1574 – 1638–40+) **Kilkenny City, 1634**

e.s. Robert Rothe (MP Kilkenny County 1585, d. 1622) and Margaret, da. Foulke Comerford (MP Callan, 1585), Callan and Rosina Rothe; m. 1) by 5 August 1608, Elizabeth, da. Sir Richard Shee, Kilkenny, and Margaret, da. John Sherlock, Mothell, Waterford;[609] 1 s., 1 da.
ed. Inner Temple, 1594; King's Inns, 1607.

605 Thomas Birch (ed.), *Collection of the State Papers of John Thurloe*, 7 vols (London, 1742), vi, p. 325.
606 Tallon (ed.), *Court of Claims*, p. 198.
607 NLI, MS 24,555 (31).
608 HL, HP, Manorial Papers, Box 78(17).
609 But possibly well before that date: NLI, GO, MS 66, Funeral Entries, Volume 3, 1604–22, fo. 13v.

Rothe was a founder member of the King's Inns, where he shared chambers with Richard Wadding*, MP for Waterford in 1613; he was described as '*in legibus eruditus*' and was a pensioner of the Inns by 1614, but lost that position when Catholic lawyers were excluded later that year. Named an alderman in Kilkenny's new charter of 1609, he was mayor in 1616, when he was deposed for refusing the oath of supremacy and nominated by the city council as candidate in the 1628 election. He was excluded from the 1624–5 Kilkenny Commission of the Peace, but was a commissioner to raise money for the army in that county in 1627 and was a commissioner for Kilkenny city and county for managing the export of corn to England in 1631.[610] He lent £250 on bond on the Dublin staple on 30 June 1602.[611] He inherited very extensive lands from his father, lived in Tullaghmaine in Kilkenny and had property also in the city, including a lease of the tithes of Rathbeagh from the corporation for 21 years at 26*s*. 8*d*. annually; one of his properties was burned by 1639. In the sale of effects from Kilkenny Castle in 1630, he bought five pieces of tapestry, five damask curtains, a chair and a cushion for £12.[612] David was close to successive earls of Ormond, witnessing deeds for them and other Butlers.[613] He also had close ties to the Everards; John Everard fitz Nicholas named his 'cozen' Rothe as a tutor to his daughters, with his uncle Sir Richard. He borrowed £100 from Cork in 1631, being described as 'my cozen' by the earl.[614]

The extent of David's legal practice is unclear after his expulsion from the King's Inns, but he did not rejoin after 1628, which suggests he concentrated on his other interests after 1614 along with a local practice including advising Ormond on legal matters; his expertise would have helped him defend a chancery case in 1633 and he was appointed a commissioner for Ormond in disputes in 1638–9.[615] The Ormond connection also led to Wandesford's employing him, despite his Catholicism, to 'deal with the Brennans' in 1638, for which he was paid £200 and explains the agreement the earl came to with the crown about the plantation of Ormond, in which he arranged for 1,000 acres each to be given to David Rothe*, John Piggott and Gerald Fennell.[616] David was an active committee man in the

610 Edwards, *Ormond lordship*, pp 275, 284; McGrath, 'Nomination of Kilkenny MPs in 1628'; TCD, MS 672, fo. 178v; Caulfield (ed.), *Youghal*, pp 160–7.

611 Ohlmeyer and Ó Ciardha (eds), *Irish statute staple*.

612 Burtchaell, *Genealogical memoirs*, p. 28; *Inq. cancel. Hib. repert.*, Kilkenny City, Jac.I (2), Car. I (17, 20); G.D. Burtchaell, 'The family of Rothe of Kilkenny', *Journal of the Royal Historical and Archaeological Association of Ireland*, 4th series, 7:67 (1886), 501–37; KCA, MSS CR/I/58, CR/K/44; William Healy, *History and antiquities of Kilkenny* (Kilkenny, 1893), appendix, pp 10, 56, 74, 78–84; Jane Fenlon (ed.), *Goods & chattels: a survey of early household inventories in Ireland* (Kilkenny, 2003), p. 27.

613 NLI, MS 11,048(9), D. 3805, D. 3939, D. 3979–80; NAI, MS RC 5/23, pp 32–5; NLI, MS 2,306, fos. 264–8.

614 Will of John Everard fitz Nicholas, 9 Aug. 1638, NAI, RC 5/23, p. 37; Grosart (ed.), *Lismore Papers*, iii, p. 83.

615 NLI, D. 4102, D. 4135, D. 4167; Rothe to Ormond with legal advice on tithes, 17 March 1635–6, MS 2,305, p. 11.

616 BL, Add. MS 46,925, fos. 121–2; Thomas Carte, *A history of the life of James, duke of Ormonde*, 2 vols (London, 1736), i, p. 59.

Commons until 25 November 1634 when he received licence to be absent on account of his sickness. He was recommended as a commissioner of the subsidies in 1640 but seems to have died shortly after that as his son Sir Robert is listed as a proprietor in 1641.[617]

PIERCE ROTHE[618] (1590 – 1654) **Kilkenny City, 1640**

s. John Rothe FitzPiers (MP Kilkenny, 1585, d. 1621), Kilkenny, and Rose Archer; m. 1610, Lettice, da. Walter Lawless and Margaret Rothe.
ed. Clifford's Inn, Inner Temple, 1612; King's Inns, 1629.

The Rothes, like the Archers, were prosperous Kilkenny merchants; Pierce's father was mayor in 1616 and the family's wealth may be judged from the house he built on the main street in Kilkenny in the 1590s. The Confederation met in a building almost opposite this house.[619] Pierce was an alderman and held lands in Kilkenny County and in Wexford (where he inherited 350 acres worth £23 annually in Bantry Barony) and 400 acres in Tipperary.[620] He was an active member of the Commons, sitting on many committees, including that which drew up articles of impeachment against Radcliffe* and others. After his expulsion for rebellion, he became equally active in the Confederation, taking the oath of association and was an adherent of Rinuccini. In 1644 he was paid £400 by the Confederation for Lord Castlehaven.[621] His will was proved in 1654.

THOMAS RYVES (Reeves, Rives) (*c.*1578 – 2 January 1652) **Monaghan, 1613**

8 s. John Ryves (*c.*1536–1609), Blandford, Dorsetshire, and Elizabeth (*c.*1537–1609), da. Sir John Mervyn, Fonthill, Wiltshire; m. 1) Elizabeth (1609–73), da. Sir Richard Waldron, Oadby, Leicester, and Farnham, Cavan, and Jane, da. John Bussey, Lincolnshire who rem. Edward Harris*.[622]
ed. Winchester School; New College, Oxford, 1598; France, BCL, 1605, D.C.L., 1610; Gray's Inn, honorary admission 10 March 1631.
Bur. St Clement Dane's, 3 January 1652.

Ryves was an advocate in Doctor's Commons in 1611 and in the following year came to Ireland, as a client of John Davies*, a family connection who promoted Thomas' career and that of his older brother William*. Thomas was registrar of the 1613 Convocation, where his dress, actions and lack of qualification as a notary public were criticized by Archbishop Christopher Hampton; he rectified the last deficiency by 1615.[623] He succeeded Doyne* as master in chancery in 1617 where

617 Burtchaell, *Genealogical memoirs*, p. 28.
618 Ibid., p. 36; John Rothe Fitz Piers was mayor of Kilkenny, and its MP in 1585. BL, Sloane MS 3,827, fo. 21v; Arthur Vicars, *Index to the Prerogative Wills of Ireland, 1536–1810* (Dublin, 1897), p. 407. Pierce should not be confused with Peter Rothe, MP for New Ross in 1634.
619 The house is still standing and is known as Rothe House.
620 *Inq. cancel. Hib. repert.*, Wexford, Car. I (34, 53); Kilkenny, Jac. I (31, 33); Car. I (21); NLI, MSS D. 3906–8; Simington (ed.), *Civil Survey*, Tipperary, i, p. 116, Wexford, p. 206; Healy, *History and antiquities of Kilkenny*, pp 381–97, Appendix, p. 68; KCA, CR/I/47.
621 Bellings and Gilbert (eds), *Confederation*, iii, p. 216; v, p. 223.
622 J.D. Davies, 'Ryves, Sir Thomas', *Oxford DNB*.
623 TCD, MS 1,062, pp 54–5; *Cal. S.P. Ire., 1615–25*, p. 49.

he was a diligent officer and was principal officer of the Consistorial Court of the Dublin Diocese in 1618–19. Ryves was also judge of the faculties and prerogative courts, although the episcopacy objected to this appointment, which he resigned. His behavour in that office gave great offence 'That whereas upon the power given to call ~~before them~~ anie Criticall person before them to show their titles, and orders to be tried and examined, Doctor Reeves … did visit most parts of the Kingdome, and al the Bishops therein with their cleargie to their great preiudice.' The episode coloured James Ussher's opinion of Thomas as dishonest.[624]

Ryves was commissioned by the Irish administration to write a reply to Rothe's *Annalecta*, which was published as *Regiminis Anglicani in Hibernia defensio adversus [David Rothe's] analecten* (1624); he had already published *The Poore Vicars Plea* (1620), which defended the Irish clergy's claims to tithes, and went on to produce *Imperatoris Justiniani defensio adversus Alemannum* (London, 1626, Frankfurt, 1628) and a history of naval affairs. He had returned to practice in the courts in London in 1622 and was an active counsel in the admiralty courts. From this time he pursued his career exclusively in England. He was instructed by the king to ascertain the circumstances of the divorce proceedings taken by Lord Cahir against his wife in 1633.[625]

WILLIAM RYVES (Reeves, Rives) (*c.*1577 – 1648) **Belturbet, 1634**

6s. John Ryves, Blandford, Dorsetshire and Elizabeth, da. Sir John Mervyn, Fonthill, Dorsetshire; m. 1) by 1620, ____ (d. 8, Bur. 11 November 1624),[626] da. ____ Jackman; sons John and Thomas and daughter Christian christened, St John's, Dublin, 19 November 1620, 30 June 1622 and 16 December 1623 respectively (Thomas Bur. 4 July 1622);[627] da. Elizabeth m. Sir Arthur Leigh, Omagh, ss William and George m. respectively Elizabeth and Ann, das. Sir Edward Bagshaw; also s. Charles; 2) after 1625, Dorothy, da. John Waldron and Jane, da. John Bussy, Haydor, Lincolnshire, who rem. Sir Edward Harris*; Dorothy also later married Captains Cole and John Farrar.[628]

ed. Middle Temple, 1593; Bar, 1600; bencher, 1619; King's Inns, 24 January 1620, 6 February 1637.

Kt. 1619.

Bur. St John's Church, Dublin.[629]

Like his brother Thomas*, William was a lawyer; he was based in Oxford in 1613, when Cork used him as counsel. He was a judge on the Carmarthen circuit in Wales before his arrival in Ireland in early November 1619 to succeed his uncle-

624 HL, HP, MS 15,743, 18 June 1617, MS 14,189, *c.*1626, Church of Ireland, exceptions against the act for the confirmation of the Court of Prerogatives and faculties. He signed many of the documents in NAI, MS Chancery bills, Box AA; McEnery and Refausé (eds), *Christ Church deeds*, nos 1477, 1479; *Oxford DNB*; Treadwell (ed.), *Irish commission of 1622*, p. 252.

625 Lodge, *Peerage*, vi, pp 230–2.

626 TCD, MS 1,216, fo. 29v.

627 Mills (ed.), *Registers of St John the Evangelist*, pp 4, 6, 8, 10, 263 records the burial of two of his children (their names and gender are not given), one between Easter 1622 and Easter 1623, and the other in the following 12 months.

628 NLI, GO, MS 225, p. 164; Edward MacLysaght (ed.), 'Commonwealth state accounts Ireland, 1650–1656', *Anal. Hib.*, 15 (Nov., 1944), 227–321; TNA, PROB/11/217/661.

629 Terry Clavin, 'Ryves, Sir William', *DIB*; Ball, *Judges in Ireland*, i, pp 336–7.

by-marriage John Davies* as attorney general (through Buckingham's patronage) and he regularly acted as a justice of assize from 1620. His other Irish family connections were Audley Mervyn and John FitzGerald and he was a cousin of the diarist and parliamentarian Symonds D'Ewes.[630] In 1620 he wrote to Essex about a case Patrick Gernon was taking about some of the earl's lands in Ireland.[631] While he had lobbied Davies hard for promotion, he was dissatisfied with his office: 'Sir I would fayne write you and my Ladye some thankes for your friendly wishinge of me to this place, but that in troth it proves not worth any, the solicitor hath all the warrants sent unto him, whiles I sitt by for a cipher, if it prove better hereafter I shall bee ready to acknowledge it, if not it is the worse bargen that ever I made.'[632] He followed this letter with another complaining that he had not been paid the full fee for his work in Wales and asking Davies to resolve the matter.

Unlike Davies, Ryves made no attempt to influence government policy and operated strictly as a crown lawyer and judge, including in supporting the work of the 1622 Commission and pursuing recusants. He was supported by Falkland, especially when he was, like so many others, victimized by Chancellor Adam Loftus; Ryves was congratulated by the former lord deputy on his 'reconcilement' with Loftus.[633] His official roles did not preclude his accepting private clients: Ormond consulted Ryves and William Talbot* about the proposed plantation of Ormond and he also worked on chancery cases. In 1633–4 he worked to secure an agreement between his 'old friend' Lord Herbert and Baltinglass. Wentworth reprimanded him for acting in cases against the crown.[634] His return for Belturbet was presumably due to the influence of his sons' father-in-law, Sir Edward Bagshaw, there. William took little recorded part in parliamentary proceedings, sitting on no committees.

Despite their earlier friendship, he prosecuted Cork in the Castle Chamber in 1634 over the College of Youghal.[635] He resigned as attorney general in 1636 to become third justice of the king's bench and was again admitted to the King's Inns. Ryves became a member of its council from early 1637 and treasurer in 1638. He was also named as a possible delegate to hear appeals from ecclesiastical courts. In

630 Boyle to Mr Dutton, 18 Aug. 1613, Ryves to Boyle, 25 Aug. 1613, Boyle to Henry Vaughan, 28 Aug. 1613, all calendared in *Calendar of the Lismore manuscripts*, i, pp 95–6; *Cal. S.P. Ire., 1625–33*, pp 493–4; Ryves to his cousin, Sir Henry Mervyn, 8 Nov. 1629, TNA, SP 63/249, fo. 26; Treadwell, *Buckingham and Ireland*, pp 56, 330n. 88, 352n. 32; Birr Castle, MS A/1/26.

631 Ryves to Essex, 23 Feb. 1620, in Owen D. Dyfnallt (ed.), *Calendar of the manuscripts of the most honourable the marquess of Bath, preserved at Longleat, Wiltshire, Volume 5, Talbot, Dudley and Devereux Papers, 1533–1659* (London, 1980), p. 284.

632 Ryves to Davies*, 1 Jan. 1620, HL, HP, MS 15,721; same to same, 23 Feb. 1620, HL, HP, MS 15,722.

633 Falkland to Ryves, 23 Feb. 1630, NAI, MS 2,445, pp 50, 62.

634 Treadwell (ed.), *Irish commission of 1622*, pp 26, 48, 83, 130–1, 189, 191, 196–7, 223, 292, 430; BL, Sloane MS 3,827, fo. 104v; Crawford, *Star Chamber*, pp 17, 113; Carte, *History of the life*, i, p. 59; Ohlmeyer, 'Records of the Irish Court of Chancery'; Smith (ed.), *Herbert correspondence*, pp 78–9, 84, 104; Empey (ed.), *Early Stuart Irish warrants*, pp 58–9.

635 Grosart (ed.), *Lismore Papers*, 1st series, iv, p 61, under 29 Nov. 1634; Crawford, *Star Chamber*, pp 371, 577–80.

November 1624 he had been allocated chambers, but was given what was clearly better accommodation in 1643; in the same year he and other members of the King's Inns' council were granted a lease of a house near the Inns.[636]

Ryves lived on Merchant's Quay in Dublin in the 1620s where he was cessed at 20 shillings in St John's Parish on 26 February 1622, but moved to a manor at Butterstown where he had acquired 240 acres by mortgage from Lord Fitzwilliam of Merrion in 1625.[637] He also obtained lands at Rathsallagh, Co. Wicklow (which he offered to sell to Cork when he stayed there in 1633), Corron, Co. Carlow (which he conveyed to his son John in 1643), and Down. He also had lands scattered around St John's College, Oxford, which Laud was anxious to buy in 1635; the archbishop wrote to Wentworth, noting that 'I hear of late [Ryves] hath richly married his son in Ireland.' He lent £1,000 on bond on the Dublin staple to Arthur Cavanagh of Ballinalagh in Carlow in 1640.[638] He had a protracted legal dispute with Richard White and Christopher Plunkett of Meath.[639]

William was appointed* Bolton's substitute as speaker of the lords in 1641 when the latter was impeached.[640] He lost his Irish lands following the October 1641 rebellion and was taking examinations relating to the outbreak of the rebellion between October 1641 and January 1642. Back in England in the following September, he intended to return to the bar, but the outbreak of the English civil war soon afterwards frustrated his plans. Ryves was a strong royalist and on 20 September 1642 was appointed one of the king's learned counsel extraordinary. He was still in England in September 1643, but he returned to Dublin and provided the Irish administration with legal advice during the negotiations with the Catholic Confederation in 1644–5. He was in England again in 1647 and died in Dublin in 1648.[641]

WILLIAM SAMBACH (Sandbatch, Sambadge) (c.1590 – d. 31 Aug. 1653–Aug. 1654)
Carrickfergus 1640

e.s. Anthony Sambach, Childs Wickham, Gloucestershire; m. by 1622 Mary____ (d. 1670); at least 1 s. William and 2 da., Mary and Brigid.[642]

636 King's Inns, MS B1/1, fos. 13r, 64r, 68v, 70r, 74r, 110v, 112r; HMC, *Various collections, Volume III*, pp 182–3; Ainsworth (ed.), 'Survey of documents in private keeping: third series', p. 3.

637 Mills (ed.), *Registers of St John the Evangelist*, p. 274; Clodagh Tait, *Death, burial and commemoration in Ireland, 1550–1650* (Basingstoke, 2002), p. 66; Simington (ed.), *Civil Survey*, Dublin, p. 260; Grosart (ed.), *Lismore Papers*, 1st series, iii, p. 197.

638 HMC, *Fifth Report of the Royal Commission on Historical Manuscripts* (London, 1876), p. 413; TNA, PROB/11/217/661; Laud to Wentworth, 4 March 1635, in Knowler (ed.), *Letters and dispatches*, i, p. 375; BL, Add. MS 19,843, fo. 47.

639 Essex County Records Office, Barrett-Lennard Muniments, MS D/DL Z9, calendared in Donovan and Edwards, *British sources for Irish history*, p. 64.

640 Dennehy, 'Speakers'; Crawford, *Star Chamber*, p. 408.

641 Clarke, *1641 Depositions, Volume IV: Dublin*, pp 33–5, 40–1, 48, 52–3, 55–7, 72–3, 101–2, 107–9; Marsh's Library, MS Z.3.2.6, fos. 331–45.

642 Daughter Brigide buried St John's, Dublin, 3 Aug. 1639. Mills (ed.), *Registers of St John the Evangelist*, p. 33; Will proved 23 Aug. 1654, TNA, PROB 11/241/63. His widow was buried in Broadway in 1670. Henry Sydney Grazebrook, *The heraldry of Worcestershire*, 2 vols (London, 1873), ii, p. 492. There are some inaccuracies in this genealogy.

ed. Middle Temple, 1606; Bar, 1626; King's Inns, 1637.
Kt. 1639.

Despite being admitted to the Middle Temple in 1606, Sambach was not called to the Bar until 1626; he may have been managing family property in the meantime. He arrived in Ireland before 1634 when Cork retained him as a lawyer (including in his lengthy dispute with Blacknall and his widow about his ironworks) and he also had legal connections with Lord Charlemont. Sambach continued to advise Cork until at least 1639.[643] At Wandesford and Radcliffe's request, he drew up Lord James Dillon's marriage settlement with Wentworth's cousin Elizabeth in 1636, which created a personal connection between Lord Dillon and the deputy.[644] Sambach became recorder of Carrickfergus in 1636 and was allowed to retain this office when he was appointed serjeant-at-law in the following year; he appointed Roger Lyndon as his deputy in 1639.[645] He acted with Catlin* and Nicholas Plunkett* as counsel for Gifford in his dispute with the Loftuses; three years later he was assisting Lady Mary Jephson to collect her granddaughter Anne Loftus' rents and was a witness at the parliamentary committee on Loftus' case in 1651.[646] In 1638 he was named as a possible delegate to hear appeals from ecclesiastical courts in Ireland and Wentworth referred Edmund Deering's petition for examination by Sambach and the attorney general.[647] In 1640 he was appointed solicitor general and with the attorney general Thomas Tempest sought to restrict James Cusack's* work in the commission of grace for Irish defective titles that threatened their interests.[648]

A resident of Dublin, he held 860 acres in Dundrum, which he rented from Lord Fitzwilliam and his heir Richard on 21 January 1639, for two years for £1,400; he also lived at Ballyna, Kildare. He claimed losses of £906, including rents of £200, for his Kildare property in March 1642. A separate deposition claimed further losses of £3,800 for his Dublin lands, and other debts and bonds.[649] Despite the distance, he continued his duties in Carrickfergus and 'when Dublin was besieged, [he] put all the writings that concerned [Carrickfergus] in Ireland into two Chests, or truncks, and sent them into the Exchequer at Dublin.'

643 Joshua Boyle to Cork, 19 Aug. 1639, NLI, MS 13,237(24).

644 Grosart (ed.), *Lismore Papers*, 1st series, iv, pp 68–9, 91, 108, 110, 136, 141–5, 150–2, 176, 183, 186, 188, 195; Wandesford to Radcliffe about the Dillon/Wentworth marriage, 12 Sept. 1636, 27 Oct. 1636, Bodl. Lib., Add. MS C. 286, fos. 5v, 14r–15v.

645 McSkimmin, *History of Carrickfergus*, p. 188 claims he was appointed recorder in 1630, but PRONI, T707|1, p. 124 records his being sworn into office in 1636; NLI, D 162/1, p. 84; Hart, *History of the king's serjeants at law*, pp 55–6.

646 HMC, *Various collections, Volume III*, pp 159, 190, 193, 208, 220–1; Essex County Records Office, Barrett-Lennard Muniments, MS D/DL C46, 12 April 1640, calendared in Donovan and Edwards, *British sources for Irish history*, p. 53.

647 HMC, *Various collections, Volume III*, p. 183; NAI, MS M. 2,448, p. 253.

648 Bodl. Lib., Carte MS 63, fo. 637.

649 Bodl. Lib., Carte MS 176, fo. 203; TCD, MS 809, fos. 258r, 339r; TCD, MS 851, fo. 106r; *Inq. cancel. Hib. repert.*, Dublin, Car. I (64); Armagh, Car. I (40); Clarke, *1641 Depositions, Volume IV: Dublin*, pp 122, 174.

When they were sought in the 1660s, it was noted that his son-in-law John Moore 'hath had the perusal of all those writings and can give a farther accountt of them'.[650] In 1644 Sambach was an agent in Oxford, advising Charles on Irish affairs. In the following year he was one of the lawyers Ormond consulted about the possibility of legalizing the saying of Mass as part of the negotiations for peace with the Confederates. He testified in 1651 in the Gifford-Loftus* case in parliament. He was living in Bretfordton, Worcestershire at the time of his death.

CHRISTOPHER SIBTHORPE (-1564 – 1631)[651] **Limavady, 1613**

2 s. John Sibthorpe (d. 1568) of Much (Great) Bardfield, Essex, and (d. by 1568), possibly Jane Berners da. John Berners, of Finchingfield, esq. and Eleanor Berners; although he married, nothing is known of his wife, *o.s.p.*[652]

ed. Queen's College, Cambridge, 1580; New Inn, Middle Temple, 1584; Bar, 1594; King's Inns, 21 June 1607.

Kt. 3 May 1618.

Sibthorpe arrived in Ireland by 21 June 1607 when he was admitted to the King's Inns as third justice of the king's bench with all the other judges and was a member of the Inns' council from its inception four days after that; two years later he was allocated a chamber which was a quarter of the old Friar's Hall, formerly the chancery and was treasurer in 1630.[653] In December 1607 he was sent into Ulster to indict Tyrone and Tirconnell and was regularly a judge on the Ulster circuit between then and 1615 and was sent twice to Ulster in 1612 to resolve disputes between planters and natives; when on 30 May he, William Parsons, George Sexton, Francis Blundell, Nicholas Pynnar and Sexton's deputy William Roules, were appointed commissioners, any two of whom were 'to deal with any controversies, complaints of differences in [the planted] counties, including deciding on church lands & suitable lands for towns, assessing numbers of men available and what burgage lands they should have &c.' Sibthorpe and Parsons were always to be one of the two and Christopher spent 52 days there trying to resolve difficulties.[654]

Given this level of official trust in his capacity and loyalty, it is no wonder that he was nominated as MP, despite being, as a judge, ineligible for membership. He was active in parliament both as a contributor to debates and as a member of many

650 Edward Conway to George Rawdon, 28 April 1668, HL, HP, MS 14,470.

651 TCD, MS 1,216, fo. 36v. a.o.ms. 68, p. 186, d. 1631. King's Inns, MS B 1/1, fos. 28r, 111r.

652 Frederick George Emmison (ed.), *Essex wills: the bishop of London's consistory court, 1558–1569* (Chelmsford, 1993), p. 221 details John Sibthorpe's will of April 1568. It makes no mention of his wife. *DIB*; Ball, *Judges in Ireland*, i, 242–3, 320–1. As Christopher's wife was not included in the guest list for St John's inauguration as deputy in August 1616, she was either dead by that date, or he was not yet married. FSL, MS X.d.607.

653 King's Inns, MS B1/1, fos. 2v, 4r, 10v, 13r, 14r, 25r, 170r, 109r; Chichester to John Davies*, warrant to draw up a fiant of the office of a justice of the chief bench, 6 May 1607, during pleasure, HL, HP, Box 1 (61).

654 James to Christopher Sibthorpe, 30 May 1612, HL, HP, Box 3 (43); McCavitt, *Arthur Chichester*, p. 158.

committees, including those on bills for the trial of felonies, taking away clergy, to defeat fraudulent conveyances, Lacy's private bill, the city and county of Londonderry, conference committees with the Lords and that appointed to examine the copies of paper bills with the original. As one of the committee dealing with Tyrone's attainder, he was also a delegate from the Commons to request Chichester to resolve the problems in the bill by an act of state. Christopher inherited lands in Fermanagh from his brother Edward who was an undertaker there. He was also a member of the 1624–5 Meath commission of the peace.[655]

Apart from his legal career, Sibthorpe was a serious theological scholar with strongly Puritan leanings (he had been expelled from the Middle Temple for his nonconformist views in 1588). One early work from *c.*1612 attracted James Ussher's interest and the latter encouraged him to publish *A friendly advertisement to the pretended Catholicks of Ireland*, described as 'a rather crude anti-Catholic polemic, which stressed that the Pope was the Antichrist described in the Book of Revelations.' It was the first instance of the use of Hebrew type in Ireland. Ussher's own *A discourse of the religion anciently professed by the Irish and British* was published with it and dedicated to Sibthorpe. That pamphlet initiated a scholarly debate with Catholic theologians and prompted two further polemics from Sibthorpe, *A reply to an answer* (1625) and *A surreplication to the rejoinder of a popish adversarie* (1627). [656] In his pamphlets Sibthorpe referred to the 'refusal and utter dislike' of Irish lawyers to take the oath of supremacy; a manuscript response dedicated to the 'lawyers of Ireland' remained unpublished thanks, according to Sibthorpe, to 'the Protestant press' in Dublin.[657]

JOHN SUTTON (1565 – 13 June 1637) **Kildare County, 1613**

s. William Sutton (d. 1590) and Margaret, da. Ald. Walter Seagrave, Dublin; m. 1) by 1590, Mary, da. John Allen (d. 20 September 1616), St Wolstan's, Kildare; 3 s., 4 da.
Bur. Kildare Abbey.[658]

Sutton and William Talbot* are described in Medhop's list of MPs as '*in legibus eruditi*' and Cregan describes him as a lawyer, although there is no evidence of his attending the Inns of Court. However, he sat on three committees, including that for the trial of felonies, which lends credence to his being a lawyer, as do his other contributions, including proposing deferring debating the subsidy bill, prophetically quoting the old adage 'little said soon amended, A subsidy granted, the Parliament ended.'[659] Sutton was a member of a gentry family, based at Tipper in Kildare; his father was a prominent member of the opposition in the 1585

655 Hill, *Historical account*, pp 488–9; TCD, MS 672, fo. 176r.
656 *DIB*.
657 Colum Kenny, 'The exclusion of Catholics from the legal profession in Ireland, 1537–1829', *IHS*, 25:100 (Nov., 1987), 337–57.
658 Fitzgerald and Lamacraft (eds), *Some funeral entries of Ireland*, p. 184; Walter FitzGerald, 'Castletown and its owners, with a genealogical table of the Sutton family and a portrait of the Rt. Hon. Thomas Conolly, d. 1803', *The Journal of the County Kildare Archaeological Society*, 2 (1896–9), 361–78.
659 Cregan, 'Irish recusant lawyers'; *Commons' Jn. Ire.*, 22 April 1615.

parliament and his grandson would represent the county in 1640. He had already been active in the Mandates campaign in 1605 and was a JP in Kildare.[660] Ald. Thomas FitzSymon of Dublin took a chancery case against him concerning the tithes of the prebend of St Kevin in County Kildare.[661] Apart from his estates in Kildare, he also inherited property in Wexford.[662]

WILLIAM SWANTON (c.1595 – 1642) **Enniscorthy, 1640**

e.s. William Swanton (d. 1618), Wincanton, Somerset and London, and Elizabeth, da. Thomas Aubrey, Chadenwich, Wiltshire; m. Margaret, da. John Harbin, Newton Sumavile, Somerset, 6 s. John, Mathew, William, Francis, Henry, Charles, at least 3 da. Margaret, Brigid, Katherine.[663]
ed. Middle Temple, 1609; Bar, 1617.

Swanton followed his father, a reader in the Middle Temple, into the law. He settled in Wexford as Henry Wallop's agent, presumably after 27 May 1637 when he drew up his will as of Brunton, Somerset. He lived near Wallop's borough of Enniscorthy and was expelled from his home at Mount Main in Wexford (which he rented from John Jessop of Clonmore, Kilkenny for £230 annually) very early in the rebellion; his son-in-law Simon Bellers of Dublin claimed losses of £4,000 in Wexford on his behalf, apart from his English property at Wincanton.[664] Swanton drowned when rebels scuttled his ship as his family escaped from Enniscorthy.[665]

WILLIAM TALBOT (? – 16 March 1634)[666] **Kildare Co., 1613**

e.s. Robert Talbot, Carton; m. 1) by 1607[667] Alison, da. John Netterville, Castletown, Meath; 8 s., including Sir Robert, 8 da.;
King's Inns, 1607.
1st. Bart. 4 February 1623; Kt. by 1628.
Bur. 1 April 1634, Maynooth Church.

The Talbots were one of the most prominent Old English families and William's grandfather was Sir Thomas Talbot of Malahide; William inherited lands in Kildare from his father. While there is no record of his legal education, he was described as '*in legibus eruditus*' on his admission to the King's Inns in May 1610 where he was assigned chambers with Edmund Nugent*.[668] He was appointed recorder of Dublin in 1602 and in the following year travelled to London to

660 Treadwell, 'Sir John Perrott'; Tallon (ed.), *Court of Claims*, pp 53, 263–4, 324–5; Griffith (ed.), *Calendar of inquisitions*, pp 312–13, 394–5; *Cal. S.P. Ire., 1603–6*, pp 362–5.
661 NAI, MS Chancery H1I.
662 *Inq. cancel. Hib. repert.*, Meath, Jac. I (12); Car. I (2, 22, 28, 33, 74, 89), Wexford, Jac. I (32, 40), Car. I (31, 73, 153).
663 George Drewry Squibb (ed.), *Wiltshire visitation pedigrees, 1623* (London, 1954), p. 4; *idem*, *The visitation of Somerset and the city of Bristol, 1672* (London, 1992), pp 15–16; TNA, PROB 11/189/205, probate 17 May 1642.
664 Jan Broadway, Richard Cust and Stephen K. Roberts (eds), *A calendar of the docquets of Lord Keeper Coventry, 1625–1640* (Kew, 2004), pp 564, 619, 626.
665 TCD, MS 810, fos. 57–8, MS 818, fos. 104–5, MS 175, 314–15.
666 Terry Clavin, 'Talbot, Sir William', *DIB*; Cokayne, *Baronetage*, i, p. 247; TCD, MS 1,216, fo. 39r.
667 Birr Castle, Rosse MS A/3.
668 King's Inns, MS B/1/1, fos. 3v, 107r.

petition that the city's charter and liberties be maintained. He was a judge on the Ulster circuit in early 1605, but later that year was displaced as recorder for recusancy. While he was unable to secure crown patronage and was disbarred as a Catholic from pleading in court after 1614, he was in great demand as a lawyer with prestigious clients including Sir Hugh Montgomery and the earls of Kildare and Ormond. Talbot was counsel in a case on *commenda* in the Court of Common Pleas in 1611 with John Haly* and Bolton* and retained by St Anne's Guild to defend it against *Quo warranto* proceedings initiated by John Davies.* He was engaged in chancery cases against John Proudfoot about a debt and a mortgage of Proudfootstown, Meath and was trustee or feoffee in land transactions with other members of the Old English gentry of the Pale. He may have been the man of that name who was involved in a violent attack on Patrick Talbot and John Quatermas of Garristown in 1592 that was the subject of a Castle Chamber case, but William was found to be innocent.[669]

As a leading Catholic lawyer, Talbot advised Dublin recusants on their parliamentary candidates in 1613 and with the rest of his political community was incensed at the rigging of elections and the illegal creation of boroughs. On parliament's opening, Talbot proposed that the house be purged before a speaker be chosen and was prominent in the moves to elect Everard* as speaker and the Catholic secession, calling Davies' election and the house illegal.[670] William was head of the Catholic delegation that met the king in July; when James asked about the Jesuit Suarez's claim that the Pope could excommunicate monarchs for spiritual and temporal offences, Talbot refused to condemn him and was imprisoned in the Tower of London as a consequence. When Talbot continued to resist James commenced legal proceedings and threatened him with execution; he was tried in the Star Chamber and fined £10,000. The fine was not collected and he was released. Moreover, despite James condemning their behaviour, he conceded many of the agents' demands.[671]

Talbot pursued a lucrative legal practice, especially to the earls of Kildare and Lettice Digby; his lands at Carton were close to their seat at Maynooth. William's involvement in Kildare's affairs extended to his unsuccessfully promoting a marriage involving the sixteenth earl and simultaneously advising the dowager Lady Kildare and Lady Lettice Digby, née FitzGerald. The dowager assured George that William was 'the only man who was employed by my [husband] and myself. Be kind to him for none can stand you in better stead.'[672] Ormond consulted William Ryves* and Sir William Talbot about the proposed plantation of Ormond.[673] He purchased

669 Davies, *Le Premier report*, fo. 83v; NAI, Chancery MSS I/279, 285 (taken from Kenneth Nicholls' calendar); Griffith (ed.), *Calendar of inquisitions*, JI 104, 120, C1 8, A5; Lennon, *Lords of Dublin*, p. 186.

670 Lodge, *Desiderata Curiosa*, i, pp 166–238, 321; Crawford, *Star Chamber*, pp 468–9.

671 Cregan, 'Irish recusant lawyers'; Crawford, *Star Chamber*, p. 305; Clarke, *Old English*, pp 44–5.

672 Clarke and McGrath (eds), *Letterbook*, pp 7–9, 13, 15–17, 31, 34, 49, 55, 60, 68–9, 71–7, 85, 97, 104–5; Digby to the earl of March, 21 Feb. 1624, FSL, MS X.c.75; Treadwell, *Buckingham and Ireland*, pp 118–21.

673 Carte, *History of the life*, p. 59.

more lands in Kildare, Meath and Wicklow and negotiated advantageous marriages for his children, including his heir Robert with Grace Calvert, daughter of Lord Baltimore and Mary and Margaret with John Dongan and Henry Talbot respectively. William formed part of the funeral procession of William Dongan, former recorder of Dublin, December 1622, was a member of the 1625 commission of the peace in Kildare and was nominated by John Bath as one of the loyal Catholics to hold a position in the trained bands he proposed for Ireland in that year. He was in London in 1628 negotiating the Graces as an agent for Leinster Catholics.[674] His will left sums of £3,800 in cash to his children, apart from the major inheritance to his eldest son and his wife's jointure and profits of leases to keep a priest to pray for his soul.[675]

JOHN TAYLOR (*c.*1612 – -1663) **Swords, 1640**

e.s. Michael Taylor (1584–1620), Swords, and Joanna Russell, Drynham; m. by 1634 Mary, da. John Fagan, Feltrim, Dublin; at least 1 s. John.[676]
ed. Gray's Inn, 1632; King's Inns, 1638.

The Taylors and Russells had long been prominent in Swords and north Dublin and John was a connection of Peppard, Nangle and the Bysses.* Michael Taylor was a trustee of the settlement of the Bysses' estates in 1614.[677] From his father John inherited over 300 acres and the manor house in Swords and other property in Drogheda. He was a member of various committees in the Commons, including that which drew up charges against Bramhall and Radcliffe.* He was indicted for rebellion and his lands declared forfeit, but his wife claimed that he had taken no part in the rebellion, describing him as 'wholly addicted to the law', and declaring that he was, in consequence, known as '*magna charta*'; Robert Bysse,* in writing to his brother John in February 1642, noted that 'My uncle Taylor is not mentioned [among the rebels], but John and Robin are.' Maurice Eustace* supported these statements and Mary's petition for the return of the lands, which were later restored.[678]

WILLIAM TEMPLE (*c.*1555 – 15 January 1627)[679] **Trinity College, Dublin, 1613**

4 s. Anthony Temple, Coughton, Warwickshire, and Jane Bargrave; m. 1) April 1599, Martha, da. Robert Harrison, Derbyshire; 2 s. Sir John Temple, Revd Thomas Temple, 3 da., including Mary.[680]
ed. Eton; King's College, Cambridge, BA, 1578, MA, 1581.

674 Fitzgerald and Lamacraft (eds), *Some funeral entries of Ireland*, p. 107; TCD, MS 672, fo. 175r; Clarke, *Old English*, pp 33, 44–5.
675 Birr Castle, MS A/3; NAI, MS Chancery G108; Bodl. Lib., Talbot MS c. 92/173; NAI, MS M. 2,448, pp 236–8; Talbot, *Into the lion's den*, pp 114, 117–19.
676 Tallon (ed.), *Court of Claims*, pp 278–9.
677 Griffith (ed.), *Calendar of inquisitions*, p. 388.
678 *Cal. S.P. Ire., 1660–2*, pp 74, 572–3; TCD, MS 840, fo. 9v.
679 Empey (ed.), 'Diary of Sir James Ware', notes his death aged 72. TCD, MS 1,216, fos. 12r, 33r.
680 da. Mary d. 24 Dec. 1627. m. Job Ward. Fitzgerald and Lamacraft (eds), *Some funeral entries of Ireland*, p. 136.

MP for Tamworth, 1597.[681]
Kt. 4 May 1622.
Bur. Trinity College Chapel.[682]

Temple studied civil law but became known as an authority on the French philosopher Pierre de la Ramée (Petrus Ramus) on whom he published a number of works between 1584 and 1611. William was a master at Lincoln grammar school in 1581, but changed career four years later to become Philip Sidney's secretary when he travelled to the Low Countries as governor of Flushing. He received an annuity of £30 in Sidney's will and the close connection between the two families continued for several generations.[683] He came to Ireland with Essex in 1599 and apparently returned with him to England; he was involved in the earl's failed coup, arrested and indicted for treason. Robert Cecil apparently prevented his execution, yet he received no preferment until 1609 when Cecil, who was chancellor of the university, apparently arranged for his appointment as provost of Trinity College, Dublin. Temple's intellectual and administrative abilities were valuable in that position and he negotiated significant grants of land and money from the crown for the college. His legal training was also useful in his producing the first set of statutes for the college. Temple's issuing of leases for college land to family members, including his wife, caused controversy, as did his Puritan stance and he owed the college £450 at his death; he certainly profited financially from his time as provost. Davies* granted him, William Crowe and Revd John Richardson lands in Mayo in 1617.[684] Temple was also appointed master in chancery in 1610 but it is unclear how he combined the duties of this position with his academic role, or how active he was in chancery.[685] The provost was returning officer for the parliamentary election and as such Temple's return was illegal. Temple was not especially active as an MP; he sat on only one committee – that for the bill to defeat fraudulent conveyances and on 12 May 1615 the Commons ordered that he and Doyne* attend the courts to administer the oath to any officer before the committees for their fees.

ROBERT TRAVERS (1590 – 1647) **Clonakilty, 1634, 1640**

e.s. John Travers (d. 30 April 1618), Isle of Wight and Ballynamona, Cork, and Sarah Spencer; m. after April 1618 1) Katherine Nangle; 2), 1638, Elizabeth (d. 1659+), da. Archbishop Richard Boyle (d. 1645), Tuam and Martha Wright; sons Richard & John, das. Martha and Eizabeth.
ed. Oxford, St John's, BA, 1604, MA, 1607.
Kt. 1625.

Travers lived at Ballynamona and Rochfordstown. His parents were New English settlers and his uncle was the poet Edmund Spencer; Robert inherited his father's

681 A.M. Mimardière, 'Temple, William' in Hasler (ed.), *History of parliament*.
682 Gilbert Library, Ware's Diary, p. 123.
683 Pierpoint Morgan Library, MS MA 1475.7, 9.
684 HL, Hastings Deeds 3573.
685 Elizabethanne Boran, 'Temple, Sir William', *Oxford DNB*; Terry Clavin, 'Temple, Sir William', *DIB*; Hughes, *Patentee officers*.

estates in Cork.[686] His second marriage linked him to the whole Boyle network, including Crowe, Boyle and the Loftuses.* Through his daughters' marriages to Robert Stannard, Kilmallock and William Meade, Ballintubber and Richard Aldworth, Newmarket, he was connected to other Munster settler families. He became a freeman of Cork in 1623, a member of the 1625 Cork commission of the peace and two years later a commissioner to raise money for the army in the county.[687] He became register of Cork diocese in 1628, a post formerly held by his father and in which he was succeeded by his brother Zachary, with whom he bought lands at Ballymack and Rochfordstown (called Castle Travers) in Cork.[688] Another brother, Joseph, became chancellor of Cloyne in 1635. Robert's civil law training was the reason for his appointment as a judge of the admiralty court in Munster by 1625 where, like Loftus* and Parsons*, he was accused of corruption. The president of Munster, Sir Edward Villiers, begged for Gosnold's* reappointment as Travers was so corrupt 'for his misdemeanours had been censured in the Star Chamber, as it is much to his Lordship's dishonour to have him employed in a place of trust.'[689] In September 1633 a warrant was issued to apprehend and arrest him, as he had ignored other summonses to answer complaints about him.

In September 1638 he wrote to Laud, citing their old acquaintance as students in Cambridge and soliciting recommendations to Wentworth and Bramhall. Laud sent a very lukewarm reference to the deputy ('My suit therefore to your Lordship must be as general as his to me, and tis only this, that if he come in your way and deserve favour, you will do what in honour and wisdom you shall think fit, and let him know that I have written to your Lordship to take notice of him').[690] In parliament, Travers sat on only two committees in 1634, those for the bills on buggery and pleading against troublesome and contentious suits. However, he emerged as a leader in 1640, sitting on many committees including those to consider possible desirable bills, how the subsidies should be assessed and grievances and drafting letters on behalf of the Commons. On the basis of these positions and his signing the November 1640 petition to the English Commons, Perceval-Maxwell regarded him as a constitutionalist despite his notorious corruption.[691]

686 His father's inquisition post mortem, 1625, RIA, MS OS EI 20, pp 47–8; TCD, MS 1,216, fos. 19v, 67r; MS 1,217, fo. 64v.

687 Caulfield (ed.), *Cork*, p. 104; TCD, MS 672, fo. 182r, MS 823, fos. 171r, 178r, 273r; *Cal. S.P. Ire., 1625–32*, pp 166, 171, 252.

688 J.J. Fitzgerald and Charles MacNeill (eds), 'Documents found at Castlewhite, Co. Cork', *JRSAI*, 60 (June, 1930), 79–83.

689 Appleby (ed.), *Calendar*, p. 307; quoted in Costello, *Court of Admiralty*, p. 16; Crawford, *Star Chamber*, pp 558–9; Treadwell, *Buckingham and Ireland*, p. 101 anticipates his Cork connection by some years. Empey (ed.), *Early Stuart Irish warrants*, p. 35; Murphy (ed.), *Calendar of material relating to Ireland from the High Court of Admiralty*, pp 70, 357, 372, 391, 566–9.

690 Laud to Wentworth, 29 Dec. 1638, in Knowler (ed.), *Letters and dispatches*, ii, pp 265–6.

691 Perceval-Maxwell, *Outbreak*, pp 88, 134.

On the outbreak of the rebellion he was in Cork and his castle at Rochfordstown was besieged by Muskerry and others at Easter 1642. His letter from Bandonbridge in May 1642 to a neighbour, James Finch, detailing events in Munster was published in London.[692] When he was partly rehabilitated as judge of the parliamentary Admiralty Court in the mid-1640s, he was back to his old ways of taking 'an unhealthy interest in prize vessels taken into Munster.'[693] He was a judge of martial causes in 1646 and in that August, with Peregrine Bannister, Anthony Stoughton, Hardress Waller, William Kingsmill and others, signed a letter of support for Inchiquin. He was killed at the battle of Knocknanuss.[694]

CHRISTOPHER VERDON (c.1573 – 25 July 1624) **Louth County, 1613**

e.s. Patrick Verdon, Clonmore, Louth (1541–1609) and Joan (d. 1625), da. Sir John Bellew and Joan Lynham; m. 1) by 1601, Mary Barnewall (d. 1625+); 4 s., eldest John (1602–59), Christopher, Patrick, Robert; 3 da., Mary, Anne, Catherine.[695]
ed. Gray's Inn, 1601; King's Inns, 1607.

Described on his admission to the King's Inns as '*in legibus eruditis*', he shared a chamber next to Sibthorpe's* in the old Friar's Hall in the King's Inns.[696] Christopher was descended from an old Norman family, settled in Louth since the twelfth century; he was well connected with other local gentry families, especially the Bellews and Barnewalls. Apart from his legal work, including in chancery cases, he acted as seneschal on Essex's estates at Farney from 1606.[697] He inherited extensive estates at Clonmore and took a lease for 41 years in 1613 of lands at Parsonstown, Louth and developed other lands at Killtalagh, which were the subject of a chancery case against him by Ald. Walter Ball of Dublin.[698] Christopher was very active in parliament, as a member of the committees on the bills to take away benefit of clergy, Tyrone's attainder and to mend highways, and the committee examining fees of clerks of the market and say-masters. He was a frequent contributor to debates and argued unsuccessfully for the subsidies bill to be committed. Verdon also objected to the preamble to the clergy subsidies bill.

RICHARD WADDING (c.1578 – 1628)[699] **Waterford, 1613**

e.s. Thomas Wadding, Waterford and Anna, da. ____ Devereux; m. 1) by 1595, Frances ____ (d. 1638); s. Paul, Gray's Inn, 1612; younger sons, Nicholas, John, Barnard, Robert; da. Mary m.

692 *Letter from a person of good quality residing in Kinsale* (London, 1646), pp 2–9; Robert Travers, *A new and trew relation from Ireland, sent in a letter … to Lievtenant James Finch* (London, 1642); *A true and good relation of the valliant exploits and victorious enterprises of Sir Simon Harcourt, and Sir Charles Coote* (London, 1641).
693 Costello, *Court of Admiralty*, p. 17; Murphy (ed.), *Calendar of material relating to Ireland from the High Court of Admiralty*, pp 73, 106, 108, 112, 119, 180.
694 *A great and bloody plot of the battell of Knocknones* (London, 1647).
695 *Inq. cancel. Hib. repert.*, Louth, Jac. I (13, 21); Pedigree of the Verdons of Clonmore, NLI, MS 9,116.
696 King's Inns, MS B1/1, fos. 4r, 109r.
697 Ohlmeyer, 'Records'; Evelyn Philip Shirley, *The history of the county of Monaghan* (London, 1879), p. 111.
698 MacNeill and Otway-Ruthven (eds), *Dowdall deeds*, nos 608, 617, 632, 643, 652; NAI, MSS Chancery G366, G375.
699 Jennings (ed.), *Wadding Papers*, pp 273, 304.

Robert Wise, Credon, Waterford, esq. (d. 23 December 1639).[700]
ed. New Inn, Middle Temple, 1594; King's Inns, 1607.
Bur. Holy Trinity Cathedral, Waterford.[701]

Wadding was a highly respected lawyer, well-integrated into Waterford City's government. He was sheriff of the city in 1604 and deposed as mayor in 1611 for refusing the oath of supremacy; he may have been the city's recorder.[702] Richard shared chambers in the cloisters in the King's Inns with David Rothe* and with Everard* acted as arbitrator for Boyle in his dispute about lands at Coneveigh in March 1613. In 1607 on his entry into King's Inn he was described as '*in legibus eruditis*.' He was one of the Catholic MPs ordered to attend James in England at the end of January 1614.[703] Richard Butler* and he were the two 'silenced lawyers' who were imprisoned in Dublin Castle for advising Waterford Corporation in its case against the administration's attack on its charter in 1617.[704] In 1623 he was one of those collecting contributions to send agents to England and was excluded from Waterford's commission of the peace in the following year.[705] In April 1627 he was involved in a chancery case with William Dobbins* and Robert Wise about a green that was disputed between Waterford Corporation and the Abbey of St John.[706]

Described as a 'known malicious papist, one of the principal disturbers of the parliament' and 'busy in the parliament … a man excommunicated and heretofore deprived of his mayorality for refusing the oath of supremacy', he was very active in the Commons, serving on the Grand Committee and many others on bills and contributing regularly to debates.[707] Outside his legal work, he borrowed £200 on bond on the staple in November 1602 and with Thomas Wale (or ?Neale), Ballymade, Tipperary, sold a house and garden in Carrickmacgriffin, Co. Tipperary, in January 1608 to Ormond's feoffees.[708] He was named guardian of Geoffrey Baron and his siblings in Laurence Baron's will and was one of the trustees chosen by John Everard* in a settlement of his estates on his eldest son in 1620.[709]

700 NLI, GO, MS 71, Funeral Entries, Volume 8, 1639–41, p. 261; TCD, MS 1,217, fo. 177v.
701 William Carrigan, 'Old Waterford wills', JWSEIAS, 9 (1906), 151–2.
702 Gilbert (ed.), 'Archives of the municipal Corporation of Waterford', p. 277; Byrne (ed.), Great Parchment Book of Waterford, p. 212; Curtis Clayton (ed.), Council book, pp 206, 212; *Cal. S.P. Ire., 1615–25*, p. 197.
703 Cal. S.P. Ire., 1611–14, p. 464.
704 King's Inns, MS B1/1, fo. 108v; Crawford, Star Chamber, pp 328–9; APC, 1616–17, pp 311–14.
705 King's Inns, MS B1/1, fo. 109v; Grosart (ed.), *Lismore Papers*, i, p. 20; *Cal. S.P. Ire., 1615–25*, pp 441–2; TCD, MS 672, fo. 183r.
706 NAI, Chancery MS AA184, taken from Kenneth Nicholls' calendar.
707 Cal. Carew, v, p. 276.
708 Ohlmeyer and Ó Ciardha (eds), *Irish statute staple*; NLI, MSS D. 3407, D. 3424; NAI, MS RC 5/23, pp 164ff.
709 Jennings (ed.), Wadding Papers, p. 239; NAI, MS RC 4/11, pp 457–60, 489, 500–1.

JAMES (Jacob) WALSHE (Walsh)[710] **(c.1580 – c.1650)** **Waterford Co., 1634**
e.s. Robert Walshe (d. 3 January 1603), Waterford, and Beale (Bess), da. James White, Kells, Kilkenny; m. 1) Katherine Sherlock; 2) 1603, Catherine, da. Piers Butler, Callan, and Jennet, da. Edward White, Ballinderry, Roscommon; e.s. Robert and two sons who died young without issue.
ed. New Inn, Middle Temple, 1600; King's Inns, 1609.
Bart. 1645.

Robert Walshe was mayor of Waterford in 1601 and 1602 and James was executor of his will and received livery of his estates in 1603. He paid a fine of £8 on a grant passed on the Commission of Defective Titles in 1611 and he held over 2,000 acres in the county at Little Island, Ballyganer, Ballybrack and Cloneluman and had property on St Peter's Street and High Street, Waterford City. He was a nephew of Richard Strange of Dunkitt, MP for Waterford in 1634.[711]

James was alderman and mayor of Waterford in 1631 and presumably mayor of the staple in the following year; his son Robert was sheriff of the county in 1634, and therefore returning officer at his father's election. In April 1636 he borrowed £100 from Cork and in November 1640 he borrowed £2,000 on bond from Thomas Porter of Waterford at that city's staple. His relationship with Boyle was not confined to this debt; Cork and St Leger acted as peacemakers in a row between Robert Walshe and Oliver Stephenson during the 1634 parliament and in 1636 Boyle sent important papers to James at Waterford for transmission to his agent and mortgaged some of Walshe's lands.[712] Curiously for a lawyer, James sat on only two parliamentary committees: that for the bill for payment of the subsidy of poundage, in the cities of Dublin, Waterford, and the towns of Drogheda and Galway (as a local MP) and a conference committee with the Lords. However, Wentworth commissioned James and his fellow Waterford men and lawyers, Sir Peter Aylward, John Sherlock and Thomas Wadding, to investigate the claims a former mayor, Robert Wise, made against Richard Butler for 'injuries, wrongs and abuses' at the election of Waterford's county members in 1634.[713]

Thomas Lluellin and John Collins deposed that the servants of several Waterford aldermen, including James, robbed them of cattle and other property in Waterford in February 1642.[714] There is no evidence of his other activities in the 1640s, but his son Robert fought with royalist forces in England, was knighted on the field at Edgehill and was a friend of Prince Rupert. This presumably explains Walsh's grant of a baronetcy in 1645.[715]

710 Spelling taken from his signature on BL, Add. MS 19,843, fo. 66r.
711 Cokayne, *Baronetage*, ii, p. 274; Bodl. Lib., Carte MS 68, fo. 127r; NAI, MS RC 5/23, pp 208ff; *Rot. Pac. Jac.*, p. 40; *Cal. S.P. Ire, 1611–14*, p. 104; Simington (ed.), *Civil Survey, Waterford*, pp 75, 152, 159, 224, 229; Tallon (ed.), *Court of Claims*, pp 81, 115, 421.
712 Byrne (ed.), *Great Parchment Book of Waterford*, p.228; McGrath, 'Thomas Wentworth's Irish electoral strategy'; Grosart (ed.), *Lismore Papers*, iv, pp 37, 178, 190–1, 206, 216–17; BL, Add. MS 19,843, fo. 66r; BL, Add. MS 19,843, fo. 66.
713 Empey (ed.), *Early Stuart Irish warrants*, pp 160–1.
714 Depositions of Thomas Lluellin, John Collins, TCD, MS 820, fos. 10–11.
715 Peter R. Newman, *The old service: royalist regimental colonels and the civil war, 1642–46* (Manchester, 1993), p. 49.

JOHN WALSHE (Walsh) (1610[716] – 1676+) **Waterford, 1640**
e.s. David Walshe, Rathronan, Tipperary[717]; m. ____; 1 s.
ed. Gray's Inn, 1631; King's Inns, 1635.[718]
Kt. 1649.

John came from a gentry background in south Tipperary and like many in this area he and his father were involved in both Waterford and Clonmel where David had some property and paid tax; John's brother James married Henry White's* sister.[719] It is probable that John spent some time in one of the chancery inns before entering Gray's Inn, as he was performing legal services for Cork in 1631. On his return home he embarked on a legal career with the earl as one of his most important clients, but the record of his admission to the King's Inns is curious and he appears to have acted as a legal counsel, rather than pleading in court. He acted in a case involving Nicholas White's father and Lord Cork in 1636. His legal practice was apparently largely confined to the southeast, including for Ormond, and combined with trade in the standard exports of hides and wool, which suggests he also served an apprenticeship as a merchant before studying law.[720]

With Waller, Roebuck Lynch*, Geoffrey Browne* and others, he signed the petition of the inhabitants of Connacht, Clare, Tipperary and Limerick concerning composition rents. He lived on High Street, Waterford and South Street, Callan. The deposition of Ambrose Aungier, chancellor of St Patrick's Cathedral, claimed losses of £120 in household goods that he confided to John's care at his dwelling there. He held lands in Tipperary and Kilkenny from Ormond at an annual rent of £32 and in 1644 he lent the earl £500. He also had property in Inistioge.[721] He had a dispute with Thomas Davills in 1640.

While John was not named to any committees in the first two sessions, he sat on three in the third and was one of the agents sent to negotiate in England in late 1640, presumably as much for his legal expertise as for his personal knowledge of the tobacco monopoly on which he gave evidence at Strafford's trial, based on his

716 TCD, MS 830, fos. 249r–50v. I am grateful to Paul Smith for information on Walshe.

717 John's father and brother-in-law, Thomas Prendergast, leased Rathronan parsonage from Boyle from November 1622. Grosart (ed.), *Lismore Papers*, 1st series, ii, pp 63, 214. The depositions record the activities of a Captain Walshe, variously described as John or James, son and heir of David Walshe, as a rebel in 1642. TCD, MS 820, fos. 71r–2v, 147r, 154v; TCD, MS 821, fo. 56r.

718 Edward Keane, P.B. Phair and Thomas U. Sadleir (eds), *King's Inns admission papers, 1607–1867* (Dublin, 1982), p. 506 notes his admission as John Welsh on 4 December 1635, but there is no entry to that effect in King's Inns, MS B1/1.

719 NAI, Chancery AA93; Simington (ed.), *Civil Survey, Tipperary*, I, pp 202, 288, 291–3, 302; Healy, *History and antiquities of Kilkenny*, appendix, p. 28.

720 NLI, MS 13,237 (11). A John Walshe was admitted to the Inner Temple in 1612, but this is improbably early for this man. Grosart (ed.), *Lismore Papers*, 1st series, iv, pp 144, 149; Rushworth (ed.), *Tryal*, p. 245; NLI, MS D 4023.

721 Edward MacLysaght (ed.), 'O'Grady Papers', *Anal. Hib.*, 15 (1944), 35–61; NLI, MS 2,308, p. 357; Simington (ed.), *Civil Survey, Waterford*, pp 228, 252; TCD, MS 809, fo. 291; Conleth Manning, 'The civil survey of Inistioge and Callan, Co. Kilkenny', *JRSAI*, 128 (1998), 48–73; David Edwards and Conleth Manning, 'A seventeenth-century map of Inistioge, Co. Kilkenny', *JRSAI*, 131 (2001), 38–55.

commercial experience.[722] He was arranging the unsuccessful transport of Irish soldiers to Spain in 1641. An active supporter of the Confederation, he signed the petition to Charles in October 1642 and that to Ormond in July 1643. With Robert Talbot and Gormanston, he was an agent to meet Ormond at Trim, Castlemartin and Gigginstown to negotiate the cessation, which he signed, in 1643. Walshe was appointed a judge in the Confederate courts in 1644 and was frequently one of the Confederation's negotiators until 1646. In February 1646 he brought letters to Kilkenny from Ormond and supported the peace treaty of that year. In October 1648 he met Theobald Taaffe and Sir Robert Talbot at Ballinakill to discuss the reorganization of the army and negotiated with Inchiquin and at Dungarvan.[723]

John represented Clonmel at the general assemblies in Waterford, Kilkenny and Limerick in 1644–6 and was a member of its town council from 1644 to 1648, despite also being mayor of Waterford in 1648–9. He was also a member of the 1647 assembly and of the 1648 Munster provincial council as substitute for his fellow Ormondist, Gerard Fennell. Both are included in a list of the 10th Supreme Council (September 1648–January 1649). He was increasingly trusted by Ormond who knighted him in 1649 and appointed him a judge under the new royalist administration; Walshe attended Ormond in 1650 (he brought the declaration of the General Assembly at Loughrea to Ormond), when his father, who was in his eighties, and his sisters, were murdered on the Clonmel–Waterford road by Sir Anthony Morgan's troops. His family was prominent in the defence of Clonmel and his wife, whose identity is unknown, died in the 1651 siege of Limerick.[724] In February 1654 he was examined about Darcy's* activities in Kilkenny in the 1640s, but he was living in Amsterdam later that year.

Walshe returned to Ireland after the Restoration and recovered his lands as reward for his loyal service to the crown. He was living in Tipperary in 1660 and as John Walshe of Ballibechan was working as Ormond's seneschal from 1660 to at least 1670.[725] Carte described Walshe as 'a very good lawyer, a wise and an honest man, who had the chief care of all his estate and affairs, and managed both with great abilities and fidelity'.[726] He signed the Catholic remonstrance of 1666, and served as Ormond's seneschal until 1670. He subscribed to the petition of other men from Wexford and Kilkenny re. appointing collectors to collect the rents of

722 Perceval-Maxwell, *Outbreak*, pp 75, 87, 90, 137, 139; Clarke, *Old English*, pp 135, 197, 222; Rushworth (ed.), *Tryal*, pp 244–5, 404.

723 McGrath (ed.), *Clonmel*, pp 310–11, 322, 333, 335, 339, 362, 377, 381; Byrne (ed.), *Great Parchment Book of Waterford*, p. 270; de Burgo, *Hibernia Dominicana*, p. 885; Ó Siochrú, *Confederate Ireland*, pp 86, 99–100, 113, 172, 188, 227, 229, 234, 263; Bellings and Gilbert (eds), *Confederation*, i, pp 123,163; ii, pp viii–cxiii, 50, 166, 219, 222–4, 286–8, 296–311, 350–79; iii, pp 42–67, 174, 216–67; iv, p. xlvii; v, pp 143–55, 206–57, 311; vi, pp 86, 93, 211–89, 374, 410; vii, pp 69, 131–69, 257, 352–9, 364; O'Ferrall and O'Connell, *Commentarius Rinuccinianus*, ii, pp 113–16, 132; vi, p. 655; Lowe (ed.), *Letter-book*, pp 208–12.

724 Micheál Ó Siochrú, *God's executioner: Oliver Cromwell and the conquest of Ireland* (London, 2008), pp 103, 109, 130, 147, 158; Burke, *History of Clonmel*, p. 82.

725 NLI, MS 11,044/121, 144–8, 151, 165, 189, 226, MS 11,045/67, MS 11,048/41, 64; MS 11,056.

726 Carte, *History of the life*, iv, pp 212–13.

the *custodium* lands there in 1677.[727] In 1676 Archbishop Oliver Plunkett met Catholic clergy in John's house at Ballyneiry, Co. Tipperary.[728]

Dr DOMINIC WHITE (Whyte) (? – d. 1654+) **Limerick City, 1634, 1640**
s. David White (?fitz Nicholas), Limerick, and ?Elinor Fagan; m ____.[729]
D.C.L.

White should not be confused with his namesakes in Limerick, Alderman Sir Dominick White fitz Bartholomew, mayor in 1636–7, or Dominic White fitz James.[730] White's father David was named mayor of Limerick in its new charter of 1609 and his mother may have been Elinor Fagan, with whom he took a number of cases in chancery in 1622 about his inheritance. White held lands worth £104 in Limerick City including a substantial house which he lost to Colonel Nelson, another and a shed in Mill Lane and a cagework house in Emblin Lane that he rented to Catherine Fanning. He inherited lands in Clare from Geoffrey Galway.*[731] It is unclear from which institution Dominic received his doctorate of civil laws, but his practice was evidently local. He was alderman of Limerick, mayor in 1629 and continued to be active in Limerick City's management, as mayor in 1643 and recorder from at least 1649 to 1651.[732] Limerick's citizens were very divided about strategy and Dominic was one of the leaders who was proclaimed a rebel by the Confederation in 1644–5 when, with Creagh and other townsmen, he opposed Lord Castleconnell's entry into the city with his troops; he accused Castleconnell of stealing his sheep and cattle, which the baron admitted but claimed he had authority to do so and returned some horses when asked by White's wife. Dominic was one of the city's councillors who urged Hugh Dubh O'Neill to yield to Henry Ireton as the population was weakened by plague and hunger and was a negotiator and hostage for the terms of surrender in October 1651. He died sometime after the Civil Survey was compiled in the mid-1650s.[733]

Ald. HENRY WHITE (Whyte) (*c.*1596[734] – 1643) **Clonmel 1628, 1634**
e.s. Nicholas White fitz Henry (d. 1623), and Barbara ____;[735] m. by April 1623 ____ da. Sir John Everard, Fethard, and Catherine, da. ____ Plunkett; 1 s. Nicholas, da. ____.[736]
ed. Clifford's Inn, Inner Temple, 10 July 1616.

727 HL, Stowe Nugent MS Manorial Box 1 (49).
728 Ciara Breathnach, 'Archbishop John Brenan (1625–1693): his life and work', *Tipperary Historical Journal*, 6 (1993), 148–59.
729 TCD, MS 829, fos. 443r–6v.
730 NLI, MS 41,677/3, 7.
731 Simington (ed.), *Civil Survey, Limerick*, pp 420, 437, 451, 453; Brown and Ó Siochrú (eds), 'Cromwellian urban civil surveys', pp 57, 68–9, 82; RIA, MS 14/C/3/2, pp 332–5.
732 NLI, MS 41,677/3, 7; Lenihan, *Limerick*, pp 153ff, 701–2, 741; NAI, MSS Chancery Papers BB34, BB57, BB110; Bodl. Lib., Carte MS 156, pp 143–5.
733 TCD, MS 829, fos. 443–6; William Layles, 'Account of surrender of Limerick, 1651', at https://celt.ucc.ie/published/E650001-023.html [accessed 21 July 2022]; Lenihan, Limerick, pp183ff; O'Ferrall and O'Connell, *Commentarius Rinuccinianus*, iv, pp 638–46.
734 NAI, MS RC 4/10, pp 137–42.
735 Walter Fitzgerald (ed.), *Association for the Preservation of Memorials of the Dead, Ireland, Volume 7* (Dublin, 1907), p. 180.
736 NLI, GO, MS 225, p. 18.

Whites had been prominent in Clonmel for many centuries, supplying at least 25 sovereigns between 1439 and 1600. Henry's father, a wealthy merchant, was mayor in 1610 and MP in 1613. Henry was John Everard's* son-in-law and John Haly's* brother-in-law. He formed part of the Countess of Cork's funeral procession in 1630.[737] White was appointed Clonmel's legal advisor on 14 October 1622 and recorder from 1624 to 1626 and again from 1634 at an annual salary of £3; he also acted in chancery cases. He was a Clonmel town councillor from 1624 until his death and mayor in 1625, 1630 and 1638. He was also a member of the 1624–5 commission of the peace for Tipperary, Clonmel's agent to the Great Assembly of April 1627 and MP in 1628; in 1634 he was admitted an honorary member of the merchant's guild. His civic standing is confirmed by his regularly being one of three councillors (including the mayor) to keep the keys of the common chest. He was a commissioner to manage the export of corn to England from Clonmel in 1631. With Geoffrey Baron and others he was appointed to settle Clonmel's chief rent due to Ormond in October 1637 and two years later as receiver and disburser of £600 due from the county to erect a house of correction within Clonmel's liberties. With Baron and other councillors, he drafted a petition for the Corporation objecting to how subsidies were cessed in the town in June 1640.[738]

Henry was Clonmel's wealthiest citizen with an annual income from property of £300; he inherited 47 acres in Tipperary and bequeathed at least 187 houses in Clonmel to his son Nicholas. In 1642 he contributed £4 quarterly (by far the largest individual sum) to the collection for the defence of Clonmel, and he was elected as Captain for Greatgate Quarter to manage the town's defence in 1642–3.[739] He took no part in the rebellion and was later described as one 'who from the beginning lived indifferently and were of known good affection to his majesties' service and died before the cessation in 1643' (although he was included in the 1644 list of Clonmel's councillors), despite which his son Nicholas was transplanted to Clare and reduced to poverty.[740]

JOHN WILKINSON (*c.*1569 – 1618) **Coleraine, 1613**

3 s. John Wilkinson, White Roodinge, Essex, gent m. ____; at least 1 da. Frances.[741]
ed. Middle Temple, 26 June 1585; Bar, 8 February 1594; subsequently of Barnard's Inn.[742]

A lawyer of some note, Wilkinson came to Ireland by 1610 when he witnessed deeds between Sir Hugh Montgomery and Conn O'Neill. Before his appointment

737 FitzGerald and Lamacraft (eds), *Some funeral entries of Ireland*, p. 118.

738 McGrath (ed.), *Clonmel*, pp 108–304; Ohlmeyer, 'Records'; TCD, MS 672, fo. 184v; Caulfield (ed.), *Youghal*, p. 162.

739 McGrath, 'Reconstructing an early-modern Irish urban economic community'; McGrath (ed.), *Clonmel*, p. 301.

740 Burke, *History of Clonmel*, pp 87–8.

741 NLI, GO, MS 71, Funeral Entries, Volume 8, 1639–41, p. 282. Frances da. John Wilkinson, counsellor at law m. Francis Aungier, one of the six clerks of his majesty's high court of chancery, d. 15 Jan. 1640.

742 Christopher W. Brookes (ed.), *The admissions registers of Barnard's Inn, 1620–1869* (London, 1995), p. 29.

as recorder in Coleraine's charter, Wilkinson was largely based at Barnard's Inn, one of the chancery inns, and he published two popular manuals on local government, *A treatise collected out of the statutes of this kingdom concerning the office and authority of coroners and sheriffs*, dedicated to Henry Montague, first earl of Manchester, recorder of London and MP for the city in 1614, an active, reforming judge, anxious to ensure that current statutes were enforced, and *An easie and plain method for the keeping of a court leet*. Both were published together in 1618, and the *Treatise* was frequently reprinted.[743]

Wilkinson was granted the use of a house and 40 acres near the church in Coleraine, in lieu of a salary, as a similar arrangement was made for Carey* in Londonderry. Wilkinson rapidly became concerned at the slow manner of Coleraine's development, and especially the activities of the town's agents Tristram Beresford and John Rowley; Josias Bodley's report in 1613 had already raised serious questions about the plantation's state and progress and Wilkinson acted as whistle-blower, supported by Coleraine's inhabitants who collected money for him to travel to England to complain to the privy council. The London companies subsequently commissioned Peter Proby and Mathias Springham to investigate Beresford and the Coleraine plantation. Their report was damning but Beresford prevailed upon the inhabitants to disavow their support for Wilkinson.[744] He once again travelled to London to deal with some matters relating to the plantation in Londonderry and 'some few matters criminal which I had against Sir James Hamilton'. He had no friends at court and readily accepted Montgomery's offer to help him through his connections which included the English attorney general Henry Yelverton whom Montgomery and Wilkinson met in London in March 1617 with another lawyer at Gray's Inn.[745] Despite clear evidence of corruption, Beresford was exonerated and Wilkinson's life became increasingly difficult. He was expelled from Barnard's Inn for having been found in his chambers with a 'lewd' woman; he sued the inn, but the outcome is unknown and he died *c.*1618.[746] While Wilkinson is listed as an MP for Coleraine, he did not sign the letter of the Protestant MPs, nor is there any record of his activities in the house, which is unusual for a lawyer, but he clearly attended, as he commented on Fulke Conway's activities in parliament to the settler Hugh Clotworthy (father of John and relative of Beresford).[747]

743 London, Printed [by Adam Islip] for the Companie of Stationers, 1618. Michael Dalton's *Countrey justice* (1618), also dedicated to Montague, is, like Wilkinson's *Treatise*, concerned to enable and empower men without a legal training to fulfil their roles as local officials and justices of the peace. Brian Quintrell, 'Montagu, Henry, first earl of Manchester', *Oxford DNB*.

744 David Heffernan (ed.), 'Three surveys of the Londonderry plantation, 1613–6', *Anal. Hib.*, 50 (2019), 1–61.

745 D.A. Chart, 'The break-up of the estate of Con O'Neill, Castlereagh, County Down, temp. James I', *Proc. RIA*, 48C (1942/43), 119–51.

746 McGrath, 'Starting from scratch'.

747 Wilkinson to Sir Hugh Clotworthy, 15 Nov. 1617, Corpus Christi College, Oxford, MS 297, fo. 155.

Bibliography

MANUSCRIPT SOURCES

Armagh

Armagh Robinson Library

Garstin's Transcriptions of Convocation Records, No. 8, 1639–41

Haynes, *Certaine Principall Matters*

Irish Parliamentary Papers

Lord Conway's Irish catalogue of printed books, *Tituli catalogi sequentis*, *c.*1639–41

MS KE.I.7

MS KH.II.7

Richard Bolton's case book

Austin, Texas

The Harry Ransom Center for the Humanities

MS 76

MS 158

MS 165

Belfast

The Public Records Office of Northern Ireland

D 162|1

Birr, County Offaly

Birr Castle

MS A/1/19

MS A/5/46

MS A/8

California

The Henry E. Huntington Library

Hastings Deeds, HAD 3,517

Hastings Papers, Box 1 (1)

Hastings Papers, Box 1 (12)

Hastings Papers, Box 3 (46)

Hastings Papers, Box 4 (1)

Hastings Papers, MS 14,058

Hastings Papers, MS 14,059

Hastings Papers, MS 14,061

Hastings Papers, MS 14,366

Hastings Papers, MS 14,368

Hastings Papers, MS 14,575
Hastings Papers, MS 14,987
Hastings Papers, MS 15,000
Hastings Papers, MS 15,076
Hastings Papers, MS 15,077
Hastings Papers, MS 15,155
Hastings Papers, MS 15,156
Hastings Papers, MS 15,158
Hastings Papers, MS 15,159
Hastings Papers, MS 15,954
Hastings Papers, MS 15,958
Hastings Papers, Religious Papers, Box 1 (16)

Chicago
The Newberry Library
Case MS Folio OJN 593 E7
MS Case fk 045.64
MS fk 0452.613

Cork
Cork City Archives
MS YTR B/1
MS YTR 1/47
MS YTR 1/68

Derbyshire
Chatsworth House
Cork Papers, Misc. Boxes, Box 3
Cork Papers, Volume 5
Cork Papers, Volume 6
Cork Papers, Volume 7
Cork Papers, Volume 18
Cork Papers, Volume 19
Cork Papers, Volume 21
Hardwick MS 78

Dublin
Gilbert Library
MS 35
MS 173
MS 205

King's Inn
King's Inns, MS B1/1
King's Inns, MS N3/2/1/7
King's Inns, MS N3/2/1/8

Marsh's Library
MS Z2.1.1
MS Z3.1.1
MS Z3.2.5

The National Archives of Ireland
Chancery G353
Ferguson MS 11
Ferguson MS 12
M 2,448
M 2,469
MS 999
MS C 59/14
MS Chancery Q 2
MS EX 1/2
MS M 10/16
MS M 31
MS RC 8/7
MS RC 8/21
MS RC 8/26
MS RCH 240/50

The National Library of Ireland
GO, MS 2
GO, MS 4
GO, MS 6
GO, MS 14
GO, MS 44
GO, MS 58
GO, MSS 64–79
GO, MS 95
MS 643
MS 835
MS 836
MS 999
MS 2,541
MS 2,656
MS 9,607
MS 11,044
MS 13,237
MS 16,085
MS 41,477
MS 41,667
MS D. 25

Representative Church Body Library
MS 23

The Royal Irish Academy
MS 12/D/1
MS 14/C/2
MS 24/Q/4
MS 24/Q/5

Trinity College Dublin
MS 581
MSS 613–15
MS 622
MS 646
MS 647
MS 672
MS 743
MS 807
MS 829
MS 836
MS 844
MS 858
MS 1,062
MS 1,178
MS 1,180
MS 1,444
MS 1,445
MS 1,739
MS MUN/1/1
MS MUN/V/1/1

University College Dublin Archives
Luke Wadding Papers, UCD-OFM, D.01

Edinburgh
The National Archives of Scotland
MS PA2/19

Kilkenny
Kilkenny Corporation Archives
MS CR/K/40
MS CR/K/52
MS CR/K/53
MS CR/K/56
MS CR/J/17
MS CR/J/39

London
The British Library
Add. MS 4,756

Add. MS 4,790
Add. MS 4,797
Add. MS 4,801
Add. MS 5,754
Add. MS 19,832
Add. MS 29,314
Add. MS 30,383
Add. MS 48,020
Add. MS 72,414
Cotton MS Caligula E VI
Egerton MS 1,048
Harleian MS 430
Harleian MS 4,892
Lansdowne MS 1,208
Sloane MS 3,827

The Inner Temple Library
MS 538.44

Lambeth Palace Library
Carew MS 603
Carew MS 629

The National Archives of the United Kingdom
MS C. 86/1
MS C. 219/44
MS E 101/241/13
MS E 179/70/145A
MS PRO 30/5
MS RC 8/27
MS RCH 262/31
PROB 11/189/205
SP 52
SP 63

The Parliamentary Archives of the United Kingdom
MS HL/PO/JO/10/1/5

New Haven, CT
Beinecke Library, Yale
Osborn MS b22
Osborn MS FB 158, III6
Osborn MS Folder 3065

Nottingham
Nottingham University Library
MS C1 C, 135–6
MS Cl LP 47

Oxford

The Bodleian Library

Add. C 286

Bankes MS 10

Bankes MS 55/65

Bankes MS 57

Bankes MSS 65–9

Carte MS 1

Carte MS 2

Carte MS 20

Carte MS 21

Carte MS 30

Carte MS 40

Carte MS 42

Carte MS 59

Carte MS 61

Carte MS 62

Carte MS 63

Carte MS 64

Carte MS 66

Carte MS 67

Carte MS 68

Carte MS 80

Carte MS 118

Carte MS 176

Carte MS 204

Laud MS Misc. 612

MS Ash Rolls 45

Rawlinson MS D 922

Tanner MS 70

Sheffield

Wentworth Woodhouse

Muniments, StrP8

Muniments, StrP14/76

Washington DC

The Folger Shakespeare Library

MS G.a.10

MS L.a.91

MS V.a.206

MS W.b.510

MS X.c.101(2–3)

MS X.d.158

MS X.d.428(185)

MS X.d.607

MS X.d.s(26)

PRINTED PRIMARY SOURCES

Act for the Kings Majesties most gracious, generall, and free pardon (Dublin, 1635).

Acts of the privy council of England, 1542–1631, 46 vols (1890–1964).

A letter, or paper, signed by Garald Fitz-gerald in behalf of an assembly of the Irish at Glanmaliroe in the province of Leinster in Ireland, to the commissioners of parliament delivered the 11 of March 1652 also a declaration thereupon made by the said commissioners of Parliament, March 12 1652 (Dublin, 1651).

An exact collection of all remonstrances, declarations, votes, orders, ordinances, proclamations, petitions, messages, answers and remarkable passages betweene the King's most excellent majesty and his high court of parliament (London, 1643).

Anno regni Caroli Regis, Angliae … decimo & undecimo, at the parliament begun and holden at Dublin, the 14 day of July [1634] and there continued untill the 18 day of Aprill 1635 (Dublin, 1635).

A word of advertisement to the Godly party in Scotland (Edinburgh, 1651).

Calendar of the Lismore manuscripts with index of matters, 1396–1774, 16 vols (Privately printed, n.d.).

Catalogue de l'Histoire de France, 9 vols (Paris, 1870–85).

Christchurch Cathedral: Dublin, 1855–1878 (Dublin, 1878).

His Majesties proclamation enent the unnecessary confluence of his Highnesse leiges to Edinburgh in the time of this parliament (Edinburgh, 1641).

In this volume are contained all the statutes from the tenthe yere of King Henrie the sixt, to the xiii yere of our moste grawious and souereaygne lady Queene Elyzabeth, made and established in her highnes realme of Irelande (London, 1572).

Inquisitionum in officio rotulorum cancellariae Hiberniae asservatarum repertorium, 2 vols (Dublin, 1826–9).

Irish patent rolls of James I: facsimile of the Irish record commission's calendar prepared prior to 1830 (Dublin, 1966).

Journal contenant ce qui s'est fait et passé en la cour de Parlement de Paris toutes les chambres assemblées et autres lieux sur le sujet des affaires du temps présent ès années 1648 et 1649 (Paris, 1649).

Journals of the House of Commons of the kingdom of Ireland, 1613–1791, 28 vols (Dublin, 1753–91).

Journals of the House of Lords of Ireland, 1634–1800, 8 vols (Dublin, 1779–1800).

'Laus Deo. Ad majorem Dei gloriam', *Journal of the Kilkenny and South-East of Ireland Archaeological Society*, new series, 5:1 (1864), 85–108.

L'ordre tenv engarde en l'assemblée des trois estats (Paris, 1558).

Novvelle extraordinaire, tovchant l'estat present des affaires dv Roy de la Grand' Bretagne. Avec devx harangves eloquentes & Zelees,…l'une prononcee par le Chevalier Richard Blaque de la part de l'Assemblee des trois Estats du party Catholique d'Irlande (Paris, 1649).

The humble and just remonstrance of the knights, citizens, and burgesses, in parliament assembled in Ireland (London, 1641).

The penny magazine of the Society for the Diffusion of Useful Knowledge, Volume 3 (London, 1834).

The plot and progresse of the Irish rebellion (London, 1644).

The prerogative of parliaments in England proved in a dialogue between a counsellour of state and a justice of the peace (London, 1664).

The priviledges and practice of parliaments in England, collected out of the common lawes of this land ([London], 1622).

The reports of the deputy keepers of the Public Records Office and keepers of the State Papers in Ireland, 52 vols (Dublin, 1868–1921).

The statutes at large, passed in the parliaments held in Ireland from the third year of Edward the second A.D. 1310, to the first year of George the third A.D. 1761, inclusive, 8 vols (Dublin, 1765).

[Alexander, Jerome], *A breviate of a sentence given against J.A. ... in the Court of Star Chamber* (London, 1644).

— *The case between Sir Jerom Alexander Knight, second justice of his majesties Court of Common Pleas in Ireland: and Sir William Ashton Knight, second justice of his majesties Court of King's Bench in Ireland concerning precedency* (s.l., 1661).

Appleby, John C. (ed.), *A calendar of material relating to Ireland from the High Court of Admiralty examinations, 1536–1641* (Dublin, 1992).

Baker, J.H., *The Inns of Chancery 1340–1640: with an edition of the surviving statutes and orders: Selden Society Supplementary Series, Volume 19* (London, 2017).

Barry, James, *Case of tenures upon the Commission of Defective Titles, argued by all the judges of Ireland* (Dublin, 1637).

Bellings, Richard and J.T. Gilbert (eds), *History of the Irish Confederation and the war in Ireland, 1641*, 7 vols (Dublin, 1882–91).

Bernard, Nicholas, *The life & death of the most reverend and learned father of our church, Dr James Ussher* (Dublin, 1656).

Berry, H.F. (ed.), *Statutes and ordinances and acts of the parliament of Ireland: King John to Henry V* (Dublin, 1907).

— *Statute rolls of the parliament of Ireland: reign of Henry the Sixth* (Dublin, 1910).

— 'Minute book of the Corporation of Dublin, known as the "Friday book", 1567–1611', *Proc. RIA*, 30C (1913), 477–514.

Bickley, Francis (ed.), *Report on the manuscripts of the late Reginald Rawdon Hastings, Volume II* (London, 1930).

— *Report on the manuscripts of the late Reginald Rawdon Hastings, Volume IV* (London, 1947).

Black, W.H., *Docquets of letters patent and other instruments passed under the great seal of King Charles at Oxford in the years 1642–1646* (London, 1837).

Blake, M.J. (ed.), *Blake family records, 1600–1700* (London, 1905).

Blake, Richard, *Sir Richard Blake his speech in the House of Commons at a Grand Committee for the bill against paper petitions: Master Brereton sitting in the chaire Iune XXVIII 1641* (London, 1641).

Bolton, Richard, *The statutes of Ireland, beginning the third yere of K. Edward the second, and continuing vntill the end of the Parliament, begunne in the eleuenth yeare of the reign of our most gratious soueraigne lord King Iames, and ended in the thirteenth yeare of his raigne of England, Fraunce, and Ireland: Newly perused and examined with the Parliament rolls; and diuerse statutes imprinted in this booke, which were not formerly printed in the olde booke. Anno Dom. MDCXXI* (Dublin, 1621).

— *A justice of the peace for Ireland* (Dublin, 1638).

Bonar, A.A. (ed.), *Letters of the Revd Samuel Rutherford* (Edinburgh, 1848).

Boran, Elizabethanne (ed.), *The correspondence of James Ussher, 1600–1656*, 3 vols (Dublin, 2015).

Borlase, Edmund, *The history of the execrable Irish rebellion* (London, 1680).

Bradford, Phil and Alison K. McHardy (eds), *Proctors for parliament: clergy, community and politics, c.1248–1539*, 2 vols (York, 2017–18).

Bradshaw, Brendan (ed.), 'A treatise for the reformation of Ireland, 1554–55', *IJ*, 16 (1981), 299–315.

Bramhall, John, *The serpent salve* (s.l., 1643).

Bray, Gerald (ed.), *Records of convocation: Ireland, 1101–1690* (Woodbridge, 2006).

— *Records of convocation: Ireland, 1690–1869, Part 1* (Woodbridge, 2006).

Breen, Martin, 'The 1626 rental of Thomond property', *North Munster Antiquarian Journal*, 54 (2014), 1–25.

Brereton, William, 'Sir William Brereton's travels in Ireland, 1635' in Caesar Litton Falkiner, *Illustrations of Irish history and topography* (London, 1904), pp 363–407.

Brewer, J.S. and William Bullen (eds), *Calendar of the Carew manuscripts, 1600–1623, preserved in the Archiepiscopal Library at Lambeth, 1515–1624*, 6 vols (London, 1867–73).

Brooks, C.W. (ed.), *The admissions registers of Barnard's Inn, 1620–1869* (London, 1995).

Brown, David and Micheál Ó Siochrú (eds), 'The Cromwellian urban civil surveys, 1653–1659 [with index]', *Archivium Hibernicum*, 69 (2016), 37–150.

Brown, William (ed.), *Yorkshire deeds*, 10 vols (Leeds, 1909–55).

de Burgo, Thomas, *Hibernia Dominicana* (Cologne, 1762).

Byrne, Niall J. (ed.), *The Great Parchment Book of Waterford: Liber antiquissimus Civitatis Waterfordiae* (Dublin, 2007).

Cadell, T. and W. Davies (eds), *A collection of scarce and valuable tracts on the most entertaining subjects: reign of King Charles I* (London, 1810).

Campion, Edmund, *A historie of Ireland written in the yeare 1571* (Dublin, 1809).

Carrigan, William, 'Old Waterford wills', *JWSEIAS*, 9 (1906), 151–2.

— 'Old Waterford wills', *JWSEIAS*, 11 (1908), 91–6.

Caulfield, Richard (ed.), *Council book of the Corporation of Cork* (Guildford, 1876).

— *Council book of the Corporation of Youghal* (Guildford, 1878).

Charles I, *A proclamation for the ease of the subiects in making their compositions for not receiving the order of knighthood, according to the law* (London, 1630).

Charles-Edwards, Gifford (ed.), 'Calendar of petitions to Ormonde in 1649 and 1650', *IG*, 6 (1980–5), 423–44, 577–600, 724–47.

Clarke, Aidan (ed.), *1641 Depositions, Volume IV: Dublin* (Dublin, 2017).

Clarke, Aidan and Bríd McGrath (eds), *The letterbook of George FitzGerald, 16th earl of Kildare* (Dublin, 2013).

Clarke, Aidan, Bríd McGrath and David Edwards (eds), *A lord justice's letterbook: the earl of Cork's letterbook, 1629–1633* (Dublin, forthcoming).

Coates, Wilson H., et al. (eds), *The private journals of the Long Parliament*, 3 vols (New Haven, 1982–92).

Collier, John Payne, Walter Caverley Trevelyan and Charles Edward Trevelyan (eds), *The Trevelyan Papers: Part III* (London, 1872).

Connolly, Philomena (ed.), *Irish exchequer payments, 1270–1446* (Dublin, 1998).

— *Statute rolls of the Irish parliament, Richard III–Henry VIII* (Dublin, 2002).

Conway Davies, James, *Catalogue of manuscripts in the library of the Honourable Society of the Inner Temple*, 2 vols (Oxford, 1972).

Cotton, Robert, *That the kings of England have been pleased usually to consult with their peers in the Great Council, and Commons in Parliament, of marriage, peace and war* (London, 1672).

Cranford, James, *The teares of Ireland* (London, 1642).

Crowley, Tony (ed.), *The politics of language in Ireland, 1366–1922: a sourcebook* (Abingdon, 2002).

Cunningham, Bernadette (ed.), 'Clanricard letters', *The Journal of the Galway Archaeological and Historical Society*, 48 (1996), 162–208.

— *Calendar of State Papers Ireland, Tudor period, 1568–1571* (Dublin, 2010).

Curtis Clayton, Margaret (ed.), *The council book for the province of Munster,* c.*1599–1649* (Dublin, 2008).

D., J., *Special newes from Ireland, newly received in a letter from a gentleman of good worth in Dublin to a friend in London* (London, 1643).

Darcy, Patrick, *An argument delivered by Patricke Darcy, esquire, by the expresse order of the House of Commons in the parliament of Ireland, 9 Junii, 1641* (Waterford, 1643; repr. Dublin, 1764).

Davies, John, *A discoverie of the true causes why Ireland was never entirely subdued, nor brought under obedience of the crowne of England untill the beginning of his majesties happy raigne* (London, 1612).

Davies, John, *Historical tracts* (Dublin, 1787).

Davila, H[enrico] C[aterino], *The historie of the civill warres of France* (London, 1647).

D'Ewes, Simonds (ed.), *The journals of all the parliaments during the reign of Queen Elizabeth* (London, 1682).

Dopping, Anthony (ed.), *Modus tenendi parliamenta* (Dublin, 1692).

Edwards, David (ed.), 'Interrogating Richard Boyle: the Savoy House proceedings of 1599', *Anal. Hib.*, 49 (2018), 79–115.

Edwards, David and Conleth Manning, 'A seventeenth-century map of Inistioge, Co. Kilkenny', *JRSAI*, 131 (2001), 38–55.

Edwards, R.D. (ed.), 'Letter book of Sir Arthur Chichester, 1612–14', *Anal. Hib.*, 8 (1938), 3–178.

Elsynge, Henry, *Modus tenendi parliamentum* (London, 1630).

— *The ancient method and manner of holding parliaments in England* (London, 1660).

— *The ancient method and manner of holding parliaments in England* (3rd ed., London, 1675).

Empey, Mark (ed.), 'The diary of Sir James Ware', *Anal. Hib.*, 45 (2014), 53–146.

— *Early Stuart Irish warrants, 1623–1639: the Falkland and Wentworth administrations* (Dublin, 2015).

Erck, J.C. (ed.), *A repertory of the inrolments on the patent rolls of chancery in Ireland, commencing with the reign of James I* (Dublin, 1846–52).

Falkiner, Caesar Litton (ed.), 'Barnaby Rich's "Remembrances of the state of Ireland"', *Proc. RIA*, 26C (1906–7), 125–42.

Farmer, William, 'A chronicle of Lord Chichester's government of Ireland' in John Lodge, *Desiderata Curiosa Hibernica*, 2 vols (Dublin, 1772), i, pp 151–326.

Fenlon, Jane (ed.), *Goods & chattels: a survey of early household inventories in Ireland* (Kilkenny, 2003).

Fincham, F.W.X. (ed.), 'Letters concerning Sir Maurice Eustace, lord chancellor of Ireland', *EHR*, 35:138 (April, 1920), 251–9.

Fitzgerald, J.J. and Charles MacNeill (eds), 'Documents found at Castlewhite, Co. Cork', *JRSAI*, 60:1 (June, 1930), 79–83.

Fitzgerald, W. and Charles T. Lamacraft (eds), *Some funeral entries of Ireland (from a manuscript in the British Museum)* (Dublin, 1910).

FitzGerald, Walter, 'Notes on the family of Patrick Crosbie of Maryborough, by whom the Seven Septs of Leix were transplanted to Tarbert in the County Kerry in 1608–9', *JRSAI*, sixth series, 13:2 (Dec. 1923), 133–50.

Fletcher, R.J. (ed.), *The pension book of Gray's Inn, 1569–1800*, 3 vols (London, 1901–10).

Fortescue, Faithful, *An account of the Rt. Honourable Sir Arthur Chichester, Lord Belfast, lord deputy of Ireland* (London, 1858).

Foster, Joseph (ed.), *London marriage licences, 1611–1828* (London, 1887).

— *Pedigrees recorded at the heralds' visitations of the counties of Cumberland and Westmorland: made by Richard St George, Norry, king of arms in 1615, and by William Dugdale, Norry, king of arms in 1666* (Carlisle, 1891).

Gernon, Luke, 'Discourse of Ireland, 1620' in Caesar Litton Falkiner, *Illustrations of Irish history and topography* (London, 1904), pp 345–62.

Gilbert, J.T. (ed.), *Calendar of ancient records of Dublin*, 18 vols (Dublin, 1889–1922).

Gillespie, Raymond (ed.), *The vestry records of the parish of St John the Evangelist, Dublin, 1595–1658* (Dublin, 2002).

Great Britain, Commissioners on municipal corporations in Ireland, *Report on municipal corporations in Ireland*, Appendix 1 (London, 1835).

Grelin, Henri, *Ordre Observé En La Convocation, & assemblée des Estats generaux de France, tenuz en la Ville de Paris, en l'Annee mil six cens quatorze, auec les Noms, surnoms, & qualitez des Deputez des trois Ordres, selon comme ils marchent aux ceremonies. Ensemble la diuision des Bailliages en douze, gouuernements, pour opiner esdictes Chambres, ainsi qu'il se peut voir par la carte & figure suiuante* (Paris, 1615).

Gressley, Walsingham, *A letter of newes from Ireland, contayning (among other thinges) the new lord deputies entertainement and taking his place there anno domini, 1633* (London, 1633).

Grimston, Harbottle, *Mr Grimston his speech at the committee sitting in Guildhall on Thuesday the 6. of Ianuary 1641[–2] concerning the breaches of the priviledges of Parliament by breaking open the chambers, studies, and trunks of the Lord Kimbolton and the rest of the members of the House of Commons* (London, 1642).

Griffith, M.C. (ed.), *Calendar of inquisitions formerly in the office of the chief remembrancer of the exchequer* (Dublin, 1991).

Grosart, Alexander B. (ed.), *The Lismore Papers*, 2 series, 10 vols (London, 1886–8).

Hakewill, William, *Modus tenendi parliamentum or the old manner of holding parliaments in England* (London, 1671).

Halliwell-Phillipps, J.O., *The autobiography and correspondence of Sir Simonds D'Ewes, bart: during the reigns of James I and Charles I*, 2 vols (London, 1845).

Hamilton, H.C., et al. (eds), *Calendar of State Papers, Ireland, 1509–1670*, 24 vols (1860–1912).

Hampton, Christopher, *An inquisition of the true church, and those that revolt from it: being a sermon pronounced at the second session of the Parliament* (Dublin, 1622).

Hardy, Thomas Duffus (ed.), *Modus tenendi parliamentum: an ancient treatise on the mode of holding the parliament in England* (London, 1846).

Heffernan, David (ed.), *'Reform' treatises on Tudor Ireland, c.1537–99* (Dublin, 2016).

Hennessy, William H. (ed.), *The Annals of Loch Cé: a chronicle of Irish affairs from AD 1014 to AD 1590*, 2 vols (London, 1871).
Hill, George (ed.), *The Montgomery manuscripts, 1603–1706* (Belfast, 1869).
HMC, *Third Report of the Royal Commission on Historical Manuscripts* (London, 1872).
— *Fourth Report of the Royal Commission on Historical Manuscripts: Part I, Report and Appendix* (London, 1874).
— *Thirteenth Report of the Royal Commission on Historical Manuscripts, Appendix 1: the manuscripts of his grace, the duke of Portland, preserved at Welbeck Abbey* (London, 1891).
— *The manuscripts of the marquis of Ormonde, preserved at the castle, Kilkenny* (London, 1895).
— *Report on manuscripts in various collections, volume III* (London, 1904).
— *Report on Franciscan manuscripts preserved at the Convent, Merchants Quay, Dublin* (Dublin, 1906).
— *Report on the manuscripts of Lord De L'Isle and Dudley preserved at Penshurst Place, Volume 1* (London, 1925).
Hobbes, Thomas, *The history of the civil wars of England from the year 1640 to 1660* (London, 1679).
Hogan, Edmund (ed.), *The description of Ireland and the state thereof as it is at this present, in anno 1598* (Dublin, 1878).
— 'Haynes' observations of the state of Ireland 1600', *Irish Ecclesiastical Record*, 3rd series, 8 (1887), 1112–22; 9 (1888), 54–5, 160–74.
Holinshed, Raphael, *The firste volume of the chronicles of England, Scotlande, and Irelande* (London, 1577).
— *The chronicles of England, Scotland and Ireland* (London, 1587).
Hooker (alias Vowell), John, *The order and vsage of keeping of the parlements in England* ([London], 1572).
Howell, James, *Epistolae Ho-Elianae: familiar letters domestic and foreign* (London, 1645).
Hughes, James L., *Patentee officers in Ireland, 1173–1826* (Dublin, 1960).
Hunter, R.J. (ed.), *'Men and arms': the Ulster settlers, c.1630* (Belfast, 2012).
Imrie, John and John G. Dunbar (eds), *Accounts of the masters of works, for building and repairing royal palaces and castles, volume II: 1616–1649* (Edinburgh, 1982).
Inderwick, F.A. (ed.), *A calendar of the Inner Temple records, 1505–1603* (London, 1896).
Irish Archaeological Society, *Tracts relating to Ireland*, 2 vols (Dublin, 1841–3).
Ireland. *Index to calendar of fiants of the reign of Queen Elizabeth*, 4 vols (Dublin, 1889–90).
Jackson, Brian (ed.), 'A document on the parliament of 1613 from St Isidore's College, Rome', *Anal. Hib.*, 33 (1986), 47–58.
Jennings, Brendan (ed.), *Wadding Papers, 1614–38* (Dublin, 1953).
Knowler, William (ed.), *The earl of Strafford's letters and dispatches*, 2 vols (London, 1739).
Lake, Edward, *Just apology for his sacred majesty* (London, 1642).
Langmead, T.P. (ed.), 'Sir Edward Lake's account of his interviews with Charles I', *Camden Miscellancy*, 4 (London, 1859).
Lascelles, Rowley, *Liber Munerum Publicorum Hiberniae, Vol. 1* (London, 1824).
Lemon, Robert, et al. (ed.), *Calendar of State Papers preserved in the Public Record Office, Domestic Series, 1547–1695*, 81 vols (London, 1856–1972).
Lodge, John, *Desiderata Curiosa Hibernica*, 2 vols (Dublin, 1732).

Lomas, Sophia Crawford (ed.), *Report on the manuscripts of the earl of Egmont*, 2 vols (London, 1905–9).
Lowe, John (ed.), *The letter-book of the earl of Clanricarde, 1643–1647* (Dublin, 1983).
MacLysaght, Edward (ed.), 'O'Grady Papers', *Anal. Hib.*, 15 (1944), 35–61.
— 'Survey of documents in private keeping: first series, Roche Papers', *Anal. Hib.*, 15 (1944), 143–52.
— 'Commonwealth state accounts Ireland, 1650–1656', *Anal. Hib.*, 15 (1944), 227–321.
Maddison, A.R. (ed.), *Lincolnshire pedigrees*, 2 vols (London, 1903).
Manning, Conleth, 'The civil survey of Inistioge and Callan, Co. Kilkenny', *JRSAI*, 128 (1998), 48–73.
Masters, Betty R. (ed.), *Chamber accounts of the sixteenth century* (London, 1984).
Maxwell, Constantia, *Irish history from contemporary sources (1509–1610)* (London, 1923).
McCavitt, John (ed.), 'An unspeakable parliamentary fracas: the Irish House of Commons, 1613', *Anal. Hib.*, 37 (1998), 223, 225–35.
McGrath, Bríd (ed.), *The minute book of the Corporation of Clonmel, 1608–1649* (Dublin, 2006).
— *Acts of the Corporation of Coleraine, 1623–1669* (Dublin, 2017).
— 'Additional Patrick Darcy Papers: letters from Anthony Martin, bishop of Meath, 1632 and to John Bramhall, with two legal opinions, 1661–2', *Anal. Hib.*, 48 (2017), 73–88.
— 'An invitation to an early modern Irish funeral or a celebration: Folger MS X.d.607', *Anal. Hib.* (forthcoming).
McInerney, Luke, 'A 1640 register of the Thomond Papers at Petworth House', *Archivium Hibernicum*, 74 (2021), 27–126.
McLaughlin, Joseph, 'Select documents XLVII: Richard Hadsor's "Discourse" on the Irish state, 1604', *IHS*, 30:119 (May, 1997), 337–53.
McNeill, Charles (ed.), 'Harris: *Collectanea de Rebus Hibernicis*', *Anal. Hib.*, 6 (Nov., 1934), 248–450.
— *The Tanner letters* (Dublin, 1943).
Merick, John, *A compendious collection and breefe abstract of all the auncient English statutes (from the beginning of Magna Charta) which now are in force within this kingdom of Ireland* (Dublin, 1617).
— *A briefe abstract of all the English statutes which are in force with in the realme of Ireland: and is verie usefull for sheriffes, iustices of the peace, escheators, coroners, and other officers in particular, as all other His Maiesties subiectes in generall* (Dublin, 1625).
Mervyn, Audley, *Captaine Audley Mervin's speech delivered in the upper house to the lords in Parliament May 24, 1641: concerning the judicature of the high court of parliament* (London, 1641).
— *Ireland's complaint against Sir George Ratcliffe knight, now prisoner in the gate-house at Westminster, delivered in parliament there by captaine Audley Mervin. VVherein is declared the grievances of that kingdome, occasioned by him, and the late earle of Strafford, the principall cause, why these late troubles are fallen upon them, whereunto is annexed the depositions and articles exhibited against him in parliament* (London, 1641).
— *Sixteene queres propounded by the Parliament of Ireland to the judges of the said kingdome: as also, another speech, made by Captaine Audley Mervin, to the House of Commons, concerning their priviledges, and their exorbitant grievances in that kingdome* (London, 1641).

— *A speech made by Captaine Audley Mervin to the Vpper House of Parliament in Ireland, March 4. 1640: Together with certaine articles (of high treason) against Sir Richard Bolton Lord Chancellor, John Lord Bishop of Derrie, Sir Gerard Lowther, Lord chiefe Justice of the Common-Pleas, and Sir George Radcliffe Knight. unto which is added an humble and just remonstrance of the Parliament* ([London], 1641).

Millar, Oliver (ed.), *The inventories and valuations of the king's goods, 1649–1651* (Glasgow, 1972).

Molyneux, C. and T. Phillipps (eds), *An account of the family and descendants of Sir Thomas Molyneux, kt., chancellor of the exchequer in Ireland* (Evesham, 1820).

de Montagut, Tomàs (ed.), *Practica, forma y estil de celebrar Corts Generals en Cathalunya y materias incidents en aquellas* (Madrid, 1998).

Moody, T.W. and J.G. Simms (eds), *The bishopric of Derry and the Irish Society of London, 1602–1705*, 2 vols (Dublin, 1968).

Morley, Henry (ed.), *Ireland under Elizabeth and James the First* (London, 1890).

de Mornay, Phillipe, *Memoires de Messire Phillippes de Mornay* (s.l., 1624).

Morrin, James (ed.), *Calendar of the patent and close rolls of chancery in Ireland, Henry VIII–Elizabeth*, 3 vols (Dublin, 1861–3).

Mountmorres, R., *The history of the principal transactions of the Irish parliament from the year 1634 to 1666*, 2 vols (London, 1792).

Moynes, Vera (ed.), *Irish Jesuit annual letters, 1604–1674*, 2 vols (Dublin, 2019).

Murray, L.P. (ed.), 'A rent-roll of all the houses and lands belonging to the see of Armagh, 1620', *Archivium Hibernicum*, 8 (1941), 99–120.

Ní Cheallacháin, Máire (ed.), *Filíocht Phádraigín Haicéad* (Baile Átha Cliath, 1962).

Nicholls, K.W. (ed.), 'The Lynch Blosse Papers', *Anal. Hib.*, 29 (1980), 115–218.

— *The O Doyne (Ó Duinn) manuscript* (Dublin, 1983).

— *The Irish fiants of the Tudor sovereigns*, 4 vols (Dublin, 1994).

Northcliffe, C.B., 'Paver's marriage licences (Part IV)', *Yorkshire Archaeological and Topographical Journal*, 10 (1898), 35–50.

O'Clery, Michael and Philip MacDermot (ed.), *The Annals of Ireland* (Dublin, 1846).

O'Donovan, John (ed.), *Annals of the kingdom of Ireland by the Four Masters*, 7 vols (Dublin, 1851).

O'Dowd, Mary (ed.), '"Irish concealed land papers" in the Hastings manuscripts in the Huntington Library, San Marino, California', *Anal. Hib.*, 31 (1984), 69–192.

O'Ferrall, Richard and Robert O'Connell, *Commentarius Rinuccinianus, de sedis apostolicae legatione ad foederatos Hiberniae catholicos per anos 1645–9*, ed. Stanislaus Kavanagh, 6 vols (Dublin, 1932–49).

Ohlmeyer, Jane and Éamonn Ó Ciardha (eds), *The Irish statute staple books, 1596–1687* (Dublin, 1998).

O'Neill, Phelim, *The true demands of the rebells in Ireland* (London, 1641).

O'Sullivan, William (ed.), *The Strafford inquisition of County Mayo* (Dublin, 1958).

de Peguera, Lluís, *Practica, forma y stil de celebrar Corts Generals en Catalvnya* (Barcelona, 1632).

Perceval-Maxwell, Michael and R.J. Hunter, 'Cavan muster roll', *Briefne*, 5:18 (1977–8), 206–22.

Phillips, C.B. (ed.), *Lowther family estate books, 1617–1675* (Woodbridge, 1979).

Pogson, Fiona (ed.), 'Financial accounts of Thomas Wentworth, earl of Strafford and Sir George Radcliffe, 1639–40', *Anal. Hib.*, 48 (2017), 89–168.

Purnell, E.K. and A.B. Hinds (eds), *Report on the manuscripts of the marquess of Downshire*, 4 vols (London, 1924–40).

Quinn, D.B., 'The bills and statutes of the Irish parliaments of Henry VII and Henry VIII', *Anal. Hib.*, 10 (July, 1941), 71–169.

Rankin, Deana (ed.), *Landgartha: a tragie-comedy by Henry Burnell* (Dublin, 2014).

Renwick, W.L. (ed.), *A view of the present state of Ireland by Edmund Spenser* (London, 1934).

Richardson, H.G., 'Irish parliament rolls of the fifteenth century', *EHR*, 58:232 (Oct. 1943), 448–61.

Richardson, H.G. and G.O. Sayles (eds), *Parliaments and councils of medieval Ireland* (Dublin, 1947).

Ridpath, George, *An historical account of the antient rights and power of the parliament of Scotland humbly offer'd to the consideration of the estates, when they come to settle limitations for the next successor* ([Edinburgh], 1703).

Routledge, F.J., 'Journal of the Irish House of Lords in Sir John Perrot's parliament (3 May 1585–13 May 1586)', *EHR*, 29:113 (Jan., 1914), 104–17.

Rushworth, John (ed.), *The tryal of Thomas, earl of Strafford* (2nd ed., London, 1700).

Sarrovira, Michel, *Ceremonial de Corts: obra compilada de Llochs, Autentichs, Lleys Del Principat De Cathalunya, Antichs y pratichs doctors per micer Michel Sarrovira, doctor en quis cun dret, y Ciutada a Honrat, de Barcelona* (Barcelona, 1599).

Scobell, Henry, *Memorials of the method and manner of proceedings in parliament, in passing bills* (London, 1670).

Shaw, W.A. (ed.), *Letters of denization and acts of naturalisation for aliens in England and Ireland, 1603–1700* (Lymington, 1911).

Simington, R.C. (ed.), *The Civil Survey*, 10 vols (Dublin, 1931–61).

– *The transplantation to Connaught, 1654–58* (Dublin, 1970).

Sims, Catherine Strateman, '"The moderne forme of the parliaments of England"', *American Historical Review*, 53:2 (Jan., 1948), 288–305.

Smith, Thomas, *The Commonwealth of England* (London, 1640).

Smith, W.J. (ed.), *Herbert correspondence* (Dublin, 1963).

Steele, Robert (ed.), *Bibliotheca Lindesiana: bibliography of royal proclamations, Vol. II, part 1, Ireland* (Oxford, 1910).

Tallon, Geraldine (ed.), *Court of Claims: submissions and evidence, 1663* (Dublin, 2006).

Temple, John, *The Irish rebellion: or, an history of the beginnings and first progresse of the general rebellion raised within the kingdom of Ireland* (London, 1646).

Thane, J., *British autography: a collection of fac-similies of the hand writing of royal and illustrious personages* (London, *c.*1788–93).

Thornton, Alice, *The autobiography of Mrs Alice Thornton of East Newton, Co. York* (Durham, 1875).

Treadwell, Victor (ed.), *The Irish Commission of 1622: an investigation of the Irish administration 1615–1622, and its consequences, 1623–1624* (Dublin, 2006).

United Kingdom, Parliament, *Accounts and papers related to representation* (s.l., 1832).

Ussher, James, *The power communicated by God to the prince* (London, 1661).

du Vair, Guillaume, *Arrest svr qvelqves qvestions notables prononcez en robbe rovge au Parlement de Prouence* (Paris, 1606).

Vallancey, Charles, *Collectanea de rebus Hibernica* (Dublin, 1774).

Walkley, Thomas, *A catalogve of the names of the knights for the counties, citizens, burgesses for the boroughs and barons for the ports for the House of Commons for this parliament, begune at Westminster the 17 of March 1627* (London, 1628).
Webster, W.F. (ed.), *Nottinghamshire hearth tax, 1664, 1674* (Nottingham, 1988).
Whitaker, T.D. (ed.), *The life and original correspondence of Sir George Radcliffe* (London, 1810).
White, Thomas, *Aviso del estado en que al presente estan las cosas de los Catholicos en el Reyno de Irlanda* (Salamanca, 1611).
Wilkinson, John, *An easie and plain method for the keeping of a court leet* (London, 1618).
— *A treatise collected out of the statutes of this kingdom concerning the office and authority of coroners and sheriffs* (London, 1618).
Wood, Herbert (ed.), *Registers of the parish of St Catherine, Dublin, 1636–1715* (Dublin, 2003).
Young, Robert Magill, *The town book of the Corporation of Belfast, 1613–1816* (Belfast, 1892).

SECONDARY SOURCES

Agnew, Hugh, *The Czechs and the lands of the Bohemian crown* (Stanford, 2008).
Ainsworth, John, 'Survey of documents in private keeping: third series', *Anal. Hib.*, 25 (1967), 1–273.
Anguez, E.G.L., *Histoire des assemblées politiques des réformés de France (1573–1622)* (Geneva, 1970).
Armstrong, Robert, *Protestant war: the 'British' of Ireland and the wars of the three kingdoms* (Manchester, 2005).
Atkins, Martyn, 'Persuading the House: the use of the Commons' journals as a source of precedent' in Paul Evans (ed.), *Essays on the history of parliamentary procedure, in honour of Thomas Erskine May* (London, 2017), pp 69–86.
Baker, Phillip, '"But private notes for my own memory"? Parliamentary diaries, parliamentary history and the politics of information in early Stuart England', *Parl. Hist.*, 39:3 (Oct., 2020), 405–22.
Ball, F.E., *A history of the county Dublin*, 6 vols (Dublin, 1902–20).
— *The judges in Ireland, 1221–1921*, 2 vols (London, 1926).
Ball, Norman, 'Representation in the English House of Commons: the new boroughs, 1485–1640', *PER*, 15:1 (1995), 117–24.
Barnard, Toby C., 'Lawyers and the law in later seventeenth-century Ireland', *IHS*, 28:111 (May, 1993), 256–82.
— *Cromwellian Ireland: English government and reform in Ireland, 1649–1660* (Oxford, 2000).
Beckett, J.C., *Protestant dissent in Ireland, 1687–1780* (London, 1948).
Bellewes, G.O., 'Robert Goodwin of Derry', *JRSAI*, 5th series, 36:4 (Dec., 1906), 422–3.
Bennett, George, *The history of Bandon and the principal towns in the west riding of County Cork* (Cork, 1869).
Berry, H.F., 'Sheriffs of the County Cork: Henry III to 1660', *JRSAI*, 5th series, 35:1 (1905), 39–52.
— 'Notes on a statement dated 1634, regarding St Thomas' Court and St Katherine's Churchyard, Dublin', *JRSAI*, fifth series, 37:4 (Dec., 1907), 393–6.

Bewley, E.T., 'Some notes on the Lowthers who held judicial office in Ireland in the seventeenth century', *Transactions of the Cumberland and Westmorland Antiquarian and Archaeological Society*, new series, 2 (1902), 1–10.

Blackall, Henry, 'The Galweys of Munster', *JCHAS*, 71 (1966), 138–58.

— 'The Galweys of Munster: Galway of Kinsale and Limerick', *JCHAS*, 72 (1967), 122–57.

Blake Butler, T., 'The officers of arms of Ireland', *IG*, 2:1 (Oct., 1943), 2–12.

Bond, M.F., *A short guide to the records of parliament* (London, 1973).

Bottigheimer, Karl S., 'The Restoration land settlement in Ireland: a structural view', *IHS*, 18:69 (March, 1972), 1–21.

Boucoyannis, Deborah, *Kings as judges: power, justice and the origins of parliament* (Cambridge, 2021).

Bowen, Lloyd, 'Wales at Westminster: parliament, principality and pressure groups, 1542–1601', *Parl. Hist.*, 22:2 (2003), 107–20.

Braddick, Michael J., *Parliamentary taxation in seventeenth-century England: local administration and response* (Woodbridge, 1994).

— *The nerves of state: taxation and the financing of the English state, 1558–1714* (Manchester, 1996).

Bradshaw, Brendan, 'The opposition to the ecclesiastical legislation in the Irish reformation parliament', *IHS*, 16:63 (March, 1969), 285–303.

— 'The beginnings of modern Ireland' in Brian Farrell (ed.), *The Irish parliamentary tradition* (Dublin, 1973), pp 68–87.

— *The Irish constitutional revolution of the sixteenth century* (Cambridge, 1979).

— *'And so began the Irish nation': nationality, national consciousness and nationalism in pre-modern Ireland* (Farnham, 2015).

Brady, Ciaran, 'Conservative subversives: the community of the Pale and the Dublin administration, 1556–1586' in Patrick J. Corish (ed.), *Historical Studies XV: radicals, rebels and establishments* (Belfast, 1985), pp 11–32.

— 'Court, castle and country: the framework of government in Tudor Ireland' in Ciaran Brady and Raymond Gillespie (eds), *Natives and newcomers: essays on the making of Irish colonial society, 1534–1641* (Dublin, 1986), pp 22–49.

— *The chief governors: the rise and fall of reform government in Tudor Ireland, 1536–1588* (Cambridge, 1994).

— 'A viceregal nervous breakdown? The collapse of the earl of Sussex in 1563' in Terence Dooley, Mary-Ann Lyons and Salvador Ryan (eds), *The historian as detective: uncovering Irish pasts, essays in honour of Raymond Gillespie* (Dublin, 2021), pp 69–73.

Brand, Paul, 'Ireland and the literature of the early common law', *IJ*, 16 (1981), 95–113.

— 'Irish law students and lawyers in late medieval England', *IHS*, 32:126 (2000), 161–73.

— 'Sir John Davies: law reporter or self-publicist?', *IJ*, new series, 43 (2008), 1–20.

Brink, Jean R., 'Sir John Davies: lawyer and poet' in Thomas Herron and Michael Potterton (eds), *Ireland in the Renaissance, c.1540–1660* (Dublin, 2007), pp 88–104.

Brown, Michael, et al. (eds), *The Irish Act of Union 1801: bicentennial essays* (Dublin, 2003).

Burtchaell, G.D., 'The family of Rothe of Kilkenny', *Journal of the Royal Historical and Archaeological Association of Ireland*, 5th series, 7:67 (1886), 501–37.

— *Genealogical memoirs of the members of parliament for the county and city of Kilkenny* (Dublin, 1888).

Burke, B., *Irish family records* (5th ed., London, 1976).

Burke, William, *History of Clonmel* (Waterford, 1906).
Burner, Sandra A., *James Shirley: a study in literary coteries and patronage in seventeenth century England* (Lanham, New Jersey, 1988).
Butterwick, Richard, *The Polish-Lithuanian Commonwealth: light and flame* (New Haven, 2021).
Byrne, Joseph, 'News not worth relating: the hanging of Walter Evers, 10 June 1642', *Ríocht na Mídhe*, 33 (2022), 85–91.
Caball, Marc, '*Pairlement Chloinne Tomáis I*: a reassessment', *Éigse*, 27 (1993), 47–57.
— 'The Bible in early modern Ireland: tradition, collaboration and alienation' in Kevin Killeen, Helen Smith and Rachel Willie (eds), *The Oxford handbook of the Bible in early modern England,* c.*1530–1700* (Oxford, 2015), pp 332–49.
Cairns, John W., 'Advocates hats, Roman law and admission to the Scots Bar, 1580–1812', *Journal of Legal History*, 20:2 (1999), 24–61.
Canavan, Tony, 'Royal Society of Antiquaries of Ireland library', *History Ireland*, 25:4 (July/Aug., 2017), 54–5.
Canny, Nicholas, *The Elizabethan conquest of Ireland: a pattern established, 1565–76* (Hassocks, 1976).
— 'English migration into and across the Atlantic during the seventeenth and eighteenth centuries' in Nicholas Canny (ed.), *Europeans on the move: studies on European migration, 1500–1800* (Oxford, 1994), pp 39–75.
— *Making Ireland British, 1580–1650* (Oxford, 2001).
Capdeferro, Josep, 'Sessions plenàries versus comissions de treball a les Corts catalanes del segle XVII' in R. Ferrero and L. Guia, *Corts i parlaments de la Corona d'Aragó: unes instituciones emblemàtiques en una monarquia composta* (Valencia, 2008), pp 307–27.
— 'Promoció, edició i difusió d'obres jurídiques a Catalunya a cavall dels segles XVI i XVII', *Ivs Fvgit*, 15 (Zaragoza, 2009), 537–59.
— 'Commissioners, ad-hoc committees and negotiators in the *Cortes* of Catalonia, 1701–02', *PER*, 39:3 (2019), 328–39.
Capp, Bernard S., *England's culture wars: Puritan reformation and its enemies in the interregnum, 1649–1660* (Oxford, 2012).
Canning, Ruth, *The Old English in early modern Ireland: the Palesmen and the Nine Years War, 1594–1603* (Woodbridge, 2019).
Carroll, Stephen, 'The Dublin parliamentary elections, 1613' in William Sheehan and Maura Cronin (eds), *Riotous assemblies: rebels, riots and revolts in Ireland* (Cork, 2011), pp 50–63.
Cathcart, Alison, 'James V, king of Scotland – and Ireland?' in Seán Duffy (ed.), *The world of the galloglass* (Dublin, 2007), pp 144–68.
—'Scots and Ulster: the late medieval context' in William P. Kelly and John R. Young (eds), *Scotland and the Ulster plantation* (Dublin, 2009), pp 62–77.
Chartier, Roger, 'La convocation aux Etats de 1614, note sur les formes politiques' in Roger Chartier and Denis Ricet (eds), *Representation & vouloir politiques autour des Etats-Generaux de 1614* (Paris, 1982), pp 53–61.
Chartier, Roger and Denis Richet (eds), *Representation & vouloir politiques autour des Etats-Generaux de 1614* (Paris, 1982).
Cherry, Jonathan, 'Colonial appropriation of Gaelic space: creating the first Ulster town', *Irish Geography*, 20:2 (2007) 112–27.

Clarke, Aidan, '28 November 1634: a detail of Strafford's administration', *JRSAI*, 93:2 (1963), 161–7.
— 'The policies of the "Old English" in parliament, 1640–41' in J.L. McCracken, *Historical Studies V: papers read before the sixth conference of Irish historians* (London, 1965).
— *The Old English in Ireland, 1625–42* (London, 1966).
— 'The history of Poynings' Law, 1615–41', *IHS*, 18:70 (1972), 207–22.
— 'The Irish economy, 1600–60' in T.W. Moody, et al. (eds), *A new history of Ireland*, 9 vols (Oxford, 1977–2005), iii, pp 168–86.
— 'Review: *Sir John Davies and the conquest of Ireland: a study in legal imperialism*, by Hans S. Pawlisch', *IHS*, 25:97 (May, 1986), 99–101.
— 'Sir Piers Crosby, 1590–1646: Wentworth's "tawney ribbon"', *IHS*, 26:102 (1988), 142–60.
— 'Colonial constitutional attitudes in Ireland, 1640–60', *Proc. RIA*, 90C (1990), 357–75.
— 'Patrick Darcy and the constitutional relationship between Ireland and Britain' in Jane Ohlmeyer (ed.), *Political thought in seventeenth-century Ireland: kingdom or colony* (Cambridge, 2000), pp 35–55.
— *Prelude to restoration in Ireland: the end of the Commonwealth, 1659–1660* (Cambridge, 2004).
Clarke, M.V., 'The manuscripts of the Irish *Modus tenendi parliamentum*', *EHR*, 48:192 (Oct., 1933), 576–600.
Cokayne, G.E. (ed.), *Complete baronetage*, 6 vols (London, 1900–9).
Cokayne, G.E. and V. Gibbs (eds), *Complete peerage of England, Scotland, Ireland, Great Britain and the United Kingdom*, 13 vols (London, 1910–40).
Collins, J.B., 'Noble political ideology and the Estates General of Orléans and Pontoise: French republicanism', *Historical Reflections/Réflexions Historiques*, 27:2 (2001), 219–40.
Copinger, Walter A., *History of the Copingers or Coppingers of the county of Cork, Ireland, and the counties of Suffolk and Kent, England* (Manchester, 1884).
Cosgrove, Art, 'Parliament and the Anglo-Irish community: the declaration of 1460' in Art Cosgrove and J.I. McGuire (eds), *Historical Studies XIV: parliament and community* (Belfast, 1983), pp 25–41.
Costello, Kevin, *The Court of Admiralty of Ireland, 1575–1893* (Dublin, 2011).
Cotton, Henry, *Fasti ecclesiae Hibernicae: the succession of the prelates and members of the cathedral bodies in Ireland*, 6 vols (Dublin, 1847–78).
Craig, Maurice, *Irish bookbindings, 1600–1800* (London, 1954).
Cramsie, John, 'Crown finance and reform: the legacy of the Addled Parliament' in Stephen Clucas and Rosalind Davies (eds), *The crisis of 1614 and the Addled Parliament: literary and historical perspectives* (Aldershot, 2003), pp 37–48.
Crawford, Jon G., *Anglicizing the government of Ireland: the Irish privy council and the expansion of Tudor rule, 1556–1578* (Dublin, 1993).
— *A Star Chamber court in Ireland: the Court of Castle Chamber, 1571–1641* (Dublin, 2005).
Cregan, Donal F., 'Some members of the Confederation of Kilkenny' in Sylvester O'Brien (ed.), *Measgra i gCuimhne Michíl Uí Chléirigh* (Dublin, 1944), pp 34–44.
— 'Irish Catholic admissions to the Inns of Court, 1558–1625', *IJ*, new series, 95 (1970), 95–114.
— 'Irish recusant lawyers in politics in the reign of James I', *IJ*, new series, 95 (1970), 306–20.

Crofton, Henry Thomas, *Crofton memoirs: an account of John Crofton, of Ballymurry, Co. Roscommon, Queen Elizabeth's escheator-general of Ireland, and of his ancestors and descendants* (York, 1911).

Crooks, Peter, 'The background to the arrest of the fifth earl of Kildare and Sir Christopher Preston in 1418: a missing membrane', *Anal. Hib.*, 40 (2007), 1–15.

— 'Representation and dissent: "Parliamentarianism" and the structure of politics in colonial Ireland', *EHR*, 125:512 (Feb., 2010), 1–34.

— 'The structure of politics in theory and practice, 1210–1541' in Brendan Smith (ed.), *The Cambridge history of Ireland*: vol. 1, *600–1550* (Cambridge, 2018), pp 441–68.

— 'Comital Ireland, 1333–1534' in David Crouch and Hugh Doherty (eds), *The earl in medieval Britain* (Woodbridge, forthcoming).

Cullen, W.D., *Parliament House: a short history and guide* (Edinburgh, 1992).

Cunningham, Bernadette, 'Native culture and political change in Ireland 1580–1640' in Ciaran Brady and Raymond Gillespie (eds), *Natives and newcomers: essays on the making of Irish colonial society, 1534–1641* (Dublin, 1986), pp 148–70.

— 'Natives and newcomers in Mayo, 1560–1603' in Raymond Gillespie and Gerard Moran (eds), *'A various country': essays in Mayo history, 1500–1900* (Westport, 1987), pp 24–43.

— *The world of Geoffrey Keating: history, myth and religion in seventeenth-century Ireland* (Dublin, 2000).

Cunningham, Jack, *James Ussher and John Bramhall: the theology and politics of two Irish ecclesiastics of the seventeenth century* (Aldershot, 2007).

Cunningham, John, *Conquest and land in Ireland: the transplantation to Connacht, 1649–1680* (Woodbridge, 2011).

Cusack, M.F., *A history of the kingdom of Kerry* (Dublin, 1995).

Damen, Mario, et al., *Political representation: communities, ideas and institutions in Europe (c.1200–c.1690)* (Leiden, 2018).

Darcy, Eamon, 'Social order in the 1641 rebellion' in Eamon Darcy, et al. (eds), *The 1641 Depositions and the Irish rebellion* (London, 2012), pp 97–111.

Dean, David, 'Public space, private affairs: committees, petitions and lobbies in the early modern English parliament' in Christopher Kyle and Jason Peacey (eds), *Parliament at work: parliamentary committees, political power and public access in early modern England* (Woodbridge, 2002), pp 169–78.

Dennehy, Coleman A., 'Some manuscript alternatives to the printed Irish parliamentary journals', *PER*, 30:2 (2010), 129–42.

— 'Speakers in the 17th-century Irish parliament' in Paul Seaward (ed.), *Speakers and the speakership: presiding officers and the management of business from the Middle Ages to the 21st century: a special issue of Parliamentary History*, 29:1 (Chichester, 2010), pp 62–74.

— 'Representation in later medieval and early modern Ireland' in Mario Damen, et al. (eds), *Political representation: communities, ideas and institutions (c.1200–c.1690)* (Leiden, 2018), pp 85–105.

— 'Appointments to the bench in early Restoration Ireland' in Coleman A. Dennehy (ed.), *Law and revolution in Ireland: law and lawyers before, during and after the Cromwellian interregnum* (Dublin, 2019), pp 265–88.

— *The Irish parliament, 1613–1689: the evolution of a colonial institution* (Manchester, 2019).

— 'The Irish parliament after the rebellion, 1642–48' in Patrick Little (ed.), *Ireland in crisis: war, politics and religion, 1641–50* (Manchester, 2019), pp 100–18.

— 'Parliamentary committees in seventeenth-century Ireland: a brief introduction', *PER*, 39:3 (2019), 316–27.
Dolley, Michael, 'The Irish coinage, 1534–1691' in T.W. Moody, et al. (eds), *A new history of Ireland*, 9 vols (Oxford, 1977–2005), iii, pp 408–19.
Donovan O'Sullivan, Mary Josephine, *Old Galway: the history of a Norman colony in Ireland* (Galway, 1942).
Drake, W.R., *Fasciculus Mervinensis: being notes historical, genealogical and heraldic of the family of Mervyn* (London, 1873).
Duccini, Hélène, *Faire voir, faire croire: l'opinion publique sous Louis XIII* (Paris, 2003).
Dudley-Edwards, R. and T.W. Moody, 'The history of Poyning's Law: part 1, 1494–1615', *IHS*, 2:8 (Sept., 1941), pp 415–24.
Duffy, Seán (ed.), *Medieval Ireland: an encyclopaedia* (London, 2005).
Dutton, Matthew, *The office and authority of sheriffs, under-sheriffs, deputies, county-clerks, and coroners, in Ireland* (Dublin, 1721).
Dutton, Richard, 'The Werburgh Street Theater, Dublin' in Adam Zucker and Andrew B. Farmer (eds), *Localizing Caroline drama: politics and economics of the early modern English stage, 1625–1642* (Basingstoke, 2006), pp 129–55.
Edwards, David, *The Ormond lordship in County Kilkenny, 1515–1642: the rise and fall of Butler feudal power* (Dublin, 2003).
— 'Fashioning service in a renaissance state: the official journals of the Elizabethan viceroys in Ireland' in Brendan Dooley (ed.), *Renaissance now: the value of the Renaissance past in contemporary culture* (Oxford, 2014), pp 139–64.
— 'Richard Boyle's private army: the creation of a colonial security force in early Stuart Munster' in David Edwards and Colin Rynne (eds), *The colonial world of Richard Boyle, first earl of Cork* (Dublin, 2018), pp 223–44.
— 'From land-thief to planter: Kerry transactions and the rise of Richard Boyle, first earl of Cork' in Maurice J. Bric (ed.), *Kerry: history and society* (Dublin, 2020), pp 141–63.
Elliott, J.H., *The revolt of the Catalans: a study in the decline of Spain* (Cambridge, 1984).
Ellis, Steven G., 'Parliament and community in Yorkist and Tudor Ireland' in Art Cosgrove and J.I. McGuire (eds), *Historical Studies XIV: parliament and community* (Belfast, 1983), pp 43–68.
— *Ireland in the age of the Tudors, 1447–1603: English expansion and the end of Gaelic rule* (London, 2014).
— 'Citizenship and the state in Ireland: from medieval lordship to early modern kingdom' in Steven G. Ellis (ed.), *Enfranchising Ireland? Identity, citizenship and state* (Dublin, 2018), pp 19–32.
Empey, Adrian, *Gowran, Co. Kilkenny: custom and conflict in a baronial town* (Dublin, 2015).
Empey, Mark, 'Power, prerogative and the politics of Sir Thomas Wentworth in England and Ireland', *The Historical Journal*, 65:2 (2022), 275–96.
Englefield, Dermott, *The printed records of the parliament of Ireland, 1613–1800* (London, 1978).
— 'Printing the journal of the Irish House of Commons' in Harry Cobb (ed.), *Parliamentary history, libraries and records* (London, 1981), pp 33–43.
Epstein, Joel J., *Francis Bacon: a political biography* (Athens, OH, 1977).
Evans, Paul (ed.), *Essays on the history of parliamentary procedure, in honour of Thomas Erskine May* (Bloomsbury, 2017).

Falkiner, Caesar Litton, 'The counties of Ireland: an historical sketch of their origin, constitution and gradual delimitation', *Proc. RIA*, 24C (1902–4), 169–94.

— 'The parliament of Ireland under the Tudor sovereigns: with some notices of the speakers of the Irish House of Commons', *Proc. RIA*, 25C (1904), 508–41.

— 'The parliament of Ireland under the Tudor sovereigns: supplementary paper', *Proc. RIA*, 25C (1904), 553–66.

— *Essays relating to Ireland: biographical, historical and topographical* (London, 1909).

Ferguson, J.F., 'The "mere English" and the "mere Irish"', *Trans. Kilkenny Arch. Soc.*, 1 (1849–51), 509–10.

Ferrell, L.A., 'Preaching and English parliaments in the 1620s' in Chris R. Kyle (ed.), *Managing Tudor and Stuart parliaments: essays in memory of Michael Graves: Parliamentary History Yearbook*, 34:1 (Chichester, 2015), pp 142–54.

Ferrall, S.A., *An exposition of the law of parliament as it relates to the power and privileges of the Commons House* (London, 1837).

Feuchter, Jörg and Johannes Helmrath, 'Oratory and representation: the rhetorical culture of political assemblies, 1300–1600', *PER*, 29:1 (2009), 53–66.

FitzGerald, Walter, 'Castletown and its owners, with a genealogical table of the Sutton family and a portrait of the Rt. Hon. Thomas Conolly, d. 1803', *The Journal of the County Kildare Archaeological Society*, 2 (1896–9), 361–78.

Fletcher, Alan J., 'The civic pageantry of Corpus Christi in fifteenth- and sixteenth-century Dublin', *IESH*, 23:1 (1996), 73–96.

— *Drama, performance and polity in pre-Cromwellian Ireland* (Cork, 2000).

Fletcher, Christopher, 'Political representation' in Christopher Fletcher, et al. (eds), *Government and political life in England and France,* c.*1300*–c.*1500* (Cambridge, 2015), pp 217–39.

Ford, Alan, 'The Protestant reformation in Ireland' in Ciaran Brady and Raymond Gillespie (eds), *Natives and newcomers: essays on the making of Irish colonial society, 1534–1641* (Dublin, 1986), pp 50–74.

Foster, Elizabeth Read, 'The painful labour of Mr Elsyng', *Transactions of the American Philosophical Society*, new series, 62:8 (1972), 1–69.

— 'Procedure and the House of Lords in the seventeenth century', *Proceedings of the American Philosophical Society*, 126:3 (June, 1982), 183–7.

— *The House of Lords, 1603–1649: structure, procedures and the nature of its business* (Chapel Hill, NC, 1983).

Fox, Harold G., 'The earl of Strafford and monopolies in Ireland' in Harold G. Fox, *Monopolies and patents: a study of the history and future of the patent monopoly* (Toronto, 1947), pp 146–50.

French, F.J., 'Nepotists and sinecurists: a history of Ulster's Office 1552–1943', *IG*, 10:3 (2000), 333–71.

Frost, Robert, 'The roads not taken: liberty, sovereignty and the idea of the republic in Poland–Lithuania and the British Isles, 1550–1660', *Transactions of the Royal Historical Society*, 32 (2022), 93–112.

Froude, James Anthony, *The English in Ireland in the eighteenth century*, 2 vols (London, 1873).

Garnham, Neal, *The courts, crime and the criminal law in Ireland, 1692–1760* (Dublin, 1996).

Giancarlo, Matthew, *Parliament and literature in late medieval England* (Cambridge, 2010).

Gibney, John, *A short history of Ireland, 1500–2000* (London, 2018).

Gibson, A.J.S. and T.C. Smout, *Prices, food and wages in Scotland, 1500–1780* (Cambridge, 2007).

Gilbert, J.T., *A history of the city of Dublin*, 3 vols (Dublin, 1854–9).

Gilbert, J.T. (ed.), *A contemporary history of affairs in Ireland from 1641–1652*, 3 vols (Dublin, 1879–80).

Gilbert, J.T. and Richard Bellings, *History of the Irish Confederation and the war in Ireland, 1641, containing a narrative of affairs of Ireland*, 7 vols (Dublin, 1882–91).

Gillespie, Raymond, 'The murder of Arthur Champion and the 1641 rising in Fermanagh', *Clogher Record*, 14:3 (1993), 52–66.

— 'Political ideas and their social contexts' in Jane Ohlmeyer (ed.), *Political thought in seventeenth-century Ireland: kingdom or colony* (Cambridge, 2000), pp 107–27.

— *Seventeenth-century Ireland* (Dublin, 2006).

— 'Preaching the reformation in early modern Ireland' in Peter McCullough, et al. (eds), *The Oxford handbook of the early modern sermon* (Oxford, 2011), pp 287–302.

Godfrey, A.M., *Civil justice in Renaissance Scotland: the origins of a central court* (Leiden, 2009).

Goodare, Julian, 'Parliamentary taxation in Scotland, 1560–1603', *Scottish Historical Review*, 68:185 (April, 1989), 23–52.

— 'The Scottish parliament of 1621', *The Historical Journal*, 38:1 (1995), 29–51.

— 'The admission of lairds to the Scottish parliament', *EHR*, 116:469 (2001), 1103–33.

— The parliament of Scotland to 1707' in Clyve Jones (ed.), *A short history of parliament: England, Great Britain, the United Kingdom, Ireland and Scotland* (Woodbridge, 2012), pp 301–20.

Goppold, Uwe, 'Norms, symbols and modes of everyday decision-making in early modern cities: the examples of Zurich and Munster' in Rudolf Schlögl, et al. (eds), *Urban elections and decision-making in early modern Europe, 1500–1800* (Newcastle-upon-Tyne, 2020), pp 52–61.

Graves, Michael, 'The management of the Elizabethan House of Commons: the council's men of business', *Parl. Hist.*, 2 (1983), pp 1–38.

— *The parliaments of early modern Europe* (Harlow, 2001).

Grazebrook, H.S., *The heraldry of Worcestershire*, 2 vols (London, 1873).

Greaves, Richard L., *God's other children: Protestant nonconformists and the emergence of denominational churches in Ireland* (Stanford, 1997).

Greene, Jack P. (ed.), *Exclusionary empire: English liberty overseas, 1600–1900* (Cambridge, 2010).

Gribbon, H.D., 'Journals of the Irish House of Commons', *An Leabharlann,* 2nd series, 2:2 (1985), 51–6.

Gross, Charles, 'The court of pie powder', *The Quarterly Journal of Economics*, 20:2 (Feb., 1906), 231–49.

Gruenfelder, John K., 'The electoral patronage of Sir Thomas Wentworth, earl of Strafford, 1614–1640', *The Journal of Modern History*, 49:4 (Dec., 1977), 557–74.

Hadfield, Andrew, 'War poetry and counsel in early modern Ireland' in Brendan Kane and Valerie McGowan-Doyle (eds), *Elizabeth I and Ireland* (Cambridge, 2011), pp 239–60.

— 'The will of William Wiseman, Edmund Spenser's son-in-law', *Notes and Queries*, 60:1 (2013), 37–40.

— 'Culture and anarchy in mid-seventeenth-century Ireland: the strange case of James Shirley at Werburgh Street', *Literature Compass*, 15:10 (2018), e12493.

Hammer, Paul, 'The use of scholarship: the secretariat of Robert Devereux, second earl of Essex, *c.*1585–1601', *EHR*, 149:430 (1994), 26–51.

Hannay, R.K. and G.P.H. Watson, 'The building of the parliament house', *Book of the Old Edinburgh Club*, 13 (1924), 1–78.

Hardiman, James, *History of the town and county of Galway* (Dublin, 1820).

Harrison, Brian and H.C.G. Matthew (eds), *The Oxford dictionary of national biography*, 60 vols (Oxford, 2004).

Hart, A.R., 'Audley Mervyn: lawyer or politician?' in W.N. Osborough (ed.), *Explorations in law and history: Irish Legal History Society discourses, 1988–1994* (Dublin, 1995), pp 83–105.

— *A history of the king's serjeants at law in Ireland: honour rather than advantage?* (Dublin, 2000).

Hasler, P.W. (ed.), *The history of parliament: the House of Commons, 1558–1603*, 3 vols (London, 1981).

Hawkyard, Alasdair D., 'The wages of members of parliament, 1509–1558', *Parl. Hist.*, 6:2 (Oct., 1987), 302–11.

— 'The enfranchisement of constituencies, 1509–1558', *Parl. Hist.*, 10 (1991), 1–25.

— 'From Painted Chamber to St Stephen's Chapel: the meeting places of the House of Commons at Westminster until 1603', *Parl. Hist.*, 21:1 (2002), 62–84.

— 'The Tudor speakers, 1485–1601: choosing, status, work', *Parl. Hist.*, 29:1 (Feb., 2010), 22–48.

— 'Inigo Jones, the surveyor of the works and the "Parliament House"', *Parl. Hist.*, 32:1 (2013), 16–59.

— 'The journals, the clerks of the parliaments and the under-clerks, 1485–1601', *Parl. Hist.*, 33:3 (2014), 389–421.

— *The House of Commons, 1509–1558: personnel procedure, precedent and change* (Oxford, 2016).

Hayden, J.M., *France and the Estates General of 1614* (Cambridge, 1974).

Hayes-McCoy, Gerard, 'The completion of the Tudor conquest and the advance of the Counter-Reformation, 1571–1603' in T.W. Moody, et al. (eds), *A new history of Ireland*, 9 vols (Oxford, 1977–2005), iii, pp 94–141.

Hazard, Benjamin, *Faith and patronage: the political career of Flaithrí Ó Maolchonaire, c.1560–1629* (Dublin, 2009).

Healy, William, *History and antiquities of Kilkenny* (Kilkenny, 1893).

Heffernan, David, 'Corruption and crown government in late Elizabethan Ireland', *Proc. RIA*, 122C (2022), 1–25.

Henning, B.D. (ed.), *The history of parliament: the House of Commons, 1660–1690* (London, 1983).

Hewer, Stephen, 'Free Gaelic people in English Ireland, *c.*1250–*c.*1327', *History Ireland*, 23:6 (Nov.–Dec., 2015), 14–17.

Higgins, Patricia, 'The reactions of women, with special reference to women petitioners' in Brian Manning (ed.), *Politics, religion and the English civil war* (New York, 1973), pp 179–222.

Hirst, Derek, *The representative of the people? Voters and voting in England under the early Stuarts* (Cambridge, 1975).

Hobsbawm, Eric, 'The general crisis of the European economy in the 17th century', *Past & Present*, 5 (May, 1954), 33–53.

Horan, P.F., 'Castledermot 1264: the first Irish parliament', *History Ireland*, 22:3 (May–June, 2014), 14–15.

Hore, Philip Herbert, *History of the town and county of Wexford*, 6 vols (London, 1900–11).

Hughes, James, 'Sir Edmund Butler of the Dullogh, knight', *JRSAI*, 4th series, 1:1 (1870), 153–92, 211–31.

Hunneyball, Paul M., 'The development of parliamentary privilege, 1604–29' in Chris R. Kyle (ed.), *Managing Tudor and Stuart parliaments: essays in memory of Michael Graves* (Chichester, 2015), pp 111–28.

Hunter, R.J., 'Towns in the Ulster Plantation', *Studia Hibernica*, 11 (1971), 40–79.

— *The Ulster plantation in the counties of Armagh and Cavan, 1608–41* (Belfast, 2012).

Jago, Charles, 'Habsburg absolutism and the *Cortes* of Castile', *American Historical Review*, 86:2 (April, 1981), 307–26.

Jansson, Maija (ed.), *Realities of representation: state building in early modern Europe and European America* (London, 2007).

Jefferies, Henry A., 'The Irish parliament of 1560: the Anglican reforms authorized', *IHS*, 26:102 (Nov., 1988), 128–41.

Johnston, W.J., 'The parliament of the Pale', *Law Quarterly Review*, 34:135 (July, 1918), 291–303.

Jones, Clyve, 'Accommodation in the Painted Chamber for conferences between the Lords and Commons from 1600 to 1834', *Parl. Hist.*, 33:2 (2014), 342–57.

Jurkowski, Maureen, Carrie L. Smith and David Crook, *Lay taxes in England and Wales, 1188–1688* (London, 1998).

Kane, Brendan, *The politics and culture of honour in Britain and Ireland, 1541–1641* (Cambridge, 2010).

— 'Scandal, Wentworth's deputyship and the breakdown of Stuart honour politics' in Brian MacCuarta (ed.), *Reshaping Ireland, 1550–1700: colonization and its consequences, essays presented to Nicholas Canny* (Dublin, 2011), pp 147–86.

Kearney, Hugh F., 'The Irish wine trade, 1614–15', *IHS*, 9:36 (Sept., 1955), 400–42.

— *Strafford in Ireland: a study in absolutism* (Manchester, 1959).

Keeler, Mary Frear, *The Long Parliament, 1640–1641: a biographical study of its members* (Philadelphia, 1954).

— 'The emergence of standing committees for privileges and returns', *Parl. Hist.*, 1 (1982), 25–46.

— 'The committee for privileges of the House of Commons, 1604–1610 and 1614', *Parl. Hist.*, 13:2 (1994), 147–69.

Kelly, James, 'The making of law in eighteenth–century Ireland: the significance and import of Poyning's Law' in N.M. Dawson (ed.), *Reflections on law and society: Irish Legal History Society discourses and other papers, 2000–2005* (Dublin, 2006), pp 259–77.

Kennedy, Allan, 'Representing the periphery: Highland commissioners in the seventeenth-century Scottish parliament, *c.*1612–1702', *PER*, 36:1 (2016), 14–34.

Kenny, Colum, 'The Four Courts in Dublin before 1796', *IJ*, new series, 21:1 (Summer, 1986), 107–24.

— 'The exclusion of Catholics from the legal profession in Ireland, 1537–1829', *IHS*, 25:100 (Nov., 1987), 337–57.

— *King's Inns and the kingdom of Ireland: the Irish Inn of Court, 1541–1800* (Dublin, 1992).
— 'Badge of servitude? The Irish at England's inns of court', *Proc. RIA*, 119C (2019), 199–227.
— 'The Black Book of King's Inns, Dublin, 1649–63: an annotated, chronological and contextualized transcription' in Coleman A. Dennehy (ed.), *Law and revolution in Ireland: law and lawyers before, during and after the Cromwellian interregnum* (Dublin, 2019), pp 128–214.
— 'Not every judge a phoenix: King's Inns under Cromwell' in Coleman A. Dennehy (ed.), *Law and revolution in Ireland: law and lawyers before, during and after the Cromwellian interregnum* (Dublin, 2019), pp 104–27.
Kershaw, R.N., 'The recruiting of the Long Parliament, 1645–7', *History*, new series, 8:31 (Oct., 1923), 169–79.
Kilroy, Phil, 'Sermon and pamphlet literature in the Irish reformed church, 1613–34', *Archivium Hibernicum*, 33 (1975), 110–21.
Kleineke, Hannes, 'The payment of members of parliament in the fifteenth century', *Parl. Hist.*, 3 (2007), 281–300.
Koenigsberger, H.G., *Estates and revolutions: essays in early modern European history* (London, 1971).
— 'Monarchies and parliaments in early modern Europe: *dominium regale* or *dominium politicum et regale*', *Theory and Society*, 5:2 (March, 1978), 191–217.
Kukhta, Joseph Francis, 'Sources for further research, Michael Kearney: a missing link to the mysterious Geoffrey Keating', *The Canadian Journal of Irish Studies*, 31:2 (Fall, 2005), 50–3.
Kyle, Chris R., 'Parliament and the palace of Westminster: an exploration of public space in the early seventeenth century', *Parl. Hist.*, 21:1 (2002), 85–98.
— 'Parliament and the theater of state: the construction of texts', *Shakespeare Studies*, 30 (2002), 31–7.
— 'From broadside to pamphlet: print and parliament in the late 1620s', *Parl. Hist.*, 26:1 (2007), 17–29.
— *Theater of state: parliament and political culture in early Stuart England* (Stanford, 2012).
— *Managing Tudor and Stuart parliaments: essays in memory of Michael Graves: Parliamentary History Yearbook*, 34:1 (Chichester, 2015).
Lambert, Sheila, 'The clerks and records of the House of Commons, 1600–1640', *Historical Research*, 43:108 (1970), 215–31.
— 'Procedure in the House of Commons in the early Stuart period', *EHR*, 95 (Oct., 1980), 753–81.
— 'The beginning of printing for the House of Commons, 1640–42', *The Library*, 6:1 (1981), 43–61.
— 'Committees, religion and parliamentary encroachment on royal authority in early Stuart England', *EHR*, 105 (Jan., 1990), 60–95.
Lambert, Sheila (ed.), *Printing for parliament 1641–1700: List and Index Society special series* (London, 1984).
Latham, R.C., 'The payment of parliamentary wages: the last phase', *EHR*, 66:258 (Jan., 1951), 27–50.
Lecky, W.E.H., *A history of Ireland in the eighteenth century*, 8 vols (London, 1898).
Lee, Patricia-Ann, 'Mistress Stagg's petitioners: February 1642', *The Historian*, 60:2 (1990), 241–56.

Legay, Marie-Laure, 'Representation: political foundations of the French province, 15th–18th century' in Joaquim Albareda and Manuel Herrero Sánchez (eds), *Political representation in the Ancien Régime* (Abingdon, 2019), pp 55–71.
Lenihan, Maurice, *Limerick, its history and antiquities, ecclesiastical, civil and military* (Dublin, 1866).
Lenihan, Padraig, *The last cavalier: Richard Talbot, 1631–1691* (Dublin, 2014).
Lennon, Colm, 'Recusancy and the Dublin Stanyhursts', *Archivium Hibernicum*, 33 (1975), 101–10.
— *The lords of Dublin in the age of reformation* (Dublin, 1989).
— 'Dublin's great explosion of 1597', *History Ireland*, 3:3 (Autumn, 1995), 29–34.
Lincoln, R., 'A list of the mayors and bailiffs of Waterford from 1365 to 1649', *JRSAI*, 7th series, 5:2 (1935), 313–19.
Little, George A., 'The Jesuit university of Dublin, *c.*1627', *Dublin Historical Record*, 13:2 (1952), 34–47.
Little, Patrick, 'The earl of Cork and the downfall of the earl of Strafford, 1638–41', *The Historical Journal*, 39:3 (Sept., 1996), 619–35.
— 'Scottish affairs at Westminster: a letter from the Union parliament of 1654–5', *Scottish Historical Review*, 84:2 (2005), 247–56.
Lodge, John, *The usage of holding parliaments and of preparing and passing bills of supply, in Ireland; annotated by C. Lucas, M.D.* (Dublin, 1770).
— *Sketches of the history of Poynings' Law and of the usage of parliament in Ireland* (Dublin, 1780).
— *The peerage of Ireland, revised by M. Archdall*, 7 vols (Dublin, 1789).
Loeber, Rolf, 'English and Irish sources for the history of Dutch economic activity in Ireland, 1600–89', *IESH*, 8:1 (1981), 70–85.
Loeber, Rolf and Magda Stouthamer-Loeber, 'Kildare Hall, the countess of Kildare's patronage of the Jesuits, and the liturgical setting of Catholic worship in early seventeenth-century Dublin' in Elizabeth FitzPatrick and Raymond Gillespie (eds), *The parish in medieval and early modern Ireland* (Dublin, 2006), pp 242–65.
Loeber, Rolf and Bríd McGrath, 'The legacy of Humphrey Farnham (d. 1624), a Dublin builder and architect', *JRSAI*, 145 (2016), 33–51.
Lynch, William, *The law of election in the ancient cities and towns of Ireland* (London, 1831).
M'Arthur, Ellen A., 'Women petitioners and the Long Parliament', *EHR*, 24:96 (Oct., 1909), 698–709.
MacCarthy, Robert, 'The Church of Ireland in Carlow 1549–2000' in Thomas McGrath (ed.), *Carlow: history and society* (Dublin, 2008), pp 331–54.
MacCarthy-Morrogh, Michael, *The Munster plantation: English migration to southern Ireland, 1583–1641* (Oxford, 1986).
Mac Cuarta, Brian, 'A planter's funeral, legacies and inventory: Sir Matthew de Renzy (1577–1634)', *JRSAI*, 127 (1997), 18–33.
— 'A Catholic funeral in county Down, 1617', *Archivium Hibernicum*, 60 (2006–7), 320–5.
Mac Curtain, Margaret, *Tudor and Stuart Ireland* (Dublin, 1972).
MacDonald, Alan R., '"Tedious to rehers?": parliament and locality in Scotland, *c.*1500–1651: the burghs of north-east Fife', *PER*, 20:1 (2000), 31–58.
— *The burghs and parliament in Scotland,* c.*1550–1651* (Aldershot, 2007).
— 'Chancellors, presidents and speakers: presiding officers in the Scottish parliament before the Restoration', *Parl. Hist.*, 29:1 (Feb., 2010), 49–61.

MacKechnie, Aonghus, 'Housing Scotland's parliament, 1603–1707', *Parl. Hist.*, 21:1 (2002), 99–130.

Maginn, Christopher, 'Contesting the sovereignty of early modern Ireland', *History Ireland*, 15:6 (Nov. – Dec., 2007), 20–5.

— 'Elizabethan Cavan: the institutions of Tudor government in an Irish county' in Brendan Scott (ed.), *Culture and society in early modern Breifne/Cavan* (Dublin, 2009), pp 69–84.

— 'The Gaelic peers, the Tudor sovereigns and English multiple monarchy', *The Journal of British Studies*, 50:3 (July, 2011), 566–86.

Maguire, J.B., 'Seventeenth-century plans of Dublin Castle', *JRSAI*, 104 (1974), 5–14.

Major, John Russell, 'The payment of deputies to the French national assemblies, 1484–1627', *The Journal of Modern History*, 27 (1955), 217–29.

— 'Bellievre, Sully and the Assembly of Notables of 1596', *Transactions of the American Philosophical Society*, 64:2 (1974), 1–34.

Malone, Nessa, 'Henry Burnell and Richard Netterville: lawyers in civic life in the English Pale, *c.*1562–1615' in Salvador Ryan and Clodagh Tait (eds), *Religion and politics in urban Ireland,* c.*1500–*c.*1750: essays in honour of Colm Lennon* (Dublin, 2016), pp 89–107.

Mann, Alastair, 'House rules: parliamentary procedure' in Keith M. Brown and Alan R. MacDonald (eds), *Parliament in context, 1235–1707* (Edinburgh, 2010), pp 122–56.

— 'A brief history of an ancient institution: the Scottish parliament', *Scottish Parliamentary Review*, 1:1 (2013), 1–50.

Mannion, Joseph, '"A mere Irish man, but good Protestant": Sir Francis Shane, 1540–1614', *History Ireland*, 25:2 (March–April, 2017), 16–19.

Martin, F.X., 'The coming of parliament' in Brian Farrell (ed.), *The Irish parliamentary tradition* (Dublin, 1973), pp 37–56.

Martin, G., 'Plantation boroughs in medieval Ireland, with a handlist of boroughs to *c.*1500' in David Harkness and Mary O'Dowd (eds), *Historical Studies XIII: the town in Ireland* (Belfast, 1981), pp 23–55.

Mayes, Charles R., 'The early Stuarts and the Irish peerage', *EHR*, 73 (1958), 227–51.

McCafferty, John, '"To follow the late precedents in England": the first Irish impeachment proceedings in 1641' in Desmond Greer and Norma Dawson (eds), *Mysteries and solutions in Irish legal history* (Dublin, 2001), pp 51–72.

— *The reconstruction of the Church of Ireland: Bishop Bramhall and the Laudian reforms, 1633–1641* (Cambridge, 2007).

McCavitt, John, '"Good planets in their several spheres": the establishment of the assize circuits in early seventeenth-century Ireland', *IJ*, 24:2 (1989), 248–78.

— *Sir Arthur Chichester, lord deputy of Ireland, 1605–16* (Belfast, 1998).

McEntee, Ann Marie, '"The [Un]Civill-Sisterhood of Oranges and Lemons": female petitioners and demonstrators, 1642–53' in James Holstun (ed.), *Pamphlet wars: prose in the English Revolution* (London, 1992), pp 92–7, 99, 108–9.

McGrath, Bríd, 'County Meath members of parliament, 1560–1613', *Riocht na Midhe*, 9:2 (1996), 60–72.

— 'Meath members of parliament, 1634–1641', *Riocht na Midhe*, 12 (2001), 90–107.

— 'Parliament men and the confederate association' in Micheál O Siochrú (ed.), *Kingdoms in crisis: Ireland in the 1640s; essays in honour of Donal Cregan* (Dublin, 2001), pp 90–105.

— 'The nomination of Kilkenny MPs in 1628', *Old Kilkenny Review*, 55 (2003), 119–25.
— 'Ireland and the third university: attendance at the Inns of Court, 1603–1649' in David Edwards (ed.), *Regions and rulers in Ireland, 1100–1650: essays for Kenneth Nicholls* (Dublin, 2004), pp 217–36.
— 'The Irish elections of 1640–1641' in Ciaran Brady and Jane Ohlmeyer (eds), *British interventions in early modern Ireland* (Cambridge, 2005), pp 186–206.
— 'Inistioge's elections in 1640', *Old Kilkenny Review*, 57 (2005), 75–82.
— 'The communities of Clonmel, 1608–1649' in Robert Armstrong and Tadhg Ó hAnnracháin (eds), *Community in early modern Ireland* (Dublin, 2006), pp 103–19.
— 'Athboy's election returns 1640 and 1641', *Riocht na Midhe*, 21 (2010), 65–72.
— 'Mount Taragh's triumph: commitment and organization in the early stages of the 1641 rebellion in Meath' in Eamon Darcy, et al. (eds), *The 1641 Depositions and the Irish Rebellion* (London, 2012), pp 51–63.
— 'A fragment of the minute book of the Corporation of New Ross, 1635', *JRSAI*, 144 (2014–15), 100–12.
— 'Sex, lies and rigged returns: the Kerry County parliamentary election of 11 June 1634 and its consequences', *PER*, 37:3 (2017), 241–55.
— 'Archbishop John Bramhall and church lands in Athboy, 1641–1663', *Ríocht na Midhe*, 28 (2017), 91–113.
— 'Managing the Windsor of Ireland: Galway town council 1603–1653', *The Journal of the Galway Archaeological and Historical Society*, 69 (2017), 61–81.
— 'Reconstructing an early-modern Irish urban economic community: Clonmel's cess list of 1642', *IESH*, 44:1 (2017), 122–42.
— 'Clonmel Corporation records, 1657–8', *Archivium Hibernicum*, 71 (2018), 34–57.
— 'Looking the part: dress and civic status and ethnicity in early-modern Ireland', *JRSAI*, 148 (2018), 101–21.
— 'Unmasking "E.S.": the author of "A Survey of the present estate of Ireland Anno 1615"', *Archivium Hibernicum*, 71 (2018), 7–33.
— 'The recruiter returns to the Irish parliament, 1642–1648' in Patrick Little (ed.), *Ireland in crisis: war, politics and religion 1641–50* (Manchester, 2019), pp 119–37.
— 'Starting from scratch: the first thirty years of Coleraine's development' in Brendan Scott (ed.), *Society and administration in Ulster's plantation towns* (Dublin, 2019), pp 36–55.
— 'Electoral law in Ireland before 1641' in Coleman A. Dennehy (ed.), *Law and revolution in Ireland: law and lawyers before, during and after the Cromwellian interregnum* (Dublin, 2019), pp 1–21.
— 'Fraternities and mysteries: early-modern provincial Irish guilds and trade companies', *JRSAI*, 150 (2020), 225–45.
— '*Obedientia Civium Urbis Felicitas*: Sir Henry Sidney's return to Dublin as depicted in Derricke's *Image of Irelande*' in Thomas Herron, Denna J. Iammarino and Maryclaire Moroney (eds), *John Derricke's The Image of Irelande: with a discoverie of Wood Karne: essays on text and context* (Manchester, 2021), pp 65–76.
— 'Poets and patronage under Falkland and Wentworth: the commendatory verses to Richard Bellings' *Arcadia* (1624) and James Shirley's *The Royal Master* (1638)', *Archivium Hibernicum*, 74 (2021), 7–27.
— 'Unconstitutional acts, violence, intimidation, vote-rigging, fraud and resistance: Cavan's parliamentary elections, 1613', *Breifne*, 15:56 (2021), 4–23.
— 'Thomas Wentworth's Irish electoral strategy', *PER*, 41:1 (March, 2021), 24–41.

— 'Town and mitre: relations between the episcopal borough of Old Leighlin and its bishops, 1635–1688', *Ossory, Laois and Leinster*, 8 (2022), 73–93.
— 'Kilkenny merchants and the 1613 parliament' in Jane Fenlon (ed.), *Magnates and merchants in early modern Ireland* (Dublin, 2023), pp 162–175.
— '"Mere Irish" in parliaments and towns, 1316–1659' in Simon Egan (ed.), *Beyond the Pale and Highland line* (Manchester, forthcoming).
— 'Kick-starting New Ross' renewal: its charter negotiations 1609–12 and subsequent economic development', *Ossory, Laois and Leinster*, 9 (forthcoming).
McGrath, Charles Ivar, 'The parliament of Ireland to 1800' in Clyve Jones (ed.), *A short history of parliament: England, Great Britain, the United Kingdom, Ireland and Scotland* (Woodbridge, 2012), pp 321–38.
McGuire, James and James Quinn (eds), *Dictionary of Irish biography*, 9 vols (Cambridge, 2009).
McInerney, Luke, 'A list of freeholders in Kilfenora diocese in 1601', *Eolas: The Journal of the American Society of Irish Medieval Studies*, 11 (2018), 60–103.
McLaughlin, Gráinne, 'Aristotle, Greco-Roman imagery and the Irish in Europe: the classical context in the seventeenth century' in Thomas O'Connor and Mary-Ann Lyons (eds), *The Ulster earls and baroque Europe: refashioning Irish identities, 1600–1800* (Dublin, 2010), pp 291–305.
Menhennet, David, *The journal of the House of Commons: a bibliographical and historical guide* (London, 1971).
Millar, Oliver, 'Strafford and Van Dyck' in Richard Ollard and Pamela Tudor-Craig (eds), *For Veronica Wedgwood these: studies in seventeenth-century history* (London, 1986), pp 109–23.
Monck Mason, H.J., *The life of William Bedell, D.D., lord bishop of Kilmore* (London, 1843).
Montano, John Patrick, *The roots of English colonialism in Ireland* (Cambridge, 2011).
Moody, T.W., 'The Irish parliament under Elizabeth and James I: a general survey', *Proc. RIA*, 45C (1939), 41–81.
Murray, James, *Enforcing the English reformation in Ireland: clerical resistance and political opposition in the diocese of Dublin, 1534–1590* (Cambridge, 2011).
Musselwhite, Paul, Peter C. Mancall and James Horn (eds), *Virginia 1619: slavery and freedom in the making of English America* (Chapel Hill, NC, 2019).
Natzler, David, 'Manuals before May: from the fourteenth to the seventeenth century' in Paul Evans (ed.), *Essays on the history of parliamentary procedure, in honour of Thomas Erskine May* (Bloomsbury, 2017), pp 87–96.
Neale, J.E., 'Parliament and the succession question in 1562/3 and 1566', *EHR*, 36:144 (Oct., 1921), 497–520.
— *The Elizabethan House of Commons* (2nd ed., London, 1976).
Newman, P.R., *Royalist officers in England and Wales, 1642–1660: a biographical dictionary* (New York, 1981).
Nicholson, William, *The English, Scotch and Irish historical libraries* (London, 1776).
Ní Mhurchadha, Maighread, *Fingal, 1603–60: contending neighbours in north Dublin* (Dublin, 2005).
— 'Documents concerning the oath of supremacy in early seventeenth-century Ireland', *Archivium Hibernicum*, 63 (2010), 264–73.
O'Brien, George, *The economic history of Ireland in the seventeenth century* (Dublin, 1919).
O'Donoghue, John, *Historical memoir of the O'Briens* (Dublin, 1860).

O'Dowd, Mary, *Power, politics and land: early modern Sligo, 1568–1688* (Belfast, 1991).

— 'The political writings and public voices of women, *c.*1500–1850' in Angela Bourke (ed.), *The Field Day anthology of Irish writing: Irish women's writing and traditions* (New York, 2002).

Ó hAnnracháin, Tadhg, *Catholic reformation in Ireland: the mission of Rinnuccini, 1645–1649* (Cambridge, 2002).

— 'Imagining political representation in seventeenth-century Ireland' in Robert Armstrong and Tadhg Ó hAnnracháin (eds), *Community in early modern Ireland* (Dublin, 2006), pp 34–50.

Ohlmeyer, Jane, 'Strafford, the "Londonderry business" and "New British history"' in J.F. Merritt (ed.), *The political world of Thomas Wentworth, earl of Strafford, 1621–1641* (Cambridge, 1996), pp 216–29.

— 'Records of the Irish Court of Chancery: a preliminary report for 1627–1634' in Desmond Greer and Norma Dawson (eds), *Mysteries and solutions in Irish legal history* (Dublin, 2001), pp 15–49.

— 'Irish recusant lawyers during the reign of Charles I' in Micheál Ó Siochrú (ed.), *Kingdoms in crisis: Ireland in the 1640s* (Dublin, 2001), pp 63–89.

— 'The Irish peers, political power and parliament, 1640–1641' in Ciaran Brady and Jane Ohlmeyer (eds), *British interventions in early modern Ireland* (Cambridge, 2005), pp 161–85.

— *Making Ireland English: the Irish aristocracy in the seventeenth century* (London, 2012).

Ó Macháin, Pádraig, 'The emergence of the Gaelic paper manuscript: a preliminary investigation' in Pádraig Ó Macháin (ed.), *Paper and the paper manuscript: a context for the transmission of Gaelic literature* (Cork, 2019), pp 21–43.

'Omurethi', 'The White Castle of Athy and its sculptured stones', *The Journal of the County Kildare Archaeological Society and Surrounding Districts*, 4 (1903–5), 47–62.

O'Riordan, Michelle, *The Gaelic mind and the collapse of the Gaelic world* (Cork, 1990).

Ó Siochrú, Micheál, *Confederate Ireland, 1642–1649: a constitutional and political analysis* (Dublin, 1999).

— *God's executioner: Oliver Cromwell and the conquest of Ireland* (London, 2008).

O'Sullivan, William, 'A finding list of Sir James Ware's manuscripts', *Proc. RIA*, 97C (1997), 69–99.

Osborough, W.N., 'Eighteenth-century Ireland's legislative deficit' in Michael Brown and Seán Patrick Donlan (eds), *The laws and other legalities of Ireland, 1689–1850* (London, 2016), pp 75–96.

Otten, Charlotte F., *English women's voices, 1540–1700* (Gainesville, FL, 1992).

Palonen, Kari, *The politics of parliamentary procedure: the formation of the Westminster Procedure as a parliamentary ideal type* (Leverkusen, 2014).

Parker, Geoffrey, *Spain and the Netherlands, 1559–1659: ten studies* (London, 1979).

— *The military revolution: military innovation and the rise of the west, 1500–1800* (Cambridge, 1988).

— *Global crisis: war, climate change and catastrophe in the seventeenth century* (New Haven CT, 2013).

Patterson, Catherine F., *Urban government and the early Stuart state: provincial towns, corporate liberties and royal authority in England, 1603–1640* (Woodbridge, 2022).

Pawlisch, Hans, *Sir John Davies and the conquest of Ireland: a study in legal imperialism* (Cambridge, 1985).

Peacey, Jason, 'The print culture of parliament, 1600–1800', *Parl. Hist.*, 26:1 (2007), 1–16.
— '"Rushworth shall not take any notes here": journals, debates and the public, 1640–60', *Parl. Hist.*, 33:3 (2014), 422–37.
— 'The street theatre of state: the ceremonial opening of parliament, 1603–60' in Chris Kyle (ed.), *Managing Tudor and Stuart parliaments: essays in memory of Michael Graves: Parliamentary History Yearbook*, 34:1 (Chichester, 2015), pp 155–72.
Peck, Linda Levy, *Northampton: patronage and policy at the court of James I* (London, 1982).
— 'Beyond the Pale: John Cusack and the language of absolutism in early Stuart Britain', *The Historical Journal*, 41:1 (March, 1998), 121–49.
Perceval-Maxwell, Michael, 'Protestant faction, the impeachment of Strafford and the origins of the Irish civil war', *The Canadian Journal of History*, 17 (1982), 235–55.
— 'Ulster 1641 in the context of political developments in the three kingdoms' in Brian Mac Cuarta (ed.), *Ulster 1641: aspects of the rising* (Belfast, 1993), pp 93–107.
— *The outbreak of the Irish rebellion of 1641* (Dublin, 1994).
Plomer, Henry R., *A dictionary of the booksellers and printers who were at work in England, Scotland and Ireland from 1641 to 1667* (London, 1907).
Pluymers, Keith, 'Cow trials, climate change and the causes of violence', *Environmental History*, 25:2 (2020), 287–309.
Pogson, Fiona, 'Public and private service at the early Stuart court: the career of William Raylton, Strafford's agent', *Historical Research*, 84:223 (Feb., 2011), 53–66.
— 'Strafford's "spirit" at the royalist court: Sir George Radcliffe and Irish affairs, 1643–5', *IHS*, 43:164 (2019), 175–93.
Pollard, A.F., 'The clerical organization of parliament', *EHR*, 57:225 (1942), 31–58.
Prendergast, J.P., 'On the projected plantation of Ormond by King Charles', *Trans. Kilkenny Arch. Soc.*, 1:3 (1851), 390–409.
— 'Further notes in the history of Sir Jerome Alexander', *Transactions of the Royal Historical Society*, 2 (1873), 117–41.
Pronay, Nicholas and John Taylor, *Parliamentary texts of the later Middle Ages* (Oxford, 1980).
Purcell, Mark, *The country house library* (London, 2017).
Quinn, David B., 'The Irish parliamentary subsidy in the fifteenth and sixteenth centuries', *Proc. RIA*, 42C (1934–5), 219–46.
— 'Government printing and the publication of the Irish statutes in the sixteenth century', *Proc. RIA*, 49C (1943–4), 45–129.
Reeves-Smith, Terence, *Irish gardens and gardening before Cromwell* (Cork, 1999).
Reid, J.S. and W.D. Killen, *A history of the Presbyterian Church in Ireland: comprising the civil history of the province of Ulster from the accession of James the First*, 2 vols (London, 1853).
Richardson, H.G. and G.O. Sayles, *The Irish parliament in the Middle Ages* (London, 1952).
Robinson, W.R.B., 'The Tudor revolution in Welsh government, 1536–1543: its effects on gentry participation', *EHR*, 103:406 (1989), 1–20.
Rogers, Charles, 'Notes in the history of Sir Jerome Alexander, second justice of the Court of Common Pleas, and founder of the Alexander Library, Trinity College, Dublin', *Transactions of the Royal Historical Society*, 2 (1873), 94–116.
Rondelez, Paul, 'The metallurgical enterprises of Richard Boyle, first earl of Cork' in David Edwards and Colin Rynne (eds), *The colonial world of Richard Boyle, first earl of Cork* (Dublin, 2018), pp 112–20.

Russell, Conrad, 'Monarchies, wars, and estates in England, France, and Spain, *c.*1580–*c.*1640', *Legislative Studies Quarterly*, 7:2 (1982), 205–20.
— 'The nature of a parliament in early Stuart England' in Howard Tomlinson (ed.), *Before the English civil war* (London, 1983), pp 123–50.
— *Unrevolutionary England, 1603–1642* (London, 1990).
Salmon, J.H.M., *Society in crisis: France in the sixteenth century* (London, 1975).
Sawyer, Jeffrey K., *Printed poison: pamphlet propaganda, faction politics and the public sphere in early seventeenth–century France* (Berkeley, CA, 1990).
Sayles, G.O., '*Modus tenendi parliamentum*: Irish or English?' in James Lydon (ed.), *England and Ireland in the later Middle Ages: essays in honour of Jocelyn Otway-Ruthven* (Dublin, 1981), pp 122–52.
Schlueter, June, 'Michael van Meer's *Album Amicorum*, with illustrations of London, 1614–15', *Huntington Library Quarterly*, 69:2 (June, 2006), 301–14.
Schroeder, Horst, *Der topos der Nine Worthies in literatur und bildender kunst* (Goettingen, 1971).
Scott, Brendan, 'Belturbet, County Cavan: the development and administration of an Ulster plantation town' in Brendan Scott (ed.), *Society and administration in Ulster's plantation towns* (Dublin, 2019), pp 56–68.
— 'Petition of the inhabitants of Cavan to the lord deputy and council, 8 July 1629', *IHS*, 43:163 (2019), 111–25.
Schreiber, Roy E., *The first Carlisle: Sir James Hay, first earl of Carlisle, as courtier, diplomat and entrepreneur, 1580–1636* (Philadelphia, 1984).
Seaward, Paul, 'Divisions, tellers and management in the 17th-century House of Commons', *Parl. Hist.*, 32:1 (2013), 79–102.
Serra, Eva, 'Butlletí bibliogràfic sobre les Corts Catalanes', *Arxiu de textos Catalans antics*, 26 (2007), 663–738.
Seymour, Edward, *Christchurch Cathedral: Dublin, 1855–1878* (Dublin, 1878).
Shagan, Ethan H., 'Protector Somerset and the 1549 rebellions: new sources and new perspectives', *EHR*, 114:455 (Feb., 1999), 34–63.
Shaw, Dougal, 'Thomas Wentworth and monarchical ritual in early modern Ireland', *The Historical Journal*, 49:2 (June, 2006), 331–55.
Simms, J.G., 'The case of Ireland stated' in Brian Farrell (ed.), *The Irish parliamentary tradition* (Dublin, 1973), pp 128–38.
— 'The establishment of Protestant ascendancy, 1691–1714' in T.W. Moody, et al. (eds), *A new history of Ireland*, 9 vols (Oxford, 1977–2005), iv, pp 1–30.
Simms, J.G. and P.H. Kelly (eds), *William Molyneux of Dublin* (Dublin, 1982).
Smith, David L., *The Stuart parliaments, 1603–1689* (London, 1999).
Snoddy, Richard, *The soteriology of James Ussher: the act and object of saving faith* (Oxford, 2014).
Spottswood, John, *The history of the church and state of Scotland* (London, 1677).
Stephen, Leslie and Sidney Lee (eds), *The dictionary of national biography*, 66 vols (London, 1885–1901).
Stevenson, Allan H., 'James Shirley and the actors at the first Irish theater', *Modern Philology*, 40:2 (Nov., 1942), 147–60.
Stevenson, David, *The government of Scotland under the Covenanters, 1637–1651* (Edinburgh, 1982).

Stewart, Laura A.M., 'Petitioning in early seventeenth-century Scotland, 1625–51', *PER*, 38:3 (2018), 307–22.
Strauss, Kathrin, 'The ceremonial mace in the House of Commons and great maces of cities and boroughs in the 16th and early 17th century', *Parl. Hist.*, 41:3 (Oct., 2022), 389–405.
Tait, Clodagh, 'Society, 1550–1700' in Jane Ohlmeyer (ed.), *The Cambridge history of Ireland: Vol. 2: Early modern Ireland, 1550–1730* (Cambridge, 2018), pp 273–98.
Tenison, Charles McCarthy, 'Cork MPs', *JCHAS*, 2nd series, 1 (1895), 230–4.
Terry, C.S., *The Scottish parliament: its constitution and procedure, 1603–1707* (Glasgow, 1905).
Thompson, I.A.A., 'The end of the Cortes of Castile', *PER*, 4:2 (Dec., 1984), 125–33.
Thorold Rogers, J.E., *A history of agriculture and prices in England: from the year after the Oxford parliament (1259) to the commencement of the continental war (1793)* (Cambridge, 2011).
Thrush, Andrew, 'The House of Lords' records repository and the clerk of the parliaments' house: a Tudor achievement', *Parl. Hist.*, 21:3 (2002), 367–73.
— 'The French marriage and the origins of the 1614 parliament' in Stephen Clucas and Rosalind Davies (eds), *The crisis of 1614 and the Addled Parliament: literary and historical perspectives* (Aldershot, 2003), pp 25–36.
Thrush, Andrew and John P. Ferris (eds), *The history of parliament: the House of Commons, 1604–1629*, 6 vols (Cambridge, 2010).
Treadwell, Victor, 'The House of Lords in the Irish parliament of 1613–1615', *EHR*, 80:314 (1965), 92–107.
— 'The Irish parliament of 1569–71', *Proc. RIA*, 65C (1966–7), 55–89.
— 'The Irish customs administration in the sixteenth century', *IHS*, 20:80 (Sept., 1977), 384–417.
— 'Sir John Perrott and the Irish parliament of 1585–6', *Proc. RIA*, 85C (1985), 259–308.
— *Buckingham and Ireland, 1616–1628: a study in Anglo-Irish politics* (Dublin, 1998).
Tricomi, Albert H., '*A dialogue betweene Pollicy and Piety* by Robert Davenport', *English Literary Renaissance*, 21:2 (1991), 190–216.
Vallee-Karcher, Aline, 'L'assemblée des notables de Saint-Germain-en-Laye (1583)', *Bibliothèque de l'école des chartes*, 114 (1956), 115–162.
Vigors, P.D., 'List of the sovereigns of the town of New Ross, County Wexford, from 1584–1841', *Journal of the Royal Historical and Archaeological Association of Ireland*, 4th series, 9 (1889), 312–17.
de Villiers, Elizabeth, 'Parliamentary boroughs restored by the House of Commons, 1621–1641', *EHR*, 67:263 (April, 1952), 175–202.
Walker, Garthine, *Crime, gender and social order in early modern England* (Cambridge, 2003).
Walsh, T.J., 'The Capuchins in Cork', *Capuchin Annual*, 21 (1952), 173–203.
Walter, John, 'Crowds and political violence in early modern Ireland: Galway and the 1641 Depositions', *IHS*, 45:168 (2021), 178–202.
Walton, Julian C., 'The Freemen of Waterford, 1542–1650', *IG*, 5:5 (1978), 560–72.
— 'The subsidy roll of County Waterford, 1662', *Anal. Hib.*, 30 (1982), 47–96.
Watt, J.A., 'The first recorded use of the word "Parliament" in Ireland?', *IJ*, 4 (1969), 123–6.

Webster, Tom, 'Preaching and parliament, 1640–1659' in Peter McCullough, Hugh Adlington and Emma Rhatigan (eds), *The Oxford handbook of the early modern sermon* (Oxford, 2011), pp 404–20.

Wedgwood, C.V., *Thomas Wentworth, first earl of Strafford, 1593–1641: a re-evaluation* (London, 1962).

Weinbaum, Martin, *British borough charters, 1370–1660* (Cambridge, 2010).

Withington, Phil, *The politics of commonwealth: citizens and freemen in early modern England* (Cambridge, 2005).

Wood, Antony A., *Athenae Oxonensis: an exact history of all the writers and bishops who have had their education in the University of Oxford* (London, 1817).

Wormald, Jenny, *Court, kirk and community: Scotland, 1470–1625* (London, 1981).

— 'James VI & I', *History Today*, 52:6 (June, 2002), 27–33.

Young, John R., *The Scottish parliament, 1639–1661: a political and constitutional analysis* (Edinburgh, 1996).

— 'Representation in the Scottish parliament to 1707 and Scottish representation in the parliament of Great Britain to the 1832 Reform Act' in Joaquim Albareda and Manuel Herrero Sánchez (eds), *Political representation in the Ancien Régime* (Abingdon, 2019), pp 123–40.

Zaller, Robert, *The discourse of legitimacy in early modern England* (Stanford, 2007).

INTERNET SOURCES

'Christmas Day in the Commons, 1656', at https://thehistoryofparliament.wordpress.com/2014/12/23/christmas-day-in-the-commons-1656/ [accessed 18 Dec. 2019].

'Constituencies, 1558–1603', at https://www.historyofparliamentonline.org/research/constituencies/constituencies-1558-1603 [accessed 19 Feb. 2021].

'Fees of office and order of dignities for the Irish parliament, 1585–1632, at http://catalogue.nli.ie/Record/vtls000529756#page/23/mode/1up [accessed 13 Jan. 2023].

'John Speed's Map of Dublin, 1610', at http://www.dublincity.ie/sites/default/files/galleries/01-speed-dublin-1610.jpg [accessed 13 March 2019].

'Members, 1509–1558', at https://www.historyofparliamentonline.org/research/members/members-1509-1558 [accessed 4 March 2019].

'New Inn – Middle Temple's lost inn of chancery', at https://www.middletemple.org.uk/archive-history/archive-month/january-2020-new-inn-middle-temple%E2%80%99s-lost-inn-chancery [accessed 22 July 2021].

'Patent Roll 5 Henry IV', at https://chancery.tcd.ie/document/patent/5-henry-iv/103 [accessed 16 June 2021].

'Records of the parliaments of Scotland to 1707', at www.rps.ac.uk [accessed 31 March 2021].

'Speakers of the House of Commons (1376–2015)', at https://doi.org/10.1093/ref:odnb/92975 [accessed 23 Feb. 2019].

'Visit the Bodleian Libraries', at https://www.bodleian.ox.ac.uk/whatson/whats-on/online/parliament-week/parliament-week-2011/Parliament-in-Oxford [accessed 15 March 2019].

Duvall, S.H., 'French political pamphlets collection at the L. Tom Perry Special Collection, Harold B. Lee Library, Brigham Young University', at http://files.lib.byu.edu/collections/french–political–pamphlets/frenchpamphlets.pdf [accessed 29 July 2019].

Fuidge, Norah M., 'Chaloner, John', at https://www.historyofparliamentonline.org/volume/1509-1558/member/chaloner-john-ii-1526-81 [accessed 1 Aug. 2019]

Hasler, P.W., 'Cinque ports', at https://www.historyofparliamentonline.org/volume/1558-1603/constituencies/cinque-ports [accessed 4 Feb. 2019]

Hawkyard, Alasdair D., 'Calais', at https://www.historyofparliamentonline.org/volume/1509-1558/constituencies/calais [accessed 1 Aug. 2019].

Larminie, Vivienne, 'Going into the country: leave, holidays and political intrigues in the 1640s', at https://thehistoryofparliament.wordpress.com/2020/07/16/going–into–the–country–leave–holidays–and–political–intrigue–in–the–1640s/ [accessed 20 Aug. 2021].

Layles, William, 'Account of surrender of Limerick, 1651', at https://celt.ucc.ie/published/E650001–023.html [accessed 14 Dec. 2022].

Little, Patrick, 'Silence and laughter in the Cromwellian House of Commons', at https://thehistoryofparliament.wordpress.com/2022/02/08/silence-and-laughter-in-the-cromwellian-house-of-commons/ [accessed 11 Feb. 2022].

McCarthy, Julia, 'Archbishop John Alen (*c.*1476–1534) and his Register', at https://www.ireland.anglican.org/news/8930/preview [accessed 6 July 2019].

McGrath, Bríd, 'The compilation of the Irish House of Commons' journals, 1613–15', Paper presented to Tudor and Stuart Ireland Annual Conference, Dublin, 2022, at https://soundcloud.com/history–hub/brid–mcgrath–journals–of–the–Irish–house–of–commons [accessed 19 Nov. 2022].

Morgan, Hiram, 'An introduction to the study of political ideas in early modern Ireland', Keynote address to 'Ireland 1598: contexts, representations and revolts', organized jointly by the departments of History and English at University College Cork, May 1998, at https://celt.ucc.ie//Ideology.pdf [accessed 3 April 2019].

Roskell, J.S., 'The composition of the House of Commons', at https://www.historyofparliamentonline.org/volume/1386-1421/survey/v-composition-house-commons [accessed 4 March 2019].

Seaward, Paul, 'Impeachment', at https://historyofparliamentblog.wordpress.com/2017/09/04/impeachment/ [accessed 10 Sept. 2019].

Seaward, Paul, 'Resignation', The History of Parliament Trust Blog, 4 Dec. 2018, at https://historyofparliamentblog.wordpress.com/2018/12/04/resignation/ [accessed 25 Feb. 2019].

Thrush, Andrew, 'The origin of the House of Lords' standing orders', at https://archives.blog.parliament.uk/2021/05/18/the-origin-of-the-house-of-lords-standing-orders/ [accessed 21 May 2021].

— 'The speaker', at https://www.historyofparliamentonline.org/volume/1604-1629/survey/viii-officers-and-servants-house [accessed 10 May 2019].

The Virtual Record Treasury of Ireland, at www.virtualtreasury.ie [accessed 15 Dec. 2022].

Wright, A.P.M., 'London', at https://www.historyofparliamentonline.org/volume/1422-1504/constituencies/london [accessed 28 Oct. 2018].

THESES AND OTHER UNPUBLISHED MATERIAL

Brownhill, Charlotte Kate, 'The personal and professional relationships between Thomas Wentworth, earl of Strafford, and his closest advisors', 2 vols (PhD, University of Sheffield, 2004).

Jones, Norm, 'Representative of what? The politics of representative institutions', Paper presented to the conference 'Rediscovering Europe's parliamentary culture, 1500–1700: concepts, methods, approaches', Krakow, 22–4 June 2022.

Lentz, Susan A., 'The Irish parliament during rebellion and civil war, 1641–1648' (MA, University of Wisconsin, 1974).

McGrath, Bríd, 'The membership of the Irish House of Commons, 1613–1615' (MLitt, University of Dublin, 1987).

— 'A biographical dictionary of the membership of the Irish House of Commons, 1640–1641', 2 vols (PhD, University of Dublin, 1998).

Moir, Thomas L., 'The Addled Parliament of 1614' (PhD, University of Dublin, 1950).

Morgan, Rhys, 'From soldier to settler: the Welsh in Ireland, 1558–1641' (PhD, University of Cardiff, 2011).

Morgan, Victor, 'A provincial perspective: the local origins of parliamentary culture in England, *c.*1530–1640', Paper presented to the conference 'Rediscovering Europe's parliamentary culture, 1500–1700: concepts, methods, approaches', Krakow, 22–4 June 2022.

Moynes, Vera, '"The written word remains as a perpetual witness …": letter-writing against all odds – the epistolary legacy of the early Irish Jesuits', Unpublished paper presented at the Irish Catholic History Society's conference, 14 Sept. 2019.

Ó Bric, Breandán, 'Galway townsmen as the owners of land in Connaught, 1585–1641' (MA, University College Galway, 1974).

Patterson, Jonathan, 'The Estates General of Blois (1588) as represented in Pierre Matthieu's *La Guisiade* (1589)', Unpublished paper given at 'Political assemblies in European historical drama, *c.*1550–1650', 23–30 June 2021.

Stapylton, Keith A.T., 'The parliamentary privilege of freedom from arrest, 1603–1629' (PhD, University College London, 2016).

Index

The names of the members of the Irish parliament are given in *italics*. The names of MPs who were lawyers are given in ***bold italics*** and indicate that they are included in the biographical notes in Appendix 3. These index references to Appendix 3 refer only to the lawyers that are the subject of biographical entries. Peers and peeresses are listed under their surnames, not their titles of honour. Additional details on these individuals' parents, place of birth, college they attended, wives, children, etc. are not listed in the index. For references to the town of Derry, please look under Derry, while references to the county are logged under Londonderry. References to Offaly and Laois are found under King's County and Queen's County, as they were known at the time.

IRISH LEGAL HISTORY SOCIETY SERIES*

1 Daire Hogan and W.N. Osborough (eds), *Brehons, serjeants and attorneys: studies in the history of the Irish legal profession* (1990)
2 Colum Kenny, *King's Inns and the kingdom of Ireland: the Irish 'inn of court', 1541–1800* (1992)
3 Jon G. Crawford, *Anglicizing the government of Ireland: the Irish privy council and the expansion of Tudor rule, 1556–1578* (1993)
4 W.N. Osborough (ed.), *Explorations in law and history: Irish Legal History Society discourses, 1988–1994* (1995)
5 W.N. Osborough, *Law and the emergence of modern Dublin: a litigation topography for a capital city* (1996)
6 Colum Kenny, *Tristram Kennedy and the revival of Irish legal training, 1835–1885* (1996)
7 Brian Griffin, *The Bulkies: police and crime in Belfast, 1800–1865* (1997)
8 Éanna Hickey, *Irish law and lawyers in modern folk tradition* (1999)
9 A.R. Hart, *A history of the king's serjeants at law in Ireland: honour rather than advantage?* (2000)
10 D.S. Greer and N.M. Dawson (eds), *Mysteries and solutions in Irish legal history: Irish Legal History Society discourses and other papers, 1996–1999* (2000)
11 Colum Kenny, *King's Inns and the battle of the books, 1972: cultural controversy at a Dublin library* (2002)
12 Desmond Greer and James W. Nicolson, *The factory acts in Ireland, 1802–1914* (2003)
13 Mary Kotsonouris, *The winding-up of the Dáil courts, 1922–1925: an obvious duty* (2004)
14 Paul Brand, Kevin Costello and W.N. Osborough (eds), *Adventures of the law: proceedings of the 16th British Legal History Conference, Dublin 2003* (2005)
15 Jon G. Crawford, *A Star Chamber court in Ireland: the Court of Castle Chamber, 1571–1641* (2005)
16 A.P. Quinn, *Wigs and guns: Irish barristers and the Great War* (2006)
17 N.M. Dawson (ed.), *Reflections on law and history: Irish Legal History Society discourses and other papers, 2000–2005* (2006)
18 James Kelly, *Poynings' Law and the making of law in Ireland, 1660–1800* (2007)
19 W.E. Vaughan, *Murder trials in Ireland, 1836–1914* (2009)
20 Kevin Costello, *The Court of Admiralty of Ireland, 1575–1893* (2011)
21 W.N. Osborough, *An island's law: a bibliographical guide to Ireland's legal past* (2013)
22 Felix M. Larkin and N.M. Dawson (eds), *Lawyers, the law and history: Irish Legal History Society discourses and other papers, 2005–2011* (2013)
23 Daire Hogan and Colum Kenny (eds), *Changes in practice and law: a selection of essays by members of the legal profession to mark twenty-five years of the Irish Legal History Society* (2013)
24 W.N. Osborough, *The Irish stage: a legal history* (2015)
25 Thomas Mohr, *Guardian of the Treaty: the Privy Council appeal and Irish sovereignty* (2016)
26 Joseph C. Sweeney, *The life and times of Arthur Browne in Ireland and America, 1756–1805* (2017)
27 Niamh Howlin, *Juries in Ireland: laypersons and law in the long nineteenth century* (2017)
28 Patrick Hyde Kelly (ed.), *The case of Ireland's being bound by acts of parliament in England, stated, Dublin 1698* (2018)
29 Mary Phelan, *Irish speakers, interpreters and the courts, 1754–1921* (2019)
30 Coleman A. Dennehy (ed.), *Law and revolution in seventeenth-century Ireland* (2020)
31 Daire Hogan and Patrick Maume (eds), *The reminiscences of Ignatius O'Brien, lord chancellor of Ireland 1913–18: a life in Cork, Dublin and Westminster* (2021)
32 Peter Crooks and Thomas Mohr (eds), *Law and the idea of liberty in Ireland: from Magna Carta to the present* (2023)
33 Bríd McGrath, *The operations of the Irish House of Commons, 1613–48* (2023)

ALSO AVAILABLE
The Irish Legal History Society (1989)
* Volumes 1–7 are published by Irish Academic Press

Irish Legal History Society

Established in 1988 to encourage the study and advance the knowledge of the history of Irish law, especially by the publication of original documents and of works relating to the history of Irish law, including its institutions, doctrines and personalities, and reprinting or editing of works of sufficient rarity or importance.